N. Garner

ENGLISH
SUPER-MINI
DICTIONARY

Rachael
Garner

Ra

CHAMBERS

ENGLISH SUPER-MINI DICTIONARY

edited by
Susan Rennie

CHAMBERS

Chambers Harrap Publishers Ltd
7 Hopetoun Crescent
Edinburgh EH7 4AY

This edition published by Chambers 1997
First published by Chambers 1995
Previously published as *Chambers Mini Dictionary* by
W & R Chambers Ltd 1978 and 1990

Reprinted 1998, 1999, 2000

We have made every effort to mark as such all words which we believe to be trademarks. We should also like to make it clear that the presence of a word in the dictionary, whether marked or unmarked, in no way affects its legal status as a trademark.

A CIP catalogue record for this book is available from the British Library

ISBN 0-550-10713-4

The editor would like to acknowledge with thanks the help of Catherine Schwarz and Megan Thomson towards the editing of this dictionary.

Typeset by Selwood Systems, Bath
Printed in Great Britain by
Caledonian International Book Manufacturing Ltd, Glasgow

Contents

Preface

In this new edition of the *Chambers Super-Mini Dictionary*, we hope you will find all you want to know about the words currently in daily use – how to spell them, what they mean, and, if the words are unusual or particularly difficult, how to pronounce them. To help distinguish between senses, many words are illustrated by phrases in which they commonly occur.

Up-to-date, modern and easy to use, this dictionary will be a reliable companion whenever and wherever everyday words are spoken or written.

Notes on using the Dictionary

The main entries (headwords) are listed alphabetically, from **a** to **zydeco**. In this list are included abbreviations (for example, **APEX**, **BAFTA** and **TUC**) and cross-references to other main entries (such as **trodden** to **tread** and **enquire** to **inquire**).

Within each main entry, related words (subheads) are listed alphabetically, together with their meanings, *eg* **highbrow** and **high tea** are listed under the main entry **high**. Phrases which include the headword (*eg* **for the high jump**) are given in a separate list at the end of the entry.

Beside each headword and subhead there is a part of speech label (for example, *noun*, *adj*, *verb*). These, as well as the labels (*informal*, *old*, *taboo* and so on) that are given before some meanings, are explained on pp x and xi. Words with direct opposites, or which are useful to compare with other words, are given a reference to other relevant entries, *eg* **heterodox** (*contrasted with*: **orthodox**).

Many verbs in English can be spelt with either *-ize* or *-ise* as their ending; their related nouns are spelt with *-ization* or *-isation*. This dictionary lists the *-z-* form, although both (*eg* **realize/realization** and **realise/realisation**) are acceptable.

Words which are often confused with each other (*eg* **complement** and **compliment**, or **flounder** and **founder**) have a warning note at the end of each entry.

Verbs which change their endings in unusual ways (*eg* **come**), as well as those which double a final consonant (*eg* **trip**), or change a final *-y* to *-i-* (*eg* **try**), are given in full in boxes after the relevant entry. The order for these verb endings is: present tense 3rd person (she *comes*), present participle (*coming*), past tense 3rd person (she *came*). If the past participle is different from the past tense, it is given also (*eg* tread*s*, tread*ing*, trod, trod*den*). All other verbs conform to the pattern: look*s*, look*ing*, look*ed*, and search*es*, search*ing*, search*ed*. Likewise, adjectives which form unusual comparatives and superlatives, or which double a final consonant *etc*, are given in boxes (*eg* **far**, **hot**). Other adjectives simply add *-er* and *-est* to the root form of the word (*eg* tall, tall*er*, tall*est*).

At the end of the book you will find additional information on punctuation, the differences between American and British English, and frequently misspelt words.

Pronunciation Guide

Accented syllables:
In most words of two or more syllables, one syllable is accented, or stressed, more strongly than the other or others. Where pronunciations are given in this dictionary, the accented syllable is shown in italics, *eg* **buffet** /*boo*feh/.

Vowels in accented syllables:

/a/	as in *bat*
/ah/	as in *far*
/ai/	as in *mine*
/aw/	as in *all*
/e/	as in *pet*
/ee/	as in *deer*
/eh/	as in *bare*
/i/	as in *bid*
/o/	as in *got*
/oh/	as in *note*
/oo/	as in *moon*
/ow/	as in *house*
/oy/	as in *boy*
/u/	as in *bud*
/uh/	as in *inter*
/yoo/	as in *pure*

Vowels in unaccented syllables:
These are often shown by a /ə/, *eg* /mə*rang*/. Unaccented /ee/ sounds which occur at the end of a word, or before a /ə/, are shown by /i/, *eg* **ceilidh** /*keh*li/, **asphyxia** /əs*fik*siə/.

Consonants:

b, *d*, *f*, *h*, *j*, *k*, *l*, *m*, *n*, *p*, *r*, *s*, *t*, *v*, *w* and *z* are pronounced as in standard English. The following other symbols are used:

/ch/	as in *cheap*
/dh/	as in *then*
/g/	as in *good*
/ng/	as in *sing*
/sh/	as in *shine*
/th/	as in *thin*
/wh/	as in *where*
/xh/	as in *loch*
/y/	as in *yet*
/zh/	as in *azure*

Additional sounds:

/anh/ and /onh/ are French nasal vowels, as in **timbre** /*tanh*brə/ and **blancmange** /blə*monhzh*/.

Abbreviations used in the Dictionary

abbrev	abbreviation
adj	adjective
adv	adverb
Austral	Australian
cap	capital letter
comp	comparative
conj	conjunction
E	East
eg	for example
esp	especially
etc	and so on, and other things
ie	that is
N	North
orig	originally
prep	preposition
S	South
sing	singular
superl	superlative
TV	television
UK	United Kingdom
US(A)	United States (of America)
W	West

Labels used in the Dictionary

All labels used in the dictionary are given below, except for unabbreviated subject labels (such as *architecture*, *golf* or *music*):

Austral	used in Australian English
biochem	biochemistry
Brit	used generally in British English, not in US or Australian *etc*
comput	computing
derog	derogatory
euphem	euphemism
exclam	exclamation
formal	used mainly in formal English
hist	historical
informal	common and generally acceptable in spoken or informal English
Irish	used in Irish English
maths	mathematics
med	medicine
offensive	a word which is offensive to the person addressed
old	no longer commonly used in modern English
photog	photography
S African	used in South African English
Scot	used in Scottish English
slang	less generally acceptable, even in informal English, than informal
taboo	not generally acceptable, even in informal use
trademark	a word which is registered as a trademark
US	used in US (and often Canadian) English

Index of Word Histories

The following headwords in the dictionary contain additional information about the history or derivation of the word, given in a box at the end of each entry:

A

or **an** *adj* **1** one: *a knock at the* *or* **2** any: *an ant has six legs* **3** in, or for each: *four times a day*

> The form *a* is used before words beginning with a consonant, *eg* knock; *an* is used before words beginning with a vowel, *eg* ant

ardvark *noun* a long-nosed S frican animal which feeds on ter- ites

back *adv*: **taken aback** surprised

bacus *noun* (*plural* **abacuses**) a rame with columns of beads for ounting

bandon *verb* **1** leave, without neaning to return to **2** give up (an dea *etc*) □ *noun* lack of inhibition □ **bandonment** *noun*

> **abandon** *verb* » abandon*s*, abandon*ing*, abandon*ed*

base *verb* humble □ **abasement** *oun*

basheđ *adj* embarrassed, con- used

abate *verb* make or grow less □ **abatement** *noun*

abattoir /abətwahr/ *noun* a (public) slaughter-house

abbess *noun* (*plural* **abbesses**) the female head of an abbey or a convent

abbey *noun* (*plural* **abbeys**) **1** a monastery or convent ruled by an abbot or an abbess **2** the church now or formerly attached to it

abbot *noun* the male head of an abbey

abbreviate *verb* shorten (a word, phrase *etc*)

abbreviation *noun* a shortened form of a word *etc* used instead of the whole word, *eg maths* for *mathematics*

abdicate *verb* give up (a position, *esp* that of king or queen) □ **abdication** *noun*

abdomen *noun* the part of the human body between the chest and the hips □ **abdominal** *adj*

abduct *verb* take away by force or fraud □ **abduction** *noun*

abet *verb* help or encourage to do wrong

> **abet** » abet*s*, abett*ing*, abett*ed*

abeyance *noun*: **in abeyance** undecided; not to be dealt with for the time being

abhor *verb* look on with horror, hate □ **abhorrence** *noun*

> **abhor** » abhor*s*, abhorr*ing*, abhorr*ed*

abhorrent *adj* hateful □ **abhorrently** *adv*

abide *verb* put up with, tolerate □ **abiding** *adj* lasting □ **abide by** keep, act according to

ability *noun* (*plural* **abilities**) **1**

power or means to do something **2** talent

abject *adj* miserable, degraded

ablaze *adj* **1** burning fiercely **2** gleaming like fire

able *adj* **1** having the power or means (to do something) **2** clever □ **ably** *adv*

ablutions *noun plural, formal* washing of the body

abnormal *adj* **1** not normal (in behaviour *etc*) **2** unusual □ **abnormality** *noun* (*plural* **abnormalities**) □ **abnormally** *adv*

aboard *adv* & *prep* on(to) or in(to) (a ship or aeroplane)

abode *noun, formal* a dwelling place

abolish *verb* do away with (*eg* a custom) □ **abolition** *noun* □ **abolitionist** *noun* someone who tries to do away with anything, *esp* slavery

abominable *adj* **1** hateful **2** very bad, terrible □ **the Abominable Snowman** (*also called* **Yeti**) a large animal believed to exist in the Himalayas □ **abominably** *adv*

abominate *verb* hate very much □ **abomination** *noun* **1** great hatred **2** anything hateful

Aboriginal or **Aborigine** a member of the original or native people of Australia □ **Aboriginal** *adj*

abort *verb* **1** of a plan *etc* come to nothing, stay undeveloped **2** remove a foetus to terminate a pregnancy □ **abortion** *noun* the removal of a foetus to terminate a pregnancy □ **abortive** *adj* coming to nothing, useless: *an aborti attempt*

abound *verb* be very plentiful **abounding in** full of, having man

about *prep* **1** around: *look abou you* **2** near (in time, size *etc*): *abou ten o'clock* **3** here and there ir *scattered about the room* □ *adv* around: *stood about waiting* **2** i motion or in action: *running abou* **3** in the opposite direction: *turne about and walked away* □ **about t** on the point of (doing something)

above *prep* **1** over, in a highe position than: *above your head* **2** greater than: *above average* **3** toc good for: *above jealousy* □ *adv* **1** overhead, on high **2** earlier on (in a letter *etc*) □ **above board** *adj* open □ *adv* openly

abrasion *noun* **1** the action of rubbing off **2** a graze on the body

abrasive *adj* **1** able to wear down **2** having a hurtful manner □ *noun* something used for rubbing or polishing □ **abrasively** *adv*

abreast *adv* side by side □ **abreast of** up to date with: *abreast of current affairs*

abridge *verb* shorten (a book, story *etc*) □ **abridgement** or **abridgment** *noun*

abroad *adv* **1** in another country **2** *formal* outside: *witches go abroad after dark*

abrupt *adj* **1** sudden, without warning **2** bad-tempered, short, curt □ **abruptly** *adv*

abscess *noun* (*plural* **abscesses**) a boil or similar collection of pus in the body

bscond *verb* run away secretly: *bsconded with the money*

bsent *adj* away, not present □ **bsence** *noun* the state of being way □ **absentee** *noun* someone ho is absent □ **absently** *adv* □ **bsent-minded** *adj* forgetful □ **bsent yourself** keep away

bsolute *adj* complete, not limited y anything: *absolute power* □ **bsolutely** *adv* completely

bsolve *verb* pardon □ **absolution** *oun* forgiveness, pardon

absorb *verb* **1** soak up (liquid) **2** ake up the whole attention of □ **bsorbed** *adj*

absorbent *adj* able to soak up iquid

absorption *noun* **1** the act of absorbing **2** complete mental concentration

abstain *verb* **1** refuse to cast a vote for or against **2** (with **from**) hold yourself back □ **abstainer** *noun* someone who abstains from something, *esp* from alcoholic drink □ **abstention** *noun*

abstemious *adj* not greedy, sparing in food, drink *etc* □ **abstemiousness** *noun*

abstention *see* **abstain**

abstinence *noun* abstaining from alcohol *etc* □ **abstinent** *adj*

abstract *adj* existing only as an idea, not as a real thing □ *noun* a summary □ **abstraction** *noun*

abstruse *adj* difficult to understand

absurd *adj* clearly wrong; ridiculous □ **absurdity** *noun* (*plural* **absurdities**)

abundance *noun* a plentiful supply □ **abundant** *adj* plentiful □ **abundantly** *adv*

abuse *verb* **1** use wrongly **2** insult or speak unkindly to; treat badly □ *noun* **1** wrongful use **2** insulting language or behaviour □ **abusive** *adj*

abysmal *adj* **1** *informal* very bad; terrible **2** bottomless □ **abysmally** *adv*

abyss *noun* (*plural* **abysses**) a bottomless depth

AC *abbrev* alternating current (*compare with*: **DC**)

a/c *abbrev* account

acacia /ə*keh*shiə/ *noun* a family of thorny shrubs and trees

academic *adj* **1** learned **2** not practical: *purely of academic interest* **3** of a university *etc* □ *noun* a university or college teacher □ **academically** *adv*

academy *noun* (*plural* **academies**) **1** a college for special study or training **2** a society for encouraging science or art **3** in Scotland, a senior school

acanthus *noun* a Mediterranean ornamental shrub

a cappella a style of singing without accompaniment, often with doubling of the voice parts

ACAS *abbrev* Advisory, Conciliation and Arbitration Service

accede *verb*: **accede to** agree to

accelerate *verb* increase in speed □ **acceleration** *noun*

accelerator *noun* a lever or pedal used to increase the speed of a car *etc*

accent *noun* **1** (a mark indicating) stress on a syllable or word **2** a mark used in written French to show the quality of a vowel **3** emphasis: *the accent must be on hard work* **4** the way in which words are pronounced in a particular area *etc*: *a Scottish accent* □ **accentuate** *verb* make more obvious; emphasize

accept *verb* **1** take something offered **2** agree or submit to □ **acceptable** *adj* satisfactory; pleasing □ **acceptance** *noun* the act of accepting

> ⚠Do not confuse with: **except**

access *noun* right or means of approach or entry □ **accession** *noun* a coming to: *accession to the throne*

> ⚠Do not confuse with: **excess**

accessible *adj* easily approached or reached □ **accessibility** *noun*

accessory *noun* (*plural* **accessories**) **1** an item chosen to match or complement dress, *eg* a piece of jewellery, a handbag *etc* **2** a helper, *esp* in crime

accident *noun* **1** an unexpected event causing injury **2** a mishap **3** chance □ **accidental** *adj* happening by chance □ **accidentally** *adv*

acclaim *verb* welcome enthusi astically □ *noun* enthusiastic recep tion: *met with critical acclaim* □ **acclamation** *noun* noisy sign o approval

acclimatize *verb* accustom tc another climate or situation □ **acclimatization** *noun*

accommodate *verb* **1** find room for **2** make suitable **3** oblige; supply (with) □ **accommodating** *adj* obliging □ **accommodation** *noun* lodgings

accompany *verb* **1** go or be with **2** play an instrument (*eg* a piano) while a singer sings *etc* □ **accompaniment** *noun* **1** something that accompanies **2** the music played while a singer sings *etc* □ **accompanist** *noun* someone who plays an accompaniment

> **accompany** » accompan*ies*, accompany*ing*, accompan*ied*

accomplice *noun* someone who helps another person, *esp* to commit a crime

accomplish *verb* **1** complete **2** bring about □ **accomplished** *adj* **1** completed **2** skilled, talented □ **accomplishment** *noun* **1** completion **2** a personal talent or skill

accord *verb* **1** agree (with) **2** give, grant □ *noun* agreement □ **accordance** *noun* agreement □ **accordingly** *adv* therefore □ **according to 1** as told by **2** in relation to: *paid according to your work* □ **of your own accord** of your own free will

accordion *noun* a musical instrument with bellows, a keyboard and metal reeds ▯ **accordionist** *noun* an accordion player

accost *verb* approach and speak to

account *verb* give a reason (for) ▯ *noun* **1** a bill **2** a record of finances **3** a description of events *etc*; an explanation ▯ **accountable** *adj* answerable, responsible ▯ **accountant** a keeper or inspector of accounts ▯ **on account of** because of

accoutrements /ə*koo*trəmənts/ *noun plural* dress and equipment, *esp* military

accredited *adj* having the official power to act

accrue *verb* **1** be given or added to **2** accumulate, collect: *the account accrued no interest* ▯ **accrued** *adj*

accumulate *verb* **1** collect **2** increase ▯ **accumulation** *noun* **1** a collection **2** a mass or pile ▯ **accumulator** *noun* a type of battery used in a car *etc*

accurate *adj* correct, exact ▯ **accuracy** *noun* ▯ **accurately** *adv*

accursed *adj*, *formal* **1** under a curse **2** hateful

accuse *verb* bring a (criminal) charge against ▯ **accusation** a charge brought against anyone ▯ **the accused** the person charged with a crime *etc* ▯ **accuser** *noun*

accustomed *adj* **1** used to: *accustomed to travel* **2** usual

AC/DC *adj*, *slang* bisexual

ace *noun* **1** the one on playing-cards **2** an expert: *a computer ace* **3** *tennis* an unreturned first serve

acetylene *noun* a gas used for giving light and heat

ache *noun* a continuous pain ▯ *verb* be in continuous pain

achieve *verb* **1** get (something) done, accomplish **2** win ▯ **achievement** *noun*

acid *adj* **1** of taste: sharp **2** sarcastic ▯ *noun* a substance containing hydrogen which will dissolve metals (*contrasted with*: **alkali**) ▯ **acidity** *noun* the state of being acid ▯ **acid rain** rain containing sulphur and nitrogen compounds and other pollutants

acidify *verb* make or become acid

> **acidify** » acidifi*es*, acidify*ing*, acidifi*ed*

acknowledge *verb* **1** admit the truth of **2** (write to) say you have received something ▯ **acknowledgement** or **acknowledgment** *noun*

acme *noun* the highest point; perfection

acne *noun* a common skin disease with pimples

acorn *noun* the fruit of the oak tree

acoustic /ə*koo*stik/ *adj* of hearing or sound ▯ **acoustics** *noun* **1** *sing* the study of sound **2** *plural* the characteristics of a room *etc* which affect the hearing of sound in it

acquaint *verb* make (someone) familiar (with) ▯ **acquaintance** *noun* **1** knowledge **2** someone whom you know slightly

acquiesce /akwee*es*/ *verb* (often

with **in**) agree (to) ▢ **acquiescence** *noun* ▢ **acquiescent** *adj*

acquire *verb* obtain, get ▢ **acquired** *adj* gained; not innate or inherited ▢ **acquisition** *noun* **1** the act of getting **2** something got

acquisitive *adj* eager to get ▢ **acquisitiveness** *noun*

acquit *verb* declare (someone) innocent of a crime ▢ **acquittal** *noun* a legal judgement of 'not guilty' ▢ **acquit yourself well** do well, be successful ▢ **acquit yourself badly** do badly, be unsuccessful

> **acquit** » acquit*s*, acquitt*ing*, acquitt*ed*

acre *noun* a land measure containing 4840 square yards or about 4000 square metres ▢ **acreage** *noun* the number of acres in a piece of land

acrid *adj* harsh, bitter

acrimony *noun* bitterness of feeling or speech ▢ **acrimonious** *adj*

acrobat *noun* someone who performs gymnastic feats, tightrope-walking *etc* ▢ **acrobatic** *adj*

acronym *noun* a word formed from the initial letters of other words, *eg radar* for *ra*dio *d*etecting *a*nd *r*anging

across *adv* & *prep* to or at the other side (of): *swam across the river/ winked at him across the table* ▢ **across the board** involving everyone or everything; sweeping

acrostic *noun* a poem *etc* in which the first or last letters of each line, taken in order, spell a word or words

acrylic *noun* a synthetically produced fibre ▢ *adj* made with this material

act *verb* **1** do something **2** behave in a particular way: *act foolishly* **3** play a dramatic role on stage, film *etc* ▢ *noun* **1** something done **2** a government law **3** a section of a play

action *noun* **1** a deed, an act **2** a law case **3** dramatic events portrayed in a film, play *etc* ▢ **actionable** *adj* likely to cause a law case: *actionable statement*

active *adj* **1** busy; lively **2** able to perform physical tasks **3** *grammar* describing the form of a verb in which the subject performs the action of the verb, *eg* 'the dog bit the postman' ▢ **activate** *verb* start (something) working ▢ **activity** *noun* (*plural* **activities**)

actor *noun* someone who acts a part in a play or film

actress *noun* (*plural* **actresses**) a female actor

actual *adj* real, existing in fact ▢ **actuality** *noun* ▢ **actually** *adv* really

actuary *noun* (*plural* **actuaries**) someone who works out the price of insurance ▢ **actuarial** *adj*

actuate *verb* **1** put into action **2** drive or urge on

acumen *noun* quickness of understanding

acupressure *noun* a method of treating illness by applying pressure to certain key points on the body

acupuncture *noun* a method of treating illness by piercing the skin with needles ▯ **acupuncturist** *noun* a practitioner of acupuncture

acute *adj* **1** quick at understanding **2** of a disease: severe, but not lasting very long **3** of an angle: less than a right angle (*contrasted with*: **obtuse**) ▯ **acute accent** a forward-leaning stroke (´) placed over letters in some languages to show their pronunciation ▯ **acuteness** *noun*

AD *abbrev* in the year of our Lord, *eg* AD1900 (from Latin *anno Domini*)

ad *noun, informal* an advertisement

adage *noun* an old saying, a proverb

adagio *noun* a slow-paced piece of music

adamant *adj* unwilling to give way ▯ **adamantly** *adv*

Adam's apple the natural lump which sticks out from the throat

adapt *verb* make suitable; alter so as to fit ▯ **adaptable** *adj* easily altered to suit new conditions ▯ **adaptation** *noun*

adaptor *noun* a device allowing an electrical plug to be used in a socket for which it was not designed, or several plugs to be used on the same socket

add *verb* **1** make one thing join another to give a sum total or whole **2** mix in: *add water to the dough* **3** say further ▯ **addition** *noun* **1** the act of adding **2** something added ▯ **additional** *adj* ▯ **additive** *noun* a chemical *etc* added to another substance

addendum *noun* (*plural* **addenda**) something added

adder *noun* the common name of the viper, a poisonous snake

addict *noun* someone who is dependent on something, often on a drug or alcohol, either physically or mentally ▯ **addictive** *adj* creating dependence, habit-forming ▯ **addicted to** dependent on

addition and **additive** *see* **add**

address *verb* **1** speak to **2** write the address on (a letter *etc*) ▯ *noun* (*plural* **addresses**) **1** the name of the house, street, and town where someone lives *etc* **2** speech

adenoids *noun plural* swellings at the back of the nose which hinder breathing

adept *adj* very skilful

adequate *adj* sufficient, enough ▯ **adequacy** *noun* ▯ **adequately** *adv*

adhere *verb* **1** stick (to) **2** give support (to) or be loyal (to) ▯ **adherence** *noun*

adherent *adj* sticking (to) ▯ *noun* a follower or supporter of a cause *etc*

adhesion *noun* the act of sticking (to)

adhesive *adj* sticky, gummed ▯ *noun* something which makes things stick to each other

ad hoc *adj* set up for a particular purpose only

ad infinitum *adv* for ever

adjacent *adj* (with **to**) lying next to

adjective *noun* a word which tells

something about a noun, *eg* 'the *black* cat,' 'times are *hard*' ▯ **adjectival** *adj*

adjoin *verb* be joined to ▯ **adjoining** *adj*

adjourn *verb* **1** stop (a meeting *etc*) with the intention of continuing it at another time or place **2** (with **to**) go to another place: *adjourn to the lounge* ▯ **adjournment** *noun*

adjudicate *verb* **1** give a judgement on (a dispute *etc*) **2** act as a judge at a competition ▯ **adjudication** *noun* ▯ **adjudicator** someone who adjudicates

adjunct *noun* something joined or added

adjust *verb* rearrange or alter to suit the circumstances ▯ **adjustable** *adj* ▯ **adjustment**

adjutant *noun* a military officer who assists a commanding officer

ad-lib *verb* speak without plan or preparation ▯ *adj* without preparation

> **ad-lib** *verb* » ad-lib*s*, ad-libb*ing*, ad-libb*ed*

administer *verb* **1** manage or govern **2** carry out (the law *etc*) **3** give (help, medicine *etc*)

administrate *verb* manage or govern ▯ **administration** *noun* **1** management **2** (the body that carries on) the government of a country *etc* ▯ **administrative** *adj* ▯ **administrator** *noun* someone involved in the administration of a country *etc*

admiral *noun* the commander of a navy ▯ **admiralty** *noun* the government office which manages naval affairs

admire *verb* **1** think very highly of **2** look at with pleasure ▯ **admirable** *adj* worthy of being admired ▯ **admirably** *adv* ▯ **admiration** *noun* ▯ **admirer** *noun*

admit *verb* **1** let in **2** acknowledge the truth of, confess **3** (with **of**) leave room for, allow: *admits of no other explanation* ▯ **admissible** *adj* allowable ▯ **admission** *noun* **1** (the price of) being let in **2** anything admitted ▯ **admittance** *noun* the right or permission to enter

> **admit** » admit*s*, admitt*ing*, admitt*ed*

admonish *verb* **1** warn **2** rebuke, scold ▯ **admonition** *noun* a warning ▯ **admonitory** *adj*

ad nauseam *adv* to a tiresome degree

ado *noun* trouble, fuss

adobe /ə*doh*bi/ *noun* clay used for buildings

adolescent *noun* someone between a child and an adult in age ▯ *adj* of this age ▯ **adolescence** *noun*

adopt *verb* take as your own (*esp* a child of other parents) ▯ **adoption** *noun* ▯ **adoptive** *adj* adopted, taken as your own: *her adoptive country*

adore *verb* **1** love very much **2** worship ▯ **adorable** *adj* very loveable ▯ **adorably** *adv* ▯ **adoration** *noun* **1** worship **2** great love

adorn *verb* decorate (with ornaments *etc*) □ **adornment** *noun* ornament

adrenaline *noun* a hormone produced in response to fear, anger *etc*, preparing the body for quick action

adrift *adv* drifting, floating

adroit *adj* skilful

adulation *noun* great flattery □ **adulatory** *adj*

adult *adj* grown up □ *noun* a grown-up person

adulterate *verb* make impure by adding something else □ **adulteration** *noun*

adultery *noun* unfaithfulness to a husband or wife □ **adulterer** or **adulteress** *noun*

advance *verb* **1** go forward **2** put forward (a plan *etc*) **3** help the progress of **4** pay before the usual or agreed time □ *noun* **1** movement forward **2** improvement **3** a loan of money □ **advanced** *adj* well forward in progress □ **advancement** *noun* progress □ **in advance** beforehand

advantage *noun* **1** a better position, superiority **2** gain or benefit □ *verb* help, benefit □ **advantageous** *adj* profitable; helpful □ **take advantage of** make use of (a situation, person *etc*) in such a way as to benefit yourself

advent *noun* **1** coming, arrival: *before the advent of television* **2** (**Advent**) in the Christian church, the four weeks before Christmas

adventitious *adj* happening by chance □ **adventitiously** *adv*

adventure *noun* a bold or exciting undertaking or experience

adventurer *noun* **1** someone who takes risks, *esp* in the hope of making a lot of money **2** a mercenary soldier

adventurous *adj* taking risks, liking adventure □ **adventurously** *adv* □ **adventurousness** *noun*

adverb *noun* a word which gives a more definite meaning to a verb, adjective, or other adverb, *eg* 'eat *slowly*,' '*extremely* hard,' '*very* carefully' □ **adverbial** *adj* of or like an adverb

adversary *noun* (*plural* **adversaries**) an enemy; an opponent

adverse *adj* unfavourable: *adverse criticism* □ **adversity** *noun* (*plural* **adversities**) misfortune

advert *noun, informal* an advertisement

advertise *verb* **1** make known to the public **2** stress the good points of (a product for sale)

advertisement *noun* a photograph, short film *etc* intended to persuade the public to buy a particular product

advice *noun* **1** something said as a help to someone trying to make a decision *etc* **2** a formal notice

⚠Do not confuse with: **advise**

advisable *adj* wise, sensible □ **advisability** *noun* □ **advisably** *adv*

advise *verb* **1** give advice to **2** recommend (an action *etc*) □

adviser *noun* ▫ **advisory** *adj* advice-giving: *advisory body*

⚠Do not confuse with: **advice**

advocate *noun* **1** someone who pleads for another **2** in Scotland, a court lawyer ▫ *verb* **1** plead or argue for **2** recommend

advt *abbrev* advertisement

adze or *US* **adz** *noun* a kind of axe used by a carpenter

adzuki or **azuki** *noun* a kind of kidney bean grown in China and Japan

aegis /eejis/ *noun* protection; patronage

aeon or **eon** /eeon/ *noun* a very long period of time, an age

aerate *verb* put air or another gas into (a liquid)

aerial *adj* **1** of, in or from the air: *aerial photography* **2** placed high up or overhead: *aerial railway* ▫ *noun* a wire or rod (or a set of these) by means of which radio or television signals are received or sent

aerobatics *noun plural* stunts performed by an aircraft

aerobics *noun sing* a system of rhythmic physical exercise which aims to strengthen the heart and lungs by increasing the body's oxygen consumption

aerodrome *noun* a landing and maintenance station for aircraft

aeronautics *noun sing* the science or art of navigation in the air

aeroplane or *US* **airplane** *noun* an engine-powered flying machine with fixed wings

aerosol *noun* a container of liquid and gas under pressure, from which the liquid is squirted as a mist

aesthetic *adj* **1** of beauty or its appreciation **2** artistic, pleasing to the eye ▫ **aesthetically** *adv*

affable *adj* pleasant, easy to speak to ▫ **affability** *noun* ▫ **affably** *adv*

affair *noun* **1** events *etc* connected with one person or thing: *the Watergate affair* **2** (**affairs**) personal concerns, transactions *etc*: *his affairs seemed to be in order* **3** business, concern: *that's not your affair* **4** a love affair

affect *verb* **1** act upon **2** have an effect on; move the feelings of **3** pretend to feel *etc* ▫ **affectation** *noun* pretence ▫ **affected** *adj* **1** moved in your feelings **2** not natural, sham ▫ **affecting** *adj* moving the feelings

⚠Do not confuse with: **effect**

affection *noun* a strong liking ▫ **affectionate** *adj* loving ▫ **affectionately** *adv*

affidavit *noun, law* a written statement made on oath

affiliated *adj* (with **with** or **to**) connected, attached ▫ **affiliation** *noun*

affinity *noun* (*plural* **affinities**) a close likeness or agreement

affirm *verb* state firmly ▫ **affirmation** *noun* a firm statement ▫ **affirmative** *adj* saying 'yes'

affix *verb* attach to

afflict *verb* give continued pain or

distress to ▯ **afflicted** *adj* suffering ▯ **affliction** *noun* great suffering, misery

affluent *adj* wealthy ▯ *noun* a stream flowing into a river or lake ▯ **affluence** *noun* wealth

afford *verb* **1** be able to pay for **2** give, yield

afforest *verb* cover land with forest ▯ **afforestation** *noun*

affray *noun* a fight, a brawl

affront *verb* insult openly ▯ *noun* an insult

aflatoxin *noun* a toxin produced in foodstuffs by a species of mould

afloat *adv* & *adj* floating

afoot *adv* happening or about to happen: *I could tell something was afoot*

aforesaid *adj* said or named before: *the aforesaid person*

afraid *adj* **1** struck with fear **2** *informal* sorry to have to admit that: *I'm afraid there are no tickets left*

afresh *adv* once again, anew

African-American *noun* an American of Black African descent

aft *adv* near or towards the stern of a vessel

after *prep* **1** later in time than: *after dinner* **2** following: *arrived one after another*; *day after day* **3** in memory or honour of: *named after his father* **4** in pursuit of: *run after the bus* **5** about: *asked after her health* **6** despite: *after all my efforts, it still didn't work* **7** in the style of: *after Rubens* ▯ *adv* later in time or place: *we left soon after* ▯ *conj* later than the time when: *after she arrived, things improved* ▯ **after(-)** *prefix* later in time or place: *in after years/ aftertaste/ afterthought* ▯ **after all 1** all things considered: *after all, he's still young* **2** despite everything said or done before: *I went after all*

afterbirth *noun* the placenta and membranes expelled from the uterus after giving birth

aftermath *noun* the bad results of something: *the aftermath of the election*

> Originally a second crop coming after the main harvest

afternoon *noun* the time between noon and evening ▯ *adj* taking place in the afternoon

aftershave *noun* a lotion used on the face after shaving

afterthought *noun* a later thought

afterwards *adv* later

again *adv* **1** once more: *say that again* **2** in or into the original state, place *etc*: *there and back again* **3** on the other hand: *again, I might be wrong* **4** *informal* at another later time: *see you again*

against *prep* **1** in opposition to: *against the law/ fight against injustice* **2** in the opposite direction to: *against the wind* **3** on a background of: *against the sky* **4** close to, touching: *lean against the wall* **5** as protection from: *guard against infection*

agate *noun* a kind of precious stone

age *noun* **1** a long period of time **2** the time someone or something has lived or existed □ *verb* grow or make visibly older □ **aged** *adj* **1** old **2** of the age of: *aged five* □ **of age** legally an adult

> **age** *verb* » ag*es*, age*ing* or ag*ing*, ag*ed*

ageism *noun* discrimination on grounds of age □ **ageist** *adj* discriminating on grounds of age

agency *noun* (*plural* **agencies**) **1** the office or business of an agent **2** action, means by which something is done

agenda *noun* a list of things to be done, *esp* at a meeting

agent *noun* **1** someone or something that acts **2** someone who acts for another **3** a spy

agent provocateur someone who deliberately incites others to violence, illegal action *etc*

aggrandize *verb* make greater □ **aggrandizement** *noun*

aggravate *verb* **1** make worse **2** *informal* annoy □ **aggravating** *adj* □ **aggravation** *noun*

aggregate *noun* a total

aggressive *adj* **1** ready to attack first **2** quarrelsome □ **aggression** *noun* □ **aggressively** *adv* □ **aggressor** *noun*

aggrieved *adj* hurt, upset

aggro /agroh/ *noun, informal* aggression, hostility

aghast *adj* struck with horror

agile *adj* active, nimble □ **agility** *noun*

agitate *verb* **1** stir up **2** excite, disturb □ **agitation** *noun* □ **agitator** *noun* someone who stirs up others

agitprop *noun* political propaganda, *esp* pro-communist

agm or **AGM** *abbrev* annual general meeting

agnostic *noun* someone who believes it is impossible to know whether God exists or not □ **agnosticism** *noun*

ago *adv* in the past: *that happened five years ago*

agog *adj* eager, excited

agony *noun* (*plural* **agonies**) great pain □ **agonized** *adj* showing great pain □ **agonizing** *adj* causing great pain □ **agony aunt** someone who gives advice in an agony column □ **agony column** a regular column in a newspaper or magazine in which readers submit and receive advice about personal problems

agoraphobia *noun* great fear of open spaces □ **agoraphobic** *noun & adj* (someone) suffering from agoraphobia

agrarian *adj* of farmland or farming

agree *verb* **1** be alike in opinions, decisions *etc* **2** say that you will do something, consent □ **agreeable** *adj* **1** pleasant **2** ready to agree □ **agreeably** *adv* □ **agreement** *noun* **1** likeness (*esp* of opinions) **2** a written statement making a bargain □ **agree with 1** suit **2** cause no problems in digestion: *the fish didn't agree with me*

agriculture *noun* the cultivation

of the land, farming ◇ **agricultural** *adj* ◇ **agriculturalist** *noun*

aground *adj* & *adv* stuck on the bottom of the sea or a river: *run aground*

ague /*ehgyoo*/ *noun, old* a fever

ahead *adv* in front; in advance: *finishing ahead of time*

AI *abbrev* **1** artificial intelligence **2** artificial insemination

aid *verb* help, assist ◇ *noun* help

aide-de-camp /ed-də-*konhp*/ *noun* (*plural* **aides-de-camp**) an officer who carries messages to and from a general on the field

aide-memoire *noun* something to help you remember; a reminder

AIDS or **Aids** *abbrev* Acquired Immune Deficiency Syndrome

aikido *noun* a Japanese martial art using pressure against the joints

ail *verb* **1** be ill **2** trouble

aileron *noun* a hinged flap on the back edge of an aeroplane's wing, used to control balance

ailment *noun* a trouble, disease

aim *verb* **1** point at (*esp* with a gun) **2** intend to do **3** have as your purpose ◇ *noun* **1** the act of, or skill in, aiming **2** the point aimed at, goal, intention ◇ **aimless** *adj* without aim or purpose ◇ **aimlessly** *adv*

air *noun* **1** the mixture of gases (mainly oxygen and nitrogen) which we breathe, the atmosphere **2** a light breeze **3** fresh air **4** space overhead **5** a tune **6** the look or manner (of a person) ◇ *verb* **1** expose to the air **2** make known (an opinion *etc*) ◇ **airbag** *noun* a bag which automatically inflates inside a car on impact to protect the driver from injury ◇ **airbed** *noun* a mattress which can be inflated ◇ **airborne** *adj* in the air, flying ◇ **air-conditioned** *adj* equipped with a system for filtering and controlling the temperature of the air ◇ **air force** the branch of the armed forces using aircraft ◇ **air-gun** *noun* a gun worked by means of compressed air ◇ **airing** *noun* the act of exposing to the air ◇ **airless** *adj* ◇ **airlock** *noun* **1** a bubble in a pipe obstructing the flow of a liquid **2** a compartment with two doors for entering and leaving an airtight spaceship *etc* ◇ **air-raid** *noun* an attack by aeroplanes ◇ **airship** *noun* a large balloon which can be steered and driven ◇ **airstream** *noun* a flow of air ◇ **airtight** *adj* made so that air cannot pass in or out ◇ **on the air** broadcasting

aircraft *noun* (*plural* **aircraft**) a flying machine

airplane *US spelling* of **aeroplane**

airport *noun* a place where aircraft land and take off, with buildings for customs, waiting-rooms *etc*

airy *adj* **1** of or like the air **2** well supplied with fresh air **3** light-hearted ◇ **airily** *adv*

aisle /*ail*/ *noun* **1** the side part of a church **2** a passage between seats in a theatre *etc*

ajar *adv* partly open: *leave the door ajar*

aka *abbrev* also known as: *Stevens, aka The Fly*

akimbo *adv* with hand on hip and elbow bent outward

From an Old Norse term meaning 'bowed' or 'curved'

akin *adj* similar

à la *prep* in the style of

à la carte *adj* & *adv* **1** according to the menu **2** each dish chosen and priced separately

alack *exclam*, *old* alas

alacrity *noun* briskness, cheerful readiness

à la mode *adj* & *adv* **1** fashionable **2** *US* served with ice-cream: *apple pie à la mode*

alarm *noun* **1** sudden fear **2** something which rouses to action or gives warning of danger ▫ *verb* frighten ▫ **alarming** *adj* ▫ **alarmist** someone who frightens others needlessly

alas! *exclam* a cry showing grief

albatross *noun* (*plural* **albatrosses**) a type of large sea-bird

albino *noun* (*plural* **albinos**) someone or an animal with no natural colour in their skin, hair and eyes

album *noun* **1** a book with blank pages for holding photographs, stamps *etc* **2** a long-playing record **3** recordings issued under one title

albumen *noun* the white of eggs

alchemy *noun* an early form of chemistry aimed at changing other metals into gold ▫ **alchemist** *noun* someone who practised alchemy

alcohol *noun* the pure spirit in strong drinks ▫ **alcoholic** *adj* of or containing alcohol ▫ *noun* someone addicted to alcohol ▫ **alcoholism** *noun* addiction to alcohol

alcove *noun* a recess in a room's wall

al dente *adj* & *adv* cooked so as to retain some firmness in texture

alder *noun* a type of tree which grows beside ponds and rivers

alderman *noun* **1** *hist* a councillor next in rank to the mayor of a town *etc* **2** *US* a member of the governing body of a city

ale *noun* a drink made from malt, hops *etc*

alert *noun* signal to be ready for action ▫ *verb* make alert, warn ▫ *adj* **1** watchful **2** quick-thinking ▫ **on the alert** on the watch (for)

alfalfa *noun* a kind of grass, often used for animal fodder (*also called*: **lucerne**

alfresco *adj* & *adv* in the open air

algae /*al*gee/ or /*al*jee/ *noun* a group of simple plants which includes seaweed

algebra *noun* a method of counting, using letters and signs

algorithm *noun*

alias *adv* also known as: *Mitchell alias Grassic Gibbon* ▫ *noun* (*plural* **aliases**) a false name

alibi *noun* **1** the plea that someone charged with a crime was elsewhere when it was done **2** the state or fact of being elsewhere when a crime was committed

lien *adj* foreign □ *noun* a foreigner **alienate** *verb* make strange or nfriendly □ **alien to** not in keeping vith: *alien to her nature*

light *verb* **1** climb *etc* down **2** ettle, land □ *adj* & *adv* on fire, urning

> **alight** *verb* » alight*s*, alight*ing*, alight*ed*

align /əlain/ *verb* **1** set in line **2** ake sides in an argument *etc* □ **alignment** *noun* arrangement in a ine

alike *adj* like one another, similar □ *adv* in the same way, similarly

alimentary *adj* of food □ **alimentary canal** the passage through the body which begins at the mouth

alimony *noun* an allowance paid by a husband to his wife, or a wife to her husband, to provide support when they are legally separated

alive *adj* **1** living **2** full of activity □ **alive to** aware of

alkali *noun* a substance such as soda or potash (*contrasted with*: **acid**) □ **alkaline** *adj*

all *adj* & *pronoun* **1** every one (of): *we are all invited/ all letters will be answered* **2** the whole (of): *painted all the house* □ *adv* wholly, completely: *dressed all in red* □ **all-rounder** *noun* someone skilled in many kinds of work, sport *etc* □ **all in 1** with everything included: *all-in price* **2** *informal* exhausted □ **all-in wrestling** wrestling in which no holds are against the rules □ **all over 1** over the whole of **2** everywhere **3** finished, ended

Allah *noun* in Islam, God

allay *verb* **1** make less, relieve: *tried to allay my fears* **2** calm

allege *verb* say without proof □ **allegation** *noun*

allegiance *noun* loyalty

allegory *noun* (*plural* **allegories**) a story or fable which deals with a subject in a way which is meant to suggest a deeper, more serious subject □ **allegorical** *adj*

allergen *noun* a substance which causes an allergic reaction

allergy *noun* (*plural* **allergies**) abnormal sensitiveness of the body to something □ **allergic** *adj*

alleviate *verb* make lighter, lessen □ **alleviation** *noun*

alley *noun* (*plural* **alleys**) **1** a narrow passage or lane **2** an enclosure for bowls or skittles

alliance *see* **ally**

alligator *noun* a large reptile like a crocodile

alliteration *noun* the repetition of the same sound at the beginning of two or more words close together, *eg* 'round and round the ragged road' □ **alliterative** *adj*

allocate *verb* give to each a share □ **allocation** *noun*

allopathic *adj* of medicine: conventional, treating disease with drugs which have an opposite effect on the body (*contrasted with*: **homeopathic**)

allot *verb* give each person a share of, distribute □ **allotment** *noun* **1** the act of distributing **2** a small plot of ground for growing vegetables *etc*

allot » allot*s*, allott*ing*, allott*ed*

allow *verb* **1** let (someone do something) **2** (with **for**) take into consideration (in sums, plans *etc*) **3** admit, confess **4** give, *esp* at regular intervals: *she allows him £40 a week* □ **allowable** *adj*

allowance *noun* a fixed sum or amount given regularly □ **make allowances for** treat differently because of taking into consideration special circumstances *etc*

alloy *noun* a mixture of two or more metals

allude to *verb* mention in passing

⚠Do not confuse with: **elude**

allure *verb* tempt, draw on by promises *etc* □ **allurement** *noun* □ **alluring** *adj*

allusion *noun* an indirect reference

⚠Do not confuse with: **delusion** and **illusion**

allusive *adj* referring indirectly, hinting □ **allusively** *adv*

⚠Do not confuse with: **elusive** and **illusive**

alluvium *noun* (*plural* **alluvia**) earth, sand *etc* brought down and left by rivers in flood □ **alluvial** *adj*

ally *verb* join yourself to by treaty *etc* □ *noun* (*plural* **allies**) someone in alliance with another; a friend □ **alliance** *noun* a joining together of two people, nations *etc*, for a common cause □ **allied** *adj*

ally *verb* » all*ies*, ally*ing*, all*ied*

alma mater someone's former university or school

almanac *noun* a calendar for any year, with information about the phases of the moon *etc*

almighty *adj* having much power □ **the Almighty** God

almond *noun* the kernel of the fruit of the almond-tree

almost *adv* very nearly but not quite: *almost five years old/ almost home*

alms *noun* gifts to the poor

aloe /aloh/ *noun* a South African plant of the lily family

aloft *adv* **1** on high **2** upward

alone *adj* not accompanied by others, solitary: *alone in the house* □ *adv* **1** only, without anything else: *that alone is bad enough* **2** not accompanied by others: *do you live alone?* □ **leave alone** let be, leave undisturbed

along *prep* over the length of: *walk along the road* □ *adv* onward: *come along!* □ **alongside** *prep* beside □ *adv* near a ship's side □ **along with** together with

aloof *adj* & *adv* **1** at a distance, apart **2** showing no interest in others □ **aloofness** *noun*

aloud *adv* so as to be heard

alpha *noun* the first letter of the Greek alphabet □ **alpha test** *comput* an initial test of software during development (*compare with*: **beta test**)

alphabet *noun* letters of a language given in a fixed order ▯ **alphabetic** or **alphabetical** *adj* in the order of the letters of the alphabet ▯ **alphabetically** *adv*

alphasort *verb* sort by computer into alphabetical order

alpine *adj* of the Alps or other high mountains

already *adv* **1** before this or that time: *I've already done that* **2** now, before the expected time: *you can't have finished already*

alsatian *noun* a German shepherd dog

also *adv* in addition, besides, too: *I also need to buy milk* ▯ **also-ran** *noun* someone or something that competed (as in a race) but was not among the winners

altar *noun* **1** a raised place for offerings to a god **2** in Christian churches, the communion table

alter *verb* change ▯ **alteration** *noun*

altercation *noun* an argument or quarrel

alter ego 1 a second self **2** a trusted friend, a confidant(e)

alternate *verb* of two things: do or happen in turn ▯ *adj* happening *etc* in turns ▯ **alternately** *adv* ▯ **alternation** *noun*

> ⚠Do not confuse: **alternate** and **alternative**

alternative *adj* offering a second possibility: *an alternative solution* ▯ *noun* a second possibility, a different course of action: *I had no alternative but to agree*

although *conj* though, in spite of the fact that

altimeter *noun* an instrument for measuring height above sea level

altitude *noun* height above sea level

alto *noun* (*plural* **altos**), *music* **1** the male voice of the highest pitch **2** the female voice of lowest pitch

> An alternative term for the female *alto* voice is **contralto**

altogether *adv* **1** considering everything, in all: *there were 20 of us altogether* **2** completely: *not altogether satisfied*

altruism *noun* unselfish concern for the good of others ▯ **altruistic** *adj* ▯ **altruistically** *adv*

aluminium or *US* **aluminum** *noun* an element, a very light metal

alumnus *noun* (*plural* **alumni**) a former student or pupil

always *adv* **1** for ever: *he'll always remember this day* **2** every time: *she always gets it wrong*

AM *abbrev* amplitude modulation (*compare with*: **FM**)

am *abbrev* before noon (from Latin *ante meridiem*)

am *see* **be**

amalgam *noun* a mixture (*esp* of metals)

amalgamate *verb* **1** join together, combine **2** mix ▯ **amalgamation** *noun*

amanuensis *noun* an assistant to an author

amaretto *noun* an almond-flavoured liqueur

amass *verb* collect in large quantity

amateur *noun* someone who takes part in a thing for the love of it, not for money (*contrasted with*: **professional)**

amateurish *adj* not done properly; not skilful □ **amateurishly** *adv*

amaze *verb* surprise greatly □ **amazement** *noun* □ **amazing** *adj* □ **amazingly** *adv*

Amazon *noun* **1** one of a nation of mythological warrior women **2** a very strong or manlike woman

ambassador *noun* **1** a government minister sent to look after the interests of one country in another country **2** a representative

amber *noun* a hard yellowish fossil resin used in making jewellery □ *adj* **1** made of amber **2** of the colour of amber

ambidextrous *adj* able to use both hands with equal skill □ **ambidexterity** *noun*

ambience *noun* environment, atmosphere □ **ambient** *adj*

ambiguity *noun* (*plural* **ambiguities**) uncertainty in meaning

ambiguous *adj* **1** having two possible meanings **2** not clear □ **ambiguously** *adv*

> ⚠Do not confuse with: **ambivalent**

ambition *noun* the desire for success, power, fame *etc* □ **ambitious** *adj* □ **ambitiously** *adv*

ambivalent *adj* having two contrasting attitudes towards something □ **ambivalence** *noun* □ **ambivalently** *adv*

> ⚠Do not confuse with: **ambiguous**

amble *verb* walk without hurrying □ *noun* an unhurried walk

ambrosia *noun* the mythological food of the gods, which gave eternal youth and beauty

ambulance *noun* a vehicle for carrying the sick or injured

ambush *noun* (*plural* **ambushes**) **1** the act of lying hidden in order to make a surprise attack **2** the people hidden in this way **3** their place of hiding □ *verb* attack suddenly from a position of hiding

amenable *adj* open to advice or suggestion □ **amenably** *adv*

amend *verb* **1** correct, improve **2** alter slightly □ **amendment** *noun* a change, often in something written □ **make amends** make up for having done wrong

> ⚠Do not confuse with: **emend**

amenity *noun* (*plural* **amenities**) a pleasant or convenient feature of a place *etc*

amethyst *noun* a precious stone of a bluish-violet colour

amiable *adj* likeable; friendly □ **amiability** *noun* □ **amiably** *adv*

amicable *adj* friendly □ **amicably** *adv*

amid or **amidst** *prep* in the middle of, among: *staying calm amidst all the confusion*

amiss *adv* wrongly; badly

amity *noun, formal* friendship

ammonia *noun* a strong-smelling gas made of hydrogen and nitrogen

ammunition *noun* gunpowder, shot, bullets, bombs *etc*

amnesia *noun* loss of memory ▫ **amnesiac** *noun* & *adj* (someone) suffering from amnesia

amnesty *noun* (*plural* **amnesties**) a general pardon of wrongdoers

amniocentesis *noun, med* the insertion of a needle into the uterus of a pregnant woman to withdraw a sample of fluid for testing

amoeba /əmeebə/ *noun* (*plural* **amoebas** or **amoebae**) a very simple form of animal life found in ponds *etc*

amok or **amuck** *adv*: **run amok** go mad and do a lot of damage, run riot

> From a Malay word meaning 'fighting frenziedly'

among or **amongst** *prep* **1** in the midst or in the middle of: *among friends* **2** in shares, in parts: *divide amongst yourselves* **3** in the group of: *among all her novels, this is the best*

amontillado *noun* a light medium-dry sherry

amoral *adj* incapable of distinguishing between right and wrong ▫ **amorality** *noun* ▫ **amorally** *adv*

> ⚠Do not confuse with: **immoral**

amorous *adj* loving; ready or inclined to love ▫ **amorously** *adv*

amount *noun* **1** total, sum **2** a quantity ▫ **amount to** add up to

amp *noun* **1** an ampère **2** *informal* an amplifier

ampère *noun* the standard unit of electric current

ampersand *noun* the character (&) representing *and*

> From phrase *and per se and*, 'and by itself and'

amphetamine *noun* a type of drug used as a stimulant

amphibian *noun* **1** an animal that lives on land and in water **2** a vehicle for use on land and in water ▫ *adj* living on land and water ▫ **amphibious** *adj* amphibian

amphitheatre *noun* a theatre with seats surrounding a central arena

ample *adj* **1** plenty of **2** large enough

amplify *verb* **1** make louder **2** make more pronounced ▫ **amplification** *noun* ▫ **amplifier** *noun* an electrical device for increasing loudness

> **amplify** » amplifi*es*, amplify*ing*, amplifi*ed*

amplitude *noun* **1** largeness **2** size

ampoule *noun* a small glass container of medicine for injection

amputate *verb* cut off (*esp* a human limb) ▫ **amputation** *noun* ▫

amputee *noun* someone who has had a limb amputated

amuck *another spelling* of **amok**

amuse *verb* **1** make to laugh **2** give pleasure to ▫ **amusement** *noun* ▫ **amusing** *adj* **1** funny **2** giving pleasure

an *see* **a**

anabolic steroids steroids used to increase the build-up of body tissue, *esp* muscle

anachronism *noun* the mention of something which did not exist or was not yet invented at the time spoken about ▫ **anachronistic** *adj*

anaconda *noun* a large South American water snake

anaemia or *US* **anemia** *noun* a shortage of red cells in the blood

anaemic *adj* **1** suffering from anaemia **2** pale or ill-looking

anaerobic *adj* not requiring oxygen to live

anaesthesia or *US* **anesthesia** *noun* loss of feeling or sensation

anaesthetic or *US* **anesthetic** *noun* a substance which produces lack of feeling for a time in a part of the body, or which makes someone unconscious ▫ **anaesthetist** *noun* a doctor trained to administer anaesthetics

anagram *noun* a word or sentence formed by reordering the letters of another word or sentence, *eg veil* is an anagram of *evil*

anal *adj* of the anus

analgesic *adj* causing insensibility to pain

analogous *adj* similar, alike in some way ▫ **analogously** *adv*

analogy *noun* (*plural* **analogies**) a likeness, resemblance in certain ways

analyse or *US* **analyze** *verb* **1** break down, separate into parts **2** examine in detail

analysis *noun* (*plural* **analyses**) **1** a breaking up of a thing into its parts **2** a detailed examination (of something)

analyst *noun* **1** someone who analyses **2** a psychiatrist or psychologist

analyze *US spelling* of **analyse**

anarchy *noun* **1** lack or absence of government **2** disorder or confusion ▫ **anarchic** or **anarchical** *adj* ▫ **anarchist** *noun* someone who advocates anarchy

anathema *noun* **1** a curse **2** a hated person or thing: *opera is anathema to him*

anatomy *noun* **1** the study of the parts of the body **2** the body ▫ **anatomist** *noun*

ancestor *noun* someone from whom someone is descended by birth; a forefather ▫ **ancestral** *adj* ▫ **ancestry** *noun* line of ancestors

anchor *noun* a heavy piece of iron, with hooked ends, for holding a ship fast to the bed of the sea *etc* ▫ *verb* **1** fix by anchor **2** let down the anchor ▫ **anchorman, anchorwoman** *noun* the main presenter of a television news programme *etc* ▫ **cast anchor** let down the anchor ▫ **weigh anchor** pull up the anchor

anchorage *noun* a place where a ship can anchor

anchorite *noun* a hermit, a recluse

anchovy *noun* (*plural* **anchovies**) a type of small fish of the herring family

ancien régime the old order, the previous arrangement

ancient *adj* **1** very old **2** of times long past

ancillary *adj* serving or supporting something more important

and *conj* **1** joining two statements, pieces of information *etc*: *black and white film/ add milk and stir* **2** in addition to: *2 and 2 make 4*

android *noun* a robot in human form

anecdote *noun* a short, interesting or amusing story, usually true ▫ **anecdotal** *adj*

anemometer *noun* an instrument for measuring the speed of the wind

anemone *noun* a type of woodland or garden flower

aneroid barometer a barometer which measures air pressure without the use of mercury

aneurism *noun* **1** dilatation of an artery **2** abnormal enlargement

angel 1 *noun* a messenger or attendant of God **2** a very good or beautiful person ▫ **angelic** *adj* ▫ **angelically** *adv*

angelica *noun* a plant whose candied leaf-stalks are used as cake decoration

anger *noun* a bitter feeling against someone, annoyance, rage ▫ *verb* make angry

anime /animeh/*noun* a type of Japanese animated film

angina *noun* a form of heart disease causing acute pains

angle *noun* **1** the V-shape made by two lines meeting at a point **2** a corner **3** a point of view ▫ *verb* try to get by hints *etc*: *angling for a job*

angler *noun* someone who fishes with rod and line ▫ **angling** *noun* the sport of fishing

Anglican *adj* of the Church of England ▫ *noun* a member of the Church of England

anglicize *verb* **1** turn into the English language **2** make English in character ▫ **anglicization** *noun*

Anglo-Saxon *adj* & *noun* **1** (of) the people of England before the Norman Conquest **2** (of) their language

angora *noun* wool made from the hair of the Angora goat or rabbit

angry *adj* feeling or showing anger ▫ **angrily** *adv*

anguish *noun* very great pain or distress

angular *adj* **1** having angles **2** thin, bony ▫ **angularity** *noun*

animal *noun* **1** a living being which can feel and move of its own accord **2** an animal other than a human ▫ *adj* of or like an animal

animate *verb* **1** give life to **2** make lively ▫ *adj* living ▫ **animated** *adj* **1** lively **2** made to move as if alive

animation *noun* **1** liveliness **2** a

film made from a series of drawings that give the illusion of movement when shown in sequence ◻ **animator** *noun* an artist who works in animation

animosity *noun* bitter hatred, enmity

aniseed *noun* a seed with a flavour like that of liquorice

ankh /angk/*noun* a cross in the shape of a T with a loop at the top

ankle *noun* the joint connecting the foot and leg

annals *noun plural* yearly historical accounts of events

anneal *verb* toughen glass or metal by heating strongly and cooling slowly

annex *verb* **1** take possession of **2** add, attach ◻ *noun* (*also spelled* **annexe**) a building added to another ◻ **annexation** *noun*

annihilate /*ənaiə*leht/ *verb* destroy completely ◻ **annihilation** *noun*

anniversary *noun* (*plural* **anniversaries**) the day of each year when a particular event is remembered

annotate *verb* **1** make notes upon **2** add notes or explanation to ◻ **annotation** *noun*

announce *verb* make publicly known ◻ **announcement** *noun* ◻ **announcer** *noun* someone who announces programmes on TV *etc*, or reads the news

annoy *verb* make rather angry; irritate ◻ **annoyance** *noun*

annual *adj* yearly ◻ *noun* **1** a plant that lives only one year **2** a book published yearly ◻ **annualize** *verb* convert to a yearly rate, amount *etc* ◻ **annually** *adv*

annuity *noun* (*plural* **annuities**) a yearly payment made for a certain time or for life

annul *verb* **1** put an end to **2** declare no longer valid ◻ **annulment** *noun*

> **annul** » annul*s*, annull*ing*, annull*ed*

anodyne *adj* soothing, relieving pain ◻ *noun* something that soothes pain

anoint *verb* smear with ointment or oil

anomaly *noun* (*plural* **anomalies**) something unusual, not according to rule ◻ **anomalous** *adj*

anon *abbrev* anonymous

anonymous *adj* without the name of the author, giver *etc* being known or given ◻ **anonymously** *adv*

anorak *noun* a hooded waterproof jacket

anorexia *noun* **1** (*also called* **anorexia nervosa**) an emotional illness causing the sufferer to refuse food and become sometimes dangerously thin **2** lack of appetite ◻ **anorexic** *adj* of or suffering from anorexia ◻ *noun* someone suffering from anorexia

another *adj* **1** a different (thing or person): *moving to another job* **2** one more of the same kind: *have another biscuit* ◻ *pronoun* an additional thing of the same kind: *do you want another?*

answer *verb* **1** speak, write *etc* in return or reply **2** find the result or solution (of a sum, problem *etc*) **3** (with **for**) be responsible **4** (with **for**) suffer, be punished ◊ *noun* something said, written *etc* in return or reply; a solution ◊ **answerable** *adj* **1** able to be answered **2** responsible: *answerable for her actions*

ant *noun* a very small insect which lives in organized colonies ◊ **ant-hill** *noun* an earth mound built by ants as a nest ◊ **have ants in your pants** be impatient or restless

antagonist *noun* **1** an enemy **2** an opponent ◊ **antagonism** *noun* hostility, opposition, enmity ◊ **antagonistic** *adj* opposed (to) unfriendly, hostile

antagonize *verb* make an enemy of, cause dislike

Antarctic *adj* of the South Pole or regions round it

ante /*an*teh/ *noun* a stake in poker *etc* ◊ **up the ante** *informal* increase the costs or risks involved

ante- *prefix* before

anteater *noun* an American animal with a long snout which feeds on ants and termites

ante-bellum *adj* of the period before a particular war

antecedent *adj* going before in time ◊ *noun* **1** someone who lived at an earlier time; an ancestor **2** (**antecedents**) previous conduct, history *etc*

antedate *verb* **1** date before the true time **2** be earlier in date than

antediluvian *adj* very old or old-fashioned

Literally 'before the flood', in allusion to the Biblical story of Noah

antelope *noun* a graceful, swift-running animal like a deer

antenatal *adj* **1** before birth **2** relating to pregnancy: *antenatal clinic*

antenna *noun* (*plural* **antennas** or **antennae**) **1** an insect's feeler **2** an aerial

anteroom *noun* a room leading into a large room

anthem *noun* **1** a piece of music for a church choir **2** any song of praise

anthology *noun* (*plural* **anthologies**) a collection of specially chosen poems, stories *etc*

anthracite *noun* coal that burns with a hot, smokeless flame

anthrax *noun* an infectious disease of cattle, sheep *etc*, sometimes tranferred to humans

anthropoid *adj* of apes: resembling humans

anthropology *noun* the study of mankind ◊ **anthropological** *adj* ◊ **anthropologist** *noun*

anti- *prefix* against, opposite: *anti-terrorist*

antibiotic *noun* a medicine taken to kill disease-causing bacteria

antibody *noun* (*plural* **antibodies**) a substance produced in the human body to fight bacteria *etc*

anticipate *verb* **1** look forward to, expect **2** see or know in advance **3** act before (someone or something) □ **anticipation** *noun* **1** expectation **2** excitement □ **anticipatory** *adj*

anticlimax *noun* a dull or disappointing ending

anticlockwise *adj* & *adv* in the opposite direction to the hands of a clock

antics *noun plural* tricks, odd or amusing actions

anticyclone *noun* a circling movement of air round an area of high air pressure, causing calm weather

antidote *noun* something given to act against the effect of poison

antifreeze *noun* a chemical with a low freezing-point, added to a car radiator to prevent freezing

antihistamine *noun* a medicine used to treat an allergy

antipathy *noun* extreme dislike

antiperspirant *noun* a substance applied to the body to reduce sweating

antipodes *noun plural* places on the earth's surface exactly opposite each other, *esp* Australia and New Zealand in relation to Europe □ **antipodean** *adj*

antique *noun* an old, interesting or valuable object from earlier times □ *adj* **1** old, from earlier times **2** old-fashioned □ **antiquarian** *noun* a dealer in antiques □ **antiquated** *adj* grown old, or out of fashion

antiquity *noun* (*plural* **antiquities**) **1** ancient times, *esp* those of the Greeks and Romans **2** great age **3** (**antiquities**) objects from earlier times

antiseptic *adj* germ-destroying □ *noun* a chemical *etc* which destroys germs

antisocial *adj* **1** not fitting in with, harmful to other people **2** disliking the company of other people

antithesis *noun* (*plural* **antitheses**) the exact opposite: *the antithesis of good taste* □ **antithetical** *adj*

antler *noun* the horn of a deer

anus /*ehnəs*/ *noun* the lower opening of the bowel through which faeces pass

anvil *noun* a metal block on which blacksmiths hammer metal into shape

anxiety *noun* (*plural* **anxieties**) worry about what may happen, apprehensiveness

anxious *adj* worried, apprehensive □ **anxiously** *adj*

any *adj* **1** some: *is there any milk?* **2** every, no matter which: *any day will suit me* □ *pronoun* some: *there aren't any left* □ *adv* at all: *I can't work any faster* □ **anybody** *pronoun* any person □ **anyhow** *adv* **1** in any case: *I think I'll go anyhow* 2 carelessly: *scattered anyhow over the floor* □ **anyone** *pronoun* any person □ **anything** *pronoun* something of any kind □ **anyway** *adv* at any rate □ **anywhere** *adv* in any place □ **at any rate** in any case, whatever happens

AOB *abbrev* (written on agendas *etc*) any other business

apart *adv* **1** aside **2** in or into pieces: *came apart in my hands* **3** in opposite directions ▫ **apart from 1** separate, or separately, from **2** except for: *who else knows apart from us?*

apartheid *noun* the political policy of keeping people of different races apart

apartment *noun* **1** a room in a house **2** *US* a flat

apathy *noun* lack of feeling or interest ▫ **apathetic** *adj* ▫ **apathetically** *adv*

ape *noun* a member of a group of animals related to monkeys, but larger, tail-less and walking upright ▫ *verb* imitate

aperitif *noun* a drink taken before a meal

aperture *noun* an opening, a hole

APEX *abbrev* **1** advance purchase excursion, a reduced fare for travel booked in advance **2** Association of Professional, Executive, Clerical and Computer Staff

apex *noun* (*plural* **apexes** or **apices**) the highest point of anything

aphasia *noun* inability to speak or express thoughts verbally

aphid /*eh*fid/ *noun* a small insect which feeds on plants

aphrodisiac *noun* a drug, food *etc* that increases sexual desire ▫ *adj* causing increased sexual desire

apiary *noun* (*plural* **apiaries**) a place where bees are kept ▫ **apiarist** *noun* someone who keeps an apiary or studies bees

apiece *adv* to or for each one: *three chocolates apiece*

aplomb *noun* self-confidence

apocalypse *noun* the destruction of the world ▫ **apocalyptic** *adj*

apocryphal /ə*pok*rifəl/ *adj* unlikely to be true

apogee /*ap*əjee/ *noun* **1** a culmination, a climax **2** the point of an orbit furthest from the earth

apologize *verb* express regret, say you are sorry

apology *noun* (*plural* **apologies**) an expression of regret for having done wrong ▫ **apologetic** *adj* expressing regret

apoplexy *noun* sudden loss of ability to feel, move *etc*, a stroke ▫ **apoplectic** *adj*

apoptosis *noun*, *biochem* cell death

apostle *noun* **1** a religious preacher, *esp* one of the disciples of Christ **2** an advocate for a cause

apostrophe *noun* **1** a mark (') indicating possession: *the minister's cat* **2** a similar mark indicating that a letter *etc* has been missed out, *eg isn't* for *is not*

apothecary *noun* (*plural* **apothecaries**) *old* a chemist or druggist

appal *verb* horrify, shock ▫ **appalling** *adj* shocking

appal » appal*s*, appall*ing*, appall*ed*

apparatchik *noun* a bureaucrat; a party political official

apparatus *noun* **1** an instrument or machine **2** instruments, tools or material required for a piece of work

apparel *noun* clothing

apparent *adj* easily seen, evident ◇ **apparently** *adv*

apparition *noun* **1** something remarkable which appears suddenly **2** a ghost

appeal *verb* **1** ask earnestly (for help *etc*) **2** *law* take a case that has been lost to a higher court **3** be pleasing (to) ◇ *noun* **1** a request for help **2** *law* the taking of a case to a higher court

appealing *adj* **1** arousing liking or sympathy **2** asking earnestly ◇ **appealingly** *adv*

appear *verb* **1** come into view **2** arrive **3** seem ◇ **appearance** *noun*

appease *verb* soothe or satisfy, *esp* by giving what was asked for

appendectomy *noun, med* surgical removal of the appendix

appendicitis *noun, med* inflammation of the appendix

appendix *noun* (*plural* **appendices** or **appendixes**) **1** a part added at the end of a book **2** a small worm-shaped part of the bowels

appertain *verb* **1** belong (to) **2** relate or pertain (to)

appetite *noun* **1** desire for food **2** taste or enthusiasm (for): *no appetite for violence*

appetizer *noun* a snack taken before a main meal

appetizing *adj* tempting to the appetite

applaud *verb* show approval of by clapping the hands

applause *noun* a show of approval by clapping

apple *noun* a round firm fruit, usually red or green

appliance *noun* a tool, instrument, machine *etc*

applicable *adj* **1** able to be applied **2** suitable, relevant

applicant *noun* someone who applies or asks

application *noun* **1** the act of applying **2** something applied, *eg* an ointment **3** a formal request, usually on paper **4** hard work, close attention

appliqué *noun* needlework in which cut pieces of fabric are sewn onto a background to form patterns

apply *verb* **1** put on (an ointment *etc*) **2** use **3** ask formally (for) **4** be suitable or relevant **5** (with **to**) affect ◇ **apply yourself** work hard

apply » appl*ies*, apply*ing*, appl*ied*

appoint *verb* **1** fix (a date *etc*) **2** place in a job: *she was appointed manager*

appointment *noun* **1** the act of appointing **2** a job, a post **3** an arrangement to meet someone

apportion *verb* divide in fair shares

apposite *adj* suitable, appropriate

appraise *verb* estimate the value or quality of ▯ **appraisal** *noun* ▯ **appraising** *adj* quickly summing up

appreciate *verb* **1** see or understand the good points, beauties *etc* of: *appreciate art* **2** understand: *I appreciate your point* **3** rise in value ▯ **appreciable** *adj* noticeable, considerable ▯ **appreciation** *noun*

apprehend *verb* **1** arrest **2** *formal* understand ▯ **apprehension** *noun*

apprehensive *adj* afraid ▯ **apprehensively** *adv*

apprentice *noun* someone who is learning a trade ▯ **apprenticeship** *noun* the time during which someone is an apprentice

appro *noun, informal* approval

approach *verb* **1** come near **2** be nearly equal to **3** speak to in order to ask for something ▯ *noun* (*plural* **approaches**) **1** a coming near to **2** a way leading to a place ▯ **approachable** *adj* **1** able to be reached **2** easy to speak to, friendly

approbation *noun* good opinion, approval

appropriate *adj* suitable, fitting ▯ *verb* **1** take possession of **2** set (money *etc*) apart for a purpose ▯ **appropriately** *adv* ▯ **appropriation** *noun*

approve *verb* **1** agree to, permit **2** think well (of): *did he approve of the new curtains?* ▯ **approval** *noun* ▯ **on approval** on trial, for return to a shop if not bought

approx *abbrev* **1** approximate **2** approximately

approximate *adj* more or less accurate ▯ *verb* be or come near (to) ▯ **approximately** *adv* ▯ **approximation** *noun* a rough estimate

APR *abbrev* annual percentage rate

après-ski *adj* taking place after a day's skiing

apricot *noun* an orange-coloured fruit like a small peach

April *noun* the fourth month of the year

a priori *adj* based on accepted principles or arguments

apron *noun* **1** a garment worn to protect the front of the clothes **2** a hard surface for aircraft to stand on ▯ **apron stage** the part of the stage in front of the curtains in a theatre

apropos *adv*: **apropos of** in connection with, concerning

apse *noun* a rounded domed section, *esp* at the east end of a church

apt *adj* **1** likely (to): *apt to change his mind* **2** suitable, fitting ▯ **aptness** *noun* suitability

aptitude *noun* talent, ability

aqualung *noun* a breathing apparatus worn by divers

aquamarine *noun* **1** a type of bluish-green precious stone **2** a bluish-green colour ▯ *adj* bluish-green

aquarium *noun* (*plural* **aquaria**) a tank or tanks for keeping fish or water animals

aquatic *adj* living, growing or taking place in water

aqueduct *noun* a bridge for taking

a canal *etc* across a valley

aquiline *adj* **1** like an eagle **2** of a nose: curved or hooked

arable *adj* of land: used for growing crops

arbiter *noun* **1** a judge, an umpire, someone chosen by opposing parties to decide between them **2** someone who sets a standard or has influence: *arbiter of good taste* ◻ **arbitrage** *noun* the practice of buying goods *etc* in one market and selling in another to make a profit

arbitrary *adj* **1** fixed according to opinion not objective rules **2** occurring haphazardly ◻ **arbitrarily** *adv* ◻ **arbitrariness** *noun*

arbitrate *verb* act as a judge between people or their claims *etc* ◻ **arbitration** *noun* **1** the act of judging between claims *etc* **2** the settlement of a dispute by an arbiter ◻ **arbitrator** *noun* someone who arbitrates

arboreal *adj* of trees, living in trees

arbour *noun* a seat in a garden shaded by tree-branches *etc*

arc *noun* part of the circumference of a circle, a curve ◻ **arc-lamp** or **arc-light** *noun* a bright lamp lit by a special kind of electric current

arcade *noun* a covered walk, *esp* one with shops on both sides

arch *noun* (*plural* **arches**) the curved part above people's heads in a gateway or the curved support for a bridge, roof *etc* ◻ *adj* mischievous, roguish ◻ *verb* raise or curve in the shape of an arch

arch- *prefix* chief, main: *arch-enemy*

archaeology *noun* the study of the people of earlier times from the remains of their buildings *etc* ◻ **archaeological** *adj* ◻ **archaeologist** *noun*

archaic *adj* no longer used, old-fashioned ◻ **archaism** *noun* an old-fashioned word *etc*

archangel *noun* a chief angel

archbishop *noun* a chief bishop

archdeacon *noun* a clergyman next in rank below a bishop

archduke *noun, hist* the title of the ruling princes of Austria

archer *noun* someone who shoots arrows from a bow ◻ **archery** *noun* the sport of shooting with a bow and arrows

archetype *noun* **archetypal** *adj*

archipelago *noun* (*plural* **archipelagoes** or **archipelagos**) a group of small islands

> From an ancient Greek term for the Aegean Sea, which translates as 'chief sea'

architect *noun* someone who plans and designs buildings

architecture *noun* **1** the study of building **2** the style of a building

archives *noun plural* **1** historical papers, written records *etc* **2** a building *etc* in which these are kept

archway *noun* a passage or road beneath an arch

Arctic *adj* of the district round the North Pole ◻ **arctic** *adj* very cold

ardent *adj* eager, passionate ▯ **ardently** *adv* ▯ **ardour** *noun*

arduous *adj* difficult ▯ **arduously** *adv* ▯ **arduousness** *noun*

are *see* **be**

area *noun* **1** the extent of a surface measured in square metres *etc* **2** a region, a piece of land or ground

arena *noun* **1** any place for a public contest, show *etc* **2** *hist* the centre of an amphitheatre *etc* where gladiators fought

argosy *noun* (*plural* **argosies**) a large trading-ship with a valuable cargo

argue *verb* **1** quarrel in words **2** try to prove by giving reasons (that) **3** suggest or urge

> **argue** » argue*s*, argu*ing*, argu*ed*

arguable *adj* that can be argued as being true ▯ **arguably** *adv*

argument *noun* **1** a heated discussion, quarrel **2** reasoning (for or against something) ▯ **argumentative** *adj* fond of arguing

aria *noun* a song for solo voice in an opera

arid *adj* dry ▯ **aridity** or **aridness** *noun*

arise *verb* **1** rise up **2** come into being

> **arise** » arise*s*, aris*ing*, ar*ose*, arise*n*

aristocracy *noun* those of the nobility and upper class ▯ **aristocrat** *noun* a member of the aristocracy ▯ **aristocratic** *adj* of the aristocracy

arithmetic *noun* a way of counting and calculating by using numbers ▯ **arithmetical** *adj*

ark *noun* the covered boat used by Noah in the Biblical story of the Flood

arm *noun* **1** the part of the body between the shoulder and the hand **2** anything jutting out like this **3** *plural* weapons ▯ *verb* equip with weapons ▯ **armchair** *noun* a chair with arms at each side ▯ **armed** *adj* carrying a weapon, now *esp* a gun ▯ **arm-pit** *noun* the hollow under the arm at the shoulder

armada *noun* a fleet of armed ships

armadillo *noun* (*plural* **armadillos**) a small American animal whose body is protected by bony plates

armageddon *noun* a final battle or devastation, an apocalypse

armaments *noun plural* equipment for war, *esp* the guns of a ship, tank *etc*

armistice *noun* a halt in fighting during war, a truce

armorial *adj* of a coat-of-arms

armour *noun, hist* a protective suit of metal worn by knights ▯ **armoured** *adj* of a vehicle: protected by metal plates ▯ **armoury** *noun* (*plural* **armouries**) an arms store

army *noun* (*plural* **armies**) **1** a large number of soldiers armed for war **2** a great number of anything

aroma *noun* a sweet smell □ **aromatic** *adj* sweet-smelling, perfumed

aromatherapy *noun* a healing therapy involving massage with plant oils □ **aromatherapist** *noun*

arose *past form* of **arise**

around *prep* **1** in a circle about **2** on all sides of, surrounding **3** all over, at several places in: *papers scattered around the room* **4** somewhere near in time, place, amount: *I left him around here/ come back around three o'clock* □ *adv* all about, in various places: *people stood around watching* □ **get around 1** of a story: become known to everyone **2** be active

arouse *verb* **1** awaken **2** stir, move (a feeling or person) □ **arousal** *noun*

arpeggio *noun, music* a chord with the notes played in rapid succession, not at the same time

arraign *verb* accuse publicly

arrange *verb* **1** put in some order **2** plan, settle □ **arrangement** *noun*

arras *noun* a screen of tapestry

array *noun* order, arrangement; clothing □ *verb* **1** put in order **2** dress, adorn

arrears *noun plural*: **in arrears** not up to date; behind with payments

arrest *verb* **1** seize, capture *esp* by power of the law **2** stop **3** catch (the attention *etc*) □ *noun* **1** capture by the police **2** stopping □ **arresting** *adj* striking, capturing the attention

arrival *noun* **1** the act of arriving **2** someone or something that arrives

arrive *verb* reach a place □ **arrive at** reach, come to (a decision *etc*)

arriviste /ari*veest*/ *noun* an upstart, a self-seeker

arrogant *adj* proud, haughty, self-important □ **arrogance** *noun* □ **arrogantly** *adv*

arrogate *verb* **1** make an unjust claim to **2** assign, attribute (to)

arrow *noun* **1** a straight, pointed weapon shot from a bow **2** an arrow-shape, *eg* on a road-sign, showing direction

arrowroot *noun* a starch used in powdered form for thickening liquids

arse *noun, taboo slang* the buttocks □ **arse around** fool about, waste time

arsenal *noun* a factory or store for weapons, ammunition *etc*

arsenic *noun* an element that, combined with oxygen, makes a strong poison

arson *noun* the crime of setting fire to a house *etc* on purpose □ **arsonist** *noun*

art *noun* **1** drawing, painting, sculpture *etc* **2** cleverness, skill; cunning **3** (**arts**) non-scientific school or university subjects □ **artful** *adj* wily, cunning □ **artless** *adj* simple, frank

artefact or **artifact** *noun* a human-made object

arteriosclerosis *noun* hardening of the arteries

artery *noun* (*plural* **arteries**) a tube which carries blood from the heart to pass through the body □ **arterial** *adj* of or like arteries □ **arterial road** a main traffic road

artesian well a well in which water rises to the surface by natural pressure

artichoke *noun* a thistle-like plant with an edible flower-head □ **Jerusalem artichoke** a type of sunflower with edible roots

article *noun* **1** a thing, object **2** a composition in a newspaper, journal *etc* **3** a section of a document **4** (**articles**) an agreement made up of clauses: *articles of apprenticeship* **5** *grammar* the name of the words *the, a, an* □ *verb* bind (an apprentice *etc*) by articles

articulate *adj* expressing thoughts or words clearly □ *verb* express clearly □ **articulation** *noun* □ **articulated lorry** a lorry with a cab which can turn at an angle to the main part of the lorry, making cornering easier

artifact *another spelling* of **artefact**

artificial *adj* not natural; human-made □ **artificiality** *noun* □ **artificially** *adv* □ **artificial insemination** the insertion of sperm into the uterus by means other than sexual intercourse

artillery *noun* **1** big guns **2** an army division that uses these

artisan *noun* a skilled worker

artist *noun* **1** someone who paints pictures **2** someone skilled in anything **3** an artiste □ **artistry** *noun* skill as an artist

artiste /ahr*teest*/ *noun* a performer in a theatre, circus *etc*

artistic *adj* **1** of artists: *the artistic community* **2** having a talent for art □ **artistically** *adv*

as *adv* & *conj* in phrases expressing comparison or similarity: *as good as his brother*; *the same as this one* □ *conj* **1** while, when: *happened as I was walking past* **2** because, since: *we stayed at home as it was raining* **3** in the same way that: *he thinks as I do* □ *adv* for instance □ **as for** concerning, regarding □ **as if** or **as though** as it would be if □ **as to** regarding □ **as well (as)** too, in addition (to)

asbestos *noun* a thread-like mineral which can be woven and which will not burn □ **asbestosis** *noun* a lung disease caused by inhaling asbestos dust

ascend *verb* **1** climb, go up **2** rise or slope upwards □ **ascendancy** or **ascendency** *noun* control (over) □ **ascendant** or **ascendent** *adj* rising □ **ascent** *noun* **1** an upward move or climb **2** a slope upwards; a rise □ **ascend the throne** be crowned king or queen

ascertain *verb* **1** find out **2** make certain

ascetic *noun* someone who keeps away from all kinds of pleasure

ascribe *verb* think of as belonging to or due to: *ascribing the blame*

ash *noun* (*plural* **ashes**) **1** a type of hard-wood tree with silvery bark **2** (**ashes**) what is left after anything is burnt □ **ashen** *adj* very pale

ashamed *adj* feeling shame

ashore *adv* on or onto the shore

aside *adv* on or to one side; apart □ *noun* words spoken which those nearby are not supposed to hear

asinine *adj* **1** of an ass **2** stupid

ask *verb* **1** request information about: *asked for my address* **2** invite: *we've asked over twenty people to come*

askance *adv* off the straight □ **look askance at** look at with suspicion

askew *adv* off the straight, to one side

asleep *adj* **1** sleeping **2** of limbs: numbed

ASLEF *abbrev* Associated Society of Locomotive Engineers and Firemen

asp *noun* a small poisonous snake

asparagus *noun* a plant whose young shoots are eaten as a vegetable

aspect *noun* **1** look, appearance **2** view, point of view **3** side of a building *etc* or the direction it faces in

aspen *noun* a kind of poplar tree

asperity *noun* **1** harshness, sharpness of temper **2** bitter coldness

asphalt *noun* a tarry mixture used to make pavements, paths *etc*

asphyxia /əsfiksiə/ *noun* suffocation by smoke or other fumes □ **asphyxiate** *verb* suffocate □ **asphyxiation** *noun*

aspidistra *noun* a kind of pot-plant with large leaves

aspire *verb* (with **to** or **after**) try to achieve or reach (something difficult, ambitious *etc*) □ **aspiration** *noun* □ **aspiring** *adj* trying or wishing to be: *an aspiring director*

aspirin *noun* a pain-killing drug

ass *noun* (*plural* **asses**) **1** a donkey **2** a stupid person **3** *US slang* the buttocks

assail *verb* attack □ **assailant** *noun* an attacker

assassin *noun* someone who assassinates, a murderer □ **assassinate** *verb* murder (*esp* a politically important person) □ **assassination** *noun*

> Literally 'hashish eater', after an Islamic sect during the Crusades who consumed the drug before assassinating Christians

assault *noun* an attack, *esp* a sudden one □ *verb* attack

assegai *noun* a South African spear, tipped with metal

assemblage *noun* a collection, a gathering

assemble *verb* **1** bring (people) together **2** put together (a machine *etc*) **3** meet together

assembly *noun* (*plural* **assemblies**) **1** a putting together **2** a gathering of people, *esp* for a special purpose □ **assembly line** series of machines and workers necessary for the manufacture of an article

assent *verb* agree □ *noun* agreement

assert *verb* **1** state firmly **2** insist on (a right *etc*) □ **assertion** *noun* □ **assertive** *adj* not shy, inclined to assert yourself □ **assert yourself** make yourself noticed, heard *etc*

assess *verb* **1** estimate the value, power of *etc* **2** fix an amount (to be paid in tax *etc*) □ **assessment**

noun □ **assessor** *noun* someone who assesses

asset *noun* **1** an advantage, a help **2** (**assets**) the property of a person, company *etc*

assiduous *adj* persevering; hard-working □ **assiduously** *adv*

assign /əsain/ *verb* **1** give to someone as a share or task **2** fix (a time or place) □ **assignation** /asig*neh*shən/ *noun* an appointment to meet □ **assignment** *noun* **1** an act of assigning **2** a task given

assimilate *verb* take in □ **assimilation** *noun*

assist *verb* help □ **assistance** *noun* □ **assistant** *noun* **1** a helper, *eg* to a senior worker **2** someone who serves in a shop *etc*

assizes *noun plural* the name of certain law courts in England

Assoc *abbrev* Association

associate *verb* **1** keep company with **2** join (with) in partnership or friendship **3** connect in thought: *I don't associate him with hard work* □ *adj* joined or connected (with) □ *noun* a friend, partner, companion

association *noun* **1** a club, society, union *etc* **2** a partnership, friendship **3** a connection made in the mind

assorted *adj* various, mixed □ **assortment** *noun* a variety, a mixture

assuage *verb* soothe, ease (pain, hunger *etc*)

assume *verb* **1** take upon yourself **2** take as true without further proof, take for granted **3** put on (a disguise *etc*) □ **assumed** *adj* **1** adopted **2** pretended: *assumed air of confidence*

assumption *noun* **1** the act of assuming **2** something taken for granted

assure *verb* **1** make (someone) sure **2** state positively (that) □ **assurance** *noun* **1** a feeling of certainty; confidence **2** a promise **3** insurance □ **assured** *adj* certain; confident

asterisk *noun* a star (*) used in printing for various purposes, *esp* to point out a footnote or insertion

astern *adv* at or towards the back of a ship

asthma *noun* an illness causing difficulty in breathing, coughing *etc* □ **asthmatic** *adj* suffering from asthma □ *noun* someone with asthma

astonish *verb* surprise greatly □ **astonishing** *adj* □ **astonishment** *noun* amazement, wonder

astound *verb* surprise greatly, amaze □ **astounding** *adj*

astrakhan *noun* lamb-skin with a curled wool

astral *adj* of the stars

astray *adv* out of the right way, straying

astride *adv* with legs apart □ *prep* with legs on each side of

astringent *noun* a lotion *etc* used for closing up the skin's pores □ *adj* **1** used for closing the pores **2** of manner: sharp, sarcastic

astrology *noun* the study of the stars and their supposed power over the lives of humans □ **astrologer** *noun*

astronaut *noun* someone who travels in space

astronomer *noun* someone who studies astronomy

astronomical *adj* **1** of astronomy **2** of a number: very large

astronomy *noun* the study of the stars and their movements

astute *adj* cunning, clever □ **astutely** *adv* □ **astuteness** *noun*

asunder *adv* apart, into pieces

asylum *noun* **1** a place of refuge or safety **2** *old* a home for the mentally ill

at *prep* **1** showing position, time *etc*: *I'll be at home/ come at 7 o'clock* **2** costing: *cakes at 25 pence each* □ **at all** in any way: *not worried at all*

ate *past form* of **eat**

atelier *noun* an artist's studio, a workshop

atheism *noun* belief that there is no God □ **atheist** *noun* someone who does not believe in a God □ **atheistic** *adj*

athlete *noun* someone good at sport, *esp* running, gymnastics *etc*

athletic *adj* **1** of athletics **2** good at sports; strong, powerful

athletics *noun plural* running, jumping *etc* or competitions in these

atlas *noun* (*plural* **atlases**) a book of maps

After the mythological *Atlas*, punished by the Greek gods by having to carry the heavens on his shoulders

ATM *abbrev* automatic teller machine

atmosphere *noun* **1** the air round the earth **2** any surrounding feeling: *friendly atmosphere*

atmospheric *adj* **1** of the atmosphere **2** with a noticeable atmosphere □ **atmospheric pressure** the pressure exerted by the atmosphere at the earth's surface, due to the weight of the air □ **atmospherics** *noun plural* air disturbances causing crackling noises on the radio *etc*

atoll *noun* a coral island or reef

atom *noun* **1** the smallest part of an element **2** anything very small □ **atom bomb** or **atomic bomb** a bomb in which the explosion is caused by nuclear energy □ **atomic energy** nuclear energy

atone *verb* make up for wrongdoing □ **atonement** *noun*

atrocious *adj* **1** cruel or wicked **2** *informal* very bad □ **atrociously** *adv* □ **atrociousness** *noun*

atrocity *noun* (*plural* **atrocities**) **1** a terrible crime **2** *informal* something very ugly

attach *verb* **1** fasten or join (to) **2** think of (something) as having: *don't atttach any importance to it* □ **attached** *adj* **1** fastened **2** (with **to**) fond (of) □ **attachment** *noun* **1** something attached **2** a joining by love or friendship

attaché /*ətasheh*/ *noun* a junior

member of an embassy staff ▯ **attaché-case** *noun* small case for papers *etc*

attack *verb* **1** fall upon suddenly or violently **2** speak or write against ▯ *noun* **1** an act of attacking **2** a fit (of an illness *etc*)

attain *verb* reach; gain ▯ **attainable** *adj* able to be attained ▯ **attainment** *noun* act of attaining; the thing attained, an achievement or accomplishment

attempt *verb* try ▯ *noun* **1** a try or effort: *first attempt* **2** an attack: *an attempt on the president's life*

attend *verb* **1** be present at **2** pay attention to **3** wait on, look after **4** *formal* accompany

attendance *noun* **1** the fact of being present: *my attendance was expected* **2** the number of people present: *good attendance at the first night*

attendant *noun* someone employed to look after a public place, shop *etc*: *cloakroom attendant* ▯ *adj* accompanying, related: *stress and its attendant health problems*

attention *noun* **1** careful notice: *pay attention* **2** concentration **3** care **4** *military* a stiffly straight standing position: *stand to attention*

attentive *adj* **1** giving or showing attention **2** polite ▯ **attentively** *adv* ▯ **attentiveness** *noun*

attic *noun* a room just under the roof of a house

From *Attica* in ancient Greece, famous for a type of square architectural column used in upper storeys of classical buildings

attire *verb* dress ▯ *noun* clothing

attitude *noun* **1** a way of thinking or feeling: *positive attitude* **2** a position of the body

attorney *noun* (*plural* **attorneys**) **1** someone with legal power to act for another **2** *US* a lawyer

attract *verb* **1** draw to or towards **2** arouse liking or interest

attraction *noun* **1** the power of attracting **2** something which attracts visitors *etc*: *tourist attraction*

attractive *adj* **1** good-looking, likeable **2** pleasing: *attractive price*

attribute /ə*trib*yoot/ *verb* **1** state or consider as the source or cause of: *attribute the accident to human error* **2** state as the author or originator of: *attributed to Rembrandt* ▯ *noun* /*a*tribyoot/ an attendant characteristic: *attributes of power* ▯ **attributable** *adj* ▯ **attributive** *adj*

aubergine /*oh*bərzheen/ *noun* an oval dark purple fruit, eaten as a vegetable

auburn *adj* of hair: reddish-brown in colour

au contraire *adv* on the contrary

au courant *adj* informed of the facts, up-to-date

auction *noun* a public sale in which articles are sold to the highest bidder ▯ *verb* sell by auction

□ **auctioneer** *noun* someone who sells by auction

audacious *adj* daring, bold □ **audaciously** *adv* □ **audacity** *noun*

audible *adj* able to be heard □ **audibility** *noun* □ **audibly** *adv*

audience *noun* **1** a number of people gathered to watch or hear a performance *etc* **2** a formal interview with someone important: *an audience with the Pope*

audio *noun* the reproduction of recorded or radio sound □ *adj* relating to such sound: *an audio tape*

audio-typist *noun* a typist able to type from a recording on a tape-recorder

audio-visual *adj* concerned with hearing and seeing at the same time □ **audio-visual aids** films, recordings *etc* used in teaching

audit *verb* examine accounts officially □ *noun* an official examination of a company's accounts □ **auditor** *noun* someone who audits accounts

audition *noun* a hearing to test an actor, singer *etc*

auditorium *noun* (*plural* **auditoria** or **auditoriums**) the part of a theatre *etc* where the audience sits

auditory *adj* of hearing

au fait /oh *feh*/ *adj* well-acquainted (with)

augment *verb* increase in size, number or amount □ **augmentation** *noun* □ **augmentative** *adj*

augur *verb*: **augur well** be a good sign for the future □ **augur ill** be a bad sign for the future

August *noun* the eighth month of the year

august *adj* full of dignity, stately

au naturel /oh naty*ərel*/ *adv* with no additions; plain, natural

aunt *noun* a father's or a mother's sister, or an uncle's wife

au pair a foreign girl who does domestic duties in return for board, lodging and pocket money

aural *adj* relating to the ear □ **aurally** *adv*

⚠Do not confuse with: **oral**

aurora borealis the Northern lights

auspices *noun plural*: **under the auspices of** under the control or supervision of

auspicious *adj* favourable; promising luck □ **auspiciously** *adv*

austere *adj* **1** severe **2** without luxury; simple, sparse □ **austerity** *noun*

authentic *adj* true, real, genuine □ **authentically** *adv* □ **authenticity** *noun*

authenticate *verb* show to be true or real □ **authentication** *noun*

author *noun* the writer of a book, poem, play *etc*

authoress *noun, old* a female author

authoritative *adj* stated by an expert or someone in authority □ **authoritatively** *adv*

authority *noun* (*plural* **authorities**) **1** power or right **2** someone whose opinion is reliable, an expert **3**

someone or a body of people having control (over something) **4** (**authorities**) people in power

authorize *verb* **1** give (a person) the power or the right to do something **2** give permission (for something to be done) ▫ **authorization** *noun*

autism *noun* a disability in children affecting their ability to relate to and communicate with other people ▫ **autistic** *adj* affected with autism

autobahn /*aw*tohban/ *noun* a motorway in Germany

autobiography *noun* (*plural* **autobiographies**) the story of someone's life, written or told by themself ▫ **autobiographer** *noun* the writer of an autobiography ▫ **autobiographical** *adj*

autocrat *noun* a ruler who has complete power ▫ **autocracy** *noun* government by such a ruler ▫ **autocratic** *adj* expecting complete obedience

autoerotism *noun* sexual gratification obtained from your own body, without external stimulation ▫ **autoerotic** *adj*

autograph *noun* **1** someone's own signature **2** someone's own handwriting ▫ *verb* write your own name on: *autograph the book*

automate *verb* make automatic by introducing machines *etc* ▫ **automation** *noun* the use of machines for controlling other machines in factories *etc*

automatic *adj* **1** of a machine *etc* self-working **2** of an action: unconscious, without thinking ▫ *noun* **1** something automatic (*eg* an automatic washing-machine) **2** a kind of self-loading gun ▫ **automatically** *adv* ▫ **automatic pilot 1** a device which can be set to control an aircraft on a course **2** the doing of anything unthinkingly or abstractedly ▫ **automatic teller machine** an electronic panel set into the exterior wall of a bank or building *etc* which dispenses cash or information about your bank account

automaton *noun* (*plural* **automatons** or **automata**) **1** a mechanical toy or machine made to look and move like a human **2** someone who acts mindlessly, like a machine

automobile *noun, US* a motor-car

autonomy *noun* the power or right of a country to govern itself ▫ **autonomous** *adj* ▫ **autonomously** *adv*

autopsy *noun* (*plural* **autopsies**) an examination of a body after death

auto-reverse *noun* a feature on a cassette player *etc* allowing it to play the second side of a tape without being changed manually

autostereogram *noun* a computer-generated picture which combines two separate images of the same subject, creating a 3-D effect when viewed

autoteller *noun* an automatic teller machine

autumn *noun* the season of the year following summer, when leaves change colour and fruits are ripe ▯ **autumnal** *adj* **1** relating to autumn **2** like those of autumn: *autumnal colours*

auxiliary *adj* supplementary, additional ▯ *noun* (*plural* **auxiliaries**) a helper, an assistant

AV *abbrev* **1** audio-visual **2** Authorized Version (of the Bible)

avail *verb* and *noun*: **avail yourself of** to make use of ▯ **to no avail** without any effect, of no use

available *adj* able or ready to be made use of ▯ **availability** *noun*

avalanche *noun* **1** a mass of snow and ice sliding down from a mountain **2** a great amount: *an avalanche of work*

avant-garde *adj* ahead of fashion, very modern: *an avant-garde writer*

avarice *noun* greed, *esp* for riches ▯ **avaricious** *adj* greedy

avatar *noun* a Hindu god in visible form

avenge *verb* take revenge for (a wrong) ▯ **avenger** *noun*

> **avenge** » avenge*s*, aveng*ing*, avenge*d*

avenue *noun* **1** a tree-lined street or approach to a house **2** a means, a way: *avenue of escape*

average *noun* the result obtained by adding several amounts and dividing the total by this number, *eg* the average of 3, 7, 9, 13 is 8 (32÷4) ▯ *adj* **1** ordinary, usual; of medium size *etc* **2** obtained by working out an average: *the average cost will be £10 each* ▯ *verb* **1** form an average **2** find the average of

averse *adj* not fond of, opposed (to)

aversion *noun* **1** extreme dislike or distaste: *an aversion to sprouts* **2** something that is hated

avert *verb*, *formal* **1** turn away or aside: *avert your eyes* **2** prevent from happening: *avert the danger*

aviary *noun* (*plural* **aviaries**) a place for keeping birds

aviation *noun* the practice of flying or piloting aircraft

aviator *noun* an aircraft pilot

avid *adj* eager, greedy: *an avid reader* ▯ **avidity** *noun* ▯ **avidly** *adv*

avocado *noun* **1** a pear-shaped fruit with a rough peel and rich, creamy flesh **2** a light, yellowish green colour

avoid *verb* escape, keep clear of ▯ **avoidable** *adj* ▯ **avoidance** *noun*

avoirdupois /avwahdoo*pwah*/ *noun* the system of measuring weights in pounds and ounces (*compare with*: **metric)**

avow *verb*, *formal* declare openly ▯ **avowal** *noun* ▯ **avowed** *adj* ▯ **avowedly** *adv*

await *verb* wait for

awake *verb* **1** rouse from sleep **2** stop sleeping ▯ *adj* not asleep

awaken *verb* **1** awake **2** arouse (interest *etc*) ▯ **awakening** *noun*

award *verb* **1** give, grant (a prize *etc*) **2** grant legally ▯ *noun* something that is awarded, a prize *etc*

aware *adj* **1** having knowledge

(of), conscious (of): *aware of the dangers* **2** alert ▫ **awareness** *noun*

away *adv* **1** to a distance from the speaker or person spoken to: *throw that ball away* **2** not here; not at home or work: *she is away all this week* **3** in the opposite direction: *he turned away and left* **4** into nothing: *the sound died away* **5** constantly; diligently: *working away* ▫ **do away with** abolish, get rid of ▫ **get away with** do (something) without being punished ▫ **make away with** steal and escape with ▫ **right away** immediately

awe *noun* wonder or admiration mixed with fear ▫ *verb* affect with awe: *awed by the occasion* ▫ **awe-struck** *adj* full of awe

awesome *adj* **1** causing fear **2** *informal* remarkable, admirable

awful *adj* **1** *informal* bad: *an awful headache* **2** *informal* very great: *an awful lot* **3** terrible: *I feel awful about what happened* ▫ **awfully** *adv*, *informal* very, extremely: *awfully good of you* ▫ **awfulness** *noun*

awkward *adj* **1** clumsy, not graceful **2** difficult to deal with: *awkward customer* ▫ **awkwardly** *adv* ▫ **awkwardness** *noun*

awl *noun* a pointed tool for boring small holes

awning *noun* a covering of canvas *etc* providing shelter

AWOL /*eh*wol/ *abbrev* absent without leave

awry /aw*rai*/ *adj* & *adv* **1** not according to plan, wrong **2** crooked

axe *noun* (*plural* **axes**) a tool for chopping ▫ *verb* **1** cancel (a plan *etc*) **2** reduce greatly (costs, services *etc*)

axiom *noun* a truth, an accepted principle

axis *noun* (*plural* **axes**) **1** the line, real or imaginary, on which a thing turns **2** the axis of the earth, from North to South Pole, around which the earth turns **3** a fixed line taken as a reference, as in a graph

axle *noun* the rod on which a wheel turns

ayatollah *noun* a religious leader of the Shiah sect of Islam

ayurveda *noun* a form of traditional Indian medicine

azalea *noun* a flowering plant related to the rhododendron

azimuth *noun* the arc of the horizon between the meridian and a circle passing through the sun *etc*

azuki *another spelling* of **adzuki**

azure *adj* sky-coloured, clear blue

B

BA *abbrev* **1** British Airways **2** Bachelor of Arts

babble *verb* talk indistinctly or foolishly □ *noun* indistinct or foolish talk

babe *noun* **1** a baby **2** *informal* a girl or young woman

baboon *noun* a large monkey with a dog-like snout

baby *noun* (*plural* **babies**) a very young child, an infant □ *verb* treat like a baby □ **babyhood** *noun* the time when someone is a baby □ **babysitter** *noun* someone who stays in the house with a child while its parents are out

> **baby** *verb* » bab*ies*, baby*ing*, bab*ied*

bachelor *noun* an unmarried man □ **Bachelor of Arts**, **Bachelor of Science** *etc* someone who has passed examinations at a certain level in subjects at a university

bacillus /bəsiləs/ *noun* (*plural* **bacilli**) a rod-shaped germ

back *noun* **1** the part of the human body from the neck to the base of the spine **2** the upper part of an animal's body **3** the part of anything situated behind: *sitting at the back of the bus* **4** *football etc* a player positioned behind the forwards □ *adj* of or at the back □ *adv* **1** to or in the place from which someone or something came: *back at the house/ walked back home* **2** to or in a former time or condition: *thinking back to their youth* □ *verb* **1** move backwards **2** bet on (a horse *etc*) **3** (often with **up**) help or support □ **back down** change your opinion *etc* □ **back out 1** move out backwards **2** excuse yourself from keeping to an agreement □ **put your back into** work hard at □ **put someone's back up** irritate someone □ **with your back to the wall** in desperate difficulties

backbone *noun* **1** the spine **2** the main support of something **3** firmness, resolve

backer *noun* a supporter

backfire *verb* **1** of a vehicle: make an explosive noise in the exhaust pipe **2** of a plan: go wrong

backgammon *noun* a game similar to draughts, played with dice

background *noun* **1** the space behind the principal figures of a picture **2** details that explain something **3** someone's family and upbringing

backhand *noun, tennis* a stroke played with the back of the hand facing the ball □ **backhanded compliment** a compliment with a double, unflattering meaning

backing *noun* **1** support **2** material used on the back of a picture *etc* **3** a musical accompaniment on a recording

backlash *noun* a violent reaction against something

backstroke *noun* a stroke used in swimming on the back

backwash *noun* a backward current, such as that caused by an outgoing wave

backwater *noun* **1** a river pool separate from the main stream **2** a place not affected by what is happening in the outside world

backward *adj* **1** to or towards the back: *backward glance* **2** slow in learning or development

backwards *adv* **1** towards the back: *walked backwards out the door* **2** in a reverse direction; back to front: *written backwards* **3** towards the past

bacon *noun* pig's flesh salted and dried, used as food

bacteria *noun plural* germs found in air, water, living and dead bodies, and especially decaying matter □ **bacterial** *adj*

bacteriology *noun* the study of bacteria □ **bacteriologist** *noun*

bad *adj* **1** not good; wicked **2** (often with **for**) hurtful: *smoking is bad for you* **3** of food: rotten, decaying **4** severe, serious: *bad dose of flu* **5** faulty **6** unwell □ **bad language** swearing □ **badly** *adv* **1** not well **2** seriously □ **badness** *noun*

badge *noun* a mark or sign or brooch-like ornament giving some information about the wearer

badger *noun* a burrowing animal of the weasel family which comes out at night □ *verb* pester or annoy

badminton *noun* a game resembling tennis, played with shuttlecocks

> Although based on a 16th-century game, this was first played in its modern form in *Badminton* House in Avon

badmouth *verb*, *informal* criticize, malign

baffle *verb* **1** be too difficult for; puzzle, confound **2** prevent from being carried out; hinder □ **baffling** *adj*

BAFTA *abbrev* British Academy of Film and Television Arts

bag *noun* **1** a holder or container, often of a soft material **2** a quantity of fish or game caught □ *verb* **1** put in a bag **2** secure possession of, claim: *bag a seat* **3** kill (game) in a hunt □ **bag lady** a homeless woman who carries her belongings with her in shopping bags

> **bag** *verb* » bag*s*, bagg*ing*, bagg*ed*

bagatelle *noun* a board game, in which balls are struck into numbered holes

bagel /*behgl*/ *noun* a ring-shaped bread roll with a dense texture

baggage *noun* luggage

baggy *adj* of clothes: large and loose □ *noun* (**baggies**) *informal* wide, knee-length shorts □ **bagginess** *noun*

bagpipes *noun plural* a wind musical instrument made up of a bag, a chanter and several pipes for producing drones

bail *noun* **1** money given to bail out a prisoner **2** *cricket* one of the crosspieces on the top of the wickets ▯ **bail out** *verb* **1** obtain temporary release of (an untried prisoner) by giving money which will be forfeited if they do not return for trial **2** bale out

> ⚠Do not confuse with: **bale**

bailie *noun, hist* a burgh magistrate in Scotland

bailiff *noun* **1** an officer who works for a sheriff **2** a landowner's agent

bain-marie /banh-ma*ree*/*noun* a double-boiler for cooking

> Originally an alchemist's pot, named after the Biblical Mary, sister of Moses

bairn *Scot* a child

Baisakhi *noun* the annual Sikh festival held at the Hindu New Year

bait *noun* **1** food put on a hook to make fish bite, or in a trap to attract animals **2** something tempting or alluring ▯ *verb* **1** put bait on a hook *etc* **2** worry, annoy

baize /behz/ *noun* a coarse woollen cloth

bake *verb* **1** cook in an oven **2** dry or harden in the sun or in an oven ▯ **baking powder** a raising agent added to flour in cake-making *etc*

baker *noun* someone who bakes or sells bread *etc* ▯ **bakery** or **bakehouse** *noun* a place used for baking in

baklava *noun* a Middle-Eastern pastry filled with nuts and honey

baksheesh *noun* a gift of money; a tip

balaklava *noun* a knitted covering for the head and neck

balalaika *noun* a traditional Russian musical instrument, like a guitar

balance *noun* **1** steadiness: *lost my balance and fell over* **2** the money needed to make the two sides of an account equal **3** a weighing machine ▯ *verb* **1** be the same in weight **2** make both sides of an account the same **3** make or keep steady: *balanced it on her head*

balcony *noun* (*plural* **balconies**) **1** a platform built out from the wall of a building **2** an upper floor or gallery in a theatre *etc*

bald *adj* **1** without hair **2** plain, frank: *a bald statement*

balderdash *noun* nonsense

bale *noun* a large tight bundle of cotton, hay *etc* ▯ **bale out** *verb* **1** escape by parachute from an aircraft in an emergency **2** scoop water out of a boat (also **bail out**)

> ⚠Do not confuse with: **bail**

baleful *adj* harmful, malevolent: *baleful influence*

balk *verb* **1** hinder, baffle **2** (with **at**) refuse to do something

ball[1] *noun* **1** anything round: *ball of wool* **2** the round object used in playing many games ▯ **ball-bearings** *noun plural* small steel balls that sit loosely in grooves and ease the revolving of one machinery part over another ▯ **on the ball** *informal* in touch with a situation, alert ▯

play ball *informal* play along, co-operate

ball[2] *noun* a formal party at which dancing takes place ▢ **have a ball** *informal* have a great time, enjoy yourself

ballad *noun* **1** a narrative poem with a simple rhyme scheme, *usu* in verses of four lines **2** a simple song

ballast *noun* sand, gravel *etc* put into a ship to steady it

ballerina *noun* a female ballet dancer

ballet *noun* a form of stylized dancing which tells a story by mime

ballistic missile a self-guided missile which falls onto its target

balloon *noun* a bag filled with gas to make it float in the air, *esp* one made of thin rubber used as a toy *etc* ▢ *verb* puff or swell out

ballot *noun* a way of voting in secret by marking a paper and putting it into a special box ▢ *verb* collect votes from by ballot

ballpark *noun, US* a sports field for ball-games ▢ *adj* rough, estimated: *ballpark figure*

ballpoint *noun* a pen with a tiny ball as the writing point

ballroom *noun* a large room used for public dances *etc*

balls *noun plural, taboo slang* **1** testicles **2** courage **3** rubbish, nonsense ▢ **balls-up** *noun* a mess

balm *noun* **1** something soothing **2** a sweet-smelling healing ointment

balmy *adj* **1** mild, gentle; soothing: *balmy air* **2** sweet-smelling ▢ **balminess** *noun*

balsam *noun* an oily sweet-smelling substance obtained from certain trees

balsawood *noun* a lightweight wood obtained from a tropical American tree

balti *noun* a style of Indian cooking in which food is cooked and served in a wok-like pan

balustrade *noun* a row of pillars on a balcony *etc*, joined by a rail

bamboo *noun* the woody, jointed stem of a very tall Indian grass

bamboozle *verb* trick, puzzle ▢ **bamboozling** *adj*

ban *noun* an order forbidding something ▢ *verb* forbid officially (the publication of a book *etc*)

> **ban** *verb* » ban*s*, bann*ing*, bann*ed*

banal *adj* lacking originality or wit, commonplace ▢ **banality** *noun* ▢ **banally** *adv*

banana *noun* the long yellow fruit of a type of tropical tree

band *noun* **1** a group of people **2** a group of musicians playing together **3** a strip of some material to put round something **4** a stripe (of colour *etc*) **5** a group of wavelengths for radio broadcasts ▢ *verb* join together

bandage *noun* a strip of cloth *etc* or special dressing for a wound

B and B *abbrev* bed and breakfast

bandeau *noun* (*plural* **bandeaux**) hairband

bandit *noun* an outlaw, robber, *esp* a member of a gang of robbers

bandolier or **bandoleer** *noun* a belt across the body for carrying cartridges

bandy *adj* of legs: bent outward at the knee ◻ **bandy words** argue

bane *noun* a cause of ruin or trouble: *the bane of my life*

baneful *adj* destructive, poisonous

bang *noun* **1** a sudden, loud noise **2** a heavy blow ◻ *verb* **1** close with a bang, slam **2** hit, strike: *banged his head on the door*

bangle *noun* a large ring worn on an arm or leg

banish *verb* **1** order to leave (a country) **2** drive away (doubts, fear *etc*) ◻ **banishment** *noun*

banister *noun* the posts and handrail of a staircase

banjo *noun* (*plural* **banjoes** or **banjos**) a stringed musical instrument like a guitar, with a long neck and a round body

bank *noun* **1** a mound or ridge of earth *etc* **2** the edge of a river **3** a place where money is put for safety, lent *etc* **4** a place where blood *etc* is stored till needed **5** a public bin for collecting items for recycling: *bottle bank* ◻ **banker** *noun* someone who manages a bank ◻ **bank holiday** a day on which all banks and many shops *etc* are closed ◻ **banknote** *noun* a piece of paper money issued by a bank ◻ **bank on** depend on, count on

bankrupt *noun* someone who has no money to pay their debts ◻ *adj* **1** unable to pay debts **2** utterly lacking in: *bankrupt of ideas* ◻ **bankruptcy** *noun* (*plural* **bankruptcies**)

banner *noun* **1** a large flag carried in processions *etc*, often hung between two poles **2** any flag

banns *noun plural* a public announcement of a forthcoming marriage

banquet *noun* a ceremonial dinner

bantam *noun* a small kind of hen

banter *verb* tease in fun ◻ *noun* light teasing

baptize *verb* **1** dip in, or sprinkle with, water as a sign of admission into the Christian church **2** christen, give a name to ◻ **baptism** *noun* ◻ **baptismal** *adj*

bar *noun* **1** a rod of solid material **2** a broad line or band **3** a piece, a cake: *bar of soap* **4** a hindrance, a block **5** a bank of sand *etc* at the mouth of a river **6** a room, or counter, where drinks are served in a public house, hotel *etc* **7** a public house **8** the rail at which prisoners stand for trial **9** the lawyers who plead in a court **10** a time division in music ◻ *prep* except: *all the runners, bar Ian, finished the race* ◻ *verb* **1** fasten with a bar **2** exclude, shut out: *barred from the competition* ◻ **barring** *prep* except for, but for

> **bar** *verb* » bar*s*, bar*ring*, bar*red*

barb *noun* the backward-pointing spike on an arrow, fish-hook *etc* ◻ **barbed** *adj* having a barb or barbs

□ **barbed wire** wire with regular clusters of sharp points, used for fencing *etc*

barbarian *noun* an uncivilized person □ *adj* uncivilized □ **barbaric** *adj* **1** uncivilized **2** extremely cruel □ **barbarity** *noun*

barbecue *noun* **1** a frame on which to grill food over an open fire **2** an outdoor party providing food from a barbecue □ *verb* cook (food) on a barbecue

From a Haitian creole term for a wooden grid or frame

barber *noun* a men's hairdresser

barbiturate *noun* a type of sedative drug

bard *noun, formal* a poet

bare *adj* **1** uncovered, naked **2** plain, simple **3** empty □ *verb* uncover, expose □ **barefaced** *adj* impudent, unashamed: *barefaced lie* □ **barely** *adv* hardly, scarcely

bargain *noun* **1** an agreement, *esp* about buying or selling **2** something bought cheaply □ *verb* argue about a price *etc* □ **bargain for** expect: *more than he bargained for* □ **into the bargain** in addition, besides

barge *noun* a flat-bottomed boat used on rivers and canals □ *verb* **1** rush clumsily **2** push or bump (into) **3** push your way (into) rudely

baritone *noun* **1** a male singing voice between tenor and bass **2** a singer with this voice

bark[1] *noun* the noise made by a dog *etc* □ *verb* **1** give a bark **2** speak sharply or angrily

bark[2] *noun* the rough outer covering of a tree's trunk and branches

barley *noun* a grain used for food and for making malt liquors and spirits □ **barley sugar** sugar candied by melting and cooling to make a sweet □ **barley water** a drink made from pearl barley

bar mitzvah a Jewish ceremony to mark a boy's coming of age

barn *noun* a building in which grain, hay *etc* is stored

barnacle *noun* a type of shellfish which sticks to rocks, ships' hulls *etc*

barometer *noun* an instrument which measures the weight or pressure of the air and shows changes in the weather

baron *noun* **1** a nobleman, the lowest in the British peerage **2** a powerful person, *esp* in a business: *drug baron* □ **baronial** *adj*

baroness *noun* (*plural* **baronesses**) a baron's wife or a female baron

baronet *noun* the lowest title that can be passed on to an heir □ **baronetcy** *noun* the rank of baronet

baroque *adj* extravagantly ornamented

barracks *noun plural* a place for housing soldiers

barracuda *noun* a voracious West Indian fish

barrage *noun* **1** heavy gunfire against an enemy **2** an overwhelming number: *barrage of questions* **3** a bar across a river to make the water deeper

barrel *noun* **1** a wooden cask with curved sides **2** the metal tube of a gun through which the shot is fired

barren *adj* not able to reproduce, infertile ◊ **barrenness** *noun*

barricade *noun* a barrier put up to block a street *etc* ◊ *verb* **1** block or strengthen against attack **2** shut behind a barrier

barrier *noun* **1** a strong fence *etc* used for enclosing or keeping out **2** an obstacle

barrister *noun* a lawyer who pleads cases in English or in Irish courts

barrow *noun* **1** a small hand-cart **2** a mound built over an ancient grave

Bart or **Bt** *abbrev* baronet

barter *verb* give one thing in exchange for another ◊ *noun* trading by exchanging goods without using money

basalt *noun* a hard, dark-coloured rock thrown up as lava from volcanoes

base *noun* **1** something on which a thing stands or rests **2** the lowest part **3** a place from where an expedition, military action *etc* is carried out ◊ *verb* use as a foundation: *based on the facts* ◊ *adj* worthless, cowardly ◊ **baseless** *adj* without foundation; untrue ◊ **basement** *noun* a storey below ground level in a building

baseball *noun* a North American ball-game in which players make a circuit of four bases on a field

bash *verb* hit hard ◊ *noun* a heavy blow ◊ **have a bash** *informal* make an attempt

bashful *adj* shy ◊ **bashfully** *adv*

basho *noun* a contest in sumo wrestling

basic *adj* **1** of or forming a base **2** necessary, fundamental ◊ **basically** *adv* fundamentally, essentially

basil *noun* an aromatic herb used in cooking

basilica *noun* a church with a large central hall

basilisk *noun* **1** a mythological reptile with a deadly look and poisonous breath **2** a type of American lizard

basin *noun* **1** a wide, open dish **2** a washhand basin **3** a large hollow holding water **4** the land drained by a river and its tributaries

basis *noun* (*plural* **bases**) **1** something on which a thing rests, a foundation: *the basis of their friendship* **2** the main ingredient

bask *verb* **1** lie in warmth **2** enjoy, feel great pleasure (in): *basking in glory*

basket *noun* **1** a container made of strips of wood, rushes *etc* woven together **2** a related group or collection: *basket of currencies*

basketball *noun* a team game in which goals are scored by throwing a ball into a raised net

basque /bask/ *noun* a woman's close-fitting under-bodice

bas-relief /bahrəleef/ *noun* sculpture carved to stand slightly out from a background

bass[1] /behs/ *noun* (*plural* **basses**) **1** the low part in music **2** a deep male singing voice **3** a singer with this voice ▫ *adj* low or deep in tone ▫ **bass clef** *see* **clef**

bass[2] /bas/ *noun* (*plural* **bass** or **basses**) a kind of fish of the perch family

bassoon *noun* a musical wind instrument with low notes

bastard *noun* **1** a child born to parents who are not married to each other **2** *informal* a general term of abuse

baste[1] *verb* spoon fat over (meat) while roasting to keep (it) from drying out

baste[2] *verb* sew loosely together with big stitches; tack

bastion *noun* **1** a defensive position, a preserve: *the last bastions of male power* **2** a tower on a castle *etc*

bat[1] *noun* a shaped piece of wood *etc* for striking a ball in some games ▫ *verb* use the bat in cricket *etc* ▫ **batsman, batswoman** *noun* someone who bats in cricket *etc*

bat *verb* » bat*s*, batt*ing*, batt*ed*

bat[2] *noun* a mouse-like flying animal

bat[3] *verb* flutter (eyelids *etc*)

bat *verb* » bat*s*, batt*ing*, batt*ed*

batch *noun* (*plural* **batches**) a quantity of things made *etc* at one time

bated *adj*: **with bated breath** anxiously

bath *noun* **1** a vessel which holds water in which to wash the body **2** the water in which to wash **3** a washing of the body in water **4** (**baths**) a public building with an artificial pool for swimming ▫ *verb* wash (oneself or another) in a bath ▫ **bathchair** *noun* an old-fashioned wheelchair

bathe *verb* **1** swim in water **2** wash gently: *bathe your eyes* **3** take a bath ▫ *noun* ▫ **bathed in** covered with

bathyscaphe or **bathysphere** *noun* a deep-sea observation chamber

batik *noun* a method of dyeing patterns on cloth by waxing certain areas so that they remain uncoloured

batman *noun* an army officer's servant

baton *noun* **1** a small wooden stick **2** a light stick used by a conductor of music

battalion *noun* a part of a regiment of foot soldiers

batten *noun* **1** a piece of sawn timber **2** a strip of wood used to fasten down a ship's hatches during a storm ▫ *verb* (with **down**) fasten down firmly

batter *verb* hit repeatedly ▫ *noun* a beaten mixture of flour, milk and eggs, for cooking ▫ **battered** *adj* **1** beaten, ill-treated **2** worn out by use ▫ **battering-ram** *noun, hist* a weapon comprising a heavy beam for breaking through walls *etc*

battery *noun* (*plural* **batteries**) **1** a number of large guns **2** a device for storing and transmitting electricity **3** a series of cages *etc* in which hens are kept for egg-laying

battle *noun* a fight, *esp* between armies *verb* fight **battleaxe** *noun* **1** *hist* a kind of axe used in fighting **2** *informal* a fierce, domineering woman **battlefield** *noun* the site of a battle **battleship** *noun* a heavily armed and armoured warship

battlement *noun* a wall on the top of a building, with openings or notches for firing

bauble *noun* a brightly-coloured ornament of little value

baud *noun* the speed at which a computer passes information along a telephone line *etc*

bawl *verb* shout or cry out loudly *noun* a loud cry

bay *noun* **1** a wide inlet of the sea in a coastline **2** a space in a room *etc* set back, a recess **3** a compartment in an aircraft **4** the laurel tree *verb* of dogs: bark **bay window** a window that forms a recess **hold at bay** fight off **stand at bay** stand and face attackers *etc*

bayonet *noun* a steel stabbing blade that can be fixed to the muzzle of a rifle *verb* stab with this

bazaar *noun* **1** a sale of goods for charity *etc* **2** an Eastern marketplace **3** a shop

BB *abbrev* Boys' Brigade

BBC *abbrev* British Broadcasting Corporation

BC *abbrev* before Christ: *55BC*

be *verb* **1** live, exist: *there may be some milk left* **2** have a position, quality *etc*: *she wants to be a dentist/ if only you could be happy*

> **be** » *pres form* **am, are, is,** *past form* **was, were,** *past participle* **been** **be** is also used to form tenses of other verbs, *eg* I *was* running for the bus/ when *will* you *be* arriving?

beach *noun* (*plural* **beaches**) the shore of the sea *etc*, *esp* when sandy or pebbly *verb* drive or haul a boat up on the beach **beachcomber** *noun* someone who searches beaches for useful or saleable articles

beacon *noun* **1** a flashing light or other warning signal **2** *hist* a fire on a hill used as a signal of danger

bead *noun* **1** a small pierced ball of glass, plastic *etc*, used in needlework or jewellery-making **2** a drop of liquid: *beads of sweat*

beadle *noun* an officer of a church or college

beagle *noun* a small hound used in hunting hares

beak *noun* **1** the hard, horny part of a bird's mouth with which it gathers food **2** a point, a projection

beaker *noun* a tall cup or glass, usually without a handle

beam *noun* **1** a long straight piece of wood or metal **2** a shaft of light **3** a radio signal **4** the greatest breadth of a ship *verb* **1** shine **2** smile broadly **3** divert by radio wave

bean *noun* **1** a pod-bearing plant **2** the seed of this used as food

bear *noun* a heavy animal with shaggy fur and hooked claws ▫ *verb* **1** *formal* carry **2** endure, put up with **3** produce (fruit, children *etc*) ▫ **bearable** *adj* able to be borne or endured ▫ **bearer** *noun* a carrier or messenger ▫ **bearskin** *noun* the high fur cap worn by the Guards in the British Army ▫ **bear in mind** remember, take into account ▫ **bear out** confirm: *this bears out my suspicions* ▫ **bear with** be patient with ▫ **bring to bear** bring into use

> **bear** *verb* » bear*s*, bear*ing*, bore, borne or born ▫ **born** is used for the past participle when referring to the birth of a child, idea *etc*: *when were you born?*; otherwise the form is **borne**: *I couldn't have borne it any longer*

beard *noun* the hair that grows on a man's chin and cheeks ▫ *verb* face up to, defy

bearing *noun* **1** behaviour **2** direction **3** connection: *it has no bearing on the issue* **4** part of a machine supporting a moving part

beast *noun* **1** a four-footed animal **2** a brutal person

beastly *adj* **1** behaving like an animal **2** horrible **3** *informal* unpleasant ▫ **beastliness** *noun*

beat *verb* **1** hit repeatedly **2** overcome, defeat **3** of a pulse: move or throb in the normal way **4** mark (time) in music **5** stir (a mixture *etc*) with quick movements **6** strike bushes *etc* to rouse birds ▫ *noun* **1** a stroke **2** the regular round of a police officer *etc* ▫ **beaten** *adj* **1** of metal: shaped **2** of earth: worn smooth by treading **3** defeated ▫ **beat up** injure by repeated hitting, kicking *etc*

> **beat** *verb* » beat*s*, beat*ing*, beat, beat*en*

beatific /behə*tif*ik/ *adj* of, or showing, great happiness

beautify *verb* make beautiful

> **beautify** » beautif*ies*, beautify*ing*, beautif*ied*

beauty *noun* (*plural* **beauties**) **1** very attractive or pleasing appearance, sound *etc* **2** a very attractive person, *esp* a woman ▫ **beautiful** *adj* ▫ **beautifully** *adv*

beaver *noun* **1** a gnawing animal that can dam streams **2** a member of the most junior branch of the Scout Association

becalmed *adj* of a sailing ship: unable to move for lack of wind

because *conj* for the reason that: *we didn't go because it was raining* ▫ *adv* (with **of**) on account of: *because of the holiday, the bank will be shut*

beck *noun*: **at someone's beck and call** obeying all their orders or requests

beckon *verb* make a sign (with the finger) to summon someone

become *verb* **1** come to be: *she became angry* **2** suit: *that tie becomes you* ▫ **becoming** *adj* **1** suiting well **2** of behaviour: appropriate, suitable

bed *noun* **1** a place on which to rest or sleep **2** a plot for flowers *etc* in a garden **3** the bottom of a river *etc* ◇ *verb* **1** plant in soil *etc* **2** provide a bed for **3** *informal* have sexual intercourse with ◇ **bedclothes** *noun plural* bedcovers ◇ **bedding** *noun* **1** mattress, bedcovers *etc* **2** straw *etc* for cattle to lie on ◇ **bedridden** *adj* kept in bed by weakness, illness *etc* ◇ **bedrock** *noun* the solid rock under the soil ◇ **bedroom** *noun* a room for sleeping ◇ **bedspread** *noun* a top cover for a bed ◇ **bedstead** *noun* a frame supporting a bed

bed *verb* » bed*s*, bedd*ing*, bedd*ed*

bedlam *noun* a place full of uproar and confusion

After St Mary of *Bethlehem* Hospital, a former mental asylum in London

bedraggled *adj* wet and untidy

bee *noun* **1** a winged insect that makes honey in wax cells **2** a gathering for combined work: *quilting bee* ◇ **beehive** *noun* a dome or box in which bees are kept ◇ **make a beeline for** go directly towards

beech *noun* (*plural* **beeches**) a forest tree with grey smooth bark

beef *noun* the flesh of an ox or cow, used as food ◇ **beefy** *adj* stout, muscular

beefeater *noun* **1** a guardian of the Tower of London **2** a member of the Queen's or King's Guard

Beelzebub *noun, old* the Devil, Satan

been *see* **be**

beer *noun* an alcoholic drink flavoured with hops

beet *noun* a plant with a carrot-like root, one type (**sugar beet**) used as a source of sugar, the other (**beetroot**) used as a vegetable

beetle *noun* an insect with four wings, the front pair forming hard covers for the back pair

beetling *adj* **1** of cliffs *etc*: overhanging **2** of eyebrows: heavy, frowning

befall *verb, formal* happen to, strike: *a disaster befell them*

befall » befall*s*, befall*ing*, be*fell*

befit *verb* be suitable or right for

befit » befit*s*, befitt*ing*, befitt*ed*

before *prep* **1** in front of: *before the entrance to the tunnel* **2** earlier than: *before three o'clock* **3** rather than, in preference to: *I'd die before telling him* ◇ *adv* **1** in front **2** earlier ◇ *conj* earlier than the time that: *before he was born* ◇ **beforehand** *adv* previously, before the time when something else is done

befriend *verb* act as a friend to, help

beg *verb* **1** ask for money *etc* from others **2** ask earnestly: *he begged her to stay* ◇ **beg the question** take as being proved the very point that needs to be proved

beg » beg*s*, begg*ing*, begg*ed*

began *past form* of **begin**

beget *verb, formal* **1** be the father of **2** cause

beget » beget*s*, begett*ing*, beg*at*, beg*otten*

beggar *noun* **1** someone who begs for money **2** a very poor person □ *verb* make poor □ **beggarly** *adj* poor; worthless □ **beggar belief** be beyond belief, be incredible

begin *verb* make a start on □ **beginning** *noun*

begin » begin*s*, beginn*ing*, beg*an*, beg*un*

begone *exclam, formal* be off, go away!

begrudge *verb* grudge, envy: *he begrudged me my success*

beguile *verb* **1** cheat **2** pass (time) pleasantly; amuse, entertain

begun *past participle* of **begin**

behalf *noun*: **on behalf of 1** as the representative of: *on behalf of my client* **2** in aid of: *collecting on behalf of the homeless*

behave *verb* **1** act (in a certain way): *he always behaves badly at parties* **2** conduct yourself well: *can't you behave for just a minute?* □ **behaviour** *noun* □ **badly-behaved** *adj* with bad manners □ **well-behaved** *adj* with good manners

behead *verb* cut off the head of

behemoth *noun* a huge beast; a monster

behest *noun, formal* command

behind *prep* **1** at or towards the back of: *behind the door* **2** after **3** in support of, encouraging: *behind him in his struggle* □ *adv* **1** at the back **2** not up to date: *behind with his work*

behold *verb, formal* look (at), see

beholden to *adj* grateful to because of a good turn

behove *verb*: **it behoves you to** you ought to

being *noun* **1** existence **2** a living person or thing

belabour *verb* beat, thrash □ **belabour the point** discuss a subject at too great length

belated *adj* arriving late

bel canto a style of operatic singing emphasizing beauty of tone

belch 1 bring up wind from the stomach through the mouth **2** of a fire *etc*: send up (smoke *etc*) violently

beleaguer /bəleegər/, *verb* besiege

belfry *noun* (*plural* **belfries**) the part of a steeple or tower in which the bells are hung

belie *verb, formal* prove to be false

belie » belie*s*, bely*ing*, beli*ed*

belief *noun* **1** what someone thinks to be true **2** faith

believe *verb* **1** think of as true or as existing **2** trust (in) **3** think or suppose □ **make believe** pretend

Belisha beacon *Brit* a pole with an orange globe on top, marking a pedestrian crossing

belittle *verb* make to seem small or unimportant

bell *noun* a hollow metal object which gives a ringing sound when struck by the tongue or clapper inside

belle époque the period of relative peace and prosperity in Europe immediately before World War I

belles lettres refined, polite literature ▯ **belletristic** *adj*

bellicose *adj* inclined to fight, quarrelsome ▯ **bellicosity** *noun*

belligerent *adj* quarrelsome, aggressive ▯ **belligerence** or **belligerency** *noun*

bellow *verb* roar like a bull ▯ *noun* a deep roar

bellows *noun plural* an instrument for making a blast of air, *eg* to increase a fire

belly *noun* (*plural* **bellies**) **1** the abdomen **2** the underpart of an animal's body **3** the bulging part of anything ▯ *verb* swell or bulge out ▯ **belly-ache** *noun* **1** a stomach pain **2** a persistent whine or complaint ▯ **belly-button** *noun, informal* the navel ▯ **belly-dance** *noun* a sensuous dance performed by women with circling movements of the stomach and hips ▯ **belly-dancer** *noun* ▯ **belly-flop** *noun* an inexpert dive landing face down on the water ▯ **bellyful** *noun* more than enough (of something) ▯ **belly-laugh** *noun* a deep laugh

> **belly** *verb* » bell*ies*, belly*ing*, bell*ied*

belong *verb* **1** be someone's property: *this book belongs to me* **2** be a member of (a club *etc*) **3** be born in or live in: *I belong to Glasgow* **4** of an object: have its place in: *those glasses belong in the kitchen* ▯ **belongings** *noun plural* what someone possesses

beloved *adj* much loved, very dear ▯ *noun* someone much loved

below *prep* lower in position than: *her skirt reached below her knees/ a captain ranks below a major* ▯ *adv* in a lower position: *looking down at the street below*

belt *noun* **1** a strip of leather, cloth *etc* worn around the waist **2** a continuous band on a machine for conveying objects in a factory *etc* **3** a broad strip, *eg* of land ▯ *verb* **1** put a belt round **2** beat with a belt **3** *informal* beat, hit ▯ **belted** *adj* wearing or having a belt

bemoan *verb* weep about, mourn

bench *noun* (*plural* **benches**) **1** a long seat **2** a work-table **3** (**the bench**) the judges of a court

bend *verb* **1** curve **2** stoop ▯ *noun* **1** a curve **2** a turn in a road

> **bend** *verb* » bend*s*, bend*ing*, bent

beneath *prep* **1** under, in a lower position than: *sitting beneath the tree reading a book* **2** covered by: *wearing a black dress beneath her coat* **3** considered too low a task *etc* for: *sweeping floors was beneath him* ▯ *adv* below

benediction *noun* a blessing

benefactor *noun* someone who does good to others

beneficial *adj* bringing gain or advantage (to) ▯ **beneficially** *adv* ▯ **beneficiary** *noun* (*plural* **beneficiaries**) someone who receives a gift, an advantage *etc*

benefit *noun* **1** something good to receive or have done to you **2**

money received from social security or insurance schemes: *unemployment benefit* ◊ *verb* **1** do good to **2** gain advantage: *benefited from the cut in interest rates*

benefit *verb* » benefit*s*, benefit*ing*, benefit*ed*

benevolence *noun* **1** tendency to do good; kindliness **2** a kind act ◊ **benevolent** *adj* kindly ◊ **benevolently** *adv*

benign /bi*nain*/ *adj* **1** gentle, kindly **2** of disease: not causing death (*contrasted with*: **malignant**)

bent *noun* a natural liking or aptitude (for something) ◊ *adj* **1** curved, crooked **2** *informal* dishonest **3** *informal, derog* homosexual ◊ **be bent on** be determined on ◊ *past form* of **bend**

bequeath *verb* leave by will

bequest *noun* money, property *etc* left in a will

berate *verb* scold

bereaved *adj* suffering from the recent death of a relative or friend ◊ **bereavement** *noun*

bereft *adj* lacking, deprived (of)

beret /*be*reh/ *noun* a flat, round hat

bergamot *noun* a citrus fruit whose rind produces an aromatic oil

Bermuda shorts loose-fitting shorts reaching almost to the knees

berry *noun* (*plural* **berries**) a small juicy fruit enclosing seeds

berserk *adv* in a frenzy, mad

berth *noun* **1** a room for sleeping in a ship *etc* **2** the place where a ship is tied up in a dock ◊ *verb* moor (a ship) ◊ **give a wide berth to** keep well away from

beryl *noun* a type of precious stone such as an emerald or aquamarine

beseech *verb* ask earnestly

beset *verb* attack from all sides; surround

beset » beset*s*, besett*ing*, beset

beside *prep* **1** by the side of, near: *the building beside the station* **2** compared with: *beside her sister she seems quite shy* **3** away from, wide of: *beside the point* ◊ **be beside yourself** lose self-control ◊ **beside the point** irrelevant

besides *prep* **1** in addition to: *he has other friends, besides me* **2** other than, except: *nothing in the fridge besides some cheese* ◊ *adv* **1** also, moreover: *besides, it was your idea* **2** in addition: *plenty more besides*

besiege *verb* **1** surround (a town *etc*) with an army **2** crowd round; overwhelm: *besieged with letters*

besiege » besiege*s*, besieg*ing*, besiege*d*

besmirch *verb* stain, dishonour

besotted *adj*: **besotted with** foolishly fond of

bespoke *adj* of clothes: ordered to be made

best *adj* good in the most excellent way ◊ *adv* in the most excellent way ◊ *verb* defeat ◊ **best man** someone who attends a man who is being married ▯ **best part** the largest or greatest part ▯ **bestseller** *noun* a book *etc* which sells exceedingly well ▯ **at best** under the most favourable circumstances ▯ **do your best** try as hard as you can ▯ **make the best of** do as well as possible with

bestial *adj* like a beast, beastly

bestir *verb* waken up, make lively

> **bestir** » bestir*s*, bestirr*ing*, bestirr*ed*

bestow *verb* give

bestride *verb* stand or sit across, straddle

bet *noun* money put down to be lost or kept depending on the outcome of a race *etc* ▯ *verb* place a bet

> **bet** *verb* » bet*s*, bett*ing*, bet or bett*ed*

beta test *comput* a second-round test of software before its release (*compare with*: **alpha test**)

betake *verb*: **betake yourself** go

bête noir /bet *nwar*/ a particular dislike

betray *verb* **1** give up (secrets, friends *etc*) to an enemy **2** show signs of: *his face betrayed no emotion* ▯ **betrayal** *noun*

betroth *verb, formal* promise in marriage ▯ **betrothal** *noun* ▯ **betrothed to** engaged to be married to

better *adj* **1** good to a greater degree, of a more excellent kind **2** healthier **3** completely recovered from illness: *don't go back to work until you're better* ▯ *adj* in a more excellent way ▯ *verb* improve ▯ **better off** in a better position, wealthier ▯ **get the better of** defeat, overcome ▯ **had better** ought to, must ▯ **think better of** change your mind about

between *prep* **1** in or through the space dividing two people or things: *there was an empty seat between us/ between 3 o'clock and 6 o'clock* **2** in parts, in shares to: *divide the chocolates between you* **3** from one thing to another: *the road between Edinburgh and Glasgow* **4** comparing one to the other: *the only difference between them is the price*

bevel *noun* a slanting edge ▯ *verb* give a slanting edge to ▯ **bevelled** *adj*

> **bevel** *verb* » bevel*s*, bevell*ing*, bevell*ed*

beverage *noun* a drink

bevy[1] *noun* (*plural* **bevies**) **1** a group of women or girls **2** a flock of quails

bevy[2] or **bevvy** *noun* (*plural* **bevies** or **bevvies**) *Brit informal* **1** an alcoholic drink **2** a drinking session

bewail *verb* mourn loudly over

beware *verb* watch out for (something dangerous)

bewilder *verb* puzzle, confuse ▯ **bewildering** *adj* ▯ **bewilderment** *noun* confusion

bewitch *verb* put under a spell; charm ▯ **bewitching** *adj* charming; very beautiful

beyond *prep* **1** on the far side of:

beyond the next set of traffic-lights **2** later than: *beyond January* **3** more than: *beyond the call of duty* **4** too far gone for: *beyond repair* **5** too difficult or confusing for: *it's beyond me!* □ *adv* on or to the far side, further away

bhajee or **bhaji** /*ba*jee/ *noun* an Indian appetizer of vegetables in batter, fried in a ball

bhangra /*bangg*rə/ *noun* music combining Western rock and traditional Punjabi styles

bi- *prefix* **1** having two: *biped/bipolar* **2** occurring twice in a certain period, or once in every two periods: *bi-monthly*

biannual *adj* happening twice a year

> Do not confuse with: **biennial**

bias *noun* **1** the favouring of one person or point of view over any others **2** a tendency to move in a particular direction **3** a weight on or in an object making it move in a particular direction □ *verb* give a bias to □ **bias binding** a piece of material cut on the slant, used for hemming

> **bias** *verb* » bias*es*, bias*ing* or biass*ing*, bias*ed* or biass*ed*

bib *noun* **1** a piece of cloth put under a child's chin to protect their clothes from food stains *etc* **2** a part of an apron, overalls *etc* above the waist, covering the chest

bibelot /*bee*bloh/ *noun* a knick-knack

Bible *noun* the holy book of the Christian Church □ **Biblical** *adj*

bibliography *noun* (*plural* **bibliographies**) **1** a list of books (about a subject) **2** the art of classifying books □ **bibliographer** *noun* someone who compiles bibliographies, or who studies book classification

bibliophile *noun* a lover of books

bicentenary *noun* (*plural* **bicentenaries**) the two-hundredth year after an event *eg* someone's birth

biceps *noun sing* the muscle in front of the upper part of the arm

bicker *verb* quarrel over small matters

bicycle *noun* a cycle with two wheels, driven by foot-pedals

bid *verb* **1** offer a price (for) **2** tell, say: *bidding her farewell* **3** command; invite □ *noun* an offer of a price; a bold attempt: *a bid for freedom*

> **bid** *verb* » bid*s*, bidd*ing*, bade or bid, bidd*en* or bid

bidet /*bee*deh/ *noun* a low wash-basin for washing the genital area

biennial *adj* lasting two years; happening once every two years □ *noun* a plant that flowers only in its second year □ **biennially** *adv*

> ⚠Do not confuse with: **biannual**

bier /beer/ *noun* a carriage or frame for carrying a dead body

big *adj* **1** large in size, amount, extent *etc* **2** important **3** boastful

> **big** » bigg*er*, bigg*est*

bigamy *noun* the crime or fact of having two wives or two husbands at once □ **bigamist** *noun* □ **bigamous** *adj*

bight *noun* a small bay

bigot *noun* someone with narrow-minded, prejudiced beliefs □ **bigoted** *adj* prejudiced □ **bigotry** *noun*

bike *noun*, *informal* a bicycle

bikini *noun* (*plural* **bikinis**) a woman's brief two-piece bathing suit

Named after *Bikini* Atoll atomic test site, because of its supposedly dynamic effect on viewers

bilateral *adj* **1** having two sides **2** affecting two sides, parties *etc*: *bilateral agreement* □ **bilaterally** *adv*

bilberry *noun* a type of plant with an edible dark-blue berry

Bildungsroman *noun* a novel about the early life and growing-up of its central character

bile *noun* a fluid coming from the liver

bilge *noun* **1** the broadest part of a ship's bottom **2** bilgewater **3** *informal* nonsense □ **bilgewater** *noun* water which lies in the ship's bottom

bilingual *adj* using or fluent in two languages

bilious *adj* **1** ill with too much bile; nauseated **2** greenish-yellow in colour □ **biliousness** *noun*

bill *noun* **1** a bird's beak **2** an account for money **3** an early version of a law before it has been passed by parliament **4** a printed sheet of information

billet *noun* a lodging, *esp* for soldiers □ *verb* lodge (soldiers) in private houses

billiards *noun* a game played with a cue and balls on a table

billion *noun* **1** a million millions (1 000 000 000 000) **2** *US* (now often in Britain) a thousand millions (1 000 000 000)

billow *noun* a great wave □ *verb* rise in billows □ **billowy** *adj*

billy *noun* (*plural* **billies**) or **billycan** a container for cooking, making tea *etc* outdoors

billy-goat *noun* a male goat

bimbo *noun* (*plural* **bimbos**) an attractive but not very clever young woman

bin *noun* a container for storing goods or rubbish □ *verb* **1** put in a bin **2** throw away

bin *verb* » bin*s*, binn*ing*, binn*ed*

binary *adj* made up of two □ **binary system** a mathematical system in which numbers are expressed by two digits only, 1 and 0

bind *verb* **1** tie with a band **2** fasten together **3** make to promise □ **binding** *noun* **1** anything that binds **2** the cover, stitching *etc* which holds a book together

bind » bind*s*, bind*ing*, bound

binge *verb* eat and drink too much □ *noun* a spell of over-eating or drinking too much

bingo *noun* a popular gambling game using numbers

binoculars *noun plural* a small double telescope

biodegradable *adj* able to be broken down into parts by bacteria

biography *noun* (*plural* **biographies**) a written account of someone's life □ **biographer** *noun* someone who writes a biography □ **biographical** *adj*

biology *noun* the study of living things □ **biological** *adj* □ **biologist** *noun*

biped *noun* an animal with two feet, *eg* a bird

birch *noun* (*plural* **birches**) **1** a type of hardwood tree **2** a bundle of birch twigs, used for beating □ *verb* beat with a birch

bird *noun* a feathered, egg-laying creature □ **birdwatching** *noun* the study of birds in their natural surroundings □ **bird of prey** a bird (*eg* a hawk) which kills and eats small animals or birds □ **bird's-eye view** a wide view, as would be seen from above □ **get the bird** *slang* be booed or hissed at; be dismissed

biretta *noun* a square cap worn by Roman Catholic clergy

biriyani *noun* an Indian dish of spiced rice

birl *verb, Scot* spin round, whirl

Biro *noun, trademark* a type of ballpoint pen

birth *noun* the very beginning of someone's life □ **birthday** *noun* **1** the day on which someone is born **2** the date of this day each year □ **birthmark** *noun* a mark on the body from birth □ **birthright** *noun* the right which someone may claim because of their parentage

biscuit *noun* dough baked hard in small cakes

bisect *verb* cut in two equal parts

bishop *noun* a high-ranking member of the clergy (next below an archbishop) in the Roman Catholic Church and the Church of England □ **bishopric** *noun* the district ruled by a bishop

bison *noun* (*plural* **bison**) a large wild ox with shaggy hair and a fat hump

bisque /beesk/ *noun* a rich shellfish soup

bistro /*bee*stroh/ *noun* (*plural* **bistros**) a small bar or restaurant

bit[1] *noun* **1** a small piece **2** a small tool for boring **3** the part of the bridle which the horse holds in its mouth **4** *comput* the smallest unit of information □ **bitty** *adj* piecemeal, scrappy □ **do your bit** do your required share □ **bit by bit** gradually □ **to bits** apart, in pieces

bit[2] *past form* of **bite**

bitch *noun* (*plural* **bitches**) **1** a female dog, wolf *etc* **2** *slang* an unpleasant woman

bitchy *adj* catty, malicious □ **bitchily** *adv* □ **bitchiness** *noun*

bite *verb* grip, cut or tear with the teeth □ *noun* **1** a grip with the teeth **2** the part bitten off **3** a nibble at a fishing bait **4** a wound caused by an animal's or insect's bite

bite *verb* » bite*s*, bit*ing*, bit, bitt*en*

bitmap *noun, comput* a method of screen display where each pixel is assigned on one or more bits of memory ▫ *verb* ▫ **bitmapped** *adj* ▫ **bitmapping** *noun*

bitmap *verb* » bitmap*s*, bitmapp*ing*, bitmapp*ed*

bitten *past participle* of **bite**

bitter *adj* **1** unpleasant to the taste; sour **2** harsh: *bitter cold* **3** resentful, angry through disappointment ▫ **bitterly** *adv* ▫ **bitterness** *noun*

bittern *noun* a bird resembling a heron

bitty *see* **bit**[1]

BIV *abbrev* bovine immuno-deficiency disease

bivouac *noun* an overnight camp outdoors without a tent ▫ *verb* sleep outdoors without a tent

bivouac *verb* » bivouac*s*, bivouack*ing*, bivouack*ed*

bi-weekly *adj* happening twice a week or once every two weeks

bizarre *adj* odd, strange ▫ **bizarrely** *adv*

blab *verb* **1** talk a lot **2** let out a secret

blab » blab*s*, blabb*ing*, blabb*ed*

black *adj* dark and colourless ▫ *noun* black colour ▫ **black-and-blue** *adj* badly bruised ▫ **blackball** *verb* ostracize, exclude from (a club *etc*) ▫ **black belt** an award for skill in judo or karate ▫ **black eye** a bruised area round the eye as result of a blow ▫ **blackguard** *noun, old* a wicked person ▫ **black ice** a thin transparent layer of ice on a road *etc* ▫ **blackleg** *noun* someone who works when other workers are on strike ▫ **black market** illegal or dishonest buying and selling ▫ **black-pudding** *noun* blood sausage ▫ **black sheep** someone who is considered a failure or outsider in a group ▫ **black tie** formal evening dress ▫ **black widow** a very poisonous American spider, the female of which often eats her mate ▫ **black out** become unconscious

blackberry *noun* (*plural* **blackberries**) a blackish-purple soft fruit growing on a prickly stem

blackbird *noun* a type of black, thrush-like bird

blackboard *noun* a dark-coloured board for writing on in chalk

blacken *verb* **1** make black or dark **2** dishonour, defame: *blackening his name*

blacklist *noun* a list of people to be refused credit, jobs *etc* ▫ *verb* put on a blacklist

blackmail *noun* the crime of threatening to reveal secrets unless money is paid ▫ *verb* threaten by blackmail ▫ **blackmailer** *noun*

blackout *noun* **1** total darkness caused by putting out or covering all lights **2** a temporary loss of consciousness

blacksmith *noun* someone who makes or repairs iron goods, *esp* horseshoes

bladder *noun* **1** the organ in which urine collects in the body **2** a bag with thin, membrane-like walls □ **bladderwrack** *noun* a common seaweed with air bladders on its strands

blade *noun* **1** the cutting part of a knife, sword *etc* **2** a leaf of grass or wheat

blame *verb* find fault with; consider responsible for □ *noun* fault; responsibility for something bad □ **blameless** *adj* □ **blameworthy** *adj* deserving blame

blancmange /blə*monhzh*/ *noun* a jelly-like pudding made with milk

bland *adj* **1** mild, not strong or irritating: *bland taste* **2** dull, insipid

blandishments *noun plural* acts or words meant to flatter

blank *adj* **1** clear, unmarked: *blank sheet of paper* **2** expressionless: *a blank look* □ *noun* **1** an empty space **2** a cartridge without a bullet □ **blank verse** non-rhyming poetry in a metre of 5 feet per line

blanket *noun* **1** a bedcovering of wool *etc* **2** a widespread, soft covering: *blanket of snow* □ *adj* covering a group of things: *blanket agreement* □ *verb* cover widely or thickly □ **blanket bombing** bombing from the air over a widespread area

blare *verb* sound loudly □ *noun* a loud sound, *eg* on a trumpet

blarney *noun* flattery or coaxing talk

blasé /blah*zeh*/ *adj* indifferent, unconcerned, *esp* because of being already familiar with something

blaspheme *verb* **1** speak irreverently of a god **2** swear, curse □ **blasphemer** *noun* □ **blasphemous** *adj* □ **blasphemy** *noun* (*plural* **blasphemies**)

blast *noun* **1** a blowing or gust of wind **2** a loud note, *eg* on a trumpet **3** an explosion □ *verb* **1** break (stones, a bridge *etc*) by explosion **2** produce a loud noise **3** *formal* wither, destroy □ *exclam* damn! □ **blast furnace** a furnace used in iron-smelting into which hot air is blown □ **blast-off** *noun* the moment of the launching of a rocket □ **at full blast** as quickly, strongly *etc* as possible

blatant *adj* very obvious; shameless: *blatant lie* □ **blatantly** *adv*

blaze *noun* a rush of light or flame □ *verb* **1** burn with a strong flame **2** throw out a strong light

blazer *noun* a light jacket often worn as part of a uniform

blazon *verb* make known publicly; display very obviously

bleach *verb* whiten, remove the colour from □ *noun* (*plural* **bleaches**) a substance which bleaches, used for cleaning, whitening clothes *etc*

bleak *adj* dull and cheerless; cold, unsheltered □ **bleakly** *adv* □ **bleakness** *noun*

bleary *adj* of eyes: tired and inflamed □ **blearily** *adv*

bleat *verb* **1** cry like a sheep **2** complain in an irritating or whining way □ *noun* **1** a sheep's cry **2** an irritating whine

bleed *verb* **1** lose blood **2** draw

blood from □ **bleeding** *noun* a flow of blood

bleed » bleed*s*, bleed*ing*, bled

bleep *noun* a high-pitched intermittent sound □ *verb* give out such a sound

blemish *noun* (*plural* **blemishes**) a stain; a fault or flaw □ *verb* stain, spoil

blend *verb* mix together □ *noun* a mixture □ **blender** *noun* an electric machine which mixes thoroughly and liquidizes food

bless *verb* **1** wish happiness to **2** make happy **3** make holy □ **blessed** *adj* or (in poetry *etc*) **blest 1** happy; fortunate **2** made holy, consecrated □ **blessing** *noun* **1** wish or prayer for happiness **2** a source of happiness or relief: *the extra money was a blessing to them* □ **blessing in disguise** something unexpectedly useful or beneficial

blether *verb, Scot* chatter; talk nonsense

blight *noun* **1** a disease which makes plants wither **2** a cause of destruction □ *verb* destroy

blimp *noun* a small airship used for observation, advertising *etc*

blind *adj* unable to see □ *noun* **1** a window screen **2** a deception, a trick □ *verb* **1** make blind **2** dazzle □ **blindness** □ **blind alley** a street open only at one end; anything which leads nowhere □ **blindfold** *adj* with the eyes bandaged or covered, so as not to see □ *verb* apply a blindfold to □ **blindman's buff** a game in which a blindfold person tries to catch others

blink *verb* close the eyes for a moment; shine unsteadily □ *noun* □ **blinkers** pieces of leather over a horse's eyes to prevent it seeing in any direction except in front

bliss *noun* very great happiness □ **blissful** *adj*

blister *noun* a thin bubble on the skin full of watery matter □ *verb* rise up in a blister

blithe *adj* happy, merry □ **blithely** adv

BLitt *abbrev* Bachelor of Literature; Bachelor of Letters

blitz *noun* (*plural* **blitzes**) **1** an air attack **2** a sudden violent attack

blizzard *noun* a fierce storm of wind and snow

bloated *adj* swollen, puffed out □ **bloater** *noun* a type of smoked herring

blob *noun* **1** a drop of liquid **2** a round spot

bloc /blok/ *noun* an alliance of countries for trade *etc*

block *noun* **1** a lump of wood, stone *etc* **2** a connected group of buildings **3** an obstruction: *road block* **4** an engraved piece of wood or metal for printing **5** *hist* the wood on which people were beheaded □ *verb* hinder, prevent from progess □ **blockhead** *noun* a stupid person □ **block letters** capital letters

blockade *verb* surround a fort or country so that food *etc* cannot reach it □ *noun* the surrounding of a place in this way

blond *adj* **1** light-coloured **2** fair-haired

blonde *adj* having fair skin and light-coloured hair □ *noun* a woman with this colouring

blood *noun* **1** the red liquid which flows in the bodies of human beings and animals **2** someone's descent or parentage: *royal blood* □ **blood donor** someone who gives blood which is stored and given to others in transfusions *etc* □ **blood group** any one of the types into which human blood is divided □ **bloodhound** *noun* a breed of large dog with a good sense of smell □ **bloodless** *adj* without bloodshed: *bloodless revuolution* □ **bloodshed** *noun* violent loss of lfe, slaughter □ **bloodshot** *adj* of eyes: inflamed with blood □ **bloodthirsty** *adj* cruel, eager to kill □ **blood-vessel** *noun* a vein or artery in which the blood circulates

bloody *adj* **1** covered with blood **2** extremely violent, gory **3** *informal* terrible, awful **bloodily** *adv*

bloom *verb* **1** of a plant: flower **2** be in good health □ *noun* **1** a flower **2** rosy colour **3** freshness, perfection **4** a powder on the skin of fresh fruits

bloomers *noun plural* **1** loose underpants with legs gathered above the knee **2** *hist* a woman's outfit of a jacket, skirt and baggy knee-length trousers

After Amelia *Bloomer*, 19th-century US feminist who promoted the use of the outfit for women

blossom *noun* **1** a flower **2** the flowers on a fruit-tree □ *verb* **1** produce flowers **2** open out, develop, flourish

blot *noun* **1** a spot of ink **2** a stain □ *verb* **1** spot, stain **2** dry writing with blotting paper □ **blotting paper** thick paper for absorbing spilled or excess ink □ **blot out** remove from sight or memory

blot *verb* » blot*s*, blott*ing*, blott*ed*

blotch *noun* (*plural* **blotches**) a spot or patch of colour *etc* □ *verb* mark with blotches □ **blotched** *adj* □ **blotchy** *adj*

blotto *adj*, *Brit slang* drunk

blouse *noun* a loose piece of clothing for the upper body

blouson /*bloo*zonh/ *noun* a loose-fitting blouse gathered at the waist

blow *noun* **1** a hard stroke or knock, *eg* with the fist **2** *informal* a sudden piece of bad luck □ *verb* **1** of wind: move around **2** drive air upon or into **3** sound (a wind instrument) **4** breathe hard or with difficulty □ **blowfly** *noun* a fly which lays its eggs in dead flesh □ **blow-job** *noun, slang* fellatio □ **blowlamp** or **blowtorch** *noun* a tool for aiming a very hot flame at a particular spot □ **blowy** *adj* windy □ **blow over** pass and be forgotten □ **blow up** destroy by explosion

blow *verb* » blow*s*, blow*ing*, blew, blown

BLT *abbrev* bacon, lettuce and tomato (sandwich)

blubber *noun* the fat of whales and other sea animals

bludgeon *noun* a short stick with a heavy end

blue *noun* the colour of a clear sky ▫ *adj* **1** of this colour **2** *informal* unhappy, depressed **3** containing sexual material: *blue film* ▫ **the blues** *noun plural* **1** a slow, sad song **2** low spirits, depression ▫ **bluebell** *noun* **1** the wild hyacinth **2** in Scotland, the harebell ▫ **blue blood** royal or aristocratic blood ▫ **bluebottle** *noun* a large fly with a blue abdomen ▫ **blue-chip** *adj* of a business company: reliable for investment; prestigious ▫ **blue funk** *informal* a state of great terror or panic ▫ **blue-pencil** *verb* edit, correct ▫ **Blue Peter** a blue flag with white centre, raised when a ship is about to sail ▫ **blueprint** *noun* a plan of work to be done ▫ **out of the blue** unexpectedly

bluff *adj* **1** rough and cheerful in manner **2** frank, outspoken ▫ *verb* try to deceive by pretending self-confidence ▫ *noun* **1** a steep bank overlooking the sea or a river **2** deception, trickery

blunder *verb* make a bad mistake ▫ *noun* a bad mistake

blunderbuss *noun* (*plural* **blunderbusses**) a short hand-gun with a wide mouth

blunt *adj* **1** having an edge or point that is not sharp **2** rough in manner ▫ *verb* make less sharp or less painful ▫ **bluntly** *adv* frankly, straightforwardly ▫ **bluntness** *noun*

blur *noun* an indistinct area of something; a smudge, a smear ▫ *verb* make indistinct, smudge ▫ **blurred** *adj*

blur *verb* » blur*s*, blurr*ing*, blurr*ed*

blurt *verb*: **blurt out** speak suddenly and without thinking

blush *noun* (*plural* **blushes**) **1** a red glow on the face caused by embarrassment *etc* **2** a reddish glow ▫ *verb* go red in the face

bluster *verb* **1** blow strongly **2** boast loudly ▫ *noun* **1** a blasting wind **2** empty boasting

BMA *abbrev* British Medical Association

BMus *abbrev* Bachelor of Music

boa *noun* a long scarf of fur or feathers ▫ **boa constrictor** a large snake which kills its prey by winding itself round it and crushing it

boar *noun* **1** a male pig **2** a wild pig

board *noun* **1** a sheet of wood **2** a group of people who run a business: *board of directors* **3** stiff card used to bind books **4** food: *bed and board* ▫ *verb* **1** cover with boards **2** supply with food at fixed terms **3** enter (a ship, aeroplane *etc*) ▫ **boarder** *noun* someone who receives food and lodging ▫ **boarding-house** *noun* a house where paying guests receive meals at a fixed price ▫ **boarding-school** *noun* a school in which food and lodging is given

boast *verb* brag, speak proudly and exaggeratedly about yourself ▯ *noun* something said in a bragging or boasting manner ▯ **boastful** *adj* fond of boasting ▯ **boastfully** *adv* ▯ **boastfulness** *noun*

boat *noun* **1** a vessel for sailing or rowing; a ship **2** a boat-shaped dish: *sauceboat* ▯ *verb* sail about in a boat

boater *noun* a straw hat with a brim

boatswain or **bosun** /*boh*sn/ *noun* an officer who looks after a ship's boats, rigging *etc*

bob[1] *verb* **1** move up and down rapidly **2** cut (hair) to about neck level ▯ *noun* a bobbed haircut

> **bob** *verb* » bob*s*, bobb*ing*, bobb*ed*

bob[2] *noun* a bobsleigh

bobbin *noun* a reel or spool on which thread is wound

bobby *noun*, *Brit informal* a police officer

> After *Robert* Peel, who introduced the Metropolitan Police Force when Home Secretary in 1828

bobsleigh *noun* a long sledge or two short sledges joined together with one long seat

bode *verb*: **bode well** or **bode ill** be a good or bad sign

bodhisattva /bodi*satv*ə/ *noun* a future Buddha

bodhran /bo*ran*/ *noun* a hand-held Irish or Scottish drum, beaten with a short stick

bodice *noun* the close-fitting part of a woman's or a child's dress above the waist

bodkin *noun, old* a large blunt needle

body *noun* (*plural* **bodies**) **1** the whole or main part of a human being or animal **2** a corpse **3** the main part of anything **4** a mass of people **5** *informal* a bodystocking ▯ **bodyguard** *noun* someone or a group of people whose job is to protect another person from harm or attack ▯ **bodily** *adj* of the body ▯ **body language** communication by means of conscious or unconscious gestures, attitudes, facial expressions *etc* ▯ **bodystocking** *noun* a one-piece woman's undergarment ▯ **bodyswerve** *verb*, *informal* bypass, avoid deliberately ▯ **bodywarmer** *noun* a padded sleeveless jacket

boffin *noun, informal* a research scientist

> Said to come from a scientist who gave his colleagues nicknames from Dickens, Mr *Boffin* being a character in *Our Mutual Friend*

bog *noun* **1** a marsh **2** *slang* a toilet ▯ **boggy** *adj* marshy ▯ **bog down** prevent from making progress ▯ **bog-standard** *adj* of the lowest grade

bogey *noun* something greatly feared

boggle *verb* be astonished at

bogle /*boh*gl/ *noun* a ghost, a ghoul

bogus *adj* false

bohemian *noun* someone who lives outside social conventions, *esp* an artist or writer ▫ *adj* of the lifestyle of a bohemian

boil *verb* **1** of a liquid: reach the temperature at which it turns to vapour **2** bubble up owing to heat **3** *informal* be hot **4** *informal* be angry ▫ *noun* a kind of inflamed swelling ▫ **boiling-point** *noun* the temperature at which a liquid turns to vapour (*eg* for water, 100°C)

boiler *noun* a container in which water is heated or steam is produced

boisterous *adj* **1** wild, noisy **2** of weather: stormy ▫ **boisterously** *adv* ▫ **boisterousness** *noun*

bold *adj* **1** daring, full of courage **2** cheeky **3** striking, well-marked: *bold colours* **4** of printing type: thick and clear ▫ **boldly** *adv* ▫ **boldness** *noun*

bolero /bo*leh*roh/ *noun*

bollard *noun* **1** a post to which ropes are fastened on a ship or quay **2** a short post on a street used for traffic control

bollocks *noun plural*, *slang* **1** the testicles **2** rubbish, nonsense ▫ **bollocking** *noun, slang* a severe reprimand

Bolshevik *noun* **1** *hist* a member of the Extreme Socialist Party in revolutionary Russia **2** *derog* a communist

> A Russian word based on *bolshe* 'greater', because of the majority held by the Bolsheviks in the Social Democratic Congress of 1903

bolshy *adj*, *informal* awkward, uncooperative ▫ **bolshiness** *noun*

> Originally a shortening of **Bolshevik**

bolster *noun* a long cylindrical pillow or cushion ▫ **bolster up** support

bolt *noun* **1** a small metal sliding bar used to fasten a door *etc* **2** a large screw or pin **3** a roll of cloth ▫ *verb* **1** fasten with a bolt **2** swallow (food) hurriedly **3** rush away, escape ▫ **bolt upright** sitting with a very straight back

bomb *noun* **1** a case containing explosive or other harmful material thrown, dropped, timed to go off automatically *etc* **2** (**the bomb**) the nuclear bomb ▫ *verb* drop bombs on ▫ **bomber** *noun* **1** an aeroplane built for bombing **2** someone who throws or plants bombs ▫ **bombshell** *noun* **1** a startling piece of news **2** a stunningly attractive woman

bombard *verb* **1** attack with artillery **2** overwhelm (with): *bombarded with letters* ▫ **bombardment** *noun*

bombast *noun* pompous language ▫ **bombastic** *adj* using pompous language

bona fide /*boh*nə *fai*deh/ *adj* real, genuine: *bona fide excuse*

bond *noun* **1** something which

binds, *eg* a rope **2** something which brings people together: *music was a bond between them* **3** a promise to pay or do something ◇ **bonded warehouse** a warehouse where goods are kept until taxes have been paid on them ◇ **in bond** in a bonded warehouse

bondage *noun* slavery

bone *noun* **1** a hard material forming the skeleton of animals **2** one of the connected pieces of a skeleton: *the hip bone* ◇ *verb* take the bones out of (meat *etc*)

bony *adj* **1** full of bones **2** not fleshy, thin **3** made of bone or bone-like substance

bonfire *noun* a large fire in the open air

bonk *noun* **1** the sound of a blow **2** *slang* an act of sexual intercourse

bon mot /bon *moh*/ a saying

bonnet *noun* **1** a decorative woman's hat, fastened under the chin **2** the covering over a motor-car engine

bonny *adj* good-looking; pretty

bonsai /*bonzai*/ *noun* a miniature or dwarf tree created by special pruning

bonus *noun* (*plural* **bonuses**) **1** an extra payment in addition to wages **2** something extra

boo *verb* make a sound of disapproval ◇ *noun* a sound of disapproval

boob *noun* **1** *informal* a mistake **2** *slang* a woman's breast

booby *noun* (*plural* **boobies**) an idiot ◇ **booby prize** a prize for the person who is last in a competition ◇ **booby trap** a device hidden or disguised as something harmless, intended to injure the first person to come near it

book *noun* **1** a number of pages bound together **2** a written work which has appeared, or is intended to appear, in the form of a book ◇ *verb* order (places *etc*) beforehand ◇ **book-keeping** *noun* the keeping of accounts ◇ **booklet** *noun* a small paperback book ◇ **bookmaker** *noun* someone who takes bets and pays winnings ◇ **bookworm** *noun* **1** an avid reader **2** a grub that eats holes in books

bookie *noun*, *informal* a bookmaker

boom *verb* **1** make a hollow sound or roar **2** increase in prosperity, success *etc* ◇ *noun* **1** a loud, hollow sound **2** a rush or increase of trade, prosperity *etc*: *oil boom/ property boom* **3** a pole along which a sail is stretched

boomerang *noun* a curved piece of wood which when thrown returns to the thrower, a traditional hunting weapon of Australian Aboriginals

boon *noun* something to be grateful for, a blessing ◇ **boon companion** a close friend who is good company

boor *noun* a rough or rude person ◇ **boorish** *adj*

boost *verb* push up, raise, increase: *boost the sales figures* ◇ *noun* an increase, a rise

booster *noun* **1** a device for

increasing the power of a machine *etc* **2** the first of several stages of a rocket

boot *noun* **1** a heavy shoe covering the foot and lower part of the leg **2** *Brit* a place for stowing luggage in a car **3** the starting of a computer from its start-up programs **4** a kick □ *verb* kick □ **bootee** *noun* a knitted boot for a baby □ **boot up** start (a computer) by running its start-up programs □ **to boot** in addition, as well

booth *noun* **1** a covered stall, *eg* at a market **2** a small compartment for telephoning, voting *etc*

bootleg *adj* of alcohol, recorded music *etc*: made illegally □ **bootlegger** *noun* a dealer in illegal drink, recordings *etc*

booty *noun* plunder, gains taken in war *etc*

border *noun* **1** the edge or side of anything **2** the boundary of a country **3** a flowerbed in a garden □ *verb* (with **on**) be near to: *bordering on the absurd*

bore[1] *verb* **1** make a hole by piercing **2** weary, be tiresome to: *this book bores me* □ *noun* **1** a pierced hole **2** the size across the tube of a gun **3** a tiresome person or thing **4** a wave that rushes up a river mouth at high tide □ **boring** *adj*

bore[2] *past form* of **bear**

boredom *noun* lack of interest, weariness

born *adj* by birth, natural: *a born actor* □ **be born 1** of a baby: come out of the mother's womb **2** come into existence

⚠Do not confuse: **born** and **borne**

borne *see* **bear**

borough *noun* **1** *hist* a town with special privileges granted by royal charter **2** a town that elects Members of Parliament

borrow *verb* get on loan

borsch or **borscht** /borsh/ *noun* an East European beetroot soup

borzoi *noun* a breed of long-haired dog

bosh *noun* nonsense

bosom *noun* the breast; midst, centre: *bosom of her family* □ *adj* of a friend: close, intimate

boss *noun* (*plural* **bosses**) a manager, a chief □ *verb* order about in a high-handed way

bossy *adj* tending to boss others, domineering □ **bossily** *adv* □ **bossiness** *noun*

bosun *see* **boatswain**

botany *noun* the study of plants □ **botanic** or **botanical** *adj* □ **botanist** *noun* someone who studies botany □ **botanic garden** a large public garden containing plants and trees from different countries

botch *verb* mend clumsily; do badly □ *noun* a badly done piece of work

both *adj* & *pronoun* the two, the one and the other: *we're both going to Paris/ both the men are dead* □ *adv* equally, together: *both willing and able*

bother *verb* **1** be a nuisance to: *stop bothering me!* **2** take time or trouble over something: *don't bother with the dishes* ◊ *noun* trouble, inconvenience

bothy *noun* (*plural* **bothies**) **1** in Scotland, a hut to give shelter to hillwalkers **2** a simply furnished hut for farm workers

bottle *noun* a hollow narrow-necked vessel for holding liquids ◊ *verb* put in a bottle ◊ **bottle up** keep in, hold back (feelings)

bottleneck *noun* **1** a narrow part of a road likely to become crowded with traffic **2** a stage in a process where progress is held up

bottom *noun* **1** the lowest part or underside of anything **2** the buttocks ◊ **bottomless** *adj* extremely deep

botulism *noun* food-poisoning caused by bacteria in infected tinned food *etc*

boudoir /*bood*wahr/ *noun* a lady's private room

bough *noun* a branch of a tree

bought *past form* of **buy**

boulder *noun* a large stone

bounce *verb* **1** jump up after striking the ground *etc* **2** make (a ball *etc*) do this ◊ *noun* a jumping back up ◊ **bouncing** *adj* full of life, lively ◊ **bounce back** recover after a setback or trouble

bouncer *noun* someone employed to force troublemakers to leave a club *etc*

bound[1] *noun* **1** a leap, a jump **2** (**bounds**) borders, limits ◊ *verb* **1** jump, leap **2** enclose, surround ◊ **boundless** *adj* having no limit, vast ◊ **bound for** ready to go to, on the way to ◊ **bound to** certain to ◊ **out of bounds** beyond the permitted limits

bound[2] *past form* of **bind**

boundary *noun* (*plural* **boundaries**) **1** an edge, a limit **2** a line *etc* marking an edge

bounteous or **bountiful** *adj* generous; plentiful

bounty *noun* (*plural* **bounties**) **1** a gift; generosity **2** money given as a help ◊ **bounty hunter** someone who tracks down people wanted by the authorities to collect the rewards offered

bouquet /boo*keh*/ *noun* **1** a bunch of flowers **2** a scent, *eg* of wine ◊ **bouquet garni** a bunch of herbs put in a stew *etc*

bourgeois /*boor*zhwah/ *adj* of the middle class ◊ **bourgeoisie** *noun*

bout *noun* **1** a round in a contest **2** a spell, a fit: *bout of flu*

boutique *noun* a small shop selling fashionable clothes *etc*

bovine *adj* **1** of or like cattle **2** stupid

bow[1] /bow/ *verb* **1** bend **2** nod the head or bend the body in greeting **3** give in: *bow to pressure* **4** weigh down, crush ◊ *noun* **1** a bending of the head or body **2** the front part of a ship

bow[2] /boh/ *noun* **1** anything in the shape of a curve or arch **2** a weapon for shooting arrows, made of a stick of springy wood bent by a string **3** a looped knot **4** a wooden rod with horsehair stretched along it, by which the strings of a violin *etc* are played □ **bow-legged** *adj* having legs curving outwards □ **bow window** a window built in a curve

bowdlerize *verb* expurgate, censor heavily

> After Thomas *Bowdler*, who produced an expurgated edition of Shakespeare in the 19th century

bowels *noun plural* **1** the large and small intestines **2** the innermost or deepest parts of anything: *in the bowels of the earth*

bower /*bowər*/ *noun* a shady spot in a garden

bowl *noun* **1** a basin for holding liquids **2** a basin-shaped hollow **3** a heavy wooden ball, used in skittles *etc* **4** (**bowls**) a game played on a green with specially weighted bowls □ *verb* **1** play at bowls **2** move speedily like a bowl **3** *cricket* send the ball at the wicket **4** *cricket* put out by knocking the wicket with the ball □ **bowl over 1** knock down **2** surprise greatly

bowler *noun* **1** someone who plays bowls **2** someone who bowls in cricket **3** a hat with a rounded top

box *noun* (*plural* **boxes**) **1** a case for holding anything **2** a hardwood tree **3** an evergreen shrub **4** an enclosure of private seats in a theatre □ *verb* **1** put in a box **2** confine in a small space **3** punch **4** engage in the sport of boxing □ **box office** an office where theatre tickets *etc* may be bought

boxer *noun* **1** someone who boxes as a sport **2** a breed of large smooth-haired dog with a head like a bulldog's □ **boxer shorts** loose-fitting men's underpants

boxing *noun* the sport of fighting with the fists wearing padded gloves □ **Boxing Day** the first weekday after Christmas Day

boy *noun* **1** a male child **2** a male servant □ **boyish** *adj* □ **boyishly** *adv* □ **boyhood** *noun* the time of being a boy

boycott *verb* refuse to do business or trade with □ *noun* a refusal to trade or do business

> After Charles *Boycott*, British estate manager ostracized by the Irish Land League in the 19th century

bpi *abbrev, comput* bits per inch

BR *abbrev* British Rail

bra *noun, informal* a brassière

brace *noun* **1** an instrument which draws things together and holds them firmly **2** a piece of wire fitted over teeth to straighten them **3** a pair of pheasant, grouse *etc* when shot **4** a carpenter's tool for boring **5** (**braces**) shoulder-straps for holding up trousers □ *verb* strengthen, give firmness to

bracelet *noun* **1** a circular ornament placed around the wrist **2** *slang* a handcuff

bracing *adj* giving strength

bracken *noun* a coarse kind of fern

bracket *noun* **1** a support for something fastened to a wall **2** each of a pair of written or printed marks, *eg* ( ), [ ], used to group together several words **3** a grouping, category: *in the same age bracket* ▫ *verb* **1** enclose in brackets **2** group together

brackish *adj* of water: rather salty

brag *verb* boast ▫ *noun* a boast

> **brag** *verb* » brag*s*, bragg*ing*, bragg*ed*

braggart *noun* someone vain and boastful

braid *verb* plait (the hair) ▫ *noun* **1** a plait of hair **2** decorative ribbon used as trimming

braille *noun* a system of raised marks on paper which blind people can read by feeling

> Named after its inventor, French teacher Louis *Braille*

brain *noun* the part of the body inside the skull, the centre of feeling and thinking ▫ *verb* knock out the brains of; hit hard on the head ▫ **brainwashing** *noun* forcing (a person) to change their views ▫ **brainwave** *noun* a good idea ▫ **brainy** *adj*, *informal* clever

braise *verb* stew (meat) in a small amount of liquid

brake *noun* a part of a vehicle used for stopping or slowing down ▫ *verb* slow down by using the brake(s)

bramble *noun* **1** the blackberry bush **2** its fruit

bran *noun* the inner husks of wheat *etc*, separated from flour after grinding

branch *noun* (*plural* **branches**) **1** an arm-like limb of a tree **2** a small shop, bank *etc* belonging to a bigger one ▫ *verb* spread out like branches

brand *noun* **1** a make of goods with a special trademark **2** a burning piece of wood **3** a permanent mark made by a red-hot iron ▫ *verb* **1** mark with a brand **2** mark permanently; impress deeply **3** mark with disgrace: *branded as a thief* ▫ **brand-new** *adj* absolutely new

brandish *verb* wave (a weapon *etc*) about

brandy *noun* (*plural* **brandies**) an alcoholic spirit made from wine

brass *noun* (*plural* **brasses**) **1** metal made by mixing copper and zinc **2** *music* brass wind instruments ▫ *adj* **1** made of brass **2** playing brass musical instruments: *brass band* ▫ **brass plate** a nameplate on a door *etc* ▫ **brassy** *adj* **1** like brass **2** of a voice: harsh

brassière *noun* an article of women's underwear for supporting the breasts

brat *noun* a disapproving name for a child

bravado *noun* a show of bravery, bold pretence

brave *adj* ready to meet danger, pain *etc* without showing fear; courageous, noble ▫ *verb* face or meet boldly and without fear ▫ *noun* a Native American warrior ▫ **bravely** *adv* ▫ **bravery** *noun*

bravo *exclam* well done!

bravura /brah*voor*ə/ *noun* boldness, spirit, dash

brawl *noun* a noisy quarrel; a fight □ *verb* quarrel or fight noisily

brawn *noun* muscle power □ **brawny** *adj* big and strong

bray *noun* **1** a cry like that of an ass **2** a pin pressing against a string on a harp to produce a buzzing effect □ *verb* cry like an ass

brazen *adj* **1** impudent, shameless: *brazen hussy* **2** of or like brass □ **brazenly** *adv* □ **brazen it out** face a difficult situation with bold impudence

brazier *noun* an iron basket for holding burning coals

brazil-nut *noun* a three-sided nut produced by a Brazilian tree

breach *noun* (*plural* **breaches**) **1** a break, a gap **2** a breaking of a law, a promise *etc* **3** a quarrel □ *verb* make a gap or opening in □ **breach of the peace** a breaking of the law by noisy, offensive behaviour

bread *noun* food made of flour or meal and baked □ **breadwinner** *noun* someone who earns a living for a family □ **daily bread** necessary food, means of living

breadth *noun* **1** distance from side to side, width **2** extent: *breadth of knowledge*

break *verb* **1** (cause to) fall to pieces or apart **2** act against (a law, promise *etc*) **3** interrupt (a silence) **4** tell (news) **5** check, soften the effect of (a fall) **6** cure (a habit) **7** of a boy's voice: drop to a deep male tone □ *noun* **1** an opening **2** a pause **3** *informal* a lucky chance □ **breakable** *adj* □ **breakage** *noun* **1** the act of breaking **2** something broken □ **breakdown** *noun* **1** a division into parts **2** a collapse from nervous exhaustion *etc* □ **breaker** *noun* a large wave □ **break-in** *noun* illegal forced entry of a house *etc* with intent to steal □ **break-through** *noun* a sudden success after some effort □ **breakwater** *noun* a barrier to break the force of waves □ **break down** **1** divide into parts **2** of an engine: fail **3** be overcome with weeping or nervous exhaustion □ **break in** tame, train (a wild horse *etc*) □ **break into** enter by force □ **break out** **1** appear suddenly **2** escape **3** (with **in**) become covered (with a rash *etc*) □ **break up** **1** (cause to) fall to pieces or apart **2** separate, leave one another

> **break** *verb* » break*s*, break*ing*, broke, broken

breakfast *noun* the first meal of the day □ *verb* eat this meal

bream *noun* a small fish

breast *noun* **1** either of the milk-producing glands on a woman's body **2** the front part of a human or animal body between neck and belly **3** a part of a jacket or coat which covers the breast □ **breastbone** *noun* the bone running down the middle of the breast; the sternum □ **breastplate** *noun* a piece of armour for the breast □ **make a clean breast** make a full confession

breath *noun* **1** the air drawn into and then sent out from the lungs **2** an instance of breathing **3** a very slight breeze

> ⚠Do not confuse: **breath** and **breathe**

breathalyser *noun* a device into which someone breathes to indicate the amount of alcohol in their blood

breathe *verb* **1** draw in and send out air from the lungs **2** whisper

> **breathe** » breath*es*, breath*ing*, breath*ed*

breather *noun* a rest or pause

breathless *adj* **1** breathing very fast, panting **2** excited □ **breathlessly** *adv* □ **breathlessness** *noun*

bred *past form* of **breed**

breech *noun* the back part, *esp* of a gun □ **breech birth** the birth of a baby feet first from the womb

breeches *noun plural* trousers reaching to just below the knee

breed *verb* **1** produce (children or a family) **2** mate and rear (animals) **3** cause: *dirt breeds disease* □ *noun* **1** a group of animals *etc* descended from the same ancestor **2** type, sort: *a new breed of salesmen*

> **breed** *verb* » breed*s*, breed*ing*, bred

breeding *noun* **1** act of producing or rearing **2** good manners; education and training

breeze *noun* a gentle wind

breezy *adj* **1** windy, gusty **2** bright, lively □ **breezily** *adv*

brethren *noun plural, old* brothers

breve /breev/ *noun* a musical note (𝅜) equivalent to double a whole note or semibreve

brevity *noun* shortness, conciseness

brew *verb* **1** make beer **2** make (tea *etc*) **3** be gathering or forming: *there's trouble brewing* **4** plot, plan: *brewing mischief* □ **brewer** *noun* someone who brews beer *etc*

brewery *noun* (*plural* **breweries**) a place where beer is made

briar or **brier** *noun* **1** the wild rose **2** a heather plant whose wood is used for making tobacco pipes

bribe *noun* a gift of money *etc* given to persuade someone to do something □ *verb* give a bribe to □ **bribery** *noun*

> **bribe** *verb* » bribe*s*, brib*ing*, brib*ed*

bric-à-brac *noun* small odds and ends

brick *noun* **1** a block of baked clay for building **2** a toy building-block of wood *etc*

bride *noun* a woman about to be married, or newly married □ **bridal** *adj* of a bride or a wedding □ **bridegroom** *noun* a man about to be married, or newly married □ **bridesmaid** *noun* an unmarried woman who attends the bride at a wedding

bridge[1] *noun* **1** a structure built to carry a track or road across a river *etc* **2** the captain's platform on a ship **3** the bony part of the nose **4** a thin piece of wood holding up the strings of a violin *etc* □ *verb* **1** be a bridge over; span **2** build a bridge over **3** get over (a difficulty)

bridge *verb* » bridge*s*, bridg*ing*, bridge*d*

bridge[2] *noun* a card game for two pairs of players

bridle *noun* the harness on a horse's head to which the reins are attached ▢ *verb* **1** put on a bridle **2** toss the head indignantly ▢ **bridle-path** *noun* a path for horseriders

Brie /bree/ *noun* a soft cheese with a yellowish centre and white rind

brief *adj* short; taking a short time ▢ *noun* a set of notes giving information or instructions, *esp* to a lawyer about a law case▢ *verb* instruct or inform ▢ **briefly** *adv* ▢ **in brief** in a few words

briefs *noun plural* close-fitting underpants

brier *another spelling* of **briar**

brig *noun* a sailing vessel with two masts and square-cut sails

brigade *noun* a body of soldiers, usually two battalions

brigadier *noun* a senior army officer

brigand *noun, old* a robber, a bandit

bright *adj* **1** shining; full of light **2** clever **3** cheerful

brighten *verb* make or grow bright

brilliant *adj* **1** very clever **2** sparkling **3** *informal* very good, excellent ▢ **brilliance** *noun* ▢ **brilliantly** *adv*

brim *noun* **1** the edge of a cup *etc*: *filled to the brim* **2** the protruding lower edge of a hat or cap ▢ *verb* be full ▢ **brimful** *adj* full to the brim

brim *verb* » brim*s*, brimm*ing*, brimm*ed*

brimstone *noun* sulphur

brine *noun* salt water ▢ **briny** *adj*

bring *verb* **1** fetch, lead or carry (to a place) **2** cause to come: *the medicine brings him relief* ▢ **bring about** cause ▢ **bring home to** make (someone) realize (something) ▢ **bring off** do (something) successfully ▢ **bring to** revive ▢ **bring up 1** rear, feed and educate: *brought up three children single-handed* **2** mention: *I'll bring it up at the meeting* **3** *informal* vomit

bring » bring*s*, bring*ing*, brought

brink *noun* the edge of a cliff *etc* ▢ **on the brink of** almost at the point of, on the verge of: *on the brink of tears* ▢ **brinkmanship** *noun* the pursuit of a policy to the very edge of disaster

brio /*bree*oh/ *noun* liveliness, spirit

brioche /bree*osh*/ *noun* a rich bread made with egg dough

briquette /bri*ket*/ *noun* a small brick of compressed charcoal *etc*

brisk *adj* **1** moving quickly: *a brisk walk* **2** lively and efficient: *a brisk manner* ▢ **briskly** *adv* ▢ **briskness** *noun*

bristle *noun* a short, stiff hair on an animal, a brush, *etc* ▢ *verb* **1** of hair *etc*: stand on end **2** show anger and indignation: *he bristled at my remark* ▢ **bristly** *adj* having bristles; rough

brittle *adj* hard but easily broken

broach *verb* **1** begin to talk about: *broached the subject* **2** open, begin using (*eg* a cask of wine)

broad *adj* **1** wide, extensive **2** of an accent *etc*: strong, obvious ▫ **broaden** *verb* make or grow broader ▫ **broadly** *adv*

broadcast *verb* transmit (a programme *etc*) on radio or television ▫ *noun* a programme transmitted on radio or television

broadsheet *noun* a large-format quality newspaper. Compare with **tabloid**

broadside 1 a strong attack in an argument *etc* **2** a shot by all the guns on one side of a ship

brocade *noun* a silk cloth on which fine patterns are sewn

broccoli *noun* a hardy variety of cauliflower with small green or purple flower-heads

brochure /broh*shoor*/ or /*broh*shər/ *noun* a booklet, a pamphlet: *holiday brochure*

brogue[1] /brohg/ *noun* a strong shoe

brogue[2] /brohg/ *noun* a broad accent in speaking: *Irish brogue*

broil *verb* **1** make or be very hot **2** *US* grill

broke *past form* of **break** ▫ *adj*, *informal* having no money

broken *past participle* of **break**

broker *noun* someone who buys and sells stocks and shares for others ▫ *verb* **1** act as a broker **2** negotiate on behalf of others: *broker a deal*

bromide *noun* **1** a chemical used as a sedative **2** a dull person **3** a platitude **4** a monochrome photographic print

bronchitis *noun* an illness affecting the windpipe, causing difficulty in breathing ▫ **bronchial** *adj* having to do with the windpipe

bronco *noun* (*plural* **broncos**) *US* a half-tamed horse

brontosaurus *noun* a large dinosaur

bronze *noun* a golden-brown mixture of copper and tin ▫ *adj* of this colour ▫ **bronzed** *adj* suntanned

brooch *noun* (*plural* **brooches**) an ornament pinned to the clothing

brood *verb* **1** of a hen *etc*: sit on eggs **2** think anxiously for some time ▫ *noun* **1** a number of young birds hatched at one time **2** young animals or children of the same family

brook *noun* a small stream ▫ *verb* put up with, endure

broom *noun* **1** a type of shrub with yellow flowers **2** a brush for sweeping ▫ **broomstick** *noun* the handle of a broom

Bros *abbrev* Brothers

brose *noun* a liquid food of boiling water poured on oatmeal *etc*

broth *noun* soup, *esp* one made with vegetables

brothel *noun* a house where prostitution is practised

Originally *brothel-house*, *brothel* being a general term of abuse that was later applied specifically to prostitutes

brother *noun* **1** a male born of the same parents as yourself **2** a companion, a fellow-worker □ **brotherhood** *noun* **1** comradeship between men **2** a men's association □ **brother-in-law** *noun* **1** the brother of your husband or wife **2** the husband of your sister or sister-in-law □ **brotherly** *adj* like a brother; affectionate

brought *past form* of **bring**

brow *noun* **1** a forehead **2** an eyebrow **3** the edge of a hill

browbeat *verb* bully

brown *noun* a dark colour made by mixing red, yellow, black *etc* □ *adj* **1** of this colour **2** *informal* suntanned □ **brown-nose** *verb, slang* fawn on, kowtow to

brownie *noun* **1** a helpful fairy or goblin **2** a Brownie Guide □ **Brownie Guide** a junior Guide

browse *verb* **1** glance through a range of books, shop merchandise *etc* **2** feed on the shoots or leaves of plants

bruise *noun* a discoloured area on the skin, the surface of fruit *etc*, where it has been struck □ *verb* cause bruises (to)

brunette *noun* a woman with dark brown hair

brunt *noun*: **bear** or **take the brunt** take the chief strain

brush *noun* (*plural* **brushes**) **1** an instrument with tufts of bristles, hair *etc* for smoothing the hair, cleaning, painting *etc* **2** a disagreement, a brief quarrel **3** the tail of a fox **4** undergrowth □ *verb* **1** pass a brush over **2** remove by sweeping **3** touch lightly in passing □ **brushwood** *noun* **1** broken branches, twigs *etc* **2** undergrowth

brusque /broosk/ *adj* sharp and short in manner, rude □ **brusquely** *adv* □ **brusqueness** *noun*

Brussels sprouts a type of vegetable with sprouts like small cabbages on the stem

brut /broot/ *adj* of wine: dry

brutal *adj* cruel, extremely harsh □ **brutality** *noun* □ **brutally** *adv*

brute *noun* **1** an animal **2** a cruel person □ **brute strength** pure physical strength □ **brutish** *adj* like a brute, savage, coarse

BSc *abbrev* Bachelor of Science

BSE *abbrev* bovine spongiform encephalopathy, a brain disease of cattle

BST *abbrev* British Summer Time

BT *abbrev* British Telecom

Bt *abbrev* baronet

bubble *noun* a thin ball of liquid blown out with air □ *verb* rise in bubbles □ **bubblejet** *noun* a kind of computer printer

bubbly *adj* **1** full of bubbles **2** lively, vivacious □ *noun, informal* champagne; sparkling wine

buccaneer *noun, old* a pirate □ **buccaneering** *adj* like a pirate

buck *noun* **1** the male of the deer, goat, hare and rabbit **2** *US informal* a dollar □ *verb* of a horse *etc*: attempt to throw a rider by rapid jumps into the air

bucket *noun* a container for water *etc*

buckle *noun* a clip for fastening straps or belts □ *verb* fasten with a buckle □ **buckler** *noun* a small shield

buckshee /buk*shee*/ *adj* free, gratuitous

buckshot *noun* large lead shot fired from a shotgun

buckwheat *noun* a plant whose seed is used to feed animals and ground into flour

bucolic *adj* of the countryside; pastoral, rural

bud *noun* the first shoot of a tree or plant □ *verb* produce buds □ **budding** *adj* showing signs of becoming: *budding author*

> **bud** *verb* » bud*s*, budd*ing*, budd*ed*

Buddhism *noun* a religion whose followers worship Buddha □ **Buddhist** *noun* & *adj*

budge *verb* move slightly, stir

> **budge** » budge*s*, budg*ing*, budge*d*

budgerigar *noun* a kind of small parrot often kept as a pet

budget *noun* **1** a government plan for the year's spending **2** any plan of their future spending □ *verb* allow for in a budget: *the project has been budgeted for*

> Originally a small bag; the parliamentary sense of *budget* stems from a political insult directed at Robert Walpole implying that he was a quack or pedlar

budgie *noun, informal* a budgerigar

buff *noun* **1** a light yellowish brown colour **2** an enthusiast, a fan: *film buff* □ *verb* polish

> The later meaning of 'enthusiast' derives from the *buff*-coloured uniforms once used by volunteer firefighters in New York

buffalo *noun* (*plural* **buffaloes**) **1** a large Asian ox, used to draw loads **2** the North American bison

buffer *noun* something which lessens the force of a blow or collision

buffet[1] *noun* /*bu*fit/ *verb* strike, knock about □ *noun* a slap or a blow

buffet[2] *noun* /*boo*fay/ **1** a counter or café serving food and drink **2** a range of dishes set out at a party, *etc* for people to serve themselves

buffoon *noun* a clown, fool □ **buffoonery** *noun*

bug *noun* **1** a small, *esp* irritating, insect **2** a disease germ: *a tummy bug* **3** a tiny hidden microphone for recording conversations **4** a problem in a computer program causing errors in its execution □ *verb* **1** conceal a microphone in (a room *etc*) **2** record with a hidden microphone **3** *US informal* annoy, harass

bug *verb* » bug*s*, bugg*ing*, bugg*ed*

bugbear *noun* something that frightens or annoys

bugger *noun, taboo slang* **1** *Brit* a general term of abuse **2** ◊ *verb* **1** have anal intercourse with **2** *Brit slang* ruin, make a mess of

buggy *noun* (*plural* **buggies**) a child's push-chair

bugle *noun* a small military trumpet ◊ **bugler** *noun* someone who plays the bugle

build *verb* put together the parts of anything ◊ *noun* physique, physical character: *a man of heavy build* ◊ **builder** *noun* ◊ **built-up** *adj* of an area: containing houses and other buildings

build *verb* » build*s*, build*ing*, built

building *noun* **1** the act or trade of building (houses *etc*) **2** a house or other built dwelling *etc* ◊ **building society** an institution like a bank which accepts investments and whose main business is to lend people money to buy a house

bulb *noun* **1** the rounded part of the stem of an onion, tulip etc, in which they store their food **2** a glass globe surrounding the element of an electric light ◊ **bulbous** *adj* bulb-shaped

bulge *noun* **1** a swelling **2** a noticeable increase ◊ *verb* swell out

bulge *verb* » bulge*s*, bulg*ing*, bulg*ed*

bulghur /bulgər/ *noun* a kind of cooked, cracked wheat

bulimia *noun* an eating disorder in which bingeing is followed by self-induced vomiting or purging ◊ **bulimic** *adj* suffering from bulimia

bulk *noun* **1** large size **2** the greater part: *the bulk of the population* ◊ **bulkhead** *noun* a wall in the inside of a ship, meant to keep out water in a collision

bulky *adj* taking up a lot of room ◊ **bulkily** *adv*

bull *noun* the male of animals of the ox family, also of the whale, elephant *etc* ◊ **bulldog** *noun* a breed of strong, fierce-looking dog ◊ **bullfight** *noun* a public entertainment in Spain *etc*, in which a bull is angered and usually killed ◊ **bullfinch** *noun* a small pink-breasted bird ◊ **bullfrog** *noun* a type of large frog ◊ **bullring** *noun* the arena in which bullfights take place ◊ **bull's-eye** *noun* **1** the mark in the middle of a target **2** a striped sweet

bulldozer *noun* a machine for levelling land and clearing away obstacles ◊ **bulldoze** *verb* **1** use a bulldozer on **2** force: *bulldozed his way into the room*

bullet *noun* the piece of metal fired from a gun ◊ **bullet-proof** *adj* not able to be pierced by bullets

bulletin *noun* a report of current news, someone's health *etc* ◊ **bulletin board** **1** a notice-board **2** *comput* a service on an electronic network providing messages and information

bullion *noun* gold or silver in the form of bars *etc*

bullock *noun* a young bull

bully *noun* (*plural* **bullies**) someone who unfairly uses their size and strength to hurt or frighten others ▫ *verb* act like a bully

> Originally a term of affection that developed to mean 'pimp' and so to someone who harasses others

bulrush *noun* (*plural* **bulrushes**) a large strong reed which grows on wet land or in water

bulwark /*bool*wərk/ *noun* **1** a strong defensive wall **2** a prop, a defence

bum[1] *noun, Brit slang* the buttocks ▫ **bumbag** *noun* a carrying pouch strapped round the waist

bum[2] *noun, US slang* a tramp ▫ *adj* useless, dud ▫ **give someone the bum's rush** get rid of them quickly

bumble-bee *noun* a type of large bee

bumf *another spelling* of **bumph**

bummer *noun, slang* something extremely annoying or disappointing

bump *verb* **1** strike heavily **2** knock by accident ▫ *noun* **1** the sound of a heavy blow **2** an accidental knock **3** a raised lump

bumper *noun* a bar round the front and back of a car's body to protect it from damage ▫ *adj* large: *bumper crop*

bumph or **bumf** *noun, Brit informal* miscellaneous, uninteresting papers, leaflets *etc*

> Originally short for 'bum-fodder', *ie* toilet paper

bumpkin *noun* a clumsy, awkward, country person

bumptious *adj* self-important

bun *noun* **1** a sweet roll made egg dough **2** hair wound into a rounded mass

bunch *noun* (*plural* **bunches**) a number of things tied together or growing together ▫ *verb* crowd together

Bundesbank *noun* the state bank of Germany

bundle *noun* a number of things loosely bound together ▫ *verb* **1** tie in a bundle **2** push roughly: *bundled the children into the car*

bung *noun* the stopper of the hole in a barrel, bottle *etc* ▫ *verb* stop up with a bung ▫ **bung-hole** *noun*

bungalow *noun* a one-storey detached house

bungle *verb* **1** do badly or clumsily **2** mishandle, mismanage ▫ *noun* a clumsy or mishandled action

bunion *noun* a lump or swelling on the joint of the big toe

bunk *noun* a narrow bed, *eg* in a ship's cabin ▫ **bunkbed** *noun* one of a pair of narrow beds one above the other

bunker *noun* **1** a sandpit on a golf course **2** an underground shelter **3** a large box for keeping coal

bunkum *noun* nonsense

From *Buncombe* county in N Carolina, whose representative once gave a rambling speech in Congress

bunny *noun* (*plural* **bunnies**) a child's name for a rabbit

Bunsen burner a gas-burner used in laboratories

bunting[1] *noun* **1** a thin cloth used for making flags **2** flags

bunting[2] *noun* a bird of the finch family

buoy /boy/ *noun* **1** a floating mark acting as a guide or warning for ships **2** a float, *eg* a lifebuoy

buoyant *adj* **1** able to float **2** cheerful, bouncy ▫ **buoyancy** *noun* ▫ **buoyantly** *adv*

bur *another spelling* of **burr**

burden *noun* **1** a load **2** something difficult to bear, *eg* poverty or sorrow **3** *old* the chorus of a song ▫ **burdensome** *adj*

burdock *noun* a type of plant with hooked leaves

bureau /*bjoo*roh/ *noun* (*plural* **bureaux** or **bureaus**) **1** a writing table **2** an office

bureaucracy /bjoo*rok*rəsi/ *noun* government by officials

bureaucrat *noun* an administrative official ▫ **bureaucratic** *adj* ▫ **bureaucratically** *adv*

burgh *noun* in Scotland, a borough

burglar *noun* someone who breaks into a house to steal ▫ **burglary** *noun* (*plural* **burglaries**)

burgle *verb* commit burglary

burial *noun* the placing of a body under the ground after death

burlesque *noun* a piece of writing, acting *etc*, making fun of somebody

burly *adj* broad and strong

burn[1] *verb* **1** set fire to **2** be on fire, or scorching **3** injure by burning ▫ *noun* an injury or mark caused by fire ▫ **burner** *noun* the part of a lamp or gas-jet from which the flame rises

burn *verb* » burn*s*, burn*ing*, burn*t* or burn*ed*

burn[2] *noun, Scot* a small stream

burnish *verb & noun* polish

burnt *past form* of **burn**

burr or **bur** *noun* the prickly seed-case or head of certain plants

burrito *noun* (*plural* **burritos**) a Mexican flour tortilla stuffed with meat, beans, *etc*

burrow *noun* a hole or passage in the ground dug by certain animals for shelter ▫ *verb* make a passage beneath the ground

burst *verb* **1** break suddenly (after increased pressure) **2** move, speak *etc* suddenly or violently

bury *verb* **1** place (a dead body *etc*) under the gound **2** cover, hide

bury » bur*ies*, bury*ing*, bur*ied*

bus *noun* (*plural* **buses**) a large road vehicle, often used for public transport ▫ **bus stop** an official stopping place for buses

busby *noun* (*plural* **busbies**) a tall fur hat worn by certain soldiers

bush *noun* (*plural* **bushes**) **1** a

growing thing between a plant and a tree in size **2** wild, unfarmed country in Africa *etc* ◊ **bush-baby** *noun* a type of small lemur ◊ **bush-ranger** *noun* in Australia, an outlaw living in the wilds ◊ **bush telegraph** the quick passing-on of news from person to person

bushy *adj* **1** growing thickly: *bushy hair* **2** full of bushes ◊ **bushily** *adv* ◊ **bushiness** *noun*

business *noun* (*plural* **businesses**) **1** someone's work or job **2** trade, commerce: *business is booming* **3** a matter of personal interest or concern: *none of your business* ◊ **businesslike** *adj* practical, methodical, alert and prompt ◊ **businessman**, **businesswoman** *noun* someone who works in commerce

busk *verb* play or sing in the street for money ◊ **busker** *noun*

bust *noun* **1** a woman's breasts **2** a sculpture of someone's head and shoulders

bustard *noun* a large, fast-running bird similar to a turkey

bustier /*bus*tieh/ *noun* a woman's strapless under-bodice

bustle *verb* busy oneself noisily ◊ *noun* **1** noisy activity, fuss **2** *hist* a stuffed pad worn under a woman's full skirt

busy *adj* having a lot to do ◊ **busily** *adv* ◊ **busybody** *noun* someone nosey about others ◊ **busy yourself with** occupy yourself with

busy *adj* » bus*ier*, bus*iest*

but *conj* **1** showing a contrast between two ideas *etc*: *my brother can swim but I can't/ that paint isn't black but brown* **2** except that, without that: *it never rains but it pours* ◊ *prep* except, with the exception of: *no one but Tom had any money/ take the next road but one* (*ie* the second road) ◊ *adv* only: *we can but hope* ◊ **but for** were it not for: *but for your car, we would have been late*

butane /*byoo*tehn/ *noun* a gas commonly used for fuel

butch *adj* of a woman: looking or behaving in a masculine way

butcher *noun* someone whose work is to kill animals for food and sell their meat ◊ *verb* **1** kill and carve up (an animal) for food **2** kill cruelly ◊ **butchery** *noun* great or cruel slaughter

butler *noun* the chief manservant in a household who looks after and serves wines *etc*

butt *noun* **1** a large cask, a barrel **2** someone of whom others make fun **3** the thick heavy end of a rifle *etc* **4** the end of a finished cigarette or cigar **5** a push with the head **6** *US slang* the buttocks ◊ *verb* strike with the head ◊ **butt in** interrupt, interfere ◊ **butt out** *slang* stop interfering

butter *noun* a fatty food made by churning cream ◊ *verb* spread over with butter ◊ **buttercup** *noun* a plant with a cup-like yellow flower ◊ **buttermilk** *noun* the milk that is left after butter has been made ◊ **butterscotch** *noun* a hard toffee made with butter ◊ **butter up** flatter, soften up

butterfly *noun* (*plural* **butterflies**) a kind of insect with large, often patterned wings

buttocks *noun plural* the two fleshy parts of the body on which you sit; the rump

button *noun* **1** a knob or disc of metal, plastic *etc* used to fasten clothing **2** a knob pressed to work an electrical device ◊ *verb* fasten by means of buttons ◊ **button up** be quiet; shut up

buttonhole *noun* a hole through which a button is passed ◊ *verb* catch the attention of (someone) and force them to listen

buttress *noun* (*plural* **buttresses**) a support on the outside of a wall ◊ *verb* support, prop up

buxom *adj* plump and pretty

buy *verb* get in exchange for money ◊ *noun* a purchase: *a good buy* ◊ **buyer** *noun*

> **buy** *verb* » buy*s*, buy*ing*, bought

buzz *verb* **1** make a humming noise like bees **2** *informal* call, telephone **3** of aircraft: fly close to ◊ *noun* **1** a humming sound **2** *informal* a phonecall ◊ **buzzer** *noun* a signalling device which makes a buzzing noise ◊ **buzzword** *noun* a word well-established in a particular jargon, its use suggesting up-to-date specialized knowledge

buzzard *noun* a large bird of prey

by *adv* **1** near: *a crowd stood by, watching* **2** past: *people strolled by* **3** aside: *money put by for an emergency* ◊ *prep* **1** next to, near: *standing by the door* **2** past: *going by the house* **3** through, along, across: *we came by the main road* **4** indicating the person who does something: *written by Burns/ played by a young actor* **5** of time: not after: *it'll be ready by four o'clock* **6** during the time of: *working by night* **7** by means of: *by train* **8** to the extent of: *taller by a head* **9** used to express measurements, compass directions etc: *6 metres by 4 metres/ north by northwest* **10** in the quantity of: *sold by the pound/ paid by the week* ◊ **by-election** *noun* an election for parliament during a parliamentary session ◊ **bygone** *adj* past ◊ **bygones** *noun plural* old grievances or events that have been, or should be, forgotten ◊ **by-law** or **bye-law** *noun* a local (not a national) law ◊ **bypass** *noun* a road built round a town *etc* so that traffic need not pass through it ◊ **by-product** *noun* something useful obtained during the manufacture of something else ◊ **byroad** or **byway** *noun* a side road ◊ **bystander** *noun* someone who stands watching an event or accident ◊ **byword** *noun* someone or something well-known for a particular quality

bye *noun, cricket* **1** a ball bowled past the wicket **2** a run made from this

byte /bait/ *noun, comput* a unit used to measure data or memory

C

°C *abbrev* degree(s) Celsius or centigrade

c or **ca** *abbrev* about (from Latin *circa*)

CAB *abbrev* Citizens Advice Bureau

cab *noun* **1** a taxi **2** *hist* a hired carriage

cabaret /kab*ə*reh/ *noun* **1** an entertainment consisting of variety acts **2** a restaurant with a cabaret

cabbage *noun* a type of vegetable with edible leaves

caber /*keh*bər/ *noun* a heavy pole tossed in competition at Highland games

cabin *noun* **1** a wooden hut **2** a small room used for living quarters in a ship **3** the part of a commercial aircraft containing passenger seating ◻ **cabin crew** the flight attendants on a commercial airline

cabinet *noun* **1** a cupboard which has shelves and doors **2** a similar container for storage *etc* **3** a wooden case with drawers **4** a selected number of government ministers who decide on policy ◻ **cabinet-maker** *noun* a maker of fine furniture

cable *noun* **1** a strong rope or thick metal line **2** a line of covered telegraph wires laid under the sea or underground **3** a telegram sent by such a line **4** an underground wire **5** *informal* cable television ◻ *verb* telegraph by cable ◻ **cable television** a service transmitting television programmes to individual subscribers by underground cable

cacao *noun* a tree from whose seeds cocoa and chocolate are made

cache /kash/ *noun* **1** a store or hiding place for ammunition, treasure *etc* **2** things hidden

cachet /ka*sheh*/ *noun* **1** prestige, credit **2** an official stamp or seal

cackle *noun* **1** the sound made by a hen or goose **2** a laugh which sounds like this

cacophony *noun* (*plural* **cacophonies**) an unpleasant noise ◻ **cacophonous** *adj* ◻ **cacophonously** *adv*

cactus *noun* (*plural* **cactuses** or **cacti**) a type of prickly plant

CAD *abbrev* computer-aided design

cad *noun*, *old* a mean, despicable person

cadaver /k*ə*dav*ə*r/ *noun* a human corpse

cadaverous *adj* corpse-like, very pale and thin ◻ **cadaverously** *adv* ◻ **cadaverousness** *noun*

caddie *noun* an assistant who carries a golfer's clubs

caddy *noun* (*plural* **caddies**) a box for keeping tea fresh

cadence *noun* **1** a fall of the voice, *eg* at the end of a sentence **2** a group of chords ending a piece of music

cadenza *noun* a musical passage at the end of a movement, concerto *etc*

cadet /ka*det*/*noun* **1** an officer trainee in the armed forces or police service **2** a school pupil who takes military training

cadge *verb* beg □ **cadger** *noun*

> **cadge** » cadge*s*, cadg*ing*, cadge*d*

Caesarean *adj* of a birth: delivered by cutting through the walls of the mother's abdomen □ *noun* a Caesarian birth or operation

caesura /*səzoorə*/ *noun* a pause, a breathing space

café *noun* a small restaurant serving coffee, tea, snacks *etc*

cafeteria *noun* a self-service restaurant

cafetière *noun* a coffee-pot with a plunger mechanism

caffeine *noun* a stimulating drug found in coffee and tea

caftan *noun* a long-sleeved, ankle-length Middle-Eastern garment

cage *noun* **1** a barred enclosure for birds or animals **2** a lift used by miners □ *verb* close up in a cage

> **cage** *verb* » cage*s*, cag*ing*, cage*d*

cagey or **cagy** *adj* unwilling to speak freely; wary □ **caginess** *noun*

cagoule *noun* a lightweight anorak

cahoots *noun plural*: **in cahoots with** in collusion with

cairn *noun* **1** a heap of stones marking a grave, or on top of a mountain **2** a breed of small terrier

cairngorm *noun* a brown or yellow variety of quartz, used for brooches *etc*

cajole *verb* coax by flattery □ **cajolery** *noun*

cake *noun* **1** a baked piece of dough made from flour, eggs, sugar *etc* **2** something pressed into a lump: *cake of soap* □ *verb* become dry and hard □ **have your cake and eat it** enjoy both of two alternative things

calamine *noun* a pink powder containing a zinc salt, used to make a skin-soothing lotion

calamity *noun* (*plural* **calamities**) a great disaster, a misfortune □ **calamitous** *adj* □ **calamitously** *adv*

calcium *noun* a metal which forms the chief part of lime

calculate *verb* **1** count, work out by mathematics **2** think out in an exact way □ **calculable** *adj* able to be counted or measured □ **calculating** *adj* thinking selfishly □ **calculation** *noun* a mathematical reckoning, a sum □ **calculator** *noun* a machine which makes mathematical calculations

calculus *noun* a mathematical system of calculation

calendar *noun* a table or list showing the year divided into months, weeks and days

calendula *noun* a preparation of

marigold flowers used in herbal medicine

calf[1] *noun* (*plural* **calves**) **1** the young of a cow or ox **2** the young of certain other mammals, *eg* an elephant or whale **3** calf's skin cured as leather

calf[2] *noun* (*plural* **calves**) the back of the lower part of the leg

calibrate *verb* **1** mark the scale on (a measuring instrument) **2** check or adjust the scale of (a measuring instrument)

calibre or *US* **caliber** *noun* **1** measurement across the opening of a tube or gun **2** of a person: quality of character, ability

calico *noun* a patterned kind of cotton cloth

> Originally *Calicut cloth*, after the port in SW India from where it was exported

call *verb* **1** cry aloud **2** name: *what is your cat called?* **3** summon **4** make a short visit **5** telephone ▯ *noun* **1** a loud cry **2** a short visit **3** a telephone conversation

calligraphy *noun* the art of handwriting ▯ **calligrapher** *noun* ▯ **calligraphic** *adj*

calling *noun* a vocation, a job

callipers or **calipers** *noun* **1** *plural* an instrument like compasses, used to measure thickness **2** *sing* a splint to support the leg, made of two metal rods

callous *adj* cruel, hardhearted ▯ **callously** *adv* ▯ **callousness** *noun*

> ⚠Do not confuse with: **callus**

callow *adj* not mature; inexperienced, naive ▯ **callowly** *adv* ▯ **callowness** *noun*

callus *noun* (*plural* **calluses**) an area of thickened or hardened skin

> ⚠Do not confuse with: **callous**

calm *adj* **1** still or quiet **2** not anxious or flustered ▯ *noun* **1** absence of wind **2** quietness, peacefulness ▯ *verb* make peaceful ▯ **calmly** *adv* ▯ **calmness** *noun*

calorie *noun* **1** a measure of heat **2** a measure of the energy-giving value of food ▯ **calorimeter** *noun* an instrument for measuring heat

calumny *noun* (*plural* **calumnies**) a false accusation or lie about a person

calve *verb* give birth to a calf

calypso *noun* (*plural* **calypsos**) a West Indian improvised song

calyx /*ka*liks/ *noun* (*plural* **calyces** or **calyxes**) the outer covering or cup of a flower

calzone /kal*tsoh*ni/ *noun* a type of folded-over pizza

CAM *abbrev* computer-aided manufacturing

camaraderie *noun* comradeship, fellowship

camber *noun* a slight curve on a road *etc* making the middle higher than the sides

camcorder *noun* a hand-held device combining a video camera and video recorder

came *past form* of **come**

camel *noun* an animal native to Asia and Africa, with a humped back, used for transport

camelopard *noun*, *old* a giraffe

cameo *noun* (*plural* **cameos**) a gem or stone with a figure carved in relief (*contrasted with*: **intaglio**)

camera[1] *noun* an instrument for taking photographs

camera[2] *noun*: **in camera** in private

> Literally 'in a room', from Latin word 'room' or 'chamber'

camisole /*kam*isohl/ *noun* a woman's undervest with thin shoulder straps

camomile *noun* a plant with pale yellow flowers, used as a medicinal herb

camouflage /*kamə*flahzh/ *noun* **1** the disguising of the appearance of something to blend in with its background **2** natural protective colouring in animals ▢ *verb* disguise by camouflage

camp[1] *noun* **1** a group of tents, caravans *etc* forming a temporary settlement **2** fixed military quarters ▢ *verb* **1** pitch tents **2** set up a temporary home ▢ **camp bed** a small portable folding bed ▢ **campsite** *noun* an area set aside for pitching tents

camp[2] *adj* effeminate ▢ **campness** *noun*

campaign *noun* **1** organized action in support of a cause or movement **2** a planned series of battles or movements during a war ▢ *verb* **1** organize support: *campaigning against the poll tax* **2** serve in a military campaign

campanile /kamp*ə*neeleh/ *noun* a bell-tower

campanology *noun* bell-ringing ▢ **campanologist** *noun*

camphor *noun* a pungent solid oil obtained from a cinnamon tree, or a synthetic substitute for it, used to repel insects *etc*

campion *noun* a plant with pink or white star-shaped flowers

campus *noun* (*plural* **campuses**) the grounds and buildings of a university or college

can[1] *verb* **1** be able to (do something): *can anybody here play the piano?* **2** have permission to (do something): *asked if I could have the day off* ▢ **can but** can only: *we can but hope*

> **can**[1] *verb* » *present form* **can**, *past form* **could**

can[2] *noun* a sealed tin container for preserving food or liquids ▢ *verb* put into a sealed tin to preserve ▢ **canned music** pre-recorded bland music

> **can**[2] *verb* » can*s*, cann*ing*, cann*ed*

canal *noun* an artificial waterway for boats

canapé /*ka*n*ə*peh/ *noun* a small piece of bread *etc* with a topping, served as an appetizer

canary *noun* (*plural* **canaries**) a songbird with yellow plumage, kept as a pet

canasta *noun* a card-game similar to rummy

cancan *noun* a high-kicking dance performed by women

cancel *verb* **1** put off permanently, call off: *cancel all engagements for the week* **2** mark for deletion by crossing with lines □ **cancel out** make ineffective by balancing each other

> **cancel** » cancel*s*, cancell*ing*, cancell*ed*

cancer *noun* a malignant growth □ **cancerous** *adj*

candid *adj* frank, open, honest □ **candidly** *adv*

candida /*kan*didə/ *noun* an infection caused by a yeastlike fungus

candidate *noun* **1** an entrant for an examination, or competition for a job, prize *etc* **2** an entrant in a political election □ **candidacy** or **candidature** *noun*

> From a Latin word meaning 'dressed in white', because of the white togas worn by electoral candidates in ancient Rome

candied *adj* cooked or coated in sugar

candle *noun* a stick of wax containing a wick, used for giving light □ **candlestick** *noun* a holder for a candle □ **candlewick** *noun* a cotton tufted material, used for bedspreads *etc* □ **not worth the candle** not worth the effort or expense needed

candour or *US* **candor** *noun* frankness, honesty

candy *noun* **1** sugar crystallized by boiling **2** *US* (*plural* **candies**) sweets, chocolate

cane *noun* **1** the woody stem of bamboo, sugar cane *etc* **2** a walking stick □ *verb* beat with a cane □ **cane sugar** sugar extracted from sugar cane

canine *adj* of dogs □ **canine tooth** a sharp-pointed tooth found on each side of the upper and lower jaw

canister *noun* a tin or other container for tea *etc*

canker *noun* **1** a spreading sore **2** a disease in trees, plants *etc*

cannabis *noun* a narcotic drug obtained from the hemp plant

cannelloni *noun plural* wide hollow tubes of pasta, stuffed with meat, cheese, vegetables *etc*

cannery *noun* (*plural* **canneries**) a factory where food is canned

cannibal *noun* **1** someone who eats human flesh **2** an animal that eats its own kind □ **cannibalism** *noun* □ **cannibalistic** *adj*

cannon *noun* a large gun mounted on a wheel-carriage

> ⚠Do not confuse with: **canon**

cannonball *noun* a solid metal ball shot from a cannon

cannot *verb* **1** used with another verb to express inability to do something: *I cannot understand this* **2** used to refuse permission: *he cannot see me today*

canny *adj* wise, shrewd, cautious

 cannily *adv* **canniness** *noun*

canoe *noun* a light narrow boat driven by paddles

canon *noun* **1** a rule used as a standard to judge by **2** a member of the Anglican clergy connected with a cathedral **3** a list of saints **4** an accepted or established list: *not in the literary canon* **5** a piece of music in which parts follow each other repeating the melody

> ⚠Do not confuse with: **cannon**

cañon *noun* another spelling of **canyon**

canonical *adj* part of an accepted canon: *canonical text*

canonize *verb* put on the list of saints **canonization** *noun*

canopy *noun* (*plural* **canopies**) a canvas or cloth covering suspended over a bed *etc*

cant[1] *noun* **1** the slang or vocabulary of a particular group: *thieves' cant* **2** insincere talk

cant[2] *noun* a slope, an incline *verb* tilt from a level position

can't *short form* of **cannot**

cantankerous *adj* crotchety, bad-tempered, quarrelsome **cantankerously** *adv* **cantankerousness** *noun*

cantata *noun* a short piece of music for a choir

canteen *noun* **1** a place serving food and drink in a workplace *etc* **2** a water-flask **3** a case for storing cutlery

canter *verb* move at an easy gallop *noun* an easy gallop

> Originally *Canterbury gallop*, referring to the pace at which pilgrims rode to the town

cantilever *noun* a large projecting bracket used to support a balcony or staircase **cantilever bridge** a bridge consisting of upright piers with cantilevers extending to meet one another

canton *noun* a federal state in Switzerland

canvas *noun* (*plural* **canvases**) **1** coarse, strong cloth used for sails, tents *etc* **2** a piece of this stretched and used for painting on

canvass *verb* go round asking for votes, money *etc* **canvasser** *noun*

canyon or **cañon** *noun* a deep, steep-sided river valley

cap *noun* **1** a peaked soft hat **2** a lid, a top **3** a contraceptive diaphragm *verb* **1** put a cap on **2** set a limit to (a budget *etc*) **3** do better than, improve on: *no-one can cap this story* **4** select for a national sports team **5** confer a university degree on

> **cap** *verb* » cap*s*, capp*ing*, capp*ed*

capable *adj* able to cope with difficulties without help **capability** *noun* (*plural* **capabilities**) **capable of** able or likely to achieve, produce *etc*: *capable of a better performance* **capably** *adv*

capacious *adj* roomy, wide **capaciously** *adv* **capaciousness** *noun*

capacitor *noun* a device for collecting and storing electricity

capacity *noun* (*plural* **capacities**) **1** power of understanding **2** ability to do something: *capacity for growth* **3** the amount that something can hold **4** post, position: *capacity as leader* ◻ **to capacity** to the greatest extent possible: *filled to capacity*

cape[1] *noun* a thick shawl or covering for the shoulders

cape[2] *noun* a point of land running into the sea

caper[1] *verb* leap, dance about ◻ *noun* **1** a leap **2** *informal* a prank, an adventure

caper[2] *noun* the flower-bud of a shrub, pickled or salted for eating

capercaillie or **capercailzie** /kapərkehli/ or /kehpərkehli/ *noun* a kind of large grouse

capillary *noun* (*plural* **capillaries**) **1** a tiny blood vessel **2** a very fine tube ◻ *adj* very fine, like a hair

capital *adj* **1** chief, most important **2** punishable by death: *capital offence* **3** *informal* excellent **4** of a letter: written or printed in upper case, *eg* A, B or C ◻ *noun* **1** the chief city of a country: *Paris is the capital of France* **2** an upper-case letter **3** money for running a business **4** money invested, accumulated wealth ◻ **capital punishment** punishment by death ◻ **make capital out of** turn to your advantage

capitalism *noun* a system in which a country's wealth is owned by individuals, not by the State ◻ **capitalist** someone who supports or practises capitalism ◻ **capitalistic** *adj*

capitalize *verb* **1** write in capital letters **2** turn to your advantage ◻ **capitalization** *noun*

capitulate *verb* give in to an enemy ◻ **capitulation** *noun*

capon *noun* a young castrated cock, fattened for eating

cappuccino *noun* white coffee made frothy with pressurized steam

caprice /kəprees/ *noun* a sudden, impulsive change of mind or mood

> Originally meaning 'horror', from an Italian word which translates as 'hedgehog head'

capricious *adj* full of caprice; impulsive, fickle ◻ **capriciously** *adv* ◻ **capriciousness** *noun*

capsize *verb* upset, overturn

capstan *noun* a device used for winding in heavy ropes on a ship or quay

capsule *noun* **1** a small gelatine case containing a dose of medicine *etc* **2** a dry seed-pod on a plant **3** a self-contained, detachable part of a spacecraft

Capt *abbrev* captain

captain *noun* **1** the commander of a company of soldiers, a ship or an aircraft **2** the leader of a sports team, club *etc* ◻ *verb* lead ◻ **captaincy** *noun* (*plural* **captaincies**) the rank of captain

caption *noun* a heading for a newspaper article, photograph *etc*

captious *adj* quick to find fault; judgemental

captivate *verb* charm, fascinate

captive *noun* a prisoner ◊ *adj* **1** taken or kept prisoner **2** not able to get away: *captive audience*

captivity *noun* **1** the state of being a prisoner **2** the enclosure of an animal in a zoo *etc*, not in the wild

captor *noun* someone who takes a prisoner

capture *verb* **1** take by force **2** get hold of; seize: *capture the imagination* ◊ *noun* **1** the act of capturing **2** something captured

car *noun* **1** a motor-car **2** *US* a train carriage ◊ **car park** a place where motor-cars *etc* may be left for a time ◊ **car pool** an arrangement between car owners to take turns at driving each other to work *etc*

carafe /*kəraf*/ *noun* a bottle for serving wine, water *etc*

caramel *noun* **1** sugar melted and browned **2** a sweet made with sugar and butter ◊ **caramelize** *verb* cook slowly in butter and sugar

carat *noun* **1** a measure of purity for gold **2** a measure of weight for gemstones

⚠Do not confuse with: **carrot**

caravan *noun* **1** a covered vehicle with living accommodation drawn behind a motor-car **1** a number of travellers *etc* crossing the desert together

caravanserai *noun* an inn where desert caravans stop

caraway *noun* a plant with spicy seeds used in cooking

carbine *noun* a short light musket

carbohydrate *noun* a compound of carbon, hydrogen and oxygen, *eg* sugar or starch

carbon *noun* an element of which charcoal is one form ◊ **carbon copy** **1** a copy of a document made by using carbon paper **2** an exact copy ◊ **carbon dioxide** a gas present in the air and breathed out by humans and animals ◊ **carbonic** *adj* of or made with carbon ◊ **carboniferous** *adj* producing or containing coal or carbon ◊ **carbon monoxide** a poisonous gas with no smell ◊ **carbon paper** paper coated with black ink, interleaved between ordinary paper when typing to produce exact copies

carbuncle *noun* **1** a fiery-red precious stone **2** an inflamed swelling under the skin

carburettor or **carburetter** or *US* **carburetor** *noun* the part of a motor-car engine which changes the petrol into vapour

carcass or **carcase** *noun* the dead body (of an animal)

carcinogen *noun* a substance that encourages the growth of cancer ◊ **carcinogenic** *adj* causing cancer

carcinoma /karsi*noh*mə/ *noun* (*plural* **carcinomas** or **carcinomata**) a cancerous growth

card *noun* **1** pasteboard or very thick paper **2** an illustrated, folded of paper sent in greeting *etc* **3** tool for combing wool *etc* **4** (**cards**) any of the many types of games played with a pack of special cards *verb* comb (wool *etc*)

cardboard *noun* stiff pasteboard

cardiac *adj* of the heart: *cardiac failure*

cardigan *noun* a knitted woollen jacket

> Named after the 19th-century Earl of *Cardigan* who advocated the use of buttonable woollen jackets

cardinal *adj* principal, important *noun* the highest rank of priest in the Roman Catholic Church **cardinal number** a number which expresses quantity, *eg* 1,2,3 (*contrasted with*: **ordinal number**)

care *noun* **1** close attention **2** worry, anxiety **3** protection, keeping: *in my care* *verb* be concerned or worried: *I don't care what happens now* **care for 1** look after **2** feel affection or liking for **carefree** *adj* having no worries **careworn** *adj* worn out by anxiety **care of** at the house of (often written as **c/o**) **take care** be careful; watch out

careful *adj* attentive, taking care **carefully** *adv* **carefulness** *noun*

careless *adj* paying little attention; not taking care **carelessly** *adv* **carelessness** *noun*

caretaker *noun* someone who looks after a building *adj* in charge temporarily; interim: *caretaker government*

career *noun* **1** life work; trade, profession **2** course, progress through life **3** headlong rush *verb* run rapidly and wildly: *careering along the road*

caress *verb* touch gently and lovingly *noun* (*plural* **caresses**) a gentle touch

carfuffle /kə*rfuf*əl/ *noun* commotion, fuss

cargo *noun* (*plural* **cargoes**) a ship's load

caribou *noun* the North American reindeer

caricature *noun* a picture of someone which exaggerates certain of their features *verb* draw a caricature of **caricaturist** *noun*

caries /*keh*rieez/ *noun* decay, *esp* of the teeth **carious** *adj* decaying

CARIFTA *abbrev* Caribbean Free Trade Area

carillon /kə*ril*yən/ *noun* **1** a set of bells on which tunes can be played **2** a tune played with bells

carmine *noun* a bright red colour *adj* of this colour

carnage *noun* slaughter, killing

carnation *noun* a type of garden flower, often pink, red or white

carnival *noun* a celebration with merriment, feasting *etc*

carnivore *noun* a flesh-eating animal

carnivorous *adj* eating meat or flesh **carnivorously** *adv* **carnivorousness** *noun*

carnyx /*kar*niks/ *noun* an ancient Celtic war trumpet

carol *noun* a hymn or song sung at Christmas **caroller** *noun* **carolling** *noun*

carouse *verb* take part in a drinking bout □ **carousal** *noun*

carousel /karəsel/ *noun* **1** *US* a merry-go-round **2** a rotating conveyor belt for luggage at an airport *etc*

carp[1] *noun* a freshwater fish found in ponds

carp[2] *verb* find fault with small errors; complain about nothing

carpe diem seize the day; make the most of the present

carpenter *noun* a worker in wood, *eg* for building □ **carpentry** *noun* the trade of a carpenter

carpet *noun* the woven covering of floors, stairs *etc* □ *verb* cover with a carpet

carriage *noun* **1** a vehicle for carrying people **2** the act or cost of carrying **3** a way of walking; bearing

carrier *noun* **1** someone who carries goods **2** a machine or container for carrying **3** someone who passes on a disease □ **carrier pigeon** a pigeon used to carry messages

carrion *noun* rotting animal flesh

carrot *noun* a vegetable with an edible orange-coloured root

> ⚠Do not confuse with: **carat**

carry *verb* **1** pick up and take to another place **2** contain and take to a destination: *cables carrying electricity* **3** bear, have as a mark: *carry a scar* **4** of a voice: be able to be heard at a distance **5** win, succeed: *carry the day* **6** keep for sale: *we don't carry cigarettes* □ **carried away** overcome by emotion; overexcited □ **carry on** continue (doing) □ **carry-on** *noun* a fuss, a to-do □ **carry out** accomplish; succeed in doing □ **carry-out** *noun* a take-away meal or alcoholic drink □ **carry the can** accept responsibility for an error □ **carry weight** have force or authority

> **carry** » carr*ies*, carry*ing*, carr*ied*

cart *noun* **1** a horse-drawn vehicle used for carrying loads **2** a small wheeled vehicle pushed by hand □ *verb* **1** carry by cart **2** drag, haul: *carted off the stage* □ **cart-horse** *noun* a large, heavy work-horse □ **cartwright** *noun* someone who makes carts

carte blanche /kart blonhsh/ freedom of action; a free hand

cartilage *noun* a strong elastic material in the bodies of humans and animals; gristle

cartography *noun* the science of map-making □ **cartographer** *noun*

carton *noun* a small container made of cardboard, plastic *etc*

cartoon *noun* **1** a comic drawing, or strip of drawings, often with a caption **2** an animated film **3** a drawing used as the basis for a large painting *etc* □ **cartoonist** *noun* someone who draws cartoons

cartridge *noun* **1** a case holding the powder and bullet fired by a gun **2** a spool of film or tape enclosed in a case **3** a tube of ink for loading a pen **4** the part of a record-player which holds the stylus

cartwheel *noun* **1** the wheel of a cart **2** a sideways somersault with hands touching the ground

carve *verb* **1** make or shape by cutting **2** cut up (meat) into slices

cascade *noun* **1** a waterfall **2** an abundant hanging display: *cascade of curls* □ *verb* fall like or in a waterfall

case *noun* **1** a container or outer covering **2** that which happens, an occurrence **3** a statement of facts, an argument **4** state of affairs, what is true: *if that is the case* **5** a trial in a law-court: *murder case*

casement *noun* **1** a window-frame **2** a window that swings on hinges

cash *noun* money in the form of coins and notes □ *verb* turn into, or change for, money □ **cash card** a card issued by a bank *etc* that allows the holder to use a cash dispenser □ **cash dispenser** an automatic teller machine □ **cash register** a machine for holding money that records the amount put in □ **cash in on** profit from

cashew *noun* a kidney-shaped nut produced by a tropical tree

cashier *noun* someone who looks after the receiving and paying of money □ *verb, military* dismiss in disgrace

cashmere *noun* fine soft goat's wool

casino /*kəseenoh*/ *noun* (*plural* **casinos**) a building in which gambling takes place

cask *noun* a barrel containing wine *etc*

casket *noun* **1** a small box for holding jewels *etc* **2** *US* a coffin

cassava *noun* a tropical plant with roots from which tapioca is obtained

casserole *noun* **1** a covered oven-proof dish for cooking and serving food **2** food cooked in a casserole

cassette *noun* **1** a small case for film, magnetic recording tape *etc* **2** the magnetic tape itself

cassock *noun* a long robe worn by priests

cassoulet /*kasəleh*/ *noun* a French stew made with beans and pork *etc*

cassowary *noun* (*plural* **cassowaries**) a large flightless bird of Australia and New Guinea

cast *verb* **1** throw, fling **2** throw off; drop, shed **3** shape in a mould **4** choose (actors) for a play or film **5** give a part to (an actor *etc*) □ *noun* **1** something shaped in a mould **2** plaster encasing a broken limb **3** the actors in a play **4** a small heap of earth thrown up by a worm **5** a type: *cast of mind* **6** an eye squint □ **cast down** *adj* depressed □ **cast iron** unpurified iron melted and moulded into shape □ **cast off** *adj* used by someone else, second-hand

> **cast** *verb* » cast*s*, cast*ing*, cast

castanets *noun plural* hollow shells of ivory or hard wood, clicked together to accompany a dance

> From a Spanish word for 'chestnuts', because of their shape

castaway *noun* a deserted or shipwrecked person

caste *noun* a class or rank of people, *esp* in the Indian subcontinent

castellated *adj* having walls, towers *etc* like those of a castle

caster *another spelling* of **castor**

castigate *verb* scold, punish ▯ **castigation** *noun* ▯ **castigator** *noun*

castle *noun* a fortified house or fortress

castor or **caster** *noun* a small wheel, *eg* on the legs of furniture ▯ **caster oil** a kind of palm oil used medicinally ▯ **castor sugar** or **caster sugar** very fine granulated sugar

castrate *verb* remove the testicles of

castrato *noun* (*pl* **castrati**) a male singer who has been castrated to preserve a high voice

casual *adj* **1** happening by chance: *casual encounter* **2** not regular, temporary: *casual labour* **3** informal: *casual clothes* **4** not careful, unconcerned: *casual attitude to work*

casualty *noun* (*plural* **casualties**) **1** someone who is killed or wounded **2** a casualty department ▯ **casualty department** a hospital department for treating accidental injuries *etc*

cat *noun* **1** a sharp-clawed furry animal kept as a pet **2** an animal of a family which includes lions, tigers *etc* ▯ **cat burglar** a burglar who breaks into houses by climbing walls *etc* ▯ **cat flap** a small door set in a larger door to allow a cat entry and exit ▯ **cat-o'-nine-tails** *noun* a whip with nine lashes ▯ **cat's cradle** a children's game of creating patterns by winding string around the fingers ▯ **cat's-eye** *noun, trademark* a small mirror fixed in a road surface to reflect light at night

cataclysm *noun* **1** a violent change; an upheaval **2** a great flood of water

catacombs *noun plural* an underground burial place

catalogue *noun* **1** an ordered list of names, books, objects for sale *etc* ▯ *verb* **1** list in order **2** compile details of (a book) for a library catalogue

catalyst *noun* **1** a substance which helps or prevents a chemical reaction without itself changing **2** something that brings about a change

catamaran *noun* a boat with two parallel hulls

catapult *noun* **1** a small forked stick with a piece of elastic attached, used for firing small stones **2** *hist* a weapon for throwing heavy stones in warfare

cataract *noun* **1** a waterfall **2** a disease of the outer eye

catarrh *noun* inflammation of the lining of the nose and throat causing a discharge

catastrophe /kə*tas*trəfi/ *noun* a sudden disaster ▯ **catastrophic** *adj* ▯ **catastrophically** *adv*

catch *verb* **1** take hold of, capture **2** take (a disease): *catch a cold* **3** be in time for: *catch the last train* **4** surprise (in an act): *caught him* *stealing* ◊ *noun* **1** a haul of fish *etc* **2** something you are lucky to have got or won **3** a hidden flaw or disadvantage: *where's the catch?* **4** a fastening: *window catch* ◊ **catching** *adj* infectious ◊ **catch-phrase** or **catchword** *noun* a phrase or word which is popular for a while ◊ **catch on** become popular ◊ **catch-22** *noun* an absurd situation with no way out ◊ **catchy** *adj* of a tune: easily remembered ◊ **catch up on 1** draw level with, overtake **2** get up-to-date with (work *etc*)

> **catch** *verb* » catch*es*, catch*ing*, caught

catchment area 1 an area from which a river or reservoir draws its water supply **2** an area from which the pupils in a school are drawn

catechism /*katə*kizm/ *noun* **1** a religious book which teaches by asking questions to which it gives the answers **2** a series of searching questions ◊ **catechize** *verb* ask many questions

categorical *adj* allowing no doubt or argument: *categorical denial* ◊ **categorically** *adv*

category *noun* (*plural* **categories**) a class or group of similar people or things ◊ **categorize** *verb* divide into categories

cater *verb* **1** provide food **2** supply what is required: *cater for all tastes* ◊ **caterer** *noun*

caterpillar *noun* the larva of an insect that feeds on plant leaves ◊ *adj* moving on rotating metal belts: *caterpillar tractor*

> Based on a Latin phrase which translates as 'hairy cat'

caterwaul *verb* howl or yell like a cat

catgut *noun* cord made from sheep's stomachs, used to make strings for violins, harps *etc*

cathedral *noun* **1** the church of a bishop **2** the chief church in a bishop's district

catherine-wheel *noun* a firework which rotates as it burns

cathode ray tube a device in a television set *etc*, which causes a narrow beam of electrons to strike against a screen

Catholic *adj* of the Roman Catholic Church

catholic *adj* wide, comprehensive: *a catholic taste in literature*

catkin *noun* a tuft of small flowers on certain trees, *eg* the willow and hazel

CAT scan computer-assisted scan, a form of X-ray which produces a three-dimensional image from a sequence of passes

catsup *noun*, *US* ketchup

cattle *noun*, *plural* animals that eat grass, *eg* oxen, bulls and cows

Caucasian *noun* a White person ◊ *adj* White

caucus /*kawkəs*/ *noun*, *US* a meeting of members of a political party to nominate candidates for election *etc*

caught *past form* of **catch**

cauldron *noun* a large pan

cauliflower *noun* a kind of cabbage with an edible white flower-head

caul *noun* a membrane sometimes covering a baby's head at birth

caulk *verb* make (a plank *etc*) watertight by filling in the seams

cause *noun* **1** that which makes something happen **2** a reason for action: *cause for complaint* **3** an aim for which a group or person works: *the cause of peace* ◊ *verb* make happen

cause célèbre a notorious controversy or controversial person

causeway *noun* a raised road over wet ground or shallow water

caustic *adj* **1** burning, corroding **2** bitter, severe: *caustic wit* ◊ **caustically** *adv*

cauterize *verb* burn away flesh with a hot iron *etc* in order to make a wound heal cleanly

caution *noun* **1** carefulness because of potential danger: *approach with caution* **2** a warning ◊ *verb* warn ◊ **cautionary** *adj* giving a warning

cautious *adj* careful, showing caution ◊ **cautiously** *adv*

cavalcade *noun* a procession on horseback, in cars *etc*

cavalier *hist* a supporter of the king in the Civil War of the 17th century ◊ *adj* offhand, careless: *cavalier fashion*

cavalry *noun* soldiers mounted on horses

cave *noun* a hollow place in the earth or in rock ◊ **caveman, cavewoman** *noun* a prehistoric cave-dweller ◊ **cave in** fall or collapse inwards

caveat /*ka*viat/ *noun* a warning

cavern *noun* a deep hollow place in the earth

cavernous *adj* **1** huge and hollow **2** full of caverns ◊ **cavernously** *adv*

caviare or **caviar** *noun* the pickled eggs of the sturgeon

cavil *verb* make objections over small, unimportant details

> **cavil** » cavil*s*, cavill*ing*, cavill*ed*

cavity *noun* (*plural* **cavities**) **1** a hollow place, a hole **2** a decayed hollow in a tooth

cavort *verb* dance or leap around

caw *verb* call like a crow ◊ *noun* a crow's call

cayenne *noun* a type of very hot red pepper

cayman *noun* (*plural* **caymans**) a South American alligator

CB *abbrev* Companion of the Order of the Bath

CBE *abbrev* Companion of the Order of the British Empire

CBI *abbrev* Confederation of British Industry

cc *abbrev* cubic centimetre(s)

CD *abbrev* compact disc

CD-I *abbrev* compact disc interactive

CD-R *abbrev* compact disc recordable

CD-ROM *abbrev* compact disc read-only memory

cease *verb* come or bring to an end

ceaseless *adj* without stopping ▫ **ceaselessly** *adv*

cedar *noun* a large evergreen tree with a hard sweet-smelling wood

cede *verb* yield, give up

ceilidh /*keh*li/ *noun* an event involving traditional Scottish dancing, sometimes combined with musical performances

ceiling *noun* **1** the inner roof of a room **2** an upper limit

celandine *noun* a small yellow wild-flower

celebrate *verb* commemorate an event (*eg* a birthday or marriage) by going out, having a party *etc* ▫ **celebrated** *adj* famous ▫ **celebration** *noun*

celebrity *noun* (*plural* **celebrities**) **1** a famous person, a star **2** fame

celery *noun* a type of vegetable with edible fibrous stalks

celestial *adj* **1** of the sky: *celestial bodies* **2** heavenly

celibate *adj* abstaining from sexual intercourse ▫ **celibacy** *noun*

cell *noun* **1** a small room in a prison, monastery *etc* **2** the smallest, fundamental part of living things **3** the part of an electric battery containing electrodes

cellar *noun* an underground room used for storing coal, wine *etc*

cellist /*che*list/ *noun* someone who plays the cello

cello /*che*loh/ *noun* (*short for* **violoncello**) a large stringed musical instrument, similar in shape to a violin

cellophane *noun, trademark* a thin transparent wrapping material

cellphone *noun* a pocket telephone for use in a cellular radio system based on a network of transmitters

cellular *adj* made of or having cells

celluloid *noun* a very hard elastic substance used for making photographic film *etc*

cellulose *noun* a substance found in plants and wood used to make paper, textiles *etc*

Celsius /*sel*siəs/ *adj* **1** of a temperature scale: consisting of a hundred degrees, on which water freezes at 0° and boils at 100° **2** of a degree: measured on this scale: *10° Celsius*

cement *noun* **1** the mixture of clay and lime used to secure bricks in a wall **2** something used to make two things stick together ▫ *verb* **1** put together with cement **2** join firmly, fix: *cemented their friendship*

cemetery *noun* (*plural* **cemeteries**) a place where the dead are buried

cenotaph *noun* a monument to someone or a group buried elsewhere

censer *noun* a container for burning incense in a church

⚠Do not confuse: **censer**, **censor** and **censure**

censor *noun* someone whose job is to examine books, films *etc* with power to delete any of the contents ▯ *verb* examine (books *etc*) in this way

censorious *adj* fault-finding; judgemental ▯ **censoriously** *adv*

censure *noun* blame, expression of disapproval ▯ *verb* blame, criticize

census *noun* (*plural* **censuses**) a periodical official count of the people who live in a country

⚠Do not confuse with: **consensus**

cent *noun* a coin which is the hundredth part of a larger coin, *eg* of a US dollar

centaur *noun* a mythological monster, half man and half horse

centenary *noun* (*plural* **centenaries**) a hundredth anniversary; the hundredth year since an event took place ▯ **centenarian** *noun* someone a hundred or more years old

centennial *adj* **1** having lasted a hundred years **2** happening every hundred years ▯ *noun* a centenary

centigrade *adj* **1** of a temperature scale: consisting of a hundred degrees **2** measured on this scale: *5° centigrade* **3** Celsius

centigramme *noun* a hundredth part of a gramme

centilitre *noun* a hundredth part of a litre

centimetre *noun* a hundredth part of a metre

centipede *noun* a small crawling insect with many legs

central *adj* **1** belonging to the centre **2** chief, main: *central point of the argument* ▯ **central heating** heating of a building by water, steam or air from a central point ▯ **central locking** a system whereby all the doors of a vehicle are locked by the locking of the driver's door

centralize *verb* **1** group in a single place **2** bring (government authority) under one central control ▯ **centralization** *noun*

centre or *US* **center** *noun* **1** the middle point or part **2** a building used for some special activity: *sports centre*/ *shopping centre* ▯ *verb* put in the centre

centre *verb* » centre*s*, centr*ing*, centre*d*

centrifugal *adj* moving away from the centre

centripetal *adj* moving towards the centre

centurion *hist* a commander of 100 Roman soldiers

century *noun* (*plural* **centuries**) **1** a hundred years **2** *cricket* a hundred runs

ceramic *adj* **1** made of pottery **2** of pottery-making ▯ *noun* **1** something made of pottery **2** (**ceramics**) the art of pottery

Cerberus *noun* the mythological three-headed dog guarding the entrance to the Greek underworld

cereal *noun* **1** grain used as food **2** a breakfast food prepared from grain

cerebral *adj* of the brain ▫ **cerebrally** *adv*

ceremonial *adj* with or of ceremony ▫ **ceremonially** *adv*

ceremonious *adj* full of ceremony ▫ **ceremoniously** *adv* ▫ **ceremoniousness**

ceremony *noun* (*plural* **ceremonies**) the formal acts that accompany an important event: *marriage ceremony*

cerise /*sərees*/ *adj* & *noun* cherry-red

CERN *abbrev* in French, *Conseil Européen pour la Recherche Nucléaire*, the European Organization for Nuclear Research (now the Europeran Laboratory for Particle Physics)

certain *adj* **1** sure; not to be doubted **2** fixed, settled **3** particular but unnamed: *stopping at certain places/ a certain look* ▫ **certainly** *adv* ▫ **certainty** *noun*

certificate *noun* a written or printed statement giving details of a birth, passed examination *etc*

certify *verb* put down in writing as an official promise or statement *etc*

> **certify** » certifi*es*, certify*ing*, certifi*ed*

cervical *adj* of the cervix ▫ **cervical smear** a collection of a sample of cells from the cervix for examination under a microscope

cervigram *noun* a photograph of the cervix used to detect early signs of cancer

cervix *noun* the neck of the womb

cessation *noun* a ceasing or stopping; an ending

cesspool *noun* a pool or tank for storing liquid waste or sewage

CET *abbrev* central European time

cf *abbrev* compare (from Latin *confer*)

CFC *abbrev* chlorofluorocarbon

chacun à son goût each to their own taste

chador /*chud*ər/ *noun* a veil worn by Islamic or Hindu women, covering the head and shoulders

chafe *verb* **1** make hot or sore by rubbing **2** wear away by rubbing **3** become annoyed

chaff *noun* **1** husks of corn left after threshing **2** something of little value **3** good-natured teasing ▫ *verb* tease jokingly

chaffinch *noun* (*plural* **chaffinches**) a small songbird of the finch family

chagrin /*shəgrin*/ *noun* annoyance, irritation ▫ **chagrined** *adj* annoyed

chain *noun* **1** a number of metal links or rings passing through one another **2** (**chains**) these used to tie a prisoner's limbs; fetters **3** a number of connected things: *mountain chain* **4** a group of shops owned by one person or company **5** a number of atoms of an element joined together ▫ *verb* fasten or imprison with a chain ▫ **chain letter** a letter containing promises or threats, requesting the recipient to send a similar letter to several other people ▫ **chain mail** armour made of iron links ▫ **chain reaction** a chemical process in which each reaction in turn causes a similar reaction □ **chain saw** a power-driven saw with teeth on a rotating chain □ **chain-smoker** *noun* someone who smokes continuously □ **chain-store** *noun* one of several shops under the same ownership

chair *noun* **1** a seat for one person with a back to it **2** a university professorship: *the chair of French literature* **3** a chairman or chairwoman □ **chairlift** *noun* a row of chairs on a rotating cable for carrying people up mountains *etc* □ **chairman, chairwoman** or **chairperson** *noun* someone who presides at or is in charge of a meeting

chakra *noun* in yoga, a centre of spiritual power in the body

chalet /*sha*leh/ *noun* **1** a small wooden house used by holiday-makers **2** a summer hut used by Swiss herdsmen in the Alps

chalice *noun* a cup for wine, used *eg* in church services

chalk *noun* **1** a type of limestone **2** a compressed stick of coloured powder used for writing or drawing □ *verb* mark with chalk □ **chalky** *adj* **1** of chalk **2** white, pale

challenge *verb* **1** question another's right to do something **2** ask (someone) to take part in a contest, *eg* to settle a quarrel □ *noun* **1** a questioning of another's right **2** a call to a contest □ **challenger** *noun* □ **challenging** *adj* interesting but difficult

chamber *noun* **1** a room **2** a place where a parliament meets **3** a room where legal cases are heard by a judge **4** an enclosed space or cavity **5** the part of a gun that holds the cartridges □ **chamber music** music for a small group of players, suitable for performance in a room rather than a large hall

chamberlain *noun* an officer appointed by the crown or a local authority to carry out certain duties

chamberpot *noun* a receptacle for urine *etc*, used in the bedroom

chameleon /k*ə*meelyən/ *noun* a small lizard able to change its colour to match its surroundings

chamois /*sham*wuh/ or /*sha*mee/ *noun* **1** a goat-like deer living in mountainous country **2** (*also called* **shammy**) a soft kind of leather made from its skin

champ *verb* chew noisily □ **champing at the bit** impatient to act

champagne /sham*pehn*/ *noun* a type of white sparkling wine

champion *noun* **1** someone who has beaten all others in a competition **2** a strong supporter of a cause: *champion of free speech* □ *verb* support the cause of

championship *noun* **1** the act of championing **2** a contest to find a champion **3** the title of champion

chance *noun* **1** a risk, a possibility **2** something unexpected or unplanned **3** an opportunity □ *verb* **1** risk **2** happen by accident □ *adj* happening by accident □ **by chance** not by arrangement, unexpectedly □ **chance upon** meet or find unexpectedly

chancel *noun* the part of a church near the altar

chancellor *noun* **1** a high-ranking government minister **2** the head of a university □ **Chancellor of the Exchequer** the minister in the British cabinet in charge of government spending □ **Lord Chancellor** the head of the English legal system

chancery *noun* (in England) the Lord Chancellor's court

chancre /*shang*kər/ *noun* a small lump occurring in the early stages of syphilis

⚠Do not confuse with: **canker**

chancy *adj* risky

chandelier /shandəleer/ *noun* a fixture hanging from the ceiling with branches for holding lights

change *verb* **1** make or become different **2** give up or leave (a job, house *etc*) for another **3** put on different clothes **4** give (money of one kind) in exchange for (money of another kind) □ *noun* **1** the act of making or becoming different **2** another set of clothing **3** money in the form of coins **4** money returned when a buyer gives more than the price of an article □ **change of life** the menopause

change *verb* » change*s*, chang*ing*, change*d*

changeable *adj* likely to change; often changing □ **changeably** *adv*

changeling *noun* a child secretly taken or left in place of another

channel *noun* **1** the bed of a stream **2** a passage for ships **3** a narrow sea **4** a groove; a gutter **5** a band of frequencies for radio or television signals □ *verb* direct into a particular course

channel *verb* » channel*s*, channell*ing*, channell*ed*

chant *verb* recite in a singing manner □ *noun* a singing recitation □ **chanter** *noun* a pipe with finger-holes on a set of bagpipes, on which the melody is played

chanterelle /shonhtə*rel*/ *noun* a yellowish edible mushroom

chanteuse *noun* a female singer

chaos /*keh*os/ *noun* disorder, confusion

chaotic *adj* disordered, confused □ **chaotically** *adv*

chap *noun*, *informal* a man

chaparral *noun* a thicket of brushwood

chapati *noun* a round of unleavened Indian bread

chapbook *noun* a small book, a pamphlet

chapel *noun* **1** a small church **2** a small part of a larger church

chaperone *noun* a woman who attends a younger one when she goes out in public □ *verb* act as a chaperone to

chaplain *noun* a member of the clergy accompanying an army, navy *etc*

chapped *adj* of skin: cracked by cold or wet weather

chapter *noun* **1** a division of a

book **2** a branch of a society or organization □ **chapter of accidents** a series of accidents

char[1] *verb* burn until black

> **char** *verb* » char*s*, charr*ing*, charr*ed*

char[2] *verb* do odd jobs of housework, cleaning *etc* □ *noun, informal* a charwoman

charabanc /*sharə*bang/ *noun* a long motor-coach with rows of seats

character *noun* **1** the nature and qualities of someone **2** the good and bad points which make up a person's nature **3** self-control, firmness **4** someone noted for eccentric behaviour **5** someone in a play, story or film

characteristic *noun* a typical and noticeable feature of someone or something □ *adj* typical □ **characteristically** *adv*

characterize *verb* **1** be typical of **2** describe (as) □ **characterization** *noun*

charade /sh*ə*rahd/ or /sh*ə*rehd/ *noun* **1** a ridiculous pretence **2** (**charades**) a game in which players have to guess a word from gestures representing its sound or meaning

charcoal *noun* wood burnt black, used for fuel or sketching

charge *verb* **1** accuse: *charged with murder* **2** ask (a price) **3** ask to do; give responsibility for **4** load (a gun) **5** attack in a rush □ *noun* **1** accusation for a crime **2** a price, a fee **3** an attack **4** the gunpowder in a shell or bullet **5** care, responsibility **6** someone looked after by another person □ **charger** *noun* a horse used in battle □ **in charge** in command or control □ **take charge of** take command of

> **charge** *verb* » charge*s*, charg*ing*, charge*d*

chariot *noun, hist* a wheeled carriage used in battle □ **charioteer** *noun* a chariot-driver

charisma /k*ə*rizm*ə*/ *noun* a personal quality that impresses others

charismatic *adj* full of charisma or charm □ **charismatically** *adv*

charitable *adj* **1** giving to the poor; kindly **2** of a charity: *charitable status* □ **charitably** *adv*

charity *noun* (*plural* **charities**) **1** donation of money to the poor *etc* **2** an organization which collects money and gives it to those in need **3** kindness, humanity

charlatan /*sharl*ət*ə*n/ *noun* someone who claims greater powers or abilities than they really have

charm *noun* **1** something thought to have magical powers **2** a magical spell **3** personal power to attract □ *verb* **1** please greatly, delight **2** put under a spell □ **charming** *adj*

chart *noun* **1** a table or diagram giving particular information: *temperature chart* **2** a geographical map of the sea **3** a rough map □ *verb* make into a chart; plot

charter *noun* a written paper showing the official granting of rights, lands *etc* □ *verb* hire (a boat, aeroplane *etc*) □ *adj* hired for a special purpose: *charter flight* □ **chartered** *adj* **1** qualified under the regulations of a professional body: *chartered surveyor* **2** hired for a purpose

charwoman *noun* a woman hired to do domestic cleaning *etc*

chary *adj* cautious, careful (of) □ **charily** *adv* □ **chariness** *noun*

chase *verb* **1** run after, pursue **2** hunt □ *noun* a pursuit, a hunt

chasm /kazm/ *noun* **1** a steep drop between high rocks *etc* **2** a wide difference; a gulf

chassis /*sha*see/ *noun* (*plural* **chassis**) **1** the frame, wheels and machinery of a motor-car **2** an aeroplane's landing carriage

chaste *adj* **1** pure, virtuous **2** virgin □ **chastely** *adv* □ **chastity** *noun*

chasten *verb* **1** make humble **2** scold □ **chastened** *adj*

chastise *verb* punish, *esp* by beating □ **chastisement** *noun*

chat *verb* talk in an easy, friendly way □ *noun* a friendly conversation □ **chat-show** *noun* a radio or TV programme in which personalities talk informally with their host

> **chat** *verb* » chat*s*, chatt*ing*, chatt*ed*

chateau /*sha*toh/ *noun* (*plural* **chateaux**) a French castle or country house

chattels *noun plural* movable possessions □ **goods and chattels** personal possessions

chatter *verb* **1** talk idly or rapidly; gossip **2** of teeth: rattle together because of cold □ **chatterbox** *noun* someone who talks a great deal

chatty *adj* willing to talk, talkative □ **chattily** *adv*

chauffeur /*shoh*fər/ *noun* someone employed to drive a motor-car

chauvinist *noun* a man who practises sexism towards women □ **chauvinism** *noun* extreme nationalism or patriotism □ **chauvinistic** *adj*

> After Nicholas *Chauvin*, Napoleonic French soldier and keen patriot

cheap *adj* **1** low in price, inexpensive **2** of little value, worthless □ **cheapen** *verb* make cheap □ **cheaply** *adv*

cheat *verb* **1** deceive **2** act dishonestly to gain an advantage □ *noun* **1** someone who cheats **2** a dishonest trick

check *verb* **1** bring to a stop **2** hold back, restrain **3** see if (a total *etc*) is correct or accurate **4** see if (a machine *etc*) is in good condition or working properly □ *noun* **1** a sudden stop **2** a restraint **3** a test of correctness or accuracy **4** a square, *eg* on a draughtboard **5** a pattern of squares □ **checked** *adj* patterned with squares □ **check in** or **check out** record your arrival at or departure from (a hotel *etc*)

> ⚠Do not confuse with: **cheque**

checkered *another spelling* of **chequered**

checkers *another spelling of* **chequers**

checkmate *noun, chess* a position from which the king cannot escape

checkout *noun* a place where payment is made in a supermarket

cheek *noun* **1** the side of the face below the eye **2** a buttock **3** insolence, disrespectful behaviour

cheeky *adj* impudent, insolent ▫ **cheekily** *adv* ▫ **cheekiness** *noun*

cheep *verb* make a faint sound like a small bird ▫ *noun* the sound of a small bird

cheer *noun* a shout of approval or welcome ▫ *verb* **1** shout approval **2** encourage, urge on **3** comfort, gladden ▫ **cheerless** *adj* sad, gloomy ▫ **cheer up** make or become less gloomy

cheerful *adj* happy, in good spirits ▫ **cheerfully** *adv* ▫ **cheerfulness** *noun*

cheerio *exclam* goodbye!

cheers *exclam* **1** good health! **2** regards, best wishes

cheery *adj* lively and merry ▫ **cheerily** *adv*

cheese *noun* a solid food made from milk ▫ **cheesecloth** *noun* loosely-woven cotton cloth ▫ **cheeseparing** *adj* mean

cheesy 1 tasting of cheese **2** of a smile: broad

cheetah *noun* a fast-running animal similar to a leopard

chef *noun* a head cook in a restaurant

chef d'oeuvre a masterpiece; a life's work

chemical *adj* relating to the reactions between elements *etc* ▫ *noun* a substance formed by or used in a chemical process

chemist *noun* **1** someone who studies chemistry **2** someone who makes up and sells medicines; a pharmacist

chemistry *noun* the study of the elements and the ways they combine or react with each other

chenille /sh*ə*neel/ *noun* a thick, velvety material or yarn

cheongsam /chong*sam*/ *noun* a traditional Chinese woman's dress, tight-fitting with a high neck

cheque or *US* **check** *noun* a written order to a banker to pay money from a bank account to another person ▫ **cheque book** a book containing cheques

⚠Do not confuse with: **check**

chequered or **checkered** *adj* **1** marked like a chessboard **2** partly good, partly bad: *a chequered career*

chequers or **checkers** *noun plural* **1** a pattern of squares, *eg* on a chessboard **2** the game of draughts

cherish *verb* **1** protect and treat with fondness or kindness **2** keep in your mind or heart: *cherish a hope*

cheroot *noun* a small cigar

cherry *noun* (*plural* **cherries**) **1** a small bright-red fruit with a stone

2 the tree that produces this fruit

cherub *noun* (*plural* **cherubs** or **cherubim**) **1** an angel with a plump, childish face and body **2** a beautiful child

chervil *noun* a feathery herb related to the carrot

chess *noun* a game for two players in which pieces are moved in turn on a board marked in alternate black and white squares ▫ **chessboard** *noun* ▫ **chessman** or **chesspiece** *noun*

chest *noun* **1** a large strong box **2** the part of the body between the neck and the stomach ▫ **chest of drawers** a piece of furniture fitted with a set of drawers

chesterfield *noun* a kind of sofa

chestnut *noun* **1** a reddish-brown nut **2** the tree that produces this nut, the **horse chestnut** or **sweet chestnut 3** a reddish-brown horse **4** an old joke

cheviot *noun* a kind of sheep

chèvre /*she*vrə/ *noun* a soft goat's cheese

chevron *noun* a V-shape, *eg* on a badge or road-sign

chew *verb* **1** break up (food) with the teeth before swallowing **2** reflect or ponder (on)

chez /sheh/ *prep* at the home of

chi /chee/ *noun another spelling* of **qi**

chiaroscuro /kyahroh*skoo*roh/ dramatic contrast between light and dark in a painting *etc*

chic /sheek/ *adj* smart and fashionable ▫ *noun* style, fashionable elegance

chicanery /shi*keh*nəree/ *noun* dishonest cleverness

chichi /*shee*shee/ *adj* fussy, affected

chick *noun* **1** a chicken **2** *slang* a girl, a young woman

chicken *noun* **1** the young of birds, *esp* of domestic poultry **2** *informal* a coward ▫ *adj*, *informal* cowardly ▫ **chicken-hearted** *adj* cowardly

chicken-feed *noun* **1** food for poultry **2** something paltry or worthless

chickenpox *noun* an infectious disease which causes red, itchy spots

chickpea *noun* a plant of the pea family with a brown edible seed

chicory *noun* **1** a plant with sharp-tasting leaves eaten in salads **2** its root, roasted and ground to mix with coffee

chide *verb* scold with words

chief *adj* **1** main, most important **2** largest ▫ *noun* **1** a leader or ruler **2** the head of a department, organization *etc*

chiefly *adv* mainly, for the most part

chieftain *noun* the head of a clan or tribe

chiffon *noun* a thin flimsy material made of silk or nylon

chignon /*sheen*yonh/ *noun* a knot or roll of hair on the back of the head

chihuahua /chi*wa*wa/ *noun* a

breed of very small dog, originally from Mexico

chilblain *noun* a painful swelling on hands and feet, caused by cold weather

child *noun* (*plural* **children**) **1** a young human being **2** a son or daughter: *is that your child?* ◻ **childhood** *noun* the time of being a child ◻ **childlike** *adj* innocent

childish *adj* **1** of or like a child **2** silly, immature ◻ **childishly** *adv* ◻ **childishness** *noun*

chile *noun another spelling* of **chilli**

chill *noun* **1** coldness **2** an illness that causes fever and shivering **3** lack of warmth or enthusiasm ◻ *adj* cold ◻ *verb* **1** make cold **2** refrigerate

chilli or **chile** *noun* **1** the hot-tasting pod of a kind of pepper, sometimes dried for cooking **2** a dish or sauce made with this

chilly *adj* cold

chime *noun* **1** the sound of bells ringing **2** (**chimes**) a set of bells, *eg* in a clock ◻ *verb* **1** ring **2** of a clock: strike

chimera /kai*meer*ə/ *noun* a wild idea or fancy ◻ **chimerical** *adj* wildly fanciful

chimney *noun* (*plural* **chimneys**) a passage allowing smoke or heated air to escape from a fire ◻ **chimneypot** *noun* a metal or earthenware pipe placed at the top of a chimney ◻ **chimneystack** *noun* **1** a tall chimney, *eg* in a factory **2** a number of chimneys built up together ◻ **chimneysweep** *noun* someone employed to clean chimneys

chimpanzee *noun* a type of African ape

chin *noun* the part of the face below the mouth

china *noun* **1** fine kind of earthenware; porcelain **2** articles made of this

chinchilla *noun* a small S American animal with soft grey fur

chink *noun* **1** a narrow opening **2** the sound of coins *etc* striking together

chintz *noun* (*plural* **chintzes**) a cotton cloth with brightly coloured patterning

> From a Hindi word for painted or multicoloured cotton

chip *verb* break or cut small pieces (from or off) ◻ *noun* **1** a small piece chipped off **2** a part damaged by chipping **3** a long thin piece of potato fried **4** *US* a potato or corn crisp

> **chip** *verb* » chip*s*, chipp*ing*, chipp*ed*

chipmunk *noun* a kind of N American squirrel

chipolata *noun* a type of small sausage

chiropodist *noun* someone who treats minor disorders and diseases of the feet ◻ **chiropody** *noun*

chiropractic *noun* a treatment for muscular pain *etc* involving manipulation of the spinal column

□ **chiropractor** *noun* a therapist who uses chiropractic

chirp or **chirrup** *verb* of a bird: make a sharp, shrill sound

chirpy *adj* merry, cheerful □ **chirpily** *adv* □ **chirpiness** *noun*

chisel *noun* a metal tool to cut or hollow out wood, stone *etc* □ *verb* cut with a chisel

> **chisel** *verb* » chisel*s*, chisell*ing*, chisell*ed*

chit *noun* **1** a short note **2** a child, a young woman: *chit of a girl*

chit-chat *noun* & *verb* gossip, talk

chivalry /*shiv*əlri/ *noun* **1** kindness, *esp* towards women or the weak **2** *hist* the standard of behaviour expected of knights in medieval times □ **chivalrous** *adj* □ **chivalrously** *adv* □ **chivalrousness** *noun*

chives *noun* an onion-like herb used in cooking

chlorine *noun* a yellowish-green gas with a sharp smell, used as a bleach and disinfectant □ **chlorinated** *adj* mixed with chlorine or a substance containing chlorine

chloroform *noun* a liquid whose vapour causes unconsciousness if inhaled

chock-a-block *adj* completely full or congested

chockfull *adj* completely full

chocolate *noun* **1** a sweet made from the seeds of the cacao tree **2** a drink made from the seeds (*also called* **cocoa**) □ *adj* dark brown in colour □ **chocolatey** *adj* tasting of chocolate

choice *noun* **1** the act or power of choosing **2** something chosen □ *adj* of a high quality: *choice vegetables*

choir *noun* **1** a group or society of singers **2** a part of a church where a choir sits

> ⚠Do not confuse with: **quire**

choke *verb* **1** stop or partly stop the breathing of **2** block or clog (a pipe *etc*) **3** have your breathing stopped or interrupted, *eg* by smoke □ *noun* a valve in a petrol engine which controls the inflow of air

cholera /*kol*ərə/ *noun* an infectious intestinal disease, causing severe vomiting and diarrhoea

cholesterol *noun* a substance found in body cells which carries fats through the bloodstream

chomp *verb*, *informal* munch noisily

choose *verb* **1** select and take from two or several things: *choose whichever book you like* **2** decide, prefer to: *we chose to leave before the film began*

> **choose** » choose*s*, choos*ing*, chose, chosen

chop *verb* **1** cut into small pieces **2** cut with a sudden blow □ *noun* **1** a chopping blow **2** a slice of meat containing a bone: *mutton chop* □ **chop and change** keep changing

> **chop** *verb* » chop*s*, chopp*ing*, chopp*ed*

chopper *noun* **1** a knife or axe for chopping **2** *informal* a helicopter

choppy *adj* of the sea: not calm, having small waves

chopsticks *noun plural* a pair of small sticks of wood, ivory *etc* used instead of a knife and fork for eating Chinese food

> Literally 'quick sticks', from Pidgin English *chop* for 'quick'

choral *adj* sung by or written for a choir

chord *noun* **1** a musical sound made by playing several notes together **2** a straight line joining any two points on a curve

> ⚠Do not confuse with: **cord**

chore *noun* **1** a dull, boring job **2** (**chores**) housework

choreography *noun* the arrangement of dancing and dance steps ▫ **choreographer** *noun*

chorister *noun* a member of a choir

chortle *verb* laugh, chuckle

chorus *noun* (*plural* **choruses**) **1** a band of singers and dancers **2** a choir or choral group **3** a part of a song repeated after each verse

chose *past form* of **choose**

chosen *past participle* of **choose**

chow *noun* a Chinese breed of dog with a bushy coat and a blue-black tongue

chowder *noun* a thick soup containing cream

christen *verb* baptize and give a name to ▫ **christening** *noun* the ceremony of baptism

Christian *noun* a believer in Christianity ▫ *adj* of Christianity ▫ **Christian name** a first or personal name

Christianity *noun* the religion which follows the teachings of Christ

Christmas *noun* an annual Christian holiday or festival, in memory of the birth of Christ, held on 25 December ▫ **Christmassy** *adj* suitable for Christmas ▫ **Christmas Eve** 24 December ▫ **Christmas tree** an evergreen tree hung with lights, decorations and gifts at Christmas

chromatic *adj* **1** of colours **2** coloured **3** *music* of or written in a scale in which each note is separated from the next by a semitone

chromium *noun* a metal which does not rust

chromosome *noun* a rod-like part of a body cell that determines the characteristics of an individual

chronic *adj* **1** of a disease: lasting a long time **2** *informal* very bad ▫ **chronically** *adv*

chronicle *noun* a record of events in order of time ▫ *verb* write down events in order ▫ **chronicler** *noun*

chronological *adj* arranged in the order of the time of happening ▫ **chronologically** *adv*

chronometer *noun* an instrument for measuring time

chrysalis *noun* an insect (*esp* a butterfly or moth) in its early stage of life, with no wings and encased in a soft cocoon

chrysanthemum *noun* a type of

garden flower with a large bushy head

chubby *adj* plump ▫ **chubbily** *adv* ▫ **chubbiness** *noun*

chubby » chubb*ier*, chubb*iest*

chuck *verb* **1** throw, toss **2** pat gently under the chin ▫ **chuck out** *informal* **1** throw away, get rid of **2** expel

chuckle *noun* a quiet laugh ▫ *verb* laugh quietly

chuffed *adj*, *informal* very pleased

chum *informal* a close friend ▫ **chummy** *adj* very friendly

chump *noun* ▫ **off your chump** *informal* off your head; mad

chunk *noun* a thick piece

chunky *adj* heavy, thick

church *noun* (*plural* **churches**) **1** a building for public, *esp* Christian, worship **2** any group of people who meet together for worship ▫ **churchyard** *noun* a burial ground next to a church

churlish *adj* bad-mannered, rude ▫ **churlishly** *adv* ▫ **churlishness** *noun*

churn *noun* a machine for making butter from milk ▫ *verb* **1** make (butter) in a churn **2** shake or stir about violently

chute /shoot/ *noun* **1** a sloping trough for sending water, parcels *etc* to a lower level **2** a sloping structure for children to slide down, with steps for climbing back up

chutney *noun* (*plural* **chutneys**) a sauce made with vegetables or fruits and vinegar

chutzpah /*hoot*spə/ *noun* brazenness, effrontery

CIA *abbrev* Central Intelligence Agency (in the USA)

cicada /si*kah*də/ *noun* a chirping insect found in warm climates

cicatrice *noun* a scar

cicely *noun* a plant related to chervil

CID *abbrev* Criminal Investigation Department

cider *noun* an alcoholic drink made from fermented apple-juice

cigar *noun* a roll of tobacco leaves for smoking

cigarette *noun* a tube of fine tobacco enclosed in thin paper

C-in-C *abbrev* Commander-in-Chief

cinder *noun* a burnt-out piece of coal

cinema *noun* **1** a place where films are shown **2** films as an art form or industry

cinnamon *noun* a yellowish-brown spice obtained from tree bark

cipher *noun* **1** a secret writing, a code **2** nought, zero **3** someone of no importance

Originally meaning 'zero' and later 'number', because of the early use of numbers in encoded documents

circa *prep* about (in dates): *circa 300BC*

circadian *adj* relating to biological rhythms repeated every 24 hours

circle *noun* **1** a figure formed from an endless curved line **2** something in the form of a circle; a ring **3** a society or group of people **4** a tier of seats in a theatre *etc* □ *verb* **1** enclose in a circle **2** move round in a circle

circlet *noun* **1** a small circle **2** an ornamental headband

circuit *noun* **1** a movement in a circle **2** a connected group of places, events *etc*: *the American tennis circuit* **3** the path of an electric current

circuitous *adj* not direct, roundabout: *by a circuitous route* □ **circuitously** *adv*

circular *adj* round, like a circle □ *noun* a letter sent round to a number of people □ **circularize** *verb* send a circular to

circulate *verb* **1** move round **2** send round: *circulate a memo*

circulation *noun* **1** the act of circulating **2** the movement of the blood **3** the total sales of a newspaper or magazine

circumference *noun* **1** the outside line of a circle **2** the length of this line

circumlocution *noun* a roundabout way of saying something

circumnavigate *verb* sail round (the world) □ **circumnavigator** *noun*

circumscribe *verb* **1** draw a line round **2** put limits on, restrict □ **circumscription** *noun*

circumspect *adj* wary, cautious □ **circumspection** *noun* caution

circumstance *noun* **1** a condition of time, place *etc* which affects someone, an action or an event **2** (**circumstances**) the state of someone's financial affairs

circumstantial *adj* of evidence: pointing to a conclusion without giving absolute proof

circumstantiate *verb* prove by giving details

circumvent *verb* **1** get round (a difficulty) **2** outwit □ **circumvention** *noun*

circus *noun* (*plural* **circuses**) **1** a travelling company of acrobats, clowns *etc* **2** a large sports arena

cirrhosis *noun* a disease of the liver

cirrus *noun* a fleecy kind of cloud

CIS *abbrev* Commonwealth of Independent States

cissy *noun*, *informal* an effeminate person

cistern *noun* a tank for storing water

citadel *noun* a fortress within a city

citation *noun* **1** something quoted **2** a summons to appear in court **3** official recognition of an achievement or action

cite *verb* **1** quote as an example or as proof **2** summon to appear in court

> ⚠Do not confuse with: **sight** and **site**

CITES *abbrev* Convention on International Trade in Endangered Species

cithara *noun* an ancient Greek stringed musical instrument

citizen *noun* someone who lives in a city or state □ **citizenry** *noun plural* the inhabitants of a city or state □ **citizenship** *noun* the rights or state of being a citizen

citric acid a sharp-tasting acid found in citrus fruits

citron *noun* a type of fruit similar to a lemon

citrus fruit one of a group of fruits including the orange, lemon and lime

cittern *noun* a metal-stringed instrument similar to a lute

city *noun* (*plural* **cities**) **1** a large town **2** a town with a cathedral □ **the City** *Brit* the part of London regarded as the centre of business

civic *adj* relating to a city or citizens □ **civics** *noun sing* the study of people's duties as citizens

civil *adj* **1** relating to a community **2** non-military, civilian **3** polite □ **civil engineer** an engineer who plans bridges, roads *etc* □ **civil law** law concerned with citizens' rights, not criminal acts □ **civil list** the expenses of the royal household □ **civil marriage** a marriage which does not take place in church □ **civil rights** the rights of a citizen □ **civil service** the paid administrative officials of the country, excluding the armed forces □ **civil war** war between citizens of the same country

civilian *noun* someone who is not in the armed forces □ *adj* non-military

civility *noun* politeness, good manners

civilization *noun* **1** making or becoming civilized **2** life under a civilized system **3** a particular culture: *a prehistoric civilization*

civilize *verb* bring (a people) under a regular system of laws, education *etc* □ **civilized** *adj* living under such a system; not savage

clachan /*kla*xhən/ *noun*, *Scot* a small village

clad *adj*, *formal* clothed: *clad in leather from head to toe*

claim *verb* **1** demand as a right **2** state as a truth; assert (that) □ *noun* an act of claiming □ **claimant** *noun* someone who makes a claim

clair de lune a bluish porcelain glaze

clairvoyant *adj* able to see into the future, or to contact the spirit world □ *noun* someone with clairvoyant powers □ **clairvoyance** *noun*

clam *noun* a large shellfish with two shells hinged together

clamber *verb* climb awkwardly or with difficulty

clammy *adj* moist and sticky

clamour *noun* a loud, continuous noise or outcry □ *verb* **1** cry aloud **2** make a loud demand (for) □ **clamorous** *adj* noisy

clamp *noun* a piece of metal, wood *etc* used to fasten things together □ *verb* bind with a clamp □ **clamp down on** suppress firmly

clan *noun* **1** a number of families with the same surname, traditionally under a single chieftain

2 a sect, a clique □ **clannish** *adj* loyal to each another, but showing little interest in others □ **clansman, clanswoman** *noun* a member of a clan

> From Scottish Gaelic *clann* meaning 'children'

clandestine *adj* hidden, secret, underhand □ **clandestinely** *adv*

clang *verb* make a loud, deep ringing sound □ *noun* a loud, deep ring

clank *noun* a sound like that made by metal hitting metal □ *verb* make this sound

clap *noun* **1** the noise made by striking together two things, *esp* the hands **2** a burst of sound, *esp* thunder □ *verb* **1** strike noisily together **2** strike the hands together to show approval **3** *informal* put suddenly, throw: *clap in jail* □ **clapper** *noun* the tongue of a bell

> **clap** *verb* » clap*s*, clapp*ing*, clapp*ed*

claptrap *noun* meaningless words, nonsense

claret *noun* a type of red wine

clarify *verb* **1** make clear and understandable **2** make (a liquid) clear and pure

> **clarify** » clarifi*es*, clarify*ing*, clarifi*ed*

clarinet *noun* a musical wind instrument, usually made of wood □ **clarinettist** *noun* someone who plays the clarinet

clarion *noun, old* **1** a kind of trumpet **2** a shrill, rousing noise □ **clarion call** a clear call to action

clarity *noun* clearness

clarsach /*klars*əxh/ *noun* the traditional Scottish Highland harp, strung with wire □ **clarsair** *noun* a clarsach player

clash *noun* (*plural* **clashes**) **1** a loud noise made by striking swords *etc* **2** a disagreement, a fight □ *verb* **1** bang noisily together **2** disagree **3** of events: take place at the same time **4** of two colours *etc*: not to look well together

clasp *noun* **1** a hook or pin for fastening: hair clasp **2** a handshake **3** an embrace □ *verb* **1** hold closely; grasp **2** fasten

class *noun* (*plural* **classes**) **1** a rank or order of people or things **2** a group of schoolchildren or students taught together **3** a group of plants or animals with something in common □ *verb* **1** place in a class **2** arrange in some order

classify *verb* **1** arrange in classes **2** put into a class or category □ **classification** *noun*

> **classify** » classifi*es*, classify*ing*, classifi*ed*

classic *noun* **1** a great book or other work of art **2** something typical and influential of its kind **3** (**classics**) the study of ancient Greek and Latin literature □ *adj* **1** excellent **2** standard, typical of its kind: *a classic example* **3** simple and elegant in style: *a classic black dress*

classical *adj* **1** of a classic or the

classics **2** of music: serious, not light

classy *adj* elegant, stylish

clatter *noun* a noise of plates *etc* banged together

clause *noun* **1** a part of a sentence containing a finite verb **2** a part of a will, act of parliament *etc*

claustrophobia *noun* an abnormal fear of enclosed spaces □ **claustrophobic** *adj*

claw *noun* **1** an animal's or bird's foot with hooked nails **2** a hooked nail on one of these feet □ *verb* scratch or tear

clay *noun* soft, sticky earth, often used to make pottery, bricks *etc* □ **clayey** *adj*

claymore *noun* *hist* a large sword used by Scottish Highlanders in battle

clean *adj* **1** free from dirt; pure **2** neat, complete: *a clean break* □ *adv* completely: *got clean away* □ *verb* make clean; free from dirt □ **cleaner** *noun* **1** someone employed to clean a building *etc* **2** a substance which cleans □ **cleanliness** *noun* □ **cleanly** *adv*

cleanse /klenz/ *verb* make clean

clear *adj* **1** bright, undimmed **2** free from mist or cloud: *clear sky* **3** transparent **4** free from difficulty or obstructions **5** easy to see, hear or understand **6** after deductions and charges have been made: *clear profit* **7** without a stain **8** without touching: *clear of the rocks* □ *verb* **1** make clear **2** empty **3** free from blame **4** leap over without touching **5** of the sky: become bright □ **clearance** *noun* □ **clear-cut** *adj* distinct, obvious □ **clearing** *noun* land free of trees □ **clearly** *adv* □ **clearness** *noun* □ **clear out** or **clear off** go away

cleave *verb* **1** divide, split **2** crack **3** stick (to)

> **cleave** » cleave*s*, cleav*ing*, clove or cleft, clove*n* or cleft

cleavage *noun* **1** splitting **2** the way in which two things are split or divided **3** the hollow between a woman's breasts

cleaver *noun* a heavy knife for splitting meat carcases *etc*

clef *noun* a musical sign, (𝄞 **treble clef**) or (𝄢 **bass clef**), placed on a stave to fix the pitch of the notes

cleft *noun* an opening made by splitting; a crack □ *past form* of **cleave** □ **cleft palate** a congenital defect causing a fissure in the roof of the mouth

cleg *noun* a type of horsefly

clematis *noun* a flowering, climbing shrub

clement *adj* mild; merciful □ **clemency** *noun* readiness to forgive; mercy

clench *verb* press firmly together: *clenching his teeth*

clergy *noun plural* the ministers of the Christian church □ **clergyman, clergywoman** *noun* a Christian minister

cleric *noun* a member of the clergy

clerk *noun* an office worker who writes letters, keeps accounts *etc* □

verb act as clerk □ **clerical** *adj* **1** relating to office work **2** of the clergy

clever *adj* **1** quick in learning and understanding **2** intelligent, skilful: *a clever answer* □ **cleverly** *adv* □ **cleverness** *noun*

cliché /*klee*sheh/ *noun* an idea, phrase *etc* that has been used too much and has little meaning

> From a French word for 'stereotype', in the sense of a fixed printing plate

click *noun* a short sharp sound like a clock's tick □ *verb* make this sound

client *noun* **1** a customer of a shop *etc* **2** someone who goes to a lawyer *etc* for advice

clientele /klaiən*tel*/ *noun* the customers of a lawyer, shopkeeper *etc*

cliff *noun* a very steep, rocky slope, *esp* by the sea

climate *noun* **1** the weather conditions of a particular area **2** general condition or situation: *in the present cultural climate* □ **climatic** *adj*

climax *noun* (*plural* **climaxes**) the point of greatest interest or importance in a situation

climb *verb* **1** go to the top of **2** go up using hands and feet **3** slope upward □ *noun* an act of climbing □ **climber** *noun* **1** someone who climbs **2** a plant which climbs up walls *etc*

clinch *verb* **1** grasp tightly **2** settle (an argument, bargain *etc*) □ *noun* (*plural* **clinches**) **1** *boxing* a position in which the boxers hold each other with their arms **2** a passionate embrace □ **clincher** *noun*

cling *verb* stick or hang on (to) □ **clingy** *adj*

> **cling** » cling*s*, cling*ing*, clung

clingfilm *noun* thin transparent plastic material used to wrap food

clinic *noun* a place or part of a hospital where a particular kind of treatment is given

clinical *adj* **1** of a clinic **2** based on observation: *clinical medicine* **3** objective, cool and unemotional: *clinical approach* □ **clinically** *adv*

clink *noun* a ringing sound of knocked glasses *etc* □ *verb*

clinker *noun* waste produced from smelting iron or burning coal

clip *verb* **1** cut (off) **2** fasten with a clip □ *noun* **1** something clipped off **2** a small fastener **3** *informal* a smart blow

> **clip** *verb* » clip*s*, clipp*ing*, clipp*ed*

clipper *noun* **1** a fast-sailing ship **2** (**clippers**) large scissors for clipping

clique /kleek/ *noun* a small group of people who help each other but keep others at a distance

clitoris *noun* a small structure at the front of the external female sex organs □ **clitoral** *adj*

cloak *noun* **1** a loose outer garment **2** something which hides: *cloak of darkness* □ *verb* **1** cover as with a cloak **2** hide □ **cloakroom** a place where coats, hats *etc* may be left for a time

cloche /klosh/ *noun* (*plural* **cloches**) a transparent frame for protecting plants

clock *noun* a machine for measuring time ◊ **clockwise** *adj* turning or moving in the same direction as the hands of a clock ◊ **clockwork** *adj* worked by machinery such as that of a clock ◊ **clock in** or **clock out** record your time of arrival at, or departure from, work ◊ **like clockwork** smoothly, without difficulties

clod *noun* **1** a thick lump of turf **2** a stupid man

clodhopper *noun* a stupid clumsy person ◊ **clodhopping** *adj*

clog *noun* a shoe with a wooden sole ◊ *verb* block (pipes *etc*)

> **clog** *verb* » clog*s*, clogg*ing*, clogg*ed*

cloisonné /*klwa*zoneh/ *noun* a form of enamelling with coloured areas divided by threads of metal

cloister *noun* **1** a covered-in walk in a monastery or convent **2** a monastery or convent ◊ **cloistered** *adj* **1** shut up in a monastery *etc* **2** sheltered

clootie dumpling a Scottish steamed pudding made with suet and dried fruit

close[1] /klohs/ *adj* **1** near in time, place *etc* **2** shut up, with no opening **3** without fresh air, stuffy **4** narrow, confined **5** mean **6** secretive **7** beloved, very dear: *a close friend* **8** decided by a small amount: *a close contest* ◊ *noun* **1** a narrow passage off a street **2** the gardens, walks *etc* near a cathedral ◊ **closely** *adv* ◊ **closeness** *noun* ◊ **close-up** *noun* a film or photograph taken very near the subject

close[2] /klohz/ *verb* **1** shut **2** finish **3** come closer to and fight (with) ◊ *noun* the end ◊ **closed-circuit television** a system of television cameras and receivers for use in shops *etc*

closet *noun*, *US* a cupboard ◊ *verb* take into a room for a private conference ◊ **closeted with** in private conference with

closure *noun* the act of closing

clot *noun* **1** a lump that forms in blood, cream *etc* **2** *informal* an idiot ◊ *verb* form into clots

> **clot** *verb* » clot*s*, clott*ing*, clott*ed*

cloth *noun* **1** woven material of cotton, wool, silk *etc* **2** a piece of this **3** a table-cover

clothe *verb* **1** put clothes on **2** provide with clothes **3** cover

clothes *noun plural* **1** things worn to cover the body and limbs, *eg* shirt, trousers, skirt **2** sheets and coverings for a bed ◊ **clothing** *noun* clothes

cloud *noun* **1** a mass of tiny drops of water or ice floating in the sky **2** a mass of anything: *cloud of bees* ◊ *verb* become dim or blurred ◊ **cloudburst** *noun* a sudden heavy fall of rain ◊ **clouded** *adj* ◊ **cloudless** *adj*

cloudy *adj* **1** darkened with clouds **2** not clear or transparent

clout *noun, informal* **1** a blow **2** *informal* influence, power ▫ *verb* hit

clove[1] *noun* **1** a flower bud of the clove tree, used as a spice **2** a small section of a bulb of garlic

clove[2] *past form* of **cleave**

cloven-hoofed *adj* having a divided hoof like an ox, sheep *etc*

clover *noun* a field plant with leaves usually in three parts ▫ **in clover** in luxury

clown *noun* **1** a comedian with a painted face and comical clothes in a circus **2** a fool ▫ **clowning** *noun* silly or comical behaviour ▫ **clownish** *adj* like a clown; awkward

cloy *verb* of something sweet: become unpleasant when too much is taken ▫ **cloying** *adj* ▫ **cloyingly** *adv*

club *noun* **1** a heavy stick **2** a stick used to hit the ball in golf **3** a group of people who meet for social events *etc* **4** the place where these people meet **5** (**clubs**) one of the four suits in playing-cards ▫ *verb* beat with a club ▫ **club together** put money into a joint fund for some purpose

> **club** *verb* » club*s*, club*bing*, club*bed*

cluck *noun* a sound like that made by a hen ▫ *verb* make this sound

clue *noun* a sign or piece of evidence that helps to solve a mystery

clump *noun* a cluster of trees or shrubs ▫ *verb* walk heavily

clumsy *adj* **1** awkward in movement or actions **2** tactless, thoughtless: *clumsy apology* ▫ **clumsily** *adv* ▫ **clumsiness** *noun*

> **clumsy** » clums*ier*, clums*iest*

clung *past form* of **cling**

clunky *adj* awkward or noisy in operation

cluster *noun* **1** a bunch of fruit *etc* **2** a crowd ▫ *verb* group together in clusters

clutch *verb* **1** hold firmly **2** seize, grasp ▫ *noun* (*plural* **clutches**) **1** a grasp **2** part of a motor-car engine used for changing gears

clutter *noun* **1** a muddled or disorded collection of things **2** disorder, confusion, untidiness ▫ *verb* **1** crowd together untidily **2** (with **up**) fill or cover in an untidy, disordered way

cm *abbrev* centimetre

CND *abbrev* Campaign for Nuclear Disarmament

CO *abbrev* **1** carbon monoxide **2** Commanding Officer

Co *abbrev* **1** Company **2** County

c/o *abbrev* care of

co- *prefix* joint, working with: *co-author/ co-driver*

coach *noun* (*plural* **coaches**) **1** a bus for long-distance travel **2** a closed, four-wheeled horse carriage **3** a railway carriage **4** a private trainer for sportspeople ▫ *verb* train or help to prepare for an examination, sports contest *etc*

coagulate *verb* thicken; clot

coal *noun* a black substance dug out of the earth and used for burning, making gas *etc* □ **coalfield** *noun* an area where there is coal to be mined □ **coal gas** the mixture of gases obtained from coal, used for lighting and heating □ **coalmine** *noun* a mine from which coal is dug

coalesce /kohəles/ *verb* come together and unite

coalition *noun* a joining together of different parts or groups

coarse *adj* **1** not fine in texture; rough, harsh **2** vulgar □ **coarsely** *adv* □ **coarsen** *verb* make coarse □ **coarseness** *noun*

coast *noun* the border of land next to the sea □ *verb* **1** sail along or near a coast **2** move without the use of power on a bike, in a car *etc* □ **coastal** *adj* of or on the coast □ **coastguard** *noun* someone who acts as a guard along the coast to help those in danger in boats *etc*

coat *noun* **1** an outer garment with sleeves **2** an animal's covering of hair or wool **3** a layer of paint □ *verb* cover with a coat or layer □ **coating** *noun* a covering □ **coat of arms** the badge or crest of a family

coax *verb* persuade to do what is wanted without using force

cob *noun* **1** a head of corn, wheat *etc* **2** a male swan

cobalt *noun* **1** a silvery metal **2** a blue colouring obtained from this

cobble *noun* **1** a rounded stone used in paving roads (*also called* **cobblestone**) □ *verb* **1** mend (shoes) **2** repair roughly or hurriedly □ **cobbler** *noun* someone who mends shoes

cobra *noun* a poisonous snake found in India and Africa

cobweb *noun* a spider's web

cocaine *noun* a narcotic drug

cochineal *noun* a scarlet dye, used to colour food, made from the dried bodies of certain insects

cock *noun* **1** the male of most kinds of bird, *esp* of the farmyard hen **2** a tap or valve for controlling the flow of liquid **3** a hammer-like part of a gun which fires the shot **4** a small heap of hay **5** *slang* the penis □ *verb* **1** draw back the cock of a gun **2** set (the ears) upright to listen **3** tilt (the head) to one side □ **cocker spaniel** a breed of small spaniel □ **cockscomb** *noun* the comb or crest of a cock's head □ **cocksure** *adj* quite sure, often without cause □ **cock-up** *noun, slang* a mess, a mistake

cockade *noun* a knot of ribbons worn on a hat

cockatoo *noun* a kind of parrot

cockatrice *noun* a mythological creature like a cock with a dragon's tail

cockerel *noun* a young cock

cockle *noun* a type of shellfish □ **cockleshell** *noun* the shell of a cockle □ **cockles of the heart** someone's inmost heart

cockney *noun* (*plural* **cockneys**) **1** someone born in the East End of London **2** the speech characteristic of this area

> Literally 'cock's egg', an old word for a misshapen egg which was later applied to an effeminate person, and so to a soft-living city-dweller

cockpit *noun* **1** the space for the pilot or driver in an aeroplane or small boat **2** a pit where game cocks fight

cockroach *noun* (plural **cockroaches**) a type of crawling insect

cocktail *noun* a mixed alcoholic drink

cocky *adj* conceited, self-confident □ **cockily** *adv* □ **cockiness** *noun*

cocoa *noun* a drink made from the ground seeds of the cacao tree

coconut *noun* the large, hard-shelled nut of a type of palm tree

> Based on a Portuguese word meaning 'grimace', because of the resemblance of the three holes on the base of the fruit to a human face

cocoon *noun* a protective covering of silk spun by the larva of a butterfly, moth *etc*

cod *noun* a fish much used as food, found in the northern seas

cod *abbrev* cash on delivery

coda *noun* a closing passage in a piece of music, book *etc*

coddle *verb* **1** pamper, over-protect **2** cook (an egg) gently over hot water

code *noun* **1** a way of signalling or sending secret messages, using letters *etc* agreed beforehand **2** a book or collection of laws, rules *etc*

codger /*ko*jər/ *noun* an old, eccentric man

codicil *noun* a note added to a will or treaty

codify *verb* arrange in an orderly way, classify

> **codify** » codifi*es*, codify*ing*, codifi*ed*

coed /*ko*hed/ *adj*, *informal* coeducational

coeducation *noun* the education of boys and girls together □ **coeducational** *adj*

coerce *verb* make to do; force, compel □ **coercion** *noun* □ **coercive** *adj* using force

coeval /koh*eev*əl/ *adj* of the same age or time

coexist *verb* exist at the same time □ **coexistence** *noun* □ **coexistent** *adj*

C of E *abbrev* Church of England

coffee *noun* **1** a drink made from the roasted, ground beans of the coffee shrub **2** a pale brown colour

coffer *noun* a chest for holding money, gold *etc* □ **coffer-dam** *noun* a watertight dam enclosing the foundations of a bridge

coffin *noun* a box in which a dead body is buried or cremated

cog *noun* a tooth on a wheel □ **cogwheel** *noun* a toothed wheel

cogent *adj* convincing, believable □ **cogency** *noun* □ **cogently** *adv*

cogitate *verb* think carefully □ **cogitation** *noun*

cognac *noun* a kind of French brandy

cognizance *noun* awareness, notice □ **take cognizance of** take notice of, take into consideration

cohere *verb* stick together

coherence *noun* connection between thoughts, ideas *etc*

coherent *adj* **1** sticking together **2** clear and logical in thought or speech □ **coherently** *adv*

cohesion *noun* the act of sticking together □ **cohesive** *adj*

cohort *noun*, *hist* a tenth part of a Roman legion

coiffure /kwah*foor*/ *noun* a style of hairdressing

coil *verb* wind in rings; twist □ *noun* **1** a wound arrangement of hair, rope *etc* **2** a contraceptive device fitted in the uterus

coin *noun* a piece of stamped metal used as money □ *verb* **1** make metal into money **2** make up (a new word *etc*)

coinage *noun* **1** the system of coins used in a country **2** a newly-made word

coincide *verb* **1** (often with **with**) be the same as: *their interests coincide/ his story coincides with mine* **2** (often with **with**) happen at the same time as: *coincided with his departure*

coincidence *noun* the occurrence of two things simultaneously without planning □ **coincidental** *adj* □ **coincidentally** *adv*

coir *noun* the outside fibre of a coconut

coitus *noun*: **coitus interruptus** deliberate withdrawal of the penis before ejaculation during intercourse

coke *noun* **1** a type of fuel made by heating coal till the gas is driven out **2** *informal* cocaine

Col *abbrev* Colonel

colander *noun* a bowl with small holes in it for straining vegetables *etc*

cold *adj* **1** low in temperature **2** lower in temperature than is comfortable **3** unfriendly □ *noun* **1** the state of being cold **2** an infectious disease causing shivering, running nose *etc* □ **cold-blooded** *adj* **1** of fishes *etc*: having cold blood **2** cruel; lacking in feelings □ **cold-calling** *noun* the contacting of potential business contacts *etc* without appointment □ **cold feet** lack of courage □ **coldly** *adv* □ **coldness** *noun* □ **cold war** a power struggle between nations without open warfare

coleslaw *noun* a salad made from raw cabbage

colic *noun* a severe stomach pain

collaborate *verb* **1** work together (with) **2** work with (an enemy) to betray your country □ **collaboration** *noun* □ **collaborator** *noun*

> ⚠Do not confuse with: **corroborate**

collage /k*ə*lazh/ *noun* a design

made of scraps of paper pasted on wood, card *etc*

collapse *verb* **1** fall or break down **2** cave or fall in **3** become unable to continue ▯ *noun* a falling down or caving in ▯ **collapsible** *adj* of a chair *etc*: able to be folded up

collar *noun* **1** a band, strip *etc* worn round the neck **2** part of a garment that fits round the neck ▯ *verb*, *informal* seize ▯ **collarbone** *noun* either of two bones joining the breast bone and shoulderblade

collate *verb* **1** examine and compare **2** gather together and arrange in order: *collate the pages for the book*

collateral *noun* an additional security for repayment of a debt

collation *noun* **1** a light, often cold meal **2** a comparison

colleague *noun* someone who works in the same company *etc* as yourself

collect *verb* **1** bring together **2** gather together

collected *adj* **1** gathered together **2** calm, composed

collection *noun* **1** the act of collecting **2** a number of objects or people **3** money gathered at a meeting, *eg* a church service

collective *adj* **1** acting together **2** of several things or people, not of one: *collective decision* ▯ *noun* a business *etc* owned and managed by the workers

collector *noun* someone who collects a particular group of things: *stamp collector*

colleen *noun*, *Irish* a young woman, a girl

college *noun* **1** a building housing students, forming part of a university **2** a higher-education institute ▯ **collegiate** *adj* of a university: divided into colleges

collide *verb* come together with great force; clash

collision *noun* **1** a crash between two moving vehicles *etc* **2** a disagreement, a clash of interests *etc*

collie *noun* a breed of long-haired dog with a pointed nose

collier *noun* **1** a coal-miner **2** a coal ship ▯ **colliery** *noun* (*plural* **collieries**) a coalmine

colloquial *adj* used in everyday speech but not in formal writing or speaking ▯ **colloquialism** *noun* an example of colloquial speech ▯ **colloquially** *adv*

collusion *noun* a secret or clandestine agreement

cologne *noun* light perfume made with plant oils and alcohol

colon[1] *noun* a punctuation mark (:) used *eg* to introduce a list of examples

colon[2] *noun* a part of the bowel

colonel /*ku*hrnəl/ *noun* a senior army officer fulfilling a staff appointment

colonial *adj* of colonies abroad ▯ **colonialism** *noun* the policy of setting up colonies abroad ▯ **colonialist** *adj*

colonnade *noun* a row of columns or pillars

colony *noun* (*plural* **colonies**) **1** a group of settlers or the settlement they make in another country **2** a group of people, animals *etc* of the same type living together ◊ **colonist** *noun* a settler ◊ **colonize** *verb* set up a colony in

coloratura *noun*, *music* a passage sung with trills

colossal *adj* huge, enormous

colossus *noun* an enormous statue

colour or *US* **color** *noun* **1** a quality that an object shows in the light, *eg* redness, blueness *etc* **2** a shade or tint **3** vividness, brightness **4** (**colours**) a flag or standard ◊ *verb* **1** put colour on **2** blush **3** influence: *coloured my attitude to life* ◊ **colour-blind** *adj* unable to distinguish certain colours, *eg* red and green ◊ **coloured** *adj* **1** having colour **2** *offensive* not white-skinned ◊ **off colour** unwell

colourful *adj* **1** brightly coloured **2** vivid, interesting ◊ **colourfully** *adv*

colouring *noun* **1** shade or combination of colours **2** complexion

colourless *adj* **1** without colour **2** dull, bland

colt *noun* a young horse

column *noun* **1** an upright stone or wooden pillar **2** something of a long or tall, narrow shape **3** a vertical line of print, figures *etc* on a page **4** a regular feature in a newspaper **5** an arrangement of troops *etc* one behind the other ◊ **columnist** *noun* someone who writes a regular newspaper column

coma *noun* unconsciousness lasting a long time

comatose *adj* **1** in or of a coma **2** drowsy, sluggish

comb *noun* **1** a toothed instrument for separating or smoothing hair, wool *etc* **2** the crest of certain birds **3** a collection of cells for honey ◊ *verb* **1** arrange or smooth with a comb **2** search through thoroughly

combat *verb* fight or struggle against ◊ *noun* a fight or struggle ◊ **combatant** *noun* someone who is fighting ◊ *adj* fighting ◊ **combative** *adj* quarrelsome; fighting

combination *noun* **1** a joining together of things or people **2** a set of things or people combined **3** a series of letters or figures dialled to open a safe **4** (**combinations**) *old* underwear for the body and legs

combine *verb* join together ◊ *noun* a number of traders *etc* who join together ◊ **combine harvester** a machine that both cuts and threshes crops

combustible *adj* liable to catch fire and burn ◊ *noun* anything that will catch fire ◊ **combustion** *noun* burning

come *verb* **1** move towards this place (*opposite* of **go**): *come here!* **2** draw near: *Christmas is coming* **3** arrive: *we'll have tea when you come* **4** happen, occur: *the index comes at the end* **5** *slang* achieve a sexual orgasm ◊ **come about** happen ◊ **come across** or **come upon** meet find accidentally ◊ **come by** obtain ◊ **come into** inherit ◊ **come of age** reach the age at which you become an adult for legal purposes □ **come round** or **come to** recover from a faint *etc* □ **come upon** come across □ **to come** in the future

> **come** » come*s*, com*ing*, *came*, *come*

comedian *noun* a performer who tells jokes, acts in comedy *etc*

comedogenic *adj* causing blackheads

comedy *noun* (*plural* **comedies**) a light-hearted or amusing play (*contrasted with*: **tragedy**)

comely *adj* good-looking, pleasing □ **comeliness** *noun*

comet *noun* a kind of star which has a tail of light

comfort *verb* help, soothe (someone in pain or distress) □ *noun* **1** ease; quiet enjoyment **2** something that brings ease and happiness

comfortable *adj* **1** at ease; free from trouble, pain *etc* **2** giving comfort □ **comfortably** *adv*

comfrey *noun* a plant with hairy leaves, used in herbal medicine

comic *adj* **1** of comedy **2** amusing, funny □ *noun* **1** a professional comedian **2** a children's magazine with illustrated stories *etc* □ **comical** *adj* funny, amusing □ **comically** *adv* □ **comic strip** a strip of small pictures outlining a story

comma *noun* a punctuation mark (,) indicating a pause in a sentence

command *verb* **1** give an order **2** be in charge of **3** look over or down upon: *commanding a view* □ *noun* **1** an order **2** control: *in command of the situation*

commandant *noun* an officer in command of a place or of troops

commandeer *verb* seize (something) *esp* for the use of an army

commander *noun* **1** someone who commands **2** a naval officer next in rank below captain

commandment *noun* an order or command

commando *noun* (*plural* **commandoes**) a soldier in an army unit trained for special tasks

commemorate *verb* **1** bring to memory by some solemn act **2** serve as a memorial of □ **commemoration** *noun*

commence *verb* begin □ **commencement** *noun*

commend *verb* **1** praise **2** give into the care of □ **commendable** *adj* praiseworthy □ **commendation** *noun* praise □ **commendatory** *adj* praising

commensurate *adj*: **commensurate with** proportionate with, appropriate to

comment *noun* **1** a remark **2** a criticism □ *verb* remark on; criticize

commentary *noun* (*plural* **commentaries**) **1** a description of an event *etc* by someone who is watching it **2** a set of explanatory notes for a book *etc*

commentator *noun* someone who gives or writes a commentary

commerce *noun* the buying and

selling of goods between people or nations; trade, dealings

commercial *adj* **1** of commerce **2** paid for by advertisements: *commercial radio* ▯ *noun* an advertisement on radio, TV *etc* ▯ **commercially** *adv*

commis /*k*omi/ *noun* an apprentice waiter or chef

commiserate *verb* sympathize (with) ▯ **commiseration** *noun* pity

commissar *noun*, *hist* the head of a government department in the former Soviet Union

commissariat *noun* a department in the army *etc* that looks after the food supply

commission *noun* **1** the act of committing **2** a document giving authority to an officer in the armed forces **3** an order for a work of art **4** a fee for doing business on another's behalf **5** a group pf people appointed to investigate something ▯ *verb* give a commission or power to ▯ **in** or **out of commission** in or not in use

commissionaire *noun* a uniformed doorkeeper

commissioner *noun* **1** someone with high authority in a district **2** a member of a commission

commit *verb* **1** give or hand over; entrust **2** make a promise to do: *committed to finishing this book* **3** do, bring about: *commit a crime*

commit » commit*s*, commit*ting*, committ*ed*

commitment *noun* **1** a promise **2** a task that must be done

committal *noun* the act of committing

committed *adj* strong in belief or support: *a committed socialist*

committee *noun* a number of people chosen from a larger body to attend to special business

commodious *adj* roomy, spacious

commodity *noun* (*plural* **commodities**) **1** an article to be bought or sold **2** (**commodities**) goods, produce

commodore *noun* an officer next above a captain in the navy

common *adj* **1** shared by all or many: *common belief* **2** seen or happening often: *common occurrence* **3** ordinary, normal ▯ *noun* land belonging to the people of a town, parish *etc* ▯ **common law** unwritten law based on custom ▯ **Common Market** the European Community, the EC ▯ **common noun** a name for any one of a class of things (*contrasted with*: **proper noun**) ▯ **common room** *noun* a sitting-room for the use of a group in a school *etc* ▯ **Commons** or **House of Commons** the lower House of Parliament ▯ **common sense** practical good sense

commoner *noun* someone who is not a noble

commonplace *adj* ordinary

commonwealth *noun* an association of self-governing states

commotion *noun* a disturbance among several people

communal *adj* common, shared □ **communally** *adv*

commune *noun* a group of people living together, sharing work *etc* □ *verb* talk together

communicable *adj* able to be passed on to others: *communicable disease*

communicate *verb* **1** make known, tell **2** pass on **3** get in touch (with) **4** have a connecting door

communication *noun* **1** a means of conveying information **2** a message **3** a way of passing from place to place

communicative *adj* willing to give information, talkative □ **communicatively** *adv*

communiqué /k*ə*m*yoo*nikeh/ *noun* an official announcement

communion *noun* **1** the act of sharing thoughts, feelings *etc*; fellowship **2** (**Communion**) in the Christian Church, the celebration of the Lord's supper

communism *noun* a form of socialism where industry is controlled by the state □ **communist** *adj* of communism □ *noun* someone who believes in communism

community *noun* (*plural* **communities**) **1** a group of people living in one place **2** the public in general □ **community charge** a local tax in the UK to pay for public services, charged according to property values

commute *verb* **1** travel regularly between two places, *eg* between home and work **2** change (a punishment) for one less severe

commuter *noun* someone who travels regularly some distance to work from their home

compact *adj* fitted or packed closely together □ *noun* a bargain or agreement □ **compact disc** a small disc on which digitally recorded sound is registered as a series of pits to be read by a laser beam

companion *noun* someone or something that accompanies; a friend □ **companionable** *adj* friendly □ **companionship** *noun* friendship; the act of accompanying □ **companionway** *noun* a staircase on a ship from deck to cabin

company *noun* (*plural* **companies**) **1** a gathering of people **2** a business firm **3** a part of a regiment **4** a ship's crew **5** companionship

compare *verb* **1** set things together to see how similar or different they are **2** liken □ **comparable** *adj* □ **beyond compare** much better than all rivals

comparative *adj* **1** judged by comparing with something else; relative: *comparative improvement* **2** near to being: *a comparative stranger* **3** *grammar* the degree of an adjective or adverb between positive and superlative, *eg* black*er*, bett*er*, *more* courageous

comparison *noun* the act of comparing

compartment *noun* a separate part or division, *eg* of a railway carriage

compass *noun* (*plural*

compasses) **1** an instrument with a magnetized needle for showing direction **2** (**compasses**) an instrument with one fixed and one movable leg for drawing circles

compassion *noun* pity for another's suffering; mercy ◊ **compassionate** *adj* pitying, merciful ◊ **compassionately** *adv*

compatible *adj* able to live with, agree with *etc* ◊ **compatibility** *noun* ◊ **compatibly** *adv*

compatriot *noun* a fellow-countryman or -countrywoman

compel *verb* force to do something

> **compel** » compel*s*, compel*ling*, compell*ed*

compensate *verb* make up for wrong or damage done, *esp* by giving money ◊ **compensation** *noun* something given to make up for wrong or damage

compère *noun* someone who introduces acts as part of an entertainment ◊ *verb* act as compère

compete *verb* try to beat others in a race *etc*

competent *adj* **1** capable, efficient **2** skilled; properly trained or qualified ◊ **competence** *noun* ◊ **competently** *adv*

competition *noun* **1** a contest between rivals **2** rivalry

competitive *adj* **1** of sport: based on competitions **2** fond of competing with others ◊ **competitively** *adv* ◊ **competitiveness** *noun*

competitor *noun* someone who competes; a rival

compile *verb* make (a book *etc*) from information that has been collected ◊ **compilation** *noun* ◊ **compiler** *noun*

complacent *adj* self-satisfied ◊ **complacence** or **complacency** *noun* ◊ **complacently** *adv*

complain *verb* **1** express dissatisfaction about something **2** grumble ◊ **complainant** *noun* **1** someone who complains **2** the plaintiff in a law suit

complaint *noun* **1** a statement of dissatisfaction **2** an illness

complement *noun* **1** something which completes or fills up **2** the full number or quantity needed to fill something **3** the angle that must be added to a given angle to make up a right angle

> ⚠Do not confuse with: **compliment**

complementary *adj* **1** together making up a whole **2** making up a right angle

> ⚠Do not confuse with: **complimentary**

complete *adj* **1** having nothing missing; whole **2** finished ◊ *verb* **1** finish **2** make whole ◊ **completely** *adv* ◊ **completeness** *noun* ◊ **completion** *noun*

complex *adj* **1** made up of many parts **2** complicated, difficult ◊ *noun* (*plural* **complexes**) **1** a set of repressed emotions and ideas which affect someone's behaviour **2** an exaggerated reaction, an obsession: *has a complex about her height* **3** a group of related buildings: *sports* *complex* ▯ **complexity** *noun* (*plural* **complexities**)

complexion *noun* **1** the colour or look of the skin of the face **2** appearance

compliance *noun* the act of complying; agreement with another's wishes

compliant *adj* yielding, giving agreement ▯ **compliantly** *adv*

complicate *verb* make difficult ▯ **complicated** *adj* difficult to understand; detailed

complication *noun* **1** a difficulty **2** a development in an illness which makes things worse

complicity *noun* (*plural* **complicities**) a share in a crime or other misdeed

compliment *noun* **1** an expression of praise or flattery **2** (**compliments**) good wishes ▯ *verb* praise, congratulate: *complimented me on my cooking*

⚠Do not confuse with: **complement**

complimentary *adj* **1** flattering, praising **2** given free: *complimentary ticket*

Do not confuse with: **complementary**

comply *verb* agree to do something that someone else orders or wishes

comply » complies, complying, complied

component *adj* forming one of the parts of a whole ▯ *noun* one of several parts, *eg* of a machine

compose *verb* **1** put together or in order; arrange **2** create (a piece of music, a poem *etc*) ▯ **composed** *adj* quiet, calm

composer *noun* someone who writes music

composite *adj* made up of parts

composition *noun* **1** the act of composing **2** a created piece of writing or music **3** a mixture of things

compositor *noun* someone who puts together the types for printing

compos mentis sane, rational

compost *noun* a mixture of natural manures for spreading on soil

composure *noun* calmness, self-possession

compound *adj* **1** made up of a number of different parts **2** not simple ▯ *noun* **1** *chemistry* a substance formed from two or more elements **2** an enclosure round a building

comprehend *verb* **1** understand **2** include ▯ **comprehensible** *adj* able to be understood ▯ **comprehensibly** *adv* ▯ **comprehension** *noun*

comprehensive *adj* taking in or including much or all ▯ **comprehensive school** a state-funded school providing all types of secondary education

compress *verb* **1** press together **2** force into a narrower or smaller space ▯ *noun* a pad used to create pressure on a part of the body or to reduce inflammation □ **compression** *noun*

comprise *verb* **1** include, contain **2** consist of

> ⚠Do not confuse with: **consist**

compromise *noun* an agreement reached by both sides giving up something □ *verb* **1** make a compromise **2** put in a difficult or embarrassing position

compulsion *noun* a force driving someone to do something

compulsive *adj* unable to stop yourself, obsessional: *compulsive liar* □ **compulsively** *adv*

> ⚠Do not confuse: **compulsive** and **compulsory**

compulsory *adj* **1** requiring to be done **2** forced upon someone □ **compulsorily** *adv*

compunction *noun* regret

computation *noun* counting, calculation

compute *verb* count, calculate

computer *noun* an electronic machine that stores and sorts information of various kinds

comrade *noun* a companion, a friend

con *verb* trick, play a confidence trick on □ *noun* a trick, a deceit □ **con-man** *noun* someone who regularly cons people □ **con-trick** *noun* a confidence trick

> **con** *verb* » con*s*, con*ning*, con*ned*

concave *adj* hollow or curved inwards (*contrasted with*: **convex**)

concavity *noun* (*plural* **concavities**) a hollow

conceal *verb* hide, keep secret □ **concealment** *noun*

concede *verb* **1** give up, yield **2** admit the truth of something: *I concede that you may be right*

conceit *noun* a too high opinion of yourself; vanity □ **conceited** *adj* full of conceit; vain □ **conceitedness** *noun*

conceive *verb* **1** form in the mind, imagine **2** become pregnant □ **conceivable** *adj* able to be imagined □ **conceivably** *adv*

concentrate *verb* **1** direct all your attention or effort towards something **2** bring together to one place □ **concentrated** *adj* made stronger or less dilute □ **concentration** *noun*

concentric *adj* of circles: placed one inside the other with the same centre point (*contrasted with*: **eccentric**)

concept *noun* a general idea about something

conception *noun* **1** the act of conceiving **2** an idea

concern *verb* **1** have to do with **2** make uneasy **3** interest, affect □ *noun* **1** anxiety **2** a cause of anxiety, a worry **3** a business □ **concerning** *prep* about: *concerning your application* □ **concern yourself with** be worried about

concert *noun* a musical performance □ **in concert** together

> ⚠Do not confuse with: **consort**

concerted *adj* planned or performed together

concertina *noun* a type of musical wind instrument, with bellows and keys

concerto *noun* (*plural* **concertos**) a long piece of music for a solo instrument with orchestral accompaniment

concession *noun* **1** a granting or allowing of something: *a concession for oil exploration* **2** something granted or allowed **3** a reduction in the price of something for children, the unemployed, senior citizens *etc*

conch *noun* (*plural* **conches**) a kind of sea-shell

concierge *noun* a warden in a residential building

conciliate *verb* win over (someone previously unfriendly or angry) ▯ **conciliation** *noun* ▯ **conciliatory** *adj*

concise *adj* brief, using few words ▯ **concisely** *adv* ▯ **conciseness** *noun*

⚠Do not confuse with: **precise**

conclude *verb* **1** end **2** reach a decision or judgement; settle ▯ **concluding** *adj* last, final

conclusion *noun* **1** end **2** decision, judgement

conclusive *adj* settling, deciding: *conclusive proof* ▯ **conclusively** *adv*

concoct *verb* **1** mix together (a dish or drink) **2** make up, invent: *concoct a story* ▯ **concoction** *noun*

concord *noun* agreement

concourse *noun* **1** a crowd **2** a large open space in a building *etc*

concrete *adj* **1** solid, real **2** made of concrete ▯ *noun* a mixture of gravel, cement *etc* used in building

concur *verb* agree ▯ **concurrence** *noun*

concur » concur*s*, concurr*ing*, concurr*ed*

concurrent *adj* **1** happening together **2** agreeing ▯ **concurrently** *adv*

concussion *noun* temporary harm done to the brain from a knock on the head

condemn *verb* **1** blame **2** sentence to (a certain punishment) **3** declare (a building) unfit for use ▯ **condemnation** *noun* ▯ **condemned cell** a cell for a prisoner condemned to death

condensation *noun* **1** the act of condensing **2** drops of liquid formed from vapour

condense *verb* **1** make to go into a smaller space **2** of steam: turn to liquid

condescend *verb* act towards someone as if you are better than them ▯ **condescending** *adj* ▯ **condescendingly** *adv* ▯ **condescension** *noun*

condiment *noun* a seasoning for food, *esp* salt or pepper

condition *noun* **1** the state in which anything is: *in poor condition* **2** something that must happen before some other thing happens **3** a point in a bargain, treaty *etc*

conditional *adj* depending on

certain things happening ▫ **conditionally** *adv*

condolence *noun* sharing in another's sorrow; sympathy

condom *noun* a contraceptive rubber sheath worn by a man

condone *verb* allow (an offence) to pass unchecked

conducive *adj* helping, favourable (to): *conducive to peace*

conduct *verb* **1** lead, guide **2** control, be in charge of **3** direct (an orchestra) **4** transmit (electricity *etc*) **5** behave: *conducted himself correctly* ▫ *noun* behaviour ▫ **conduction** *noun* transmission of heat, electricity *etc*

conductor *noun* **1** someone who directs an orchestra **2** someone who collects fares on a bus *etc* **3** something that transmits heat, electricity *etc*

conduit /*kon*dit/ *noun* a channel or pipe to carry water, electric wires *etc*

cone *noun* **1** a shape that is round at the bottom and comes to a point **2** the fruit of a pine or fir-tree *etc* **3** an ice-cream cornet

coney *noun another spelling* of **cony**

confectioner *noun* someone who makes or sells sweets, cakes *etc* ▫ **confectionery** *noun* **1** sweets, cakes *etc* **2** the shop or business of a confectioner

confederacy *noun* (*plural* **confederacies**) **1** a league, an alliance **2** (**Confederacy**) *US hist* the union of Southern states in the American Civil War

confederate *adj* **1** joined together by treaty **2** *US hist* supporting the Confederacy ▫ *noun* someone acting in an alliance with others

confederation *noun* a union, a league

confer *verb* **1** talk together **2** give, grant: *confer a degree*

> **confer** » confer*s*, conferr*ing*, conferr*ed*

conference *noun* a meeting for discussion

confess *verb* own up, admit to (wrong) ▫ **confessed** *adj* admitted, not secret ▫ **confession** *noun* an admission of wrong-doing

confetti *noun plural* small pieces of coloured paper thrown at weddings or other celebrations

confide *verb*: **confide in 1** tell secrets to **2** hand over to someone's care

confidant *noun* someone trusted with a secret

> ⚠Do not confuse with: **confident**

confidante *noun* a female confidant

confidence *noun* **1** trust, belief **2** self-assurance, boldness **3** something told privately ▫ **confidence trick** a trick to get money *etc* from someone by first gaining their trust

confident *adj* **1** very self-assured **2** certain of an outcome: *confident that they would win* ▫ **confidently** *adv*

⚠Do not confuse with: **confidant** and **confidante**

confidential *adj* **1** to be kept as a secret: *confidential information* **2** entrusted with secrets ▫ **confidentially** *adv*

confiding *adj* trusting

confine *verb* **1** shut up, imprison **2** keep within limits ▫ **confines** *noun plural* limits

confinement *noun* **1** the state of being confined **2** imprisonment **3** the time of a woman's labour and childbirth

confirm *verb* **1** make firm, strengthen **2** make sure **3** show to be true **4** admit into full membership of a church

confirmation *noun* **1** a making sure **2** proof **3** the ceremony by which someone is made a full member of a church

confirmed *adj* settled in a habit *etc*: *a confirmed bachelor*

confiscate *verb* take away, as a punishment ▫ **confiscation** *noun*

conflagration *noun* a large, widespread fire

conflict *noun* **1** a struggle, a contest **2** a battle **3** disagreement ▫ *verb* of statements *etc*: contradict each other ▫ **conflicting** *adj*

confluence *noun* a place where rivers join

conform *verb* follow the example of most other people in behaviour, dress *etc* ▫ **conformation** *noun*

conformity *noun* (*plural* **conformities**) **1** likeness **2** the act of conforming

confound *verb* puzzle, confuse

confront *verb* **1** face, meet: *confronted the difficulty* **2** bring face to face (with): *confronted with the evidence* ▫ **confrontation** *noun*

confuse *verb* **1** mix up, disorder **2** puzzle, bewilder ▫ **confusion** *noun*

confusing *adj* puzzling, bewildering ▫ **confusingly** *adv*

congeal *verb* **1** become solid, *esp* by cooling **2** freeze

congenial *adj* agreeable, pleasant ▫ **congenially** *adv*

congenital *adj* of a disease: present in someone from birth

conger /*kongər*/ *noun* a kind of large sea-eel

congested *adj* **1** overcrowded **2** clogged **3** of part of the body: too full of blood ▫ **congestion** *noun*

conglomeration *noun* a heap or collection

congratulate *verb* express joy to (someone) at their success ▫ **congratulations** *noun plural* an expression of joy at someone's success ▫ **congratulatory** *adj*

congregate *verb* come together in a crowd ▫ **congregation** *noun* a gathering, *esp* of people in a church

congress *noun* (*plural* **congresses**) **1** a large meeting of people from different countries *etc* for discussion **2** (**Congress**) the parliament of the United States, consisting of the Senate and the House of Representatives

congruent *adj* of triangles: exactly matching

congruous *adj* suitable, appropriate **congruity** *noun* **congruously** *adv*

conical *adj* cone-shaped

conifer *noun* a cone-bearing tree **coniferous** *adj*

conjecture *noun* a guess *verb* guess **conjectural** *adj*

conjugal *adj* of marriage

conjugate *verb* give the different grammatical parts of (a verb) **conjugation** *noun*

conjunction *noun* **1** *grammar* a word that joins sentences or phrases, *eg* and, but **2** a union, a combination **in conjunction with** together with, acting with

conjunctivitis *noun* inflammation of the inside of the eyelid and surface of the eye

conjure *verb* perform tricks that seem magical **conjuror** or **conjurer** *noun* someone who performs conjuring tricks

conker *noun* **1** a horse-chestnut **2** (**conkers**) a game in which players try to hit and destroy each other's chestnut, held on the end of a string

connect *verb* join or fasten together

connection *noun* **1** something that connects **2** a state of being connected **3** a train, aeroplane *etc* which takes you to the next part of a journey **4** an acquaintance, a friend **in connection with** concerning

conning-tower *noun* the place on a warship or submarine from which orders for steering are given

connive *verb*: **connive at** disregard (a misdeed) **connivance** *noun*

connoisseur /kon*ə*suhr/ *noun* someone with an expert knowledge of a subject: *wine connoisseur*

connotation *noun* **1** a meaning **2** what is suggested by a word in addition to its simple meaning

connubial *adj* of marriage

conquer *verb* **1** gain by force **2** overcome: *conquered his fear of heights*

conqueror *noun* someone who conquers

conquest *noun* **1** something won by force **2** an act of conquering

conquistador /k*ə*n*kee*st*ə*dor/ *noun, hist* a soldier fighting for the Spanish crown in the New World

conscience *noun* an inner sense of what is right and wrong

conscientious *adj* careful and diligent in work *etc* **conscientiously** *adv* **conscientiousness** *noun*

conscious *adj* **1** aware of yourself and your surroundings; awake **2** aware, knowing **3** deliberate, intentional: *conscious decision* **consciously** *adv* **consciousness** *noun*

conscript *noun* someone obliged by law to serve in the armed forces *verb* compel to serve in the armed forces **conscription** *noun*

consecrate *verb* set apart for sacred use **consecration** *noun*

consecutive *adj* coming in order, one after the other

consensus *noun* an agreement of opinion

⚠Do not confuse with: **census**

consent *verb* agree (to) □ *noun* **1** agreement **2** permission □ **age of consent** the age at which someone is legally able to consent to sexual intercourse

consequence *noun* **1** something that follows as a result **2** importance

consequent *adj* following as a result □ **consequently** *adv*

consequential *adj* **1** following as a result **2** important □ **consequentially** *adv*

conservation *noun* the maintaining of old buildings, the countryside *etc* in an undamaged state □ **conservationist** *noun* someone who encourages and practises conservation

conservative *adj* **1** resistant to change **2** moderate, not extreme: *conservative estimate* □ *noun* **1** someone of conservative views **2** (**Conservative**) a supporter of the Conservative Party □ **Conservative Party** a right-wing political party in the UK

conservatory *noun* (*plural* **conservatories**) a glass-house for plants

conserve *verb* keep from being wasted or lost; preserve

consider *verb* **1** think about carefully **2** think of as, regard as **3** pay attention to the wishes of (someone)

considerable *adj* fairly large, substantial □ **considerably** *adv*

considerate *adj* taking others' wishes into account; thoughtful

consideration *noun* **1** serious thought **2** thoughtfulness for others **3** a small payment

considering *prep* taking into account: *considering your age*

consign /*kənsain*/ *verb* give into the care of □ **consignment** *noun* a load, *eg* of goods

consist *verb* be made up (of)

⚠Do not confuse with: **comprise**

consistency *noun* (*plural* **consistencies**) **1** thickness, firmness **2** the quality of always being the same

consistent *adj* **1** not changing, regular **2** of statements *etc*: not contradicting each other □ **consistently** *adv*

consolation *noun* something that makes trouble *etc* more easy to bear

console *verb* comfort, cheer up

consolidate *verb* **1** make or become strong **2** unite □ **consolidation** *noun*

consonant *noun* a letter of the alphabet that is not a vowel, *eg* b, c, d

consort *noun* **1** a husband or wife **2** a companion □ *verb* keep company (with)

⚠Do not confuse with: **concert**

conspicuous *adj* clearly seen, noticeable ▯ **conspicuously** *adv* ▯ **conspicuousness** *noun*

conspiracy *noun* (*plural* **conspiracies**) a plot by a group of people ▯ **conspirator** *noun* someone who takes part in a conspiracy

conspire *verb* plan or plot together

constable *noun* **1** a policeman **2** *hist* a high officer of state

constabulary *noun* the police force

constant *adj* **1** never stopping **2** never changing **3** faithful ▯ **constancy** *noun* ▯ **constantly** *adv* always

constellation *noun* a group of stars

consternation *noun* dismay, astonishment

constipation *noun* sluggish working of the bowels ▯ **constipate** *verb* cause constipation in

constituency *noun* (*plural* **constituencies**) **1** a district which has a member of parliament **2** the voters in such a district

constituent *adj* making or forming ▯ *noun* **1** a necessary part **2** a voter in a constituency

constitute *verb* **1** step up, establish **2** form, make up **3** be the equivalent of: *this action constitutes a crime*

constitution *noun* **1** the way in which something is made up **2** the natural condition of a body in terms of health *etc*: *a weak constitution* **3** a set of laws or rules governing a country or organization ▯ **constitutional** *adj* of a constitution ▯ *noun* a short walk for the sake of your health

constrain *verb* force to act in a certain way

constraint *noun* **1** compulsion, force **2** restraint, repression

constrict *verb* **1** press together tightly **2** surround and squeeze

construct *verb* build, make ▯ **construction** *noun* **1** the act of constructing **2** something built **3** the arrangement of words in a sentence **4** meaning

constructive *adj* **1** of construction **2** helping to improve: *constructive criticism* ▯ **constructively** *adv*

consul *noun* **1** someone who looks after their country's affairs in a foreign country **2** *hist* a chief ruler in ancient Rome ▯ **consular** *adj*

consulate *noun* **1** the official residence of a consul **2** the duties and authority of a consul

consult *verb* seek advice or information from ▯ **consultation** *noun* ▯ **consulting room** a room where a doctor sees patients

consultant *noun* **1** someone who gives professional or expert advice **2** the senior grade of hospital doctor

consume *verb* **1** eat up **2** use (up) **3** destroy ▯ **consumer** *noun* someone who buys, eats or uses goods

consummate /*kon*səmeht/ *verb* **1** complete **2** make (marriage) legally complete by sexual intercourse □ *adj* /*kon*səmət/ complete, perfect

consumption *noun* **1** the act of consuming **2** an amount consumed **3** *old* tuberculosis

cont or **contd** *abbrev* continued

contact *noun* **1** touch **2** meeting, communication **3** an acquaintance; someone who can be of help: *business contact* **4** someone who has been with someone suffering from an infectious disease □ *verb* get into contact with □ **contact lens** a plastic lens worn in contact with the eyeball instead of spectacles

contagious *adj* of disease: spreading from person to person, *esp* by touch

contain *verb* **1** hold or have inside **2** hold back: *couldn't contain her anger*

container *noun* a box, tin, jar *etc* for holding anything

contaminate *verb* make impure or dirty □ **contamination** *noun*

contd *another spelling* of **cont**

contemplate *verb* **1** look at or think about attentively **2** intend: *contemplating suicide* □ **contemplation** *noun*

contemporary *adj* belonging to the same time □ *noun* someone of roughly the same age as yourself

contempt *noun* complete lack of respect; scorn □ **contempt of court** deliberate disobedience to and disrespect for the law and those who carry it out

contemptible *adj* deserving scorn, worthless

> ⚠Do not confuse: **contemptible** and **contemptuous**

contemptuous *adj* scornful

contend *verb* **1** struggle against **2** hold firmly to a belief; maintain (that)

content /kən*tent*/ *adj* happy, satisfied □ *noun* happiness, satisfaction □ *verb* make happy, satisfy □ *noun* (**contents** /*kon*tents/) that which is contained in anything □ **contented** *adj* happy, content □ **contentment** *noun* happiness, content

contention *noun* **1** an opinion strongly held **2** a quarrel, a dispute

contentious *adj* quarrelsome □ **contentiously** *adv*

contest *verb* fight for, argue against □ *noun* a fight, a competition □ **contestant** *noun* a participant in a contest

context *noun* **1** the place in a book *etc* to which a certain part belongs **2** the background of an event, remark *etc*

contiguous *adj* touching, close □ **contiguity** *noun* □ **contiguously** *adv*

continent *noun* one of the five large divisions of the earth's land surface (Europe, Asia, Africa, Australia, America) □ **continental** *adj* **1** of a continent **2** *Brit* European □ **the Continent** *Brit* the mainland of Europe

contingency *noun* (*plural* **contingencies**) a chance happening

□ **contingency plan** a plan of action in case something does not happen as expected

contingent *adj* depending (on) □ *noun* a group, *esp* of soldiers

continue *verb* keep on, go on (doing something)

continual *adj* going on without stop □ **continually** *adv*

> ⚠Do not confuse with: **continuous**

continuation *noun* **1** the act of continuing **2** a part that continues, an extension

continuity *noun* the state of having no gaps or breaks

continuous *adj* coming one after the other without a gap or break □ **continuously** *adv*

> ⚠Do not confuse with: **continual**

contort *verb* twist or turn violently □ **contortion** *noun* a violent twisting □ **contortionist** *noun* someone who can twist their body violently

contour *noun* (often **contours**) outline, shape □ **contour line** a line drawn on a map through points all at the same height above sea-level

contraband *noun* **1** goods legally forbidden to be brought into a country **2** smuggled goods

contraception *noun* the prevention of conceiving children

contraceptive *adj* used to prevent the conceiving of children □ *noun* a contraceptive device or drug

contract *verb* **1** become or make smaller **2** bargain for **3** promise in writing □ *noun* a written agreement

contraction *noun* **1** a shortening **2** a shortened form of a word **3** a muscle spasm, *eg* during childbirth

contractor *noun* someone who promises to do work, or supply goods, at an arranged price

contradict *verb* say the opposite of; deny □ **contradiction** *noun* □ **contradictory** *adj*

contralto *noun* (*plural* **contraltos**) the lowest singing voice in women

contraption *noun* a machine, a device

contrapuntal see **counterpoint**

contrary[1] /*kon*trəri/ *adj* opposite □ *noun* the opposite □ **on the contrary** just the opposite

contrary[2] /kən*treh*ri/ *adj* always doing or saying the opposite, perverse □ **contrariness** noun

contrast *verb* **1** compare so as to show differences **2** show a marked difference from □ *noun* a difference between (two) things

contravene *verb* break (a law *etc*) □ **contravention** noun

contretemps /*konh*trətonh/ *noun* a mishap at an awkward moment

contribute *verb* **1** give (money, help *etc*) along with others **2** supply (articles *etc*) for a publication **3** help to cause: *contributed to a nervous breakdown* □ **contribution** *noun* □ **contributor** *noun*

contrite *adj* very sorry for having done wrong □ **contrition** *noun*

contrive *verb* **1** plan **2** bring

about, manage: *contrived to be out of the office* □ **contrivance** *noun* an act of contriving; an invention

control *noun* **1** authority to rule, manage, restrain *etc* **2** (often **controls**) means by which a driver keeps a machine powered or guided □ *verb* **1** exercise control over **2** have power over □ **controlled** *adj* □ **controller** *noun* □ **control tower** an airport building from which landing and take-off instructions are given

controversial *adj* likely to cause argument □ **controversially** *adv*

controversy *noun* (*plural* **controversies**) an argument, a disagreement

conundrum *noun* a riddle, a question

conurbation *noun* a group of towns forming a single built-up area

convalesce *verb* recover health gradually after being ill □ **convalescence** *noun* a gradual return to health and strength □ **convalescent** *noun* someone convalescing from illness

convection *noun* the spreading of heat by movement of heated air or water □ **convector** *noun* a heater which works by convection

convene *verb* call or come together □ **convener** *noun* **1** someone who calls a meeting **2** the chairman or chairwoman of a committee

convenience *noun* **1** suitableness, handiness **2** a means of giving ease or comfort **3** *informal* a public lavatory □ **at your convenience** when it suits you best

convenient *adj* easy to reach or use, handy □ **conveniently** *adv*

convent *noun* a building accommodating an order of nuns

conventicle *noun, hist* a secret religious meeting

convention *noun* **1** a way of behaving that has become usual, a custom **2** a large meeting, an assembly **3** a treaty or agreement □ **conventional** *adj* done by habit or custom □ **conventionally** *adv*

converge *verb* come together, meet at a point □ **convergence** *noun* □ **convergent** *adj*

conversation *noun* talk, exchange of ideas, news *etc* □ **conversational** *adj* **1** of conversation **2** talkative

converse[1] /kən*vers*/ *verb* talk □ *noun* conversation

converse[2] /*kon*vers/ *noun* the opposite □ *adj* opposite

convert *verb* **1** change (from one thing into another) **2** turn from one religion to another □ *noun* someone who has been converted □ **conversion** *noun* □ **convertible** *adj* able to be changed from one thing to another □ *noun* a car with a folding roof

convex *adj* curved on the outside (*contrasted with*: **concave**) □ **convexity** *noun* (*plural* **convexities**)

convey *verb* **1** carry, transport **2** send **3** *law* hand over: *convey property* □ **conveyance** *noun* **1** the act of conveying **2** a vehicle □ **conveyor**

or **conveyor belt** an endless moving mechanism for conveying articles, *esp* in a factory

convict *verb* declare or prove that someone is guilty ▫ *noun* someone found guilty of a crime and sent to prison ▫ **conviction** *noun* **1** the passing of a guilty sentence on someone in court **2** a strong belief

convince *verb* **1** make (someone) believe that something is true **2** persuade (someone) by showing

convivial *adj* jolly, festive ▫ **conviviality** *noun*

convocation *noun* a meeting, *esp* of bishops or heads of a university

convolvulus *noun* a twining plant with trumpet-shaped flowers

convoy *verb* go along with and protect ▫ *noun* **1** merchant ships protected by warships **2** a line of army lorries with armed guard

convulse *verb* cause to shake violently: *convulsed with laughter* ▫ **convulsion** *noun* **1** a sudden stiffening or jerking of the muscles **2** a violent disturbance ▫ **convulsive** *adj*

cony or **coney** *noun* **1** a rabbit **2** rabbit fur

coo *noun* a sound like that of a dove ▫ *verb* make this sound

cook *verb* **1** prepare (food) by heating **2** *informal* alter (accounts *etc*) dishonestly ▫ *noun* someone who cooks and prepares food ▫ **cooker** *noun* **1** a stove for cooking **2** an apple *etc* used in cooking, not for eating raw ▫ **cookery** *noun* the art of cooking

cool *adj* **1** slightly cold **2** calm, not excited **3** *informal* acceptable ▫ *verb* make or grow cool; calm ▫ **coolly** *adj* ▫ **coolness** *noun*

coop *noun* a box or cage for hens *etc* ▫ *verb* shut (up) as in a coop ▫ **cooper** *noun* someone who makes barrels

cooperate *verb* work or act together ▫ **cooperation** *noun* **1** a working together **2** willingness to act together ▫ **cooperative** *noun* a business or farm *etc* owned by the workers ▫ **cooperative society** or **co-op** a trading organization in which the profits are shared among members

co-opt *verb* choose (someone) to join a committee or other body

co-ordinate *verb* make things fit in or work smoothly together ▫ **co-ordination** *noun*

coot *noun* a water-bird with a white spot on the forehead

cop *noun, Brit slang* a police officer ▫ *verb* catch, seize ▫ **cop it** land in trouble ▫ **cop out** avoid responsibility

cop *verb* » cop*s*, copp*ing*, copp*ed*

cope *verb* struggle or deal successfully (with), manage

coping *noun* the top layer of stone in a wall ▫ **coping-stone** *noun* the top stone of a wall

copious *adj* plentiful ▫ **copiously** *adj*

copper *noun* **1** a hard reddish-brown metal **2** a reddish-brown colour **3** a coin made from copper **4** a large vessel made of copper, for boiling water ▯ **copperplate** *noun* a style of very fine and regular handwriting

copra *noun* the dried kernel of the coconut, yielding coconut oil

copse or **coppice** *noun* a wood of low-growing trees

copy *noun* (*plural* **copies**) **1** an imitation **2** a print or reproduction of a picture *etc* **3** an individual example of a certain book *etc* ▯ *verb* **1** make a copy of **2** imitate ▯ **copyright** *noun* the right of one person or body to publish a book, perform a play, print music *etc* ▯ *adj* of or protected by the law of copyright

coquette *noun* a flirtatious woman ▯ **coquettish** *adj* flirtatious

coral *noun* a hard substance made from the skeletons of a tiny animal ▯ **coral reef** a rock-like mass of coral built up gradually from the sea-bed

cord *noun* **1** thin rope or strong string **2** a thick strand of anything

⚠Do not confuse with: **chord**

cordial *adj* cheery, friendly ▯ *noun* a refreshing drink ▯ **cordiality** *noun*

cordite *noun* a kind of explosive

cordon *noun* a line of guards, police *etc* to keep people back

cordon bleu *adj* of a cook or cooking: first-class, excellent

Literally 'blue ribbon' in French, after the ribbon worn by the Knights of the Holy Ghost

corduroy *noun* a ribbed cotton cloth resembling velvet

core *noun* the inner part of anything, *esp* fruit ▯ *verb* take out the core of (fruit)

corespondent *noun* a man or woman charged with having committed adultery with a wife or husband (the **respondent**)

⚠Do not confuse with: **correspondent**

corgi *noun* a breed of short-legged dog

cork *noun* **1** the outer bark of a type of oak found in southern Europe *etc* **2** a stopper for a bottle *etc* made of cork ▯ *adj* made of cork ▯ *verb* plug or stop up with a cork ▯ **corkscrew** *noun* a tool with a screw-like spike for taking out corks ▯ *adj* shaped like a corkscrew

corm *noun* the bulb-like underground stem of certain plants

cormorant *noun* a type of big seabird

corn *noun* **1** wheat, oats or maize **2** a small lump of hard skin, *esp* on a toe ▯ **corncrake** *noun* a kind of bird with a harsh croaking cry ▯ **corned beef** salted tinned beef ▯ **cornflour** *noun* finely ground maize flour ▯ **cornflower** *noun* a type of plant, with a blue flower

cornea *noun* the transparent covering of the eyeball

corner *noun* **1** the point where two walls, roads *etc* meet **2** a small secluded place **3** *informal* a difficult situation ▯ *verb* force into a position from which there is no escape ▯

cornerstone *noun* **1** the stone at the corner of a building's foundations **2** something upon which much depends

cornet *noun* **1** a musical instrument like a small trumpet **2** an ice-cream in a cone-shaped wafer

cornice *noun* an ornamental border round a ceiling

corolla *noun* the petals of a flower

corollary *noun* (*plural* **corollaries**) something which may be taken for granted when something else has been proved; a natural result

coronary *noun* (*plural* **coronaries**) (*short for* **coronary thrombosis**) a heart disease caused by blockage of one of the arteries supplying the heart

coronation *noun* the crowning of a king or queen

coroner *noun* a government officer who holds inquiries into the causes of sudden or accidental deaths

coronet *noun* **1** a small crown **2** a crown-like head-dress

corporal[1] *noun* the rank next below sergeant in the British army

corporal[2] *adj* of the body ◊ **corporal punishment** physical punishment by beating

corporate *adj* of or forming a whole, united ◊ **corporation** *noun* a body of people acting as one for administrative or business purposes

corps /kohr/ or /kawr/ *noun* (*plural* **corps**) **1** a division of an army **2** an organized group

⚠Do not confuse: **corps** and **corpse**

corpse *noun* a dead body

corpulence *noun* obesity, fatness ◊ **corpulent** *adj*

corpus *noun* (*plural* **corpora**) a collection of writing *etc*

corpuscle *noun* **1** a very small particle **2** a blood cell, red or white ◊ **corpuscular** *adj*

corral *noun*, *US* a fenced enclosure for animals ◊ *verb* enclose, pen

corral *verb* » corral*s*, corral*ling*, corrall*ed*

correct *verb* **1** remove errors from **2** set right **3** punish ◊ *adj* **1** having no errors **2** true ◊ **correction** *noun* **1** the putting right of a mistake **2** punishment ◊ **corrective** *adj*

correspond *verb* **1** write letters to **2** be similar (to), match ◊ **correspondence** *noun* **1** letters **2** likeness, similarity

correspondent *noun* **1** someone who writes letters **2** someone who contributes reports to a newspaper *etc*

⚠Do not confuse with: **co-respondent**

corridor *noun* a passageway

corrigendum *noun* (*plural* **corrigenda**) a correction to a book *etc*

corroborate *verb* give evidence which strengthens evidence already given ◊ **corroboration** *noun* ◊ **corroborative** *adj*

> ⚠Do not confuse with: **collaborate**

corrode *verb* **1** rust **2** eat away at, erode ◊ **corrosion** *noun* ◊ **corrosive** *adj*

corrugated *adj* folded or shaped into ridges: *corrugated iron*

corrupt *verb* **1** make evil or rotten **2** make dishonest, bribe ◊ *adj* **1** dishonest, taking bribes **2** bad, rotten ◊ **corruptible** *adj* ◊ **corruption** *noun*

corsair *noun, old* **1** a pirate **2** a pirate-ship

corset *noun* a tight-fitting undergarment to support the body

cortège /kor*tezh*/ *noun* a funeral procession

corvette *noun* a small swift warship, used against submarines

cosh *noun* (*plural* **coshes**) a short heavy stick ◊ *verb* hit with a cosh

cosmetic *noun* something designed to improve the appearance, *esp* of the face ◊ *adj* **1** applied as a cosmetic **2** superficial, for appearances only

cosmic *adj* **1** of the universe or outer space **2** *informal* excellent

cosmonaut *noun, hist* an astronaut of the former USSR

cosmopolitan *adj* **1** including people from many countries **2** familiar with, or comfortable in, many different countries

cosmos *noun* the universe

cosset *verb* treat with too much kindness, pamper

cost *verb* **1** be priced at **2** cause the loss of: *the war cost many lives* ◊ *noun* what must be spent or suffered in order to get something

> **cost** *verb* » cost*s*, cost*ing*, cost

costly *adj* high-priced, valuable ◊ **costliness** *noun*

costume *noun* **1** a set of clothes **2** clothes to wear in a play **3** fancy dress **4** a swimsuit ◊ **costume jewellery** inexpensive, imitation jewellery

cosy *adj* warm and comfortable ◊ *noun* (*plural* **cosies**) a covering to keep a teapot *etc* warm

cot *noun* **1** a small high-sided bed for children **2** *US* a small collapsible bed; a camp bed ◊ **cot death** the sudden unexplained death in sleep of an apparently healthy baby

coterie /*koh*tәri/ *noun* a number of people interested in the same things who tend to exclude other people

cottage *noun* a small house, *esp* in the countryside or a village ◊ **cottage cheese** a soft, white cheese made from skimmed milk ◊ **cottager** *noun* someone who lives in a cottage ◊ **cottaging** *noun, slang* homosexual soliciting in public toilets

cotton *noun* **1** a soft fluffy substance obtained from the seeds of the cotton plant **2** cloth made of cotton ◊ *adj* made of cotton ◊ **cottonwool** *noun* cotton in a fluffy state, used for wiping or absorbing

couch *noun* (*plural* **couches**) a sofa ◊ *verb* express verbally:

couched in archaic language □ **couch grass** a kind of grass, a troublesome weed □ **couch potato** someone who spends their free time watching TV *etc*

couchette /koo*shet*/ *noun* a sleeping berth on a train, convertible into an ordinary seat

cougar *noun*, *US* the puma

cough *noun* a noisy effort of the lungs to throw out air and harmful matter from the throat □ *verb* make this effort

could *verb* **1** the form of the verb **can** used to express a condition: *he could afford it if he tried/ I could understand a small mistake, but this is ridiculous* **2** *past form* of the verb **can**

coulis /*koo*li/ *noun* a thin puréed sauce

coulomb *noun* a unit of electric charge

council *noun* a group of people elected to discuss or give advice about policy, government *etc* □ **councillor** *noun* a member of a council

> ⚠Do not confuse with: **counsel**

counsel *noun* **1** advice **2** someone who gives legal advice; a lawyer □ *verb* give advice to □ **counsellor** *noun* someone who gives advice

> **counsel** » counsel*s*, counsell*ing*, counsell*ed*

> ⚠Do not confuse with: **council**

count[1] *verb* **1** find the total number of, add up **2** say numbers in order (1, 2, 3 *etc*) **3** think, consider: *count yourself lucky!* □ *noun* **1** the act of counting **2** the number counted, *eg* of votes at an election **3** a charge, an accusation **4** a point being considered □ **countless** *adj* too many to be counted, very many □ **count on** rely on, depend on

count[2] *noun* a nobleman in certain countries

countenance *noun* **1** the face **2** the expression on someone's face □ *verb* allow, encourage

counter[1] *verb* answer or oppose (a move, act *etc*) by another □ *adv* in the opposite direction □ *adj* opposed; opposite

counter[2] *noun* **1** a token used in counting **2** a small plastic disc used in ludo *etc* **3** a table across which payments are made in a shop

counter- *prefix* **1** against, opposing: *counter-argument* **2** opposite

counteract *verb* block or defeat (an action) by doing the opposite

counterattack *noun* an attack made by the defenders upon an attacking enemy □ *verb* launch a counterattack

counterattraction *noun* something which draws away the attention from something else

countercharge *noun* a charge against someone who has accused you □ *verb* make a countercharge against

counterfeit *adj* **1** not genuine, not real **2** made in imitation for criminal purposes: *counterfeit money* □ *verb* make a copy of

counterfoil *noun* a part of a cheque, postal order *etc* kept by the payer or sender

countermand *verb* give an order which goes against one already given

counterpane *noun* a top cover for a bed

counterpart *noun* someone or something which is just like or which corresponds to another person or thing

counterpoint *noun* the combining of two or more melodies to make a piece of music □ **contrapuntal** *adj* of or in counterpoint

counterpoise *noun* a weight which balances another weight

countersign *verb* sign your name after someone else's signature to show that a document is genuine

counter-tenor *noun* the highest alto male voice

countess *noun* **1** a woman of the same rank as a count or earl **2** the wife or widow of a count or earl

country *noun* (*plural* **countries**) **1** a nation **3** a land under one government **3** the land in which someone lives **4** a district which is not in a town or city **5** an area or stretch of land □ *adj* belonging to the country □ **countryside** *noun* the parts of a country other than towns and cities

county *noun* (*plural* **counties**) a division of a country

coup /koo/ *noun* **1** a sudden outstandingly successful move or act **2** a coup d'état

coup de grâce /koo də *grahs*/ a final blow, a last straw

coup d'état /koo deh*tah*/ a sudden and violent change in government

couple *noun* **1** a pair, two of a kind together **2** a husband and wife □ *verb* join together □ **couplet** *noun* two lines of rhyming verse □ **coupling** *noun* a link for joining railway carriages *etc*

coupon *noun* a piece of paper which may be exchanged for goods or money □ **football coupon** a form on which people guess the results of football matches in the hope of winning money

courage *noun* bravery, lack of fear

courageous *adj* brave, fearless □ **courageously** *adv*

courgette *noun* a type of small marrow

courier *noun* **1** someone who acts as guide for tourists **2** a messenger

course *noun* **1** a path in which anything moves **2** movement from point to point **3** a track along which athletes *etc* run **4** a direction to be followed: *the ship held its course* **5** line of action: *the best course to follow* **6** a part of a meal **7** a number of things following each other: *a course of twelve lectures* **8** one of the rows of bricks in a wall □ *verb* **1** move quickly **2** hunt □ **courser** *noun* a fast horse □ **coursing** *noun* the hunting of hares with greyhounds □ **in due course** after a while, in its proper time □ **in the course of** during

court *noun* **1** an open space surrounded by houses **2** an area marked out for playing tennis *etc* **3** the people who attend a monarch *etc* **4** a royal residence **5** a room or building where legal cases are heard or tried □ *verb* **1** woo as a potential lover **2** try to gain: *courting her affections* **3** come near to achieving: *courting disaster* □ **courtly** *adj* having fine manners □ **courtship** *noun* the act or time of courting or wooing □ **courtyard** *noun* a court or enclosed space beside a house

courtesy *noun* politeness □ **courteous** *adj* polite; obliging □ **courteously** *adv*

courtier *noun* a member of a royal court

court-martial *noun* (*plural* **courts-martial**) an internal court held to try those who break navy or army laws □ *verb* try in a court-martial

couscous /*koos*koos/ *noun* hard wheat semolina

cousin *noun* the son or daughter of an uncle or aunt

cove *noun* a small inlet on the sea coast; a bay

coven *noun* a gathering of witches

covenant *noun* an important agreement between people to do or not to do something

cover *verb* **1** put or spread something on or over **2** hide **3** stretch over: *the hills were covered with heather/ my diary covers three years* **3** include, deal with: *covering the news story* **4** be enough for: *five pounds should cover the cost* **5** travel over: *covering 3 kilometres a day* **6** point a weapon at: *had the gangster covered* □ *noun* something that covers, hides or protects □ **coverage** *noun* **1** an area covered **2** the extent of news covered by a newspaper *etc* **3** the amount of protection given by an insurance policy □ **coverlet** *noun* a bed cover □ **cover up 1** cover completely **2** conceal deliberately □ **cover-up** *noun* a deliberate concealment, *esp* by people in authority

covert *adj* secret, not done openly □ *noun* a hiding place for animals or birds when hunted □ **covertly** *adv*

covet *verb* desire eagerly, *esp* something belonging to another person □ **covetous** *adj* □ **covetously** *adv* □ **covetousness** *noun*

covey *noun* (*plural* **coveys**) a flock of birds, *esp* partridges

cow *noun* **1** the female animal of the ox kind used for giving milk **2** the female of an elephant, whale *etc* □ *verb* frighten, subdue □ **cowed** *adj* □ **cowboy, cowgirl** *noun* a man or woman who works with cattle on a ranch □ **cowherd** *noun* someone who looks after cows

coward *noun* someone who has no courage and shows fear easily □ **cowardice** *noun* lack of courage □ **cowardly** *adj*

cowed *past form* of **cow**

cower *verb* crouch down or shrink back through fear

cowl *noun* **1** a hood, *esp* that of a monk **2** a cover for a chimney

cowslip *noun* a yellow wild flower

cox *noun* (*pl* **coxes**) the person who steers a racing crew

coxcomb *noun* **1** *hist* a head-covering notched like a cock's comb, worn by a jester **2** a vain or conceited person

coxswain *noun* **1** someone who steers a boat **2** an officer in charge of a boat and crew

coy *adj* too modest or shy

coyote /kai*oh*ti/ *noun* (*plural* **coyote** or **coyotes**) a type of small North American wolf

coypu *noun* a large, beaverlike animal living in rivers and marshes

crab *noun* a sea creature with a shell and five pairs of legs, the first pair of which have large claws □ **crab apple** a type of small, bitter apple □ **crabbed** /*kra*bid/ *adj* bad-tempered □ **crabwise** *adv* sideways like a crab

crack *verb* **1** (cause to) make a sharp, sudden sound **2** break partly without falling to pieces **3** break into (a safe) **3** decipher (a code) **4** break open (a nut) **5** make (a joke) □ *noun* **1** a sharp sound **2** a split, a break **3** a narrow opening **4** *informal* a sharp, witty remark **5** *informal* a pure form of cocaine □ *adj* excellent: *a crack tennis player* □ **cracked** *adj* **1** split, damaged **2** mad, crazy □ **crack up** go to pieces, collapse

cracker *noun* **1** a hollow paper tube containing a small gift, which breaks with a bang when the ends are pulled **2** a thin, crisp biscuit **3** *informal* something excellent: *a cracker of a story*

crackle *verb* make a continuous cracking noise

crackling *noun* **1** a cracking sound **2** the rind or outer skin of roast pork

cradle *noun* **1** a baby's bed, *esp* one which can be rocked **2** a frame under a ship that is being built

craft *noun* **1** a trade, a skill **2** a boat, a small ship **3** slyness, cunning □ **craftsman, craftswoman** or **craftworker** *noun* someone who works at a trade, *esp* with their hands

crafty *adj* cunning, sly □ **craftily** *adv* □ **craftiness** *noun*

crag *noun* a rough steep rock

craggy *adj* **1** rocky **2** of a face: well-marked, lined

cram *verb* **1** fill full, stuff **2** learn up facts for an examination in a short time

> **cram** » cram*s*, cramm*ing*, cramm*ed*

cramp *noun* **1** a painful stiffening of the muscles **2** (**cramps**) an acute stomach pain □ *verb* **1** confine in too small a space **2** hinder, restrict

cramped *adj* **1** without enough room **2** of handwriting: small and closely-written

crampon *noun* a metal plate with spikes, fixed to boots for climbing on ice or snow

cranberry *noun* (*plural* **cranberries**) a type of red, sour berry

crane *noun* **1** a large wading bird with long legs, neck and bill **2** a machine for lifting heavy weights □

verb stretch out (the neck) to see round or over something

cranium *noun* (*plural* **crania** or **craniums**) the skull

crank *noun* **1** a handle for turning an axle **2** a lever which converts a horizontal movement into a rotating one **3** an eccentric □ *verb* start (an engine) with a crank

cranky *adj* **1** odd, eccentric **2** cross, irritable

cranny *noun* (*plural* **crannies**) a small opening or crack

crap *noun, taboo slang* **1** faeces **2** something worthless, rubbish □ *adj* poor, low-quality

crape *another spelling* of **crêpe**

craps *noun sing* a gambling game in which a player rolls two dice

crapulent *adj* drinking excessively, intemperate

crash *noun* (*plural* **crashes**) **1** a noise of heavy things breaking or banging together **2** a collision causing damage, *eg* between vehicles **3** the failure of a business □ *adj* short but intensive: *crash course in French* □ *verb* **1** be involved in a crash **2** of a business: fail **3** of a computer program: break down, fail **4** *informal* attend (a party) uninvited (*also called* **gatecrash**) □ **crash-helmet** *noun* a protective covering for the head worn by motor-cyclists *etc* □ **crash-land** *verb* land (an aircraft) in an emergency, causing some structural damage □ **crash-landing** *noun*

crass *adj* stupid □ **crassly** *adv* □ **crassness** *noun*

crate *noun* a container for carrying goods, often made of wooden slats

crater *noun* **1** the bowl-shaped mouth of a volcano **2** a hole made by an explosion

cravat /krəvat/ *noun* a scarf worn in place of a tie

> From a French word for 'Croat', because of the linen neckbands worn by 17th-century Croatian soldiers

craven *adj, old* cowardly

crawfish *noun* same as **crayfish**

crawl *verb* **1** move on hands and knees **2** move slowly **3** be covered (with): *crawling with wasps* **4** be obsequious, fawn □ *noun* **1** the act of crawling **2** a swimming stroke of kicking the feet and alternating the arms □ **crawler** *noun, informal* an obsequious, fawning person

crayfish or **crawfish** *noun* a shellfish similar to a small lobster

crayon *noun* a coloured pencil or stick for drawing

craze *noun* a temporary fashion or enthusiasm

crazy *adj* mad, unreasonable □ **crazily** *adv* □ **craziness** *noun* □ **crazy patchwork** patchwork made with irregular shapes of fabric □ **crazy paving** paving with stones of irregular shape

creak *verb* make a sharp, grating sound like a hinge in need of oiling

cream *noun* **1** the fatty substance which forms on milk **2** something like this in texture: *cleansing cream/shaving cream* **3** the best part:

cream of society □ *verb* **1** take the cream from **2** take away (the best part) □ **creamy** *adj* full of or like cream

crease *noun* **1** a mark made by folding **2** *cricket* a line showing the position of a batsman and bowler □ *verb* **1** make creases in **2** become creased

create *verb* **1** bring into being; make **2** *informal* make a fuss □ **creation** *noun* **1** the act of creating **2** something created □ **creator** *noun* □ **the Creator** God

creative *adj* having the ability to create, artistic □ **creatively** *adv* □ **creativity** *noun*

creature *noun* an animal or person

crèche *noun* a nursery for children

credentials *noun plural* documents carried as proof of identity, character *etc*

credible *adj* able to be believed □ **credibility** *noun*

> ⚠Do not confuse with: **credulous**

credit *noun* **1** recognition of good qualities, achievements *etc*: *give him credit for some common sense* **2** good qualities **3** a source of honour: *a credit to the family* **4** trustworthiness in ability to pay for goods **5** the sale of goods to be paid for later **6** the side of an account on which payments received are entered **7** a sum of money in a bank account **8** belief, trust **9** (**credits**) the naming of people who have helped in a film *etc* □ *verb* **1** believe **2** enter on the credit side of an account **3** (with **with**) believe to have: *I credited him with more sense* □ **credit card** a card allowing the holder to pay for purchased articles at a later date

creditable *adj* bringing honour or good reputation to □ **creditably** *adv*

creditor *noun* someone to whom money is due

credulous *adj* believing too easily □ **credulity** *noun* □ **credulously** *adv*

> ⚠Do not confuse with: **credible**

creed *noun* a belief, *esp* a religious one

creek *noun* **1** a small inlet or bay on the sea coast **2** a short river

creep *verb* **1** move slowly and silently **2** move with the body close to the ground **3** shiver with fear or disgust: *makes your flesh creep* **4** of a plant: grow along the ground or up a wall □ *noun* **1** a move in a creeping way **2** *informal* an unpleasant person □ **creep up on** approach silently from behind □ **the creeps** *informal* a feeling of disgust or fear

> **creep** *verb* » creep*s*, creep*ing*, crept

creeper *noun* a plant growing along the ground or up a wall

creepy *adj* unsettlingly sinister □ **creepy-crawly** *noun, informal* a crawling insect

cremate *verb* burn (a dead body) □ **cremation** *noun*

crematorium *noun* a place where dead bodies are burnt

crème fraîche cream thickened with a culture of bacteria

crenellated *adj* of a building: with battlements

Creole /*kree*ohl/ *noun* **1** a West Indian of mixed European and Black African descent **2** *hist* a French or Spanish settler in Louisiana **3** a hybrid or pidgin language

creosote *noun* an oily liquid made from wood tar, used to keep wood from rotting

crêpe *noun* **1** a type of fine, crinkly material **2** a thin pancake □ **crêpe paper** paper with a crinkled appearance

crept *past form* of **creep**

crepuscular *adj* **1** relating to twilight **2** dark, dim

crescendo *noun* **1** a musical passage of increasing loudness **2** a climax

crescent *adj* shaped like the new or old moon; curved □ *noun* **1** something in a curved shape **2** a curved road or street

cress *noun* a plant with small, slightly bitter-tasting leaves, used in salads

crest *noun* **1** a tuft on the head of a cock or other bird **2** the top of a hill, wave *etc* **3** feathers on top of a helmet **4** a badge

crestfallen *adj* down-hearted, discouraged

cretin *noun, informal* an idiot, a fool

crevasse /*krəvas*/ *noun* a deep split in snow or ice

> ⚠Do not confuse: **crevasse** and **crevice**

crevice /*kre*vis/ *noun* a crack, a narrow opening

crew[1] *noun* **1** the people who man a ship, aircraft *etc* **2** a gang, a mob □ *verb* act as a member of a crew □ **crewcut** *noun* an extremely short hairstyle

crew[2] *past form* of **crow**

crib *noun* **1** a manger **2** a child's bed **3** a ready-made translation of a school text *etc* □ *verb* copy someone else's work

> **crib** *verb* » crib*s*, cribb*ing*, cribb*ed*

cribbage *noun* a type of card game in which the score is kept with a pegged board

crick *noun* a sharp pain, *esp* in the neck □ *verb* produce a crick in

cricket *noun* **1** a game played with bats, ball and wickets, between two sides of 11 each **2** an insect similar to a grasshopper □ **cricketer** *noun* someone who plays cricket

cri de coeur a cry from the heart

cried *past form* of **cry**

crime *noun* an act or deed which is against the law

criminal *adj* **1** forbidden by law **2** very wrong □ *noun* someone guilty of a crime

crimson *noun* a deep red colour □ *adj* of this colour

cringe *verb* **1** crouch or shrink back in fear **2** behave in too humble a way

crinkle *verb* **1** wrinkle, crease **2** make a crackling sound ▫ **crinkly** *adj* wrinkled

crinoline *noun* a wide petticoat or skirt shaped by concentric hoops

cripple *noun* a disabled person ▫ *verb* **1** make lame **2** make less strong, less efficient *etc*: *their policies crippled the economy*

crisis *noun* (*plural* **crises**) **1** a deciding moment, a turning point **2** a time of great danger or suspense

crisp *adj* **1** stiff and dry; brittle **2** cool and fresh: *crisp air* **3** firm and fresh: *crisp lettuce* **4** sharp ▫ *noun* a thin crisp piece of fried potato eaten cold ▫ **crispness** *noun* ▫ **crispy** *adj*

criss-cross *adj* having a pattern of crossing lines ▫ *verb* move across and back: *railway lines criss-cross the landscape*

> Based on the phrase *Christ's cross*

criterion *noun* (*plural* **criteria**) a means or rule by which something can be judged; a standard

critic *noun* **1** someone who judges the merits or faults of a book, film *etc* **2** someone who finds faults in a thing or person

critical *adj* **1** fault-finding **2** of criticism: *critical commentary* **3** of or at a crisis **4** very ill **5** serious, very important

criticism *noun* **1** a judgement or opinion on (something) *esp* one showing up faults **2** the act of criticizing

criticize *verb* **1** find fault with **2** give an opinion or judgement on

croak *verb* make a low, hoarse sound ▫ *noun* a low, hoarse sound ▫ **croakily** *adv* ▫ **croaky** *adj*

crochet /*kroh*sheh/ *noun* a form of knitting done with one hooked needle ▫ *verb* work in crochet

crock *noun* **1** an earthenware pot or jar **2** a worthless, old and decrepit person or thing

crockery *noun* china or earthenware dishes

crocodile *noun* **1** a large reptile found in rivers in Asia, Africa *etc* **2** a procession of children walking two by two ▫ **crocodile tears** pretended tears

crocus *noun* (*plural* **crocuses**) a yellow, purple or white flower which grows from a bulb

croft *noun* a small farm with a cottage, *esp* in the Scottish Highlands ▫ **crofter** *noun* someone who farms on a croft ▫ **crofting** *noun* farming on a croft

croissant *noun* a curved roll of rich bread dough

crone *noun* an ugly old woman

crony *noun* (*plural* **cronies**) *informal* a close friend

crook *noun* **1** a shepherd's or bishop's stick bent at the end **2** a criminal ▫ *verb* bend or form into a hook

crooked /*krook*əd/ *adj* **1** bent, hooked **2** dishonest, criminal ▫ **crookedly** *adv* ▫ **crookedness** *noun*

croon *verb* sing or hum in a low voice ▫ **crooner** *noun* ▫ **crooning** *noun*

crop *noun* **1** natural produce gathered for food from fields, trees or bushes **2** a part of a bird's stomach **3** a riding whip **4** the hair on the head **5** a short haircut □ *verb* **1** cut short **2** gather a crop (of wheat *etc*) □ **come a cropper 1** fail badly **2** have a bad fall □ **crop up** happen unexpectedly

> **crop** *verb* » crop*s*, cropp*ing*, cropp*ed*

croquet /*kroh*keh/ *noun* a game in which players use long-handled mallets to drive wooden balls through hoops in the ground

croquette /kroh*ket*/ *noun* a ball of potato *etc* coated in breadcrumbs

cross *noun* **1** a shape (×) or (+) formed of two lines intersecting in the middle **2** a crucifix **3** a street monument marking the site of a market *etc* **4** the result of breeding an animal or plant with one of another kind: *a cross between a horse and a donkey* **5** a trouble that must be endured □ *verb* **1** mark with a cross **2** go to the other side of (a room, road *etc*) **3** lie or pass across **4** meet and pass **5** go against the wishes of **6** draw two lines across to validate (a cheque) **7** breed (one kind) with (another) □ *adj* bad-tempered, angry □ **cross-country** *adj* of a race: across fields *etc*, not on roads □ **cross-examine** *verb* question closely in court to test accuracy of a statement *etc* □ **cross-eyed** *adj* having a squint □ **crossly** *adv* angrily □ **crossness** *noun* bad temper, sulkiness □ **cross-reference** *noun* a statement in a reference book directing the reader to further information in another section

crossbow *noun* a bow fixed crosswise to a wooden stand with a device for pulling back the bowstring

crossing *noun* **1** a place where a street, river *etc* may be crossed **2** a journey over the sea

crossroads *noun sing* a place where roads cross each other

cross-section *noun* **1** a section made by cutting across something **2** a sample taken as representative of the whole: *a cross-section of voters*

crossword *noun* a puzzle in which letters are written into blank squares to form words

crotch *noun* the area between the tops of the legs

crotchet *noun* a musical note (♩) equivalent to a quarter of a whole note or semibreve

crotchety *adj* bad-tempered

crouch *verb* **1** stand with the knees well bent **2** of an animal: lie close to the ground

croup[1] /kroop/ *noun* a children's disease causing difficulty in breathing and a harsh cough

croup[2] /kroop/ *noun* the hindquarters of a horse

croupier *noun* someone who collects the money and pays the winners at gambling

croûton /*kroo*ton/ *noun* a small piece of fried bread, sprinkled on soup *etc*

crow *noun* **1** a large bird, generally black **2** the cry of a cock **3** the happy sounds made by a baby ▫ *verb* **1** cry like a cock **2** boast **3** of a baby: make happy noises ▫ **crow's feet** fine wrinkles around the eye, produced by ageing ▫ **crow's-nest** *noun* a sheltered and enclosed platform near the mast-head of a ship from which a lookout is kept ▫ **as the crow flies** in a straight line

> **crow** *verb* » crow*s*, crow*ing*, crew or crow*ed* ▫ **crew** is used as the past form for the first sense only: *the cock crew*; otherwise the form is **crowed**: *crowed about his exam results*

crowbar *noun* a large iron bar used as a lever

crowd *noun* a number of people or things together ▫ *verb* **1** gather into a crowd **2** fill too full **3** keep too close to, impede

crowdie *noun* a creamy Scottish curd cheese

crown *noun* **1** a jewelled head-dress worn by monarchs on ceremonial occasions **2** the top of the head **3** the highest part of something **4** *Brit hist* a coin worth five shillings ▫ *verb* **1** put a crown on **2** make a monarch **3** *informal* hit on the head **4** reward, finish happily: *crowned with success*

crucial *adj* extremely important, critical: *crucial question* ▫ **crucially** *adv*

crucible *noun* a small container for melting metals *etc*

crucifix *noun* (*plural* **crucifixes**) a figure or picture of Christ fixed to the cross ▫ **crucifixion** *noun* **1** the act of crucifying **2** death on the cross, *esp* that of Christ

crucify *verb* put to death by fixing the hands and feet to a cross

> **crucify** » crucifi*es*, crucify*ing*, crucifi*ed*

cruddy *adj, slang* worthless, shoddy

crude *adj* **1** not purified or refined: *crude oil* **2** roughly made or done **3** rude, blunt, tactless ▫ **crudely** *adv* ▫ **crudity** *noun*

crudités /*kroo*diteh/ *noun plural* raw vegetables served as an appetizer

cruel *adj* **1** causing pain or distress **2** having no pity for others' sufferings ▫ **cruelly** *adv* ▫ **cruelty** *noun* (*plural* **cruelties**)

cruet /*krooə*t/ *noun* **1** a small jar for salt, pepper, mustard *etc* **2** two or more such jars on a stand

cruise *verb* travel by car, ship *etc* at a steady speed ▫ *noun* a journey by ship made for pleasure ▫ **cruiser** *noun* a middle-sized warship

crumb *noun* a small bit of anything, *esp* bread

crumble *verb* **1** break into crumbs or small pieces **2** fall to pieces ▫ *noun* a dish of stewed fruit *etc* topped with crumbs ▫ **crumbly** *adj*

crumpet *noun* a soft cake, baked on a griddle and eaten with butter

crumple *verb* **1** crush into creases or wrinkles **2** become creased **3** collapse ▫ **crumple zone** a buffer area in a car *etc* to absorb the impact of a crash

crunch *verb* **1** chew hard so as to make a noise **2** crush ▯ *noun* **1** a noise of crunching **2** *informal* a testing moment, a turning-point

crusade *noun* **1** a movement undertaken for some good cause **2** *hist* a Christian expedition to regain the Holy Land from the Turks ▯ **crusader** *noun* someone who goes on a crusade

crush *verb* **1** squeeze together **2** beat down, overcome **3** crease, crumple ▯ *noun* **1** a violent squeezing **2** a pressing crowd of people **3** a drink made by squeezing fruit

crushed *adj* **1** squeezed, squashed **2** completely defeated or miserable

crust *noun* a hard outside coating, *eg* on bread, a pie, a planet

crustacean /krə*steh*shən/ *noun* one of a large group of animals with a hard shell, including crabs, lobsters, shrimps *etc*

crusty *adj* **1** having a crust **2** cross, irritable

crutch *noun* (*plural* **crutches**) **1** a stick held under the armpit or elbow, used for support in walking **2** a support, a prop

crux *noun* the most important or dificult part of a problem

cry *verb* **1** make a loud sound in pain or sorrow **2** weep **3** call loudly ▯ *noun* (*plural* **cries**) a loud call ▯ **cry off** cancel ▯ **cry over spilt milk** be worried about a misfortune that is past

cry » cri*es*, cry*ing*, cri*ed*

crying *adj* **1** weeping **2** calling loudly **3** requiring notice or attention: *a crying need*

crypt *noun* an underground cell or chapel, *esp* one used for burial

cryptic *adj* mysterious, difficult to understand: *cryptic remark* ▯ **cryptically** *adv*

cryptography *noun* the art of coding and reading codes ▯ **cryptographer** *noun*

crystal *noun* **1** very clear glass often used for making drinking glasses *etc* **2** the regular shape taken by each small part of certain substances, *eg* salt or sugar

crystalline *adj* made up of crystals

crystallize *verb* **1** form into the shape of a crystal **2** take a form or shape, become clear ▯ **crystallization** *noun*

CSA *abbrev* Child Support Agency

cub *noun* **1** the young of certain animals, *eg* foxes **2** a Cub Scout ▯ **Cub Scout** a junior Scout

cube *noun* **1** a solid body having six equal square sides **2** the answer to a sum in which a number is multiplied by itself twice: *8 is the cube of 2*

cubic *adj* **1** of cubes **2** in the shape of a cube

cubicle *noun* a small room closed off in some way from a larger one

cubit *noun, hist* the distance from elbow to middle-finger tip, used as a measurement

cuckoo *noun* a bird which visits Britain in summer and lays its eggs in the nests of other birds

cucumber *noun* a creeping plant with a long green fruit used in salads

cud *noun* food regurgitated by certain animals, *eg* sheep and cows

cuddle *verb* put your arms round, hug ◊ *noun* a hug, an embrace

cudgel *noun* a heavy stick, a club ◊ *verb* beat with a cudgel

> **cudgel** *verb* » cudgel*s*, cudgell*ing*, cudgell*ed*

cue[1] *noun* **1** a sign to tell an actor when to speak *etc* **2** a hint, an indication

cue[2] *noun* the stick used to hit a ball in billiards and snooker

cuff *noun* **1** the end of a sleeve near the wrist **2** the turned-back hem of a trouser leg **3** a blow with the open hand ◊ *verb* hit with the hand ◊ **off the cuff** without planning or rehearsal

cufflinks *noun plural* a pair of ornamental buttons *etc* used to fasten a shirt cuff

cuisine /kwi*zeen*/ *noun* **1** the art of cookery **2** a style of cooking: *Mexican cuisine*

cul-de-sac /*kul*dəsak/ *noun* a street closed at one end

culinary *adj* of or used for cookery

cull *verb* **1** gather **2** choose from a group **3** pick out (seals, deer *etc*) from a herd and kill for the good of the herd ◊ *noun* such a killing

culminate *verb* **1** reach the highest point **2** reach the most important or greatest point, end (in): *culminated in divorce* ◊ **culmination** *noun*

culottes *noun plural* a divided skirt

culpable *adj* guilty, blameworthy

culprit *noun* **1** someone who is to blame for something **2** *English* and *US law* a prisoner accused but not yet tried

cult *noun* **1** a religious sect **2** a general strong enthusiasm for something: *the cult of physical fitness*

cultivate *verb* **1** grow (vegetables *etc*) **2** plough, sow **3** try to develop and improve: *cultivated my friendship* ◊ **cultivated** *adj* **1** farmed, ploughed **2** educated, informed ◊ **cultivation** *noun* ◊ **cultivator** *noun*

culture *noun* **1** a type of civilization with its associated customs: *Mediterranean culture* **2** development of the mind by education **3** educated tastes in art, music *etc* **4** cultivation of plants ◊ **cultured** *adj* well-educated in literature, art *etc*

culvert *noun* an arched drain for carrying water under a road or railway

cum *prep* used for both of two stated purposes: *a newsagent-cum-grocer*

cumbersome *adj* awkward to handle

cummerbund *noun* a sash worn around the waist

cumulative *adj* increasing with

additions: *cumulative effect* ▢ **cumulatively** *adv*

cumulus *noun* a kind of cloud common in summer, made up of rounded heaps

cunnilingus *noun* oral stimulation of a woman's genitals

cunning *adj* **1** sly, clever in a deceitful way **2** skilful, clever ▢ *noun* **1** slyness **2** skill, knowledge

cunt *noun, taboo slang* **1** the vagina **2** a general term of abuse

cup *noun* **1** a hollow container holding liquid for drinking **2** an ornamental vessel given as a prize in sports events ▢ *verb* make (hands *etc*) into the shape of a cup ▢ **cupful** *noun* (*plural* **cupfuls**) as much as fills a cup ▢ **cup-tie** *noun* a game in a sports competition for which the prize is a cup

cup *verb* » *cups*, cupp*ing*, cupp*ed*

cupboard *noun* a shelved recess, or a box with drawers, used for storage

Cupid *noun* the Roman god of sexual love

cupidity *noun* greed

cupola /*kyoo*pələ/ *noun* a curved ceiling or dome on the top of a building

cur *noun* **1** a dog of mixed breed **2** a cowardly person

curable *adj* able to be treated and cured

curate *noun* a Church of England cleric assisting a rector or vicar

curative *adj* likely to cure

curator *noun* someone who has charge of a museum, art gallery *etc*

curb *verb* hold back, restrain ▢ *noun* a restraint

⚠Do not confuse with: **kerb**

curd *noun* **1** milk thickened by acid **2** the cheese part of milk, as opposed to the **whey**

curdle *verb* turn into curd ▢ **curdle someone's blood** shock or terrify them

cure *noun* **1** freeing from disease, healing **2** something which frees from disease ▢ *verb* **1** heal **2** get rid of (a bad habit *etc*) **3** preserve by drying, salting *etc*

curfew *noun* an order forbidding people to be out of their houses after a certain hour

curio *noun* (*plural* **curios**) an article valued for its oddness or rarity

curiosity *noun* (*plural* **curiosities**) **1** strong desire to find something out **2** something unusual, an oddity

curious *adj* **1** anxious to find out **2** unusual, odd ▢ **curiously** *adv*

curl *verb* **1** twist (hair) into small coils **2** of hair: grow naturally in small coils **3** of smoke: move in a spiral **4** twist, form a curved shape **5** play at the game of curling ▢ *noun* a small coil or roll, *eg* of hair

curlew *noun* a wading bird with very long slender bill and legs

curler *noun* **1** something used to make curls **2** someone who plays the game of curling

curling *noun* a game played by

throwing round, flat stones along a sheet of ice

curly *adj* having curls □ **curliness** *noun*

curmudgeon *noun* a miser

currant *noun* **1** a small black raisin **2** a berry of various kinds of soft fruit: *redcurrant*

> ⚠Do not confuse: **currant** and **current**

currency *noun* (*plural* **currencies**) **1** the money used in a particular country **2** the state being generally known: *the story gained currency*

current *adj* **1** belonging to the present time: *the current year* **2** generally known and talked about: *that story is current* □ *noun* a stream of water, air or electrical power moving in one direction □ **current account** a bank account from which money may be withdrawn by cheque

curriculum *noun* the course of study at a university, school *etc* □ **curriculum vitae** a brief account of the main events of a person's life

curry[1] *noun* (*plural* **curries**) a dish containing a mixture of spices with a strong, peppery flavour □ *verb* make into a curry by adding spices □ **curry powder** a selection of ground spices used in making curry

> **curry** *verb* » *curries*, curry*ing*, curri*ed*

curry[2] *verb* rub down (a horse) □ **curry favour** try hard to be someone's favourite

curse *verb* **1** use swear words **2** wish evil towards □ *noun* **1** a wish for evil or a magic spell **2** an evil or a great misfortune or the cause of this □ **cursed** *adj* under a curse; hateful

cursor *noun* a flashing device that appears on a VDU screen to show the position for entering data

cursory *adj* hurried □ **cursorily** *adv*

curt *adj* impolitely short, abrupt □ **curtly** adv □ **curtness** *noun*

curtail *verb* make less, reduce □ **curtailment** *noun*

curtain *noun* a piece of material hung to cover a window, stage *etc*

curtsy or **curtsey** *noun* (*plural* **curtsies**) a bow made by bending the knees

curvature *noun* **1** a curving or bending **2** a curved piece **3** an abnormal curving of the spine

curve *noun* **1** a rounded line, like part of the edge of a circle **2** a bend: *a curve in the road*

cushion *noun* **1** a casing stuffed with feathers, foam *etc*, for resting on **2** a soft pad

cushy *adj*, *informal* easy and comfortable: *a cushy job*

cusp *noun* **1** a point **2** a division between signs of the zodiac

custard *noun* a sweet sauce made from eggs, milk and sugar

custodian *noun* **1** a keeper **2** a caretaker, *eg* of a museum

custody *noun* **1** care, guardianship **2** imprisonment

custom *noun* **1** something done

by habit **2** the regular or frequent doing of something; habit **3** the buying of goods at a shop **4** (**customs**) taxes on goods coming into a country **5** (**customs**) the government department that collects these **custom-built** *adj* built to suit a particular purpose

customary *adj* usual

customer *noun* **1** someone who buys from a shop **2** *informal* a person: *an awkward customer*

cut *verb* **1** make a slit in, or divide, with a blade: *cut a hole/ cut a slice of bread* **2** wound **3** trim with a blade *etc*: *cut the grass/ my hair is needing cut* **4** reduce in amount **5** shorten (a play, book *etc*) by removing parts **6** refuse to acknowledge (someone you know) **7** divide (a pack of cards) in two **8** stop filming **9** *informal* play truant from (school) *noun* **1** a slit made by cutting **2** a wound made with something sharp **3** a stroke, a blow **4** a thrust with a sword **5** the way something is cut **6** the shape and style of clothes **7** a piece of meat **cut-and-dried** *adj* arranged carefully and exactly **cut glass** glass with ornamental patterns cut on the surface **cut-price** *adj* sold at a price lower than usual **cut-throat** *noun* a ruffian *adj* fiercely competitive: *cut-throat business* **cut-up** *adj* distressed **cut down 1** take down by cutting **2** reduce **cut down on** reduce the intake of **cut in** interrupt **cut off 1** separate, isolate: *cut off from the mainland* **2** stop: *cut off supplies* **cut out 1** shape (a dress *etc*) by cutting **2** *informal* stop **3** of an engine: fail

cut *verb* » *cuts*, cutt*ing*, cut

cute *adj* **1** smart, clever **2** pretty and pleasing

cuticle *noun* the skin at the bottom and edges of finger and toe nails

cutlass *noun* (*plural* **cutlasses**) a short broad sword

cutlery *noun* knives, forks, spoons *etc*

cutlet *noun* a slice of meat with the bone attached

cutting *noun* **1** a piece cut from a newspaper **2** a trench cut in the earth or rock for a road *etc* **3** a shoot of a tree or plant *adj* wounding, hurtful: *cutting remark*

cuttlefish *noun* a type of sea creature like a squid

cv *abbrev* curriculum vitae

cwt *abbrev* hundredweight

cyanide *noun* a kind of poison

cyber- /*sai*bər/ *prefix* relating to computers or electronic media: *cyberspace/ cyber-selling*

cyborg /*sai*borg/ *noun* a robot in human form, an android

cycle *noun* **1** a bicycle **2** a round of events following on from one another repeatedly: *the cycle of the seasons* **3** a series of poems, stories *etc* written about a single person or event *verb* **1** ride a bicycle **2** move in a cycle; rotate

cyclist *noun* someone who rides a bicycle

cyclone *noun* **1** a whirling windstorm **2** a system of winds blowing in a spiral **cyclonic** *adj*

cygnet /*sig*nət/ *noun* a young swan

⚠Do not confuse with: **signet**

cylinder *noun* a solid or hollow tube-shaped object; in machines, motor-car engines *etc*, the hollow tube in which a piston works

cylindrical *adj* shaped like a cylinder

cymbals /*sim*bəlz/ *noun plural* brass, plate-like musical instruments, beaten together in pairs

cynic /*si*nik/ *noun* someone who believes the worst about people □ **cynicism** *noun*

cynical *adj* sneering; believing the worst of people □ **cynically** *adv*

cynosure *noun* centre of attraction

cypress *noun* a type of evergreen tree

cyst /sist/ *noun* a liquid-filled blister within the body or just under the skin

cystitis *noun* inflammation of the bladder, often caused by infection

czar *another spelling* of **tsar**

czarina *another spelling* of **tsarina**

D

D *abbrev* Deutschmark(s)

dab *verb* touch gently with a pad *etc* to soak up moisture □ *noun* **1** the act of dabbing **2** a small lump of something soft **3** a gentle blow, a pat **4** a small kind of flounder □ **dab-hand** *noun, informal* an expert

> **dab** *verb* » *dabs*, dabb*ing*, dabb*ed*

dabble *verb* **1** play in water with hands or feet **2** do in a half-serious way or as a hobby: *he dabbles in computers* □ **dabbler** *noun*

da capo *music* an instruction to return to the beginning of the piece

dace *noun* a type of small river fish

dachshund /*daks*hoont/ *noun* a breed of dog with short legs and a long body

dad or **daddy** *noun, informal* father

dado /*deh*doh/ *noun* (*plural* **dadoes**) the lower part of an inside wall, decorated in a different way from the rest

daffodil *noun* a type of yellow flower which grows from a bulb

daft *adj* silly □ **daftly** *adv* □ **daftness** *noun*

dagger *noun* a short sword for stabbing

dahlia *noun* a type of garden plant with large flowers

> Named after Anders *Dahl*, 18th-century Swiss botanist

daikon *noun* a long white Japanese root vegetable

Dáil /doyl/ *noun* the lower house of parliament in the Republic of Ireland

daily *adj* & *adv* every day □ *noun* (*plural* **dailies**) **1** a paper published every day **2** someone employed to clean a house regularly

dainty *adj* **1** small and neat **2** pleasant-tasting □ *noun* (*plural* **dainties**) a tasty morsel of food □ **daintily** *adv* □ **daintiness** *noun*

dairy *noun* (*plural* **dairies**) **1** a building for storing milk and making butter and cheese **2** a shop which sells milk, butter, cheese *etc* □ **dairy cattle** cows kept for their milk, not their meat □ **dairy farm** a farm concerned with the production of milk, butter *etc* □ **dairymaid** or **dairyman** *noun* a woman or man working in a dairy □ **dairy products** food made of milk, butter or cheese

dais *noun* (*plural* **daises**) a raised floor at the upper end of a hall

daisy *noun* (*plural* **daisies**) a small common flower with white petals □ **daisy-chain** *noun* a string of daisies threaded through each other's stems □ **daisy-wheel** *noun* a flat printing wheel with characters at the end of spokes

Literally 'day's eye', so called because of its opening during the day

dalai lama the spiritual leader of Tibetan Buddhism

dale *noun* low ground between hills

dally *verb* **1** waste time idling or playing **2** play (with) □ **dalliance** *noun*

dally » dalli*es*, dally*ing*, dalli*ed*

Dalmatian *noun* a breed of large spotted dog

dam *noun* **1** a wall of earth, concrete *etc* to keep back water **2** water kept in like this □ *verb* **1** keep back by a dam **2** hold back, restrain (tears *etc*)

dam » dam*s*, damm*ing*, damm*ed*

damage *noun* **1** hurt, injury **2** (damages) money paid by one person to another to make up for injury, insults *etc* □ *verb* spoil, make less effective or unusable

damask *noun* silk, linen or cotton cloth, with figures and designs in the weave

After *Damascus* in Syria, from where it was exported in the Middle Ages

dame *noun* **1** a comic woman in a pantomime, played by a man in drag **2** (**Dame**) the title of a woman of the same rank as a knight

damn *verb* **1** sentence to unending punishment in hell **2** condemn as wrong, bad *etc* □ *exclam* an expression of annoyance

damnable *adj* **1** deserving to be condemned **2** hateful □ **damnably** *adv*

damnation *noun* **1** unending punishment in hell **2** condemnation

damning *adj* leading to conviction or ruin: *damning evidence*

damp *noun* **1** moist air **2** wetness, moistness □ *verb* **1** wet slightly **2** make less fierce or intense □ *adj* moist, slightly wet □ **damper** *noun* □ **dampness** *noun*

dampen *verb* **1** make or become damp; moisten **2** lessen (enthusiasm *etc*)

damsel *noun, old* an unmarried girl

damson *noun* a type of small dark-red plum

dan *noun* a grade awarded for skill in judo or karate

dance *verb* move in time to music □ *noun* **1** a sequence of steps in time to music **2** a social event with dancing □ **dancer** *noun*

dandelion *noun* a type of common plant with a yellow flower

From the French phrase *dent de lion*, meaning 'lion's tooth'

dandruff *noun* dead skin which collects under the hair and falls off in flakes

dandy *noun* (*plural* **dandies**) a man who pays great attention to his dress and looks

danger *noun* **1** something potentially harmful: *the canal is a danger to children* **2** potential harm: *unaware of the danger*

dangerous *adj* **1** unsafe, likely to cause harm **2** full of risks □ **dangerously** *adv*

dangle *verb* hang loosely

dank *adj* moist, wet □ **dankness** *noun*

dapper *adj* small and neat

dappled *adj* marked with spots or splashes of colour

dare *verb* **1** be brave or bold enough (to): *I didn't dare tell him* **2** lay yourself open to, risk **3** challenge: *dared him to cross the railway line* □ **dare-devil** *noun* a rash person fond of taking risks □ *adj* rash, risky □ **daring** *adj* bold, fearless □ *noun* boldness □ **daringly** *adv* □ **I dare say** I suppose: *I dare say you're right*

dark *adj* **1** without light **2** black or near to black **3** gloomy **4** evil: *dark deeds* □ **dark** or **darkness** *noun* □ **darken** *verb* make or grow dark or darker □ **dark-haired** *adj* having dark-brown or black hair □ **a dark horse** someone about whom little is known □ **in the dark** knowing nothing about something □ **keep dark** keep (something) secret

darling *noun* **1** a word showing affection **2** someone dearly loved; a favourite

darn *verb* mend (clothes) with crossing rows of stitches □ *noun* a patch mended in this way

dart *noun* **1** a pointed weapon for throwing or shooting **2** something which pierces □ *verb* move quickly and suddenly

darts *noun sing* a game in which small darts are aimed at a board marked off in circles and numbered sections □ **dartboard** *noun* the board used in playing darts

dash *verb* **1** throw or knock violently, *esp* so as to break **2** ruin (hopes) **3** depress, sadden (spirits) **4** rush with speed or violence □ *noun* (*plural* **dashes**) **1** a rush **2** a short race **3** a small amount of a drink *etc* **4** liveliness **5** a short line (-) to show a break in a sentence *etc* □ **dashing** *adj* **1** hasty **2** smart, elegant

dastardly *adj, formal* cowardly

DAT or **Dat** *abbrev* digital audio tape

data *noun plural* (*sing* **datum**) **1** available facts from which conclusions may be drawn **2** facts stored in a computer

database *noun, comput* a collection of systematically stored files that are often connected with each other

date[1] *noun* **1** a statement of time in terms of the day, month and year, *eg* 23 December 1995 **2** the time at which an event occurs **3** the period of time to which something belongs **4** an appointment □ *verb* **1** give a date to **2** belong to a certain time: *dates from the 12th century* **3** become old-fashioned: *that dress will date quickly* □ **out-of-date** *adj* **1** old-fashioned **2** no longer valid □ **up-to-date** *adj* **1** in fashion, modern **2** including or aware of the latest information **3** at the appropriate point in a schedule

date[2] *noun* **1** a type of palm tree **2** its blackish, shiny fruit with a hard stone

datum *sing* of **data**

daub *verb* **1** smear **2** paint roughly

daughter *noun* a female child ▫ **daughter-in-law** *noun* a son's wife

daunt *verb* **1** frighten **2** be discouraging ▫ **dauntless** *adj* unable to be frightened

Davy-lamp *noun* an early kind of safety lamp for coalminers

dawdle *verb* move slowly ▫ **dawdler** *noun*

dawn *noun* **1** daybreak **2** a beginning: *dawn of a new era* ▫ *verb* **1** become day **2** begin to appear ▫ **dawning** *noun* dawn ▫ **dawn chorus** the singing of birds at dawn ▫ **dawn on** become suddenly clear to (someone)

day *noun* **1** the time of light, from sunrise to sunset **2** twenty-four hours, from one midnight to the next **3** the time or hours spent at work **4** (often **days**) a particular time or period: *in the days of steam* ▫ **daylight** *noun* **1** the light of day, sunlight **2** a clear space ▫ **day-release** *noun* time off from work for training or education ▫ **day in, day out** on and on, continuously ▫ **the other day** recently: *saw her just the other day*

daydream *noun* an imagining of pleasant events while awake ▫ *verb* imagine in this way

dayglo *noun, trademark* a luminously bright colour

daze *verb* **1** stun with a blow **2** confuse, bewilder

dazzle *verb* **1** shine on so as to prevent from seeing clearly **2** shine brilliantly **3** fascinate, impress deeply

dB *abbrev* decibel(s)

DC *abbrev* **1** District of Columbia (US) **2** detective constable **3** direct current (*compare with*: **AC**) **4** *music* da capo

DCC *abbrev* digital compact cassette

deacon *noun* **1** the lowest rank of clergy in the Church of England **2** a church official in other churches

deaconess *noun* a woman deacon

dead *adj* **1** not living, without life **2** cold and cheerless **3** numb **4** not working; no longer in use **5** complete, utter: *dead silence* **6** exact: *dead centre* **7** certain: *a dead shot* ▫ *adv* **1** completely: *dead certain* **2** suddenly and completely: *stop dead* ▫ *noun* **1** those who have died: *speak well of the dead* **2** the time of greatest stillness *etc*: *the dead of night* ▫ **dead-and-alive** *adj* dull, having little life ▫ **dead-beat** *adj* having no strength left ▫ **dead end** **1** a road *etc* closed at one end **2** a job *etc* not leading to promotion ▫ **dead heat** a race in which two or more runners finish equal ▫ **dead ringer** *informal* someone looking exactly like someone else

deaden *verb* lessen (pain *etc*)

deadline *noun* a date by which something must be done

> Originally a line in a military prison, the penalty for crossing which was death

deadlock *noun* a standstill resulting from a complete failure to agree

deadly *adj* **1** likely to cause death, fatal **2** intense, very great: *deadly hush* □ *adv* intensely, extremely □ **deadliness** *noun*

deadpan *adj* without expression on the face

deaf *adj* **1** unable to hear **2** refusing to listen □ **deaf-mute** *noun* someone who is both deaf and dumb □ **deafness** *noun*

deafen *verb* **1** make deaf **2** be unpleasantly loud **3** make (walls *etc*) soundproof □ **deafening** *adj*

deal *noun* **1** an agreement, *esp* in business **2** an amount or quantity: *a good deal of paper* **3** the dividing out of playing-cards in a game **4** a kind of softwood □ *verb* **1** divide, give out **2** trade (in) **3** do business (with) □ **dealer** *noun* **1** someone who deals out cards at a game **2** a trader **3** a stock-broker □ **deal with** take action concerning, cope with

dean *noun* **1** the chief religious officer in a cathedral church **2** the head of a faculty in a university

dear *adj* **1** high in price **2** highly valued; much loved □ *noun* **1** someone who is loved **2** someone who is lovable or charming □ *adv* at a high price □ **dearly** *adv* □ **dearness** *noun*

dearth /duhrth/ *noun* a scarcity, shortage

death *noun* **1** the state of being dead, the end of life **2** the end of something: *the death of steam railways* □ **death-blow** *noun* **1** a blow that causes death **2** an event that causes something to end □ **death-knell** *noun* **1** a bell announcing a death **2** something indicating the end of a scheme, hope *etc* □ **death-mask** *noun* a plastercast taken of a dead person's face □ **death rattle** a rattling in the throat sometimes heard before someone dies □ **death roll** a list of the dead □ **deathwatch beetle** an insect that makes a ticking noise and whose larva destroys wood □ **death wish** a conscious or unconscious desire to die

deathly *adj* **1** very pale or ill-looking **2** deadly

debar *verb* keep from, prevent

> **debar** » debar*s*, debarr*ing*, debarr*ed*

debase *verb* **1** lessen in value **2** make bad, wicked *etc* □ **debased** *adj* □ **debasement** *noun*

debatable *adj* arguable, doubtful: *a debatable point* □ **debatably** *adv*

debate *noun* **1** a discussion, *esp* a formal one before an audience **2** an argument □ *verb* engage in debate, discuss

debauchery *noun* excessive indulgence in drunkenness, lewdness *etc* □ **debauched** *adj* inclined to debauchery

debilitate *verb* make weak

debility *noun* weakness of the body

debit *noun* a debt □ *verb* mark down as a debt

debonair *adj* of pleasant and cheerful appearance and behaviour

debouch /dəbowch/ *verb* come out

from a narrow or confined place

debrief *verb* gather information from an astronaut, spy *etc* after a mission ◇ **debriefing** *noun*

debris /*de*bree/ *noun* **1** the remains of something broken, destroyed *etc* **2** rubbish

debt /det/ *noun* what one person owes to another ◇ **debtor** *noun* someone who owes a debt ◇ **in debt** owing money ◇ **in someone's debt** under an obligation to them

début /*deh*byoo/ *noun* the first public appearance, *eg* of an actor ◇ *adj* first before the public: *début concert*

débutante *noun* a young woman making her first appearance in upper-class society

decade *noun* **1** a period of ten years **2** a set or series of ten

decadence *noun* a falling from high to low standards in morals, the arts *etc* ◇ **decadent** *adj*

decaff *adj*, *informal* decaffeinated

decaffeinated *adj* with the caffeine removed

decamp *verb* run away

decant *verb* pour (wine *etc*) from a bottle into a decanter

decanter *noun* an ornamental bottle with a glass stopper for wine, whisky *etc*

decapitate *verb* cut the head from ◇ **decapitation** *noun*

decathlon *noun* an athletics competition combining contests in ten separate disciplines

decay *verb* become bad, worse or rotten ◇ *noun* the process of rotting or worsening ◇ **decayed** *adj*

decease *noun*, *formal* death

deceased *adj*, *formal* dead ◇ *noun* (**the deceased**) a dead person

deceit *noun* the act of deceiving

deceitful *adj* inclined to deceive; lying ◇ **deceitfully** *adv* ◇ **deceitfulness** *noun*

deceive *verb* tell lies to so as to mislead ◇ **deceiver** *noun*

decelerate *verb* slow down ◇ **deceleration** *noun*

December *noun* the twelfth month of the year

decent *adj* **1** respectable **2** good enough, adequate: *decent salary* **3** kind: *decent of you to help* ◇ **decency** *noun* ◇ **decently** *adv*

deception *noun* **1** the act of deceiving **2** something that deceives or is intended to deceive

deceptive *adj* misleading: *appearances may be deceptive* ◇ **deceptively** *adv*

decibel *noun* a unit of loudness of sound

decide *verb* **1** make up your mind to do something: *I've decided to take your advice* **2** settle (an argument *etc*)

decided *adj* **1** clear: *decided difference* **2** with mind made up: *he was decided on the issue* ◇ **decidedly** *adv* definitely

deciduous *adj* of a tree: having leaves that fall in autumn

decimal *adj* **1** numbered by tens **2** of ten parts or the number 10 ◇

noun a decimal fraction ▯ **decimal currency** a system of money in which each coin or note is either a tenth of another or ten times another in value ▯ **decimal fraction** a fraction expressed in tenths, hundredths, thousandths *etc*, separated by a decimal point ▯ **decimal point** a dot used to separate units from decimal fractions, *eg* 0.1 = 1/10, 2.33 = 2 33/100 ▯ **decimalize** *verb* convert (figures or currency) to decimal form ▯ **decimalization** *noun*

decimate *verb* make much smaller in numbers by destruction

Literally 'reduce by a tenth'

decipher *verb* **1** translate (a code) into ordinary, understandable language **2** make out the meaning of: *can't decipher his handwriting*

decision *noun* **1** the act of deciding **2** clear judgement, firmness: *acting with decision*

decisive *adj* **1** final, putting an end to a contest *etc*: *a decisive defeat* **2 showing decision and firmness:** *a decisive manner* ▯ **decisively** *adv*

deck *noun* **1** a platform forming the floor of a ship, bus *etc* **2** a pack of playing-cards **3** the turntable of a record-player ▯ *verb* decorate, adorn ▯ **deckchair** *noun* a collapsible chair of wood and canvas *etc* ▯ **clear the decks** get rid of old papers, work *etc* before starting something fresh

deckle-edge *noun* a ragged edge on handmade paper

declaim *verb* **1** make a speech in impressive dramatic language **2** speak violently (against) ▯ **declamation** *noun* ▯ **declamatory** *adj*

declare *verb* **1** make known (goods or income on which tax is payable) **2** announce formally or publicly: *declare war* **3** say firmly **4** *cricket* end an innings before ten wickets have fallen ▯ **declaration** *noun*

decline *verb* **1** say 'no' to, refuse: *I had to decline his offer* **2** weaken, become worse **3** slope down ▯ *noun* **1** a downward slope **2** a gradual worsening of health *etc*

declivity *noun* (*plural* **declivities**) a downward slope

decode *verb* translate (a coded message) into ordinary, understandable language

decompose *verb* **1** rot, decay **2** separate in parts or elements ▯ **decomposition** *noun*

décor /*deh*kor/ *noun* the decoration of, and arrangement of objects in, a room *etc*

decorate *verb* **1** add ornament to **2** paint or paper the walls of (a room *etc*) **3** pin a badge or medal on (someone) as a mark of honour ▯ **decoration** *noun* ▯ **decorative** *adj* **1** ornamental **2** pretty ▯ **decorator** *noun* someone who decorates houses, rooms *etc*

decorous *adj* behaving in an acceptable or dignified way

decorum *noun* good behaviour

découpage /dehcoo*pazh*/ *noun* the application of paper cut-outs to wood for decoration

decoy *verb* lead into a trap or into

evil □ *noun* something or someone intended to lead another into a trap

decrease *verb* make or become less in number □ *noun* a growing less

decree *noun* **1** an order, a law **2** a judge's decision □ *verb* give an order

> **decree** *verb* » decree*s*, decree*ing*, decree*d*

decrepit *adj* **1** weak and infirm because of old age **2** in ruins or disrepair □ **decrepitude** *noun*

decry *verb* **1** make to seem worthless, belittle **2** express disapproval of

> **decry** » decri*es*, decry*ing*, decri*ed*

dedicate *verb* **1** devote yourself (to): *dedicated to his music* **2** set apart for a sacred purpose **3** inscribe or publish (a book *etc*) in tribute to someone or something: *I dedicate this book to my father* □ **dedication** *noun*

deduce *verb* find out something by putting together all that is known □ **deduction** *noun*

> ⚠Do not confuse: **deduce** and **deduct**

deduct *verb* subtract, take away (from) □ **deduction** *noun* a subtraction

deed *noun* **1** something done, an act **2** *law* a signed statement or bargain

deed poll a document by which someone legally changes their name

> From an old meaning of *poll* as 'cut' or 'trimmed', because these were written on paper with cut edges

deep *adj* **1** being or going far down **2** hard to understand; cunning **3** involved to a great extent: *deep in debt/ deep in thought* **4** intense, strong: *a deep red colour/ deep affection* **5** low in pitch □ *noun* (with **the**) the sea □ **deepen** *verb* make deep □ **deep freeze** a low-temperature refrigerator that can freeze and preserve food frozen for a long time □ **deep-seated** *adj* firmly fixed, not easily removed □ **in deep water** in serious trouble

deer *noun (plural* **deer**) an animal with antlers in the male, such as the reindeer

deface *verb* spoil the appearance of, disfigure □ **defacement** *noun*

de facto *adj* actual, but often not legally recognized

defame *verb* try to harm the reputation of □ **defamation** *noun* □ **defamatory** *adj*

default *verb* fail to do something you ought to do, *eg* to pay a debt □ **defaulter** *noun* □ **by default** because of a failure to do something

defeat *verb* beat, win a victory over □ *noun* a win, a victory

defect *noun* /*dee*fekt/ a lack of something needed for completeness or perfection; a flaw □ *verb* /di*fekt*/ desert a country, political party *etc* to join or go to another □ **defection** *noun* **1** failure in duty **2** desertion

defective *adj* **1** faulty; incomplete **2** not having normal mental or physical ability

> ⚠Do not confuse with: **deficient**

defence or *US* **defense** *noun* **1** the act of defending against attack **2** a means or method of protection **3** *law* the argument defending the accused person in a case (*contrasted with*: **prosecution**) **4** *law* the lawyer(s) putting forward this argument □ **defenceless** *adj* without defence

defend *verb* **1** guard or protect against attack **2** *law* conduct the defence of □ **defendant** *noun* **1** someone who resists attack **2** *law* the accused person in a law case □ **defensible** *adj* able to be defended

defensive *adj* **1** used for defence **2** expecting criticism, ready to justify actions □ **on the defensive** prepared to defend yourself against attack or criticism

defer *verb* **1** put off to another time **2** give way (to): *he deferred to my wishes* □ **deference** *noun* **1** willingness to consider the wishes *etc* of others **2** the act of giving way to another □ **deferential** *adj* showing deference, respectful

> **defer** » defer*s*, deferr*ing*, deferr*ed*

defiance *noun* open disobedience or opposition □ **defiant** *adj* □ **defiantly** *adv*

defibrillator *noun* a machine which applies an electric current to stop irregular beating of the heart

deficiency *noun* (*plural* **deficiencies**) **1** lack, want **2** an amount lacking

deficient *adj* lacking in what is needed

> ⚠Do not confuse with: **defective**

deficit *noun* an amount by which a sum of money *etc* is too little

defile *verb* **1** make dirty, soil **2** corrupt, make bad □ **defilement** *noun*

define *verb* **1** fix the bounds or limits of **2** outline or show clearly **3** state the exact meaning of

definite *adj* **1** having clear limits, fixed **2** exact **3** certain, sure □ **definitely** *adv* □ **definiteness** *noun* □ **definite article** the name given to the adjective *the*

definition *noun* **1** an explanation of the exact meaning of a word or phrase **2** sharpness or clearness of outline

definitive *adj* **1** fixed, final **2** not able to be bettered: *definitive biography* **definitively** *adv*

deflate *verb* **1** let the air out of (a tyre *etc*) **2** reduce in self-importance or self-confidence □ **deflation** *noun* **deflationary** *adj*

deflect *verb* turn aside (from a fixed course) □ **deflection** *noun*

deform *verb* **1** spoil the shape of **2** make ugly □ **deformed** *adj* badly or abnormally formed □ **deformity** *noun* (*plural* **deformities**) **1** something abnormal in shape **2** the fact of being badly shaped

defraud *verb* **1** cheat **2** (with **of**) take by cheating or fraud

defray *verb* pay for (expenses)

defrost *verb* remove frost or ice (from); thaw

deft *adj* clever with the hands, handy □ **deftly** *adv* □ **deftness** *noun*

defunct *adj* no longer active or in use

defy *verb* **1** dare to do something, challenge **2** resist openly **3** make impossible: *its beauty defies description*

defy » defi*es*, defy*ing*, defi*ed*

degenerate *adj* having become immoral or very bad □ *verb* become or grow bad or worse □ **degeneration** *noun*

degrade *verb* **1** lower in grade or rank **2** disgrace □ **degrading** *adj* □ **degradation** *noun*

degree 1 a step or stage in a process **2** rank or grade **3** amount, extent: *a degree of certainty* **4** a unit of temperature **5** a unit by which angles are measured, one 360th part of the circumference of a circle **6** a certificate given by a university, gained by examination or given as an honour

dehydrate *verb* **1** remove water from (food *etc*) **2** lose excessive water from the body □ **dehydrated** *adj* □ **dehydration** *noun*

deify *verb* worship as a god

deify » deifi*es*, deify*ing*, deifi*ed*

deign *verb* act as if doing a favour: *she deigned to answer us*

deity *noun* (*plural* **deities**) a god or goddess

déjà vu /dehzhah *voo*/ the feeling of having experienced something before

dejected *adj* gloomy, dispirited □ **dejection** *noun*

delay *verb* **1** put off, postpone **2** keep back, hinder □ *noun* **1** a postponement **2** a hindrance

delectable *adj* delightful, pleasing □ **delectably** *adv*

delectation *noun* delight, enjoyment

delegate *verb* give (a task) to someone else to do □ *noun* someone acting on behalf of another; a representative □ **delegation** *noun* a group of delegates

delete *verb* rub or strike out (*eg* a piece of writing) □ **deletion** *noun*

deleterious *adj* harmful

deli /*de*lee/ *noun*, *informal* a delicatessen

deliberate *verb* think carefully or seriously (about) □ *adj* **1** intentional, not accidental **2** slow in deciding **3** not hurried □ **deliberately** *adv*

deliberation *noun* **1** careful thought **2** calmness, coolness **3** (**deliberations**) formal discussions

delicacy *noun* (*plural* **delicacies**) **1** tact **2** something delicious to eat

delicate *adj* **1** not strong, frail **2** easily damaged **3** fine, dainty: *delicate features* **4** pleasant to taste **5** tactful **6** requiring skill or care: *delicate operation*

delicatessen *noun* a shop selling food cooked or prepared ready for eating

delicious *adj* **1** very pleasant to taste **2** giving pleasure □ **deliciously** *adv*

delight *verb* **1** please greatly **2** take great pleasure (in) □ *noun* great pleasure □ **delighted** *adj* □ **delightful** *adj* very pleasing □ **delightfully** *adv*

delinquency *noun* **1** wrongdoing, misdeeds **2** failure in duty

delinquent *adj* **1** guilty of an offence or misdeed **2** not carrying out your duties □ *noun* **1** someone guilty of an offence **2** someone who fails in their duty

delirious *adj* **1** raving, wandering in the mind **2** wildly excited □ **deliriously** *adv*

delirium *noun* **1** a delirious state, *esp* caused by fever **2** wild excitement □ **delirium tremens** a delirious disorder of the brain caused by excessive alcohol

deliver *verb* **1** hand over **2** give out (*eg* a speech, a blow) **3** set free, rescue **4** assist at the birth of (a child) □ **deliverance** *noun*

delivery *noun* (*plural* **deliveries**) **1** a handing over, *eg* of letters **2** the birth of a child **3** a style of speaking

delphinium *noun* a branching garden plant with blue flowers

> From a Greek word translating as 'little dolphin', because of the shape of the flowerheads

delta *noun* the triangular stretch of land at the mouth of a river

> Originally from a Hebrew word meaning 'tent door'

delude *verb* deceive

deluge *noun* **1** a great flood of water **2** an overwhelming amount: *deluge of work* □ *verb* **1** flood, drench **2** overwhelm

delusion *noun* a false belief, *esp* as a symptom of mental illness □ **delusionary** *adj*

> ⚠Do not confuse with: **allusion** and **illusion**

delve *verb* **1** dig **2** rummage, search through: *delved in her bag for her keys*

demagogue *noun* a popular leader

demand *verb* **1** ask, or ask for, firmly **2** insist: *I demand that you listen* **3** require, call for: *demanding attention* □ *noun* **1** a forceful request **2** an urgent claim: *many demands on his time* **3** a need for certain goods *etc*

demean *verb* lower, degrade

demeanour *noun* behaviour, conduct

demented *adj* mad, insane

demesne /d*ə*mehn/ or /d*ə*meen/ *noun* an estate

demise *noun*, *formal* death

demob *verb* and *noun*, *informal* **1** demobilize **2** demobilization

demobilize *verb* **1** break up an army after a war is over **2** free (a soldier) from army service □ **demobilization** *noun*

democracy *noun* government of

the people by the people through their elected representatives

democrat *noun* **1** someone who believes in democracy **2** (**Democrat**) *US* a member of the American Democratic Party

democratic *adj* **1** of or governed by democracy **2** (**Democratic**) *US* belonging to one of the two chief political parties in the USA □ **democratically** *adv*

démodé /dehmo*deh*/ *adj* no longer in fashion

demography *noun* the study of population size and movement □ **demographer** *noun* □ **demographic** *adj*

demolish *verb* **1** destroy completely **2** pull down (a building *etc*) □ **demolition** *noun*

demon *noun* an evil spirit, a devil □ **demonic** *adj*

demonstrate *verb* **1** show clearly; prove **2** show (a machine *etc*) in action **3** express an opinion by marching, showing placards *etc* in public □ **demonstrable** *adj* able to be shown clearly □ **demonstrator** *noun*

demonstration *noun* **1** a showing, a display **2** a public expression of opinion by a procession, mass-meeting *etc*

demonstrative *adj* **1** pointing out; proving **2** inclined to show feelings openly

demoralize *verb* take away the confidence of □ **demoralization** *noun*

demote *verb* reduce to a lower rank or grade □ **demotion** *noun*

demur *verb* object, say 'no'

> **demur** » demur*s*, demur*ring*, demur*red*

demure *adj* shy and modest □ **demurely** *adv*

den *noun* **1** the lair of a wild animal **2** a small private room for working *etc*

dendrochronology *noun* the dating of events by counting the rings in trees of the same age □ **dendrochronologist** *noun*

denial *noun* the act of denying □ **in denial** doggedly refusing to accept something

denier /*den*ier/ *noun* a unit of weight of nylon, silk *etc*

denigrate *verb* attack the reputation of, defame

denim *noun* a hard-wearing cotton cloth used for jeans, overalls *etc*

denizen *noun* a dweller, an inhabitant

denomination *noun* **1** name, title **2** a value of a coin, stamp *etc* **3** a religious sect □ **denominational** *adj*

denominator *noun* the lower number in a vulgar fraction by which the upper number is divided, *eg* the 3 in $\frac{2}{3}$

denote *verb* mean, signify

dénouement *noun* the ending of a story where mysteries *etc* are explained

> Literally 'untying' or 'unravelling', from French

denounce *verb* **1** accuse publicly

of a crime **2** inform against: *denounced him to the enemy* ▯ **denunciation** *noun*

dense *adj* **1** closely packed together; thick **2** very stupid ▯ **densely** *adv*

density *noun* (*plural* **densities**) **1** thickness **2** weight (of water) in proportion to volume **3** *comput* the extent to which data can be held on a floppy disk

dent *noun* a hollow made by a blow or pressure ▯ *verb* make a dent in

dental *adj* of or for a tooth or teeth

dentist *noun* a doctor who examines teeth and treats dental problems ▯ **dentistry** *noun* the work of a dentist

dentures *noun plural* a set of false teeth

denude *verb* make bare, strip: *denuded of leaves* ▯ **denudation** *noun*

denunciation *see* **denounce**

deny *verb* **1** declare to be untrue: *he denied that he did it* **2** refuse, forbid: *denied the right to appeal* ▯ **deny yourself** do without things you want or need

deny » deni*es*, deny*ing*, deni*ed*

deodorant *noun* something that hides unpleasant smells

depart *verb* **1** go away **2** turn aside from: *departing from the plan* ▯ **departure** *noun* ▯ **a new departure** a new course of action

department *noun* a self-contained section within a shop, university, government *etc*

depend *verb* **1** rely (on) **2** (with **on**) receive necessary financial support from **3** (with **on**) be controlled or decided by: *it all depends on the weather* ▯ **dependable** *adj* to be trusted

dependant *noun* someone who is kept or supported by another

⚠Do not confuse: **dependant** and **dependent**

dependent *adj* relying or depending (on) ▯ **dependence** *noun* the state of being dependent

depict *verb* **1** draw, paint *etc* **2** describe

depilatory *adj* hair-removing: *depilatory cream* ▯ *noun* a hair-removing substance

deplete *verb* make smaller in amount or number ▯ **depletion** *noun*

deplore *verb* disapprove of, regret: *deplored his use of language* ▯ **deplorable** *adj* regrettable; very bad

deploy *verb* place in position ready for action

depopulate *verb* reduce greatly in population ▯ **depopulated** *adj*

deport *verb* send (someone) out of a country ▯ **deportation** *noun* ▯ **deportment** *noun* behaviour, bearing

depose *verb* remove from a high position, *esp* a monarch from a throne ▯ **deposition** *noun*

deposit *verb* **1** put or set down **2**

put in for safe keeping, *eg* money in a bank □ *noun* **1** money paid in part payment of something **2** money put in a bank account **3** a solid that has settled at the bottom of a liquid **4** a layer of coal, iron *etc* occurring naturally in rock □ **deposit account** a bank account from which money must be withdrawn in person, not by cheque □ **deposition** *noun* a written piece of evidence □ **depository** (*plural* **depositories**) a place where anything is deposited

depot /*de*poh/ *noun* **1** a storehouse **2** a building where railway engines, buses *etc* are kept and repaired

deprave *verb* make wicked □ **depraved** *adj* wicked □ **depravity** *noun*

deprecate *verb* show disapproval of, condemn □ **deprecation** *noun*

⚠Do not confuse: **deprecate** and **depreciate**

depreciate *verb* **1** lessen the value of **2** fall in value □ **depreciation** *noun*

depredations *noun plural* plundering

depress *verb* **1** make gloomy or unhappy **2** press down **3** lower in value □ **depressing** *adj*

depression *noun* **1** low spirits, gloominess **2** a hollow **3** a lowering in value **4** a low period in a country's economy with unemployment, lack of trade *etc* **5** a region of low atmospheric pressure

deprive *verb*:**deprive of** take away from □ **deprivation** *noun* □ **deprived** *adj* suffering from hardship; disadvantaged

Dept *abbrev* department

depth *noun* **1** deepness **2** a deep place **3** the deepest part: *from the depth of her soul* **4** the middle: *depth of winter* **5** intensity, strength: *depth of colour* □ **in depth** thoroughly, carefully □ **out of your depth** concerned in problems too difficult to understand

deputation *noun* a group of people chosen and sent as representatives

deputy *noun* (*plural* **deputies**) **1** a delegate, a representative **2** a second-in-command □ **deputize** *verb* take another's place, act as substitute

derail *verb* cause to leave the rails □ **derailment** *noun*

derange *verb* put out of place, or out of working order □ **deranged** *adj* mad, insane □ **derangement** *noun*

derelict *adj* broken-down, abandoned □ **dereliction** *noun* neglect of what should be attended to: *dereliction of duty*

deride *verb* laugh at, mock □ **derision** *noun* □ **derisive** *adj*

de rigueur *adj* required by custom or fashion

derive *verb* **1** be descended or formed (from) **2** trace (a word) back to the beginning of its existence **3** receive, obtain: *derive satisfaction* □ **derivation** *noun* □ **derivative** *adj* not original □ *noun* **1** a word formed on the base of another word, *eg fabulous* from *fable* **2** (**derivatives**) stock market trading in futures and options

dermatitis *noun* inflammation of the skin

dermatology *noun* the study and treatment of skin diseases ▯ **dermatologist** *noun*

derogatory *adj* **1** harmful to reputation, dignity *etc* **2** scornful, belittling, disparaging

derrick *noun* **1** a crane for lifting weights **2** a framework over an oil well that holds the drilling machinery

> Named after Derrick, a famous 17th-century hangman in Tyburn, England

derring-do *noun* daring action, boldness

> Based on a misprint of a medieval English phrase *dorring do*, meaning 'daring to do'

dervish *noun* a member of an austere Islamic sect

descant *noun*, *music* a tune played or sung above the main tune

descend *verb* **1** go or climb down **2** slope downwards **3** (with **from**) have as an ancestor: *claims he's descended from Napoleon* **4** go from a better to a worse state ▯ **descendant** *noun* someone descended from another

descent *noun* **1** an act of descending **2** a downward slope

describe *verb* **1** give an account of in words **2** draw the outline of, trace

description *noun* **1** the act of describing **2** an account in words **3** sort, kind: *people of all descriptions* ▯ **descriptive** *adj*

descry *verb* notice, see

> **descry** » descri*es*, descry*ing*, descri*ed*

desecrate *verb* **1** spoil (something sacred) **2** treat without respect ▯ **desecration** *noun*

> ⚠Do not confuse with: **desiccate**

desert[1] *verb* **1** run away from (the army) **2** leave, abandon: *deserted his wife/ his courage deserted him* ▯ **deserter** *noun* ▯ **desertion** *noun*

desert[2] *noun* a stretch of barren country with very little water ▯ **desert island** an uninhabited island in a tropical area

> ⚠Do not confuse with: **dessert**

deserve *verb* have earned as a right, be worthy of: *you deserve a holiday* ▯ **deservedly** *adv* justly ▯ **deserving** *adj*

desiccate *verb* **1** dry up **2** preserve by drying: *desiccated coconut*

> ⚠Do not confuse with: **desecrate**

design *verb* **1** make a plan of (*eg* a building) before it is made **2** intend ▯ *noun* **1** a plan, a sketch **2** a painted picture, pattern *etc* **3** an intention ▯ **designing** *adj* crafty, cunning ▯ **have designs on** plan to get for yourself

designate *verb* **1** point out, indicate **2** name **3** appoint, select ▯ *adj* appointed to a post but not yet occupying it: *director designate* □ **designation** *noun* a name, a title

desirable *adj* pleasing; worth having □ **desirability** *noun*

desire *verb* wish for greatly □ *noun* **1** a longing for **2** a wish

desist *verb*, *formal* stop (doing something)

desk *noun* a table for writing, reading *etc*

desolate *adj* **1** deeply unhappy **2** empty of people, deserted **3** barren □ **desolated** *adj* overcome by grief □ **desolation** *noun* **1** deep sorrow **2** barren land **3** ruin

despair *verb* give up hope □ *noun* **1** lack of hope **2** a cause of despair: *she was the despair of her mother* □ **despairing** *adj*

despatch *another spelling* of **dispatch**

desperado *noun* (*plural* **desperadoes** or **desperados**) a violent criminal

desperate *adj* **1** without hope, despairing **2** very bad, awful **3** reckless; violent □ **desperately** *adv* □ **desperation** *noun*

despicable *adj* contemptible, hateful

despise *verb* look on with contempt

despite *prep* in spite of: *we had a picnic despite the weather*

despoil *verb* rob, plunder □ **despoliation** *noun*

despondent *adj* downhearted, dejected □ **despondency** *noun*

despot /*de*spot/ *noun* a ruler with unlimited power, a tyrant □ **despotic** *adj* □ **despotism** *noun*

dessert *noun* fruits, sweets *etc* served at the end of a meal

⚠Do not confuse with: **desert**

destination *noun* the place to which someone or something is going

destine *verb* set apart for a certain use □ **destined** *adj* **1** bound (for) **2** intended (for) by fate: *destined to succeed*

destiny *noun* (*plural* **destinies**) what is destined to happen; fate

destitute *adj* **1** in need of food, shelter *etc* **2** (with **of**) completely lacking in: *destitute of wit* □ **destitution** *noun*

destroy *verb* **1** pull down, knock to pieces **2** ruin **3** kill □ **destroyer** *noun* **1** someone who destroys **2** a type of fast warship □ **destructible** *adj* able to be destroyed

destruction *noun* **1** the act of destroying or being destroyed **2** ruin **3** death

destructive *adj* **1** doing great damage **2** of criticism: pointing out faults without suggesting improvements □ **destructively** *adv* □ **destructiveness** *noun*

desultory *adj* **1** moving from one thing to another without a fixed plan **2** changing from subject to subject, rambling □ **desultorily** *adv* □ **desultoriness** *noun*

detach *verb* unfasten, remove (from) □ **detachable** *adj* able to be taken off: *detachable lining* □

detached *adj* **1** standing apart, by itself: *detached house* **2** not personally involved, showing no emotion ▯ **detachment** *noun* **1** the state of being detached **2** a body or group (*eg* of troops on special service)

detail *noun* a small part, fact, item *etc* ▯ *verb* **1** describe fully, give particulars of **2** set to do a special job or task: *detailed to wash the dishes* ▯ **detailed** *adj* with nothing left out ▯ **in detail** giving attention to details, item by item

detain *verb* **1** hold back **2** keep late **3** keep under guard

detect *verb* **1** discover **2** notice ▯ **detection** *noun*

detective *noun* someone who tries to find criminals or watches suspects

détente /deh*tonht*/ *noun* a lessening of hostility between nations

detention *noun* **1** imprisonment **2** a forced stay after school as punishment

deter *verb* discourage or prevent through fear ▯ **deterrent** *noun* something which deters

> **deter** » deter*s*, deterr*ing*, deterr*ed*

detergent *noun* a soapless substance used with water for washing dishes *etc*

deteriorate *verb* grow worse: *her health is deteriorating rapidly* ▯ **deterioration** *noun*

determine *verb* **1** decide (on) **2** fix, settle: *determined his course of action* ▯ **determination** *noun* **1** the fact of being determined **2** stubbornness, firmness of purpose ▯ **determined** *adj* **1** decided on a result: *determined to succeed* **2** fixed, settled

deterrent *see* **deter**

detest *verb* hate greatly ▯ **detestable** *adj* very hateful ▯ **detestation** great hatred

dethrone *verb* remove from a throne ▯ **dethronement** *noun*

detonate *verb* (cause to) explode ▯ **detonation** *noun* an explosion ▯ **detonator** *noun* something which sets off an explosive

detour *noun* a circuitous route

detract *verb* take away (from), lessen ▯ **detraction** *noun*

detriment *noun* harm, damage, disadvantage ▯ **detrimental** *adj* disadvantageous (to), causing harm or damage

de trop /də *troh*/ *adj* in the way, unwelcome

deuce *noun* **1** a playing-card with two pips **2** *tennis* a score of forty points each

deus ex machina a contrived solution or way out

> Literally a 'god from a machine' referring to the pulley device used in ancient Greek theatres to lower the character of a god onto the stage

Deutschmark *noun* the main unit of currency of Germany

devanagari *noun* the script used for written Sanskrit and Hindi

devastate *verb* **1** lay in ruins **2** overwhelm with grief *etc* □ **devastation** *noun*

develop *verb* **1** (make to) grow bigger or more advanced **2** acquire gradually: *developed a taste for opera* **3** become active or visible **4** unfold gradually **5** use chemicals to make (a photograph) appear □ **developer** *noun* a chemical mixture used to make an image appear from a photograph □ **development** *noun*

deviate *verb* turn aside, *esp* from a standard course □ **deviation** *noun*

device *noun* **1** a tool, an instrument **2** a plan **3** a design on a coat of arms

⚠Do not confuse with: **devise**

devil *noun* **1** an evil spirit **2** Satan **3** a wicked person □ **devilish** *adj* very wicked □ **devil-may-care** *adj* not caring what happens □ **devilment** or **devilry** *noun* mischief □ **devil's advocate** someone who argues against a proposal

devious *adj* **1** not direct, roundabout **2** not straightforward □ **deviousness** *noun*

devise *verb* **1** make up, put together **2** plan, plot

⚠Do not confuse with: **device**

devoid *adj* (with **of**) empty of, free from: *devoid of curiosity*

devolution *noun* the delegation of certain legislative powers to regional or national assemblies □ **devolutionist** *noun* a supporter of devolution

devolve *verb* **1** fall as a duty (on) **2** delegate (power) to a regional or national assembly

devote *verb* give up wholly (to) □ **devoted** *adj* **1** loving and loyal **2** given up (to): *devoted to her work* □ **devotee** *noun* a keen follower □ **devotion** *noun* great love

devour *verb* **1** eat up greedily **2** destroy

devout *adj* **1** earnest, sincere **2** religious □ **devoutly** *adv* □ **devoutness** *noun*

dew *noun* tiny drops of water which form from the air as it cools at night □ **dewy** *adj* covered in dew; moist

dexterity *noun* skill, quickness □ **dexterous** or **dextrous** *adj*

DHSS *abbrev the former name* for **DSS**

DI *abbrev* donor insemination

diabetes *noun* a disease in which there is too much sugar in the blood □ **diabetic** *noun* & *adj* (someone) suffering from diabetes

diabolic or **diabolical** *adj* devilish, very wicked □ **diabolically** *adv*

diadem *noun* a kind of crown

diagnose *verb* identify (a cause of illness) after making an examination □ **diagnosis** *noun* (*plural* **diagnoses**) □ **diagnostic** *adj*

diagonal *adj* going from one corner to the opposite corner □ *noun* a line from one corner to the opposite corner □ **diagonally** *adv*

diagram *noun* a drawing to explain something □ **diagrammatic** or **diagrammatical** *adj* in the form of a diagram

dial *noun* **1** the face of a clock or watch **2** a rotating disc over the numbers on some telephones □ *verb* call (a number) on a telephone using a dial or buttons

> **dial** *verb* » dial*s*, dial*ling*, dial*led*

dialect *noun* a way of speaking found only in a certain area or among a certain group of people

dialogue *noun* a talk between two or more people

diameter *noun* a line which dissects a circle, passing through its centre

diamond *noun* **1** a very hard, precious stone **2** an elongated, four-cornered shape (♦) **3** a playing-card with red diamond pips

diaper *noun*, *US* a baby's nappy

> Originally a kind of decorated white silk. The current US meaning was used in British English in the 16th century

diaphragm *noun* **1** a layer of muscle separating the lower part of the body from the chest **2** a thin dividing layer **3** a contraceptive device that fits over the cervix

diarrhoea *noun* frequent emptying of the bowels, with too much liquid in the faeces

diary *noun* (*plural* **diaries**) **1** a record of daily happenings **2** a book detailing these

diaspora *noun* a widespread dispersion or migration of people

diatribe *noun* an angry attack in words

dice or **die** *noun* (*plural* **dice**) a small cube with numbered sides or faces, used in certain games □ *verb* (**dice**) cut (food) into small cubes

dick *noun, taboo slang* **1** the penis **2** (also **dickhead**) an idiot, a fool

dictate *verb* **1** speak the text of (a letter *etc*) for someone else to write down **2** give firm commands □ *noun* an order, a command □ **dictation** *noun*

dictator *noun* an all-powerful ruler □ **dictatorial** *adj* like a dictator; domineering

diction *noun* **1** manner of speaking **2** choice of words

dictionary *noun* (*plural* **dictionaries**) **1** a book giving the words of a language in alphabetical order, together with their meanings **2** any alphabetically ordered reference book

did *see* **do**

die[1] *verb* **1** lose life **2** wither □ **diehard** *noun* an obstinate or determined person

> **die** *verb* » die*s*, dy*ing*, di*ed*

die[2] *noun* **1** a stamp or punch for making raised designs on money *etc* **2** *sing* form of **dice**

dieresis *noun* a mark (¨) placed over a vowel to show it must be pronounced separately from the vowel immediately before it

diesel *noun* an internal combustion engine in which heavy oil is ignited by heat generated by compression

diet[1] *noun* **1** food **2** a course of

recommended foods, *eg* to lose weight □ *verb* eat certain kinds of food only, *esp* to lose weight □ **dietetic** *adj*

diet[2] *noun* **1** a council, an assembly **2** (**Diet**) the national legislature of Japan

differ *verb* **1** (with **from**) be unlike **2** disagree

> **differ** » differ*s*, differ*ing*, differ*ed*

difference *noun* **1** a point in which things differ **2** the amount by which one number is greater than another **3** a disagreement □ **different** *adj* unlike □ **differentiate** *verb* make a difference or distinction between

difficult *adj* **1** not easy, hard to do, understand or deal with **2** hard to please □ **difficulty** *noun* (*plural* **difficulties**) **1** lack of easiness, hardness **2** anything difficult **3** anything which makes something difficult; an obstacle, hindrance *etc* **4** (*plural*) troubles

diffident *adj* shy, not confident □ **diffidence** *noun*

diffuse *verb* spread in all directions □ *adj* widely spread

dig *verb* **1** turn up (earth) with a spade *etc* **2** make (a hole) by this means **3** poke or push (something) into □ *noun* **1** a poke, a thrust **2** an archaeological excavation □ **digger** *noun* a machine for digging

> **dig** *verb* » dig*s*, digg*ing*, dug

digest *verb* **1** break down (food) in the stomach into a form that the body can make use of **2** think over □ *noun* **1** a summing-up **2** a collection of written material □ **digestible** *adj* able to be digested □ **digestion** *noun* the act or power of digesting □ **digestive** *adj* aiding digestion

digit *noun* **1** a finger or toe **2** any of the numbers 0–9 □ **digital** *adj* of a clock *etc*: using the numbers 0–9 □ **digital audio tape** a magnetic audio tape on which sound has been recorded digitally □ **digital recording** the recording of sound by storing electrical pulses representing the audio signal on compact disc, digital audio tape *etc*

digitalis *noun* a family of plants, including the foxglove, from which a medicine used to treat heart disease is obtained

dignified *adj* stately, serious

dignitary *noun* (*plural* **dignitaries**) someone of high rank or office

dignity *noun* **1** manner showing a sense of your own worth or the seriousness of the occasion **2** high rank

digress *verb* wander from the point in speaking or writing □ **digression** *noun*

dike[1] or **dyke** *noun* **1** a wall; an embankment **2** a ditch

dike[2] or **dyke** *noun, informal* a lesbian

dilapidated *adj* falling to pieces, needing repair

dilate *verb* make or grow larger, swell out □ **dilatation** or **dilation** *noun*

dilatory *adj* slow to act, inclined to delay

dildo *noun* (*plural* **dildos**) an artificial penis for sexual stimulation

dilemma *noun* a situation offering a difficult choice between two options

dilettante *noun* someone with a slight but not serious interest in several subjects

diligent *adj* hard-working, industrious ▫ **diligence** *noun* ▫ **diligently** *adv*

dilly-dally *verb* loiter, waste time

> **dilly-dally** » dilly-dalli*es*, dilly-dally*ing*, dilly-dalli*ed*

dilute *verb* lessen the strength of a liquid *etc, esp* by adding water ▫ Also *adj* ▫ **diluted** *adj* ▫ **dilution** *noun*

dim *adj* **1** not bright or clear **2** not understanding clearly, stupid ▫ *verb* make or become dim ▫ **dimly** *adv* ▫ **dimness** *noun*

> **dim** *verb* » dim*s*, dimm*ing*, dimm*ed*

dime *noun* a tenth of a US or Canadian dollar, ten cents

dimension *noun* **1** a measurement of length, width or thickness **2** (**dimensions**) size, measurements

diminish *verb* make or grow less ▫ **diminution** *noun* a lessening ▫ **diminutive** *adj* very small

diminuendo *noun* a fading or falling sound

dimple *noun* a small hollow, *esp* on the cheek or chin

dim sum a Chinese meal made up of many small portions of steamed dumplings *etc*

din *noun* a loud, lasting noise ▫ *verb* put (into) someone's mind by constant repetition

> **din** *verb* » din*s*, dinn*ing*, dinn*ed*

dine *verb* eat dinner

dinghy *noun* (*plural* **dinghies**) a small rowing boat

dingy *adj* dull, faded or dirty-looking ▫ **dinginess** *noun*

dinner *noun* **1** a main evening meal **2** a midday meal, lunch

dinosaur *noun* any of various types of extinct giant reptile

> Coined in the 19th century, from Greek words which translate as 'terrible lizard'

dint *noun* a hollow made by a blow, a dent ▫ **by dint of** by means of

diocese *noun* a bishop's district

Dip *abbrev* diploma

dip *verb* **1** plunge into a liquid quickly **2** lower (*eg* a flag) and raise again **3** slope down **4** look briefly into (a book *etc*) ▫ *noun* **1** a liquid in which anything is dipped **2** a creamy sauce into which biscuits *etc* are dipped **3** a downward slope **4** a hollow **5** a short bathe or swim

> **dip** *verb* » dip*s*, dipp*ing*, dipp*ed*

DipEd *abbrev* Diploma in Education

diphtheria *noun* an infectious throat disease

diphthong *noun* two vowel-sounds pronounced as one syllable (for example *out*)

diploma *noun* a written statement conferring a degree, confirming a pass in an examination *etc*

> From a Greek word meaning a letter folded double

diplomacy *noun* **1** the business of making agreements, treaties *etc* between countries **2** skill in making people agree, tact

diplomat *noun* someone engaged in diplomacy □ **diplomatic** *adj* **1** of diplomacy **2** tactful

dire *adj* dreadful: *in dire need*

direct *adj* **1** straight, not roundabout **2** frank, outspoken □ *verb* **1** point or aim at **2** show the way **3** order, instruct **4** control, organize **5** put a name and address on (a letter) □ **directly** *adv* □ **directness** *noun* □ **direct speech** speech reported in the speaker's exact words □ **direct tax** a tax on income or property

direction *noun* **1** the act of directing **2** the place or point to which someone moves, looks *etc* **3** an order **4** guidance **5** (**directions**) instructions on how to get somewhere

director *noun* **1** a manager of a business *etc* **2** the person who controls the shooting of a film *etc*

directory *noun* (*plural* **directories**) **1** a book of names and addresses *etc* **2** a named group of files on a computer disk

dirge *noun* a lament; a funeral hymn

dirk *noun* a kind of dagger

dirt *noun* any unclean substance, such as mud, dust, dung *etc* □ **dirt track** an earth track for motor-cycle racing

dirty *adj* **1** not clean, soiled **2** obscene, lewd □ *verb* soil with dirt □ **dirtily** *adv* □ **dirtiness** *noun*

> **dirty** » dirti*es*, dirty*ing*, dirti*ed*

disable *verb* take away power or strength from, cripple □ **disability** *noun* (*plural* **disabilities**) something which disables □ **disabled** *adj* □ **disablement** *noun*

disabuse *verb* set right about a wrong belief or opinion: *she soon disabused him of that idea*

disadvantage *noun* an unfavourable circumstance, a drawback □ **disadvantaged** *adj* suffering a disadvantage, *esp* poverty or homelessness □ **disadvantageous** *adj* not advantageous

disaffected *adj* discontented, rebellious □ **disaffection** *noun*

disagree *verb* **1** (often with **with**) hold different opinions (from) **2** quarrel **3** of food: make to feel ill □ **disagreeable** *adj* unpleasant □ **disagreement** *noun*

disallow *verb* not to allow

disappear *verb* go out of sight, vanish □ **disappearance** *noun*

disappoint *verb* **1** fail to come up to the hopes or expectations (of) **2** fail to fulfil □ **disappointed** *adj* □ **disappointment** *noun*

disapprove *verb* have an unfavourable opinion (of) □ **disapproval** *noun*

disarm *verb* **1** take (a weapon) away from **2** get rid of war weapons **3** make less angry, charm □ **disarmament** *noun* the removal or disabling of war weapons □ **disarming** *adj* gaining friendliness, charming: *disarming smile*

disarrange *verb* throw out of order, make untidy □ **disarrangement** *noun*

disarray *noun* disorder

disaster *noun* an extremely unfortunate happening, often causing great damage or loss □ **disastrous** *adj* □ **disastrously** *adv*

disband *verb* break up, separate: *the gang disbanded* □ **disbandment** *noun*

disbelieve *verb* not to believe □ **disbelief** *noun* □ **disbeliever** *noun*

disburse *verb* pay out □ **disbursement** *noun*

disc *noun* **1** a flat, round shape **2** a pad of cartilage between vertebrae **3** a gramophone record □ **disc brakes** vehicle brakes which use pads that are hydraulically forced against discs on the wheels □ **disc jockey** someone who introduces and plays recorded music on radio *etc*

discard *verb* throw away as useless

discern *verb* see, realize □ **discernible** *adj* noticeable: *discernible difference* □ **discerning** *adj* quick at noticing; discriminating: *a discerning eye* □ **discernment** *noun*

discharge *verb* **1** unload (cargo) **2** set free **3** dismiss **4** fire (a gun) **5** perform (duties) **6** pay (a debt) **7** give off (*eg* smoke) **8** let out (pus) □ *noun* **1** a discharging **2** dismissal **3** pus *etc* discharged from the body **4** performance (of duties) **5** payment

disciple *noun* **1** someone who believes in another's teaching **2** *hist* one of the followers of Christ

discipline *noun* **1** training in an orderly way of life **2** order kept by means of control **3** punishment **4** a subject of study or training □ *verb* **1** bring to order **2** punish □ **disciplinarian** *noun* someone who insists on strict discipline □ **disciplinary** *adj*

disclaim *verb* refuse to have anything to do with, deny □ **disclaimer** *noun* a denial

disclose *verb* uncover, reveal, make known □ **disclosure** *noun* **1** the act of disclosing **2** something disclosed

disco *noun* (*plural* **discos**) an event or place where recorded music is played for dancing

discography *noun* a history or catalogue of musical recordings □ **discographer** *noun*

discolour or *US* **discolor** *verb* spoil the colour of; stain □ **discoloration** *noun*

discombobulate *verb, informal* confuse greatly

discomfit *verb* **1** disconcert **2** thwart, defeat □ **discomfiture** *noun*

discomfort *noun* lack of comfort, uneasiness

discommode *verb* inconvenience

disconcert *verb* upset, confuse

disconnect *verb* separate, break the connection between ▯ **disconnected** *adj* **1** separated, no longer connected **2** of thoughts *etc*: not following logically, rambling

disconsolate *adj* sad, disappointed

discontent *noun* dissatisfaction ▯ **discontented** *adj* dissatisfied, cross ▯ **discontentment** *noun*

discontinue *verb* stop, cease to continue

discord *noun* **1** disagreement, quarrelling **2** *music* a jarring of notes ▯ **discordant** *adj*

discotheque *noun* a disco

discount *noun* a small sum taken off the price of something: *10% discount* ▯ *verb* **1** leave out, not consider: *completely discounted my ideas* **2** allow for exaggeration in (*eg* a story)

discourage *verb* **1** take away the confidence, hope *etc* of **2** try to prevent by showing dislike or disapproval: *discouraged his advances* ▯ **discouragement** *noun* ▯ **discouraging** *adj* giving little hope or encouragement

discourse *noun* **1** a speech, a lecture **2** an essay **3** a conversation ▯ *verb* talk, *esp* at some length

discourteous *adj* not polite, rude ▯ **discourteously** *adv* ▯ **discourtesy** *noun*

discover *verb* **1** find out **2** find by chance, *esp* for the first time ▯ **discoverer** *noun* ▯ **discovery** *noun* (*plural* **discoveries**) **1** the act of finding or finding out **2** something discovered

discredit *verb* **1** refuse to believe **2** cause to doubt **3** disgrace ▯ *noun* **1** disgrace **2** disbelief ▯ **discreditable** *adj* disgraceful

discreet *adj* wisely cautious, tactful ▯ **discreetly** *adv* ▯ **discretion** *noun*

> ⚠Do not confuse with: **discrete**

discrepancy *noun* (*plural* **discrepancies**) a difference or disagreement between two things: *some discrepancy in the figures*

discrete *adj* separate, distinct

> ⚠Do not confuse with: **discreet**

discretion *see* **discreet**

discriminate *verb* **1** make differences (between), distinguish **2** treat (people) differently because of their gender, race *etc* ▯ **discriminating** *adj* showing good judgement ▯ **discrimination** *noun* **1** ability to discriminate **2** adverse treatment on grounds of gender, race *etc*

discus *noun* a heavy disc thrown in an athletic competition

discuss *verb* talk about ▯ **discussion** *noun*

disdain *verb* **1** look down on, scorn **2** be too proud to do ▯ *noun* scorn ▯ **disdainful** *adj*

disease *noun* illness ▯ **diseased** *adj*

disembark *verb* put or go ashore ▯ **disembarkation** *noun*

disembodied *adj* of a soul *etc*: separated from the body

disengage *verb* separate, free ◇ **disengaged** *adj*

disentangle *verb* free from entanglement, unravel

disfavour or *US* **disfavor** *noun* dislike, disapproval

disfigure *verb* spoil the beauty or appearance of ◇ **disfigurement** *noun*

disfranchise *verb* take away the right to vote from

disgorge *verb* **1** throw out **2** give up (something previously taken)

disgrace *noun* the state of being out of favour; shame ◇ *verb* bring shame on ◇ **disgraceful** *adj* shameful; very bad ◇ **disgracefully** *adv*

disgruntled *adj* sulky, discontented

disguise *verb* **1** change the appearance of **2** hide (feelings *etc*) ◇ *noun* **1** a disguised state **2** a costume *etc* which disguises

disgust *noun* **1** strong dislike, loathing **2** indignation ◇ *verb* **1** cause loathing, revolt **2** make indignant ◇ **disgusting** *adj* sickening; causing disgust

dish *noun* (*plural* **dishes**) **1** a plate or bowl for food **2** food prepared for eating ◇ *verb* **1** serve (food) **2** deal (out), distribute ◇ *noun* a saucer-shaped aerial for receiving information from a satellite

dishearten *verb* take away courage or hope from ◇ **disheartened** *adj* ◇ **disheartening** *adj*

dishevelled *adj* untidy, with hair *etc* disordered

dishonest *adj* not honest, deceitful ◇ **dishonesty** *noun*

dishonour disgrace, shame ◇ *verb* cause shame to ◇ **dishonourable** *adj* disgraceful

disillusion *verb* take away a false belief from ◇ **disillusioned** *adj* ◇ **disillusionment** *noun*

disinclined *adj* unwilling

disinfect *verb* destroy disease-causing germs in ◇ **disinfectant** *noun* a substance that kills germs

disinherit *verb* take away the rights of an heir ◇ **disinheritance** *noun* ◇ **disinherited** *adj*

disintegrate *verb* fall into pieces; break down ◇ **disintegration** *noun*

disinterested *adj* unbiased, not influenced by personal feelings

> ⚠Do not confuse with: **uninterested**

disjointed *adj* of speech *etc*: not well connected together

disk *noun* **1** *US spelling* of **disc 2** *comput* a flat round magnetic plate used for storing data ◇ **disk drive** *comput* part of a computer that records data onto and retrieves data from disks

dislike *verb* not like, disapprove of ◇ *noun* disapproval

dislocate *verb* **1** put (a bone) out of joint **2** upset, disorder ◇ **dislocation** *noun*

dislodge *verb* **1** drive from a place of rest, hiding or defence **2** knock out of place accidentally

disloyal *adj* not loyal, unfaithful □ **disloyalty** *noun*

dismal *adj* gloomy; sorrowful, sad

> Based on a Latin phrase *dies mali* 'evil days', referring to two days each month which were believed to be unusually unlucky

dismantle *verb* **1** remove fittings, furniture *etc* from **2** take to pieces

dismay *verb* make to feel hopeless, upset □ *noun*

dismember *verb* **1** tear to pieces **2** cut the limbs from

dismiss *verb* **1** send or put away **2** remove (someone) from a job, sack **3** close (a law case) □ **dismissal** *noun*

dismount *verb* come down off a horse, bicycle *etc*

disobey *verb* fail or refuse to do what is commanded □ **disobedience** *noun* □ **disobedient** *adj* refusing or failing to obey

disobliging *adj* not willing to carry out the wishes of others

disorder *noun* **1** lack of order, confusion **2** a disease □ *verb* throw out of order □ **disorderly** *adj* **1** out of order **2** behaving in a lawless (noisy) manner □ **disorderliness** *noun*

disown *verb* refuse or cease to recognize as your own

disparage *verb* speak of as being of little worth or importance, belittle □ **disparagement** *noun* □ **disparaging** *adj*

disparity *noun* (*plural* **disparities**) great difference, inequality

dispassionate *adj* **1** favouring no one, unbiased **2** calm, cool □ **dispassionately** *adv*

dispatch or **despatch** *verb* **1** send off (a letter *etc*) **2** kill, finish off **3** do or deal with quickly □ *noun* (*plural* **dispatches** or **despatches)** **1** the act of sending off **2** a report to a newspaper **3** speed in doing something **4** killing **5** (**dispatches**) official papers (*esp* military or diplomatic) □ **dispatch box 1** a case for official papers **2** the box beside which members of parliament stand to make speeches in the House of Commons □ **dispatch rider** a courier who delivers military dispatches by motor-cycle

dispel *verb* drive away, make disappear

> **dispel** » dispel*s*, dispell*ing*, dispell*ed*

dispense *verb* **1** give out **2** prepare (medicines) for giving out □ **dispensable** *adj* able to be done without □ **dispensary** *noun* (*plural* **dispensaries**) a place where medicines are given out □ **dispensation** *noun* special leave to break a rule *etc* □ **dispenser** *noun* □ **dispense with** do without

disperse *verb* **1** scatter; spread **2** (cause to) vanish □ **dispersal** or **dispersion** *noun* a scattering

dispirited *adj* sad, discouraged

displace *verb* **1** put out of place **2** disorder, disarrange **3** put (someone) out of office □ **displaced person** someone forced to leave his or her own country because of war, political reasons *etc* □ **displacement** *noun*

display *verb* set out for show □ *noun* a show, exhibition

displease *verb* not to please; to offend, annoy □ **displeasure** *noun* annoyance, disapproval

dispose *verb* **1** arrange, settle **2** get rid (of): *they disposed of the body* **3** make inclined □ **disposable** *adj* intended to be thrown away □ **disposal** *noun* □ **disposed** *adj* inclined, willing □ **at your disposal** available for your use

disposition *noun* **1** arrangement **2** nature, personality **3** *law* the handing over of property *etc* to another

dispossess *verb* take away from, deprive (of)

disproportionate *adj* too big or too little, not in proportion

disprove *verb* prove to be false

dispute *verb* argue about □ *noun* an argument, quarrel □ **disputable** *adj* not certain, able to be argued about □ **disputation** *noun* an argument

disqualify *verb* **1** put out of a competition for breaking rules **2** take away a qualification or right □ **disqualification** *noun*

disqualify » disqualifi*es*, disqualify*ing*, disqualifi*ed*

disquiet *noun* uneasiness, anxiety

disregard *verb* pay no attention to, ignore □ *noun* neglect

disrepair *noun* a state of bad repair

disrepute *noun* bad reputation □ **disreputable** *adj* having a bad reputation, not respectable

disrespect *noun* rudeness, lack of politeness □ **disrespectful** *adj*

disrobe *verb, formal* undress

disrupt *verb* **1** break up **2** throw (a meeting *etc*) into disorder □ **disruption** *noun* □ **disruptive** *adj* causing disorder

dissatisfy *verb* bring no satisfaction, displease □ **dissatisfaction** *noun* □ **dissatisfied** *adj*

dissatisfy » dissatisfi*es*, dissatisfy*ing*, dissatisfi*ed*

dissect *verb* **1** cut into parts for examination **2** study and criticize □ **dissection** *noun*

dissemble *verb* hide, disguise (intentions *etc*) □ **dissembler** *noun*

disseminate *verb* scatter, spread □ **dissemination** *noun*

dissension *noun* disagreement, quarrelling

dissent *verb* **1** have a different opinion **2** refuse to agree □ *noun* disagreement □ **dissenter** *noun* a member of a church that has broken away from the officially established church

dissertation *noun* a long piece of writing or talk on a particular (often academic) subject

disservice *noun* harm, a bad turn

dissident *noun* someone who disagrees, *esp* with a political regime

dissimilar *adj* not the same □ **dissimilarity** *noun* (*plural* **dissimilarities**)

dissipate *verb* **1** (cause to) disappear **2** waste, squander ▯ **dissipated** *adj* worn out by indulging in pleasures; dissolute ▯ **dissipation** *noun*

dissociate *verb* separate ▯ **dissociate yourself from** refuse to be associated with

dissolute *adj* having loose morals; debauched

dissolve *verb* **1** melt **2** break up **3** put an end to ▯ **dissoluble** *adj* able to be dissolved ▯ **dissolution** *noun*

dissonance *noun* **1** discord, *esp* used deliberately for musical effect **2** disagreement ▯ **dissonant** *adj*

dissuade *verb* persuade not to do something ▯ **dissuasion** *noun*

distaff *noun* a stick used to hold flax or wool being spun ▯ **the distaff side** the female side or line of descent (*contrasted with*: **spear side**)

distance *noun* **1** the space between things **2** a far-off place or point: *in the distance* **3** coldness of manner

distant *adj* **1** far off or far apart in place or time: *distant era/ distant land* **2** not close: *distant cousin* **3** cold in manner ▯ **distantly** *adv*

distaste *noun* dislike ▯ **distasteful** *adj* disagreeable, unpleasant

distemper *noun* **1** a kind of paint used chiefly for walls **2** a viral disease of dogs, foxes *etc* ▯ *verb* paint with distemper

distend *verb* swell; stretch outwards ▯ **distension** *noun*

distil *verb* **1** purify (liquid) by heating to a vapour and cooling **2** extract the spirit or essence from **3** (cause to) fall in drops ▯ **distillation** *noun* ▯ **distiller** *noun* ▯ **distillery** *noun* (*plural* **distilleries**) a place where whisky, brandy *etc* is distilled

> **distil** » distil*s*, distill*ing*, distill*ed*

distinct *adj* **1** clear; easily seen or noticed: *a distinct improvement* **2** different: *the two languages are quite distinct* ▯ **distinction** *noun* **1** a difference **2** outstanding worth or merit

> ⚠Do not confuse: **distinct** and **distinctive**

distinctive *adj* different, special ▯ **distinctively** *adv* ▯ **distinctiveness** *noun*

distinguish *verb* **1** recognize a difference (between) **2** mark off as different **3** recognize **4** give distinction to ▯ **distinguished** *adj* **1** outstanding, famous **2** dignified

distort *verb* **1** twist out of shape **2** turn or twist (a statement *etc*) from its true meaning **3** make (a sound) unclear and harsh ▯ **distortion** *noun*

distract *verb* **1** divert (the attention) **2** trouble, confuse **3** make mad ▯ **distracted** *adj* mad with pain, grief *etc* ▯ **distraction** *noun* **1** something which diverts your attention **2** anxiety, confusion **3** amusement **4** madness

distraught *adj* extremely agitated or anxious

distress *noun* **1** pain, trouble, sorrow **2** a cause of suffering ▯ *verb* cause pain or sorrow to ▯ **distressed** *adj* ▯ **distressing** *adj*

distribute *verb* **1** divide among several **2** spread out widely □ **distribution** *noun*

district *noun* a region of a country or town

distrust *noun* lack of trust, suspicion □ *verb* have no trust in □ **distrustful** *adj*

disturb *verb* **1** confuse, worry, upset **2** interrupt □ **disturbance** *noun* □ **disturbing** *adj*

disuse *noun* the state of being no longer used □ **disused** *adj* no longer used

ditch *noun* (*plural* **ditches**) a long narrow hollow trench dug in the ground, *esp* to carry water

dither *verb* **1** hesitate, be undecided **2** act in a nervous, uncertain manner □ *noun* a state of indecision

dithyrambic *adj* rapturous, passionate

ditsy *adj, US informal* scatterbrained, flighty

ditto *noun* (often written as **do**) the same as already written or said □ **ditto marks** a character (") written below a word in a text, meaning it is to be understood as repeated

ditty *noun* (*plural* **ditties**) a simple, short song

diuretic *adj* increasing the flow of urine □ *noun* a medicine with this effect

diva *noun* a leading female opera singer, a prima donna

divan *noun* **1** a long, low couch without a back **2** a bed without a headboard

dive *verb* **1** plunge headfirst into water **2** swoop through the air **3** go down steeply and quickly □ *noun* an act of diving □ **dive-bomb** *verb* bomb from an aircraft in a steep downward dive □ **dive-bomber** *noun* □ **diver** *noun* **1** someone who works under water using special breathing equipment **2** a type of diving bird

> **dive** *verb* » dive*s*, div*ing*, div*ed* or *US* dove

diverge *verb* separate and go in different directions; to differ □ **divergence** *noun* □ **divergent** *adj*

diverse *adj* different, various

diversify *verb* to make or become different or varied

> **diversify** » diversifi*es*, diversify*ing*, diversifi*ed*

diversion *noun* **1** turning aside **2** an alteration to a traffic route **3** an amusement

diversity *noun* difference; variety

divertimento *noun* a light piece of chamber music

divert *verb* **1** turn aside, change the direction of **2** entertain, amuse □ **diverting** *adj* entertaining, amusing

divest *verb* strip or deprive of: *divested him of his authority*

divide *verb* **1** separate into parts **2** share (among) **3** (cause to) go into separate groups **4** *maths* find out how many times one number contains another □ **dividers** *noun plural* measuring compasses

dividend *noun* **1** an amount to be divided (*compare with*: **divisor**) **2** a share of profits from a business

divine *adj* **1** of a god; holy **2** *informal* splendid, wonderful □ *verb* **1** guess **2** foretell, predict □ **divination** *noun* the art of foretelling □ **diviner** *noun* someone who claims special powers in finding hidden water or metals □ **divining rod** a forked stick used by diviners to guide them to hidden water *etc*

divinity *noun* (*plural* **divinities**) **1** a god **2** the nature of a god **3** religious studies

division *noun* **1** the act of dividing **2** a barrier, a separator **3** a section, *esp* of an army **4** separation **5** disagreement □ **divisible** *adj* able to be divided □ **divisibility** *noun* □ **divisional** *adj* of a division □ **divisor** *noun* the number by which another number (the **dividend**) is divided

divorce *noun* **1** the legal ending of a marriage **2** a complete separation □ *verb* **1** end a marriage with **2** separate (from)

divot *noun* a piece of turf

divulge *verb* let out, make known (a secret *etc*)

Diwali or **Dewali** *noun* the Hindu and Sikh festival of lamps, celebrated in October or November

Dixie *noun*, *US informal* the Southern states of the USA □ **dixieland** *noun* an early style of jazz music from New Orleans

DIY *abbrev* do-it-yourself

dizzy *adj* **1** giddy, confused **2** causing giddiness: *from a dizzy height* □ **dizzily** *adv* □ **dizziness** *noun*

DJ *abbrev* disc jockey

djellabah *noun* a Middle-Eastern hooded cloak with wide sleeves

djinn /jeen/ or /jin/ *noun plural* (*sing* **djinni**) a group of spirits in Islamic folklore

dl *abbrev* decilitre(s)

DLitt *abbrev* Doctor of Letters; Doctor of Literature

DMus *abbrev* Doctor of Music

DNA *abbrev* deoxyribonucleic acid, a compound carrying genetic instructions for passing on hereditary characteristics

DNB *abbrev* Dictionary of National Biography

do *verb* **1** carry out, perform (a job *etc*) **2** perform an action on, *eg* clean (dishes), arrange (hair) *etc* **3** *slang* swindle **4** act: *do as you please* **5** get on: *I hear she's doing very well/ how are you doing?* **6** be enough: *a pound will do* **7** used to avoid repeating a verb: *I seldom see him now, and when I do, he ignores me* **8** used with a more important verb (1) in questions: *do you see what I mean?* (2) in sentences with **not**: *I don't know*; or (3) for emphasis: *I do hope she'll be there* □ *noun* (*plural* **dos**) *informal* a social event, a party □ **doer** *noun* □ **do-gooder** *noun* someone who tries to help others in a self-righteous way □ **doings** *noun plural* actions □ **done** *adj* finished □ **doneness** *noun* □ **do away with** put an end to, destroy □ **do down** *informal* get the better of □ **do in** *informal* **1** exhaust, wear out **2** murder □ **done to death** too often repeated □ **do or die** a desparate final attempt at something whatever the consequences □ **do out of**

swindle out of □ **do someone proud** *see* **proud** □ **do up 1** fasten **2** renovate

> **do** *verb* » do*es*, do*ing*, did, done

do *abbrev* ditto

docent /*dohs*ənt/ *noun US* a teacher, a lecturer

docile *adj* tame, easy to manage □ **docilely** *adv* □ **docility** *noun*

dock *noun* **1** (often **docks**) a deepened part of a harbour where ships go for loading, repair *etc* **2** the box in a law court where the accused person stands **3** a weed with large leaves □ *verb* **1** put in or enter a dock **2** clip or cut short **3** of a spacecraft: join onto another craft in space □ **docker** *noun* someone who works in the docks □ **dockyard** *noun* a naval harbour with docks, stores *etc*

docket *noun* a label listing the contents of something

doctor *noun* **1** someone trained in and licensed to practise medicine **2** someone with the highest university degree in any subject □ *verb* **1** treat as a patient **2** tamper with, alter

doctrinaire *adj* dogmatic, inflexible or obstinate in beliefs

doctrine *noun* a belief that is taught □ **doctrinal** *adj*

document *noun* a written statement giving proof, information *etc*

documentary *noun* (*plural* **documentaries**) a film giving information about real people or events □ *adj* **1** of or in documents: *documentary evidence* **2** of a documentary

dodder *verb* shake, tremble, *esp* as a result of old age

doddery *adj* shaky or slow because of old age

doddle *noun, informal* an easy task

dodge *verb* avoid by a sudden or clever movement □ *noun* a trick

dodo *noun* (*plural* **dodoes** or **dodos**) a type of large extinct bird

doe *noun* the female of certain animals, *eg* a deer, rabbit or hare

doer and **does** *see* **do**

doff *noun* take off (a hat) in greeting

dog *noun* **1** a four-footed animal often kept as a pet **2** one of the dog family which includes wolves, foxes *etc* □ *adj* of an animal: male □ *verb* **1** follow and watch constantly **2** hamper, plague: *dogged by ill health* □ **dog-collar** *noun* **1** a collar for dogs **2** a clerical collar □ **dog-eared** *adj* of a page: turned down at the corner □ **dog-eat-dog** *adj* viciously competitive □ **dogfight** *noun* a fight between aeroplanes at close quarters □ **dogfish** *noun* a kind of small shark □ **dogleg** *noun* a sharp bend □ **dog-rose** *noun* the wild rose □ **dogsbody** *noun, informal* someone who is given unpleasant or dreary tasks to do □ **the Dogstar** *noun* Sirius □ **dog-tag** *noun* **1** a dog's identity disc **2** an identity disc worn by soldiers *etc* □ **dog-tired** *adj* completely worn out □ **dog-watch** *noun* the period of lookout from 4 to 6 pm or 6 to

8 pm on a ship ▯ **dog in the manger** someone who stands in the way of a plan or proposal ▯ **dog's breakfast** or **dog's dinner** a complete mess ▯ **dog's life** a life of misery ▯ **go to the dogs** be ruined

> **dog** *verb* » dog*s*, dogg*ing*, dogg*ed*

dogged /*dog*id/ *adj* determined, stubborn: *dogged refusal* ▯ **doggedly** *adv* ▯ **doggedness** *noun*

doggerel *noun* badly-written poetry

doggy *noun, informal* of or for dogs ▯ **doggy-bag** *noun* a bag used to take away left-over food from a restaurant meal ▯ **doggy-paddle** *noun* a simple style of swimming

dogma *noun* an opinion, *esp* religious, accepted or fixed by an authority ▯ **dogmatic** *adj* **1** of dogma **2** stubbornly forcing your opinions on others ▯ **dogmatically** *adv*

doily or **doyley** *noun* (*plural* **doilies** or **doyleys**) a perforated paper napkin put underneath cakes *etc*

> Originally a light summer fabric, named after Doily's drapery shop in 17th-century London

Dolby *noun, trademark* a system for reducing background noise, used in recording music or soundtracks

doldrums *noun plural* low spirits: *in the doldrums*

> The *doldrums* take their name from an area of the ocean about the equator famous for calms and variable winds

dole *verb* deal (out) in small amounts ▯ *noun, informal* unemployment benefit ▯

doleful *adj* sad, unhappy ▯ **dolefully** *adv* ▯ **dolefulness** *noun*

doll *noun* a toy in the shape of a small human being

dollar *noun* the main unit of currency in several countries, *eg* the USA, Canada, Australia and New Zealand

dolma *noun* (*plural* **dolmades**) a stuffed vine leaf or cabbage leaf

dolmen *noun* an ancient tomb in the shape of a stone table

dolphin *noun* a type of sea animal like a porpoise

dolt *noun* a stupid person ▯ **doltish** *adj*

domain *noun* **1** a kingdom **2** a country estate **3** an area of interest or knowledge

dome *noun* **1** the shape of a half sphere or ball **2** the roof of a building *etc* in this shape ▯ **domed** *adj*

domestic *adj* **1** of the home or house **2** of an animal: tame, domesticated **3** not foreign, of your own country: *domestic products* ▯ *noun* a live-in maid *etc* ▯ **domesticated** *adj* **1** of an animal: tame, used for farming *etc* **2** fond of doing housework, cooking *etc* ▯ **domestic help** (someone paid to give) assistance with housework ▯ **domesticity** *noun* home life ▯ **domestic science**

old cookery, needlework *etc*, taught as a subject

domicile *noun* the country *etc* in which someone lives permanently

dominant *adj* ruling; most powerful or important ◊ **dominance** *noun*

dominate *verb* **1** have command or influence over **2** be most strong, or most noticeable: *the castle dominates the skyline* **3** tower above, overlook ◊ **domination** *noun*

domineering *adj* overbearing, like a tyrant

dominion *noun* **1** rule, authority **2** an area with one ruler or government

domino *noun* (*plural* **dominoes**) **1** a piece used in the game of dominoes **2** *hist* a long silk cloak worn at masked balls ◊ **dominoes** *noun sing* a game played on a table with pieces marked with dots, each side of which must match a piece placed next to it

don *noun* a college or university lecturer ◊ *verb* put on (a coat *etc*)

> **don** *verb* » don*s*, donn*ing*, donn*ed*

donation *noun* a gift of money or goods ◊ **donate** *verb* present a gift

done *past participle* of **do**

donkey *noun* (*plural* **donkeys**) (*also called* **ass**) a type of animal with long ears, related to the horse

donor *noun* **1** a giver of a gift **2** someone who agrees to let their body organs be used for transplant operations

don't *short for* do not

doom *noun* **1** judgement; fate **2** ruin ◊ **doomed** *adj* **1** destined, condemned **2** bound to fail or be destroyed

door *noun* **1** a hinged barrier which closes the entrance to a room or building **2** the entrance itself ◊ **doorstep** *noun* the step in front of the door of a house ◊ **doorway** *noun* the space filled by a door, the entrance

dope *noun, informal* **1** drugs; a drug **2** an idiot ◊ *verb* drug

doric *noun* a dialect, *esp* of Scots

dormant *adj* sleeping, inactive: *a dormant volcano*

dormer *noun* or **dormer window** a small window jutting out from a sloping roof

dormitory *noun* (*plural* **dormitories**) a room with beds for several people

dormouse *noun* (*plural* **dormice**) a small animal which hibernates

dorsal *adj* of the back: *dorsal fin*

DOS /dos/ *abbrev, comput* disk operating system

dose *noun* **1** a quantity of medicine to be taken at one time **2** a bout of something unpleasant: *dose of flu* ◊ *verb* give medicine to

doss *verb, informal* lie down to sleep somewhere temporary ◊ **doss-house** *noun, informal* a cheap lodging-house

dossier /*dosieh*/ *noun* a set of papers containing information about someone or subject

dot *noun* a small, round mark ◊ *verb* **1** mark with a dot **2** scatter ◊

on the dot exactly on time

> **dot** *verb* » dot*s*, dott*ing*, dott*ed*

dotage *noun* the foolishness and childishness of old age

dote *verb*: **dote on** be foolishly fond of

double *verb* **1** multiply by two **2** fold ◇ *noun* twice as much: *he ate double the amount* **2** someone so like another as to be mistaken for them ◇ *adj* **1** containing twice as much: *a double dose* **2** made up of two of the same sort **3** folded over **4** deceitful ◇ **doubly** *adv* ◇ **double agent** a spy paid by each of two rival countries, but loyal to only one of them ◇ **double bass** a type of large stringed musical instrument ◇ **double-breasted** *adj* of a coat: with one half of the front overlapping the other ◇ **double-cross** *verb* cheat ◇ **double-dealer** *noun* a deceitful, cheating person ◇ **double-dealing** *noun* ◇ **double-decker** *noun* a bus with two floors ◇ **double-Dutch** *noun* incomprehensible talk, gibberish ◇ **double glazing** two sheets of glass in a window to keep in the heat or keep out noise ◇ **double-take** *noun* a second look at something surprising or confusing ◇ **double-think** *noun* the holding of two contradictory opinions or ideas ◇ **double-time** *noun* payment for overtime work *etc* at twice the usual rate ◇ **at the double** very quickly ◇ **double back** turn sharply and go back the way you have come ◇ **double up 1** writhe in pain **2** share accommodation (with)

double entendre a word or phrase with two meanings, one of them usually sexual

doublet *noun*, *hist* a man's close-fitting jacket

doubloon *noun*, *hist* an old Spanish gold coin

doubt *verb* **1** be unsure or undecided about **2** think unlikely: *I doubt that we'll be able to go* ◇ *noun* a lack of certainty or trust; suspicion ◇ **doubtful** *adj* ◇ **doubtless** *adv* ◇ **no doubt** probably

douche /doosh/ *noun* an instrument which injects water into the body for cleansing

dough *noun* **1** a mass of flour, moistened and kneaded **2** *informal* money

doughnut *noun* a ring-shaped cake fried in fat

doughty /*dow*ti/ *adj* strong; brave

dour /door/ *adj* dull, humourless

dove[1] *noun* a pigeon ◇ **dovecote** *noun* a pigeon-house

dove[2] *US past form* of **dive**

dovetail *verb* fit one thing exactly into another

dowdy *adj* not smart, badly dressed

down[1] *adv* **1** towards or in a lower position: *fell down/ sitting down* **2** to a smaller size: *grind down* **3** to a later generation: *handed down from mother to daughter* **4** on the spot, in cash: *£10 down* ◇ *prep* **1** towards or in the lower part of: *rolled back down the hill* **2** along: *strolling down the road* ◇ *adj* going downwards: *the down escalator* ◇ **down-at-heel** *adj* worn down, shabby ◇ **downcast**

adj sad ▯ **downfall** *noun* ruin, defeat ▯ **downhearted** *adj* discouraged ▯ **downpour** *noun* a heavy fall of rain ▯ **downstairs** *adj* on a lower floor of a building ▯ *adv* to a lower floor ▯ **downstream** *adv* further down a river, in the direction of its flow ▯ **downtrodden** *adj* kept in a lowly, inferior position ▯ **downwards** *adv* moving or leading down ▯ **go down with** or **be down with** become or be ill with

down[2] *noun* light, soft feathers ▯ **Downie** *noun*, *trademark* a duvet ▯ **downy** *adj* soft, feathery

downs *noun plural* low, grassy hills

dowry *noun* (*plural* **dowries**) money and property brought by a woman to her husband on their marriage

doyley *noun another spelling* of **doily**

doz *abbrev* dozen

doze *verb* sleep lightly ▯ *noun* a light, short sleep

dozen *adj* twelve

DPhil *abbrev* Doctor of Philosophy

DPU *abbrev* data processing unit

Dr *abbrev* doctor

drab *adj* dull, monotonous ▯ **drabness** *noun*

draft *noun* **1** a rough outline, a sketch **2** a group of people selected for a special purpose **3** *US* conscription into the army **4** an order for payment of money **5** *US* spelling of **draught** ▯ *verb* **1** make a rough plan **2** select for a purpose **3** *US* conscript

⚠Do not confuse with: **draught**

draftsman, **draftswoman** *US spellings* of **draughtsman, draughtswoman**

drag *verb* **1** pull roughly **2** move slowly and heavily **3** trail along the ground **4** search (a river-bed *etc*) with a net or hook ▯ *noun*, *informal* **1** a dreary task **2** a tedious person **3** clothes for one sex worn by the other ▯ **drag your feet** or **drag your heels** be slow to do something

dragon *noun* **1** an imaginary fire-breathing, winged reptile **2** a fierce, intimidating person

dragonfly *noun* a winged insect with a long body and double wings

dragoon *noun* a heavily-armed horse soldier ▯ *verb* force or bully (into)

drain *verb* **1** clear (land) of water by trenches or pipes **2** drink the contents of (a glass *etc*) **3** use up completely ▯ *noun* a channel or pipe used to carry off water *etc* ▯ **drainage** *noun* the drawing-off of water by rivers, pipes *etc* ▯ **drained** *adj* **1** emptied of liquid **2** sapped of strength

drake *noun* a male duck

drama 1 a play for acting in the theatre **2** exciting or tense action ▯ **dramatist** *noun* a playwright

dramatic *adj* **1** relating to plays **2** exciting, thrilling **3** unexpected, sudden ▯ **dramatically** *adv*

dramatis personae the characters in a play

dramatize *verb* **1** turn into a play

for the theatre **2** make vivid or sensational □ **dramatization** *noun*

drank *verb past form* of **drink**

drape *verb* arrange (cloth) to hang gracefully □ *noun* (**drapes**) *US* curtains □ **draper** *noun* a dealer in cloth □ **drapery** *noun* **1** cloth goods **2** a draper's shop

drastic *adj* severe, extreme □ **drastically** *adv*

draught /draft/ *noun* **1** the act of drawing or pulling **2** something drawn out **3** a drink taken all at once **4** a current of air **5** (**draughts**) a game for two, played by moving pieces on a squared board □ **draughty** *adj* full of air currents, chilly

⚠Do not confuse with: **draft**

draughtsman,draughtswoman *noun* **1** someone employed to draw plans **2** someone skilled in drawing

draw *verb* **1** make a picture with pencil, crayons *etc* **2** pull after or along **3** attract: *drew a large crowd* **4** obtain money from a fund: *drawing a pension* **5** require (a depth) for floating: *this ship draws 20 feet* **6** approach, come: *night is drawing near* **7** score equal points in a game □ *noun* **1** an equal score **2** a lottery □ **draw a blank** get no result □ **draw a conclusion** form an opinion from evidence heard □ **drawn and quartered** *hist* cut in pieces after being hanged □ **draw on 1** approach **2** use as a resource: *drawing on experience* □ **draw out 1** lengthen **2** persuade (someone) to talk and be at ease □ **draw the line at** refuse to allow or accept □ **draw up 1** come to a stop **2** move closer **3** plan, write out (a contract *etc*)

draw *verb* » draw*s*, draw*ing*, drew, drawn

drawback *noun* a disadvantage

drawbridge *noun* a bridge at the entrance to a castle which can be drawn up or let down

drawer *noun* **1** someone who draws **2** a sliding box fitting into a chest, table *etc*

drawing *noun* a picture made by pencil, crayon *etc* □ **drawing-pin** *noun* a pin with a large flat head for fastening paper on a board *etc* □ **drawing-room** *noun* a sitting-room

drawl *verb* speak in a slow, lazy manner □ *noun* a drawling voice

drawn *past participle* of **draw**

dread *noun* great fear □ *adj* terrifying □ *verb* be greatly afraid of □ **dreaded** *adj*

dreadful *adj* **1** terrible **2** *informal* very bad □ **dreadfully** *adv*

dreadlock *noun* a thick, twisted strand of hair

dreadnought *noun, hist* a kind of battleship

dream *noun* **1** a series of images and sounds in the mind during sleep **2** something imagined, not real **3** something very beautiful **4** a hope, an ambition: *her dream was to go to Mexico* □ *verb* have a dream □ **dream ticket** an ideal combination of candidates for election □ **dream up** invent

dream *verb* » dream*s*, dream*ing*, dream*t* or dream*ed*

dreamy *adj* **1** sleepy, half-awake **2** vague, dim **3** *informal* beautiful ▫ **dreamily** *adv*

dreary *adj* gloomy, cheerless ▫ **drearily** *adv* ▫ **dreariness** *noun*

dredge *verb* **1** drag a net or bucket along a river- or sea-bed to bring up fish, mud *etc* **2** sprinkle with (sugar or flour) ▫ *noun* an instrument for dredging a river *etc* ▫ **dredger** *noun* **1** a ship which digs a channel by lifting mud from the bottom **2** a perforated jar for sprinkling sugar or flour

dregs *noun plural* **1** sediment on the bottom of a liquid: *dregs of wine* **2** last remnants **3** a worthless or useless part

dreich /dreexh/ *adj, Scot* dreary, miserable

drench *verb* soak

dress *verb* **1** put on clothes or a covering **2** prepare (food *etc*) for use **3** arrange (hair) **4** treat and bandage (wounds) ▫ *noun* (*plural* **dresses**) **1** clothes **2** a one-piece woman's garment combining skirt and top **3** a style of clothing: *formal dress* ▫ *adj* of clothes: for formal use ▫ **dress-coat** *noun* a black tailcoat ▫ **dressing-gown** *noun* a loose, light coat worn indoors over pyjamas *etc* ▫ **dress rehearsal** the final rehearsal of a play, in which the actors wear their costumes ▫ **dressy** *adj* stylish, smart

dresser *noun* a kitchen sideboard for dishes

dressing *noun* **1** a covering **2** a seasoned sauce poured over salads *etc* **3** a bandage

drew *past form* of **draw**

drey *noun* (*plural* **dreys**) a squirrel's nest

dribble *verb* **1** (cause to) fall in small drops **2** let saliva run down the chin **3** *football* move the ball forward by short kicks

dried *see* **dry**

drift *noun* **1** snow, sand *etc* driven by the wind **2** the direction in which something is driven **3** the general meaning of someone's words ▫ *verb* **1** go with the tide or current **2** be driven into heaps by the wind **3** wander about **4** live aimlessly ▫ **drifter** *noun* **1** someone who drifts **2** a fishing boat that uses drift-nets ▫ **drift-net** *noun* a fishing net which stays near the surface of the water ▫ **driftwood** *noun* wood driven onto the seashore by winds or tides

drill *verb* **1** make a hole in **2** make with a drill **3** exercise (soldiers) **4** sow (seeds) in rows ▫ *noun* **1** a tool for making holes in wood *etc* **2** military exercise **3** a row of seeds or plants

drink *verb* **1** swallow (a liquid) **2** take alcoholic drink, *esp* excessively ▫ *noun* **1** liquid to be drunk **2** alcoholic liquids ▫ **drink in** listen to eagerly ▫ **drink to** drink a toast to ▫ **drink up** finish a drink

drink *verb* » drink*s*, drink*ing*, drank, drunk

drip *verb* **1** fall in drops **2** let (water *etc*) fall in drops ▫ *noun* **1** a drop **2**

a continual dropping, *eg* of water **3** a device for adding liquid slowly to a vein *etc* □ **drip-dry** *verb* dry (a garment) by hanging it up to dry without wringing it first □ **dripping** *noun* fat from roasting meat

> **drip** *verb* » drip*s*, dripp*ing*, dripp*ed*

drive *verb* **1** control or guide (a car *etc*) **2** go in a vehicle: *driving to work* **3** force or urge along **4** hurry on **5** hit hard (a ball, nail *etc*) **6** bring about: *drive a bargain* □ *noun* **1** a journey in a car **2** a private road to a house **3** an avenue or road **4** energy, enthusiasm **5** a campaign: *a drive to save the local school* **6** a games tournament: *whist drive* **7** a hard stroke with a club or bat □ **driver** *noun* **1** someone who drives a car *etc* **2** a wooden-headed golf club □ **drive-in** *noun*, *US* a cinema where the audience watches the screen while staying in their cars □ **what are you driving at?** what are you suggesting or implying?

> **drive** » drive*s*, driv*ing*, drove, driven

drivel *noun*, *informal* nonsense □ *verb* talk nonsense

> **drivel** *verb* » drivel*s*, drivel*ling*, drivel*led*

driven *past participle* of **drive**

drizzle *noun* light rain □ *verb* rain lightly □ **drizzly** *adj*

droll *adj* **1** funny, amusing **2** odd

dromedary *noun* (*plural* **dromedaries**) an Arabian camel with one hump

drone *verb* **1** make a low humming sound **2** speak in a dull boring voice □ *noun* **1** a low humming sound **2** a dull boring voice **3** the low-sounding pipe of a bagpipe **4** a male bee **5** a lazy, idle person

drool *verb* **1** produce saliva **2** anticipate something in an obvious way

droop *verb* **1** hang down: *your hem is drooping* **2** grow weak or discouraged

drop *noun* **1** a small round or pear-shaped blob of liquid **2** a small quantity: *a drop of whisky* **3** a fall from a height: *a drop of six feet* **4** a small flavoured sweet: *pear drop* □ *verb* **1** fall suddenly **2** let fall **3** fall in drops **4** set down from a motor-car *etc*: *drop me at the corner* **5** give up, abandon (a friend, habit *etc*) □ **droplet** *noun* a tiny drop □ **droppings** *noun plural* animal or bird dung □ **drop off** fall asleep □ **drop out** withdraw from a class, the rat-race *etc*

> **drop** » drop*s*, dropp*ing*, dropp*ed*

dross *noun* **1** scum produced by melting metal **2** waste material, impurities **3** anything worthless

drought *noun* a period of time when no rain falls

drove *noun* **1** a number of moving cattle or other animals **2** (**droves**) a great number of people □ *past form* of **drive** □ **drover** *noun* someone who drives cattle

drown *verb* **1** die by suffocating in water **2** kill (someone) in this way **3** flood or soak completely **4** block out (a sound) with a louder one

drowsy *adj* sleepy ▢ **drowsily** *adv* ▢ **drowsiness** *noun*

drub *verb* beat, thrash ▢ **drubbing** *noun* a thrashing

drub » drub*s*, drubb*ing*, drubb*ed*

drudge *verb* do very humble or boring work ▢ *noun* someone who does such work ▢ **drudgery** *noun* hard, uninteresting work

drug *noun* **1** a substance used in medicine to treat illness, kill pain *etc* **2** a stimulant or narcotic substance taken habitually for its effects ▢ *verb* **1** administer drugs to **2** make to lose consciousness by drugs ▢ **druggist** *noun* a chemist ▢ **drugstore** *noun*, *US* a shop selling newspapers, soft drinks *etc* as well as medicines

drug » drug*s*, drugg*ing*, drugg*ed*

drum *noun* **1** a musical instrument of skin *etc* stretched on a round frame and beaten with sticks **2** a cylindrical container: *oil drum/ biscuit drum* ▢ *verb* **1** beat a drum **2** tap continuously with the fingers ▢ **drummer** *noun*

drum » drum*s*, drumm*ing*, drumm*ed*

drumstick *noun* **1** a stick for beating a drum **2** the lower part of the leg of a cooked chicken *etc*

drunk *adj* showing the effects (giddiness, unsteadiness *etc*) of drinking too much alcohol ▢ *noun* someone who is drunk, or habitually drunk ▢ *past participle* of **drink** ▢ **drunkard** *noun* a drunk

drunken *adj* **1** habitually drunk **2** caused by too much alcohol: *drunken stupor* **3** involving much alcohol: *drunken orgy* ▢ **drunkenly** *adv* ▢ **drunkenness** *noun*

dry *adj* **1** not moist or wet **2** thirsty **3** uninteresting: *makes very dry reading* **4** reserved, matter-of-fact **5** of wine: not sweet ▢ *verb* make or become dry ▢ **dryly** or **drily** *adv* ▢ **dry-clean** *verb* clean (clothes *etc*) with chemicals, not with water ▢ **dryness** *noun* ▢ **dry-rot** *noun* a disease causing wood to become dry and crumbly ▢ **dry-stane** *Scot* or **dry-stone** *adj* built of stone without cement or mortar

dry *verb* » dri*es*, dry*ing*, dri*ed*

dryad /*drai*ad/ *noun* a mythological wood nymph

DSO *abbrev* Distinguished Service Order

DSS *abbrev* Department of Social Services (previously **DHSS** Department of Health and Social Security)

DTI *abbrev* Department of Trade and Industry

DTP *abbrev* desktop publishing

dual *adj* double; made up of two ▢ **dual carriageway** a road divided by a central barrier or boundary, with each side used by traffic moving in one direction ▢ **dual-purpose** *adj* able to be used for more than one purpose

⚠Do not confuse with: **duel**

dub *verb* **1** declare (a knight) by touching each shoulder with a sword **2** name or nickname **3** add sound effects to a film **4** give (a film) a new sound-track in a different language

> **dub** » dub*s*, dubb*ing*, dubb*ed*

dubbin or **dubbing** *noun* a grease for softening or waterproofing leather

dubious *adj* **1** doubtful, uncertain **2** probably dishonest: *dubious dealings* □ **dubiety** *noun*

ducal *adj* of a duke

ducat *noun, hist* an old European gold coin

duchess *noun* (*plural* **duchesses**) **1** a woman of the same rank as a duke **2** the wife or widow of a duke

duchy *noun* (*plural* **duchies**) the land owned by a duke or duchess

duck *noun* **1** a web-footed bird, with a broad flat beak **2** *cricket* a score of no runs □ *verb* **1** lower the head quickly as if to avoid a blow **2** push (someone's head) under water □ **duckling** *noun* a baby duck □ **duck out (of)** avoid responsibility (for) □ **lame duck** an inefficient, useless person or organization

> The meaning in cricket comes from the use of 'duck's egg' to mean a nought on a scoring sheet

duck-billed platypus *see* **platypus**

duct *noun* a pipe for carrying liquids, electric cables *etc*

ductile *adj* easily led, yielding

dud *adj, informal* useless, broken

dudgeon *noun*: **in high dudgeon** very angry, indignant

duds *noun plural, informal* clothes

due *adj* **1** owed, needing to be paid: *the rent is due next week* **2** expected to arrive *etc*: *they're due here at six* **3** proper, appropriate: *due care* □ *adv* directly: *due south* □ **1** something you have a right to: *give him his due* **2** (**dues**) the amount of money charged for belonging to a club *etc* □ **due to** brought about by, caused by

duel *noun, hist* a formalized fight with pistols or swords between two people □ *verb* fight in a duel □ **duellist** *noun* someone who fights in a duel

> ⚠Do not confuse with: **dual**

duenna *noun* a chaperone

duet /dyoo*et*/ *noun* a piece of music for two singers or players

duff *adj, informal* useless, broken

duffel bag a cylindrical canvas bag tied with a drawstring

duffel coat a heavy woollen coat, fastened with toggles

> After *Duffel*, a town in Belgium where the fabric was first made

duffer *noun, informal* a stupid or incompetent person

dug *past form* of **dig**

dugout *noun* **1** a boat made by hollowing out the trunk of a tree **2** a rough shelter dug out of a slope or bank or in a trench **3** *football* a bench beside the pitch for team managers, trainers, and extra players

duke *noun* a nobleman next in rank below a prince **dukedom** *noun* the title, rank or lands of a duke

dulcet *adj, formal* sounding pleasant, melodious

dulcimer *noun* a musical instrument with stretched wires which are struck with small hammers

dull *adj* **1** not lively **2** slow to understand or learn **3** not exciting or interesting **4** of weather: cloudy, not bright or clear **5** not bright in colour **6** of sounds: not clear or ringing **7** blunt, not sharp *verb* make dull **dullness** *noun* **dully** *adv*

dulse *noun* a type of edible seaweed

duly *adv* at the proper or expected time; as expected: *he duly arrived*

dumb *adj* **1** without the power of speech **2** silent **3** *informal* stupid **dumbly** *adv* in silence **dumb show** acting without words

dumbfound *verb* astonish

dummy *noun* (*plural* **dummies**) **1** a mock-up of something used for display **2** a model used for displaying clothes *etc* **3** an artificial teat used to comfort a baby **4** *slang* a stupid person **dummy run** a try-out, a practice

dump *verb* **1** throw down heavily **2** unload and leave (rubbish *etc*) **3** sell at a low price *noun* a place for leaving rubbish **in the dumps** feeling low or depressed

dumpling *noun* a cooked ball of dough

dumpy *adj* short and thick or fat

dun *adj* greyish-brown, mouse-coloured *verb* demand payment

> **dun** *verb* » dun*s*, dunn*ing*, dunn*ed*

dunce *noun* a stupid or slow-learning person

> Originally a term of abuse applied to followers of the medieval Scottish philosopher, John *Duns Scotus*

dunderhead *noun, informal* a stupid person

dune *noun* a low hill of sand

dung *noun* animal faeces, manure **dunghill** *noun* a heap of dung in a farmyard etc

dungarees *noun plural* trousers made of coarse, hard-wearing material with a bib

dungeon *noun* a dark underground prison

dunt *noun, Scot* a thump, a knock

duodecimo *noun* a book made from sheets of paper folded into twelve leaves

duodenary *adj* made up of twelve; twelvefold

duodenum *noun* the first part of the small intestine

dupe *noun* someone easily cheated *verb* deceive, trick

duplicate *adj* exactly the same *noun* an exact copy *verb* make a copy or copies of **duplication** *noun*

duplicity *noun* deceit, double-dealing □ **duplicitous** *adj* □ **duplicitously** *adv* □ **duplicitousness** *noun*

durable *adj* lasting, able to last; wearing well □ **durability** *noun*

duration *noun* the time a thing lasts □ **for the duration** *informal* for a long time, for ages

duress /dyoo*res*/ *noun* illegal force used to make someone do something □ **under duress** under the influence of force, threats *etc*

during *prep* **1** throughout all or part of: *we lived here during the war* **2** at a particular point within: *she died during the night*

dusk *noun* twilight, partial dark

dusky *adj* dark-coloured □ **duskiness** *noun*

dust *noun* **1** fine grains or specks of earth, sand *etc* **2** fine powder □ *verb* **1** free from dust: *dusted the table* **2** sprinkle lightly with powder □ **dustbin** *noun* a container for household rubbish □ **dust-bowl** *noun* an area with little rain in which the wind raises storms of dust □ **duster** *noun* a cloth for removing dust □ **dust jacket** a paper cover on a book □ **dustman** *noun* someone employed to collect household rubbish □ **dusty** *adj* covered with dust

dutiable *adj* of goods: liable for tax

dutiful *adj* obedient □ **dutifully** *adv*

duty *noun* (*plural* **duties**) **1** something a person ought to do **2** an action required to be done **2** a tax **3** (**duties**) the various tasks involved in a job □ **duty-free** *adj* not taxed

duvet /*doo*veh/ *noun* a quilt stuffed with feathers or synthetic material, used instead of blankets

dux *noun* (*plural* **duxes**) the top boy or girl in some Scottish schools

DV *abbrev* if God is willing (from Latin *deo volente*)

dwarf *noun* (*plural* **dwarfs** or **dwarves**) an undersized person, animal or plant □ *verb* make to appear small by comparison □ *adj* not growing to full or usual height: *dwarf cherry-tree*

dwell *verb* **1** live, inhabit, stay **2** (with **on**) think habitually about something: *dwelling on the past*

dwindle *verb* grow less, waste away

dye *verb* give a colour to (fabric *etc*) □ *noun* a powder or liquid for colouring □ **dyeing** *noun* the putting of colour into cloth □ **dyestuff** *noun* a substance used for dyeing

dying *present participle* of **die**

dyke *another spelling* of **dike**

dynamic *adj* forceful, energetic □ **dynamically** *adv*

dynamics *noun sing* the scientific study of movement and force

dynamite *noun* a type of powerful explosive

dynamo *noun* (*plural* **dynamos**) a machine for turning the energy produced by movement into electricity

dynasty *noun* (*plural* **dynasties**) a succession of monarchs, leaders *etc* of the same family □ **dynastic** *adj*

dysentery *noun* an infectious disease causing fever, pain and diarrhoea

dyslexia *noun* difficulty in learning to read and in spelling □ **dyslexic** *noun* & *adj* (someone) suffering from dyslexia

dyspepsia *noun* indigestion □ **dyspeptic** *adj*

E

E *abbrev* **1** east; eastern **2** the drug Ecstasy

each *adj* **1** of two or more things: every one taken individually: *there is a postbox on each side of the road/ she was late on each occasion* □ *pronoun* every one individually: *each of them won a prize* □ **each other** used when an action takes place between two (loosely, between more than two) people: *we don't see each other very often*

eager *adj* keen, anxious to do or get (something) □ **eagerly** *adv* □ **eagerness** *noun*

eagle *noun* a kind of large bird of prey □ **eaglet** *noun* a young eagle

ear *noun* **1** the part of the body through which you hear sounds **2** a head (of corn *etc*) □ **eardrum** *noun* the membrane in the middle of the ear □ **ear-lobe** *noun* □ **earmark** *verb* mark or set aside for a special purpose □ **ear-muffs** *noun plural* □ **earphones** *noun plural* a pair of tiny speakers fitting in or against the ear for listening to a radio *etc* □ **earplugs** *noun plural* a pair of plugs placed in the ears to block off outside noise □ **ear-piercing** *adj* very loud or shrill □ **earshot** *noun* the distance at which a sound can be heard □ **a good ear** the ability to tell one sound from another □ **lend an ear** listen

earl *noun* a member of the British aristocracy between a marquis and a viscount □ **earldom** *noun* the lands or title of an earl

early *adj* **1** in good time **2** at or near the beginning: *in an earlier chapter* **3** sooner than expected: *you're early!* □ *adv* □ **earliness** *noun* □ **early bird 1** an early riser **2** someone who gains an advantage by acting more quickly than rivals

> **early** » earli*er*, earli*est*

earn *verb* **1** receive (money) for work **2** deserve □ **earnings** *noun plural* pay for work done

earnest *adj* serious, serious-minded □ *noun* **1** seriousness **2** money *etc* given to make sure that a bargain will be kept □ **earnestly** *adv* □ **earnestness** *noun* □ **in earnest** meaning what you say or do

earth *noun* **1** the third planet from the sun; our world **2** its surface **3** soil **4** the hole of a fox, badger *etc* **5** an electrical connection with the ground □ *verb* connect electrically with the ground □ **earthen** *adj* made of earth or clay □ **earthenware** *noun* pottery, dishes made of clay □ **earthly** *adj* of the earth as opposed to heaven □ **earthquake** *noun* a shaking of the earth's crust □ **earthshattering** *adj* of great importance □ **earth-tremor** *noun* a slight earthquake □ **earthwork** *noun* an artificial bank of earth □ **earthworm** *noun* the common worm

earthy *adj* **1** like soil **2** covered in

soil **3** coarse, not refined □ **earthily** *adv* □ **earthiness** *noun*

earwig *noun* a type of insect with pincers at its tail

ease *noun* **1** freedom from difficulty: *finished the race with ease* **2** freedom from pain, worry or embarrassment **3** rest from work □ *verb* **1** make or become less painful or difficult **2** move carefully and gradually: *ease the stone into position* □ **at ease** comfortable, relaxed □ **stand at ease** stand with your legs apart and arms behind your back

easel *noun* a stand for an artist's canvas while painting *etc*

east *noun* one of the four chief directions, that in which the sun rises □ *adj* in or from the east: *an east wind* □ **easterly** *adj* coming from or facing the east □ **eastern** *adj* of the east □ **eastward** or **eastwards** *adj* & *adv* towards the east

Easter *noun* **1** the Christian celebration of Christ's rising from the dead **2** the weekend when this is celebrated each year, sometime in spring

easy *adj* **1** not hard to do **2** free from pain, worry or discomfort □ **easily** *adv* □ **easiness** *noun*

easy » easi*er*, easi*est*

eat *verb* **1** chew and swallow (food) **2** destroy gradually, waste away □ **eatable** *adj* fit to eat, edible

eat » eat*s*, eat*ing*, ate, eate*n*

eaves *noun plural* the edge of a roof overhanging the walls □ **eavesdrop** *verb* listen secretly to a private conversation □ **eavesdropper** *noun*

ebb *noun* **1** the flowing away of the tide after high tide **2** a lessening, a worsening □ *verb* **1** flow away **2** grow less or worse

ebony *noun* a type of black, hard wood □ *adj* **1** made of ebony **2** black

ebullient *adj* lively and enthusiastic □ **ebullience** *noun* □ **ebulliently** *adv*

EC *abbrev* European Community

eccentric *adj* **1** odd, acting strangely **2** of circles: not having the same centre (*contrasted with*: **concentric**) □ **eccentricity** *noun* (*plural* **eccentricities**) oddness of manner or conduct

ecclesiastic or **ecclesiastical** *adj* of the church or clergy

ECG *abbrev* electrocardiogram; electrocardiograph

echelon /*esh*əlon/ *noun* **1** a level, a rank **2** a formation of soldiers, planes *etc*

echidna /*ekidnə*/ *noun* a spiny, toothless Australian animal with a long snout

echo *noun* (*plural* **echoes**) **1** the repetition of a sound by its striking a surface and coming back **2** something that evokes a memory: *echoes of the past* □ *verb* **1** send back sound **2** repeat (a thing said) **3** imitate

echt /exht/ *adj* genuine, authentic

éclair /ə*klehr*/ *noun* an oblong sweet pastry filled with cream

eclampsia *noun* a toxic condition that can occur in the final months of pregnancy

éclat /eh*klah*/ *noun* an impressive effect

eclectic *noun* broadly based, wide-ranging: *eclectic tastes*

eclipse *noun* **1** the covering of the whole or part of the sun or moon, *eg* when the moon comes between the sun and the earth **2** loss of position or prestige ▯ *verb* **1** throw into the shade **2** blot out (someone's achievement) by doing better

eco- *prefix* relating to the environment: *ecofriendly/ eco-summit*

ecology *noun* the study of plants, animals *etc* in relation to their natural surroundings ▯ **ecological** *adj* ▯ **ecologically** *adv* ▯ **ecologist** *noun*

economic *adj* **1** concerning economy **2** making a profit ▯ **economical** *adj* thrifty, not wasteful ▯ **economics** *noun sing* the study of how money is created and spent ▯ **economist** *noun* someone who studies or is an expert on economics

economy *noun* (*plural* **economies**) **1** the management of a country's finances **2** the careful use of something, *esp* money ▯ **economize** *verb* be careful in spending or using

ecstasy *noun* (*plural* **ecstasies**) **1** very great joy or pleasure **2** (**Ecstasy**) a hallucinogenic drug ▯ **ecstatic** *adj* ▯ **ecstatically** *adv*

ECT *abbrev* electro-convulsive therapy

ectoplasm *noun* a substance believed by spiritualists to surround mediums

ecu *abbrev* European currency unit, a reserve currency with a rate based on a range of European currencies

ecumenical *adj* concerned with the unity of the whole Christian church

eczema /*ek*simə/ *noun* a skin disease causing red swollen patches on the skin ▯ **eczematic** *adj*

Edam *noun* a mild Dutch cheese with a red outer skin

eddy *noun* (*plural* **eddies**) a circling current of water or air running against the main stream ▯ *verb* flow in circles

edelweiss /*eh*dəlvais/ *noun* an Alpine plant with white flowers

edge *noun* **1** the border of anything, farthest from the middle **2** the cutting side of a blade **3** sharpness: *put an edge on my appetite* **4** advantage: *Brazil had the edge at half-time* ▯ *verb* **1** put a border on **2** move little by little: *edging forward* ▯ **edgeways** *adv* sideways ▯ **edging** *noun* a border, a fringe ▯ **edgy** *adj* unable to relax, irritable ▯ **on edge** nervous, edgy ▯ **set someone's teeth on edge** grate on their nerves, make them wince

edible *adj* fit to be eaten

edict *noun* an order, a command

edifice *noun* a large building

edify *verb* improve the mind, enlighten ▯ **edifying** *adj* ▯ **edification** *noun*

edify » edifi*es*, edify*ing*, edifi*ed*

edit *verb* prepare (a text, film *etc*) for publication or broadcasting

edition *noun* **1** the form in which a book *etc* is published after being edited **2** the copies of a book, newspaper *etc* printed at one time **3** a special issue of a newspaper, *eg* for a local area

editor *noun* **1** someone who edits a book, film *etc* **2** the chief journalist of a newspaper or section of a newspaper: *the sports editor* ◇ **editorial** *adj* of editing ◇ *noun* a newspaper column written by the chief editor

educate *verb* **1** teach (people), *esp* in a school or college ◇ **education** *noun* ◇ **educational** *adj* of education ◇ **educated guess** a guess based on knowledge of the subject involved

EEC *abbrev* European Economic Community

EEG *abbrev* electroencephalogram; electroencephalograph

eel *noun* a long, ribbon-shaped fish

eerie *adj* causing fear of the unknown

Originally a Scots word meaning 'afraid' or 'cowardly'

efface *verb* rub out ◇ **efface yourself** keep from being noticed

effect *noun* **1** the result of an action **2** strength, power: *the pills had little effect* **3** an impression produced: *the effect of the sunset* **4** general meaning **5** use, operation: *that law is not yet in effect* **6** (**effects**) goods, property ◇ *verb* bring about ◇ **effective** *adj* **1** producing the desired effect **2** actual ◇ **effectual** *adj* able to do what is required ◇ **effectually** *adv*

⚠Do not confuse with: **affect**

effeminate *adj* unmanly, womanish

effervesce *verb* **1** froth up **2** be very lively, excited *etc* ◇ **effervescence** *noun* ◇ **effervescent** *adj*

effete *adj* weak, feeble

efficacious *adj* effective ◇ **efficacy** *noun*

efficient *adj* able to do things well; capable ◇ **efficiency** *noun* ◇ **efficiently** *noun*

effigy *noun* (*plural* **effigies**) a likeness of a person carved in stone, wood *etc*

effluent *noun* **1** a stream flowing from another stream or lake **2** liquid industrial waste; sewage

effort *noun* **1** an attempt using a lot of strength or ability **2** hard work

effrontery *noun* impudence

effulgent *adj* shining, radiant

effusive *adj* speaking freely, gushing ◇ **effusively** *adv*

EFL *abbrev* English as a foreign language

eg *abbrev* for example (from Latin *exempli gratia*)

egg *noun* **1** an oval shell containing the embryo of a bird, insect or reptile **2** (*also called* **ovum**) a human reproductive cell **3** a hen's egg used for eating ▫ **egg on** urge, encourage

eggplant *noun, US* an aubergine

ego *noun* **1** the conscious self **2** self-conceit, egotism

egoism or **egotism** *noun* the habit of considering only your own interests, selfishness ▫ **egoist** or **egotist** *noun* ▫ **egoistic** or **egotistic** *adj*

egregious *adj* outrageous, notoriously bad

egress *noun* exit, way out

egret *noun* a type of white heron

eider or **eider-duck** *noun* a northern sea duck ▫ **eiderdown** *noun* **1** soft feathers from the eider **2** a feather quilt

eight *noun* the number 8 ▫ *adj* 8 in number ▫ **eighth** *adj* the last of a series of eight ▫ *noun* one of eight equal parts

eighteen *noun* the number 18 ▫ *adj* 18 in number ▫ **eighteenth** *adj* the last of a series of eighteen ▫ *noun* one of eighteen equal parts

eighty the number 80 ▫ *adj* 80 in number ▫ **eightieth** *adj* the last of a series of eighty ▫ *noun* one of eighty equal parts

EIS *abbrev* Educational Institute of Scotland

either *adj* & *pronoun* **1** one or other of two: *either bus will go there/ either of the dates would suit me* **2** each of two, both: *there is a crossing on either side of the road* ▫ *conj* used with **or** to show alternatives: *either he goes or I do* ▫ *adv* any more than another: *that won't work either*

ejaculate *verb* **1** emit semen **2** shout out, exclaim ▫ **ejaculation** *noun*

eject *verb* **1** throw out **2** force to leave a house, job *etc* ▫ **ejection** *noun*

eke *verb*: **eke out** make last longer by adding to: *eked out the stew with more vegetables*

elaborate *verb* **1** work out in detail: *you must elaborate your escape plan* **2** (often with **on**) explain fully ▫ *adj* highly detailed or decorated ▫ **elaboration** *noun*

élan *noun* enthusiasm, dash

eland *noun* a type of African deer

elapse *verb* of time: pass

elastic *adj* able to stretch and spring back again, springy ▫ *noun* a piece of cotton *etc* interwoven with rubber to make it springy ▫ **elasticity** *noun*

elated *adj* in high spirits, very pleased ▫ **elation** *noun*

elbow *noun* the joint where the arm bends ▫ *verb* push with the elbow, jostle ▫ **elbow grease 1** vigorous rubbing **2** hard work, effort ▫ **elbow-room** *noun* plenty of room to move

El Dorado an imaginary land of great wealth

elder[1] *adj* older ▫ *noun* **1** someone who is older **2** an office-bearer in the Presbyterian church ▫ **elderly** *adj* nearing old age ▫ **eldest** *adj* oldest

elder[2] *noun* a type of tree with purple-black berries ▫ **elderberry**

noun (*plural* **elderberries**) a berry from the elder tree

elect *verb* **1** choose by voting **2** choose (to) □ *adj* **1** chosen **2** chosen for a post but not yet in it: *president elect* □ **electorate** *noun* all those who have the right to vote

election *noun* the choosing by vote of people to sit in parliament *etc* □ **electioneer** *verb* campaign for votes in an election

electricity *noun* a form of energy used to give light, heat and power □ **electric** or **electrical** *adj* produced or worked by electricity □ **electrician** *noun* someone skilled in working with electricity □ **electrify** *verb* **1** supply with electricity **2** excite greatly □ **electrocute** *verb* kill by an electric current

electrify » electrifi*es*, electrify*ing*, electrifi*ed*

electrode *noun* a conductor through which an electric current enters or leaves a battery *etc*

electron *noun* a very light particle within an atom, having the smallest possible charge of electricity

electronic *adj* of or using electrons or electronics □ **electronics** *noun sing* a branch of physics dealing with electrons and their use in machines *etc*

elegant *adj* **1** graceful, well-dressed, fashionable **2** of clothes *etc*: well-made and tasteful □ **elegance** *noun* □ **elegantly** *adv*

elegy *noun* (*plural* **elegies**) a poem written on someone's death

element *noun* **1** a part of anything **2** a substance that cannot be split chemically into simpler substances, *eg* oxygen, iron *etc* **3** circumstances which suit someone best: *she is in her element when singing* **4** a heating wire carrying the current in an electric heater **5** (**elements**) first steps in learning **6** (**elements**) the powers of nature, the weather □ **elemental** *adj* of the elements □ **elementary** *adj* **1** at the first stage **2** simple

elephant *noun* a very large animal with a thick skin, a trunk and two ivory tusks □ **elephantine** *adj* big and clumsy

elevate *verb* **1** raise to a higher position **2** cheer up **3** improve (the mind) □ **elevation** *noun* **1** the act of raising up **2** rising ground **3** height **4** a drawing of a building as seen from the side **5** an angle measuring height: *the sun's elevation* □ **elevator** *noun*, *US* a lift in a building

eleven the number 11 □ *adj* 11 in number □ *noun* a team of eleven players, *eg* for cricket □ **elevenses** *noun plural* coffee, biscuits *etc* taken around eleven o'clock in the morning

eleventh *adj* the last of a series of eleven □ *noun* one of eleven equal parts

elf *noun* (*plural* **elves**) a tiny, mischievous supernatural creature □ **elfin**, **elfish** or **elvish** *adj* like an elf

elicit *verb* draw out (information *etc*)

⚠Do not confuse with: **illicit**

eligible *adj* fit or worthy to be chosen □ **eligibility** *noun*

eliminate *verb* **1** get rid of **2** exclude, omit □ **elimination** *noun*

élite or **elite** /eh*leet*/ *noun* a part of a group selected as, or believed to be, the best

elixir *noun* a liquid believed to give eternal life, or to be able to turn iron *etc* into gold

elk *noun* a very large deer found in N Europe and Asia, related to the moose

ell *noun* an old measure of length

ellipse *noun* (*plural* **ellipses**) an oval shape □ **ellipsis** *noun* **1** the omission of a word or words in a text **2** marks (...) indicating missing words in a text □ **elliptic** or **elliptical** *adj* **1** oval **2** having part of the words or meaning left out

elm *noun* a tree with a rough bark and leaves with saw-like edges

elocution *noun* **1** the art of what is thought to be correct speech **2** style of speaking

elongate *verb* stretch out lengthwise, make longer □ **elongation** *noun*

elope *verb* run away from home to get married □ **elopement** *noun*

eloquent *adj* **1** good at expressing thoughts **2** persuasive □ **eloquence** *noun*

else *adv* otherwise: *come inside or else you will catch cold* □ *adj* other than the person or thing mentioned: *someone else has taken her place* □ **elsewhere** *adv* in or to another place

elucidate *verb* make (something) easy to understand

elude *verb* **1** escape by a trick **2** be too difficult to remember or understand

⚠Do not confuse with: **allude**

elusive *adj* hard to catch

⚠Do not confuse with: **allusive** and **illusive**

elver *noun* a young eel

elves and **elvish** *see* **elf**

Elysium *noun* paradise

emaciated *adj* very thin, like a skeleton

E-mail *noun* electronic mail

emanate *verb* flow, come out from □ **emanation** *noun*

emancipate *verb* set free, *eg* from slavery or repressive social conditions □ **emancipation** *noun*

emasculate **1** castrate **2** deprive of power, weaken

embalm *verb* preserve (a dead body) from decay by treating it with spices or drugs

embankment *noun* a bank of earth or stone to keep back water, or carry a railway over low-lying places

embargo *noun* (*plural* **embargoes**) an official order forbidding something, *esp* trade with another country

embark *verb* **1** go on board ship **2** (with **on**) start (a new career *etc*) □ **embarkation** *noun*

embarrass *verb* make to feel uncomfortable and self-conscious □ **embarrassing** *adj* □ **embarrassment** *noun*

embassy *noun* (*plural* **embassies**) the offices and staff of an ambassador in a foreign country

embellish *verb* **1** decorate **2** add details to (a story *etc*) □ **embellishment** *noun*

ember *noun* a piece of wood or coal glowing in a fire

embezzle *verb* use for yourself money entrusted to you □ **embezzlement** *noun*

emblazon *verb* **1** decorate, adorn **2** show in bright colours or conspicuously

emblem *noun* **1** an image which represents something: *the dove is the emblem of peace/ the leek is the emblem of Wales* **2** a badge

embody *verb* **1** include **2** express, give form to: *embodying the spirit of the age* □ **embodiment**

> **embody** » embodi*es*, embody*ing*, embodi*ed*

embolism *noun* an obstructing clot in a blood vessel

emboss *verb* make a pattern in leather, metal *etc*, which stands out from a flat surface □ **embossed** *adj*

embrace *verb* **1** throw your arms round in affection **2** include **3** accept, adopt eagerly □ *noun* an affectionate hug

embrocation *noun* an ointment for rubbing on the body, *eg* to relieve stiffness

embroider *verb* **1** decorate with designs in needlework **2** add false details to (a story) □ **embroiderer** *noun* □ **embroidery** *noun*

embroil *verb* **1** get (someone) into a quarrel, or into a difficult situation **2** throw into confusion

embryo *noun* (*plural* **embryos**) **1** the young of an animal or plant in its earliest stage **2** the beginning of anything □ **embryonic** *adj* in an early stage of development

emend *verb* remove faults or errors from □ **emendation** *noun*

> ⚠Do not confuse with: **amend**

emerald *noun* a bright green precious stone

emerge *verb* **1** come out **2** become known or clear □ **emergence** *noun* □ **emergent** *adj* **1** arising **2** newly formed or newly independent: *emergent nation*

emergency *noun* (*plural* **emergencies**) an unexpected event requiring very quick action □ **emergency exit** a way out of a building for use in an emergency

emery *noun* a very hard mineral, used for smoothing and polishing

emetic *adj* causing vomiting □ *noun* an emetic medicine

emigrate *verb* leave your country to settle in another □ **emigrant** *noun* someone who emigrates □ **emigration** *noun*

> ⚠Do not confuse with: **immigrate**

émigré *noun* someone who emigrates for political reasons

éminence grise someone who exercises power from behind the scenes

eminent *adj* famous, notable □ **eminence** *noun* **1** distinction, fame **2** a title of honour **3** a hill □ **eminently** *adv* very, obviously: *eminently suitable*

> ⚠Do not confuse with: **imminent**

emissary *noun* (*plural* **emissaries**) someone sent on private, often secret, business

emit *verb* send or give out (light, sound *etc*) □ **emission** *noun*

> **emit** » emit*s*, emitt*ing*, emitt*ed*

Emmy *noun* an annual award given by the American Academy of Television Arts and Sciences

emollient *adj* softening and smoothing □ *noun* an emollient substance

emolument *noun, formal* wages, salary

emotion *noun* a feeling that disturbs or excites the mind, *eg* fear, love, hatred □ **emotional** *adj* **1** moving the feelings **2** of a person: having feelings easily excited □ **emotionally** *adv* □ **emotive** *adj* causing emotion rather than thought

empathy *noun* the ability to share another person's feelings *etc* □ **empathize** *verb*

emperor *noun* the ruler of an empire

emphasis *noun* **1** stress placed on a word or words in speaking **2** greater attention or importance: *the emphasis is on playing, not winning* □ **emphasize** *verb* put emphasis on; call attention to □ **emphatic** *adj* spoken strongly: *an emphatic 'no'* □ **emphatically** *adv*

emphysema /emfi*seem*ə/ *noun* a lung disease causing breathing difficulties

empire *noun* **1** a group of nations *etc* under the same ruling power **2** a large business organization including several companies

empirical *adj* based on experiment and experience, not on theory alone □ **empirically** *adv* □ **empiricism** *noun* □ **empiricist** *noun*

employ *verb* **1** give work to **2** use **3** occupy the time of □ *noun* employment □ **employee** *noun* someone who works for an **employer** *noun* □ **employment** *noun* work, occupation

emporium *noun* (*plural* **emporia** or **emporiums**) a large shop; a market

empower *verb* **1** authorize **2** give self-confidence to

empress *noun* the female ruler of an empire

empty *adj* **1** containing nothing or no one **2** unlikely to result in anything: *empty threats* □ *verb* make or become empty □ *noun* (*plural* **empties**) an empty bottle *etc* □ **emptiness** *noun* □ **empty-handed** *adj* bringing or gaining nothing □ **empty-headed** *adj* flighty, irresponsible

> **empty** » empti*es*, empty*ing*, empti*ed*

EMS *abbrev* European Monetary System

EMU *abbrev* European Monetary Union

emu *noun* a type of Australian bird which cannot fly

emulate *verb* try to do as well as, or better than ◊ **emulation** *noun*

emulsion *noun* a milky liquid, *esp* that made by mixing oil and water

enable *verb* make it possible for, allow: *the money enabled him to retire*

enact *verb* **1** act, perform **2** make a law

enamel *noun* **1** a glassy coating fired onto metal **2** a paint with a glossy finish **3** the smooth white coating of the teeth ◊ *verb* coat or paint with enamel ◊ **enamelling** *noun*

> **enamel** *verb* » enamel*s*, enamell*ing*, enamell*ed*

enamoured *adj*: **enamoured of** fond of

encampment *noun* a military camp

encapsulate *verb* capture the essence of; describe briefly and accurately

encephalitis *noun* inflammation of the brain

enchant *verb* **1** delight, please greatly **2** put a spell or charm on ◊ **enchanter**, **enchantress** *noun* ◊ **enchantment** *noun*

enchilada a Mexican tortilla stuffed and cooked in a chilli sauce

enclave *noun* an area enclosed within foreign territory

enclose *verb* **1** put inside an envelope with a letter *etc* **2** put (*eg* a wall) around ◊ **enclosure** *noun* **1** the act of enclosing **2** something enclosed

encomium *noun* a speech full of praise; a eulogy

encompass *verb* surround; to include

encore /ong*kawr*/ *noun* **1** an extra performance of a song *etc* in reply to audience applause **2** a call for an encore

encounter *verb* **1** meet by chance **2** come up against (a difficulty, enemy *etc*) ◊ *noun* a meeting, a fight

encourage *verb* **1** give hope or confidence to **2** urge (to do) ◊ **encouragement** *noun* ◊ **encouraging** *adj*

encroach *verb* go beyond your rights or land and interfere with someone else's ◊ **encroachment** *noun*

encumber *verb* burden, load down ◊ **encumbrance** *noun* a heavy burden, a hindrance

encyclopedia or **encylopaedia** *noun* a reference book containing information on many subjects, or on a particular subject ◊ **encyclopedic** or **encyclopaedic** *adj* giving complete information

end *noun* **1** the last point or part **2** death **3** the farthest point of the length of something: *at the end of the road* **4** a result aimed at **5** a small piece left over ◊ *verb* bring or come to an end ◊ **ending** *noun* the last part ◊ **on end 1** standing on one end **2** in a series, without a stop: *he has been working for days on end*

endanger *verb* put in danger or at risk

endear *verb* make dear or more dear □ **endearing** *adj* appealing □ **endearment** *noun*

endeavour *verb* try hard (to) □ *noun* a determined attempt

endemic *adj* of a disease: found regularly in a certain area

endive *noun* a plant with curly leaves eaten as a salad

endocrine *noun* of a gland: secreting hormones *etc* into the blood

endorse *verb* **1** give your support to something said or written **2** sign the back of a cheque to confirm receiving money for it **3** indicate on a motor licence that the owner has broken a driving law □ **endorsement** *noun*

endow *verb* **1** give money for the buying and upkeep of: *he endowed a bed in the hospital* **2** give a talent, quality *etc* to: *nature endowed her with a good brain* □ **endowment** *noun*

endure *verb* bear without giving way; last □ **endurable** *adj* bearable □ **endurance** *noun* the power of enduring

enema *noun* the injection of fluid into the bowels

enemy *noun* (*plural* **enemies**) **1** someone hostile to another; a foe **2** someone armed to fight against another **3** someone who is against something: *an enemy of socialism* □

enmity *noun* (*plural* **enmities**)

energy *noun* (*plural* **energies**) **1** strength to act, vigour **2** a form of power, *eg* electricity, heat *etc* □ **energetic** *adj* active, lively □ **energetically** *adv*

enervate *verb* weaken, enfeeble

enfant terrible someone who behaves outrageously or unconventionally

enfold *verb* enclose, embrace

enforce *verb* cause (a law *etc*) to be carried out

enfranchise 1 set free **2** give the right to vote to

engage *verb* **1** begin to employ (workers *etc*) **2** book in advance **3** take or keep hold of (someone's attention *etc*) **4** be busy with, be occupied (in) **5** of machine parts: fit together **6** begin fighting □ **engaged** *adj* **1** bound by a promise of marriage **2** busy with something **3** of a telephone: in use □ **engagement** *noun* **1** a promise of marriage **2** an appointment to meet **3** a fight: *naval engagement* □ **engaging** *adj* pleasant, charming

engine *noun* **1** a machine which converts heat or other energy into motion **2** the part of a train which pulls the coaches

engineer *noun* **1** someone who works with, or designs, engines or machines **2** someone who designs or makes bridges, roads *etc* □ *verb* bring about by clever planning □ **engineering** *noun* the science of designing machines, roadmaking *etc*

engrave *verb* **1** draw with a special

tool on glass, metal *etc* **2** make a deep impression on: *engraved on his memory* □ **engraving** *noun* a print made from a cut-out drawing in metal or wood

engross *verb* take up the whole interest or attention

engulf *verb* swallow up wholly

enhance *verb* improve, make greater or better

enigma *noun* something or someone difficult to understand, a mystery □ **enigmatic** *adj*

enjoy *verb* **1** take pleasure in **2** experience, have (something beneficial): *enjoying good health* □ **enjoyable** *adj* □ **enjoyment** *noun* □ **enjoy yourself** have a pleasant time

enlarge *verb* **1** make larger **2** (with **on**) say much or more about something □ **enlargement** *noun* **1** an increase in size **2** a larger photograph made from a smaller one

enlighten *verb* give more knowledge or information to □ **enlightenment** *noun*

enlist *verb* **1** join an army *etc* **2** obtain the support and help of

enliven *verb* make more active or cheerful

en masse /onh *mas*/ *adv* all together, in a body

enmesh *verb* entangle, trap

enmity *see* **enemy**

ennui /on*wee*/ *noun* boredom

enormity *noun* **1** hugeness **2** extreme badness

enormous *adj* very large □ **enormously** *adv*

enough *adj & pronoun* (in) the number or amount wanted or needed: *I have enough coins/ do you have enough money?* □ *adv* as much as is wanted or necessary: *she's been there often enough to know the way*

enquire, enquiry *etc see* **inquire**

enrage *verb* make angry

enrol or **enroll** *verb* enter (a name) in a register or list □ **enrolment** *noun*

enrol » enrol*s*, enroll*ing*, enroll*ed*

en route /onh *root*/ *adv* on the way

ensconce *verb*: **ensconce yourself** settle comfortably

ensemble *noun* **1** the parts of a thing taken together **2** an outfit of clothes **3** a group of musicians

enshrine *verb* treat as sacred, cherish

ensign *noun* **1** the flag of a nation, regiment *etc* **2** *hist* a young officer who carried the flag

enslave *verb* make a slave of

ensue *verb* **1** follow, come after **2** result (from)

ensure *verb* make sure

⚠Do not confuse with: **insure**

entail *verb* **1** leave land so that the heir cannot sell any part of it **2** bring as a result, involve: *the job entailed extra work*

entangle *verb* **1** make tangled or complicated **2** involve (in difficulties)

entente /onh*tont*/ *noun* a treaty

enter *verb* **1** go or come in or into **2** put (a name *etc*) onto a list **3** take part (in) **4** begin (on)

enterprise *noun* **1** an undertaking, *esp* if risky or difficult **2** boldness in trying new things **3** a business concern □ **enterprising** *adj*

entertain *verb* **1** amuse **2** receive as a guest **3** give a party **4** consider (*eg* a suggestion) **5** hold in the mind: *entertain a belief* □ **entertainer** *noun* someone who entertains professionally □ **entertaining** *adj* amusing □ **entertainment** *noun* a theatrical show

enthral *verb* give great delight to

> **enthral** » enthral*s*, enthrall*ing*, enthrall*ed*

enthuse *verb* be enthusiastic (about)

enthusiasm *noun* great interest and keenness □ **enthusiast** *noun* □ **enthusiastic** *adj* greatly interested, very keen □ **enthusiastically** *adv*

entice *verb* attract with promises, rewards *etc* □ **enticement** *noun* a bribe, an attractive promise □ **enticing** *adj*

entire *adj* whole, complete □ **entirely** *adv* □ **entirety** *noun*

entitle *verb* **1** give a name to (a book *etc*) **2** give (someone) a right to

entity *noun* (*plural* **entities**) something which exists; a being

entomology *noun* the study of insects □ **entomologist** *noun*

entourage /*onh*toorahzh/ *noun* followers, attendants

entr'acte *noun* **1** an interval between acts in a play **2** a piece of music *etc* performed between acts

entrails *noun plural* the inner parts of an animal's body, the bowels

entrance[1] /*en*trəns/ *noun* **1** a place for entering, *eg* a door **2** the act of coming in **3** the right to enter □ **entrant** *noun* someone who goes in for a race, competition *etc*

entrance[2] /in*trans*/ *verb* **1** delight, charm **2** bewitch □ **entrancing** *adj*

entreat *verb* ask earnestly □ **entreaty** *noun* (*plural* **entreaties**)

entrecote /*onh*trəkoht/ *noun* a steak cut from between two ribs

entrée /*on*treh/ *noun* **1** *Brit* a dish served between courses **2** *US* a main course

entrenched *adj* **1** firmly established **2** unmoving, inflexible

entre nous /onhtrə *noo*/ *adv* between ourselves

entrepreneur /onhtrəprə*nuhr*/ *noun* someone who undertakes an enterprise, often with financial involvement □ **entrepreneurial** *adj*

entresol /*onh*trəsol/ *noun* a low storey between two others in a building

entropy *noun* the tendency of all energy to become inert

entrust or **intrust** *verb* place in someone else's care

entry (*plural* **entries**) **1** the act of entering **2** a place for entering, a doorway **3** a name or item in a record book

E-number *noun* an identification

code for food additives, *eg* E102 for tartrazine

enumerate *verb* **1** count **2** mention individually ▯ **enumeration** *noun*

enunciate *verb* **1** pronounce distinctly **2** state formally ▯ **enunciation** *noun*

envelop *verb* **1** cover by wrapping **2** surround entirely: *enveloped in mist*

envelope *noun* a wrapping or cover, *esp* for a letter

environment *noun* surroundings, circumstances in which someone or an animal lives

environs /in*vair*ənz/ *noun plural* surrounding area, neighbourhood

envisage *verb* **1** visualize, picture in the mind **2** consider, contemplate

envoy *noun* a messenger, *esp* one sent to deal with a foreign government

envy *noun* (*plural* **envies**) greedy desire for someone else's property, qualities *etc* ▯ *verb* feel envy for ▯ **enviable** *adj* worth envying, worth having ▯ **envious** *adj* feeling envy ▯ **enviously** *adv*

> **envy** *verb* » envi*es*, envy*ing*, envi*ed*

enzyme *noun* a substance produced in a living body which affects the speed of chemical changes

eon *another spelling* of **aeon**

epaulet or **epaulette** *noun* a shoulder ornament on a uniform

ephemeral *adj* very short-lived, fleeting ▯ **ephemerality** *noun*

epic *noun* a long poem, story, film *etc* about heroic deeds ▯ *adj* **1** of an epic; heroic **2** large-scale, impressive

epicene *noun* common to both sexes

epicentre or *US* **epicenter** *noun* the centre of an earthquake

epicure *noun* a gourmet ▯ **epicurean** *adj*

epidemic *noun* a widespread outbreak of a disease *etc*

epidermis *noun* the top covering of the skin ▯ **epidermal** or **epidermic** *adj*

epidural *noun* (short for **epidural anaesthetic**) the injection of anaesthetic into the spine to ease pain in the lower half of the body

epiglottis *noun* a piece of skin at the back of the tongue which closes the windpipe during swallowing

epigram *noun* a short, witty saying ▯ **epigrammatic** *adj*

epilepsy *noun* an illness causing attacks of unconsciousness and convulsions ▯ **epileptic** *adj* **1** suffering from epilepsy **2** of epilepsy: *an epileptic fit* ▯ *noun* someone suffering from epilepsy

epilogue or *US* **epilog** *noun* **1** the very end part of a book, programme *etc* **2** a speech at the end of a play

epiphany *noun* **1** a Christian festival celebrated on 6 January **2** a sudden revelation or insight

episcopal *adj* of or ruled by

bishops ◇ **episcopalian** *adj* belonging to a church ruled by bishops ◇ **episcopacy** *noun*

episode *noun* **1** one of several parts of a story *etc* **2** an interesting event ◇ **episodic** *adj* happening at irregular intervals

epistle *noun* a formal letter, *esp* one from an apostle of Christ in the Bible ◇ **epistolary** *adj* written in the form of letters

epitaph *noun* words on a gravestone about a dead person

epithet *noun* a word used to describe someone; an adjective

epitome /*əpitə*mi/ *noun* **1** a perfect example or representative of something: *the epitome of good taste* **2** a summary of a book *etc* ◇ **epitomize** *verb* be the epitome of something

EPNS *abbrev* electroplated nickel silver

epoch *noun* an extended period of time, often marked by a series of important events ◇ **epochal** *adj* ◇ **epochmaking** *adj* marking an important point in history

epoxy resin a type of synthetic adhesive

EPROM /*ee*prom/ *abbrev*, *comput* electrically programmable read-only memory

Epsom salts a purgative medicine

equable *adj* **1** of calm temper **2** of climate: neither very hot nor very cold ◇ **equably** *adv*

equal *adj* **1** of the same size, value, quantity *etc* **2** evenly balanced **3** (with **to**) able, fit for: *not equal to the job* ◇ *noun* someone of the same rank, cleverness *etc* as another ◇ *verb* **1** be or make equal to **2** be the same as ◇ **equality** *noun* ◇ **equalize** *verb* make equal ◇ **equalizer** *noun* a goal *etc* which draws the score in a game ◇ **equally** *adv*

> **equal** *verb* » equal*s*, equall*ing*, equall*ed*

equanimity *noun* evenness of temper, calmness

equate *verb* **1** regard or treat as the same **2** state as being equal ◇ **equation** *noun* a statement, *esp* in mathematics, that two things are equal

equator *noun* an imaginary line around the earth, halfway between the North and South Poles ◇ **equatorial** *adj* on or near the equator

equerry *noun* (*plural* **equerries**) *noun* a royal attendant

equestrian *adj* **1** of horse-riding **2** on horseback ◇ *noun* a horse-rider

equi- *prefix* equal ◇ **equidistant** *adj* equally distant ◇ **equilateral** *adj* of a triangle: with all sides equal (*compare with*: **isosceles**)

equilibrium *noun* **1** equal balance between weights, forces *etc* **2** a balanced state of mind or feelings

equine *adj* of or like a horse

equinox *noun* either of the times (about 21 March and 23 September) when the sun crosses the equator, making night and day equal in length ◇ **equinoctial** *adj*

equip *verb* supply with everything needed for a task ◇ **equipage** *noun* attendants, retinue ◇ **equipment**

noun a set of tools *etc* needed for a task; an outfit

> **equip** » equip*s*, equipp*ing*, equipp*ed*

equipoise *noun* balance

equitable *adj* fair, just ▯ **equitably** *adv*

equity *noun* **1** fairness, just dealing **2** (**Equity**) the trade union for the British acting profession ▯ **negative equity** *see* **negative**

equivalent *adj* equal in value, power, meaning *etc* ▯ *noun* something that is the equal of another

equivocal *adj* having more than one meaning; ambiguous, uncertain ▯ **equivocally** *adv*

equivocate *verb* use ambiguous words in order to mislead ▯ **equivocation** *noun*

era *noun* a period in history: *the Jacobean era/ the era of steam*

eradicate *verb* get rid of completely ▯ **eradication** *noun*

erase *verb* **1** rub out **2** remove ▯ **eraser** *noun* something which erases, a rubber ▯ **erasure** *noun*

ere *prep & conj* before: *ere long*

erect *verb* **1** build **2** set upright ▯ *adj* standing straight up ▯ **erection** *noun* **1** the act of erecting **2** something erected **3** an erect penis

erg *noun* a unit of energy

ergo /*er*goh/ *adv* therefore

ergonomic /ergoh*nom*ik/ *adj* of a workplace, machine *etc*: adapted to suit human needs and comfort ▯ **ergonomically** *adv* ▯ **ergonomics** *noun sing* ▯ **ergonomist** *noun*

ermine *noun* **1** a stoat **2** its white fur

ERNIE *abbrev* electronic random number indicator equipment, a computer that chooses winning premium bond numbers at random

erode *verb* wear away, destroy gradually ▯ **erosion** *noun*

erotic *adj* of or arousing sexual desire ▯ **erotica** *noun plural* erotic art or literature ▯ **eroticism** *noun* ▯ **eroticize** *verb* make erotic

err *verb* **1** make a mistake **2** sin

errand *noun* a short journey to carry a message, buy something *etc*

errant *adj* **1** doing wrong **2** wandering in search of adventure: *knight errant*

erratic *adj* **1** irregular, not following a fixed course **2** not steady or reliable in behaviour ▯ **erratically** *adv*

erratum *noun* (*plural* **errata**) an error in a book

erroneous *adj* wrong ▯ **erroneously** *adv*

error *noun* **1** a mistake **2** wrongdoing

ersatz *adj* **1** imitation, fake **2** second-rate, shoddy

erudite *adj* well-educated or well-read, learned ▯ **erudition** *noun*

erupt *verb* break out or through ▯ **eruption** *noun* **1** an outburst from a volcano **2** a rash or spot on the skin

escalate *verb* increase in amount, intensity *etc* ◊ **escalation** *noun* ◊ **escalator** *noun* a moving stairway

escalope *noun* a slice of meat beaten to make it thinner before cooking

escape *verb* **1** get away safe or free **2** of gas *etc*: leak **3** slip from memory: *his name escapes me* ◊ *noun* the act of escaping ◊ **escapade** *noun* an adventure ◊ **escapement** *noun* a device which controls the movement of a watch or clock ◊ **escapism** *noun* the tendency to escape from reality by daydreaming *etc* ◊ **escapist** *noun* & *adj*

escarpment *noun* a steep side of a hill or rock

eschew *verb, formal* shun, avoid

escort *noun* someone who accompanies others for protection, courtesy *etc* ◊ *verb* act as escort to

escritoire *noun* a writing desk

escudo *noun* the main currency unit of Portugal

escutcheon *noun* a shield with a coat of arms

Eskimo *noun* (*plural* **Eskimos**) Inuit

esoteric *adj* understood by a small number of people

ESP *abbrev* extrasensory perception

esparto *noun* a strong grass grown in Spain and N Africa, used for making paper and ropes

Esperanto *noun* an international language created in the 19th century

especial *adj* **1** special, extraordinary **2** particular ◊ **especially** *adv*

espionage *noun* spying, *esp* by one country to find out the secrets of another

esplanade *noun* a level roadway, *esp* along a seafront

espouse *verb* adopt, embrace (a cause)

espresso *noun* strong coffee made by extraction under high pressure

esprit de corps loyalty to, or among, a group

espy /espai/ *verb, old* watch, observe

Esq *abbrev* or **Esquire** *noun* a courtesy title written after a man's name: *Robert Brown, Esq*

essay *noun* **1** a written composition **2** an attempt ◊ *verb* try ◊ **essayist** *noun* a writer of essays

essence *noun* **1** the most important part or quality of something **2** a concentrated extract from a plant *etc*: *vanilla essence*

essential *adj* absolutely necessary ◊ *noun* an absolute requirement ◊ **essentially** *adv* **1** basically **2** necessarily

establish *verb* **1** settle in position **2** found, set up **3** show to be true, prove (that) ◊ **established** *adj* **1** firmly set up **2** accepted, recognized **3** of a church: officially recognized as national ◊ **establishment** *noun* a place of business, residence *etc* ◊ **The Establishment** the people holding influential positions in a community

estate *noun* **1** a large piece of private land **2** someone's total possessions **3** land built on with houses, factories *etc*: *housing estate/ industrial estate* □ **estate agent** someone who sells and leases property for clients □ **estate car** a car with an inside luggage compartment and a rear door □ **the fourth estate** the press, the media

esteem *verb* think highly of; value □ *noun* high value or opinion □ **esteemed** *adj*

estimate *verb* judge roughly the size, amount or value of something □ *noun* a rough judgement of size *etc* □ **estimation** *noun* opinion, judgement

estranged *adj* no longer friendly; separated

estuary *noun* (*plural* **estuaries**) the wide lower part of a river, up which the tide travels

et al *abbrev* and others (from Latin *et alii*, *aliae* or *alia*)

etc or **&c** *abbrev* and other things of the same sort (from Latin *et cetera*)

etch *verb* draw on metal or glass by eating out the lines with acid □ **etching** *noun* a picture printed from an etched metal plate

eternal *adj* **1** lasting for ever **2** seemingly endless □ **eternally** *adv* □ **eternity** *noun* **1** time without end **2** the time or state after death

ether *noun* a colourless liquid used as an anaesthetic, or to dissolve fats

ethereal *adj* delicate, airy, spirit-like □ **ethereally** *adv* □ **ethereality** *noun*

ethical *adj* having to do with right behaviour, justice, duty; right, just, honourable □ **ethically** *adv* □ **ethics** *noun sing* the study of right and wrong; (belief in) standards leading to right, ethical behaviour

ethnic *adj* **1** of race or culture **2** of the culture of a particular race or group □ **ethnically** *adv* □ **ethnicity** *noun*

ethnocentric *adj* believing in the superiority of your own culture □ **ethnocentrism** *noun*

ethnology *noun* the study of human cultures and civilizations □ **ethnological** *adj* □ **ethnologist** *noun*

etiolate *verb* **1** of a plant: grow pale through lack of light **2** make feeble □ **etiolated** *adj*

etiquette *noun* rules governing correct social behaviour

etymology *noun* (*plural* **etymologies**) **1** the study of the history of words **2** the history of a word □ **etymological** *adj* □ **etymologist** *noun*

eucalyptus *noun* (*plural* **eucalyptuses** or **eucalypti**) a large Australian evergreen tree whose leaves produce a pungent oil

eucharist *noun* **1** the Christian sacrament of the Lord's Supper **2** bread and wine *etc* taken as a sacrament

eugenics *noun sing* the science of trying to improve a race or stock by selective breeding *etc* □ **eugenicist** *noun & adj*

eulogy *noun* (*plural* **eulogies**) a speech, poem *etc* in praise of someone □ **eulogize** *verb* praise greatly

eunuch /*yoo*nək/ *noun* a castrated man

euphemism *noun* a vague word or phrase used to refer to an unpleasant subject, *eg* 'passed on' for 'died' □ **euphemistic** *adj*

euphonious *adj* pleasant in sound, harmonious □ **euphonium** *noun* a brass musical instrument with a low tone □ **euphony** *noun*

euphorbia *noun* a flowering plant with a milky, poisonous sap

euphoria *noun* a feeling of great happiness, joy □ **euphoric** *adj*

euphuism *noun* florid writing style □ **euphuistic** *adj*

eurhythmics *noun sing* the art of graceful movement of the body, *esp* to music

Euro- *prefix* of Europe or the European community: *Euro-budget/ Eurocrat* □ **Eurosceptic** *noun & adj*, *Brit* (someone) opposed to strengthening the powers of the European community

euthanasia *noun* the killing of someone painlessly, *esp* to end suffering

evacuate *verb* (cause to) leave *esp* because of danger; make empty □ **evacuation** *noun* □ **evacuee** *noun* someone who has been evacuated (from danger)

evade *verb* avoid or escape *esp* by cleverness or trickery □ **evasion** *noun* □ **evasive** *adj* with the purpose of evading; not straightforward: *an evasive answer*

evaluate *verb* find or state the value of

evanescent *adj* passing away quickly

evangelical *adj* **1** spreading Christian teaching **2** strongly advocating some cause □ **evangelist** *noun* □ **evangelistic** *adj*

evaporate *verb* **1** change into vapour **2** vanish □ **evaporation** *noun*

evasion *see* **evade**

eve *noun* **1** the evening or day before a festival: *New Year's Eve* **2** the time just before an event: *the eve of the revolution*

even *adj* **1** level, smooth **2** of a number: able to be divided by 2 without a remainder (*contrasted with*: **odd**) **3** calm □ *adv* **1** used to emphasize another word: *even harder than before/ even a child would understand* **2** exactly, just □ *verb* make even or smooth □ **even-handed** *adv* fair, unbiased □ **evenly** *adv* □ **evenness** *noun* □ **even out** become equal □ **get even with** get revenge on

evening *noun* the last part of the day and early part of the night

evensong *noun* an evening service in the Anglican church

event *noun* **1** an important happening **2** an item in a sports programme *etc* □ **eventful** *adj* exciting

eventide home a residential home for the elderly

eventual *adj* **1** final **2** happening as a result ▯ **eventuality** *noun* (*plural* **eventualities**) a possible happening ▯ **eventually** *adv* at last, finally

ever *adv* **1** always, for ever **2** at any time, at all: *I won't ever see her again* **3** that has existed, on record: *the best ever* ▯ **evergreen** *noun* a tree with green leaves all the year round ▯ **everlasting** *adj* lasting for ever, eternal ▯ **evermore** *adv, old* forever

every *adj* each of several things without exception ▯ **everybody** or **everyone** *pronoun* each person without exception ▯ **everyday** *adj* **1** daily **2** common, usual ▯ **everything** *pronoun* all things ▯ **everywhere** *adv* in every place ▯ **every other** one out of every two, alternate

evict *verb* force (someone) out of their house, *esp* by law ▯ **eviction** *noun*

evidence *noun* **1** a clear sign; proof **2** information given in a law case

evident *adj* easily seen or understood ▯ **evidently** *adv*

evil *adj* wicked, very bad; malicious ▯ *noun* wickedness ▯ **evilly** *adv*

evince *verb* show, display: *they evinced no surprise*

eviscerate *verb* tear out the bowels of; gut

evoke *verb* draw out, produce: *evoking memories of their childhood* ▯ **evocative** *adj* evoking memories or atmosphere

evolution *noun* **1** gradual development **2** the belief that the higher forms of life have gradually developed out of the lower ▯ **evolutionary** *adj*

evolve *verb* **1** develop gradually **2** work out (a plan *etc*)

ewe *noun* a female sheep

ewer *noun* a large jug with a wide spout

ex *noun, informal* a former husband, wife or lover

ex- *prefix* **1** no longer, former: *ex-husband/ ex-president* **2** outside, not in: *ex-directory number*

exacerbate *verb* make worse or more severe

> ⚠Do not confuse with: **exasperate**

exact *adj* **1** accurate, precise **2** punctual **3** careful ▯ *verb* compel to pay, give *etc*: *exacting revenge* ▯ **exactly** *adv* ▯ **exactness** *noun* accuracy, correctness

exacting *adj* **1** asking too much **2** wearying, tiring

exaggerate *verb* make to seem larger or greater than reality ▯ **exaggeration** *noun*

exalt *verb* **1** raise in rank **2** praise **3** make joyful ▯ **exaltation** *noun*

exam *noun* an examination

examination *noun* **1** a formal test of knowledge or skill: *driving examination* **2** a close inspection or inquiry **3** formal questioning

examine *verb* **1** put questions to (pupils *etc*) to test knowledge **2** question (a witness) **3** look at closely, inquire into **4** look over (someone's body) for signs of illness □ **examiner** *noun*

example *noun* **1** something taken as a representative of its kind: *an example of early French glass* **2** a warning

exasperate *verb* make very angry □ **exasperation** *noun*

> ⚠Do not confuse with: **exacerbate**

ex-cathedra *adj* **1** spoken with authority **2** of a papal decree: infallible

excavate *verb* **1** dig, scoop out **2** uncover by digging □ **excavation** *noun* **1** the act of digging out **2** a hollow made by digging □ **excavator** *noun* a machine used for excavating

exceed *verb* go beyond, be greater than

exceedingly *adv* very

excel *verb* **1** do very well **2** be better than

> **excel** » excel*s*, excel*ling*, excel*led*

excellence *noun* the fact of being excellent, very high quality

Excellency *noun* (*plural* **Excellencies**) a title of ambassadors *etc*

excellent *adj* unusually or extremely good

except *prep* leaving out, not counting □ *conj* with the exception (that) □ *verb* leave out, not to count □ **except for** with the exception of □ **excepting** *prep* except

exception *noun* **1** something left out **2** something unlike the rest: *an exception to the rule* □ **take exception to** object to, be offended by

exceptional *adj* standing out from the rest □ **exceptionally** *adv* very, extremely

excerpt /*ek*sert/ *noun* a part chosen from a whole work: *excerpt from a play*

> ⚠Do not confuse with: **exert**

excess *noun* **1** a going beyond what is usual or proper **2** the amount by which one thing is greater than another **3** (**excesses**) very bad behaviour □ *adj* beyond the amount allowed

> ⚠Do not confuse with: **access**

excessive *adj* too much, too great *etc* □ **excessively** *adv*

exchange *verb* give (one thing) and get another in return □ *noun* **1** the act of exchanging **2** exchanging money of one country for that of another **3** the difference between the value of money in different places: *rate of exchange* **4** a central office or building: *telephone exchange* **5** a place where business shares are bought and sold

exchequer a government office concerned with a country's finances □ **Chancellor of the Exchequer** see **chancellor**

> From the chequered cloth used to aid calculation in medieval revenue offices

excise[1] *verb* cut off or out ▯ **excision** *noun*

excise[2] tax on goods *etc* made and sold within a country and on certain licences *etc*

excite *verb* **1** rouse the feelings of **2** move to action ▯ **excitable** *adj* easily excited ▯ **excitement** *noun* ▯ **exciting** *adj*

exclaim *verb* cry or shout out

exclamation *noun* a sudden shout ▯ **exclamation mark** a punctuation mark (!) used for emphasis, or to indicate surpise *etc*

exclamatory *adj* exclaiming, emphatic

exclude *verb* **1** shut out **2** prevent from sharing **3** leave out of consideration ▯ **exclusion** *noun*

exclusive *adj* **1** only open to certain people, select: *an exclusive club* **2** not obtainable elsewhere: *exclusive offer* ▯ **exclusive of** not including

excommunicate *verb* expel from membership of a church ▯ **excommunication** *noun*

excoriate *verb* **1** strip the skin from **2** criticize strongly

excrement *noun* the waste matter cast out by humans or animals

excrescence *noun* an unwelcome growth, *eg* a wart

excrete *verb* discharge (waste matter) from the body ▯ **excreta** *noun plural* discharged waste products

excruciating *adj* **1** of pain *etc*: very severe **2** painfully bad: *an excruciating performance*

exculpate *verb* absolve from a crime; vindicate ▯ **exculpation** *noun* ▯ **exculpatory** *adj*

excursion *noun* an outing for pleasure, *eg* picnic

excuse *verb* **1** forgive, pardon **2** set free from a duty or task ▯ *noun* an explanation for having done something wrong ▯ **excusable** *adj* pardonable

execrable *adj* very bad

execrate *verb* curse, denounce

execute *verb* **1** perform: *execute a dance step* **2** carry out: *execute commands* **3** put to death legally

execution *noun* **1** a doing or performing **2** killing by order of the law ▯ **executioner** *noun* someone with the job of putting condemned prisoners to death

executive *adj* having power to act or carry out laws ▯ *noun* **1** the part of a government with such power **2** a business manager

executor *noun* someone who sees that the requests stated in a will are carried out

exegesis *noun* a critical discussion of a literary text

exemplary *adj* **1** worth following as an example: *exemplary conduct* **2** acting as a warning: *exemplary punishment*

exemplify *verb* **1** be an example of **2** demonstrate by example

> **exemplify** » exemplifi*es*, exemplify*ing*, exemplifi*ed*

exempt *verb* **1** grant freedom from an unwelcome task, payment *etc* ▯

adj free (from), not liable for payment *etc* ▯ **exemption** *noun*

exercise *noun* **1** a task for practice **2** a physical routine for training muscles *etc* ▯ *verb* **1** give exercise to **2** use: *exercise great care*

⚠Do not confuse with: **exorcize**

exert *verb* bring into action, use: *exerting great influence* ▯ **exert yourself** make a great effort

⚠Do not confuse with: **excerpt**

exertion *noun* or **exertions** *noun plural* effort(s); hard work

exeunt *verb* leave the stage (a direction printed in a playscript): *exeunt Rosencrantz and Guildenstern*

exhale *verb* breathe out ▯ **exhalation** *noun*

exhaust *verb* **1** tire out **2** use up completely: *we've exhausted our supplies* **3** say all that can be said about (a subject *etc*) ▯ *noun* a device for expelling waste fumes from fuel engines ▯ **exhausted** *adj* **1** tired out **2** emptied; used up ▯ **exhaustion** *noun* ▯ **exhaustive** *adj* extremely thorough: *exhaustive research* ▯ **exhaustively** *adv*

exhibit *verb* show; put on public display ▯ *noun* something on display in a gallery *etc* ▯ **exhibitor** *noun*

exhibition *noun* a public show, an open display

exhibitionism *noun* a tendency to try to attract people's attention ▯ **exhibitionist** *noun*

exhilarate *verb* make joyful or lively, refresh ▯ **exhilarating** *adj* ▯ **exhilaration** *noun*

exhort *verb* urge (to do) ▯ **exhortation** *noun*

exhume *verb* dig out (a buried body) ▯ **exhumation** *noun*

exigency *noun* (*plural* **exigencies**) an urgent need or demand

exigent *adj* demanding immediate attention; urgent

exiguous *adj* meagre, scanty

exile *noun* **1** someone who lives outside their own country, by choice or unwillingly **2** a period of living in a foreign country ▯ *verb* drive (someone) away from their own country; banish

exist *verb* **1** be, have life; live **2** live in poor circumstances ▯ **existence** *noun* ▯ **existent** *adj*

exit *noun* **1** a way out **2** the act of going out: *a hasty exit*

exodus *noun* a going away of many people (*esp* those leaving a country for ever)

exonerate *verb* free from blame ▯ **exoneration** *noun*

exorbitant *adj* going beyond what is usual or reasonable: *exorbitant price* ▯ **exorbitance** *noun*

exorcize *verb* **1** drive out (an evil spirit) **2** free from possession by an evil spirit ▯ **exorcism** *noun* the act of driving away evil spirits ▯ **exorcist** *noun*

⚠Do not confuse with: **exercise**

exotic *adj* **1** coming from a foreign country **2** unusual, colourful

expand *verb* **1** grow wider or bigger **2** open out

expanse *noun* a wide stretch of land *etc*

expansion *noun* a growing, stretching or spreading

expansive *adj* **1** spreading out **2** talkative, telling much ◊ **expansively** *adv*

expat *noun, informal* an expatriate

expatiate *verb* talk a great deal (about something)

expatriate *adj* living outside your native country ◊ *noun* someone living abroad

expect *verb* **1** think of as likely to happen or arrive soon: *what did you expect her to say?* **2** think, assume: *I expect he's too busy* ◊ **expectancy** *noun* ◊ **expectant** *adj* **1** hopeful, expecting **2** waiting to become: *expectant mother* ◊ **expectation** *noun* ◊ **expecting** *adj, informal* pregnant

expedient *adj* done for speed or convenience rather than fairness or truth ◊ *noun* something done to get round a difficulty ◊ **expedience** or **expediency** *noun*

expedite *verb* hasten, hurry on

expedition *noun* **1** a journey with a purpose, often for exploration **2** people making such a journey ◊ **expeditionary** *adj* of or forming an expedition

expeditious *adj* swift, speedy ◊ **expeditiously** *adv*

expel *verb* **1** drive or force out **2** send away in disgrace, *eg* from a school ◊ **expulsion** *noun*

expel » expel*s*, expell*ing*, expell*ed*

expend *verb* spend, use up ◊ **expenditure** *noun* an amount spent or used up, *esp* money

expense *noun* **1** cost **2** a cause of spending: *the house was a continual expense* **3** (**expenses**) money spent in carrying out a job *etc*

expensive *adj* costing a lot of money ◊ **expensively** *adv*

experience *noun* **1** an event in which you are involved: *a horrific experience* **2** knowledge gained from events, practice *etc* ◊ *verb* go through, undergo ◊ **experienced** *adj* skilled, knowledgeable

experiment *noun* a trial, a test (of an idea, machine *etc*) ◊ *verb* carry out experiments ◊ **experimental** *adj* ◊ **experimentally** *adv*

expert *adj* highly skilful or knowledgeable (in a particular subject) ◊ *noun* someone who is highly skilled or knowledgeable ◊ **expertise** /ekspərteez/ *noun* skill

expiate *verb* make up for (a crime *etc*) ◊ **expiation** *noun*

expire *verb* **1** die **2** come to an end, become invalid: *your visa has expired* ◊ **expiry** *noun* the end or finish

explain *verb* **1** make clear **2** give reasons for: *please explain your behaviour*

explanation *noun* a statement which makes clear something difficult or puzzling; a reason (*eg* for your behaviour)

explanatory *adj* intended to make clear

expletive *noun* an exclamation, *esp* a swear word

explicable *adj* able to be explained □ **explicably** *adv*

explicit *adj* plainly stated or shown; outspoken, frank □ **explicitly** *adv* □ **explicitness** *noun*

explode *verb* **1** blow up like a bomb with loud noise **2** prove to be wrong or unfounded: *that explodes your theory*

exploit *noun* a daring deed; a feat □ *verb* **1** make use of selfishly **2** make good use of (resources *etc*) □ **exploitation** *noun*

explore *verb* make a journey of discovery □ **exploration** *noun* □ **explorer** *noun*

explosion *noun* a sudden violent burst or blow-up

explosive *adj* **1** liable to explode **2** hot-tempered □ *noun* something that will explode, *eg* gunpowder □ **explosively** *adv*

exponent *noun* someone who shows skill in a particular art or craft: *an exponent of karate* □ **exponential** *adj*

export *verb* sell goods *etc* in a foreign country □ *noun* **1** an act of exporting **2** something exported □ **exportation** *noun*

expose *verb* **1** place in full view **2** show up (a hidden crime *etc*) **3** lay open to the sun or wind **4** allow light to reach and act on (a film) □ **exposition** *noun* **1** a public display **2** a statement explaining a writer's meaning □ **exposure** *noun*

exposé /eks*poh*zeh/ *noun* a report *etc* exposing a scandal or crime

expostulate *verb* protest □ **expostulation** *noun*

exposure *see* **expose**

expound *verb* explain fully

express *verb* **1** show by action **2** put into words **3** press or squeeze out □ *adj* **1** clearly stated: *express instructions* **2** sent in haste: *express messenger* □ *noun* a fast train, bus *etc*

expression *noun* **1** the look on someone's face: *expression of horror* **2** showing meaning or emotion through language, art *etc* **3** a show of emotion in an artistic performance *etc* **4** a word or phrase: *idiomatic expression* **5** pressing or squeezing out

expressive *adj* expressing meaning or feeling clearly □ **expressively** *adv*

expropriate *verb* take (property *etc*) away from its owner

expulsion *see* **expel**

expunge *verb* rub out, remove

expurgate *noun* remove offensive material from (a book *etc*), censor

exquisite *adj* **1** extremely beautiful **2** excellent **3** very great, utter: *exquisite pleasure*

extempore /iks*tem*pəreh/ *adv* & *adj* at a moment's notice, without preparation □ **extemporize** *verb* make up on the spot, improvise

extend *verb* **1** stretch, make longer **2** hold out: *extended a hand* **3** last, carry over: *my holiday extends into next week*

extension *noun* **1** a part added to a building **2** an additional amount of time on a schedule, holiday *etc* **3** a telephone connected with a main one

extensive *adj* **1** wide; covering a large space **2** happening in many places **3** wide-ranging, sweeping: *extensive changes* □ **extensively** *adv*

extent *noun* **1** the space something covers **2** degree: *to a great extent*

extenuate *verb* **1** lessen **2** make to seem less bad: *extenuating circumstances* □ **extenuation** *noun*

exterior *adj* on the outside; outer: *exterior wall* □ *noun* the outside of a building *etc*

exterminate *verb* kill off completely (a race, a type of animal *etc*), wipe out □ **extermination** *noun*

external *adj* **1** outside; on the outside **2** not central: *external considerations*

extinct *adj* **1** no longer active: *extinct volcano* **2** no longer found alive: *the dodo is now extinct* □ **extinction** *noun* making or becoming extinct

extinguish *verb* **1** put out (fire *etc*) **2** put an end to □ **extinguisher** *noun* a spray containing chemicals for putting out fires

extirpate *verb* destroy completely, exterminate

> ⚠Do not confuse with: **extricate** and **extrapolate**

extol *verb* praise greatly

> **extol** » extol*s*, extoll*ing*, extoll*ed*

extort *verb* take by force or threats □ **extortion** *noun* □ **extortionate** *adj* of a price: much too high

extra *adj* more than is usual or necessary; additional □ *adv* unusually; more than is average: *extra large* □ *noun* **1** something extra **2** someone employed to be one of a crowd in a film

extra- *prefix* outside, beyond

extract *verb* **1** draw or pull out, *esp* by force: *extract a tooth* **2** remove selected parts of a book *etc* **3** draw out by pressure or chemical action □ *noun* **1** an excerpt from a book *etc* **2** a substance obtained by extraction: *vanilla extract* □ **extraction** *noun* **1** the act of extracting **2** someone's descent or lineage: *of Irish extraction*

extracurricular *adj* done outside school or college hours

extradite *verb* hand over (someone wanted for trial) to the police of another country □ **extradition** *noun*

extramarital *adj* happening outside a marriage: *extramarital affair*

extramural *adj* of a university department: teaching courses outwith the regular degree courses

extraneous *adj* having nothing to do with the subject: *extraneous information* □ **extraneously** *adv*

extraordinary *adj* **1** not usual,

exceptional **2** very surprising **3** specially employed: *ambassador extraordinary* □ **extraordinarily** *adv*

extrapolate *verb* infer or predict on the basis of known facts

> ⚠Do not confuse with: **extirpate** and **extricate**

extrasensory *adj* beyond the range of the ordinary senses: *extrasensory perception*

extraterrestrial *adj* from outside the earth □ *noun* a being from another planet

extravagant *adj* **1** spending too freely; wasteful **2** too great, overblown: *extravagant praise* □ **extravagantly** *adv* □ **extravagance** *noun*

extravaganza *noun* an extravagant creation or production

extravert or **extrovert** *noun* an outgoing, sociable person

extreme *adj* **1** far from the centre **2** far from the ordinary or usual **3** very great: *extreme sadness* □ *noun* an extreme point □ **extremely** *adv*

extremist *noun* someone who carries ideas foolishly far □ **extremism** *noun*

extremity *noun* (*plural* **extremities**) **1** a part or place furthest from the centre **2** great distress or pain **3** (**extremities**) the hands and feet

extricate *verb* free from (difficulties *etc*)

> ⚠Do not confuse with: **extirpate** and **extrapolate**

extrovert *another spelling of* **extravert**

extrude *verb* protrude, stick out

exuberant *adj* in very high spirits □ **exuberantly** *adv* □ **exuberance** *noun*

exude *verb* give off in large amounts: *exuding sweat/ exuded happiness*

exult *verb* be very glad, rejoice greatly: *exulting in their victory* □ **exultant** *adj* □ **exultation** *noun*

eye *noun* **1** the part of the body with which you see **2** the ability to notice: *an eye for detail* **3** sight **4** something the shape of an eye, *eg* the hole in a needle □ *verb* look at with interest: *eyeing the last slice of cake* □ **eyeball** *noun* the round part of the eye; the eye itself (the part between the eyelids) □ **eyebrow** *noun* the hairy ridge above the eye □ **eyeglass** *noun* a lens to correct faulty eyesight □ **eyelash** *noun* one of the hairs on the edge of the eyelid □ **eyelet** *noun* a small hole for a lace *etc* □ **eyelid** *noun* the skin covering of the eye □ **eye-opener** *noun* that which shows up something unexpected □ **eyesore** *noun* anything that is ugly (*esp* a building) □ **eye-wash** *noun* □ **eye-witness** *noun* someone who sees a thing done (*eg* a crime committed)

> **eye** *verb* » eye*s*, eye*ing*, eye*d*

eyrie or **eyry** /eeri/ or /airi/ *noun* the nest of an eagle or other bird of prey

F

°F *abbrev* degree(s) Fahrenheit

FA *abbrev*, *Brit* Football Association

fable *noun* a story about animals *etc*, including a lesson or moral

fabric *noun* **1** cloth **2** framework; the external parts of a building *etc*

fabricate *verb* make up (lies) ◊ **fabrication** *noun*

fabulous *adj* **1** *informal* very good, excellent **2** imaginary, mythological ◊ **fabulously** *adv* ◊ **fabulousness** *noun*

façade /fə*sahd*/ *noun* **1** the front of a building **2** a deceptive appearance or act; a mask

face *noun* **1** the front part of the head **2** the front of anything **3** appearance ◊ *verb* **1** turn or stand in the direction of **2** stand opposite to **3** put an additional surface on ◊ **face pack** a cosmetic paste applied to the face and left to dry ◊ **face-powder** cosmetic powder for the face ◊ **face up to** meet or accept boldly: *facing up to responsibilities*

facet *noun* **1** a side of a many-sided object, *eg* a cut gem **2** an aspect; a characteristic

facetious *adj* not meant seriously; joking ◊ **facetiously** *adv* ◊ **facetiousness** *noun*

facial *adj* of the face ◊ **facially** *adv*

facile /*fa*sail/ *adj* **1** not deep or thorough; superficial, glib **2** fluent ◊ **facilely** *adv*

facilitate *verb* make easy ◊ **facilitator** *noun*

facility *noun* **1** ease **2** skill, ability **3** (**facilities**) buildings, equipment *etc* provided for a purpose: *sports facilities*

facsimile *noun* an exact copy

fact *noun* **1** something known or held to be true **2** reality **3** *law* a deed ◊ **in fact** actually, really

faction *noun* a group that is part of a larger group, acting together: *rival factions*

factious *adj* trouble-making, riotous ◊ **factiously** *adv* ◊ **factiousness** *noun*

factitious *adj* produced artificially ◊ **factitiously** *adv* ◊ **factitiousness** *noun*

factoid *noun* an unproved statement accepted as a fact

factor *noun* **1** something affecting the course of events **2** someone who does business for another **3** a number which exactly divides into another (*eg* 3 is a factor of 6) ◊ **factorize** *verb* find factors of

factory *noun* (*plural* **factories**) a workshop producing goods in large quantities

factotum *noun* someone employed to do all kinds of work

factual *adj* consisting of facts; real, not fictional: *factual account*

faculty *noun* (*plural* **faculties**) **1** power of the mind, *eg* reason **2**

a natural power of the body, *eg* hearing **3** ability, aptitude **4** a department of study in a university: *Faculty of Arts*

fad *noun* **1** an odd like or dislike **2** a temporary fashion ◻ **faddist** *noun* a follower of a fad ◻ **faddy** *adj*

fade *verb* **1** (make to) lose colour or strength **2** disappear gradually, *eg* from sight or hearing

faeces */feeseez/ noun plural* solid excrement

faff *verb, informal* dither, fumble: *don't faff about*

fag *noun* **1** tiring work **2** *slang* a cigarette **3** *informal* a young schoolboy forced to do jobs for an older one **4** *US slang, derogatory* a male homosexual ◻ **fag end** *informal* **1** a cigarette butt **2** the very end, the tail end ◻ **fagged out** *informal* exhausted, tired out

faggot or *US* **fagot** *noun* **1** a bundle of sticks **2** a meatball **3** *US slang, derogatory* a male homosexual

Fahrenheit *noun* a temperature scale on which water freezes at 32° and boils at 212° ◻ *adj* measured on this scale: *70° Fahrenheit*

fail *verb* **1** (declare to) be unsuccessful **2** break down, stop **3** lose strength **4** be lacking or insufficient **5** disappoint ◻ **fail-safe** *adj* made to correct automatically, or be safe, if a fault occurs ◻ **without fail** certainly, for sure

failing *noun* a fault; a weakness

failure *noun* **1** the act of failing **2** someone or something which fails

fain *adv, old* willingly: *I would fain go with you*

faint *adj* **1** lacking in strength, brightness *etc* **2** about to lose consciousness: *feel faint* ◻ *verb* **1** become faint **2** fall down unconscious ◻ *noun* a loss of consciousness ◻ **faintly** *adv* dimly, not clearly ◻ **faintness** *noun*

⚠Do not confuse with: **feint**

fair[1] *adj* **1** of a light colour: *fair hair* **2** of weather: clear and dry **3** unbiased, just: *fair assessment* **4** good enough but not excellent **5** beautiful ◻ **fair-haired** *adj* having light-coloured hair; blond ◻ **fairly** *adv* ◻ **fairness** *noun* ◻ **fair-weather friend** someone who is a friend only when things are going well

fair[2] *noun* **1** a large market held at fixed times **2** an exhibition of goods from different producers *etc*: *craft fair* **3** a travelling collection of merry-go-rounds, stalls *etc*

fairway *noun* **1** the mown part on a golf course, between the tee and the green **2** the deep-water part of a river

fairy *noun* (*plural* **fairies**) a small imaginary creature, human in shape, with magical powers ◻ **fairy light** a small coloured light for decorating Christmas trees *etc* ◻ **fairy story** or **fairy tale 1** a traditional story of fairies, giants *etc* **2** *informal* a lie

fait accompli */fet əkomplee/* (*plural* **faits accomplis**) something already done, an accomplished fact

faith *noun* **1** trust **2** belief in a religion or creed **3** loyalty to a promise: *kept faith with them* ▯ **faithless** *adj*

faithful *adj* **1** loyal; keeping your promises **2** true, accurate: *faithful account of events* **3** believing in a particular religion or creed ▯ **faithfully** *adv* ▯ **faithfulness** *noun*

fake *adj* not genuine, forged ▯ *noun* **1** someone who is not what they pretend to be **2** a forgery ▯ *verb* make an imitation or forgery of

fakir *noun* an Islamic or Hindu holy man

falcon *noun* a kind of bird of prey

falconry *noun* the training of falcons for hunting ▯ **falconer** *noun*

falderal or **falderol** *noun* meaningless nonsense

fall *verb* **1** drop down **2** become less **3** of a fortress *etc*: be captured **4** die in battle **5** happen, occur: *Christmas falls on a Monday this year* ▯ *noun* **1** a dropping down **2** something that falls: *a fall of snow* **3** lowering in value *etc* **4** *US* autumn **5** an accident involving falling **6** ruin, downfall, surrender **7** (**falls**) a waterfall ▯ **fall guy** a scapegoat ▯ **fallout** *noun* radioactive dust resulting from the explosion of an atomic bomb *etc* ▯ **fall flat** fail to have the intended effect ▯ **fall in love** begin to be in love ▯ **fall out with** quarrel with ▯ **fall through** of a plan: fail, come to nothing

> **fall** *verb* » falls, fall*ing*, fallen, fell

fallacy *noun* (*plural* **fallacies**) a false belief; something believed to be true but really false ▯ **fallacious** *adj*

fallible *adj* liable to make a mistake or to be wrong ▯ **fallibility** *noun*

fallopian tubes two tubes along which egg cells pass from a woman's ovaries to her uterus

fallow[1] *adj* of land: left unsown for a time after being ploughed

fallow[2] *adj* of a yellowish-brown colour ▯ **fallow deer** a type of yellowish-brown deer

false *adj* **1** untrue **2** not real, fake **3** not natural: *false teeth* ▯ **falsehood** *noun* a lie, an untruth ▯ **falseness** or **falsity** *noun* quality of being false ▯ **falsies** *noun plural, slang* artificial breasts made of padding

falsetto *noun* a singing voice forced higher than its natural range

falsify *verb* make false, alter for a dishonest purpose: *falsified his tax forms*

> **falsify** » falsifi*es*, falsify*ing*, falsifi*ed*

falter *verb* stumble or hesitate

fame *noun* the quality of being well-known, renown ▯ **famed** *adj* famous

familiar *adj* **1** well-known **2** seen, known *etc* before **3** well-acquainted (with) **4** over-friendly, cheeky ▯ **familiarity** *noun* ▯ **familiarize** *verb* make quite accustomed or acquainted (with)

family *noun* (*plural* **families**) **1** a

couple and their children **2** the children alone **3** a group of people related to one another **4** a group of animals, languages, *etc* with common characteristics

famine *noun* a great shortage of food or water

famished *adj* very hungry

famous *adj* well-known, having fame □ **famously** *adv*, *informal* very well: *get along famously*

fan[1] *noun* **1** a device or appliance for making a rush of air **2** a small hand-held device for cooling the face □ *verb* **1** cause a rush of air with a fan **2** increase the strength of: *fanning her anger* □ **fanlight** *noun* a window above a door, usually semi-circular □ **fan out** spread out in the shape of a fan

> **fan** *verb* » fan*s*, fann*ing*, fann*ed*

fan[2] *noun* an admirer, a devoted follower: *a fan of traditional music*

fanatic *noun* someone who is over-enthusiastic about something □ **fanatic** or **fanatical** *adj* wildly or excessively enthusiastic □ **fanatically** *adv*

fancy *noun* (*plural* **fancies**) **1** a sudden liking or desire: *he had a fancy for ice-cream* **2** imagination **3** something imagined □ *adj* not plain, elaborate □ *verb* **1** picture, imagine **2** have a sudden wish for **3** think without being sure □ **fancier** *noun* someone whose hobby is to keep prize animals, birds *etc* □ **fanciful** *adj* **1** inclined to have fancies **2** imaginary, not real □ **fancifully** *adv* □ **fancy dress** an elaborate costume worn *eg* for a party, often representing a famous character

> **fancy** *verb* » fanci*es*, fancy*ing*, fanci*ed*

fandango *noun* (*plural* **fandangos**) a Spanish dance for two with castanets

fanfare *noun* a loud flourish from a trumpet or bugle

fang *noun* **1** a long tooth of a wild animal **2** the poison-tooth of a snake

fankle *noun*, *Scot* a muddle, a tangle

fanny *noun*, *taboo slang* **1** *Brit* the vagina **2** *US* the buttocks

fantastic *adj* **1** very unusual, strange **2** *informal* very great **3** *informal* excellent

fantasy *noun* (*plural* **fantasies**) **1** an imaginary scene, story *etc* **2** an idea not based on reality

fanzine *noun*, *informal* **1** a magazine for a particular group of fans **2** a small-circulation magazine

FAO *abbrev* for the attention of

far *adv* **1** at or to a long way: *far off* **2** very much: *far better* □ *adj* **1** a long way off, distant: *a far country* **2** more distant: *the far side* □ **far-fetched** *adj* very unlikely: *a far-fetched story* □ **far-flung** *adj* extending over a great distance □ **far-sighted** *adj* foreseeing what is likely to happen and preparing for it □ *See* also **further**

> **far** *adj* » farth*er*, farth*est*

farce *noun* **1** a play with far-fetched characters and plot **2** a ridiculous situation ▫ **farcical** *adj* absurd, ridiculous

fardel *noun* a burden, a pack

fare *verb* get on (either well or badly): *they fared well in the competition* ▫ *noun* **1** the price of a journey **2** a paying passenger in a taxi *etc* **3** food ▫ **farewell** *exclam* & *noun* goodbye

farinaceous *adj* floury, mealy

farm *noun* **1** an area of land for growing crops, breeding and feeding animals *etc* **2** a place where certain animals, fish *etc* are reared: *a salmon farm* ▫ *verb* work on a farm ▫ **farmer** *noun* the owner or tenant of a farm ▫ **farmhouse** *noun* the house attached to a farm ▫ **farmstead** *noun* a farm and farmhouse ▫ **farmyard** *noun* the yard surrounded by farm buildings ▫ **farm out** give (work) to others to do for payment

farrago *noun* (*plural* **faragoes** a confused mixture

farrow *noun* a litter of baby pigs ▫ *verb* give birth to a litter of pigs

Farsi *noun* the modern Persian language

fart *noun, taboo slang* **1** an outburst of wind from the anus **2** a despised person ▫ *verb* expel wind from the anus

farther and **farthest** *see* **far**

farthing *noun, hist* an old coin, worth ¼ of an old penny

farthingale *noun* a wide whalebone underskirt for a woman's dress

fascia /*feh*sheeə/ *noun* a signboard above a shop *etc*

fascinate *verb* **1** charm, attract irresistibly **2** hypnotize ▫ **fascinating** *adj* ▫ **fascination** *noun*

fascism *noun* a form of authoritarian government characterized by extreme nationalism and suppression of individual freedom ▫ **fascist** *noun* **1** a supporter of fascism **2** a right-wing extremist

From Italian word, *fascio* meaning 'bundle' or 'group'

fashion *noun* **1** the style in which something is made, *esp* clothes **2** a way of behaving or dressing which is popular for a time **3** a manner, a way: *acting in a strange fashion* ▫ *verb* shape, form ▫ **fashionable** *adj* up-to-date, agreeing with the latest style ▫ **after a fashion** to some extent, in a way ▫ **in fashion** fashionable

fast *adj* **1** quick-moving **2** of a clock: showing a time in advance of the correct time **3** of dyed colour: fixed, not likely to wash out ▫ *adv* **1** quickly **2** firmly: *stand fast* **3** soundly, completely: *fast asleep* ▫ *verb* go without food voluntarily, *eg* for religious reasons or as a protest ▫ *noun* abstinence from food ▫ **fastness** *noun* ▫ **fast-track** *adj* of a career: liable for quick promotion ▫ **in the fast lane** having an exciting but stressful lifestyle

fasten *verb* fix; make firm by tying, nailing *etc*

fastidious *adj* difficult to please **fastidiously** *adv* **fastidiousness** *noun*

fat *noun* an oily substance made by the bodies of animals and by plants *adj* **1** having a lot of fat; plump **2** thick, wide **fatten** *verb* make or become fat **fatty** *adj* containing a lot of fat

fatal *adj* causing death or disaster **fatality** *noun* (*plural* **fatalities**) a death, *esp* caused by accident or disaster

fate *noun* **1** what the future holds; fortune, luck **2** end, death: *met his fate bravely* **fated** *adj* doomed **fateful** *adj* with important consequences; crucial, significant

father *noun* **1** a male parent **2** a priest **3** the creator or inventor of something: *Poe is the father of crime fiction* *verb* be the father of **father-in-law** *noun* the father of someone's husband or wife **fatherland** *noun* someone's native country

fathom *noun* a measure of depth of water (6 feet, 1.83 metres) *verb* understand, get to the bottom of

fatigue /fəteeg/ *noun* **1** great tiredness **2** weakness or strain caused by use: *metal fatigue* *verb* tire out

fatuous *adj* very foolish **fatuously** *adv* **fatuousness** *noun*

fatwa *noun* an edict issued by an Islamic authority

faucet *noun*, *US* a tap

fault *noun* **1** a mistake **2** a flaw, something bad or wrong, *eg* with a machine **faultless** *adj* perfect **faultlessly** *adv* **faulty** *adj* having a fault or faults

faun *noun* a mythological creature, half human and half animal

fauna *noun* the animals of a district or country as a whole

faux /foh/ *adj* imitation: *faux leather*

faux pas /*foh* pah/ an embarrassing mistake, a blunder

favour *noun* **1** a kind action **2** goodwill, approval **3** a gift, a token *verb* **1** show preference for **2** be an advantage to: *the darkness favoured our escape* **in favour of 1** in support of **2** for the benefit of

favourable *adj* **1** showing approval **2** advantageous, helpful (to) **favourably** *adv*

favourite *adj* best liked *noun* **1** a liked or best-loved person or thing **2** a competitor, horse, *etc* expected to win a race **favouritism** *noun* showing favour towards one person *etc* more than another

fawn[1] *noun* **1** a young deer **2** a light yellowish-brown colour *adj* of this colour

fawn[2] *verb* **1** show affection as a dog does **2** (with **on**) flatter in a grovelling fashion

fax *noun* **1** a machine that scans a document electronically and transfers the information by a telephone line to a receiving machine that produces a corresponding copy **2** a document copied and sent in this way *verb* **1** send by fax **2** send a fax message to

FBI *abbrev*, *US* Federal Bureau of Investigation

FE *abbrev* Further Education

fear *noun* an unpleasant feeling caused by danger, evil *etc* ▫ **fearful** *adj* **1** timid, afraid **2** terrible **3** *informal* very bad: *a fearful headache* ▫ **fearfully** *adv* ▫ **fearless** *adj* brave, daring ▫ **fearlessly** *adv*

feasible *adj* able to be done, likely ▫ **feasibility** *noun* ▫ **feasibly** *adv*

feast *noun* **1** a rich and plentiful meal **2** a festival day commemorating some event ▫ *verb* eat or hold a feast

feat *noun* a deed requiring some effort

feather *noun* one of the growths which form the outer covering of a bird ▫ **feathery** *adj* **1** covered in feathers **2** soft **3** light

feature *noun* **1** an identifying mark, a characteristic **2** a special article in a newspaper *etc* **3** the main film in a cinema programme **4** a special attraction **5** (**features**) the various parts of someone's face, *eg* eyes, nose *etc* ▫ *verb* **1** have as a feature **2** take part (in) **3** be prominent in

February *noun* the second month of the year

fecund *adj* fertile ▫ **fecundity** *noun*

fed *past form* of **feed**

federal *adj* joined by treaty or agreement ▫ **federated** *adj* joined after an agreement is made ▫ **federation** *noun* a group of states *etc* joined together for a common purpose, a league

fee *noun* a price paid for work done, or for a special service

feeble *adj* weak ▫ **feebleness** *noun* ▫ **feebly** *adv*

feed *verb* **1** give food to **2** eat food **3** supply with necessary materials ▫ *noun* food for animals: *cattle feed* ▫ **fed up** *adj* tired, bored and disgusted

> **feed** *verb* » feed*s*, feed*ing*, fed

feel *verb* **1** explore by touch **2** experience, be aware of: *he felt no pain* **3** believe, consider **4** think (yourself) to be: *I feel ill* **5** be sorry (for): *we felt for her in her grief* ▫ *noun* an act of touching ▫ **feelgood** *adj* causing a feeling of comfort or security: *feelgood movie* ▫ **feel like** want, have an inclination for: *do you feel like going out tonight?*

> **feel** *verb* » feel*s*, feel*ing*, felt

feeler *noun* one of two thread-like parts on an insect's head for sensing danger *etc*

feeling *noun* **1** sense of touch **2** emotion: *spoken with great feeling* **3** affection **4** an impression, belief ▫ **feelings** *noun plural* what someone feels inside; emotions

feet *plural* of **foot**

feign /fehn/ *verb* pretend to feel or be: *feigning illness*

feint *noun* **1** a pretence **2** a move to put an enemy off guard ▫ *verb*

> ⚠Do not confuse with: **faint**

feis /fehsh/ *noun* (*plural* **feisean**) an arts festival based around classes in traditional music, dancing *etc*

feisty *adj, informal* **1** irritable, touchy **2** spirited

felafel *noun* a fried ball of chick-peas and spices

felicity *noun* happiness □ **felicitations** *noun plural* good wishes, congratulations □ **felicitous** *adj* **1** lucky **2** well-chosen, suiting well

feline *adj* **1** of or relating to cats **2** like a cat

fell[1] *noun* a barren hill

fell[2] *verb* cut down (a tree)

fell[3] *adj, old* cruel, ruthless

fell[4] *past form* of **fall**

fellatio /fə*leh*shioh/ *noun* oral sexual stimulation of the penis

fellow *noun* **1** an equal **2** one of a pair **3** a member of an academic society, college *etc* **4** a man, a boy □ **fellowship** *noun* **1** comradeship, friendship **2** an award to a university graduate

felon *noun* a committer of a serious crime □ **felony** *noun* (*plural* **felonies**) a serious crime

felt[1] *noun* a type of rough cloth made of rolled and pressed wool

felt[2] *past form* of **feel**

female *adj* of the sex which produces children □ *noun* a human or animal of this sex

feminine *adj* **1** of or relating to women **2** characteristic of women □ **femininity** *noun*

feminism *noun* a social and cultural movement aiming to win equal rights for women □ **feminist** *noun* a supporter of feminism □ *adj* relating to this movement: *feminist literature*

femme fatale an irresistibly attractive woman who brings disaster on men

femoral *adj* relating to the thigh or thigh bone

femur *noun* the thigh bone

fen *noun* low marshy land, often covered with water

fence *noun* **1** a railing, hedge *etc* for closing in animals or land **2** *slang* a receiver of stolen goods □ *verb* **1** close in with a fence **2** fight with swords **3** give evasive answers when questioned □ **fencing** *noun* **1** material for fences **2** the sport of fighting with swords, using blunted weapons

fend *verb*: **fend for yourself** look after and provide for yourself

fender *noun* **1** a low guard round a fireplace to keep in coal *etc* **2** a piece of matting over a ship's side acting as a buffer against the quay **3** *US* the bumper of a car

ferment *verb* **1** change by fermentation **2** stir up (trouble *etc*) □ *noun*

> ⚠Do not confuse with: **foment**

fermentation *noun* **1** a reaction caused by bringing certain substances together, *eg* by adding yeast to dough in bread-making **2** great excitement or agitation

fern *noun* a plant with no flowers and feather-like leaves

ferocious *adj* fierce, savage ▯ **ferociously** *adv* ▯ **ferocity** *noun*

ferret *noun* a small weasel-like animal used to chase rabbits out of their warrens ▯ *verb* search busily and persistently

ferrule *noun* a metal tip on a walking stick or umbrella

ferry *verb* **1** carry over water by boat, or overland by aeroplane ▯ *noun* (*plural* **ferries**) **1** a crossing place for boats **2** a boat which carries passengers and cars *etc* across a channel

> **ferry** *verb* » ferri*es*, ferry*ing*, ferri*ed*

fertile *adj* **1** able to produce children or young **2** full of ideas, creative, productive ▯ **fertility** *noun*

fertilize *verb* make (soil *etc*) fertile ▯ **fertilization** *noun* ▯ **fertilizer** *noun* manure or chemicals used to make soil more fertile

fervent *adj* very eager; intense ▯ **fervently** *adv*

fervour *noun* ardour, zeal

fest *noun* or **-fest** *suffix* a gathering or festival around some subject: *news-fest/ trade fest*

fester *verb* of a wound: produce pus because of infection

festival *noun* **1** a celebration; a feast **2** a season of musical, theatrical or other performances

festive *adj* **1** of a feast **2** in a happy, celebrating mood ▯ **festivity** *noun* (*plural* **festivities**) a celebration, a feast

festoon *verb* decorate with chains of ribbons, flowers *etc*

feta *noun* a crumbly white cheese made from ewes' milk

fetch *verb* **1** go and get **2** bring in (a price): *fetched £100 at auction*

fete or **fête** *noun* a public event with stalls, competitions *etc* to raise money ▯ *verb* entertain lavishly, make much of

fetid *adj* having a rotten smell, stinking

fetish (*plural* **fetishes**) **1** a sacred object believed to carry supernatural power **2** an object of excessive fixation or (*esp* sexual) obsession ▯ **fetishist** *noun* ▯ **fetishistic** *adj*

fetlock *noun* the part of a horse's leg just above the foot

fetters *noun plural, formal* chains for imprisonment

fettle *noun*: **in fine fettle** in good health or condition

fettuccine *noun* pasta shaped in flat, wide strips

feu /fyoo/ *noun, Scot* a right to use land, a house *etc* indefinitely in return for an annual payment

feud *noun* a private, drawn-out war between families, clans, *etc*

feudal *adj, hist* of a social system under which tenants were bound to give certain services to the overlord in return for their tenancies ▯ **feudalism** *noun* ▯ **feudalist** *adj*

fever *noun* an above-normal body temperature and quickened pulse ▯ **fevered** *adj* **1** having a fever **2** very excited ▯ **feverish** *adj* **1** having a slight fever **2** excited **3** too eager, frantic: *feverish pace*

few *adj* not many: *only a few tickets left* ▯ **a good few** or **quite a few** several, a considerable number

few » few*er*, few*est*

fey /feh/ *adj* **1** clairvoyant **2** eccentric, whimsical

fez *noun* (*plural* **fezzes**) a brimless flowerpot-shaped hat, usually with a top tassel

FF *abbrev* franc(s)

ff *abbrev* following pages, lines *etc*

fiancé /fee*onh*seh/ *noun* the man a woman is engaged to marry

fiancée /fee*onh*seh/ *noun* the woman a man is engaged to marry

fiasco *noun* (*plural* **fiascos**) a complete failure

Based on an Italian phrase *far fiasco* 'make a bottle', meaning forget your lines on stage

fib *verb* lie about something unimportant ▯ *noun* an unimportant lie

fib *verb* » fib*s*, fibb*ing*, fibb*ed*

fibre *noun* **1** a thread or string **2** the essence or material of something: *the fibre of her being* **3** roughage in foods ▯ **fibrous** *adj* thread-like, stringy

fibreglass *noun* a lightweight material made of very fine threads of glass, used for building boats *etc*

fibre-optic *adj* of a cable: made of glass or plastic filaments which transmit light signals

fibula *noun* the thinner, outer bone in the lower leg (*compare with*: **tibia**)

fickle *adj* changeable; not stable or loyal

fiction *noun* **1** stories about imaginary characters and events **2** a lie

fictional *adj* imagined, created for a story: *fictional character*

⚠Do not confuse: **fictional** and **fictitious**

fictitious *adj* **1** not real, imaginary **2** untrue

fiddle *noun*, *informal* **1** a violin **2** a tricky or delicate operation **3** a cheat, a swindle ▯ *verb* **1** play the violin **2** play aimlessly (with) **3** interfere, tamper (with) **4** *informal* falsify (accounts *etc*) with the intention of cheating ▯ **fiddly** *adj* needing delicate or careful handling

fidelity *noun* **1** faithfulness **2** truth, accuracy

fidget *verb* move about restlessly

field *noun* **1** a piece of enclosed ground for pasture, crops, sports *etc* **2** an area of land containing a natural resource: *goldfield/ coalfield* **3** a branch of interest or knowledge **4** those taking part in a race ▯ *verb*, *cricket* catch the ball and return it ▯ **field-day** *noun* a day of unusual activity or success ▯ **fieldglasses** *noun plural* binoculars ▯ **field-gun** *noun* a light, mobile cannon ▯ **field-marshal** *noun* the highest ranking army officer

fiend *noun* **1** an evil spirit **2** a wicked person **3** an extreme enthusiast: *a crossword fiend* ▯ **fiendish** *adj*

fierce *adj* **1** very angry-looking, hostile, likely to attack **2** intense, strong: *fierce competition* ▯ **fiercely** *adv* ▯ **fierceness** *noun*

fiery *adj* **1** like fire **2** quick-tempered, volatile ▯ **fiery cross** *hist* a charred cross carried round Scottish Highland clans as a call to arms

fiesta *noun* a festival, a carnival

FIFA /*feefə*/ *abbrev* (in French) *Fédération Internationale de Football Association*, the International Football Federation

fife *noun* a small flute

fifteen *noun* the number 15 ▯ *adj* 15 in number ▯ **fifteenth** *adj* the last of a series of fifteen ▯ *noun* one of fifteen equal parts

fifth *adj* the last of a series of five ▯ *noun* one of five equal parts

fifty *noun* the number 50 ▯ *adj* 50 in number ▯ **fiftieth** *adj* the last of a series of fifty ▯ *noun* one of fifty equal parts

fig *noun* **1** a soft roundish fruit with thin, dark skin and red pulp containing many seeds **2** the tree which bears it

fight *verb* **1** struggle with fists, weapons *etc* **2** quarrel **3** go to war with ▯ *noun* a struggle; a battle ▯ **fighter** *noun* **1** someone who fights **2** a fast military aircraft armed with guns

> **fight** *verb* » fight*s*, fight*ing*, fought

figment *noun* an imaginary story or idea

figurative *adj* of a word: used not in its ordinary meaning but to show likenesses, *eg* 'she was a tiger' for 'she was as ferocious as a tiger'; metaphorical (*contrasted with*: **literal**) ▯ **figuratively** *adv*

figure *noun* **1** outward form or shape **2** a number **3** a geometrical shape **4** an unidentified person: *a shadowy figure approached* **5** a diagram or drawing on a page **6** a set of movements in skating *etc* ▯ *verb* appear, take part: *he figures in the story* ▯ **figured** *adj* marked with a design: *figured silk* ▯ **figurehead** a leader who has little real power ▯ **figure out** work out, understand

filament *noun* a slender thread, *eg* of wire in a light bulb

filch *verb*, *informal* steal

file *noun* **1** a loose-leaf book *etc* to hold papers **2** an amount of computer data held under a single name **3** a line of soldiers *etc* walking one behind another **4** a steel tool with a roughened surface for smoothing wood, metal *etc* ▯ *verb* **1** put (papers *etc*) in a file **2** rub with a file **3** walk in a file

filet mignon a small boneless cut of beef

filial *adj* of or characteristic of a son or daughter

filibeg *noun* a kilt

filibuster *noun* a long speech given in parliament to delay the passing of a law

filigree *noun* very fine gold or silver work in lace or metal

fill *verb* **1** put (something) into until there is no room for more: *fill the bucket with water* **2** become full: *her eyes filled with tears* **3** satisfy, fulfil (a requirement *etc*) **4** occupy: *fill a post* **5** appoint someone to (a job *etc*): *have you filled the vacancy?* **6** put something in a hole to stop it up □ *noun* as much as is needed to fill: *we ate our fill* □ **filler** *noun* **1** a funnel for pouring liquids through **2** a substance added to increase bulk **3** a material used to fill up holes in wood, plaster *etc* □ **filling-station** *noun* a garage which sells petrol □ **fill in 1** fill (a hole) **2** complete (a form *etc*) **3** do another person's job while they are absent: *I'm filling in for Anne* □ **fill up** fill completely

fillet *noun* a piece of meat or fish with bones removed □ *verb* remove the bones from

> **fillet** *verb* » fillet*s*, fillet*ing*, fillet*ed*

filling *noun* something used to fill a hole or gap □ *adj* of food: satisfying

fillip *noun* an encouragement

filly *noun* (*plural* **fillies**) a young female horse

film *noun* **1** a thin skin or coating **2** a chemically-coated strip of celluloid on which photographs are taken **3** a narrative photographed on celluloid and shown in a cinema, on television *etc* □ *verb* **1** photograph on celluloid **2** develop a thin coating: *his eyes filmed over* □ **filmstar** *noun* a famous actor or actress in films

filo /*fee*loh/ *noun* Middle-Eastern pastry in the form of paper-thin sheets

Filofax *noun*, *trademark* a personal organizer

filter *noun* **1** a strainer for removing solid material from liquids **2** a green arrow on a traffic light signalling one lane of traffic to move while the main stream is held up □ *verb* **1** strain through a filter **2** move or arrive gradually: *the news filtered through* **3** of cars *etc*: join gradually a stream of traffic **4** of a lane of traffic: move in the direction shown by a filter

> **filter** *verb* » filter*s*, filter*ing*, filter*ed*

filth *noun* dirt □ **filthily** *adv* □ **filthiness** *noun* □ **filthy** *adj* **1** very dirty **2** obscene, lewd

fin *noun* a flexible projecting part of a fish's body used for balance and swimming

final *adj* **1** last **2** allowing of no argument: *the judge's decision is final* □ *noun* the last contest in a competition: *World Cup final* □ **finality** *noun* the quality of being final and decisive □ **finalize** *verb* put (*eg* plans) in a final or finished form □ **finally** *adv*

finale /fi*nah*leh/ *noun* the last part of anything (*eg* a concert)

finance *noun* **1** money affairs **2** the study or management of these **3** (**finances**) the money someone has to spend □ *verb* supply with sums of money □ **financial** *adj* □ **financially** *adv* □ **financier** *noun* someone who manages (public) money

finch *noun* (*plural* **finches**) a small bird

find *verb* **1** come upon accidentally or after searching: *I found an earring in the street* **2** discover **3** judge to be: *finds it hard to live on her pension* □ *noun* something found, *esp* something of interest or value □ **find out** discover, detect

find *verb* » find*s*, find*ing*, found

fine[1] *adj* **1** made up of very small pieces, drops *etc* **2** not coarse: *fine linen* **3** thin, delicate **4** slight: *a fine distinction* **5** beautiful, handsome **6** of good quality; pure **7** bright, not rainy **8** well, healthy □ **fine arts** painting, sculpture, music □ **finery** *noun* splendid clothes *etc*

fine[2] *noun* money to be paid as a punishment □ *verb* compel to pay (money) as punishment

fines herbes a mixture of herbs as a garnish

finesse /fi*nes*/ *noun* cleverness and subtlety in handling situations *etc*

finger *noun* one of the five branching parts of the hand □ *verb* touch with the fingers □ **fingering** *noun* **1** the positioning of the fingers in playing a musical instrument **2** the showing of this by numbers □ **fingerprint** *noun* the mark made by the tip of a finger, used by the police as a means of identification

finish *verb* **1** end or complete the making of **2** stop: *when do you finish work today?* □ *noun* **1** the end (*eg* of a race) **2** the last coating of paint, polish *etc* □ **finished** *adj* **1** ended, complete **2** of a person: ruined, not likely to achieve further success *etc*

finite *adj* having an end or limit

fiord or **fjord** *noun* a long narrow inlet between steep hills, *esp* in Norway

fir *noun* a kind of cone-bearing tree □ **fir-cone** *noun*

fire *noun* **1** the heat and light given off by something burning **2** a mass of burning material, objects *etc* **3** a heating device: *electric fire* **4** eagerness, keenness □ *verb* **1** set on fire **2** make eager: *fired by his enthusiasm* **3** make (a gun) explode, shoot □ **fire alarm** a device to sound a bell *etc* as a warning of fire □ **firearm** *noun* a gun *eg* a pistol □ **fire brigade** a company of firemen □ **fire-damp** *noun* a dangerous gas found in coal mines □ **fire engine** a vehicle carrying firefighters and their equipment □ **fire escape** a means of escape from a building in case of fire □ **firefly** *noun* a type of insect which glows in the dark □ **fire-guard** *noun* a framework of iron placed in front of a fireplace for safety □ **fireman, firewoman** *noun* someone whose job it is to put out fires □ **fireplace** *noun* a recess in a room below a chimney for a fire □ **firewood** *noun* wood for burning on a fire □ **fireworks** *noun plural* **1** squibs, rockets *etc* sent up at night for show **2** *informal* angry behaviour

fire *verb* » fire*s*, fir*ing*, fir*ed*

firkin *noun, old* a small barrel

firm *adj* **1** not easily moved or

shaken **2** with mind made up □ *noun* a business company

firmament *noun, formal* the heavens, the sky

first *adj* & *adv* before all others in place, time or rank □ *adj* before doing anything else □ **first-aid** *noun* treatment of a wounded or sick person before the doctor's arrival □ **first-born** *noun* the eldest child □ **first-class** *adj* of the highest standard, best kind *etc* □ **first-hand** *adj* direct □ **first name** a person's name that is not their surname □ **first-rate** *adj* first-class

firth *noun* a narrow arm of the sea, *esp* at a river mouth

fiscal *adj* **1** of the public revenue **2** of financial matters

fish *noun* (*plural* **fish** or **fishes**) a kind of animal that lives in water, and breathes through gills □ *verb* **1** try to catch fish with rod, nets *etc* **2** search (for): *fishing for a handkerchief in her bag* **3** try to obtain: *fish for compliments* □ **fisherman** *noun* a man who fishes, *esp* for a living □ **fishmonger** *noun* someone who sells fish for food □ **fishy** *adj* **1** like a fish **2** doubtful, arousing suspicion

fission *noun* splitting

fissure *noun* a crack

fist *noun* a tightly-shut hand □ **fisticuffs** *noun plural, old* a fight with the fists

fit *adj* **1** suited to a purpose; proper **2** in good training or health □ *noun* a sudden attack or spasm of laughter, illness *etc* □ *verb* **1** be of the right size or shape **2** be suitable □ **fitful** *adj* coming or doing in bursts or spasms □ **fitfully** *adv* □ **fitness** *noun* □ **fitting** *adj* suitable □ *noun* something fixed or fitted in a room, house *etc* □ **fittingly** *adv*

fit *verb* » fit*s*, fitt*ing*, fitt*ed*

five *noun* the number 5 □ *adj* 5 in number

fives *noun plural* a handball game played in a walled court

fix *verb* **1** make firm; fasten **2** mend, repair □ **fixed** *adj* settled; set in position □ **fixedly** *adv* steadily, intently: *staring fixedly*

fixture *noun* **1** a piece of furniture *etc* fixed in position **2** an arranged sports match or race

fizz *verb* make a hissing sound □ *noun* a hissing sound □ **fizzy** *adj* of a drink: forming bubbles on the surface

fizzle or **fizzle out** *verb* fail, coming to nothing

fjord *another spelling* of **fiord**

flabbergasted *adj* very surprised

flabby *adj* not firm, soft, limp; weak, feeble □ **flabbily** *adv* □ **flabbiness** *noun*

flaccid /*fla*sid/ *adj* **1** hanging loosely **2** limp, not firm

flag *noun* **1** a banner, standard, or ensign **2** a flat paving-stone □ *verb* become tired or weak

flag *verb* » flag*s*, flagg*ing*, flagg*ed*

flagellate *verb*, *formal* whip, lash □ **flagellation** *noun* whipping

flageolet[1] *noun* a variety of kidney bean

flageolet[2] *noun* a small high-pitched flute

flagon *noun* a large container for liquid

flagrant *adj* **1** conspicuous **2** openly wicked □ **flagrancy** *noun* □ **flagrantly** *adv*

flail *verb* wave or swing in the air □ *noun, old* a tool for threshing corn

flair *noun* talent, skill: *a flair for languages*

flak *noun* **1** anti-aircraft fire **2** strong criticism

flake *noun* **1** a thin slice or chip of anything **2** a very small piece of snow *etc* □ *verb* form into flakes □ **flaky** *adj* **1** forming flakes, crumbly: *flaky pastry* **2** *US informal* eccentric □ **flake off** break off in flakes

flambé /*flom*beh/ or **flambéed** *adj, cookery* cooked or served in flaming alcohol

flamboyant *adj* **1** splendidly coloured **2** too showy, gaudy

flame *noun* the bright leaping light of a fire □ *verb* **1** burn brightly **2** *comput slang* send abusive electronic mail (to) □ **flaming** *adj* **1** burning **2** red **3** violent: *a flaming temper*

flamingo *noun* (*plural* **flamingoes**) a type of long-legged bird of pink or bright-red colour

flammable *adj* easily set on fire

flan *noun* a flat, open tart

flange *noun* a raised edge on the rim of a wheel

flank *noun* the side of an animal's body, of an army *etc* □ *verb* **1** go by the side of **2** be situated at the side of

flannel *noun* **1** loosely woven woollen fabric **2** a small towel or face cloth

flannelette *noun* cotton fabric imitating flannel

flannels *noun plural* trousers made of flannel or similar material

flap *noun* **1** anything broad and loose-hanging: *tent flap* **2** the sound of a wing *etc* moving through air **3** a panic: *getting in a flap over nothing* □ *verb* **1** hang down loosely **2** move with a flapping noise **3** get into a panic

> **flap** *verb* » flap*s*, flapp*ing*, flapp*ed*

flapjack *noun* **1** *Brit* a biscuit made with rolled oats, butter and sugar **2** *US* a pancake

flapper *noun, hist* an emancipated woman of the 1920s

flare *verb* blaze up □ *noun* a bright light, *esp* one used at night as a signal, to show the position of a boat in distress *etc*

> **flare** *verb* » flare*s*, flar*ing*, flar*ed*

flash *noun* (*plural* **flashes**) **1** a quick burst of light **2** a moment, an instant **3** a distinctive mark on a uniform □ *verb* **1** shine out suddenly **2** pass quickly □ **flashlight** *noun* **1** a burst of light in which a photograph is taken **2** an electric torch □ **in a flash** very quickly or suddenly

flasher *noun, slang* someone who

exposes their genitals in public

flashy *adj* showy, gaudy

flask *noun* **1** a narrow-necked bottle **2** a small flat bottle **3** an insulated bottle or vacuum flask

flat *adj* **1** level: *a flat surface* **2** of a drink: no longer fizzy **3** leaving no doubt, downright: *a flat denial* **4** below the right musical pitch **5** of a tyre: punctured **6** dull, uninteresting ▯ *adv* stretched out: *lying flat on her back* ▯ *noun* **1** an apartment on one storey of a building **2** *music* a sign (♭) which lowers a note by a semitone **3** a punctured tyre ▯ **flatfish** *noun* a sea fish with a flat body, *eg* a sole ▯ **flatly** *adv* ▯ **flatness** *noun* ▯ **flat race** a race over level ground without hurdles ▯ **flat rate** a rate which is the same in all cases ▯ **flat out** *adv* as fast as possible, with as much effort as possible

flatten *verb* make or become flat

flatter *verb* praise insincerely ▯ **flattery** *noun*

flatulence *noun* wind in the stomach ▯ **flatulent** *adj*

flaunt /flont/ *verb* display in an obvious way: *flaunted his wealth*

⚠Do not confuse with: **flout**

flautist /*flo*tist/ a flute player

flavour *noun* **1** taste: *lemon flavour* **2** quality or atmosphere: *an exotic flavour* ▯ *verb* give a taste to ▯ **flavouring** *noun* an ingredient used to give a particular taste: *chocolate flavouring*

flaw *noun* a fault, an imperfection ▯ **flawless** *adj* with no faults or blemishes ▯ **flawlessly** *adv*

flax *noun* a plant whose fibres are woven into linen cloth ▯ **flaxen** *adj* **1** made of or looking like flax **2** of hair: fair

flay *verb* strip the skin off

flea *noun* a small, wingless, blood-sucking insect with great jumping power

fleck *noun* a spot, a speck ▯ **flecked** *adj* marked with spots or patches

fled *past form* of **flee**

fledgling *noun* a young bird with fully-grown feathers

flee *verb* run away from danger *etc*

flee » flee*s*, flee*ing*, fled

fleece *noun* a sheep's coat of wool ▯ *verb* **1** clip wool from **2** *informal* rob by cheating ▯ **fleecy** *adj* soft and fluffy like wool

fleet *noun* **1** a number of ships **2** a number of cars or taxis ▯ *adj* swift; nimble, quick in movement ▯ **fleeting** *adj* passing quickly: *fleeting glimpse* ▯ **fleetness** *noun* swiftness

flesh *noun* **1** the soft tissue which covers the bones of humans and animals **2** meat **3** the body **4** the soft eatable part of fruit ▯ **fleshy** *adj* fat, plump ▯ **flesh and blood 1** relations, family **2** human, mortal

flew *past form* of **fly**

flex *verb* bend ▯ *noun* a length of covered wire attached to electrical devices ▯ **flexitime** *noun* a system in which an agreed number of hours' work is done at times chosen by the worker

flexible *adj* **1** easily bent **2** willing

to adapt to new or different conditions □ **flexibility** *noun* □ **flexibly** *adv*

flick *verb* **1** strike lightly with a quick movement **2** remove (dust *etc*) with a movement of this kind □ *noun* a quick, sharp movement: *a flick of the wrist* □ **flick-knife** *noun* a knife with a blade which springs out at the press of a button

flicker[1] *verb* **1** flutter **2** burn unsteadily □ *noun*

flicker[2] *noun, US* a woodpecker

flight *noun* **1** the act of flying **2** a journey by plane **3** the act of fleeing or escaping **4** a flock (of birds) **5** a number (of steps) □ **flighty** *adj* changeable, impulsive

flimsy *adj* **1** thin; easily torn or broken *etc* **2** weak: *a flimsy excuse*

flinch *verb* move or shrink back in fear, pain *etc*

fling *verb* throw □ *noun* **1** a throw **2** a casual attempt **3** a period of time devoted to pleasure **4** a brief romantic affair

> **fling** *verb* » fling*s*, fling*ing*, flung

flint *noun* a kind of hard stone □ *adj* made of flint □ **flintlock** *noun* a gun fired by sparks from a flint

flip *verb* toss lightly □ *noun* a light toss or stroke □ **flip side** **1** the reverse side of a record *etc* **2** the converse of anything

> **flip** *verb* » flip*s*, flipp*ing*, flipp*ed*

flippant *adj* joking, not serious □ **flippancy** *noun* □ **flippantly** *adv*

flipper *noun* **1** a limb of a seal, walrus *etc* **2** a webbed rubber shoe worn by divers

flirt *verb* play at courtship without any serious intentions □ *noun* someone who flirts □ **flirtation** *noun* □ **flirtatious** *adj* fond of flirting

flit *verb* **1** move quickly and lightly from place to place **2** *Scot* move house

> **flit** » **flit***s*, **flitt***ing*, **flitt***ed*

float *verb* **1** keep on the surface of a liquid without sinking **2** set going: *float a fund* □ **1** a cork *etc* on a fishing line **2** a raft **3** a van delivering milk *etc* **4** a large lorry for transporting cattle **5** a platform on wheels, used in processions **6** a sum of money set aside for giving change

flock[1] *noun* **1** a number of animals or birds together **2** a large number of people **3** the congregation of a church; □ *verb* (with **together**) gather or move in a crowd

flock[2] *noun* **1** a shred or tuft of wool **2** wool or cotton waste

floe /floh/ *noun* a sheet of floating ice

flog *verb* **1** beat, lash **2** *slang* sell □ **flogging** *noun*

> **flog** » flog*s*, flogg*ing*, flogg*ed*

flood *noun* **1** a great flow, *esp* of water **2** the rise or flow of the tide **3** a great quantity: *a flood of letters* □ *verb* **1** (cause to) overflow **2** cover or fill with water □ **floodlight** *verb* illuminate with floodlighting □ *noun* a light used to floodlight ▯ **flood-lighting** *noun* strong artificial lighting to illuminate an exterior or stage

floodlight *verb* » floodlight*s*, floodlight*ing*, floodlit

floor *noun* **1** the base level of a room on which people walk **2** a storey of a building: *a third-floor flat* ▯ *verb* **1** make a floor **2** *informal* knock flat **3** *informal* puzzle: *floored by the question*

floozie *noun, informal* a sexually promiscuous woman

flop *verb* **1** sway or swing about loosely **2** fall or sit down suddenly and heavily **3** move about clumsily **4** fail badly ▯ *noun* **1** an act of flopping **2** a complete failure ▯ **floppy** *adj* flopping, soft and flexible ▯ **floppy disk** a flexible computer disk, often in a harder case, used to store data

flop » flop*s*, flopp*ing*, flopp*ed*

flora *noun* the plants of a district or country as a whole

floral *adj* (made) of flowers

florid *adj* **1** with a flushed or ruddy complexion **2** too ornate

florist *noun* a seller or grower of flowers ▯ **floristry** *noun*

floss *noun* **1** fine silk thread **2** thin, often waxed thread for passing between the teeth to clean them ▯ *verb* clean (teeth) with dental floss

flotilla *noun* a fleet of small ships

flotsam *noun* floating objects washed from a ship or wreck

flounce[1] *verb* walk away suddenly and impatiently, *eg* in anger

flounce[2] *noun* a gathered decorative strip sewn onto the hem of a dress

flounder[1] *verb* **1** struggle to move your legs and arms in water, mud *etc* **2** have difficulty speaking or thinking clearly, or in acting efficiently

⚠Do not confuse with: **founder**

flounder[2] *noun* a small flatfish

flour *noun* **1** finely-ground wheat **2** any grain crushed to powder: *rice flour*

flourish *verb* **1** be successful, *esp* financially **2** grow well, thrive **3** be healthy **4** wave or brandish as a show or threat ▯ *noun* (*plural* **flourishes**) **1** fancy strokes in writing **2** a sweeping movement with the hand, sword *etc* **3** showy splendour **4** an ornamental passage in music

floury *adj* **1** covered with flour **2** powdery

⚠Do not confuse with: **flowery**

flout *verb* treat with contempt, defy openly: *flouted the speed limit*

⚠Do not confuse with: **flaunt**

flow *verb* **1** run, as water **2** move or come out in an unbroken run **3** of the tide: rise ▯ *noun* a smooth or unbroken run: *flow of ideas*

flower *noun* **1** the part of a plant or tree from which fruit or seeds grow **2** the best of anything ▯ *verb* **1** of plants *etc*: produce a flower **2**

be at your best, flourish ▫ **flowering** *noun*

flowery *adj* **1** full of or decorated with flowers **2** using fine-sounding, fancy language: *flowery prose style*

⚠Do not confuse with: **floury**

flown *see* **fly**

fl oz *abbrev* fluid ounce(s)

flu *noun, informal* influenza

fluctuate *verb* **1** vary in number, price *etc* **2** be always changing ▫ **fluctuation** *noun*

flue *noun* a passage for air and smoke in a stove or chimney

fluent *adj* finding words easily in speaking or writing without any awkward pauses ▫ **fluency** *noun*

fluff *noun* **1** soft, downy material **2** *informal* a mistake ▫ **fluffy** *adj*

fluid *noun* a substance whose particles can move about freely, a liquid or gas ▫ *adj* **1** flowing **2** not settled or fixed: *my plans for the weekend are fluid*

fluke[1] *noun* a small worm which harms sheep

fluke[2] *noun* the part of an anchor which holds fast in sand

fluke[3] *noun* an accidental or unplanned success

flume *noun* a water chute

flummox *verb* bewilder, confuse totally

flung *past form* of **fling**

flunk *verb, slang* fail

flunky *noun* **1** a servant **2** a servile person

fluoride *noun* a chemical added to water or toothpaste to prevent tooth decay ▫ **fluoridize** or **fluoridate** *verb* add fluoride to

flurry *noun* (*plural* **flurries**) a sudden rush of wind *etc* ▫ *verb* excite

flurry *verb* » flurri*es*, flurry*ing*, flurri*ed*

flush *noun* (*plural* **flushes**) **1** a reddening of the face **2** freshness, glow ▫ *verb* **1** become red in the face **2** clean by a rush of water ▫ *adj* **1** (with **with**) having the surface level with the surface around **2** *informal* well supplied with money

fluster *noun* excitement caused by hurry ▫ *verb* harass, confuse

flute *noun* **1** a high-pitched musical wind instrument **2** a tall narrow wine glass ▫ **fluted** *adj* decorated with grooves

flutter *verb* move (eyelids, wings, *etc*) back and forth quickly ▫ *noun* **1** a quick beating of pulse *etc* **2** nervous excitement: *in a flutter*

flux *noun* an ever-changing flow: *in a state of flux*

fly *noun* (*plural* **flies**) **1** a small winged insect **2** a fish-hook made to look like a fly to catch fish **3** a flap of material with buttons or a zip *esp* at the front of trousers ▫ *verb* **1** move through the air on wings or in an aeroplane **2** run away ▫ **flying saucer** a disc-shaped object believed to be an alien spacecraft ▫ **flying squad** a group of police officers organized for fast action or movement ▫ **flyover** *noun* a road built on pillars to cross over another □ **flysheet** *noun* the outer covering of a tent □ **flywheel** *noun* a heavy wheel which enables a machine to run at a steady speed

fly *verb* » flie*s*, fly*ing*, flew, flown

flyer *noun* a small poster or advertising sheet

FM *abbrev* frequency modulation (*compare with*: **AM**)

foal *noun* a young horse □ *verb* give birth to a foal

foam *noun* a mass of small bubbles on liquids □ *verb* produce foam □ **foam rubber** sponge-like form of rubber for stuffing chairs, mattresses *etc*

fob[1] *noun* **1** a small watch pocket **2** an ornamental chain hanging from such a pocket

fob[2] *verb* force to accept (something worthless): *I won't be fobbed off with a silly excuse*

focaccia /foh*ka*chə/ *noun* a flat round of Italian bread topped with olive oil and herbs

focal *adj* central, pivotal: *focal point*

fo'c'sle *another spelling of* **forecastle**

focus *noun* (*plural* **focuses** or **foci**) **1** the meeting point for rays of light **2** point to which light, a look, attention, is directed □ *verb* **1** get the right length of ray of light for a clear picture **2** direct (one's attention *etc*) to one point

focus *verb* » focuse*s*, focus*ing*, focus*ed*

fodder *noun* dried food, *eg* hay or oats, for farm animals

foe *noun, formal* an enemy

foetal *adj* relating to a foetus □ **foetal alcohol syndrome** a range of birth defects caused by an excessive alcohol intake during pregnancy

foetus *noun* a young human being or animal in the womb or egg

fog *noun* thick mist □ *verb* **1** cover in fog **2** bewilder, confuse □ **foggy** *adj* □ **foghorn** *noun* a horn used as a warning to or by ships in fog

fogy or **fogey** *noun* someone with old-fashioned views

foie gras fattened goose liver, used for making pâté

foil *verb* defeat, disappoint □ *noun* **1** metal in the form of paper-thin sheets **2** a dull person against which someone else seems brighter **3** a blunt sword with a button at the end, used in fencing practice

foist *verb* **1** pass off as genuine **2** palm off (something undesirable) on someone

fold *noun* **1** a part laid on top of another **2** an enclosure for sheep *etc* □ *verb* lay one part on top of another □ **folder** *noun* a cover to hold papers

foliage *noun* leaves

folio *noun* (*plural* **folios**) **1** a leaf (two pages back to back) of a book **2** a page number **3** a sheet of paper folded once

folk *noun* **1** people **2** a nation, race **3** (**folks**) family or relations □ **folkie** *noun, informal* a folk music fan □ **folk music** traditional music of a particular culture ▯ **folksong** *noun* a traditional song passed on orally

folklore *noun* the study of the customs, beliefs, stories *etc* of a people ▯ **folklorist** *noun* someone who studies or collects folklore

follicle *noun* the pit surrounding a root of hair

follow *verb* **1** go or come after **2** happen as a result **3** act according to: *follow your instincts* **4** understand: *I don't follow you* **5** work at (a trade)

follower *noun* **1** someone who follows **2** a supporter, disciple: *a follower of Jung*

following *noun* supporters: *the team has a large following* ▯ *adj* next in time: *we left the following day* ▯ *prep* after, as a result of: *following the fire, the house collapsed*

folly *noun* (*plural* **follies**) **1** foolishness **2** a purposeless building

foment *verb* stir up, encourage growth of (a rebellion *etc*)

> ⚠Do not confuse with: **ferment**

fond *adj* loving; tender ▯ **fondly** *adv* ▯ **fondness** *noun* ▯ **fond of** having a liking for

fondle *verb* caress

font *noun* **1** a basin holding water for baptism **2** a main source: *a font of knowledge*

food *noun* that which living beings eat ▯ **foodie** *noun, informal* someone who takes great interest in food ▯ **food processor** an electrical appliance for chopping, blending *etc* food ▯ **foodstuff** *noun* something used for food

fool *noun* **1** a silly person **2** *hist* a court jester **3** a dessert made of fruit, sugar and whipped cream ▯ *verb* deceive; play the fool ▯ **fool about** behave in a playful or silly manner

foolhardy *adj* rash, taking foolish risks

foolish *adj* unwise, ill-considered ▯ **foolery** or **foolishness** *noun* foolish behaviour ▯ **foolishly** *adv*

foolproof *adj* unable to go wrong

foolscap *noun* paper for writing or printing, 17 x 13 in (43 x 34 cm)

> Referring to the original watermark used on this size of paper, showing a jester's cap and bells

foot *noun* (*plural* **feet**) **1** the part of the leg below the ankle **2** the lower part of anything **3** twelve inches, 30 cm ▯ *verb* pay (a bill *etc*) ▯ **football** *noun* **1** a game played by two teams of 11 on a field with a round ball **2** *US* a game played with an oval ball which can be handled or kicked **3** a ball used in football ▯ **foothill** *noun* a smaller hill at the foot of a mountain ▯ **foothold** *noun* **1** a place to put the foot in climbing **2** a firm position from which to begin something ▯ **footing** *noun* balance; degree of friendship, seniority *etc* ▯ **footlight** *noun* a light at the front of a stage, which shines on the actors ▯ **footloose** *adj* unattached, with no responsibilities ▯ **footnote** *noun* a note at the bottom of a page ▯

footplate *noun* a driver's platform on a railway engine ▯ **footprint** *noun* a mark of a foot ▯ **footsore** *adj* tired out from too much walking ▯ **footstep** *noun* the sound of someone's foot when walking ▯ **footwear** *noun* shoes *etc* ▯ **foot the bill** pay up ▯ **my foot!** *exclam* used to express disbelief ▯ **put a foot wrong** make a mistake, act inappropriately

Footsie *informal another name* for **FTSE**

footsie *noun*, *informal* the rubbing of a foot against someone's leg *etc* in sexual play

fop *noun* a man who is vain about his dress ▯ **foppish** *adj*

for *prep* **1** sent to or to be given to: *there is letter for you* **2** towards: *headed for home* **3** during (an amount of time): *waited for three hours* **4** on behalf of: *for me* **5** because of: *for no good reason* **6** as the price of: *£5 for a ticket* **7** in order to obtain: *only doing it for the money*

forage food for horses and cattle ▯ *verb* search for food, fuel *etc*

foray *noun* **1** a sudden raid **2** a brief journey

forbade *past form* of **forbid**

forbearance *noun* control of temper ▯ **forbearing** *adj* patient

forbid *verb* order not to ▯ **forbidden** *adj* ▯ **forbidding** *adj* rather frightening

> **forbid** » forbid*s*, forbidd*ing*, forbade, forbidd*en*

force *noun* **1** strength, violence **2** the police **3** a group of workers, soldiers *etc* **4** (**forces**) those in the army, navy and airforce ▯ *verb* **1** make, compel: *forced him to go* **2** get by violence: *force an entry* **3** break open **4** hurry on **5** make vegetables *etc* grow more quickly ▯ **forced** *adj* done unwillingly, with effort: *a forced laugh* ▯ **forceful** *adj* acting with power ▯ **forcefully** *adv* ▯ **forcible** *adj* done by force ▯ **forcibly** *adv*

forceps *noun* surgical pincers for holding or lifting

ford *noun* a shallow crossing-place in a river ▯ *verb* cross (water) on foot

fore- *prefix* **1** before **2** beforehand **3** in front

forearm[1] *noun* the part of the arm between elbow and wrist

forearm[2] *verb* prepare beforehand

foreboding *noun* a feeling of coming evil

forecast *verb* tell about beforehand, predict ▯ *noun* a prediction

forecastle or **fo'c'sle** (both /fohksl/) **1** a raised deck at the front of a ship **2** the part of a ship under the deck containing the crew's quarters

foreclose *verb* **1** prevent, preclude **2** bar from redeeming (a mortgage)

forefather *noun*, *formal* an ancestor

forefinger *noun* the finger next to the thumb

forefront *noun* the very front

foregone: **a foregone conclusion** a result that can be guessed rightly in advance ▯ *see also* **forgo**

foreground *noun* the part of a view or picture nearest the person looking at it

forehead *noun* the part of the face above the eyebrows

foreign *adj* **1** belonging to another country **2** not belonging naturally in a place *etc*: *a foreign body in an eye* **3** not familiar ▫ **foreigner** *noun* **1** someone from another country **2** somebody unfamiliar

foreleg *noun* an animal's front leg

forelock *noun* the lock of hair next to the forehead

foreman *noun* (*plural* **foremen**) **1** an overseer of a group of workers **2** the leader of a jury

foremast *noun* a ship's mast nearest the bow

foremost *adj* the most famous or important

forensic *adj* relating to courts of law or criminal investigation: *forensic medicine*

forerunner *noun* an earlier example or sign of what is to follow: *the forerunner of cinema*

foresee *verb* see or know beforehand

> **foresee** » foresee*s*, foresee*ing*, foreseen, foresaw

foreshore *noun* the part of the shore between high and low tidemarks

foresight *noun* **1** ability to see what will happen later **2** a fitting on the front of the barrel of a gun to help the aim

forest *noun* **1** a large piece of land covered with trees **2** a stretch of country kept for game ▫ **forester** *noun* a worker in a forest ▫ **forestry** *noun* the science of forest-growing

forestall *verb* upset someone's plan by acting earlier than they expect

foretaste *noun* a sample of what is to come

foretell *verb* tell in advance, prophesy

> **foretell** » foretell*s*, foretell*ing*, foretold

forethought *noun* thought or care for the future

foretold *past form* of **foretell**

forewarn *verb* warn beforehand ▫ **forewarning** *noun*

forewent *past form* of **forgo**

forewoman *noun* **1** a woman overseer **2** a head woman in a shop or factory

foreword *noun* a piece of writing at the beginning of a book

> ⚠Do not confuse with: **forward**

forfeit *verb* lose (a right) as a result of doing something: *forfeit the right to appeal* ▫ *noun* something given in compensation or punishment for an action, *eg* a fine ▫ **forfeiture** *noun* the loss of something as a punishment

forge *noun* **1** a blacksmith's workshop **2** a furnace in which metal is heated ▫ *verb* **1** hammer (metal) into shape **2** imitate for criminal purposes **3** move steadily on: *forged ahead with the plan* ▫ **forger** *noun*

> **forge** *verb* » forge*s*, forg*ing*, forg*ed*

forgery *noun* (*plural* **forgeries**) **1** something imitated for criminal purposes **2** the act of criminal forging

forget *verb* lose or put away from the memory □ **forgetful** *adj* likely to forget □ **forgetfully** *adv* □ **forgetfulness** *noun*

> **forget** » forget*s*, forgett*ing*, forgot, forgott*en*

forgive *verb* **1** be no longer angry with **2** overlook (a fault, debt *etc*) □ **forgiveness** *noun* pardon □ **forgiving** *adj*

> **forgive** » forgive*s*, forgiv*ing*, forgave, forgiv*en*

forgo *verb* give up, do without

> **forgo** » forgo*es*, forgo*ing*, forewent or forwent, foregone or forgone

forgot and **forgotten** *see* **forget**

fork *noun* **1** a pronged tool for piercing and lifting things **2** the point where a road, tree *etc* divides into two branches □ *verb* divide into two branches *etc* □ **fork-lift truck** a power-driven truck with steel prongs that can lift and carry heavy packages

forlorn *adj* pitiful, unhappy □ **forlorn hope** a wish which seems to have no chance of being granted

form *noun* **1** shape or appearance **2** kind, type **3** a paper with printed questions and space for answers **4** a long seat **5** a school class **6** the nest of a hare □ *verb* **1** give shape to **2** make

formal *adj* **1** of manner: cold, business-like **2** done according to custom or convention □ **formally** *adv* □ **formal dress** clothes required to be worn on formal social occasions, *eg* balls and banquets □ **formality** *noun* (*plural* **formalities**) **1** something which must be done but has little meaning: *the nomination was only a formality* **2** cold correctness of manner

format *noun* **1** the size, shape *etc* of a printed book **2** the design or arrangement of an event, *eg* a television programme **3** *comput* the description of the way data is arranged on a disk □ *verb* **1** arrange into a specific format **2** *comput* arrange data for use on a disk **3** *comput* prepare (a disk) for use by dividing it into sectors

> **format** » format*s*, formatt*ing*, formatt*ed*

formation *noun* **1** the act of forming **2** arrangement, *eg* of aeroplanes in flight

former *adj* **1** of an earlier time **2** of the first-mentioned of two (*contrasted with*: **latter**) □ **formerly** *adv* in earlier times; previously

formic *adj* relating to ants □ **formic acid** an acid found in ants

formica *noun, trademark* a tough, heat-resistant material used for covering work surfaces

formidable *adj* **1** fearsome, frightening **2** difficult to overcome

formula *noun* (*plural* **formulae** or

formulas) **1** a set of rules to be followed **2** an arrangement of signs or letters used in chemistry, arithmetic *etc* to express an idea briefly, *eg* H_2O = water ◊ **formulate** *verb* **1** set down clearly: *formulate the rules* **2** make into a formula

fornicate *verb*, *formal* have sexual intercourse outside marriage ◊ **fornication** *noun* ◊ **fornicator** *noun*

forsake *verb* desert ◊ **forsaken** *adj* deserted; miserable

> **forsake** » forsake*s*, forsak*ing*, forsook, forsak*en*

forswear *verb*, *formal* give up

fort *noun* a place of defence against an enemy

forte /*for*teh/ *noun* someone's particular talent or specialty

forth *adv* forward, onward ◊ **forthcoming** *adj* **1** happening soon **2** willing to share knowledge; friendly and open ◊ **forthright** *adj* outspoken, straightforward ◊ **forthwith** *adv* immediately

fortieth *adj* the last of a series of forty ◊ *noun* one of forty equal parts

fortifications *noun plural* walls *etc* built to strengthen a position

fortify *verb* strengthen against attack

> **fortify** » fortifi*es*, fortify*ing*, fortifi*ed*

fortitude *noun* courage in meeting danger or bearing pain

fortnight *noun* two weeks ◊ **fortnightly** *adj* or *adv* once a fortnight

FORTRAN *noun* a computer language

fortress *noun* (*plural* **fortresses**) a fortified place

fortuitous *adj* happening by chance ◊ **fortuitously** *adv* ◊ **fortuitousness** *noun*

fortunate *adj* lucky ◊ **fortunately** *adv*

fortune *noun* **1** luck (good or bad) **2** large sum of money

forty *noun* the number 40 ◊ *adj* 40 in number

forum *noun* **1** a public place where speeches are made **2** a meeting to talk about a particular subject **3** *hist* a market-place in ancient Rome

forward *adj* **1** advancing: *a forward movement* **2** near or at the front **3** of fruit: ripe earlier than usual **4** too quick to speak or act, pert ◊ *verb* **1** help towards success: *forwarded his plans* **2** send on (letters) ◊ **forward** or **forwards** *adv* onward, towards the front

> Do not confuse with: **foreword**

forwent *past form* of **forgo**

fossil *noun* the hardened remains of the shape of a plant or animal found in rock ◊ **fossilize** *verb* change into a fossil

foster *verb* **1** bring up or nurse (a child not your own) **2** help on, encourage ◊ **foster-child** *noun* a child fostered by a family ◊ **foster-parent** *noun* someone who brings up a fostered child

fought *past form* of **fight**

foul *adj* **1** very dirty **2** smelling or tasting bad **3** stormy: *foul weather/ in a foul temper* □ *verb* **1** become entangled with **2** dirty **3** play unfairly □ *noun* a breaking of the rules of a game □ **foul play** a criminal act

found[1] *verb* **1** establish, set up **2** shape by pouring melted metal into a mould □ **foundation** *noun* **1** that on which anything rests **2** a sum of money left or set aside for a special purpose **3** an organization *etc* supported in this way □ **founder** *noun* someone who founds □ **foundry** *noun* (*plural* **foundries**) a workshop where metal founding is done

found[2] *past form* of **find**

founder[1] *verb* **1** of a ship: sink **2** of a horse: stumble, go lame

> ⚠Do not confuse with: **flounder**

founder[2] *see* **found**

foundling *noun* a child abandoned by its parents

fountain *noun* **1** a rising jet of water **2** the pipe or structure from which it comes **3** the beginning of anything

four the number 4 □ *adj* 4 in number

fourteen *noun* the number 14 □ *adj* 14 in number

fourteenth *adj* the last of a series of fourteen □ *noun* one of fourteen equal parts

fourth *adj* the last of a series of four □ *noun* **1** one of four equal parts **2** *music* an interval of four notes

fowl *noun* a bird, *esp* a domestic cock or hen

fox *noun* (*plural* **foxes**) a wild animal related to the dog, with reddish-brown fur and a long bushy tail □ *verb* **1** trick by cleverness **2** puzzle, baffle □ **foxhound** *noun* a breed of dog trained to chase foxes □ **fox terrier** a breed of dog trained to drive foxes from their earths

foxglove *noun* a tall wild flower

foxtrot *noun* a ballroom dance made up of walking steps and turns

foxy *adj* **1** cunning **2** *US informal* sexually attractive

foyer /*foi*eh/ *noun* an entrance hall to a theatre, hotel *etc*

FP *abbrev* Former Pupil(s)

fps *abbrev* frames (of photographic film) per second

fracas /*fra*kah/ *noun* **1** uproar **2** a noisy quarrel

fraction *noun* **1** a part, not a whole number, *eg* $\frac{1}{4}$, $\frac{4}{5}$ **2** a small part

fractious *adj* cross, quarrelsome

fracture *noun* a break in something hard, *esp* in a bone of the body

fragile *adj* easily broken □ **fragility** *noun*

fragment *noun* a part broken off; something not complete □ *verb* break into pieces □ **fragmentary** *adj* broken □ **fragmentation** *noun*

fragrant *adj* sweet-smelling □ **fragrance** *noun* sweet scent □ **fragrantly** *adv*

frail *adj* weak; easily tempted to do wrong □ **frailty** (*plural* **frailties**) weakness

frame *verb* **1** put a frame round **2** put together, construct **3** *slang* make (someone) appear to be guilty of a crime □ *noun* **1** a case or border round anything **2** build of human body **3** state (of mind) □ **framework** *noun* the outline or skeleton of something

> **frame** *verb* » frame*s*, fram*ing*, frame*d*

franc *noun* the standard unit of French, Belgian and Swiss money

franchise *noun* **1** the right to vote in a general election **2** a right to sell the goods of a particular company □ *verb* give a business franchise to

Franco- *prefix* of France, French: *Francophile*

frangipani *noun* perfume from red jasmine flowers

franglais *noun* French sprinkled with words borrowed from English

frank *adj* open, speaking your mind □ *verb* mark a letter by machine to show that postage has been paid □ **frankly** *adv* □ **frankness** *noun*

frankfurter *noun* a kind of smoked sausage

frankincense *noun* a sweet-smelling resin used as incense

frantic *adj* wildly excited or anxious □ **frantically** *adv*

fraternal *adj* brotherly; of a brother □ **fraternally** *adv*

fraternity (*plural* **fraternities**) **1** a society, a brotherhood **2** a North American male college society (*compare with*: **sorority**)

fraternize *verb* make friends with

fratricide *noun* **1** the murder of a brother **2** someone who murders their brother

fraud *noun* **1** deceit, dishonesty **2** an impostor; a fake □ **fraudulence** or **fraudulency** *noun* □ **fraudulent** *adj* □ **fraudulently** *adv*

fraught *adj* **1** anxious, tense **2** (with **with**) filled

fray *verb* wear away □ *noun* a fight, a brawl

freak *noun* **1** an unusual event **2** an odd or eccentric person **3** *informal* a keen fan: *film freak*

freckle *noun* a small brown spot on the skin

free *adj* **1** not bound or shut in **2** generous **3** frank, open **4** costing nothing □ *verb* **1** make or set free **2** (with **from** or **of**) get rid □ **freebase** *noun, slang* refined cocaine □ **freehand** *adj* of drawing: done without the help of rulers, tracing *etc* □ **freehold** *adj* of an estate: belonging to the holder or their heirs for all time □ **freelance** or **freelancer** *noun* someone working independently (such as a writer who is not employed by any one newspaper) □ **freeloader** *noun, informal* a sponger □ **Freemason** *noun* a member of a certain men's society, sworn to secrecy □ **free radical** an atom containing an unpaired electron ◇ **free-range** *adj* **1** of poultry: allowed to move about freely and feed out of doors **2** of eggs: laid by poultry of this kind ◇ **free speech** the right to express opinions of any kind ◇ **freestyle** *adj* of swimming, skating *etc*: in which any style may be used ◇ **freeware** *noun* computer software which can legally be copied and distributed, but not resold for profit

-free *suffix* not containing or involving: *additive-free/ cruelty-free*

freebie *informal* a free event, performance *etc*

freedom *noun* liberty

freeze *verb* **1** turn into ice **2** make (food) very cold in order to preserve **2** go stiff with cold, fear *etc* **3** fix (prices or wages) at a certain level ◇ **freezing-point** *noun* the point at which liquid becomes a solid (of water, 0°C)

freeze *verb* » freeze*s*, freez*ing*, froze, froz*en*

freezer *noun* a type of cabinet in which food is made, or kept, frozen

freight *noun* **1** load, cargo **2** a charge for carrying a load ◇ *verb* load with goods ◇ **freighter** *noun* a ship or aircraft that carries cargo ◇ **freight train** a goods train

French *adj*: **French fries** *US* fried potatoes ◇ **French letter** *Brit slang* a condom ◇ **French polish** a kind of varnish for furniture ◇ **French toast** bread dipped in egg and fried ◇ **French window** a long window also used as a door ◇ **take French leave** go or stay away without permission

frenetic *adj* frantic ◇ **frenetically** *adv*

frenzy *noun* **1** a fit of madness **2** wild excitement ◇ **frenzied** *adj* mad ◇ **frenziedly** *adv*

frequent *adj* happening often ◇ *verb* visit often ◇ **frequency** *noun* (*plural* **frequencies**) **1** the rate at which something happens **2** the number per second of vibrations, waves *etc*

fresco *noun* (*plural* **frescoes** or **frescos**) a picture painted on a wall while the plaster is still damp

fresh *adj* **1** new, unused: *fresh sheet of paper* **2** newly made or picked; not preserved: *fresh fruit* **3** cool, refreshing: *fresh breeze* **4** not tired **5** cheeky, impertinent ◇ *adv* newly: *fresh-laid eggs* ◇ **freshen** *verb* make fresh; to grow strong ◇ **freshly** *adv* ◇ **freshness** *noun* ◇ **freshwater** *adj* of inland rivers, lakes *etc*, not of the sea

fresher or **freshman** *noun* a first-year university student

fret[1] *verb* worry or show discontent ◇ **fretful** *adj* ◇ **fretfully** *adv*

fret *verb* » fret*s*, frett*ing*, frett*ed*

fret[2] *noun* one of the ridges on the fingerboard of a guitar

fretsaw *noun* a narrow-bladed, fine-toothed saw for fretwork

fretwork *noun* decorated cut-out work in wood

friar *noun* a member of one of the

Roman Catholic brotherhoods, *esp* someone who has vowed to live in poverty □ **friary** *noun* (*plural* **friaries**) the friars' house

friction *noun* **1** rubbing of two things together **2** the wear caused by rubbing **3** quarrelling, bad feeling

Friday *noun* the sixth day of the week

fridge *noun, informal* refrigerator

fried *see* **fry**

friend *noun* **1** someone who likes and knows well another person **2** sympathizer, helper

friendly *adj* **1** kind **2** (with **with**) on good terms □ *noun* (*plural* **friendlies**) a sports match that is not part of a competition □ **friendliness** *noun*

-friendly *suffix* **1** not harmful towards: *dolphin-friendly* **2** compatible with or easy to use for: *child-friendly*

friendship *noun* the state of being friends; mutual affection

frieze *noun* **1** a part of a wall below the ceiling, often ornamented with designs **2** a picture on a long strip of paper *etc*, often displayed on a wall

frig *verb, slang* **1** masturbate **2** have sexual intercourse with □ **frigging** *adj*

> **frig** » frig*s*, frigg*ing*, frigg*ed*

frigate *noun* a small warship

fright *noun* sudden fear: *gave me a fright/ took fright and ran away* □ **frighten** *verb* make afraid □ **frightening** *adj* □ **frighteningly** *adv*

frightful *adj* **1** causing terror **2** *informal* very bad □ **frightfully** *adv*

frigid *adj* **1** frozen, cold **2** cold in manner **3** sexually unresponsive □ **frigidity** *noun* □ **frigidly** *adv*

frill *noun* **1** an ornamental edging **2** an unnecessary ornament

fringe *noun* **1** a border of loose threads **2** hair cut to hang over the forehead **3** a border of soft material, paper *etc* □ *verb* edge round

Frisbee *noun, trademark* a plastic plate-like object skimmed through the air as a game

frisk *verb* **1** skip about playfully **2** *informal* search someone closely for concealed weapons *etc* □ **friskily** *adv* □ **friskiness** *noun* □ **frisky** *adj*

frisson /*free*sonh/ *noun* a shiver, a thrill

fritter *noun* a piece of fried batter containing fruit *etc*

fritter away *verb* waste, squander

fritillary *noun* (*plural* **fritillaries**) **1** a type of lily with chequered, bell-shaped flowers **2** a butterfly with similar markings

frivolity *noun* (*plural* **frivolities**) levity, lack of seriousness

frivolous *adj* playful, not serious □ **frivolously** *adv*

frizzy *adj* of hair: massed in small curls

fro *adv*: **to and fro** forwards and backwards

frock *noun* **1** a woman's or girl's

dress **2** a monk's wide-sleeved garment □ **frock-coat** *noun* a man's long coat

frog *noun* a small greenish jumping animal living on land and in water □ **frogmarch** *verb* seize (someone) from behind and push them forward while holding their arms tight behind their back □ **frogman** *noun, informal* an underwater diver with flippers and breathing apparatus

frolic *noun* a merry, lighthearted playing □ *verb* play lightheartedly □ **frolicsome** *adj*

> **frolic** *verb* » frolic*s*, frolick*ing*, frolick*ed*

from *prep* **1** used before the place, person *etc* that is the starting point of an action *etc*: *sailing from England to France/ the office is closed from Friday to Monday* **2** used to show separation: *warn them to keep away from there*

fromage frais /fromazh *fre*/ a low-fat cheese with the consistency of whipped cream

frond *noun* a leaf-like growth, *esp* a branch of a fern or palm

front *noun* **1** the part of anything nearest the person who sees it **2** the part which faces the direction in which something moves **3** the fighting line in a war □ *adj* at or in the front □ **frontage** *noun* the front part of a building □ **frontman** *noun* the main person in a group, TV programme *etc* □ **in front of** at the head of, before

frontier *noun* a boundary between countries

frontispiece *noun* a picture at the very beginning of a book

frost *noun* **1** frozen dew **2** the coldness of weather needed to form ice □ *verb* **1** cover with frost **2** *US* ice (a cake) □ **frosted** *adj* □ **frosting** *noun, US* icing on a cake *etc* □ **frosty** *adj* cold, unwelcoming: *gave me a frosty look*

froth *noun* foam on liquids □ *verb* throw up foam □ **frothy** *adj*

frown *verb* wrinkle the brows in deep thought, disapproval *etc* □ *noun* **1** a wrinkling of the brows **2** a disapproving look □ **frown on** look upon with disapproval

frowzy *adj* rough and tangled

froze and **frozen** *see* **freeze**

frugal *adj* **1** careful in spending, thrifty **2** costing little, small: *a frugal meal* □ **frugality** *noun* □ **frugally** *adv*

fruit *noun* **1** the part of a plant containing the seed **2** result: *all their hard work bore fruit* □ **fruitarian** *noun* someone who eats only fruit □ **fruiterer** *noun* someone who sells fruit □ **fruitful** *adj* **1** producing plenty of fruit **2** producing good results: *a fruitful meeting* □ **fruitless** *adj* useless, done in vain □ **fruit machine** a gambling machine into which coins are put

fruition *noun* **1** ripeness **2** a good result

frump *noun* a plain, badly or unfashionably dressed woman □ **frumpish** *adj*

frustrate *verb* **1** make to feel powerless **2** bring to nothing: *frustrated his wishes* □ **frustration** *noun*

fry[1] *verb* cook in hot fat ▯ *noun* food cooked in hot fat

fry *verb* » fri*es*, fry*ing*, fri*ed*

fry[2] *noun* a young fish ▯ **small fry** unimportant people or things

ft *abbrev* foot, feet

ftp *abbrev*, *comput* file transfer protocol, by which large files and programs are accessed from a remote computer

FTSE *abbrev* the Financial Times Stock Exchange 100-Share Index, recording share prices of the 100 top UK companies

fuchsia */fyooshiə/ noun* a plant with long hanging flowers

fuck *verb*, *taboo slang* have sexual intercourse (with) ▯ *noun* **1** an act of sexual intercourse **2** a sexual partner **3** something of little or no value ▯ **fucker** *noun* a general term of abuse ▯ **fuck about** or **around** play around, act foolishly ▯ **fuck all** nothing ▯ **fuck off** go away ▯ **fuck up** spoil, mess up

fuddle *verb* confuse, muddle

fuddy-duddy *noun* an old fogy, a stick-in-the-mud

fudge[1] *noun* a soft, sugary sweet

fudge[2] *verb* cheat ▯ *noun* a cheat

fuel *noun* a substance such as coal, gas or petrol, used to keep a fire or engine going

fugitive *adj* running away, on the run ▯ *noun* someone who is running away from the police *etc*: *a fugitive from justice*

fugue /fyoog/ *noun* a piece of music with several interwoven tunes

fulcrum *noun* (*plural* **fulcrums** or **fulcra**) the point on which a lever turns, or a balanced object rests

fulfil *verb* carry out (a task, promise *etc*) ▯ **fulfilment** *noun*

fulfil » fulfil*s*, fulfill*ing*, fulfill*ed*

full *adj* **1** holding as much as can be held **2** plump: *full face* ▯ *adv* (used with *adjs*) fully: *full-grown* ▯ **fullness** *noun* ▯ **fully** *adv* ▯ **full moon** the moon when it appears at its largest ▯ **full of** *adj* having a great deal or plenty ▯ **full stop** a punctuation mark (.) placed at the end of a sentence

fullback *noun* a defensive player in football *etc*, the nearest to their team's goal-line

fulmar *noun* a white sea bird

fulminate *verb*, *formal* **1** speak angrily or passionately against something **2** flash like lightning ▯ **fulmination** *noun*

fulsome *adj*, *formal* overdone: *fulsome praise*

fumble *verb* **1** use the hands awkwardly **2** drop (a thrown ball *etc*)

fume *verb* **1** give off smoke or vapour **2** be in a silent rage

fume *verb* » fum*es*, fum*ing*, fum*ed*

fumes *noun plural* smoke, vapour

fumigate *verb* kill germs by means of strong fumes ▯ **fumigation** *noun*

fun *noun* enjoyment, a good time: *are you having fun?* ▯ **funfair** *noun* an amusement park ◊ **make fun of** tease, make others laugh at

function *noun* **1** a special job, use or duty of a machine, person, part of the body *etc* **2** an arranged public gathering ◊ *verb* **1** work, operate: *the engine isn't functioning properly* **2** carry out usual duties: *I can't function at this time in the morning* ◊ **functionary** *noun* (*plural* **functionaries**) an office holder, an official

fund *noun* **1** a sum of money for a special purpose: *charity fund* **2** a store or supply

fundamental *adj* **1** of great or far-reaching importance **2** basic, essential: *fundamental to her happiness* ◊ *noun* **1** a necessary part **2** (**fundamentals**) the groundwork, the first stages

funeral *noun* the ceremony of burial or cremation ◊ **funereal** *adj* mournful

fungus *noun* (*plural* **fungi** /*fung*gee/) **1** a soft, spongy plant growth, *eg* a mushroom **2** disease-growth on animals and plants

funicular railway a railway with carriages which are pulled uphill by a cable

funk *noun*, *informal* fear, panic

funky *adj*, *informal* **1** fashionable, trendy **2** odd, eccentric

funnel *noun* **1** a cone ending in a tube, for pouring liquids into bottles **2** a tube or passage for escape of smoke, air *etc* ◊ *verb* pass through a funnel; channel

funnel *verb* » funnel*s*, funnel*ling*, funnell*ed*

funny *adj* **1** amusing **2** odd ◊ **funnily** *adv* ◊ **funny bone** part of the elbow which gives a prickly feeling when knocked

fur *noun* **1** the short fine hair of certain animals **2** their skins covered with fur **3** a coating on the tongue, on the inside of kettles *etc* ◊ *verb* line or cover with fur ◊ **furrier** *noun* someone who trades in or works with furs

fur *verb* » fur*s*, furr*ing*, furr*ed*

furbish *verb* rub until bright; burnish

furious *adj* extremely angry ◊ **furiously** *adv*

furlong *noun* one-eighth of a mile (220 yards, 201.17 metres)

furnace *noun* a very hot oven for melting iron ore, making steam for heating *etc*

furnish *verb* **1** fit up (a room or house) completely **2** supply: *furnished with enough food for a week* ◊ **furnishings** *noun plural* fittings, furniture

furniture *noun* movable articles in a house, *eg* tables, chairs

furore /fyoo*raw*reh/ *noun* uproar; excitement

furrow *noun* **1** a groove made by a plough **2** a deep groove **3** a deep wrinkle ◊ *verb* **1** cut deep grooves in **2** wrinkle: *furrowed brow*

furry *adj* covered with fur

further *adv* & *adj* to a greater distance or degree; in addition ◊ *verb* help on or forward □ **furthermore** *adv* in addition to what has been said □ **furthest** *adv* to the greatest distance or degree

furtive *adj* stealthy, sly: *furtive glance* □ **furtively** *adv*

fury *noun* violent anger

furze *another name* for **gorse**

fuse *verb* **1** melt **2** join together **3** put a fuse in (a plug *etc*) **4** of a circuit *etc*: stop working because of the melting of a fuse □ *noun* **1** easily-melted wire put in an electric circuit for safety **2** any device for causing an explosion to take place automatically

> **fuse** *verb* » fuse*s*, fus*ing*, fus*ed*

fuselage *noun* the body of an aeroplane

fusion *noun* **1** melting **2** a merging: *a fusion of musical traditions*

fuss *noun* **1** unnecessary activity, excitement or attention, often about something unimportant: *making a fuss about nothing* **2** strong complaint □ *verb* **1** be unnecessarily concerned about details **2** worry too much

fussy *adj* **1** over-elaborate **2** choosy, finicky **3** partial, in favour of one thing over another: *either will do; I'm not fussy* □ **fussily** *adv* □ **fussiness** *noun*

fusty *adj* mouldy; stale-smelling

futile *adj* useless; having no effect □ **futility** *noun* uselessness

futon /*foo*ton/ *noun* a sofa bed with a low frame and detachable mattress

future *adj* happening later in time □ *noun* **1** the time to come: *foretell the future* **2** the part of your life still to come: *planning for their future* **3** *grammar* the future tense in verbs

fuzz *noun* **1** fine, light hair or feathers **2** *Brit slang* the police □ **fuzzy** *adj* **1** covered with fuzz, fluffy **2** tightly curled: *fuzzy hairdo*

fx *informal* effects (in film-making, *etc*)

G

g *abbrev* gramme; gram

gabble *verb* talk fast, chatter □ *noun* fast talk

gaberdine *noun* **1** a heavy overcoat **2** a heavy fabric

gable *noun* the triangular area of wall at the end of a building with a ridged roof

gadabout *noun* someone who loves going out or travelling

gadfly *noun* a fly which bites cattle

gadget *noun* a small simple machine or tool

Gaelic *noun* **1** the language of the Scottish Highlands **2** the Irish language; Erse □ *adj* written or spoken in Gaelic

gaff *noun* **1** a large hook used for landing fish, such as salmon **2** a spar made from a mast, for raising the top of a sail □ **blow the gaff** *informal* let out a secret

gag *verb* silence by stopping the mouth □ *noun* **1** a piece of cloth *etc* put in or over someone's mouth to silence them **2** *informal* a joke

> **gag** *verb* » gag*s*, gagg*ing*, gagg*ed*

gaggle *noun* a flock of geese

gaiety and **gaily** *see* **gay**

gain *verb* **1** win; earn **2** reach **3** get closer, *esp* in a race: *gaining on the leader* **4** of a clock: go ahead of correct time **5** take on (*eg* weight) □ *noun* **1** something gained **2** profit

gainsay *verb*, *formal* deny

gait *noun* way or manner of walking

> ⚠Do not confuse with: **gate**

gaiter *noun* a cloth ankle-covering, fitting over the shoe, sometimes reaching to the knee

gala *noun* **1** a public festival **2** a sports meeting: *swimming gala*

galaxy *noun* (*plural* **galaxies**) **1** a system of stars **2** an impressive gathering □ **the Galaxy** the Milky Way

gale *noun* a strong wind

gall /gaẉl/ *noun* **1** bile, a bitter fluid produced by the liver and stored in the **gallbladder** **2** bitterness of feeling **3** a growth caused by insects on trees and plants □ *verb* annoy □ **galling** *adj* annoying, frustrating

gallant *adj* **1** brave; noble **2** polite or attentive towards women □ *noun* a gallant man □ **gallantry** *noun*

galleon *noun, hist* a large Spanish sailing ship

gallery *noun* (*plural* **galleries**) **1** a long passage **2** the top floor of seats in a theatre **3** a room or building for showing artworks

galley *noun* (*plural* **galleys**) **1** *hist* a long, low-built ship driven by oars **2** a ship's kitchen □ **galley-slave** *noun, hist* a prisoner condemned to row in a galley

gallivant *verb* travel or go out for pleasure

gallon *noun* a measure for liquids (8 pints, 3.636 litres)

gallop *verb* **1** move by leaps **2** (cause to) move very fast ▫ *noun* a fast pace

gallows *noun sing* a wooden framework on which criminals were hanged

gallus /galəs/ *adj, Scot* spirited, perky; bold

galore *adv* in plenty: *whisky galore*

> Based on an Irish Gaelic phrase *go leōr*, meaning 'sufficient'

galosh or **golosh** *noun* (*plural* **galoshes** or **goloshes**) a rubber shoe worn over ordinary shoes in wet weather

galvanic *adj* electricity produced by the action of acids or other chemicals on metal ▫ **galvanism** *noun* ▫ **galvanometer** *noun* an instrument for measuring electric currents

> Named after the Italian physicist, Luigi *Galvani*

galvanize *verb* **1** stir into activity **2** stimulate by electricity **3** coat (iron *etc*) with zinc

gambit *noun* **1** *chess* a first move involving sacrificing a piece to make the player's position stronger **2** an opening move in a transaction, or an opening remark in a conversation

gamble *verb* **1** play games for money **2** risk money on the result of a game, race *etc* **3** take a wild chance ▫ *noun* a risk; a bet on a result

gambol *verb* leap playfully

> **gambol** » gambol*s*, gambol*ling*, gambol*led*

game *noun* **1** a contest played according to rules **2** (**games**) athletic competition **3** wild animals and birds hunted for sport ▫ *adj* **1** plucky **2** of a limb: lame ▫ **gamekeeper** *noun* someone who looks after game birds, animals, fish *etc* ▫ **gaming** *noun* & *adj* gambling ▫ **big game** large hunted animals, *eg* lions

gammon *noun* leg of a pig, salted and smoked

gamut *noun* **1** the whole range or extent of anything **2** the range of notes of an individual voice or musical instrument

> From the name of a medieval 6-note musical scale, two notes of which were *gamma* and *ut*

gander *noun* a male goose

gang *noun* **1** a group of people who meet regularly **2** a team of criminals **3** a number of labourers

gangrene *noun* the rotting of some part of the body ▫ **gangrenous** *adj*

gangsta *noun* **1** a style of rap music with violent lyrics **2** a singer of this kind of music

gangster *noun* a member of a gang of criminals

gangway *noun* **1** a passage between rows of seats **2** a movable bridge leading from a quay to a ship

gannet *noun* a large white sea bird

gantry *noun* (*plural* **gantries**) a platform or structure for supporting a travelling crane *etc*

gaol *another spelling* of **jail**

gaoler *another spelling* of **jailer**

gap *noun* an opening or space between things

gape *verb* **1** open the mouth wide (as in surprise) **2** be wide open

garage *noun* **1** a building for storing a car (or cars) **2** a shop which carries out car repairs and sells petrol, oil *etc*

garam masala a mixture of ground spices used in Asian cookery

garb *noun, formal* dress ▯ *verb* clothe

garbage *noun* rubbish

garbanzo *noun* (*plural* **garbanzos**) *US* a chickpea

garble *verb* mix up, muddle: *garbled account of events*

> Originally meaning 'sift', which gradually developed into the sense of confusing by leaving out too much

Garda *noun* **1** the police force of the Republic of Ireland **2** a police officer in the Garda

garden *noun* a piece of ground on which flowers or vegetables are grown ▯ *verb* work in a garden ▯ **gardener** *noun* someone who tends a garden ▯ **garden party** a large tea party, held out of doors

gardenia *noun* a tropical plant producing large, waxy white flowers

gargantuan *adj* extremely large, huge

> Named after *Gargantua*, a giant with an enormous appetite in a 16th-century French novel by Rabelais

gargle *verb* rinse the throat with a liquid, without swallowing

gargoyle *noun* a grotesque carving of a human or animal head, jutting out from a roof

garish *adj* tastelessly over-bright: *garish book cover* ▯ **garishness** *noun*

garland *noun* flowers or leaves tied or woven into a circle

garlic *noun* an onion-like plant with a strong smell and taste, used in cooking

garment *noun* an article of clothing

garner *verb, formal* gather; collect and store

garnet *noun* a semi-precious stone, usually red in colour

garnish *verb* decorate (a dish of food) ▯ *noun* (*plural* **garnishes**) a decoration on food ▯ **garnishing** *noun*

garret *noun* an attic room

garrison *noun* a body of troops for guarding a fortress

garrotte *verb* strangle by tightening a noose *etc* round someone's neck (originally by tightening an iron collar)

garrulous *adj* fond of talking ▯ **garrulity** or **garrulousness** *noun*

garter *noun* broad elastic band to keep a stocking up

gas *noun* (*plural* **gases**) **1** a substance like air (though some gases may be smelled) **2** natural or manufactured form of this which will burn and is used as a fuel **3** *US* petrol ▯ *verb* poison with gas ▯ **gaseous** *adj* ▯ **gas mask** a covering for the face to prevent breathing in poisonous gas ▯ **gasometer** *noun* a tank for storing gas ▯ **gasworks** *noun* place where gas is made

> **gas** *verb* » gas*es*, gass*ing*, gass*ed*

gash *noun* (*plural* **gashes**) a deep, open cut ▯ *verb* cut deeply into

gasket *noun* a layer of padding used to make air-tight or gas-tight joints

gasoline *noun, US* petrol

gasp *noun* the sound made by a sudden intake of breath ▯ *verb* **1** breathe with difficulty **2** say breathlessly **3** *informal* want badly: *gasping for a cup of tea*

gastric *adj* relating to the stomach: *gastric ulcer*

gate *noun* **1** a door across an opening in a wall, fence *etc* **2** the number of people at a football match **3** the total entrance money paid by those at a football match

> ⚠Do not confuse with: **gait**

gateau /*ga*toh/ *noun* (*plural* **gateaus** or **gateaux**) a rich cake, usually layered and filled with cream

gatecrash *verb* go to a party uninvited ▯ **gatecrasher** *noun*

gateway *noun* **1** an opening containing a gate **2** an entrance **3** *comput* a connection between networks

gather *verb* **1** bring together, or meet, in one place **2** pick (flowers *etc*) **3** increase in: *gather speed* **4** learn, come to the conclusion (that): *I gather you don't want to go* ▯ **gathering** *noun* a crowd

GATT /gat/ *abbrev* General Agreement on Tariffs and Trade (now **WTO**)

gauche /gohsh/ *adj* awkward and clumsy in people's company

> Taken from the French word for 'left', because of the supposed awkwardness of using the left hand

gaucho *noun* (*plural* **gauchos**) a cowboy of the South American plains, noted for horse-riding

gaudy *adj* showy; vulgarly bright in colour ▯ **gaudily** *adv* ▯ **gaudiness** *noun*

gauge *verb* **1** measure **2** make a guess ▯ *noun* a measuring device ▯ **broad-gauge** or **narrow-gauge** *adj* of a railway: having the distance between rails greater or less than the *standard gauge* (4ft 8in, 1.435 metre)

gaunt *adj* thin, haggard

gauntlet[1] *noun* **1** a long glove (often of leather) with a guard for the wrist used by motor-cyclists *etc* **2** *hist* an iron glove worn with armour □ **take up the gauntlet** accept a challenge □ **throw down the gauntlet** offer a challenge

gauntlet[2] *noun*: **run the gauntlet** expose yourself to criticism, hostility *etc*

> The *gauntlet* was an old military punishment of being made to run past a line of soldiers armed with sticks; the word is of Swedish origin and unrelated to **gauntlet**[1]

gauze *noun* thin cloth that can be seen through

gavotte *noun* a lively type of dance

gawky *adj* awkward

gay *adj* **1** homosexual **2** lively; merry, full of fun **3** brightly coloured □ *noun* a homosexual □ **gaiety** *noun* □ **gaily** *adv*

gaze *verb* look steadily □ *noun* a fixed look

gazelle *noun* a small deer

gazette *noun* a newspaper, *esp* one having lists of government notices □ **gazetteer** *noun* a geographical dictionary

gazpacho *noun* a Spanish chilled soup of crushed garlic, tomatoes and peppers

gazump *verb*, *informal* raise the price of property after accepting an offer, but before contracts are signed

gazunder *verb*, *informal* lower an offer for property just before contracts are signed

GB *abbrev* Great Britain

GBH or **gbh** *abbrev* grievous bodily harm

GC *abbrev* George Cross

GCE *abbrev* General Certificate of Education

GDP *abbrev* gross domestic product

gear *noun* **1** clothing and equipment needed for a particular job, sport *etc* **2** a connection by means of a set of toothed wheels between a car engine and the wheels □ *verb* (with **to**) adapt to, design for what is needed

geese *plural* of **goose**

geisha /*geh*shə/ *noun* a Japanese girl trained to entertain

gelatine *noun* a jelly-like substance made from hooves, animal bones *etc*, and used in food

gelatinous *adj* jelly-like

geld *verb* castrate (an animal)

gelding *noun* a castrated horse

gem *noun* **1** a precious stone, *esp* when cut **2** something greatly valued

gender *noun* (in grammar, *esp* in languages other than English) any of three types of noun, masculine, feminine or neuter

gene *noun* the basic unit of heredity responsible for passing on specific characteristics from parents to offspring

genealogy *noun* (*plural*

genealogies) **1** the history of families from generation to generation **2** a personal family history ▯ **genealogical** *adj* ▯ **genealogist** *noun* someone who studies or makes genealogies

general *adj* **1** not detailed, broad: *a general idea of the person's interests* **2** involving everyone: *a general election* **3** to do with several different things: *general knowledge* **4** of most people: *the general opinion* ▯ *noun* a high-ranking army officer ▯ **generally** *adv* **1** usually, in most cases **2** by most people: *generally known* ▯ **general practitioner** a doctor who treats most ordinary illnesses ▯ **in general** generally

generalize *verb* make a broad general statement, meant to cover all individual cases ▯ **generalization** a too general view, statement *etc*

generate *verb* produce, bring into being: *generate electricity/ generate good will* ▯ **generator** *noun* a machine for making electricity *etc*

generation *noun* **1** creation, making **2** a step in family descent **3** people born at about the same time: *90s generation*

generic *adj* general, applicable to any member of a group or class

generous *adj* giving plentifully; kind ▯ **generosity** *noun* ▯ **generously** *adv*

genesis *noun* beginning, origin

genetic *adj* **1** relating to genes **2** inherited through genes: *genetic disease* ▯ **genetically** *adv*

genial *adj* good-natured ▯ **geniality** *noun* ▯ **genially** *adv*

genie *noun* (*plural* **genii**) a guardian spirit

genitals *noun plural* the organs of sexual reproduction

genius *noun* (*plural* **geniuses**) **1** unusual cleverness **2** someone who is unusually clever

genocide *noun* the deliberate extermination of a race of people ▯ **genocidal** *adj*

genome *noun* the full set of chromosomes of one person

genotype *noun* the genetic make-up of an individual

gent *noun, informal* a man ▯ **the gents** *informal* a men's public toilet

genteel *adj* good-mannered, *esp* excessively

gentile /*jen*tail/ *noun* a non-Jew

gentility *noun* **1** aristocracy **2** good manners, refinement, often in excess

gentle *adj* **1** mild-mannered, not brutal **2** mild, not extreme: *gentle breeze* ▯ **gently** *adv* ▯ **gentleness** *noun*

gentleman *noun* (*plural* **gentlemen**) **1** a man, *esp* one of noble birth **2** a well-mannered man ▯ **gentlemanly** *adj* behaving in a polite manner

gentry *noun* a wealthy, land-owning class of people

genuine *adj* **1** real, not fake: *genuine antique* **2** honest and straightforward ▯ **genuinely** *adv* ▯ **genuineness** *noun*

genus *noun* (*plural* **genera**) a

group of living things made up of a number of kinds

geography *noun* the study of the surface of the earth and its inhabitants ◻ **geographer** *noun* someone who studies geography ◻ **geographic** or **geographical** *adj*

geology *noun* the study of the earth's history as shown in its rocks and soils ◻ **geological** *adj* ◻ **geologist** *noun* someone who studies geology

geometric or **geometrical** *adj* of a shape or pattern: made up of angles and straight lines

geometry *noun* the branch of mathematics which deals with the study of lines, angles, and figures ◻ **geometrician** *noun* someone who studies geometry

Geordie *noun, Brit informal* someone who was born or lives in Newcastle

geranium *noun* a plant with thick leaves and bright red or pink flowers

gerbil /*jer*bil/ *noun* a small, rat-like desert animal, often kept as a pet

germ *noun* **1** a small living organism which can cause disease **2** the earliest or initial form of something, *eg* a fertilized egg **3** that from which anything grows: *germ of an idea* ◻ **germicide** *noun* a germ-killing substance

germane *adj* closely related; very relevant ◻ **germanely** *adv*

German shepherd dog (*also called* **Alsatian**) a breed of large wolf-like dog

germinate *verb* begin to grow; sprout ◻ **germination** *noun*

gerrymander *verb* rearrange (voting districts *etc*) to suit a political purpose ◻ **gerrymandering**

> After US governor, Elbridge *Gerry*, who rearranged the map of Massachusetts in 1811 to a shape resembling that of a sala*mander*

gerund *noun* a noun with the ending *-ing*, *eg* watch*ing*, wait*ing*

gesso /*jes*oh/ *noun* (*plural* **gessoes**) **1** plaster of Paris **2** a plastered surface for painting on

Gestalt therapy a form of psychotherapy emphasizing self-analysis and self-expression

gesticulate *verb* wave hands and arms about in excitement *etc* ◻ **gesticulation** *noun* ◻ **gesticulatory** *adj*

gesture *noun* **1** a meaningful action with the hands, head *etc* **2** an action expressing your feelings or intent: *gesture of good will*

get *verb* **1** obtain, go or move **2** cause to be done: *get your hair cut* **3** receive: *get a letter* **4** cause to be in some condition: *get the car started* **5** arrive: *what time did you get home?* **6** catch or have (a disease): *I think I've got flu* **7** become: *get rich* ◻ **get at 1** reach: **2** hint at: *what are you getting at?* **3** criticize continually: *stop getting at me* **4** effect badly, distress: *the pressure is getting to him* **5** *slang* try to influence by bribes or threats ◻ **get away with** escape punishment for ◻ **get on with** be on friendly terms with ◻ **get over** recover from

□ **get up 1** stand up **2** get out of bed

> **get** » get*s*, gett*ing*, got
> *US* get*s*, gett*ing*, got, gott*en*

geyser /*geez*ər/ *noun* **1** a natural hot spring **2** a device which heats domestic water when the tap is turned on

ghastly *adj* **1** very ill: *feeling ghastly* **2** horrible, ugly **3** very pale, death-like **4** very bad □ **ghastliness**

ghee /gee/ *noun* clarified butter, used in Asian cookery

gherkin *noun* a small pickled cucumber

ghetto *noun* (*plural* **ghettos**) a poor residential part of a city in which a certain group (*esp* of immigrants) lives

ghost *noun* the spirit of a dead person □ **ghostly** *adj* like a ghost □ **ghostliness** *noun*

ghoul /gool/ *noun* **1** an evil spirit which robs dead bodies **2** someone unnaturally interested in death and disaster □ **ghoulish** *adj*

GHQ *abbrev* general headquarters

giant *noun* **1** an imaginary being, like a human but enormous **2** a very tall or large person □ *adj* huge

giantess *noun* a female giant

gibber *verb* **1** speak nonsense **2** make meaningless noises; babble

gibberish *noun* words without meaning; rubbish

gibbet *noun*, *hist* a gallows where criminals were executed, or hung up after execution

gibbon *noun* a large, tailless ape

gibe *another spelling* of **jibe**

giblets *noun plural* eatable organs from the inside of a chicken *etc*

giddy *adj* **1** unsteady, dizzy **2** causing dizziness: *from a giddy height* □ **giddily** *adv* □ **giddiness** *noun*

gift 1 something freely given, *eg* a present **2** a natural talent: *a gift for music* **3** *informal* something easily done: *the exam paper was a gift* □ **gifted** *adj* having special natural power or ability □ **look a gift horse in the mouth** find fault with a gift

gigantic *adj* huge, of giant size □ **gigantically** *adv*

giggle *verb* laugh in a nervous or silly manner □ *noun* a nervous or silly laugh

gigolo /*jig*əloh/ *noun* a male lover kept by a woman at her expense

gigot /*jig*ət/ *noun* a leg of mutton, lamb *etc*

gild *verb* **1** cover with beaten gold **2** make bright □ **gild the lily** try to improve something already beautiful enough

> ⚠Do not confuse with: **guild**

gill[1]/jil/ *noun* a measure ($\frac{1}{4}$ pint, 11.36 centilitres) for liquids

gill[2] /gil/ *noun* one of the openings on the side of a fish's head through which it breathes

gillie *noun* an assistant and guide to someone fishing or shooting on a Scottish estate

gilt *noun* beaten gold used for gilding □ *adj* **1** covered with thin gold **2** gold in colour ▫ **gilt-edged** *adj* not risky, safe to invest in: *gilt-edged stocks*

⚠Do not confuse with: **guilt**

gimcrack *adj* cheap and badly-made

gimlet *noun* a small tool for boring holes by hand

gimmick *noun* something meant to attract attention

gin[1] *noun* an alcoholic drink made from grain, flavoured with juniper berries

gin[2] *noun* a trap or snare

ginger *noun* a hot-tasting root, used as a seasoning in food ▫ *adj* **1** flavoured with ginger **2** reddish-brown in colour: *ginger hair*

gingerbread *noun* cake flavoured with ginger

gingerly *adv* very carefully and gently: *opened the door gingerly*

gingham *noun* a striped or checked cotton cloth

gingival /jin*jai*vəl/ *adj* relating to the gums

gingivitis *noun* inflammation of the gums

ginkgo *noun* (*plural* **ginkgoes**) a Chinese tree with fan-shaped leaves

ginseng /jin*seng*/ *noun* a root grown in the Far East believed to have restorative powers

gipsy *another spelling* of **gypsy**

giraffe *noun* an African animal with very long legs and neck

Called a *camelopard* until the 17th century

gird *verb, formal* bind round

girder *noun* a beam of iron, steel or wood used in building

girdle *noun* **1** a belt for the waist **2** a tight-fitting piece of underwear to slim the waist

girl *noun* a female child or young woman ▫ **girlhood** the state or time of being a girl ▫ **girlie** *adj* **1** girlish **2** pornographic: *girlie magazines* ▫ **girlish** *adj* like a girl

giro /*jai*roh/ *noun* (*plural* **giros**) **1** a system by which payment may be made through banks, post offices *etc* **2** (*also called* **girocheque**) a form like a cheque by which such payment is made **3** *informal* social security paid by girocheque

girth *noun* **1** measurement round the middle **2** a strap tying a saddle on a horse

gismo or **gizmo** *noun* (*plural* **gismos** or **gizmos**), *informal* a gadget, a thingumajig

gist /jist/ *noun* the main points or ideas of a story, argument *etc*: *give me the gist of the story*

give *verb* **1** hand over freely or in exchange **2** utter (a shout or cry) **3** break, crack: *the bridge gave under the weight of the train* **4** produce: *this lamp gives a good light* ▫ **giver** *noun* ▫ **give away 1** hand over (something) to someone without payment **2** betray ▫ **give in** yield ▫ **give over** *informal* stop (doing something) ▫ **give rise to** cause ▫ **give up 1** hand over **2** yield **3** stop, abandon (a habit *etc*) ▫ **give way 1**

yield **2** collapse **3** let traffic crossing your path go before you

> **give** » give*s*, giv*ing*, gave, give*n*

GLA *abbrev* gamma linolenic acid

glacé *adj* iced or sugared: *glacé cherries*

glacial *adj* **1** of ice or glaciers **2** icy, cold: *glacial expression*

glacier *noun* a slowly-moving river of ice in valleys between high mountains

glad *adj* **1** pleased: *I'm glad you were able to come* **2** giving pleasure: *glad tidings* ▯ **gladly** *adv* ▯ **gladness** *noun* ▯ **glad eye** an ogle ▯ **glad hand** a ready but insincere welcome ▯ **glad rags** best clothes

gladden *verb* make glad

glade *noun* an open space in a wood

gladiator *noun, hist* in ancient Rome, a man trained to fight with other men or with animals for the amusement of spectators ▯ **gladiatorial** *adj*

glaikit *adj, Scot* stupid, daft

glam *adj, slang* glamorous

glamour *noun* fascination, charm, beauty, *esp* artificial ▯ **glamorous** *adj* ▯ **glamorously** *adv*

glance *noun* a quick look ▯ *verb* take a quick look at ▯ **glance off** hit and fly off sideways

gland *noun* a part of the body which takes substances from the blood and stores them for later use or elimination by the body ▯ **glandular** *adj*

glare *noun* **1** an unpleasantly bright light **2** an angry or fierce look ▯ *verb* **1** shine with an unpleasantly bright light **2** look angrily

glaring *adj* **1** dazzling **2** very clear, obvious: *glaring mistake* ▯ **glaringly** *adv*

glasnost *noun* a political policy of openness and forthrightness, originally in the Soviet Union in the 1980s

glass *noun* (*plural* **glasses**) **1** a hard transparent substance made from metal and other oxides **2** (**glasses**) spectacles **3** a drinking vessel made of glass **4** *old* a mirror ▯ *adj* made of glass ▯ **glass ceiling** a barrier to promotion at work experienced by some women but not officially recognized ▯ **glasshouse** *noun* a greenhouse

glassy *adj* of eyes: without expression ▯ **glassily** *adv*

glaucoma *noun* an eye disease causing dimness in sight

glaze *verb* **1** cover with a thin coating of glass or other shiny stuff **2** ice (a cake *etc*) **3** put panes of glass in a window **4** of eyes: become glassy ▯ *noun* **1** a shiny surface **2** sugar icing ▯ **glazier** *noun* someone who sets glass in window-frames

gleam *verb* **1** glow **2** flash ▯ *noun* **1** a beam of light **2** brightness

glean *verb* **1** collect, gather **2** *old* gather corn in handfuls after the reapers

glee *noun* **1** joy **2** a song in parts

gleeful *adj* merry ▯ **gleefully** *adv*

glen *noun* in Scotland, a long narrow valley

glib *adj* **1** speaking smoothly and fluently (often insincerely and superficially) **2** quick and ready, but showing little thought: *glib reply* ▯ **glibly** *adv* ▯ **glibness** *noun*

glide *verb* **1** move smoothly and easily **2** travel by glider ▯ *noun* the act of gliding

glider *noun* an aeroplane without an engine

glimmer *noun* **1** a faint light **2** a faint indication: *a glimmer of hope* ▯ *verb* burn or shine faintly

glimpse *noun* a brief view ▯ *verb* get a brief look at

glint *verb* sparkle, gleam ▯ *noun* a sparkle, a gleam

glisten *verb* sparkle

glitter *verb* sparkle ▯ *noun* **1** sparkling **2** shiny granules used for decorating paper *etc* ▯ **glittery** *adj*

glitz *noun* showiness, garishness ▯ **glitzy** *adj*

> Originally a Yiddish word meaning 'glitter'

gloaming *noun* twilight, dusk

gloat *verb* look at or think about with malicious joy: *gloating over their rivals' defeat*

global *adj* **1** of or affecting the whole world: *global warming* **2** applying generally: *global increase in earnings*

globe *noun* **1** the earth **2** a ball with a map of the world drawn on it **3** a ball, a sphere **4** a glass covering for a lamp

globule *noun* **1** a droplet **2** a small ball-shaped piece ▯ **globular** *adj* ball-shaped

gloom *noun* dullness, darkness; sadness ▯ **gloomy** *adj* **1** sad, depressed **2** dimly lighted ▯ **gloomily** *adv*

glorify *verb* **1** make glorious **2** praise highly

> **glorify** » glorifi*es*, glorify*ing*, glorifi*ed*

glorious *adj* **1** spendid **2** deserving great praise **3** delightful ▯ **gloriously** *adv*

glory *noun* (*plural* **glories**) **1** fame, honour **2** great show, splendour ▯ *verb* rejoice, take great pleasure (in)

gloss *noun* brightness on the surface ▯ *verb* **1** make bright **2** explain **3** (with **over**) try to hide (a fault *etc*) by treating it quickly or superficially ▯ **glossy** *adj* shiny, highly polished

glossary *noun* (*plural* **glossaries**) a list of words with their meanings

glove *noun* **1** a covering for the hand with a separate covering for each finger **2** a boxing glove

glow *verb* **1** burn without flame **2** give out a steady light **3** be flushed from heat, cold *etc* **4** be radiant with emotion: *glow with pride* ▯ *noun* **1** a glowing state **2** great heat **3** bright light ▯ **glowing** *adj* **1** giving out a steady light **2** flushed **3** radiant **4** full of praise: *glowing report* ▯ **glow-worm** *noun* a kind of beetle which glows in the dark

glower *verb* stare (at) with a frown

□ **glowering** *adj* **1** scowling **2** threatening

glucose *noun* a sugar found in fruits *etc*

glue *noun* a substance for sticking things together □ *verb* join with glue □ **gluey** *adj* sticky

glum *adj* sad, gloomy □ **glumly** *adv* □ **glumness** *noun*

glut *verb* **1** feed greedily till full **2** supply too much to (a market) □ *noun* an over-supply: *a glut of fish on the market*

glut *verb* » glut*s*, glutt*ing*, glutt*ed*

gluten *noun* a sticky protein found in wheat, oats and other cereals

glutinous *adj* sticky, gluey

glutton *noun* **1** someone who eats too much **2** someone who is eager for anything: *a glutton for punishment* □ **gluttonous** *adj* **1** fond of overeating **2** eating greedily □ **gluttony** *noun* greediness in eating

glycerine *noun* a colourless, sticky, sweet-tasting liquid

GMT *abbrev* Greenwich Mean Time

GMWU *abbrev* General and Municipal Workers Union

gnarled /narld/ *adj* knotty, twisted

gnash /nash/ *verb* grind (the teeth)

gnat /nat/ *noun* a small blood-sucking fly, a midge

gnaw /naw/ *verb* bite at with a scraping action

gnome /nohm/ *noun* a small imaginary human-like creature who lives underground, often guarding treasure

GNP *abbrev* gross national product

gnu /noo/ *noun* a type of African antelope

GNVQ *abbrev* General National Vocational Qualification

go *verb* **1** to move: *I want to go home/ when are you going to Paris?* **2** leave: *time to go* **3** lead: *that road goes north* **4** become: *go mad* **5** work: *the car is going at last* **6** intend (to do): *I'm going to have a bath* **7** be removed or taken: *the best seats have all gone now* **8** be given, awarded *etc*: *the first prize went to Janet* □ *noun* **1** the act or process of going **2** energy, spirit **3** *informal* an attempt, a try: *have a go* **4** *informal* fashion, style: *all the go* □ **go-ahead** *adj* eager to succeed □ *noun* permission to act □ **go-between** *noun* someone who helps two people to communicate with each other □ **go-kart** *noun* a small low-powered racing car □ **go-slow** *noun* a slowing of speed at work as a form of protest □ **from the word go** from the start □ **go about** try, set about □ **go ahead** proceed (with), begin on □ **go along with** agree with □ **go back on** fail to keep (a promise *etc*) □ **go for 1** aim to get **2** attack □ **go off 1** explode **2** become rotten **3** come to dislike □ **go on 1** continue **2** talk too much □ **go round** be enough for everyone: *will the trifle go round?* □ **go steady with** court, go out with □ **go the whole hog** do something thoroughly □ **go under** be ruined □ **on the go** very active

go *verb* » goes, going, went, gone

goad *noun* **1** a sharp-pointed stick for driving animals **2** something used to urge action □ *verb* urge on by annoying

goal *noun* **1** the upright posts between which the ball is to be driven in football and other games **2** a score in football and other games **3** anything aimed at or wished for: *my goal is to get to Z*

goat *noun* an animal of the sheep family with horns and a long-haired coat

gob *slang* the mouth □ **gobsmacked** *adj, slang* shocked, astonished □ **gobstopper** *noun* a hard round sweet for sucking

gobble *verb* **1** eat quickly **2** make a noise like a turkey

goblet *noun, hist* **1** a large cup without handles **2** a drinking glass with a stem

goblin *noun* a mischievous, ugly spirit in folklore

god, **goddess** *noun* a supernatural being who is worshipped □ **God** *noun* the creator and ruler of the world in the Christian, Jewish *etc* religions □ **godly** *adj* holy, good living □ **godspeed** *exclam* a wish for success or for a safe journey

godfather, **godmother** *noun* someone who agrees to see that a child is brought up according to the beliefs of the Christian Church

godsend *noun* a very welcome piece of unexpected good fortune

goggle-eyed *adj* with staring eyes

goggles *noun plural* spectacles for protecting the eyes from dust, sparks *etc*

goitre *noun* a swelling in the neck

gold *noun* **1** a precious yellow metal **2** riches □ *adj* **1** made of gold **2** golden in colour □ **goldfield** *noun* a place where gold is found □ **goldfinch** *noun* a small multi-coloured bird □ **gold-leaf** *noun* gold beaten to a thin sheet □ **goldsmith** *noun* a maker of gold articles

golden *adj* **1** of or like gold **2** very fine □ **golden handshake** money given by a firm to a retiring employee □ **golden rule** a guiding principle □ **golden share** a large share in a company that prevents it being taken over □ **golden wedding** a 50th anniversary of a wedding *etc*

goldfish *noun* a golden-yellow Chinese carp, often kept as a pet

golf *noun* a game in which a ball is struck with a club and aimed at a series of holes on a large open course □ **golfer** *noun* someone who plays golf □ **golf club 1** a club used in golf **2** a society of golf players **3** the place where they meet

golosh *another spelling* of **galosh**

gondola *noun* **1** a canal boat used in Venice **2** a car suspended from an airship, cable railway *etc* **3** a shelved display unit in a supermarket □ **gondolier** *noun* a boatman who rows a gondola

gone *past participle* of **go**

gong *noun* a metal plate which makes a booming sound when struck, used to summon people to meals *etc*

good *adj* **1** having desired or positive qualities: *a good butcher will bone it for you* **2** virtuous: *a good person* **3** kind: *she was good to me* **4** pleasant, enjoyable: *a good time* **5** substantial, sufficiently large: *a good income* □ **good-for-nothing** *adj* useless, lazy □ **goodly** *adj* **1** large **2** ample, plentiful □ **good morning, good-day, good afternoon, good evening, good night** or **good-bye** words used as greeting when meeting or leaving someone □ **good name** good reputation □ **good-natured** *adj* kind, cheerful □ **goodness** *noun* the quality of being good □ **goods** *noun plural* **1** personal belongings **2** things to be bought and sold □ **good taste** good judgement for what is aesthetically pleasing or socially acceptable □ **goodwill** *noun* **1** kind wishes **2** a good reputation in business

goof around *verb* behave in a stupid or irresponsible way □ **goofy** *adj, US* stupid, silly

goose *noun* (*plural* **geese**) a web-footed bird larger than a duck □ **goosebumps** or **goosepimples** *noun plural* small bumps on the skin caused by cold or fear □ **goosestep** *noun* a military march with knees locked □ **goosestepping** *noun*

gooseberry *noun* a sour-tasting, pale green berry

gopher *noun* a piece of software used to search or index services on the Internet

gore[1] *noun* a mass of blood □ *verb* run through with horns, tusks *etc*: *gored by an elephant*

gore[2] *noun* a triangular-shaped piece of cloth in a garment *etc*

gorge *noun* **1** the throat **2** a narrow valley between hills □ *verb* eat greedily till full: *gorging himself on chocolate biscuits*

> **gorge** *verb* » gorg*es*, gorg*ing*, gorg*ed*

gorgeous *adj* **1** beautiful, very attractive **2** showy, splendid **3** *informal* excellent, very enjoyable

gorgon *noun* **1** a mythological monster whose glance turned people to stone **2** a very stern-looking person

gorgonzola *noun* a strong-flavoured Italian cheese

gorilla *noun* the largest kind of ape

> ⚠Do not confuse with: **guerrilla**

gormless *adj, Brit* stupid, senseless

gorse *noun* a prickly bush with yellow flowers

gory *adj* full of gore; bloody: *a very gory film*

goshawk *noun* a short-winged hawk

gosling *noun* a young goose

gospel *noun* **1** the teaching of Christ **2** *informal* the absolute truth

gossamer *noun* **1** fine spider-threads floating in the air or lying on bushes **2** a very thin material

gossip *noun* **1** talk, not necessarily true, about other people's personal affairs *etc* **2** someone who listens to and passes on gossip ▢ *verb* **1** engage in gossip **2** chatter

> **gossip** *verb* » gossip*s*, gossip*ing*, gossip*ed*

> Originally *godsibb*, meaning 'godparent'

got *past form* of **get**

gothic *adj*

gouache /goo*ash*/ *noun* **1** a paint containing water, gum and honey **2** a painting done with this paint

Gouda /gowdə/ *noun* a mild-flavoured round Dutch cheese

gouge /gowj/ *noun* a chisel with a hollow blade for cutting grooves ▢ *verb* scoop (out)

> **gouge** *verb* » gouge*s*, goug*ing*, goug*ed*

goulash *noun* (*plural* **goulashes**) a stew of meat and vegetables, flavoured with paprika

gourd *noun* **1** a large fleshy fruit **2** the skin of a gourd used to carry water *etc*

gourmand *noun* a glutton

gourmet /*goor*meh/ *noun* someone with a taste for good wines or food

gout *noun* a painful swelling of the smaller joints, especially of the big toe ▢ **gouty** *adj* suffering from gout

govern *verb* **1** rule, control **2** put into action the laws *etc* of a country

governess *noun* a woman who teaches young children at their home

government *noun* **1** rule; control **2** those who rule and administer the laws of a country

governor *noun* someone who rules a state or country *etc*

gown *noun* **1** a woman's formal dress **2** a loose robe worn by members of the clergy, lawyers, teachers *etc*

goy *noun* (*plural* **goyim**) a non-Jew, a Gentile

GP *abbrev* general practitioner

GPO *abbrev* General Post Office

grab *verb* **1** seize or grasp suddenly: *grabbed me by the arm* **2** secure possession of quickly: *grab a seat* **3** get in a hurry: *grab a bite to eat* ▢ *noun* a sudden grasp or catch ▢ **grab-bag** *noun* a miscellaneous collection: *grab-bag of ideas*

> **grab** *verb* » grab*s*, grabb*ing*, grabb*ed*

grace *noun* **1** beauty of form or movement **2** a short prayer at a meal **3** the title of a duke or archbishop **4** favour, mercy: *by God's grace* ▢ **graceful** *adj* **1** elegant or beautiful in appearance **2** done in a neat way ▢ **gracefully** *adv* ▢ **grace-note** *music* a short note played before the main note in a melody ▢ **gracious** *adj* kind, polite ▢ **graciously** *adv* ▢ **graciousness** *noun* ▢ **with good** (or **bad**) **grace** willingly (or unwillingly)

grade *noun* a step or placing according to quality or rank; class ▢ *verb* arrange in order, *eg* from easy to difficult ▢ **gradation** *noun* arrangement in order of rank, difficulty *etc* □ **gradient** *noun* a slope on a road, railway *etc* □ **gradual** *adj* step by step; going slowly but steadily □ **gradually** *adv* □ **make the grade** do as well as is necessary

graduate *verb* **1** divide into regular spaces **2** pass university examinations and receive a degree □ *noun* someone who has done so □ **graduation** *noun* the act of getting a degree from a university

graffiti *noun plural* words or drawings scratched or painted on a wall *etc*

graft *verb* **1** fix a shoot or twig of one plant onto another for growing **2** fix (skin) from one part of the body onto another part **3** transfer (a part of the body) from one person to another **4** get illegal profit □ *noun* **1** living tissue (*eg* skin) which is grafted **2** a shoot grafted **3** hard work **4** profit gained by illegal or unfair means

Grail *noun* the plate or cup believed to have been used by Christ at the Last Supper

grain *noun* **1** a seed *eg* of wheat, oats **2** corn in general **3** a very small quantity **4** a very small measure of weight **5** the run of the lines of fibre in wood, leather *etc* □ **against the grain** against your natural feelings or instincts

gram *another spelling* of **gramme**

grammar *noun* **1** the correct use of words in speaking or writing: *his grammar is very bad* **2** the rules applying to a particular language: *French grammar* □ **grammarian** *noun* an expert on grammar □ **grammar school** a kind of secondary school □ **grammatical** *adj* correct according to rules of grammar □ **grammatically** *adv*

gramme or **gram** *noun* the basic unit of weight in the metric system

Grammy *noun* an annual award given by the American National Academy of Recording Arts and Sciences

gramophone *noun, old* a record-player

granary *noun* (*plural* **granaries**) a storehouse for grain

grand *adj* great; noble; fine □ **grandchild, grand-daughter** or **grandson** *noun* a son's or daughter's child □ **grand duke** a duke of specially high rank □ **grandfather** *noun* a father's or mother's father □ **grand master** a chess-player of the greatest ability □ **grandmother** *noun* a father's or mother's mother □ **grand opera** opera without spoken dialogue □ **grand piano** a piano with a large flat top □ **grandstand** *noun* rows of raised seats at a sports ground giving a good view

grandee *noun* a man of high rank

grandeur /*grandy*ər/ *noun* greatness

grandiloquent *adj* speaking in a high-sounding language

grandiose *adj* planned on a large scale

granita *noun* a dessert of flavoured crushed ice

granite *noun* a hard rock of greyish or reddish colour

granny *noun* (*plural* **grannies**) *informal* a grandmother

grant *verb* **1** give, allow (something asked for) **2** admit as true ▯ *noun* money awarded for a special purpose ▯ **granted** or **granting** *conj* (often with **that**) even if, assuming: *granted that you are right* ▯ **take for granted 1** assume that something will happen without checking **2** treat (someone) casually, without respect or kindness

granule *noun* a tiny grain or part ▯ **granular** *adj* made up of grains ▯ **granulated** *adj* broken into grains

grape *noun* the green or black smooth-skinned berry from which wine is made ▯ **grapefruit** *noun* a sharp-tasting fruit like a large yellow orange ▯ **grapeshot** *noun* shot which scatters when fired

graph *noun* lines drawn on squared paper to show changes in quantity, *eg* in temperature, money spent

graphic *adj* **1** relating to writing, drawing or painting **2** vivid, well told **3** explicit: *graphic violence* ▯ *noun* a painting, print, illustration or diagram ▯ **graphically** *adv*

graphite *noun* a form of carbon used in making pencils

grapple *verb*: **grapple with 1** struggle with **2** try to deal with (a problem *etc*)

grasp *verb* **1** clasp and grip with the fingers or arms **2** understand ▯ *noun* **1** a grip with the hand or arms **2** someone's power of understanding ▯ **grasping** *adj* greedy, mean

grass *noun* (*plural* **grasses**) **1** the plant covering fields of pasture **2** a kind of plant with long narrow leaves, *eg* wheat, reeds, bamboo **3** *slang* marijuana ▯ **grasshopper** *noun* a type of jumping insect ▯ **grass-snake** *noun* a type of green harmless snake ▯ **grass-widow** *noun* a woman whose husband is temporarily away ▯ **grass-widower** *noun* a man whose wife is temporarily away ▯ **grassy** *adj* covered with grass

grate *noun* a framework of iron bars for holding a fire ▯ *verb* **1** rub down into small pieces **2** make a harsh, grinding sound **3** irritate ▯ **grater** *noun* an instrument with a rough surface for rubbing cheese *etc* into small pieces ▯ **grating** *noun* a frame of iron bars

grateful *adj* **1** feeling thankful **2** showing or giving thanks ▯ **gratefully** *adv*

gratify *verb* please; satisfy ▯ **gratification** *noun* pleasure; satisfaction

> **gratify** » gratifi*es*, gratify*ing*, gratifi*ed*

gratis *adv* for nothing, without payment

gratitude *noun* thankfulness; desire to repay kindness

gratuitous *adj* uncalled-for, done without good reason: *gratuitous violence* ▯ **gratuitously** *adv*

gratuity *noun* (*plural* **gratuities**) a money gift in return for a service; a tip

grave *noun* a pit in which a dead person is buried ▯ *adj* **1** serious, important: *grave error* **2** not cheerful, solemn ▯ **gravely** *adv* ▯ **graveness** or **gravity** *noun* ▯ **gravestone** *noun* a stone placed to mark a grave ▯ **graveyard** *noun* a place where the dead are buried, a cemetery

gravel *noun* small stones or pebbles

graven *adj*, *old* carved: *graven images*

gravitate *verb* move towards as if strongly attracted (to) ▯ **gravitation** *noun*

gravity *noun* **1** seriousness, importance: *gravity of the situation* **2** lack of levity, solemnity **3** weight **4** the force which attracts things towards earth and causes them to fall to the ground

gravy *noun* (*plural* **gravies**) a sauce made from juices of meat that is cooking ▯ **gravy train** a situation producing large, easy profits

gray *US spelling* of **grey**

graze *verb* **1** feed on (growing grass) **2** scrape the skin of **3** touch lightly in passing ▯ *noun* **1** a scraping of the skin **2** a light touch ▯ **grazing** *noun* grass land for animals to graze on

grease *noun* **1** thick animal fat **2** an oily substance ▯ *verb* smear with grease, apply grease to ▯ **greasepaint** *noun* theatrical make-up

greasy *adj* ▯ **greasily** *adv* ▯ **greasiness** *noun*

great *adj* **1** very large **2** powerful **3** very important, distinguished **4** very talented: *a great singer* **5** of high rank, noble **6** *informal* excellent, very good ▯ **great-grandchild** *noun* the son or daughter of a grandson or grand-daughter ▯ **great-grandfather**, **great-grandmother** *noun* the father and mother of a grandfather or grandmother ▯ **greatly** *adv* very much ▯ **greatness** *noun*

grebe *noun* a fresh-water diving bird

greed *noun* great and selfish desire for food, money *etc*

greedy *adj* full of greed ▯ **greedily** *adv* ▯ **greediness** *noun*

green *adj* **1** of the colour of growing grass *etc* **2** inexperienced, naive **3** concerned with care of the environment ▯ *noun* **1** the colour of growing grass **2** a piece of ground covered with grass **3** a member of the Green Party, an environmentalist **4** (**greens**) green vegetables for food ▯ **green belt** open land surrounding a city ▯ **greenery** *noun* green plants ▯ **greenfly** *noun* the aphid ▯ **greengage** *noun* a kind of plum, green but sweet ▯ **greengrocer** *noun* someone who sells fresh vegetables ▯ **greenhouse** *noun* a building with large glass panes in which plants are grown ▯ **Green Party** a political party concerned with conserving natural resources and decentralizing political and economic power ▯ **greenhouse effect** the warming-up of the earth's surface due to excess carbon dioxide in the atmosphere ▯ **have green fingers** be a skilful gardener ▯ **the green light** permission to go ahead with a plan

greet *verb* **1** meet someone with kind words **2** say hello *etc* to **3**

react to, respond to: *greeted the news with relief* **4** become evident to □ **greeting** *noun* **1** words of welcome or kindness **2** reaction, response

gregarious *adj* **1** sociable, liking the company of others **2** living in flocks and herds

grenade *noun* a small bomb thrown by hand

> From a French word for 'pomegranate', because of its shape

grew *past form* of **grow**

grey or *US* **gray** *adj* **1** of a colour between black and white **2** grey-haired, old □ *noun* **1** grey colour **2** a grey horse □ **grey matter** *informal* brains

greyhound *noun* a breed of fast-running dog

grid *noun* **1** a grating of bars **2** a network of lines, *eg* for helping to find a place on a map **3** a network of wires carrying electricity over a wide area □ **grid-iron** *noun* **1** a frame of iron bars for cooking food over a fire **2** *US* a football field

grief *noun* deep sorrow, *esp* after bereavement □ **come to grief** meet with misfortune

grievance *noun* a cause for complaining

grieve *verb* feel grief or sorrow

grievous *adj* **1** painful; serious **2** causing grief

griffin or **griffon** *noun* a mythological animal with the body and legs of a lion and the beak and wings of an eagle

grill *verb* **1** cook directly under heat (provided by an electric or gas cooker) **2** cook on a grid-iron over a fire **3** question closely □ *noun* **1** a frame of bars for grilling food on **2** grilled food **3** the part of a cooker used for grilling **4** a restaurant serving grilled food

grille *noun* a metal grating over a door, window *etc*

grim *adj* **1** stern, fierce-looking **2** terrible; very unpleasant: *a grim sight* **3** unyielding, stubborn: *grim determination* □ **grimly** *adv* □ **grimness** *noun*

grimace *noun* a twisting of the face in fun or pain □ *verb* a twisted facial expression

grime *noun* dirt □ **grimy** *adj* □ **grimily** *adv* □ **griminess** *noun*

grin *verb* smile broadly □ *noun* a broad smile □ **grin and bear it** suffer something without complaining

> **grin** *verb* » grin*s*, grinn*ing*, grinn*ed*

grind *verb* **1** crush to powder **2** sharpen by rubbing **3** rub together: *grinding his teeth* □ *noun* hard or unpleasant work □ **grinder** *noun* someone or something that grinds

> **grind** *verb* » grind*s*, grind*ing*, ground

grindstone *noun* a revolving stone for grinding or sharpening tools □ **back to the grindstone** back to work □ **keep your nose to the grindstone** work hard without stopping

grip *noun* **1** a firm hold, a grasp: *these shoes have a good grip* **2** a way of holding or grasping; control: *a loose grip* **3** a handle or part for holding **4** a travelling bag, a holdall ▫ *verb* take a firm hold of ▫ **gripping** *adj* commanding attention, compelling

> **grip** *verb* » grip*s*, gripp*ing*, gripp*ed*

gripe *noun* **1** a sharp stomach pain **2** *informal* a complaint ▫ *verb* complain

grisly *adj* frightful, hideous

> ⚠Do not confuse with: **grizzly**

grist *noun* corn for grinding ▫ **grist to the mill** something which brings profit or advantage

gristle *noun* a tough elastic substance in meat ▫ **gristly** *adj*

grit *adj* **1** a mixture of rough sand and gravel, spread on icy surfaces **2** courage ▫ *verb* **1** apply grit to (an icy surface): *has the road been gritted?* **2** clench: *grit your teeth* ▫ **gritty** *adj* ▫ **grittily** *adv* ▫ **grittiness** *noun*

> **grit** *verb* » grit*s*, gritt*ing*, gritt*ed*

grits *noun plural, US* coarsely ground maize

grizzled *adj* grey; mixed with grey

grizzly *adj* grey in colour ▫ *noun* (*plural* **grizzlies**) *informal* a grizzly bear ▫ **grizzly bear** a type of large bear of North America

> ⚠Do not confuse with: **grisly**

groan *verb* **1** moan in pain, disapproval *etc* **2** be full or loaded: *a table groaning with food*

groats *noun plural* oat grains without the husks

grocer *noun* a dealer in certain kinds of food and household supplies ▫ **groceries** *noun plural* food *etc* sold by grocers

groggy *adj* weak and light-headed after illness or blows

> Originally meaning 'drunk', from *grog*, a mixture of rum and water

groin *noun* the part of the body where the inner thigh joins the torso

groom *noun* **1** a bridegroom **2** someone in charge of horses ▫ *verb* **1** look after (a horse) **2** make smart and tidy

groove *noun* a furrow, a long hollow ▫ *verb* cut a groove (in)

grope *verb* search (for) by feeling as if blind: *groping for his socks in the dark*

gross *adj* **1** coarse **2** very fat **3** great, obvious: *gross error* **4** of money: total, before any deductions for tax etc: *gross profit* **5** *US informal* disgusting, revolting ▫ *noun* **1** the whole taken together **2** twelve dozen ▫ **grossly** *adv* ▫ **grossness** *noun* coarseness

grotesque *adj* very odd or unnatural-looking

grotto *noun* (*plural* **grottoes** or **grottos**) a cave

ground[1] *noun* **1** the surface of the earth **2** (also **grounds**) a good reason: *ground for complaint* **3** (**grounds**) lands surrounding a large house *etc* **4** (**grounds**) dregs:

coffee grounds ▯ *verb* **1** of a ship: strike the sea-bed and become stuck **2** prevent (aeroplanes) from flying ▯ **grounded** *adj* of aeroplanes: unable to fly ▯ **ground floor** the storey of a building at street level ▯ **groundhog** *same as* **marmot** ▯ **grounding** *noun* the first steps in learning something ▯ **groundless** *adj* without reason ▯ **groundnut** *same as* **peanut** ▯ **groundswell** *noun* **1** broad ocean waves **2** a growing general feeling or opinion ▯ **groundwork** *noun* the first stages of a task

ground[2] *past form* of **grind**

groundsel *noun* a common wild plant with small yellow flowers

group *noun* a number of people or things together ▯ *verb* **1** form or gather into a group **2** classify

grouse[1] *noun* (*plural* **grouse**) a game bird hunted on moors and hills

grouse[2] (*plural* **grouses**) a grumble, a complaint ▯ *verb* grumble, complain

grove *noun* a small group of trees

grovel *verb* **1** crawl or lie on the ground **2** be overly humble

> **grovel** » grovel*s*, grovell*ing*, grovell*ed*

grow *verb* **1** become bigger or stronger: *the local population is growing* **2** become: *grow old* **3** rear, cause to grow (plants, trees *etc*): *grow from seed*

> **grow** » grow*s*, grow*ing*, grown, grew

growl *verb* utter a deep sound like a dog ▯ *noun* a dog's deep sound

grown *past form* of **grow**

growth *noun* **1** growing **2** increase: *growth in market shares* **3** something that grows **4** something abnormal that grows on the body

grub *noun* **1** the form of an insect after being hatched from the egg, *eg* a caterpillar **2** *informal* food ▯ *verb* dig

> **grub** *verb* » grub*s*, grubb*ing*, grubb*ed*

grubby *adj* dirty ▯ **grubbily** *adv* ▯ **grubbiness** *noun*

grudge *verb* **1** be unwilling to grant or allow: *I grudge him his success* **2** give unwillingly or reluctantly ▯ *noun* a feeling of resentment: *she bears a grudge against me*

gruel *noun* a thin mixture of oatmeal boiled in water ▯ **gruelling** *adj* straining, exhausting

gruesome *adj* horrible

> Originally a Scots word, from *grue* 'be terrified', popularized by Walter Scott

gruff *adj* **1** rough in manner **2** of a voice: deep and harsh

grumble *verb* complain in a bad-tempered, discontented way ▯ *noun* a complaint

grumpy *adj* cross, bad-tempered ▯ **grumpily** *adv* ▯ **grumpiness** *noun*

grunge *noun, informal* grime, dirt ▯ **grungy** *adj*

grunt *verb* make a sound like that of a pig ▯ *noun* a pig-like snort

guacamole /gwakə*moh*leh/ *noun* a Mexican dish of mashed avocado and chillies *etc*

guarantee *noun* **1** a promise to do something **2** a statement by the maker that something will work well **3** money put down which will be forfeited if a promise is broken □ *verb* give a guarantee

guarantor *noun* someone who promises to pay if another person fails to keep an agreement to pay

guard *verb* keep safe from danger or attack □ *noun* **1** someone or a group whose duty it is to protect **2** a screen *etc* which protects from danger **3** someone in charge of a railway train or coach **4** *sport* a position of defence □ **guarded** *adj* careful, not revealing much: *guarded comments* □ **guardedly** *adv*

guardian *noun* **1** someone with the legal right to take care of an orphan **2** someone who protects or guards

guava *noun* **1** a yellow pear-shaped fruit **2** the tree that bears this fruit

gubbins *noun, informal* a stupid person, a fool

gubernatorial *adj, US* relating to a state governor: *gubernatorial election*

guddle *verb, Scot* fish with the hands by groping under the stones in a river

gudgeon *noun* a type of small freshwater fish

guerrilla *noun* one of a small band which makes sudden attacks on a larger army but does not fight openly □ *adj* of fighting: in which many small bands acting independently make sudden raids on an enemy

⚠Do not confuse with: **gorilla**

guess *verb* **1** say without sure knowledge: *I can only guess the price* **2** *US* suppose: *I guess I'll go* □ *noun* (*plural* **guesses**) an estimate □ **guesswork** *noun* guessing

guest *noun* a visitor received and entertained in another's house or in a hotel *etc*

guff *noun, informal* rubbish, nonsense

guffaw *verb* laugh loudly □ *noun* a loud laugh

GUI /*gooee*/ *abbrev, comput* graphic user interface

guide *verb* **1** show the way to, lead, direct **2** influence □ *noun* **1** someone who shows tourists around **2** someone who leads travellers on a route unfamiliar to them **3** a guidebook **4** (**Guide**) a girl belonging to the Guides organization □ **guidance** *noun* help or advice towards doing something □ **guidebook** *noun* a book with information for tourists about a place □ **guided missile** an explosive rocket which after being fired can be guided to its target by radio waves

guild *noun* **1** an association for those working in a particular trade or profession **2** a society, a social club

⚠Do not confuse with: **gild**

guile *noun* cunning, deceit

guillemot *noun* a diving sea bird

guillotine *noun* **1** *hist* an instrument with a falling blade used for executing by beheading **2** a machine with a blade for cutting paper **3** the limiting of discussion time in parliament by prearranging voting times ▫ *verb* **1** behead with the guillotine **2** cut (paper) with a guillotine **3** use a parliamentary guillotine on

> Named after Joseph *Guillotin*, a French doctor who recommended its use during the French Revolution

guilt *noun* **1** a sense of shame **2** blame for wrongdoing, *eg* breaking the law ▫ **guiltily** *adv* ▫ **guilty** *adj*

> ⚠Do not confuse with: **gilt**

guinea *noun* **1** *hist* a British gold coin **2** a sum of money equal to £1.05, sometimes used in expressing prices, fees *etc*

guinea-fowl *noun* a bird resembling a pheasant, with white-spotted feathers

guinea-pig *noun* **1** a rodent about the size of a rabbit **2** someone used as the subject of an experiment

guise *noun* appearance, dress, *esp* in disguise: *in the guise of a priest* ▫ **guiser** *noun* a child who dresses up and goes round houses collecting money in return for performing ▫ **guising** *noun*

guitar *noun* a stringed musical instrument with frets and a waisted body

gulag /*goo*lag/*noun, hist* a labour camp for political prisoners in the former Soviet Union

gulch *noun* (*plural* **gulches**) a narrow rocky valley

gulf *noun* a large inlet of the sea

gull *noun* a seagull

gullet *noun* a passage by which food goes down into the stomach

gullible *adj* easily tricked

gully *noun* (*plural* **gullies**) a channel worn by water

gulp *verb* swallow quickly and in large mouthfuls ▫ *noun* a sudden fast swallowing

gum 1 the firm flesh in which the teeth grow **2** sticky juice got from some trees and plants **3** a flavoured gummy sweet, chewing gum ▫ *verb* stick with gum ▫ **gummy** *adj* sticky

> **gum** *verb* » gum*s*, gumm*ing*, gumm*ed*

gumbo *noun* a thick soup containing okra

gumption *noun* good sense

gum tree *noun*: **up a gum tree** in a mess

gun *noun* any weapon firing bullets or shells ▫ **gunboat** *noun* a small warship with heavy guns ▫ **gun-carriage** *noun* a wheeled support for a field-gun ▫ **gun dog** a dog trained to fetch birds *etc* after they have been shot ▫ **gunfire** *noun* the firing of guns ▫ **gun-metal** *noun* a mixture of copper and tin ▫ **gunpowder** *noun* an explosive in powder form ▫ **gun-running** *noun* bringing guns into a country illegally ▫ **stick to your guns** keep determinedly to your opinion

gung-ho *adj* boisterously enthusiastic

Based on a Chinese phrase meaning 'work together'

gunk *noun, informal* unpleasantly sticky or dirty material

gunwale or **gunnel** (both /*gunəl*/) *noun* the upper edge of a boat's side

gurgle *verb* **1** of water: make a bubbling sound **2** make such a sound, *eg* in pleasure ▫ *noun*

guru *noun* **1** a Hindu spiritual teacher **2** a revered instructor, a mentor

gush *verb* **1** flow out in a strong stream **2** talk at length with exaggerated emotions: *gushing on about the wedding* ▫ *noun* (*plural* **gushes**) a strong or sudden flow: *gush of tears*

gusset *noun* a piece of material sewn into a seam join to strengthen or widen part of a garment

gussy up *verb, informal* dress up

gust *noun* a sudden blast of wind ▫ **gusty** *adj* windy

gusto *noun* enthusiasm ▫ **with gusto** enthusiastically

gut *noun* **1** a narrow passage in the lower part of the body **2** animal intestines used as strings for musical instruments **3** (**guts**) spirit, courage ▫ *verb* **1** take out the inner parts of: *gut a fish* **2** destroy completely, *esp* by fire: *gutted the building*

gut *verb* » gut*s*, gutt*ing*, gutt*ed*

guttapercha *noun* a waterproof material, less elastic than rubber, used for clothing

gutter *noun* a water channel on a roof, at the edge of a roadside *etc* ▫ **gutter press** that part of the press that specializes in sensational journalism ▫ **guttersnipe** *noun, old* a poor child living in the streets

guttural *adj* harsh in sound, as if formed in the throat

guy[1] *noun* **1** *Brit* an effigy of Guy Fawkes, traditionally burned on 5 November **2** *informal* a man

guy[2] *noun* a steadying rope for a tent *etc*

guzzle *verb* eat or drink greedily

gym *informal* **1** a gymnasium **2** gymnastics

gymkhana *noun* a meeting for competitions, *esp* in horse-riding

gymnasium *noun* (*plural* **gymnasiums** or **gymnasia**) a building or room equipped for physical exercises

gymnast *noun* someone who does gymnastics ▫ **gymnastic** *adj* ▫ **gymnastics** *noun plural* exercises to strengthen the body

gypsum *noun* a softish chalk-like mineral

gypsy or **gipsy** *noun* (*plural* **gypsies** or **gipsies**) a member of a wandering people; a Romany

Based on *Egyptian*, because of the belief that the Romanies came originally from Egypt

gyrate *verb* whirl round ▫ **gyration** *noun* ▫ **gyratory** *adj*

H

haar *noun* a cold mist or fog, *esp* from the sea

haberdashery *noun* materials for sewing, mending *etc* ▯ **haberdasher** *noun* someone who sells haberdashery

habeas corpus a request to produce a prisoner in person and give the reasons for their detention

habit *noun* **1** something you are used to doing: *nasty habits* **2** someone's usual behaviour **3** the dress of a monk or nun ▯ **make a habit of** do regularly or frequently

habitable *adj* fit to live in

habitat *noun* the natural home of an animal or plant

habitation *noun* a dwelling place

habitual *adj* usual, formed by habit ▯ **habitually** *adv*

habituate *verb* make accustomed

habitué *noun* a frequent visitor or attender: *a habitué of nightclubs*

hacienda *noun* a large house on a ranch in Mexico *etc*

hack *verb* **1** cut or chop up roughly **2** ride on horseback, *esp* along ordinary roads ▯ *noun* **1** a writer who does hard work for low pay **2** a riding horse kept for hire **3** a rough cut, a gash

hackamore *noun* a horse's bridle without a bit

hacker *noun* **1** a skilled computer operator **2** someone who breaks into government or commercial computer systems

hackles *noun plural* **1** the feathers on the neck of a farmyard cock **2** the hair on a dog's neck ▯ **make someone's hackles rise** make them angry

hackneyed *adj* over-used, not fresh or original: *hackneyed phrase*

hacksaw *noun* a saw for cutting metal

haddock *noun* (*plural* **haddock** or **haddocks**) a small edible N Atlantic fish

Hades *noun* the ancient Greek underworld, home of the dead

hadj *noun* a Muslim pilgrimage to Mecca

haemoglobin or *US* **hemoglobin** /heem*əgloh*bin/ *noun* the oxygen-carrying substance in red blood cells

haemophilia or *US* **hemophilia** /heem*əfili*ə/ *noun* a hereditary disease causing extreme bleeding when cut ▯ **haemophiliac** *noun* someone suffering from haemophilia

haemorrhage or *US* **hemorrhage** /*hem*ərij/ *noun* a large amount of bleeding

haft *noun* a handle of a knife *etc*

hag *noun* **1** an ugly old woman **2** a witch

haggard *adj* gaunt and hollow-eyed, from tiredness

> Originally a falconer's term for an untamed hawk

haggis *noun* (*plural* **haggises**) a Scottish dish made from chopped sheep's offal and oatmeal, traditionally cooked in a sheep's stomach

haggle *verb* argue determinedly over a price

hagiography *noun* a biography of a saint ◻ **hagiographer** *noun* a saint's biographer ◻ **hagiographic** *adj* **1** of a hagiography **2** highly praising, eulogistic

ha-ha *noun* a sunken fence

haiku *noun* a Japanese form of poem written in three lines of 5, 7 and 5 syllables

hail[1] *verb* **1** greet, welcome **2** call to, attract the attention of ◻ *noun* **1** a call from a distance **2** greeting, welcome ◻ **hail-fellow-well-met** *adj* friendly and familiar on first meeting ◻ **hail from** come from, belong to

hail[2] *noun* **1** frozen raindrops **2** a falling mass: *a hail of bullets* ◻ *verb* **1** shower with hail **2** descend in a mass ◻ **hailstone** *noun* a piece of hail

hair *noun* a thread-like growth on the skin of an animal; the whole mass of these (as on the head) ◻ **hair-breadth** or **hair's-breadth** *noun* a very small distance ◻ **hairdresser** *noun* someone who cuts, washes and sets hair ◻ **hairdryer** *noun* an electrical device which blows hot air to dry hair ◻ **hair-raising** *adj* terrifying ◻ **hairspray** *noun* a fine spray to fix a hairstyle ◻ **hairspring** *noun* a very fine spring in a watch *etc* ◻ **split hairs** worry about unimportant details; nitpick

hairy *adj* **1** covered with hair **2** risky, dangerous

hake *noun* an edible sea-fish similar to a cod

halal *noun* meat from animals that have been slaughtered according to Islamic law ◻ *adj* from animals slaughtered in this way

halberd *noun, hist* a battleaxe fixed on a long pole

halcyon /*hal*siən/ *adj*: **halcyon days** a time of peace and happiness

> From the Greek word for 'kingfisher' in the phrase 'kingfisher days', a period of calm weather in mid-winter

hale *adj*: **hale and hearty** healthy

half *noun* (*plural* **halves**) one of two equal parts ◻ *adj* **1** being one of two equal parts: *a half bottle of wine* **2** not full or complete: *a half smile* ◻ *adv* partly, to some extent ◻ **half-baked** *adj* not properly thought out, incomplete ◻ **half-board** *noun* a hotel charge for bed, breakfast and another meal ◻ **half-breed** or **half-caste** *noun, derog offensive* someone with a father and mother of different races ◻ **half-brother** or **half-sister** *noun* a brother or sister sharing only one parent ◻ **half-crown** *noun, hist* a British coin before decimal currency, worth two shillings and sixpence ($12\frac{1}{2}$ pence) ◻ **half-hearted** *adj* not eager ◻ **half-life** *noun* the time in which the radioactivity of a substance falls to half its original value

▫ **half-mast** *adv* of a flag: hoisted half-way up the mast to show that someone important has died ▫ **half-penny** /*heh*pni/ *noun, hist* a coin worth half of a penny ▫ **half-time** *noun* an interval half-way through a sports game ▫ **half-way** *adv & adj* at or to a point equally far from the beginning and the end ▫ **half-wit** *noun* an idiot, a fool ▫ **half-witted** *adj* stupid, idiotic ▫ **at half-cock** not completely ready, unprepared

halibut *noun* a large edible flatfish

halitosis *noun* bad breath

hall *noun* **1** a passage at the entrance to a house **2** a large public room **3** a large country house

hallmark *noun* **1** a mark put on gold and silver articles to show quality **2** a characteristic sign: *the hallmark of a good editor*

hallo *another spelling* of **hello**

hallowed *adj, old* holy, sacred

Hallowe'en *noun* the evening of 31 October, traditionally a time when spirits are believed to be around

hallucination *noun* the seeing of something that is not really there ▫ **hallucinatory** *adj* causing hallucinations

hallucinogen *noun* a substance that causes hallucinations ▫ **hallucinogenic** *adj*

halo *noun* (*plural* **haloes** or **halos**) **1** a circle of light surrounding *eg* the sun or moon **2** a circle of light depicted around the head of a saint *etc* as a sign of holiness

halogen *noun* one of a group of elements that includes chlorine and iodine

halt *verb* **1** come or bring to a stop **2** be lame, limp **3** hesitate, be uncertain ▫ *adj* lame ▫ *noun* **1** a stop, a standstill: *call a halt* **2** stopping place ▫ **halting** *adj* hesitant, uncertain ▫ **haltingly** *adv*

halter *noun* a head-rope for holding and leading a horse ▫ **halterneck** *noun* a woman's sleeveless dress or top with a single strap around the neck

halva *noun* a Middle-Eastern sweet made from pounded sesame seeds

halve *verb* divide in two

halyard *noun* a rope for raising or lowering a sail or flag

ham[1] *noun* **1** a pig's thigh salted and dried **2** the back of the thigh ▫ **ham-fisted** *adj* clumsy

ham[2] *informal* **1** an actor who overacts **2** an amateur radio operator

hamburger *noun* a round cake of minced beef, cooked by frying or grilling

hamlet *noun* a small village

hammer *noun* **1** a tool with a heavy metal head for beating metal, driving nails *etc* **2** a striking piece in a clock, piano, pistol *etc* ▫ *verb* **1** drive or shape with a hammer **2** defeat overwhelmingly ▫ **hammer and tongs** determinedly, violently

hammock *noun* a length of netting, canvas *etc* hung up by the corners, and used as a bed

hammy *adj, informal* **1** overacted

2 badly done, inexpert □ **hammily** *adv*

hamper[1] *verb* hinder, impede

hamper[2] *noun* a large basket with a lid

hamster *noun* a small rodent with large cheek pouches, often kept as a pet

hamstring *noun* a tendon at the back of the knee □ *verb* **1** make lame by cutting the hamstring **2** make ineffective or powerless

hand *noun* **1** the part of the human body at the end of the arm **2** a pointer, *eg* on a clock **3** help, aid: *can you give me a hand?* **4** a measure (four inches, 10.16 centimetres) for the height of horses **5** a worker, a labourer **6** a style of handwriting **7** side, direction: *left-hand side* **8** a group of playing-cards dealt to someone **9** clapping, applause: *a big hand* □ *verb* **1** pass (something) with the hand **2** (with **over**) give □ **handbag** *noun* a small bag for personal belongings □ **handbill** *noun* a small printed notice □ **handbook** *noun* a small book giving information or directions □ **handcuffs** *noun plural* steel bands joined by a short chain, put round the wrists of prisoners □ **handhold** *noun* something which the hand can grip (*eg* in climbing) □ **hand-in-hand** *adj* **1** holding hands **2** in partnership □ **hand-me-down** *noun* a secondhand piece of clothing, *esp* one that used to belong to another member of the family □ **handout** *noun* a sheet or bundle of information given out at a lecture *etc* □ **hand-picked** *adj* chosen carefully □ **hands-on** *adj* **1** hand-operated **2** involving practical experience □ **hand-to-hand** *adj* of fighting: at close quarters □ **hand-to-mouth** *adj* with barely enough to live on and nothing to spare □ **handwriting** *noun* writing with pen or pencil □ **at hand** nearby □ **at first hand** directly from the source □ **change hands** pass to another owner □ **hand over fist** progressing quickly and steadily □ **in hand 1** in your possession: *cash in hand* **2** in preparation, under control □ **out of hand 1** out of control **2** at once □ **out of someone's hands** no longer their concern □ **take in hand** take charge of □ **try your hand at** have a go at, attempt □ **wash your hands of** give up all responsibility for

handful *noun* (*plural* **handfuls**) **1** as much as can be held in one hand **2** a small amount **3** a demanding child, pet *etc*

handicap *noun* **1** something that makes an action more difficult **2** a disadvantage, such as having to run a greater distance, given to the best competitors in a race **3** a race in which handicaps are given **4** a physical or mental disability □ *verb* **1** give a handicap to **2** burden, impede

> Originally a gambling game in which wagers were drawn by *hand* from a *cap*

handicapped *adj* **1** having or given a handicap **2** physically or mentally disabled

handicraft *noun* skilled work done by hand, not machine

handiwork *noun* **1** thing(s) made by hand **2** something done by a particular person *etc*: *the handiwork of a sick mind*

handkerchief *noun* a small cloth for wiping the nose *etc*

handle *verb* **1** touch, hold or use with the hand **2** manage, cope with □ *noun* **1** the part of anything meant to be held in the hand **2** a way of understanding something

handlebars *noun plural* a steering bar at the front of a bicycle with a handle at each end

handsome *adj* **1** good-looking **2** generous: *a handsome gift*

handy *adj* **1** useful or convenient to use **2** easily reached, near **3** clever with the hands □ **handily** *adv* □ **handiness** *noun* □ **handyman** *noun* a man who does odd jobs

hang *verb* **1** fix or be fixed to a point off the ground **2** be suspended in the air **3** (with **down**) droop or fall downwards **4** attach (wallpaper) to a wall **5** (*past form* **hanged**) put a prisoner to death by putting a rope round their neck and letting them fall □ **hangdog** *adj* guilty-looking □ **hang-gliding** *noun* a form of gliding by hanging in a harness under a large kite □ **hanging** *noun* an execution in which the prisoner is hanged □ **hangman** *noun* an executioner who hangs people □ **get the hang of** understand, learn how to use □ **hang about** or **hang around** remain near, loiter □ **hang back** hesitate □ **hang fire** delay □ **hang on 1** depend on **2** wait, linger

> **hang** » hang*s*, hang*ing*, hung or hang*ed*

hangar *noun* a shed for aeroplanes

> ⚠Do not confuse: **hangar** and **hanger**

hanger *noun* that on which a coat *etc* is hung □ **hanger-on** *noun* (*plural* **hangers-on**) someone who stays near someone in the hope of gaining some advantage

hangnail *noun* a torn shred of skin beside a fingernail

hangover *noun* **1** uncomfortable after-effects of being drunk **2** something remaining: *a hangover from the 60s* □ **hungover** *adj* suffering from a hangover

hank *noun* a coil or loop of string, rope, wool *etc*

hanker *verb* long for: *hankering after a chocolate biscuit*

hankie or **hanky** *noun* (*plural* **hankies**) *informal* a handkerchief

Hansard *noun* the printed record of debates in the British parliament

hansom cab a light two-wheeled cab with the driver's seat raised behind

Hanukkah *noun* the Jewish festival of lights held in mid-December

haphazard *adj* depending on chance, without planning or system □ **haphazardly** *adv*

hapless *adj* unlucky

happen *verb* **1** take place **2** occur by chance **3** chance to do: *did you happen to see the news?* □ **happening** *noun* an event

happy *adj* **1** joyful **2** contented **3** fortunate, lucky: *a happy coincidence* **4** willing: *happy to help* ◊ **happily** *adv* ◊ **happiness** *noun* ◊ **happy-go-lucky** *adj* easy-going, taking things as they come

happy » happi*er*, happi*est*

hara-kiri *noun* a Japanese form of ritual suicide by slitting the stomach with a sword

harangue *noun* a loud aggressive speech ◊ *verb* deliver a harangue

harass *verb* annoy persistently, pester ◊ **harassment** *noun*

harbinger *noun* a sign of something to come: *harbinger of spring*

harbour *noun* **1** a place of shelter for ships **2** a shelter, a place of safety ◊ *verb* **1** give shelter or refuge **2** store in the mind: *harbouring ill will*

hard *adj* **1** solid, firm **2** not easily broken or put out of shape **3** not easy to do, understand *etc* **4** not easy to please **5** not easy to bear **6** having no kind or gentle feelings **7** of water: containing many minerals and so not forming a good lather **8** of drugs: habit-forming ◊ *adv* strongly, violently ◊ **harden** *verb* make hard ◊ **hardcore** *adj* of pornography *etc*: very explicit, graphic ◊ **hard disk** *comput* a hard-cased disk able to store large amounts of data, fixed into a base unit ◊ **hard-headed** *adj* clever, shrewd ◊ **hard-hearted** *adj* having no kind feelings ◊ **hard hit** *adj* badly affected ◊ **hard labour** tiring work given to prisoners as part of their punishment ◊ **hard lines** or **hard luck** bad luck ◊ **hardly** *adv* scarcely; only just; with difficulty ◊ **hardness** *noun* the state of being hard ◊ **hard-nosed** *adj* tough, unsentimental ◊ **hardship** *noun* something difficult to bear ◊ **hard shoulder** the surfaced strip on the outer edges of a motorway, used when stopping in an emergency ◊ **hard up** *adj* short of money ◊ **hardware** *noun* **1** ironmongery **2** the casing, processor, disk drives *etc* of a computer, not the programs which it runs (*contrasted with*: **software**) ◊ **hardwood** *noun* the wood of certain trees including oak, ash, elm *etc* ◊ **hard and fast** strict, rigid ◊ **hard of hearing** rather deaf

hardy *adj* strong, robust, tough ◊ **hardiness** *noun*

hare *noun* a fast-running animal, like a large rabbit ◊ **harebell** *noun* a plant with blue, bell-shaped flowers ◊ **hare-brained** *adj* mad, foolish ◊ **harelip** *noun* a split in the upper lip at birth, resembling that of a hare

harem /*hehr*əm/ or /*hahr*əm/ *noun* **1** the women's rooms in an Islamic house **2** a set of wives and concubines

haricot /*har*ikoh/ *noun* a type of bean

hark *exclam* listen! ◊ **hark back to** recall or refer to (a previous time, remark *etc*)

harlequin *noun* a comic pantomime character wearing a multi-coloured costume

harlot *noun, old* a prostitute

harm *noun* hurt, damage ◊ *verb* **1**

wound, damage **2** do wrong to □ **harmful** *adj* □ **harmfully** *adv* □ **harmless** *adj* □ **harmlessly** *adv*

harmony *noun* (*plural* **harmonies**) **1** agreement of one part, colour or sound with another **2** agreement between people: *living in harmony* **3** *music* a part intended to agree in sound with the melody □ **harmonic** *adj* relating to harmony □ *noun, music* a ringing sound produced by lightly touching a string being played

harmonica *noun* a mouth organ

harmonious *adj* **1** pleasant-sounding **2** peaceful, without disagreement □ **harmoniously** *adv*

harmonium *noun* a musical wind instrument like a small organ

harmonize *verb* **1** bring into harmony **2** agree, go well (with) **3** *music* add the different parts to a melody □ **harmonization** *noun*

harness *noun* **1** the leather and other fittings for a workhorse **2** an arrangement of straps *etc* attaching something to the body: *parachute harness* □ *verb* **1** put a harness on a horse **2** use as a resource: *harnessing the power of the wind* □ **in harness** working, not on holiday or retired

harp *noun* a triangular, stringed musical instrument played upright by plucking with the fingers □ *verb* play the harp □ **harper** or **harpist** *noun* a harp player □ **harp on about** talk too much about

harpoon *noun* a spear tied to rope, used for killing whales □ *verb* strike with a harpoon

harpsichord *noun* an early musical instrument with keys, played like a piano

harpy *noun* (*plural* **harpies**) **1** a mythological creature with a woman's body, and the wings, feet and claws of a bird of prey **2** a cruel woman

harridan *noun* a bullying woman, a scold

harrier *noun* **1** a breed of small dog for hunting hares **2** a bird of prey **3** a cross-country runner

harrow *noun* a frame with iron spikes for breaking up lumps of earth □ *verb* **1** drag a harrow over **2** distress greatly

harrowing *adj* very distressing

harry *verb* **1** plunder, lay waste **2** harass, worry

> **harry** » harri*es*, harry*ing*, harri*ed*

harsh *adj* rough, bitter; cruel □ **harshly** *adv* □ **harshness** *noun*

hart *noun* the stag or male deer, *esp* from the age of six years

hartebeest or **hartbeest** *noun* a type of S African antelope

harum-scarum *adj* flighty, scatty

harvest *noun* **1** the time of the year when ripened crops are gathered in **2** the crops gathered at this time □ *verb* gather in (a crop) □ **harvester** *noun* **1** a farm worker who helps with the harvest **2** (*also called* **combine harvester**) a large machine that cuts and threshes grain **3** a creature like a spider □ **harvest home** a feast held after a harvest is gathered in

has *see* **have** □ **has-been** *noun* someone no longer important or popular

hash *noun* a dish of chopped meat *etc* □ **make a hash of** spoil completely

hashish *noun* the strongest form of the drug made from hemp

hasp *noun* a clasp, *eg* on a padlock

hassle *verb* cause problems for □ *noun* difficulty, trouble

hassock *noun* a thick cushion used as a footstool or for kneeling on

haste *noun* speed, hurry □ **hasten** *verb* **1** hurry (on) **2** drive forward □ **hastily** *adv* □ **make haste** hurry

hasty *adj* hurried; done without thinking

hat *noun* a covering for the head □ **hatter** *noun* someone who makes or sells hats □ **keep something under your hat** keep it secret

hatch *noun* (*plural* **hatches**) a door or cover over an opening in a floor, wall *etc* □ *verb* **1** produce young from eggs **2** form and set working: hatch (a plan/evil); to shade (part of a picture *etc*) with fine lines □ **hatchback** *noun* a car with a sloping rear door which opens upwards □ **hatchery** *noun* (*plural* **hatcheries**) a place for hatching eggs (*esp* of fish) □ **hatchway** *noun* an opening in a floor or ship's deck

hatchet *noun* a small axe □ **hatchet-faced** *adj* thin-faced, with sharp features □ **hatchet job 1** a severe critical attack on someone or their good reputation **2** a severe reduction □ **bury the hatchet** put an end to a quarrel

hate *verb* dislike very much □ *noun* great dislike □ **hateful** *adj* causing hatred □ **hatred** *noun* extreme dislike

hat-trick *noun* **1** *cricket* the putting out of three batsmen by three balls in a row **2** *football* three goals scored by the same player **3** any action performed three times in a row

haughty *adj* proud, looking on others with scorn □ **haughtily** *adv* □ **haughtiness** *noun*

haul *verb* drag, pull with force □ *noun* **1** a strong pull **2** *informal* a difficult or tiring job: *a long haul* **3** an amount gathered at one time: *a haul of fish* **4** a rich find, booty □ **haulage** *noun* **1** the carrying of goods **2** money charged for this □ **haulier** *noun* a transporter of goods

haunch *noun* (*plural* **haunches**) **1** the fleshy part of the hip **2** a leg and loin of meat, *esp* venison

haunt *verb* **1** visit often **2** of a ghost: inhabit, linger in (a place) □ a place often visited □ **haunted** *adj* inhabited by ghosts

haute couture high fashion; the fashion industry

haute cuisine cooking of the highest standard

have *verb* **1** used with another verb to show that an action is in the past and completed: *we have decided to move house* **2** own, possess: *do you have a cat?* **3** hold, contain: *the* *hotel has a swimming pool* **4** give birth to: *have a baby* **5** suffer from: *have a cold* **6** cause to be done: *have your hair cut* **7** put up with: *I won't have him being so rude* □ **have done with** finish □ **have it out** settle by argument

have » ha*s*, hav*ing*, ha*d*

haven *noun* a place of safety

haver *verb, Scot* **1** speak nonsense **2** dawdle, potter

haversack *noun* a bag made of canvas *etc* with shoulder-straps, for carrying on the back

havoc *noun* great destruction

haw *noun* a berry of the hawthorn tree

hawk *noun* a bird of prey like a falcon □ *verb* **1** hunt birds with trained hawks **2** carry goods about for sale □ **hawker** *noun* a door-to-door salesman

hawthorn *noun* a prickly tree with white flowers and small red berries

hay *noun* cut and dried grass, used as cattle food □ **hay-fever** *noun* an illness with effects like a bad cold, caused by pollen *etc* □ **hayrick** or **haystack** *noun* hay built up into a mound

haywire *adj* tangled, in a state of disorder

hazard *noun* **1** chance **2** risk of harm or danger □ *verb* **1** risk **2** put forward (a guess) at the risk of being wrong □ **hazardous** *adj* dangerous, risky

haze *noun* a thin mist □ **hazy** *adj* **1** misty **2** not clear, vague □ **hazily** *adv* □ **haziness** *noun*

hazel *noun* a nut-producing tree of the birch family □ *adj* light, greenish brown in colour □ **hazelnut** *noun* a light brown nut produced by the hazel tree

H-bomb *noun* a hydrogen bomb

he *pronoun* a male person or animal already spoken about (used only as the subject of a verb): *he ate a banana*

head *noun* **1** the uppermost part of the body, containing the brain, skull *etc* **2** someone's mind: *can't get that tune out of my head* **3** a person in charge, a chief □ *verb* **1** lead **2** go in front of **3** go in the direction of: *heading for home* **4** hit (a ball) with the head **5** (with **off**) turn aside, deflect: *head off an attack* □ **headache** *noun* **1** a pain in the head **2** a worrying problem □ **headband** *noun* a band worn round the head □ **headboard** *noun* a board across the top end of a bed □ **head-dress** *noun* a covering for the head □ **header** *noun, football* a shot at goal striking the ball with the head □ **headfirst** *adv* **1** with the head first: *fall headfirst down the stairs* **2** rashly, without thinking □ **heading** *noun* the title of a book or chapter □ **headland** *noun* a point of land running out into the sea, a cape □ **headlight** *noun* a strong light on the front of a motor car *etc* □ **headline** *noun* a line in large letters at the top of a newspaper page □ **headlong** *adj & adv* headfirst □ **headmaster, headmistress** or **headteacher** *noun* the principal teacher of a school □ **head-on** *adj &*

adv with the head or front first □ **headphones** *noun plural* a listening device that fits over the ears □ **headquarters** *noun sing* and *noun plural* place from which the chief officers of an army *etc* control their operations; the chief office (of a business *etc*) □ **headrest** *noun* a support for the head in a vehicle *etc* □ **headstone** *noun* a gravestone □ **headstrong** *adj* determined, stubborn □ **headway** *noun* forward movement □ **headwind** *noun* a wind blowing straight in your face □ **heady** *adj* exciting □ **head over heels** completely, thoroughly □ **off your head** mad, crazy □ **per head** per person

heal *verb* make or become healthy or sound; cure

health *noun* **1** someone's physical condition: *how's your health?* **2** good or natural physical condition □ **healthy** *adj* **1** in good health or condition **2** encouraging good health **your** *etc* **health** (as a toast) a wish that someone may have good health

heap *noun* **1** a pile of things thrown one on top of another **2** a great many (of) □ *verb* throw in a pile

hear *verb* **1** receive (sounds) by the ear **2** listen to **3** be told, understand: *I hear you want to speak to me* □ **hearing** *noun* **1** the act or power of listening **2** a court case □ **hearsay** *noun* gossip, rumour □ **hear! hear!** *exclam* a cry to show agreement with a speaker □ **will not hear of** will not allow: *he wouldn't hear of her going there alone*

hear » hear*s*, hear*ing*, heard

hearse *noun* a car for carrying a dead body to the grave *etc*

heart *noun* **1** the part of the body which acts as a blood pump **2** the inner or chief part of anything: *the heart of the problem* **3** courage: *take heart* **4** will, enthusiasm: *his heart isn't in it* **5** love, affection: *with all my heart* **6** a sign (♥) representing a heart, or often love **7** this sign used in one of the suits on playing-cards □ **heartache** *noun* sorrow, grief □ **heartbroken** *adj* very upset, very sad □ **heartburn** *noun* a burning feeling in the chest after eating, indigestion □ **hearten** *verb* cheer on, encourage □ **heart-failure** *noun* the sudden stopping of the heart's beating □ **heartfelt** *adj* felt deeply, sincere □ **heartless** *adj* cruel □ **heart-rending** *adj* very moving, very upsetting □ **heartstrings** *noun plural* inmost feelings of love □ **heart-throb** *noun* a sexually attractive person, with whom others fall in love □ **heart-to-heart** *noun* a frank, intimate discussion

hearth *noun* a fireplace

hearty *adj* **1** strong, healthy **2** of a meal: large, satisfying **3** eager, over-cheerful □ **heartily** *adv*

heat *noun* **1** high temperature **2** anger **3** a round in a competition, race *etc* □ *verb* make or become hot □ **heat wave** *noun* a period of hot weather □ **in heat** of a female animal: ready for mating in the breeding season

heath *noun* **1** barren, open country **2** heather

heathen *noun* someone who does not believe in an established religion, *esp* someone who worships idols ◊ *adj* of heathens, pagan

heather *noun* a plant with small purple or white flowers growing on moorland ◊ *adj* of the colour of purple heather

heave *verb* **1** lift by force **2** throw **3** rise and fall **4** produce, let out (*esp* a sigh)

heaven *noun* **1** the sky (often **the heavens**) **2** the dwelling place of God; paradise **3** any place of great happiness ◊ **heavenly** *adj* **1** living in heaven **2** *informal* delightful ◊ **heavenly bodies** the sun, moon and stars

heavy *adj* **1** of great weight **2** great in amount, force *etc*: *heavy rainfall* **3** not easy to bear **4** slow; sleepy ◊ **heavyhanded** *adj* clumsy, awkward ◊ **heavily** *adv* ◊ **heaviness** *noun* ◊ **heavy metal** a very loud repetitive form of rock music ◊ **heavyweight** *noun* **1** a boxer in the highest weight category **2** someone very important or powerful

hebdomadal *adj, formal* weekly

heckle *verb* ask awkward questions of a public speaker ◊ **heckler** *noun* someone who heckles

hectare *noun* 10 000 square metres

hectic *adj* rushed; feverish

hector *verb* bully

> After *Hector*, the Trojan hero in the *Iliad*

hedge *noun* a fence of bushes, shrubs *etc* ◊ *verb* **1** make a hedge **2** shut in with a hedge **3** avoid giving a straight answer ◊ **hedgehog** *noun* a small animal with prickly spines on its back ◊ **hedgerow** *noun* a row of bushes forming a hedge ◊ **hedge your bets** keep open two or more possible courses of action

heebie-jeebies *noun plural* **1** a fit of nerves **2** the creeps

heed *verb* give attention to, listen to ◊ **heedless** *adj* careless ◊ **pay heed to** take notice of

heel *noun* the back part of the foot ◊ *verb* **1** hit (*esp* a ball) with the heel **2** put a heel on (a shoe) **3** of a ship: lean over ◊ **take to your heels** or **show a clean pair of heels** run away

hefty *adj* **1** powerful, muscular **2** heavy

hegemony *noun* complete influence or power over others ◊ **hegemonous** *adj*

Hegira *noun* the Islamic era, dating from AD 622

heifer /*hefər*/ *noun* a young cow

height *noun* **1** the state of being high **2** distance from bottom to top **3** the highest point **4** (often **heights**) a high place ◊ **heighten** *verb* make higher

heinous /*heenəs*/ *adj* extremely bad, atrocious: *heinous crime* ◊ **heinously** *adv* ◊ **heinousness** *noun*

heir, **heiress** *noun* the legal inheritor of a title or property on the death of the owner ◊ **heir-apparent** *noun* someone expected to receive a title or property when the present holder dies ◊ **heirloom** *noun* something that has been handed down in a family from generation to generation

heist *noun, slang* an armed robbery

held *past form* of **hold**

helicopter *noun* a flying machine kept in the air by propellers rotating on a vertical axis

> A coinage based on Greek words meaning 'spiral wing'

heliograph *noun* a means of signalling, using the sun's rays

heliotrope *noun* **1** a plant with small, sweet-smelling, lilac-blue flowers **2** a light purple colour

helium *noun* a very light gas

helix *noun* a screw-shaped coil

hell *noun* **1** a place of punishment of the wicked after death **2** the dwelling place of the Devil **3** any place of great misery or pain □ **hellish** *adj* □ **hellishly** *adv* □ **hellbent on** determined to

hello or **hallo** or **hullo** *noun* (*plural* **hellos** or **helloes** *etc*) a greeting used between people: *I said hello to him/ Hello! How are you?*

helm *noun* the wheel or handle by which a ship is steered □ **helmsman** *noun* the person who steers

helmet *noun* an armoured or protective covering for the head

help *verb* **1** aid, do something useful for **2** give the means for doing something to **3** stop yourself from (doing): *I can't help liking him* □ **1** aid, assistance **2** someone who assists □ **helpful** *adj* useful, able to help □ **helpfully** *adv* □ **helping** *noun* a share, *esp* of food □ **helpless** *adj* useless; powerless □ **helplessly** *adv* □ **helpmate** *noun* a partner □ **help yourself** serve yourself, take what you want

helter-skelter *adv* in a great hurry, in confusion □ *noun* a spiral slide in a fairground *etc*

hem *noun* the border of a garment doubled down and stitched □ *verb* put or form a hem on □ **hem in** surround

> **hem** *verb* » hem*s*, hemm*ing*, hemm*ed*

hemisphere *noun* **1** a half of a sphere or ball-shape **2** half of the earth: *western hemisphere/ southern hemisphere* □ **hemispherical** *adj* like half a ball in shape

hemlock *noun* a poisonous plant with spotted leaves

hemoglobin *US spelling* of **haemoglobin**

hemophilia *US spelling* of **haemophilia**

hemorrhage *US spelling* of **haemorrhage**

hemp *noun* a plant used for making ropes, bags, sails *etc* and the drug cannabis

hen *noun* **1** a female bird **2** a female domestic fowl □ **henpecked** *adj* of a husband: dominated by his wife

hence *adv* **1** from this place or time: *ten years hence* **2** for this reason: *hence, I am unable to go* □ **henceforth** or **henceforward** *adv* from now on

henchman *noun* a follower; a servant

hendiadys /hen*daiə*dis/ *noun* the

use of two nouns to describe something instead of an adjective and a noun, *eg* 'wearing silk and green' for 'wearing green silk'

henna *noun* a reddish plant dye used for colouring the hair *etc*

hepatitis *noun* inflammation of the liver caused by one of several viruses

heptagon *noun* a seven-sided figure ◊ **heptagonal** *adj*

her *pronoun* a female person already spoken about (used only as the object in a sentence): *have you seen her?* ◊ *adj* belonging to such a person: *her house* ◊ **hers** *pronoun* something belonging to such a person: *the idea was hers* ◊ **herself** *pronoun* **1** used reflexively: *she washed herself* **2** used for emphasis: *she herself won't be there but her brother will*

herald *noun* **1** something that is a sign of future things **2** *hist* someone who carries and reads important notices ◊ *verb* **1** announce loudly **2** be a sign of ◊ **heraldic** *adj* of heraldry ◊ **heraldry** *noun* the study of coats of arms, crests *etc*

herb *noun* a plant used in the making of medicines or in cooking

herbaceous *adj* **1** of a plant: with a stem which dies every year **2** of a flower-bed: filled with such plants

herbal *adj* of or using herbs: *herbal remedy* ◊ **herbalism** *noun* the study and use of plants in medicine ◊ **herbalist** *noun*

herbivore *noun* an animal which feeds on grass *etc* ◊ **herbivorous** *adj*

Herculean *adj* requiring tremendous strength or effort: *a Herculean task*

> After the Greek hero, *Hercules*, who was given twelve seemingly impossible tasks to do by the gods

herd *noun* **1** a group of animals of one kind **2** (**the herd**) most people ◊ *verb* group together like a herd of animals

here *adv* at, in or to this place: *he's here already/ come here!* ◊ **hereabouts** *adv* approximately in this place ◊ **hereafter** *adv* after this ◊ **hereby** *adv* by this means ◊ **the hereafter** life after death

heredity *noun* the passing on of physical qualities from parents to children ◊ **hereditary** *adj* passed on in this way

heresy /*her*isee/ *noun* (*plural* **heresies**) an opinion which goes against the official (*esp* religious) view ◊ **heretic** *noun* someone who holds or teaches such an opinion ◊ **heretical** *adj*

heritage *noun* something passed on by or inherited from an earlier generation

hermaphrodite /her*ma*frədait/ *noun* an animal which has the qualities of both male and female sexes

hermeneutic *adj* relating to interpretation, *esp* of Biblical texts

hermetically *adv*: **hermetically sealed** closed completely and airtight

hermit *noun* someone who lives alone, often for religious reasons ◊

hermitage *noun* the dwelling of a hermit ◊ **hermit crab** a kind of crab which lives in the abandoned shell of a shellfish

hernia *noun* the bursting out of part of an internal organ through a weak spot in surrounding body tissue

hero *noun* (*plural* **heroes**), **heroine** *noun* **1** someone much admired for their bravery **2** the chief character in a story, film *etc* ◊ **heroic** *adj* **1** brave as a hero **2** of heroes ◊ **heroically** *adv* ◊ **heroism** *noun* bravery

heroin *noun* a drug derived from morphine

heron *noun* a large water bird, with long legs and neck

herpes *noun* a name for various types of a skin disease

herring *noun* (*plural* **herring** or **herrings**) an edible sea fish with silvery colouring, which moves in large shoals

hers and **herself** *see* **her**

hertz *noun* a unit of frequency for radio waves *etc*

hesitate *verb* **1** pause because of uncertainty **2** be unwilling (to do something): *I hesitate to ask* ◊ **hesitancy** *noun* ◊ **hesitant** *adj* ◊ **hesitation** *noun*

hessian *noun* a type of coarse cloth

heterodox *noun* heretical, having an opinion other than the accepted one (*contrasted with*: **orthodox** ◊ **heterodoxy** *noun*

heterogeneous *adj* composed of many different kinds (*contrasted with*: **homogeneous**)

heterosexual *noun* someone who is sexually attracted to the opposite sex ◊ *adj* attracted to the opposite sex ◊ **heterosexuality** *noun*

het up *adj, informal* excited

heuristic *adj* based on trial and error

hew *verb* cut or shape with an axe *etc*

> **hew** » hew*s*, hew*ing*, hew*ed*, hew*n* or hew*ed*

hex *noun* a spell to bring bad luck; a curse

hexagon *noun* a six-sided figure ◊ **hexagonal** *adj*

heyday *noun* the time of greatest strength, the prime

> From an old English expression *heyda*, meaning 'hurrah'. The *-day* ending and current sense developed much later

HGV *abbrev* heavy goods vehicle

hi *exclam, informal* **1** hello **2** hey

hiatus /hai*eh*təs/ *noun* a gap, a rift

hibachi *noun* a small portable barbecue

hibernate *verb* of an animal: pass the winter in a dormant state ◊ **hibernation** *noun* ◊ **hibernator** *noun*

hibiscus *noun* a tropical tree with large colourful flowers

hiccup *noun* **1** a sharp gasp, caused by laughing, eating, drinking **2** (**hiccups**) a fit of such gasping **3** a minor setback or difficulty □ *verb* make a hiccuping sound

hick *noun, derog* a country bumpkin

hickory *noun* (*plural* **hickories**) a N American tree

hide[1] *verb* put or keep out of sight □ *noun* a concealed place from which to watch birds *etc* □ **hidden** *adj* **1** concealed, out of sight **2** unknown: *hidden meaning* □ **hidebound** *adj* not open to new ideas

> **hide** *verb* » hide*s*, hid*ing*, hid, hidd*en*

hide[2] the skin of an animal □ **hiding** *noun* a beating

hideous *adj* **1** horrible, ghastly **2** very ugly □ **hideously** *adv* □ **hideousness** *noun*

hie /hai/ *verb, old* hurry, hasten

hierarchy *noun* a number of people or things arranged in order of rank □ **hierarchical** *adj*

hieratic *adj* of a priest or priests

hieroglyphics *noun plural* ancient Egyptian writing, in which pictures are used as letters

hi-fi *adj* short for **high fidelity** □ *noun, informal* high-quality equipment for reproducing recorded sound

higgledy-piggledy *adv & adj* in a complete muddle

high *adj* **1** raised far above **2** extending far upwards, tall **3** well up on any scale of measurement, rank *etc* **4** great, large: *high hopes/ high prices* **5** of sound: shrill, acute in pitch **6** of meat: beginning to go bad □ *adv* **1** far above in the air **2** well up on any scale **3** to a high degree □ **highball** *noun, US* an alcoholic drink and mixer (*eg* whisky and soda) with ice in a tall glass □ **highbrow** *adj* intellectual, very literary (*contrasted with*: **lowbrow**) □ **High Court** a supreme court □ **Higher** *noun* an examination in Scottish secondary schools, usually taken at the end of the 5th year □ **high-fidelity** *adj* reproducing sound very clearly □ **high-five** *noun* a sign of greeting made by slapping together one another's raised palms □ **high-flier** *noun* a highly ambitious person □ **high-flown** *adj* (of language, style) using words that sound too grand or pompous □ **high-handed** *adj* thoughtless, overbearing □ **high jinks** lively games or play □ **Highlander** *noun* someone who comes from the Highlands □ **highly** *adv* very: *highly delighted* □ **highly-strung** *adj* nervous, easily excited □ **Highness** *noun* a title of a monarch □ **highroad** *noun* a main road □ **high-spirited** *adj* bold, lively □ **high tea** a cooked meal in the late afternoon □ **high tide** or **high water** the time when the tide is farthest up the shore □ **high treason** the crime of acting against the safety of your own country □ **highway** *noun* the public road □ **highwayman** *noun, hist* a robber who attacked people on the public road □ **Highway Code** a set of official rules for road users in Britain □ **for the high jump** expecting trouble or punishment □ **the Highlands** a mountainous region, *esp* the north of Scotland □ **the high seas** the open seas □ **on your high horse**

behaving with exaggerated pride or superiority

highlight *noun* **1** a bright spot or area in a picture **2** a lighter patch in hair *etc* made obvious by bright light **3** the most memorable part or experience: *the highlight of the week* ◇ *verb* emphasize, make the focus of attention ◇ **highlighter** *noun* a coloured felt-tip pen used to mark but not obscure lines of text

hijack *verb* steal (a car, aeroplane *etc*) while it is moving, forcing the driver or pilot to take a new route ◇ *noun* the action of hijacking a vehicle *etc* ◇ **hijacker** *noun*

hike *verb* travel on foot through countryside ◇ *noun* a country walk ◇ **hiker** *noun*

hilarious *adj* extremely funny ◇ **hilariously** *adv* ◇ **hilarity** *noun*

hill *noun* a mound of high land, less high than a mountain ◇ **hilly** *adj*

hillock *noun* a small hill

hilt *noun* the handle of a sword ◇ **up to the hilt** thoroughly, completely

him *pronoun* a male person already spoken about (used only as the object in a sentence): *I saw him yesterday/ what did you say to him?* ◇ **himself** *pronoun* **1** used reflexively: *he cut himself shaving* **2** used for emphasis: *he wrote it himself*

hind *noun* a female deer ◇ *adj* placed behind ◇ **hindmost** *adj* farthest behind ◇ **hindsight** *noun* wisdom or knowledge got only after something has happened

hinder *verb* keep back, delay, prevent ◇ **hindrance** *noun* something that hinders

hinge *noun* a joint on which a door, lid *etc* turns ◇ *verb* **1** move on a hinge **2** depend (on): *everything hinges on the weather*

hint *noun* **1** a remark which suggests a meaning without stating it clearly: *I'll give you a hint* **2** a slight impression, a suggestion: *a hint of panic in her voice* ◇ *verb* suggest without stating clearly: *he hinted that he might be there*

hinterland *noun* an area lying inland from the coast

hip[1] *noun* the part of the side of the body just below the waist ◇ **hip-flask** *noun* a small pocket flask for alcohol

hip[2] *noun* the fruit of the wild rose

hip[3] *adj* very fashionable, trendy

hippie *noun* a member of a youth movement rebelling against conventional society, dress codes *etc*

Hippocratic oath an oath taken by a doctor agreeing to observe a code of medical ethics

hippodrome *noun* **1** an arena for horse-racing **2** a large theatre

hippopotamus *noun* (*plural* **hippopotami** or **hippopotamuses**) a large African animal living in and near rivers

> Based on a Greek word which translates as 'river horse'

hire *noun* money paid for work done, or for the use of something belonging to another person ◇ *verb* give or get the use of by paying money ▫ **hire-purchase** *noun* a way of buying an article by paying for it in instalments

hirsute *adj* hairy, shaggy

his *adj* belonging to him: *his book* ▫ *pronoun*: *that jacket is his*

Hispanic *adj* **1** Spanish **2** Spanish-American

hiss *verb* make a sound like a snake ▫ *noun* (*plural* **hisses**) such a sound, made to show anger or displeasure

histamine *noun* a chemical present in pollen *etc* which can cause an allergic reaction

histology *noun* the study of animal tissue ▫ **histological** *adj* ▫ **histologist** *noun*

history *noun* (*plural* **histories**) **1** the study of the past **2** a description of past events, society *etc* ▫ **historian** *noun* someone who studies or writes history ▫ **historic** *adj* important, likely to be remembered ▫ **historical** *adj* **1** of history **2** true of something in the past

histrionic *adj* relating to stage-acting or actors ▫ **histrionics** *noun plural* an exaggerated show of strong feeling

hit *verb* **1** strike with a blow **2** occur suddenly to: *it finally hit me* ▫ *noun* **1** a blow, a stroke **2** a shot which hits a target **3** a success **4** a successful song, recording *etc* **5** *slang* a murder by criminals **6** *slang* a dose of a drug ▫ **hit-and-miss** *adj* haphazard, sometimes working and sometimes not ▫ **hit-and-run** *adj* of a driver: driving away after causing injury without reporting the accident ▫ **hitman** *noun, slang* someone employed to kill or attack others ▫ **hit the ceiling** or **hit the roof** explode with anger ▫ **hit the ground running** react immediately and efficiently ▫ **hit the nail on the head** identify the important point, be exactly right ▫ **hit upon** come upon, discover

hit *verb* » hit*s*, hitt*ing*, hit

hitch *verb* **1** fasten with a hook *etc* **2** lift with a jerk **3** hitch-hike ▫ *noun* (*plural* **hitches**) **1** a jerk **2** an unexpected stop or delay **3** a type of knot

hitchhike *verb* travel by getting lifts in other people's vehicles ▫ **hitchhiker** *noun*

hither *adv* to this place ▫ **hitherto** *adv* up till now ▫ **hither and thither** back and forwards

Hitler *noun*: **little Hitler** *noun, derog* an authoritarian

HIV *abbrev* human immuno-deficiency virus ▫ **HIV-positive** *adj* carrying HIV

hive *noun* **1** place where bees live **2** a busy place: *hive of industry*

hives /haivz/ *noun sing* nettle rash

HM *abbrev* Her or His Majesty

HMS *abbrev* **1** Her or His Majesty's Service **2** Her or His Majesty's Ship

HMSO *abbrev* Her or His Majesty's Stationery Office

hoard *noun* a hidden store of treasure, food *etc* ▫ *verb* store up secretly

⚠Do not confuse with: **horde**

hoarding *noun* a fence of boards

hoarse *adj* having a harsh voice, *eg* from a cold or cough

hoary *adj* **1** white with age **2** very old ▫ **hoar-frost** *noun* white frost

hoax *noun* (*plural* **hoaxes**) a trick played to deceive ▫ *verb* play a hoax on

hob *noun* **1** the top of a cooker, with rings for heating *etc* **2** a small shelf next to a fireplace for keeping pans *etc* hot

hobble *verb* **1** walk with short unsteady steps **2** tie the legs of (a horse *etc*) loosely **3** impede, hamper

hobby *noun* (*plural* **hobbies**) a favourite way of passing your spare time

> Originally *hobby-horse*, a horse used in morris dances and therefore for amusement or pleasure

hobby-horse *noun* **1** a toy wooden horse **2** a favourite subject of discussion

hobgoblin *noun* a mischievous fairy

hobnail *noun* a large nail used for horseshoes and in the soles of heavy boots

hobnob *verb* be on friendly terms (with); socialize (with)

> **hobnob** » hobnob*s*, hobnobb*ing*, hobnobb*ed*

hobo *noun* (*plural* **hoboes**) a tramp

Hobson's choice the choice of having something as offered, or nothing at all

> Named after *Hobson*, a Cambridge horsekeeper who reputedly gave customers the choice of the horse nearest the door or none at all

hock[1] *noun* a joint on the hind leg of an animal, below the knee

hock[2] *noun* a white German wine

hock[3] *verb, slang* pawn ▫ **in hock** pawned

hockey *noun* an eleven-a-side ball-game played with clubs curved at one end

hocus-pocus *noun* deception, trickery

hod *noun* **1** a wooden trough on a pole, for carrying bricks and mortar **2** a container for coal

hodge-podge *noun same as* **hotchpotch**

hoe *noun* a tool used for weeding, loosening earth *etc* ▫ *verb* use a hoe

hog *noun* a pig ▫ *verb, informal* take or use selfishly ▫ **hogwash** nonsense, rubbish ▫ **road hog** an inconsiderate driver who refuses to let others pass *etc*

> **hog** *verb* » hog*s*, hogg*ing*, hogg*ed*

Hogmanay *noun* the name in Scotland for 31 December and the celebrations held that night

> From an old French word *aguillanneuf*, a gift given at New Year

hoick *verb* jerk, hitch (up)

hoi polloi the masses, the rabble

> Taken from a Greek phrase for 'the people'

hoisin /*hoy*sin/ *noun* a sweet, hot Chinese sauce made with soy beans, chilli *etc*

hoist *verb* lift, to raise □ *noun* a lift, an elevator for goods

hoity-toity *adj* haughty, superior

hokum /*hoh*kəm/ *noun, US* pretentious rubbish, claptrap

hold *verb* **1** keep in your possession or power; have **2** contain **3** occupy (a position *etc*) **4** think, believe **5** put on, organize: *hold a meeting* **6** apply: *that rule doesn't hold any longer* **7** celebrate: *hold Christmas* □ *noun* **1** grip, grasp **2** influence: *a hold over the others* **3** a large space for carrying a ship's cargo □ **holdall** *noun* a large carrying bag with a zip □ **holder** *noun* **1** container **2** someone who holds (a position *etc*) □ **holding** *noun* an amount of land, shares *etc* held □ **hold-up** *noun* an armed attempt at robbery □ **hold forth** speak at length □ **hold good** be true □ **hold out** refuse to give in □ **hold over** keep till later □ **hold up** **1** support **2** hinder **3** attack and demand money from

> **hold** *verb* » hold*s*, hold*ing*, held

hole *noun* **1** an opening in something solid **2** a pit, a burrow **3** a miserable place □ **in a hole** in a difficult situation

Holi *noun* a Hindu Spring festival

holiday *noun* **1** a day when businesses *etc* are closed **2** a period away from work for rest

holistic *adj* of medicine: treating the patient as a whole rather than the individual disease or symptoms □ **holism** *noun*

hollow *adj* **1** having empty space inside, not solid **2** false, unreal: *hollow victory/ hollow smile* □ *noun* **1** a sunken place **2** a dip in the land □ *verb* scoop (out)

holly *noun* (*plural* **hollies**) an evergreen shrub with scarlet berries and prickly leaves

hollyhock *noun* a tall garden plant

Hollywood *noun* the American cinema industry, based in Hollywood, California

holocaust *noun* a great destruction (by fire)

hologram *noun* a 3-D image created by laser beams

holograph *noun* a document written entirely by one person

holster *noun* a case for a pistol

holt *noun* an otter's den

holus-bolus *adv* all at once, altogether

holy *adj* **1** of or like God **2** religious, righteous **3** for religious use; sacred □ **holiness** *noun* □ **holy of holies** an inner sanctum □ **holy week** the week before Easter □ **holy writ** the Bible □ **holier than thou** superior

> **holy** » holi*er*, holi*est*

homage *noun* a show of respect; an acknowledgement of debt:

paying homage to the pioneers of cinema

home *noun* **1** the place where someone lives **2** the house of someone's family **3** a centre or place of origin: *Nashville is the home of country music* **4** a place where children, the elderly *etc* live and are looked after ▫ *adj* **1** of someone's house or family: *home comforts* **2** domestic, not foreign: *home affairs* ▫ *adv* **1** towards home **2** to the full length: *drive the nail home* ▫ **home economics** the study of how to run a home ▫ **homely** *adj* **1** plain but pleasant **2** *US* plain, not attractive ▫ **home-made** *adj* made at home ▫ **home rule** government of a country *etc* by its own parliament ▫ **Home Secretary** *Brit* the government minister who deals with domestic issues, *eg* law and order, immigration *etc* ▫ **homesick** *adj* longing for home ▫ **homespun** *adj* plain, unelaborate ▫ **homestead** *noun* a farmhouse ▫ **home truth** a frank statement of something true but unpleasant ▫ **homewards** *adv* towards home ▫ **homework** *noun* work for school *etc* done at home ▫ **homing** *adj* of a pigeon: having the habit of making for home ▫ **bring home to** make (someone) realize

homeopathy or **homoeopathy** *noun* the treatment of illness by small quantities of substances that produce symptoms similar to those of the illness ▫ **homeopath** *noun* a practitioner of homeopathy ▫ **homeopathic** *adj* of or using homeopathy (*contrasted with*: **allopathic**)

homicide *noun* **1** the killing of a human being **2** someone who kills a person ▫ **homicidal** *adj*

homily *noun* **1** a plain, practical sermon **2** a talk giving advice

homoeopathy *another spelling* of **homeopathy**

homoeostasis *noun* a tendency towards health or stable condition ▫ **homoeostatic** *adj*

homoerotic *adj* relating to homosexual desire ▫ **homoeroticism** *noun*

homogeneous *adj* composed of parts of the same kind (*contrasted with*: **heterogeneous**) ▫ **homogeneity** *noun*

homogenize *verb* treat (milk) so that the cream does not separate and rise to the surface ▫ **homogenization** *noun*

homograph *noun* a word which has the same spelling as, but a different meaning from, another, *eg keen* meaning 'eager' is a homograph of *keen* meaning 'lament'

homonym *noun* a word which has the same sound as, but a different meaning from another, *eg pair* is a homonym of *pear*

homo sapiens a human being

homosexual *noun* someone who is sexually attracted to the same sex ▫ *adj* sexually attracted to the same sex ▫ **homosexuality** *noun*

Hon *abbrev* **1** Honourable **2** Honorary

hone *verb* sharpen (a knife *etc*)

honest *adj* truthful; not inclined to steal, cheat *etc* ▫ **honestly** *adv* ▫ **honesty** *noun*

honey *noun* **1** a sweet, thick fluid made by bees from the nectar of flowers **2** *informal* sweetheart, dear □ **honey trap** a planned sexual seduction to trap someone into blackmail *etc*

honeycomb *noun* a network of wax cells in which bees store honey □ **honeycombed** *adj* patterned with holes like honey cells

honeydew *noun* a sweet-tasting melon with a smooth rind

honeymoon *noun* a holiday spent immediately after marriage □ *verb* spend a honeymoon □ **honeymooner** *noun*

honeysuckle *noun* a climbing shrub with sweet-smelling flowers

honk *noun* a noise like the cry of the wild goose or the sound of a motor horn □ *verb* make this sound

honky-tonk *noun* a jangly style of piano music

honorary *adj* **1** done to give honour **2** without payment □ **honorarium** *noun* a fee for services not paid for by wages

honour or *US* **honor** *noun* **1** respect for truth, honesty *etc* **2** fame, glory **3** reputation, good name **4** a title of respect, *esp* to a judge: *Your Honour* **5** a privilege **6** (**honours**) recognition given for exceptional achievements □ *verb* **1** give respect to **2** give high rank to **3** pay money when due: *honour a debt* □ **honourable** *adj* worthy of honour □ **honourably** *adv* □ **do the honours** perform a ceremonial task

hood *noun* **1** a covering for the head **2** a protective cover for anything **3** *US* the bonnet of a car

hoodwink *verb* deceive

hoof *noun* (*plural* **hoofs** or **hooves**) the horny part on the feet of certain animals (*eg* horses) □ **on the hoof** *informal* on the move, while moving

hoo-ha *noun, informal* a noisy fuss

hook *noun* **1** a bent piece of metal *etc* for hanging things on **2** a piece of metal on the end of a line for catching fish □ *verb* hang or catch with a hook □ **hooked** *adj* **1** curved, bent **2** caught by a hook **3** *slang* addicted to, fascinated by □ **by hook or by crook** by one means or another, whatever the cost

hookah or **hooka** *noun* a tobacco pipe in which the smoke is drawn through water

hooker *noun, slang* a prostitute

hookey *noun*: **play hookey** *US* play truant

hooligan *noun* a wild, unruly person □ **hooliganism** *noun* unruly behaviour

hoop *noun* a thin ring of wood or metal

hoopoe /*hoo*poo/ *noun* a bird with a large crest

hooray *another spelling* of **hurrah**

hoot *verb* **1** sound (a siren, car horn *etc*) **2** of an owl: call, cry **3** laugh loudly □ *noun* **1** the sound made by a car horn, siren or owl **2** a shout of scorn or disgust **3** *informal* someone or something extremely funny □ **hooter** *noun* **1** a siren or horn which makes a hooting sound **2** *slang* a large nose

Hoover *noun, trademark* a vacuum cleaner □ **hoover** *verb* vacuum (a floor *etc*)

hop[1] *verb* leap on one leg □ *noun* a short jump on one leg □ **hopper** *noun* a funnel for shaking down corn to a grinding machine

> **hop** *verb* » hop*s*, hopp*ing*, hopp*ed*

hop[2] *noun* a climbing plant with bitter-tasting fruits which are used in brewing beer

hope *noun* **1** the state of expecting or wishing something good to happen **2** something desired □ *verb* expect or wish good to happen □ **hopeful** *adj* □ **hopefully** *adv* □ **hopeless** *adj* **1** without hope **2** very bad □ **hopelessly** *adv*

hoplite *noun, hist* an armed Greek foot-soldier

hopscotch *noun* a hopping game over lines drawn on the ground

horde *noun* a large crowd or group

> ⚠Do not confuse with: **hoard**

horizon *noun* **1** the imaginary line formed where the earth meets the sky **2** the limit of someone's experience or understanding □ **horizontal** *adj* lying level or flat □ **horizontally** *adv*

hormone *noun* a substance produced by certain glands of the body, which acts on a particular organ □ **hormonal** *adj*

horn *noun* **1** a hard growth on the heads of certain animals, *eg* deer, sheep **2** something curved or sticking out like an animal's horn **3** part of a motor car which gives a warning sound **4** a brass wind instrument (originally made of horn) □ **horned** *adj* having horns □ **horny** *adj* **1** hard like horn **2** *slang* sexually aroused

hornbill *noun* a bird with a horny growth on its bill

hornet *noun* a kind of large wasp □ **stir up a hornet's nest** cause a commotion or violent reaction

hornpipe *noun* a lively sailor's dance

horoscope *noun* a prediction of someone's future based on the position of the stars at their birth

horrendous *adj, informal* awful, terrible □ **horrendously** *adv*

horrific *adj* **1** terrifying **2** awful, very bad □ **horrifically** *adv*

horror *noun* **1** great fear, terror **2** something which causes fear **3** an unruly or demanding child

horrible *adj* **1** very unpleasant **2** very bad, awful □ **horribly** *adv*

horrid *adj* hateful; very unpleasant

horrify *verb* frighten greatly, shock: *we were horrified by his behaviour* □ **horrifying** *adj* □ **horrifyingly** *adv*

> **horrify** » horrifi*es*, horrify*ing*, horrifi*ed*

hors de combat not fit to fight

hors d'oeuvre an appetizer

horse *noun* **1** a four-footed animal with hooves and a mane **2** a wooden frame for drying clothes on **3** a piece of gymnastic equipment for vaulting ◊ **horse-chestnut** *noun* a tree which produces a shiny, bitter-tasting nut ◊ **horsefly** *noun* a large fly which bites ◊ **horse laugh** a loud, harsh laugh ◊ **horseplay** *noun* rough play, fooling around ◊ **horsepower** *noun* a unit of mechanical power for car engines (*short form* **hp**) ◊ **horseradish** *noun* a plant with a sharp-tasting root which is used in sauces ◊ **horseshoe** *noun* **1** a shoe for horses, made of a curved piece of iron **2** a horseshoe-shaped thing ◊ **horsy** or **horsey** *adj* fond of horses ◊ **from the horse's mouth** directly from the source, first-hand ◊ **horses for courses** people will do best in situations that suit them individually

horticulture *noun* the study and art of gardening ◊ **horticultural** *adj* ◊ **horticulturist** *noun*

hosanna *noun* an exclamation of praise to God

hose *noun* **1** (*plural* **hose**) a covering for the legs or feet, *eg* stockings **2** (*plural* **hoses**) a rubber tube for carrying water ◊ **hosiery** *noun* stockings, tights *etc*

hospice *noun* a home providing special nursing care for incurable invalids

hospitable *adj* showing kindness to guests or strangers ◊ **hospitably** *adv* ◊ **hospitality** *noun*

hospital *noun* a building for the treatment of the sick and injured

host[1], **hostess** *noun* **1** someone who welcomes and entertains guests **2** an innkeeper or hotel-keeper

host[2] *noun* a very large number

hostage *noun* someone held prisoner by an enemy to make sure that an agreement will be kept to

hostel *noun* a building providing rooms for students *etc* ◊ **hostelry** *noun* (*plural* **hostelries**), *old* an inn ◊ **hostler** or **ostler** *noun*, *hist* a servant in charge of horses at an inn

hostile *adj* **1** of an enemy **2** not friendly **3** showing dislike or opposition (to) ◊ **hostility** *noun* **1** unfriendliness, dislike **2** (*plural* **hostilities**) acts of warfare

hot *adj* **1** very warm **2** spicy **3** passionate **4** radioactive **5** *slang* stolen **6** *slang* not safe ◊ **hot air** meaningless talk ◊ **hotbed** *noun* a centre or breeding ground for anything: *a hotbed of rebellion* ◊ **hot-blooded** *adj* passionate, easily angered ◊ **hotdog** *noun* a hot sausage in a roll ◊ **hotfoot** *adv* in great haste ◊ **hot-headed** *adj* inclined to act rashly without thinking ◊ **hothouse** *noun* a heated glasshouse for plants ◊ *verb* give (a child) intensive schooling at an early age ◊ **hotline** *noun* a direct telephone line between heads of government ◊ **hot potato** a touchy subject ◊ **hot seat** a position of responsibility ◊ **hot on someone's heels** following them closely ◊ **hot under the collar** indignant, enraged ◊ **in hot water** in trouble ◊ **sell like hot cakes** sell very quickly

hot » hott*er*, hott*est*

hotchpotch *noun* (*plural* **hotchpotches**) a confused mixture

hotel *noun* a building with several rooms which people can pay to stay in for a number of nights

hound *noun* a dog used in hunting □ *verb* hunt, pursue

hour *noun* **1** sixty minutes, the 24th part of a day **2** a time or occasion: *the hour of reckoning* □ **hour-glass** *noun* an instrument which measures the hours by the running of sand from one glass into another □ **hourly** *adj* happening or done every hour □ *adv* every hour

houri *noun* a female spirit in the Islamic paradise

house *noun* **1** a building in which people live **2** a household **3** a business firm **4** a building where school boarders stay □ *verb* provide a house for; accommodate □ **house arrest** confinement under guard in a private house, hospital *etc* □ **houseboat** *noun* a river barge with a cabin for living in □ **housebreaker** *noun* someone who breaks into a house to steal □ **housecoat** *noun* a dressing-gown □ **household** *noun* the people who live together in a house □ **householder** *noun* someone who owns or pays the rent of a house □ **housekeeper** *noun* someone employed to look after the running of a house □ **house-proud** *adj* proud of keeping your house clean and tidy □ **house-trained** *adj* of a pet: trained to urinate and defecate outdoors □ **housewarming** *noun* a party held when someone moves into a new house □ **housewife** *noun* a woman who looks after a house and her family □ **housing** *noun* **1** accommodation, *eg* houses, flats *etc* **2** a casing for a machine *etc* □ **a household name** or **a household word** someone or something which everyone is talking about □ **like a house on fire** very successfully, extremely well □ **on the house** free, complimentary

hovel *noun* a small squalid dwelling

hover *verb* **1** stay in the air in the same spot **2** stay near, linger (about) **3** be undecided or uncertain

hovercraft *noun* a craft able to travel over land or sea supported on a cushion of air

how *adv* **1** in what manner: *how are they getting there?* **2** to what extent: *how old are you?/ how cold is it outside?* **3** to a great extent: *how young he seems/ how well you play* **4** by what means: *how do you switch this on?* **5** in what condition: *how is she?* □ **however** *adv* **1** no matter how **2** in spite of that

howdah *noun* a seat fixed on an elephant's back

howitzer *noun* a short cannon used to attack a besieged town or trench

howk *verb, Scot* dig out

howl *verb* **1** make a long, loud sound like that of a dog or wolf **2** yell in pain, anger *etc* **3** laugh loudly □ *noun* a howling sound □ **howler** *noun, informal* a ridiculous mistake

hoyden *noun* a tomboy □ **hoydenish** *adj*

HP or **hp** *abbrev* **1** hire-purchase **2** horsepower

HQ *abbrev* headquarters

hr *abbrev* hour

HRH *abbrev* Her or His Royal Highness

HRT *abbrev* hormone replacement therapy

hub *noun* **1** the centre part of a wheel through which the axle passes **2** a thriving centre of anything: *the hub of the entertainment industry*

hubbub *noun* a confused sound of many voices

> Originally meaning 'battle' or 'war cry', based on an Irish Gaelic word

hubby *noun, informal* a husband

huddle *verb* crowd together □ *noun* a close group

hue *noun* colour, shade

hue and cry a commotion, a fuss

huff *noun* a fit of bad temper and sulking □ **huffily** *adv* □ **huffiness** *noun* □ **huffy** *adj* inclined to sulk; peevish

hug *verb* **1** hold tightly with the arms **2** keep close to: *hugging the kerb* □ *noun* a tight embrace

> **hug** *verb* » hug*s*, hugg*ing*, hugg*ed*

huge *adj* extremely big □ **hugeness** *noun*

hugger-mugger *adj* secret, hush-hush

hula-hoop *noun* a light hoop for spinning round the waist

hulk *noun* **1** an old ship unfit for use **2** something big and clumsy □ **hulking** *adj* big and clumsy

hull *noun* the body or framework of a ship

hullabaloo *noun* a noisy disturbance

hullo *another spelling* of **hello**

hum *verb* **1** make a buzzing sound like that of bees **2** sing with the lips shut **3** of a place: be noisily busy □ *noun* **1** the noise of bees **2** any buzzing, droning sound □ **humming-bird** *noun* a small brightly-coloured bird which beats its wings rapidly making a humming noise

> **hum** *verb* » hum*s*, humm*ing*, humm*ed*

human *adj* **1** relating to people as opposed to animals or gods **2** having natural qualities, feelings *etc* □ *noun* a man, woman or child □ **humanism** *noun* a set of ideas about or interest in ethics and mankind, not including religious belief □ **humanist** *noun* □ **humanitarian** *adj* kind to fellow human beings □ **humanity** *noun* **1** men and women in general **2** kindness, gentleness

humane *adj* kind, showing mercy, gentle □ **humanely** *adv*

humble *adj* **1** modest, meek **2** not of high rank, unimportant □ *verb* make to feel low and unimportant □ **eat humble pie** admit a mistake openly

humbug *noun* **1** nonsense, rubbish **2** a kind of hard minty sweet

humdinger *noun, informal*

someone or something exceptional

humdrum *adj* dull, not exciting

humdudgeon *noun, Scot* an unnecessary fuss

humerus *noun* the bone of the upper arm

humid *adj* of air *etc*: moist, damp ◇ **humidifier** *noun* a device which controls the amount of humidity in the air ◇ **humidity** *noun*

humiliate *noun* make to feel humble or ashamed, hurt someone's pride ◇ **humiliating** *adj* ◇ **humiliation** *noun*

humility *noun* humble state of mind, meekness

hummus *noun* a paste made from ground chick-peas and olive oil

humongous or **humungous** *adj, informal* enormous, huge

humour or *US* **humor** *noun* **1** the ability to see things as amusing or ridiculous **2** funniness; the amusing side of anything: *failed to see the humour of the situation* 3 state of mind; temper, mood ◇ *verb* do as someone else wishes in order to please them ◇ **humorist** *noun* a comedian, a comic writer

humorous *adj* funny, amusing ◇ **humorously** *adv*

hump *noun* **1** a lump, a mound **2** a lump on the back ◇ **humpback** *noun* **1** a back with a hump **2** someone with a hump on their back ◇ **humpbacked** *adj* **1** with a hump on the back **2** of a bridge: rising and falling so as to form a hump shape

humungous *another spelling* of **humongous**

humus /*hyoo*məs/ *noun* soil made of rotted leaves *etc*

hunch *noun* (*plural* **hunches**) a suspicion that something is untrue or is going to happen *etc* ◇ **hunchback** *noun* humpback ◇ **hunchbacked** *adj* humpbacked

hundred the number 100 ◇ *adj* 100 in number ◇ **hundredth** *adj* the last of a hundred (things *etc*) ◇ *noun* one of a hundred equal parts ◇ **hundredweight** *noun* 112 lb, 50.8 kilogrammes (often written **cwt**)

hunger *noun* **1** a desire for food **2** a strong desire for anything ◇ *verb* **1** go without food **2** long (for) ◇ **hunger-strike** *noun* a refusal to eat as a protest ◇ **hungrily** *adv* ◇ **hungry** *adj* wanting or needing food

hunk *noun, informal* a muscular, sexually attractive man ◇ **hunky** *adj*

hunker *verb*: **hunker down** squat

hunky-dory *adj* in a good situation; well, fine

hunt *verb* **1** chase animals or birds for food or sport **2** search (for) ◇ *noun* **1** chasing wild animals **2** a search ◇ **huntsman, huntswoman** *noun* someone who hunts

hurdle *noun* **1** a light frame to be jumped over in a race **2** a difficulty which must be overcome

hurdygurdy *noun* a barrel organ

hurl *verb* throw with force

hurlyburly *noun* a great stir, uproar

hurrah or **hurray** *exclam* a shout of joy, approval *etc*

hurricane *noun* a violent storm of wind blowing at a speed of over 75 miles (120 kilometres) per hour **hurricane lamp** a lamp specially made to keep alight in strong wind

hurry *verb* **1** act or move quickly **2** make (someone) act quickly *noun* eagerness to act quickly, haste **hurried** *adj* done in a hurry **hurriedly** *adv*

> **hurry** *verb* » hurri*es*, hurry*ing*, hurri*ed*

hurt *verb* **1** cause pain or distress to **2** injure physically, wound **3** damage, spoil *noun* **1** pain, distress **2** damage **hurtful** *adj* causing pain, distress or damage **hurtfully** *adv*

hurtle *verb* rush at great speed

husband *noun* a married man (the partner of a **wife**) *verb* spend or use (*eg* money, strength) carefully **husbandry** *noun* **1** farming **2** management **3** care with money, thrift

hush *exclam* be quiet! *noun, informal* silence, quiet *verb* make quiet **hush-hush** *adj, informal* top secret **hush up** stop (a scandal *etc*) becoming public

husk *noun* the dry thin covering of certain fruits and seeds

husky[1] *adj* **1** of a voice: deep and rough **2** big and strong **huskily** *adv* **huskiness** *noun*

husky[2] *noun* (*plural* **huskies**) a Canadian sledge-dog

hussar /*həzahr*/ *noun* a light-armed horse soldier

hussy *noun* (*plural* **hussies**) a forward, cheeky girl

hustings *noun plural* political campaigning just before an election

hustle *verb* **1** push rudely **2** hurry

hut *noun* a small wooden building

hutch *noun* (*plural* **hutches**) a box in which pet rabbits are housed

hyacinth *noun* a sweet-smelling flower which grows from a bulb

hyaena *another spelling* of **hyena**

hybrid *noun* **1** an animal or plant bred from two different kinds, *eg* a mule, which is a hybrid from a horse and an ass **2** a word formed of parts from different languages

hydra *noun* **1** a mythological many-headed snake that grew two heads for each one cut off **2** a sea creature that can divide and re-divide itself

hydrant *noun* a connection to which a hose can be attached to draw water off the main water supply

hydraulic *adj* **1** carrying water **2** worked by water or other fluid

hydro *noun* (*plural* **hydros**) a hotel with a swimming pool and gymnasium *etc*

hydro- *prefix* water

hydroelectricity *noun* electricity obtained from water-power **hydroelectric** *adj*

hydrogen *noun* the lightest gas, which with oxygen makes up water **hydrogen bomb** an extremely powerful bomb using hydrogen

hydrophobia *noun* **1** a fear of water, a symptom of rabies **2** rabies **hydrophobic** *adj*

hyena or **hyaena** *noun* a dog-like wild animal with a howl sounding like laughter

hygiene /*hai*jeen/ *noun* the maintaining of cleanliness as a means to health ▫ **hygienic** *adj*

hymen *noun* the thin membrane that partially closes the vagina of a virgin

hymn *noun* a religious song of praise ▫ **hymnal** or **hymnary** *noun* (*plural* **hymnaries**) a book of hymns

hype /haip/ *informal noun* **1** extravagant advertisement or publicity **2** a hypodermic syringe ▫ *verb* **1** promote extravagantly **2** inject yourself with a drug ▫ **hype up** hype

hyper- *prefix* to a greater extent than usual, excessive: *hypersensitive*

hyperbole /hai*puhr*bəli/ *noun* exaggeration ▫ **hyperbolical** *adj*

hypermarket *noun* a large self-service store stocking a wide range of goods

hypernym *noun* a general word whose meaning contains several specific words, *eg dance* is a hypernym of *waltz* and *reel* (*contrasted with*: **hyponym**)

hypertension *noun* high blood pressure

hypertext *noun* electronic text containing cross-references which can be accessed by keystrokes *etc*

hyphen *noun* a short stroke (-) used to link or separate parts of a word or phrase: *touch-and-go/ re-elect*

hypnosis *noun* **1** a sleep-like state in which suggestions are obeyed **2** hypnotism ▫ **hypnotic** *adj* **1** of hypnosis or hypnotism **2** causing a sleep-like state ▫ **hypnotically** *adv* ▫ **hypnotism** *noun* the putting of someone into hypnosis ▫ **hypnotist** *noun* ▫ **hypnotize** *verb* put someone into hypnosis

hypo- *prefix* below, under

hypoallergenic *adj* specially formulated in order to reduce the risk of allergy

hypochondria *noun* over-anxiety about your own health ▫ **hypochondriac** *noun & adj*

hypocorism *noun* a pet-name ▫ **hypocoristic** *adj*

hypocrite /*hi*pohkrit/ *noun* someone who pretends to be something they are not, or to believe something they do not ▫ **hypocrisy** *noun* ▫ **hypocritical** *adj*

hypodermic *adj* used for injecting drugs just below the skin: *hypodermic syringe/ hypodermic needle* ▫ *noun* a hypodermic syringe

hypoglycaemia *noun* an abnormally low amount of sugar in the blood ▫ **hypoglycaemic** *adj*

hyponym *noun* one of a group of words whose meanings are included in a more general term, *eg guitar* and *piano* are hyponyms of *musical instrument* (*contrasted with*: **hypernym**)

hypostyle *adj* of a roof: supported by pillars

hypotenuse *noun* the longest side of a right-angled triangle

hypothermia *noun* an abnormally

low body temperature caused by exposure to cold

hypothesis *noun* (*plural* **hypotheses**) something taken as true for the sake of argument □ **hypothetical** *adj* supposed □ **hypothetically** *adv*

hyssop *noun* an aromatic plant used in perfumes and herbal medicine

hysterectomy *noun* (*plural* **hysterectomies**) surgical removal of the womb

hysteria *noun* **1** a nervous excitement causing uncontrollable laughter, crying *etc* **2** a nervous illness □ **hysterical** *adj* □ **hysterically** *adv* □ **hysterics** *noun plural* a fit of hysteria

> Based on a Greek word for 'womb', because originally thought to be caused by womb disease or abnormalities

Hz *abbrev* hertz

I

I *pronoun* the word used by a speaker or writer in mentioning themselves (as the subject of a verb): *you and I/ I, myself*

IBA *abbrev* Independent Broadcasting Authority

ibex *noun* (*plural* **ibexes**) a wild mountain goat

ibid *adv* in the same book, article *etc*

IBS *abbrev* irritable bowel syndrome

ice *noun* **1** frozen water **2** ice-cream □ *verb* **1** cover with icing **2** freeze □ **ice age** an age when the earth was mostly covered with ice □ **iceberg** *noun* a huge mass of floating ice □ **icebox** *noun*, *US* refrigerator □ **ice-cap** *noun* a permanent covering of ice, as at the north and south poles □ **ice-cream** *noun* a sweet creamy mixture, flavoured and frozen □ **ice floe** a piece of floating ice □ **ice hockey** hockey played with a rubber disc (called a **puck**) on an ice rink □ **ice-skate** *noun* a skate for moving on ice □ **ice-skating** *noun* □ **dry ice** solid carbon dioxide

ichthyology *noun* the study of fishes □ **ichthyologist** *noun*

icicle *noun* a hanging, pointed piece of ice formed by the freezing of dropping water

icing *noun* powdered sugar, mixed with water or egg-white, spread on cakes or biscuits □ **icing on the cake** something added but not really necessary

icky *adj, informal* disgusting, repulsive

icon *noun* **1** a painted or mosaic image of Christ or a saint (*also* **ikon**) **2** *comput* a small graphic image which is clicked to access a particular program

iconoclasm *noun* **1** the act of breaking images **2** the attacking of long-established beliefs □ **iconoclast** *noun* □ **iconoclastic** *adj*

iconography *noun* □ **iconographer** *noun*

icy *adj* **1** covered with ice **2** very cold □ **icily** *adv* □ **iciness** *noun*

ID *abbrev* identification □ *noun*, *US* a means of identification, *eg* a driving licence

I'd *short for* I would, I should or I had: *I'd sooner go than stay*

id *noun* the unconscious part of the personality, the source of instincts and dreams

idea *noun* **1** a thought, a notion **2** a plan

ideal *adj* **1** perfect **2** existing in imagination only (*contrasted with*: **real**) □ *noun* the highest and best; a standard of perfection □ **idealism** *noun* □ **idealist** *noun* someone who thinks that perfection can be reached □ **idealistic** *adj* □ **idealization** *noun* □ **idealize** *verb* think of as perfect □ **ideally** *adv* in ideal circumstances: *ideally all children* *should have a place in nursery school*

identical *adj* the same in all details ▯ **identically** *adv*

identify *verb* claim to recognize, prove to be the same: *he identified the man as his attacker* ▯ **identification** *noun* ▯ **identify with 1** feel close to or involved with **2** think of as the same, equate: *identifying money with happiness*

identify » identifi*es*, identify*ing*, identifi*ed*

identikit picture a rough picture of a wanted person which police put together from descriptions

identity *noun* (*plural* **identities**) **1** who or what someone or something is **2** the state of being the same

ideogram *noun* a written character that represents an idea rather than a sound

ideolect *noun* the language spoken by an individual person, including their vocabulary, pronunciation *etc*

ideology *noun* (*plural* **ideologies**) a set of ideas, often political or philosophical ▯ **ideological** *adj* ▯ **ideologically** *adv*

idiocy *see* **idiot**

idiom *noun* a common expression whose meaning cannot be guessed from the individual words, *eg* 'I'm feeling *under the weather*' ▯ **idiomatic** *adj* ▯ **idiomatically** *adv*

idiosyncrasy *noun* (*plural* **idiosyncrasies**) a personal oddness of behaviour ▯ **idiosyncratic** *adj* ▯ **idiosyncratically** *adv*

idiot *noun* a feeble-minded person; a fool ▯ **idiocy** *noun* feeble-mindedness, foolishness ▯ **idiotic** *adj* ▯ **idiotically** *adv*

idle *adj* **1** not working **2** lazy **3** meaningless: *idle chatter* ▯ *verb* **1** spend time in doing nothing **2** of an engine: run without doing any work ▯ **idleness** *noun* ▯ **idler** *noun* ▯ **idly** *adv*

idol *noun* **1** an image worshipped as a god **2** someone much loved or honoured ▯ **idolater** *noun* ▯ **idolatrous** *adj* ▯ **idolatry** *noun* ▯ **idolize** *verb* adore, worship

idyll *noun* **1** a poem on a pastoral theme **2** a time of pleasure and contentment

idyllic *adj* very happy and content, blissful ▯ **idyllically** *adv*

ie *abbrev* that is, that means (from Latin *id est*)

if *conj* **1** on condition that, supposing that: *If you go, I'll go* **2** whether: *do you know if she'll be there?*

iffy *adj*, *informal* dubious, uncertain

igloo *noun* an Inuit snow hut

igneous *adj* **1** relating to fire **2** of rock: formed by the action of great heat within the earth

ignite *verb* **1** set on fire **2** catch fire

ignition *noun* **1** the act of setting on fire or catching fire **2** the sparking part of a motor engine

ignoble *adj* dishonourable; of low birth

ignominy /ignəmini/ *noun* disgrace, dishonour ▯ **ignominious** *adj* ▯ **ignominiously** *adv*

ignoramus /ignə*reh*məs/ *noun* an ignorant person

ignorant *adj* knowing very little ▯ **ignorance** *noun* ▯ **ignorant of** unaware of

ignore *verb* take no notice of

iguana /ig*wah*nə/ *noun* a type of tree lizard

ikat *noun* a patterned cloth woven from hand-died yarn

ikebana *noun* the Japanese art of flower arranging

ikon *another spelling* of **icon**

I'll *short for* I shall, I will

ill *adj* **1** unwell, sick **2** evil, bad **3** unlucky ▯ *adv* badly ▯ *noun* **1** evil **2** (**ills**) misfortunes, troubles ▯ **ill-at-ease** *adj* uncomfortable ▯ **ill-gotten** *adj* got in a dishonest or unethical way ▯ **ill-humoured** or **ill-natured** *adj* bad-tempered ▯ **ill-starred** *adj* unlucky ▯ **ill-treat** or **ill-use** *verb* treat badly ▯ **ill-will** or **ill-feeling** *noun* dislike, resentment

illegal *adj* against the law ▯ **illegality** *noun* (*plural* **illegalities**)

illegible *adj* impossible to read, indistinct ▯ **illegibility** *noun* ▯ **illegibly** *adv*

illegitimate *adj* born of parents not married to each other

illicit *adj* unlawful, forbidden ▯ **illicitly** *adv*

⚠Do not confuse with: **elicit**

illiterate *adj* not able to read or write ▯ **illiteracy** *noun*

illness *noun* disease, sickness

illogical *adj* not logical, not showing sound reasoning ▯ **illogicality** *noun* ▯ **illogically** *adv*

illuminate *verb* **1** light up **2** make more clear ▯ **illuminated** *adj* of a manuscript: decorated with ornamental lettering ▯ **illuminations** *noun plural* a decorative display of lights

illusion *noun* **1** something which deceives the mind or eye **2** a mistaken belief ▯ **illusory** *adj*

⚠Do not confuse with: **allusion** and **delusion**

illusive *adj* misleading, deceptive

⚠Do not confuse with: **allusive** and **elusive**

illustrate *verb* **1** draw pictures for (a book *etc*) **2** explain, show by example ▯ **illustration** *noun* **1** a picture in a book *etc* **2** an example which illustrates ▯ **illustrative** *adj* ▯ **illustrator** *noun* someone who illustrates books *etc*

illustrious *adj* famous, distinguished

I'm *short for* I am

image *noun* **1** a likeness made of someone or something **2** a striking likeness: *she is the image of her mother* **3** a picture in the mind **4** public reputation

imagery *noun* words that suggest images, used to make a piece of writing more vivid

imaginary *adj* existing only in the imagination, not real

⚠Do not confuse with: **imaginative**

imagination *noun* the power of forming pictures in the mind of things not present or experienced

imagine *verb* **1** form a picture in the mind, *esp* of something that does not exist **2** think, suppose

imaginative *adj* **1** having a lively imagination **2** done with imagination: *an imaginative piece of writing* ▫ **imaginatively** *adv*

⚠Do not confuse with: **imaginary**

imago *another word* for **pupa**

imam *noun* **1** the priest who leads the prayers in a mosque **2 (Imam)** an Islamic leader

IMAX *noun, trademark* a kind of widescreen cinema for projecting 70mm film

imbecile *noun* a feeble-minded person; a fool ▫ **imbecility** *noun* feeble-mindedness, stupidity

imbibe *verb* drink (in)

imbroglio /imbrohlyoh/ *noun* (*plural* **imbroglios**) a confused situation, a tangle

imbue *verb* fill or affect (with): *imbued her staff with enthusiasm*

IMF *abbrev* International Monetary Fund

imitate *verb* try to be the same as, copy ▫ **imitation** *noun* a copy ▫ *adj* made to look like: *imitation leather* ▫ **imitator** *noun*

immaculate *adj* spotless; very clean and neat ▫ **immaculately** *adv*

immaterial *adj* of little importance

immature *adj* not mature ▫ **immaturely** *adv* ▫ **immaturity** *noun*

immediate *adj* **1** happening straight away: *immediate reaction* **2** close: *immediate family* **3** direct: *my immediate successor* ▫ **immediacy** *noun* ▫ **immediately** *adv* without delay

immemorial *adj* going further back in time than can be remembered ▫ **immemorially** *adv*

immense *adj* very large ▫ **immensely** *adv* ▫ **immensity** *noun*

immerse *verb* plunge into liquid ▫ **immersion** *noun* ▫ **immersion heater** an electric water-heater inside a hot-water tank ▫ **immerse yourself in** give your whole attention to

immigrate *verb* come into a country and settle there ▫ **immigrant** *noun* someone who immigrates ▫ **immigration** *noun*

⚠Do not confuse with: **emigrate**

imminent *adj* about to happen: *imminent danger* ▫ **imminently** *adv*

⚠Do not confuse with: **eminent**

immiscible *adj* not able to be mixed, as *eg* water and oil

immobile *adj* **1** without moving **2** not easily moved ▫ **immobility** *noun* ▫ **immobilize** *verb* put out of action

immoderate *adj* going beyond reasonable limits ▫ **immoderately**

adv □ **immoderation** *noun*

immolate *verb* sacrifice □ **immolation** *noun*

immoral *adj* **1** wrong, unscrupulous **2** sexually improper □ **immorally** *adv* □ **immorality** *noun*

⚠Do not confuse with: **amoral**

immortal *adj* **1** living for ever **2** famous for ever □ **immortality** *noun* unending life or fame □ **immortalize** *verb* make immortal or famous for ever

immovable *adj* not able to be moved or changed □ **immovably** *adv*

immune *adj* **1** not likely to catch a particular disease: *immune to measles* **2** not able to be affected by: *she is immune to his charm* □ **immune system** the natural defensive system of an organism that identifies and neutralizes harmful matter within itself □ **immunity** *noun* □ **immunize** *verb* make someone immune to (a disease), *esp* by inoculation □ **immunodeficiency** *noun* weakened ability to produce antibodies □ **immunosuppressant** *noun* a drug which prevents the body producing antibodies and so rejecting a transplanted organ *etc*

immunology *noun* the study of the human immune system □ **immunological** *adj* □ **immunologist** *noun*

imp *noun* **1** a small malignant spirit **2** a mischievous child □ **impish** *adj*

impact *noun* **1** the blow of one thing striking another; a collision **2** strong effect: *made an impact on the audience* □ *verb* press firmly together □ **impact on** affect strongly

impair *verb* damage, weaken □ **impairment** *noun*

impala *noun* a large African antelope

impale *verb* pierce through with a spear *etc*

impart *verb* tell (information, news *etc*) to others

impartial *adj* not favouring one side over another; unbiased □ **impartiality** *noun* □ **impartially** *adv*

impassable *adj* of a road: not able to be driven through

impasse /*anh*pas/ *noun* a situation from which there seems to be no way out

impassioned *adj* moved by strong feeling

impassive *adj* not easily moved by strong feeling □ **impassively** *adv*

impatient *adj* **1** restlessly eager **2** irritable, short-tempered □ **impatience** *noun* □ **impatiently** *adv*

impeach *verb* accuse publicly of, or charge with, misconduct □ **impeachment** *noun*

impeccable *adj* faultless, perfect □ **impeccably** *adv*

impecunious *adj* having little or no money

impede *verb* hinder, keep back □ **impediment** *noun* **1** a hindrance **2** a speech defect, *eg* a stutter or stammer

impel *verb* **1** urge **2** drive on

impel » impel*s*, impell*ing*, impell*ed*

impending *adj* about to happen: *an impending storm*

impenetrable *adj* **1** not allowing light *etc* through **2** incomprehensible, inscrutable

impenitent *adj* not sorry for wrongdoing, unrepentant

imperative *adj* **1** necessary, urgent **2** *gram* expressing command, *eg look!* or *read this* □ **imperatively** *adv*

imperceptible *adj* so small as not to be noticed □ **imperceptibly** *adv*

imperfect *adj* having a fault or flaw, not perfect □ **imperfection** *noun* a fault or a flaw □ **imperfectly** *adv*

imperial *adj* **1** of an emperor or empire **2** commanding, superior □ **imperialism** *noun* the policy of annexing the territory of, and ruling, other nations and people □ **imperialist** *adj*

imperil *verb* put in danger

imperil » imperil*s*, imperill*ing*, imperill*ed*

imperious *adj* having an air of authority, haughty □ **imperiously** *adv*

impermanence *noun* lack of permanence, transitoriness □ **impermanent** *adj* □ **impermanently** *adv*

impermeable *adj* not able to be passed through: *impermeable by water*

impersonal *adj* **1** not influenced by personal feelings **2** not connected with any person □ **impersonally** *adv*

impersonate *verb* dress up as, or act the part of, someone □ **impersonation** *noun* □ **impersonator** *noun* someone who impersonates others

impertinent *adj* **1** cheeky, impudent **2** not pertinent, irrelevant □ **impertinence** *noun* □ **impertinently** *adv*

imperturbable *adj* not easily worried, calm □ **imperturbably** *adv*

impervious *adj*: **impervious to** not able to be affected by: *impervious to suggestions*

impetigo /imp*ə*t*ai*goh/ *noun* a kind of skin disease

impetuous *adj* rushing into action, rash □ **impetuosity** *noun* □ **impetuously** *adv*

impetus *noun* **1** moving force, motivation **2** impulse

impiety *noun* lack of respect for holy things □ **impious** *adj* □ **impiously** *adv*

impinge *verb* (with **on** or **upon**) **1** come in contact with **2** trespass on, interfere with

impious *see* **impiety**

implacable *adj* not able to be soothed or calmed □ **implacably** *adv*

implant *verb* fix in, plant firmly □ *noun* an artificial organ, graft *etc* inserted into the body

implement *noun* a tool □ *verb* carry out, fulfil (*eg* a promise) □ **implementation** *noun*

implicate *verb* bring in, involve:

the statement implicates you in the crime □ **implication** *noun* something meant though not actually said

implicit *adj* **1** understood, meant though not actually said **2** unquestioning: *implicit obedience* □ **implicitly** *adv*

implode *verb* collapse inwards suddenly □ **implosion** *noun*

implore *verb* beg, entreat

imply *verb* suggest: *her silence implies disapproval*

Do not confuse with: **infer**

impolite *adj* not polite, rude □ **impolitely** *adv* □ **impoliteness** *noun*

imponderable *adj* not able to be judged or evaluated

import *verb* bring in (goods) from abroad for sale □ *noun* **1** the act of importing **2** goods imported **3** meaning, significance □ **importation** *noun* □ **importer** *noun*

important *adj* worthy of attention; special □ **importance** *noun* □ **importantly** *adv*

importune *verb* keep asking for something □ **importunate** *adj* repeatedly asking □ **importunity** *noun*

impose *verb* **1** place (a tax *etc*) on **2** (with **on**) take advantage of, inconvenience □ **imposing** *adj* impressive, commanding attention □ **imposition** *noun* a burden, an inconvenience

impossible *adj* **1** not able to be done or to happen **2** extremely difficult to deal with, intolerable □ **impossibility** *noun* □ **impossibly** *adv*

impostor *noun* someone who pretends to be someone else in order to deceive □ **imposture** *noun* deceiving in this way

impotent *adj* **1** without power or effectiveness **2** of a male: unable to achieve or maintain an erection □ **impotence** *noun* □ **impotently** *adv*

impound *verb* seize possession of (something) by law

impoverish *verb* **1** make financially poor **2** lessen in quality: *an impoverished culture* □ **impoverishment** *noun*

impracticable *adj* not able to be done □ **impracticability** *noun*

⚠Do not confuse: **impracticable** and **impractical**

impractical *adj* lacking common sense □ **impracticality** *noun*

imprecation *noun* a curse

imprecise *adj* not precise, vague □ **imprecisely** *adv*

impregnable *adj* too strong to be taken by attack

impregnate *verb* **1** make pregnant **2** saturate: *impregnated with perfume*

impresario *noun* (*plural* **impresarios**) the organizer of an entertainment

impress *verb* **1** arouse the interest or admiration of **2** mark by pressing upon **3** fix deeply in the mind

impression *noun* **1** someone's thoughts or feelings about something: *my impression is that it's* *likely to rain* **2** a deep or strong effect: *the film left a lasting impression on me* **3** a mark made by impressing **4** a quantity of copies of a book printed at one time □ **impressionable** *adj* easily influenced or affected □ **impressionably** *adv* □ **impressionism** *noun* an artistic or literary style aiming to reproduce personal impressions of things or events □ **impressionist** *noun* **1** a follower of impressionism **2** an entertainer who impersonates people □ **impressive** *adj* having a strong effect on the mind □ **impressively** *adv*

imprimatur *noun* a licence to print or publish

imprint *verb* **1** stamp, press **2** fix in the mind □ *noun* **1** the printer's or publisher's name *etc* on a book **2** a common title for a series of related books from one publisher

imprison *verb* shut up as in a prison □ **imprisonment** *noun*

improbable *adj* not likely to happen □ **improbability** *noun*

impromptu *adj & adv* without preparation or rehearsal

improper *adj* **1** not suitable; wrong **2** indecent □ **improper fraction** a fraction greater than **1** (as $\frac{5}{4}$, $\frac{11}{8}$) □ **impropriety** *noun* (*plural* **improprieties**) something improper

improve *verb* make or become better □ **improvement** *noun*

improvident *adj* taking no thought for future needs □ **improvidence** *noun* □ **improvidently** *adv*

improvise *verb* **1** put together from available materials: *we improvised a stretcher* **2** create (a tune, script *etc*) spontaneously: *the actors had to improvise their lines* □ **improvisation** *noun*

impudent *adj* cheeky, insolent □ **impudence** *noun* □ **impudently** *adv*

impugn *verb* attack in words; criticize

impulse *noun* **1** a sudden force or push **2** a sudden urge resulting in sudden action □ **impulsive** *adj* acting on impulse, without taking time to consider □ **impulsively** *adv* □ **impulsiveness** *noun*

impunity *noun* freedom from punishment, injury or loss

impure *adj* mixed with other substances; not clean □ **impurity** *noun* (*plural* **impurities**)

impute *verb* think of as being caused, done *etc* by someone: *imputing the blame to others* □ **imputation** *noun* suggestion of fault; blame

in *prep* **1** showing position in space or time: *sitting in the garden/ born in the 60s* **2** showing state, manner *etc*: *in part/ in cold blood* □ *adv* **1** towards the inside, not out **2** in power **3** *informal* in fashion □ *adj* **1** that is in, inside or coming in **2** *informal* fashionable □ *abbrev* inch(es) □ **be in for 1** be trying to get (a prize *etc*) **2** be about to receive (trouble, punishment)

in- *prefix* **1** into, on, towards: *inshore* **2** not: *inaccurate*

inability *noun* (*plural* **inabilities**) lack of power, means *etc* (to do something)

in absentia in the absence of (someone receiving a degree *etc*)

inaccessible *adj* not able to be easily reached or obtained

inaccurate *adj* **1** not correct **2** not exact ▯ **inaccuracy** *noun* (*plural* **inaccuracies**)

inactive *adj* **1** not active **2** not working, doing nothing ▯ **inaction** *noun* lack of action ▯ **inactivity** *noun* idleness; rest

inadequate *adj* **1** not enough **2** unable to cope with a situation

inadmissible *adj* not allowable: *inadmissible evidence*

inadvertent *adj* unintentional

inadvisable *adj* not advisable, unwise

inalienable *adj* not able to be removed or transferred: *inalienable rights*

inalterable *adj* not able to be altered

inane *adj* silly, foolish ▯ **inanity** *noun* (*plural* **inanities**) an empty, meaningless remark

inanimate *adj* without life

inapplicable *adj* not applicable

inapposite *adj* not suitable, not relevant

inappropriate *adj* not suitable

inapt *adj* unsuitable, unfit ▯ **inaptitude** or **inaptness** *noun* unfitness, awkwardness

⚠Do not confuse with: **inept**

inarticulate *adj* **1** unable to express yourself clearly **2** said indistinctly

inasmuch as *conj* because, since

inattentive *adj* not paying attention ▯ **inattention** *noun*

inaudible *adj* not loud enough to be heard

inaugurate *verb* mark the beginning of (*eg* a presidency) with a ceremony ▯ **inaugural** *adj* ▯ **inauguration** *noun*

inauspicious *adj* unlucky, unlikely to end in success

inauthentic *adj* not authentic, false

inborn *adj* innate, natural: *inborn talent*

inbred *adj* **1** inborn **2** resulting from inbreeding ▯ **inbreeding** *noun* repeated mating within the same family

inc *abbrev* **1** incorporated **2** inclusive **3** including

Inca *noun* a member of a complex pre-Columbian civilization in Peru ▯ **Incan** *adj*

incalculable *adj* not able to be counted or estimated

incandescent *adj* white-hot

incantation *noun* a spell

incapable *adj* **1** unable (to do what is expected) **2** helpless (through drink *etc*)

incapacitate *verb* **1** take away power, strength or rights **2** disable ▯ **incapacity** *noun* **1** inability **2** disability

incarcerate *verb* imprison ▯ **incarceration** *noun*

incarnate *adj* having human form ▯ **incarnation** *noun* appearance in the form of a human body

incendiary *adj* meant for setting (buildings *etc*) on fire: *an incendiary bomb*

incense *verb* make angry □ *noun* a mixture of resins, gums, *etc* burned to give off fumes, *esp* in religious ceremonies

incentive *noun* something which encourages someone to do something

inception *noun* beginning

incessant *adj* going on without pause □ **incessantly** *adv*

incest *noun* illegal sexual intercourse between close relatives □ **incestuous** *adj* **1** involving incest **2** done within a closely-knit group

inch *noun* (*plural* **inches**) one twelfth of a foot (about 2.5 centimetres) □ *verb* move very gradually

inchoate /in*koh*eht/ *adj* in the early stages, rudimentary

incidence *noun* **1** the frequency of something occurring **2** a falling of a ray of light *etc*

incident *noun* a happening

incidental *adj* **1** happening in connection with something: *an incidental expense* **2** casual □ **incidentally** *adv* by the way

incinerate *verb* burn to ashes □ **incineration** *noun* □ **incinerator** *noun* an apparatus for burning rubbish *etc*

incipient *adj* beginning to exist: *an incipient dislike*

incise *verb* cut into, engrave

incision *noun* **1** cutting into something **2** a cut, a gash

incisive *adj* sharp, clear, firm

incisor *noun* a front tooth

incite *verb* move to action; urge on □ **incitement** *noun*

incivility *noun* (*plural* **incivilities**) impoliteness

inclement *adj* of weather: stormy □ **inclemency** *noun*

incline *verb* **1** lean, slope (towards) **2** bend, bow **3** have a liking for □ *noun* a slope □ **inclination** *noun* **1** liking, tendency **2** a slope, an angle □ **inclined** *adj*

include *verb* count in, along with others □ **inclusion** *noun* □ **inclusive** *adj* including everything mentioned: *from Tuesday to Thursday inclusive is 3 days*

incognito /ink*ə*g*nee*toh/ *adj & adv* in disguise, with identity concealed □ *noun* (*plural* **incognitos**) a disguise

incoherent *adj* **1** unconnected, rambling **2** speaking in an unconnected, rambling way □ **incoherence** *noun*

incombustible *adj* not able to be burned by fire

income *noun* **1** personal earnings **2** gain, profit

incoming *adj* approaching, next

incommode *verb* inconvenience, trouble

incommunicado *adj & adv* without means of communicating with others

incomparable *adj* without equal

incompatible *adj* **1** of statements:

contradicting each other **2** of people: not suited, bound to disagree □ **incompatibility** *noun*

incompetent *adj* not good enough at doing a job □ **incompetence** *noun* □ **incompetently** *adv*

incomplete *adj* not finished

incomprehensible *adj* not able to be understood, puzzling □ **incomprehensibly** *adv* □ **incomprehension** *noun*

inconceivable *adj* not able to be imagined or believed

inconclusive *adj* not leading to a definite decision or conclusion □

incongruous *adj* **1** not matching well **2** out of place, unsuitable □ **incongruity** (*plural* **incongruities**)

inconsequential *adj* unimportant □ **inconsequence** *noun* □ **inconsequentially** or **inconsequently** *adv*

inconsiderable *adj* slight, unimportant

inconsiderate *adj* not thinking of others

inconsistent *adj* not consistent, contradicting

inconsolable *adj* not able to be comforted

inconspicuous *adj* not noticeable

inconstant *adj* often changing □ **inconstancy** *noun*

incontinent *adj* **1** unable to control the bladder or bowels **2** uncontrolled, unrestrained □ **incontinence** *noun*

incontrovertible *adj* not to be doubted

inconvenient *adj* causing awkwardness or difficulty □ **inconvenience** *noun* □ *verb* cause trouble or difficulty to

incorporate *verb* **1** contain as parts of a whole: *the new building incorporates a theatre, cinema and restaurant* **2** include, take account of: *the new text incorporates the author's changes* □ **incorporated** *adj* (*short form* **inc**) formed into a company or society

incorrect *adj* wrong

incorrigible *adj* too bad to be put right or reformed

incorruptible *adj* **1** not able to be bribed **2** not likely to decay

increase *verb* grow, make greater or more numerous □ *noun* **1** growth **2** the amount added by growth □ **increasingly** *adv* more and more

incredible *adj* impossible to believe □ **incredibility** *noun* □ **incredibly** *adv*

> ⚠Do not confuse: **incredible** and **incredulous**

incredulous *adj* not believing what is said □ **incredulity** *noun* □ **incredulously** *adv*

increment *noun* an annual increase in a salary

incriminate *verb* show that (someone) has taken part in a crime

incubator *noun* **1** a large heated box for hatching eggs **2** a hospital crib for rearing premature babies □ **incubate** *verb* brood, hatch □ **incubation period** the time that it takes for a disease to develop from infection to the first symptoms

incubus *noun* an evil spirit in the shape of a man believed to have sexual intercourse with women in their sleep (*compare with*: **succubus**)

inculcate *verb* impress something on (the mind) by constant repetition

incumbent *adj* resting on (someone) as a duty: *it is incumbent upon me to warn you* ◊ someone who holds an official position

incunabula *noun plural* early printed books

incur *verb* bring (blame, debt *etc*) upon yourself

incur » incur*s*, incurr*ing*, incurr*ed*

incurable *adj* unable to be cured

incurious *adj* not curious, uninterested

incursion *noun* an invasion, a raid

indebted *adj* having cause to be grateful: *we are indebted to you for your kindness* ◊ **indebtedness** *noun*

indecent *adj* offending against normal or usual standards of (*esp* sexual) behaviour ◊ **indecency** *noun* ◊ **indecent assault** an assault involving indecency but not rape

indecipherable *adj* **1** illegible **2** incomprehensible

indecision *noun* slowness in making up your mind, hesitation ◊ **indecisive** *adj* **1** not coming to a definite result **2** unable to make up your mind

indecorous *adj* unseemly, inappropriate ◊ **indecorousness** or **indecorum** *noun*

indeed *adv* **1** in fact: *she is indeed a splendid cook* **2** (used for emphasis) really: *did he indeed?* ◊ *exclam* expressing surprise

indefatigable *adj* untiring

indefensible *adj* **1** unable to be defended **2** inexcusable

indefinable *adj* not able to be stated or described clearly

indefinite *adj* **1** not fixed, uncertain **2** without definite limits ◊ **indefinite article** the name given to the adjectives *a* and *an* ◊ **indefinitely** *adv* for an indefinite period of time

indehiscent *adj* of fruit: not opening when mature

indelible *adj* unable to be rubbed out or removed

indelicate *adj* impolite, rude ◊ **indelicacy** *noun*

indemnify *verb* **1** compensate for loss **2** exempt (from)

indemnify » indemnifi*es*, indemnify*ing*, indemnifi*ed*

indemnity *noun* **1** security from damage or loss **2** compensation for loss

indemonstrable *adj* not proveable

indent *verb* **1** begin a new paragraph by going in from the margin **2** (with **for**) apply for (stores, equipment *etc*) ◊ **indentation** *noun* **1** a hollow, a dent **2** an inward curve in an outline, coastline *etc*

indenture *noun* a written agreement □ *verb* bind by a written agreement

independent *adj* **1** free to think or act for yourself **2** not relying on someone else for support, guidance *etc* **3** of a country: self-governing □ **independence** *noun*

indescribable *adj* not able to be described

indestructible *adj* not able to be destroyed

indetectable *adj* not able to be detected

indeterminate *adj* not fixed, indefinite □

index *noun* (*plural* **indexes**) **1** an alphabetical list giving the page number of subjects mentioned in a book **2** an indication **3** (*plural* **indices**) *maths* an upper number which shows how many times a number is multiplied by itself (*eg* 4^3 means 4 x 4 x 4) **4** a numerical scale showing changes in the cost of living, wages *etc* □ **index-linked** *adj* of pensions *etc*: directly related to the cost-of-living index

Indian *adj*: **Indian corn** maize □ **Indian ink** a very black ink used by artists □ **Indian summer** a period of summer warmth in autumn

indiarubber *noun* a rubber eraser

indicate *verb* point out, show □ **indication** *noun* a sign □ **indicative** *adj* pointing out, being a sign of: *indicative of his attitude* □ **indicator** *noun* **1** something which indicates; a pointer **2** a flashing light on either side of a vehicle for signalling to other drivers

indices *plural* of **index** (sense **3**)

indict /in*dait*/ *verb* accuse formally of a crime □ **indictment** *noun*

indie *noun, informal* an independent record, film or television company

indifferent *adj* **1** neither very good nor very bad **2** (with **to**) showing no interest in □ **indifference** *noun*

indigenous *adj* native to a country or area

indigent *adj* poor, impoverished □ **indigence** *noun*

indigestion *noun* discomfort or pain experienced in digesting food □ **indigestible** *adj* difficult to digest

indignant *adj* angry, *esp* because of wrong done to yourself or others □ **indignation** *noun* □ **indignity** *noun* (*plural* **indignities**) **1** loss of dignity **2** insult

indigo *noun* a purplish-blue colour □ *adj* purplish-blue

indirect *adj* **1** not straight or direct **2** not affecting or affected directly □ **indirect speech** speech reported not in the speaker's actual words, *eg* they said *that they'd leave this morning* (*contrasted with*: **direct speech**) □ **indirect tax** a tax on particular goods, paid by the customer in the form of a higher price

indiscreet *adj* **1** rash, not cautious **2** giving away too much information □ **indiscretion** *noun* a rash or unwise remark or act

indiscriminate *adj* making no distinction between one person (or thing) and another: *indiscriminate buying/ indiscriminate killing*

indispensable *adj* not able to be done without, necessary

indisposed *adj* unwell ▯ **indisposition** *noun*

indisputable *adj* not able to be denied

indistinct *adj* not clear

indistinguishable *adj* **1** difficult to make out **2** too alike to tell apart

individual *adj* **1** relating to a single person or thing **2** distinctive, unusual ▯ *noun* a single person or thing ▯ **individualist** *noun* someone with an independent or distinctive lifestyle ▯ **individualistic** *adj* ▯ **individuality** *noun* **1** separate existence **2** the quality of standing out from others

indivisible *adj* not able to be divided

indoctrinate *verb* fill with a certain teaching or set of ideas

indolent *adj* lazy ▯ **indolence** *noun*

indomitable *adj* unconquerable, unyielding

indoor *adj* done *etc* inside a building ▯ **indoors** *adv* in or into a building *etc*

indubitable *adj* not to be doubted

induce *verb* **1** persuade **2** bring on, cause ▯ **inducement** *noun* something which encourages or persuades: *money is an inducement to work*

induct *verb* introduce, install

induction *noun* **1** the formal installation of someone in a new post **2** the production of electricity in something by placing it near an electric source **3** the drawing of conclusions from particular cases ▯ **inductive** *adj*

indulge *verb* **1** be inclined to give into the wishes of; spoil: *she indulges that child too much* **2** give way to, not restrain: *indulging his sweet tooth* ▯ **indulgence** *noun* **1** the act of indulging **2** a pardon for a sin ▯ **indulgent** *adj* not strict, kind

industrious *adj* hard-working

industry *noun* (*plural* **industries**) **1** a branch of trade or manufacture: *the clothing industry* **2** steady attention to work ▯ **industrial** *adj* ▯ **industrialist** *noun* someone involved in organizing an industry

inebriated *adj* drunk

inedible *adj* not eatable

ineffable *adj* not able to be described

ineffective *adj* useless, having no effect

ineffectual *adj* achieving nothing

inefficient *adj* **1** not efficient, not capable **2** wasting time, energy *etc* ▯ **inefficiency** *noun* (*plural* **inefficiencies**)

inelegant *adj* not graceful ▯ **inelegance** *noun*

ineligible *adj* not qualified, not suitable to be chosen

ineluctable *adj* unavoidable

inept *adj* clumsy, badly done ▯ **ineptitude** *noun*

⚠Do not confuse with: **inapt**

inequality *noun* (*plural*

inequalities) **1** lack of equality, unfairness **2** unevenness

inert *adj* **1** not moving or able to move **2** disinclined to move or act **3** not lively **4** chemically inactive □ **inertia** *noun* □ **inertness** *noun*

inescapable *adj* unable to be avoided

inessential *adj* not essential, unnecessary

inestimable *adj* too good to be estimated

inevitable *adj* not able to be avoided □ **inevitability** *noun*

inexact *adj* not exact, approximate

inexcusable *adj* not to be excused

inexhaustible *adj* very plentiful; not likely to be used up

inexorable *adj* not able to be persuaded; relentless

inexpensive *adj* cheap in price

inexperience *noun* lack of (skilled) knowledge or experience □ **inexperienced** *adj*

inexpert *adj* unskilled, amateurish

inexplicable *adj* not able to be explained

inexplicit *adj* not clear

inexpressible *adj* not able to be described in words

inextirpable *adj* not able to be destroyed

in extremis *adv* in desperate circumstances

inextricable *adj* not able to be disentangled

infallible *adj* **1** never making an error **2** certain to produce the desired result: *infallible cure* □ **infallibility** *noun*

infamous *adj* having a very bad reputation; notorious, disgraceful □ **infamy** *noun* public disgrace, notoriety

infant *noun* a baby □ **infancy** *noun* **1** early childhood, babyhood **2** the beginning of anything: *when psychiatry was in its infancy* □ **infanticide** *noun* **1** the murder of a child **2** a child murderer □ **infantile** *adj* **1** of babies **2** childish

infantry *noun* foot-soldiers

infatuated *adj* filled with foolish love □ **infatuation** *noun*

infect *verb* **1** fill with disease-causing germs **2** pass on disease to **3** pass on, spread (*eg* enthusiasm) □ **infection** *noun* **1** a disease which can be spread to others **2** something that spreads widely and affects many people □ **infectious** *adj* likely to spread from person to person

infelicitous *adj* unfortunate, inappropriate: *an infelicitous remark*

infer *verb* **1** reach a conclusion from facts or reasoning **2** hint □ **inference** *noun*

infer » infer*s*, inferr*ing*, inferr*ed*

⚠Do not confuse with: **imply**

inferior *adj* **1** lower in any way **2** not of best quality □ *noun* someone lower in rank *etc* □ **inferiority** *noun* □ **inferiority complex** a constant feeling that you are less good in some way than others

infernal *adj* **1** of hell **2** *informal* annoying, blasted ▫ **inferno** *noun* **1** hell **2** (*plural* **infernos**) a raging fire

infertile *adj* **1** of soil: not producing much **2** not able to bear children or young ▫ **infertility** *noun*

infest *verb* swarm over: *infested with lice*

infibulation *noun* the partial closing of the entrance to a woman's vagina to prevent sexual intercourse

infidel *adj* someone who does not believe in a particular religion (*esp* Christianity) ▫ **infidelity** *noun* unfaithfulness, disloyalty

infighting *noun* rivalry or quarrelling between members of the same group

infiltrate *verb* enter (an organization *etc*) secretly to spy or cause damage ▫ **infiltration** *noun*

infinite *adj* without end or limit ▫ **infinitesimal** *adj* very small ▫ **infinitive** *noun*, *grammar* the part of a verb which expresses the action but has no subject, *eg* I hate *to lose* ▫ **infinity** *noun* space or time without end

infirm *adj* feeble, weak ▫ **infirmary** *noun* (*plural* **infirmaries**) a hospital ▫ **infirmity** *noun* (*plural* **infirmities**) **1** a physical weakness **2** a character flaw

in flagrante delicto *adv* in the act, red-handed

inflame *verb* **1** make hot or red **2** arouse passion in ▫ **inflamed** *adj*

inflammable *adj* **1** easily set on fire **2** easily excited ▫ **inflammation** *noun* heat in a part of the body, with pain, redness and swelling

inflammatory *adj* arousing passion (*esp* anger)

inflate *verb* **1** blow up (a balloon, tyre *etc*) **2** puff up (with pride), exaggerate: *an inflated sense of her own importance* **3** increase to a great extent ▫ **inflation** *noun* **1** the act of inflating **2** an economic situation in which prices and wages keep forcing each other to increase

inflect *verb* **1** change the tone of (your voice) **2** vary the endings of (a verb) to show tense, number *etc* ▫ **inflection** *noun* ▫ **inflectional** *adj*

inflexible *adj* not yielding, unbending ▫ **inflexibility** *noun*

inflict *verb* bring down (blows, punishment *etc*) on ▫ **infliction** *noun*

in-flight *adj* happening or used during an air flight: *in-flight movie*

inflorescence *noun* a blossoming of flowers on a plant

inflow *noun* a flowing in, influx

influence *noun* the power to affect other persons or things ▫ *verb* have power over ▫ **influential** *adj*

influenza *noun* an infectious illness with fever, headache, muscle pains *etc*

influx *noun* **1** a flowing in **2** the arrival of large numbers of people

info *noun*, *informal* information

inform *verb* **1** give knowledge to **2** (with **on**) tell on, betray ▫ **informant** *noun* someone who informs ▫ **informer** *noun* someone who gives information to the police or authorities

informal *adj* not formal; relaxed, friendly ▫ **informality** *noun*

information *noun* knowledge, news ▫ **informative** *adj* giving information

infra- *prefix* below, beneath

infraction *noun* a violation, a breach

infra-red *adj* of rays of heat: with wavelengths longer than visible light

infrastructure *noun* inner structure, framework

infrequent *adj* rare, happening seldom ▫ **infrequently** *adv*

infringe *verb* break (a rule or law) ▫ **infringement** *noun*

infuriate *verb* drive into a rage ▫ **infuriating** *adj*

infuse *verb* **1** pour on or over **2** fill the mind (with a desire *etc*) ▫ **infusion** *noun* **1** the act of infusing **2** a tea formed by steeping a herb *etc* in water

ingenious *adj* **1** skilful in inventing **2** cleverly thought out ▫ **ingenuity** *noun* cleverness; quickness of ideas

> ⚠Do not confuse with: **ingenuous**

ingénue /unhzhehnoo/ *noun* a naive young girl

ingenuous *adj* frank; without cunning ▫ **ingenuousness** *noun*

> ⚠Do not confuse with: **ingenious**

inglenook *noun* a fireside corner

inglorious *adj* shameful, dishonourable

ingot *noun* a block of metal (*esp* gold or silver) cast in a mould

ingrained *adj* deeply fixed: *ingrained laziness*

ingratiate *verb* work your way into someone's favour by flattery *etc* ▫ **ingratiating** *adj*

ingratitude *noun* lack of gratitude or thankfulness

ingredient *noun* one of the things of which a mixture is made

ingrown *adj* of a nail: growing into the flesh

inhabit *verb* live in ▫ **inhabitant** *noun* someone who lives permanently in a place

inhale *verb* breathe in ▫ **inhalant** *noun* a medicine which is inhaled ▫ **inhalation** *noun* **1** the act of inhaling **2** a medicine which is inhaled ▫ **inhaler** *noun* a device for breathing in medicine, steam *etc*

inhere *verb* stick, be fixed (in)

inherent *adj* inborn, belonging naturally

inherit *verb* **1** receive property *etc* as an heir **2** get (a characteristic) from your parents *etc*: *she inherits her sense of humour from her father* ▫ **inheritance** *noun* something received by will when a relative dies ▫ **inheritor** *noun* an heir

inhibit *verb* hold back, prevent ▫ **inhibited** *adj* unable to let yourself go ▫ **inhibition** *noun* a holding back of natural impulses *etc*, restraint

inhospitable *adj* unwelcoming, unfriendly

inhuman *adj* not human; brutal ▫ **inhumanity** *noun*

inhumane *adj* cruel

inimical *adj* unfriendly, hostile

inimitable *adj* impossible to imitate

iniquity *noun* (*plural* **iniquities**) wickedness; a sin ▫ **iniquitous** *adj* unjust; wicked

initial *adj* of or at a beginning: *initial difficulties* ▫ *noun* the letter beginning a word, *esp* someone's name ▫ *verb* sign with the initials of your name

> **initial** *verb* » initial*s*, initial-l*ing*, initiall*ed*

initiate *verb* **1** begin, start: *initiate the reforms* **2** give first lessons to **3** admit formally to a society *etc* ▫ **initiation** *noun* ▫ **initiative** *noun* **1** the right to take the first step **2** readiness to take a lead

inject *verb* **1** force (a fluid *etc*) into the veins or muscles with a syringe **2** put (*eg* enthusiasm) into ▫ **injection** *noun*

in-joke *noun* a joke only understood by a particular group

injudicious *adj* unwise

injunction *noun* an official order or command

injure *verb* harm, damage, wrong ▫ **injured** *adj* hurt; offended ▫ **injury** *noun* (*plural* **injuries**) **1** hurt, damage, harm **2** a wrong

injustice *noun* **1** unfairness **2** a wrong

ink *noun* a coloured liquid used in writing, printing *etc* ▫ *verb* mark with ink ▫ **inkjet** *adj* a computer printer which forms characters by squirting a fine jet of ink at the paper ▫ **inky** *adj* **1** of or covered in ink **2** very dark

inkling *noun* a hint or slight sign

inlaid *past form* of **inlay**

inland *adj* **1** not beside the sea **2** happening inside a country ▫ *adv* towards the inner part of a country ▫ **inland revenue** taxes *etc* collected within a country

inlay *noun* decoration made by fitting pieces of different shapes and colours into a background ▫ *verb* fit into a background as decoration ▫ **inlaid** *adj*

> **inlay** *verb* » inlay*s*, inlay*ing*, inlaid

inlet *noun* a small bay

in loc cit *adv* in the place mentioned (from Latin *in loco citato*)

in loco parentis *adv* in the place of a parent

inmate *noun* a resident, an occupant (*esp* of an institution): *the inmates of the prison*

inmost *adj* the most inward, the farthest in

inn *noun* a small country hotel ▫ **innkeeper** *noun* someone who keeps an inn

innards *noun plural* **1** internal parts **2** entrails

innate *adj* inborn, natural

inner *adj* **1** farther in **2** of feelings

etc: hidden □ **innermost** *adj* farthest in; most secret

innings *noun sing* **1** a team's turn for batting in cricket **2** a turn, a go at something

innocent *adj* **1** not guilty, blameless **2** harmless **3** (with **of**) lacking, without □ **innocence** *noun*

innocuous *adj* not harmful

innovation *noun* something new

innuendo *noun* (*plural* **innuendoes**) an indirect reference, a hint

innumerable *adj* too many to be counted

innumerate *adj* not understanding arithmetic or mathematics □ **innumeracy** *noun*

inoculate *verb* inject (someone) with a mild form of a disease to prevent them later catching it □ **inoculation** *noun*

inoffensive *adj* harmless, giving no offence

inoperative *adj* not active, not working

inopportune *adj* at a bad or inconvenient time

inordinate *adj* going beyond the limit, unreasonably great

inorganic *adj* not of animal or vegetable origin

in-patient *noun* a patient who stays in a hospital during their treatment (*contrasted with*: **out-patient**)

input *noun* **1** an amount (of energy, labour *etc*) put into something **2** data fed into a computer (*contrasted with*: **output**)

inquest *noun* a legal inquiry into a case of sudden death

inquire or **enquire** *verb* ask □ **inquirer** or **enquirer** *noun* □ **inquiring** or **enquiring** *adj* questioning, curious: inquiring mind □ **inquiry** or **enquiry** *noun* (*plural* **inquiries** or **enquiries**) **1** a question; a search for information **2** an official investigation

inquisition *noun* a careful questioning or investigation □ **inquisitor** *noun* an official investigator

inquisitive *adj* **1** very curious **2** fond of prying, nosy □ **inquisitively** *adv* □ **inquisitiveness** *noun*

inroad *noun* a raid, an advance □ **make inroads into** use up large amounts of: *the holiday made inroads into their savings*

insane *adj* mad, not sane □ **insanity** *noun*

insanitary *adj* not sanitary; encouraging the spread of disease

insatiable *adj* not able to be satisfied: *insatiable appetite* □ **insatiably** *adv*

inscribe *verb* write or engrave (*eg* a name) on a book, monument *etc* □ **inscription** *noun* the writing on a book, monument *etc*

inscrutable *adj* not able to be understood, mysterious

insect *noun* a small six-legged creature with wings and a body divided into sections □ **insecticide** *noun* powder or liquid for killing insects ▢ **insectivorous** *adj* feeding on insects

insecure *adj* **1** not safe; not firm **2** lacking confidence, not feeling settled ▢ **insecurity** *noun*

inseminate *verb* **1** plant, introduce (into) **2** impregnate, *esp* artificially ▢ **insemination** *noun*

insensate *adj* without feeling, insensible

insensible *adj* **1** unconscious, unaware (of) **2** not having feeling

insensitive *adj* **1** (with **to**) not feeling: *insensitive to cold* **2** unsympathetic (to): *insensitive to her grief* **3** unappreciative, crass ▢ **insensitivity** *noun*

inseparable *adj* not able to be separated or kept apart ▢ **inseparably** *adv*

insert *verb* put in or among ▢ *noun* **1** a special feature added to a television programme *etc* **2** a separate leaflet or pullout section in a magazine *etc* ▢ **insertion** *noun*

in-service *adj* happening as part of someone's work: *in-service training*

insessorial *adj* of a bird's foot: adapted for perching

inset *noun* **1** an insert **2** a small picture, map *etc* in a corner of a larger one

inshore *adj* carried on near the shore ▢ *adv* to or near the shore

inside *noun* **1** the side, space or part within **2** indoors ▢ *adj* **1** being on or in the inside **2** indoor **3** coming from or done by someone within an organization: *inside information* ▢ *adv* to, in or on the inside ▢ *prep* to the inside of; within

insidious *adj* **1** likely to trap those who are not careful, treacherous **2** of a disease: coming on gradually and unnoticed

insight *noun* ability to consider a matter and understand it clearly

insignia *noun plural* signs or badges showing that someone holds an office, award *etc*

insignificant *adj* of little importance ▢ **insignificance** *noun* ▢ **insignificantly** *adv*

insincere *adj* not sincere ▢ **insincerity** *noun*

insinuate *verb* **1** hint (at a fault) **2** put in gradually and secretly **3** work yourself into (someone's favour *etc*) ▢ **insinuation** *noun* a sly hint

insipid *adj* **1** dull, without liveliness **2** tasteless, bland

insist *verb* **1** urge something strongly: *insist on punctuality* **2** refuse to give way, hold firmly to your intentions: *he insists on walking there* **3** go on saying (that): *she insists that she saw a UFO*

insistent *adj* **1** holding fast to what you claim **2** compelling attention ▢ **insistence** *noun* ▢ **insistently** *adv*

in situ *adv* in position, in place

insolent *adj* rude, impertinent, insulting ▢ **insolence** *noun*

insoluble *adj* **1** not able to be dissolved **2** of a problem: not able to be solved

insolvent *adj* not able to pay your debts, impoverished □ **insolvency** *noun*

insomnia *noun* sleeplessness □ **insomniac** *noun* someone who suffers from insomnia

insouciant *adj* indifferent, unconcerned □ **insouciance** *noun*

inspect *verb* **1** look carefully into, examine **2** look over (troops *etc*) ceremonially □ **inspection** *noun* careful examination □ **inspector** *noun* **1** an official who inspects **2** a police officer below a superintendent and above a sergeant in rank

inspiration *noun* **1** something or someone that influences or encourages others **2** a brilliant idea **3** breathing in □ **inspirational** *adj* inspiring

inspire *verb* **1** encourage, rouse **2** be the source of creative ideas **3** breathe in □ **inspired** *adj* **1** seeming to be aided by higher powers **2** brilliantly good

inst *abbrev* this month: *10th inst*

instability *noun* lack of steadiness or stability (*esp* in the personality)

install or **instal** *verb* **1** place in position, ready for use: *has the electricity being installed?* **2** introduce formally to a new job *etc* □ **installation** *noun*

install » install*s* or instal*s*, install*ing*, install*ed*

instalment *noun* **1** a part of a sum of money paid at fixed times until the whole amount is paid **2** one part of a serial story

instance *noun* an example, a particular case □ *verb* mention as an example □ **at the instance of** at the request of

instant *adj* **1** immediate, urgent **2** able to be prepared almost immediately: *instant coffee* □ *noun* **1** a very short time, a moment **2** point or moment of time: *I need it this instant* □ **instantaneous** *adj* done or happening very quickly □ **instantly** *adv* immediately

instead *adv* in place of someone or something: *you can go instead* □ **instead of** in place of

instep *noun* the arching, upper part of the foot

instigate *verb* stir up, encourage □ **instigation** *noun*

instil or **instill** *verb* put in little by little (*esp* ideas into the mind)

instil » instil*s* or instill*s*, instil*ling*, instill*ed*

instinct *noun* a natural feeling or knowledge which someone has without thinking and without being taught □ **instinctive** *adj* due to instinct

institute *verb* set up, establish, start □ *noun* a society, organization *etc* or the building it uses □ **institution** *noun* **1** an organization, building *etc* established for a particular purpose (*esp* care or education) **2** an established custom □ **institutional** *adj*

instruct *verb* **1** teach **2** direct, command □ **instruction** *noun* **1** teaching **2** a command **3** (**instructions**) rules showing how something is to be used □ **instructive** *adj* containing or giving information or knowledge □ **instructor** *noun*

instrument *noun* **1** something used for a particular purpose, a tool **2** a device for producing musical sounds, *eg* a piano, a harp □ **instrumental** *adj* **1** helpful in bringing (something) about **2** written for or played by musical instruments, without voice accompaniment □ **instrumentalist** *noun* someone who plays on a musical instrument

insubordinate *adj* rebellious, disobedient □ **insubordination** *noun*

insufferable *adj* not able to be endured

insufficient *adj* not enough □ **insufficiency** *noun*

insular *adj* **1** of an island or islands **2** narrow-minded, prejudiced □ **insularity** *noun*

insulate *verb* **1** cover with a material that will not let through electrical currents, heat, frost *etc* **2** cut off, isolate □ **insulation** *noun*

insulin *noun* a substance used in the treatment of diabetes

> Based on the Latin word for 'island', because insulin is secreted by cells called the *islets* of Langerhans

insult *verb* treat with scorn or rudeness □ *noun* a rude or scornful remark □ **insulting** *adj* scornful, rude

insuperable *adj* that cannot be overcome

insure *verb* arrange for payment of a sum of money on (something) if it should be lost, damaged, stolen *etc* □ **insurance** *noun*

> ⚠Do not confuse with: **ensure**

insurgent *adj* rising up in rebellion □ *noun* a rebel □ **insurgency** *noun*

insurmountable *adj* not able to be got over

insurrection *noun* a rising up in rebellion

intact *adj* whole, unbroken

intaglio *noun* **1** sculpture carved into a background, not raised from the surface (*contrasted with*: **relief**) **2** a gemstone with a hollowed-out design (*contrasted with*: **cameo**)

intake *noun* an amount of people or things taken in: *this year's intake of students*

intangible *adj* **1** not able to be felt by touch **2** difficult to define or describe, not clear

integer *noun* a whole number, not a fraction □ **integral** *adj* **1** of or essential to a whole: *an integral part of the machine* **2** made up of parts forming a whole

integrate *verb* **1** fit parts together to form a whole **2** enable (racial groups) to mix freely and live on equal terms □ **integration** *noun*

integrity *noun* **1** honesty **2** wholeness, completeness

integument *noun* an external layer, a covering

intellect *noun* the thinking power of the mind □ **intellectual** *adj* showing or requiring intellect □

noun someone of natural ability or with academic interests

intelligent *adj* clever, quick at understanding □ **intelligence** *noun* **1** mental ability **2** information sent, news □ **intelligible** *adj* able to be understood

intelligentsia *noun* the intellectuals within a particular society

intemperate *adj* **1** going beyond reasonable limits, uncontrolled **2** tending to drink too much alcohol □ **intemperance** *noun*

intend *verb* mean or plan to (do something)

intense *adj* **1** very great **2** tending to feel strongly, deeply emotional □ **intensely** *adv* □ **intensity** *noun* (*plural* **intensities**) strength, *eg* of feeling, colour *etc*

intensify *verb* increase, make more concentrated

intensify » intensifi*es*, intensify*ing*, intensifi*ed*

intensive *adj* very thorough, concentrated □ **intensive care** a unit in a hospital where a patient's condition is carefully monitored

intent *noun* purpose □ *adj* **1** with all your concentration (on), attentive **2** determined (on) □ **intention** *noun* **1** what someone means to do, an aim **2** meaning □ **intentional** *adj* done on purpose □ **intentionally** *adv*

inter- *prefix* between, among, together: *intermingle/ interplanetary*

inter *verb* bury □ **interment** *noun*

inter » inter*s*, interr*ing*, interr*ed*

interact *verb* act on one another □ **interactive** *adj* allowing two-way communication, *eg* between a computer and its user

inter alia *adv* among other things

intercede *verb* act as peacemaker between two people, nations *etc* □ **intercession** *noun* □ **intercessor** *noun*

intercept *verb* **1** stop or seize on the way **2** cut off, interrupt (a view, the light *etc*)

interchange *verb* **1** put each in the place of the other **2** alternate □ *noun* **1** the act of interchanging **2** a junction of two or more major roads on separate levels □ **interchangeable** *adj* able to be used one for the other

intercom *noun* a telephone system within a building, aeroplane *etc*

intercourse *noun* **1** communication **2** dealings between people *etc* **3** sexual intercourse

interdict *noun* an order forbidding something

interest *noun* **1** special attention, curiosity **2** someone's personal concern or field of study **3** advantage, benefit **4** a sum paid for the loan of money □ *verb* catch or hold the attention of □ **interested** *adj* having or taking an interest □ **interesting** *adj* holding the attention

interface *noun, comput* a connection between two parts of the same system

interfere *verb* **1** (with **in**) take part

in what is not your business, meddle **2** (with **with**) get in the way of, hinder: *interfering with her work* ▢ **interference** *noun* **1** the act of interfering **2** the spoiling of radio or television reception by another station or disturbance from traffic *etc*

interim *noun* time between; the meantime ▢ *adj* temporary

interior *adj* **1** inner **2** inside a building **3** inland ▢ *noun* **1** the inside of anything **2** the inland part of a country

interject *verb* **1** make a sudden remark in a conversation **2** exclaim ▢ **interjection** *noun* a word or phrase of exclamation, *eg* Ah! Oh dear!

interlock *verb* **1** lock or clasp together **2** fit into each other

interlocution *noun* dialogue, conversation ▢ **interlocutor** *noun* someone taking part in a conversation

interloper *noun* someone who enters without permission, an intruder

interlude *noun* **1** an interval **2** a short piece of music played between the parts of a play, film *etc*

intermarry *verb* **1** marry with members of another race *etc* **2** marry with members of the same group, race *etc*

intermediary *noun* (*plural* **intermediaries**) someone who acts between two people in trying to settle a quarrel

intermediate *adj* in the middle; coming between

interment *see* **inter**

> ⚠Do not confuse with: **internment**

intermezzo *noun* (*plural* **intermezzos**), *music* a short movement separating sections of a symphony

interminable *adj* never-ending, boringly long

intermission *noun* an interval, a pause

intermittent *adj* stopping every now and then and starting again

intern *verb* keep (someone from an enemy country) prisoner during a war ▢ **internee** *noun* someone who is confined in this way ▢ **internment** *noun*

> ⚠Do not confuse with: **interment**

internal *adj* **1** of the inner part, *esp* of the body **2** inside, within a country, organization *etc*: *internal affairs*

international *adj* **1** happening between nations **2** concerning more than one nation **3** world-wide ▢ *noun* a sports match between teams of two countries

internecine *adj* causing deaths on both sides: *internecine feud*

Internet *noun* an international computer network linking users through telephone lines

interplanetary *adj* between planets

interplay *noun* the action of one thing on another

interpose *verb* **1** place or come between **2** make (a remark *etc*) which interrupts someone

interpret *verb* **1** explain the meaning of something **2** translate **3** bring out the meaning of (music, a part in a play *etc*) in performance **4** take the meaning of something to be □ **interpretation** *noun* □ **interpreter** *noun* someone who translates (on the spot) the words of a speaker into another language

interregnum *noun* the time between the end of one reign and the beginning of the next

interrogate *verb* examine by asking questions □ **interrogation** *noun* □ **interrogative** *noun* a word used in asking a question, *eg* who? where? □ *adj* questioning □ **interrogator** *noun*

interrupt *verb* **1** stop (someone) while they are saying or doing something **2** stop doing (something) **3** get in the way of, cut off (a view *etc*) □ **interruption** *noun*

intersect *verb* of lines: meet and cross □ **intersection** *noun* **1** the point where two lines cross **2** a crossroads

intersperse *verb* scatter here and there in □ **interspersion** *noun*

interstice /in*tuhr*stis/ *noun* a small gap between things, a chink

intertwine *verb* twine or twist together

interval *noun* **1** a time or space between two things **2** a short pause in a programme *etc*

intervene *verb* **1** come or be between, or in the way **2** join in (in order to stop) a fight or quarrel between other persons or nations □ **intervention** *noun*

interview *noun* a formal meeting of one person with others to apply for a job, give information to the media *etc* □ *verb* **1** ask questions *etc* of in an interview **2** conduct an interview

intestate *adj* without having made a will: *he died intestate*

intestines *noun plural* the inside parts of the body, *esp* the bowels and passages leading to them □ **intestinal** *adj*

intimacy *noun* (*plural* **intimacies**) **1** close friendship **2** familiarity **3** sexual intercourse

intimate *adj* **1** knowing a lot about, familiar (with) **2** of friends: very close **3** private, personal: *intimate details* **4** having a sexual relationship (with) □ *noun* a close friend □ *verb* **1** hint **2** announce □ **intimately** *adv* □ **intimation** *noun* **1** a hint **2** announcement

intimidate *verb* frighten or threaten into submission □ **intimidating** *adj* □ **intimidation** *noun*

into *prep* **1** to the inside: *into the room* **2** towards: *into the millennium* **3** to a different state: *a tadpole changes into a frog* **4** *maths* expressing the idea of division: *2 into 4 goes twice*

intolerable *adj* not able to be endured

intolerant *adj* not willing to put up with (people of different ideas, religion *etc*) ▫ **intolerance** *noun*

intone *verb* speak in a singing manner, chant ▫ **intonation** *noun* the rise and fall of the voice

intoxicate *verb* **1** make drunk **2** enthuse, excite ▫ **intoxicant** *noun* a strong drink ▫ **intoxication** *noun* drunkenness

intra- *prefix* within

intractable *adj* difficult, stubborn ▫ **intractability** *noun*

intransigent *adj* refusing to come to an agreement ▫ **intransigence** *noun*

intransitive *adj*, *gram* of a verb: not needing an object, *eg* to *go*, to *fall*

in-tray *noun* an office tray for letters and work still to be dealt with (*contrasted with*: **out-tray**)

intrepid *adj* without fear, brave ▫ **intrepidity** *noun*

intricate *adj* complicated, having many twists and turns ▫ **intricacy** *noun* (*plural* **intricacies**)

intrigue *noun* **1** a secret plot **2** a secret love affair ▫ *verb* **1** plot, scheme **2** rouse the curiosity of, fascinate ▫ **intriguing** *adj*

intrinsic *adj* belonging to something as part of its nature

introduce *verb* **1** bring in or put in **2** make (someone) known to another person ▫ **introduction** *noun* **1** the introducing of someone or thing **2** an essay at the beginning of a book *etc* briefly explaining its contents ▫ **introductory** *adj* coming at the beginning

introspective *adj* inward-looking, fond of examining your own thoughts and feelings ▫ **introspection** *noun*

intrude *verb* thrust yourself into somewhere uninvited ▫ **intruder** *noun* someone who breaks in or intrudes ▫ **intrusion** *noun* ▫ **intrusive** *adj*

intuition *noun* **1** ability to understand something without thinking it out **2** an instinctive feeling or belief

Inuit *noun* **1** the Eskimo people, *esp* those in Greenland, Canada and N Alaska **2** their language

Inuktitut *noun* the Inuit language spoken in the Canadian Arctic

inundate *verb* **1** flood **2** overwhelm: *inundated with work* ▫ **inundation** *noun*

inure *verb* make accustomed (to): *inured to pain*

invade *verb* **1** enter (a country *etc*) as an enemy to take possession **2** interfere with (someone's rights, privacy *etc*) ▫ **invader** *noun* ▫ **invasion** *noun*

invalid[1] /in*va*lid/ *adj* not valid, not legally effective ▫ **invalidate** *verb* make invalid ▫ **invalidity** *noun*

invalid[2] /*inv*əlid/ *noun* someone who is ill or disabled ▫ *adj* ▫ *verb* **1** make an invalid of **2** (with **out**) discharge from the army as an invalid

invaluable *adj* priceless, essential

invariable *adj* unchanging □ **invariably** *adv* always

invasion *see* **invade**

invective *noun* abusive words; scorn

inveigle *verb* coax, entice □ **inveiglement** *noun*

invent *verb* **1** make or think up for the first time **2** make up (a story, an excuse) □ **invention** *noun* something invented □ **inventive** *adj* good at inventing, resourceful □ **inventor** *noun*

inventory *noun* (*plural* **inventories**) a detailed list of contents

invert *verb* **1** turn upside down **2** reverse the order of □ **inverse** *adj* opposite, reverse □ *noun* the opposite □ **inversely** *adv* □ **inversion** *noun* **1** a turning upside-down **2** a reversal □ **inverted commas** *noun plural* commas written or printed upside down (‘ ’ or “ ”) to show where direct speech begins and ends

invertebrate *adj* of an animal: not having a backbone □ *noun* an animal with no backbone, *eg* a worm or insect

invest *verb* **1** put money in a firm, property *etc* to make a profit **2** give a particular quality to **3** *old* besiege □ **investiture** *noun* a ceremony before taking on an important office □ **investment** *noun* **1** money invested **2** something in which money is invested **3** *old* a siege □ **investor** *noun* someone who invests

investigate *verb* search into with care □ **investigation** *noun* a careful search □ **investigator** *noun*

inveterate *adj* **1** firmly fixed in a habit: *an inveterate gambler* **2** deep-rooted □ **inveteracy** *noun*

invidious *adj* likely to cause ill-will or envy

invigilate *verb* supervise (an examination *etc*) □ **invigilator** *noun*

invigorate *verb* strengthen, refresh □ **invigorating** *adj*

invincible *adj* not able to be defeated or overcome □ **invincibility** *noun*

inviolable *adj* sacred, not to be disregarded or harmed □ **inviolability** *noun* □ **inviolate** *adj* not violated, free from harm *etc*

invisible *adj* not able to be seen □ **invisibility** *noun*

invite *verb* **1** ask (someone) to do something, *esp* to come for a meal *etc* **2** seem to ask for: *inviting punishment* □ **invitation** *noun* a request to do something □ **inviting** *adj* tempting, attractive

in vitro *adj* of fertilization: carried out in a test tube, in a laboratory

invocation *see* **invoke**

invoice *noun* a letter sent with goods with details of price and quantity □ *verb* make such a list

invoke *verb* **1** call upon in prayer **2** ask for (*eg* help) □ **invocation** *noun*

involuntary *adj* not done willingly or intentionally □ **involuntarily** *adv*

involve *verb* **1** have as a consequence, require **2** take part (in), be concerned (in): *involved in* *publishing/ involved in the scandal* ▫ **involved** *adj* complicated ▫ **involvement** *noun*

invulnerable *adj* not vulnerable, not able to be hurt ▫ **invulnerability** *noun*

inward *adj* **1** placed within **2** situated in the mind or soul ▫ *adv* (also **inwards**) towards the inside ▫ **inwardly** *adv* **1** within **2** in your heart, privately

in-your-face *adj, slang* aggressive, demanding attention

IOC *abbrev* International Olympic Committee

iodine *noun* a liquid chemical used to kill germs

ion *noun* an electrically-charged atom or group of atoms ▫ **ionizer** *noun* a device which sends out negative ions to improve the quality of the air

iota *noun* a little bit, a jot

IOU *short for* I owe you, a note given as a receipt for money borrowed

IPA *abbrev* International Phonetic Alphabet

ipso facto *adv* by that fact, thereby

IQ *abbrev* intelligence quotient

IRA *abbrev* Irish Republican Army

irascible *adj* easily made angry ▫ **irascibility** *noun*

irate *adj* angry

ire *noun, formal* anger

iridescent *adj* **1** coloured like a rainbow **2** shimmering with changing colours ▫ **iridescence** *noun*

iridology *noun* diagnosis of illness by examining the irises of someone's eyes ▫ **iridologist** *noun*

iris *noun* (*plural* **irises**) **1** the coloured part of the eye around the pupil **2** a lily-like flower which grows from a bulb

irk *verb* weary, annoy ▫ **irksome** *adj* tiresome

iron *noun* **1** a common metal, widely used to make tools *etc* **2** an iron instrument: *a branding iron* **3** a golf club (originally with an iron head) **4** an appliance for pressing clothes **5** (**irons**) a prisoner's chains ▫ *adj* **1** made of iron **2** stern, resolute: *iron will* **3** of a rule: not to be broken ▫ *verb* **1** press (clothes) with an iron **2** (with **out**) smooth out (difficulties) ▫ **Iron Age** human culture at the stage of using iron for tools *etc* ▫ **Iron Curtain** *hist* the border separating the West from the countries of the former Soviet bloc

ironmonger *noun* a shopkeeper selling household tools, gardening equipment *etc* ▫ **ironmongery** *noun* goods sold by an ironmonger

irony *noun* (*plural* **ironies**) **1** a form of humour in which someone says the opposite of what is obviously true **2** an absurd contradiction or paradox: *the irony of it was that she would have given him the money if he hadn't stolen it* ▫ **ironic** or **ironical** *adj* ▫ **ironically** *adv*

irrational *adj* against logic or common-sense ▫ **irrationality** *noun*

irregular *adj* **1** uneven, variable **2** against the rules ▫ **irregularity** *noun* (*plural* **irregularities**)

irrelevant *adj* not having to do with what is being spoken about □ **irrelevancy** *noun* (*plural* **irrelevancies**)

irreparable *adj* not able to be repaired

irreplaceable *adj* too good or rare to be replaced

irrepressible *adj* not restrainable or controllable

irreproachable *adj* not able to be criticized or blamed

irresistible *adj* too strong or too charming to be resisted

irresolute *adj* not able to make up your mind or keep to a decision

irrespective *adj* taking no account of: *irrespective of the weather*

irresponsible *adj* having no sense of responsibility, thoughtless

irreverent *adj* having no respect, *eg* for holy things □ **irreverence** *noun*

irrevocable *adj* not to be changed

irrigate *verb* supply (land) with water by canals *etc* □ **irrigation** *noun*

irritate *verb* **1** annoy **2** cause discomfort to (the skin, eyes *etc*) □ **irritable** *adj* cross, easily annoyed □ **irritation** *noun*

ISBN *abbrev* International Standard Book Number, an identification number given to a published book

Islam *noun* **1** the Muslim religion, founded by the prophet Mohammed **2** the Muslim world □ **Islamic** *adj*

island *noun* **1** an area of land surrounded by water **2** an isolated place, a haven □ **islander** *noun* an inhabitant of an island □ **traffic island** a platform in the middle of a road for pedestrians to stand on while waiting to cross

isle *noun, formal* an island

-ism *suffix* **1** indicating a system, set of beliefs *etc*: *socialism/ Catholicism* **2** indicating prejudice against a particular group: *racism/ sexism*

ISO *abbrev* International Standards Organization

isobar *noun* a line on the map connecting places where atmospheric pressure is the same

isolate *verb* **1** place or keep separate from other people or things **2** consider (something) by itself: *isolate the problem* □ **isolation** *noun*

isomer *noun* a chemical substance with the same molecular weight as another, but with its atoms in a different arrangement □ **isomeric** *adj*

isosceles *adj* of a triangle: having two sides equal (*compare with*: **equilateral**)

isotherm *noun* a line on the map connecting places which have the same temperature

isotope *noun* an atom with the same atomic number as, but different mass number from, another

issue *verb* **1** go or come out **2** give out (orders *etc*) **3** publish ▯ *noun* **1** a flowing out **2** *formal* children: *he died without issue* **3** the copies of a book published at one time **4** one number in a series of magazines *etc* **5** result, consequence **6** the matter which is being discussed ▯ **take issue with** disagree with

isthmus *noun* (*plural* **isthmuses**) a narrow neck of land connecting two larger portions

it *pronoun* **1** the thing spoken of: *I meant to bring the book, but I left it at home* **2** used in sentences with no definite subject: *it snowed today/ it is too late now* **3** used in phrases as a kind of object: *go it alone/ brave it out*

italics *noun plural* a kind of type which *slopes to the right* ▯ **italicize** *verb* print in italics

itch *noun* **1** an irritating feeling in the skin, made better by scratching **2** a strong desire ▯ *verb* **1** have an itch **2** be impatient (to do), long (to): *itching to open his presents* ▯ **itchy** *adj*

item *noun* a separate article or detail in a list ▯ **itemize** *verb* list item by item, detail

itinerant *adj* travelling from place to place, *esp* on business ▯ *noun* someone who travels around, *esp* a tramp, pedlar *etc*

itinerary *noun* (*plural* **itineraries**) a route or plan of a journey

its *adj* belonging to it: *keep the hat in its box*

⚠Do not confuse: **its** and **it's**

it's *short for* it is

itself *pronoun* **1** used reflexively: *the cat licked itself* **2** used for emphasis or contrast: *after I've read the introduction, I'll begin the book itself*

ITV *abbrev* Independent Television

IU or **IUD** *abbrev* intra-uterine (contraceptive) device

IV *abbrev* intravenous (drip)

IVF *abbrev* in vitro fertilization

ivory *noun* (*plural* **ivories**) the hard white substance which forms the tusks of the elephant, walrus *etc*

ivy *noun* (*plural* **ivies**) a creeping evergreen plant

J

jab *verb* poke, stab □ *noun* **1** a poke, a stab **2** *informal* an injection

> **jab** *verb* » jab*s*, jabb*ing*, jabb*ed*

jabber *verb* talk rapidly and indistinctly

jabot /*zha*boh/ *noun* a lace frill on the front of a blouse or shirt

jacinth *noun* **1** a type of precious stone **2** a reddish-orange colour

jack *noun* **1** a device with a lever for raising heavy weights **2** (*also called* **knave** the playing-card between ten and queen □ **jackboots** *noun plural* large boots reaching above the knee □ **jack-in-the-box** *noun* a doll fixed to a spring inside a box that leaps out when the lid is opened □ **jack-knife** *noun* **1** a large folding knife **2** a dive forming a sharp angle and then straightening □ *verb* of a vehicle and its trailer: swing together to form a sharp angle □ **jack up 1** raise with a jack **2** raise (prices *etc*) steeply

jackal *noun* a dog-like wild animal

jackass *noun* **1** a male ass **2** *informal* an idiot □ **laughing jackass** (*also called* **kookaburra**) the Australian giant kingfisher

jackdaw *noun* a type of small crow

jacket *noun* **1** a short coat **2** a loose paper cover for a book □ **jacket potato** a baked potato

jackpot *noun* a fund of prize money which increases until someone wins it

Jacobean *noun, hist* relating to the period of James VI of Scotland, I of England (1603–1625)

Jacobite *noun, hist* a supporter of James VII of Scotland, II of England and his descendants

jacuzzi *noun, trademark* a bath fitted with a device that agitates the water

jade *noun* a hard green mineral substance used for ornaments □ **jaded** *adj* tired

jagged *adj* rough-edged, uneven

jaguar *noun* a S American animal like a leopard

jail *noun* a prison □ **jailbird** *noun* a convict or ex-convict □ **jailer** *noun* someone in charge of a jail or prisoners

Jain *noun* a member of an ascetic Indian religion similar to Buddhism

jalapeño /hal*ə*pehnyoh/ *noun* a hot Mexican chilli pepper

jalopy /j*ə*lopee/ *noun* an old motor car or aeroplane

jam *noun* **1** fruit boiled with sugar till it is set **2** a crush **3** a blockage caused by crowding **4** *informal* a difficult situation □ *verb* **1** press or squeeze tight **2** crowd full **3** stick and so be unable to move: *the back wheel has jammed* **4** cause interference with another radio station's broadcast **5** *music* play with other musicians in an improvised style □ **jam-packed** *adj* packed tightly, congested ▯ **jam session** an informal gathering to play improvised music

jam *verb* » jam*s*, jamm*ing*, jamm*ed*

jamb *noun* the side post of a door

jamboree *noun* **1** a large, lively gathering **2** a rally of Scouts

JANET /*janət*/ *abbrev* Joint Academic Network, a computer network linking universities in the UK

jangle *verb* **1** make a harsh ringing noise **2** irritate

janitor *noun* **1** a caretaker **2** a doorkeeper

January *noun* the first month of the year

jape *noun, informal* a trick, a practical joke

japonica *noun* a Japanese flowering plant

jar *noun* a glass or earthenware bottle with a wide mouth ▯ *verb* **1** have a harsh, startling effect **2** be discordant, not agree ▯ **jarring** *adj* harsh, startling

jar *verb* » jar*s*, jarr*ing*, jarr*ed*

jargon *noun* special words used within a particular trade, profession *etc*

jasmine *noun* a shrub with white or yellow sweet-smelling flowers

jaundice *noun* a disease which causes the skin and eyes to turn yellow ▯ **jaundiced** *adj* **1** having jaundice **2** discontented, bitter

jaunt *noun* a short journey for pleasure

jaunty *adj* cheerful, gay ▯ **jauntily** *adv*

javelin *noun* a long spear for throwing

jaw *noun* **1** the lower part of the face, including the mouth and chin **2** (**jaws**) an animal's mouth

jay *noun* a brightly-coloured bird like a crow

jaywalker *noun* someone who walks carelessly among traffic

jazz *noun* a style of music with a strong rhythm, syncopation, improvisation *etc*, based on African-American folk music ▯ **jazzy** *adv* colourful, flamboyant ▯ **jazz something up** make it more lively or colourful

jealous *adj* **1** wanting to have what someone else has; envious **2** guarding closely (possessions *etc*) ▯ **jealousy** *noun*

jeans *noun plural* denim trousers

jeep *noun* a small army motor vehicle

jeer *verb* make fun of, scoff ▯ *noun* a scoff

Jehovah *noun* the Hebrew God of the Old Testament

jejune /*jəjoon*/ *adj* naive, inexperienced

From a Latin word meaning 'hungry' or 'fasting'

jelly *noun* (*plural* **jellies**) **1** fruit juice boiled with sugar till it becomes firm **2** a transparent wobbly food, often fruit-flavoured

3 an extremely nervous person

jellyfish *noun* a sea animal with a jelly-like body

jemmy *noun* (*plural* **jemmies**) a burglar's iron tool

jeopardy *noun* danger **jeopardize** *verb* put in danger or at risk

> Originally a gambling term, based on French *jeu parti* meaning 'even chance'

jerboa *noun* a small rat-like desert animal with very long hindlegs

jeremiad *noun* a long, woeful story

jerk *verb* give a sudden sharp movement *noun* a sudden sharp move **jerkily** *adv* **jerky** *adj* moving or coming in jerks

jerkin *noun* a type of short coat

jeroboam *noun* a bottle of wine equivalent to 6 standard bottles, or to 4 bottles of champagne

jerry-built *adj* hastily and badly built

jersey *noun* (*plural* **jerseys**) a sweater, pullover

jest *noun* a joke *verb* joke

jester *noun*, *hist* a fool employed to amuse a royal court *etc*

jet *noun* **1** a hard black mineral, used for ornaments and jewellery **2** a spout of flame, air or liquid **3** a jet plane **jet-black** *adj* very black **jet lag** tiredness caused by the body's inability to cope with being in a new time zone **jet plane** an aeroplane driven by jet propulsion **jet propulsion** high speed forward motion produced by sucking in air or liquid and forcing it out from behind **jet set** rich people who enjoy frequent expensive holidays **jet stream 1** a band of high-speed winds far above the earth **2** the exhaust of a jet engine

jetsam *noun* goods thrown overboard and washed ashore

jettison *verb* **1** throw overboard **2** abandon

jetty *noun* (*plural* **jetties**) a small pier

Jew *noun* someone who is of the race or religion of the Israelites **Jewish** *adj* of the Jews **Jew's harp** a small harp-shaped musical instrument played between the teeth

jewel *noun* **1** a precious stone **2** someone or something highly valued **jewelled** or *US* **jeweled** *adj* set with jewels **jeweller** or *US* **jeweler** *noun* someone who makes or sells articles made of precious jewels and metals **jewellery** or *US* **jewelry** *noun* articles made or sold by a jeweller

Jezebel *noun* a wicked, scheming woman

jib *noun* **1** a three-cornered sail in front of a ship's foremast **2** the jutting-out arm of a crane **jib at** refuse to do, object to

> **jib** *verb* » jib*s*, jibb*ing*, jibb*ed*

jibe or **gibe** *verb* jeer, scoff *noun* a jeer

Jiffy bag *trademark* a padded envelope for posting

jig *noun* a lively dance or tune *verb* jump about

jig *verb* » jig*s*, jigg*ing*, jigg*ed*

jiggery-pokery *noun, informal* trickery, deceit

jigsaw *noun* or **jigsaw puzzle** a puzzle consisting of many different shaped pieces that fit together to form a picture

jihad /jee*had*/ *noun* an Islamic holy war

jilt *verb* cast aside (a lover) after previously encouraging them

jingle *noun* **1** a clinking sound like that of coins **2** a simple rhyme

jingoism *noun* chauvinism, narrow-minded nationalism ◊ **jingoistic** *adj*

jinx *noun* someone or something thought to bring bad luck

Probably from the *Jynx* bird which was once invoked in spells and charms

jitterbug *noun* a dance to rock music

jitters *noun plural*: **have the jitters** be very nervous

jittery *adj* very nervous, shaking with nerves

jive *noun* a style of fast dancing to jazz music

jo *noun, Scot* sweetheart, dear

job *noun* **1** someone's daily work **2** any piece of work ◊ **jobbing** *adj* doing odd jobs of work for payment: *jobbing gardener* ◊ **job centre** a government office where information about available jobs is shown ◊ **job-lot** *noun* a collection of odds and ends ◊ **job-share** *noun* the division of one job between two people, each working part-time

jock *noun, slang* **1** *derog* a Scotsman or Scotswoman **2** *US* an athletic college student

jockey *noun* (*plural* **jockeys**) someone who rides a horse in a race ◊ *verb* push your way into a good position

jockstrap *noun* a genital support for men while playing sports

jocose *adj* humorous, jokey ◊ **jocosity** *noun*

jocular *adj* joking, merry ◊ **jocularity** *noun* ◊ **jocularly** *adv*

jodhpurs *noun plural* riding breeches, fitting tightly from knee to ankle

joey *noun* (*plural* **joeys**), *Austral informal* a young kangaroo

jog *verb* **1** nudge, push slightly **2** run at a gentle pace ◊ *noun* ◊ **jogger** *noun* someone who runs gently to keep fit ◊ **jogging** *noun*

jog *verb* » jog*s*, jogg*ing*, jogg*ed*

joggle *verb* shake slightly

joie de vivre enthusiasm for life; sparkle, spirit

join *verb* **1** put or come together **2** connect, fasten **3** become a member of **4** come and meet ◊ *noun* the place where two or more things join ◊ **joiner** *noun* someone who makes wooden fittings, furniture *etc* ◊ **joint** *noun* **1** the place where two or more things join **2** the place where two bones are joined, *eg* an elbow or knee **3** meat containing a bone ◊ *adj* **1** united **2** shared among more than one ◇ **jointly** *adv* together ◇ **join battle** begin fighting in battle

joist *noun* the beam to which the boards of a floor or the laths of a ceiling are nailed

jojoba /hoh*hoh*bə/ *noun* a desert shrub with edible seeds whose oil is used in cosmetics

joke *noun* something said or done to cause laughter ◇ *verb* make a joke, tease ◇ **joker** *noun* **1** someone who jokes **2** an extra playing-card in a pack

jolly *adj* merry ◇ **jollification** *noun* noisy festivity or celebration ◇ **jolliness** or **jollity** *noun* merriment

jollyboat *noun* a small boat belonging to a ship

jolt *verb* **1** shake suddenly **2** go forward with sudden jerks ◇ *noun* a sudden jerk

joss-stick *noun* a stick of gum which gives off a sweet smell when burned

jostle *verb* push or knock against

jot *noun* a very small part ◇ *verb* write down hurriedly or briefly ◇ **jotter** *noun* a book for taking notes

jot *verb* » jot*s*, jott*ing*, jott*ed*

joule *noun* a unit of energy

journal *noun* **1** a personal account of each day's events; a diary **2** a newspaper, a magazine ◇ **journalism** *noun* the business of recording daily events for the media ◇ **journalist** *noun* ◇ **journalistic** *adj*

journey *noun* (*plural* **journeys**) a distance travelled ◇ *verb* travel ◇ **journeyman** *noun* someone whose apprenticeship is finished

journo *noun* (*plural* **journos**), *informal* a journalist

joust *noun, hist* the armed contest between two knights on horseback at a tournament ◇ *verb* fight on horseback at a tournament

jovial *adj* cheerful, good-humoured ◇ **joviality** *noun*

jowl *noun* the lower part of the jaw or cheek

joy *noun* gladness ◇ **joyful** or **joyous** *adj* full of joy ◇ **joyless** *adj* dismal ◇ **joy-ride** *noun* a reckless trip for amusement in a stolen car ◇ **joystick** *noun*

JP *abbrev* Justice of the Peace

Jr *abbrev* Junior: *John Brown Jr*

jubilant *adj* full of rejoicing, triumphant ◇ **jubilation** *noun*

jubilee *noun* celebrations arranged for the anniversary of a wedding, coronation *etc*

From a Hebrew word for 'ram's horn', which was blown to announce the start of a celebratory Jewish year

Judaism *noun* the Jewish religion or way of life ◇ **Judaic** *adj*

Judas *noun* a traitor

judder *noun* a strong vibration or jerky movement

judge *verb* **1** make a decision on (a law case) after hearing all the evidence **2** form an opinion **3** decide the winners in a competition *etc* ◇ *noun* **1** an official who hears cases in the law-courts and decides on them according to the country's or state's laws **2** someone skilled in evaluating anything: *a good judge of character* □ **judgement** or **judgment** *noun* **1** a decision in a law case **2** an opinion **3** good sense in forming opinions

judicial *adj* of a judge or court of justice □ **judicially** *adv*

judiciary *noun* the judges of a country or state

judicious *adj* wise □ **judiciously** *adv*

judo *noun* a Japanese form of wrestling for self-defence

jug *noun* a dish for liquids with a handle and a shaped lip for pouring

juggernaut *noun* a large articulated lorry

> From a Hindi word for a large wagon used to carry the image of the god Krishna in religious processions

juggle *verb* **1** toss a number of things (balls, clubs *etc*) into the air and catch them in order **2** handle or present in a deceitful way □ **juggler** *noun*

jugular vein the large vein at the side of the neck

juice *noun* the liquid in vegetables, fruits *etc* □ **juicy** *adj* **1** full of juice **2** sensational, scandalous

jujitsu *noun* a Japanese martial art similar to judo

jujube /*joo*joob/ *noun* a spiny shrub with a dark red fruit

jukebox *noun* a coin-operated machine which plays selected records automatically

julep *noun, US* a sweet cocktail made with alcohol, sugar and mint

julienne *verb* cut (vegetables *etc*) into thin strips for cooking

July *noun* the seventh month of the year

Juma *noun* the Islamic Sabbath, held on Friday

jumble *verb* throw together without order, muddle □ *noun* a confused mixture □ **jumble sale** a sale of odds and ends, cast-off clothing *etc*

jumbo *noun* (*plural* **jumbos**) a child's name for an elephant □ *adj* very large □ **jumbo jet** a large jet aircraft

jump *verb* **1** leap **2** make a sudden startled movement □ *noun* **1** a leap **2** a sudden start □ **jumpily** *adv* □ **jumpy** *adj* easily startled □ **jumpsuit** *noun* a one-piece garment combining trousers and top

jumper *noun* a sweater, a jersey

junction *noun* a place or point of joining, *esp* of roads or railway lines

juncture *noun* point: *it's too early to decide at this juncture*

June *noun* the sixth month of the year

jungle *noun* a dense growth of trees and plants in tropical areas

junior *adj* **1** younger **2** in a lower class or rank □ *noun* someone younger: *he is my junior*

juniper *noun* an evergreen shrub

with berries and prickly leaves

junk[1] *noun* worthless articles, rubbish □ **junk bond** a bond offering a high yield but low security □ **junk food** convenience food with little nutritional value □ **junkie** or **junky** *noun* (*plural* **junkies**) a drug addict □ **junk mail** unsolicited mail, *esp* advertising material

junk[2] *noun* a Chinese flat-bottomed sailing ship, high in the bow and stern

junket *noun* a dish made of curdled milk sweetened and flavoured □ **junketing** *noun* feasting, merriment

junta /hoontə/ *noun* a government formed following a successful coup d'état

jurisdiction *noun* **1** a legal authority or power **2** the district over which a judge, court *etc* has power

jurisprudence *noun* the study or knowledge of law

jury *noun* (*plural* **juries**) **1** a group of men or women selected to reach a decision on whether an accused prisoner is guilty or not **2** a group of judges for a competition *etc* □ **juror, juryman** or **jurywoman** *noun* someone who serves on a jury

just *adj* **1** fair in judgement; unbiased **2** correct □ *adv* **1** exactly: *just right* **2** not long since: *only just arrived* **3** merely, only **4** really: *just beautiful* □ **justly** *adv*

justice *noun* **1** fairness in making judgements **2** what is right or rightly deserved **3** a judge □ **Justice of the Peace** (*short form* **JP**) a citizen who acts as a judge for certain matters

justifiable *adj* able to be justified or defended □ **justifiably** *adv*

justify *verb* **1** prove or show to be right or desirable **2** *printing* make (text) form an even margin down the page □ **justification** *noun* good reason

> **justify** » justifi*es*, justify*ing*, justifi*ed*

jut *verb* stand or stick out

> **jut** » jut*s*, jutt*ing*, jutt*ed*

jute *noun* fibre from certain plants for making sacking, canvas *etc*

juvenile *adj* **1** young; of young people **2** childish □ *noun* a young person

juxtapose *verb* place side by side □ **juxtaposition** *noun*

K

k *abbrev* kilo-; one thousand

kabaddi *noun* an Asian game resembling tag, played barefoot by teams of seven

kabuki *noun* a stylized form of Japanese theatre

kaftan *another spelling* of **caftan**

kaiser *noun, hist* a German emperor

kalanchoe /kə*lan*kohee/ *noun* a plant with flower clusters on long stems

kale *noun* a cabbage with open curled leaves

kaleidoscope *noun* a tube held to the eye and turned, so that loose, coloured shapes reflected in two mirrors change patterns

kaleidoscopic *adj* **1** with changing colours **2** changing quickly **kaleidoscopically** *adv*

kamikaze *noun, hist* a Japanese pilot trained to make a suicidal attack ▯ *adj* suicidal, self-destructive

kangaroo *noun* a large Australian animal with long hindlegs and great jumping power, the female carrying its young in a pouch on the front of her body

kaolin *noun* China clay

kapok *noun* light waterproof fibre fluff from the seeds of a tropical tree, used for padding

kaput /kə*poot*/ *adj, slang* broken, not working

karaoke *noun* an entertainment of singing well-known songs against pre-recorded backing music

karate *noun* a Japanese form of unarmed fighting using blows and kicks

karma *noun* in Buddhist belief, someone's destiny as determined by their actions in a previous life

kayak *noun* **1** an Inuit sealskin canoe **2** a lightweight canoe for one person, manoeuvred with a single paddle

KB *abbrev* **1** *comput* kilobyte **2** King's Bench

KBE *abbrev* Knight Commander of the British Empire

KC *abbrev* King's Counsel

kcal *abbrev* kilocalorie

kebab *noun* small pieces of meat or vegetables cooked on a skewer

kedgeree *noun* a dish made with rice, fish and hard-boiled eggs

keel *noun* the piece of a ship's frame that lies lengthways along the bottom ▯ **keelhaul** *verb, hist* punish by hauling under the keel of a ship with ropes ▯ **keelson** *noun* a ship's inner keel ▯ **keel over** overturn, fall over

keek *verb, Scot* look, peep

keen[1] *adj* **1** eager, enthusiastic **2** very sharp; bitingly cold ▯ **keenly** *adv* ▯ **keenness** *noun*

keen[2] *verb* wail in grief; lament ▯ **keening** *noun*

keep *verb* **1** hold on to, not give or throw away **2** look after; feed and clothe **3** have or use **4** fulfil (a promise) **5** remain in a position or state **6** (also with **on**) continue (doing something): *keep taking the tablets* **7** of food: stay in good condition **8** celebrate: *keep Christmas* ▫ *noun* **1** food, board **2** a castle stronghold ▫ **keeper** *noun* someone who looks after something: *zoo-keeper* ▫ **keeping** *noun* care, charge ▫ **keepsake** *noun* a gift in memory of an occasion *etc* ▫ **in keeping with** suited to ▫ **keep out 1** exclude **2** stay outside ▫ **keep up** go on with, continue ▫ **keep up with** go as fast *etc* as

> **keep** *verb* » keep*s*, keep*ing*, kept

keg *noun* a small cask or barrel

kelp *noun* a type of large brown seaweed

kelpie *noun* a Celtic water-sprite in the shape of a horse

kelvin *noun* a measure of temperature

ken *noun* the extent of someone's knowledge or understanding: *beyond the ken of the average person* ▫ *verb*, *Scot* know

kendo *noun* a Japanese martial art using bamboo staves

kennel *noun* **1** a hut for a dog **2** (**kennels**) a place where dogs can be looked after

kept *past form* of **keep**

keratin *noun* the substance from which horns and nails are made

kerb *noun* the edge of something, *esp* a pavement ▫ **kerb-crawling** *noun* driving a car slowly in order to pick up prostitutes

> ⚠Do not confuse with: **curb**

kerchief *noun* a square of cloth used as a headscarf

kernel *noun* **1** a soft substance in the shell of a nut, or inside the stone of a fruit **2** the important part of anything

kerosine *noun* paraffin oil

kestrel *noun* a type of small falcon which hovers

ketch *noun* (*plural* **ketches**) a two-masted sailing ship

ketchup *noun* a flavouring sauce made from tomatoes *etc*

> Originally spelt *catsup*, as it still is in US English; based on a Chinese word for 'fish brine'

kettle *noun* a pot with a spout for heating liquids

kettledrum *noun* a drum made of a metal bowl covered with stretched skin *etc*

key *noun* **1** a device which is turned in a corresponding hole to lock or unlock, tighten, tune *etc* **2** a lever pressed on a piano *etc* to produce a note **3** a button on a typewriter or computer keyboard which is pressed to type letters **4** the chief note of a piece of music **5** something which explains a mystery or deciphers a code **6** a book containing answers to exercises ▫ *verb* type on a typewriter or computer ▫ *adj* important, essential ▫ **keyboard** *noun* **1** the keys in a piano or organ arranged along a flat board **2** the keys of a typewriter or computer **3** an electronic musical instrument with keys arranged as on a piano *etc* ▯ **keyhole** *noun* the hole in which a key of a door is placed ▯ **keynote** *noun* **1** the chief note of a piece of music **2** the chief point about anything ▯ **keypad** *noun* a device with buttons that can be pushed to operate a television, telephone *etc* ▯ **keystone** *noun* the stone at the highest point of an arch holding the rest in position ▯ **keyed-up** *adj* excited

kg *abbrev* kilogramme(s)

KGB *abbrev, hist* Committee of State Security (in Russian, *Komitet Gosudarstvennoi Bezopasnosti*)

khaki *adj* greenish-brown in colour ▯ *noun* **1** greenish-brown **2** cloth of this colour used for military uniforms

From an Urdu word meaning 'dusty'

kibbutz *noun* (*plural* **kibbutzim**) a farming settlement in Israel in which all share the work

kibosh *verb, informal* destroy, get rid of

kick *verb* **1** hit or strike out with the foot **2** of a gun: spring back violently when fired ▯ *noun* **1** a blow with the foot **2** the springing-back of a gun when fired ▯ **kick-off** *noun* the start (of a football game) ▯ **for kicks** *informal* for fun

kid 1 *informal* a child **2** a young goat **3** the skin of a young goat ▯ *adj* made of kid leather ▯ **kids' stuff** *informal* something very easy or tame ▯ **with kid gloves** very carefully or tactfully

kidnap *verb* carry off (someone) by force, often demanding money in exchange ▯ **kidnapper** *noun* ▯ **kidnapping** *noun*

kidnap » kidnap*s*, kidnapp*ing*, kidnapp*ed*

kidney *noun* (*plural* **kidneys**) either of a pair of organs in the lower back which filter waste from the blood and produce urine ▯ **kidney bean** a bean with a curved shape like a kidney

kilim *noun* a Middle-Eastern woven rug

kill *verb* **1** put to death **2** put an end to ▯ *noun* **1** the act of killing **2** the animals killed by a hunter ▯ **killer** *noun* ▯ **be in at the kill** be there at the most exciting moment

kiln *noun* a large oven or furnace for baking pottery, bricks *etc* or for drying grain, hops *etc*

kilobyte *noun, comput* a measure of capacity equal to 1024 bytes

kilocalorie *noun* a measure of energy equal to 1000 calories

kilogramme *noun* a measure of weight equal to 1000 grammes (about 2 lb)

kilometre *noun* a measure of length equal to 1000 metres (about $\frac{5}{8}$ of a mile)

kilowatt *noun* a measure of electrical power equal to 1000 watts

kilt *noun* a pleated tartan skirt reaching to the knee, part of traditional Scottish dress

kilter *noun*: **out of kilter** out of sequence, off balance

kimono *noun* (*plural* **kimonos**) a loose Japanese robe, fastened with a sash

kin *noun* members of the same family, relations ▯ **kith and kin** *see* **kith** ▯ **next of kin** your nearest relative

kind *noun* **1** a sort, type **2** goods, not money: *paid in kind* ▯ *adj* having good feelings towards others; generous, gentle ▯ **kindhearted** *adj* kind ▯ **kindliness** *noun* ▯ **kindly** *adv* in a kind way ▯ *adj* kind, warm-hearted ▯ **kindness** *noun*

kindergarten *noun* a nursery school

kindle *verb* **1** light a fire **2** catch fire **3** stir up (feelings)

kindling *noun* material for starting a fire

kindred *noun* relatives, relations ▯ *adj* of the same sort; related: *a kindred spirit*

kinesiology *noun* the study of human movement and posture

kinesis *noun* movement, change in position

kinetic *adj* of or expressing motion: *kinetic sculpture*

king *noun* **1** the inherited male ruler of a nation **2** a playing-card with a picture of a king **3** the most important chess piece ▯ **kingdom** *noun* **1** the area ruled by a king **2** any of the three major divisions of natural objects, *ie* animal, vegetable or mineral ▯ **kingly** *adj* like a king; royal ▯ **kingpin** *noun* the most important person in an organization

kingcup *noun* marsh marigold

kingfisher *noun* a type of fish-eating bird with brightly coloured feathers

kink *noun* **1** a bend or curl in a rope, hair *etc* **2** a peculiarity of the mind

kinky *adj* **1** twisted, contorted **2** *informal* sexually unusual or perverted

kinsfolk *noun plural* relations, relatives

kinsman, kinswoman *noun* a close relation

kiosk *noun* **1** a small stall for the sale of papers, sweets *etc* **2** a telephone box

kip *slang* a bed ▯ *verb* go to bed, sleep

kipper *noun* a smoked and dried herring

kir /keer/ *noun* a drink of white wine mixed with blackcurrant syrup or liqueur

kirk *noun*, *Scot* a church

kirsch /keersh/ *noun* a liqueur made from cherries

kismet *noun* destiny, fate

kiss *verb* **1** touch lovingly with the lips **2** touch gently ▯ *noun* (*plural* **kisses**) ▯ **kiss of life** a mouth-to-mouth method of restoring breathing

kit *noun* an outfit of clothes, tools *etc* necessary for a particular job

kitchen *noun* a room where food is cooked ▯ **kitchenette** *noun* a small kitchen ▯ **kitchen-garden** *noun* a vegetable garden

kite *noun* **1** a light frame, covered with paper or other material, for flying in the air **2** a kind of hawk

kith *noun*: **kith and kin** friends and relatives

kitsch *noun* vulgarly tasteless art *etc*

kitten *noun* a young cat ▯ **kittenish** *adj* behaving like a kitten, playful ▯ **have kittens** *informal* make a great fuss

kittiwake *noun* a type of gull

kitty[1] *noun* (*plural* **kitties**) a sum of money set aside for a purpose

kitty[2] *noun* (*plural* **kitties**) *informal* a kitten

kiwi *noun* **1** a fast-running almost wingless bird of New Zealand **2** a kiwi fruit ▯ **kiwi fruit** an edible fruit with a thin hairy skin and bright green flesh

kleptomania *noun* an uncontrollable desire to steal ▯ **kleptomaniac** *noun* & *adj*

klondyker *noun* a factory ship processing fish for sale in a foreign country

> After the famous *Klondyke* gold rush in Canada, because these ships originally traded in the lucrative herring market

km *abbrev* kilometre(s)

knack /nak/ *noun* a special clever ability

knacker /*nak*ər/ *noun* a buyer of old horses for slaughter ▯ *verb, informal* exhaust, tire out

knapsack /*nap*sak/ *noun* a bag for food, clothes *etc* slung on the back

knave /nehv/ *noun* **1** a cheating rogue **2** in playing-cards, the jack ▯ **knavery** *noun* dishonesty ▯ **knavish** *adj* cheating, wicked

knead /need/ *verb* **1** work (dough *etc*) by pressing with the fingers **2** massage

knee /nee/ *noun* the joint at the bend of the leg ▯ **kneecap** *noun* the flat round bone on the front of the knee joint ▯ *verb* cause to suffer ▯ **kneecapping** *noun* a form of torture or punishment in which the victim is shot or otherwise injured in the kneecap

kneel /neel/ *verb* go down on one or both knees

> **kneel** » kneel*s*, kneel*ing*, knelt

knell /nel/ *noun* **1** the tolling of a bell for a death or funeral **2** a warning of a sad end or failure

knickerbockers *noun plural* loose breeches tucked in at the knee

> Named after Diedrich *Knickerbocker*, a fictional Dutchman invented by US author Washington Irving in the 19th century

knickers /*nik*ərz/ *noun plural* women's or girls' underpants

knick-knack /*nik*nak/ *noun* a small, ornamental article

knife /naif/ *noun* (*plural* **knives**) a tool for cutting ▯ *verb* stab ▯ **at knife point** under threat of injury

knight /nait/ *noun* **1** *hist* an aristocrat trained to use arms **2** a rank, with the title *Sir*, which is not inherited by a son **3** a piece used in chess ▯ *verb* raise to the rank of knight ▯ **knight-errant** *hist* a knight who travelled in search of adventures ▯ **knighthood** *noun* the rank of a knight ▯ **knightly** *adj* **1** of knights **2** gallant, courageous

knit /nit/ *verb* **1** form a garment from yarn or thread by means of knitting needles **2** join closely ▯ **knitting** *noun* work done by knitting ▯ **knitting needles** *noun plural* a pair of thin pointed rods used in knitting

knit » knit*s*, knitt*ing*, knitt*ed*

knob /nob/ *noun* **1** a small rounded projection **2** a round door-handle

knock /nok/ *verb* **1** strike, hit **2** drive or be driven against **3** tap on a door to have it opened ▯ *noun* **1** a sudden stroke **2** a tap (on a door) ▯ **knocker** *noun* a hinged weight on a door for knocking with ▯ **knock back** *informal* eat or drink greedily ▯ **knock down 1** demolish **2** *informal* reduce in price ▯ **knock-kneed** *adj* having knees that touch in walking ▯ **knock off** *informal* **1** stop work for the day **2** plagiarize, copy illegally ▯ **knock out** hit (someone) hard enough to make them unconscious ▯ **knock up 1** put together hastily **2** *slang* make pregnant

knoll /nohl/ *noun* a small rounded hill

knot /not/ *noun* **1** a hard lump, *eg* one made by tying string, or found in wood at the join between trunk and branch **2** a tangle **3** a small gathering, a cluster of people **4** a measure of speed for ships (about 1.85 kilometre per hour) ▯ *verb* tie in a knot

knot *verb* » knot*s*, knott*ing*, knott*ed*

knotted *adj* full of knots ▯ **get knotted!** *exclam, informal* expressing anger or defiance towards someone

knotty *adj* **1** having knots **2** difficult, complicated: *knotty problem*

know /noh/ *verb* **1** be aware or sure of **2** recognize ▯ **knowing** *adj* clever; cunning ▯ **knowingly** *adv* intentionally

know » know*s*, know*ing*, known, knew

knowledge *noun* **1** that which is known **2** information **3** ability, skill

knowledgeable *adj* showing or having knowledge ▯ **knowledgeably** *adv*

knuckle /nukl/ *noun* a joint of the fingers ▯ **knuckleduster** *noun* a metal covering worn on the knuckles as a weapon ▯ **knucklehead** *noun, informal* an idiot ▯ **knuckle under** give in, yield

koala bear an Australian tree-climbing animal resembling a small bear

kofta *noun* an Indian dish of balls of minced, spiced meat

kohl *noun* a black powder used as an eyeliner

kohlrabi *noun* a type of cabbage with a turnip-shaped stem

kookaburra *another word* for **jackass**

kooky *adj, informal* eccentric

kopeck *noun* a Russian coin, equal to a hundredth of a rouble

kora *noun* a West African string instrument like a harp

Koran *noun* the sacred book of Islam

kosher *adj* **1** pure and clean according to Jewish law **2** acceptable, all right

kowtow to *verb* treat with too much respect

Based on a Chinese phrase meaning to prostrate yourself before the emperor

kraal *noun* a South African village

krill *noun* a small shrimplike creature eaten by whales *etc*

Krugerrand *noun* a South African coin used only for investment

krypton *noun* an inert gas present in the air, used in fluorescent lighting

Kt *abbrev* Knight

kudos /*kyoo*dos/ *noun* fame, glory

kulfi *noun* Indian ice-cream made with boiled, reduced milk

kumquat *noun* a small Chinese orange with a sweet rind

kung-fu *noun* a Chinese form of self-defence

kyrie /*kee*riyeh/ *noun* **1** a prayer in the Roman Catholic mass following the opening anthem **2** a musical setting for this

kw *abbrev* kilowatt(s)

L

l *abbrev* litre

lab *noun, informal* a laboratory

label *noun* a small written note fixed onto something listing its contents, price *etc* □ *verb* **1** fix a label to **2** call something by a certain name

> **label** *verb* » label*s*, label*ling*, label*led*

labial *adj* of the lips

laboratory *noun* (*plural* **laboratories**) a scientist's workroom

labour or *US* **labor** *noun* **1** hard work **2** workers on a job **3** the process of childbirth □ *verb* **1** work hard to move slowly or with difficulty **2** emphasize (a point) too greatly □ **laborious** *adj* requiring hard work; wearisome □ **laboured** *adj* showing signs of effort □ **labourer** *noun* someone who does heavy unskilled work □ **Labour Party** one of the chief political parties of Great Britain

labrador *noun* a large black or fawn-coloured dog, often used for retrieving game

laburnum *noun* a tree with large clusters of yellow flowers and poisonous seeds

labyrinth *noun* a maze

lace *noun* **1** a cord for fastening shoes *etc* **2** decorative openwork fabric made with fine thread □ *verb* **1** fasten with a lace **2** add alcohol to (a drink)

lacerate *verb* **1** tear, rip **2** wound □ **laceration** *noun*

lachrymal *adj* of tears

lack *verb* **1** be in want **2** be without □ *noun* want, need

lackadaisical *adj* bored, half-hearted □ **lackadaisically** *adv*

lackey *noun* (*plural* **lackeys**) **1** a manservant **2** someone who acts like a slave

lacklustre or *US* **lackluster** *adj* dull, insipid

laconic *adj* using few words to express meaning □ **laconically** *adv*

lacquer *noun* a varnish □ *verb* varnish

lacrosse *noun* a twelve-a-side ball-game played with sticks having a shallow net at the end

lactate *verb* produce or secrete milk

lactic *adj* of milk

lactobacillus *noun* a bacterium which converts carbohydrates to lactic acid

lactose *noun* (*also called* **milk sugar**) a sugar obtained by evaporating whey

lacuna *noun* (*plural* **lacunae**) a gap, a space

lad *noun* a boy, a youth

ladder *noun* **1** a set of rungs or steps between two supports, for climbing up or down **2** a run from a broken stitch, in a stocking *etc*

lade *noun* a channel for carrying water to a millwheel

laden *adj* loaded, burdened

lading *noun* a load; cargo

ladle *noun* a large spoon for lifting out liquid □ *verb* lift with a ladle

lady *noun* (*plural* **ladies**) **1** a woman of good manners **2** a title for the wife of a knight, lord or baronet, or a daughter of a member of the aristocracy **3** (**ladies**) a public lavatory for women □ **Her Ladyship** the title used in addressing a titled lady

ladybird *noun* a small beetle, usually red with black spots

lag *verb* **1** move slowly and fall behind **2** cover (a boiler or pipes) with a warm covering □ *noun* a delay □ **lagging** *noun* material for covering pipes *etc*

lag » lag*s*, lagg*ing*, lagg*ed*

lager *noun* a light beer □ **lager lout** a drunken pugnacious youth

laggard *noun* someone who lags behind □ *adj* lagging behind

lagoon *noun* a shallow stretch of water separated from the sea by low sandbanks, rocks *etc*

laid *past form* of **lay**[1] □ **get laid** *slang* have sexual intercourse

lain *past participle* of **lie**[2]

lair *noun* the den of a wild beast

⚠Do not confuse with: **layer**

laird *noun* in Scotland, a landowner

laissez-faire /lesay-*fer*/ *noun* a general principle of not interfering

laity *see* **lay**[2]

lake *noun* a large stretch of water surrounded by land

Lallans *noun* the Scots language, *esp* as used in literature

lama *noun* a Buddhist priest of Tibet

lamb *noun* **1** a young sheep **2** the meat of this animal **3** a gentle person

lambast *noun* beat or reprimand severely

lame *adj* **1** unable to walk, crippled **2** not good enough: *a lame excuse* □ *verb* make lame □ **lame duck** an inefficient or weak person or organization □ **lamely** *adv* □ **lameness** *noun*

lamé *noun* a fabric interwoven with metallic thread

lament *verb* **1** mourn, feel or express grief for **2** regret □ *noun* **1** a show of grief **2** a mournful poem or piece of music □ **lamentation** *noun*

lamentable *adj* **1** pitiful **2** very bad □ **lamentably** *adv*

laminated *adj* made by putting layers together: *laminated glass*

Lammas *noun* 1 August, an old feast day celebrating the beginning of the harvest

lamp *noun* a device to give out light, containing an electric bulb, candle *etc* □ **lamp-post** *noun* a pillar supporting a street lamp

lampoon *noun* a piece of ridicule

or satire directed at someone ▯ *verb* ridicule, satirize

lamprey *noun* (*plural* **lampreys**) a type of fish like an eel

LAN /lan/ *abbrev, comput* local area network

lance *noun* a long shaft of wood, with a spearhead ▯ *verb* cut open (a boil *etc*) with a knife ▯ **lance-corporal** *noun* a soldier with rank just below a corporal

lancer *noun* a light cavalry soldier

lancet *noun* a sharp surgical instrument

land *noun* **1** the solid portion of the earth's surface **2** ground **3** soil **4** a part of a country ▯ *verb* **1** arrive on land or on shore **2** set (an aircraft, ship *etc*) on land or on shore ▯ **landed** *adj* owning lands and estates: *landed gentry* ▯ **landfall** *noun* **1** an approach to land after a voyage **2** the land approached ▯ **landlocked** *adj* almost shut in by land ▯ **landlubber** *noun* someone who works on land and knows little about the sea ▯ **landmark** *noun* **1** an object on land that serves as a guide **2** an important event ▯ **landmine** *noun* a bomb laid on or near the surface of the ground which explodes when someone passes over it

landau *noun, hist* a horse-drawn carriage with a removable top

landing *noun* **1** a coming ashore or to ground **2** a place for getting on shore **3** the level part of a staircase between the flights of steps

landlord, **landlady** *noun* **1** the owner of land or accommodation for rent **2** the owner or manager of an inn *etc*

landscape *noun* a painting, photograph *etc* of inland scenery ▯ **landscape gardening** gardening for picturesque effect

landslide *noun* a mass of land that slips down from the side of a hill ▯ **landslide victory** a win in an election in which a great mass of votes goes to one side

lane *noun* **1** a narrow street or passage **2** a part of the road, sea or air to which cars, ships, aircraft *etc* must keep

lang syne /lang sain/ *adv, Scot* long since, long ago

language *noun* **1** human speech **2** the speech of a particular people or nation

languid *adj* lacking liveliness and spirit

languish *verb* **1** grow weak, droop **2** long (for) ▯ **languishing** *adj*

languor *noun* a languid state, listlessness

laniard *another spelling* of **lanyard**

lank *adj* **1** tall and thin **2** of hair: straight and limp

lanky *adj* tall and thin

lanolin *noun* a fat extracted from sheep's wool

lantern *noun* a case for holding or carrying a light ▯ **lantern-jawed** *adj* hollow-cheeked, long-jawed

lanyard or **laniard** *noun* **1** a short rope used for fastening on a ship **2** a cord for hanging a whistle *etc* round the neck

lap *verb* **1** lick up with the tongue **2** wash or flow against **3** (with **up**) accept (praise *etc*) greedily **4** wrap round, surround **5** get a lap ahead of other competitors in a race □ *noun* **1** the front part, from waist to knees, of someone seated **2** a fold **3** one round of a racetrack or competition course □ **lapdog** *noun* a small pet dog □ **laptop** *noun* a compact portable computer combining screen, keyboard and processor in one unit

> **lap** *verb* » lap*s*, lapp*ing*, lapp*ed*

laparoscope *noun* a long optical tube used for examining internal organs without cutting □ **laparoscopy** *noun* surgical examination with a laparoscope

lapel *noun* the part of a coat joined to the collar and folded back on the chest

lapidary *noun* (*plural* **lapidaries**) someone who cuts, polishes and shapes gems and stones □ *adj* engraved on stone

lapis lazuli a deep-blue stone containing several minerals

lapsang souchong a Chinese tea with a smoky flavour

lapse *verb* **1** fall into bad habits **2** cease, be no longer valid □ *noun* **1** a mistake, a failure **2** a period of time passing

lapwing *noun* (*also called* **peewit**) a type of bird of the plover family

larceny *noun* stealing, theft

larch *noun* (*plural* **larches**) a cone-bearing deciduous tree

lard *noun* the melted fat of a pig □ *verb* **1** put strips of bacon in meat before cooking **2** smear, lay on thickly

larder *noun* **1** a room or place where food is kept **2** stock of food

large *adj* great in size, amount *etc* □ **largely** *adv* mainly, to a great extent □ **largeness** *noun* □ **at large** **1** at liberty, free **2** in general: *the public at large*

largesse /lar*zhes*/ *noun* a generous giving away of money *etc*

largo *adj* & *adv*, *music* (to be played) broad and slow

lariat *noun* **1** a rope for fastening horses while they are grazing **2** a lasso

lark *noun* **1** a general name for several kinds of singing bird **2** a piece of fun or mischief □ *verb* fool about, behave mischievously

larkspur *noun* a tall plant with blue, white or pink spurred flowers, a kind of delphinium

larva *noun* (*plural* **larvae**) an insect in its first stage after coming out of the egg, a grub

laryngitis *noun* inflammation of the larynx

larynx *noun* (*plural* **larynxes** or **larynges**) the upper part of the windpipe containing the cords that produce the voice

lasagne *noun plural* flat sheets of pasta □ *noun sing* (or **lasagna**) a baked dish made with this

lascar *noun* an East Indian sailor

lascivious *adj* lustful; indecent, lewd □ **lasciviously** *adv* □ **lasciviousness** *noun*

laser *noun* **1** a very narrow powerful beam of light **2** an instrument that concentrates light into such a beam

> An acronym of '*l*ight *a*mplification by *s*timulated *e*mission of *r*adiation'

lash *noun* (*plural* **lashes**) **1** a thong or cord of a whip **2** a stroke with a whip **3** an eyelash □ *verb* **1** strike with a whip **2** fasten tightly with a rope *etc* **3** attack with bitter words □ **lash out 1** kick or swing out without thinking **2** speak angrily **3** spend extravagantly

lass *noun* (*plural* **lasses**) a girl

lassitude *noun* lack of energy, weariness

lasso *noun* (*plural* **lassoes** or **lassos**) a long rope with a loop that tightens when the rope is pulled, used for catching wild horses *etc* □ *verb* catch with a lasso

> **lasso** *verb* » lasso*es*, lasso*ing*, lasso*ed*

last *adj* **1** coming after all the others: *last person to arrive* **2** the final one remaining: *last ticket* **3** most recent: *my last employer* □ *adv* □ *verb* **1** continue, go on **2** remain in good condition □ *noun* a foot-shaped tool on which shoes are made or repaired □ **lastly** *adv* finally □ **last rites** religious ceremonies performed for the dying □ **last straw** the last in a series of unpleasant events, which makes a situation unbearable □ **last word** the final comment or decision about something □ **at last** in the end □ **on your last legs** completely worn out, about to collapse □ **to the last** to the end

latch *noun* (*plural* **latches**) **1** a wooden or metal catch used to fasten a door **2** a light door-lock □ *verb* fasten with a latch □ **latchkey** *noun* a key to raise the latch of a door □ **latchkey child** a child who regularly returns home to an empty house

late *adj* & *adv* **1** coming after the expected time: *his train was late* **2** far on in time: *it's getting late* **3** recent: *our late disagreement* **4** recently dead: *the late author* **5** recently, but no longer, holding an office or position: *the late chairman* □ **lately** *adv* recently □ **lateness** *noun* □ **of late** recently

latent *adj* hidden, undeveloped as yet: *latent ability/ latent hostility*

lateral *adj* of, at, to or from the side □ **lateral thinking** thinking which seeks new ways of looking at a problem and does not merely proceed in logical stages

latex *noun* the milky juice of plants, *esp* of the rubber tree

lath /lahth/ *noun* a thin narrow strip of wood

> ⚠Do not confuse: **lath** and **lathe**

lathe /lehdh/ *noun* a machine for turning and shaping articles of wood, metal *etc*

lather *noun* **1** a foam or froth, *eg* from soap and water **2** *informal* a state of agitation □ *verb* cover with lather

Latin *noun* the language of ancient Rome

latitude *noun* **1** the distance, measured in degrees, of a place north or south of the equator (*compare with*: **longitude**) **2** freedom of action or choice: *the new job allows him far more latitude than his previous one*

latrine *noun* a toilet in a camp, barracks *etc*

latter *adj* **1** the last of two things mentioned (*contrasted with*: **former**): *between working and sleeping, I prefer the latter* **2** recent □ **latter-day** *adj* of recent times □ **latterly** *adv* recently

lattice *noun* **1** a network of crossed wooden *etc* strips **2** a window constructed this way

laud *verb, formal* praise □ **laudatory** *adj* expressing praise

laudable *adj* worthy of being praised □ **laudably** *adv*

laudanum /*lodənəm*/ *noun* tincture of opium

laugh *verb* make sounds with the voice in showing amusement, scorn *etc* □ *noun* the sound of laughing □ **laughable** *adj* comical, ridiculous □ **laughably** *adv* □ **laughing stock** an object of scornful laughter

laughter *noun* the act or noise of laughing

launch *verb* **1** slide a boat or ship into water, *esp* on its first voyage **2** fire off (a rocket *etc*) **3** start off on a course **4** put (a product) on the market with publicity **5** throw, hurl □ *noun* (*plural* **launches**) **1** the act of launching **2** a large motor boat

launder *verb* wash and iron clothes *etc*

launderette *noun* a shop where customers may wash clothes *etc* in washing machines

laundry *noun* (*plural* **laundries**) **1** a place where clothes are washed **2** clothes to be washed

laurel *noun* **1** the bay tree, from which ceremonial wreaths were made **2** (**laurels**) honours or victories gained □ **rest on your laurels** be content with past successes and not try for any more

lava *noun* molten rock *etc* thrown out by a volcano, becoming solid as it cools

lavatory *noun* (*plural* **lavatories**) a toilet

lavender *noun* **1** a sweet-smelling plant with small pale purple flowers **2** a pale-purple colour

lavish *verb* spend or give very freely □ *adj* very generous

law *noun* **1** the official rules that apply in a country or state **2** one such rule **3** a scientific rule stating the conditions under which certain things always happen □ **law-abiding** *adj* obeying the law □ **law court** a place where people accused of crimes are tried □ **lawful** *adj* allowed by law □ **lawfully** *adv* □ **lawless** *adj* paying no attention to, and not observing, the laws □ **lawsuit** a quarrel or dispute to be settled by a court of law

lawn *noun* an area of smooth grass *eg* as part of a garden; a kind of fine linen □ **lawnmower** *noun* a machine for cutting grass □ **lawn tennis** tennis played on a hard or grass court

lawyer *noun* someone whose work it is to give advice in matters of law

lax *adj* **1** not strict **2** careless, negligent □ **laxity** or **laxness** *noun*

laxative *noun* a medicine which loosens the bowels

lay[1] *verb* **1** place or set down **2** put (*eg* a burden, duty) on (someone) **3** beat down **4** make to leave or subside: *lay a ghost* **5** set in order, arrange **6** of a hen: produce eggs **7** bet, wager □ **laid-back** *adj, informal* relaxed, easy-going □ **laid-up** *adj* ill in bed □ **layabout** *noun* a lazy idle person □ **layby** *noun* a parking area at the side of a road □ **lay about someone** beat them all over □ **lay down 1** assert: *laying down the law* **2** store (*eg* wine) □ **lay off 1** dismiss (workers) temporarily **2** *informal* stop: *lay off arguing* □ **lay up** store for future use □ **lay waste** ruin, destroy

> **lay** *verb* » lays, lay*ing*, laid

> ⚠Do not confuse with: **lie**

lay[2] *adj* **1** not of the clergy **2** without special training in a particular subject □ **laity** *noun* ordinary people, not clergymen □ **layman, laywoman** *noun* someone without special training in a subject

lay[3] *noun, old* a short poem or song

layer *noun* a thickness forming a covering or level □ **layered** *adj* having a number of distinct layers: *layered cake*

> ⚠Do not confuse with: **lair**

layette *noun* a complete outfit for a baby

lay-figure *noun* a jointed model of a human figure used by artists

laze *verb* be lazy; idle

lazy *adj* not inclined to work; idle □ **lazily** *adj* □ **laziness** *noun* □ **lazy-bones** *informal* an idler

> **lazy** *adj* » laz*ier*, laz*iest*

lb *abbrev* pound(s) (in weight)

lbw *abbrev, cricket* leg before wicket

LCD *abbrev* liquid crystal display

lea *noun, old* a meadow

leach *noun* seep slowly through or out of something

> ⚠Do not confuse with: **leech**

lead[1] *verb* **1** show the way by going first **2** direct, guide **3** persuade **4** live (a busy, quiet *etc* life) **5** of a road: go (to) □ *noun* **1** the first or front place **2** guidance, direction **3** a leash for a dog *etc* □ **leading question** one asked in such a way as to suggest the desired answer

> **lead** *verb* » lead*s*, lead*ing*, led

lead[2] *noun* **1** a soft bluish-grey metal **2** the part of a pencil that writes, really made of graphite **3** a weight used for sounding depths at sea *etc* □ **lead-free** *adj* of petrol: unleaded

leaden *adj* **1** made of lead **2** lead-coloured **3** dull, heavy

leader *noun* **1** someone who leads or goes first; a chief **2** a column in a newspaper expressing the editor's opinions □ **leadership** *noun* **1** the state of being a leader **2** the ability to lead

leaf *noun* (*plural* **leaves**) **1** a part of a plant growing from the side of a stem **2** a page of a book **3** a hinged flap on a table *etc* □ **leafy** *adj* □ **turn over a new leaf** begin again and do better

leaflet *noun* a small printed sheet

league *noun* **1** a union of people, nations *etc* for the benefit of each other **2** an association of clubs for games **3** *old* a measure of distance, approximately 3 miles (about 4.8 kilometres) □ **in league with** allied with

leak *noun* **1** a hole through which liquid passes **2** an escape of gas *etc* **3** a release of secret information □ *verb* **1** escape, pass out **2** give (secret information) to the media *etc* □ **leakage** *noun* a leaking

lean *verb* **1** slope over to one side **2** rest (against) **3** rely (on) □ *adj* **1** thin **2** poor, scanty **3** of meat: not fat □ **leaning** *noun* a liking for, or interest in, something □ **lean-burn** *adj* of an engine: able to run on a reduced amount of fuel □ **lean-to** *noun* a shed *etc* built against another building or wall

> **lean** *verb* » lean*s*, lean*ing*, leant

leap *verb* **1** move with jumps **2** jump (over) □ *noun* a jump □ **leap-frog** *noun* a game in which one player leaps over another's bent back □ **leap year** a year which has 366 days (February having 29), occurring every fourth year

> **leap** *verb* » leap*s*, leap*ing*, leapt

learn *verb* **1** get to know (something) **2** gain skill □ **learned** *adj* having or showing great knowledge □ **learner** *noun* □ **learning** *noun* knowledge

> **learn** » learn*s*, learn*ing*, learnt or learn*ed*

lease *noun* **1** an agreement giving the use of a house *etc* on payment of rent **2** the period of this agreement □ *verb* let or rent □ **lease-back** *noun* an arrangement in which the buyer of a property leases it back to the seller □ **leasehold** *noun* property or land held by lease

leash *noun* (*plural* **leashes**) a lead by which a dog *etc* is held □ *verb* put (a dog *etc*) on a leash

least *adj* the smallest amount of anything: *he had the least money* □ *adv* (often with **the**) the smallest or lowest degree: *I like her least* □ **at least** at any rate, anyway □ **not in the least** not at all

leather *noun* the skin of an animal, prepared by tanning for use □ *verb* beat □ **leathering** *noun* a thrashing □ **leathery** *adj* like leather; tough

leave *noun* **1** permission to do something (*eg* to be absent) **2** a holiday □ *verb* **1** allow to remain **2** abandon, forsake **3** depart (from) **4** hand down to someone in a will **5** give over to someone's responsibility, care *etc*: *leave the choice to* *her* **leavings** *noun plural* things left over **take your leave of 1** part from **2** say goodbye to

> **leave** *verb* » leave*s*, leav*ing*, left

leaven *noun* yeast **leavened** *adj* raised with yeast

lecher *noun* a lustful man **lecherous** *adj* lustful in a sexual way **lechery** *noun*

lectern *noun* a stand for a book to be read from

lecture *noun* **1** a discussion of a certain subject, written or read to an audience **2** a scolding *verb* **1** deliver a lecture **2** scold **lecturer** *noun* someone who lectures, *esp* to students

LED *abbrev* light-emitting diode

led *past form* of **lead**[1]

ledge *noun* **1** a shelf or projecting rim: *window-ledge* **2** an underwater ridge

ledger *noun* the accounts book of an office or shop

lee *noun* the side away from the wind, the sheltered side **leeward** *adj* & *adv* in the direction towards which the wind blows **leeway** *noun* **1** a ship's drift off course **2** lost time, ground *etc*: *a lot of leeway to make up* **3** room to manoeuvre, latitude

leech *noun* (*plural* **leeches**) a kind of blood-sucking worm

> ⚠Do not confuse with: **leach**

leek *noun* a long green and white vegetable of the onion family

leer *noun* a sly, sidelong or lustful look *verb* look sideways or lustfully (at)

leery *adj*: **leery of** wary of

lees *noun plural* dregs that settle at the bottom of liquid *esp* wine

left[1] *adj* on or of the side of the body that in most people has the less skilful hand (*contrasted with*: **right**) *adv* on or towards the left side *noun* **1** the left side **2** a political grouping with left-wing ideas *etc* **left-field** *adj, informal* odd, eccentric **left-handed** *adj* **1** using the left hand rather than the right **2** awkward **left-wing** *adj* of or holding socialist or radical political views, ideas *etc*

left[2] *past form* of **leave**

leg *noun* **1** one of the limbs by which humans and animals walk **2** a long slender support for a table *etc* **3** one stage in a journey, contest *etc* **leggings** *noun plural* outer coverings for the lower legs **leggy** *adj* having long legs **legless** *adj, informal* drunk **legroom** *noun* room to move the legs

legacy *noun* (*plural* **legacies**) **1** something which is left by will **2** something left behind by the previous occupant of a house, job *etc* **legatee** *noun* someone to whom a legacy is left

legal *adj* **1** allowed by law, lawful **2** of law **legality** *noun* (*plural* **legalities**) the state of being legal **legalize** *verb* make lawful

legalism *noun* rigid adherence to the law or rules **legalist** *noun*

□ **legalistic** *adj* sticking rigidly to the law or rules

legate *noun* an ambassador, *esp* from the Pope

legation *noun* an official body of people acting on behalf of their government abroad

legato *adj & adv, music* (to be played) smoothly

legend *noun* **1** a traditional story handed down, a myth **2** a caption □ **legendary** *adj* **1** of legend; famous **2** not to be believed

legerdemain /lejərdə*mehn*/ *noun* conjuring by quickness of the hand

leggings, leggy *see* **leg**

legible *adj* able to be read easily □ **legibility** *noun*

legion *noun, hist* **1** a body of from three to six thousand Roman soldiers **2** a great many □ **legionary** *noun* (*plural* **legionaries**) a soldier of a legion

legionnaire's disease a serious disease similar to pneumonia caused by a bacterium

So called after an outbreak of the disease at an American *Legion* convention in 1976

legislate *verb* make laws □ **legislation** *noun* □ **legislative** *adj* lawmaking □ **legislator** *noun* someone who makes laws □ **legislature** *noun* the part of the government which has the powers of making laws

legitimate *adj* **1** lawful **2** of a child: born of parents married to each other **3** correct, reasonable □ **legitimacy** *noun*

legume *noun* a plant of the pea or bean family

leisure *noun* time free from work, spare time □ **leisured** *adj* not occupied with business □ **leisurely** *adj* unhurried: *leisurely pace*

leitmotiv /*lait*mohteef/ *noun* **1** a musical theme in an opera associated with a particular character *etc* **2** a recurring theme

lemming *noun* **1** a small rat-like animal of the arctic regions, reputed to follow others of its kind over sea-cliffs *etc* when migrating **2** someone who follows others unquestioningly

lemon *noun* **1** an oval fruit with pale yellow rind and sour juice **2** the tree that bears this fruit

lemonade *noun* a soft drink flavoured with lemons

lemur *noun* an animal related to the monkey but with a pointed nose

lend *verb* **1** give use of (something) for a time **2** give, add (a quality) to someone or something: *his presence lent an air of respectability to the occasion* □ **lend itself to** be suitable for, adapt easily to

lend » lend*s*, lend*ing*, lent

length *noun* **1** extent from end to end in space or time **2** the quality of being long **3** a great extent **4** a piece of cloth *etc* □ **lengthen** *verb* make or grow longer □ **lengthways** or **lengthwise** *adv* in the direction of the length □ **lengthy** *adj* **1** long **2** tiresomely long □ **at length 1** in detail **2** at last

lenient *adj* merciful, punishing

only lightly ▯ **lenience** or **leniency** *noun*

lenitive *adj* soothing, mitigating

lens *noun* (*plural* **lenses**) **1** a piece of glass curved on one or both sides, used in spectacles, cameras *etc* **2** a part of the eye

Lent *noun* in the Christian church, a period of fasting before Easter lasting forty days

lent *past form* of **lend**

lentil *noun* the seed of a pod-bearing plant, used in soups *etc*

leonine *adj* like a lion

leopard *noun* an animal of the cat family with a spotted skin ▯ **leopardess** *noun* a female leopard

leotard *noun* a tight-fitting garment worn for dancing, gymnastics *etc*

leper *noun* **1** someone with leprosy **2** an outcast ▯ **leprosy** *noun* a contagious skin disease causing thickening or numbness in the skin

lepidopterology *noun* the study of butterflies and moths ▯ **lepidopterist** *noun*

leprechaun *noun* a creature in Irish folklore

lesbian *noun* a female homosexual ▯ *adj* of a woman: homosexual

lese-majesty *noun* an offence against the state, treason

lesion *noun* a wound

less *adj* **1** not as much: *take less time* **2** smaller: *think of a number less than 40* ▯ *adv* not as much, to a smaller extent: *he goes less often than he should* ▯ *noun* a smaller amount: *he has less than I have* ▯ *prep* minus: *5 less 2 equals 3* ▯ **lessen** *verb* make smaller ▯ **lesser** *adj* smaller

lessee /lesee/ *noun* someone with a lease for a property, business *etc*

lesson *noun* **1** something which is learned or taught **2** a part of the Bible read in church **3** a period of teaching

lest *conj* for fear that, in case

let *verb* **1** allow **2** grant use of (*eg* a house, shop, farm) in return for payment ▯ **let down** fail to act as expected, disappoint ▯ **let off** excuse, not punish ▯ **let up** become less

let *verb* » let*s*, lett*ing*, let

lethal *adj* causing death

lethargy *noun* a lack of energy or interest; sleepiness ▯ **lethargic** *adj*

LETS /lets/ *abbrev* local exchange trading system

letter *noun* **1** a mark expressing a sound **2** a written message **3** (**letters**) learning: *a woman of letters* ▯ **lettering** *noun* the way in which letters are formed ▯ **to the letter** according to the exact meaning of the words: *following instructions to the letter*

lettuce *noun* a kind of green plant whose leaves are used in a salad

leucocyte *noun* a white blood corpuscle

leukaemia *noun* a cancerous disease of the white blood cells in the body

levee[1] *noun, old* a reception held by a king or queen

levee[2] *noun, US* a river embankment

level *noun* **1** a flat, smooth surface **2** a height, position *etc* in comparison with some standard: *water level* **3** an instrument for showing whether a surface is level: *spirit level* **4** personal rank or degree of understanding: *a bit above my level* ▫ *adj* **1** flat, even, smooth **2** horizontal ▫ *verb* **1** make flat, smooth or horizontal **2** make equal **3** aim (a gun *etc*) **4** pull down (a building *etc*) ▫ **level crossing** a place where a road crosses a railway track ▫ **level-headed** *adj* having good sense ▫ **level playing-field** a position of equality from which to compete fairly

level *verb* » level*s*, levell*ing*, levell*ed*

lever *noun* **1** a bar of metal, wood *etc* used to raise or shift something heavy **2** a handle for operating a machine **3** a method of gaining advantage ▫ **leverage** *noun* **1** the use of a lever **2** power, influence

leveret *noun* a young hare

leviathan *noun* **1** a huge mythological sea monster **2** anything huge or powerful

levitation *noun* the illusion of raising a heavy body in the air without support ▫ **levitate** *verb* float in the air

levity *noun* lack of seriousness, frivolity

levy *verb* collect by order (*eg* a tax, army conscripts) ▫ *noun* (*plural* **levies**) money, troops *etc* collected by order

levy » levi*es*, levy*ing*, levi*ed*

lewd *adj* taking delight in indecent thoughts or acts ▫ **lewdness** *noun*

lexical *adj* of words

lexicographer *noun* someone who compiles or edits a dictionary ▫ **lexicography** *noun*

lexicon *noun* **1** a dictionary **2** a glossary of terms

liable *adj* **1** legally responsible (for) **2** likely or apt (to do something or happen) **3** (with **to**) likely to have, suffer from: *liable to colds* ▫ **liability** *noun* (*plural* **liabilities**) **1** legal responsibility **2** a debt **3** a disadvantage

liaise *verb* make a connection (with), be in touch (with)

liaison /leee*h*zon/ *noun* **1** contact, communication **2** a sexual affair

liana *noun* a climbing tropical plant

liar *see* **lie**[1]

Lib Dem *short for* Liberal Democrat

lib *noun, informal* liberation: *women's lib*

libation *noun* wine poured to honour a god

libel *noun* something written to hurt another's reputation ▫ *verb* write something libellous about ▫ **libellous** *adj* ▫ **libellously** *adv*

libel *verb* » libel*s*, libell*ing*, libell*ed*

liberal *adj* generous; broad-minded, tolerant ▯ **Liberal** a member of the former Liberal Party ▯ **liberality** *noun* ▯ **Liberal Democrats** one of the chief political parties of Great Britain

liberate *verb* set free ▯ **liberation** *noun*

libertine *noun* someone who lives a wicked, immoral life

liberty *noun* (*plural* **liberties**) **1** freedom, *esp* of speech or action **2** (**liberties**) rights, privileges ▯ **take liberties** behave rudely or impertinently

libido *noun* sexual drive or urge ▯ **libidinous**

library *noun* (*plural* **libraries**) **1** a collection of books, records *etc* **2** a building or room housing these ▯ **librarian** *noun* the keeper of a library

libretto *noun* (*plural* **libretti** or **librettos**) the words of an opera, musical show *etc*

lice *plural* of **louse**

licence *noun* **1** a form giving permission to do something, *eg* to keep a television set, drive a car *etc* **2** too great freedom of action

⚠Do not confuse: **licence** and **license**

license *verb* permit ▯ **licensee** *noun* someone to whom a licence is given

licentious *adj* given to behaving immorally or improperly ▯ **licentiousness** *noun*

lichen /*lai*kən/ *noun* a large group of moss-like plants that grow on rocks *etc*

licit *adj* legal, allowable

lick *verb* **1** pass the tongue over **2** of flames: reach up, touch ▯ *noun* **1** the act of licking **2** a tiny amount ▯ **lick into shape** make vigorous improvements on

licorice *another spelling* of **liquorice**

lid *noun* **1** a cover for a box, pot *etc* **2** the cover of the eye

lido /*lee*doh/ *noun* **1** a bathing beach **2** an open-air swimming pool

lie[1] *noun* a false statement meant to deceive ▯ *verb* tell a lie ▯ **liar** *noun* someone who tells lies

lie[1] *verb* » lie*s*, ly*ing*, li*ed*

lie[2] *verb* **1** rest in a flat position **2** be or remain in a state or position ▯ *noun* the position or situation in which something lies ▯ **lie in wait** keep hidden in order to surprise someone ▯ **lie low** keep quiet or hidden ▯ **the lie of the land** the present state of affairs

lie[2] *verb* » lie*s*, ly*ing*, lay or li*ed*, lain

⚠Do not confuse with: **lay**

liege /leezh/ *noun* **1** a loyal subject **2** a lord or superior

lieu *noun*: **in lieu of** instead of

Lieut *abbrev* Lieutenant

lieutenant *noun* **1** an army officer next below captain **2** in the navy, an officer below a lieutenant-commander **3** a rank below a higher officer: *lieutenant-colonel*

life *noun* (*plural* **lives**) **1** the period between birth and death **2** the state of being alive **3** liveliness **4** manner of living **5** the story of someone's life **6** living things: *animal life* □ **lifebelt** *noun* a ring of cork or filled with air for keeping someone afloat □ **lifeboat** *noun* a boat for rescuing people in difficulties at sea □ **lifeblood** *noun* a source of necessary strength or life □ **lifebuoy** *noun* a float to support someone awaiting rescue at sea □ **life-cycle** *noun* the various stages through which a living thing passes □ **life drawing** drawing from a live human model □ **life-jacket** *noun* a buoyant jacket for keeping someone afloat in water □ **lifeless** *adj* **1** dead **2** not lively, spiritless □ **life-like** *adj* like a living person □ **lifeline** *noun* a vital means of communication □ **lifelong** *adj* lasting the length of a life □ **life-size** *adj* full size, as in life □ **lifespan** *noun* the length of someone's life □ **lifestyle** *noun* the way in which someone lives □ **life-support machine** a device for keeping a human being alive during severe illness, space travel *etc* □ **lifetime** *noun* the period during which someone is alive

lift *verb* **1** raise, take up **2** *informal* steal **3** of fog: disappear, disperse □ *noun* **1** a moving platform carrying goods or people between floors in a large building **2** a ride in someone's car *etc* **3** a boost □ **lift-off** *noun* the take-off of a rocket, spacecraft *etc*

ligament *noun* a tough substance that connects the bones of the body

ligature *noun* **1** something which binds **2** a printed character formed or two or more letters, *eg* æ or ﬃ

light[1] *noun* **1** the brightness given by the sun, moon, lamps *etc* that makes things visible **2** a source of light, *eg* a lamp **3** a flame on a cigarette lighter **4** knowledge □ *adj* **1** bright **2** of a colour: pale **3** having light, not dark □ *verb* **1** give light to **2** set fire to □ **lighten** *verb* **1** make or become brighter **2** of lightning: to flash □ **lightening** *noun* a making or becoming lighter or brighter □ **lighter** *noun* a device with a flame *etc* for lighting □ **lighthouse** *noun* a tower-like building with a flashing light to warn or guide ships □ **lighting** *noun* a means of providing light □ **lightship** *noun* a ship anchored in a fixed position to serve as a lighthouse □ **light-year** *noun* the distance light travels in a year (6 billion miles) □ **bring to light** reveal, cause to be noticed □ **come to light** be revealed or discovered □ **in the light of** taking into consideration (information *etc*)

> **light** *verb* » light*s*, light*ing*, lit or light*ed*

light[2] *adj* **1** not heavy **2** easy to bear or do **3** easy to digest **4** nimble **5** lively **6** not grave, cheerful **7** not serious: *light music* **8** of rain *etc*: little in quantity □ **lighten** *verb* make less heavy □ **lighter** a large open boat used in unloading and loading ships □ **light-fingered** *adj* apt to steal □ **light-headed** *adj* dizzy □ **light-hearted** *adj* cheerful □ **lightly** *adv* □ **lightweight** *noun* a weight category in boxing

light[3] *verb, old* (with **on**) **1** land,

settle on **2** come upon by chance

> light » light*s*, light*ing*, lit or light*ed*

lightning *noun* an electric flash in the clouds ▯ **lightning conductor** a metal rod that on a building *etc* which conducts electricity down to earth

> ⚠Do not confuse with: **lightening**

ligneous *adj* woody; wooden

lignite *noun* brown, woody coal

like[1] *adj* the same as or similar to ▯ *adv* in the same way as: *he sings like an angel* ▯ *noun* something or someone that is the equal of another: *you won't see her like again* ▯ **likelihood** *noun* probability ▯ **likely** *adj* **1** probable **2** liable (to do something) ▯ *adv* probably ▯ **liken** *verb* think of as similar, compare ▯ **likeness** *noun* **1** similarity, resemblance **2** a portrait, photograph *etc* of someone ▯ **likewise** *adv* **1** in the same way **2** also

like[2] *verb* **1** be pleased with **2** be fond of ▯ **likeable** or **likable** *adj* attractive, lovable ▯ **liking** *noun* **1** fondness **2** satisfaction: *to my liking*

lilac *noun* a small tree with hanging clusters of pale purple or white flowers ▯ *adj* of pale purple colour

lilliputian *adj* tiny, minuscule

> After *Lilliput*, a country on a tiny scale in Jonathan Swift's 18th-century satirical novel, *Gulliver's Travels*

lilt *noun* a striking rhythm or swing ▯ *verb* have this rhythm

lily *noun* (*plural* **lilies**) a tall plant grown from a bulb with large white or coloured flowers ▯ **lily-of-the-valley** *noun* a plant with small white bell-shaped flowers

limb *noun* **1** a leg or arm **2** a branch

limber *adj* easily bent, supple ▯ **limber up** exercise so as to become supple

limbo[1] *noun* the borderland of Hell, reserved for those unbaptized before death ▯ **in limbo** forgotten, neglected

limbo[2] *noun* a W Indian dance in which the dancer passes under a low bar

lime *noun* **1** (*also called* **quicklime**) a white substance left after heating limestone, used in making cement **2** a tree related to the lemon **3** its greenish-yellow fruit **4** another name for **linden** ▯ **in the limelight** attracting publicity or attention

limerick *noun* a type of humorous rhymed poetry in five-line verses

> After *Limerick* in Ireland, the name of which was repeated in nonsense songs in an old Victorian parlour game

limit *noun* **1** the farthest point or place **2** a boundary **3** largest (or smallest) extent, degree *etc* **4** restriction ▯ *verb* set or keep to a limit ▯ **limitation** *noun* **1** something which limits **2** a weak point, a flaw

limo *noun, informal* a limousine

limousine *noun* a kind of large motor car, *esp* one with a separate compartment for the driver

> Named after a type of cloak worn in *Limousin* in France, because the car's roof was supposedly similar in shape

limp *adj* **1** not stiff, floppy **2** weak □ *verb* **1** walk lamely **2** of a damaged ship *etc:* move with difficulty □ *noun* **1** the act of limping **2** a limping walk

limpet *noun* **1** a small cone-shaped shellfish that clings to rocks **2** someone who is difficult to get rid of

limpid *adj* clear, transparent

linchpin *noun* a pin-shaped rod used to keep a wheel on an axle

linctus *noun* a syrupy medicine for sore throats *etc*

linden *noun* (*also called* **lime**) a lime tree with small flowers and heart-shaped leaves

line *noun* **1** a cord, rope *etc* **2** a long thin stroke or mark **3** a wrinkle **4** a row of people, printed words *etc* **5** a service of ships or aircraft **6** a railway **7** a telephone connection **8** a short letter **9** a family from generation to generation **10** course, direction **11** a subject of interest, activity *etc* **12** (**lines**) army trenches **13** (**lines**) a written school punishment exercise □ *verb* **1** mark out with lines **2** (often with **up**) place in a row or alongside of **3** form lines along (a street) **4** cover on the inside: *line a dress* □ **lineage** *noun* descent, traced back to your ancestors □ **lineal** *adj* directly descended through the father, grandfather *etc* □ **lineament** *noun* a feature, *esp* of the face □ **linear** *adj* **1** made of lines **2** in one dimension (length, breadth or height) only □ **liner** *noun* a ship or aeroplane working on a regular service □ **linesman, lineswoman** *noun* an umpire at a boundary line □ **lining** *noun* a covering on the inside

linen *noun* **1** cloth made of flax **2** articles made of linen: *tablelinen/ bedlinen*

ling[1] *noun* a long slender fish like the cod

ling[2] *noun* heather

linger *verb* **1** stay for a long time or for longer than expected **2** loiter, delay

lingerie *noun plural* women's underwear

lingo *noun* (*plural* **lingoes**) a language, a dialect

lingua franca a language used amongst people from different nations *etc* so that they can communicate

linguini *noun plural* pasta in long thin flat strands

linguist *noun* **1** someone skilled in languages **2** someone who studies language □ **linguistic** *adj* □ **linguistics** *noun sing* the scientific study of languages and of language in general

liniment *noun* an oil or ointment rubbed into the skin to cure stiffness in the muscles, joints *etc*

link *noun* **1** a ring of a chain **2** a single part of a series **3** anything connecting two things □ *verb* **1** connect with a link **2** to join closely **3** be connected □ **linkage** *noun*

links *noun plural* **1** a stretch of flat or slightly hilly ground near the seashore **2** a golf course

linnet *noun* a small songbird of the finch family

lino *noun, informal* linoleum ▫ **linocut** *noun* a design for printing cut into a block of linoleum

linoleum *noun* a type of smooth, hard-wearing covering for floors

linseed *noun* flax seed ▫ **linseed oil** oil from flax seed

lint *noun* **1** a soft woolly material for putting over wounds **2** fine pieces of fluff

lintel *noun* a timber or stone over a doorway or window

lion *noun* a powerful animal of the cat family, the male of which has a shaggy mane ▫ **lioness** *noun* a female lion ▫ **lionize** *verb* treat as a celebrity ▫ **the lion's share** the largest share

lip *noun* **1** either of the two fleshy flaps in front of the teeth forming the rim of the mouth **2** the edge of a container *etc* ▫ **lip-reading** *noun* reading what someone says from the movement of their lips ▫ **lip-service** *noun* saying one thing but believing another: *paying lip-service to the rules* ▫ **lipstick** *noun* a stick of red, pink *etc* colouring for the lips

liposuction *noun* a surgical operation to remove unwanted body fat

liquefy *verb* make or become liquid ▫ **liquefaction** *noun*

> **liquefy** » liquef*ies*, liquefy*ing*, liquefi*ed*

liqueur *noun* a strong alcoholic drink, strongly flavoured and sweet

> ⚠Do not confuse with: **liquor**

liquid *noun* a flowing, water-like substance ▫ *adj* **1** flowing **2** looking like water **3** soft and clear

liquidate *verb* **1** close down, wind up the affairs of (a bankrupt business company) **2** *slang* kill, murder ▫ **liquidation** *noun* ▫ **liquidator** *noun* ▫ **liquidize** *verb* **1** make liquid **2** make into a purée ▫ **liquidizer** *noun* a machine for liquidizing

liquor *noun* an alcoholic drink, *esp* a spirit (*eg* whisky)

> ⚠Do not confuse with: **liqueur**

liquorice or **licorice** *noun* **1** a plant with a sweet-tasting root **2** a black, sticky sweet flavoured with this root

lira /leerB/ *noun* the standard unit of Italian money

lisp *verb* **1** say *th* for *s* or *z* because of being unable to pronounce these letters correctly **2** speak imperfectly, like a child ▫ *noun* a speech disorder of this kind

lissome *adj* nimble, bending easily

list[1] *noun* a series of names, numbers, prices *etc* written down one after the other ▫ *verb* write (something) down in this way ▫ **listed building** one protected from being knocked down because it is of architectural or historical interest

list[2] *verb* of a ship: lean over to one side ▫ *noun* a slope to one side

listen *verb* hear, pay attention to ◊ **listener** *noun*

listeria *noun* a bacterium found in certain foods which can damage the nervous system if not killed during cooking ◊ **listeriosis** *noun* a brain disease caused by eating food contaminated with listeria bacteria

listless *adj* weary, without energy or interest ◊ **listlessness** *noun*

lists *noun plural*, *hist* the ground enclosed for a battle between knights on horseback

lit *past form* of **light**[1] and **light**[3]

litany *noun* (*plural* **litanies**) **1** a set form of prayer **2** a long list or catalogue

liter *US spelling* of **litre**

literal *adj* following the exact or most obvious meaning ◊ **literally** *adv* exactly as stated: *he was literally blinded by the flash*

literary *adj* **1** relating to books, authors *etc* **2** knowledgeable about books ◊ **literacy** *noun* ability to read and write ◊ **literate** *adj* able to read and write

literature *noun* **1** the books *etc* that are written in any language **2** anything in written form on a subject

lithe *adj* bending easily, supple, flexible

lithium *noun* a metallic element whose salts are used in treating some mental illnesses

lithograph *noun* a picture made from a drawing done on stone or metal ◊ **lithographer** *noun* ◊ **lithography** *noun* printing done by this method

litigation *noun* a law case

litigious *adj* fond of taking your grievances to court

litmus paper treated paper which changes colour when dipped in an acid or alkaline solution ◊ **litmus test** something which indicates underlying attitudes *etc*

litre *noun* a metric measure of liquids (1.76 pint)

litter *noun* **1** an untidy mess of paper, rubbish *etc* **2** a heap of straw as bedding for animals **3** a number of animals born at one birth **4** *hist* a bed for carrying the sick and injured ◊ *verb* **1** scatter rubbish carelessly about **2** produce a litter of young

little *adj* small in quantity or size ◊ *adv* **1** in a small quantity or degree **2** not much **3** not at all: *little does she know* ◊ *pronoun* a small amount, distance *etc*: *have a little more/ move a little to the right*

liturgy *noun* (*plural* **liturgies**) the form of service of a church ◊ **liturgical** *adj*

live[1] /liv/ *verb* **1** have life **2** dwell **3** pass your life **4** continue to be alive **5** survive **6** to be lifelike or vivid ◊ **livelihood** *noun* someone's means of living, *eg* their daily work ◊ **live and let live** allow others to live as they please ◊ **live down** live until (an embarrassment *etc*) is forgotten by others ◊ **live on 1** keep yourself alive **2** be supported by ◊ **live up to** be as good as expected

live[2] /laiv/ *adj* **1** having life, not dead **2** full of energy **3** of a television broadcast *etc*: seen as the event takes place, not recorded **4** charged with electricity and apt to give an electric shock □ **liven** *verb* make lively □ **livestock** *noun* farm animals □ **liveware** *noun, comput informal* the people operating a system, as opposed to the hardware and equipment □ **livewire** *noun* a very lively, energetic person

livelong *adj, old* whole: *the livelong day*

lively *adj* full of life, high spirits □ **liveliness** *noun*

liver *noun* a large gland in the body that carries out several important functions including purifying the blood

livery *noun* (*plural* **liveries**) the uniform of a manservant *etc* □ **livery stable** a stable where horses are kept for hire

livid *adj* **1** of a bluish lead-like colour **2** very angry

living *adj* **1** having life **2** active, lively **3** of a likeness: exact □ *noun* means of living □ **living-room** *noun* an informal sitting-room □ **living wage** a wage on which it is possible to live comfortably

lizard *noun* a four-footed reptile

llama *noun* a S American animal of the camel family without a hump

lo *exclam, old* look

loach *noun* (*plural* **loaches**) a type of small river fish

load *verb* **1** put on what is to be carried **2** put the ammunition in (a gun) **3** put a film in (a camera) **4** weight for some purpose: *loaded dice* □ *noun* **1** as much as can be carried at once **2** cargo **3** a heavy weight or task **4** the power carried by an electric circuit □ **loaded question** one meant to trap someone into making a damaging admission □ **loadline** *noun* a line along a ship's side to mark the waterline when fully loaded

loaf *noun* (*plural* **loaves**) a shaped mass of bread □ *verb* pass time idly or lazily □ **loafer** *noun* **1** an idler **2** (**loafers**) casual shoes

loam *noun* a rich soil □ **loamy** *adj*

loan *noun* something lent, *esp* a sum of money □ *verb* lend

loath or **loth** /lohth/ *adj* unwilling (to)

> ⚠Do not confuse: **loath** and **loathe**

loathe *verb* /lohdh/ dislike greatly □ **loathing** *noun* great hate or disgust □ **loathsome** *adj* causing loathing or disgust, horrible

loaves *plural* of **loaf**

lob *noun* **1** *cricket* a slow, high ball bowled underhand **2** *tennis* a ball high overhead dropping near the back of the court □ *verb* **1** send such a ball **2** *informal* throw

> **lob** *verb* » lob*s*, lobb*ing*, lobb*ed*

lobby *noun* (*plural* **lobbies**) **1** a small entrance hall **2** a passage off which rooms open **3** a group of people who try to influence the government or other authority □ *verb* **1** try to influence (public officials) **2** conduct a campaign to influence public officials

lobby *verb* » lobbi*es*, lobby*ing*, lobbi*ed*

lobe *noun* **1** the hanging-down part of an ear **2** a division of the brain, lungs *etc*

lobelia *noun* a garden plant with flowers twisted upside-down

lobotomy *noun* **1** surgical incision into a lobe or gland **2** a surgical operation on the front lobes of the brain in cases of schizophrenia *etc* ▯ **lobotomize** *verb* **1** perform a lobotomy on **2** make bland or spiritless

lobster *noun* a kind of shellfish with large claws, used for food ▯ **lobster pot** a basket in which lobsters are caught

local *adj* of or confined to a certain place ▯ *noun*, *informal* **1** the public house nearest someone's home **2** (**locals**) the people living in a particular place or area ▯ **local colour** details in a story which make it more interesting and realistic ▯ **locale** *noun* scene, location ▯ **local government** administration of the local affairs of a district *etc* by elected inhabitants ▯ **locality** *noun* a particular place and the area round about ▯ **localize** *verb* confine to one area, keep from spreading ▯ **locate** *verb* **1** find **2** set in a particular place: *a house located in the Highlands* ▯ **location** *noun* **1** the act of locating **2** situation ▯ **on location** of filming *etc*: in natural surroundings, not in a studio

loch *noun* **1** in Scotland, a lake **2** an arm of the sea

lock *noun* **1** a fastening for doors *etc* needing a key to open it **2** a part of a canal for raising or lowering boats **3** the part of a gun by which it is fired **4** a tight hold **5** a section of hair **6** (**locks**) hair ▯ *verb* **1** fasten with a lock **2** become fastened **3** (with **up**) shut in with a lock ▯ **locker** *noun* a small cupboard ▯ **locker-room** *noun* a room for changing clothes and storing personal belongings ▯ **locket** *noun* a little ornamental case hung round the neck ▯ **lockjaw** *noun* a form of tetanus which stiffens the jaw muscles ▯ **lockout** *noun* the locking out of workers by their employer during wage disputes ▯ **locksmith** *noun* a smith who makes locks ▯ **lock-up** *noun* a lockable garage ▯ **lock, stock and barrel** completely

locomotion *noun* movement from place to place ▯ **locomotive** *noun* a railway engine ▯ *adj* of or capable of locomotion

locum *noun* (*plural* **locums**) a doctor, dentist *etc* taking another's place for a time

locus *noun* (*plural* **loci**) a place, a locality ▯ **locus classicus** a standard or stock quotation

locust *noun* a large insect of the grasshopper family which destroys growing plants

lode *noun* a vein containing metallic ore ▯ **lodestone** *noun* **1** a form of the mineral magnetite with magnetic properties **2** a magnet ▯ **lodestar** *noun* the Pole star

lodge *noun* **1** a small house, often

at the entrance to a larger building **2** a beaver's dwelling **3** a house occupied during the shooting or hunting season **4** a branch of a society ◊ *verb* **1** live in rented rooms **2** become fixed (in) **3** put in a safe place **4** make (a complaint, appeal, *etc*) officially ◊ **lodger** *noun* someone who stays in rented rooms ◊ **lodging** *noun* **1** a place to stay, sleep *etc* **2** (**lodgings**) a room or rooms rented in someone else's house

loess /*loh*is/ *noun* a loamy deposit found in river valleys

loft *noun* **1** a room just under a roof **2** a gallery in a hall, church *etc*

lofty *adj* **1** high up **2** noble, proud ◊ **loftily** *adv* ◊ **loftiness** *noun*

log *noun* **1** a thick, rough piece of wood, part of a felled tree **2** a device for measuring a ship's speed **3** a logbook ◊ *verb* write down (events) in a logbook ◊ **log-jam** *noun* **1** a piling up of floating logs **2** congestion which brings traffic *etc* to a standstill

log *verb* » log*s*, logg*ing*, logg*ed*

loganberry *noun* a kind of fruit like a large raspberry

logbook *noun* **1** an official record of a ship's or aeroplane's progress **2** a record of progress, attendance *etc* **3** the registration documents of a motor vehicle

loggerhead *noun*: **at loggerheads** quarrelling

loggia /*loh*jə/ *noun* (*plural* **loggie** or **loggias**) a covered arcade

logic *noun* **1** the study of reasoning correctly **2** correctness of reasoning ◊ **logical** *adj* according to the rules of logic or sound reasoning ◊ **logically** *adv*

logo *noun* (*plural* **logos**) a symbol of a business firm *etc* consisting of a simple picture or lettering

loin *noun* **1** the back of an animal cut for food **2** (**loins**) the lower part of the back ◊ **loincloth** *noun* a piece of cloth worn round the hips, *esp* in India and south-east Asia

loiter *verb* **1** proceed, move slowly **2** linger **3** stand around

loll *verb* **1** lie lazily about **2** of the tongue: hang down or out

lollipop *noun* a large boiled sweet on a stick ◊ **lollipop man, lollipop woman** *Brit* someone employed to stop cars to allow schoolchildren to cross the street, who carries a pole with a disc at the top

lollop *verb* **1** bound clumsily **2** lounge, idle

lolly *noun, informal* **1** a lollipop **2** money

lone *adj* alone; standing by itself

lonely *adj* **1** lone **2** lacking or needing companionship **3** of a place: having few people ◊ **loneliness** *noun* ◊ **lonesome** *adj* **1** lone **2** feeling lonely

long *adj* **1** not short, measuring a lot from end to end **2** measuring a certain amount: *cut a strip 2 cm long/ the film is 3 hours long* **3** far-reaching **4** slow to do something ◊ *adv* **1** for a great time **2** through the whole time: *all day long* ◊ *verb* wish very much (for): *longing to see* *him again* □ **longbow** *noun* a large bow bent by the hand in shooting □ **longhand** *noun* writing in full (*contrasted with*: **shorthand**) □ **longing** *noun* a strong desire □ **long johns** men's under-trousers reaching to the ankles □ **long jump** □ **long-range** *adj* **1** able to reach a great distance **2** looking a long way into the future □ **longship** *noun, hist* a Viking sailing ship □ **long-sighted** *adj* able to see things at a distance but not those close at hand □ **long-standing** *adj* begun a long time ago, having lasted a long time □ **long-suffering** *adj* putting up with troubles without complaining □ **long-term** *adj* **1** extending over a long time **2** taking the future, not just the present, into account □ **long-wave** *adj* of radio: using wavelengths over 1000 metres (*compare with*: **short wave**) □ **long-winded** *adj* using too many words □ **before long** soon □ **in the long run** in the end □ **so long** *informal* goodbye

longevity *noun* great length of life

longitude *noun* the distance, measured in degrees, of a place east or west of the Greenwich meridian (*compare with*: **latitude**)

longueur /long*guhr*/ *noun* a tedious, over-long part of a book, film *etc*

loo *noun*, *informal* a toilet

loofah *noun* the fibrous fruit of a tropical plant, used as a rough sponge

look *verb* **1** turn the eyes towards so as to see **2** appear, seem: *you look tired/ it looks as if I can go after all* **3** face: *his room looks south* □ *noun* **1** the act of looking **2** the expression on someone's face **3** appearance **4** (**looks**) personal appearance □ **look-alike** *noun* someone who looks physically like another □ **looker** *noun, informal* someone attractive or good-looking □ **look-in** *noun* a chance of doing something □ **looking-glass** *noun* a mirror □ **lookout** *noun* **1** (someone who keeps) a careful watch **2** a high place for watching from **3** concern, responsibility □ **look alive** *informal* rouse yourself, get ready for action □ **look down on** think of as being inferior □ **look for** search for □ **look forward to** anticipate with pleasure □ **look into** investigate □ **look on 1** stand by and watch **2** think of (as): *he looks on her as his mother* □ **look out!** be careful! □ **look over** examine briefly □ **look sharp** *informal* be quick, hurry up

loom *noun* a machine for weaving cloth □ *verb* appear indistinctly, often threateningly

loony *noun, informal* a lunatic, an insane person □ *adj* mad, insane

loop *noun* **1** a doubled-over part in a piece of string *etc* **2** a U-shaped bend □ **loophole** *noun* **1** a narrow slit in a wall **2** a way of avoiding a difficulty □ **loop the loop** fly (an aircraft) upwards, back and down as if going round a circle

loose *adj* **1** not tight, slack **2** not tied, free **3** not closely packed **4** vague, not exact **5** careless □ *verb* **1** make loose, slacken **2** untie □ **loose-leaf** *adj* having a cover that allows pages to be inserted or removed ▫ **loosely** *adv* ▫ **loosen** *verb* make loose or looser ▫ **break loose** escape ▫ **on the loose** free

⚠Do not confuse with: **lose**

loot *noun* goods stolen or plundered ▫ *verb* plunder, ransack

lop *verb* cut off the top or ends of ▫ **lop-eared** *adj* of an animal: having ears hanging down ▫ **lop-sided** *adj* leaning to one side, not symmetrical

lop » lop*s*, lopp*ing*, lopp*ed*

lope *verb* run with a long stride

loquacious *adj* talkative ▫ **loquaciousness** or **loquacity** *noun*

loquat *noun* a small edible yellow fruit from a Chinese ornamental tree

lord *noun* **1** the owner of an estate **2** a title for a male member of the aristocracy, bishop, judge *etc* **3** *old* a master, a ruler **4** (**Lord**: with **the**) God or Christ ▫ **lordly** *adj* **1** relating to a lord **2** noble, proud ▫ **Lord's day** Sunday ▫ **lordship** *noun* **1** power, rule **2** used in addressing a lord: *his lordship* ▫ **drunk as a lord** extremely drunk ▫ **House of Lords** the upper (non-elected) house of the British parliament ▫ **lord it over someone** act in a domineering manner towards them

lore *noun* knowledge, beliefs *etc* handed down

lorelei /*lor*əlai/ *noun* a mythological siren in the Rhine who lured sailors to their death

lorgnette *noun* eyeglasses with a handle

lorry *noun* (*plural* **lorries**) a motor vehicle for carrying heavy loads

lose *verb* **1** cease to have, have no longer **2** have (something) taken away from **3** put (something) where it cannot be found **4** waste (time) **5** miss (a train, a chance *etc*) **6** not win (a game) ▫ **loser** *noun* someone unlikely to succeed at anything

lose » lose*s*, los*ing*, lost

⚠Do not confuse with: **loose**

loss *noun* (*plural* **losses**) **1** the act of losing **2** something which is lost **3** waste, harm, destruction ▫ **at a loss** uncertain what to do or say

lost *adj* **1** not able to be found **2** no longer possessed; thrown away **3** not won **4** ruined ▫ **lost in** completely taken up by, engrossed in: *lost in thought*

lot *noun* **1** a large number or quantity **2** someone's fortune or fate **3** a separate portion ▫ **draw lots** decide who is to do something by drawing names out of a hat *etc*

loth *another spelling* of **loath**

lotion *noun* a liquid for treating or cleaning the skin or hair

lottery *noun* (*plural* **lotteries**) an event in which money or prizes are won through drawing lots

lotus *noun* (*plural* **lotuses**) **1** a kind of water-lily **2** a mythical tree whose fruit caused forgetfulness

louche /loosh/ *adj* shady, disreputable

loud *adj* **1** making a great sound; noisy **2** showy, over-bright ▫ **loud** or **loudly** *adv* ▫ **loudhailer** *noun* a megaphone with microphone and amplifier ◊ **loudmouth** *noun, informal* someone who talks offensively and too much ◊ **loudness** *noun* ◊ **loudspeaker** *noun* a device for converting electrical signals into sound

lounge *verb* **1** lie back in a relaxed way **2** move about lazily ◊ *noun* a sitting-room ◊ **lounger** *noun* a lazy person ◊ **lounge lizard** someone who spends a lot of time aimlessly at social events ◊ **lounge suit** a man's suit for everyday (but not casual) wear

lour *see* **lower**[2]

louse *noun* (*plural* **lice**) a small blood-sucking insect sometimes found on the bodies of animals and people

lousy *adj* **1** swarming with lice **2** *informal* inferior, of poor quality

lout *noun* a clumsy or boorish man

louvre or *US* **louver** *noun* a slat set at an angle ◊ **louvre door** a slatted door allowing air and light to pass through ◊ **louvre window 1** a window covered with sloping slats **2** a window with narrow panes that can be set open at an angle

love *noun* **1** a great liking or affection **2** a loved person **3** *tennis* no score, zero ◊ *verb* be very fond of; like very much ◊ **lovable** *adj* worthy of love ◊ **love affair** a relationship between people in love but not married ◊ **lovebite** *noun* a mark on the skin caused by biting during lovemaking ◊ **love-child** *noun* an illegitimate child ◊ **lovemaking** *noun* **1** courtship **2** sexual play and intercourse ◊ **lovesick** *adj* languishing with love ◊ **loving** *adj* full of love ◊ **lovingly** *adv* ◊ **in love (with) 1** feeling love and desire (for) **2** having a great liking (for): *in love with his own voice* ◊ **make love to 1** have sexual intercourse with **2** make sexual advances to, court

lovely *adj* beautiful; delightful ◊ **loveliness** *noun*

lover *noun* **1** someone who loves another **2** an admirer, an enthusiast: *an art lover* **3** someone who is having a love affair

low *adj* **1** not high; not lying or reaching far up **2** of a voice: not loud **3** cheap: *low air-fare* **4** feeling sad, depressed **5** humble **6** mean, unworthy ◊ *verb* make the noise of cattle; bellow, moo ◊ *adv* **1** in or to a low position **2** not loudly **3** cheaply ◊ **lowbrow** *adj* populist, not intellectual (*contrasted with*: **highbrow**) ◊ **lowdown** *noun* damaging information ◊ **lowkey** *adj* not elaborate, unpretentious ◊ **lowland** *noun* flattish country, without high hills ◊ **lowness** *noun* ◊ **keep a low profile** not make your feelings or presence known

lower[1] */lohər/ adj* less high ◊ *verb* **1** make less high: *lower the price* **2** let or come down: *lower the blinds* ◊ **lower-case** *adj* of a letter: not a capital, *eg a* not *A* (*contrasted with*: **upper-case**)

lower[2] or **lour** */lowər/ verb* **1** of the sky: become dark and cloudy **2** frown ◊ **lowering** *adj*

lowly *adj* low in rank, humble ◊ **lowliness** *noun*

loyal *adj* faithful, true ◊ **loyalist** *noun* someone loyal to their sovereign or country ◊ **loyally** *adv* ◊

loyalty (*plural* **loyalties**) *noun*

lozenge *noun* **1** a diamond-shaped figure **2** a small sweet for sucking

LP *noun* a long-playing record

LSD *abbrev* **1** lysergic acid diethylamide, a hallucinogenic drug **2** pounds, shillings and pence (British coinage before decimalization)

Lt *abbrev* Lieutenant

Ltd *abbrev* limited liability

lubricate *verb* **1** apply oil *etc* to (something) to overcome friction and make movement easier **2** *informal* ply with alcohol □ **lubricant** *noun* something which lubricates; an oil □ **lubrication** *noun* □ **lubricator** *noun*

lucerne *noun* a type of plant used for feeding cattle, alfalfa

lucid *adj* **1** easily understood **2** clear in mind; not confused □ **lucidity** *noun* □ **lucidly** *adv*

Lucifer *noun* Satan, the Devil

luck *noun* **1** fortune, either good or bad **2** chance: *as luck would have it* **3** good fortune: *have any luck?* □ **luckless** *adj* unfortunate, unhappy

lucky *adj* **1** fortunate, having good luck **2** bringing good luck: *lucky charm* □ **luckily** *adv*

lucky » luck*ier*, luck*iest*

lucrative *adj* profitable

lucre /*look*r/ *noun* gain; money

Luddite *noun* an opponent of technological innovation

Originally a group of protesters against the Industrial Revolution in the early 19th century, who based their name on Ned *Ludd*, an earlier opponent of machines for weaving stockings

ludicrous *adj* ridiculous □ **ludicrously** *adv*

ludo *noun* a game played with counters on a board

lug[1] *verb* pull or drag with effort □ **lugger** *noun* a small sailing vessel

lug » lug*s*, lugg*ing*, lugg*ed*

lug[2] *noun, informal* the ear □ **lughole** *noun, informal* the earhole

luggage *noun* suitcases and other travelling baggage

lugubrious *adj* mournful, dismal □ **lugubriously** *adv* □ **lugubriousness** *noun*

lugworm *noun* a large worm found on the seashore, used for fishing bait

lukewarm *adj* **1** neither hot nor cold **2** not very keen, unenthusiastic

lull *verb* soothe or calm □ *noun* a period of calm

lullaby *noun* (*plural* **lullabies**) a song to lull children to sleep

lumbago *noun* a pain in the lower part of the back

lumbar *adj* of or in the lower part of the back

lumber *noun* **1** sawn-up timber **2** discarded old furniture *etc* □ *verb* move about clumsily

lumberjack *noun* someone who fells, saws and shifts trees

luminary *noun* (*plural* **luminaries**) **1** the sun, moon *etc* as a source of light **2** an exemplary teacher or leader

luminescent *adj* giving out light □ **luminescence** *noun*

luminous *adj* **1** giving light **2** shining; clear □ **luminosity** *noun* □ **luminously** *adv*

lump *noun* **1** a small, solid mass of indefinite shape **2** a swelling **3** the whole taken together: *considered in a lump* **4** a heavy, dull person □ *verb* **1** form into lumps **2** treat as being alike: *lumped all of us together* □ **lumpectomy** *noun* surgery to remove a lump in the breast □ **lumpish** *adj* heavy, dull □ **lump sum** an amount of money given all at once □ **lumpy** *adj* full of lumps

lumpen proletariat the poorest social class; the underclass

lunacy *noun* madness, insanity

lunar *adj* of the moon: *lunar eclipse*

lunatic *noun* someone who is insane or crazy □ *adj* insane, mad

lunch *noun* (*plural* **lunches**) a midday meal □ *verb* eat lunch

luncheon *noun* lunch

lung *noun* either of the two bag-like organs which fill with and expel air in the course of breathing

lunge *noun* a sudden thrust or push □ *verb* thrust or plunge forward suddenly

lupin *noun* a type of plant with flowers on long spikes

lurch *verb* roll or pitch suddenly to one side; stagger □ *noun* a pitch to one side □ **leave in the lurch** leave in a difficult position without help

lure *noun* something which entices; a bait □ *verb* attract, entice away

lurex *noun, trademark* a plastic-coated aluminium thread

lurid *adj* **1** glaring, garish: *lurid book cover* **2** horrifying, sensational: *lurid story* **3** pale, ghostly

lurk *verb* **1** keep out of sight; be hidden **2** move or act secretly and slyly □ **lurker** *noun* □ **lurking** *adj* vague, hidden

luscious *adj* sweet, delicious, juicy

lush *adj* of grass *etc*: thick and plentiful

lust *noun* **1** a greedy desire for power, riches *etc* **2** a strong sexual desire □ *verb* have a strong desire (for) □ **lustful** *adj* □ **lustfully** *adv*

luster *US spelling* of **lustre**

lustre or *US* **luster** *noun* brightness, shine, gloss □ **lustrous** *adj* bright, shining

lusty *adj* lively, strong □ **lustily** *adv* □ **lustiness** *noun*

lute *noun* a stringed musical instrument with a pear-shaped, round-backed body and fretted fingerboard □ **lutar** *Scot* or **lutenist** *noun* a lute player

lutein *noun* the yellow pigment in egg-yolks

luxuriant *adj* **1** thick with leaves, flowers *etc* **2** richly ornamented

> ⚠Do not confuse with: **luxurious**

luxuriate *verb* **1** be luxuriant **2** enjoy; take delight (in)

luxurious *adj* full of luxuries; very comfortable ▯ **luxuriously** *adv* ▯ **luxuriousness** *noun*

⚠Do not confuse with: **luxuriant**

luxury *noun* (*plural* **luxuries**) **1** something very pleasant or expensive but not necessary: *having a car is a luxury* **2** the use or enjoyment of such things

lycanthropy *noun* the ability to change into a werewolf

lycée /*lee*seh/ *noun* a state secondary school in France

lychee /*lai*chee/ *noun* a small Chinese fruit with rough skin and translucent flesh

lychgate *noun* a churchyard gate with a porch

lycra *noun, trademark* a lightweight synthetic elastic fabric

lying *see* **lie**

lymph *noun* a colourless fluid in the body ▯ **lymph gland** one of the glands carrying lymph

lynch *verb* condemn and put to death without legal trial

Named after William *Lynch*, 19th-century Virginian planter who organized unofficial trials of suspected criminals

lynx *noun* (*plural* **lynxes**) a wild animal of the cat family, noted for its keen sight

lyre *noun* an ancient stringed musical instrument, played like a harp

lyrebird *noun* an Australian bird with a lyre-shaped tail

lyric *noun* **1** a short poem, often expressing the poet's feelings **2** (**lyrics**) the words of a song ▯ *adj* **1** of a lyric **2** full of joy

lyrical *adj* **1** lyric **2** song-like **3** full of enthusiastic praise ▯ **lyrically** *adv*

M

M *abbrev* a thousand (from Latin *mille*)

m *abbrev* **1** metre(s) **2** mile(s) **3** married **4** male **5** masculine

MA *abbrev* Master of Arts

macabre *adj* gruesome, horrible

macadamia *noun* an edible nut from an Australian evergreen tree

macadamize *verb* surface (a road) with small broken stones

> Named after the 19th-century Scottish engineer John *McAdam* who invented the process

macaroni *noun* pasta shaped into short hollow tubes

macaroon *noun* a sweet cake or biscuit made with ground almonds and sugar

macassar *noun* oil obtained from ylang-ylang flowers, once popular as a hair oil

macaw *noun* a long-tailed brightly-coloured parrot

mace[1] *noun* a heavy staff with an ornamental head, carried as a sign of office

mace[2] *noun* a spice made from the covering of a nutmeg

macerate *verb* **1** make into pulp by steeping **2** emaciate

machair /*ma*xhər/ *noun* a low-lying sandy beach used for grazing

machete /mə*sheti*/ *noun* a heavy knife used to cut through foliage *etc*

machinations *noun plural* a crafty scheme, a plot

machine *noun* **1** a working arrangement of wheels, levers *etc* **2** a (motor) bicycle **3** a political party organization ▫ *verb* sew *etc* with a machine ▫ **machine code** a system of symbols that can be understood by a computer ▫ **machinegun** *noun* an automatic rapid-firing gun ▫ **machinist** *noun* a machine maker or operator

machinery *noun* **1** machines in general **2** the working parts of a machine **3** organization: *machinery of local government*

machismo *noun* overt or aggressive masculinity

Mach number the ratio of the speed of an aircraft to the velocity of sound (*eg* Mach 5 = 5 times the speed of sound)

macho /*ma*choh/ *adj* overtly or aggressively masculine

mackerel *noun* an edible seafish with wavy markings

mackintosh *noun* (*plural* **mackintoshes**) a waterproof overcoat

macramé *noun* ornamental knotted threadwork

macro *noun*, *comput* a single instruction that prompts a computer to carry out a series of short instructions embedded in it

macrobiotic *adj* of diet: consisting of organic unprocessed food, especially vegetables

macula *noun* a spot or mark, *eg* on the skin

mad *adj* **1** out of your mind, insane **2** wildly foolish **3** furious with anger ▯ **madhouse** *noun* **1** a place of confusion and noise **2** *hist* an insane asylum ▯ **madman, madwoman** *noun* someone who is mad ▯ **madness** *noun* ▯ **like mad** very quickly or energetically

madam *noun* a polite form of address to a woman

madcap *noun* a rash, hot-headed person ▯ *adj* foolishly rash: *madcap scheme*

madden *verb* make angry or mad ▯ **maddening** *adj* extremely annoying

made *past form* of **make**

madeira *noun* **1** a kind of fortified white wine **2** a plain rich sponge cake

madly *adv* **1** insanely **2** extremely: *madly in love*

Madonna *noun* the Virgin Mary as depicted in art

madrigal *noun* a part-song for several voices

maelstrom /*mehl*strom/ *noun* **1** a whirlpool **2** any place of great confusion

maestro /*mai*stroh/ *noun* (*plural* **maestros**) someone highly skilled in an art, especially music

MAFF *abbrev* Ministry of Agriculture, Fisheries and Food

magazine *noun* **1** a periodical paper containing articles, stories and pictures **2** a storage place for military equipment **3** a place for extra cartridges in a rifle

> The sense of *magazine* as a periodical developed from the military use, being intended as a storehouse or treasury of information

magenta *noun* a reddish-purple colour ▯ *adj* of this colour

maggot *noun* a small worm-like creature, the grub of a bluebottle *etc* ▯ **maggoty** *adj* full of maggots

Maghreb *noun* the countries of NW Africa as a group, sometimes including Libya

Magi *see* **magus**

magic *noun* **1** a process which produces results which cannot be explained or which are remarkable **2** conjuring tricks ▯ *adj* **1** using magic **2** used in magic **3** magical ▯ **black magic** magic performed for an evil purpose; witchcraft

magical *adj* **1** of or produced by magic **2** very wonderful or mysterious ▯ **magically** *adv*

magician *noun* someone skilled in magic

magisterial *adj* **1** of magistrates **2** having an air of authority ▯ **magisterially** *adv*

magistrate *noun* someone with the power to enforce the law, *eg* a provost or justice of the peace

magma *noun* molten rock

magnanimity *noun* generosity ▯

magnanimous *adj* very generous □ **magnanimously** *adv*

magnate *noun* someone with great power or wealth

magnesia *noun* a white powder formed from magnesium

magnesium *noun* a white metal which burns with an intense white light

magnet *noun* **1** a piece of iron, steel *etc* which has the power to attract other pieces of metal **2** someone or something that attracts strongly

magnetic *adj* **1** having the powers of a magnet **2** strongly attractive: *magnetic personality* □ **magnetic north** the direction in which the magnetized needle of a compass points □ **magnetic tape** tape on which sound, pictures, computer material *etc* can be recorded

magnetism *noun* **1** the attractive power of a magnet **2** attraction, great charm

magnetize *verb* **1** make magnetic **2** attract, influence

magneto *noun* (*plural* **magnetos**) a device producing electric sparks, *eg* for lighting the fuel in a car engine

magnificent *adj* **1** splendid in appearance or action **2** excellent, very fine □ **magnificence** *noun* □ **magnificently** *adv*

magnify *verb* **1** make to appear larger by using special lenses **2** exaggerate □ **magnification**

> **magnify** » magnif*ies*, magnif*ying*, magnifi*ed*

magniloquent *adj* of speech: overly grand; pompous □ **magniloquence** *noun*

magnitude *noun* great size

magnolia *noun* a tree which produces large white or purplish sweet-scented flowers

magnum *noun* a bottle of wine or champagne equal to two ordinary bottles

magnum opus a great work, a masterpiece

magpie *noun* a black-and-white bird of the crow family, known for its habit of collecting objects

> Originally *maggot pie*, meaning 'pied Margaret'

magus *noun* (*plural* **magi**) an ancient Persian priest or astrologer □ **the Magi** the three wise men who brought gifts to the infant Christ

Magyar *noun* the Hungarian language

Maharajah *noun* an important Indian prince, especially the ruler of a state

Maharani *noun* a Maharajah's wife

maharishi *noun* a Hindu sage or religious leader

Mahdi *noun* the Islamic messiah

mah-jong *noun* a Chinese table game played with small painted bricks

mahogany *noun* **1** a tropical American hardwood tree **2** its hard reddish-brown wood, often used for furniture

maid *noun* **1** a female servant **2** *old* an unmarried woman; a young girl

maiden *noun*, *old* an unmarried girl; a virgin ▢ *adj* **1** of a maiden **2** unmarried: *maiden aunt* **3** first, initial: *maiden speech/ maiden voyage* ▢ **maiden name** the surname of a married woman before her marriage ▢ **maiden over** *cricket* an over in which no runs are made

mail[1] *noun* letters, parcels *etc* carried by post ▢ *verb* post ▢ **mail order** an order for goods to be sent by post ▢ **mail shot** unsolicited advertising material sent by post

mail[2] *noun* body armour of steel rings or plates

maim *verb* cripple, disable

main *adj* chief, most important ▢ *noun*, *old* **1** the ocean **2** (**the mains**) a chief pipe, wire *etc* supplying gas, water or electricity ▢ **mainframe** *noun* the central processing unit and storage unit of a computer ▢ *adj* of a computer: of the large, powerful type rather than the small-scale kind ▢ **mainland** *noun* a large piece of land off whose coast smaller islands lie ▢ **mainline** *verb*, *slang* inject drugs intravenously ▢ **mainly** *adv* chiefly, mostly ▢ **mainsail** *noun* the principal sail of a ship or boat ▢ **mainstay** *noun* the chief support ▢ **in the main** for the most part

mainspring *noun* **1** the chief spring causing the wheels to move in a watch or clock **2** the chief cause of any action: *mainspring of the revolution*

maintain *verb* **1** keep (something) as it is **2** continue to keep in good working order **3** support (a family *etc*) **4** state (an opinion) firmly

maintenance *noun* **1** the act of maintaining; upkeep, repair **2** means of support, *esp* money for food, clothing *etc*

maize *noun* a cereal crop grown in N and S America

Maj *abbrev* Major

majesty *noun* (*plural* **majesties**) **1** a title used in addressing a king or queen: *Your Majesty* **2** greatness of rank or manner ▢ **majestic** *adj* stately, regal

Majlis /maj*lis*/ *noun* the Iranian parliament

majolica *noun* tin-glazed decorative earthenware

major *adj* great in size, importance *etc* (*contrasted with*: **minor**) ▢ *noun* a senior army officer

majority *noun* (*plural* **majorities**) **1** the greater number or quantity **2** the difference in amount between the greater and the lesser number **3** the age when someone becomes legally an adult (18 in the UK)

make *verb* **1** form, construct **2** cause to be: *he makes me mad at times* **3** bring about: *make trouble* **4** amount to: *2 and 2 make 4* **5** earn: *she made £300 last week* **6** force: *I made him do it* **7** undergo (a journey *etc*) **8** prepare (a meal *etc*): *I'll make some tea* ▢ *noun* **1** kind, shape, form **2** brand ▢ **maker** *noun* ▢ **makeshift** *adj* used for a time for want of something better ▢ **make-up** *noun* cosmetics ▢ **make believe** pretend ▢ **make good 1** do well **2** carry out (a promise) **3** make up for (a loss) □ **make light of** treat as unimportant □ **make much of** fuss over, treat as important □ **make nothing of 1** be unable to understand, do *etc* **2** make light of □ **make off** run away □ **make out 1** see in the distance or indistinctly **2** declare, prove **3** write out (a bill *etc*) formally □ **make up 1** form a whole: *eleven players make up the side* **2** put together, invent (a false story) **3** put make-up on the face **4** be friendly again after a quarrel □ **make up for** give or do something in return for damage done □ **on the make** *informal* **1** looking for personal gain **2** looking for a sexual partner

> **make** *verb* » mak*es*, mak*ing*, made

malachite *noun* a green mineral, basic copper carbonate

maladjusted *adj* unable to fit in happily in your environment, society *etc*

maladministration *noun* bad management, especially of public affairs

maladroit *adj* **1** clumsy, awkward **2** tactless

malady *noun* (*plural* **maladies**) illness, disease

malaise *noun* a feeling or general air of depression or despondency

malapropism *noun* the use of a wrong word which sounds similar to the one intended, *eg contemptuous* for *contemporary*

> After Mrs *Malaprop* in Sheridan's play, *The Rivals* (1775), who habitually used the wrong word

malaria *noun* a fever caused by the bite of a particular mosquito □ **malarial** *adj*

> From an Italian phrase meaning 'bad air', malarial fever being originally thought to be caused by poisonous marsh gases

male *adj* of the sex that is able to father children or young, masculine □ *noun* a member of this sex

malediction *noun* a curse; cursing □ **maledictory** *adj*

malefactor *noun* an evildoer

malevolent *adj* wishing ill to others; spiteful □ **malevolence** *noun* □ **malevolently** *adv*

malformation *noun* faulty or wrong shape

malfunction *verb* fail to work or operate properly □ *noun* failure to operate

malice *noun* ill will; spite

malicious *adj* intending harm; spiteful □ **maliciously** *adv* □ **maliciousness** *noun*

malign /m*ə*lain/ *verb* speak ill of

malignant *adj* **1** wishing harm, spiteful **2** of a disease: likely to cause death (*contrasted with*: **benign**) □ **malignantly** *adv*

malinger *verb* pretend to be ill to avoid work *etc* □ **malingerer** *noun*

mall /mol/ *noun, US* a shopping centre

mallard *noun* the male of the common wild duck

malleable *adj* **1** of metal: able to be beaten out by hammering **2** of people: easy to influence ▯ **malleability** *noun*

mallet *noun* a heavy wooden hammer

malnutrition *noun* lack of sufficient or proper food; undernourishment

malodorous *adj* having a bad smell

malpractice *noun* **1** wrongdoing **2** professional misconduct

malt *noun* **1** barley or other grain prepared for making beer or whisky **2** a malt whisky

maltreat *verb* treat roughly or unkindly ▯ **maltreatment** *noun*

mama or **mamma** *noun, informal* mother

mamba *noun* a large deadly African snake, black or green in colour

mammal *noun* a member of the class of animals of which the female parent feeds the young with her own milk ▯ **mammalian** *adj*

mammary *adj* of a female breast or breasts: *mammary gland*

mammogram *noun* an X-ray taken of a woman's breast to detect early signs of cancer

mammon *noun* money considered as the root of evil

mammoth *noun* a very large elephant, now extinct ▯ *adj* enormous, huge: *mammoth savings*

man *noun* (*plural* **men**) **1** a grown-up human male **2** a human being **3** the human race **4** *informal* a husband **5** a piece in chess or draughts ▯ *verb* supply with workers, crew *etc*: *man the boats* ▯ **manful** *adj* courageous ▯ **manfully** *adv* ▯ **manhandle** *verb* handle roughly ▯ **manhole** *noun* a hole (into a drain, sewer *etc*) large enough to let a man through ▯ **manhood** *noun* the state of being a man ▯ **mankind** *noun* the human race ▯ **mannish** *adj* of a woman: behaving, looking like a man ▯ **man-of-war** *noun* a warship ▯ **manpower** *noun* the number of people available for work ▯ **the man in the street** the ordinary person ▯ **to a man** every single one

man *verb* » mans, mann*ing*, mann*ed*

manacle *noun, formal* a handcuff ▯ *verb* handcuff

manage *verb* **1** have control or charge of **2** deal with, cope: *can't manage on his own* **3** succeed: *managed to finish on time*

manageable *adj* easily managed or controlled ▯ **manageably** *adv*

management *noun* **1** those in charge of a business *etc* **2** the art of managing a business *etc*

manager *noun* someone in charge of a business *etc*

manageress *noun, old* a woman manager

mañana /man*yah*na/ *noun* tomorrow; sometime in the future

Mancunian *noun* someone born or living in Manchester

mandarin *noun* **1** a small orange-like citrus fruit **2** *hist* a senior Chinese official

mandate *noun* **1** power to act on someone else's behalf **2** a command

mandatory *adj* compulsory □ **mandatorily** *adv*

mandible *noun* the jaw or lower jawbone

mandolin or **mandoline** *noun* a round-backed stringed instrument similar to a lute

mandore or **mandora** *noun* a large mandolin

mandrake *noun* a poisonous plant of the potato family with a forked root

mandrill *noun* a large baboon from W Africa with a red and blue muzzle

mane *noun* **1** long hair on the head and neck of a horse or male lion **2** a long or thick head of hair

maneuver *US spelling of* **manoeuvre**

manga *noun* a Japanese adult comic book

manganese *noun* a hard easily-broken metal of a greyish-white colour

mange /mehnj/ *noun* a skin disease of dogs, cats *etc*

mangel-wurzel *noun* a kind of beetroot used as cattle food

manger *noun* a box or trough holding dry food for horses and cattle

mangetout /*monhzh*too/ *noun* a thin pea with an edible pod

mangle *noun* a machine for squeezing water out of clothes or for smoothing them □ *verb* **1** squeeze (clothes) through a mangle **2** crush, tear, damage badly

mango *noun* (*plural* **mangoes**) **1** the fruit of a tropical Indian tree, with juicy orange flesh **2** the tree which produces mangoes

mangosteen *noun* a round tropical fruit with thick red skin and juicy flesh

mangrove *noun* a type of tree which grows in swamps in hot countries

mangy *adj* **1** shabby, squalid **2** of an animal: suffering from mange

mania *noun* **1** a form of mental illness in which the sufferer is over-active, over-excited and unreasonably happy **2** extreme fondness or enthusiasm: *a mania for stamp-collecting*

maniac *noun* **1** a mad person **2** a very rash or over-enthusiastic person

manic *adj* **1** suffering from mania **2** very energetic or excited □ **manically** *adv*

manicure *noun* **1** the care of hands and nails **2** professional treatment for the hands and nails □ *verb* perform a manicure on □ **manicurist** *noun* someone who performs manicures

manifest *adj* easily seen or understood □ *verb* show plainly □ **manifestation** *noun* □ **manifestly** *adv* obviously, clearly

manifesto *noun* (*plural* **manifestoes** or **manifestos**) a public announcement of intentions, *eg* by a political party

manifold *adj* many and various

manila *noun* strong brown paper used for stationery *etc*

manioc *noun* tapioca

manipulate *verb* handle so as to turn to your own advantage

manky *adj, slang* dirty, grubby □ **mankiness** *noun*

manly *adj* brave, strong □ **manliness** *noun*

manna *noun* an unexpected or delicious treat

> The name given in the Bible to the food miraculously provided for the Israelites in the wilderness

mannequin *noun* **1** someone who models clothes for prospective buyers **2** a display dummy

manner *noun* **1** the way in which something is done **2** the way in which someone behaves **3** (**manners**) polite behaviour towards others □ **mannerism** *noun* an odd and obvious habit or characteristic □ **mannerly** *adj* polite □ **all manner of** all kinds of

manoeuvre or *US* **maneuver** *noun* **1** a planned movement of troops, ships or aircraft **2** a trick, a cunning plan □ *verb* **1** perform a manoeuvre **2** manipulate

manor *noun* **1** a large house, usually attached to a country estate **2** *hist* the land belonging to a lord or squire □ **manorial** *adj*

manqué *adj* unfulfilled in a particular ambition: *poet manqué*

mansard roof a roof with a divided slope which is steeper in the lower part

manse *noun* the house of a minister in certain Christian churches, *eg* the Church of Scotland

mansion *noun* a large house

manslaughter *noun* killing someone without deliberate intent

mantelpiece *noun* a shelf over a fireplace

mantis *noun* an insect of the cockroach family, with large spiny forelegs (*also called*: **praying mantis**)

mantle *noun* **1** a cloak or loose outer garment **2** a covering: *mantle of snow* **3** a thin, transparent shade around the flame of a gas or paraffin lamp

mantra *noun* a word or phrase, chanted or repeated inwardly in meditation

manual *adj* **1** of the hand or hands **2** worked by hand **3** working with the hands: *manual worker* □ *noun* a handbook giving instructions on how to use something: *a car manual* □ **manually** *adv*

manufacture *verb* make (articles or materials) in large quantities, *usu* by machine □ *noun* **1** the process of manufacturing **2** a manufactured article ▢ **manufacturer** *noun*

manure *noun* a substance, especially animal dung, spread on soil to make it more fertile ▢ *verb* treat with manure

manuscript *noun* **1** the prepared material for a book *etc* before it is printed **2** a book or paper written by hand

Manx cat a tailless breed of cat

many *adj* a large number of: *many people were present* ▢ *pronoun* a large number: *many survived* ▢ **many a** a large number of: *many a voice was raised*

map *noun* a flat drawing of all or part of the earth's surface, showing geographical features ▢ *verb* **1** make a map of **2** (**map out**) plan

> **map** *verb* » map*s*, mapp*ing*, mapp*ed*

maple *noun* **1** a tree related to the sycamore, one variety of which produces sugar **2** its hard light-coloured wood used for furniture *etc*

maquette *noun* an artist's scaled-down model of a piece of sculpture *etc*

mar *verb* spoil, deface

> **mar** » mar*s*, marr*ing*, marr*ed*

maracas *noun plural* a pair of filled gourds shaken as a percussion instrument

maraschino /mar*əsheen*oh/ *noun* a liqueur distilled from cherries

marathon *noun* a long-distance foot-race, usually covering 26 miles 385 yards

> After the distance run by a Greek soldier from *Marathon* to Athens with news of the victory over the Persians

maraud *verb* plunder, raid ▢ **marauder** *noun* a plundering robber ▢ **marauding** *adj*

marble *noun* **1** limestone that takes a high polish, used for sculpture, decorating buildings *etc* **2** a small glass ball used in a children's game

marcasite *noun* crystals formed from iron and used in jewellery

March *noun* the third month of the year

march[1] *verb* **1** (cause) to walk in time with regular step **2** go on steadily ▢ *noun* (*plural* **marches**) **1** a marching movement **2** a piece of music for marching to **3** the distance covered by marching **4** a steady progression of events: *the march of time*

march[2] *noun* a boundary or border ▢ **riding the marches** the traditional ceremony of riding around the boundaries of a town *etc*

marchioness *noun* (*plural* **marchionesses**) a woman marquess

Mardi Gras a carnival held on Shrove Tuesday in certain countries

mare *noun* a female horse

margarine *noun* an edible spread similar to butter, made mainly of vegetable fats

margarita *noun* a cocktail made with tequila and lime juice *etc*

margin *noun* **1** an edge, a border **2** the blank edge on the page of a book **3** additional space or room; allowance: *margin for error*

marginal *adj* **1** of or in a margin **2** borderline, close to a limit **3** of a political constituency: without a clear majority for any one candidate or party **4** of little effect or importance: *marginal improvement* ▫ *noun* a marginal political constituency ▫ **marginalize** *verb* make less important or central ▫ **marginally** *adv*

marguerite *noun* a kind of large daisy

mariachi *noun* one of a band of musicians playing traditional Mexican dance music

marigold *noun* a kind of plant with a yellow flower

marijuana *noun* a drug made from the plant hemp

marimba *noun* an African instrument like a xylophone, often used in jazz music

marina *noun* a place with moorings for yachts, dinghies *etc*

marinade *noun* a mixture of oil, wine, herbs, spices *etc* in which food is steeped for flavour ▫ **marinade** or **marinate** *verb* steep in a marinade

marine *adj* of the sea ▫ *noun* a soldier serving on board a ship

mariner /*marinər*/ *noun, old* a sailor

marionette *noun* a puppet moved by strings

marital *adj* of marriage ▫ **maritally** *adv*

maritime *adj* **1** of the sea or ships **2** lying near the sea

marjoram *noun* a sweet-smelling herb used in cooking

Mark *noun* a Deutschmark, the standard unit of German money

mark *noun* **1** a sign that can be seen **2** a stain, spot *etc* **3** a target aimed at **4** trace **5** a point used to assess the merit of a piece of schoolwork *etc* **6** the starting-line in a race: *on your marks!* ▫ *verb* **1** make a mark on; stain **2** observe, watch **3** stay close to (an opponent in football *etc*) **4** award marks to (a piece of schoolwork *etc*) **5** (**mark off**) separate, distinguish ▫ **marked** *adj* easily noticed: *marked improvement* ▫ **markedly** *adv* noticeably ▫ **marker** *noun* **1** someone who marks the score at games **2** a counter *etc* used to mark a score ▫ **marksman, markswoman** *noun* someone who shoots well ▫ **mark time 1** move the feet up and down, as if marching, but without going forward **2** keep things going without progressing ▫ **up to the mark** coming up to the required standard

market *noun* **1** a public place for buying and selling **2** (a country, place *etc* where there is) a need or demand (for certain types of goods) ▫ *verb* put on sale ▫ **market forces** commerce not restricted by government intervention ▫ **market garden**

a garden in which fruit and vegetables are grown to be sold ◇ **marketing** *noun* the act or practice of advertising and selling ◇ **market leader** a company, or brand of goods, that outsells its competitors ◇ **on the market** for sale

marlin *noun* a large ocean fish related to the swordfish

marlinspike *noun* a spike for separating the strands of a rope *etc*

marmalade *noun* a jam made from citrus fruit, *esp* oranges

marmite *noun, trademark* a savoury spread made from yeast and vegetable extracts

marmoset *noun* a type of small monkey found in America

marmot *noun* a burrowing animal of the squirrel family (*also called*: **woodchuck** or **groundhog**)

maroon[1] *noun* **1** a brownish-red colour **2** a firework used as a distress signal ◇ *adj* brownish-red

maroon[2] *verb* **1** abandon on an island *etc* without means of escape **2** leave in a helpless or uncomfortable position

marquee /mar*kee*/ *noun* a large tent used for large gatherings, *eg* a wedding reception or circus

marquess or **marquis** /*mar*kwis/ *noun* (*plural* **marquesses** or **marquises**) a nobleman below a duke in rank

marquetry *noun* the inlaying of wood with small pieces of different coloured wood, ivory *etc*

marriage *noun* **1** the ceremony by which two people become husband and wife **2** a joining together: *marriage of minds* ◇ **marriageable** *adj* suitable or old enough for marriage

marrow *noun* **1** the soft substance in the hollow part of bones **2** a long thick-skinned vegetable

marry *verb* join, or be joined, together in marriage

marry » marr*ies*, marry*ing*, marri*ed*

marsh *noun* (*plural* **marshes**) a piece of low-lying wet ground ◇ marsh-gas *see* **methane** ◇ **marsh marigold** a marsh plant with yellow flowers (*also called*: **kingcup**)

marshal *noun* **1** a high-ranking officer in the army or air force **2** someone who directs processions *etc* **3** *US* a law-court official **4** *US* the head of a police force ◇ *verb* **1** arrange (troops, facts, arguments *etc*) in order **2** show the way, conduct, lead

marshal *verb* » marshal*s*, marshall*ing*, marshall*ed*

marshmallow *noun* **1** a spongy jellylike sweet made from sugar and egg-whites *etc* **2** a marsh plant with pink flowers, similar to the hollyhock

marshy *adj* wet underfoot; boggy

marsupial *noun* an animal which carries its young in a pouch, *eg* the kangaroo

martello tower a round coastal fort

marten *noun* an animal related to the weasel

martial *adj* **1** of war or battle **2**

warlike ◊ **martial art** a combative sport or method of self-defence ◊ **martial law** the government of a country by its army

Martian *noun* a potential or imaginary being from the planet Mars

martin *noun* a bird of the swallow family

martinet *noun* someone who keeps strict order; a disciplinarian

Named after Jean *Martinet*, a 17th-century French officer who invented a type of military drill

martini *noun* (*plural* **martinis**) a cocktail made with gin and vermouth

Martinmas *noun* 11 November, the feast of St Martin

martyr *noun* someone who suffers death or hardship for their beliefs ◊ *verb* execute or make suffer for beliefs ◊ **martyrdom** *noun* the death or suffering of a martyr

marvel *noun* something astonishing or wonderful ◊ *verb* feel amazement (at)

marvel *verb* » marvel*s*, marvell*ing*, marvell*ed*

marvellous *adj* **1** astonishing, extraordinary **2** *informal* excellent, very good ◊ **marvellously** *adv*

Marxist *noun* a follower of the theories of Karl Marx; a communist ◊ **Marxism** *noun*

marzipan *noun* a mixture of ground almonds, sugar *etc*, used in cake-making and confectionery

mascara *noun* a cosmetic paint used to colour the eyelashes

mascot *noun* a person, animal or thing believed to bring good luck

masculine *adj* **1** of the male sex **2** manly ◊ **masculinity** *noun*

mash *verb* beat or crush into a pulp ◊ *noun* **1** mashed potato **2** a mixture of bran, meal *etc*, used as animal food

mask *noun* **1** a cover for the face for disguise or protection **2** a pretence, a disguise ◊ *verb* **1** hide, disguise **2** cover the face with a mask

masochism *noun* an unnatural pleasure taken in being dominated or treated cruelly ◊ **masochist** *noun* someone who takes such pleasure ◊ **masochistic** *adj*

After Leopold von Sacher-*Masoch*, 19th-century Austrian novelist

mason *noun* **1** someone who carves stone **2** a Freemason ◊ **masonic** *adj*

masonry *noun* stonework

masque *noun* an old type of theatre performance with actors wearing masks

masquerade *noun* **1** a dance at which masks are worn **2** pretence ◊ *verb* pretend to be someone else: *masquerading as a journalist*

mass *noun* (*plural* **masses**) **1** a lump or quantity gathered together **2** a large quantity **3** the main part or body **4** a measure of quantity of matter in an object (**Mass**) **5** (in some Christian churches) the celebration of Christ's last supper with his disciples (**Mass**) **6** music for a Mass *adj* **1** of a mass **2** of or consisting of large numbers or quantities *verb* form into a mass **mass media** means of communicating information to a large number of people, *eg* television **mass production** production in large quantities of articles all exactly the same **the masses** ordinary people

massacre *noun* the merciless killing of a large number of people *verb* kill (a large number) in a cruel way

massage *noun* the rubbing of parts of the body to remove pain or tension *verb* perform massage on

masseur *noun* someone who performs massage

masseuse *noun* a female masseur

massif *noun* a central mountain mass

massive *adj* bulky, heavy, huge **massively** *adv*

mast *noun* a long upright pole holding up the sails *etc* in a ship, or holding an aerial, flag *etc*

mastectomy *noun* the surgical removal of a woman's breast or breasts

master *noun* **1** someone who controls or commands **2** an owner of a dog *etc* **3** an employer **4** a male teacher **5** the commander of a merchant ship **6** someone who is very skilled in something, an expert **7** a degree awarded by universities: *Master of Arts* *adj* chief, controlling: *master switch* *verb* **1** overcome, defeat **2** become able to do or use properly: *I've finally mastered this computer program* **masterful** *adj* strong-willed **masterkey** *noun* a key which is so made that it opens a number of different locks **masterly** *adj* showing the skill of an expert or master, clever **mastermind** *verb* plan, work out the details of (a scheme *etc*) *noun* **masterpiece** *noun* the best example of someone's work, *esp* a very fine picture, book, piece of music *etc* **masterstroke** *noun* a clever act or move **master of ceremonies** someone who directs the form and order of events at a public occasion; a compère

mastery *noun* **1** victory (over) **2** control (of) **3** great skill (in)

mastic *noun* a gum resin from Mediterranean trees, used as a varnish or glue

masticate *verb, formal* chew **mastication** *noun*

mastiff *noun* a breed of large, powerful dog

mastodon *noun* an extinct animal similar to an elephant

masturbate *verb* stimulate the sexual organs to a state of orgasm **masturbation** *noun* **masturbator** *noun*

mat *noun* **1** piece of material (coarse plaited plant fibre, carpet *etc*) for wiping shoes on, covering the floor *etc* **2** a piece of material, wood *etc* put below dishes at table *adj, another spelling* of **matt** **matted** *adj* thickly tangled

matting *noun* material from which mats are made

matador *noun* the person who kills the bull in bullfights

match[1] *noun* (*plural* **matches**) a small stick of wood *etc* tipped with a substance which catches fire when rubbed against an abrasive surface ▫ **matchbox** *noun* a box for holding matches ▫ **matchstick** *noun* a single match ▫ **matchwood** *noun* wood broken into small pieces

match[2] *noun* (*plural* **matches**) **1** someone or thing similar to or the same as another **2** someone or thing agreeing with or suiting another **3** an equal **4** someone suitable for marriage **5** a contest or game ▫ *verb* **1** be of the same make, size, colour *etc* **2** set (two things, teams *etc*) against each other **3** hold your own with, be equal to ▫ **matchless** *adj* having no equal ▫ **matchmaker** *noun* someone who tries to arrange marriages or partnerships

mate *noun* **1** a friend, a companion **2** an assistant worker: *plumber's mate* **3** a husband or wife **4** the sexual partner of an animal, bird *etc* **5** a merchant ship's officer, next in rank to the captain ▫ *verb* **1** marry **2** bring or come together to breed

material *adj* **1** made of matter, able to be seen and felt **2** not spiritual, concerned with physical comfort, money *etc*: *a material outlook on life* **3** important, essential: *material difference* ▫ *noun* **1** something out of which anything is, or may be, made **2** cloth, fabric ▫ **materially** *adv* to a large extent, greatly

materialism *noun* **1** a tendency to attach too much importance to material things (*eg* physical comfort, money) **2** the belief that only things we can see or feel really exist or are important ▫ **materialist** *noun* ▫ **materialistic** *adj*

materialize *verb* **1** appear in bodily form **2** happen, come about

maternal *adj* **1** of a mother **2** like a mother, motherly **3** related through your mother: *maternal grandmother* ▫ **maternally** *adv*

maternity *noun* the state of being a mother, motherhood ▫ *adj* of or for a woman having or about to have a baby: *maternity clothes*

math *noun*, *US informal* mathematics

mathematics *noun sing* the study of measurements, numbers and quantities ▫ **mathematical** *adj* **1** of or done by mathematics **2** very exact ▫ **mathematician** *noun* an expert in mathematics

maths *noun*, *informal* mathematics

matinée *noun* an afternoon performance in a theatre or cinema ▫ **matinée coat** a baby's short jacket

matins *noun plural* the morning service in certain churches

matriarch *noun* a woman who controls a family or community ▫ **matriarchal** *adj*

matrices *plural* of **matrix**

matricide *noun* **1** the killing of your own mother **2** someone who kills their own mother

matriculate *verb* admit, or be admitted, to a university ▫ **matriculation** *noun*

matrilineal *adj* of family descent: progressing through the female line ▫ **matrilineally** *adv*

matrimony *noun, formal* marriage ▫ **matrimonial** *adj* relating to marriage ▫ **matrimonially** *adv*

matrix *noun* (*plural* **matrices**) **1** a mould in which metals *etc* are shaped **2** a mass of rock in which gems *etc* are found **3** a rectangular table of data

matron *noun* **1** a married woman **2** a senior nurse in charge of a hospital **3** *old* a woman in charge of housekeeping or nursing in a school, hostel *etc* ▫ **matronly** *adj* **1** of a woman: dignified, staid **2** rather plump

matt or **mat** *adj* having a dull surface; not shiny or glossy

matter *noun* **1** anything that takes up space, can be seen, felt *etc*; material, substance **2** a subject written or spoken about **3** (**matters**) affairs, business **4** trouble, difficulty: *what is the matter?* **5** importance: *of no great matter* **6** pus ▫ *verb* **1** be of importance: *it doesn't matter* **2** give out pus ▫ **matter-of-fact** *adj* keeping to the actual facts; unimaginative, uninteresting ▫ **a matter of course** something that is to be expected ▫ **a matter of opinion** a subject on which different opinions are held ▫ **as a matter of fact** in fact

mattock *noun* a tool like a pickaxe

mattress *noun* (*plural* **mattresses**) a thick layer of padding covered in cloth, usually as part of a bed

mature *adj* **1** fully grown or developed **2** ripe, ready for use ▫ *verb* **1** (cause to) become mature **2** of an insurance policy *etc*: be due to be paid out ▫ **maturely** *adv* ▫ **maturity** *noun* ripeness

matzo *noun* (*plural* **matzos** or **matzoth**) a wafer or cracker eaten during Passover

maudlin *adj* silly, sentimental

> From Mary *Magdalene*, who was frequently depicted crying in paintings

maul *verb* hurt badly by rough or savage treatment

maulstick *noun* an artist's stick tipped with a small pad, used to steady the hand during painting

Maundy Thursday the day before Good Friday in the Christian calendar

mausoleum *noun* a large or elaborate tomb

mauve *adj* of a purple colour

maverick *noun* someone who refuses to conform; a determined individualist

> After Samuel *Maverick*, Texas rancher who never branded his cattle

mavin *noun, US slang* an expert, a pundit

mavis *noun* the song thrush

maw *noun* **1** an animal's jaws or gullet **2** a wide or gaping cavity

mawkish *adj* weak and sentimental ▯ **mawkishly** *adv*

maxi- *prefix* very large or long: *maxi-skirt*

maxim *noun* a general truth or rule about behaviour *etc*

maximum *adj* greatest, most ▯ *noun* (*plural* **maxima**) **1** the greatest number or quantity **2** the highest point or degree

May *noun* the fifth month of the year

may *verb* **1** used with another verb to express permission or possibility: *you may watch the film/ I thought I might find him there* **2** used to express a wish: *may your wishes come true*

may » may, might

maybe *adv* perhaps

Mayday *noun* the first day of May

mayday *noun* an international distress signal

mayfly *noun* a short-lived insect that appears in May

mayhem *noun* widespread chaos or confusion

mayo /*meh*oh/ *noun*, *informal* mayonnaise

mayonnaise /mehə*nehz*/ *noun* a sauce made of eggs, oil and vinegar or lemon juice

mayor *noun* the chief elected public official of a city or town ▯ **mayoress** a mayor's wife

Note: *mayor* is used for a woman mayor, never *mayoress*

maypole *noun* a decorated pole traditionally danced around on Mayday

maze *noun* **1** a series of winding paths in a park *etc*, planned to make exit difficult **2** something complicated and confusing: *maze of regulations*

mazurka *noun* a lively Polish dance or dance music

MB *abbrev* Bachelor of Medicine (in Latin, *Medicinae Baccalaureus*)

Mb *abbrev* megabyte(s)

MBE *abbrev* Member of the Order of the British Empire

MBO *abbrev* management buyout

MC *abbrev* **1** Master of Ceremonies **2** Military Cross

MCC *abbrev* Marylebone Cricket Club

MCP *abbrev* male chauvinist pig

MD *abbrev* **1** Doctor of Medicine (from Latin *Medicinae Doctor*) **2** Managing Director

MDMA *abbrev* methylene-dioxymethamphetamine, the drug Ecstasy

ME *abbrev* myalgic encephalomyelitis, a condition of chronic fatigue and muscle pain following a viral infection

me *pronoun* the word used by a speaker or writer in mentioning themselves: *she kissed me/ give it to me*

mea culpa my fault

mead *noun* an alcoholic drink made with honey

meadow *noun* a field of grass

meadowsweet *noun* a wild flower with sweet-smelling cream-coloured flowers

meagre or *US* **meager** *adj* **1** thin **2** poor in quality **3** scanty, not enough □ **meagreness** *noun*

meal[1] *noun* the food taken at one time, *eg* breakfast or dinner

meal[2] *noun* grain ground to a coarse powder

mealy-mouthed *adj* not frank and straightforward in speech

mean[1] *adj* **1** not generous with money *etc* **2** unkind, selfish **3** lowly, humble □ **meanly** *adv* □ **meanness** *noun*

mean[2] *adj* **1** midway between two other points, quantities *etc*; middle **2** average □ *noun* □ **meanwhile** *adv* in the time between two happenings □ **in the meantime** meanwhile

mean[3] *verb* **1** intend to express; indicate: *what do you mean?/ when I say no, I mean no* **2** intend: *how do you mean to do that?* □ **meaning** *noun* **1** what is intended to be expressed or conveyed **2** purpose, intention □ **meaningful** *adj* full of significance; expressive □ **meaningfully** *adv* □ **meaningless** *adj* □ **mean well** have good intentions

> **mean** » mean*s*, mean*ing*, meant

meander *verb* **1** of a river: flow in a winding course **2** wander about slowly and aimlessly

> After the winding *Maeander* river in Turkey

means *noun plural* **1** an action or instrument by which something is brought about **2** money, property *etc*: *a woman of means* □ **by all means 1** certainly, of course **2** in every way possible □ **by no means** certainly not; not at all

measles *noun* an infectious disease causing red spots

measly *adj*, *informal* mean, stingy

measure *noun* **1** size or amount (found by measuring) **2** an instrument or container for measuring **3** musical time **4** (**measures**) a plan of action: *measures to prevent crime* **5** a law brought before parliament to be considered □ *verb* **1** find out the size, quantity *etc* by using some form of measure **2** be of a certain length, amount *etc* **3** indicate the measurement of **4** mark (off) or weigh (out) in portions □ **measured** *adj* steady, unhurried □ **measurement** *noun* **1** the act of measuring **2** the size, amount *etc* found by measuring □ **for good measure** as a bonus

meat *noun* animal flesh used as food

meaty *adj* **1** full of meat; tasting of meat **2** of a book *etc*: full of information

MEBO *abbrev* management and employee buyout

Mecca *noun* **1** the birthplace of Mohammed **2** a place of pilgrimage

mechanic *noun* a skilled worker with tools or machines

mechanical *adj* **1** of machinery: *mechanical engineering* **2** worked by machinery **3** done without thinking □ **mechanically** *adv*

mechanics *noun* **1** *sing* the study and art of constructing machinery **2** *plural* the actual details of how something works: *the mechanics of the plan are beyond me*

mechanism *noun* **1** a piece of machinery **2** the way a piece of machinery works **3** an action by which a result is produced

mechanize *verb* **1** equip (a factory *etc*) with machinery **2** supply (troops) with armoured vehicles □ **mechanization** *noun*

Med *noun*, *informal* the Mediterranean

medal *noun* a metal disc stamped with a design, inscription *etc*, made to commemorate an event or given as a prize □ **medallion** *noun* a large medal or piece of jewellery like one □ **medallist** *noun* someone who has gained a medal

meddle *verb* **1** concern yourself with things that are not your business **2** interfere or tamper (with) □ **meddler** *noun* □ **meddlesome** *adj* fond of meddling

media *noun*: **the media** television, newspapers *etc* as a form of communication □ **mediagenic** *adj* presenting well on television *etc*

mediaeval *another spelling* of **medieval**

median *noun* **1** a straight line from an angle of a triangle to the centre of the opposite side **2** the middle value or point of a series □ *adj* mid, middle

mediate *verb* act as a peacemaker (between) □ **mediation** *noun* □ **mediator** *noun* someone who tries to make peace between people who are quarrelling

medic *noun*, *informal* a medical student

medical *adj* of doctors or their work □ *noun* a health check, a physical examination

medicate *verb* give medicine to □ **medicated** *adj* including medicine or disinfectant

medication *noun* **1** medical treatment **2** a medicine

medicinal *adj* **1** used in medicine **2** used as a medicine □ **medicinally** *adv*

medicine *noun* **1** something given to a sick person to make them better **2** the science of the treatment of illness □ **medicine man** a tribal healer or shaman

medieval *adj* of or in the Middle Ages

mediocre *adj* not very good, ordinary □ **mediocrity** *noun*

meditate *verb* **1** think deeply and in quietness **2** contemplate religious or spiritual matters **3** consider, think about □ **meditative** *adj* thoughtful □ **meditatively** *adv*

meditation *noun* **1** deep, quiet thought **2** contemplation on a religious or spiritual theme

medium *noun* (*plural* **media** or **mediums**) **1** a means or substance through which an effect is produced **2** (*plural* **mediums**) someone through whom spirits (of dead people) are said to speak □ *adj* middle or average in size, quality *etc* □ **the media** *see* **media**

medley *noun* (*plural* **medleys**) **1** a mixture **2** a piece of music put together from a number of other pieces

meek *adj* gentle, uncomplaining ▫ **meekly** *adv* ▫ **meekness** *noun*

meemies *noun plural*: **screaming meemies** *informal* a fit of hysterics

meerkat *noun* a South African animal related to the mongoose

meerschaum *noun* **1** a fine white clay used to make tobacco pipes **2** a pipe made of this

meet *verb* **1** come face to face (with) **2** come together, join **3** make the acquaintance of **4** pay (bills *etc*) fully **5** be suitable for, satisfy: *able to meet the demand* ▫ *noun* a gathering for a sports event ▫ *adj* proper, suitable ▫ **meeting** *noun* a gathering of people for a particular purpose

> **meet** *verb* » meet*s*, meet*ing*, met

mega *adj*, *slang* **1** huge **2** excellent, very good

mega- *prefix* great, huge

megalith *noun* a huge stone erected in prehistoric times

megalomania *noun* an exaggerated idea of your own importance or abilities ▫ **megalomaniac** *noun* someone suffering from megalomania

megaphone *noun* a portable cone-shaped device with microphone and amplifier to increase sound

megaton *adj* of a bomb: having an explosive force equal to a million tons of TNT

melancholy *noun* lowness of spirits, sadness ▫ *adj* sad, depressed ▫ **melancholic** *adj*

mélange *noun* a mixture, a medley

melanin *noun* the dark pigment in human skin or hair

melanoma *noun* a skin tumour which usually develops from a mole

melba toast thin curled slices of toasted bread

meld *verb* merge, blend

mêlée /*me*lay/ *noun* a confused fight between two groups of people

mellifluous *adj* sweet-sounding ▫ **mellifluously** *adv* ▫ **mellifluousness** *noun*

mellow *adj* **1** of fruit: ripe, juicy, sweet **2** having become pleasant or agreeable with age **3** of light, colour *etc*: soft, not harsh ▫ *verb* make or become mellow ▫ **mellowness** *noun*

melodeon *noun* a type of accordion

melodious *adj* pleasant sounding; tuneful ▫ **melodiously** *adv* ▫ **melodiousness** *noun*

melodrama *noun* a type of play with a sensational or exaggerated plot

melodramatic *adj* exaggerated, sensational, over-dramatic ▫ **melodramatically** *adv*

melody *noun* (*plural* **melodies**) **1** a tune **2** pleasant music ▫ **melodic** *adj* of melody ▫ **melodically** *adv*

melon *noun* a large round fruit with soft juicy flesh

melt *verb* **1** make or become liquid, *eg* by heating **2** disappear gradually: *the crowd melted away* **3** soften in feeling: *his heart melted at the sight* □ **meltdown** *noun* the process in which the radioactive fuel in a nuclear reactor overheats and melts through the insulation into the environment

member *noun* **1** someone who belongs to a group or society **2** a limb or organ of the body □ **Member of Parliament** (shortened to **MP**) someone elected to the House of Commons □ **membership** *noun* **1** the number of members **2** the state of being a member

membrane *noun* a thin skin or covering, especially as part of a human or animal body, plant *etc*

memento *noun* (*plural* **mementos**) something by which an event is remembered □ **memento mori** an object used as a reminder of human mortality

memo *noun* (*plural* **memos**) *short for* **memorandum**

memoirs *noun plural* a personal account of someone's life; an autobiography □ **memoirist** *noun* a writer of memoirs

memorable *adj* worthy of being remembered; famous □ **memorably** *adv*

memorandum *noun* (*plural* **memoranda**) **1** a note which acts as a reminder **2** a written statement of something under discussion **3** a brief note sent to colleagues in an office *etc*

memorial *noun* a monument commemorating an historical event or people □ *adj* commemorating an event or person

memorize *verb* learn by heart

memory *noun* (*plural* **memories**) **1** the power to remember **2** the mind's store of remembered things **3** something remembered **4** *comput* a store of information **5** what is remembered about someone □ **in memory of** in remembrance of, as a memorial of

menace *noun* **1** potential harm or danger **2** someone persistently threatening or annoying □ *verb* be a danger to; threaten

menacing *adj* looking evil or threatening

ménage *noun* a household

menagerie /*mənajəree*/ *noun* **1** a collection of wild animals **2** a place where these are kept

mend *verb* repair; make or grow better □ *noun* a repaired part □ **on the mend** getting better, recovering

mendacious *adj* not true; lying □ **mendaciously** *adv* □ **mendacity** *noun*

mendicant *noun* a beggar □ *adj* begging

menhir /*men*heer/ *noun* a prehistoric standing stone

menial *adj* of work: unskilled, unchallenging

meningitis *noun* an illness caused by inflammation of the covering of the brain

menopause *noun* the ending of menstruation in middle age

menorah *noun* a candelabrum used in Jewish ceremonies

menses *noun plural* the discharge of blood *etc* during menstruation

menstruation *noun* the monthly discharge of blood from a woman's womb □ **menstrual** *adj* of menstruation □ **menstruate** *verb* undergo menstruation

mensurable *adj* measurable

mensuration *noun* measurement of length, height *etc*

mental *adj* **1** of the mind **2** done, made, happening *etc* in the mind: *mental arithmetic* **3** of illness: affecting the mind □ **mental hospital** a hospital for people suffering from mental illness □ **mentally** *adv*

mentality *noun* (*plural* **mentalities**) **1** mental power **2** type of mind; way of thinking

menthol *noun* a sharp-smelling substance obtained from peppermint oil

mention *verb* **1** speak of briefly **2** remark (that) □ *noun* a mentioning, a remark

mentor *noun* someone who gives advice as a tutor or supervisor

> After *Mentor*, a friend of Odysseus, who guides Telemachus in his search for his father

menu *noun* (*plural* **menus**) **1** (a card with) a list of dishes to be served at a meal **2** *comput* a list of options

MEP *abbrev* Member of the European Parliament

mercantile *adj* of buying and selling; trading

Mercator's projection a map of the globe in the form of a rectangle evenly marked with lines of latitude and longitude

mercenary *adj* **1** working for money **2** influenced by the desire for money □ *noun* (*plural* **mercenaries**) a soldier paid by a foreign country to fight in its army

mercerized *adj* of thread *etc*: treated with caustic soda to increase its strength and absorbency

merchandise *noun* goods to be bought and sold □ **merchandiser** *noun*

merchant *noun* someone who carries on a business in the buying and selling of goods, a trader □ *adj* of trade □ **merchant bank** a bank providing *esp* commercial banking services □ **merchantman** *noun* a trading ship □ **merchant navy** ships and crews employed in trading

merciful *adj* willing to forgive or be lenient □ **mercifully** *adv*

merciless *adj* showing no mercy; cruel □ **mercilessly** *adv*

mercury *noun* an element, a heavy, silvery liquid metal (also **quicksilver**) □ **mercurial** *adj* changeable, volatile

mercy *noun* (*plural* **mercies**) lenience or forgiveness towards an enemy *etc*; pity □ **at someone's mercy** in their power

mere *adj* nothing more than: *mere nonsense*

merely *adv* only, simply

meretricious *adj*, *formal* superficially attractive, flashy

⚠Do not confuse with: **meritorious**

merge *verb* **1** combine or join together **2** blend, come together gradually

merger *noun* a joining together, *eg* of business companies

meridian *noun* **1** an imaginary line around the globe passing through the north and south poles **2** the highest point of the sun's path **3** *Chinese med* a main energy channel in the body

meringue /mərang/ *noun* a baked cake or shell made of sugar and egg-white

merino *noun* (*plural* **merinos**) **1** a sheep with very fine soft wool **2** its wool, or a soft fabric made from it

merit *noun* **1** positive worth or value **2** a commendable quality ▯ *verb* deserve

meritorious *adj*, *formal* deserving honour or reward

⚠Do not confuse with: **meretricious**

mermaid *noun* an imaginary sea creature with a woman's upper body and a fish's tail

merry *adj* **1** full of fun; cheerful and lively **2** slightly drunk ▯ **merrily** *adv*

merry-go-round *noun*, *Brit* a fairground roundabout with wooden horses *etc* for riding on

mesh *noun* (*plural* **meshes**) **1** network, netting **2** the opening between the threads of a net ▯ *verb* of gears *etc*: interconnect, engage

mesmeric *adj* **1** hypnotic **2** commanding complete attention, fascinating ▯ **mesmerically** *adv*

mesmerize *verb* **1** hypnotize **2** hold the attention of completely; fascinate

An earlier term than *hypnotize*, the word comes from the name of the 18th-century Austrian doctor, Franz Anton Mesmer, who claimed to be able to cure disease through the influence of his will on patients

mesolithic *adj* referring to the period between paleolithic and neolithic

meson *noun* a particle with a mass between that of a proton and an electron

mess (*plural* **messes**) **1** an untidy or disgusting sight **2** disorder, confusion **3** a group of soldiers *etc* who take their meals together, or the place where they eat ▯ **mess up** make untidy, dirty or muddled ▯ **mess with** *US informal* interfere with, fool with

message *noun* **1** a piece of news or information sent from one person to another **2** a lesson, a moral ▯ **get the message** *informal* understand, get the point

messenger *noun* someone who carries a message

messiah *noun* a saviour, a deliverer

Messrs *plural* of **Mr**

messy *adj* **1** dirty **2** untidy, disordered □ **messily** *adv* □ **messiness** *noun*

metabolic *adj* of metabolism □ **metabolically** *adv*

metabolism *noun* **1** the combined chemical changes in the cells of a living organism that provide energy for living processes and activity **2** the conversion of nourishment into energy

metal *noun* any of a group of substances (*eg* gold, silver, iron *etc*) able to conduct heat and electricity

⚠Do not confuse with: **mettle**

metallic *adj* **1** made of metal **2** shining like metal: *metallic thread*

metallurgy *noun* the study of metals □ **metallurgic** or **metallurgical** *adj* □ **metallurgist** *noun*

metamorphose *verb* change completely in appearance or character

metamorphosis *noun* (*plural* **metamorphoses**) **1** a complete change in appearance or character; a transformation **2** a physical change that occurs during the growth of some creatures, *eg* from a tadpole into a frog

metaphor *noun* a way of describing something by suggesting that it is, or has the qualities of, something else, *eg the camel is the ship of the desert*

metaphorical *adj* using a metaphor or metaphors □ **metaphorically** *adv*

metaphysics *noun* **1** the study of being and knowledge **2** any abstruse or abstract philosophy □ **metaphysical** *adj* □ **metaphysician** *noun*

meteor *noun* a small piece of matter moving rapidly through space, becoming bright as it enters the earth's atmosphere

meteoric *adj* **1** of a meteor **2** extremely rapid: *meteoric rise to fame*

meteorite *noun* a meteor which falls to the earth as a piece of rock

meteorologist *noun* someone who studies or forecasts the weather

meteorology *noun* the study of weather and climate □ **meteorological** *adj*

mete out *verb*, *formal* deal out (punishment *etc*)

meter[1] *noun* an instrument for measuring the amount of gas, electricity, *etc* used □ *verb* measure with a meter

meter[2] *US spelling* of **metre**

⚠Do not confuse with: **metre**

methadone *noun* a synthetic drug similar to morphine, used to treat addiction

methane *noun* a colourless gas produced by rotting vegetable matter (*also called*: **marsh-gas**)

methanol *noun* methyl alcohol (*also called*: **wood spirit**)

method *noun* **1** a planned or regular way of doing something **2** orderly arrangement

methodical *adj* orderly, done or acting according to some plan ▫ **methodically** *adv*

meths *noun*, *informal* methylated spirits

methyl *noun* a poisonous alcohol found in nature

methylated spirits an alcohol with added violet dye, used as a solvent or fuel

meticulous *adj* careful and accurate about small details ▫ **meticulously** *adv* ▫ **meticulousness** *noun*

métier /*meh*tieh/ *noun*, *formal* occupation, profession

metonym *noun* the use of the name of part of a thing to stand for the whole, *eg the ring* for *boxing* ▫ **metonymy** *noun*

metre or *US* **meter** *noun* **1** the chief unit of length in the metric system (about 1.1 yards) **2** the arrangement of syllables in poetry, or of musical notes, in a regular rhythm

⚠Do not confuse with: **meter**

metric *adj* **1** of the metric system **2** metrical ▫ **metric system** the system of weights and measures based on tens (1 metre = 10 decimetres = 100 centimetres *etc*)

metrical *adj* **1** of poetry: of or in metre **2** arranged in the form of verse

metrication *noun* the change-over of a country's units of measurements to the metric system

metronome *noun* an instrument that keeps a regular beat, used for music practice

metropolis *noun* (*plural* **metropolises**) a large city, usually the capital city of a country ▫ **metropolitan** *adj*

mettle *formal* courage, pluck ▫ **on your mettle** out to do your best

⚠Do not confuse with: **metal**

mew *noun* a whining cry made by a cat *etc* ▫ *verb* cry in this way

mews *noun* buildings (originally stables) built around a yard or in a lane

Originally a cage for hawks, *mews* took on its present meaning after royal stables were built in the 17th century on a site formerly used to house the King's hawks

mezzanine *noun* **1** a low storey between two main storeys **2** *US* a balcony in a theatre

mezzo *noun*, *informal* (*plural* **mezzos**) a mezzo-soprano

mezzo-soprano *noun* (*plural* **mezzo-sopranos**) **1** a singer whose voice is between alto and soprano **2** a singing voice between alto and soprano

mg *abbrev* milligram(s)

MHz *abbrev* megahertz

MI5 *informal* a British government counter-espionage agency

MI6 *informal* a British espionage and intelligence agency

miaow *noun* the sound made by a cat ▫ *verb* make the sound of a cat

miasma /maiazmə/ *noun* an unhealthy or depressing atmosphere

mica *noun* a mineral which glitters and divides easily into thin transparent layers

mice *plural* of **mouse**

Michaelmas *noun* the festival of St Michael, 29 September

mickey *noun*: **take the mickey** *informal* tease, make fun of someone

micro *noun, informal* (*plural* **micros**) **1** a microwave oven **2** a microcomputer

micro- *prefix* very small

microbe *noun* a minute living organism

microchip *noun* a tiny piece of silicon designed to act as a complex electronic circuit

microcomputer *noun* a small desktop computer containing a microprocessor

microcosm *noun* a version on a small scale: *a microcosm of society*

microfiche /*mai*krohfeesh/ *noun* a sheet of microfilm suitable for filing

microfilm *noun* narrow photographic film on which books, newspapers, *etc* are recorded in miniaturized form ▫ *verb* record on microfilm

microphone *noun* an instrument which picks up sound waves for broadcasting, recording or amplifying

microprocessor *noun* a computer processor consisting of one or more microchips

microscope *noun* a scientific instrument which magnifies very small objects placed under its lens

microscopic *adj* tiny, minuscule ▫ **microscopically** *adv*

microsecond *noun* a millionth of a second

microsurgery *noun* delicate surgery carried out under a microscope ▫ **microsurgeon** *noun* a surgeon who performs microsurgery

microwave *noun* **1** a microwave oven **2** a very short radio wave ▫ **microwave oven** an oven which cooks food by passing microwaves through it

mid- *prefix* placed or occurring in the middle: *mid-morning*

midday *noun* noon

midden *noun* a rubbish or dung heap

middle *noun* the point or part of anything equally distant from its ends or edges; the centre ▫ *adj* **1** occurring in the middle or centre **2** coming between extreme positions *etc*: *trying to find a middle way* ▫ **in the middle of** in the midst of doing, busy doing ▫ **middle-aged** *adj* between youth and old age ▫ **Middle Ages** the time roughly between AD 500 and AD 1500 ▫ **middle class** the class of people between the working and upper classes ▫

middle-of-the-road *adj* bland, unadventurous

middling *adj* **1** of middle size or quality **2** neither good nor bad; mediocre

midge *noun* a small biting insect

midget *noun* an abnormally small person or thing □ *adj* very small

midnight *noun* twelve o'clock at night □ *adj* occurring at midnight

midriff *noun* the middle of the body, just below the ribs

midst *noun* the middle □ **in our midst** among us

midsummer *noun* the time around 21 June, which is the longest day in the year

midway *adv* half-way

midwife *noun* (*plural* **midwives**) a nurse trained to assist women during childbirth □ **midwifery** *noun* the practice or occupation of being a midwife

> Meaning literally 'with woman'

midwinter *noun* the time around 21 December, the winter solstice and shortest day in the year

mien /meen/ *noun*, *formal* look, appearance, aspect

might[1] *noun* power, strength

might[2] *past tense* of **may**

mighty *adj* very great or powerful □ *adv*, *US informal* very □ **mightily** *adv* □ **mightiness** *noun*

> **mighty** » mighti*er*, mighti*est*

migraine /*mee*grehn/ *noun* a severe form of headache

migrant *noun* **1** someone migrating, or recently migrated, from another country **2** a bird that migrates annually

migrate *verb* **1** change your home to another area or country **2** of birds: fly to a warmer region for the winter □ **migration** *noun*

migratory *adj* **1** migrating **2** wandering

mike *noun*, *informal* a microphone

milch cow **1** a cow kept for milk production **2** a ready source of money

mild *adj* **1** not harsh or severe; gentle **2** of taste: not sharp or bitter **3** of weather: not cold □ **mildly** *adv* □ **mildness** *noun*

mildew *noun* a whitish mark on plants, fabric *etc* caused by fungus □ **mildewed** *adj*

mile *noun* a measure of length (1.61 kilometre or 1760 yards) □ **mileage** *noun* **1** distance in miles **2** travel expenses (counted by the mile) □ **milestone** *noun* **1** a stone beside the road showing the number of miles to a certain place **2** something which marks an important event

milieu /meel*yuh*/ *noun* surroundings

militant *adj* **1** fighting, warlike **2** aggressive, favouring or taking part in forceful action □ *noun* someone who is militant

military *adj* of soldiers or warfare □ *noun* (**the military**) the army

militate *verb* **1** fight or work

(against) **2** act to your disadvantage

> ⚠Do not confuse with: **mitigate**

militia *noun* a group of fighters, not regular soldiers, trained for emergencies

milk *noun* **1** a white liquid produced by female animals as food for their young **2** this liquid, *esp* from cows, used as a drink □ *verb* **1** draw milk from **2** take (money *etc*) from □ **milk float** a vehicle that makes deliveries of milk to homes □ **milkmaid** *noun, old* a woman who milks cows □ **milkman** *noun* a man who sells or delivers milk □ **milk-tooth** *noun* a tooth from the first set of teeth in humans and mammals □ **milky** *adj* **1** like milk, creamy **2** white □ **Milky Way** a bright band of stars seen in the night sky

mill *noun* **1** a machine for grinding or crushing grain, coffee *etc* **2** a building where grain is ground **3** a factory □ *verb* **1** grind **2** cut grooves round the edge of (a coin) **3** move round and round in a crowd □ **miller** *noun* someone who grinds grain □ **millrace** *noun* the stream of water which turns a millwheel □ **millstone** *noun* **1** one of two heavy stones used to grind grain **2** something felt as a burden or hindrance □ **millwheel** *noun* a water-wheel which drives the machinery of a mill

millennium *noun* (*plural* **millennia**) a period of a thousand years

millet *noun* a type of grain used for food

milli- *prefix* thousand; a thousandth part of

milligramme *noun* a thousandth of a gramme

millilitre *noun* a thousandth of a litre

millimetre *noun* a thousandth of a metre

milliner *noun* someone who makes and sells women's hats □ **millinery** *noun* the goods sold by a milliner

million *noun* a thousand thousands (1 000 000)

millionaire *noun* someone who has a million pounds (or dollars) or more

millipede *noun* a small crawling insect with a long body and many pairs of legs

millisecond *noun* a thousandth of a second

mime *noun* **1** a theatrical art using body movements and facial expressions in place of speech **2** a play performed through mime □ *verb* **1** perform a mime **2** express through mime

mimic *verb* imitate, especially in a mocking way □ *noun* someone who mimics □ **mimicry** *noun*

> **mimic** *verb* » mimics, mimick*ing*, mimick*ed*

mimosa *noun* a tree producing bunches of yellow, scented flowers

min *abbrev* **1** minimum **2** minute (of time)

minaret *noun* a slender tower on an Islamic mosque

mince *verb* **1** cut or chop into small pieces **2** walk primly with short steps □ *noun* meat chopped finely □ **mince-pie** *noun* a pie filled with mincemeat □ **mincer** *noun* a machine for mincing food □ **not mince matters** not try to soften an unpleasant fact or statement

mincemeat *noun* a chopped-up mixture of dried fruit, suet *etc* □ **make mincemeat of** pulverize, destroy

mind *noun* **1** consciousness, intelligence, understanding **2** intention: *I've a good mind to tell him so* □ *verb* **1** see to, look after: *mind the children* **2** watch out for, be careful of: *mind the step* **3** object to: *do you mind if I open the window?* □ **change your mind** change your opinion or intention □ **in two minds** undecided □ **make up your mind** decide □ **mindful of** paying attention to □ **out of your mind** mad, crazy □ **presence of mind** ability to act calmly and sensibly □ **speak your mind** speak frankly

minder *noun* **1** someone who looks after a child *etc* **2** an aide or adviser to a public figure

mindless *adj* foolish, unthinking; pointless □ **mindlessly** *adv*

mine[1] *noun* **1** an underground pit or system of tunnels from which metals, coal *etc* are dug **2** a heavy charge of explosive material □ *verb* **1** dig or work a mine **2** lay explosive mines in □ **minefield** *noun* an area covered with explosive mines □ **miner** *noun* someone who works in a mine □ **minesweeper** or **minelayer** *noun* a ship which removes or places explosive mines

mine[2] *pronoun* a thing or things belonging to me: *that drink is mine*

mineral *noun* a natural substance mined from the earth, *eg* coal, metals, gems *etc* □ *adj* of or containing minerals □ **mineral water 1** water containing small amounts of minerals **2** *informal* carbonated water

mineralogy *noun* the study of minerals □ **mineralogist** *noun*

minestrone *noun* a thick Italian vegetable soup containing rice or pasta

mingle *verb* mix

mingy /*min*jee/ *adj*, *informal* stingy, mean

Mini *noun, trademark* a small, two-doored British car

mini- *prefix* smaller than average; compact: *minibus*/ *minicab*

miniature *noun* **1** a small-scale painting **2** a small bottle of spirits □ *adj* on a small scale

minibus *noun* (*plural* **minibuses**) a type of small bus

minim *music* a note (♪) equal to two crotchets, or half a semibreve, in length

minimize *verb* **1** make to seem small or unimportant **2** make as small as possible

minimum *noun* (*plural* **minima**) the smallest possible quantity □ *adj* the least possible

minion *noun* a slave-like follower

miniscule *noun another spelling* of **minuscule**

> The **miniscule** spelling is not yet standard

minister *noun* **1** the head of a government department: *minister of trade* **2** a member of the clergy **3** an agent, a representative □ *verb* (**minister to**) help, supply the needs of □ **ministerial** *adj* of a minister

ministry *noun* (*plural* **ministries**) **1** a government department or its headquarters **2** the work of a member of the clergy

mink *noun* a small weasel-like kind of animal or its fur

minneola *noun* a hybrid fruit grown from a tangerine and a grapefruit

minnow *noun* a type of very small river or pond fish

minor *adj* **1** of less importance, size *etc* **2** small, unimportant (*contrasted with*: **major**) □ *noun* someone not yet legally of age (*ie* in the UK, under 18) □ **minority** *noun* (*plural* **minorities**) **1** the smaller number or part **2** the state of being a minor

Minotaur *noun* a mythological creature with a bull's head, living in the Cretan labyrinth

minster *noun* a large church or cathedral

minstrel *noun* **1** *hist* a medieval travelling musician **2** a singer, an entertainer □ **minstrelsy** a collection of songs

mint[1] *noun* a plant with strong-smelling leaves, used as flavouring

mint[2] *noun* **1** a place where coins are made **2** *informal* a large sum of money: *cost a mint* □ *verb* make coins □ **in mint condition** in perfect condition

minuet *noun* **1** a kind of slow, graceful dance **2** the music for this

minus *prep* **1** used to show subtraction, represented by the sign (−): *five minus two equals three* or *5−2=3* **2** *informal* without: *I'm minus my car today* □ *adj* of a quantity less than zero

minuscule *noun* a small cursive script originally used by monks for manuscripts □ *adj* **1** written in minuscule **2** tiny, minute

minute[1] /*min*ət/ *noun* **1** a sixtieth part of an hour **2** in measuring an angle, the sixtieth part of a degree **3** a very short time **4** (**minutes**) notes taken of what is said at a meeting

minute[2] /mai*nyoot*/ *adj* **1** very small **2** very exact

minutiae *noun plural* minute or exact details

minx *noun* (*plural* **minxes**) a cheeky young girl

miracle *noun* **1** a wonderful act beyond normal human powers **2** a fortunate happening with no natural cause or explanation □ **miraculous** *adj* □ **miraculously** *adv*

mirage *noun* something imagined but not really there, *eg* an oasis seen by travellers in the desert

MIRAS *abbrev* mortgage interest relief at source

mire *noun* deep mud □ **miry** *adj*

mirepoix /*meer*pwa/ *noun* diced vegetables used for sauces *etc*

mirror *noun* a backed piece of glass which shows the image of someone looking into it ▯ *verb* **1** reflect like a mirror **2** copy exactly

mirth *noun* merriment, laughter ▯ **mirthful** *adj* ▯ **mirthless** *adj*

mis- *prefix* wrong(ly), bad(ly): *mispronounce*/ *misapply*

misadventure *noun* an unlucky happening

misandry *noun* hatred of men

misanthropist *noun* someone who hates humanity ▯ **misanthropic** *adj* ▯ **misanthropy** *noun*

misappropriate *verb* put to a wrong use, *eg* use (someone else's money) for yourself

misbehave *verb* behave badly ▯ **misbehaviour** *noun*

misc *abbrev* miscellaneous

miscarriage *noun* **1** a going wrong, failure: *miscarriage of justice* **2** the accidental loss of a foetus during pregnancy

miscarry *verb* **1** go wrong or astray **2** be unsuccessful **3** have a miscarriage in pregnancy

> **miscarry** » miscarri*es*, miscarry*ing*, miscarri*ed*

miscegenation *noun* intermarriage or interbreeding between different races

miscellaneous *adj* assorted, made up of several kinds ▯ **miscellaneously** *adv*

miscellany *noun* (*plural* **miscellanies**) a mixture or collection of things, *eg* pieces of writing

mischance *noun* an unlucky accident

mischief *noun* **1** naughtiness **2** *old* harm, damage ▯ **mischievous** *adj* naughty, teasing; causing trouble ▯ **mischievously** *adv*

misconceive *verb* misunderstand ▯ **misconception** *noun* a wrong idea, a misunderstanding

misconduct *noun* bad or immoral behaviour

misconstrue *verb* misunderstand ▯ **misconstruction** *noun*

miscreant *noun* a wicked person

misdeed *noun* a bad deed; a crime

misdemeanour *noun* a minor offence

mise-en-scène *noun* the arrangement of scenery for a film or play

miser *noun* someone who hoards money and spends very little ▯ **miserly** *adj* stingy, mean

misery *noun* (*plural* **miseries**) great unhappiness, pain, poverty *etc* ▯ **miserable** *adj* very unhappy; wretched

misfire *verb* **1** of a gun: fail to go off **2** of a plan: go wrong

misfit *noun* **1** someone who cannot fit in happily in society *etc* **2** something that fits badly

misfortune *noun* **1** bad luck **2** an unlucky accident

misgiving *noun* fear or doubt, *eg* about the result of an action

misguided *adj* led astray, mistaken ▫ **misguidedly** *adv*

mishandle *verb* treat badly or roughly

mishap *noun* an unlucky accident

mishmash *noun* a hotchpotch, a medley

misinform *verb* inform wrongly

misinterpret *verb* interpret wrongly

misjudge *verb* judge unfairly or wrongly

mislay *verb* put (something) aside and forget where it is; lose

> **mislay** » mislay*s*, mislay*ing*, mislaid

mislead *verb* **1** give a false idea (to); deceive ▫ **misleading** *adj*

> **mislead** » mislead*s*, mislead*ing*, misled

mismatch *noun* an unsuitable match

misnomer *noun* a wrong or unsuitable name

miso /*mee*soh/ *noun* fermented soy bean paste

misogynist /mi*so*jinist/ *noun* a man who hates women

misplace *verb* put in the wrong place; mislay

misprint *noun* a mistake in printing

misquote *verb* make a mistake in repeating something written or said

misrepresent *verb* give a wrong idea of (someone's words, actions *etc*)

Miss *noun* (*plural* **Misses**) **1** a form of address used before the surname of an unmarried woman **2** (**miss**) a young woman or girl

miss *verb* **1** fail to hit, see, hear, understand *etc* **2** discover the loss or absence of **3** feel the lack of: *missing old friends* ▫ *noun* (*plural* **misses**) **1** the act of missing **2** a failure to hit a target **3** a loss ▫ **missing** *adj* lost ▫ **miss out 1** leave out **2** be left out of something worthwhile or advantageous

missal *noun* the Mass book of the Roman Catholic Church

misshapen *adj* badly or abnormally shaped

missile *noun* a weapon or other object that is thrown or fired

mission *noun* **1** a task that someone is sent to do **2** a group of representatives sent to another country **3** a group sent to spread a religion **4** the headquarters of such groups **5** someone's chosen task or purpose: *his only mission is to make money*

missionary *noun* (*plural* **missionaries**) someone sent abroad *etc* to spread a religion

missive *noun* something sent, *eg* a letter

misspell *verb* spell wrongly ▫ **misspelling** *noun*

> **misspell** » misspell*s*, misspell*ing*, misspell*ed* or misspelt

misspent *adj* spent unwisely, wasted: *misspent youth*

mist *noun* a cloud of moisture in the air; thin fog or drizzle ▫ **mist**

up or **mist over** cover or become covered with mist ▫ **misty** *adj*

mistake *verb* **1** misunderstand, be wrong or make an error about **2** take (one thing or person) for another ▫ *noun* a wrong action or statement; an error ▫ **mistaken** *adj* making an error, unwise: *mistaken belief* ▫ **mistakenly** *adv*

> **mistake** *verb* » mistake*s*, mistak*ing*, mistaken, mistook

mister *noun full form* of **Mr**

mistletoe *noun* a plant with white berries, used as a Christmas decoration

mistreat *verb* treat badly; abuse

mistress *noun* (*plural* **mistresses**) **1** a female teacher **2** a female owner of a dog *etc* **3** a woman skilled in an art **4** a woman who is the lover though not the legal wife of a man **5** *full form* of **Mrs**

mistrust *noun* a lack of trust or confidence in ▫ *verb* have no trust or confidence in

misunderstand *verb* take a wrong meaning from what is said or done ▫ **misunderstanding** *noun* **1** a mistake about a meaning **2** a slight disagreement

misuse *noun* bad or wrong use ▫ *verb* **1** use wrongly **2** treat badly

MIT *abbrev* Massachusetts Institute of Technology

mite *noun* **1** something very small, *eg* a tiny child **2** a very small spider **3** *hist* a very small coin

mithridate an antidote to poison

> Named after *Mithridates*, king of Pontus, who acquired immunity to poison by taking gradual doses

mitigate *verb* make (punishment, anger *etc*) less great or severe ▫ **mitigation** *noun*

> ⚠Do not confuse with: **militate**

mitre *noun* **1** the pointed headdress worn by archbishops and bishops **2** a slanting joint between two pieces of wood

mitt or **mitten** *noun* a glove without separate divisions for the four fingers

Mittel-Europa *noun* Central Europe ▫ **Mittel-European** *adj*

mix *verb* **1** unite or blend two or more things together **2** (**mix up**) confuse, muddle **3** associate with other people ▫ *noun* a mixture, a blending

mixed *adj* **1** jumbled together **2** confused, muddled **3** consisting of different kinds **4** for both sexes: *mixed doubles* ▫ **mixed-up** *adj* confused, bewildered

mixer *noun* **1** a machine that mixes food **2** someone who mixes socially **3** a soft drink added to alcohol

mixture *noun* **1** a number of things mixed together **2** a medicine

mizzen-mast *noun* the mast nearest the stern of a ship

ml *abbrev* millilitre(s)

MLitt *abbrev* Master of Letters or Literature (from Latin *Magister Litterarum*)

Mlle *abbrev* mademoiselle

MLR *abbrev* minimum lending rate

mm *abbrev* millimetre(s)

Mme *abbrev* madame

mnemonic /ni*mon*ik/ *noun* a rhyme *etc* which helps you to remember something

MO *abbrev* medical officer

moan *noun* a low sound of grief or pain ▫ *verb* make this sound

moat *noun* a deep trench round a castle *etc*, often filled with water

mob *noun* a noisy crowd ▫ *verb* crowd round, or attack, in disorder

mob » mob*s*, mobb*ing*, mobb*ed*

mobile *adj* **1** able to move or be moved easily **2** not fixed, changing quickly **3** portable, not relying on fixed cables *etc*: *mobile phone* ▫ *noun* **1** a decoration or toy hung so that it moves slightly in the air **2** *informal* a mobile phone ▫ **mobility** *noun*

mobilize *verb* gather (troops *etc*) together ready for active service ▫ **mobilization** *noun*

Möbius strip *maths* a one-sided surface made by twisting and joining together the ends of a rectangular strip

moccasin *noun* a soft leather shoe of the type originally worn by Native Americans

mocha /*moh*kə/ *noun* **1** a fine coffee **2** coffee and chocolate mixed together **3** a deep brown colour

mock *verb* laugh at, make fun of ▫ *adj* false, pretended, imitation: *mock battle* ▫ **mockery** *noun* **1** the act of mocking **2** a ridiculous imitation

MOD *abbrev* Ministry of Defence

Mod *noun* an annual festival of Gaelic music and literature

modal verb *grammar* a verb which modifies the sense of a main verb, *eg* can, may, must *etc*

mode *noun* **1** a manner of doing or acting **2** kind, sort; fashion

model *noun* **1** a design or pattern to be copied **2** a small-scale copy of something: *model railway* **3** a living person who poses for an artist **4** someone employed to wear and display new clothes ▫ *adj* **1** acting as a model **2** fit to be copied, perfect: *model behaviour* ▫ *verb* **1** make a model of **2** shape according to a particular pattern **3** wear and display (clothes)

model *verb* » model*s*, modell*ing*, modell*ed*

modem *noun* a device which transmits information from a computer along telephone cables

moderate *verb* make or become less great or severe ▫ *adj* **1** keeping within reason, not going to extremes **2** of medium or average quality, ability *etc* ▫ **moderately** *adv* ▫ **moderation** *noun* **1** a lessening or calming down **2** the practice of not going to extremes

modern *adj* belonging to the present or to recent times; not old ▫ **modernity** *noun* ▫ **modernize** *verb* bring up to date

modest *adj* **1** not exaggerating

achievements; not boastful **2** not very large: *modest salary* **3** behaving decently; not shocking □ **modesty** *noun*

modicum *noun* (*plural* **modicums**) a small quantity or amount: *a modicum of kindness*

modify *verb* **1** make a change in: *modified my design* **2** make less extreme: *modified his demands* □ **modification** *noun*

modify » modifi*es*, modify*ing*, modifi*ed*

modish *adj* fashionable, smart □ **modishly** *adv* □ **modishness** *noun*

modular *adj* of or composed of modules

modulate *verb* **1** vary or soften in tone or pitch **2** *music* change key □ **modulation** *noun*

module *noun* **1** a set course forming a unit in an educational scheme **2** a separate, self-contained section of a spacecraft **3** *architecture* a standard unit of size

modus operandi a method of working

modus vivendi a way of life or living

mogul *noun* **1** a mound of hard snow forming an obstacle on a ski-slope **2** an influential person; a magnate

mohair *noun* **1** the long silky hair of an Angora goat **2** fabric made from this

Mohammed *noun* a prophet, the founder of Islam

moiety *noun* a half share or division

moiré /*mwa*reh/ *adj* of silk: marked with a wavy pattern; watered

moist *adj* damp, very slightly wet □ **moisten** *verb* make slightly wet or damp

moisture *noun* slight wetness; water or other liquid in tiny drops in the atmosphere or on a surface

moisturize *verb* add moisture to □ **moisturizer** *noun* a cosmetic cream that restores moisture to the skin

mola *noun* a brightly coloured piece of embroidery from S America

molar *noun* a back tooth used for grinding food

molasses *noun sing* a thick dark syrup left when sugar is refined

mole[1] *noun* **1** a small burrowing animal, with tiny eyes and soft fur **2** a spy who successfully infiltrates a rival organization □ **molehill** *noun* a small heap of earth created by a burrowing mole

mole[2] *noun* a small dark spot on the skin, often raised

molecule *noun* the smallest part of a substance that has the same qualities as the substance itself

molest *verb* **1** annoy or torment **2** injure or abuse sexually □ **molester** *noun*

moll *noun* a gangster's girlfriend

mollify *verb* calm down; lessen the anger of

mollify » mollifi*es*, mollify*ing*, mollifi*ed*

mollusc *noun* one of a group of boneless animals, usually with hard shells, *eg* shellfish and snails

mollycoddle *verb* pamper, over-protect

molten *adj* of metal *etc*: melted

moment *noun* **1** a very short space of time; an instant **2** importance, consequence

momentary *adj* lasting for a moment □ **momentarily** *adv*

momentous *adj* of great importance

momentum *noun* (*plural* **momenta**) the force of a moving body

monarch *noun* a king, queen, emperor or empress □ **monarchist** *noun* someone who believes in government by a monarch

monarchy *noun* (*plural* **monarchies**) **1** government by a monarch **2** an area governed by a monarch

monastery *noun* (*plural* **monasteries**) a building housing a group of monks □ **monastic** *adj* of or like monasteries or monks □ **monasticism** *noun* the way of life in a monastery

Monday *noun* the second day of the week

monetarism *noun* an economic policy based on control of a country's money supply □ **monetarist** *noun & adj*

monetary *adj* of money or coinage

money *noun* **1** coins and bank-notes used for payment **2** wealth □ **moneyed** or **monied** *adj* wealthy

mongoose *noun* (*plural* **mongooses**) a small weasel-like animal which kills snakes

mongrel *noun* an animal of mixed breed

monicker *noun* a nickname, an alias

monitor *noun* **1** an instrument used to check the operation of a system or apparatus **2** a screen in a television studio showing the picture being transmitted **3** a computer screen **4** a school pupil given certain responsibilities □ *verb* **1** keep a check on **2** listen to and report on foreign broadcasts *etc*

monk *noun* a member of a male religious group living secluded in a monastery

monkey *noun* (*plural* **monkeys**) **1** a long-tailed mammal which walks on four legs **2** a mischievous child □ **monkey about** fool about □ **monkey-nut** *noun* a peanut □ **monkey-puzzle** *noun* a pine tree with prickly spines along its branches □ **monkey-wrench** *noun* an adjustable spanner

monkfish *noun* a type of sea-fish, used as food

mono- *prefix* one, single

monoboard *noun* a wide single ski, controlled with both feet

monochrome *adj* **1** in one colour **2** black and white

monocle *noun* a single eyeglass

monogamy *noun* marriage to one spouse at a time □ **monogamous** *adj*

monogram *noun* two or more

letters, usually initials, made into a single design

monolith *noun* **1** an upright block of stone **2** something unmovable or intractable ▯ **monolithic** *adj* intractable, obstinate

monologue *noun* a long speech by one person

monoplane *noun* an aeroplane with a single pair of wings

monopolize *verb* **1** have exclusive rights to **2** take up the whole of: *monopolizing the conversation*

monopoly *noun* (*plural* **monopolies**) **1** an exclusive right to make or sell something **2** complete unshared possession, control *etc*

monorail *noun* a railway on which the trains run along a single rail

monosyllable *noun* a word of one syllable ▯ **monosyllabic** *adj*

monotone *noun* a single, unchanging tone

monotonous 1 in a single tone **2** unchanging, dull ▯ **monotonously** *adv*

monotony *noun* lack of variety

monsoon *noun* **1** a wind that blows in the Indian Ocean **2** the rainy season caused by the south-west monsoon in summer

mons pubis the soft mound of tissue above the human genitals

monster *noun* **1** something of unusual size or appearance **2** a huge terrifying creature **3** an evil person ▯ *adj* huge

monstrosity *noun* (*plural* **monstrosities**) **1** something unnatural **2** something very ugly

monstrous *adj* huge, horrible

montage /mon*tazh*/ *noun* **1** a composite picture **2** a film made up of parts of other films

month *noun* a twelfth part of a year, approximately four weeks

monthly *adj* & *adv* happening once a month ▯ *noun* (*plural* **monthlies**) a magazine *etc* published once a month

monument *noun* a building, pillar, tomb *etc* built in memory of someone or an event ▯ **ancient monument** a building, grave *etc* remaining from ancient times

monumental *adj* **1** of a monument **2** huge, enormous ▯ **monumentally** *adv*

moo *noun* the sound made by a cow

mooch *verb* slouch, skulk

mood *noun* the state of a person's feelings or temper

moody *adj* **1** often changing in mood **2** ill-tempered, cross ▯ **moodily** *adv* ▯ **moodiness** *noun*

mooli *noun* a long white root vegetable from E Africa

moon *noun* the heavenly body which travels round the earth once each month and reflects light from the sun ▯ *verb* **1** wander (about) **2** gaze dreamily (at) ▯ **moonbeam** *noun* a beam of light from the moon ▯ **moonlight** *noun* the light of the moon ▯ **moonshine** *noun* **1** the shining of the moon **2** rubbish, foolish ideas or talk ▯ **moonstone**

noun a precious stone with a pearly shine

moor *noun* a large stretch of open ground, often covered with heather □ *verb* tie up or anchor (a ship *etc*) □ **moorhen** *noun* a kind of water bird, a female coot □ **moorings** *noun plural* **1** the place where a ship is moored **2** the anchor, rope *etc* holding it □ **moorland** *noun* a stretch of moor

moose *noun* (*plural* **moose**) a large deer-like animal, found in N America

moot point a debatable point; a question with no obvious solution

mop *noun* **1** a pad of sponge or a bunch of short pieces of coarse yarn *etc* on a handle for washing or cleaning **2** a thick head of hair □ *verb* **1** clean with a mop **2** clean or wipe: *mopped his brow* □ **mop up** clean up

> **mop** *verb* » mop*s*, mopp*ing*, mopp*ed*

mope *verb* be unhappy and gloomy

moped *noun* a pedal bicycle with a motor

moquette *noun* fabric with a velvety pile and canvas backing, used for upholstery

moraine *noun* a line of rocks and gravel left by a glacier

moral *adj* **1** relating to standards of behaviour and character **2** of correct or acceptable behaviour or character □ *noun* **1** the lesson of a story **2** (**morals**) principles and standards of (*esp* sexual) behaviour □ **morality** *noun* moral standards □ **moralize** *verb* draw a lesson from a story or event □ **moral support** encouragement without active help □ **moral victory** a failure that can really be seen as a success

morale /mor*ahl*/ *noun* spirit and confidence

morass *noun* (*plural* **morasses**) **1** a marsh or bog **2** a bewildering mass of something: *a morass of regulations*

moratorium *noun* (*plural* **moratoria**) an official suspension or temporary ban

morbid *adj* **1** too concerned with gloomy, unpleasant things **2** diseased, unhealthy □ **morbidity** *noun* □ **morbidly** *adv*

mordant *noun* a substance used to fix dye or make paint stick to a surface

more *adj* a greater number or amount of: *more money* □ *adv* to a greater extent: *more beautiful/ more than I can say* □ *noun* **1** a greater proportion or amount **2** a further or additional number: *more where this came from*

moreish *adj* of food *etc*: enjoyable, making you want more

morel /mo*rel*/ *noun* a mushroom with a honeycombed cap

morello /mə*rel*oh/ *noun* a sour-tasting cherry

moreover *adv* besides

morganatic *adj* of a marriage: in which the woman has no claim to the title or property of her husband

From early German *morgengabe* 'morning gift', a present given to a spouse on the morning after the wedding

morgue *noun* a place where dead bodies are laid, awaiting identification *etc*

MORI *abbrev* Market and Opinion Research Institute

moribund *adj* **1** dying **2** stagnant

morn *noun, formal* morning

morning *noun* the part of the day before noon □ *adj* of or in the morning □ **morning star** Venus when it rises before the sun

morocco *noun* a fine goatskin leather first brought from Morocco

moron *noun* someone of low mental ability; an idiot □ **moronic** *adj*

morose *adj* bad-tempered, gloomy □ **morosely** *adv* □ **morosity** *noun*

morphia *noun* morphine

morphine *noun* a drug which causes sleep or deadens pain (*also called* **morphia**)

morphology *noun* the study of the forms of words □ **morphological** *adj* □ **morphologist** *noun*

morris dance a traditional English country dance in which male dancers carry sticks and wear bells

Originally a *Moorish* dance brought from Spain

morrow *noun, old*: **the morrow** tomorrow, the day after

morse *noun* a signalling code of signals made up of dots and dashes

morsel *noun* a small piece, *eg* of food

mortal *adj* **1** liable to die **2** causing death; deadly: *mortal injury* □ *noun* a human being □ **mortally** *adv* fatally: *mortally wounded*

mortality *noun* (*plural* **mortalities**) **1** the state of being mortal **2** death **3** frequency of death; death-rate: *infant mortality*

mortar *noun* **1** a heavy bowl for crushing and grinding substances with a pestle **2** a short gun for throwing shells **3** a mixture of lime, sand and water, used for fixing stones *etc*

mortarboard *noun* a university or college cap with a square flat top

mortgage *noun* a sum of money lent through a legal agreement for buying buildings, land *etc* □ *verb* offer (buildings *etc*) as security for money borrowed

mortice *another spelling of* **mortise**

mortician *noun, US* an undertaker

mortify *verb* **1** make to feel ashamed or humble **2** of a part of the flesh: die □ **mortification** *noun*

mortify » mortifi*es*, mortify*ing*, mortifi*ed*

mortise or **mortice** *noun* a hole in a piece of wood to receive the shaped end (**tenon**) of another piece □ **mortise-lock** or **mortice-lock** a lock whose mechanism is sunk into the edge of a door

mortuary *noun* (*plural* **mortuaries**) a place where dead bodies are kept before burial or cremation

mosaic *noun* a picture or design made up of many small pieces of coloured glass, stone *etc*

Moses basket a portable cot for babies

Moslem *another spelling* of **Muslim**

mosque *noun* an Islamic place of worship

mosquito *noun* (*plural* **mosquitoes** or **mosquitos**) a biting or blood-sucking insect, often carrying disease

moss *noun* (*plural* **mosses**) a very small flowerless plant, found in moist places ▫ **mossy** *adj* covered with moss

most *adj* the greatest number or amount of: *most children attend school regularly* ▫ *adv* **1** very, extremely: *most grateful* **2** to the greatest extent: *the most ill of the family* ▫ *noun* the greatest number or amount: *he got most* ▫ **mostly** *adv* mainly, chiefly ▫ **at most** not more than ▫ **for the most part** mostly

MOT *noun* a compulsory annual check on behalf of the *M*inistry *o*f *T*ransport on vehicles over a certain age

mote *noun* a particle of dust; a speck

motel *noun* a hotel built to accommodate motorists and their vehicles

moth *noun* **1** a flying insect, seen mostly at night **2** the cloth-eating grub of the clothes-moth ▫ **moth-eaten** *adj* **1** full of holes made by moths **2** tatty, shabby

mothball *noun* a small ball of chemical used to protect clothes from moths ▫ *verb* (*also* **put in mothballs**) put aside for later use *etc*

mother *noun* **1** a female parent **2** the female head of a convent ▫ *verb* **1** be the mother of **2** care for like a mother ▫ **motherboard** *noun, comput* a printed circuit board into which other boards can be slotted ▫ **motherhood** *noun* the state of being a mother ▫ **mother-in-law** the mother of your husband or wife ▫ **mother-in-law's tongue** a houseplant with thick spiky leaves ▫ **motherland** *noun* the country of your birth ▫ **motherly** *adj* of or like a mother ▫ **mother-of-pearl** *noun* a hard shiny substance which forms inside certain shells ▫ **mother tongue** a native language

motif *noun* (*plural* **motifs**) a distinctive feature or idea in a piece of music, a play *etc*

⚠Do not confuse with: **motive**

motion *noun* **1** the act or state of moving **2** a single movement **3** a suggestion put before a meeting for discussion ▫ *verb* **1** make a signal by a movement or gesture **2** direct (someone) in this way: *the policeman motioned us forward* ▫ **motionless** *adj* not moving

motive *noun* the cause of someone's actions; a reason ▫ **motivate** *verb* cause (someone) to act in a certain way

> ⚠Do not confuse with: **motif**

motley *adj* made up of different colours or kinds

motocross *noun* the sport of motorcycle racing across rough terrain

motor *noun* **1** an engine which causes motion **2** a motor-car □ *verb* travel by motor vehicle □ **motorcade** *noun* a procession of cars carrying a head of state *etc* □ **motorist** *noun* someone who drives a motor-car □ **motorize** *verb* supply with an engine

motorbike or **motorcycle** *noun* a bicycle with a petrol-driven engine □ **motorbiker** *noun* □ **motorcyclist** *noun*

motorway *noun* a dual carriageway on which traffic is allowed to drive faster than on other roads

mottled *adj* marked with spots or blotches

motto *noun* (*plural* **mottoes**) a phrase which acts as a guiding principle or rule

mould[1] *noun* a shape into which a liquid is poured to take on that shape when it cools or sets: *jelly mould* □ *verb* **1** form in a mould **2** shape

mould[2] *noun* **1** a fluffy growth on stale food *etc* **2** soil containing rotted leaves *etc* □ **mouldy** *adj* affected by mould; stale

moulder *verb* crumble away to dust

moulding *noun* a decorated border of moulded plaster round a ceiling *etc*

moult *verb* of a bird: shed its feathers

mound *noun* **1** a bank of earth or stones **2** a hill; a heap

mount *verb* **1** go up, ascend **2** climb on to (a horse, bicycle *etc*) **3** fix (a picture *etc*) on to a backing or support **4** fix (a gemstone) in a casing **5** organize (an exhibition) □ *noun* **1** a support or backing for display **2** a horse, bicycle *etc* to ride on **3** *old* a mountain □ **The Mounties** *informal* the Canadian mounted police

mountain *noun* **1** a large hill **2** a large quantity □ **mountaineer** *noun* a mountain climber □ **mountain-ash** *noun* the rowan tree

mountainous *adj* **1** having many mountains **2** huge

mountebank *noun* a charlatan, a quack

> Originally a street pedlar who climbed on a mound or bench to sell his goods

mourn *verb* **1** grieve for **2** be sorrowful □ **mourner** *noun* □ **mournful** *adj* sad

mourning *noun* **1** the showing of grief **2** the period during which someone grieves **3** dark-coloured clothes traditionally worn by mourners

mouse *noun* (*plural* **mice**) **1** a small gnawing animal, found in houses and fields **2** a shy, timid, uninteresting person **3** *comput* a device moved by hand which causes corresponding cursor movements on a screen

moussaka *noun* a Greek dish of minced lamb topped with a cheese sauce

mousse *noun* a frothy set dish including eggs, cream *etc*, either sweet or savoury

moustache *noun* unshaved hair above a man's upper lip

mousy *adj* **1** of a light-brown colour **2** shy, timid, uninteresting

mouth *noun* **1** the opening in the head through which an animal or person eats and makes sounds **2** the point of a river where it flows into the sea **3** an opening, an entrance ◊ *verb* **1** speak **2** shape (words) in an exaggerated way ◊ **mouthful** *noun* (*plural* **mouthfuls**) as much as fills the mouth ◊ **mouth-organ** *noun* a small wind instrument, moved across the lips

mouthpiece *noun* **1** the part of a musical instrument, tobacco-pipe *etc* held in the mouth **2** someone who speaks for others

move *verb* **1** (cause to) change place or position **2** change your house **3** rouse or affect the feelings of **4** rouse into action **5** propose, suggest ◊ *noun* **1** an act of moving **2** a step, an action **3** a shifting of pieces in a game of chess *etc* ◊ **movable** *adj* able to be moved, changed *etc*

movement *noun* **1** the act or manner of moving **2** a change of position **3** a division of a piece of music **4** a group of people united in a common aim: *the peace movement* **5** an organized attempt to achieve an aim: *the movement to reform the divorce laws*

movie *noun* a cinema film ◊ **the movies** the cinema

moving *adj* **1** in motion **2** causing emotion ◊ **movingly** *adv*

mow *verb* **1** cut (grass, hay *etc*) with a scythe or machine **2** (**mow down**) destroy in great numbers ◊ **mower** *noun* a machine for mowing

moxa *noun* a pithy substance burned for cauterization *etc* in traditional Chinese medicine

mozzarella *noun* a mild-tasting spongy Italian cheese

MP *abbrev* **1** Member of Parliament **2** Military Police

mpg *abbrev* miles per gallon

mph *abbrev* miles per hour

MPhil *abbrev* Master of Philosophy

Mr *noun* (*short* for **mister**) the form of address used before a man's surname

Mrs *noun* (*short* for **mistress**) the form of address used before a married woman's surname

MS *abbrev* **1** multiple sclerosis **2** manuscript

Ms *noun* a form of address used before the surname of a married or unmarried woman

MSc *abbrev* Master of Science

MSG *abbrev* monosodium glutamate

much *adj* a great amount of ◊ *adv* to or by a great extent: *much loved/ much faster* ◊ *pronoun* **1** a great amount **2** something important: *made much of it* ◊ **much the same** nearly the same

mucilage *noun* a sticky or gluey substance

muck *noun* dung, dirt, filth ▫ **muck-raking** *noun* looking for scandals to expose

mucous *adj* like or covered by mucus

> ⚠Do not confuse: **mucous** and **mucus**

mucus *noun* slimy fluid secreted from the nose *etc*

mud *noun* wet, soft earth ▫ **mud-guard** *noun* a shield or guard over wheels to catch mud splashes

muddle *verb* **1** confuse, bewilder **2** mix up **3** make a mess of ▫ *noun* **1** a mess **2** a state of confusion

muddy *adj* **1** covered with mud **2** unclear, confused

muesli *noun* a mixture of grains, nuts and fruit eaten with milk

muezzin *noun* an Islamic priest who calls out the hour of prayer from a mosque

muff[1] *noun* a tube of warm fabric to cover and keep the hands warm

muff[2] *verb* fail in an opportunity, *eg* to catch a ball

muffin *noun* **1** a round, flat spongy cake, toasted and eaten hot with butter **2** *US* a small sweet cake made of flour, cornmeal *etc*

muffle *verb* **1** wrap up for warmth *etc* **2** deaden (a sound)

muffler *noun* **1** a scarf **2** *US* a silencer for a car

mufti *noun* clothes worn by soldiers *etc* when off duty

mug[1] *noun* **1** a straight-sided cup **2** *informal* a stupid person **3** *informal* the face

mug[2] *verb* attack and rob (someone) in the street ▫ **mugger** *noun*

> **mug** » **mug**s, mugg*ing*, mugg*ed*

mug[3] *verb*: **mug up** *informal* study hard; swot up

muggy *adj* of weather: close and damp ▫ **mugginess** *noun*

mugwump *noun*, *US* **1** a big chief, a boss **2** a political independant or maverick

mulatto *noun* (*plural* **mulattoes**) *old* someone with one Black and one White parent

mulberry *noun* **1** a tree on whose leaves silkworms are fed **2** its purple berry

mulch *noun* loose straw *etc* laid down to protect plant roots ▫ *verb* cover with mulch

mule[1] *noun* an animal bred from a horse and an ass

mule[2] *noun* a backless slipper

mulish *adj* stubborn

mullah *noun* an Islamic teacher

mulled *adj* of wine, *etc*: mixed with spices and served warm

mullet *noun* an edible small sea-fish

mulligatawny *noun* an East Indian curried soup

mullion *noun* an upright division in a window

mull over *verb* think over, ponder over

multi- *prefix* many

multi-coloured *adj* many-coloured

multifarious *adj* of many kinds

multimedia *adj* of a computer: able to run various sound and visual applications

multimillionaire *noun* someone who has property worth several million pounds (or dollars)

multinational *adj* of a company: having branches in several different countries

multiple *adj* **1** affecting many parts: *multiple injuries* **2** involving many things of the same sort, *eg* vehicles in a *multiple crash* □ *noun* a number or quantity which contains another an exact number of times □ **multiple sclerosis** a progressive nerve disease resulting in paralysis (shortened to **MS**)

multiplex *adj* of a cinema: including several screens and theatres in one building

multiply *verb* **1** increase **2** increase a number by adding it to itself a certain number of times: *2 multiplied by 3 is 6* □ **multiplication** *noun* the act of multiplying □ **multiplier** *noun* the number by which another is to be multiplied □ **a multiplicity of** a great number of

> **multiply** » multipli*es*, multiply*ing*, multipli*ed*

multitasking *noun*, *comput* the action of running several processes simultaneously

multitude *noun* a great number; a crowd □ **multitudinous** *adj* very many

mum[1] *noun*, *informal* mother

mum[2] *adj* silent

mumble *verb* speak indistinctly

mummy[1] *noun* (*plural* **mummies**) *informal* mother

mummy[2] *noun* (*plural* **mummies**) a dead body preserved by wrapping in bandages and treating with wax, spices *etc* □ **mummify** *verb* make into a mummy

> **mummify** » mummifi*es*, mummify*ing*, mummifi*ed*

mumps *noun sing* an infectious disease affecting glands at the side of the neck, causing swelling

munch *verb* chew noisily □ **the munchies** hunger pangs

mundane *adj* dull, ordinary

municipal *adj* of or owned by a city or town □ **municipality** *noun* a city or town; an area covered by local government

munificent *adj* very generous □ **munificence** *noun*

munitions *noun plural* weapons and ammunition used in war

Munro *noun* (*plural* **Munros**) a British or Irish mountain above 3000 feet □ **Munro-bagger** *noun* someone who aims to climb every Munro

> Originally applied only to mountains in Scotland, from a list prepared by the Scottish mountaineer, Hugh *Munro*

mural *adj* of or on a wall □ *noun* a painting or design on a wall

murder *verb* kill someone unlawfully and on purpose □ *noun* the act of murdering □ **murderer** *noun* someone who commits murder □ **murderess** *noun, old* a woman murderer □ **murderous** *adj* capable or guilty of murder; wicked

murky *adj* dark, gloomy □ **murkiness** *noun*

murmur *noun* **1** a low indistinct continuous sound **2** a hushed speech or tone □ *verb* **1** make a murmur **2** complain, grumble

Murphy's Law the law that if something can go wrong, it will

muscat *noun* a musky variety of grape, used to make wine

muscle *noun* **1** fleshy tissue which contracts and stretches to cause body movements **2** an area of this in the body **3** physical strength or power

muscular *adj* **1** of muscles **2** strong □ **muscular dystrophy** a hereditary disease in which the muscles gradually deteriorate

Muse *noun* one of the nine goddesses of poetry, music, dancing *etc* in classical mythology

muse *verb* think (over) in a quiet, leisurely way

museum *noun* (*plural* **museums**) a building for housing and displaying objects of artistic, scientific or historic interest

mush *noun* **1** something soft and pulpy **2** an overly sentimental film, song *etc*

mushroom *noun* an edible fungus, usually umbrella-shaped □ *verb* grow very quickly: *buildings mushroomed all over town*

mushy *adj* **1** soft and pulpy **2** overly sentimental □ **mushiness** *noun*

music *noun* **1** the art of arranging, combining *etc* certain sounds able to be produced by the voice, or by instruments **2** an arrangement of such sounds or its written form **3** a sweet or pleasant sound

musical *adj* **1** of music **2** sounding sweet or pleasant **3** having a talent for music □ **musically** *adv*

musician *noun* **1** a specialist in music **2** someone who plays a musical instrument

musicology *noun* the study of music □ **musicologist** *noun*

musk *noun* a strong perfume, obtained from the male musk deer or artificially □ **musky** *adj* □ **musk deer** a small hornless deer found in Central Asia □ **musk rat** a musquash

musket *noun* a kind of gun once used by soldiers □ **musketeer** *noun* a soldier armed with a musket

Muslim *noun* a follower of the Islamic religion □ *adj* Islamic

muslin *noun* a fine, soft cotton cloth

musquash *noun* (*plural* **musquashes**) a large North American water-rat

mussel *noun* an edible shellfish with two separate halves to its shell

must *verb* **1** used with another

verb to express necessity: *I must finish this today* **2** expressing compulsion: *you must do as you're told* **3** expressing certainty or probability: *that must be the right answer* □ *noun* something that must be done; a necessity

mustache *US spelling* of **moustache**

mustang *noun* a North American wild horse

mustard *noun* **1** a plant with sharp-tasting seeds **2** a hot yellow paste made from its seeds

muster *verb* gather up or together (*eg* troops, courage) □ **pass muster** be accepted as satisfactory

musty *adj* smelling old and stale □ **mustiness** *noun*

mutable *adj* changeable

mute *adj* **1** not able to speak; dumb **2** silent **3** of a letter in a word: not pronounced □ *noun* a mute person

muted *adj* **1** of a sound: made quieter, hushed **2** of a colour: not bright

mutilate *verb* **1** inflict great physical damage on; maim **2** damage greatly □ **mutilation** *noun*

mutiny *verb* **1** rise against those in power **2** refuse to obey the commands of military officers □ *noun* (*plural* **mutinies**) refusal to obey commands; rebellion □ **mutineer** *noun* someone who takes part in a mutiny □ **mutinous** *adj* rebellious; refusing to obey orders

> **mutiny** *verb* » mutini*es*, mutiny*ing*, mutini*ed*

mutt *noun, informal* an idiot

mutter *verb* speak in a low voice; mumble

mutton *noun* meat from a sheep, used as food

mutual *adj* **1** given by each to the other(s): *mutual help* **2** shared by two or more: *mutual friend* □ **mutually** *adv*

Muzak *noun, trademark* recorded music played in shops *etc*

muzzle *noun* **1** an animal's nose and mouth **2** a fastening placed over an animal's mouth to prevent it biting **3** the open end of a gun □ *verb* **1** put a muzzle on (a dog *etc*) **2** prevent from speaking freely

muzzy *adj* cloudy, confused □ **muzziness** *noun*

my *adj* belonging to me: *this is my book*

mycology *noun* the study of fungi □ **mycologist** *noun*

mynah *noun* a black Asiatic bird which can be trained to imitate human speech

myopia *noun* short-sightedness □ **myopic** *adj* short-sighted

myriad *noun* a very great number □ *adj* very many, countless

myrmidon *noun* someone who carries out orders ruthlessly or fearlessly

> After the *Myrmidons*, Greek warriors who accompanied Achilles to Troy

myrrh *noun* a bitter-tasting resin used in medicines, perfumes *etc*

myrtle *noun* a type of evergreen shrub

myself *pronoun* **1** used reflexively: *I can see myself in the mirror* **2** used for emphasis: *I wrote this myself*

mysterious *adj* **1** puzzling, difficult to understand **2** secret, hidden ▫ **mysteriously** *adv* ▫ **mysteriousness** *noun*

mystery *noun (plural* **mysteries***)* **1** something that cannot be or has not been explained; something puzzling **2** a deep secret

mystic *noun* someone who seeks knowledge of sacred or mystical things by going into a state of spiritual ecstasy ▫ **mystical** *adj* having a secret or sacred meaning beyond ordinary human understanding

mystify *verb* **1** puzzle greatly **2** confuse, bewilder

mystify » mystifi*es*, mystify*ing*, mystifi*ed*

mystique /mis*teek*/ *noun* an atmosphere of mystery about someone or something

myth *noun* **1** a story about gods, heroes *etc* of ancient times; a fable **2** something imagined or untrue ▫ **mythical** *adj* **1** of a myth **2** invented, imagined

mythology *noun* **1** the study of myths **2** a collection of myths ▫ **mythological** *adj* of myth or mythology; mythical ▫ **mythologist** *noun*

myxomatosis *noun* a contagious disease of rabbits

N

N *abbrev* **1** north **2** northern

nab *verb, informal* **1** snatch, seize **2** arrest

> **nab** » nab*s*, nabb*ing*, nabb*ed*

nabob *noun, hist* a local governor in India

nacre *noun* mother-of-pearl

nadir *noun* **1** the point of the heavens opposite the zenith **2** the lowest point of anything

naevus or *US* **nevus** /*neev*əs/ *noun* a birthmark

naff *adj, slang* inferior, crass, tasteless

NAFTA *abbrev* North American Free Trade Agreement

nag *verb* find fault with constantly ◇ *noun* a horse

> **nag** *verb* » nag*s*, nagg*ing*, nagg*ed*

Nahuatl *noun* the Aztec language of ancient Mexico

naiad *noun* a mythological river nymph

nail *noun* **1** a horny covering protecting the tips of the fingers and toes **2** a thin pointed piece of metal for fastening wood *etc* ◇ *verb* **1** fasten with nails **2** enclose in a box *etc* with nails **3** *informal* catch, trap

naive or **naïve** /nai*eev*/ *adj* **1** simple in thought, manner or speech **2** inexperienced and lacking knowledge of the world ◇ **naiveté** *noun*

NALGO *abbrev* National and Local Government Officers Association

naked *adj* **1** without clothes **2** having no covering **3** bald, blatant: *naked lie* ◇ **nakedly** *adv* ◇ **nakedness** *noun*

namby-pamby *adj* childish, feeble

> Originally a nickname of the 18th-century sentimental English poet, *Ambrose* Philips

name *noun* **1** a word by which a person, place or thing is known **2** fame, reputation: *making a name for himself* **3** an offensive description: *don't call people names* **4** authority: *I arrest you in the name of the king* ◇ *verb* **1** give a name to **2** speak of by name, mention **3** appoint ◇ **nameless** *adj* without a name, not named ◇ **namely** *adv* that is to say ◇ **nameplate** *noun* a small panel having on it the name of a person, house *etc* ◇ **namesake** *noun* someone with the same name as another

nan *noun* a flat round Indian bread

nanny *noun* (*plural* **nannies**) a children's nurse

nanny-goat *noun* a female goat

nano- *prefix* **1** a thousand millionth: *nanosecond* **2** microscopic in size

nap *noun* **1** a short sleep **2** a woolly

or fluffy surface on cloth **3** a kind of card game ▫ *verb* take a short sleep ▫ **caught napping** taken unawares

nap *verb* » nap*s*, napp*ing*, napp*ed*

napalm *noun* petroleum jelly, used to make bombs

nape *noun* the back of the neck

naphtha *noun* a highly flammable, clear liquid, obtained from coal and other substances

napkin *noun* a small piece of cloth or paper for wiping the lips at meals

nappy *noun* (*plural* **nappies**) a piece of cloth, or thick pad, put between a baby's legs to absorb urine and faeces

narcissus *noun* (*plural* **narcissi** or **narcissuses**) a plant like a daffodil with a white, star-shaped flower

narcotic *noun* a type of drug that brings on sleep or stops pain

nark *noun* a persistent complainer ▫ **narky** *adj* irritable, complaining

narrate *verb* tell a story ▫ **narration** *noun* the telling of a story ▫ **narrative** *noun* a story ▫ *adj* telling a story ▫ **narrator** *noun*

narrow *adj* **1** of small extent from side to side, not wide: *a narrow road* **2** with little to spare: *a narrow escape* **3** lacking wide interests or experience: *narrow views* ▫ *verb* make or become narrow ▫ **narrowly** *adv* closely; barely ▫ **narrow-minded** *adj* unwilling to accept or tolerate new ideas ▫ **narrows** *noun plural* a narrow sea passage, a strait

narwal or **narwhal** *noun* a kind of whale with a large tusk

NASA *abbrev, US* National Aeronautics and Space Administration

nasal *adj* **1** of the nose **2** sounded through the nose

nascent *adj* beginning to develop, in an early stage ▫ **nascency** *noun*

nasturtium *noun* a climbing plant with brightly-coloured flowers

nasty *adj* **1** very disagreeable or unpleasant **2** of a problem *etc*: difficult to deal with ▫ **nastily** *adv* ▫ **nastiness** *noun*

natal *adj* of birth

nation *noun* **1** the people living in the same country, or under the same government **2** a race of people: *the Jewish nation*

national *adj* of or belonging to a nation or race ▫ *noun* someone belonging to a nation: *a British national* ▫ **national anthem** a nation's official song or hymn ▫ **national call** a long-distance, but not international, telephone call ▫ **nationally** *adv*

nationalism *noun* the desire to bring the people of a nation together under their own government ▫ **nationalist** *noun* & *adj* ▫ **nationalistic** *adj* ▫ **nationality** *noun* membership of a particular nation

nationalize *verb* place (industries *etc*) under the control of the government ▫ **nationalization** *noun*

native *adj* **1** born in a person: *native intelligence* **2** of someone's birth: *my native land* ▫ *noun* **1** someone born in a certain place: *a* *native of Scotland* **2** an inhabitant of a country from earliest times before the discovery by explorers, settlers *etc* □ **the Nativity** the birth of Christ

NATO *abbrev* North Atlantic Treaty Organization

natty *adj* trim, tidy, smart □ **nattily** *adv*

natural *adj* **1** of nature **2** produced by nature, not artificial **3** of a quality *etc*: present at birth, not learned afterwards **4** unpretentious, simple **5** of a result *etc*: expected, normal □ *noun* **1** an idiot **2** someone with a natural ability **3** *music* a note which is neither a sharp nor a flat, shown by the sign (♮) □ **natural gas** gas suitable for burning found in the earth or under the sea □ **natural history** the study of animals and plants □ **natural selection** evolution by survival of the fittest, who pass their characteristics onto the next generation □ **naturalist** *noun* someone who studies animal and plant life □ **naturalize** *verb* give the rights of a citizen to (someone born in another country) □ **naturally** *adv* **1** by nature **2** simply **3** of course □ **natural resources** the natural wealth of a country in its forests, minerals, water *etc*

nature *noun* **1** the things which make up the physical world, *eg* animals, trees, rivers, mountains *etc* **2** the qualities which characterize someone or something: *a kindly nature* □ **-natured** *adj* (added to another word) having a certain temper or personality: *good-natured*

naturism *noun* the belief in nudity practised openly □ **naturist** *noun*

naturopathy *noun* treatment of disease through a combination of herbs, diet, exercise *etc* □ **naturopath** *noun* a practitioner of naturopathy

naught *noun* nothing: *plans came to naught*

> ⚠Do not confuse with: **nought**

naughty *adj* bad, misbehaving □ **naughtily** *adv* □ **naughtiness** *noun*

nausea *noun* a feeling of sickness □ **nauseate** *verb* make sick, fill with disgust □ **nauseated** *adj* sickened, disgusted □ **nauseous** *adj* sickening; disgusting

nautical *adj* of ships or sailors □ **nautical mile** 1.85 kilometre (6080 ft)

nautilus *noun* (*plural* **nautiluses** or **nautili**) a small sea creature related to the octopus

naval *see* **navy**

nave *noun* the middle or main part of a church

navel *noun* the small hollow in the centre of the front of the belly

navigate *verb* **1** steer or pilot a ship, aircraft *etc* on its course **2** sail on, over or through □ **navigable** *adj* able to be used by ships □ **navigation** the art of navigating □ **navigator** someone who steers or sails a ship *etc*

navvy *noun* (*plural* **navvies**) a labourer working on roads *etc*

navy *noun* (*plural* **navies**) **1** a

nation's fighting ships **2** the men and women serving on these □ **naval** *adj* of the navy □ **navy blue** dark blue

nay *adv*, *old* no

Nazi /*na*tsee/ *noun, hist* a member of the German National Socialist Party, a fascist party ruling Germany in 1933–45 □ **Nazism** *noun*

NB or **nb** *abbrev* note well (from Latin *nota bene*)

NCO *abbrev* non-commissioned officer

NE *abbrev* north-east; north-eastern

neap *adj* of the tide: at its smallest extent between low and high level

near *adj* **1** not far away in place or time **2** close in relationship, friendship *etc* **3** barely avoiding or almost reaching (something): *a near disaster* □ *adv* to or at a short distance; nearby □ *prep* close to □ *verb* approach □ **nearby** *adv* to or at a short distance: *do you live nearby?* □ **nearly** *adv* **1** almost: *nearly four o'clock* **2** closely: *nearly related* □ **nearness** *noun* □ **nearside** *adj* of the side of a vehicle: furthest from the centre of the road (*contrasted with*: **offside**) □ **near-sighted** *adj* short-sighted

neat *adj* **1** trim, tidy **2** skilfully done **3** of an alcoholic drink: not diluted with water *etc*

neb *noun, Scot* a nose

nebula *noun* (*plural* **nebulae**) a shining cloud-like appearance in the night sky, produced by very distant stars or by a mass of gas and dust

nebulous *adj* hazy, vague

necessary *adj* not able to be done without □ *noun* (*plural* **necessaries**) something that cannot be done without, such as food, clothing *etc* □ **necessarily** *adv* □ **necessitate** *verb* make necessary; force □ **necessity** (*plural* **necessities**) **1** something necessary **2** great need; want, poverty

neck *noun* **1** the part between the head and body **2** a narrow passage or area: *neck of a bottle/ neck of land* □ **necktie** *noun*, *US* a man's tie □ **neck and neck** running side by side, staying exactly equal

necklace *noun* a string of beads or precious stones *etc* worn round the neck

necromancer *noun* someone who works with black magic □ **necromancy** *noun*

necropolis *noun* (*plural* **necropolises**) a cemetery

nectar *noun* **1** the sweet liquid collected from flowers by bees to make honey **2** the drink of the ancient Greek gods **3** a delicious drink

nectarine *noun* a kind of peach with a smooth skin

née *adj* born (in stating a woman's surname before her marriage): *Mrs Janet Brown, née Phillips*

need *verb* **1** be without, be in want of **2** require □ *noun* **1** necessity, needfulness **2** difficulty, want, poverty □ **needful** *adj* necessary □

needless *adj* unnecessary □ **needlessly** *adv* □ **needy** *adj* poor

needle *noun* **1** a small, sharp piece of steel used in sewing, with a small hole (**eye**) at the top for thread **2** a long thin piece of metal, wood *etc* used *eg* in knitting **3** a thin hollowed-out piece of steel attached to a hypodermic syringe *etc* **4** the moving pointer in a compass **5** the long, sharp-pointed leaf of a pine, fir *etc* **6** a stylus on a record-player □ **needle bank** a place where drug-users can exchange used hypodermic needles for new ones, to help prevent the spread of disease

neep *noun, Scot* a turnip

ne'er *adj, formal* never □ **ne'er-do-well** or *Scot* **ne'er-do-weel** *noun* a lazy, worthless person who makes no effort

nefarious *adj* very wicked; villainous, shady

negate *verb* **1** prove the opposite **2** refuse to accept, reject (a proposal *etc*)

negative *adj* **1** meaning or saying 'no', as an answer (contrasted with: **positive**) **2** of a person, attitude *etc*: timid, lacking spirit or ideas □ *noun* **1** a word or statement by which something is denied **2** the photographic film, from which prints are made, in which light objects appear dark and dark objects appear light

neglect *verb* **1** treat carelessly **2** fail to give proper attention to **3** fail to do □ *noun* lack of care and attention □ **neglectful** *adj*

negligée *noun* a women's loose dressing-gown made of thin material

negligent *adj* careless □ **negligence** *noun* □ **negligently** *adv*

⚠Do not confuse: **negligent** and **negligible**

negligible *adj* not worth thinking about, very small: *a negligible amount*

negotiate *verb* **1** discuss a subject (with) in order to reach agreement **2** arrange (a treaty, payment *etc*) **3** get past (an obstacle or difficulty) □ **negotiable** *adj* able to be negotiated □ **negotiation** *noun* □ **negotiator** *noun*

Negro *noun* (*plural* **Negroes**) a Black African, or Black person of African descent □ **Negress** *noun* a Black woman □ **negroid** *adj* Black, dark-skinned

neigh *verb* cry like a horse □ *noun* a horse's cry

neighbour or *US* **neighbor** *noun* someone who lives near another □ **neighbourhood** *noun* surrounding district or area: *in the neighbourhood of Paris/ a poor neighbourhood* □ **neighbouring** *adj* near or next in position □ **neighbourly** *adj* friendly □ **in the neighbourhood of** approximately, nearly

neither *adj & pronoun* not either: *neither bus goes that way/ neither of us can afford it* □ *conj* (sometimes with **nor**) used to show alternatives in the negative: *neither Bill or David knew the answer/ she is neither eating nor sleeping*

nematode *noun* (*also called*

threadworm) a parasitic worm with a cylindrical body

nem con *abbrev* unanimously (from Latin *nemine contradicente*)

nemesis *noun* fate, punishment that is bound to follow wrongdoing

neo- *prefix* new □ **neonatal** *adj* of newborn babies

Neolithic *adj* relating to the later Stone Age

neologism *noun* a new word or expression □ **neologistic** *adj*

neon lighting a form of lighting in which an electric current is passed through a small quantity of gas

neophyte *noun* **1** a new convert **2** a novice, a beginner

nephew *noun* the son of a brother or sister, or of a brother-in-law or sister-in-law

nerd *noun* a socially inept, irritating person □ **nerdish** *adj*

neroli *noun* oil distilled from orange flowers

nerve *noun* **1** one of the fibres which carry feeling from all parts of the body to the brain **2** courage, coolness **3** *informal* impudence, cheek □ *verb* strengthen the nerve or will of □ **nervy** *adj* excitable, jumpy

nervous *adj* **1** of the nerves **2** easily excited or frightened; timid □ **nervously** *adv* □ **nervousness** *noun* □ **nervous system** the brain, spinal cord and nerves of an animal or human being

nest *noun* **1** a structure in which birds (and some animals and insects) live and rear their young **2** a shelter, a den □ *verb* build a nest and live in it □ **nestling** *noun* a young newly hatched bird

nestle /nesl/ *verb* **1** lie close together as in a nest **2** settle comfortably

Net *noun*: **the Net** *informal* the Internet

net *noun* **1** a loose arrangement of crossed and knotted cord, string or thread, used for catching fish, wearing over the hair *etc* **2** fine meshed material, used to make curtains, petticoats *etc* □ *adj* (*also* **nett**) **1** of profit *etc*: remaining after expenses and taxes have been paid **2** of weight: not including packaging □ *verb* **1** catch or cover with a net **2** put (a ball) into a net **3** make by way of profit □ **netball** *noun* a team game in which a ball is thrown into a high net □ **netting** *noun* fabric of netted string, wire *etc* □ **network** *noun* **1** an arrangement of lines crossing one another **2** a widespread organization **3** a system of linked computers, radio stations *etc*

net *verb* » net*s*, nett*ing*, nett*ed*

nether *adj* lower □ **nethermost** *adj* lowest

netsuke *noun* a small Japanese carving, originally used as a fastening

nett *see* **net**

nettle *noun* a plant covered with hairs which sting sharply □ *verb* make angry, provoke □ **nettlerash** *noun* a skin rash, like that caused by a sting from a nettle

neur- or **neuro-** *prefix* of the nerves

neuralgia *noun* a pain in the nerves, *esp* in those of the head and face

neurosis *noun* a type of mental illness in which the patient suffers from extreme anxiety □ **neurotic** *adj* **1** suffering from neurosis **2** in a bad nervous state □ *noun* someone suffering from neurosis □ **neurotically** *adv*

neuter *adj* **1** *grammar* neither masculine nor feminine **2** of an animal: neither male nor female **3** of an animal: infertile, sterile □ *verb* sterilize (an animal)

neutral *adj* **1** taking no side in a quarrel or war **2** of a colour: not strong or definite □ *noun* **1** someone or a nation that takes no side in a war *etc* **2** the gear position used when a vehicle is remaining still □ **neutrality** *noun* □ **neutralize** *verb* **1** make neutral **2** make useless or harmless

neutrino *noun* (*plural* **neutrinos**) an uncharged particle with zero mass when at rest

neutron *noun* one of the uncharged particles which, together with protons, make up the nucleus of an atom □ **neutron bomb** a nuclear bomb that kills people by intense radiation but leaves buildings intact

never *adv* **1** not ever; at no time **2** under no circumstances □ **nevertheless** *adv* in spite of that: *I hate opera, but I shall come with you nevertheless*

nevus *US spelling* of **naevus**

new *adj* **1** recent; not seen or known before **2** not used or worn; fresh □ **newcomer** *noun* someone lately arrived □ **newfangled** *adj* new and not thought very good □ **newly** *adv* □ **newness** *noun*

news *noun sing* **1** report of a recent event **2** new information □ **newsagent** *noun* a shopkeeper who sells newspapers □ **newsgroup** *noun, comput* a special-interest group of Internet users □ **newspaper** *noun* a paper printed daily or weekly containing news

newt *noun* a small lizard-like animal, living on land and in water

next *adj* nearest, closest in place, time *etc*: *the next page* □ *adv* in the nearest place or at the nearest time: *she won and I came next*/ *do that sum next*

nexus *noun* a bond, a connection

NHS *abbrev* National Health Service

nib *noun* a pen point

nibble *verb* take little bites (of) □ *noun* a little bite

Nibelung /*nee*bəloong/ *noun* a mythological German dwarf

nicad *adj* containing *ni*ckel-*cad*mium, used in rechargeable batteries

NICAM or **Nicam** *noun* *n*ear-*i*nstantaneous *c*ompanded *a*udio *m*ultiplexing, a system for transmitting digital sound with standard TV signals

nice *adj* **1** agreeable, pleasant **2**

careful, precise, exact: *a nice distinction* ▯ **nicely** *adv* pleasantly; very well

nicety *noun* (*plural* **niceties**) a small fine detail ▯ **to a nicety** with great exactness

niche /neesh/ *noun* **1** a hollow in a wall for a statue, vase *etc* **2** a suitable place in life: *she hasn't yet found her niche* **3** a gap in a market for a type of product

nick *noun* **1** a little cut, a notch **2** *slang* prison, jail ▯ *verb* **1** cut notches in **2** *slang* steal

nickel *noun* a greyish-white metal used for mixing with other metals and for plating **2** *US* a 5-cent coin

nickname *noun* an informal name used instead of someone's real name, *eg* for fun or as an insult

nicky-tams *noun plural, Scot* ties to keep trouser legs from getting dirty, flapping *etc*

nicotine *noun* a poisonous substance contained in tobacco

> Named after Jean *Nicot*, 16th-century French ambassador who sent tobacco samples back from Portugal

niece *noun* the daughter of a brother or sister, or of a brother-in-law or sister-in-law

niff *noun, slang* a bad smell

nifty *adj, slang* **1** fine, smart, neat **2** speedy, agile

niggardly *adj* mean, stingy

nigger *noun, offensive* a Black man or woman

niggle *verb* irritate, rankle ▯ *noun* **1** an irritation **2** a minor criticism ▯ **niggling** *adj* **1** unimportant, trivial, fussy **2** of a worry or fear: small but always present

nigh *adj, old* near

night *noun* **1** the period of darkness between sunset and sunrise **2** darkness ▯ *adj* **1** of or for night **2** happening, active *etc* at night ▯ **nightdress** or **nightgown** *noun* a garment worn in bed ▯ **nightfall** *noun* the beginning of night ▯ **nightjar** *noun* a kind of bird like a swallow which is active at night ▯ **nightly** *adj* & *adv* **1** by night **2** every night ▯ **night-watchman** *noun* someone who looks after a building during the night

nightingale *noun* a small bird, the male of which sings beautifully by night and day

nightmare *noun* a frightening dream

> The *-mare* ending comes from an old English word meaning 'incubus', nightmares being thought to be caused by an evil spirit pressing on the body

nightshade *noun* a family of plants some of which have poisonous berries, *eg* deadly nightshade

nihilism *noun* belief in nothing, extreme scepticism ▯ **nihilist** *noun* ▯ **nihilistic** *adj*

nil *noun* nothing

nimble *adj* quick and neat, agile ▯ **nimbleness** *noun* ▯ **nimbly** *adv*

nimbus *noun* a rain cloud

NIMBY *abbrev* not in my back yard, *ie* not wanting something to take place in your neighbourhood

nincompoop *noun* a weak, foolish person

nine *noun* the number 9 □ *adj* 9 in number □ **ninth** *adj* the last of a series of nine □ *noun* one of nine equal parts

ninepins *noun* a game in which nine bottle-shaped objects are set up and knocked down by a ball

nineteen *noun* the number 19 □ *adj* 19 in number □ **nineteenth** *adj* the last of a series of nineteen □ *noun* one of nineteen equal parts

ninety *noun* the number 90 □ *adj* 90 in number □ **ninetieth** *adj* the last of a series of ninety □ *noun* one of ninety equal parts

ninja *noun, hist* an assassin in feudal Japan, trained in martial arts

ninny *noun* (*plural* **ninnies**) a fool

nip *verb* **1** pinch, squeeze tightly **2** be stingingly painful **3** bite, cut (off) **4** check the growth of, damage (plants *etc*) **5** *informal* go nimbly or quickly □ *noun* **1** a pinch **2** a sharp coldness in the weather: *a nip in the air* **3** a small amount: *nip of whisky*

> **nip** *verb* » nip*s*, nipp*ing*, nipp*ed*

nipper *noun, informal* **1** a child, a youngster **2** (**nippers**) pincers, pliers

nipple *noun* the pointed part of the breast from which a baby sucks milk

nippy *adj, informal* **1** speedy, nimble **2** frosty, very cold

Nirvana *noun* the state to which a Buddhist or Hindu aspires as the best attainable □ **nirvana** a blissful state

nit *noun* **1** the egg of a louse or other small insect **2** *informal* an idiot, a nitwit

nitrate *noun* a substance formed from nitric acid, often used as a soil fertilizer

nitric acid a strong acid containing nitrogen

nitrogen *noun* a gas forming nearly four-fifths of ordinary air □ **nitro-glycerine** *noun* a powerful kind of explosive

nitwit *noun* a very stupid person

No or **no** *abbrev* number

no *adj* **1** not any: *they have no money* **2** not a: *she is no beauty* □ *adv* not at all: *the patient is no better* □ *exclam* expressing a negative: *are you feeling better today? No* □ *noun* (*plural* **noes**) **1** a refusal **2** a vote against □ **no-ball** *noun, cricket* a bowled ball disallowed by the rules □ **nobody** *pronoun* not any person □ *noun* someone of no importance: *just a nobody* □ **no one** or **no-one** *pronoun* not any person, nobody □ **no-show** *noun* someone expected who does not arrive □ **no-win** *adj* of a situation: in which you are bound to lose or fail □ **no dice** no answer, no success □ **no doubt** surely □ **no go** not possible, futile □ **no joke** not something to laugh about or dismiss □ **no way** *informal* under no circumstances

nobble *verb, slang* **1** get hold of **2**

persuade, coerce **3** seize, arrest

Nobel prize an annual international prize awarded for achievements in arts, science, politics *etc*

noble *adj* **1** great and good, fine **2** of aristocratic birth □ *noun* an aristocrat □ **nobility** *noun* **1** the aristocracy **2** goodness, greatness of mind or character □ **nobleman, noblewoman** *noun* □ **nobly** *adv*

noblesse oblige rank imposes obligations

nobody *see* **no**

nocturnal *adj* happening or active at night □ **nocturnally** *adv*

nocturne *noun* a piece of music intended to have an atmosphere of night-time

nod *verb* **1** bend the head forward quickly, often as a sign of agreement **2** let the head drop in weariness □ *noun* an action of nodding □ **nodding acquaintance with** a slight knowledge of □ **nod off** fall asleep

> **nod** *verb* » nod*s*, nodd*ing*, nodd*ed*

noddle *noun, slang* head; intelligence

node *noun* **1** the swollen part of a branch or twig where leaf-stalks join it **2** a swelling

nodule *noun* a small rounded lump

Noël *noun* Christmas

noise *noun* a sound, often one which is loud or harsh □ *verb, old* spread (a rumour *etc*) □ **noiseless** *adj* □ **noisy** *adj* making a loud sound

> **noisy** » nois*ier*, nois*iest*

nomad *noun* **1** one of a group of people without a fixed home who wander with their animals in search of pasture **2** someone who wanders from place to place □ **nomadic** *adj*

no-man's-land *noun* land owned by no one, *esp* that lying between two opposing armies

nom de plume *noun* (*plural* **noms de plume**) a pen-name

nomenclature *noun* **1** a system of naming **2** names

nomenklatura *noun* those holding power, *esp* in a communist regime

nominal *adj* **1** in name only **2** very small: *a nominal fee*

nominate *verb* propose (someone) for a post or for election; appoint □ **nomination** *noun* □ **nominee** *noun* someone whose name is put forward for a post

non- *prefix* not (used with many words to change their meaning to the opposite): *non-aggression/ non-event/ non-smoking*

nonagenarian *noun* someone from ninety to ninety-nine years old

nonce *noun*: **for the nonce** for the moment, in the meantime

nonchalant *adj* not easily roused or upset, cool □ **nonchalance** *noun* □ **nonchalantly** *adv*

non-commissioned *adj* belonging to the lower ranks of army officers, below second-lieutenant

non-committal *adj* unwilling to express, or not expressing, an opinion

nonconformist *noun* someone

who does not agree with those in authority, *esp* in church matters ◇ *adj* not agreeing with authority

nondescript *adj* not easily described, lacking anything noticeable or interesting

none *adv* not at all: *none the worse* ◇ *pronoun* not one, not any

nonentity *noun* (*plural* **nonentities**) someone of no importance

non-existent *adj* not existing, not real

nonplussed *adj* taken aback, confused

nonsense *noun* **1** words that have no sense or meaning **2** foolishness ◇ **nonsensical** *adj* ◇ **nonsensically** *adv*

non sequitur a remark unconnected with what has gone before

non-stop *adj* going on without a stop

noodle *noun* a long thin strip of pasta, eaten in soup or served with a sauce

nook *noun* **1** a corner **2** a small recess ◇ **every nook and cranny** *informal* everywhere

nooky *noun, slang* sexual intercourse

noon *noun* twelve o'clock midday

no one *see* **no**

noose *noun* a loop in a rope *etc* that tightens when pulled

nor *conj* used (often with **neither**) to show alternatives in the negative: *neither James nor I can speak Japanese*

Nordic *adj* **1** relating to Finland or Scandinavia **2** of skiing: involving cross-country and jumping events

norm *noun* a pattern or standard to judge other things from

normal *adj* ordinary, usual according to a standard ◇ **normality** *noun* ◇ **normally** *adv*

north *noun* **1** one of the four chief directions, that to the left of someone facing the rising sun ◇ *adj & adv* in or to the north ◇ **northerly** *adj* of, from or towards the north ◇ **northern** *adj* of the north ◇ **north-east** *noun* the point of the compass midway between north and east ◇ **north pole** *see* **pole** ◇ **northward** or **northwards** *adj & adv* towards the north ◇ **north-west** *noun* the point of the compass midway between north and west

nose *noun* **1** the part of the face by which people and animals smell and breathe **2** a jutting-out part, *eg* the front of an aeroplane ◇ *verb* **1** track by smelling **2** *informal* interfere in other people's affairs, pry (into) **3** push a way through: *the ship nosed through the ice* **4** move forward cautiously ◇ **nosedive** *noun* a headfirst dive by an aeroplane ◇ *verb* dive headfirst ◇ **nosegay** *noun, old* a bunch of flowers ◇ **nosey** or **nosy** *adj* inquisitive, fond of prying

nostalgia *noun* **1** a longing for past times **2** a longing for home ◇ **nostalgic** *adj* ◇ **nostalgically** *adv*

nostril *noun* either of the two openings of the nose

not *adv* expressing a negative, refusal or denial: *I am not going/*

give it to me, not to him/ I did not break the window

notable *adj* worth taking notice of; important, remarkable □ *noun* an important person □ **notability** *noun* (*plural* **notabilities**) a well-known person □ **notably** *adv* **1** in a notable or noticeable way **2** particularly

notary *noun* (*plural* **notaries**) an official who sees that written documents are drawn up in a way required by law

notation *noun* **1** the showing of numbers, musical sounds *etc* by signs: *sol-fa notation* **2** a set of such signs

notch *noun* (*plural* **notches**) a small V-shaped cut □ *verb* make a notch □ **notched** *adj*

note *noun* **1** a sign or piece of writing to draw someone's attention **2** (**notes**) details for a speech, from a talk *etc* set down in a short form **3** a short explanation **4** a short letter **5** a piece of paper used as money: *£5 note* **6** a single sound or the sign standing for it in music **7** a key on the piano *etc* □ *verb* **1** make a note of **2** notice □ **notebook** *noun* **1** a small book for taking notes **2** a small laptop computer □ **noted** *adj* well-known □ **notepaper** *noun* writing paper □ **noteworthy** *adj* notable, remarkable □ **of note** well-known, distinguished □ **take note of** notice particularly

nothing *noun* **1** no thing, not anything **2** nought, zero **3** something of no importance □ *adv* not at all: *he's nothing like his father* □

nothingness *noun* **1** non-existence **2** space, emptiness

notice *noun* **1** a public announcement **2** attention: *the colour attracted my notice* **3** a warning given before leaving, or before dismissing someone from, a job □ *verb* see, observe, take note of □ **noticeable** *adj* easily noticed, standing out

notify *verb* **1** inform **2** give notice of □ **notifiable** *adj* that must be reported: *a notifiable disease* □ **notification** *noun*

> **notify** » notifi*es*, notify*ing*, notifi*ed*

notion *noun* **1** an idea **2** a vague belief or opinion

notorious *adj* well known because of badness: *a notorious criminal* □ **notoriety** *noun*

notwithstanding *prep* in spite of: *notwithstanding his poverty, he refused all help*

nougat /*noo*gah/ or /*nug*ət/ *noun* a sticky kind of sweet containing nuts *etc*

nought *noun* the figure 0, zero

> ⚠Do not confuse with: **naught**

noun *noun*, *grammar* the word used as the name of someone or something, *eg John* and *tickets* in the sentence *John bought the tickets*

nourish *verb* **1** feed **2** encourage the growth of □ **nourishing** *adj* giving the body what is necessary for health and growth ▫ **nourishment** *noun* **1** food **2** an act of nourishing

nous /nows/ *noun* common sense

nouveau riche /noovoh *reesh*/ someone who has recently acquired wealth but not good taste

nouvelle cuisine a style of cooking using light sauces and fresh ingredients

nova *noun* (*plural* **novae** or **novas**) a star that suddenly increases in brightness for a period

novel /*nov*l/ *adj* new and strange ▫ *noun* a book telling a long story ▫ **novelist** *noun* a writer of novels

novelty *noun* (*plural* **novelties**) **1** something new and strange **2** newness **3** a small, cheap souvenir or toy

November *noun* the eleventh month of the year

novice *noun* a beginner

now *adv* **1** at the present time: *I can see him now* **2** immediately before the present time: *I thought of her just now* **3** in the present circumstances: *I can't go now because my mother is ill* ▫ *conj* (often with **that**) because, since: *you can't go out now that it's raining* ▫ **nowadays** *adv* in present times, these days ▫ **now and then** or **now and again** sometimes, from time to time

nowhere *adv* not in, or to, any place

noxious *adj* harmful: *noxious fumes*

⚠Do not confuse with: **obnoxious**

nozzle *noun* a spout fitted to the end of a pipe, tube *etc*

NSPCC *abbrev* National Society for the Prevention of Cruelty to Children

nuance *noun* a slight difference in meaning or colour *etc*

nub *noun* a small lump, a knob

nubile *adj* of a woman: sexually attractive ▫ **nubility** *noun*

nuclear *adj* **1** of a nucleus, *esp* that of an atom **2** produced by the splitting of the nuclei of atoms ▫ **nuclear energy** energy released or absorbed during reactions taking place in atomic nuclei ▫ **nuclear family** the family unit made up of the mother and father with their children ▫ **nuclear fission** the splitting of atomic nuclei ▫ **nuclear fusion** the creation of a new nucleus by merging two lighter ones, with release of energy ▫ **nuclear missile** a missile whose warhead is an atomic bomb ▫ **nuclear reactor** apparatus for producing nuclear energy

nucleus *noun* (*plural* **nuclei**) **1** the central part of an atom **2** the central part round which something collects or from which it grows: *the nucleus of my book collection* **3** the part of a plant or animal cell that controls its development

nude *adj* without clothes, naked ▫ *noun* **1** an unclothed human figure **2** a painting or statue of such a figure ▫ **nudism** *noun* ▫ **nudist** *noun* someone who advocates going without clothes in public ▫ **nudity**

noun the state of being nude ▯ **in the nude** naked

nudge *noun* a gentle push, *eg* with the elbow or shoulder ▯ *verb*

nugatory *adj* insignificant, trifling

nugget *noun* a lump, *esp* of gold

nuisance *noun* someone or something annoying or troublesome

NUJ *abbrev* National Union of Journalists

nuke *noun, slang* a nuclear weapon ▯ *verb* **1** attack with a nuclear weapon **2** cook in a microwave

null *adj*: **null and void** having no legal force

nullify *verb* **1** make useless or of no effect **2** declare to be null and void

nullify » nullifi*es*, nullify*ing*, nullifi*ed*

NUM *abbrev* National Union of Mineworkers

numb *adj* having lost the power to feel or move ▯ *verb* make numb

number *noun* **1** a word or figure showing how many, or showing a position in a series **2** a collection of people or things **3** a single issue of a newspaper or magazine **4** a popular song or piece of music ▯ *verb* **1** count **2** give numbers to **3** amount to in number ▯ **numberless** *adj* more than can be counted

numeral *noun* a figure (*eg* 1, 2 *etc*) used to express a number ▯ **numerator** *noun* the number above the line in vulgar fractions, *eg* 2 in $\frac{2}{3}$ ▯ **numerical** *adj* of, in, using or consisting of numbers ▯ **numerous** *adj* many

numerate *adj* having some understanding of mathematics and science

numerology *noun* prediction of future events by studying numbers ▯ **numerologist** *noun*

numinous *adj* producing spiritual or deeply religious feelings

numismatics *noun sing* the study of coins ▯ **numismatist** *noun* someone who collects and studies coins

numskull *noun* a stupid person

nun *noun* a member of a female religious group living in a convent ▯ **nunnery** *noun* (*plural* **nunneries**) a house where a group of nuns live

nuncio *noun* (*plural* **nuncios**) **1** an ambassador from the Pope **2** a messenger

NUPE *abbrev* National Union of Public Employees

nuptial *adj* of marriage ▯ **nuptials** *noun plural* a wedding ceremony

NUR *abbrev* National Union of Railway-workers

nurse *noun* someone who looks after sick or injured people, or small children ▯ *verb* **1** look after sick people *etc* **2** give (a baby) milk from the breast **3** hold or look after with care: *he nurses his tomato plants* **4** encourage (feelings) in yourself: *nursing her wrath*

nursery (*plural* **nurseries**) **1** a room for young children **2** a place where young plants are reared **3** a nursery school ▯ **nursery school** a school for very young children ▫ **nursing home** a small private hospital

nurture *verb* bring up, rear; to nourish: *nurture tenderness* ▫ *noun* care, upbringing; food, nourishment

NUS *abbrev* National Union of Students

NUT *abbrev* National Union of Teachers

nut *noun* **1** a fruit with a hard shell which contains a kernel **2** a small metal block with a hole in it for screwing on the end of a bolt ▫ **nutcrackers** *noun plural* an instrument for cracking nuts open ▫ **nuthatch** *noun* (*plural* **nuthatches**) a small bird living on nuts and insects ▫ **nutty** *adj* **1** containing, or having the flavour of nuts **2** *informal* mad, insane ▫ **in a nutshell** expressed very briefly

nutmeg *noun* a hard aromatic seed used as a spice in cooking

nutrient *noun* a substance which provides nourishment ▫ **nutriment** *noun* nourishment, food ▫ **nutrition** *noun* nourishment; food ▫ **nutritious** or **nutritive** *adj* valuable as food, nourishing

nuzzle *verb* **1** press, rub or caress with the nose **2** lie close to, snuggle, nestle

NVQ *abbrev, Brit* National Vocational Qualification

NW *abbrev* north-west; north-western

NY *abbrev* New York (city or state)

nylon *noun* **1** a synthetic material made from chemicals **2** (**nylons**) stockings made of nylon

nymph *noun* **1** a mythological female river or tree spirit **2** a beautiful girl **3** an insect not yet fully developed

nymphomania *noun* excessively strong sexual desire in women ▫ **nymphomaniac** *noun* someone suffering from nymphomania

NZ *abbrev* New Zealand

O

O! or **Oh!** *exclam* expressing surprise, admiration, pain *etc*

oaf *noun* (*plural* **oafs**) a stupid or clumsy person

oak *noun* **1** a tree which produces acorns as fruit **2** its hard wood ▯ **oak** or **oaken** *adj* made of oak ▯ **oak apple** a growth on the leaves and twigs of oaks, caused by insects

OAP *abbrev* **1** Old Age Pension **2** Old Age Pensioner

oar *noun* a pole for rowing, with a flat blade on the end ▯ *verb* row ▯ **oarsman, oarswoman** *noun* someone who rows ▯ **put your oar in** interfere in

oasis *noun* (*plural* **oases**) a place in a desert where water is found and trees *etc* grow

oast *noun* a large oven to dry hops ▯ **oast-house** *noun* a building containing this

oath *noun* (*plural* **oaths**) **1** a solemn promise to speak the truth, keep your word, be loyal *etc* **2** a swear word

oatcake *noun* a thin flat cake made of oatmeal

oatmeal *noun* meal made by grinding down oat grains

oats *noun plural* a type of grassy plant or its grain, used as food

obbligato *noun* (*plural* **obbligatos**), *music* an instrumental accompaniment

obdurate *adj* stubborn, firm, unyielding

OBE *abbrev* Officer of the Order of the British Empire

obedience and **obedient** *see* **obey**

obeisance *noun* a bow or curtsy showing respect

obelisk *noun* a tall four-sided pillar with a pointed top

obese *adj* very fat ▯ **obesity** *noun*

obey *verb* do what you are told to do: *obey the instructions* ▯ **obedience** *noun* **1** the act of obeying **2** willingness to obey ▯ **obedient** *adj* ▯ **obediently** *adv*

obfuscate *verb* make unclear; obscure, confuse

obi *noun* a broad Japanese sash, worn with a kimono

obiter dictum a passing remark

obituary *noun* (*plural* **obituaries**) a notice in a newspaper *etc* of someone's death, sometimes with a brief biography

object *noun* **1** something that can be seen or felt **2** an aim, a purpose: *our main object is not to make money* **3** *grammar* the word in a sentence which stands for the person or thing on which the action of the verb is done, *eg me* in the sentence *he gave me some good advice* ▯ *verb* (often with **to**) feel or show disapproval of ▯ **objection** *noun* **1** the act of objecting **2** a reason for objecting ◊ **objectionable** *adj* nasty, disagreeable ◊ **objective** *adj* not influenced by personal interests, fair ◊ *noun* aim, purpose, goal

objet d'art an article with artistic value

oblige *verb* **1** force, compel: *we were obliged to go home* **2** do a favour or service to: *oblige me by shutting the door* ◊ **obligation** *noun* **1** a promise or duty by which someone is bound: *under an obligation to help* **2** a debt of gratitude for a favour received ◊ **obligatory** *adj* **1** compulsory **2** required as a duty ◊ **obliged** *adj* owing or feeling gratitude ◊ **obliging** *adj* ready to help others

oblique *adj* **1** slanting **2** indirect, not straight or straightforward: *an oblique reference* ◊ **obliquely** *adv* ◊ **obliqueness** *noun*

obliterate *verb* **1** blot out (writing *etc*), efface **2** destroy completely ◊ **obliteration** *noun*

oblivion *noun* **1** forgetfulness **2** the state of being forgotten ◊ **oblivious** *adj* **1** unaware (of), not paying attention (to) **2** forgetful

oblong *noun* a rectangle with touching sides unequal in length, forming this shape: ▭ ◊ *adj* of the shape of an oblong

obloquy *noun* strong criticism, censure

obnoxious *adj* offensive, causing dislike ◊ **obnoxiously** *adv*

> ⚠Do not confuse with: **noxious**

oboe *noun* (*plural* **oboes**) a high-pitched woodwind instrument ◊ **oboist** *noun* someone who plays the oboe

obscene *adj* **1** sexually indecent, lewd **2** disgusting, repellent ◊ **obscenity** *noun* (*plural* **obscenities**)

obscure *adj* **1** dark **2** not clear or easily understood **3** unknown, not famous: *an obscure poet* ◊ *verb* **1** darken **2** make less clear ◊ **obscurity** *noun*

obsequies *noun plural* funeral rites

obsequious *adj* trying to win favour by flattery, willingness to agree *etc* ◊ **obsequiousness** *noun*

observe *verb* **1** notice **2** watch with attention **3** remark (that) **4** obey (a law *etc*) **5** keep, preserve: *observe a tradition* ◊ **observance** *noun* the act of keeping (a law, tradition *etc*) ◊ **observant** *adj* good at noticing ◊ **observation** *noun* **1** the act of seeing and noting; attention **2** a remark ◊ **observatory** *noun* (*plural* **observatories**) a place for making observations of the stars, weather *etc* ◊ **observer** *noun* someone sent to listen to, but not take part in, a discussion *etc*

obsess *verb* fill the mind completely ◊ **obsession** *noun* **1** a feeling or idea which someone cannot stop thinking about **2** the state of being obsessed ◊ **obsessive** *adj* **1** forming an obsession **2** having or likely to have an obsession

obsidian *noun* a glassy black volcanic rock

obsolete *adj* gone out of use

> ⚠Do not confuse: **obsolete** and **obsolescent**

obsolescent *adj* going out of date □ **obsolescence** *noun*

obstacle *noun* something which stands in the way and hinders □ **obstacle race** a race in which obstacles have to be passed, climbed *etc*

obstetrics *noun sing* the study of helping women before, during and after childbirth □ **obstetric** or **obstetrical** *adj* of obstetrics □ **obstetrician** *noun* a doctor trained in obstetrics

obstinate *adj* stubborn; not yielding □ **obstinacy** *noun* stubbornness

obstreperous *adj* noisy, unruly

obstruct *verb* **1** block up, keep from passing **2** hold back □ **obstruction** *noun* **1** a hindrance **2** something which blocks up

obtain *verb* **1** get, gain **2** be in use, be valid: *that rule still obtains* □ **obtainable** *adj* able to be got

obtrude *verb* **1** thrust (something unwanted) on someone **2** thrust (yourself) forward when not wanted □ **obtrusion** *noun*

obtrusive *adj* **1** too noticeable **2** pushy, impudent □ **obtrusiveness** *noun*

obtuse *adj* **1** of an angle: greater than a right angle (*contrasted with*: **acute**) **2** blunt, not pointed **3** stupid, not quick to understand □ **obtuseness** *noun*

obverse *noun* the side of a coin showing the head or main design

obviate *verb* remove, prevent or get round (a difficulty *etc*)

obvious *adj* easily seen or understood; plain, evident □ **obviously** *adv*

OC *abbrev* Officer Commanding

ocarina *noun* a musical toy with holes, played like a flute

occasion *noun* **1** a particular time: *on that occasion* **2** a special event: *a great occasion* **3** a cause, a reason **4** opportunity □ *verb* cause

occasional *adj* happening or used now and then □ **occasionally** *adv*

Occident *noun* the West □ **occidental** *adj*

occlude *verb* **1** shut out, exclude **2** of the teeth: bite or come together □ **occlusion** *noun*

occult *adj* **1** secret, mysterious **2** supernatural

occupy *verb* **1** dwell in **2** keep busy **3** take up, fill (space, time *etc*) **4** seize, capture (a town, fort *etc*) □ **occupancy** *noun* (*plural* **occupancies**) the act, fact or period of occupying □ **occupant** *noun* □ **occupation** *noun* **1** the state of being occupied **2** something which occupies **3** someone's trade or job **4** possession of a house *etc* □ **occupier** *noun* someone who has possession of a house *etc*

> **occupy** » occupi*es*, occupy*ing*, occupi*ed*

occur *verb* **1** happen **2** appear, be found **3** (with **to**) come into the mind of: *that never occurred to me*

□ **occurrence** *noun* **1** a happening, an event **2** the act or fact of occurring

> **occur** » occur*s*, occurr*ing*, occurr*ed*

ocean *noun* **1** the stretch of salt water surrounding the land of the earth **2** one of five main divisions of this, *ie* the Atlantic, Pacific, Indian, Arctic or Antarctic

ocelot *noun* a wild American cat like a small leopard

oche /oki/ *noun* the line or groove behind which a darts player must stand to throw

ochre *noun* a fine pale-yellow or red clay, used for colouring

octa- or **octo-** or **oct-** *prefix* eight

octagon *noun* an eight-sided figure □ **octagonal** *adj* having eight sides

octane *noun* a colourless liquid found in petroleum and used in petrol

octave *noun, music* a range of eight notes, *eg* from one C to the C next above or below it

octavo *noun* (*plural* **octavos**) a book folded to give eight leaves to each sheet of paper

octet *noun* a group of eight lines of poetry, singers *etc*

October *noun* the tenth month of the year

octogenarian *noun* someone from eighty to eighty-nine years old

octopus *noun* (*plural* **octopuses**) a deep-sea creature with eight arms

ocular *adj* of the eye

oculist *noun* someone who specializes in diseases and defects of the eye

OD /oh*dee*/ *noun, slang* an overdose of drugs □ *verb* take an overdose

> **OD** *verb* » OD'*s*, OD'*ing*, OD'*d*

odd *adj* **1** of a number: leaving a remainder of one when divided by two, *eg* the numbers 3, 17, 31 (*contrasted with*: **even**) **2** unusual, strange **3** not one of a matching pair or group, left over: *an odd glove/ odd screw* **4** (**odds**) chances or probability: *the odds are that they will win* **5** (**odds**) difference: *it makes no odds* □ **oddity** *noun* (*plural* **oddities**) **1** queerness, strangeness **2** a strange person or thing □ **odd jobs** jobs of different kinds, not part of regular employment □ **oddments** *noun plural* scraps □ **at odds** quarrelling □ **odds and ends** objects, scraps *etc* of different kinds

ode *noun* a type of poem, often written to someone or something: *ode to autumn*

odious *adj* hateful □ **odiously** *adv* □ **odium** *noun* dislike, hatred

odour *noun* smell, either pleasant or unpleasant □ **odourless** *adj* without smell

OED *abbrev* Oxford English Dictionary

oedema /ee*dee*mə/ or *US* **edema** /i*dee*mə/ *noun* an accumulation of fluid in body tissue, causing swelling

oenology /ee*nol*əji/ *noun* the study

of wines ◊ **oenological** *adj* ◊ **oenologist** *noun*

oesophagus /eesofəgəs/ or *US* **esophagus** /isofəgəs/ *noun* the gullet

oestrogen /eestrəjən/ or *US* **estrogen** /estrəjən/ *noun* a female sex hormone which regulates the menstrual cycle, prepares the body for pregnancy *etc* ◊ **oestrogenic** *adj*

oestrus /eestrəs/ or *US* **estrus** /estrəs/ *noun* the period during which a female mammal is ready for conceiving; heat

oeuvre *noun* the complete works of an artist, writer *etc*

of *prep* **1** belonging to: *the house of my parents* **2** from (a place, person *etc*): *within two miles of his home* **3** from among: *one of my pupils* **4** made from, made up of: *a house of bricks* **5** indicating an amount, measurement *etc*: *a gallon of petrol* **6** about, concerning: *talk of old friends* **7** with, containing: *a class of twenty children/ a cup of coffee* **8** as a result of: *die of hunger* **9** indicating removal or taking away: *robbed her of her jewels* **10** indicating a connection between an action and its object: *the joining of the pieces* **11** indicating character, qualities *etc*: *a man of good taste/ it was good of you to come* **12** *US* (in telling the time) before, to: *ten of eight*

off *adv* **1** away from a place, or from a particular state, position *etc*: *he walked off rudely/ your work has gone off/ switch the light off* **2** entirely, completely: *finish off your work* ◊ *adj* **1** cancelled: *the holiday is off* **2** rotten, bad: *the meat is off* **3** not working, not on: *the control is in the off position* **4** not quite pure in colour: *off-white* ◊ *prep* **1** not on, away from: *fell off the table* **2** taken away: *10% off the usual price* **3** below the normal standard: *off his game* ◊ **badly off** poor ◊ **be off** go away, leave quickly ◊ **off and on** occasionally ◊ **off the cuff** *see* **cuff** ◊ **off the wall** *see* **wall** ◊ **well off** rich

offal *noun* **1** the parts of an animal unfit for use as food **2** certain internal organs of an animal (heart, liver *etc*) that are eaten

off-beam *adj* mistaken, misguided

off-beat *adj* not standard, eccentric

off-chance *noun* a slight chance ◊ **on the off-chance** just in case

off-colour *adj* not feeling well

offcut *noun* a piece of wood, fabric *etc* remaining from a larger piece

offence or *US* **offense 1** displeasure, hurt feelings **2** a crime, a sin ◊ **take offence at** be angry or feel hurt at

offend *verb* **1** hurt the feelings of; insult, displease **2** do wrong ◊ **offender** *noun*

offensive *noun* **1** the position of someone who attacks **2** an attack ◊ *adj* **1** insulting, disgusting **2** used for attack or assault: *an offensive weapon*

offer *verb* **1** put forward (a gift, payment *etc*) for acceptance or refusal **2** lay (a choice, chance *etc*) before **3** say that you are willing to do something ▯ *noun* **1** an act of offering **2** a bid of money **3** something proposed ▯ **offering** *noun* **1** a gift **2** a collection of money in church

offhand *adj* **1** said or done without thinking or preparation **2** rude, curt ▯ *adv* without preparation; impromptu

office *noun* **1** a place where business is carried on **2** the people working in such a place **3** a duty, a job **4** a position of authority, *esp* in the government **5** (**offices**) services, helpful acts ▯ **officer** *noun* **1** someone who carries out a public duty **2** someone holding a commission in the armed forces

official *adj* **1** done or given out by those in power: *official announcement/ official action* **2** forming part of the tasks of a job or office: *official duties* **3** having full and proper authority ▯ *noun* someone who holds an office in the service of the government *etc* ▯ **officially** *adv* **1** as an official, formally **2** as announced or said in public (though not necessarily truthfully)

⚠Do not confuse with: **officious**

officiate *verb* perform a duty or service, *esp* as a clergyman at a wedding *etc*

officious *adj* fond of interfering *esp* in a pompous way ▯ **officiously** *adv* ▯ **officiousness** *noun*

⚠Do not confuse with: **official**

offie *noun, slang* an off-licence

offing *noun*: **in the offing** expected to happen soon, forthcoming

off-licence *noun* a shop selling alcohol which must not be drunk on the premises

offload *verb* **1** unload **2** get rid of (something) by passing onto someone else

offpeak *adj* not at the time of highest use or demand

off-putting *adj* causing aversion

offset *verb* weigh against, make up for: *the cost of the project was partly offset by a government grant*

offshoot *noun* **1** a shoot growing out of the main stem **2** a small business, project *etc* created out of a larger one: *an offshoot of an international firm*

offshore *adj & adv* **1** in or on the sea close to the coast **2** at a distance from the shore **3** from the shore: *offshore winds*

offside *adj & adv, sport* **1** illegally ahead of the ball, *eg* in football, in a position between the ball and the opponent's goal **2** of the side of a vehicle: nearest to the centre of the road (*contrasted with*: **nearside**)

offspring *noun* **1** someone's child or children **2** the young of animals *etc*

OFGAS or **Ofgas** *abbrev* Office of Gas Supply

OFT *abbrev* Office of Fair Trading

oft *adv, formal* often

OFTEL or **Oftel** *abbrev* Office of Telecommunications

often *adv* many times

ogle *verb* eye (someone) impudently in order to show admiration

ogre *noun* **1** a mythological man-eating giant **2** someone extremely frightening or threatening

Oh! *another spelling* of **O!**

ohm *noun* a unit of electrical resistance □ **ohmage** *noun* electrical resistance measured in ohms

OHMS *abbrev* On Her (or His) Majesty's Service

-oid *suffix* indicating something with a particular shape or resemblance: *deltoid/ anthropoid*

oil *noun* **1** a greasy liquid obtained from plants (*eg* olive oil), from animals (*eg* whale oil), and from minerals (*eg* petroleum) **2** (**oils**) oil colours for painting □ *verb* smear with oil, put oil on or in □ **oil colour** paint made by mixing a colouring substance with oil □ **oilfield** *noun* an area where mineral oil is found □ **oil painting** a picture painted in oil colours □ **oilrig** *noun* a structure set up for drilling an oil-well □ **oilskin** *noun* **1** cloth made waterproof with oil **2** a heavy coat made of this □ **oil-well** *noun* a hole drilled into the earth's surface or into the sea bed to extract petroleum □ **oily** *adj* **1** of or like oil **2** obsequious, too friendly or flattering

oink *noun* the noise of a pig □ *verb* make this noise

ointment *noun* a greasy substance rubbed on the skin to soothe, heal *etc*

OK or **okay** *exclam, adj* & *adv* all right □ **okay** *verb* mark or pass as being all right

okay *verb* » okay*s*, okay*ing*, okay*ed*

okapi *noun* a Central African animal related to the giraffe

okra *noun* a tropical plant with edible pods

old *adj* **1** advanced in age, aged **2** having a certain age: *ten years old* **3** not new, having existed a long time: *an old joke* **4** belonging to far-off times **5** worn, worn-out **6** out-of-date, old-fashioned □ **old age** the later part of life □ **old-fashioned** *adj* in a style common in the past, out-of-date □ **old guard** the conservative element in an organization *etc* □ **old hand** someone with long experience in a job *etc* □ **old maid 1** *derog* a spinster **2** a game played by passing and matching playing cards □ **old timer 1** an old person **2** a veteran, someone with experience □ **of old** long ago

oleander *noun* an evergreen shrub with spiky leaves and red or white flowers

olfactory *adj* of or used for smelling: *olfactory glands*

oligarchy *noun* government by a small exclusive group □ **oligarch** *noun* a member of an oligarchy □ **oligarchic** or **oligarchical** *adj*

olive *noun* **1** a small oval fruit with a hard stone, which is pressed to produce a cooking oil **2** the Mediterranean tree that bears this fruit □ *adj* of a yellowish-green colour □ **olive branch** a sign of a wish for peace

ombudsman *noun* an official

appointed to look into complaints against the government

> From a Swedish word meaning 'administration man', introduced into English in the 1960s

omega *noun* the last letter of the Greek alphabet

omelette or **omelet** *noun* beaten eggs fried in a single layer in a pan

omen *noun* a sign of future events

ominous *adj* suggesting future trouble

omit *verb* **1** leave out **2** fail to do ▫ **omission** *noun* **1** something omitted **2** the act of omitting

> **omit** » omit*s*, omitt*ing*, omitt*ed*

omnibus *noun* (*plural* **omnibuses**) *old* a bus ▫ *adj* **1** widely comprehensive **2** of miscellaneous contents ▫ **omnibus edition** a radio or TV programme made up of material from preceding editions of the series

omnipotent *adj* having absolute, unlimited power: *omnipotent ruler* ▫ **omnipotence** *noun*

omnipresent *adj* being present everywhere at the same time ▫ **omnipresence** *noun*

omniscient *adj* knowing everything ▫ **omniscience** *noun*

omnivorous *adj* feeding on all kinds of food ▫ **omnivorousness** *noun*

on *prep* **1** touching or fixed to the outer or upper side: *on the table* **2** supported by: *standing on one foot* **3** receiving, taking *etc*: *suspended on half-pay/ on antibiotics* **4** occurring in the course of a specified time: *on the following day* **5** about: *a book on Scottish history* **6** with: *do you have your cheque book on you?* **7** next to, near: *a city on the Rhine* **8** indicating membership of: *on the committee* **9** in the process or state of: *on sale/ on show* **10** by means of: *can you play that on the piano?* **11** followed by: *disaster on disaster* ▫ *adv* **1** so as to be touching or fixed to the outer or upper side: *put your coat on* **2** onwards, further: *they carried on towards home* **3** at a further point: *later on* ▫ *adj* **1** working, performing: *the television is on* **2** arranged, planned: *do you have anything on this afternoon?* ▫ **from now on** after this time, henceforth ▫ **on and off** occasionally, intermittently ▫ **you're on!** I agree, accept the challenge *etc*

once *adv* **1** at an earlier time in the past: *people once lived in caves* **2** for one time only: *I've been to Paris once in the last two years* ▫ *noun* one time only: *do it just this once* ▫ *conj* when: *once you've finished, you can go* ▫ **all at once** suddenly ▫ **at once 1** immediately: *come here at once!* **2** (sometimes with **all**) at the same time, together: *trying to do several things all at once* ▫ **once and for all** for the last time ▫ **once upon a time** at some time in the past

oncogen *noun* something that causes cancerous tumours ▫ **oncogene** *noun* a gene involved in the onset and development of cancer ▫ **oncogenic** *adj*

oncology *noun* the study of

tumours □ **oncological** *adj* □ **oncologist** *noun* someone who studies tumours

oncoming *adj* approaching from the front: *oncoming traffic*

one *noun* **1** the number 1 **2** a particular member of a group: *she's the one I want to meet* □ *pronoun* **1** a single person or thing: *one of my cats* **2** in formal or pompous English used instead of **you**, meaning anyone: *one must do what one can* □ *adj* **1** 1 in number, a single: *we had only one reply* **2** identical, the same: *we are all of one mind* **3** some, an unnamed (time *etc*): *one day soon* □ **oneself** *pronoun* **1** used reflexively: *wash oneself* **2** used for emphasis: *one usually has to finish the job oneself* □ **one-sided** *adj* with one person, side *etc* having a great advantage over the other □ **one-way** *adj* meant for traffic moving in one direction only □ **one another** used when an action takes place between two or more people: *they looked at one another*

onerous *adj* heavy, hard to bear or do: *onerous task*

ongoing *adj* continuing: *ongoing talks*

onion *noun* a bulb vegetable with a strong taste and smell □ **oniony** *adj* tasting of onions □ **know your onions** *informal* know your subject or job well

onlooker *noun* someone who watches an event, but does not take part in it

only *adv* **1** not more than: *only two weeks left* **2** alone, solely: *only you are invited* **3** not longer ago than: *I saw her only yesterday* **4** indicating an unavoidable result: *he'll only be offended if you ask* **5** (with **too**) extremely: *only too pleased to help* □ *adj* single, solitary: *an only child* □ *conj, informal* but, except that: *I'd like to go, only I have to work*

ono *abbrev* or nearest offer

onomatopoeia *noun* the forming of a word which sounds like the thing it refers to, *eg* moo, swish □ **onomatopoeic** *adj*

onrush *noun* a rush forward

onset *noun* **1** beginning **2** a fierce attack

onslaught *noun* a fierce attack

ontology *noun* the study of pure being or essence □ **ontologic** or **ontological** *adj* □ **ontologist** *noun*

onus *noun* burden; responsibility

onward *adj* going forward in place or time □ **onward** or **onwards** *adv*

onyx *noun* a precious stone with layers of different colours

oodles *noun plural, informal* lots (of), many

ooze *verb* flow gently or slowly □ *noun* **1** soft mud **2** a gentle flow

op *abbrev* **1** opus **2** optical: *op art*

opacity *see* **opaque**

opal *noun* a bluish-white precious stone, with flecks of various colours

opalescent *noun* milky and iridescent □ **opalescence** *noun*

opaque *adj* not able to be seen through □ **opacity** *noun*

op cit in the book *etc* cited

OPEC *abbrev* Organization of Petroleum-Exporting Countries

open *adj* **1** not shut, allowing entry or exit **2** not enclosed or fenced **3** showing the inside or inner part; uncovered **4** not blocked **5** free for all to enter **6** honest, frank **7** of land: without many trees ▯ *verb* **1** make open; unlock **2** begin ▯ **open air** any place not indoors or underground ▯ **open-air** *adj* happening outside ▯ **open book** something that can be easily seen or understood ▯ **open-cast** *adj* of a mine: excavating in the open, above ground ▯ **open-ended** *adj* without definite limits ▯ **opener** *noun* something that opens: *tin opener* ▯ **open-heart** *adj* of surgery: performed on a heart which has been temporarily stopped, with blood being circulated by a heart-lung machine ▯ **opening** *noun* **1** a hole, a gap **2** an opportunity **3** a vacant job ▯ **openly** *adv* without trying to hide or conceal anything ▯ **open-minded** *adj* ready to take up new ideas ▯ **open-plan** *adj* of an office: with desks *etc* in the same room, not divided by walls or partitions ▯ **open verdict** a verdict of death, with no cause stated, given by a coroner's jury ▯ **in the open 1** out-of-doors, in the open air **2** widely known, not secret ▯ **open to** likely or willing to receive: *open to attack/open to suggestions* ▯ **with open arms** warmly, enthusiastically

opera[1] *noun* a play in which the characters sing accompanied by an orchestra ▯ **operatic** *adj*

opera[2] *plural* of **opus**

operate *verb* **1** act, work **2** bring about an effect **3** perform an operation ▯ **operating** *adj* of or for an operation on someone's body

operation *noun* **1** action **2** method or way of working **3** the cutting of a part of the human body to examine or treat disease **4** (**operations**) movements of armies, troops

operative *adj* **1** working, in action **2** of a rule *etc*: in force, having effect ▯ *noun* a workman in a factory *etc*

operator *noun* **1** someone who works a machine **2** someone who connects telephone calls

operetta *noun* a play with music and singing

ophthalmic *adj* relating to the eye: *an ophthalmic surgeon* ▯ **ophthalmologist** *noun* a doctor who specializes in eye diseases and injuries

opiate *noun* **1** a drug containing opium used to make someone sleep **2** anything that calms or dulls the mind or feelings

opine *verb, formal* give as an opinion

opinion *noun* **1** what someone thinks or believes **2** professional judgement or point of view: *he wanted another opinion on his son's case* **3** judgement of the value of someone or something: *I have a low opinion of her* ▯ **opinionated** *adj* having and expressing strong opinions

opium *noun* a drug made from the dried juice of a type of poppy

opossum *noun* a small American

animal that carries its young in a pouch

opponent *noun* someone who opposes; an enemy, a rival

opportune *adj* coming at the right or convenient time

opportunist *noun* someone who takes advantage of an advantageous situation □ **opportunism** *noun* □ **opportunistic** *adj*

opportunity *noun* (*plural* **opportunities**) a chance (to do something)

oppose *verb* **1** struggle against, resist **2** stand against, compete against

opposite *adj* **1** facing, across from **2** lying on the other side (of) **3** as different as possible □ *prep* **1** facing, across from: *he lives opposite the post office* **2** acting a role in a play, opera *etc* in relation to another: *she played Ophelia opposite his Hamlet* □ *noun* something as different as possible (from something else): *black is the opposite of white*

opposition *noun* **1** resistance **2** those who resist **3** the political party which is against the governing party

oppress *verb* **1** govern harshly like a tyrant **2** treat cruelly **3** distress, worry greatly □ **oppression** *noun* □ **oppressive** *adj* **1** oppressing **2** cruel, harsh **3** of weather: close, tiring □ **oppressively** *adv*

opprobrium *noun* **1** a great or public disgrace **2** something that brings great disgrace □ **opprobrious** *adj* disgraceful; scornful

opt *verb* **1** (with **for**) choose **2** decide (to do) □ **opt out** decide not to (do something)

optic or **optical** *adj* relating to the eyes or sight □ **optical illusion** an impression that something seen is different from what it is □ **optics** *noun sing* the science of light

optician *noun* someone who makes and sells spectacles

optimal *adj* very best, optimum

optimism *noun* the habit of taking a bright, hopeful view of things (*contrasted with*: **pessimism**) □ **optimist** *noun* someone who tends to take a positive view of things □ **optimistic** *adj*

optimum *adj* best, most favourable: *optimum conditions*

option *noun* **1** choice; the right or power to choose **2** something chosen □ **optional** *adj* left to choice, not compulsory

opulent *adj* wealthy; luxurious □ **opulence** *noun* riches

opus *noun* (*plural* **opera**) an artistic work, *esp* a musical composition

or *conj* **1** used (often with **either**) to show alternatives: *would you prefer tea or coffee?* **2** because if not: *you'd better go or you'll miss your bus*

oracle *noun* **1** someone thought to be very wise or knowledgeable **2** *hist* a sacred place where a god answered questions **3** someone through whom such answers were made known □ **oracular** *adj*

oral *adj* **1** spoken, not written: *oral literature* **2** relating to the mouth □ *noun* an oral examination or test □ **orally** *adv* by mouth

⚠Do not confuse with: **aural**

orange *noun* a juicy citrus fruit, with a thick reddish-yellow skin

orang-utan *noun* a large man-like ape

Based on a Malay phrase which translates as 'wild man'

oration *noun* a public speech, *esp* one in fine formal language ▫ **orator** *noun* a public speaker ▫ **oratory** *noun* the art of speaking well in public

oratorio *noun* (*plural* **oratorios**) a sacred story set to music, performed by soloists, choir and often orchestra

orb *noun* anything in the shape of a ball, a sphere

orbit *noun* **1** the path of a planet or moon round a sun, or of a space capsule round the earth **2** range or area of influence: *within his orbit* ▫ *verb* go round the earth *etc* in space

Orcadian *adj* of or from Orkney ▫ *noun* someone born or living in Orkney

orchard *noun* a large garden of fruit trees

orchestra *noun* a group of musicians playing together under a conductor ▫ **orchestrate** *verb* **1** arrange (a piece of music) for an orchestra **2** organize so as to produce the best effect

orchid *noun* a plant with unusually shaped, often brightly coloured, flowers

ordain *verb* **1** declare something to be law **2** receive (a member of the clergy) into the Church ▫ **ordinance** *noun* a command; a law ▫ **ordination** *noun*

ordeal *noun* **1** a hard trial or test **2** suffering, painful experience

order *noun* **1** an instruction to act made by someone in authority **2** a request or list of requests: *put an order in with the grocer* **3** an arrangement according to a system **4** an accepted way of doing things **5** a tidy or efficient state **6** peaceful conditions: *law and order* **7** rank, position, class **8** a society or brotherhood, *eg* of monks ▫ *verb* **1** give an order to, tell to do **2** put in an order for: *I've ordered another copy of the book* **3** arrange ▫ **in order 1** correct according to what is regularly done **2** in a tidy arrangement ▫ **in order to** for the purpose of: *in order to live you must eat* ▫ **out of order 1** not working **2** not the correct way of doing things **3** not in a tidy arrangement

orderly *adj* **1** in proper order **2** well-behaved, quiet ▫ *noun* (*plural* **orderlies**) **1** a soldier who carries the orders and messages of an officer **2** a hospital attendant who does routine jobs

ordinal *adj* of or in an order ▫ **ordinal number** a number which shows order in a series, *eg* first, second, third (*compare with*: **cardinal number**)

ordinance *see* **ordain**

ordinary *adj* **1** common, usual **2** normal; not exceptional ▫ **ordinarily** *adv* ▫ **ordinariness** *noun* ▫ **out of the ordinary** unusual

ordination *see* **ordain**

Ordnance Survey a government office which produces official detailed maps

ordure *noun* excrement, dung

ore *noun* a mineral from which a metal is obtained: *iron ore*

oregano /ori*gah*noh/ or *US* /o*reg*ənoh/ *noun* a Mediterranean herb used in cooking

organ *noun* **1** an internal part of the body, *eg* the liver **2** a large musical wind instrument with a keyboard **3** a means of spreading information or propaganda, *eg* a newspaper: *an organ of conservatism* □ **organism** *noun* any living thing □ **organist** *noun* someone who plays the organ

organdie *noun* a fine thin stiff muslin

organic *adj* **1** of or produced by the bodily organs **2** of living things **3** made up of parts each with its separate function **4** of food: grown without the use of artificial fertilizers *etc* □ **organically** *adv*

organize *verb* **1** arrange, set up (an event *etc*) **2** form into a whole □ **organization** *noun* **1** the act of organizing **2** a group of people working together for a purpose

orgasm *noun* the climax of sexual excitement □ *verb* experience an orgasm □ **orgasmic** *adj*

orgy *noun* (*plural* **orgies**) a drunken or other unrestrained celebration □ **orgiastic** *adj*

oriel *noun* a small room with a bay window built out from a wall

Orient *noun, old* the countries of the East □ **oriental** *adj* eastern; from the East

orientate *verb* **1** find your position and sense of direction **2** set or put facing a particular direction □ **orientation** *noun*

orienteering *noun* the sport of finding your way across country with the help of map and compass

orifice *noun, formal* an opening

origami *noun* the Japanese art of folding paper

origin *noun* **1** the starting point **2** the place from which someone or something comes **3** cause

original *adj* **1** first in time **2** not copied **3** able to think or do something new □ *noun* **1** the earliest version **2** a model from which other things are made □ **originally** *adv*

originate *verb* **1** bring or come into being **2** produce

Orion *noun* a constellation containing seven bright stars, forming the shape of a hunter

orison *noun* a prayer

ormolu *noun* gilded bronze or other metal, used for ornamentation

ornament *noun* something added to give or enhance beauty □ *verb* adorn, decorate □ **ornamental** *adj* used for ornament; decorative □ **ornamentation** *noun*

ornate *adj* richly decorated □ **ornately** *adv*

ornery *adj, US informal* cantankerous, touchy

ornithologist *noun* someone who

studies or is an expert on birds □ **ornithological** *adj* □ **ornithology** *noun*

orotund *adj* of a voice: full, round

orphan *noun* a child who has lost one or both parents □ **orphanage** *noun* a home for orphans

orthodox *adj* agreeing with the prevailing or established religious, political *etc* views (*contrasted with*: **heterodox**) □ **orthodoxy** *noun*

orthography *noun* an established system of spelling □ **orthographic** or **orthographical** *adj*

orthopaedics or *US* **orthopedics** *noun sing* the branch of medicine which deals with bone diseases and injuries □ **orthopaedic** *adj*

Oscar *noun* an annual award given by the American Academy of Motion Picture Arts and Sciences

oscillate *verb* **1** swing to and fro like the pendulum of a clock **2** keep changing your mind □ **oscillation** *noun*

> From Latin *oscillum*, literally 'small face', a mask of the god Bacchus which hung in Roman vineyards and swayed in the wind

osier *noun* **1** a type of willow tree whose twigs are used for weaving baskets *etc* **2** a twig from this tree

osmosis *noun* **1** diffusion of liquids through a membrane **2** gradual absorption or assimilation

osprey *noun* (*plural* **ospreys**) a type of eagle which eats fish

ostensible *adj* of a reason *etc*: apparent, but not always real or true

ostentatious *adj* showy, meant to catch the eye □ **ostentation** *noun*

osteopath *noun* someone who treats injuries to bones, muscles *etc* by manipulating the patient's body, not by drugs or surgery □ **osteopathy** *noun*

osteoporosis *noun* a disease which makes bones porous and brittle, caused by lack of calcium

ostler *another spelling* of **hostler**

ostracize *verb* banish (someone) from the company of a group of people □ **ostracism** *noun*

> Based on *ostrakon*, a piece of pottery used in ancient Greece to cast votes to decide if someone was to be exiled

ostrich *noun* (*plural* **ostriches**) a large African bird with showy plumage, which cannot fly but runs very fast □ **ostrich-like** *adj* avoiding facing up to difficulties (after the ostrich's supposed habit of burying its head in the sand when chased)

other *adj* **1** the second of two: *where is the other sock?* **2** remaining, not previously mentioned: *these are for the other children* **3** different, additional: *there must be some other reason* **4** (with **every**) second: *every other day* **5** recently past: *the other day* □ *pronoun* **1** the second of two **2** those remaining, those not previously mentioned: *the others arrived the next day* **3** the previous one: *one after the other* □ **other than** except: *no hope other* *than to retreat* □ **someone or other** or **something or other** someone or something not named or specified: *there's always someone or other here*

otiose *adj* superfluous, redundant

OTT *abbrev* over-the-top, extravagant

otter *noun* a type of river animal living on fish

Ottoman *adj, hist* relating to the Turkish empire from the 14th to the 19th centuries

ottoman *noun* a low, cushioned seat without a back

ought *verb* **1** used with other verbs to indicate duty or need: *we ought to set an example/ I ought to practise more* **2** to indicate what can be reasonably expected: *the weather ought to be fine*

ounce *noun* a unit of weight, one-sixteenth of a pound, 28.35 grammes

our *adj* belonging to us: *our house* □ **ours** *pronoun* something belonging to us: *the green car is ours* □ **ourselves** *pronoun* **1** used reflexively: *we exhausted ourselves swimming* **2** used for emphasis: *we ourselves don't like it, but other people may*

oust *verb* **1** drive out (from) **2** take the place of: *she ousted him as leader of the party*

out *adv* **1** into or towards the open air: *go out for a walk* **2** from within: *take out a handkerchief* **3** not inside: *out of prison* **4** far from here: *out in the Far East* **5** not at home, not in the office *etc*: *she's out at the moment* **6** aloud: *shouted out* **7** to or at an end: *hear me out* **8** inaccurate: *the total was five pounds out* **9** *informal* on strike **10** published: *is the book not out yet?* **11** no longer hidden: *the secret is out* **12** openly admitting to being homosexual **13** dismissed from a game of cricket, baseball *etc* **14** finished, having won at cards *etc* **15** no longer in power or office **16** determined: *out to win* □ **outer** *adj* nearer the edge, surface *etc*; further away □ **outermost** *adj* nearest the edge; furthest away □ **outing** *noun* a trip, excursion □ **out-and-out** *adj* complete, total, thorough

outback *noun* the wild interior parts of Australia

outbid *verb* offer a higher price than (somebody else)

> **outbid** » outbid*s*, outbidd*ing*, outbid

outboard *adj* on the outside of a ship or boat: *an outboard motor*

outbreak *noun* a beginning, a breaking out, *eg* of war or disease

outbuilding *noun* a building that is separate from the main buildings

outburst *noun* a bursting out, *esp* of angry feelings

outcast *noun* someone driven away from friends and home

outcome *noun* result

outcrop *noun* the part of a rock formation that can be seen at the surface of the ground

outcry *noun* (*plural* **outcries**) a widespread show of anger, disapproval *etc*

outdo *verb* do better than

outdo » outdo*es*, outdo*ing*, outdid, outdone

outdoor *adj* of or in the open air ◇ **outdoors** *adv* **1** outside the house **2** in or into the open air

outfit *noun* a set of clothes worn together, often for a special occasion *etc* ◇ **outfitter** *noun* a seller of outfits, *esp* men's clothes

outgoings *noun plural* money spent or being spent

outgrow *verb* get too big or old for (clothes, toys *etc*)

outgrow » outgrow*s*, outgrow*ing*, outgrew, outgrown

out-house *noun* a shed

outlandish *adj* looking or sounding very strange

outlaw *noun* someone put outside the protection of the law; a robber or bandit ◇ *verb* **1** place beyond the protection of the law **2** ban, forbid

outlay *noun* money paid out

outlet *noun* **1** a passage to the outside, *eg* for a water-pipe **2** a means of expressing or getting rid of (a feeling, energy *etc*) **3** a market for goods

outline *noun* **1** the outer line of a figure in a drawing *etc* **2** a sketch showing only the main lines **3** a rough sketch **4** a brief description ◇ *verb* draw or describe an outline of

outlive *verb* live longer than

outlook *noun* **1** a view from a window *etc* **2** what is thought likely to happen: *the weather outlook*

outlying *adj* far from the centre, distant

outnumber *verb* be greater in number than: *their team outnumbered ours*

out-of-date *adj* or **out of date** obsolete, no longer valid: *this voucher is out of date/ an out-of-date ticket*

out-patient *noun* a patient who does not stay in a hospital while receiving treatment (*contrasted with*: **in-patient**)

outpost *noun* a military station in front of or far from the main army; an outlying settlement

output *noun* the goods produced by a machine, factory *etc*; the amount of work done by a person **2** data produced by a computer program (*contrasted with*: **input**)

outrage *noun* **1** an act of great violence **2** an act which shocks or causes offence ◇ *verb* **1** injure, hurt by violence **2** insult, shock ◇ **outrageous** *adj* **1** violent, very wrong **2** not moderate, extravagant

outré /*ootreh*/ *adj* beyond what is normal, extravagant

outright *adv* completely ◇ *adj* complete, thorough

outset *noun* start, beginning

outside *noun* **1** the outer surface or place: *the outside of the box* ◇ *adj* **1** in, on or of the outer surface or place: *the outside seat* **2** relating to leisure rather than your full-time job: *outside interests* **3** slight: *an outside chance of winning* ◇ *adv* **1**

beyond the limits of: *go outside the building/ locked outside working hours* **2** out-of-doors; in or into the open air: *let's eat outside* ▫ *prep* beyond the range of, not within ▫ **outsider** *noun* **1** someone not included in a particular social group **2** a runner *etc* whom no one expects to win ▫ **at the outside** at the most: *ten miles at the outside*

outsize *adj* of a very large size

outskirts *noun plural* the outer borders of a city *etc*

outspoken *adj* bold and frank in speech

outstanding *adj* **1** well-known **2** excellent **3** of a debt: unpaid

outstretched *adj* reaching out

out-tray *noun* an office tray for letters and work already dealt with (*contrasted with*: **in-tray**)

outvote *verb* defeat by a greater number of votes

outward *adj* **1** towards or on the outside **2** of a journey: away from home, not towards it ▫ **outwardly** or **outwards** *adv* on the outside, externally

outweigh *verb* be more important than: *the advantages outweigh the disadvantages*

outwit *verb* defeat by cunning

outwit » outwit*s*, outwitt*ing*, outwitt*ed*

outwith *prep, Scot* outside of

ouzo /*oo*zoh/ *noun* a Greek aniseed-flavoured liqueur

ova *plural* of **ovum**

oval *adj* having the shape of an egg ▫ *noun* an egg shape

ovary *noun* (*plural* **ovaries**) one of two organs in the female body in which eggs are formed

ovation *noun* an outburst of cheering, hand-clapping *etc*

oven *noun* a covered place for baking; a small furnace

over *prep* **1** higher than, above: *the number is over the door/ she won over £200/ we've lived here for over thirty years* **2** across: *going over the bridge* **3** on the other side of: *the house over the road* **4** on top of: *threw his coat over the body* **5** here and there on: *paper scattered over the carpet* **6** about: *they quarrelled over their money* **7** by means of: *over the telephone* **8** during, throughout: *over the years* **9** while doing, having *etc*: *fell asleep over his dinner* ▫ *adv* **1** above, higher up: *two birds flew over our heads* **2** across a distance: *he walked over and spoke* **3** downwards: *did you fall over?* **4** above in number *etc*: *aged four and over* **5** as a remainder: *three left over* **6** through: *read the passage over* ▫ *adj* finished: *the sale is over* ▫ *noun, cricket* a fixed number of balls bowled from one end of the wicket ▫ **over again** once more ▫ **overly** *adv* too, excessively

over- *prefix* too much, to too great an extent: *overcook/ over-excited*

overall *noun* **1** a garment worn over ordinary clothes to protect them against dirt **2** hard-wearing trousers with a bib worn as work clothes ▫ *adj* **1** from one end to the other: *overall length* **2** including everything: *overall cost* ▫ **over all** altogether

overawe *verb* frighten or astonish into silence

overbalance *verb* lose your balance and fall

overbearing *adj* over-confident, domineering

overboard *adv* out of a ship into the water: *man overboard*

overcast *adj* of the sky: cloudy

overcharge *verb* **1** charge too great a price **2** fill or load too heavily

overcoat *noun* an outdoor coat worn over all other clothes

overcome *verb* get the better of, defeat ▫ *adj* helpless from exhaustion, emotion *etc*

overdo *verb* **1** do too much **2** exaggerate: *they rather overdid the sympathy* **3** cook (food) too long

overdose *noun* too great an amount (of medicine, a drug *etc*) ▫ *verb* give or take too much medicine *etc*

overdraw *verb* draw more money from the bank than you have in your account ▫ **overdraft** *noun* the amount of money overdrawn from a bank

overdue *adj* **1** later than the stated time: *the train is overdue* **2** of a bill *etc*: still unpaid although the time for payment has passed

overflow *verb* **1** flow or spill over: *the river overflowed its banks/ the crowd overflowed into the next room* **2** be so full as to flow over ▫ *noun* **1** a running-over of liquid **2** a pipe or channel for getting rid of excess water *etc*

overgrown *adj* **1** covered with wild plant growth **2** grown too large

overhang *verb* jut out over

overhaul *verb* examine carefully and carry out repairs ▫ *noun* a thorough examination and repair

overhead *adv* directly above: *the aeroplane flew overhead* ▫ *adj* placed high above the ground: *overhead cables* ▫ *noun* (**overheads**) the general expenses of a business *etc*

overhear *verb* hear what you were not meant to hear

overjoyed *adj* filled with great joy

overland *adv* & *adj* on or by land, not sea

overlap *verb* **1** extend over and partly cover: *the two pieces of cloth overlapped* **2** cover a part of the same area or subject as another; partly coincide ▫ *noun* the amount by which something overlaps

overleaf *adj* on the other side of a leaf of a book

overload *verb* load or fill too much

overlook *verb* **1** look down on from a higher point; have or give a view of: *the house overlooked the village* **2** fail to see, miss **3** pardon, not punish

overlord *noun*, *hist* a lord with power over other lords

overmuch *adv* too much

overnight *adv* **1** during the night: *staying overnight with a friend* **2**

in a very short time: *he changed completely overnight* □ *adj* **1** for the night: *an overnight bag* **2** got or made in a very short time: *an overnight success*

overpass *noun* a road going over above another road, railway, canal *etc*

overpower *verb* **1** defeat through greater strength **2** overwhelm, make helpless □ **overpowering** *adj* **1** unable to be resisted **2** overwhelming, very strong: *overpowering smell*

overrate *verb* value more highly than is deserved: *his new film is overrated*

overreach *verb*: **overreach yourself** try to do or get more than you can and so fail

override *verb* ignore, set aside: *overriding the teacher's authority*

overrule *verb* go against or cancel an earlier judgement or request

overrun *verb* **1** grow or spread over: *overrun with weeds* **2** take possession of (a country)

overseas *adj* & *adv* abroad; beyond the sea

oversee *verb* watch over, supervise □ **overseer** *noun*

overshadow *verb* lessen the importance of by doing better than

oversight *noun* **1** something left out or forgotten by mistake **2** failure to notice

overstep *verb* go further than (a set limit, rules *etc*)

overt *adj* not hidden or secret; openly done

overtake *verb* catch up with and pass

overthrow *verb* defeat

overtime *noun* **1** time spent working beyond the agreed normal hours **2** payment for this, usually at a higher rate

overtone *noun* an additional meaning or association, not directly stated

overture *noun* **1** a proposal intended to open discussions: *overtures of peace* **2** a piece of music played as an introduction to an opera

overweening *adj* **1** arrogant, extremely conceited **2** of pride: excessive

overwhelm *verb* **1** defeat completely **2** load with too great an amount: *overwhelmed with work* **3** overcome, make helpless: *overwhelmed with grief* □ **overwhelming** *adj*

overwork *verb* work more than is good for you □ **overworked** *adj*

overwrought *adj* excessively nervous or excited, agitated

oviparous *adj*

ovoid *adj*

ovum *noun* (*plural* **ova**) the egg from which the young of animals and people develop

owe *verb* **1** be in debt to: *I owe Peter three pounds* **2** have (someone or thing) to thank for: *he owes his success to his family* □ **owing to** because of

owl *noun* a bird of prey which

comes out at night □ **owlet** *noun* a young owl

own *verb* **1** have as a possession **2** admit, confess to be true □ *adj* belonging to the person mentioned: *is this all your own work?* □ **own goal** a goal scored by mistake against your own side □ **hold your own** keep your place or position, not weaken □ **on your own 1** by your own efforts **2** alone

owner *noun* someone who possesses anything □ **ownership** *noun* possession

ox *noun* (*plural* **oxen**) a male cow, usually castrated, used for drawing loads *etc*

Oxbridge *noun* Oxford and Cambridge Universities □ *adj* of or typical of Oxbridge

oxide *noun* a compound of oxygen and another element

oxidize *verb* **1** combine with oxygen **2** become rusty

oxygen *noun* a gas with no taste, colour or smell, forming part of the air and of water □ **oxygenate** *verb*

oyster *noun* a type of eatable shellfish □ **oystercatcher** *noun* a black and white wading bird which eats limpets and mussels □ **oyster mushroom** an edible mushroom often found on dead wood

oz *abbrev* ounce(s)

ozone *noun* a form of oxygen □ **ozone layer** a layer of the upper atmosphere which protects the earth from the sun's ultraviolet rays

P

p *abbrev* **1** page **2** pence

PA *abbrev* **1** public address (system) **2** personal assistant

pa *abbrev* per annum

pace *noun* **1** a step **2** rate of walking, running *etc* □ *verb* **1** measure by steps **2** walk backwards and forwards □ **pacemaker** *noun* **1** someone who sets the pace in a race **2** a device used to correct weak or irregular heart rhythms

pachyderm *noun* a thick-skinned animal such as an elephant

pacify *verb* **1** make peaceful **2** calm, soothe □ **pacifist** *noun* someone who is against war and works for peace

> **pacify** » pacifi*es*, pacify*ing*, pacifi*ed*

pack *noun* **1** a bundle, *esp* one carried on the back **2** a set of playing-cards **3** a group of animals, *esp* dogs or wolves □ *verb* **1** place (clothes *etc*) in a case or trunk for a journey **2** press or crowd together closely □ **pack animal** an animal which carries loads on its back □ **pack-ice** *noun* a mass of large pieces of floating ice driven together by wind, currents *etc* □ **pack in** cram in tightly

package *noun* a bundle, a parcel □ *verb* **1** put into a container **2** wrap □ **package holiday** or **package tour** a holiday or tour arranged by an organizer with all travel and accommodation included in the price

packet *noun* **1** a small parcel **2** a container made of paper, cardboard *etc*

packing *noun* **1** the act of putting things in cases, parcels *etc* **2** material for wrapping goods to pack **3** something used to fill an empty space □ **packing case** a wooden box for transporting goods □ **send packing** send (someone) away forcefully

pact *noun* **1** an agreement **2** a treaty, a contract

pad *noun* **1** a soft cushion-like object to prevent jarring or rubbing *etc* **2** a bundle of sheets of paper fixed together **3** the paw of certain animals **4** a rocket-launching platform □ *verb* **1** stuff or protect with a soft material **2** (often with **out**) fill up with unnecessary material **3** walk making a dull, soft, noise □ **padding** *noun* **1** stuffing material **2** words included in a speech, book *etc* just to fill space or time

> **pad** *verb* » pad*s*, padd*ing*, padd*ed*

paddle *verb* **1** move forward by the use of paddles; row **2** wade in shallow water □ *noun* a short, broad spoon-shaped oar □ **paddle-steamer** *noun* a steamer driven by two large wheels made up of paddles

paddock *noun* a small closed-in field used for pasture

paddy-field *noun* a muddy field in which rice is grown

padlock *noun* a removable lock with a hinged hook

paean /*peeə*n/ *noun* a song of praise or thanksgiving

paediatrics or *US* **pediatrics** *noun sing* the treatment of children's diseases ▫ **paediatrician** *noun*

paedophile or *US* **pedophile** *noun* someone who has sexual desire for children

pagan *noun* someone who does not believe in any religion; a heathen ▫ *adj* heathen ▫ **paganism** *noun*

page *noun* **1** one side of a blank, written or printed sheet of paper **2** a boy servant **3** a boy who carries the train of the bride's dress in a marriage service

pageant *noun* **1** a show or procession made up of scenes from history **2** an elaborate parade or display ▫ **pageantry** *noun* elaborate show or display

pagoda *noun* an Eastern temple, *esp* in China or India

paid *past form* of **pay**

pail *noun* an open vessel of tin, zinc, plastic *etc* for carrying liquids; a bucket

pain *noun* **1** feeling caused by hurt to mind or body **2** threat of punishment: *under pain of death* **3** (**pains**) care: *takes great pains with his work* ▫ *verb* cause suffering to, distress ▫ **pained** *adj* showing pain or distress ▫ **painful** *adj* ▫ **painfully** *adv* ▫ **painkiller** *noun* a medicine taken to lessen pain ▫ **painless** *adj* ▫ **painlessly** *adv* ▫ **painstaking** *adj* very careful ▫ **painstakingly** *adv*

paint *verb* **1** apply colour to in the form of liquid or paste **2** describe in words ▫ *noun* a liquid substance used for colouring and applied with a brush, a spray *etc* ▫ **painter** *noun* **1** someone whose trade is painting **2** an artist who works in paint **3** a rope used to fasten a boat ▫ **painting** *noun* **1** the act or art of creating pictures with paint **2** a painted picture

pair *noun* **1** two of the same kind **2** a set of two ▫ *verb* **1** join to form a pair **2** go in twos **3** mate

pajamas *another spelling* of **pyjamas**

pakora *noun* an Indian dish of balls of chopped vegetables coated in batter and fried

pal *noun*, *informal* a friend

palace *noun* the house of a king, queen, archbishop or aristocrat

palaeography *noun* the study of historical styles of handwriting ▫ **palaeographer** *noun* ▫ **palaeographic** or **palaeographical** *adj*

palaeolithic or **paleolithic** *adj* relating to the early Stone Age when people used stone tools

palaeontology *noun* the study of fossils ▫ **palaeontological** *adj* ▫ **palaeontologist** *noun*

palanquin *noun* a carriage consisting of a box for one passenger, carried on men's shoulders

palatable *adj* **1** pleasant to the taste **2** acceptable, pleasing: *the truth is often not palatable*

palate *noun* **1** the roof of the mouth **2** taste

⚠Do not confuse with: **palette** and **pallet**

palatial *adj* like a palace, magnificent

palaver *noun* an unnecessary fuss

pale[1] *noun* a wooden stake used in making a fence to enclose ground ▫ **paling** *noun* a row of wooden stakes forming a fence

pale[2] *adj* **1** light or whitish in colour **2** not bright ▫ *verb* make or turn pale

palette *noun* a board or plate on which an artist mixes paints

⚠Do not confuse with: **pallet** and **palate**

palfrey *noun*, *old* a horse for riding, not one used in battle

palimpsest *noun* a manuscript written, or drawing made, on top of an earlier work which has been erased

palindrome *noun* a word or phrase that reads the same backwards as forwards, *eg* level

From Greek *palindromos*, meaning 'running back'

paling *see* **pale**

palisade *noun* a fence of pointed wooden stakes

pall /pawl/ *noun* **1** the cloth over a coffin at a funeral **2** a dark covering or cloud: *a pall of smoke* ▫ *verb* become dull or uninteresting ▫ **pallbearer** *noun* one of those carrying or walking beside the coffin at a funeral

pallet *noun* **1** a straw bed or mattress **2** a platform that can be lifted by a fork-lift truck for stacking goods

⚠Do not confuse with: **palette** and **palate**

palliative *adj* making less severe or harsh ▫ *noun* something which lessens pain, *eg* a drug

pallid *adj* pale

pallor *noun* paleness

palm *noun* **1** a tall tree with broad fan-shaped leaves, which grows in hot countries **2** the inner surface of the hand between the wrist and the start of the fingers ▫ **palmist** *noun* someone who claims to tell fortunes by the lines and markings of the hand ▫ **palmistry** *noun* the telling of fortunes in this way ▫ **palm off** give with the intention of cheating: *that shopkeeper palmed off a foreign coin on me*

palpable *adj* **1** able to be touched or felt **2** easily noticed, obvious

palpate *verb* examine by touch ▫ **palpation** *noun*

palpitate *verb* of the heart: beat rapidly, throb ▫ **palpitations** *noun plural* uncomfortable rapid beating of the heart

palsy *noun* a loss of power and feeling in the muscles ▫ **palsied** *adj*

paltry *adj* of little value

pampas *noun plural* the vast treeless plains of South America

pamper *verb* spoil (a child *etc*) by giving too much attention to

pamphlet *noun* a small book, stitched or stapled, often with a light paper cover □ **pamphleteer** *noun* a writer of pamphlets

pan *noun* **1** a broad shallow pot used in cooking, a saucepan **2** a shallow dent in the ground **3** the bowl of a toilet □ *verb* move a television or film camera so as to follow an object or give a wide view □ **panhandle** *verb, US* beg on the streets □ **pan out 1** turn out (well or badly) **2** come to an end

> **pan** *verb* » pan*s*, pann*ing*, pann*ed*

pan- *prefix* all, whole □ **Pan American** including all America or Americans, North and South

panacea /pan*ə*see*ə*/ *noun* a cure for all things

panache *noun* a sense of style, swagger

pancake *noun* a thin cake of flour, eggs, sugar and milk, fried in a pan

panda *noun* **1** a large black-and-white bear-like animal found in Tibet *etc* **2** a raccoon-like animal found in the Himalayas □ **panda car** *Brit informal* a police patrol car

pandemic *adj* of a disease *etc*: occurring over a wide area and affecting a large number of people

pandemonium *noun* a state of confusion and uproar

> The name of the capital of Hell in Milton's *Paradise Lost* (1667)

pander *noun* a pimp □ **pander to** indulge, easily comply with

> After *Pandarus*, who acts as a go-between in the story of Troilus and Cressida

Pandora's box something which causes unexpected havoc

> After the story of *Pandora*, who disobeyed the Greek gods and opened a box containing all the troubles of the world

p and p or **p & p** *abbrev* postage and packing

pane *noun* a sheet of glass

panegyric /pani*j*irik/ *noun* a speech praising highly someone, an achievement *etc*

panel *noun* **1** a flat rectangular piece of wood such as is set into a door or wall **2** a group of people chosen to judge a contest, take part in a television quiz *etc* □ **panelled** *adj*

pang *noun* a sudden sharp pain; a twinge

panic *noun* **1** a sudden and great fright **2** fear that spreads from person to person □ *verb* **1** throw into panic **2** act wildly through fear

> **panic** *verb* » panic*s*, panick*ing*, panick*ed*

pannier *verb* **1** a basket slung on a horse's back **2** a light container attached to a bicycle *etc*

panoply *verb* (*plural* **panoplies**) **1**

the ceremonial dress, equipment *etc* associated with a particular event: *the panoply of a military funeral* **2** *hist* a full suit of armour

panorama *verb* a wide view of a landscape, scene *etc*

pansy *verb* (*plural* **pansies**) a flower like the violet but larger

pant *verb* **1** gasp for breath **2** say breathlessly **3** wish eagerly (for)

pantechnicon *noun* a large van for transporting furniture

pantheism *noun* **1** the belief that all things in the physical universe are part of God **2** belief in many gods ▯ **pantheist** *noun* a believer in pantheism ▯ **pantheistic** or **pantheistical** *adj*

panther *noun* **1** a large leopard **2** *US* a puma

pantomime *noun* a Christmas play, with songs, jokes *etc*, based on a popular fairy tale *eg* Cinderella

pantry *noun* (*plural* **pantries**) a room for storing food

pants *noun plural* **1** underpants **2** women's short-legged knickers **3** *US* trousers ▯ **panties** *noun plural* women's or children's knickers with short legs ▯ **pantihose** *noun plural, US* tights

papa *noun* a child's name for **father**

papacy *noun* the position or power of the Pope ▯ **papal** *adj*

paparazzo *noun* (*plural* **paparazzi**) a press photographer who hounds celebrities *etc*

papaya *noun* (*also called*: **pawpaw**) a green-skinned edible fruit from S America

paper *noun* **1** a material made from rags, wood *etc* used for writing or wrapping **2** a single sheet of this **3** a newspaper **4** an essay on a learned subject **5** a set of examination questions **6** (**papers**) documents proving someone's identity, nationality *etc* ▯ *verb* cover up (*esp* walls) with paper ▯ **paperback** *noun* a book bound in a flexible paper cover ▯ **paper-chase** *noun* a game in which one runner leaves a trail of paper so that others may track them ▯ **paper-tiger** *noun* someone who appears to be powerful but really is not ▯ **paperweight** *noun* a heavy glass, metal *etc* object used to keep a pile of papers in place

papier-mâché /papyeh-*ma*sheh/ *noun* a substance consisting of paper pulp and some sticky liquid or glue, shaped into models, bowls *etc*

papoose *noun, old* a Native American baby

paprika *noun* a type of ground red pepper

papyrus *noun* (*plural* **papyri** or **papyruses**) a reed used by the ancient Egyptians *etc* to make paper

par *noun* **1** an accepted standard, value *etc* **2** *golf* the number of strokes allowed for each hole if the play is perfect ▯ **below par 1** not up to standard **2** not feeling very well ▯ **on a par with** equal to or comparable with

parable *noun* a story (*eg* in the

Bible) which teaches a moral lesson

parabola *noun* **1** a curve **2** the intersection of a cone with a plane parallel to its side

paracetamol *noun* a pain-relieving drug

parachute *noun* an umbrella-shaped device made of light material and rope which supports someone or something dropping slowly to the ground from an aeroplane □ *verb* drop by parachute □ **parachutist** *noun* someone dropped by parachute from an aeroplane

parade *noun* **1** an orderly arrangement of troops for inspection or exercise **2** a procession of people, vehicles *etc* in celebration of some event □ *verb* **1** arrange (troops) in order **2** march in a procession **3** display in an obvious way

paradigm /parədaim/ *noun* an example showing a certain pattern

paradise *noun* **1** heaven **2** a place or state of great happiness

paradox *noun* (*plural* **paradoxes**) a saying which seems to contradict itself but which may be true □ **paradoxical** *adj* □ **paradoxically** *adv*

paraffin *noun* an oil which burns and is used as a fuel (for heaters, lamps *etc*)

paragliding *noun* the sport of gliding, supported by a modified type of parachute

paragon *noun* a model of perfection or excellence: *a paragon of good manners*

paragraph *noun* **1** a division of a piece of writing shown by beginning the first sentence on a new line **2** a short item in a newspaper

parakeet *noun* a type of small parrot

parallel *adj* **1** of lines: going in the same direction and never meeting, always remaining the same distance apart **2** similar or alike in some way: *parallel cases* □ *noun* **1** a parallel line **2** something comparable in some way with something else **3** a line to mark latitude, drawn east and west across a map or round a globe at a set distance from the equator

parallelogram *noun* a four-sided figure, the opposite sides of which are parallel and equal in length

paralyse or *US* **paralyze** *verb* **1** affect with paralysis **2** make helpless or ineffective **3** bring to a halt □ **paralysis** *noun* loss of the power to move and feel in part of the body □ **paralytic** *adj* **1** suffering from paralysis **2** *informal* helplessly drunk □ *noun* a paralysed person

paramedic *noun* someone helping doctors and nurses, *eg* a member of an ambulance crew □ **paramedical** *adj*

parameter *noun* a boundary, a limit

> ⚠Do not confuse with: **perimeter**

paramilitary *adj* **1** on military lines and intended to supplement the military **2** organized illegally as a military force □ *noun* a member of a paramilitary force

paramount *adj* **1** above all others in rank or power **2** very greatest: *of paramount importance*

paramour *noun*, *old* a lover

paranoia *noun* **1** a form of mental disorder characterized by delusions of grandeur, persecution *etc* **2** intense, irrational fear or suspicion

paranormal *adj* beyond what is normal in nature; supernatural, occult

parapet *noun* a low wall on a bridge or balcony to prevent people falling over the side

paraphernalia *noun plural* belongings; gear, equipment

> Originally a woman's property outwith her dowry, which remained her own after marriage

paraphrase *verb* express (a piece of writing) in other words □ *noun* an expression in different words

paraplegia *noun* paralysis of the lower part of the body and legs □ **paraplegic** *adj* of paraplegia □ *noun* someone who suffers from paraplegia

parasite *noun* an animal, plant or person living on another without being any use in return □ **parasitic** *adj*

parasol *noun* a light umbrella used as a sunshade

paratroops *noun plural* soldiers carried by air to be dropped by parachute into enemy country □ **paratrooper** *noun*

paravane *noun* a device with fins or vanes towed behind by a ship to disconnect mines

parboil *verb* boil (food) slightly

parcel *noun* a wrapped and tied package to be sent by post □ *verb* **1** (with **out**) divide into portions **2** (with **up**) wrap up as a package □ **part and parcel** an absolutely necessary part

> **parcel** *verb* » parcel*s*, parcell*ing*, parcell*ed*

parch *verb* **1** make hot and very dry **2** make thirsty □ **parched** *adj*

parchment *noun* **1** the dried skin of a goat or sheep used for writing on **2** paper resembling this

pardon *verb* **1** forgive **2** free from punishment **3** allow to go unpunished □ *noun* **1** forgiveness **2** the act of pardoning □ **pardonable** *adj* able to be forgiven

pare *verb* **1** peel or cut off the edge or outer surface of **2** make smaller gradually □ **parings** *noun plural* small pieces cut away or peeled off

parent *noun* a father or mother □ **parentage** *noun* descent from parents or ancestors □ **parental** *adj* **1** of parents **2** with the manner or attitude of a parent

parenthesis *noun* (*plural* **parentheses**) **1** a word or group of words in a sentence forming an explanation or comment, often separated by brackets or dashes, *eg* he and his wife (*so he said*) were separated **2** (**parentheses**) brackets □ **parenthetical** *adj*

par excellence *adj* superior to all others of the kind

pariah *noun* someone driven out from a community or group; an outcast

> Originally a member of a low caste in southern India

parish *noun* (*plural* **parishes**) a district with its own church and minister or priest ▯ **parishioner** *noun* a member of a parish

parity *noun* equality

park *noun* **1** a public place for walking, with grass and trees **2** an enclosed piece of land surrounding a country house ▯ *verb* stop and leave (a car *etc*) in a place for a time

parka *noun* a type of thick jacket with a hood

Parkinson's disease a disease causing trembling in the hands *etc* and rigid muscles

parley *verb* hold a conference, *esp* with an enemy ▯ *noun* (*plural* **parleys**) a meeting between enemies to settle terms of peace *etc*

> **parley** *verb* » parley*s*, parley*ing*, parley*ed*

parliament *noun* **1** the chief law-making council of a nation **2** *Brit* the House of Commons and the House of Lords ▯ **parliamentary** *adj*

parlour *noun* a sitting room in a house ▯ **parlourmaid** *noun* a woman or girl whose job is to wait at table

Parma ham an Italian smoked ham

Parmesan *noun* a hard Italian cheese, often grated over dishes

parochial *adj* **1** relating to a parish **2** interested only in local affairs; narrow-minded ▯ **parochially** *adv*

parody *noun* (*plural* **parodies**) an amusing imitation of someone's writing style, subject matter *etc* ▯ *verb* make a parody of

> **parody** *verb* » parodi*es*, parody*ing*, parodi*ed*

parole *noun* the release of a prisoner before the end of a sentence on condition that they will have to return if they break the law ▯ *verb* release on parole

> From French *parole* meaning 'word' because prisoners are released on their word of honour

paroxysm *noun* a fit of pain, rage, laughter *etc* ▯ **paroxysmal** *adj*

parquet *noun* a floor covering of wooden blocks arranged in a pattern

parr *noun* a young salmon before it leaves a river for the sea

parricide *noun* **1** the murder of a parent or close relative **2** someone who commits such a crime

parrot *noun* a bird found in warm countries with a hooked bill and often brightly coloured feathers

parry *verb* deflect, turn aside (a blow, question *etc*)

> **parry** » parri*es*, parry*ing*, parri*ed*

parse *verb* name the parts of speech of (words in a sentence) and say how the words are connected with each other

Parsee or **Parsi** *noun* a member of an Indian religious sect descended from the Persian Zoroastrians

parsimony *noun* great care in spending money, meanness ◊ **parsimonious** *adj*

parsley *noun* a bright green leafy herb, used in cookery

parsnip *noun* a plant with an edible yellowish root shaped like a carrot

parson *noun* a member of the clergy, *esp* one in charge of a parish ◊ **parsonage** *noun* a parson's house ◊ **parson's nose** the piece of flesh at the tail-end of a cooked chicken or other bird

part *noun* **1** a portion, a share **2** a piece forming part of a whole: *the various parts of a car engine* **3** a character taken by an actor in a play **4** a role in an action or event: *played a vital part in the campaign* **5** *music* the notes to be played or sung by a particular instrument or voice **6** (**parts**) talents: *a man of many parts* ◊ *verb* **1** divide **2** separate, send or go in different ways **3** put or keep apart ◊ **partly** *adv* not wholly or completely ◊ **part-song** *noun* a song in which singers sing different parts in harmony ◊ **in good part** without being hurt or taking offence ◊ **part of speech** one of the grammatical groups into which words are divided, *eg* noun, verb, adjective, preposition ◊ **part with** let go, be separated from ◊ **take someone's part** support them in an argument *etc*

partake *verb*: **partake of 1** eat or drink some of something **2** take a part in

> **partake** » partake*s*, partak*ing*, partook, partak*en*

parthenogenesis reproduction from an unfertilized egg

partial *adj* **1** in part only, not total or complete: *partial payment* **2** having a liking for (someone or something): *partial to cheese* ◊ **partiality** *noun* **1** the favouring of one thing more than another, bias **2** a particular liking (for something) ◊ **partially** *adv*

participate *verb* **1** take part (in) **2** have a share in ◊ **participant** or **participator** *noun* someone who takes part in anything ◊ **participation** *noun* ◊ **participatory** *adj*

participle *noun* **1** a form of a verb which can be used with other verbs to form tenses, *eg* 'he was *eating*' or 'she has *arrived*' **2** used as an adjective, *eg* '*stolen* jewels' **3** used as a noun, *eg* '*running* makes me tired'

particle *noun* a very small piece: *a particle of sand*

parti-coloured *adj* variegated

particular *adj* **1** relating to a single definite person, thing *etc* considered separately from others: *I want this particular colour* **2** special: *take particular care of the china* **3** fussy, difficult to please: *particular about her food* ◊ *noun* (**particulars**) the facts or details about someone or something

parting *noun* **1** the act of separating or dividing **2** a place of separation **3** a going away (from each other), a leave-taking **4** a line dividing hair on the head brushed in opposite directions

partisan *adj* giving strong support or loyalty to a particular cause, theory *etc*, often without considering other points of view □ *noun* someone with partisan views

partition *noun* **1** a division **2** something which divides, *eg* a wall between rooms □ *verb* **1** divide into parts **2** divide by making a wall *etc*

partner *noun* **1** someone who shares the ownership of a business *etc* with another or others **2** one of a pair in games, dancing *etc* **3** a husband, wife or lover □ *verb* act as someone's partner □ **partnership** *noun*

partridge *noun* a type of bird which is shot as game

parturient *adj* **1** relating to childbirth **2** giving or about to give birth

party *noun* (*plural* **parties**) **1** a gathering of guests: *birthday party/ dinner party* **2** a group of people travelling together: *party of tourists* **3** a number of people with the same plans or ideas: *a political party* **4** someone taking part in, or approving, an action □ **party line 1** a shared telephone line **2** policy laid down by the leaders of a political party

parvenu *noun* (*plural* **parvenus**) an upstart, someone with newly acquired wealth or power

PASCAL *noun* a high-level computer programming language

pas de bas a step in Scottish traditional dancing

pas de deux a ballet sequence involving two dancers

paso doble a Spanish dance like a two-step

pass *verb* **1** go, move, travel *etc*: *he passed out of sight over the hill* **2** move on or along: *pass the salt* **3** go by: *I saw the bus pass our house* **4** overtake **5** of parliament: put (a law) into force **6** be successful in an examination **7** be declared healthy or in good condition after an inspection **8** come to an end: *the feeling of dizziness soon passed* **9** hand on, give: *he passed the story onto his son* **10** spend (time): *passing a pleasant hour by the river* **11** make, utter (*eg* a remark) □ *noun* **1** a narrow passage over or through a range of mountains **2** a ticket or card allowing someone to go somewhere **3** success in an examination **4** a sexual advance □ **pass-back** *noun, hockey* a move to put the ball back into play.□ **passer-by** *noun* (*plural* **passers-by**) someone who happens to pass by when something happens □ **passkey** *noun* a key which can open several locks □ **pass off** present (a forgery *etc*) as genuine □ **pass on 1** go forward, proceed **2** hand on **3** die □ **pass out** faint □ **pass up** fail to take up (an opportunity)

> **pass** *verb* » pass*es*, pass*ing*, pass*ed*

passable *adj* **1** fairly good **2** of a river *etc*: able to be crossed □ **passably** *adv*

passage *noun* **1** the act of passing: *passage of time* **2** a journey in a ship **3** a corridor **4** a way through **5** a part of the text of a book ▯ **passageway** *noun* a passage, a way through

passé /pa*seh*/ *adj* no longer used or done, out of date

passenger *noun* a traveller, not a member of the crew, in a train, ship, aeroplane *etc*

passing *adj* **1** going by: *a passing car* **2** not lasting long: *passing interest* **3** casual: *passing remark* ▯ *noun* **1** the act of someone or something which passes **2** a going away, a coming to an end **3** death

passion *noun* strong feeling, *esp* anger or love ▯ **passionate** *adj* **1** easily moved to passion **2** full of passion ▯ **passionately** *adv* ▯ **passionflower** *noun* a tropical climbing plant with flowers thought to resemble a crown of thorns ▯ **passionfruit** *noun* the edible, oblong fruit of the passionflower ▯ **the Passion** the sufferings and death of Christ

passive *adj* **1** making no resistance **2** acted upon, not acting ▯ **passively** *adv* ▯ **passiveness** or **passivity** *noun* ▯ **passive smoking** the involuntary inhaling of smoke from tobacco smoked by others

Passover *noun* a Jewish festival celebrating the exodus of the Israelites from Egypt

passport *noun* a card or booklet which gives someone's name and description, and which is needed to travel in another country

password *noun* **1** a secret word which allows those who know it to pass **2** a word typed into a computer to allow access to restricted data

past *noun* **1** (**the past**) the time gone by **2** someone's previous life or career **3** *grammar* the past tense ▯ *adj* **1** of an earlier time: *past kindnesses* **2** just over, recently ended: *the past year* **3** gone, finished: *the time for argument is past* ▯ *prep* **1** after: *it's past midday* **2** up to and beyond, further than: *go past the traffic lights* ▯ *adv* by: *she walked past, looking at no one*

pasta *noun* **1** a dough used in making spaghetti, macaroni *etc* **2** the prepared shapes of this, *eg* spaghetti

paste *noun* **1** pastry dough **2** a gluey liquid for sticking paper *etc* together **3** any soft, kneadable mixture: *almond paste* **4** fine glass used to make imitation gems ▯ **pasteboard** *noun* cardboard

pastel *adj* of a colour: soft, pale ▯ *noun* **1** a chalk-like crayon used for drawing **2** a drawing made with this

pasteurize *verb* heat food (*esp* milk) in order to kill harmful germs in it

> Named after Louis *Pasteur*, the 19th-century French chemist who invented the process

pastiche /pas*teesh*/ *noun* a humorous imitation, a parody

pastille *noun* a small sweet, sometimes sucked as a medicine

pastime *noun* a hobby, a spare-time interest

pastor *noun* a member of the clergy ◊ **pastoral** *adj* **1** relating to country life **2** of a pastor or clerical work

pastrami *noun* a smoked, seasoned cut of beef

pastry *noun* (*plural* **pastries**) **1** a flour paste used to make the bases and crusts of pies, tarts *etc* **2** a small cake

pasture *noun* ground covered with grass on which cattle graze ◊ **pasturage** *noun* grazing land

pasty[1] *adj* **1** like paste **2** pale

pasty[2] *noun* a pie containing meat and vegetables in a covering of pastry

pat *noun* **1** a light, quick blow or tap with the hand **2** a small lump of butter *etc* **3** a cake of animal dung ◊ *verb* strike gently, tap ◊ **off pat** memorized thoroughly, ready to be said when necessary

> **pat** *verb* » pat*s*, patt*ing*, patt*ed*

patch *verb* **1** mend (clothes) by putting in a new piece of material to cover a hole **2** (with **up**) mend, *esp* hastily or clumsily **3** (with **up**) settle (a quarrel) ◊ *noun* (*plural* **patches**) **1** a piece of material sewn on to mend a hole **2** a small piece of ground ◊ **patchwork** *noun* fabric formed of small patches or pieces of material sewn together

patchouli *noun* a perfume oil obtained from the dried branches of an Asian tree

patchy *adj* uneven, mixed in quality ◊ **patchily** *adv* ◊ **patchiness** *noun*

pate /peht/ *noun, formal* the head: *a bald pate*

pâté *noun* a paste made of finely minced meat, fish or vegetable, flavoured with herbs, spices *etc*

patella *noun* the knee-cap

patent *noun* an official written statement granting someone the sole right to make or sell something that they have invented ◊ *adj* **1** protected from copying by a patent **2** open, easily seen ◊ *verb* obtain a patent for ◊ **patent leather** leather with a very glossy surface ◊ **patently** *adv* openly, clearly: *patently obvious*

paterfamilias *noun* the male head of a family or household

paternal *adj* **1** of a father **2** like a father, fatherly **3** on the father's side of the family: *my paternal grandfather* ◊ **paternalism** *noun* ◊ **paternalistic** *adj*

paternity *noun* the state or fact of being a father ◊ **paternity leave** leave of absence from work for a father after the birth of a child

path *noun* **1** a way made by people or animals walking on it, a track **2** the route to be taken by someone or vehicle: *in the lorry's path* **3** a course of action, a way of life ◊ **pathway** *noun* a path

pathetic *adj* **1** causing pity **2** causing contempt; feeble, inadequate: *a pathetic attempt* ◊ **pathetically** *adv*

pathology *noun* the study of diseases ◊ **pathological** *adj* **1** relating to disease **2** *informal* compulsive, obsessive: *pathological liar* □ **pathologist** *noun* **1** a doctor who studies the causes and effects of disease **2** a doctor who makes post-mortem examinations

pathos /*peh*thos/ *noun* a quality that arouses pity: *the pathos of the situation made me weep*

patience *noun* **1** the ability or willingness to be patient **2** (*also called*: **solitaire**) a card game played by one person

patient *adj* suffering delay, discomfort *etc* without complaint or anger □ *noun* someone under the care of a doctor *etc* □ **patiently** *adv*

patina *noun* a film that forms on the surface of exposed metals *etc*

patio *noun* (*plural* **patios**) a paved open yard attached to a house

patisserie *noun* a shop selling French pastries and cakes

patois /*pat*wah/ *noun* a dialect of language spoken by the ordinary people of a certain area

patriarch *noun* **1** the male head of a family or tribe **2** the head of the Greek Orthodox Church □ **patriarchal** *adj* □ **patriarchy** *noun*

patrician *adj* aristocratic

patricide *noun* **1** the murder of your own father **2** someone who commits such a murder □ **patricidal** *adj*

patrimony *noun* property handed down from a father or ancestors

patriot *noun* someone who loves and is loyal to their country □ **patriotic** *adj* □ **patriotically** *adv* □ **patriotism** *noun* love of and loyalty to your country

patrol *verb* keep guard or watch by moving regularly around an area *etc* □ *noun* **1** the act of keeping guard in this way **2** the people keeping watch **3** a small group of Scouts or Guides □ **patrol car** a police car used to patrol an area

> **patrol** *verb* » patrol*s*, patrol*ling*, patroll*ed*

patron *noun* **1** someone who protects or supports (an artist, a form of art *etc*) **2** a customer of a shop *etc* □ **patronage** *noun* the support given by a patron □ **patronize** *verb* **1** be a patron towards: *patronize your local shops* **2** treat (someone) as an inferior, look down on: *don't patronize me* □ **patron saint** a saint chosen as the protector of a country *etc*

patronymic *noun* a name derived from a father or male ancestor

patter[1] *verb* of rain, footsteps *etc*: make a quick tapping sound □ *noun* the sound of falling rain, of footsteps *etc*

patter[2] *noun* **1** chatter, rapid talk, *esp* that used by salesmen to encourage people to buy their goods **2** the jargon of a particular group

pattern *noun* **1** an example suitable to be copied **2** a model or guide for making something **3** a decorative design **4** a sample: *a book of tweed patterns* □ **patterned**

adj having a design, not self-coloured

patty *noun* (*plural* **patties**) a small flat cake of chopped meat *etc*

paucity *noun* smallness of number or quantity

paunch *noun* (*plural* **paunches**) a fat stomach

pauper *noun* a very poor person

pause *noun* **1** a short stop, an interval **2** a break or hesitation in speaking or writing **3** *music* a symbol (𝄐) showing the holding of a note or rest ◊ *verb* stop for a short time

pave *verb* lay (a street) with stone or concrete to form a level surface for walking on ◊ **pave the way for** prepare or make the way easy for

pavement *noun* a paved footway at the side of a road for pedestrians

pavilion *noun* **1** a building in a sports ground with facilities for changing clothes **2** a large ornamental building **3** a large tent

paw *noun* the foot of an animal ◊ *verb* **1** of an animal: scrape with one of the front feet **2** handle or touch roughly or rudely **3** strike out wildly with the hand: *paw the air*

pawn *verb* put (an article of some value) in someone's keeping in exchange for a sum of money which, when repaid, buys back the article ◊ *noun* **1** *chess* a small piece of the lowest rank **2** someone who lets themselves be used by another for some purpose ◊ **pawnbroker** *noun* someone who lends money in exchange for pawned articles ◊ **pawnshop** *noun* a pawnbroker's place of business ◊ **in pawn** having been pawned

pawpaw *another word* for **papaya**

pay *verb* **1** give (money) in exchange for (goods *etc*): *I paid £30 for it* **2** suffer the punishment (for) **3** be advantageous or profitable: *it pays to be prepared* **4** give (*eg* attention) ◊ *noun* money given or received for work; wages ◊ **payable** *adj* requiring to be paid ◊ **pay-as-you-earn** *adj* of income tax: deducted from a salary before it is given to the worker ◊ **payee** *noun* someone to whom money is paid ◊ **payment** *noun* **1** the act of paying **2** money paid for goods *etc* ◊ **payphone** *noun* a coin- or card-operated public telephone ◊ **pay-roll** *noun* a list of people entitled to receive pay ◊ **payroll** *noun* the money for paying wages ◊ **pay off 1** pay in full and discharge (workers) owing to lack of work **2** have good results: *his hard work paid off* ◊ **pay out 1** spend **2** give out (a length of rope *etc*)

pay *verb* » pay*s*, pay*ing*, paid

PAYE *abbrev* pay as you earn

PC *abbrev* **1** police constable **2** privy councillor **3** political correctness

pc *abbrev* **1** personal computer **2** postcard **3** percent

PCC *abbrev* Press Complaints Commission

PE *abbrev* physical education

pea *noun* **1** a climbing plant which produces round green seeds in pods

2 the seed itself, eaten as a vegetable ◻ **pea-shooter** *noun* a small toy tube for blowing peas through

peace *noun* **1** quietness, calm **2** freedom from war or disturbance **3** a treaty bringing this about ◻ **peaceable** *adj* of a quiet nature, fond of peace ◻ **peaceful** *adj* quiet; calm ◻ **peacefully** *adv* ◻ **peace-offering** *noun* something offered to bring about peace

peach *noun* (*plural* **peaches**) **1** a juicy, velvet-skinned fruit **2** the tree that bears it **3** an orangey-pink colour

peacock *noun* a large bird, the male of which has brightly coloured, patterned tail feathers

peahen *noun* a female peacock

peak *noun* **1** the pointed top of a mountain or hill **2** the highest point **3** the jutting-out part of the brim of a cap ◻ *verb* **1** rise to a peak **2** reach the highest point: *prices peaked in July and then fell steadily* ◻ **peaked** *adj* **1** pointed **2** of a cap: having a peak ◻ **peaky** *adj* looking pale and unhealthy

peal *noun* **1** a set of bells tuned to each other **2** the changes rung on such bells **3** a succession of loud sounds: *peals of laughter* ◻ *verb* sound loudly

⚠Do not confuse with: **peel**

peanut *noun* **1** a type of nut similar to a pea in shape (*also called* **groundnut, monkey-nut**) ◻ **peanut butter** a paste of ground roasted peanuts, spread on bread *etc*

pear *noun* **1** a fruit which narrows towards the stem and bulges at the end **2** the tree that bears it ◻ **pear-shaped** *adj*

pearl *noun* **1** a gem formed in the shell of the oyster and several other shellfish **2** a valuable remark *etc*: *pearls of wisdom* ◻ **pearly gates** the entrance to heaven

peasant *noun* someone who works and lives on the land, *esp* in an underdeveloped area

pease pudding a dish of boiled, mashed peas

peat *noun* turf cut out of boggy places, dried and used as fuel

pebble *noun* a small, roundish stone ◻ **pebble dash** a coating for outside walls with small stones set into the mortar ◻ **pebbly** *adj* **1** full of pebbles **2** rough, knobbly

pecan *noun* **1** an oblong, thin-shelled nut common in N America **2** the tree bearing this nut

peccadillo *noun* (*plural* **peccadilloes** or **peccadillos**) a slight misdemeanour or wrong

peccary *noun* (*plural* **peccaries**) a South American animal like a pig

peck *verb* **1** strike with the beak **2** pick up with the beak **3** eat little, nibble (at) **4** kiss quickly and briefly ◻ *noun* **1** a sharp blow with the beak **2** a brief kiss ◻ **peckish** *adj* slightly hungry

pectoral *adj* of the breast or chest: *pectoral muscles*

peculiar *adj* **1** belonging to one person or thing only: *a custom peculiar to England* **2** strange, odd: *He* *is a very peculiar person* ◊ **peculiarity** (*plural* **peculiarities**) that which marks someone or something off from others in some way; something odd ◊ **peculiarly** *adv*

pecuniary *adj* of money

pedagogue *noun* a teacher ◊ **pedagogic** or **pedagogical** *adj* of a teacher or of education

pedal *noun* **1** a lever worked by the foot on a bicycle, piano, harp *etc* **2** a key worked by the foot on an organ ◊ *verb* **1** work the pedals of **2** ride on a bicycle

pedal *verb* » pedal*s*, pedall*ing*, pedall*ed*

pedant *noun* **1** someone who makes a great show of their knowledge **2** someone overly fussy about minor details ◊ **pedantic** *adj* ◊ **pedantry** *noun* **1** fussiness about unimportant details **2** a display of knowledge

peddle *verb* travel from door to door selling goods

pederasty *noun* anal sexual intercourse betwen a man and a boy ◊ **pederast** *noun* someone who practises pederasty

pedestal *noun* the foot or support of a pillar, statue *etc*

pedestrian *adj* **1** going on foot **2** for those on foot **3** unexciting, dull: *a pedestrian account* ◊ someone who goes or travels on foot ◊ **pedestrian crossing** a place where pedestrians may cross the road when the traffic stops

pediatrics, pediatrician *US spelling* of **paediatrics, paediatrician**

pedicure *noun* a treatment for the feet including treating corns, cutting nails *etc* ◊ **pedicurist** *noun* someone who gives a pedicure

pedigree *noun* **1** a list of someone's ancestors **2** the ancestry of a pure-bred animal **3** a distinguished descent or ancestry ◊ *adj* of an animal: pure-bred, from a long line of ancestors of the same breed

Literally 'crane's foot', because the forked feet of the bird were thought to resemble the lines of a family tree

pediment *noun* a triangular structure over the front of an ancient Greek building

pedlar *noun* someone who peddles, a hawker

pedometer *noun* an instrument for measuring the distance covered by a walker

pee *verb, informal* urinate ◊ *noun* **1** the act of urinating **2** urine

pee *verb* » pee*s*, pee*ing*, pee*d*

peek *verb* peep, glance *esp* secretively ◊ *noun* a secret look

peel *verb* **1** strip off the outer covering or skin of: *peel an apple* **2** of skin, paint *etc*: come off in small pieces **3** lose skin in small flakes, *eg* as a result of sunburn ◊ *noun* skin, rind

⚠Do not confuse with: **peal**

peelie-wally *adj, Scot* pale-looking, off-colour

peep *verb* **1** look through a narrow opening, round a corner *etc* **2** look slyly or quickly (at) **3** begin to appear: *the sun peeped out* **4** make a high, small sound ▯ *noun* **1** a quick look, a glimpse, often from hiding **2** a high, small sound ▯ **peeping Tom** someone who spies secretly on others, a voyeur

peer *verb* look at with half-closed eyes, as if with difficulty ▯ *noun* **1** someone's equal in rank, merit or age **2** a nobleman of the rank of baron upwards **3** a member of the House of Lords ▯ **peerage** *noun* **1** a peer's title **2** the peers as a group ▯ **peerless** *adj* without any equal, better than all others

peeve *verb, informal* irritate ▯ **peeved** *adj* annoyed

peevish *adj* cross, bad-tempered, irritable

peewit *noun* the lapwing

peg *noun* **1** a pin or stake of wood, metal *etc* **2** a hook fixed to a wall for hanging clothes *etc* ▯ *verb* **1** fasten with a peg **2** fix (prices *etc*) at a certain level

> **peg** *verb* » peg*s*, pegg*ing*, pegg*ed*

peignoir *noun* a woman's light dressing-gown

pejorative *adj* showing disapproval, scorn *etc*: *a pejorative remark* ▯ **pejoratively** *adv*

Pekinese or **Pekingese** *noun* a breed of small dog with a long coat and flat face

pelagic *adj* living near the surface or middle layer of the sea

pelf *noun, old* riches, money

pelican *noun* a large waterbird with a pouched bill for storing fish

pelican crossing a street-crossing where the lights are operated by pedestrians

> Taken from the phrase '*pe*destrian *li*ght *con*trolled crossing'

pellagra *noun* a disease marked by shrivelled skin and paralysis caused by the lack of certain vitamins

pellet 1 a small ball of shot *etc* **2** a small pill

pell-mell *adv* in great confusion; headlong

pellucid *adj* clear, transparent

Pelmanism *noun* a card-game in which cards are spread out face down and must be picked up in matching pairs

> Named after a form of memory training devised by the *Pelman* Institute

pelmet *noun* a strip or band hiding a curtain rail

pelota *noun* a Basque ball-game played against a marked wall with a basket-like racket strapped to the players' wrists

peloton *noun* the leading group of cyclists in a race

pelt *noun* the untreated skin of an animal ▯ *verb* **1** throw (things) at **2** run fast **3** of rain: fall heavily ▯ **at full pelt** at top speed

pelvis *noun* the frame of bone which circles the body below the waist

pemmican *noun* dried meat, pressed hard into cakes

pen[1] *noun* an instrument with a nib for writing in ink □ *verb* write (*eg* a letter) □ **pen-friend** *noun* someone you have never seen (*usu* living abroad) with whom you exchange letters □ **penknife** *noun* a pocket knife with folding blades □ **pen-name** *noun* a name adopted by a writer instead of their own name

> **pen** » pen*s*, penn*ing*, penn*ed*

pen[2] *noun* a small enclosure for sheep, cattle *etc* □ *verb* enclose in a pen

pen[3] *noun* a female swan

penal *adj* of or as punishment □ **penalize** *verb* **1** punish **2** put under a disadvantage □ **penal servitude** imprisonment with hard labour as an added punishment

penalty *noun* (*plural* **penalties**) **1** punishment **2** a disadvantage put on a player or team which breaks a rule of a game

penance *noun* punishment willingly suffered by someone to make up for a wrong

penates *noun plural* ancient Roman household gods

pence *plural* of **penny**

penchant *noun* an inclination (for), a bias

pencil *noun* an instrument containing a length of graphite or other substance for writing, drawing *etc* □ *verb* draw, mark *etc* with a pencil

> **pencil** *verb* » pencil*s*, pencill*ing*, pencill*ed*

pendant *noun* **1** an ornament hung from a necklace *etc* **2** a necklace with such an ornament

pendent *adj* hanging

pending *adj* awaiting a decision or attention: *this matter is pending* □ *prep* awaiting, until the coming of: *pending confirmation*

pendulous *adj* hanging down, drooping □ **pendulosity** *noun*

pendulum *noun* a swinging weight which drives the mechanism of a clock

penetrate *verb* **1** pierce or pass into or through **2** enter by force □ **penetrating** *adj* of a sound: piercing **2** keen, probing: *penetrating question* □ **penetration** *noun*

penguin *noun* a large sea bird of Antarctic regions, which cannot fly

penicillin *noun* a medicine obtained from mould, which kills many bacteria

penile *adj* of or for the penis

peninsula *noun* a piece of land almost surrounded by water □ **peninsular** *adj*

penis *noun* the part of the body of a male human or animal used in sexual intercourse and for urinating

penitent *adj* sorry for your sins □ *noun* a penitent person □ **penitential** *adj* □ **penitentiary** *noun*, *US* a prison

pennant *noun* a long flag coming to a point at the end

pennate *adj* wing-shaped

penny *noun* **1** a coin worth $\frac{1}{100}$ of £1 **2** (*plural* **pence**) used to show an amount in pennies: *the newspaper costs forty-two pence* **3** (*plural* **pennies**) used for a number of coins: *I need five pennies for the coffee machine* ◇ **penniless** *adj* having no money ◇ **penny-farthing** *noun* a old type of bicycle with a large front wheel and small rear wheel ◇ **penny-pinching** *adj* mean, stingy

pension *noun* a sum of money paid regularly to a retired person, a widow, someone wounded in war *etc* ◇ **pensionable** *adj* having or giving the right to a pension: *pensionable age* ◇ **pensioner** *noun* someone who receives a pension ◇ **pension off** dismiss or allow to retire with a pension

pensive *adj* thoughtful ◇ **pensively** *adv* ◇ **pensiveness** *noun*

pent or **pent-up** *adj* **1** shut up, not allowed to go free **2** of emotions: not freely expressed

pentagon *noun* a five-sided figure ◇ **pentagonal** *adj* ◇ **the Pentagon** the headquarters of the US armed forces in Washington, DC

pentathlon *noun* a five-event contest in the Olympic Games *etc* ◇ **pentathlete** *noun* an athlete who takes part in this event

pentatonic *adj, music* of a scale: consisting of five notes, *ie* a major scale omitting the fourth and seventh

Pentecost *noun* **1** a Jewish festival held fifty days after Passover **2** a Christian festival held seven weeks after Easter

penthouse *noun* a luxurious flat at the top of a building

penultimate *adj* last but one

penumbra *noun* a light shadow surrounding the main shadow of an eclipse

penury *noun* poverty, want ◇ **penurious** *adj* impoverished, penniless

peon *noun* an agricultural labourer in S America

peony *noun* (*plural* **peonies**) a type of garden plant with large red, white or pink flowers

people *noun plural* **1** the men, women and children of a country or nation **2** persons generally ◇ *verb* **1** fill with people **2** inhabit, make up the population of

PEP *abbrev* personal equity plan

pep *noun, informal* spirit, verve ◇ **pep pill** a pill containing a stimulating drug ◇ **pep talk** a talk meant to encourage or arouse enthusiasm ◇ **pep up** invigorate, enliven

pepper *noun* **1** a plant whose berries are dried, powdered and used as seasoning **2** the spicy powder it produces **3** a hot-tasting hollow fruit containing many seeds, eaten raw, cooked or pickled ◇ *verb* **1** sprinkle with pepper **2** (with **with**) throw at or hit: *peppered with bullets* ◇ **pepper-and-salt** *adj* mixed black and white: *pepper-and-salt hair* ◇ **peppercorn** *noun* the dried berry of the pepper plant ◇ **pepper mill** a small device for grinding peppercorns over food

peppermint *noun* **1** a type of plant with a powerful taste and smell **2** a flavouring taken from this and used in sweets *etc* ◊ **peppery** *adj* **1** containing much pepper **2** inclined to be hot-tempered

pepperoni *noun* a spicy beef and pork sausage

peptic *adj* of the digestive system: *peptic ulcer*

per *prep* **1** in, out of: *five per cent* (*ie* five out of every hundred) **2** for each: *£2 per dozen* **3** in each: *six times per week* ◊ **per annum** in each year ◊ **per capita** or **per head** for each person

peradventure *adv*, *old* by chance

perambulator *full form* of **pram**

percale *noun* a closely woven fine French linen

perceive *verb* **1** become aware of through the senses **2** see **3** understand ◊ **perceptible** *adj* able to be seen or understood ◊ **perception** *noun* the ability to perceive; understanding ◊ **perceptive** *adj* able or quick to perceive or understand ◊ **perceptively** *adv*

percentage *noun* the rate per hundred

perch[1] *noun* (*plural* **perches**) **1** a rod on which birds roost **2** a high seat or position ◊ *verb* roost

perch[2] *noun* (*plural* **perches**) a type of freshwater fish

perchance *adv*, *old* by chance; perhaps

percolate *verb* **1** of a liquid: drip or drain through small holes **2** cause (a liquid) to do this **3** of news *etc*: pass slowly down or through ◊ **percolator** *noun* a device for percolating: *a coffee percolator*

percussion *noun* **1** a striking of one object against another **2** musical instruments played by striking, *eg* drums, cymbals *etc* ◊ **percussionist** *noun* a musician who plays percussion ◊ **percussive** *adj* making the noise of percussion; loud, striking

perdition *noun* **1** utter loss or ruin **2** everlasting punishment

peregrinations *noun plural* wanderings

peregrine *noun* a type of falcon used in hawking

peremptory *adj* **1** urgent **2** of a command: to be obeyed at once **3** domineering, dictatorial

perennial *adj* **1** lasting through the year **2** everlasting, perpetual **3** of a plant: growing from year to year without replanting or sowing ◊ *noun* a perennial plant

perestroika *noun* reconstruction, restructuring of the state (originally in the former Soviet Union)

perfect *adj* **1** complete, finished **2** faultless **3** exact ◊ *verb* **1** make perfect **2** finish ◊ **perfection** *noun* **1** the state of being perfect **2** the highest state or degree ◊ **perfectionist** *noun* someone who is satisfied only by perfection

perfidious *adj* treacherous, unfaithful ◊ **perfidiousness** *noun* ◊ **perfidy** *noun*

perforate *verb* make a hole or holes through ◊ **perforated** *adj* pierced with holes

perforce *adv*, *old* of necessity, unavoidably

perform *verb* **1** do, act **2** act (a part) on the stage **3** provide entertainment for an audience **4** play (a piece of music) ◊ **performance** *noun* **1** an entertainment in a theatre *etc* **2** the act of doing something **3** the level of success of a machine, car *etc* ◊ **performer** *noun* someone who acts or performs

perfume *noun* **1** smell, fragrance **2** a fragant liquid put on the skin, scent ◊ *verb* **1** put scent on or in **2** give a sweet smell to ◊ **perfumery** *noun* a shop or factory where perfume is sold or made

perfunctory *adj* done carelessly or half-heartedly: *perfunctory inspection* ◊ **perfunctorily** *adv*

perhaps *adv* it may be (that), possibly: *perhaps she'll resign*

peri- *prefix* around

peril *noun* a great danger ◊ **perilous** *adj* very dangerous ◊ **perilously** *adv* ◊ **at your peril** at your own risk

perimeter *noun* **1** the outside line enclosing a figure or shape **2** the outer edge of any area

⚠Do not confuse with: **parameter**

perinatal *adj* relating to the period between the seventh month of pregnancy and the first week of the baby's life

perineum *noun* the part of the body between the genitals and the anus ◊ **perineal** *adj*

period *noun* **1** a stretch of time **2** a stage in the earth's development or in history **3** a full stop after a sentence **4** a time of menstruation

periodic *adj* **1** of a period **2** happening at regular intervals, *eg* every month or year **3** happening every now and then: *a periodic clearing out of rubbish*

periodical *adj* issued or done at regular intervals; periodic ◊ *noun* a magazine which appears at regular intervals

peripatetic *adj* moving from place to place; travelling

peripheral *adj* **1** of or on a periphery; away from the centre **2** not essential, of little importance

periphery *noun* (*plural* **peripheries**) **1** the line surrounding something **2** an outer boundary or edge

periphrastic *adj* roundabout, using more words than necessary

periscope *noun* a tube with mirrors by which a viewer in a submarine *etc* is able to see objects on the surface

perish *verb* **1** be destroyed, pass away completely; die **2** decay, rot ◊ **perishable** *adj* liable to go bad quickly

peristyle *noun* a group of columns surrounding a building

peritoneum *noun* a membrane in the stomach and pelvis ◊ **peritonitis** *noun* inflammation of the peritoneum

periwig *noun, hist* a wig

periwinkle *noun* **1** a small shellfish, shaped like a small snail, eaten as food when boiled **2** a creeping evergreen plant with a small blue flower

perjure *verb* (with **yourself** *etc*) tell a lie when you have sworn to tell the truth, *esp* in a court of law ▫ **perjurer** *noun* ▫ **perjury** *noun*

perk[1] *noun* something of value allowed in addition to payment for work; a side benefit

perk[2] *verb*: **perk up** recover energy or spirits ▫ **perky** *adj* jaunty, in good spirits ▫ **perkily** *adv* ▫ **perkiness** *noun* ▫

perm *noun short for* **permanent wave** ▫ *verb* give a permanent wave to (hair)

permaculture *noun* farming without using artificial fertilizers and with minimal weeding

permafrost *noun* permanently frozen subsoil

permanent *adj* lasting, not temporary ▫ **permanence** or **permanency** *noun* (*plural* **permanencies**) ▫ **permanently** *adv* ▫ **permanent wave** a wave or curl put into the hair by a special process and *usu* lasting for some months

permeate *verb* **1** pass into through small holes, soak into **2** fill every part of ▫ **permeable** *adj*

permit *verb* **1** agree to an action, allow **2** make possible ▫ *noun* a written order, allowing someone to do something: *a fishing permit* ▫ **permissible** *adj* allowable ▫ **permission** *noun* freedom given to do something ▫ **permissive** *adj* **1** allowing something to be done **2** too tolerant ▫ **permissiveness** *noun*

permutation *noun* **1** the arrangement of numbers, letters *etc* in a certain order **2** the act of changing the order of things

pernicious *adj* destructive ▫ **perniciousness** *noun*

pernickety *adj* fussy about small details

peroration *noun* **1** the closing part of a speech **2** a speech

peroxide a chemical (hydrogen peroxide) used for bleaching hair *etc* ▫ **peroxide blonde** *informal* a woman whose hair has been bleached

perpendicular *adj* **1** standing upright, vertical **2** at right angles (to) ▫ *noun* a line at right angles to another

perpetrate *verb* commit (a sin, error *etc*) ▫ **perpetration** *noun* ▫ **perpetrator** *noun*

⚠Do not confuse with: **perpetuate**

perpetual *adj* everlasting, unending ▫ **perpetually** *adv*

perpetuate *verb* make to last for ever or for a long time ▫ **perpetuity** *noun* ▫ **in perpetuity 1** for ever **2** for the length of someone's life

⚠Do not confuse with: **perpetrate**

perplex *verb* **1** puzzle, bewilder **2** make more complicated ▫ **perplexity** *noun* **1** a puzzled state of mind **2** something which puzzles

perquisite *noun* a perk

per se *adv* in itself, essentially

persecute *verb* **1** harass over a period of time **2** make to suffer, *esp* because of religious beliefs □ **persecution** *noun* □ **persecutor** *noun*

⚠Do not confuse with: **prosecute**

persevere *verb* keep trying to do a thing (in spite of difficulties) □ **perseverance** *noun* the act of persevering

persimmon *noun* a plum-like fruit from an African or American tree

persist *verb* **1** hold fast to (*eg* an idea) **2** continue to do something in spite of difficulties **3** survive, last □ **persistence** *noun* □ **persistent** *adj* **1** obstinate, refusing to be discouraged **2** lasting, not dying out □ **persistently** *adv*

person *noun* **1** a human being **2** someone's body: *jewels hidden on his person* **3** form, shape: *trouble arrived in the person of Gordon* □ **personable** *adj* good-looking □ **personage** *noun* a well-known person

persona *noun* the outward part of the personality presented to others; social image

personal *adj* **1** your own; private: *personal belongings* **2** of a remark: insulting, offensive to the person it is aimed at □ **personal column** a newspaper column containing personal messages, advertisements *etc*

⚠Do not confuse with: **personnel**

personality *noun* (*plural* **personalities**) **1** all of a person's characteristics as seen by others **2** a well-known person □ **personal organizer** a small loose-leaf filing system containing a diary and an address book, maps, indexes *etc* □ **personal stereo** a small portable cassette player with earphones

personally *adv* **1** speaking from your own point of view **2** by your own action, not using an agent or representative: *he thanked me personally*

persona non grata someone disliked or out of favour

personify *verb* **1** talk about things, ideas *etc* as if they were living persons (*eg* 'Time marches on') **2** typify, be a perfect example of □ **personification** *noun* □ **in person** personally, not represented by someone else

personify » personifi*es*, personify*ing*, personifi*ed*

personnel *noun* the people employed in a firm *etc*

⚠Do not confuse with: **personal**

perspective *noun* **1** a point of view **2** the giving of a sense of depth, distance *etc* in a painting like that in real life □ **in perspective 1** of an object in a painting *etc*: of a size in relation to other things that it would have in real life **2** of an event: in its true degree of importance when considered in relation to other events: *keep things in perspective*

Perspex *noun, trademark* a transparent plastic which looks like glass

perspicacious *adj* of clear or sharp understanding □ **perspicacity**

noun keenness of understanding

perspicuity *noun* clearness in expressing thoughts ▯ **perspicuous** *adj*

perspire *verb* sweat ▯ **perspiration** *noun* sweat

persuade *verb* bring someone to do or think something, by arguing with them or advising them ▯ **persuasion** *noun* **1** the act of persuading **2** a firm belief *esp* a religious belief ▯ **persuasive** *adj* having the power to convince ▯ **persuasiveness** *noun*

pert *adj* saucy, cheeky

pertain *verb* (with **to**) to belong, have to do with: *duties pertaining to the job*

pertinacious *adj* holding strongly to an idea, obstinate ▯ **pertinacity** *noun*

pertinent *adj* connected with the subject spoken about, to the point

perturb *verb* disturb greatly; to make anxious or uneasy ▯ **perturbation** *noun* great worry, anxiety

peruse *verb* read (with care) ▯ **perusal** *noun*

pervade *verb* spread through: *silence pervaded the room*

perverse *adj* obstinate in holding to the wrong point of view; unreasonable ▯ **perverseness** or **perversity** *noun* stubbornness

pervert *verb* **1** turn away from what is normal or right: *pervert the course of justice* **2** turn (someone) to crime or evil; corrupt ▯ *noun* someone who commits unnatural or perverted acts ▯ **perversion** *noun* **1** the act of perverting **2** an unnatural or perverted act

peseta *noun* the standard unit of Spanish currency

pessary *noun* a cotton plug containing medicine *etc* inserted into the vagina

pessimism *noun* the habit of thinking that things will always turn out badly (*contrasted with*: **optimism**) ▯ **pessimist** *noun* someone who tends to think in this way ▯ **pessimistic** *adj* ▯ **pessimistically** *adv*

pest *noun* **1** a troublesome person or thing **2** a creature that is harmful or destructive, *eg* a mosquito ▯ **pesticide** *noun* any substance which kills animal pests ▯ **pestilence** *noun* a deadly, spreading disease ▯ **pestilent** or **pestilential** *adj* **1** very unhealthy **2** troublesome

pester *verb* annoy continually

pestle *noun* a tool for pounding things to powder

pesto *noun* a sauce made with ground pine nuts, basil, olive oil and parmesan cheese

pet *noun* **1** a tame animal kept in the home, such as a cat **2** a favourite **3** a fit of sulks ▯ *adj* **1** kept as a pet **2** favourite **3** chief: *my pet hate* ▯ *verb* fondle ▯ **pettish** *adj* sulky ▯ **pet name** one used to express affection or love

pet *verb* » pets, pett*ing*, pett*ed*

petal *noun* one of the leaf-like parts of a flower

petard *noun*: **hoist with your own**

petard caught in a trap of your own making

peter *verb*: **peter out** fade or dwindle away to nothing

petite *adj* small and neat in appearance

petit fours small fancy cakes or biscuits

petition *noun* a request or note of protest signed by many people and sent to a government or authority □ *verb* send a petition to □ **petitioner** *noun*

petrel *noun* a small, long-winged sea-bird

petrify *verb* **1** turn into stone **2** turn (someone) stiff with fear □ **petrifaction** *noun*

petrify » petrifi*es*, petrify*ing*, petrifi*ed*

petrissage *noun* massage with long strokes up and down the body

petroglyph *noun* an ancient carving on a rock face

petrol *noun* petroleum when refined as fuel for use in motor-cars *etc*

petroleum *noun* oil in its raw, unrefined form, extracted from natural wells below the earth's surface

petticoat *noun* an underskirt worn by women

pettifogger *noun* a lawyer who deals in trivial cases

petty *adj* of little importance, trivial □ **pettiness** *noun* □ **petty cash** money paid or received in small sums □ **petty officer** a rank of officer in the navy (equal to a non-commissioned officer in the army)

petulant *adj* **1** cross, irritable **2** unreasonably impatient □ **petulance** *noun*

petunia *noun* a S American flowering plant related to tobacco

pew *noun* a seat or bench in a church

pewter *noun* a mixture of tin and lead

PG *abbrev* parental guidance (certificate awarded to a film denoting possible unsuitability for young children)

pH *abbrev*

phagocyte *noun* a white blood corpuscle that surrounds and destroys bacteria

phalanx *noun* (*plural* **phalanxes**) **1** a company of foot soldiers in an oblong-shaped formation **2** a group of supporters

phallus *noun* a representation of a penis □ **phallic** *adj*

phantasm *noun* a vision, an illusion

phantasmagoria *noun* a dream-like series of visions or hallucinations

phantom *noun* a ghost

Pharaoh *noun*, *hist* a ruler of ancient Egypt

pharmaceutical *adj* relating to the making up of medicines and drugs □ **pharmacist** *noun* someone who prepares and sells medicines □ **pharmacy** *noun* (*plural* **pharmacies**) **1** the art of preparing medicines **2** a chemist's shop

pharmacology *noun* the scientific study of drugs and their effects □ **pharmacological** *adj* □ **pharmacologist** *noun*

pharmacopoeia *noun* a list of drugs with directions for their preparation

pharynx *noun* the back part of the throat behind the tonsils □ **pharyngitis** *noun* inflammation of the pharynx

phase *noun* **1** one in a series of changes in the shape or appearance of something (*eg* the moon) **2** a stage in the development of something (*eg* a war, a scheme *etc*)

phatic *adj* of speech: used for communication or social exchange

PhD *abbrev* Doctor of Philosophy

pheasant *noun* a bird with brightly coloured feathers which is shot as game

phenobarbitone *noun* a sedative and hypnotic drug

phenol *noun* an acid used as a powerful disinfectant

phenomenon *noun* (*plural* **phenomena**) **1** an event (*esp* in nature) that is observed by the senses: *the phenomenon of lightning* **2** something remarkable or very unusual, a wonder □ **phenomenal** *adj* very unusual, remarkable □ **phenomenally** *adv* extremely: *phenomenally successful*

pheronome *noun* a chemical secreted by the body which attracts or influences other people or animals

phew *exclam* used to express relief

phial *noun* a small glass bottle

philabeg *noun* a kilt

philander *verb* make love, flirt □ **philanderer** *noun*

philanthropy *noun* love of mankind, often shown by giving money for the benefit of others □ **philanthropic** *adj* □ **philanthropist** *noun* someone who does good to others

philately *noun* the study and collecting of stamps □ **philatelist** *noun*

philharmonic *adj* (in names of orchestras *etc*) music-loving

philistine *noun* someone ignorant of, or hostile to, culture and the arts

> After a people of ancient Palestine, enemies of the Israelites

philodendron *noun* a tropical American climbing plant

philology *noun* the study of words and their history □ **philologist** *noun*

philosopher *noun* someone who studies philosophy □ **philosophic** or **philosophical** *adj* **1** of philosophy **2** calm, not easily upset

philosophy *noun* (*plural* **philosophies**) **1** the study of the nature of the universe, or of human behaviour **2** someone's personal view of life

philtre *noun* a love potion

phlegm /flem/ *noun* **1** thick slimy matter brought up from the throat by coughing **2** coolness of temper, calmness □ **phlegmatic** *adj* not easily aroused

phlox /floks/ *noun* a garden plant with flat white or purplish flowers

phobia *noun* an intense, often irrational, fear or dislike

phoenix /*fee*niks/ *noun* a mythological bird believed to burn itself and to rise again from its ashes

phone *noun short* for **telephone** □ **phonecard** *noun* a card that can be used instead of cash to operate certain public telephones

phoneme *noun* the smallest meaningful unit of sound in any language

phonetic *adj* **1** relating to the sounds of language **2** of a word: spelt according to sound, *eg flem* for 'phlegm' □ **phonetics** *noun sing* **1** the study of the sounds of language **2** a system of writing according to sound

phoney or **phony** *adj*, *informal* fake, not genuine

phosphorus *noun* a wax-like, poisonous substance that gives out light in the dark □ **phosphate** *noun* a soil fertilizer containing phosphorus □ **phosphorescence** *noun* faint glow of light in the dark □ **phosphorescent** *adj*

photic *noun* relating to light

photo *noun* (*plural* **photos**) *informal* a photograph

photocopy *noun* a copy of a document made by a device which photographs and develops images of the document □ *verb* make a photocopy of

photofit *noun*, *trademark* a method of making identification pictures by combining photographs of individual features

photogenic *adj* being a good subject for a photograph; photographing well

photography *noun* the art of taking pictures with a camera □ **photograph** *noun* a picture taken with a camera □ *verb* take a picture with a camera □ **photographer** *noun*

photosensitive *adj* affected by light

photostat *noun*, *trademark* **1** a special camera for making photographic copies of documents, pages of books *etc* **2** a photographic copy so made

photosynthesis *noun* the conversion of light into complex compounds by plants

phrase *noun* **1** a small group of words expressing a single idea, *eg* 'after dinner', 'on the water' **2** a short saying or expression **3** *music* a short group of bars forming a distinct unit □ *verb* express in words: *he could have phrased it more tactfully* □ **phraseology** *noun* someone's personal choice of words and phrases

phrenology *noun* the study of the surface of the skull as a sign of personality *etc* □ **phrenologist** *noun*

phut /fut/ *adj* not working, broken

phylactery *noun* a small box containing a piece of Scripture worn on the wrist or forehead by Orthodox Jews

phylum *noun* a main division of the animal or vegetable kingdoms

physical *adj* **1** relating to the body: *physical strength/ physical exercises* **2** relating to things that can be seen or felt □ **physically** *adv*

physician *noun* a doctor specializing in medical rather than surgical treatment

physics *noun sing* the science which includes the study of heat, light, sound, electricity, magnetism *etc* □ **physicist** *noun* someone who specializes in physics

physiognomy *noun* the features or expression of the face

physiology *noun* the study of the way in which living bodies work, including blood circulation, food digestion *etc* □ **physiological** *adj* □ **physiologist** *noun*

physiotherapy *noun* the treatment of disease by bodily exercise, massage *etc* rather than by drugs □ **physiotherapist** *noun*

physique *noun* **1** the build of someone's body **2** bodily strength

PI *abbrev* private investigator

piano *noun* (*plural* **pianos**) a large musical instrument played by striking keys □ **pianist** *noun* someone who plays the piano

piazza *noun* a market-place or town square surrounded by buildings

pibroch *noun* bagpipe music which is free in rhythm, consisting of a theme and variations

picador *noun* a bullfighter armed with a lance and mounted on a horse

piccalilli *noun* a vegetable pickle

piccolo *noun* (*plural* **piccolos**) a small, high-pitched flute

pick *verb* **1** choose **2** pluck, gather (flowers, fruit *etc*) **3** peck, bite, nibble (at) **4** poke, probe (teeth *etc*) **5** open (a lock) with a tool other than a key □ *noun* **1** choice: *take your pick* **2** the best or best part **3** a pickaxe **4** an instrument for picking, *eg* a toothpick □ **pick a quarrel** start a quarrel deliberately □ **pick on 1** single out for criticism *etc* **2** nag at □ **pick up 1** lift up **2** learn (a language, habit *etc*) **3** give (someone) a lift in a car **4** find or get by chance **5** improve, gain strength

pickaxe *noun* a heavy tool for breaking ground, pointed at one end or both ends

picket *noun* **1** a pointed stake **2** a small sentry-post or guard **3** a number of workers on strike who prevent others from going into work □ *verb* **1** fasten (a horse *etc*) to a stake **2** place a guard or a group of strikers at (a place)

pickle *noun* **1** a liquid in which food is preserved **2** vegetables preserved in vinegar **3** *informal* an awkward, unpleasant situation □ *verb* preserve with salt, vinegar *etc*

pickpocket *noun* someone who robs people's pockets or handbags

picky *adj* choosy, fussy □ **pickiness** *noun*

picnic *noun* a meal eaten out-of-doors, often during an outing *etc* □ *verb* have a picnic

picnic *verb* » picnic*s*, picnick*ing*, picnick*ed*

picot *noun* an ornamental loop in a lace edging

pictorial *adj* **1** having pictures **2** consisting of pictures **3** calling up pictures in the mind

picture *noun* **1** a painting or drawing **2** a portrait **3** a photograph **4** a film **5** (**pictures**) the cinema **6** a vivid description ▫ *verb* **1** make a picture of **2** see in the mind, imagine

picturesque *adj* such as would make a good or striking picture; pretty, colourful

PID *abbrev* pelvic inflammatory disease

piddling *adj* trifling, minor

pidgin *noun* a language made up of two others in a distorted form

> ⚠Do not confuse with: **pigeon**

pie *noun* meat, fruit or other food baked in a casing or covering of pastry ▫ **pie-eyed** *adj, informal* drunk

piebald *adj* white and black in patches

piece *noun* **1** a part or portion of anything **2** a single article or example: *a piece of paper* **3** an artistic work: *a piece of popular music* **4** a coin **5** a man in chess, draughts *etc* ▫ *verb* put (together)

pièce de résistance /pyesdə rehsis*tonns*/ the best item or work

piecemeal *adv* by pieces, little by little

piecework *noun* work paid according to how much is done, not to the time spent on it

pied *adj* with two or more colours in patches

pied à terre /pyehda *ter*/ a second home in a city

pier *noun* **1** a platform stretching from the shore into the sea as a landing place for ships **2** a pillar supporting an arch, bridge *etc*

pierce *verb* make a hole through; force a way into; move (the feelings) deeply ▫ **piercing** *adj* shrill, loud; sharp

pierrot /*pee*roh/ *noun* a comic entertainer with a white face and loose white clothes

pietà *noun* a painting *etc* of the Virgin Mary with the dead Christ

piety *see* **pious**

piffle *noun* nonsense

pig *noun* **1** a farm animal, from whose flesh ham and bacon are made **2** an oblong moulded piece of metal (*eg* pig-iron) ▫ **piggery** *noun* (*plural* **piggeries**) or **pigsty** *noun* (*plural* **pigsties**) a place where pigs are kept ▫ **piggy-back** *noun* a ride on someone's back with your arms round their neck ▫ **piggy-bank** *noun* a china pig with a slit along its back to insert coins for saving ▫ **pig-headed** *adj* stubborn ▫ **pigskin** *noun* leather made from a pig's skin ▫ **pigtail** *noun* hair formed into a plait

pigeon *noun* a bird of the dove family ▫ **pigeon-hole** *noun* a small division in a case or desk for papers *etc* ▫ *verb* **1** lay aside **2** classify, put into a category

pigment *noun* **1** paint or other substance used for colouring **2** a substance in animals and plants that gives colour to the skin *etc* **pigmentation** *noun* colouring of skin *etc*

pigmy *another spelling* of **pygmy**

pike *noun* **1** a freshwater fish **2** a weapon like a spear, with a long shaft and a sharp head

pilau or **pilaff** *noun* an Indian dish of rice, meat and spices

pilchard *noun* a small sea-fish like a herring, often tinned

pile *noun* **1** a number of things lying one on top of another, a heap **2** a great quantity **3** a large building **4** a large stake or pillar driven into the earth as a foundation for a building, bridge *etc* **5** the thick, soft surface on carpets and on cloth such as velvet *verb* (often with **up**) make or form a pile or heap

pilfer *verb* steal small things **pilfering** *noun*

pilgrim *noun* a traveller to a holy place **pilgrimage** *noun* a journey to a holy place

pill *noun* **1** a tablet of medicine **2** (often with **the**) a contraceptive in the form of a small tablet taken by mouth

pillage *verb* seize goods and money, *esp* as loot in war *noun* the act of plundering in this way

pillar *noun* **1** an upright support for roofs, arches *etc* **2** an upright post or column as a monument **3** someone or something that gives support: *a pillar of the community* **pillarbox** *noun* a tall box with a slot through which letters *etc* are posted

pillion *noun* **1** a seat for a passenger on a motor-cycle **2** *old* a light saddle for a passenger on horseback, behind the main saddle

pillory *noun* (*plural* **pillories**) *hist* a wooden frame fitted over the head and hands of wrongdoers as a punishment *verb* mock in public

> **pillory** *verb* » pillori*es*, pillory*ing*, pillori*ed*

pillow *noun* a soft cushion for the head *verb* rest or support on a pillow **pillowcase** or **pillowslip** *noun* a cover for a pillow

pilot *noun* **1** someone who steers a ship in or out of a harbour **2** someone who flies an aeroplane **3** a guide, a leader *verb* steer, guide **pilot-light** *noun* **1** a small gaslight from which larger jets are lit **2** an electric light showing that a current is switched on **pilot scheme** a scheme introduced on a small scale to act as a guide to a full-scale one

pimento *noun* (*plural* **pimentos**) a mild type of red pepper

pimp *noun* a man who manages prostitutes and takes money from them

pimpernel *noun* a plant of the primrose family, with small pink or scarlet flowers

pimple *noun* a small round infected swelling on the skin **pimpled** or **pimply** *adj* having pimples

PIN /pin/ *abbrev* personal identification number (for automatic teller machines *etc*)

pin *noun* **1** a short pointed piece of metal with a small round head, used for fastening fabric **2** a wooden or metal peg **3** a skittle □ *verb* **1** fasten with a pin **2** hold fast, pressed against something: *the bloodhound pinned him to the ground*

> **pin** *verb* » pin*s*, pinn*ing*, pinn*ed*

piña colada a drink of pineapple juice, rum and coconut

pinafore *noun* **1** an apron to protect the front of a dress **2** a sleeveless dress worn over a jersey, blouse *etc*

pinball *noun* a game played on a slot-machine in which a ball runs down a sloping board between obstacles

pince-nez /panhs-*neh*/ *noun* a pair of eyeglasses with a spring for gripping the nose

pincers *noun plural* **1** a tool like pliers, but with sharp points for gripping, pulling out nails *etc* **2** the claw of a crab or lobster

pinch *verb* **1** squeeze (*esp* flesh) between the thumb and forefinger, nip **2** grip tightly, hurt by tightness **3** *informal* steal □ *noun* (*plural* **pinches**) **1** a squeeze, a nip **2** a small amount (*eg* of salt) □ **pinched** *adj* of a face: looking cold, pale or thin □ **at a pinch** if really necessary or urgent □ **feel the pinch** suffer from lack of money

pinchbeck *adj* sham, in poor imitation

> From Christopher *Pinchbeck*, a 17th-century watchmaker who invented a copper alloy to imitate gold

pine *noun* **1** an evergreen tree with needle-like leaves which produces cones **2** the soft wood of such a tree used for furniture *etc* □ *verb* **1** waste away, lose strength **2** long (for something)

pineal gland a gland in the brain that releases a hormone at night which causes sleepiness

pineapple *noun* a large tropical fruit shaped like a pine-cone

ping *noun* a whistling sound such as that of a bullet □ *verb* make a whistling sound □ **ping-pong** *noun, trademark* table-tennis

pinion *noun* **1** a bird's wing **2** a small toothed wheel □ *verb* **1** hold (someone) fast by binding or holding their arms **2** cut or fasten the wings of (a bird)

pink *noun* **1** a pale red colour **2** a sweet-scented garden flower like a carnation **3** a healthy or good state: *feeling in the pink* □ *verb* **1** of an engine: make a faint clinking noise **2** cut (cloth *etc*) with pinking scissors □ **pinking scissors** or **pinking shears** scissors with blades which give cloth a zig-zag edge

pinkie *noun, informal* the little finger

pinnacle *noun* **1** a slender spire or turret **2** a high pointed rock or mountain **3** the highest point

pinnie *noun, informal* an apron or overall

pinochle *noun* a card game played with two packs with the lowest cards removed

pint *noun* a liquid measure equal to just over $\frac{1}{2}$ litre

Pinyin *noun* a system for transcribing Chinese using Roman characters

pioneer *noun* **1** an explorer **2** an inventor, or an early exponent of something: *pioneers of the cinema* ▯ *verb* act as a pioneer

pious *adj* respectful in religious matters ▯ **piety** *noun*

pip *noun* **1** a seed of a fruit **2** a spot or symbol on dice or cards **3** a star on an army officer's tunic **4** a short bleep as part of a time signal *etc* on the radio or telephone

pipe *noun* **1** a tube for carrying water, gas *etc* **2** a tube with a bowl at the end, for smoking tobacco **3** (**pipes**) a musical instrument made of several small pipes joined together **4** (**pipes**) bagpipes ▯ *verb* **1** play (notes, a tune) on a pipe or pipes **2** whistle, chirp **3** speak in a shrill high voice **4** convey (*eg* water) by pipe ▯ **pipe clay** a fine white clay used to whiten leather and in making clay pipes ▯ **piped music** continuous background music played throughout a building ▯ **pipeline** *noun* a long line of pipes, *eg* to carry oil from an oil-field ▯ **piper** *noun* someone who plays a pipe, *esp* the bagpipes ▯ **in the pipeline** in preparation, soon to become available ▯ **pipe down** become silent, stop talking ▯ **pipe up** speak up, express an opinion

pipette *noun* a small glass tube used in laboratories

piping *adj* high-pitched, shrill ▯ **piping hot** very hot ▯ *noun* **1** a length of tubing **2** a system of pipes **3** a narrow ornamental cord for trimming clothes **4** a strip of decorative icing round a cake

pippin *noun* a kind of apple

pipsqueak *noun, informal* an insignificant, or very small, person

piquant /*pee*kənt/ *adj* **1** sharp-tasting, spicy **2** arousing interest

pique /peek/ *noun* anger caused by wounded pride, spite, resentment ▯ *verb* **1** wound the pride of **2** arouse (curiosity)

piranha *noun* a S American river-fish which eats flesh

pirate *noun* **1** someone who robs ships at sea **2** someone who steals or plagiarizes another's work ▯ **piracy** *noun* ▯ **piratical** *adj*

pirouette *noun* a rapid whirling on the toes in dancing ▯ *verb* twirl in a pirouette

piss *verb slang* urinate ▯ *noun* **1** urine **2** an act of urinating ▯ **pissed** *adj, slang* extremely drunk ▯ **piss about** or **piss around** *slang* behave foolishly, waste time ▯ **pissed off** *slang* annoyed, fed up ▯ **piss off** *exclam, slang* go away

pistachio *noun* (*plural* **pistachios**) a greenish nut, often used as a flavouring

piste /peest/ *noun* a ski trail

pistil *noun* the seed-bearing part of a flower

pistol *noun* a small gun held in the hand

piston *noun* a round piece of metal that moves up and down inside a cylinder, *eg* in an engine □ **piston-rod** *noun* the rod to which the piston is fitted

pit *noun* **1** a hole in the ground **2** a place from which coal and other minerals are dug **3** the ground floor of a theatre behind the stalls **4** (often **pits**) a place beside the racecourse for repairing and refuelling racing cars *etc* □ *verb* set one thing or person against another: *pitting my wits against his* □ **pitted** *adj* marked with small holes

pit *verb* » pit*s*, pitt*ing*, pitt*ed*

pitch *verb* **1** fix a tent *etc* in the ground **2** throw **3** fall heavily; lurch: *pitch forward* **4** set the level or key of a tune □ *noun* (*plural* **pitches**) **1** a thick dark substance obtained by boiling down tar **2** a throw **3** an attempt at selling or persuading: *sales pitch* **4** the height or depth of a note **5** a peak, an extreme point: *reach fever pitch* **6** the field for certain sports **7** *cricket* the ground between wickets **8** the slope of a roof *etc* **9** the spot reserved for a street seller or street-entertainer □ **pitchblende** *noun* a black mineral made up of uranium oxides □ **pitch-dark** *adj* very dark □ **pitched battle** a battle on chosen ground between sides arranged in position beforehand □ **pitchfork** *verb* a fork for lifting and throwing hay □ *verb* throw suddenly and violently

pitcher *noun* a kind of large jug

piteous *see* **pity**

pitfall *noun* a trap, a possible danger

pith *noun* **1** the soft substance in the centre of plant stems **2** the white substance under the rind of an orange, lemon *etc* **3** the important part of anything □ **pithy** *adj* **1** full of pith **2** full of meaning, to the point: *a pithy saying*

pitiable *see* **pity**

piton *noun* an iron peg for attaching a rope to in mountaineering

pitta *noun* a flat round Mediterranean bread

pittance *noun* a very small wage or allowance

pituitary gland a gland in the brain affecting growth

pity *noun* **1** feeling for the sufferings of others, sympathy **2** a cause of grief **3** a regrettable fact □ *verb* feel sorry for □ **piteous** or **pitiable** *adj* deserving pity; wretched □ **pitiful** *adj* poor, wretched

pity *verb* » piti*es*, pity*ing*, piti*ed*

pivot *noun* **1** the pin or centre on which anything turns **2** something or someone greatly depended on □ *verb* **1** turn on a pivot **2** depend (on) □ **pivotal** *adj*

pixel *noun, comput* the smallest element in a screen display

pixy or **pixie** *noun* (*plural* **pixies**) a kind of fairy

pizza *noun* a flat piece of dough spread with tomato, cheese *etc* and baked

pizzazz *noun* flamboyant style, panache

pizzicato *adv, music* played by plucking the strings rather than bowing

placard *noun* a printed notice (as an advertisement *etc*) placed on a wall *etc*

placate *verb* calm, soothe, make less angry *etc*

place *noun* **1** a physical location; any area or building **2** a particular spot **3** an open space in a town: *market place* **4** a seat in a theatre, train, at a table *etc* **5** a position in football *etc* **6** a position on a course, in a job *etc* **7** rank ▯ *verb* **1** put in a particular place **2** find a place for **3** give (an order for goods *etc*) **4** remember who someone is: *I can't place him at all* ▯ **placed** *adj* **1** having a place **2** among the first three in a competition ▯ **in place 1** in the proper position **2** suitable ▯ **in place of** instead of ▯ **out of place 1** not in the proper position **2** unsuitable

> **place** *verb* » plac*es*, plac*ing*, plac*ed*

placebo *noun* (*plural* **placebos**) an inactive medicine given to humour a patient, or used in drug trials

placenta *noun* a part of the womb that connects an unborn mammal to its mother, shed at birth

placid *adj* calm, not easily disturbed ▯ **placidity** *noun*

plagiarize *verb* steal or borrow from the writings or ideas of someone else without permission ▯ **plagiarism** *noun* ▯ **plagiarist** *noun*

plague *noun* **1** a fatal infectious disease carried by rat fleas **2** a great and troublesome quantity: *a plague of flies* ▯ *verb* pester or annoy continually

plaice *noun* a type of edible flatfish

plaid *noun* a long piece of cloth (*esp* tartan) worn over the shoulder

plain *adj* **1** flat, level **2** simple, ordinary **3** without ornament or decoration **4** clear, easy to see or understand **5** not good-looking, not attractive ▯ *noun* a level stretch of land ▯ **plain-clothes** *adj* of a police detective: wearing ordinary clothes, not uniform ▯ **plain-spoken** *adj* speaking your thoughts frankly

plaintiff *noun* someone who takes action against another in the law courts

plaintive *adj* sad, sorrowful

plait *noun* **1** a length of hair arranged by intertwining three or more separate pieces **2** threads *etc* intertwined in this way ▯ *verb* form into a plait

plan *noun* **1** a diagram of a building, town *etc* as if seen from above **2** a scheme or arrangement to do something ▯ *verb* **1** make a sketch or plan of **2** decide or arrange to do (something)

> **plan** *verb* » plan*s*, plann*ing*, plann*ed*

plane[1] *short* for **aeroplane**

plane[2] *noun* **1** a level surface **2** a carpentry tool for smoothing wood **3** a standard (of achievement *etc*) □ *adj* flat, level □ *verb* **1** smooth with a plane **2** glide over water *etc*

plane[3] *noun* a type of tree with broad leaves

planet *noun* any of the bodies (*eg* the earth, Venus) which move round the sun or round another fixed star □ **planetary** *adj*

plangent *adj* resonant, resounding

plank *noun* a long, flat piece of timber

plankton *noun* tiny living creatures floating in seas, lakes *etc*

plant *noun* **1** a living growth from the ground, with a stem, root and leaves **2** a factory or machinery □ *verb* **1** put (something) into the ground so that it will grow **2** put (an idea) into the mind **3** put in position: *plant a bomb* **4** set down firmly: *plant your feet on the floor* **5** *informal* place (something) as false evidence

plantain *noun* a coarse green-skinned tropical fruit like a banana

plantation *noun* **1** an area planted with trees **2** an estate for growing cotton, sugar, rubber, tobacco *etc* □ **planter** *noun* the owner of a plantation

planxty *noun* an Irish dance tune, slower than a jig

plaque *noun* **1** a decorative plate of metal, china *etc* for fixing to a wall **2** a film of saliva and bacteria which forms on the teeth

plasma *noun* the liquid part of blood and certain other fluids

plaster *noun* **1** a mixture of lime, water and sand which sets hard, for covering walls *etc* **2** (*also called* **plaster of Paris**) a fine mixture containing gypsum used for moulding, making casts for broken limbs *etc* **3** a small dressing which can be stuck over a wound □ *adj* made of plaster □ *verb* **1** apply plaster to **2** cover too thickly (with) □ **plastered** *adj, slang* drunk □ **plasterer** *noun* someone who plasters walls

plastic *adj* **1** easily moulded or shaped **2** made of plastic □ *noun* a chemically manufactured substance that can be moulded when soft, formed into fibres *etc* □ **plastic bullet** a cylinder of PVC fired from a gun □ **plastic explosive** mouldable explosive material □ **plasticity** *noun* the quality of being easily moulded □ **plastic surgery** an operation to repair or replace damaged areas of skin, or to improve the appearance of a facial feature

Plasticine *noun, trademark* a soft clay-like substance used for modelling

plate *noun* **1** a shallow dish for holding food **2** a flat piece of metal, glass, china *etc* **3** gold and silver articles **4** a sheet of metal used in printing **5** a book illustration **6** the part of false teeth that fits to the mouth □ *verb* cover with a coating of metal □ **plate-glass** *noun* glass in thick sheets, used for shop windows, mirrors *etc* □ **plating** *noun* a thin covering of metal

plateau *noun* (*plural* **plateaus** or **plateaux**) **1** a broad level stretch of high land **2** a steady, unchanging state: *prices have now reached a plateau*

platelet *noun* a tiny blood particle which plays a part in clotting

platform *noun* **1** a raised level surface for passengers at a railway station **2** a raised floor for speakers, entertainers *etc*

platinum *noun* a heavy and very valuable steel-grey metal

platitude *noun* a dull, ordinary remark made as if it were important

platonic *adj* of a relationship: not sexual

platoon *noun* a section of a company of soldiers

platter *noun* a large, flat plate

platypus *noun* (*plural* **platypuses**) a small water animal of Australia that has webbed feet and lays eggs (*also called* **duck-billed platypus**)

plaudits *noun plural* applause, praise

plausible *adj* **1** seeming to be truthful or honest **2** seeming probable or reasonable ◊ **plausibility** *noun*

play *verb* **1** amuse yourself **2** take part in a game **3** gamble **4** act (on a stage *etc*) **5** perform on (a musical instrument) **6** carry out (a trick) **7** trifle or fiddle (with): *don't play with your food* **8** move over lightly: *the firelight played on his face* ◊ *noun* **1** amusement, recreation **2** gambling **3** a story for acting, a drama **4** a way of behaving: *foul play* **5** freedom of movement ◊ **playboy** *noun* an irresponsible rich man only interested in pleasure ◊ **player** *noun* **1** an actor **2** someone who plays a game, musical instrument *etc*: *a lute player* ◊ **playground** *noun* an open area for playing at school, in a park *etc* ◊ **playgroup** *noun* a group of young children who play together supervised by adults ◊ **playing-card** *noun* one of a pack of cards used in playing card games ◊ **playmate** *noun* a friend with whom you play ◊ **play-off** *noun* **1** a game to decide a tie **2** a game between the winners of other competitions ◊ **playschool** *noun* a nursery school or playgroup ◊ **plaything** *noun* a toy ◊ **playwright** *noun* a writer of plays ◊ **play at** treat in a light-hearted, not serious way: *he only plays at being a business man* ◊ **play off** set off (one person) against another to gain some advantage for yourself ◊ **play on** make use of (someone's feelings) to turn to your own advantage ◊ **a play on words** a pun ◊ **play the game** act fairly and honestly

playful *adj* **1** wanting to play: *a playful kitten* **2** fond of joking, not serious ◊ **playfully** *adv* ◊ **playfulness** *noun*

PLC *abbrev* public limited company

plea *noun* **1** an excuse **2** an accused person's answer to a charge in a law-court **3** an urgent request ◊ **plea bargaining** the arranging of lenient terms for an accused person willing to plead guilty *etc*, before their trial begins

plead *verb* **1** state your case in a

lawcourt **2** (with **with**) beg earnestly **3** give as an excuse □ **plead guilty** or **not guilty** admit or deny guilt in a law court

pleasant *adj* giving pleasure; agreeable □ **pleasantness** *noun* □ **pleasantry** *noun* (*plural* **pleasantries**) a good-humoured joke □ **pleasurable** *adj* delightful, pleasant

please *verb* **1** give pleasure or delight to **2** satisfy **3** choose, like (to do): *do as you please* □ *exclam* added for politeness to a command or request: *please keep off the grass* □ **if you please** please

pleasure *noun* **1** enjoyment, joy, delight **2** what you wish: *what is your pleasure?* □ **at your pleasure** when or if you please

pleat *noun* a fold in cloth, which has been pressed or stitched down □ *verb* put pleats in □ **pleated** *adj*

pleb *noun, informal* someone of no taste or culture, a boor

plebeian *adj* **1** of the ordinary or common people **2** vulgar, lacking culture or taste

plebiscite *noun* a vote by everyone in an area on a special issue, for or against

plectrum *noun* a small piece of horn, metal *etc* used for plucking the strings of a guitar

pledge *noun* **1** something handed over as security for a loan **2** a solemn promise □ *verb* **1** give as security, pawn **2** promise solemnly: *pledged himself to carry out the plan* **3** drink to the health of, toast

plenary *adj* full, complete

plenty *noun* **1** a full supply, as much as is needed **2** a large number or quantity (of) □ **plenteous** or **plentiful** *adj* not scarce, abundant

plethora *noun* too large a quantity of anything: *a plethora of politicians*

pleurisy *noun* an illness in which the covering of the lungs becomes inflamed

pliable *adj* **1** easily bent or folded **2** easily persuaded □ **pliant** *adj* pliable

plié *noun* a ballet movement with the knees bent and body upright

pliers *noun plural* a tool used for gripping, bending and cutting wire *etc*

plight *noun* a bad state or situation □ *verb, old* promise solemnly, pledge

plimsoll *noun* a light rubber-soled canvas shoe for sports □ **Plimsoll line** a ship's loadline

plink *noun* a short, high-pitched sound

plinth *noun* **1** the square slab at the foot of a column **2** the base or pedestal of a statue, vase *etc*

PLO *abbrev* Palestine Liberation Organization

plod *verb* **1** travel slowly and steadily **2** work on steadily □ **plodder** *noun* a dull but hard-working person

> **plod** » plod*s*, plodd*ing*, plodd*ed*

plonk *noun, informal* cheap wine

plop *noun* the sound made by a small object falling into water □ *verb* make this sound

plop *verb* » plop*s*, plopp*ing*, plopp*ed*

plot *verb* **1** a small piece of ground **2** a plan for an illegal or malicious action **3** the story of a play, novel *etc* □ *verb* **1** plan secretly **2** make a chart, graph *etc* of **3** mark points on one of these □ **plotter** *verb*

plot *verb* » plot*s*, plott*ing*, plott*ed*

plough *noun* a farm tool for turning up the soil □ *verb* **1** turn up the ground in furrows **2** work through slowly: *ploughing through the ironing* □ **ploughman's lunch** a cold dish of bread, cheese and pickle *etc* □ **ploughshare** *noun* the blade of a plough □ **the Plough** a group of seven stars forming a shape like an old plough

plover *noun* any of several kinds of bird that nest on the ground in open country

ploy *noun* an activity, an escapade

pluck *verb* **1** pull out or off **2** pick (flowers, fruit *etc*) **3** strip off the feathers of (a bird) before cooking □ *noun* courage, spirit □ **plucky** *adj* brave, determined □ **pluck up courage** prepare yourself to face a danger or difficulty

plug *noun* **1** an object fitted into a hole to stop it up **2** a fitting on an appliance put into a socket to connect with an electric current **3** *informal* a brief advertisement □ *verb* **1** stop up with a plug **2** *informal* advertise, publicize

plug » plug*s*, plugg*ing*, plugg*ed*

plum *noun* **1** a soft fruit, often dark red or purple, with a stone in the centre **2** the tree that produces this fruit □ *adj* very good, very profitable *etc*: *a plum job* □ **plum cake** or **plum pudding** a rich cake or pudding containing dried fruit

plumage *see* **plume**

plumb *noun* a lead weight hung on a string (**plumbline**), used to test if a wall has been built straight up □ *adj & adv* standing straight up, vertical □ *verb* test the depth of (the sea *etc*)

plumber *noun* someone who fits and mends water, gas and sewage pipes □ **plumbing** *noun* **1** the work of a plumber **2** the drainage and water systems of a building *etc*

plume *noun* **1** a feather, *esp* an ornamental one **2** something looking like a feather: *a plume of smoke* □ **plumage** *noun* the feathers of a bird

plummet *noun* a weight of lead hung on a line, for taking depths at sea □ *verb* plunge

plump *adj* fat, rounded, well filled out □ *verb* **1** grow fat, swell **2** beat or shake (cushions *etc*) back into shape **3** sit or sink down heavily **4** (with **for**) choose, vote for

plunder *verb* carry off goods by force, loot, rob □ *noun* goods seized by force

plunge *verb* **1** dive (into water *etc*) **2** rush or lurch forward **3** thrust suddenly (into): *he plunged the knife into its neck* □ *noun* a thrust; a dive

pluperfect *noun, grammar* showing an action which took place before the main past actions being described, *eg* he *had already left*, when you phoned

plural *adj* more than one ▫ *noun, grammar* the form which shows more than one, *eg mice* is the plural of *mouse* ▫ **plurality** *noun*

plus *prep* used to show addition and represented by the sign (+): *five plus two equals seven* ▫ *adj* of a quantity more than zero ▫ *adv, informal* and a bit extra: *she earns £20 000 plus*

plus fours *noun plural* baggy trousers reaching to just below the knees

So called from the four additional inches of cloth needed for their length

plush *noun* cloth with a soft velvety surface on one side ▫ *adj* luxurious

plutocrat *noun* someone who is powerful because of their wealth ▫ **plutocratic** *adj*

ply *verb* **1** work at steadily **2** make regular journeys: *the ferry plies between Oban and Mull* **3** use (a tool) energetically **4** keep supplying with (food, questions to answer *etc*) ▫ **plywood** *noun* a board made up of thin sheets of wood glued together ▫ **two-** or **three-** *etc* **ply** having two or three *etc* layers or strands

ply » pli*es*, ply*ing*, pli*ed*

PM *abbrev* prime minister

pm *abbrev* after noon (from Latin *post meridiem*)

PMS *abbrev* premenstrual syndrome

PMT *abbrev* premenstrual tension

pneumatic /nyoo*ma*tik/ *adj* **1** filled with air **2** worked by air: *pneumatic drill*

pneumonia /nyoo*moh*niə/ *noun* a disease in which the lungs become inflamed

PO *abbrev* **1** post office **2** postal order

poach *verb* **1** cook gently in boiling water or stock **2** catch fish or hunt game illegally ▫ **poacher** *noun* someone who hunts or fishes illegally

pocket *noun* **1** a small pouch or bag, *esp* as part of a garment **2** a personal supply of money: *well beyond my pocket* **3** a small isolated area: *a pocket of unemployment* ▫ *verb* **1** put in a pocket **2** steal ▫ **pocket-book** *noun* a wallet ▫ **pocket money** an allowance of money for personal spending ▫ **in** or **out of pocket** having gained or lost money on a deal *etc*

pockmark *noun* a scar or small hole in the skin left by disease

pod *noun* a long seed-case of the pea, bean *etc* ▫ *verb* **1** remove from a pod **2** form pods

pod *verb* » pod*s*, podd*ing*, podd*ed*

podgy *adj* short and fat

podium *noun* a low pedestal, a platform

poem *noun* a piece of imaginative writing set out in lines which often have a regular rhythm or rhyme

poesy *noun, old* poetry

poet *noun* someone who writes poetry ▯ **poetaster** *noun* a writer of bad poetry

poetic *adj* of or like poetry ▯ **poetically** *adv* ▯ **poetic justice** a fitting reward or punishment ▯ **poetic licence** a departure from truth, logic *etc* for the sake of effect

poetry *noun* **1** the art of writing poems **2** poems

po-faced *adj* stupidly solemn, humourless

pogo stick a child's stick with a spring in it for jumping up and down

pogrom *noun* an organized killing or massacre of a group of people

poignant *adj* **1** sharp, keen **2** very painful or moving; pathetic ▯ **poignancy** *noun*

poinsettia *noun* a plant, originally from Mexico, with large scarlet or white petal-like leaves

point *noun* **1** a sharp end of anything **2** a headland **3** a dot: *decimal point* **4** a full stop in punctuation **5** an exact place or spot **6** an exact moment of time **7** the chief matter of an argument **8** the meaning of a joke **9** a mark in a competition **10** a purpose, an advantage: *there is no point in going* **11** a movable rail to direct a railway engine from one line to another **12** an electrical wall socket **13** a mark of character: *he has many good points* ▯ *verb* **1** make pointed: *point your toes* **2** direct, aim **3** indicate with a gesture: *pointing to the building* **4** fill (wall joints) with mortar ▯ **point-blank** *adj* **1** of a shot: fired from very close range **2** of a question: direct ▯ **pointed** *adj* **1** having a point, sharp **2** of a remark: obviously aimed at someone ▯ **pointer** *noun* **1** a rod for pointing **2** a type of dog used to show where game has fallen ▯ **pointless** *adj* having no meaning or purpose

poise *verb* **1** balance, keep steady **2** hover in the air ▯ *noun* **1** a state of balance **2** dignity, self-confidence ▯ **poised** *adj* **1** balanced, having poise **2** prepared, ready: *poised for action*

poison *noun* **1** a substance which, when taken into the body, kills or harms **2** anything harmful ▯ *verb* **1** kill or harm with poison **2** add poison to **3** make bitter or bad: *poisoned her mind* ▯ **poisonous** *adj* **1** harmful because of containing poison **2** causing evil ▯ **poison ivy** a N American plant whose juice causes a skin rash ▯ **poison pen** a writer of malicious anonymous letters ▯ **poison pill** *informal* a merger of companies to prevent a threatened takeover bid

poke *verb* **1** push (*eg* a finger or stick) into something **2** prod, thrust at **3** search about inquisitively ▯ *noun* **1** a nudge, a prod **2** a prying search ▯ **poker** *noun* **1** a rod for stirring up a fire **2** a card game in which players bet on their chance of winning ▯ **poky** *adj* cramped and shabby

polar and **polarity** *see* **pole**

polarize *verb* **1** give polarity to **2** split into opposing sides

polaroid *noun, trademark* **1** a

plastic through which light is seen less brightly **2** (**polaroids**) sunglasses **3** a camera that develops individual pictures in a few seconds

polder *noun* land below sea-level reclaimed for use

pole *noun* **1** a long rounded rod or post **2** the north or south end of the earth's axis (**the north** or **south pole**) **3** either of the opposing points of a magnet or electric battery ◇ **polar** *adj* of the regions round the north or south poles ◇ **polarity** *noun* the state of having two opposite poles ◇ **pole-star** *noun* the star most directly above the north pole ◇ **pole vault** a sport in which an athlete jumps over a bar with the aid of a flexible pole

polecat *noun* **1** a large kind of weasel **2** *US* a skunk

polemic or **polemical** *adj* expressing strong, often controversial views ◇ **polemicist** *noun* someone who writes polemic material

police *noun* the body of men and women whose work it is to see that laws are obeyed *etc* ◇ *verb* keep law and order in (a place) by use of police ◇ **policeman, policewoman** *noun* ◇ **police station** the headquarters of the police in a district

policy *noun* (*plural* **policies**) **1** an agreed course of action **2** a written agreement with an insurance company

polio *short for* **poliomyelitis**

poliomyelitis *noun* a disease of the spinal cord, causing weakness or paralysis of the muscles

polish *verb* **1** make smooth and shiny by rubbing **2** improve (a piece of writing *etc*) **3** make more polite ◇ *noun* **1** a gloss on a surface **2** a substance used for polishing **3** fine manners, style *etc*

polite *adj* having good manners, courteous ◇ **politely** *adv* ◇ **politeness** *noun*

politic *adj* wise, cautious

political *adj* of government, politicians or politics ◇ **politician** *noun* someone involved in politics, *esp* a member of parliament ◇ **politics** *noun sing* the art or study of government ◇ **politicize** *verb* make aware of political issues ◇ **politicking** *noun* working in politics, vote-seeking ◇ **politico** *noun* (*plural* **politicos** or **politicoes**), *informal* a politician

polka *noun* a lively dance or the music for it

poll *noun* **1** a counting of voters at an election **2** total number of votes **3** (*also called* **opinion poll**) a test of public opinion by questioning ◇ *verb* **1** cut or clip off (hair, branches *etc*) **2** receive (votes): *they polled 5000 votes* ◇ **polling station** a place where voting is done ◇ **poll tax** *Brit* the community charge

pollard *noun* a tree with its top cut off to allow new growth ◇ *verb* cut the top off (a tree)

pollen *noun* the fertilizing powder of flowers ◇ **pollinate** *verb* fertilize with pollen ◇ **pollination** *noun*

pollute *verb* **1** make dirty or impure **2** make (the environment) harmful to life ◇ **pollutant** *noun* something that pollutes □ **pollution** *noun* **1** the act of polluting **2** dirt

polo *noun* a game like hockey played on horseback □ **polo neck 1** a close-fitting neck with a part turned over at the top **2** a jumper with a neck like this

polonaise *noun* a slow Polish dance

poltergeist *noun* a kind of ghost believed to move furniture and throw objects around a room

poly- *prefix* many, much

polyanthus *noun* a hybrid plant which produces many flowers

polycarpous *noun* of a tree: producing fruit year after year

polyester *noun* a synthetic material often used in clothing

polygamy *noun* the fact of having more than one wife or husband at the same time □ **polygamist** *noun* □ **polygamous** *adj*

polyglot *adj* speaking, or written in, many languages □ *noun* someone fluent in many languages

polygon *noun* a figure with many angles and sides □ **polygonal** *adj*

polygraph *noun* an instrument which measures pulse rate *etc*, used as a lie-detector

polymath *noun* someone with knowledge of a wide range of subjects

polymer *noun* a chemical compound with large molecules

polymorphous *noun* occurring in several different forms

polyp *noun* **1** a small sea-animal with arms or tentacles **2** a kind of tumour

polyphony *noun* musical composition in parts, each with a separate melody □ **polyphonic** *adj*

polystyrene *noun* a synthetic material which resists moisture, used for packing and disposable cups *etc*

polysyllable *noun* a word of three or more syllables □ **polysyllabic** *adj*

polytechnic *noun* a college which teaches technical and vocational subjects

polythene *noun* a type of plastic that can be moulded when hot

polyunsaturated *adj* of oil: containing no cholesterol

polyurethane *noun* a resin used to produce foam materials

pomegranate *noun* a fruit with a thick skin, many seeds and pulpy edible flesh

pommel *noun* **1** the knob on the hilt of a sword **2** the high part of a saddle

pomp *noun* solemn and splendid ceremony, magnificence

pompous *adj* self-important, excessively dignified □ **pomposity** *noun*

poncho *noun* (*plural* **ponchos**) a S American cloak made of a blanket with a hole for the head

pond *noun* a small lake or pool

ponder *verb* think over, consider □ **ponderous** *adj* **1** weighty **2** clumsy **3** sounding very important

poniard *noun* a kind of small dagger

pontiff *noun* **1** a Roman Catholic bishop **2** the Pope □ **pontifical** *adj* **1** of a pontiff **2** pompous in speech □ **pontificate** *verb* speak in a pompous manner

pontoon[1] *noun* a flat-bottomed boat used to support a temporary bridge (a **pontoon bridge**)

pontoon[2] *noun* a card-game in which players try to collect 21 points

pony *noun* (*plural* **ponies**) a small horse □ **pony-trekking** *noun* riding cross-country in small parties

poodle *noun* a breed of dog, with curly hair often clipped in a fancy way

pool *noun* **1** a small area of still water **2** a deep part of a river **3** a joint fund or stock (of money, typists *etc*) **4** the money played for in a gambling game □ *verb* put (money *etc*) into a joint fund □ **football pools** organized betting on football match results

poop *noun* **1** a ship's stern, or back part **2** a high deck in the stern

poor *adj* **1** having little money or property **2** not good: *this work is poor* **3** lacking (in): *poor in sports facilities* **4** deserving pity: *poor Tom has broken his leg* □ **poorly** *adj* in bad health, ill □ **the poor** those with little money

pop *noun* **1** a sharp quick noise, *eg* that made by a cork coming out of a bottle **2** a fizzy soft drink **3** popular music □ *verb* **1** make a pop **2** move quickly, dash: *pop in/ pop along the road* □ *adj* of music: popular

> **pop** *verb* » pop*s*, popp*ing*, popp*ed*

popadom or **popadum** *noun* a thin circle of dough fried in oil until crisp

popcorn *noun* a kind of maize that bursts open when heated

pope *noun* the bishop of Rome, head of the Roman Catholic Church

popinjay *noun* someone who is conceited about their clothes

poplar *noun* a tall, narrow quick-growing tree

poplin *noun* strong cotton cloth

poppy *noun* (*plural* **poppies**) a plant growing wild in fields *etc* with large scarlet flowers

populace *noun* the people of a country or area

popular *adj* **1** of the people: *popular vote* **2** liked by most people **3** widely held or believed: *popular belief* □ **popularity** *noun* the state of being generally liked □ **popularize** *verb* make popular or widely known □ **popularly** *adv*

population *noun* the number of people living in a place □ **populate** *verb* fill (an area) with people

populist *adj* appealing to the mass of people □ **populism** *noun*

populous *adj* full of people □ **populousness** *noun*

porcelain *noun* a kind of fine china

porch *noun* (*plural* **porches**) a

covered entrance to a building

porcupine *noun* a large gnawing animal, covered with sharp quills

pore *noun* **1** a tiny hole **2** the hole of a sweat gland in the skin

⚠Do not confuse with: **pour**

pore over study closely or eagerly

pork *noun* the flesh of the pig, prepared for eating

porn *noun, informal* pornography

pornography *noun* literature or art that is sexually explicit and often offensive ◇ **pornographic** *adj*

porous *adj* **1** having pores **2** allowing fluid to pass through ◇ **porosity** *noun*

porpoise *noun* a blunt-nosed sea animal of the dolphin family

porridge *noun* a food made from oatmeal boiled in water or milk

porringer *noun* a small bowl for soup, porridge *etc*

port *noun* **1** a harbour **2** a town with a harbour **3** the left side of a ship as you face the front **4** a strong, dark-red sweet wine

port a beul /pohrsh *ə beel*/ a rhythmic Gaelic song sung without accompaniment

portable *adj* able to be lifted and carried ◇ *noun* a computer, telephone *etc* that can be carried around ◇ **portability** *noun*

portal *noun* a grand entrance or doorway

portcullis *noun* (*plural* **portcullises**) a grating which is let down quickly to close a gateway

portend *verb* give warning of, foretell

portent *noun* a warning sign ◇ **portentous** *adj* **1** strange, wonderful **2** important, weighty ◇ **portentousness** *noun*

porter *noun* **1** someone employed to carry luggage, push hospital trolleys *etc* **2** a doorkeeper **3** a kind of dark brown beer

portfolio *noun* (*plural* **portfolios**) **1** a case for carrying papers, drawings *etc* **2** the job of a government minister

port-hole *noun* a small round window in a ship's side

portico *noun* (*plural* **porticoes** or **porticos**) a row of columns in front of a building forming a porch or covered walk

portion *noun* **1** a part **2** a share, a helping ◇ *verb* divide into parts

portly *adj* stout and dignified

portmanteau *noun* a large leather travelling bag

portrait *noun* **1** a drawing, painting, or photograph of a person **2** a description of a person, place *etc*

portray *verb* **1** make a painting or drawing of **2** describe in words **3** act the part of ◇ **portrayal** *noun*

portray » portray*s*, portray*ing*, portray*ed*

Portuguese man-of-war a stinging jellyfish

pose *noun* **1** a position of the body: *a relaxed pose* **2** behaviour put on to impress others, a pretence ◇ *verb* **1** position yourself for a photograph *etc* **2** (with **as**) pretend or claim to be what you are not: *posing as an expert* **3** put forward (a problem, question *etc*) ◊ **poser** *noun* **1** someone who poses to impress others **2** a difficult question ◊ **poseur** *noun* a poser

posh *adj, informal* high-class; smart

posit *verb* postulate, assume as true for the sake of argument

position *noun* **1** place, situation **2** manner of standing, sitting *etc*, posture: *in a crouching position* **3** a rank or job: *a high position in a bank* ◊ *verb* place

positive *adj* **1** meaning or saying 'yes': *a positive answer* (*contrasted with*: **negative**) **2** not able to be doubted: *positive proof* **3** certain, convinced: *I am positive that she did it* **4** definite: *a positive improvement* **5** greater than zero **6** *grammar* of an adjective or adverb: of the first degree of comparison, *eg big*, not *bigger* or *biggest*

positron *noun* a particle with a positive electrical charge

posse /*posi*/ *noun* a body of police *etc*

possess *verb* **1** own, have **2** take hold of your mind: *anger possessed her* ◊ **possessed** *adj* **1** in the power of an evil spirit **2** obsessed **3** self-possessed, calm ◊ **possession** *noun* the state of possessing; the state of being possessed; something owned ◊ **possessive** *adj* **1** *grammar* of an adjective: showing possession, *eg* the adjectives *my, mine, your, their etc* **2** over-protective and jealous in attitude ◊ **possessor** *noun* an owner

posset *noun* a drink of milk curdled with wine or vinegar

possible *adj* **1** able to happen or to be done **2** not unlikely ◊ **possibility** *noun* (*plural* **possibilities**) something that may happen or that may be done ◊ **possibly** *adv* perhaps

possum *noun*: **play possum** pretend to be asleep or dead

post *noun* **1** an upright pole or stake **2** the service which delivers letters and other mail **3** a job: *teaching post* **4** a place of duty: *the soldier remained at his post* **5** a settlement, a camp: *military post/ trading post* ◊ *verb* **1** put (a letter) in a postbox for collection **2** send or station somewhere: *posted abroad* **3** put up, stick up (a notice *etc*) ◊ **postage** *noun* money paid for sending a letter *etc* by post ◊ **postage stamp** a small printed label to show that postage has been paid ◊ **postal** *adj* of or by post ◊ **postal order** a document bought at a post office which can be exchanged for a stated amount of money ◊ **postbox** *noun* a box with an opening in which to post letters *etc* ◊ **postcard** *noun* a card for sending a message by post ◊ **post code** a short series of letters and numbers, used for sorting mail by machine ◊ **post-date** *verb* mark (a cheque) with a date in the future, so that it cannot be cashed immediately ◊ **poster** *noun* **1** a large notice or placard **2** a large printed picture ◊ **post-free** *adv* without charge for postage ◊ **post-haste** *adv* with great speed ◊ **postie** *noun, informal* a postman or postwoman ▫ **postman, postwoman** *noun* someone who delivers letters ▫ **postmark** *noun* a date stamp put on a letter at a post office ▫ **postmaster, postmistress** *noun* an official in charge of a post office ▫ **post office** an office for receiving and sending off letters by post *etc*

post- *prefix* after

posterior *adj* situated behind, coming after ▫ *noun* the buttocks

posterity *noun* **1** all future generations **2** someone's descendants

postern *noun* a back door or gate to a castle *etc*

postgraduate *adj* of study *etc*: following on from a first university degree ▫ *noun* someone continuing to study after a first degree

posthumous *adj* **1** of a book: published after the author's death **2** of a child: born after the father's death

postilion or **postillion** *noun*, *old* a carriage driver who rides on one of the horses

postmortem *noun* an examination of a dead body to find out the cause of death

postpone *verb* put off to a future time, delay ▫ **postponement** *noun*

postscript *noun* an added remark at the end of a letter, after the sender's name

postulant *noun* someone applying to enter a religious order

postulate *verb* assume or take for granted (that)

posture *noun* **1** the manner in which someone holds themselves in standing or walking **2** a position, a pose

postwar *adj* relating to the time after a war

posy *noun* (*plural* **posies**) a small bunch of flowers

pot *noun* **1** a deep vessel used in cooking, as a container, or for growing plants **2** *slang* marijuana **3** (**pots**) *informal* a great deal: *pots of money* ▫ *verb* **1** plant in a pot **2** make articles of baked clay ▫ **pot belly** a protruding stomach ▫ **potboiler** *noun* a book with a sensational plot, written to sell ▫ **pothole** *noun* **1** a deep cave **2** a hole worn in a road surface ▫ **potholer** *noun* someone who explores caves ▫ **pot plant** a household plant kept in a pot ▫ **pot shot** a casual or random shot ▫ **potted** *adj* **1** of meat: pressed down and preserved in a jar **2** condensed and simplified: *potted history* ▫ **take pot-luck** take whatever is available or offered

pot *verb* » pot*s*, pott*ing*, pott*ed*

potash *noun* potassium carbonate, obtained from the ashes of wood

potassium *noun* a type of silvery-white metal

potato *noun* (*plural* **potatoes**) **1** a plant with round starchy roots which are eaten as a vegetable **2** the vegetable itself ▫ **couch potato** *see* **couch**

poteen *noun* illicit Irish whiskey

potent *adj* powerful, strong ▫ **potency** *noun*

potentate *noun* a powerful ruler

potential *adj* that may develop, possible □ *noun* the possibility of further development □ **potentiality** *noun* (*plural* **potentialities**) a possibility

potion *noun* a drink, often containing medicine or poison

potpourri *noun* **1** a scented mixture of dried petals *etc* **2** a mixture or medley

potter *noun* someone who makes articles of baked clay □ *verb* do small odd jobs, dawdle

pottery *noun* **1** articles made of baked clay **2** (*plural* **potteries**) a place where such things are made **3** the art of making them

potty[1] *adj, informal* mad, eccentric

potty[2] *noun, informal* a child's chamberpot

pouch *noun* (*plural* **pouches**) **1** a pocket or small bag **2** a bag-like fold on the front of a kangaroo, for carrying its young

pouffe *noun* a low, stuffed seat without back or arms

poultice *noun* a wet dressing spread on a bandage and put on inflamed skin □ *verb* put a poultice on

poultry *noun* farmyard fowls, *eg* hens, ducks, geese, turkeys □ **poulterer** *noun* someone who sells poultry and game

pounce *verb* (with **on**) seize, attack □ *noun* **1** a sudden attack **2** a bird's claw

pound *noun* **1** the standard unit of money in Britain, shown by the sign (£), equal to 100 new pence **2** a measure of weight, written lb, equal to 16 ounces (about $\frac{1}{2}$ kilogramme) **3** an enclosure for animals □ *verb* **1** beat into powder **2** beat heavily **3** walk or run with heavy steps

pour *verb* **1** flow in a stream: *the blood poured out* **2** make flow : *pour the tea* **3** rain heavily

⚠Do not confuse with: **pore**

pout *verb* push out the lips sulkily to show displeasure □ *noun* a sulky look

poverty *noun* **1** the state of being poor **2** lack, want: *poverty of ideas*

POW *abbrev* prisoner of war

powder *noun* **1** a substance made up of very fine particles **2** gunpowder **3** cosmetic facepowder □ *verb* **1** sprinkle or dab with powder **2** grind down to powder □ **powdered** *adj* **1** in fine particles **2** covered with powder □ **powdery** *adj* **1** covered with powder **2** like powder: *powdery snow*

power *noun* **1** strength, force **2** ability to do things **3** authority or legal right **4** a strong nation **5** someone in authority **6** the force used for driving machines: *electric power/ steam power* **7** *maths* the product obtained by multiplying a number by itself a given number of times (*eg* 2 x 2 x 2 or 2^3 is the third power of 2) □ **power-driven** or **powered** *adj* worked by electricity, not by hand □ **powerful** *adj* □ **powerless** *adj* without power or ability □ **power station** a building where electricity is produced

pow-wow *noun* **1** *hist* a Native

American gathering for debate **2** *informal* a conference, a debate

pp *abbrev* pages

PR *abbrev* **1** proportional representation **2** public relations

practicable *adj* able to be used or done

practical *adj* **1** preferring action to thought **2** efficient **3** learned by practice, rather than from books: *practical knowledge* □ **practical joke** a joke consisting of action, not words □ **practically** *adv* **1** in a practical way **2** in effect, in reality **3** almost: *practically empty*

practice *noun* **1** habit: *it is my practice to get up early* **2** the actual doing of something: *I always intend to get up early but in practice I stay in bed* **3** repeated performance to improve skill: *piano practice/ in practice for the race* **4** the business of a doctor, lawyer *etc*

⚠Do not confuse: **practice** and **practise**

practise or *US* **practice** *verb* **1** perform or exercise repeatedly to improve a skill: *he practises judo nightly* **2** make a habit of: *practise self-control* **3** follow (a profession): *practise dentistry* □ **practitioner** *noun* someone engaged in a profession: *a medical practitioner*

pragmatic or **pragmatical** *adj* relating to fact, rather than ideas or theories, practical □ **pragmatism** *noun* □ **pragmatist** *noun*

prairie *noun* a stretch of level grassland in N America

praise *verb* **1** speak highly of **2** glorify (God) by singing hymns *etc* □ *noun* an expression of approval □ **praiseworthy** *adj* deserving to be praised

pram *noun* a small wheeled carriage for a baby, pushed by hand (*short for* **perambulator**)

prance *verb* **1** strut or swagger about **2** dance about **3** of a horse: spring from the hind legs

prank *noun* a trick played for mischief

prat *noun, informal* an idiot

prate *verb* talk foolishly

prattle *verb* talk or chatter meaninglessly □ *noun* meaningless talk

prawn *noun* a type of shellfish like the shrimp

pray *verb* **1** ask earnestly, beg **2** speak to God in prayer □ **praying mantis** *see* **mantis**

⚠Do not confuse with: **prey**

prayer *noun* **1** an earnest request for something **2** a request, or thanks, given to God

pre- *prefix* before

preach *verb* **1** give a sermon **2** teach, speak in favour of: *preach caution* □ **preacher** *noun* a religious teacher

preamble *noun* something said as an introduction

prearrange *verb* arrange beforehand

precarious *adj* uncertain, risky, dangerous

precaution *noun* care taken

beforehand to avoid an accident *etc* □ **precautionary** *adj*

precede *verb* go before in time, rank or importance □ **precedence** *noun* the right to go before; priority □ **preceding** *adj* going before; previous

> ⚠Do not confuse with: **proceed**

precedent *noun* a past action which serves as an example or rule for the future

precentor *noun* someone who leads the singing in a church

precept *noun* a guiding rule, a commandment

precinct *noun* **1** an area enclosed by the boundary walls of a building **2** (**precincts**) the area closely surrounding any place **3** *US* an administrative district □ **shopping precinct** a shopping centre, often closed to traffic

precious *adj* **1** highly valued or valuable **2** over-fussy or precise

precipice *noun* a steep cliff

precipitate *verb* **1** throw head foremost **2** force into (hasty action *etc*) **3** hasten (death, illness *etc*) □ *adj* **1** headlong **2** hasty, rash □ *noun* sediment at the bottom of a liquid □ **precipitation** *noun* **1** great hurry **2** rainfall

precipitous *adj* very steep □ **precipitousness** *noun*

précis /*prehsee*/ *noun* (*plural* **précis**) a summary of a piece of writing

precise *adj* **1** definite **2** exact, accurate □ **precisely** *adv* □ **precision** *noun* **1** preciseness **2** exactness, accuracy

> ⚠Do not confuse with: **concise**

preclude *verb* prevent, make impossible □ **preclusion** *noun* □ **preclusive** *adj*

precocious *adj* of a child: unusually advanced or well-developed □ **precocity** *noun*

precognitive *adj* knowing beforehand, foretelling □ **precognition** *noun*

preconceive *verb* form (ideas *etc*) before having actual knowledge or experience □ **preconception** *noun* an idea formed without actual knowledge

precondition *noun* a condition that must be met before something can happen

precursor *noun* someone or thing which goes before, an early form of something: *the precursor of jazz*

predate *verb* happen before in time

predator *noun* a bird or animal that kills others for food □ **predatory** *adj* **1** of a predator **2** using other people for your own advantage

predecease *verb* die before (someone)

predecessor *noun* the previous holder of a job or office

predestine *verb* destine beforehand, preordain

predetermine *verb* settle beforehand

predicament *noun* an unfortunate or difficult situation

predicate *noun, grammar* something said about the subject of a sentence, *eg has green eyes* in the sentence *Anne has green eyes*

predict *verb* foretell, forecast □ **predictable** *adj* able to be foretold □ **prediction** *noun* an act of predicting; something predicted

predilection *noun* a preference, a liking for something

predispose *verb* **1** make (someone) in favour of something beforehand: *we were predisposed to believe her* **2** make liable (to): *predisposed to colds* □ **predisposition** *noun*

predominate *verb* **1** be the strongest or most numerous **2** have control (over) □ **predominance** *noun* □ **predominant** *adj* **1** ruling **2** most noticeable or outstanding □ **predominantly** *adv*

pre-eminent *adj* outstanding, excelling all others □ **pre-eminence** *noun* □ **pre-eminently** *adv*

pre-empt *verb* block or stop by making a first move □ **pre-emptive** *adj*

preen *verb* **1** of a bird: arrange its feathers **2** smarten your appearance in a conceited way □ **preen yourself** show obvious pride in your achievements

prefabricated *adj* made of parts made beforehand, ready to be fitted together

preface *noun* an introduction to a book *etc* □ *verb* precede or introduce (with)

prefect *noun* **1** the head of an administrative district in France *etc* **2** a senior pupil in some schools with certain powers □ **prefecture** *noun* an area controlled by a prefect

prefer *verb* **1** like better: *I prefer tea to coffee* **2** put forward (a claim or request) □ **preferable** *adj* more desirable □ **preference** *noun* **1** greater liking **2** something preferred: *what is your preference?* □ **preferential** *adj* giving preference □ **preferment** *noun* promotion

> **prefer** » prefer*s*, preferr*ing*, preferr*ed*

prefix *noun* (*plural* **prefixes**) a syllable or word at the beginning of a word which adds to its meaning, *eg dis-, un-, re-*, in *dis*like, *un*happy, *re*gain

pregnant *adj* **1** carrying a foetus in the womb **2** full of meaning: *pregnant pause* □ **pregnancy** *noun* (*plural* **pregnancies**) the state of being pregnant

prehensile *adj* able to grasp or hold: *prehensile tail*

prehistoric *adj* relating to the time before history was written down □ **prehistory** *noun*

prejudge *verb* decide (something) before hearing the facts of a case

prejudice *noun* **1** an unfair feeling for or against anything **2** an opinion formed without careful thought **3** harm, injury □ *verb* **1** fill with prejudice **2** do harm to, damage: *his late arrival prejudiced his chances of success* ▯ **prejudiced** *adj* showing prejudice ▯ **prejudicial** *adj* damaging, harmful

prelate *noun* a bishop or archbishop ▯ **prelacy** (*plural* **prelacies**) the office of a prelate

preliminary *adj* going before, preparatory: *preliminary investigation* ▯ *noun* (*plural* **preliminaries**) something that goes before

prelude *noun* **1** a piece of music played as an introduction to the main piece **2** a preceding event: *a prelude to a brilliant career*

premarital *adj* before marriage

premature *adj* coming, born *etc* before the right, proper or expected time

premeditate *verb* think out beforehand, plan: *premeditated murder* ▯ **premeditation** *noun*

premenstrual *adj* before menstruation

premier *adj* first, leading, foremost ▯ *noun* a prime minister

⚠Do not confuse: **premier** and **première**

première *noun* a first performance of a play, film *etc*

premise or **premiss** *noun* (*plural* **premises** or **premisses**) something assumed from which a conclusion is drawn

premises *noun plural* a building and its grounds

premium *noun* (*plural* **premiums**) **1** a reward **2** a payment on an insurance policy ▯ **at a premium** very desirable and therefore difficult to obtain

premonition *noun* a feeling that something is going to happen; a forewarning

prenatal *adj* before birth, or before giving birth

preoccupy *verb* completely engross the attention of (someone) ▯ **preoccupation** *noun* ▯ **preoccupied** *adj* deep in thought

preordain *verb* determine beforehand

prep *noun, informal* preparation ▯ **prep school** a preparatory school

prepaid *past form* of **prepay**

preparatory *adj* **1** acting as an introduction or first step **2** (with **to**) before, in preparation for ▯ **preparatory school** a private school educating children of primary-school age

prepare *verb* **1** make or get ready **2** train, equip ▯ **preparation** *noun* **1** an act of preparing **2** study for a lesson **3** something prepared for use, *eg* a medicine ▯ **prepared** *adj* **1** ready **2** willing

prepay *verb* pay beforehand ▯ **prepayment** *noun*

prepay » prepay*s*, prepay*ing*, prepaid

preponderance *noun* greater amount or number: *a preponderance of young people in the audience*

preposition *noun, grammar* a word placed before a noun or pronoun to show its relation to another word, *eg* '*through* the door', '*in* the town', 'written *by* me'

⚠Do not confuse with: **proposition**

prepossessing *adj* pleasant, making a good impression

preposterous *adj* very foolish, absurd

prequel *noun* a book *etc* which deals with events happening before an existing book

pre-Raphaelite *noun* one of a group of 19th-century British artists who painted in a naturalistic style

prerequisite *noun* something necessary before another thing can happen

prerogative *noun* a right enjoyed by someone because of rank or position

presage *verb* foretell, warn of

presbyter *noun* a minister or elder in a Presbyterian church

Presbyterian *adj* **1** of a church: managed by ministers and elders **2** belonging to such a church ◊ *noun* a member of a Presbyterian church

presbytery *noun* (*plural* **presbyteries**) **1** a body of presbyters **2** the house of a Roman Catholic priest

prescient *adj* having foresight ◊ **prescience** *noun*

prescribe *verb* **1** lay down as a rule **2** order the use of (a medicine) ◊ **prescriptive** *adj* laying down rules

⚠Do not confuse with: **proscribe**

prescription *noun* **1** a doctor's written instructions for preparing a medicine **2** something prescribed

⚠Do not confuse with: **proscription**

presence *noun* **1** the state of being present (*contrasted with*: **absence**) **2** someone's personal appearance, manner *etc* ◊ **in your presence** while you are present ◊ **presence of mind** calmness, ability to act sensibly in an emergency, difficulty *etc*

present[1] *adj* **1** here, in this place **2** happening or existing now: *present rates of pay/ the present situation* ◊ *noun* **1** the time now **2** *grammar* the tense describing events happening now, *eg* 'we *are* on holiday' ◊ **presently** *adv* soon

present[2] *noun* a gift ◊ *verb* **1** hand over (a gift) formally **2** offer, put forward **3** introduce (someone) to another ◊ **present yourself 1** introduce yourself **2** arrive

presentation *noun* **1** the giving of a present **2** something presented **3** a formal talk or demonstration **4** a showing of a play *etc*

presentiment *noun* a feeling that something bad is about to happen, a foreboding

preserve *verb* **1** keep safe from harm **2** keep in existence, maintain **3** treat (food) so that it will not go bad ◊ *noun* **1** a place where game animals, birds *etc* are protected **2** jam ◊ **preservation** *noun*

preservative *noun* a substance

added to food to prevent it from going bad

preside *verb* be in charge at a meeting *etc*

president *noun* **1** the leading member of a society *etc* **2** the head of a republic □ **presidency** *noun* (*plural* **presidencies**) the office of a president

press *verb* **1** push on, against or down **2** urge, force **3** iron (clothes *etc*) □ *noun* **1** a crowd **2** a printing machine **3** the news media, journalists □ **pressing** *adj* requiring immediate action, insistent

pressgang *noun, hist* a group of men employed to carry off people by force into the army or navy □ *verb* **1** *hist* carry off in a pressgang **2** force (someone) to do something: *pressganged into joining the committee*

pressure *noun* **1** force on or against a surface **2** strong persuasion, compulsion **3** stress, strain **4** urgency □ **pressure cooker** a pan in which food is cooked quickly by steam under pressure □ **pressure group** a group of people who try to influence the authorities on a particular issue □ **pressurize** *verb* **1** fit (an aeroplane *etc*) with a device that maintains normal air pressure **2** force (someone) to do something

prestidigitation *noun* conjuring, magic tricks □ **prestidigitator** *noun* a conjurer

prestige *noun* reputation, influence due to rank, success *etc* □ **prestigious** *adj* having or giving prestige

presume *verb* **1** take for granted, assume (that) **2** (with **on**) take advantage of (someone's kindness *etc*) □ **presumably** *adv* probably □ **presumption** *noun* **1** a strong likelihood **2** impertinent behaviour □ **presumptuous** *adj* unsuitably bold □ **presumptuousness** *noun*

presuppose *verb* take for granted

pretend *verb* **1** make believe, fantasize **2** make a false claim: *pretending to be ill* □ **pretence** *noun* **1** the act of pretending **2** a false claim □ **pretender** *noun* someone who lays claim to something (*esp* to the crown)

pretension *noun* **1** a claim (whether true or not) **2** self-importance

pretentious *adj* self-important; showy, ostentatious □ **pretentiousness** *noun*

preterite *noun, grammar* the past tense in verbs

preternatural *adj* beyond what is natural, abnormal

pretext *noun* an excuse

pretty *adj* pleasing or attractive to see, listen to *etc* □ *adv* fairly, quite: *pretty good* □ **prettiness** *noun*

pretzel *noun* a crisp salted biscuit, twisted in shape

prevail *verb* **1** (with **against** or **over**) gain control over **2** win, succeed **3** (with **on**) persuade: *she prevailed on me to stay* **4** be most usual or common □ **prevailing** *adj* **1** controlling **2** most common: *the prevailing mood* □ **prevalent** *adj* common, widespread □ **prevalence** *noun*

prevaricate *verb* avoid telling the truth □ **prevarication** *noun* □ **prevaricator** *noun*

prevent *verb* hinder, stop happening □ *noun* the act of preventing □ **preventive** *adj* of medicine: helping to prevent illness

preview *noun* a view of a performance, exhibition *etc* before its official opening

previous *adj* going before in time; former □ **previously** *adv*

prey *noun* **1** an animal killed by others for food **2** a victim □ *verb* (with **on**) **1** seize and eat: *preying on smaller birds* **2** stalk and harass

⚠Do not confuse with: **pray**

price *noun* **1** the money for which something is bought or sold, the cost **2** something that must be given up in order to gain something: *the price of fame* □ **priceless** *adj* **1** very valuable **2** *informal* very funny

prick *verb* **1** pierce slightly **2** give a sharp pain to **3** stick up (the ears) □ *noun* **1** a pricking feeling on the skin **2** *slang* the penis **3** *slang* an idiot

prickle *noun* a sharp point on a plant or animal □ *verb* **1** be prickly **2** feel prickly □ **prickly** *adj* **1** full of prickles **2** stinging, pricking

pride *noun* **1** too great an opinion of yourself **2** pleasure in having done something well **3** dignity **4** a group of lions □ **pride yourself on** feel or show pride in

priest *noun* **1** a member of the clergy in the Roman Catholic and Anglican churches **2** an official in a non-Christian religion □ **priestess** *noun* a female, non-Christian priest □ **priesthood** *noun* those who are priests

prig *noun* a smug, self-righteous person □ **priggish** *adj* □ **priggishly** *adv*

prim *adj* unnecessarily formal and correct

prima ballerina the leading female dancer of a ballet company

prima donna **1** a leading female opera singer **2** a woman who is over-sensitive and temperamental

primaeval *another spelling* of **primeval**

prima facie /praimə *feh*shi/ *adj* of evidence: enough to bring a case to court

primary *adj* **1** first **2** most important, chief □ **primary colours** those from which all others can be made *eg* red, blue and yellow □ **primary school** a school for the early stages of education

primate *noun* **1** a member of the highest order of mammals including humans, monkeys and apes **2** an archbishop

prime *adj* **1** first in time or importance **2** best quality, excellent □ *noun* the time of greatest health and strength: *the prime of life* □ *verb* **1** prepare the surface of for painting: *prime a canvas* **2** supply with detailed information: *she was well primed before the meeting* □ **prime minister** the head of a government

◆ **primer** *noun* **1** a simple introductory book on a subject **2** a substance for preparing a surface for painting

primeval or **primaeval** *adj* **1** relating to the beginning of the world **2** primitive, instinctive

primitive *adj* **1** belonging to very early times **2** old-fashioned **3** not skilfully made, rough

primogeniture *noun* **1** the fact of being born first **2** the rights of a first-born child

primrose *noun* a pale-yellow spring flower common in woods and hedges

Primus stove *trademark* a portable oil cooking stove

prince *noun* **1** the son of a king or queen **2** a ruler of certain states ◆ **princely** *adj* splendid, impressive: *a princely reward*

princess *noun* (*plural* **princesses**) the daughter of a king or queen

principal *adj* most important, chief ◆ *noun* **1** the head of a school or university **2** a leading part in a play *etc* **3** money in a bank on which interest is paid ◆ **principality** (*plural* **principalities**) a state ruled by a prince ◆ **principally** *adv* chiefly, mostly

⚠Do not confuse: **principal** and **principle**

principle *noun* **1** a general truth or law **2** the theory on which the working of a machine is based **3** (**principles**) someone's personal rules of behaviour, sense of right and wrong *etc*

print *verb* **1** mark letters on paper with type **2** write in capital letters **3** publish in printed form **4** stamp patterns on (cloth *etc*) **5** make a finished photograph ◆ *noun* **1** a mark made by pressure: *footprint* **2** printed lettering **3** a photograph made from a negative **4** a printed reproduction of a painting *etc* **5** cloth printed with a design ◆ **printout** *noun* the printed information produced by a computer ◆ **in print** of a book: published and available to buy

printer *noun* **1** someone who prints books, newspapers *etc* **2** a machine that prints, attached to a computer system

prior[1] *adj* **1** earlier **2** previous (to)

prior[2] *noun* the head of a priory ◆ **prioress** *noun* the female head of a priory ◆ **priory** *noun* (*plural* **priories**) a building where a community of monks or nuns live

priority *noun* (*plural* **priorities**) **1** first position **2** the right to be first: *ambulances must have priority in traffic* **3** something that must be done first: *our priority is to get him into hospital*

prise *verb* force open or off with a lever: *prised off the lid*

prism *noun* a glass tube with triangular ends that breaks light into different colours

prison *noun* **1** a building for holding criminals **2** a place where someone is confined against their will ◆ **prisoner** *noun* someone held under arrest or locked up ◆ **prisoner of war** someone captured by the enemy forces during war

pristine *adj* in the original or unspoilt state

privacy *noun* freedom from observation; secrecy

private *adj* **1** relating to an individual, not to the general public; personal **2** not open to the public **3** secret, not generally known □ *noun* the lowest rank of ordinary soldier (not an officer) □ **private eye** *informal* a detective □ **privately** *adv* □ **private parts** *euphem* the external sexual organs

privation *noun* **1** want, poverty, hardship **2** taking away, loss

privatize *verb* transfer from state to private ownership, denationalize

privet *noun* a type of shrub used for hedges

privilege *noun* a right available to one person or to only a few people □ **privileged** *adj* having privileges

privy *adj*: **privy council** an appointed group of advisers to a king or queen □ **privy to** knowing about (something secret)

prize *noun* **1** a reward **2** something won in a competition **3** something captured **4** something highly valued □ *adj* very fine, worthy of a prize □ *verb* value highly □ **prize fight** a boxing match fought for money

pro *short* for **professional**

pro- *prefix* **1** before, forward, front **2** in favour of: *pro-devolution* □ **pros and cons** the arguments for and against anything

probable *adj* **1** likely to happen **2** likely to be true □ **probability** *noun* (*plural* **probabilities**) **1** likelihood **2** something likely to happen □ **probably** *adv* very likely

probation *noun* **1** a trial period in a new job *etc* **2** a system of releasing prisoners on condition that they commit no more offences and report regularly to the authorities □ **probationer** *noun* someone who is training to be a member of a profession

probe *noun* **1** a long, thin instrument used to examine a wound **2** a thorough investigation **3** a spacecraft for exploring space □ *verb* **1** examine very carefully **2** investigate thoroughly to find out information

probity *noun* honesty, goodness of character

problem *noun* a question to be solved; a matter which is difficult to deal with □ **problematic** or **problematical** *adj* doubtful, uncertain

proboscis *noun* (*plural* **proboscises**) **1** an animal's nose, *esp* an elephant trunk **2** an insect's mouth

procedure *noun* **1** method of doing business **2** a course of action

proceed *verb* **1** go on with, continue **2** begin (to do something) **3** take legal action (against) □ **proceeds** *noun plural* profit made from a sale *etc*

> ⚠Do not confuse with: **precede**

proceeding *noun* **1** a step forward **2** (**proceedings**) a record of the meetings of a society *etc* **3** a law action

process *noun* (*plural* **processes**) **1** a series of operations in manufacturing goods **2** a series of events producing change or development **3** a law-court case ▫ **in the process of** in the course of

procession *noun* a line of people or vehicles moving forward in order

proclaim *verb* announce publicly, declare openly ▫ **proclamation** *noun* an official announcement made to the public

procrastinate *verb* put things off, delay doing something till a later time ▫ **procrastination** *noun*

procure *verb* obtain; to bring about ▫ **procurator-fiscal** *noun* the law officer of a district in Scotland

prod *verb* poke; urge on

prod » prod*s*, prodd*ing*, prodd*ed*

prodigal *adj* spending money recklessly, wasteful ▫ **prodigality** *noun*

prodigy (*plural* **prodigies**) **1** a wonder **2** someone astonishingly clever: *child prodigy* ▫ **prodigious** *adj* **1** strange, astonishing **2** enormous

produce *verb* **1** bring into being **2** bring about, cause **3** prepare (a play *etc*) for the stage **4** make, manufacture ▫ *noun* food grown or produced on a farm or in a garden ▫ **producer** *noun* someone who produces a play, film *etc*

product *noun* **1** something produced **2** a result **3** *maths* the number that results from the multiplication of two or more numbers ▫ **production** *noun* ▫ **productive** *adj* fruitful, producing results ▫ **productivity** *noun* the rate of work done

Prof *abbrev* Professor

profane *adj* **1** not sacred **2** treating holy things without respect ▫ **profanity** *noun* (*plural* **profanities**) **1** swearing **2** lack of respect for sacred things

profess *verb* **1** declare (a belief *etc*) openly **2** pretend, claim: *he professes to be an expert on Scott* ▫ **professed** *adj* **1** declared **2** pretended

profession *noun* **1** an occupation requiring special training, *eg* that of a doctor, lawyer, teacher *etc* **2** an open declaration

professional *adj* **1** of a profession **2** earning a living from a game or an art (*contrasted with*: **amateur**) **3** skilful, competent ▫ *noun* **1** someone who works in a profession **2** someone who earns money from a game or art ▫ **professionalism** *noun* ▫ **professionally** *adv*

professor *noun* **1** a teacher of the highest rank in a university **2** *US* a university teacher

proffer *verb* offer

proficiency *noun* skill ▫ **proficient** *adj* skilled, expert

profile *noun* **1** an outline **2** a side view of a face, head *etc* **3** a short description of someone's life, achievements *etc*

profit *noun* **1** gain, benefit **2** money got by selling an article for a higher price than was paid for it ▫ *verb* gain (from), benefit ▫ **profitable** *adj* bringing profit or gain

profiteer *noun* someone who makes large profits unfairly ▫ *verb* make large profits

profligate *adj* **1** living an immoral life **2** very extravagant ▫ *noun* a profligate person ▫ **profligacy** *noun*

pro forma or **pro-forma** *adj* of an invoice: showing the market price of specified goods, with goods being paid for before dispatch

profound *adj* **1** very deep **2** deeply felt **3** showing great knowledge or understanding: *a profound comment* ▫ **profundity** *noun*

profuse *adj* abundant, lavish, extravagant ▫ **profusion** *noun*

progenitor *noun* an ancestor ▫ **progeny** *noun* children

progesterone *noun* a female sex hormone that maintains pregnancy

prognosis *noun* a prediction of the course of a disease

prognosticate *verb* foretell ▫ **prognostication** *noun*

program *noun* a set of instructions telling a computer to carry out certain actions ▫ *verb* **1** give instructions to **2** prepare instructions to be carried out by a computer

> **program** *verb* » program*s*, programm*ing*, programm*ed*

programme or *US* **program** *noun* **1** a booklet with details of an entertainment, ceremony *etc* **2** a scheme, a plan

progress *noun* **1** advance, forward movement **2** improvement ▫ *verb* **1** go forward **2** improve ▫ **progression** *noun* ▫ **progressive** *adj* **1** going forward **2** favouring reforms

prohibit *verb* **1** forbid **2** prevent ▫ **prohibition** *noun* the forbidding by law of making and selling alcoholic drinks ▫ **prohibitive** *adj* **1** prohibiting **2** of price: too expensive, discouraging

project *noun* **1** a plan, a scheme **2** a task **3** a piece of study or research ▫ *verb* **1** throw out or up **2** jut out **3** cast (an image, a light *etc*) onto a surface **4** plan, propose ▫ **projectile** *noun* a missile ▫ **projection** *noun* an act of projecting; something projected; something which juts out ▫ **projector** *noun* a machine for projecting cinema pictures on a screen ▫ **projectionist** *noun* someone who operates a film projector

prolapse *verb* of a body organ: fall out of place

prole *noun, informal* a proletarian

proletariat *noun* the ordinary working people ▫ **proletarian** *noun* a member of the proletariat

proliferate *verb* grow or increase rapidly ▫ **prolific** *adj* producing a lot, fruitful

prolix *adj* using too many words, tiresomely long ▫ **prolixity** *noun*

prologue *noun* a preface or introduction to a play *etc*

prolong *verb* make longer

prom *informal, short for* **1** promenade **2** promenade concert

promenade *noun* **1** a level roadway or walk, *esp* by the seaside **2** a walk, a stroll ▫ *verb* walk for pleasure ▢ **promenade concert** a concert at which a large part of the audience stands instead of being seated

prominent *adj* **1** standing out, easily seen **2** famous, distinguished ▢ **prominence** *noun*

promiscuous *adj* **1** having many sexual relationships **2** mixed in kind **3** not making distinctions between people or things ▢ **promiscuity** *noun*

promise *verb* **1** give your word (to do or not do something) **2** show signs for the future: *the weather promises to improve* ▢ *noun* **1** a statement of something promised **2** a sign of something to come **3** a sign of future success: *his painting shows great promise* ▢ **promising** *adj* showing signs of being successful

promontory *noun* (*plural* **promontories**) a headland jutting out into the sea

promote *verb* **1** raise to a higher rank **2** help onwards, encourage **3** advertise, encourage the sales of ▢ **promotion** *noun* ▢ **promotional** *adj*

prompt *adj* **1** quick, immediate **2** punctual ▢ *verb* **1** move to action **2** supply words to an actor who has forgotten their lines ▢ **prompter** *noun* ▢ **promptly** *adv* ▢ **promptness** *noun*

promulgate *verb* make widely known ▢ **promulgation** *noun*

prone *adj* **1** lying face downward **2** inclined (to): *prone to laziness*

prong *noun* the spike of a fork ▢ **pronged** *adj* having prongs

pronoun *noun* a word used instead of a noun, *eg* I, you, who

pronounce *verb* **1** speak (words, sounds) **2** announce (an opinion), declare ▢ **pronounced** *adj* noticeable, marked ▢ **pronouncement** *noun* a statement, an announcement ▢ **pronunciation** *noun* the way a word is said

pronto *adv, informal* quickly

proof *noun* **1** evidence that makes something clear beyond doubt **2** the standard strength of whisky *etc* **3** a copy of a printed sheet for correction before publication ▢ *adj* able to keep out or withstand: *proof against attack/ waterproof* ▢ **proofread** *verb* read printed page proofs of a text ▢ **proofreader** *noun*

prop *noun* **1** a support **2** *short for* propeller **3** *short for* stage property ▢ *verb* hold up, support

prop *verb* » prop*s*, propp*ing*, propp*ed*

propaganda *noun* **1** the spreading of ideas to influence public opinion **2** material used for this, *eg* posters, leaflets ▢ **propagandist** *noun* someone who spreads propaganda

propagate *verb* **1** spread **2** produce seedlings or young ▢ **propagator** *noun*

propane *noun* a gas used as fuel

propel *verb* drive forward ▢ **propellant** *noun* **1** an explosive for firing a rocket **2** the gas in an aerosol spray ▢ **propeller** *noun* a shaft with revolving blades which drives forward a ship, aircraft *etc* ▢

propulsion *noun* an act of driving forward

propel » propel*s*, propell*ing*, propell*ed*

propensity *noun* (*plural* **propensities**) a natural inclination: *a propensity for bumping into things*

proper *adj* **1** right, correct: *the proper way to do it* **2** full, thorough: *a proper search* **3** prim, well-behaved ▫ **properly** *adv* **1** in the right way **2** thoroughly ▫ **proper noun** or **proper name** *grammar* a name for a particular person, place or thing, *eg Shakespeare, the Parthenon* (*contrasted with*: **common noun**)

property *noun* (*plural* **properties**) **1** land or buildings owned **2** a quality **3** (**properties**) the furniture *etc* required by actors in a play

prophecy *noun* (*plural* **prophecies**) **1** foretelling the future **2** something prophesied

⚠Do not confuse: **prophecy** and **prophesy**

prophesy *verb* foretell the future, predict

prophesy » prophesi*es*, prophesy*ing*, prophesi*ed*

prophet *noun* **1** someone who claims to foretell events **2** someone who tells what they believe to be the will of God

prophylactic *noun* **1** something that helps to prevent disease **2** a condom

propinquity *noun* nearness

propitiate *verb* calm the anger of ▫ **propitious** *adj* favourable: *propitious circumstances*

proponent *noun* someone in favour of a thing, an advocate

proportion *noun* **1** a part of a total amount: *a large proportion of income is taxed* **2** relation in size, number *etc* compared with something else: *the proportion of girls to boys is small* ▫ **proportional** or **proportionate** *adj* in proportion ▫ **proportional representation** a voting system in which parties are represented in proportion to their voting strength ▫ **in** or **out of proportion** appropriate or inappropriate in size or degree when compared with other things

propose *verb* **1** put forward for consideration, suggest **2** intend **3** make an offer of marriage (to) ▫ **proposal** *noun* **1** an act of proposing **2** anything proposed **3** an offer of marriage

proposition *noun* **1** a proposal, a suggestion **2** a statement **3** a situation that must be dealt with: *a tough proposition*

⚠Do not confuse with: **preposition**

propound *verb* state, put forward for consideration

proprietor, proprietress *noun* an owner, *esp* of a hotel

propriety *noun* (*plural* **proprieties**) **1** fitness, suitability **2** correct behaviour, decency

propulsion *see* **propel**

pro rata *adv* in proportion

prorogue *verb* discontinue meetings of (parliament *etc*) for a period □ **prorogation** *noun*

prosaic *adj* dull, not interesting □ **prosaically** *adv*

proscenium /proh*seen*iəm/ *noun* the front part of a stage

prosciutto *noun* cured, uncooked Italian ham

proscribe *verb* ban, prohibit □ **proscription** *noun* □ **proscriptive** *adj*

> ⚠Do not confuse with: **prescribe**

prose *noun* **1** writing which is not in verse **2** ordinary written or spoken language

prosecute *verb* **1** bring a lawcourt action against **2** carry on (studies, an investigation *etc*)

> ⚠Do not confuse with: **persecute**

prosecution *noun* **1** an act of prosecuting **2** *law* those bringing the case in a trial (*contrasted with*: **defence**)

proselyte *noun* a convert □ **proselytize** *verb* make converts

prosody *noun* study of the rhythms and construction of poetry

prospect *noun* **1** a view, a scene **2** a future outlook or expectation: *the prospect of a free weekend/ a job with good prospects* □ *verb* search for gold or other minerals □ **prospective** *adj* soon to be, likely to be: *the prospective election* □ **prospector** *noun* someone who prospects for minerals

prospectus *noun* (*plural* **prospectuses**) a booklet giving information about a school, organization *etc*

prosper *verb* get on well, succeed □ **prosperity** *noun* success, good fortune □ **prosperous** *adj* successful, wealthy

prostate *noun* a gland in a man's bladder which releases a fluid used in semen

prosthesis *noun* (*plural* **prostheses**) an artificial replacement part for the body □ **prosthetics** *noun sing* the study and use of artificial body parts

prostitute *noun* someone who offers sexual intercourse for payment

prostrate *adj* **1** lying flat face downwards **2** worn out, exhausted □ *verb* **1** lie on the ground as a sign of respect: *prostrated themselves before the emperor* **2** exhaust, tire out completely □ **prostrated** *adj* worn out by grief, tiredness *etc* □ **prostration** *noun*

protagonist *noun* a chief character in a play *etc*

protean *adj* changing shape often and easily

protect *verb* shield from danger, keep safe □ **protective** *adj* giving protection; intended to protect □ **protector** *noun* a guardian, a defender □ **protectorate** *noun* a country which is partly governed and defended by another country

protection *noun* **1** the act of protecting **2** safety, shelter ▯ **protectionism** *noun* ▯ **protectionist** *noun*

protégé, **protégée** *noun* a pupil or employee who is taught or helped in their career by someone important or powerful

protein *noun* a substance present in milk, eggs, meat *etc* which is a necessary part of a human or animal diet

pro tem *adj & adv* temporary, to be used in the meantime

protest *verb* **1** object strongly **2** declare solemnly: *protesting his innocence* ▯ *noun* a strong objection ▯ **protestation** *noun* **1** a solemn declaration **2** a protest

Protestant *noun* a member of one of the Christian churches that broke away from the Roman Catholic Church at the time of the Reformation

protocol *noun* correct procedure

proton *noun* a particle with a positive electrical charge, forming part of the nucleus of an atom (*compare with*: **electron**)

protoplasm *noun* a semi-liquid substance which is the chief material of all living cells

prototype *noun* the original model from which something is copied

protozoan *noun* a tiny creature made up of a single cell

protract *verb* lengthen in time ▯ **protractor** *noun* an instrument for drawing and measuring angles on paper

protrude *verb* stick out, thrust forward ▯ **protrusion** *noun*

protuberance *noun* a swelling, a bulge ▯ **protuberant** *adj*

proud *adj* **1** thinking too highly of yourself, conceited **2** feeling pleased at an achievement *etc* **3** dignified, self-respecting: *too proud to accept the money*

prove *verb* **1** show to be true or correct **2** try out, test **3** turn out (to be): *his prediction proved correct*

provenance *noun* source, origin

provender *noun* food, *esp* for horses and cattle

proverb *noun* a well-known wise saying, *eg* 'nothing ventured, nothing gained' ▯ **proverbial** *adj* well-known, widely spoken of

provide *verb* supply ▯ **providing that** on condition that

providence *noun* **1** foresight; thrift **2** (**Providence**) God ▯ **provident** *adj* thinking of the future; thrifty ▯ **providential** *adj* fortunate, coming as if by divine help

province *noun* **1** a division of a country **2** the extent of someone's duties or knowledge **3** (**provinces**) all parts of a country outside the capital ▯ **provincial** *adj* **1** of a province or provinces **2** narrow-minded, parochial

provision *noun* **1** an agreed arrangement **2** a rule or condition **3** (**provisions**) a supply of food ▯ **provisional** *adj* used for the time being; temporary

proviso *noun* (*plural* **provisos**) a condition laid down beforehand

provoke *verb* **1** cause, result in **2** rouse to anger or action: *don't let him provoke you* □ **provocation** *noun* □ **provocative** *adj* **1** tending to rouse anger **2** likely to arouse sexual interest □ **provoking** *adj* annoying

provost *noun* the chief magistrate of a burgh in Scotland

prow *noun* the front part of a ship

prowess *noun* skill, ability

prowl *verb* go about stealthily

proximity *noun* nearness

proxy *noun* (*plural* **proxies**) someone who acts or votes on behalf of another

prude an over-modest, priggish person □ **prudery** *noun* □ **prudish** *adj*

prudent *adj* wise and cautious □ **prudently** *adv* □ **prudence** *noun*

prune[1] *verb* **1** trim (a tree) by cutting off unneeded twigs **2** shorten, reduce

prune[2] *noun* a dried plum

prurient *adj* excessively concerned with sexual matters □ **prurience** *noun*

pry *verb* look closely into things that are not your business □ **prying** *adj*

pry » pries, pry*ing*, pri*ed*

PS *abbrev* postscript

psalm *noun* a sacred song □ **psalmist** *noun* a writer of psalms

psalter *noun* a book of psalms

psaltery *noun* a medieval stringed instrument played by plucking

p's and q's correct social manners

psephologist *noun* someone who studies elections and voting trends

Coined in the 1950s, based on Greek *psephos*, a pebble used in the ancient Greek system of casting votes

pseud- or **pseudo-** /*soo*doh/ *prefix* false

pseudo /*soo*doh/ or **pseud** /sood/ *adj informal* false, fake, pretended: *His Spanish accent is pseudo* □ **pseud** *noun, informal* a fraud

pseudonym *noun* a false name used by an author

psoriasis *noun* a skin disease causing red scaly patches

psychedelic *adj* bright and multicoloured

psychiatry *noun* the treatment of mental illness □ **psychiatric** *adj* □ **psychiatrist** *noun* someone who treats mental illness

psychic /*sai*kik/ or **psychical** *adj* **1** relating to the mind **2** able to read other people's minds, or tell the future

psycho- /*sai*koh/ *prefix* relating to the mind

psychoanalysis *noun* a method of treating mental illness by discussing with the patient its possible causes in their past □ **psychoanalyse** *verb* treat by psychoanalysis □ **psychoanalyst** *noun*

psychology *noun* the science which studies the human mind □ **psychological** *adj* of psychology or the mind □ **psychologist** *noun*

psychosis *noun* a mental illness **psychotic** *adj*

psychosomatic *adj* of an illness: having a psychological cause

psychotherapy *noun* treatment of mental illness by psychoanalysis *etc* □ **psychotherapist** *noun*

PT *abbrev* physical training

pt *abbrev* **1** part **2** pint

PTA *abbrev* parent teacher association

ptarmigan /*tar*məgən/ *noun* a mountain-dwelling bird of the grouse family, which turns white in winter

Pte *abbrev* Private (military)

pterodactyl /terə*dak*til/ *noun* an extinct flying reptile

PTO *abbrev* please turn over

pub *short for* public house

puberty *noun* the time during youth when the body becomes sexually mature

pubic *adj* of the lowest part of the abdomen: *pubic hair*

public *adj* **1** relating to or shared by the people of a community or nation in general: *public opinion/ public library* **2** generally or widely known: *a public figure* □ *noun* people in general □ **publican** *noun* the keeper of an inn or public house □ **publication** *noun* **1** the act of making news *etc* public **2** the act of publishing a book, newspaper *etc* **3** a published book, magazine *etc* □ **public house** a building where alcoholic drinks are sold and consumed □ **publicist** *noun* an advertising agent □ **publicity** *noun* advertising; bringing to public notice or attention □ **publicize** *verb* make public, advertise □ **public relations 1** the relations between a business *etc* and the public **2** a department of a business *etc* dealing with this □ **in public** in front of or among other people □ **public address system** a system of microphones, amplifiers and loudspeakers used to enable an audience to hear voices, music *etc*

publish *verb* **1** make generally known **2** prepare and put out (a book *etc*) for sale □ **publisher** *noun* someone who publishes books

puce *adj* of a brownish-purple colour

pucker *verb* wrinkle □ *noun* a wrinkle, a fold

pudding *noun* **1** the sweet course of a meal **2** a sweet dish made with eggs, flour, milk *etc* **3** a type of sausage: *mealy pudding*

puddle *noun* a small, often muddy, pool

pudendum *noun* (*plural* **pudenda**) the female external sex organs

puerile *adj* childish, silly □ **puerility** *noun*

puerperal *adj, formal* relating to childbirth

puff *verb* **1** blow out in small gusts **2** breathe heavily, *eg* after running **3** blow up, inflate **4** swell (up or out) □ *noun* **1** a short, sudden gust of wind, breath *etc* **2** a powder puff **3** a piece of advertising □ **puffball** *noun* a ball-shaped mushroom containing a powdery mass of spores □ **puff pastry** a light, flaky kind of pastry ▯ **puffy** *adj* **1** swollen, flabby **2** breathing heavily

puffin *noun* a type of sea bird, with a short, thick beak

pug *noun* a breed of small dog with a snub nose

pugilist *noun* a boxer ▯ **pugilism** *noun* boxing

pugnacious *adj* quarrelsome, fond of fighting ▯ **pugnacity** *noun*

puissant *adj, formal* powerful

puke *noun* & *verb, slang* vomit

pulchritude *noun, formal* beauty ▯ **pulchritudinous** *adj*

pull *adj* **1** move or try to move (something) towards yourself by force **2** drag, tug **3** stretch, strain: *pull a muscle* **4** tear: *pull to pieces* ▯ *noun* **1** the act of pulling **2** a pulling force, *eg* of a magnet **3** a handle for pulling **4** *informal* advantage, influence ▯ **pull yourself together** regain self-control or self-possession ▯ **pull through** get safely to the end of a difficult or dangerous experience ▯ **pull up** stop, halt

pullet *noun* a young hen

pulley *noun* (*plural* **pulleys**) a grooved wheel fitted with a cord and set in a block, used for lifting weights *etc*

Pullman *noun* luxurious or superior seating on a train, in a cinema *etc*

> Named after George M *Pullman*, an American who made the first luxury sleeping car for railways in the 19th century

pullover *noun* a knitted garment for the top half of the body, a jersey

pulmonary *adj* relating to the lungs

pulp *noun* **1** the soft fleshy part of a fruit **2** a soft mass of wood *etc* which is made into paper **3** any soft mass ▯ *verb* reduce to pulp

pulpit *noun* an enclosed platform in a church for the minister or priest

pulque *noun* a Mexican fermented alcoholic drink

pulsar *noun* a distant source of regular radio signals in space, possibly a star

pulsate *verb* beat, throb

pulse *noun* the beating or throbbing of the heart and blood vessels as blood flows through them ▯ *verb* throb, pulsate

pulses *noun plural* beans, peas, lentils and other edible seeds

pulverize *verb* make or crush into powder

puma *noun* an American wild animal like a large cat

pumice *noun* or **pumice stone** a piece of light solidified lava used for smoothing skin and for rubbing away stains

pummel *verb* beat with the fists

> **pummel** » pummel*s*, pummel*ling*, pummell*ed*

pump *noun* **1** a machine used for making water rise to the surface **2** a machine for drawing out or forcing in air, gas *etc*: *bicycle pump*

3 a kind of thin- or soft-soled shoe for dancing, gymnastics *etc* ◊ *verb* **1** raise or force with a pump **2** *informal* draw out information from by clever questioning

pumpernickel *noun* a coarse dark rye-bread

pumpkin *noun* a large roundish, thick-skinned, yellow fruit, with stringy edible flesh

pun *noun* a play upon words which sound similar but have different meanings, *eg* 'two *pears* make a *pair*' ◊ *verb* make a pun

> **pun** *verb* » pun*s*, pun*ning*, pun*ned*

punch[1] *verb* **1** hit with the fist **2** make a hole in with a tool: *punch a ticket* ◊ *noun* (*plural* **punches**) **1** a blow with the fist **2** a tool for punching holes ◊ **punchy** *adj* having a powerful effect, striking ◊ **punch-drunk** *adj* dizzy from being hit ◊ **punch line** the words that give the main point to a joke

punch[2] *noun* a drink made of spirits or wine, water, sugar *etc* ◊ **punch-bowl** *noun* a bowl for mixing punch

punctilious *adj* paying attention to details, *esp* in behaviour; fastidious

punctual *adj* **1** on time, not late **2** strict in keeping the time of appointments ◊ **punctuality** *noun*

punctuate *verb* **1** divide up sentences by commas, full stops *etc* **2** interrupt at intervals: *the silence was punctuated by occasional coughing* ◊ **punctuation** *noun* the use of punctuation marks ◊ **punctuation marks** the symbols used in punctuating sentences, *eg* full stop, comma, colon, question mark *etc*

puncture *noun* **1** an act of pricking or piercing **2** a small hole made with a sharp point **3** a hole in a tyre

pundit *noun* an expert

pungent *adj* **1** sharp-tasting or sharp-smelling **2** of a remark: strongly sarcastic

punish *verb* **1** make (someone) suffer for a fault or crime **2** inflict suffering on **3** treat roughly or harshly ◊ **punishable** *adj* likely to bring punishment ◊ **punishment** *noun* pain or constraints inflicted for a fault or crime ◊ **punitive** *adj* inflicting punishment or suffering

punnet *noun* a small basket for holding fruit

punt *noun* a flat-bottomed boat with square ends ◊ *verb* move (a punt) by pushing a pole against the bottom of a river

punter *noun* **1** a professional gambler **2** a customer, a client **3** an ordinary person

puny *adj* little and weak ◊ **puniness** *noun*

pup *noun* **1** a young dog (also **puppy**) **2** the young of certain other animals, *eg* a seal ◊ **puppy fat** temporary fat in childhood or adolescence ◊ **puppy love** immature love when very young

pupa *noun* (*plural* **pupae**) the stage in the growth of an insect in which it changes from a larva to its mature form, *eg* from a caterpillar into a butterfly ▯ **pupate** *verb* become a pupa

pupil *noun* **1** someone who is being taught by a teacher **2** the round opening in the middle of the eye through which light passes

puppet *noun* **1** a doll which is moved by strings or wires **2** a doll that fits over the hand and is moved by the fingers **3** someone who acts exactly as they are told to

puppy *see* **pup**

purblind *adj, old* nearly blind, dim-sighted

purchase *verb* buy ▯ *noun* **1** the act of buying **2** something which is bought **3** the power to lift by using a lever *etc* **4** firm grip or hold ▯ **purchaser** *noun* someone who buys

purdah *noun, hist* the seclusion of Hindu or Islamic women from strangers, behind a screen or under a veil

pure *adj* **1** clean, spotless **2** free from dust, dirt *etc* **3** not mixed with other substances **4** free from faults or sin, innocent **5** utter, absolute, nothing but: *pure nonsense* ▯ **purely** *adv* **1** in a pure way **2** wholly, entirely: *purely on merit* **3** merely, only: *purely for the sake of appearance* ▯ **purist** *noun* someone who insists on correctness ▯ **purity** *noun* the state of being pure

purée *noun* food made into a pulp by being put through a sieve or liquidizing machine ▯ *verb* make into a purée, pulp

purgative *noun* a medicine which clears waste matter out of the body ▯ *adj*

purgatory *noun* **1** in the Roman Catholic Church, a place where souls are made pure before entering heaven **2** a state of suffering for a time

purge *verb* **1** make clean, purify **2** clear (something) of anything unwanted: *purged the party of those who disagreed with her*

purify *verb* make pure ▯ **purification** *noun*

purify » purifi*es*, purify*ing*, purifi*ed*

puritan *noun* **1** someone of strict, often narrow-minded, morals **2** (**Puritan**) *hist* one of a group believing in strict simplicity in worship and daily life ▯ **puritanical** *adj* ▯ **puritanism** *noun*

purity *see* **pure**

purl *verb* knit in stitches made with the wool in front of the work

purlieus *noun plural* **1** someone's usual haunts **2** outskirts, borders

purloin *verb* steal

purple *noun* a dark colour formed by the mixture of blue and red

purport *noun* meaning ▯ *verb* **1** mean **2** seem, pretend: *he purports to be a film expert*

purpose *noun* **1** aim, intention **2** use, function (of a tool *etc*) ▯ *verb* intend ▯ **purposely** *adv* intentionally ▯ **on purpose** intentionally ▯ **to the purpose** to the point

purr *noun* the low, murmuring sound made by a cat when pleased ▯ *verb* of a cat: make this sound

purse *noun* **1** a small bag for carrying money **2** *US* a handbag □ *verb* close (the lips) tightly □ **purser** *noun* the officer who looks after a ship's money □ **purse strings** the control of a source of money

pursue *verb* **1** follow after (in order to overtake or capture), chase **2** be engaged in, carry on (studies, an enquiry *etc*) **3** follow (a route, path *etc*) □ **pursuer** *noun* someone who pursues □ **pursuit** *noun* **1** the act of pursuing **2** an occupation or hobby

purulent *adj* full of, or like, pus

purvey *verb* supply (food *etc*) as a business □ **purveyor** *noun*

pus *noun* a thick yellowish liquid produced from infected wounds

push *verb* **1** press hard against **2** thrust (something) away with force, shove **3** urge on **4** make a big effort □ *noun* **1** a thrust **2** effort **3** *informal* energy and determination □ **push-chair** *noun* a folding chair on wheels for a young child □ **pushy** *adj* aggressively assertive

pusillanimous *adj* cowardly □ **pusillanimity** *noun*

pussy *noun, informal* a cat, a kitten □ **pussy-foot** *verb* act timidly or non-committally □ **pussy-willow** *noun* an American willow tree with silky catkins

pustule *noun* a small pimple containing pus

put *verb* **1** place, lay, set: *put the book on the table* **2** bring to a certain position or state: *put the light on/ put it out of your mind* **3** express: *put the question more clearly* □ **put about 1** change course at sea **2** spread (news) □ **put by** set aside, save up □ **put down** defeat □ **put in for** make a claim for, apply for □ **put off 1** delay **2** turn (someone) away from their plan or intention □ **put out 1** extinguish (a fire, light *etc*) **2** annoy, embarrass □ **put up 1** build **2** propose, suggest (a plan, candidate *etc*) **3** let (someone) stay in your house *etc* **4** stay as a guest in someone's house □ **put-up job** *informal* a dishonest scheme □ **put up with** bear patiently, tolerate

put » put*s*, putt*ing*, put

putative *adj* supposed, commonly accepted □ **putatively** *adv*

putrefy *verb* go bad, rot □ **putrefaction** *noun* □ **putrid** *adj* rotten; stinking □ **putrescence** *noun* the state of going bad □ **putrescent** *adj* going bad

putrefy » putrefi*es*, putrefy*ing*, putrefi*ed*

putt *verb, golf* send a ball gently forward □ **putter** *noun* a golf club used for this

putty *noun* a cement made from ground chalk, used in putting glass in windows *etc*

puzzle *verb* **1** present with a difficult problem or situation *etc* **2** be difficult (for someone) to understand: *her moods puzzled him* **3** (with **out**) consider long and carefully in order to solve (a problem) □ *noun* **1** a difficulty which needs a lot of thought **2** a toy or riddle to test knowledge or skill: *crossword puzzle/ jigsaw puzzle*

PVC *abbrev* polyvinyl chloride

pygmy or **pigmy** (*plural* **pygmies** or **pigmies**) *noun* one of a race of very small human beings

pyjamas or **pajamas** *noun plural* a sleeping suit consisting of trousers and a jacket

pylon *noun* **1** a high, steel tower supporting electric power cables **2** a guiding mark at an airfield

pyramid *noun* **1** a solid shape with flat sides which come to a point at the top **2** *hist* a building of this shape used as a tomb in ancient Egypt

pyre *noun* a pile of wood on which a dead body is burned

Pyrex *noun, trademark* a type of glassware for cooking that will withstand heat

pyromaniac *noun* someone who gets pleasure from starting fires ◊ **pyromania** *noun*

pyrotechnics *noun plural* a display of fireworks

Pyrrhic victory a victory gained at so great a cost that it is equal to a defeat

> After the costly defeat of the Romans by *Pyrrhus*, king of Epirus, in 280 BC

python *noun* a large, non-poisonous snake which crushes its victims

Q

QC *abbrev* Queen's Counsel

qed *abbrev quod erat demonstrandum,* which was to be demonstrated (from Latin)

qi /chee/ *noun* in Chinese medicine, the life-force in each person

qt[1] *abbrev* quart

qt[2] *noun*: **on the qt** *informal* on the quiet, secretly

qua *adv* in the capacity of, thought of as

quack *noun* **1** the cry of a duck **2** someone who falsely claims to have medical knowledge or training ▫ *verb* make the noise of a duck

quad *short for* **1** quadruplet **2** quadrangle

quadrangle *noun* **1** *maths* a figure with four equal sides and angles **2** a four-sided courtyard surrounded by buildings in a school, college *etc* ▫ **quadrangular** *adj*

quadrant *noun* **1** one quarter of the circumference or area of a circle **2** an instrument used in astronomy, navigation *etc* for measuring heights

quadraphonic *adj* of recorded sound: relayed through a minimum of four speakers

quadrennial *adj* happening every four years

quadri- *prefix* four

quadrilateral *noun* a four-sided figure or area ▫ *adj* four-sided

quadrille *noun* a dance for four couples arranged to form a square

quadriplegia *noun* paralysis of both arms and both legs ▫ **quadriplegic** *noun* someone suffering from quadriplegia

quadruped *noun* a four-footed animal

quadruple *adj* **1** four times as much or many **2** made up of four parts ▫ *verb* make or become four times greater: *quadrupled the price* ▫ **quadruplet** *noun* one of four children born to the same mother at one birth

quaff *verb* drink up eagerly

quagmire *noun* wet, boggy ground

quaich /kwehxh/ *noun, Scot* a shallow ornamental cup with two handles

quail *verb* shrink back in fear ▫ *noun* a type of small bird like a partridge

quaint *adj* pleasantly odd, *esp* because of being old-fashioned

quake *verb* shake, tremble with fear ▫ *noun, informal* an earthquake

> **quake** *verb* » *quakes*, quak*ing*, quake*d*

Quaker *noun* a member of a religious group opposed to violence and war, founded in the 17th century

Originally a nickname given to the group because their founder, George Fox, told them to *quake* at the word of God

qualify *verb* **1** be suitable for a job or position **2** pass a test **3** lessen the force of (a statement) by adding or changing words **qualification** *noun* **1** a qualifying statement **2** a skill that makes someone suitable for a job **qualified** *adj* having the necessary qualifications for a job

quality *noun* (*plural* **qualities**) **1** an outstanding feature of someone or thing: *kindness is a quality admired by all* **2** degree of worth: *cloth of poor quality* **qualitative** *adj* relating to quality rather than quantity

qualm *noun* doubt about whether something is right

quandary *noun* (*plural* **quandaries**) **1** a state of uncertainty **2** a situation in which it is difficult to decide what to do

quango *noun* (*plural* **quangos**) an official body, funded and appointed by government, that supervises some national activity *etc*

quantify *verb* state the quantity of **quantifiable** *adj* **quantification** *noun*

quantify » quantifi*es*, quantify*ing*, quantifi*ed*

quantity *noun* (*plural* **quantities**) **1** amount: *a large quantity of paper* **2** a symbol which represents an amount: *x is the unknown quantity* **quantitative** *adj* relating to quantity, not quality

quantum leap a huge, dramatic jump

quarantine *noun* the isolation of people or animals who might be carrying an infectious disease *verb* put in quarantine

quark *noun*, *physics* a sub-atomic particle

A word invented by James Joyce in *Finnegans Wake* (1939)

quarrel *noun* an angry disagreement or argument *verb* **1** disagree violently or argue angrily (with) **2** find fault (with) **quarrelsome** *adj* fond of quarrelling, inclined to quarrel

quarrel *verb* » quarrel*s*, quarrell*ing*, quarrell*ed*

quarry *verb* (*plural* **quarries**) **1** a pit from which stone is taken for building **2** a hunted animal **3** someone or something eagerly looked for *verb* **1** dig (stone *etc*) from a quarry

quarry *verb* » quarri*es*, quarry*ing*, quarri*ed*

quart *noun* a measure of liquids, 1.136 litre (2 pints)

quarter *noun* **1** one of four equal parts of something **2** a fourth part of a year, three months **3** direction: *no help came from any quarter* **4** a district **5** mercy shown to an enemy: *no quarter was given by either side* **6** (**quarters**) lodgings, accommodation *verb* **1** divide into four equal parts **2** accommodate **quarter-deck** *noun* the upper deck of a ship between the stern and the mast nearest it ▯ **quarter-final** *noun* a match in a competition immediately before a semi-final ▯ **quartermaster** *noun* an officer who looks after soldiers' accommodation and supplies

quarterly *adj* happening every three months ▯ *adv* every three months ▯ *noun* (*plural* **quarterlies**) a magazine *etc* published every three months

quartet *noun* **1** a group of four players or singers **2** a piece of music written for such a group

quarto *noun* (*plural* **quartos**) a book folded to give four leaves to each sheet of paper

quartz *noun* a hard substance often in crystal form, found in rocks

quasar *noun* a star-like object (not really a star) which gives out light and radar waves

quash *verb* **1** crush, put down (*eg* a rebellion) **2** wipe out, annul (*eg* a judge's decision)

quasi- *prefix* to some extent, but not completely: *quasi-historical*

quatrain *noun* a poetic stanza of four lines

quaver *verb* **1** shake, tremble **2** speak in a shaking voice ▯ *noun* **1** a trembling of the voice **2** *music* a note (♪) equal to half a crotchet in length

quay /kee/ *noun* a solid landing place for loading and unloading boats

queasy *adj* **1** feeling nauseous **2** easily shocked or disgusted ▯ **queasiness** *noun*

queen *noun* **1** a female monarch **2** the wife of a king **3** the most powerful piece in chess **4** a high value playing-card with a picture of a queen **5** an egg-laying female bee, ant or wasp ▯ **queenly** *adj* of or like a queen ▯ **queen bee 1** an egg-laying female bee **2** a woman who is the centre of attention ▯ **queen mother** the mother of the reigning king or queen who was once herself queen

Queensberry rules standards of proper behaviour in a fight

queer *adj* **1** odd, strange **2** *informal* (sometimes *derog*) homosexual ▯ *noun*, *informal* (sometimes *derog*) a homosexual

quell *verb* **1** crush (a rebellion *etc*) **2** remove (fears, suspicions *etc*)

quench *verb* **1** drink and so satisfy (thirst) **2** put out (*eg* a fire)

quenelle *noun* a poached dumpling of chicken, fish *etc*

querulous *adj* complaining

query *noun* (*plural* **queries**) **1** a question **2** a question mark (?) ▯ *verb* question (*eg* a statement)

> **query** *verb* » queri*es*, query*ing*, queri*ed*

quest *noun* a search

question *noun* **1** something requiring an answer, *eg* 'where do you live?' **2** a subject, matter *etc*: *the energy question/ a question of ability* **3** a matter for dispute or doubt: *there's no question of him leaving* ▯ *verb* **1** ask questions of (someone)

2 express doubt about □ **questionable** *adj* doubtful □ **question mark** a symbol (?) put after a question in writing □ **questionnaire** *noun* a written list of questions to be answered by several people to provide information for a survey □ **out of the question** not even to be considered, unthinkable

queue *noun* a line of people waiting, *eg* for a bus □ *verb* stand in, or form, a queue

quibble *verb* avoid an important part of an argument by quarrelling over details □ *noun* a petty argument or complaint

quiche /keesh/ *noun* an open pastry case filled with beaten eggs, cheese *etc* and baked

quick *adj* **1** done or happening in a short time **2** acting without delay, fast-moving: *a quick brain* □ *noun* a tender area of skin under the nails □ *adv, informal* quickly □ **quicken** *verb* speed up, become or make faster □ **quicklime** *noun* lime which has not been mixed with water □ **quickly** *adv* without delay, rapidly □ **quicksand** *noun* sand that sucks in anyone who stands on it □ **quicksilver** *noun* mercury □ **quickstep** *noun* a ballroom dance like a fast foxtrot □ **quick-tempered** *adj* easily made angry □ **the quick** *old* the living

quid *noun, slang* a pound (£1)

quiddity *noun* **1** the essence or nature of something **2** a quibble

quid pro quo 1 a returned favour **2** a retaliation

quiescent *adj* not active □ **quiescence** *noun*

quiet *adj* **1** making little or no noise **2** calm: *a quiet life* □ *noun* **1** the state of being quiet **2** lack of noise, peace □ *verb* make or become quiet □ **quieten** *verb* make or become quiet □ **quietly** *adv* □ **quietness** *noun*

⚠Do not confuse with: **quite**

quiff *noun* a tuft of hair brushed up and back from the forehead

quill *noun* **1** a large feather of a goose or other bird made into a pen **2** one of the sharp spines of a porcupine

quilt *noun* a bedcover filled with down, feathers *etc* □ **quilted** *adj* made of two layers of material with padding between them

quin *short for* **quintuplet**

quince *noun* a pear-like fruit with a sharp taste, used to make jams *etc*

quincunx *noun* an arrangement of five things, one at each corner and one in the centre of a square

quinine *noun* a bitter drug taken from the bark of a S American tree, used to treat malaria

quinoa *noun* a S American plant whose seeds are cooked like rice

quinquennial *adj* **1** happening once every five years **2** lasting five years

quinsy *noun* acute inflammation of the tonsils with pus forming round them

quintessence *noun* **1** the most

important part of anything **2** the purest part or form of something ▫ **quintessential** *adj* ▫ **quintessentially** *adv*

> Literally 'fifth essence', sought after by medieval alchemists as the highest essence or ether

quintet *noun* **1** a group of five players or singers **2** a piece of music written for such a group

quintuplet *noun* one of five children born to a mother at the same time

quip *noun* a witty remark or reply ▫ *verb* make a witty remark

> **quip** *verb* » quip*s*, quipp*ing*, quipp*ed*

quipu *noun* an ancient Peruvian memory-aid consisting of knotted coloured cords

quire *noun* a set of 24 sheets of paper

> ⚠Do not confuse with: **choir**

quirk *noun* **1** an odd feature of someone's behaviour **2** a trick, a sudden turn: *quirk of fate*

quirky *adj* full of sudden twists; unpredictable, inconsistent ▫ **quirkily** *adv* ▫ **quirkiness** *noun*

quirt *noun* a South American braided riding-whip

quisling *noun* someone who collaborates with an enemy, *esp* a puppet ruler

> After Vidkun *Quisling*, head of the Norwegian fascist party during the German occupation

quit *verb* **1** give up, stop: *I'm going to quit smoking* **2** *informal* leave, resign from (a job) ▫ **be quits** be even with each other

> **quit** » quit*s*, quitt*ing*, quit or quitt*ed*

quite *adv* **1** completely, entirely: *quite empty* **2** fairly, moderately: *quite good*

> ⚠Do not confuse with: **quiet**

quiver[1] *noun* a tremble, a shake ▫ *verb* tremble, shake

quiver[2] *noun* a carrying case for arrows

qui vive: **on the qui vive** on the alert, ready for action

quixotic *adj* having noble but foolish and unrealistic aims ▫ **quixotically** *adv*

> After Don *Quixote*, the knight in Cervantes's 16th-century Spanish romance

quiz *verb* question ▫ *noun* (*plural* **quizzes**) a competition to test knowledge ▫ **quizzical** *adj* of a look: as if asking a question, *esp* mockingly

> **quiz** *verb* » quizz*es*, quizz*ing*, quizz*ed*

quoits *noun sing* a game in which heavy flat rings (**quoits**) are thrown onto small rods

quorum *noun* the least number of people who must be present at a meeting before any business can be done

From Latin phrase *quorum vos .. esse volumus* 'of whom we wish that you be (one, two etc)', used in legal commissions

quota *noun* a part or share to be given or received by each member of a group

quotation *noun* **1** the act of repeating something said or written **2** the words repeated **3** a price stated ◇ **quotation marks** marks used in writing to show that someone's words are being repeated exactly, *eg* 'he said "I'm going out"'

quote *verb* **1** repeat the words of (someone) exactly as said or written **2** state (a price for something)

quoth *verb*, *old* said

quotidian *adj, formal* daily

quotient *noun, maths* the result obtained by dividing one number by another, *eg* 4 is the quotient when 12 is divided by 3

qv *abbrev* which see (from Latin *quod vide*)

qwerty *noun* (*plural* **qwertys**) a standard arrangement of keys on a typewriter keyboard, with the top line of letters beginning Q,W,E,R,T,Y

R

R *abbrev* King or Queen (from Latin *rex* or *regina*)

RA *abbrev* Royal Academy

rabbi *noun* (*plural* **rabbis**) a Jewish priest or teacher of the law □ **rabbinical** *adj*

rabbit *noun* a small, burrowing, long-eared animal

rabble *noun* a disorderly, noisy crowd

rabid *adj* **1** of a dog: suffering from rabies **2** violently enthusiastic or extreme: *a rabid nationalist*

rabies *noun* (*also called*: **hydrophobia**) a disease transmitted by the bite of an infected animal, causing fear of water and madness

raccoon or **racoon** *noun* a small furry animal of N America

race[1] *noun* **1** a group of people with the same ancestors and physical characteristics **2** descent: *of noble race*

race[2] *noun* a competition to find the fastest person, animal, vehicle *etc* □ *verb* **1** run fast **2** take part in a race □ **racecourse** or **racetrack** *noun* a course over which races are run □ **racehorse** *noun* a horse bred and used for racing □ **racy** *adj* of a story: full of action, and often involving sexual exploits

raceme *noun* a plant stalk with flowers growing along it

racial *adj* of or according to race □ **racism** or **racialism** *noun* **1** the belief that some races of people are superior to others **2** prejudice on the grounds of race □ **racist** or **racialist** *noun* someone who believes in, or practises, racialism □ *adj* involving racism

rack *noun* **1** a framework for holding letters, plates, coats *etc* **2** *hist* an instrument for torturing victims by stretching their joints **3** a bar with teeth which fits into and moves a toothed wheel □ **rack and ruin** a state of neglect and decay □ **rack your brains** think hard about something

racket[1] or **racquet** *noun* **1** a bat made up of a strong frame strung with gut or nylon for playing tennis, badminton *etc* **2** (**rackets**) a form of tennis played against a wall

racket[2] *noun* **1** a great noise, a din **2** *informal* a dishonest way of making a profit □ **racketeer** *noun* someone who makes money dishonestly

raconteur *noun* someone who tells stories, *esp* in an entertaining way

racoon *another spelling* of **raccoon**

racquet *another spelling* of **racket**

RADA *abbrev* Royal Academy of Dramatic Art

radar *noun* a method of detecting solid objects using radio waves which bounce back off the object and form a picture of it on a screen

radiant *adj* **1** sending out rays of light, heat *etc* **2** showing joy and happiness: *a radiant smile* □ **radiance** *noun* brightness, splendour

radiate *verb* **1** send out rays of light, heat *etc* **2** spread or send out from a centre

radiation *noun* **1** the giving off of rays of light, heat *etc* or of those from radioactive substances **2** radioactivity

radiator *noun* **1** a device (*esp* a series of connected hot-water pipes) which sends out heat **2** the part of a motor-car which cools the engine

radical *adj* **1** thorough: *a radical change* **2** basic, deep-seated: *radical differences* **3** advocating dramatic changes in the method of government □ *noun* someone who has radical political views

radicchio *noun* a purple-leaved variety of chicory

radio *noun* (*plural* **radios**) a device for sending and receiving signals by means of electromagnetic waves □ *verb* send a message to (someone) in this way

> **radio** *verb* » radio*s*, radio*ing*, radio*ed*

radioactive *adj* giving off rays which are often dangerous but which can be used in medicine □ **radioactivity** *noun*

radiography *noun* photography of the interior of the body by X-rays □ **radiographer** *noun*

radiology *noun* **1** the study of radioactive substances and radiation **2** the branch of medicine involving the use of X-rays and radium □ **radiologist** *noun*

radiotherapy *noun* the treatment of certain diseases by X-rays or radioactive substances □ **radiotherapist** *noun*

radish *noun* (*plural* **radishes**) a plant with a sharp-tasting root, eaten raw in salads

radium *noun* a radioactive metal used in radiotherapy

radius *noun* (*plural* **radii**) **1** a straight line from the centre to the circumference of a circle **2** an area within a certain distance from a central point

RAF *abbrev* Royal Air Force

raffia *noun* strips of fibre from the leaves of a palm tree, used in weaving mats *etc*

raffish *adj* flashy, dashing

raffle *noun* a way of raising money by selling numbered tickets, one or more of which wins a prize □ *verb* give as a prize in a raffle

raft *noun* a number of logs *etc* fastened together and used as a boat

rafter *noun* one of the sloping beams supporting a roof

rag *noun* **1** a torn or worn piece of cloth **2** (**rags**) worn-out, shabby clothes □ *adj* made of rags: *a rag doll* □ *verb* tease, play tricks on □ **rag-bag** *noun* a random or confused collection □ **rag-doll** *noun* a floppy doll made of scrap material □ **ragged** *adj* **1** in torn, shabby clothes **2** torn and tattered □ **rag-rolling** *noun* a technique of decorating by rolling a folded cloth over a freshly painted surface □ **rag-trade** *noun* the fashion or clothes industry

> **rag** *verb* » rag*s*, ragg*ing*, ragg*ed*

ragamuffin *noun* a ragged, dirty child

rage *noun* great anger, fury □ *verb* **1** be violently angry **2** of a storm, battle *etc*: be violent □ **all the rage** very fashionable or popular

ragga *noun* a style of rap music

raglan *noun* a cardigan or coat with the sleeves in one piece with the shoulders

> Named after Lord *Raglan*, British commander in the Crimean war

ragout /ragoo/ *noun* a highly seasoned meat-and-vegetable stew

ragtime *noun* a style of jazz music with highly syncopated melody

ragwort *noun* a large coarse weed with a yellow flower

raid *noun* **1** a short, sudden attack **2** an unexpected visit by the police to catch a criminal, recover stolen goods *etc* □ *verb* make a raid on □ **raider** *noun*

rail *noun* **1** a bar of metal used in fences **2** (**rails**) strips of steel which form the track on which trains run **3** the railway: *I came here by rail* □ *verb* (with **against** or **at**) speak angrily or bitterly □ **railing** *noun* a fence or barrier of rails □ **railway** or *US* **railroad** *noun* a track laid with steel rails on which trains run

raiment *noun*, *old* clothing

rain *noun* **1** water falling from the clouds in drops **2** a great number of things falling □ *verb* pour or fall in drops: *It's raining today* □ **rainbow** *noun* **1** the brilliant coloured bow or arch sometimes to be seen in the sky opposite the sun when rain is falling **2** a member of the most junior branch of the Guides □ **raincheck** *noun*, *US* an arrangement to keep an appointment *etc* at a later, postponed date □ **raincoat** *noun* a waterproof coat to keep out the rain □ **rainfall** *noun* the amount of rain that falls in a certain time □ **rain-forest** *noun* a tropical forest with very heavy rainfall □ **rainy** *adj* **1** full of rain: *rainy skies* **2** showery, wet: *a rainy day*

raise *verb* **1** lift up: *raise the flag* **2** make higher: *raise the price* **3** bring up (a subject) for consideration **4** bring up (a child, family *etc*) **5** breed or grow (*eg* pigs, crops) **6** collect, get together (a sum of money)

> ⚠Do not confuse with: **raze**

raisin *noun* a dried grape

raison d'être reason for existing

Raj *noun*, *hist* the time of British rule in India, 1858–1947

rajah *noun*, *hist* an Indian prince

rake[1] *noun* a tool, like a large comb with a long handle, for smoothing earth, gathering hay *etc* □ *verb* **1** draw a rake over **2** scrape (together) **3** aim gunfire at (*eg* a ship) from one end to the other

rake[2] *noun, old* someone who lives an immoral life ▫ **rakish** *adj* at a slanting, jaunty angle

raku *noun* Japanese lead-glazed pottery fired at a low temperature

rally *verb* **1** gather again: *rally troops* **2** come together for a joint action or effort: *the club's supporters rallied to save it* **3** recover from an illness ▫ *noun* (*plural* **rallies**) **1** a gathering **2** a political mass meeting **3** an improvement in health after an illness **4** *tennis* a long series of shots before a point is won or lost **5** a competition to test driving skills over an unknown route ▫ **rallying** *noun* long-distance motor-racing over public roads

> **rally** *verb* » rall*ies*, rally*ing*, rall*ied*

RAM *abbrev, comput* random access memory

ram *noun* **1** a male sheep **2** something heavy, *esp* as part of a machine, for ramming ▫ *verb* **1** press or push down hard **2** of a ship, car *etc*: run into and cause damage to ▫ **ram-raid** *noun* a raid by smashing into a shop window with a stolen car

> **ram** *verb* » ram*s*, ramm*ing*, ramm*ed*

Ramadan *noun* **1** the ninth month of the Islamic calendar, a period of fasting by day **2** the fast itself

ramble *verb* **1** walk about for pleasure, *esp* in the countryside **2** speak in an aimless or confused way ▫ *noun* a country walk for pleasure ▫ **rambler** *noun* **1** someone who rambles **2** a climbing rose or other plant

rambunctious *adj* boisterous, exuberant

rambutan *noun* a SE Asian fruit with a thick red shell and edible translucent flesh

ramekin *noun* **1** a baked mixture of cheese and eggs **2** a baking dish for a single portion

ramification *noun* **1** a branch or part of a subject, plot *etc* **2** a consequence, usually indirect and one of several

ramp *noun* a sloping surface (*eg* of a road) ▫ **ramping** *noun* the pushing up of prices (*esp* of shares) illegally or dishonestly

rampage *verb* rush about angrily or violently ▫ **on the rampage** rampaging

rampant *adj* **1** widespread and uncontrolled **2** *heraldry* standing on the left hind leg: *lion rampant*

rampart *noun* a mound or wall built as a defence

ramrod *noun* **1** a rod for pushing the charge down a gun barrel **2** someone strict or inflexible in their views

ramshackle *adj* badly made, falling to pieces

ran *past form* of **run**

ranch *noun* (*plural* **ranches**) a large farm in North America for rearing cattle or horses

rancid *adj* of butter: smelling or tasting stale

rancour *noun* ill-will, hatred □ **rancorous** *adj*

rand *noun* the standard unit of South African money

R and B *abbrev* rhythm and blues

R and D *abbrev* research and development

random *adj* done without any aim or plan; chance: *a random sample* □ **at random** without any plan or purpose □ **random access memory** a computer memory in which data can be directly located

randy *adj* lustful

range *noun* **1** a line or row: *a range of mountains* **2** extent, number: *a wide range of goods* **3** a piece of ground with targets for shooting or archery practice **4** the distance which an object can be thrown, or across which a sound can be heard **5** the distance between the top and bottom notes of a singing voice **6** a large kitchen stove with a flat top □ *verb* **1** set in a row or in order **2** wander (over) **3** stretch, extend □ **ranger** *noun* a keeper who looks after a forest or park □ **Ranger Guide** an older member of the Guide movement

rank *noun* **1** a row or line (*eg* of soldiers) **2** class, order: *the upper ranks of society/ the rank of captain* **3** (**ranks**) private soldiers, not officers □ *verb* **1** place in order of importance, merit *etc* **2** have a place in an order: *apes rank above dogs in intelligence* □ *adj* **1** of a plant: growing too plentifully **2** having a strong, unpleasant taste or smell **3** absolute: *rank nonsense* □ **rank and file 1** soldiers of the rank of private **2** ordinary people, the majority

rankle *verb* cause lasting annoyance, bitterness *etc*

ransack *verb* search thoroughly; plunder

ransom *noun* the price paid for the freeing of a captive □ *verb* pay money to free (a captive)

rant *verb* talk foolishly and angrily for a long time

rap[1] *noun* **1** a sharp blow or knock **2** *slang* a criminal charge □ *verb* **1** (often with **on**) strike with a quick, sharp blow **2** (with **out**) speak sharply

> **rap** *verb* » rap*s*, rapp*ing*, rapp*ed*

rap[2] *noun* **1** *informal* an informal talk or discussion **2** a style of music accompanied by a rhythmic monologue

rapacious *adj* greedy, eager to seize as much as possible

rape[1] *verb* have sexual intercourse with (someone) against their will, usually by force □ *noun* **1** the act of raping **2** the act of seizing and carrying off by force □ **rapist** *noun* someone who commits rape

rape[2] *noun* a type of plant like the turnip whose seeds give oil

rapid *adj* quick, fast: *a rapid rise to fame* □ **rapidity** *noun* swiftness □ **rapidly** *adv* □ **rapids** *noun plural* a part in a river where the current flows swiftly

rapier *noun* a type of light sword with a narrow blade

rapport /ra*pawr*/ *noun* a good relationship, sympathy

rapprochement *noun* a drawing together; a renewal of contact

rapt *adj* having the mind fully occupied, engrossed: *rapt attention*

rapture *noun* great delight □ **rapturous** *adj*

rare *adj* **1** seldom found, uncommon **2** of meat: lightly cooked

> ⚠Do not confuse with: **unique**

rarefy or **rarify** *verb* make thin or less dense

> **rarefy** or **rarify** » rarefi*es* or rarifi*es*, rarefy*ing* or rarify*ing*, rarefi*ed* or rarifi*ed*

raring *adj*: **raring to go** very keen to go, start *etc*

rarity *noun* (*plural* **rarities**) **1** something uncommon **2** uncommonness

rascal *noun* a naughty or wicked person

rash *adj* acting, or done, without thought □ *noun* redness or outbreak of spots on the skin □ **rashness** *noun* the state of being rash

rasher *noun* a thin slice (of bacon or ham)

rasp *noun* **1** a coarse file **2** a rough, grating sound □ *verb* **1** rub with a file **2** make a rough, grating noise **3** say in a rough voice □ **rasping** *adj* of a sound: rough and unpleasant

raspberry *noun* **1** a type of red berry similar to a blackberry **2** the bush which bears this fruit

rat *noun* a gnawing animal, larger than a mouse □ *verb* hunt or kill rats □ **rat-race** *noun* a fierce, unending competition for success or wealth □ **ratty** *adj* irritable □ **rat on** inform against

> **rat** *verb* » rat*s*, ratt*ing*, ratt*ed*

ratatouille /rat*ə*twee/ or /rat*ə*tooi/ *noun* a Mediterranean vegetable stew

ratchet *noun* a toothed wheel, *eg* in a watch

rate *noun* **1** the frequency with which something happens or is done: *a high rate of road accidents* **2** speed: *speak at a tremendous rate* **3** level of cost, price *etc*: *paid at a higher rate* **4** (**rates**) the sum of money to be paid by the owner of a shop *etc* to pay for local public services □ *verb* **1** work out the value of for taxation *etc* **2** value: *I don't rate his work very highly* □ **rateable value** a value of a shop *etc* used to work out the rates to be paid on it

rather *adv* **1** somewhat, fairly: *It's rather cold today* **2** more willingly: *I'd rather talk about it now than later* **3** more correctly speaking: *He agreed, or rather he didn't say no*

ratify *verb* approve officially and formally: *ratified the treaty* □ **ratification** *noun*

> **ratify** » ratifi*es*, ratify*ing*, ratifi*ed*

rating *noun* a sailor below the rank of an officer

ratio *noun* (*plural* **ratios**) the proportion of one thing to another: *a ratio of two parts flour to one of sugar*

ratiocination *noun* reasoning

ration *noun* **1** a measured amount of food given out at intervals **2** an allowance ▫ *verb* **1** deal out (*eg* food) in measured amounts **2** allow only a certain amount to (someone)

rational *adj* **1** able to reason **2** sensible; based on reason: *rational arguments* ▫ **rationality** *noun* ▫ **rationally** *adv*

rationalize *verb* think up a good reason for (an action or feeling) so as not to feel guilty about it ▫ **rationalization** *noun*

rattle *verb* **1** give out short, sharp, repeated sounds: *the coins rattled in the tin* **2** fluster or irritate (someone) ▫ *noun* **1** a sharp noise, quickly repeated **2** a toy or instrument which makes such a sound ▫ **rattler** *noun* a rattlesnake ▫ **rattle off** go through (a list of names *etc*) quickly

rattlesnake *noun* a poisonous snake with bony rings on its tail which rattle when shaken

ratty *see* **rat**

raucous *adj* hoarse, harsh: *a raucous voice*

raunchy *adj* sexually suggestive, lewd

ravage *verb* cause destruction or damage to; plunder ▫ *noun plural* damaging effects: *the ravages of time*

rave *verb* **1** talk wildly, as if mad **2** *informal* talk very enthusiastically (about) ▫ *noun* a large party held in a warehouse *etc* with electronic music ▫ **raver** *noun* someone who attends a rave party ▫ **raving** *adj* mad, crazy

raven *noun* a type of large black bird of the crow family ▫ *adj* of hair: black and glossy

ravenous *adj* very hungry

ravine *noun* a deep, narrow valley between hills

ravioli *noun plural* little pasta cases with savoury fillings

ravish *verb* **1** plunder **2** rape **3** delight, enrapture ▫ **ravishing** *adj* filling with delight

raw *adj* **1** not cooked **2** not prepared or refined, in its natural state: *raw cotton/ raw text* **3** of weather: cold **4** sore ▫ **a raw deal** unjust treatment

ray *noun* **1** a line of light, heat *etc* **2** a small degree or amount: *a ray of hope* **3** one of several lines going outwards from a centre **4** a kind of flat-bodied fish

rayon *noun* a type of artificial silk

raze *verb* destroy, knock flat (a town, house *etc*)

⚠Do not confuse with: **raise**

razor *noun* a sharp-edged instrument for shaving ▫ **razorbill** *noun* a type of seabird of the auk family ▫ **razorfish** *noun* a type of long narrow shellfish

razzmatazz *noun* showiness, glamorous or extravagant show

RC *abbrev* Roman Catholic

re *prep* concerning, about

re- *prefix* **1** again, once more: *recreate* **2** back: *reclaim*

reach *verb* **1** arrive at: *reach the summit/ your message never reached* *me* **2** stretch out (the hand) so as to touch: *I couldn't reach the top shelf* **3** extend ▯ *noun* **1** a distance that can be travelled easily: *within reach of home* **2** the distance someone can stretch their arm **3** a straight part of a stream or river between bends

react *verb* **1** act or behave in response to something done or said **2** undergo a chemical change: *metals react with sulphuric acid* ▯ **reaction** *noun* **1** behaviour as a result of action **2** a chemical change **3** a movement against a situation or belief: *a reaction against Victorian morality* ▯ **reactionary** *adj* favouring a return to old ways, laws *etc* ▯ *noun* (*plural* **reactionaries**) someone who holds reactionary views

read *verb* **1** look at and understand, or say aloud written or printed words **2** study a subject in a university or college: *reading law* ▯ **readable** *adj* quite interesting ▯ **read-out** *noun* **1** data from a computer; output **2** data from a radio transmitter ▯ **read only memory** *comput* a memory device that can only be read, not written to

read » read*s*, read*ing*, read

reader *noun* **1** someone who reads books *etc* **2** someone who reads manuscripts for a publisher **3** a senior university lecturer **4** a reading book for children

ready *adj* **1** prepared: *packed and ready to go* **2** willing: *always ready to help* **3** quick: *too ready to find fault* **4** available for use: *your coat is ready for collection* ▯ **readiness** *noun* ▯ **readily** *adv* easily; willingly ▯ **readymade** *adj* of clothes: made for general sale, not made specially for one person

real *adj* **1** actually existing, not imagined (*contrasted with*: **ideal**) **2** not imitation, genuine: *real leather* **3** sincere: *a real love of music* ▯ **realism** *noun* the showing or viewing of things as they really are ▯ **realist** *noun* someone who claims to see life as it really is ▯ **reality** *noun* (*plural* **realities**) that which is real and not imaginary; truth ▯ **really** *adv* **1** in fact **2** very: *really dark hair* ▯ **the real Mackay** or **the real McCoy** the genuine article, the real thing

realistic *adj* **1** life-like **2** viewing things as they really are ▯ **realistically** *adv*

realize *verb* **1** come to understand, know: *I never realized you could sing* **2** make real, accomplish: *realize an ambition* **3** get (money) for: *realized £16 000 on the sale of the house* ▯ **realization** *noun*

realm *noun* **1** a kingdom, a country **2** an area of activity or interest

realpolitik *noun* politics based on practical realities, not idealism

realty *noun* real estate ▯ **realtor** *noun* an estate agent

ream *noun* **1** a measure for paper, 20 quires **2** (**reams**) a large quantity, *esp* of paper: *she wrote reams in her English exam*

reap *verb* **1** cut and gather (corn *etc*) **2** gain: *reap the benefits of hard work* ▯ **reaper** *noun* **1** someone who reaps **2** a machine for reaping

rear *noun* **1** the back part of anything **2** the last part of an army or fleet □ *verb* **1** bring up (children) **2** breed (animals) **3** of an animal: stand on its hindlegs □ **rear-admiral** *noun* an officer who commands the rear division of the fleet □ **rearguard** *noun* troops which protect the rear of an army □ **bring up the rear** come or be last in a series

reason *noun* **1** cause, excuse: *what is the reason for this noise?* **2** purpose: *what is your reason for visiting America?* **3** the power of the mind to form opinions, judge right and truth *etc* **4** common sense □ *verb* **1** think out (opinions *etc*) **2** (with **with**) try to persuade (someone) by arguing □ **reasonable** *adj* **1** sensible **2** fair

reassure *verb* take away (someone's) doubts or fears □ **reassurance** *noun* □ **reassuring** *adj*

rebarbative *adj* repellent

rebate *noun* a part of a payment or tax which is given back to the payer

rebel *noun* someone who opposes or fights against those in power □ *verb* take up arms against or oppose those in power □ **rebellion** *noun* **1** an open or armed fight against those in power **2** a refusal to obey □ **rebellious** *adj* □ **rebelliousness** *noun*

rebel *verb* » rebel*s*, rebell*ing*, rebell*ed*

reboot *verb* restart (a computer) using its start-up programs

rebound *verb* bounce back: *the ball rebounded off the wall* □ *noun* **1** the act of rebounding **2** a reaction following an emotional situation or crisis

rebuff *noun* a blunt refusal or rejection □ *verb* reject bluntly

rebuke *verb* scold, blame □ *noun* a scolding

rebut *verb* deny (what has been said) □ **rebuttal** *noun*

rebut » rebut*s*, rebutt*ing*, rebutt*ed*

recalcitrant *adj* stubborn; disobedient □ **recalcitrance** *noun*

recall *verb* **1** call back: *recalled to headquarters* **2** remember □ *noun* **1** a signal or message to return **2** the act of recalling or remembering

recant *verb* **1** take back what you have said **2** reject publicly your beliefs □ **recantation** *noun*

recap *short for* **1** recapitulation **2** recapitulate

recap » recap*s*, recapp*ing*, recapp*ed*

recapitulate *verb* go over again quickly the chief points of anything (*eg* a discussion) □ **recapitulation** *noun*

recapture *verb* capture (what has escaped or been lost)

recast *verb* shape in a new form

recast » recast*s*, recast*ing*, recast

recede *verb* **1** go back **2** become more distant **3** slope backwards □ **receding** *adj* **1** going or sloping backwards **2** becoming more distant

receipt *noun* **1** the act of receiving (*esp* money or goods) **2** a written note saying that money has been received

receive *verb* **1** have something given or brought to you: *receive a gift/ receive a letter* **2** meet and welcome: *receiving visitors* **3** take goods, knowing them to be stolen

receiver *noun* **1** someone who receives stolen goods **2** the part of a telephone through which words are heard and into which they are spoken **3** an apparatus through which television or radio broadcasts are received

recent *adj* happening, done or made only a short time ago □ **recently** *adv*

receptacle *noun* an object to receive or hold things, a container

reception *noun* **1** a welcome: *a warm reception* **2** a large meeting to welcome guests **3** the quality of radio or television signals □ **receptionist** *noun* someone employed in an office or hotel to answer the telephone *etc*

receptive *adj* quick to take in or accept ideas *etc* □ **receptivity** *noun*

recess *noun* (*plural* **recesses**) **1** part of a room set back from the rest, an alcove **2** the time during which parliament or the law courts do not work **3** remote parts: *in the recesses of my memory*

recession *noun* **1** the act of moving back **2** a temporary fall in a country's or world business activities □ **recessive** *adj*

recherché *adj* carefully chosen, choice

recidivism *noun* the habit of relapsing into crime □ **recidivist** *noun & adj*

recipe *noun* instructions on how to prepare or cook a certain kind of food

recipient *noun* someone who receives

reciprocal *adj* both given and received: *reciprocal affection*

reciprocate *verb* feel or do the same in return: *I reciprocate his dislike of me*

recite *verb* repeat aloud from memory □ **recital** *noun* **1** the act of reciting **2** a musical performance **3** the facts of a story told one after the other □ **recitation** *noun* a poem *etc* recited

reckless *adj* rash, careless □ **recklessly** *adj* □ **recklessness** *noun*

reckon *verb* **1** count **2** consider, believe □ **reckoning** *noun* **1** the settling of debts, grievances *etc* **2** payment for sins **3** a bill **4** a sum, calculation

reclaim *verb* **1** claim back **2** win back (land from the sea) by draining, building banks *etc* **3** make waste land fit for use □ **reclamation** *noun*

réclame /reh*klahm*/ *noun* publicity

recline *verb* lean or lie on your back or side □ **reclining** *adj*

recluse *noun* someone who lives alone and avoids other people □ **reclusive** *adj*

recognize *verb* **1** know from a

previous meeting *etc* **2** admit, acknowledge: *everyone recognized his talent* **3** show appreciation of: *they recognized his courage by giving him a medal* ▫ **recognizable** *adj* ▫ **recognition** *noun* act of recognizing

recoil *verb* **1** shrink back in horror or fear **2** of a gun: jump back after a shot is fired ▫ *noun* a shrinking back

recollect *verb* remember ▫ **recollection** *noun* **1** the act or power of remembering **2** a memory, something remembered

recommend *verb* **1** urge, advise: *I recommend that you take a long holiday* **2** speak highly of ▫ **recommendation** *noun* **1** the act of recommending **2** a point in favour of someone or something

recompense *verb* pay money to or reward (a person) to make up for loss, inconvenience *etc* ▫ *noun* payment in compensation

reconcile *verb* **1** bring together in friendship, after a quarrel **2** show that two statements, facts *etc* do not contradict each other **3** (with **to**) make to accept patiently: *I became reconciled to her absence* ▫ **reconciliation** *noun*

recondite *adj* secret, little-known

reconnaissance *noun* a survey to obtain information, *esp* before a battle

reconnoitre *verb* make a reconnaissance of

reconstitute *verb* **1** put back into its original form: *reconstitute the milk* **2** make up, form in a different way

record *verb* **1** write down for future reference **2** put (music, speech *etc*) on tape or disc so that it can be listened to later **3** show in writing (*eg* a vote) **4** show, register: *the thermometer recorded 30°C yesterday* ▫ *noun* **1** a written report of facts **2** a round, flat piece of plastic on which sounds are recorded for playing on a record-player **3** the best known performance: *John holds the school record for the mile* ▫ **record-player** *noun* a machine for playing records ▫ **break** or **beat the record** do better than any previous performance ▫ **off the record** of a remark *etc*: not to be made public

recorder *noun* **1** someone who records **2** a type of simple musical wind instrument **3** a judge in certain courts

recording *noun* **1** the act of recording **2** recorded music, speech *etc*

recount *verb* **1** count again **2** tell (the story of) ▫ *noun* a second count, *esp* of votes in an election

recoup *verb* make good, recover (expenses, losses *etc*)

> ⚠Do not confuse with: **recuperate**

recourse *noun*: **have recourse to** make use of in an emergency

recover *verb* **1** get possession of again **2** become well again after an illness ▫ **recoverable** *adj* able to be recovered

re-cover *verb* cover again

recovery *noun* (*plural* **recoveries**) **1** a return to health **2** the regaining of something lost *etc*

recreant *noun, old* a coward

recreate *verb* describe or create again (something past)

recreation *noun* a sport, hobby *etc* done in your spare time

recriminate *verb* accuse your accuser in return ▯ **recriminations** *noun plural* accusations made by someone who is themselves accused ▯ **recriminatory** *adj*

recruit *noun* a newly-enlisted soldier, member *etc* ▯ *verb* enlist (someone) in an army, political party *etc* ▯ **recruitment** *noun*

rectangle *noun* a four-sided figure with all its angles right angles and its opposite sides equal in length, an oblong ▯ **rectangular** *adj*

rectify *verb* put right ▯ **rectifiable** *adj*

> **rectify** » rectifi*es*, rectify*ing*, rectifi*ed*

rectilineal or **rectilinear** *adj* in a straight line or lines

rectitude *noun* honesty; correctness of behaviour

recto *noun* the right-hand page of an open book (*compare with*: **verso**)

rector *noun* **1** a member of the Anglican clergy in charge of a parish **2** the headmaster of some Scottish secondary schools **3** a Scottish university official elected by the students ▯ **rectory** *noun* (*plural* **rectories**) the house of an Anglican rector

rectum *noun* the lower part of the alimentary canal

recumbent *adj* lying down

recuperate *verb* recover strength or health ▯ **recuperation** *noun*

> ⚠Do not confuse with: **recoup**

recur *verb* happen again ▯ **recurrence** *noun* ▯ **recurrent** *adj* happening every so often

> **recur** » recur*s*, recurr*ing*, recurr*ed*

recycle *verb* **1** remake into something different **2** treat (material) by some process in order to use it again

red *adj* **1** of the colour of blood ▯ *noun* this colour ▯ **redbreast** *noun* the robin ▯ **red deer** a type of reddish-brown deer ▯ **redden** *verb* make or grow red ▯ **red-handed** *adv* in the act of doing wrong: *caught red-handed* ▯ **red herring** something mentioned to lead a discussion away from the main subject; a false clue ▯ **Red Indian** *offensive* a Native American ▯ **red-letter** *adj* of a day: especially important or happy for some reason ▯ **red light 1** a danger signal **2** a signal to stop ▯ **redness** *noun* ▯ **redskin** *noun, offensive* a Native American ▯ **red tape** unnecessary and troublesome rules about how things are to be done ▯ **redwood** *noun* a North American tree which grows to a great height ▯ **see red** become very angry

redeem *verb* **1** buy back (*eg* articles from a pawnbroker) **2** save from sin or condemnation **3** make amends for ▫ **the Redeemer** *noun* Jesus Christ ▫ **redeeming** *adj* making up for other faults: *a redeeming feature* ▫ **redemption** *noun*

redeploy *verb* move (*eg* soldiers, workers) to a different place where they will be more useful

redolent *adj* **1** sweet-smelling **2** smelling (of) **3** suggestive, making one think (of): *redolent of earlier times*

redouble *verb* make twice as great: *redouble your efforts*

redoubtable *adj* brave, bold

redress *verb* set right, make up for (a wrong *etc*) ▫ *noun* something done or given to make up for a loss or wrong, compensation

reduce *verb* **1** make smaller **2** lessen **3** bring to the point of by force of circumstances: *reduced to begging in the streets* **4** bring to a lower rank or state **5** change into other terms: *reduce pounds to pence* ▫ **reducible** *adj* ▫ **reduction** *noun*

reductio ad absurdum reduction to absurdity

redundant *adj* **1** more than what is needed **2** of a worker: no longer needed because of the lack of a suitable job ▫ **redundance** or **redundancy** *noun* (*plural* **redundancies**)

reduplicate *verb* double, repeat

reed *noun* **1** a tall stiff grass growing in moist or marshy places **2** a part (originally made of reed) of certain wind instruments which vibrates when the instrument is played ▫ **reedy** *adj* **1** full of reeds **2** like a reed **3** sounding like a reed instrument: *a reedy voice*

reef *noun* a chain of rocks lying at or near the surface of the sea ▫ **reef knot** a square, very secure knot

reefer *noun* **1** a short coat, as worn by sailors **2** *slang* a marijuana cigarette

reek *noun* **1** a strong, unpleasant smell **2** smoke ▫ *verb* **1** send out smoke **2** smell strongly

reel *noun* **1** a cylinder of plastic, metal or wood on which thread, film, fishing lines *etc* may be wound **2** a length of cinema film **3** a lively Scottish or Irish dance ▫ *verb* **1** wind on a reel **2** (with **in**) draw, pull in (a fish on a line) **3** stagger ▫ **reel off** repeat or recite quickly, without pausing

reeve *noun, hist* a chief magistrate, a bailiff

ref *abbrev* **1** referee **2** reference

refectory *noun* (*plural* **refectories**) a communal dining hall for monks, students *etc*

refer *verb* **1** (with **to**) mention **2** turn (to) for information **3** relate, apply (to) **4** direct (to) for information, consideration *etc*: *I refer you to the managing director*

> **refer** » refer*s*, referr*ing*, referr*ed*

referee *noun* **1** someone to whom a matter is taken for settlement **2** a judge in a sports match **3** someone willing to provide a note about someone's character, work record *etc*

reference *noun* **1** the act of referring **2** a mention **3** a note about a person's character, work *etc* □ **reference book** a book to be consulted for information, *eg* an encyclopedia □ **reference library** a library of books to be looked at for information but not taken away

referendum *noun* (*plural* **referenda** or **referendums**) a vote given by the people of a country about some important matter

refine *verb* **1** purify **2** improve, make more exact *etc* □ **refined** *adj* **1** purified **2** polite in manners, free of vulgarity □ **refinement** *noun* **1** good manners, taste, learning **2** an improvement □ **refinery** *noun* (*plural* **refineries**) a place where sugar, oil *etc* are refined

refit *verb* repair damages (*esp* to a ship)

refit » refit*s*, refitt*ing*, refitt*ed*

reflation *noun* an increase in the amount of currency, economic activity *etc* after deflation

reflect *verb* **1** throw back (light or heat): *reflecting the sun's heat* **2** give an image of: *reflected in the mirror* **3** (with **on**) throw blame: *her behaviour reflects on her mother* **4** (with **on**) think over something carefully □ **reflection** *noun* **1** the act of throwing back **2** the image of someone *etc* reflected in a mirror **3** blame, unfavourable criticism □ **reflective** *adj* thoughtful □ **reflector** *noun* something (*eg* a piece of shiny metal) which throws back light

reflex *noun* (*plural* **reflexes**) an action which is automatic, not intended, *eg* jerking the leg when the kneecap is struck □ *adj* done as a reflex, unthinking

reflexive *adj, grammar* showing that the object (**reflexive pronoun**) of the verb (**reflexive verb**) is the same as its subject, *eg* in 'he cut himself', *himself* is a *reflexive pronoun* and *cut* a *reflexive verb*

reflexology *noun* a way of treating illness or stress by massaging particular areas on the soles of the feet □ **reflexologist** *noun* a practitioner of reflexology

reform *verb* **1** improve, remove faults from **2** give up bad habits, evil *etc* □ *noun* an improvement □ **reformer** *noun* someone who wishes to bring about improvements

reformation *noun* a change for the better □ **the Reformation** *noun* the religious movement in the Christian Church in the 16th century from which the Protestant Church arose

re-form *verb* form again (*eg* a society)

refract *verb* change the direction of (a ray of light) □ **refraction** *noun*

refractory *adj* unruly, not easily controlled

refrain *noun* a chorus coming at the end of each verse of a song □ *verb* keep yourself back (from doing something): *please refrain from smoking*

refresh *verb* give new strength, power or life to □ **refreshing** *adj* **1** bringing back strength **2** cooling □

refresher course a course of study intended to keep up or increase existing knowledge of a subject □ **refreshments** *noun plural* food and drink □ **refresh your memory** go over facts again so that they are clear in your mind

refrigerator *noun* a storage machine which keeps food cold and so prevents it from going bad □ **refrigerate** *verb* □ **refrigeration** *noun*

refuel *verb* supply with, or take in, fresh fuel

> **refuel** » refuel*s*, refuell*ing*, refuell*ed*

refuge *noun* a place of safety (from attack, danger *etc*) □ **refugee** *noun* someone who seeks shelter from persecution in another country

refulgent beaming, giving off light

refund *verb* pay back □ *noun* a payment returned, *eg* for unsatisfactory goods

refuse[1] *verb* **1** say that you will not do something: *he refused to leave the room* **2** withhold, not give (*eg* permission) □ **refusal** *noun* □ **refusenik** *noun* someone who refuses to comply with a political *etc* regime

refuse[2] *noun* something which is thrown aside as worthless, rubbish

refute *verb* prove wrong (something that has been said or written) □ **refutation** *noun*

regain *verb* **1** win back again **2** get back to: *regain the shore*

regal *adj* kingly, royal □ **regalia** *noun plural* symbols of royalty, *eg* a crown and sceptre

regale /ra*gehl*/ *verb* entertain lavishly

regard *verb* **1** look upon, consider: *I regard you as a nuisance* **2** look at carefully **3** pay attention to □ *noun* **1** concern **2** affection **3** respect **4** (**regards**) good wishes □ **regarding** *prep* concerning, to do with: *a reply regarding his application* □ **regardless of** paying no care or attention to □ **with regard to** or **in regard to** concerning

regatta *noun* a meeting for yacht or boat races

> From the name of a gondola race held on the Grand Canal in Venice

regency *see* **regent**

regenerate *verb* make new and good again □ **regeneration** *noun*

regent *noun* someone who governs in place of a king or queen □ **regency** *noun* (*plural* **regencies**) **1** rule by a regent **2** the period of a regent's rule **3** *Brit hist* the period during which George IV was regent, 1715–1723

reggae *noun* a strongly rhythmic type of rock music, originally from the West Indies

regicide *noun* **1** the killing of a monarch **2** someone who kills a monarch

régime or **regime** *noun* method or system of government or administration

regimen *noun* diet and habits to be followed

regiment *noun* a body of soldiers, commanded by a colonel □ *verb* organize or control too strictly □ **regimental** *adj* of a regiment □ **regimentation** *noun* too strict control

region *noun* an area, a district □ **regional** *adj* □ **in the region of** somewhere near: *in the region of £10*

register *noun* **1** a written list (*eg* of attendances at school, of those eligible to vote *etc*) **2** the distance between the highest and lowest notes of a voice or instrument □ *verb* **1** write down in a register **2** record, cast (a vote *etc*) **3** show, record: *a thermometer registers temperature* □ **registered letter** one insured against loss by the post office □ **registrar** *noun* a public official who keeps a register of births, deaths and marriages □ **registry** *noun* (*plural* **registries**) an office where a register is kept □ **registry office** one where records of births, marriages and deaths are kept and where marriages may be performed

regius *adj* of a university professor: holding a chair created by the crown

regress *verb* go back to an earlier state

regret *verb* be sorry about: *I regret any inconvenience you have suffered* **2** be sorry (to have to say something): *we regret to inform you* □ *noun* sorrow for anything □ **regretful** *adj* □ **regretfully** *adv* □ **regrettable** *adj* to be regretted, unwelcome □ **regrettably** *adv*

> **regret** *verb* » regret*s*, regret*ting*, regrett*ed*

regular *adj* **1** done according to rule or habit; usual **2** arranged in order; even: *regular teeth* **3** happening at certain fixed times **4** having normal bowel movements □ *noun* a soldier of the regular army □ **regularity** *verb* □ **regularly** *adv* □ **regular army** the part of the army which is kept always in training, even in peacetime

regulate *verb* **1** control by rules **2** adjust to a certain order or rate □ **regulation** *verb* a rule, an order □ **regulator** *verb* someone or thing that regulates

regurgitate *verb* bring back into the mouth after swallowing □ **regurgitation** *noun*

rehabilitate *verb* **1** give back rights, powers or health to **2** train or accustom (a disabled person *etc*) to live a normal life □ **rehabilitation** *noun*

rehash *verb* express in different words, do again

rehearsal *noun* **1** a private practice of a play, concert *etc* before performance in public **2** a practice for a future event or action □ **rehearse** *verb* **1** practise beforehand **2** recount (facts, events *etc*) in order

Reich *noun, hist* a period of German empire

reify *verb* make material, manifest

reign *noun* **1** rule **2** the time during which a king or queen rules □ *verb* **1** rule **2** prevail: *silence reigned at last*

reimburse *verb* pay (someone) an

amount to cover expenses ▯ **reimbursement** *noun*

rein *noun* **1** one of two straps attached to a bridle for guiding a horse **2** (**reins**) a simple device for controlling a child when walking ▯ *verb* control with reins

reincarnation *noun* the rebirth of the soul in another body after death

reindeer *noun* (*plural* **reindeer**) a type of deer found in the far North

reinforce *verb* strengthen (*eg* an army with men, concrete with iron) ▯ **reinforcement** *noun* **1** the act of reinforcing **2** something which strengthens **3** (**reinforcements**) additional troops

reinstate *verb* put back in a former position ▯ **reinstatement** *noun*

reiterate *verb* repeat several times ▯ **reiteration** *noun*

reject *verb* **1** throw away, cast aside **2** refuse to take: *she rejected his offer of help* **3** turn down (*eg* an application, request) ▯ *noun* something discarded or refused ▯ **rejection** *noun*

rejig *verb* rearrange, *esp* in an unexpected way

rejig » rejig*s*, rejigg*ing*, rejigg*ed*

rejoice *verb* feel or show joy ▯ **rejoicing** *noun*

rejoinder *noun* an answer to a reply

rejuvenate *verb* make young again ▯ **rejuvenation** *noun*

relapse *verb* fall back (*eg* into ill health, bad habits) ▯ *noun* a falling back

relate *verb* **1** show a connection between (two or more things) **2** tell (a story) ▯ **related** *adj* **1** (often with **to**) of the same family (as): *I'm related to him/ we are not related* **2** connected

relation *noun* **1** someone who is of the same family, either by birth or marriage **2** a connection between two or more things ▯ **relationship** *noun* connection

relative *noun* someone who is of the same family *etc* ▯ *adj* comparative: *relative merits* ▯ **relatively** *adv* more or less: *relatively happy* ▯ **relativity** *noun*

relax *verb* **1** become or make less tense **2** slacken (*eg* your grip or control) **3** make (laws or rules) less severe ▯ **relaxation** *noun* **1** a slackening **2** rest from work, leisure

relay *verb* **1** receive and pass on (*eg* a message, a television programme) ▯ *noun* **1** the sending out of a radio or television broadcast received from another station **2** a fresh set of people to replace others at a job *etc* ▯ **relay race** a race in which members of each team take over from each other, each running a set distance ▯ **in relays** in groups which take over from one another in series

relay *verb* » relay*s*, relay*ing*, relay*ed*

release *verb* **1** set free; let go **2** allow (news *etc*) to be made public ▯ *noun* a setting free

relegate *verb* **1** put down (to a

lower position, group *etc*) **2** leave (a task *etc*) to someone else ▯ **relegation** *verb*

relent *verb* treat (someone) less severely or strictly ▯ **relentless** *adj* **1** without pity **2** refusing to be turned from a purpose ▯ **relentlessly** *adv*

relevant *adj* having to do with what is being spoken about ▯ **relevance** *noun*

reliable and **reliance** *see* **rely**

relic *noun* something left over from a past time; an antiquity

relief *noun* **1** a lessening of pain or anxiety **2** release from a post or duty **3** people taking over someone's duty *etc* **4** help given to those in need: *famine relief* **5** the act of freeing (a town *etc*) from a siege **6** a way of carving or moulding in which the design stands out from its background

relieve *verb* **1** lessen (pain or anxiety) **2** take over a duty from (someone else) **3** come to the help of (a town *etc* under attack)

religion *noun* belief in, or worship of, a god ▯ **religious** *adj*

relinquish *verb* give up, abandon: *relinquish control*

reliquary *noun* a container for religious relics

relish *verb* **1** enjoy **2** like the taste of ▯ *noun* (*plural* **relishes**) **1** enjoyment **2** flavour **3** something which adds flavour

relocate *verb* move to another position, residence *etc*

reluctant *adj* unwilling ▯ **reluctance** *noun*

rely *verb* have full trust in, depend (on) ▯ **reliability** or **reliance** *noun* trust ▯ **reliable** *adj* able to be trusted or counted on ▯ **reliant** *adj*

rely » reli*es*, rely*ing*, reli*ed*

REM *abbrev* rapid-eye movement, the movement of the eyes behind the eyelids during dreaming

remain *verb* **1** stay, not leave **2** be left: *only two tins of soup remained* **3** be still the same: *the problem remains unsolved* ▯ **remainder** *noun* **1** something which is left behind after removal of the rest **2** *maths* the number left after subtraction or division ▯ **remains** *noun plural* **1** that which is left **2** a dead body

remake *noun* a second making of a film *etc* ▯ *verb* make again

remand *verb* put (someone) back in prison until more evidence is found ▯ **on remand** having been remanded

remark *verb* **1** say **2** comment (on) **3** notice ▯ *noun* something said ▯ **remarkable** *adj* deserving notice, unusual ▯ **remarkably** *adv*

remedial *adj* **1** remedying **2** relating to the teaching of slow-learning children ▯ **remedially** *adv*

remedy *noun* (*plural* **remedies**) a cure for an illness, evil *etc* ▯ *verb* **1** cure **2** put right

remember *verb* **1** keep in mind **2** recall after having forgotten **3** send your best wishes (to): *remember me to your mother* **4** reward, give a present to: *he remembered her in his* *will* ▢ **remembrance** *noun* **1** the act of remembering **2** memory **3** something given to remind someone of a person or event, a keepsake **4** (**remembrances**) a friendly greeting

remind *verb* **1** bring (something) back to a person's mind: *remind me to post that letter* **2** cause (someone) to think about (someone or something) by resemblance: *she reminds me of her sister* ▢ **reminder** *noun* something which reminds

reminiscence *noun* **1** something remembered from the past **2** (**reminiscences**) memories, *esp* told or written ▢ **reminiscent** *adj* **1** reminding (of): *reminiscent of Paris* **2** in a mood to remember and think about past events *etc* ▢ **reminisce** *verb* think and talk about things remembered from the past

remiss *adj* careless, unthinking

remission *noun* **1** a shortening of a prison sentence **2** a lessening of a disease or illness

remit *verb* **1** pardon, excuse (a crime *etc*) **2** wipe out, cancel (a debt *etc*) **3** lessen, become less intense **4** send (money) **5** hand over (*eg* a prisoner to a higher court) ▢ **remittance** *noun*

> **remit** » remit*s*, remitt*ing*, remitt*ed*

remnant *noun* a small piece or number left over

remonstrate *verb* protest (about) ▢ **remonstrance** *noun*

remorse *noun* regret about something done in the past ▢ **remorseful** *adj* ▢ **remorseless** *adj* having no remorse; cruel

remote *adj* **1** far away in time or place **2** isolated, far from other people **3** slight: *a remote chance*

removal *noun* the act of removing, *esp* of moving furniture to a new home

remove *verb* **1** take (something) from its place **2** dismiss from a job **3** take off (clothes *etc*) **4** get rid of: *remove a stain* ▢ *noun* a stage away (from): *one remove from anarchy* ▢ **removed** *adj* **1** distant (from) **2** of cousins: separated by a generation: *first cousin once removed* (a cousin's child)

remunerate *verb* pay (someone) for something done ▢ **remuneration** *noun* pay, salary ▢ **remunerative** *adj* profitable

renaissance *noun* **1** a rebirth **2** a period of cultural revival and growth

renal *adj* of the kidneys

rend *verb* tear (apart), divide

> **rend** » rend*s*, rend*ing*, rent

render *verb* **1** give (*eg* thanks) **2** translate into another language **3** perform (music *etc*) **4** cause to be: *his words rendered me speechless* ▢ **rendering** *noun* **1** a translation **2** a performance

rendezvous /*ron*dehvoo/ *noun* (*plural* **rendezvous**) **1** a meeting place fixed beforehand **2** an arranged meeting

renegade *noun* someone who deserts their own side, religion or beliefs

renew *verb* **1** make as if new again **2** begin again: *renew your efforts* **3** make valid for a further period (*eg* a driving licence) **4** replace: *renew the water in the tank* ◇ **renewal** *noun*

rennet *noun* a substance used in curdling milk for making cheeses *etc*

renounce *verb* give up publicly or formally ◇ **renunciation** *noun*

renovate *verb* make (something) like new again, mend ◇ **renovation** *noun*

renown *noun* fame ◇ **renowned** *adj* famous

rent[1] *noun* payment made for the use of property or land ◇ *verb* (also with **out**) pay or receive rent for (a house *etc*) ◇ **rental** *noun* money paid as rent ◇ **rent-boy** *noun* a young male homosexual prostitute

rent[2] *noun* a tear, a split ◇ *verb past form* of **rend**

renunciation *see* **renounce**

reorganize *verb* put in a different order ◇ **reorganization** *noun*

rep *noun, short for* **1** representative: *sales rep* **2** repertory

repair *verb* **1** mend **2** make up for (a wrong) **3** *old* go, move: *repair to the drawing room* ◇ *noun* **1** state, condition: *in bad repair* **2** mending: *in need of repair* **3** a mend, a patch ◇ **reparation** *noun* compensation for a wrong

repartee *noun* **1** an exchange of witty remarks **2** skill in witty conversation

repast *noun, old* a meal

repatriate *verb* send (someone) back to their own country ◇ **repatriation** *noun*

repay *verb* **1** pay back **2** give or do something in return: *he repaid her kindness with a gift* ◇ **repayment** *noun*

> **repay** » repay*s*, repay*ing*, repaid

repeal *verb* do away with, cancel (*esp* a law) ◇ *noun* a cancellation of a law *etc*

repeat *verb* **1** say or do over again **2** say from memory **3** pass on (someone's words) ◇ *noun* a musical passage, television programme *etc* played or shown for a second time ◇ **repeatedly** *adv* again and again ◇ **repeater** *noun* a gun which fires several shots ◇ **repetition** *noun* ◇ **repetitive** *adj* repeating too often, predictable

repel *verb* **1** drive back or away **2** disgust ◇ **repellent** *adj* disgusting ◇ *noun* something that repels: *insect repellent*

> **repel** » repel*s*, repell*ing*, repell*ed*

repent *verb* **1** be sorry for your actions **2** (with **of**) regret ◇ **repentance** *noun* ◇ **repentant** *adj* repenting

repercussion *noun* an indirect or resultant effect of something which has happened

repertoire *noun* the range of works performed by a musician, theatre company *etc*

repertory *noun* (*plural* **repertories**) repertoire ◇ **repertory**

theatre a theatre with a permanent company which performs a series of plays

répétiteur *noun* a coach for opera singers

repetition and **repetitive** *see* **repeat**

repine *verb, formal* be unhappy or discontented

replace *verb* **1** put (something) back where it was **2** put in place of another

replenish *verb* refill (a stock, supply)

replete *adj* full

replica *noun* an exact copy of a work of art

replicant *noun* an android

reply *verb* speak or act in answer to something □ *noun* (*plural* **replies**) an answer

> **reply** *verb* » repli*es*, reply*ing*, repli*ed*

report *verb* **1** pass on news **2** give a description of (an event) **3** give information about events for a newspaper **4** make a formal complaint against □ *noun* **1** a statement of facts **2** an account, a description **3** a news article **4** a rumour **5** a written description of a school pupil's work **6** a loud noise □ **reporter** *noun* a news journalist

repose *noun, formal* sleep, rest □ *verb* **1** rest **2** place (*eg* trust in a person)

repository *noun* (*plural* **repositories**) a storage place for safe keeping

repossess *verb* take back (goods, property), *esp* because of non-payment

reprehensible *adj* deserving blame □ **reprehension** *noun*

represent *verb* **1** speak or act on behalf of others: *representing the tenants' association* **2** stand for, be a symbol of: *each letter represents a sound* **3** claim to be **4** explain, point out □ **representation** *noun* **1** an image, a picture **2** a strong claim or appeal

representative *adj* **1** typical, characteristic: *a representative specimen* **2** standing or acting for others □ *noun* **1** someone who acts or speaks on behalf of others **2** a travelling salesman for a company

repress *verb* **1** keep down by force **2** keep under control □ **repression** *noun* □ **repressive** *adj*

reprieve *verb* **1** pardon (a criminal) **2** relieve from trouble or difficulty □ *noun* a pardon, a relief

reprimand *verb* scold severely, censure □ *noun* a censure

reprint *verb* print more copies of (a book *etc*) □ *noun* another printing of a book

reprisal *noun* a return of wrong for wrong, a repayment in kind

reproach *verb* scold, blame □ *noun* **1** blame, discredit **2** a cause of blame or censure □ **reproachful** *adj*

reprobate *noun* someone of evil or immoral habits □ *adj* immoral

reproduce *verb* **1** produce a copy of **2** produce (children or young) □ **reproduction** *noun*

reprography *noun* reproduction by photocopying

reproof *noun* a scolding, criticism for a fault ▫ **reprove** *verb* scold, blame ▫ **reproving** *adj*

reptile *noun* a creeping, cold-blooded animal, such as a snake, lizard *etc* ▫ **reptilian** *adj*

republic *noun* a form of government in which power is in the hands of elected representatives with a president at its head ▫ **Republican** *adj* belonging to the more conservative of the two chief political parties in the United States

repudiate *verb* refuse to acknowledge or accept: *repudiate a suggestion* ▫ **repudiation** *noun*

repugnant *adj* hateful, distasteful ▫ **repugnance** *noun*

repulse *verb* **1** drive back **2** reject, snub ▫ **repulsion** *noun* disgust

repulsive *adj* causing disgust, loathsome ▫ **repulsiveness** *noun*

reputation *noun* **1** opinion held by people in general of a particular person **2** good name ▫ **reputable** *adj* having a good reputation, well thought of ▫ **repute** *noun* reputation ▫ **reputed** *adj* **1** considered, thought (to be something): *reputed to be dangerous* **2** supposed: *the reputed author of the book* ▫ **reputedly** *adv* in the opinion of most people

request *verb* ask for ▫ *noun* **1** an asking for something **2** something asked for

requiem *noun* a hymn or mass sung for the dead

require *verb* **1** need **2** demand, order ▫ **requirement** *noun* **1** something needed **2** a demand

requisite *adj* required; necessary ▫ *noun* something needed or necessary ▫ **requisition** *noun* a formal request for supplies, *eg* for a school or army ▫ *verb* put in a formal request for

requite *verb* **1** repay, give back in return **2** avenge (one action) by another ▫ **requital** *noun* payment in return

reremouse *noun* (*plural* **reremice**) *old* a bat

rerun *verb* run again ▫ *noun* a repeated television programme

rescind *verb* do away with, repeal (a law)

rescue *verb* **1** save from danger **2** free from capture ▫ *noun* an act of saving from danger or capture

research *noun* (*plural* **researches**) close and careful scientific study to try to find out new facts: *cancer research* ▫ *verb* study carefully ▫ **researcher** *noun* someone who does research

resemble *verb* look like or be like: *he doesn't resemble his sister* ▫ **resemblance** *noun* likeness

resent *verb* feel injured, annoyed or insulted by ▫ **resentful** *adj* ▫ **resentment** *noun* annoyance

reservation *noun* **1** the act of reserving, booking **2** an exception or condition: *she agreed to the plan, but with certain reservations* **3** doubt, objection: *I had reservations about his appointment* **4** an area of land set aside by treaty for Native

American people in the United States

reserve *verb* **1** set aside for future use **2** book, have kept for you (*eg* a seat, a table) □ *noun* **1** something reserved **2** (**reserves**) troops outside the regular army kept ready to help those already fighting **3** a piece of land set apart for some reason: *nature reserve* **4** shyness, reluctance to speak or act openly □ **reserved** *adj* **1** shy, reluctant to speak openly **2** kept back for a particular person or purpose □ **reservist** *noun* a member of a military reserve

reservoir *noun* an artificial lake where water is kept in store

reshuffle *verb* rearrange ministerial posts within (a government cabinet) □ *noun* a rearrangement of a cabinet

reside *verb* **1** live, stay (in) **2** of authority *etc*: be placed (in) □ **residence** *noun* **1** the building where someone lives **2** living, or time of living, in a place

resident *noun* someone who lives in a particular place: *a resident of Dublin* □ *adj* **1** living in (a place) **2** living in a place of work: *resident caretaker* □ **residential** *adj* **1** of an area: containing houses rather than shops, offices *etc* **2** providing accommodation: *a residential course*

residue *noun* what is left over □ **residual** *adj*

resign *verb* give up (a job, position *etc*) □ **resigned** *adj* patient, not actively complaining □ **resignedly** *adv* □ **resign yourself to** accept (a situation) patiently and calmly

resignation *noun* **1** the act of resigning **2** a letter to say you are resigning **3** patient, calm acceptance of a situation

resilient *adj* **1** able to recover easily from misfortune, hurt *etc* **2** of an object: readily recovering its original shape after being bent, twisted *etc* □ **resilience** *noun*

resin *noun* a sticky substance produced by certain plants (*eg* firs, pines) □ **resinous** *adj*

resist *verb* **1** struggle against, oppose **2** stop yourself from (doing something)

resistance *noun* **1** the act of resisting **2** an organized opposition, *esp* to an occupying force **3** ability to turn a passing electrical current into heat □ **resistant** *adj*

resit *verb* sit (an examination) again □ *noun* a retaking of an examination

resit *verb* » resit*s*, resitt*ing*, resat

resolute *adj* determined, with mind made up □ **resolutely** *adv*

resolution *noun* **1** determination of mind or purpose **2** a firm decision (to do something) **3** a proposal put before a meeting **4** a decision expressed by a public meeting

resolve *verb* **1** decide firmly (to do something) **2** solve (a difficulty) **3** break up into parts □ *noun* a firm purpose

resonate *verb* echo □ **resonance**

noun a deep, echoing tone ▯ **resonant** *adj* echoing, resounding

resort *verb* **1** begin to use **2** turn (to) in a difficulty: *resorting to bribery* ▯ *noun* a popular holiday destination ▯ **in the last resort** when all else fails

resound *verb* **1** sound loudly **2** echo ▯ **resounding** *adj* **1** echoing **2** thorough: *a resounding victory*

resources *noun plural* **1** a source of supplying what is required **2** the natural sources of wealth in a country *etc* **3** money or other property **4** an ability to handle situations skilfully and cleverly ▯ **resourceful** *adj* good at finding ways out of difficulties

respect *verb* **1** feel a high regard for **2** treat with consideration: *respect his wishes* ▯ *noun* **1** high regard, esteem **2** consideration **3** a detail, a way: *alike in some respects* **4** (**respects**) good wishes ▯ **respectful** *adj* showing respect ▯ **respective** *adj* belonging to each (person or thing mentioned) separately: *my brother and his friends went to their respective homes* (*eg* each went to their own home) ▯ **respectively** *adv* in the order given: *James, Andrew and Ian were first, second and third respectively* ▯ **in respect of** concerning, as regards ▯ **with respect to** with reference to

respectable *adj* **1** worthy of respect **2** having a good reputation **3** considerable, fairly good: *a respectable score* ▯ **respectability** *noun*

respire *verb* breathe ▯ **respiration** *noun* breathing ▯ **respirator** *noun* **1** a mask worn over the mouth and nose to purify the air taken in **2** a device to help people breathe when they are too ill to do so naturally

respite *noun* a pause, a rest: *no respite from work*

resplendent *adj* very bright or splendid in appearance

respond *verb* **1** answer **2** react in response to: *I waved but he didn't respond* **3** show a positive reaction to: *responding to treatment* ▯ **respondent** *see* **corespondent**

response *noun* **1** a reply **2** an action, feeling *etc* in answer to another **3** an answer made during a church service

responsible *adj* **1** (sometimes with **for**) being the cause of: *responsible for this mess* **2** liable to be blamed (for): *responsible for the conduct of his staff* **3** involving making important decisions *etc*: *a responsible post* **4** trustworthy ▯ **responsibility** *noun* (*plural* **responsibilities**)

responsive *adj* quick to react, to show sympathy *etc* ▯ **responsiveness** *noun*

rest *noun* **1** a break in work **2** a sleep **3** *music* a pause in playing or singing for a given number of beats **4** a support, a prop: *book rest* **5** what is left, the remainder **6** the others, those not mentioned: *I went home but the rest went to the cinema* ▯ *verb* **1** stop working for a time **2** be still **3** sleep **4** depend (on), be based on: *the case rests on your evidence* **5** stop, develop no further: *I can't let the matter rest there* **6** lean or place on a support ▯ **restful**

adj **1** relaxing **2** relaxed ▯ **restive** *adj* restless, impatient ▯ **restless** *adj* **1** unable to keep still **2** agitated ▯ **rest with** be the responsibility of: *the choice rests with you*

restaurant *noun* a place where meals may be bought and eaten ▯ **restaurateur** *noun* the owner or manager of a restaurant

restitution *noun* **1** the return of what has been lost or taken away **2** compensation for harm or injury done

restive *see* **rest**

restore *verb* **1** put or give back **2** repair (a building, a painting *etc*) so that it looks as it used to **3** cure (a person) ▯ **restoration** *noun* ▯ **restorative** *adj* curing, giving strength

restrain *verb* **1** hold back (from) **2** keep under control ▯ **restraint** *noun* **1** the act of restraining **2** self-control **3** a tie or bond used to restrain

restrict *verb* **1** limit, keep within certain bounds: *restricted space for parking* **2** open only to certain people: *restricted area* ▯ **restriction** *noun* ▯ **restrictive** *adj* restricting

result *noun* **1** a consequence of something already done or said **2** the answer to a sum **3** a score in a game ▯ *verb* **1** (with **from**) be the result or effect of **2** (with **in**) have as a result: *result in a draw* ▯ **resultant** *adj* happening as a result

resume *verb* **1** begin again after an interruption: *resume a discussion* **2** take again: *he resumed his seat* ▯ **resumption** *noun*

résumé /rehz*oo*meh/ *noun* **1** a summary **2** *US* a curriculum vitae

resurgent *adj* rising again, becoming prominent again ▯ **resurgence** *noun*

resurrection *noun* **1** a rising from the dead **2** (**Resurrection**) the rising of Christ from the dead **3** the act of bringing back into use ▯ **resurrect** *verb* bring back to life or into use

resuscitate *verb* bring back to consciousness, revive ▯ **resuscitation** *noun*

retail *verb* **1** sell goods to someone who is going to use them (not to another seller) **2** tell (*eg* a story) fully and in detail ▯ *noun* the sale of goods to the actual user ▯ **retailer** *noun* a shopkeeper, a trader

retain *verb* **1** keep possession of **2** keep (something) in mind **3** reserve (someone's services) by paying a fee in advance **4** hold back, keep in place ▯ **retainer** *noun* **1** a fee for services paid in advance **2** *old* a servant (to a family)

retake *verb* take or capture again ▯ *noun* the filming of part of a film again

retaliate *verb* return like for like, hit back ▯ **retaliation** *noun*

retard *verb* **1** keep back, hinder **2** make slow or late ▯ **retardation** *noun* ▯ **retarded** *adj* slow in mental or physical growth

retch *verb* make the actions and sound of vomiting, without actually vomiting

retd *abbrev* retired

retention *noun* **1** the act of holding in or keeping **2** the act of retaining the services of (*eg* a lawyer) ▯ **retentive** *adj* able to hold or retain well: *retentive memory*

reticent *adj* unwilling to speak openly and freely, reserved ▯ **reticence** *noun*

retina *noun* (*plural* **retinas** or **retinae**) the part of the back of the eye that receives the image of what is seen

retinue *noun* the attendants of someone important

retire *verb* **1** give up work permanently, usually because of age **2** go to bed **3** draw back, retreat ▯ **retiral** *noun* retirement ▯ **retired** *adj* **1** having given up work **2** out-of-the-way, quiet ▯ **retirement** *noun* **1** the act of retiring from work **2** someone's life after they have given up work ▯ **retiring** *adj* shy, avoiding being noticed

retort *verb* make a quick and witty reply ▯ *noun* **1** a quick, witty reply **2** a bottle of thin glass used for distilling liquids

retouch *verb* improve or repair with artwork

retrace *verb* go over again: *retrace your steps*

retract *verb* **1** take back (something said or given) **2** draw back: *the cat retracted its claws* ▯ **retractable** *adj* able to be retracted ▯ **retraction** *noun*

retread *noun* a remoulded tyre

retreat *verb* **1** draw back, withdraw **2** go away ▯ *noun* **1** a movement backwards before the advance of an enemy **2** a withdrawal **3** a quiet, peaceful place

retrenchment *noun* economizing in spending

retrial *noun* a new hearing of a law case

retribution *noun* punishment

retrieve *verb* **1** get back, recover (something lost) **2** search for and fetch ▯ **retriever** *noun* a breed of dog trained to find and fetch shot birds

retro *adj* recreating the past for effect

retroflex *adj* bent backwards

retrograde *adj* **1** going backward **2** going from a better to a worse stage

retrospect *noun*: **in restrospect** considering or looking back on the past

retrospective *adj* **1** looking back on past events **2** of a law: applying to the past as well as the present and the future

retroussé *adj* of a nose: turned up

retsina *noun* a Greek wine flavoured with resin

return *verb* **1** go or come back **2** give, send, pay *etc* back **3** elect to parliament ▯ *noun* **1** the act of returning **2** a profit: *return on your investment* **3** a statement of income for calculating income tax ▯ **return match** a second match played between the same team or players ▯ **return ticket** a ticket which covers a journey both to and from a place ▯ **by return** sent by the first post back

reunion *noun* a meeting of people who have been apart for some time □ **reunite** *verb* join after having been separated

Rev or **Revd** *abbrev* Reverend

rev *noun* a revolution of an engine □ *verb* (often with **up**) increase the speed of (an engine)

> **rev** *verb* » rev*s*, revv*ing*, revv*ed*

revamp *verb* renovate, renew the appearance of

reveal *verb* **1** make known **2** show

reveille /ri*va*li/ *noun* a bugle call at daybreak to waken soldiers

revel *verb* **1** take great delight (in) **2** celebrate □ *noun* (**revels**) festivities □ **reveller** *noun* □ **revelry** *noun*

> **revel** *verb* » revel*s*, revell*ing*, revell*ed*

revelation *noun* **1** the act of revealing **2** something unexpected which is made known

revenge *noun* **1** harm done to someone in return for harm they themselves have committed **2** the desire to do such harm □ *verb* **1** inflict punishment in return for harm done: *revenging his father's murder* **2** (with **yourself**) take revenge: *he revenged himself on his enemies*

revenue *noun* **1** money received as payment **2** a country's total income

reverberate *verb* echo and re-echo, resound □ **reverberation** *noun*

revere *verb* look upon with great respect □ **reverence** *noun* great respect □ **reverent** or **reverential** *adj* showing respect

reverend *adj* **1** worthy of respect **2** (**Reverend**) a title given to a member of the clergy (*short form*: **Rev** or **Revd**)

> ⚠Do not confuse: **reverend** and **reverent**

reverie *noun* a daydream

reverse *verb* **1** turn upside down or the other way round **2** move backwards **3** undo (a decision, policy *etc*) □ *noun* **1** the opposite (of) **2** the other side (of a coin *etc*) **3** a defeat □ **reversal** *noun* the act of reversing or being reversed □ **reversible** *adj* of clothes: able to be worn with either side out

revert *verb* **1** go back to an earlier topic **2** return to a previous owner □ **reversion** *noun*

review *verb* **1** give an opinion or criticism of (an artistic work) **2** consider again: *review the facts* **3** inspect (*eg* troops) □ *noun* **1** a critical opinion of a book *etc* **2** a magazine consisting of reviews **3** a second look, a reconsideration **4** an inspection of troops *etc* □ **reviewer** *noun* someone who reviews, a critic

> ⚠Do not confuse with: **revue**

revile *verb* say harsh things about

revise *verb* **1** correct faults in and make improvements **2** study notes *etc* in preparation for an examination **3** change (*eg* an opinion) □ **revision** *noun* **1** the act of revising **2** a revised version of a book *etc*

revive *verb* bring or come back to life, use or fame □ **revival** *noun* **1** a return to life, use *etc* **2** a fresh show of interest: *a religious revival* □ **revivalist** *noun* someone who helps to create a religious revival

revivify *verb* put new life into

revoke *verb* **1** cancel (a decision *etc*) **2** fail to follow suit in a card-game □ **revocation** *noun*

revolt *verb* **1** rise up (against), rebel **2** feel disgust (at) **3** disgust □ *noun* a rising, a rebellion □ **revolting** *adj* causing disgust

revolution *noun* **1** a full turn round a centre **2** the act of turning round a centre **3** a general uprising against those in power **4** a complete change in ideas, way of doing things *etc* □ **revolutionize** *verb* bring about a complete change in

revolutionary *adj* **1** relating to a revolution **2** bringing about great changes **3** turning □ *noun* (*plural* **revolutionaries**) someone who is involved in, or is in favour of, revolution

revolve *verb* roll or turn round □ **revolver** *noun* a kind of pistol

revue *noun* a light theatre show, with short topical plays or sketches

⚠Do not confuse with: **review**

revulsion *noun* **1** disgust **2** a sudden change of feeling

reward *noun* **1** something given in return for work done or for good behaviour *etc* **2** a sum of money offered for helping to find a criminal, lost property *etc* □ *verb* **1** give a reward to **2** give a reward for (a service) □ **rewarding** *adj* giving pleasure or satisfaction

rewind *verb* wind back (a spool, cassette *etc*) to the beginning

rewrite *verb* write again

RGN *abbrev* Registered General Nurse

Rh *abbrev* rhesus

rhapsody *noun* music or poetry which expresses strong feeling □ **rhapsodize** *verb* talk or write enthusiastically (about) □ **go into rhapsodies over** show wild enthusiasm for

rhesus factor a substance normally present in human blood □ **rhesus-negative** *adj* not having this substance in the blood □ **rhesus-positive** *adj* having this substance

rhetoric *noun* **1** the art of good speaking or writing **2** language which is too showy, consisting of unnecessarily long or difficult words *etc* □ **rhetorical** *adj* □ **rhetorical question** one which the asker answers, or which does not need an answer

rheumatism *noun* a disease which causes stiffness and pain in the joints □ **rheumatic** *adj*

rhinestone *noun* an artificial paste diamond

rhino (*plural* **rhinos**) *short for* rhinoceros

rhinoceros (*plural* **rhinoceros** or **rhinoceroses**) a large, thick-skinned animal, with a horn (or two) on its nose

rhinoplasty *noun* plastic surgery on the nose

rhizome *noun* an underground

plant stem producing roots and shoots

rhododendron *noun* a flowering shrub with thick evergreen leaves and large flowers

rhomboid *noun* a parallelogram

rhombus *noun* (*plural* **rhombi** or **rhombuses**) a geometrical figure with four equal straight sides

rhotic *adj* of an accent: pronouncing the letter 'r'

rhubarb *noun* a plant with long red-skinned stalks, edible when cooked

rhyme *noun* **1** a similarity in sounds between words or their endings, *eg humble* and *crumble,* or *convention* and *prevention* **2** a word which sounds like another **3** a short poem ▫ *verb* (sometimes with **with**) sound like, be rhymes: *harp rhymes with carp*

rhythm *noun* **1** a regular repeated pattern of sounds or beats in music or poetry **2** a regularly repeated pattern of movements ▫ **rhythmic** or **rhythmical** *adj* ▫ **rhythm and blues** a type of music combining the styles of rock-and-roll and the blues ▫ **rhythm method** a method of contraception by abstaining from intercourse when a woman is most fertile

rial *another spelling* of **riyal**

rib *noun* **1** any of the bones which curve round and forward from the backbone, enclosing the heart and lungs **2** a spar of wood in the framework of a boat, curving up from the keel **3** a ridged knitting pattern ▫ **ribbed** *adj* arranged in ridges and furrows

ribald *adj* of a joke *etc*: coarse, vulgar

ribbon *noun* a narrow strip of silk or other material, used for decoration, tying hair *etc*

riboflavin *noun* a vitamin found in milk, liver *etc*

rice *noun* the seeds of a plant, grown for food in well-watered ground in tropical countries ▫ **rice cake** a light cake made with puffed rice grains ▫ **rice paper** thin edible paper often put under baking to prevent it sticking

rich *adj* **1** having a lot of money or valuables, wealthy **2** valuable: *a rich reward* **3** (with **in**) having a lot of: *rich in natural resources* **4** of food: containing a lot of fat, eggs *etc* **5** of material: heavily decorated or textured, lavish **6** of a colour: deep in tone ▫ **riches** *noun plural* wealth ▫ **richly** *adv* ▫ **richness** *noun*

Richter scale a scale for measuring the intensity of earthquakes

rickets *noun sing* a children's disease caused by lack of calcium, with softening and bending of the bones ▫ **rickety** *adj* **1** suffering from rickets **2** unsteady: *a rickety table*

rickshaw *noun* a two-wheeled carriage pulled by a man, used in Japan *etc*

ricochet /rĭkəsheh/ *verb* of a bullet: rebound at an angle from a surface

ricochet » ricochet*s*, ricochet*ing*, ricochet*ed* or ricochett*ed*

ricotta *noun* a soft Italian sheep's-milk cheese

rictus *noun* a gaping of the mouth, *eg* in horror

rid *verb* free from, clear of: *rid the city of rats* ▫ **get rid of** free yourself of ▫ **good riddance to** I am happy to have got rid of

rid » rid*s*, ridd*ing*, rid

riddle *noun* **1** a puzzle in the form of a question which describes something in a misleading way **2** something difficult to understand **3** a tray with holes for separating large objects from smaller ones

ride *verb* **1** travel on a horse or bicycle, or in a vehicle **2** travel on and control (a horse) **3** of a ship: float at anchor ▫ *noun* **1** a journey on horseback, bicycle *etc* **2** a path through a wood, for riding horses ▫ **rider** *noun* **1** someone who rides **2** something added to what has already been said ▫ **ride up** of a skirt *etc*: work itself up out of position

ride *verb* » ride*s*, rid*ing*, rode, ridd*en*

ridge *noun* **1** a raised part between furrows **2** a long crest on high ground

ridicule *verb* laugh at, mock ▫ *noun* mockery ▫ **ridiculous** *adj* deserving to be laughed at, very silly

rife *adj* very common: *disease was rife in the country*

riff-raff *noun* worthless people

rifle[1] *verb* **1** search through and rob **2** steal

rifle[2] *noun* a gun fired from the shoulder

rift *noun* **1** a crack **2** a disagreement between friends ▫ **rift valley** a long valley formed by the fall of part of the earth's crust

rig *verb* **1** (with **out**) clothe, dress **2** fix (an election result) illegally or dishonestly ▫ **rigging** *noun* ship's spars, ropes *etc* ▫ **rig up** **1** fit (a ship) with sails and ropes **2** make or build hastily

rig » rig*s*, rigg*ing*, rigg*ed*

right *adj* **1** on or belonging to the side of the body which in most people has the more skilful hand (*contrasted with*: **left**) **2** correct, true **3** just, good **4** straight ▫ *adv* **1** to or on the right side **2** correctly **3** straight **4** all the way: *right along the pier and back* ▫ *noun* **1** something good which ought to be done **2** something you are entitled to: *a right to a fair trial* **3** the right-hand side, direction *etc* **4** the conservative side in politics ▫ *verb* mend, set in order ▫ **right angle** an angle like one of those in a square, an angle of 90° ▫ **rightful** *adj* by right, proper: *the rightful owner* ▫ **right-handed** *adj* using the right hand more easily than the left ▫ **Right Honourable** *adj* used before the names of cabinet ministers in the British government ▫ **right-of-way** *noun* a road or path over private land along which people may go as a right ▫ **right-wing** *adj* of conservative views in politics ▫ **by right** because you have the right

□ **in your own right** not because of anyone else, independently

righteous *adj* living a good life; just □ **righteousness** *noun*

rigid *adj* **1** not easily bent, stiff **2** strict □ **rigidity** *noun*

rigmarole *noun* a long, rambling speech

> Originally *ragman roll*, a Scots term for a long list or catalogue

rigor mortis stiffening of the body after death

rigour *noun* strictness; harshness □ **rigorous** *adj* very strict

rill *noun* a small stream

rim *noun* an edge or border, *eg* the top edge of a cup

rime *noun* thick white frost

rind *noun* a thick firm covering, *eg* fruit peel, bacon skin, the outer covering of cheese

ring *noun* **1** a small hoop worn on the finger, on the ear *etc* **2** a hollow circle **3** an enclosed space for boxing, circus performances *etc* **4** the sound of a bell being struck **5** a small group of people formed for business or criminal purposes: *a drug ring* □ *verb* **1** (*past* **ringed**) encircle, go round **2** mark (a bird *etc*) by putting on a ring **3** (*past* **rang**) make the sound of a bell **4** strike (a bell *etc*) **5** telephone □ **ringleader** *noun* someone who takes the lead in mischief *etc* □ **ringlet** *noun* a long curl of hair □ **ringmaster** *noun* someone who is in charge of the performance in a circus ring □ **ring road** a road that circles a town *etc* avoiding the centre □ **ringworm** *noun* a skin disease causing circular red patches

> **ring** » ring*s*, ring*ing*, rang or ring*ed*, rung or ring*ed*

rink *noun* a sheet of ice, often artificial, for skating or curling

rinse *verb* **1** wash lightly to remove soap *etc* **2** clean (a cup, your mouth *etc*) by swilling with water □ *noun* **1** the act of rinsing **2** liquid colour for the hair

riot *noun* **1** a noisy disturbance by a crowd **2** a striking display: *a riot of colour* **3** a hilarious event □ *verb* take part in a riot □ **riotous** *adj* noisy, uncontrolled

RIP *abbrev* may he or she rest in peace

rip *verb* **1** tear apart or off **2** come apart □ *noun* a tear □ **rip-off** *noun, slang* a cheat, a swindle □ **ripstop** *adj* of fabric: woven so as to prevent tearing □ **let rip** express yourself fully, without restraint

> **rip** *verb* » rip*s*, ripp*ing*, ripp*ed*

ripe *adj* **1** of fruit *etc*: ready to be picked or eaten **2** fully developed, mature □ **ripen** *verb* make or become ripe □ **ripeness** *noun*

riposte *noun* a quick return or reply

ripple *noun* **1** a little wave or movement on the surface of water **2** a soft sound *etc* that rises and falls quickly and gently: *a ripple of laughter*

RISC *abbrev* reduced instruction set computer

rise *verb* **1** to get up from bed **2** stand up **3** move upwards **4** of a river: have its source (in): *the Rhone rises in the Alps* **5** rebel (against) ▫ *noun* **1** a slope upwards **2** an increase in wages, prices *etc* ▫ **rising** *noun* **1** an act of rising **2** a rebellion ▫ **give rise to** cause

> **rise** *verb* » rise*s*, ris*ing*, rose, rise*n*

risible *adj* laughable

risk *noun* a chance of loss or injury; a danger ▫ *verb* **1** take the chance of: *risk death* **2** take the chance of losing: *risk one's life, health etc* ▫ **risky** *adj* possibly resulting in loss or injury

risotto *noun* a dish made with rice

risqué /ris*keh*/ *adj* slightly lewd or suggestive

rissole *noun* a fried cake or ball of minced meat, fish *etc*

rite *noun* a solemn ceremony, *esp* a religious one

ritual *noun* a traditional way of carrying out religious worship *etc* ▫ *adj* relating to a rite or ceremony ▫ **ritualistic** *adj* done in a set, unchanging way

rival *noun* someone who tries to equal or beat another ▫ *verb* try to equal ▫ **rivalry** *noun* (*plural* **rivalries**)

> **rival** *verb* » rival*s*, rivall*ing*, rivall*ed*

riven *adj*, *old* split

river *noun* a large stream of water flowing across land

rivet *noun* a bolt for fastening plates of metal together ▫ *verb* **1** fasten with a rivet **2** fix firmly (someone's attention *etc*): *riveted to the spot*

riviera *noun* a warm coastal area

rivulet *noun* a small stream

riyal or **rial** *noun* the main unit of currency in Saudia Arabia and the Yemen

RN *abbrev* Royal Navy

RNIB *abbrev* Royal National Institute for the Blind

RNLI *abbrev* Royal National Lifeboat Institution

roach *noun* (*plural* **roaches**) a type of freshwater fish

road *noun* **1** a hard, level surface for vehicles and people **2** a way of getting to (somewhere), a route **3** (**roads**) a place where ships may lie at anchor (*also called*: **roadstead**) ▫ **roadie** *noun* a member of the crew who transport, set up and dismantle equipment for rock, jazz *etc* musicians ▫ **road hog** a reckless or selfish driver ▫ **road movie** a film showing the travels of a character or characters ▫ **roadway** *noun* the part of a road used by cars *etc* ▫ **roadworthy** *adj* (of a vehicle) fit to be used on the road

roam *verb* wander about

roan *noun* a horse with a dark-brown coat spotted with grey or white

roar *verb* **1** give a loud, deep sound **2** laugh loudly **3** say (something) loudly ▫ *noun* a loud, deep sound or laugh

roast *verb* cook or be cooked in

an oven or over a fire □ *adj* roasted: *roast beef* □ *noun* **1** meat roasted **2** meat for roasting

rob *verb* steal from □ **robber** *noun* □ **robbery** *noun* (*plural* **robberies**) the act of stealing

> **rob** » rob*s*, robb*ing*, robb*ed*

robe *noun* **1** a long loose garment **2** *US* a dressing-gown **3** (**robes**) the official dress of a judge *etc* □ *verb, formal* dress

robin *noun* a type of small bird, known by its red breast

robot *noun* **1** a mechanical man or woman **2** a machine that can do the work of a person □ **robotic** *adj*

robust *adj* strong, healthy □ **robustness** *noun*

rock *noun* **1** a large lump of stone **2** a hard sweet made in sticks **3** music with a heavy beat and simple melody (*also called*: **rock music**) □ *verb* sway backwards and forwards or from side to side □ **rock-and-roll** or **rock'n'roll** *noun* a simpler, earlier form of rock music □ **rock cake** a small rough-textured cake □ **rocker** *noun* a curved support on which a chair, cradle *etc* rocks □ **rockery** *noun* (*plural* **rockeries**) a collection of stones amongst which small plants are grown □ **rocking-chair** or **rocking-horse** *noun* a chair or a toy horse which rocks backwards and forwards on rockers □ **rocky** *adj* **1** full of rocks **2** inclined to rock, unsteady

rocket *noun* **1** a tube containing inflammable materials, used for launching a spacecraft, signalling and as a firework **2** a spacecraft □ *verb* **1** move upwards rapidly: *prices are rocketing*

rococo *adj* extravagantly ornamented, grotesque

rod *noun* **1** a long thin stick **2** a fishing rod **3** *hist* a measure of distance, about 5 metres

rode *past form* of **ride**

rodent *noun* a gnawing animal, such as a rat, beaver *etc*

rodeo *noun* (*plural* **rodeos**) **1** a round-up of cattle for marking **2** a show of riding by cowboys

roe *noun* **1** the eggs of fishes **2** (also **roe deer**) a small kind of deer **3** a female red deer □ **roebuck** *noun* the male roe deer

rogue *noun* a dishonest or mischievous person, a rascal □ **roguery** *noun* dishonesty; mischief □ **roguish** *adj*

roisterer *noun* a reveller

rôle *noun* a part played by an actor

roll *verb* **1** move along by turning over like a wheel **2** of a ship: rock from side to side **3** of thunder *etc*: rumble **4** wrap round and round: *roll up a carpet* **5** flatten with a roller: *roll the lawn* □ *noun* **1** a sheet of paper, length of cloth *etc* rolled into a cylinder **2** a very small loaf of bread **3** a rocking movement **4** a list of names **5** a long, rumbling sound □ **rollcall** *noun* the calling of names from a list □ **roller** *noun* **1** a cylindrical tool for flattening **2** a tube over which hair is rolled and styled **3** a small solid wheel **4** a long heavy wave on the sea □ **rollerblades** *noun plural* rollerskates with the wheels in a single line □

rollerskates *noun plural* skates with wheels at each corner of the shoe ◊ **rolling pin** a roller for flattening dough ◊ **rolling stock** the stock of engines, carriages *etc* that run on a railway

rollicking *adj* noisy and full of fun

rollmop *noun* a rolled fillet of herring, pickled in vinegar

ROM *abbrev, comput* read-only memory

Roman *adj* of a number: written in letters, as I, II, III, IV *etc* for 1, 2, 3, 4 *etc* ◊ **Roman Catholic Church** the Church whose head is the Pope, the Bishop of Rome

romance *noun* **1** a story about heroic events not likely to happen in real life **2** a love story **3** a love affair ◊ *verb* write or tell imaginative stories ◊ **romantic** *adj* **1** of romance **2** full of feeling and imagination **3** relating to love ◊ **romanticism** *noun*

Romanesque *adj* of architecture: in a style between Roman and Gothic

Romany *noun* **1** a gypsy **2** the gypsy language

romp *verb* **1** play in a lively way **2** move quickly and easily ◊ *noun* a lively game ◊ **rompers** *noun plural* a short suit for a baby

rondel *noun* a poem written in stanzas of thirteen or fourteen lines

rondo *noun* (*plural* **rondos**) a musical composition with a recurring section

rood *noun, old* **1** a measure of area, equal to a quarter of an acre **2** a cross carrying an image of Christ

roof *noun* (*plural* **roofs**) **1** the top covering of a building, car *etc* **2** the upper part of the mouth ◊ *verb* cover with a roof

rook *noun* **1** a kind of crow **2** *chess* the castle ◊ **rookery** *noun* (*plural* **rookeries**) **1** a nesting place of rooks **2** a breeding place of penguins or seals ◊ **rookie** *noun informal* a new recruit

room *noun* **1** an inside compartment in a house **2** space: *room for everybody* **3** (**rooms**) lodgings ◊ **roomy** *adv* having plenty of space

roost *noun* a perch on which a bird rests at night ◊ *verb* sit or sleep on a roost ◊ **rooster** *noun* a farmyard cock

root *noun* **1** the underground part of a plant **2** the base of anything, *eg* a tooth **3** a cause, a source **4** a word from which other words have developed ◊ *verb* **1** form roots and begin to grow **2** be fixed **3** of an animal: turn up ground in a search for food **4** to search (about) ◊ **root-and-branch** *adj & adv* thorough(ly), complete(ly) ◊ **rooted** *adj* firmly planted ◊ **root out** or **root up 1** tear up by the roots **2** get rid of completely ◊ **take root 1** form roots and grow firmly **2** become firmly fixed

rope *noun* **1** a thick cord, made by twisting strands together **2** anything resembling a thick cord ◊ *verb* **1** fasten or catch with a rope **2** enclose, mark off with a rope ◊ **ropy** *adj* **1** like ropes, stringy **2** *informal* bad, not well

rorqual *noun* a finbacked whale

Rorschach test a psychological

test in which someone must interpret the shapes made by ink-blots

rosary *noun* (*plural* **rosaries**) **1** a set of prayers **2** a string of beads used in saying prayers **3** a rose garden

rosé *noun* a pink-coloured wine produced by removing red grape-skins during fermentation

rose[1] *see* **rise**

rose[2] *noun* **1** a type of flower, often scented, growing on a *usu* prickly bush **2** a deep pink colour ▫ **rosehip** *noun* the fruit of the rose ▫ **rosewood** *noun* a dark Brazilian or Indian wood, which smells of roses when cut **rosy** *adj* **1** red, pink **2** (of the future *etc*) bright, hopeful

rosemary *noun* an evergreen sweet-smelling shrub, used as a cooking herb

rosette *noun* a badge shaped like a rose, made of ribbons

roster *noun* a list showing a repeated order of duties *etc*

rostrum *noun* (*plural* **rostrums** or **rostra**) a platform for public speaking

rot *verb* go bad, decay ▫ *noun* **1** decay **2** *informal* nonsense ▫ **rotten** *adj* **1** decayed, bad **2** worthless, disgraceful ▫ **rotter** *noun, informal* a very bad, worthless person

rot *verb* » rot*s*, rott*ing*, rott*ed*

rota *noun* a list of duties *etc* to be repeated in a set order

rotary *adj* turning round like a wheel

rotate *verb* **1** turn round like a wheel **2** go through a repeating series of changes ▫ **rotation** *noun*

rotavator *noun, trademark* a machine for tilling soil

rote *noun*: **by rote** off by heart, automatically

rotisserie *noun* a spit for roasting meat

rotor a turning part of a motor, dynamo *etc*

rotten and **rotter** *see* **rot**

rottweiler *noun* a large, powerful German dog with a smooth coat

rotund *adj* round; plump ▫ **rotundity** *noun*

rouble or **ruble** *noun* a standard unit of Russian coinage

roué *noun* a debauched person, a rake

rouge *noun* a powder or cream used to add colour to the cheeks

rough *adj* **1** not smooth **2** uneven **3** coarse, harsh **4** boisterous, wild **5** not exact: *a rough guess* **6** stormy ▫ *noun* **1** a hooligan, a bully **2** rough ground ▫ **roughage** *noun* bran or fibre in food ▫ **roughcast** *noun* plaster mixed with fine gravel, for coating outside walls ▫ **roughen** *verb* make rough ▫ **rough and ready** not fine or carefully made, but effective ▫ **rough out** sketch or shape roughly

roulade *noun* a meat or vegetable dish shaped into a long roll

roulette *noun* a gambling game, played with a ball which is placed on a wheel

round *adj* **1** shaped like a circle **2**

plump **3** even, exact: *a round dozen* □ *adv* & *prep* **1** on all sides (of), around: *look round the room* **2** in a circle (about): *the earth moves round the sun* **3** from one (person, place *etc*) to another: *the news went round* □ *noun* **1** a circle, something round in shape **2** a single bullet or shell **3** a burst of firing, cheering *etc* **4** a song in which the singers take up the tune in turn **5** a usual route: *a postman's round* **6** a series of calls or deliveries **7** each stage of a contest □ *verb* **1** make or become round **2** of a ship: go round (*eg* a headland) □ **rounders** *noun sing* a ball game played with a bat in which players run around a series of stations □ **Roundhead** *noun* a supporter of Parliament during the English Civil War □ **roundly** *adv* boldly, plainly □ **round trip** *US* a journey to a place and back □ **round on** make a sudden attack on □ **round up** gather or drive together

roundabout *noun* **1** a revolving machine for children to ride on in a park *etc* **2** a meeting place of roads, where traffic must move in a circle □ *adj* not straight or direct: *a roundabout route*

roundel *noun* a round painting, glass panel *etc*

roundelay *noun* a song with a refrain

rouse *verb* **1** awaken **2** stir up, excite □ **rousing** *adj* stirring, exciting

rout *noun* a complete defeat □ *verb* defeat utterly

route *noun* the course to be followed, a way of getting to somewhere □ *verb* fix the route of

routine *noun* a fixed, unchanging order of doing things □ *adj* regular, usual: *routine enquiries*

roux /roo/ *noun* a paste of flour and water used to thicken sauces *etc*

rove *verb* wander or roam □ **rover** **1** a wanderer; an unsettled person **2** (*hist*) a pirate □ **Rover Scout** an older member of the Scout Association

row[1] *noun* **1** a line of people or things **2** a trip in a rowing boat □ *verb* drive (a boat) by oars □ **rower** *noun* someone who rows □ **rowing boat** a boat rowed by oars

row[2] *noun* **1** a noisy quarrel **2** a noise **3** *informal* a scolding

rowan *noun* (*also called*: **mountain ash**) a tree with clusters of bright red berries

rowdy *adj* noisy, disorderly □ **rowdyism** *noun*

rowlock *noun* a place to rest an oar on the side of a rowing boat

royal *adj* **1** relating to a king or queen **2** splendid, magnificent: *royal welcome* □ **royal blue** a deep, bright blue □ **royal icing** stiff cake icing made with egg-white □ **royalist** *noun* someone who supports a king or queen □ **royalty** *noun* (*plural* **royalties**) **1** the state of being royal **2** royal people as a whole **3** a sum paid to the author of a book for each copy sold □ **royal jelly** a jelly secreted by worker bees to feed developing larvae

RP *abbrev* Received Pronunciation, the accepted accent of standard English

rpm *abbrev* revolutions per minute

rps *abbrev* revolutions per second

RSA *abbrev* **1** Royal Society of Arts **2** Royal Scottish Academy

RSAMD *abbrev* Royal Scottish Academy of Music and Drama

RSI *abbrev* repetitive strain injury

RSPB *abbrev* Royal Society for the Protection of Birds

RSPCA *abbrev* Royal Society for the Prevention of Cruelty to Animals

RSSPCC *abbrev* Royal Scottish Society for Prevention of Cruelty to Children

RSVP *abbrev* please reply (from French *répondez, s'il vous plaît*)

Rt Hon *abbrev* Right Honourable

Rt Rev *abbrev* Right Reverend

rub *verb* **1** move one thing against the surface of another **2** clean, polish (something) **3** (with **out** or **away**) remove (a mark) ▫ *noun* **1** the act of rubbing **2** a wipe ▫ **rub in 1** work into (a surface) by rubbing **2** keep reminding someone of (something unpleasant)

> **rub** *verb* » rub*s*, rubb*ing*, rubb*ed*

rubber *noun* **1** a tough elastic substance made from plant juices **2** a piece of rubber used for erasing pencil marks **3** an odd number (three or five) of games in cards, cricket *etc* ▫ **rubber bullet** a hard rubber pellet fired by police in riot control ▫ **rubberneck** *noun, informal* a tourist ▫ **rubber stamp** an instrument with rubber figures or letters for stamping dates *etc* on paper ▫ **rubber-stamp** *verb* authorize, approve

rubbish *noun* **1** waste material, litter **2** nonsense

rubble *noun* small rough stones, bricks *etc* left from a building

rubella *noun* German measles

Rubicon *noun*: **cross the Rubicon** take a decisive step

> After Caesar's crossing of the *Rubicon* river which meant declaring war on his neighbouring province

rubicund *adj* red or rosy-faced

ruble *another spelling* of **rouble**

rubric *noun* **1** a heading **2** a guiding rule

> From a Latin word for red ink, originally an entry in a Biblical text written in red ink

ruby *noun* (*plural* **rubies**) a type of red, precious stone

ruche *noun* a frill

ruck *noun* a wrinkle, a crease

rucksack *noun* a bag carried on the back by walkers, climbers *etc*

ruckus *noun, US* an uproar, a rumpus

ructions *noun plural* a row, a disturbance

rudder *noun* a device fixed to the stern of a boat, or tail of an aeroplane, for steering

ruddy *adj* **1** red **2** of the face: rosy, in good health

rude *adj* **1** showing bad manners, not polite **2** roughly made: *a rude shelter* **3** rough, not refined **4** startling and sudden: *a rude awakening* **5** coarse, vulgar, lewd ▯ **rudely** *adv* ▯ **rudeness** *noun*

rudiments *noun plural* the first simple rules or facts of anything ▯ **rudimentary** *adj* in an early stage of development

rue *noun* a shrub with bitter-tasting leaves ▯ *verb* be sorry for, regret ▯ **rueful** *adj* sorrowful, regretful

ruff *noun* **1** *hist* a pleated frill worn round the neck **2** a band of feathers round a bird's neck

ruffian *noun* a rough, brutal person ▯ **ruffianly** *adj*

ruffle *verb* **1** make unsmooth, crumple (*eg* hair, a bird's feathers) **2** annoy, offend

rug *noun* **1** a floor mat **2** a blanket

Rugby or **rugby** *noun* a form of football using an oval ball which can be handled

Named after *Rugby* School in Warwickshire, where the game was supposedly invented

rugged *adj* **1** having a rough, uneven appearance **2** strong, robust **3** stern, harsh

ruin *noun* **1** complete loss of money *etc* **2** a downfall **3** (**ruins**) broken-down remains of buildings ▯ *verb* **1** destroy **2** spoil completely: *ruin your chances* **3** make very poor ▯ **ruination** *noun* ▯ **ruined** *adj* in ruins, destroyed ▯ **ruinous** *adj* **1** ruined **2** likely to cause ruin

rule *noun* **1** government: *under military rule* **2** a regulation: *school rules* **3** what usually happens **4** a guiding principle **5** a measuring ruler ▯ *verb* **1** govern, be in power **2** decide (that) **3** draw (a line) **4** mark with lines ▯ **ruler** *noun* **1** someone who rules **2** a marked tool for measuring length and drawing straight lines ▯ **ruling** *adj* governing; most important ▯ *noun* a decision, a rule ▯ **as a rule** usually ▯ **rule out** leave out, not consider

rum[1] *noun* an alcoholic spirit made from sugar-cane

rum[2] *adj, informal* strange, odd

rumba *noun* an Afro-Cuban dance in a square pattern

rumble *verb* make a low rolling noise like that of thunder *etc* ▯ *noun* a low rolling noise

rumbustious *noun* boisterous ▯ **rumbustiousness** *noun*

ruminant *noun* an animal, such as a cow, that chews the cud ▯ **ruminate** *verb* **1** chew the cud **2** be deep in thought ▯ **rumination** *noun* deep thought

rummage *verb* turn things over in search ▯ *noun* a thorough search

rummy *noun* a card game played with hands of seven cards

rumour *noun* **1** general talk **2** a story passed from person to person which may not be true ▯ *verb* **1** spread a rumour of **2** tell widely

rump *noun* **1** the hind part of an animal **2** the meat from this part

rumple *verb* **1** make untidy **2** crease

rumpus *noun* an uproar, a clamour

rumpy-pumpy *noun, slang* sexual intercourse

run *verb* **1** move swiftly, hurry **2** race **3** travel: *the train runs every day* **4** of water: flow **5** of a machine: work **6** spread (rapidly): *this colour is running* **7** continue, extend: *the programme runs for two hours* **8** operate (machinery *etc*) **9** organize, conduct (a business *etc*) ◊ *noun* **1** a trip **2** a distance run **3** a spell of running **4** a continuous period: *a run of good luck* **5** a ladder in a stocking *etc* **6** free use of: *the run of the house* **7** a single score in cricket **8** an enclosure for hens *etc* ◊ **runaway** *noun* a person, animal or vehicle that runs away ◊ **run-down** *adj* in poor health or condition ◊ **run-of-the-mill** *adj* ordinary ◊ **runway** *noun* a path for aircraft to take off from or land on ◊ **run a risk** take a chance of loss, failure *etc* ◊ **run down 1** knock (someone) down **2** speak ill of ◊ **run into 1** bump into, collide with **2** meet accidentally ◊ **run out of** become short of ◊ **run over** knock down or pass over with a car

rune *noun* a letter of an early alphabet used in ancient writings ◊ **runic** *adj* written in runes

rung[1] *noun* a step of a ladder

rung[2] *see* **ring**

runnel *noun* a small stream

runner *noun* **1** someone who runs **2** a messenger **3** a rooting stem of a plant **4** a blade of a skate or sledge ◊ **runner-up** *noun* (*plural* **runners-up**) someone who comes second in a race or competition ◊ **do a runner** *slang* leave without paying a bill

running *noun* **1** the act of moving fast **2** management, control ◊ *adj* **1** for use in running **2** giving out fluid: *running sore* **3** carried on continuously: *running commentary* ◊ *adv* one after another: *three days running* ◊ **in (out of) the running** having (or not having) a chance of success

runrig *noun, Scot* a system of dividing land into strips for leasing to tenants

rupee *noun* the standard currency of India, Pakistan and Sri Lanka

rupture *noun* **1** a breaking, *eg* of a friendship **2** a tear in a part of the body ◊ *verb* break, burst

rural *adj* of the country (*contrasted with*: **urban**)

ruse *noun* a trick, a cunning plan

rush[1] *verb* **1** move quickly, hurry **2** make (someone) hurry **3** take (a fort *etc*) by a sudden attack ◊ *noun* (*plural* **rushes**) **1** a quick, forward movement **2** a hurry

rush[2] *noun* (*plural* **rushes**) a tall grasslike plant growing near water

rusk *noun* a hard dry biscuit like toast

russet *adj* reddish-brown ◊ *noun* a type of apple of russet colour

rust *noun* a reddish-brown coating

on metal, caused by air and moisture *verb* form rust **rustproof** *adj* resistant to rust

rustic *adj* **1** relating to the country **2** roughly made **3** simple, unsophisticated *noun* someone who lives in the country **rusticate** *verb* live in the country **rusticity** *noun* **1** country living **2** simplicity

rustle *verb* **1** of silk *etc*: make a soft, whispering sound **2** steal (cattle) **3** *informal* (with **up**) prepare quickly: *rustle up a meal* *noun* a soft, whispering sound **rustler** *noun* someone who steals cattle

rusty *adj* **1** covered with rust **2** *informal* showing lack of practice: *my French is rusty*

rut *noun* a deep track made by a wheel *etc* **rutted** *adj* full of ruts **in a rut** having a dull, routine way of life

rutabaga *noun, US* a yellow turnip, a swede

ruthless *adj* without pity, cruel **ruthlessness** *noun*

RV *abbrev, US* recreational vehicle

rye *noun* a kind of grain **rye-bread** *noun* bread made with flour from this grain **rye-grass** *noun* a grass grown for cattle-feeding

S

s *abbrev* second(s)

Sabbath *noun* the day of the week regularly set aside for religious services and rest (among Muslims, Friday; Jews, Saturday; and Christians, Sunday)

sabbatical *noun* a period of paid leave from work

sable *noun* a small weasel-like animal with dark brown or blackish fur ▯ *adj* black or dark brown in colour

sabotage *noun* deliberate destruction of machinery, an organization *etc* by enemies or dissatisfied workers ▯ *verb* destroy or damage deliberately ▯ **saboteur** *noun* someone who carries out sabotage

> Originally meaning the destruction of machinery by factory workers, from French *sabot* 'clog'

sabre *noun, hist* a curved sword used by cavalry ▯ **sabre-rattling** *noun* an obvious display of force to frighten an enemy

sac *noun* a bag containing a liquid, part of a plant or animal body

saccharine *noun* a very sweet substance used as a sugar substitute

sacerdotal *noun* of a priest; priestly

sachet /*sa*sheh/ *noun* **1** a small bag to hold handkerchiefs *etc* **2** a small sealed packet containing powder or liquid, *eg* shampoo

sack[1] *noun* **1** a large bag of coarse cloth for holding flour *etc* **2** (**the sack**) *informal* dismissal from your job ▯ *verb, informal* dismiss from a job ▯ **sackcloth** *noun* **1** coarse cloth for making sacks **2** a garment made of this worn as a sign of repentance ▯ **sacking** *noun* sackcloth ▯ **get the sack** *informal* be dismissed from your job

sack[2] *noun* the plundering of a captured town ▯ *verb* plunder

sackbut *noun* an early wind instrument with a slide like a trombone

sacral *adj* of the sacrum

> ⚠Do not confuse with: **sacred**

sacralize *verb* make sacred

sacrament *noun* a religious ceremony, *eg* baptism or communion ▯ **sacramental** *adj*

sacred *adj* **1** holy **2** dedicated to some purpose or person: *sacred to her memory* **3** religious: *sacred music*

> ⚠Do not confuse with: **sacral**

sacrifice *noun* **1** the offering of an animal killed for the purpose to a god **2** an animal *etc* offered to a god **3** the giving up of something for the benefit of another person, or to gain something more important **4** something given up for this purpose ▯ *verb* **1** offer (an animal *etc*) as a sacrifice to a god **2** give up (something) for someone or something else

sacrificial *adj* of or for sacrifice □ **sacrificially** *adv*

sacrilege *noun* the use of something holy in a blasphemous way □ **sacrilegious** *adj* □ **sacrilegiously** *adv*

sacrosanct *adj* **1** very sacred **2** not to be harmed or touched

sacrum /*seh*krəm/ *noun* a triangular bone forming part of the human pelvis

SAD *abbrev* seasonal affective disorder, a form of depression caused by lack of sunlight in winter

sad *adj* **1** sorrowful, unhappy **2** showing sorrow **3** causing sorrow: *sad story* **4** *informal* pitiful, feeble

sadden *verb* make or become sad

saddle *noun* **1** a seat for a rider on the back of a horse or bicycle **2** a cut or joint of meat from the back of an animal □ *verb* put a saddle on (an animal) □ **saddlebag** *noun* a bag attached to a horse saddle □ **saddler** *noun* a maker of saddles and harnesses □ **saddle with** burden with: *saddled with debts*

saddo /*sa*doh/ *noun*, *slang* (*plural* **saddoes**) someone with an inadequate personality or lifestyle

sadhu /*sa*doo/ *noun* (*plural* **sadhus**) a Hindu ascetic

sadism /*seh*dizm/ *noun* taking pleasure in cruelty to others □ **sadist** *noun* □ **sadistic** *adj*

SAE or **sae** *abbrev* stamped addressed envelope

safari *noun* an expedition for observing or hunting wild animals □ **safari park** an enclosed area where wild animals are kept outdoors and on view to visitors

safe *adj* **1** unharmed **2** free from harm or danger **3** reliable, trustworthy □ *noun* **1** a lockable box for keeping money and valuables **2** a storage place for meat *etc*

safeguard *noun* anything that gives protection or security □ *verb* protect □ **safety** *noun* freedom from harm or danger □ *adj* giving protection or safety: *safety belt* □ **safety belt** a seat-belt □ **safety-pin** *noun* a curved pin in the shape of a clasp, with a guard covering its point □ **safe and sound** unharmed

safflower *noun* an Indian thistle-like plant whose dried leaves produce a red dye

saffron *noun* a type of crocus from which is obtained a yellow food dye and flavouring agent

sag *verb* droop or sink in the middle

sag » sag*s*, sagg*ing*, sagg*ed*

saga *noun* **1** an ancient story about heroes *etc* **2** a novel or series of novels about several generations of a family **3** a long detailed story

sagacious *adj* very wise, quick at understanding □ **sagaciously** *adv* □ **sagacity** *noun*

sage *noun* **1** a type of herb with grey-green leaves which are used for flavouring **2** a wise man □ *adj* wise □ **sagebrush** *noun* a desert shrub of N America □ **sagely** *adv*

sago *noun* a white starchy substance obtained from a palm-tree, often used in puddings

sahib *noun* a term of respect used in India

said *adj* mentioned before: *the said shopkeeper* □ *past form* of **say**

sail *noun* **1** a sheet of canvas spread out to catch the wind and drive forward a ship or boat **2** a journey in a ship or boat **3** an arm of a windmill □ *verb* **1** travel in a ship or boat (with or without sails) **2** navigate or steer a ship or boat **3** begin a sea voyage **4** glide along easily □ **sailboard** *noun* a surfboard fitted with a mast and sail □ **set sail** set out on a sea voyage

sailor *noun* **1** someone who sails **2** a member of a ship's crew

saint *noun* **1** a very good or holy person **2** a title conferred after death on a holy person by the Roman Catholic Church (*short form*: **St**) □ **sainted** or **saintly** *adj* very holy or very good

Saint Bernard or **St Bernard** a breed of large dog, famous for its use in mountain rescues

sake[1] *noun* **1** cause, purpose: *for the sake of making money* **2** benefit, advantage: *for my sake*

sake[2] /*sa*ki/ *noun* a Japanese alcoholic drink made from fermented rice

salaam *noun* a low bow with the right palm on the forehead, a form of Eastern greeting □ *verb* perform this greeting

salacious *adj* lustful, lecherous □ **salaciously** *adv* □ **salaciousness** *noun*

salad *noun* a dish of raw vegetables, *eg* lettuce, cucumber *etc* □ **salad cream** or **salad dressing** sauce for putting on salad □ **salad days** youth, early days

salamander *noun* a kind of small lizard-like animal

salami *noun* a type of highly seasoned sausage

salary *noun* (*plural* **salaries**) fixed wages regularly paid for work

> Based on Latin *salarium*, ration money given to Roman legionaries for buying salt

salchow /*sal*koh/ *noun, ice-skating* a jump in which a skater takes off from one foot, spins, and lands on the other foot

sale *noun* **1** the exchange of anything for money **2** a selling of goods at reduced prices **3** an auction □ **saleroom** *noun* an auction room □ **salesman**, **saleswoman** *noun* someone who sells or shows goods to customers

salient *adj* **1** pointing outwards: *salient angle* **2** outstanding, chief: *salient points of the speech*

saline *adj* containing salt, salty: *saline solution*

saliva *noun* the liquid that forms in the mouth to help digestion; spittle □ **salivary** *adj* of or producing saliva □ **salivate** *verb* **1** produce saliva **2** anticipate keenly

sallow[1] *adj* of complexion: pale, yellowish

sallow[2] *noun* a type of willow tree

sally *noun* (*plural* **sallies**) **1** a sudden rush forward **2** a trip, an excursion **3** a witty remark or retort ▫ *verb* rush out suddenly ▫ **sally forth** go out, emerge

> **sally** *verb* » sallie*s*, sally*ing*, sallie*d*

salmon *noun* a large fish with yellowish-pink flesh

salmonella *noun* a bacterium which causes food poisoning

salon *noun* **1** a shop in which hairdressing *etc* is done **2** a large room for receiving important guests **3** a gathering of such people

saloon *noun* **1** a passengers' dining-room in a ship **2** a covered-in motor-car **3** a public-house, a bar

salopettes *noun plural* quilted trousers held up by shoulder-straps, worn for skiing

salsa *noun* **1** a type of Latin American dance. music **2** a spicy sauce made from tomatoes, chillies *etc*

salsify *noun* a plant with an edible root which tastes of oysters

salt *noun* **1** a substance used for seasoning, either mined from the earth or obtained from sea water **2** a substance formed from a metal and an acid **3** *informal* a sailor ▫ *adj* **1** containing salt: *salt water* **2** tasting of salt **3** preserved in salt: *salt herring* ▫ *verb* **1** sprinkle with salt **2** preserve with salt ▫ **salt cellar** a small container for salt ▫ **salt-pan** *noun* a dried-up hollow near the sea where salt can be found

saltire /*sol*tair/ *noun* the flag of Scotland, a white cross on a blue background

saltpetre or *US* **saltpeter** *noun* potassium nitrate

salty *adj* **1** tasting of salt **2** piquant, racy

salubrious *adj* **1** health-giving **2** pleasant, respectable

salutary *adj* **1** giving health or safety **2** beneficial, useful: *salutary lesson*

salute *verb* **1** greet with words, an embrace *etc* **2** *military* raise the hand to the forehead to show respect to **3** honour someone by a firing of guns *etc* ▫ *noun* an act or way of saluting ▫ **salutation** *noun* an act of greeting

salvage *noun* **1** goods saved from destruction or waste **2** the act of saving a ship's cargo, goods from a fire *etc* **3** payment made for this act ▫ *verb* save from loss or ruin

salvation *noun* **1** an act, means or cause of saving: *the arrival of the police was his salvation* **2** the saving of humanity from sin

salve *noun* an ointment for healing or soothing ▫ *verb* soothe (pride, conscience *etc*)

salver *noun* a small tray, often of silver

salvo *noun* (*plural* **salvos**) a great burst of gunfire, clapping etc

Samaritans *noun plural* an organization that provides a telephone help-line for people in distress

same *adj* **1** exactly alike, identical: *we both had the same feeling* **2** not different, unchanged: *he still looks the same* **3** mentioned before: *the same person came again* ▯ *pronoun* the thing just mentioned ▯ **sameness** *noun* lack of change or variety ▯ **all the same** or **just the same** in spite of that ▯ **at the same time** still, nevertheless

samizdat *noun* underground literature, forbidden by the state *etc*

samosa *noun* a fried Indian pastry with a spicy filling

samovar *noun* a Russian tea-urn

sampan *noun* a kind of small boat used in Far Eastern countries

sample *noun* a small part extracted to show what the whole is like ▯ *verb* test a sample of: *sample a cake* ▯ **sampler** *noun* **1** someone who samples **2** a piece of needlework *etc* showing skill in different techniques

samurai *noun, hist* a member of the military caste in feudal Japan

sanatorium *noun* **1** a hospital, *esp* for people suffering from respiratory diseases **2** a sick-room in a school *etc*

sanctify *verb* make holy or sacred ▯ **sanctification** *noun*

sanctify » sanctifi*es*, sanctify*ing*, sanctifi*ed*

sanctimonious *adj* self-righteous, priggish

sanction *noun* **1** permission, approval **2** a penalty for breaking a law or rule **3** (**sanctions**) measures applied to force another country *etc* to stop a course of action

sanctity *noun* holiness; sacredness

sanctuary *noun* (*plural* **sanctuaries**) **1** a sacred place **2** the most sacred part of a temple or church **3** a place of safety from arrest or violence **4** a protected reserve for birds or animals

sanctum *noun:* **inner sanctum** a very sacred or private room *etc*

sand *noun* **1** a mass of tiny particles of crushed rocks *etc* **2** (**sands**) a stretch of sand on the seashore ▯ *verb* **1** sprinkle with sand **2** add sand to **3** smooth or polish with sandpaper ▯ **sandbag** *noun* a bag filled with sand, used as a protective barrier ▯ **sand dune** a ridge of sand blown up by the wind ▯ **sand martin** a small bird which nests in sandy banks ▯ **sandpaper** *noun* paper with a layer of sand glued to it for smoothing and polishing ▯ **sandpiper** *noun* a type of wading bird ▯ **sandshoe** *noun* a light shoe with a rubber sole ▯ **sandstone** *noun* a soft rock made of layers of sand pressed together

sandal *noun* a shoe with straps to hold the sole onto the foot

sandalwood *noun* a fragrant E Indian wood

sandwich *noun* (*plural* **sandwiches**) two slices of bread, or a split roll, stuffed with a filling ▯ *verb* fit between two other objects

After the 18th-century Earl of *Sandwich*, said to have invented it to allow him to gamble without interruption for meals

sandy *adj* **1** covered with sand **2**

like sand **3** of hair: yellowish-red in colour

sane *adj* **1** of sound mind, not mad **2** sensible **sanely** *adv* **sanity** *noun*

sang *past form* of **sing**

sangfroid /sonh*frwah*/ *noun* coolness, composure

sanguinary *adj* bloodthirsty, bloody

⚠Do not confuse: **sanguinary** and **sanguine**

sanguine *adj* **1** hopeful, cheerful **2** of a complexion: red, ruddy

sanitary *adj* **1** promoting good health, *esp* by having good drainage and sewage disposal **2** free from dirt, infection *etc* **sanitary towel** a pad of absorbent material worn to soak up menstrual blood

sanitation *noun* arrangements for protecting health, *esp* drainage and sewage disposal

sanity *noun* **1** soundness of mind **2** mental health **3** good sense or judgement

sank *past form* of **sink**

sanserif /san*s*erif/ *noun* a printing type without serifs

Sanskrit *noun* the ancient literary language of India

sap *noun* **1** the juice in plants, trees *etc* **2** *informal* a weakling, a fool *verb* weaken (someone's strength *etc*)

sap *verb* » sap*s*, sapp*ing*, sapp*ed*

sapling *noun* a young tree

saponaceous *adj* soapy; soap-like

sapphire *noun* a precious stone of a deep blue colour

sappy *adj* foolishly weak or sentimental

Saracen *noun, hist* an Islamic opponent of the Crusaders; a Moor

sarcasm *noun* **1** a hurtful remark made in scorn **2** the use of such remarks

sarcastic *adj* **1** containing sarcasm **2** often using sarcasm, scornful **sarcastically** *adv*

sarcoma *noun* a tumour

sarcophagus *noun* a stone coffin

sardine *noun* a young pilchard, often tinned in oil **like sardines** crowded closely together

sardonic *adj* bitter, mocking, scornful

sari *noun* a long cloth wrapped round the waist and brought over the shoulder, traditionally worn by Indian women

sarnie *noun, informal* a sandwich

sarong *noun* a skirt traditionally worn by Malay men and women

sarsaparilla /sarsp*ə*ri*l*ə/ *noun* **1** a tropical American plant whose root is used in medicine **2** a soft drink flavoured with its root

sarsen *noun* a large eroded block of sandstone

sartorial *adj* relating to dress or clothes: *sartorial elegance*

SAS *abbrev* Special Air Service

sash[1] *noun* (*plural* **sashes**) a decorative band worn round the waist or over the shoulder

sash[2] *noun* (*plural* **sashes**) a sliding frame for window panes

sashimi *noun* a Japanese dish of thin slices of raw fish

sassafras *noun* a N American laurel tree whose bark is used as a stimulant

Sassenach *noun, Scot derog* an English person

sat *past form* of **sit**

Satan *noun* the Devil □ **Satanic** *adj* of Satan, devilish □ **satanism** *noun* devil worship □ **satanist** *noun*

satchel *noun* a small bag for carrying schoolbooks *etc*

sate *verb, old* satisfy fully; give more than enough to □ **sated** *adj*

satellite *noun* **1** a moon orbiting a larger planet **2** a man-made object fired into space to orbit a planet **3** a state controlled by a more powerful neighbour □ **satellite television** the broadcasting of television programmes via satellite

satiate *verb* satisfy fully; to give more than enough to □ **satiety** *noun*

satin *noun* a closely woven silk with a glossy surface □ **satinwood** *noun* a smooth kind of wood

satire *noun* **1** a piece of writing *etc* which makes fun of particular people or events **2** ridicule, scorn □ **satirical** *adj* □ **satirist** *noun* a writer of satire

satisfaction *noun* **1** the act of satisfying or being satisfied **2** a feeling of pleasure or comfort **3** something that satisfies **4** compensation for damage *etc*

satisfactory *adj* **1** satisfying **2** fulfilling the necessary requirements □ **satisfactorily** *adv*

satisfy *verb* **1** give enough (of something) to **2** please, make content **3** give enough to lessen or quieten: *satisfied her curiosity* **4** convince: *satisfied that he was innocent* **5** fulfil: *satisfy all our requirements*

> **satisfy** » satisf*ies*, satisfy*ing*, satisf*ied*

satrap *noun* a provincial governor, *esp* in ancient Persia

satsuma *noun* a small seedless orange

saturate *verb* **1** soak or immerse in water **2** cover or fill completely (with): *saturated with information* □ **saturation** *noun*

Saturday *noun* the seventh day of the week

saturnine *adj* gloomy, sullen

satyr /satər/ *noun* a mythological creature, half man, half goat, living in the woods

sauce *noun* **1** a liquid seasoning added to food to improve flavour **2** *informal* cheek, impudence

saucepan *noun* a deep-sided cooking pan with a long handle

saucer *noun* a small, shallow dish for placing under a cup

saucy *adj* impudent, cheeky

sauerkraut *noun* a dish of finely-cut cabbage pickled in salt *etc*

sauna *noun* a room filled with dry steam to induce sweating

saunter *verb* stroll about without hurrying ▢ *noun* a leisurely stroll

sausage *noun* minced meat seasoned and stuffed into a tube of animal gut *etc*

sauté /*soh*teh/ *verb* fry quickly in a small amount of oil or butter

savage *adj* **1** wild, untamed **2** fierce and cruel **3** uncivilized **4** very angry ▢ *noun* **1** an uncivilized person **2** someone fierce or cruel ▢ *verb* attack very fiercely ▢ **savagely** *adv* ▢ **savagery** *noun*

savanna or **savannah** *noun* a grassy, treeless plain

save *verb* **1** bring out of danger, rescue **2** protect from harm, damage or loss **3** keep from spending or using: *saving money/ saves time* **4** put money aside for the future ▢ *prep* except (for): *all the records were scratched save this one* ▢ **saving grace** a good quality that makes up for faults ▢ **savings** *noun plural* money put aside for the future ▢ **save up** put money aside for future use

saviour *noun* **1** someone who saves others from harm or evil **2** (**Saviour**) Christ

savour *noun* **1** characteristic taste or flavour **2** an interesting quality ▢ *verb* **1** taste or smell of **2** taste with enjoyment **3** have a trace or suggestion (of): *his reaction savours of jealousy* **4** experience

savoury *adj* **1** having a pleasant taste or smell **2** salt or sharp in flavour; not sweet ▢ *noun* (*plural* **savouries**) a savoury dish or snack

savoy *noun* a type of winter cabbage

savvy *adj, slang* wise, shrewd ▢ *verb* understand

saw[1] *noun* **1** a tool with a toothed edge for cutting wood *etc* **2** *old* a wise saying ▢ *verb* cut with a saw

saw *verb* » saw*s*, saw*ing*, sawn, saw*ed*

saw[2] *past form* of **see**

sawdust *noun* a dust of fine fragments of wood, made in sawing

sawmill *noun* a mill where wood is sawn up

sax *noun, informal* a saxophone

saxifrage *noun* a type of rock plant

Saxon *noun, hist* one of a Germanic people who invaded Britain in the 5th century

saxophone *noun* a wind instrument with a curved metal tube and keys for the fingers ▢ **saxophonist** *noun* a player of the saxophone

say *verb* **1** speak, utter: *why don't you say 'Yes'?* **2** express in words, state: *they said they knew him* ▢ *noun* **1** the right to speak: *no say in the matter* **2** the opportunity to speak: *I've had my say* ▢ **I say!** *interj* **1** expressing surprise or protest **2** used to try to attract attention ▢ **that is to say** in other words

say *verb* » say*s*, say*ing*, said

saying *noun* something often said; a proverb

scab *noun* **1** a crust formed over

a sore **2** any of several diseases of animals or plants **3** *informal* a blackleg

scabbard *noun* the sheath in which the blade of a sword is kept

scabby *adj* **1** covered in scabs **2** *informal* disgusting, revolting

scabies *noun* an itchy skin disease

scabious *noun* a plant of the teasel family

scabrous *adj* **1** rough, harsh **2** indecent, rude

scaffold *noun* a platform on which people are put to death

scaffolding *noun* a framework of poles and platforms used by people doing repairs on a building *etc*

scald *verb* **1** burn with hot liquid or steam **2** heat (milk *etc*) just short of boiling point ◊ *noun* a burn caused by hot liquid or steam

scale *noun* **1** a set of regularly spaced marks for measurement on a thermometer *etc* **2** a series or system of increasing values: *salary scale* **3** *music* a group of notes going up or down in order **4** the measurements of a map compared with the actual size of the area shown: *drawn to the scale 1:50000* **5** the size of a business *etc*: *manufacture on a small scale* **6** a small thin flake on the skin of a fish or snake **7** (**scales**) a weighing machine ◊ *verb* **1** climb up **2** clear of scales **3** remove in thin layers ◊ **scaly** *adj* having scales; flaky

scallion *noun* a spring onion

scallop *noun* a shellfish with a pair of hinged fan-shaped shells ◊ **scalloped** *adj* of an edge: cut into curves or notches

scallywag *noun* a rogue

scalp *noun* **1** the outer covering of the skull **2** the skin and hair on top of the head ◊ *verb* cut the scalp from

scalpel *noun* a small, thin-bladed knife, used in surgery

scam *noun*, *US informal* a swindle, a trick

scamp *noun* a rascal

scamper *verb* **1** run about playfully **2** run off in haste

scampi *noun plural* Norway lobsters (large prawns) cooked for eating

scan *verb* **1** count the beats in a line of poetry **2** of poetry: have the correct number of beats **3** examine carefully **4** *informal* read quickly, skim over **5** pass an X-ray, ultrasonic wave *etc* over ◊ *noun* an act of scanning ◊ **scanner** *noun* a machine which scans ◊ **scansion** *noun* scanning of poetry

> **scan** *verb* » scan*s*, scann*ing*, scann*ed*

scandal *noun* **1** something disgraceful or shocking **2** talk or gossip about people's (supposed) misdeeds ◊ **scandalize** *verb* shock, horrify ◊ **scandalmonger** *noun* someone who spreads gossip or scandal

scandalous *adj* **1** shameful, disgraceful **2** containing scandal ◊ **scandalously** *adv*

scansorial *adj* having feet adapted for climbing

scant *adj* not plentiful, hardly enough: *pay scant attention*

scanty *adj* little or not enough in amount: *scanty clothing* ▫ **scantily** *adv*

scapegoat *noun* someone who bears the blame for the wrongdoing of others

> Literally 'escape goat', after an ancient Jewish ritual of transferring the people's sins to a goat which was afterwards let free in the wilderness

scapula *noun* the shoulderblade

scar *noun* **1** the mark left by a wound or sore **2** a mark, a blemish ▫ *verb* mark with a scar

> **scar** *verb* » scar*s*, scarr*ing*, scarr*ed*

scarab *noun* a beetle regarded as sacred by the ancient Egyptians

scarce *adj* **1** not plentiful, not enough **2** rare, seldom found ▫ **make yourself scarce** go, run away

scarcely *adv* **1** only just, barely: *could scarcely hear* **2** surely not: *you can scarcely expect me to eat that*

scarcity *noun* (*plural* **scarcities**) want, shortage

scare *verb* **1** drive away with fear **2** startle, frighten ▫ *noun* a sudden fright or alarm

scarecrow *noun* a figure set up to scare birds away from crops

scarey *adj another spelling* of **scary**

scarf *noun* (*plural* **scarves** or **scarfs**) a strip of material worn round the neck, shoulders or head

scarlatina *noun* a mild form of scarlet fever

scarlet *noun* a bright red colour ▫ *adj* bright red ▫ **scarlet fever** an infectious illness, causing a rash

scarper *verb, slang* run away

scary or **scarey** *adj* frightening

scat *interj, informal* go away!

scathing *adj* cruel, hurtful: *scathing remark*

scatological *adj* full of references to faeces or defecation: *scatological humour*

scatter *verb* **1** throw loosely about; sprinkle **2** spread widely **3** flee in all directions ▫ **scatterbrain** *noun* someone who frequently forgets things ▫ **scattered** *adj* thrown or spread about widely ▫ **scattering** *noun* a small amount thinly spread or scattered

scatty *adj* scatterbrained

scavenger *noun* an animal which feeds on dead flesh

SCE *abbrev* Scottish Certificate of Education

scenario /sə*na*reeoh/ *noun* **1** a scene-by-scene outline of a play, film *etc* **2** an outline of a plan or project

> ⚠Do not confuse with: **scene**

scene *noun* **1** the place where something happens: *scene of the* *accident* **2** a view, a landscape **3** a division of a play or opera **4** an area of activity: *the music scene* **5** a show of bad temper: *don't create a scene*

scenery *noun* **1** the painted background on a theatre stage **2** the general appearance of a stretch of country

scenic *adj* **1** of scenery **2** picturesque

scent *verb* **1** discover by the smell **2** have a suspicion of, sense: *scent danger* **3** give a pleasant smell to: *roses scented the air* ▫ *noun* **1** perfume **2** an odour, a smell **3** the trail of smell used to track an animal *etc*

sceptic /*skep*tik/ *noun* someone who doubts what they are told ▫ **sceptical** *adj* unwilling to believe, doubtful ▫ **sceptically** *adv* ▫ **scepticism** *noun*

⚠Do not confuse with: **septic**

sceptre /*sep*tər/ *noun* an ornamental rod carried by a monarch on ceremonial occasions

schadenfreude /*sha*dənfroidə/ *noun* pleasure in the misfortunes of others

schedule /*she*dyool/ or /*ske*dyool/ *noun* **1** the time set for doing something: *I'm two weeks behind schedule* **2** a written statement of details **3** a form for filling in information ▫ *verb* **1** form into a schedule **2** plan, arrange

schema /*skee*mə/ *noun* a scheme, a plan

schematic *adj* according to a plan ▫ **schematically** *adv*

scheme /skeem/ *noun* **1** a plan, a systematic arrangement **2** a dishonest or crafty plan ▫ *verb* make schemes, plot ▫ **scheming** *adj* crafty, cunning

scherzo /*skuhrt*soh/ *noun* (*plural* **scherzos**), *music* a lively movement in triple time

schism /sizm/ or /skizm/ *noun* a breaking away from the main group

schist /shist/ *noun* a type of rock that splits easily into layers

schizo /*skit*soh/ *noun* (*plural* **schizos**) & *adj*, *slang* (a) schizophrenic

schizophrenia /skitsoh*freen*yə/ *noun* a mental illness involving a complete change in personality and behaviour ▫ **schizophrenic** *noun* & *adj* (someone) suffering from schizophrenia

schlock *noun, informal* tacky or shoddy goods ▫ **schlocky** *adj*

schmaltz *noun, informal* sentimentality

schmuck *noun, informal* an idiot, a fool

schnapps *noun* a German liqueur

schnitzel *noun* a veal cutlet

scholar *noun* **1** someone of great learning **2** someone who has been awarded a scholarship **3** a pupil, a student ▫ **scholarship** *noun* **1** learning **2** a sum of money given to help a clever student to carry on further studies ▫ **scholastic** *adj* of schools or scholars

scholarly *adj* showing or having knowledge, high intelligence and love of accuracy ▯ **scholarliness** *noun*

school *noun* **1** a place for teaching, *esp* children **2** a group of artists *etc* who share the same ideas **3** a large number of fish, whales *etc* ▯ *verb* **1** educate in a school **2** train by practice ▯ **schooling** *noun* **1** education in a school **2** training ▯ **schoolmate** *noun* someone taught at the same school as yourself ▯ **schoolmaster**, **schoolmistress** *noun* a teacher at a school

schooner *noun* **1** a two-masted sailing ship **2** a large sherry glass **3** *US & Austral* a large beer glass

schwa *noun* an unstressed vowel sound, written (ə)

sciatic /sai*a*tik/ *adj* relating to the hip

sciatica /sai*a*tikə/ *noun* severe pain in the upper part of the leg

SCID *abbrev* severe combined immuno-deficiency disease

science *noun* **1** knowledge obtained by observation and experiment **2** a branch of this knowledge, *eg* chemistry, physics, biology *etc* **3** these sciences considered together ▯ **science fiction** stories dealing with future life on earth, space travel, other planets *etc*

scientific *adj* **1** of science **2** done according to the methods of science **scientifically** *adv*

scientist *noun* someone who studies one or more branches of science

sci fi *abbrev* science fiction

scimitar *noun* a sword with a short curved blade

scintillate *verb* **1** sparkle **2** show brilliant wit *etc*

scion /*sai*ən/ *noun* **1** a young member of a family **2** a descendant **3** a cutting for grafting on another plant

scissors *noun plural* a cutting instrument with two hinged blades

sclerosis *noun* hardening, *esp* of the arteries

scoff *verb* **1** express scorn **2** (**scoff at**) make fun of, mock

scold *verb* blame or rebuke with angry words ▯ *noun* a bad-tempered person ▯ **scolding** *noun*

scone *noun* a small plain cake made with flour and water

scoop *noun* **1** a hollow instrument used for lifting loose material, water *etc* **2** an exclusive news story ▯ *verb* lift or dig out with a scoop

scooter *noun* **1** a two-wheeled toy vehicle pushed along by foot **2** a low-powered motor-cycle

scope *noun* **1** opportunity or room to do something: *scope for improvement* **2** extent, range: *outside the scope of this dictionary*

scorch *verb* **1** burn slightly, singe **2** dry up with heat

scorching *adj* **1** burning, singeing **2** very hot **3** harsh, severe: *scorching criticism*

score *noun* **1** a gash, a notch **2** an account, a debt: *settle old scores* **3** the total number of points gained in a game **4** a written piece of music showing separate parts for voices and instruments **5** a set of twenty **6** (**scores**) a great many: *scores of people* **7** a reason, account: *don't worry on that score* □ *verb* **1** mark with lines or notches **2** gain (points) **3** keep a note of points gained in a game □ **score out** cross out

scorn *verb* **1** look down on, despise **2** refuse (help *etc*) because of pride □ *noun* despisal □ **scornful** *adj* full of scorn □ **scornfully** *adv*

scorpion *noun* a spider-like creature with a poisonous sting in its tail

scotch *verb* stamp out, suppress

Scotch *noun, informal* whisky □ **Scotch tape** *US, trademark* adhesive tape □ **Scotch terrier** a breed of small rough-coated dog

scot-free *adj* unhurt; unpunished

SCOTVEC *abbrev* Scottish Vocational Education Council

scoundrel *noun* a rascal

scour *verb* **1** clean by hard rubbing; scrub **2** search thoroughly

scourge *noun* **1** a whip **2** a cause of great suffering □ *verb* **1** whip, lash **2** afflict, cause to suffer

Scouse *noun, Brit* a native or inhabitant of Liverpool

scout *noun* **1** a guide or spy sent ahead to bring back information **2** (**Scout**) a member of the Scout Association

scowl *verb* wrinkle the brows in displeasure or anger □ *noun* a frown

Scrabble *noun, trademark* a word-building game

scrabble *verb* scratch or grope about

scraggy *adj* **1** long and thin **2** uneven, rugged

scram *exclam* go away!

scramble *verb* **1** struggle to seize something before others **2** wriggle along on hands and knees **3** mix or toss together: *scrambled eggs* **4** jumble up (a message) to make it unintelligible without decoding □ *noun* **1** a rush and struggle to get something **2** a motor-cycle race over rough country

scrap *noun* **1** a small piece, a fragment **2** a picture for pasting in a scrapbook **3** *informal* a fight **4** parts of a car *etc* no longer required: *sold as scrap* **5** (**scraps**) small pieces, odds and ends □ *verb* **1** abandon as useless **2** *informal* fight, quarrel □ **scrapbook** *noun* a blank book in which to stick pictures *etc* □ **scrap metal** metal for melting and re-using

> **scrap** *verb* » scrap*s*, scrap*ping*, scrap*ped*

scrape *verb* **1** rub and mark with something sharp **2** drag or rub against or across a surface with a harsh grating sound **3** (with **up** or **together**) collect (money *etc*) with difficulty □ *noun* **1** an act of scraping **2** a mark or sound made by scraping **3** *informal* a difficult situation □ **scrape through** only just avoid failure

scrap-heap *noun* a heap of old metal *etc*, a rubbish heap □ **on the scrap-heap** no longer needed

scrapie *noun* a disease of sheep

scrappy *adj* made up of odd scraps, not well put together □ **scrappily** *adv*

scratch *verb* **1** draw a sharp point across the surface of **2** mark by doing this **3** tear or dig with claws, nails *etc* **4** rub with the nails to relieve or stop itching **5** withdraw from a competition □ *noun* (*plural* **scratches**) **1** a mark or sound made by scratching **2** a slight wound □ *adj* **1** *golf* too good to be allowed a handicap **2** of a team: made up of players hastily got together □ **come up to scratch** be satisfactory □ **start from scratch** start from nothing, right at the beginning

scrawl *verb* write or draw untidily or hastily □ *noun* **1** untidy, hasty or bad writing **2** something scrawled

scrawny *adj* thin, skinny

scream *verb* utter a shrill, piercing cry as in pain, fear *etc;* shriek □ *noun* a shrill cry

scree *noun* loose stones covering a steep mountain side

screech *verb* utter a harsh, shrill and sudden cry □ *noun* a harsh shrill cry

screed *noun* a long boring speech or letter

screen *noun* **1** a flat covered framework to shelter from view or protect from heat, cold *etc* **2** something that shelters from wind, danger, difficulties *etc* **3** the surface on which cinema films are projected **4** the surface on which a television picture, or computer data, appears □ *verb* **1** shelter, hide **2** make a film of **3** show on a screen **4** sift, sieve **5** sort out (the good from the bad) by testing **6** conduct examinations on someone to test for disease □ **screen off** hide behind, or separate by, a screen

screw *noun* **1** a nail with a slotted head and a winding groove or ridge (called the **thread**) on its surface **2** a kind of propeller (a **screw-propeller**) with spiral blades, used in ships and aircraft **3** a turn or twist (of a screw *etc*) □ *verb* **1** fasten or tighten with a screw **2** fix (*eg* a stopper) in place with a twisting movement **3** twist, turn round (your head *etc*) **4** twist up, crumple, pucker □ **screwdriver** *noun* a tool for turning screws

scribble *verb* **1** write carelessly **2** make untidy or meaningless marks with a pencil *etc* □ **1** careless writing **2** meaningless marks, a doodle

scribe *noun, hist* **1** a clerk who copied out manuscripts **2** a Jewish teacher of law

scrimp *verb* be sparing or stingy with money: *scrimping and saving for a holiday*

scrimshaw *noun* decorative engraving on shells or bone, traditionally done by sailors

script *noun* **1** the text of a play, talk *etc* **2** handwriting like print

scripture *noun* **1** sacred writings **2** (**Scripture**) the Christian Bible

scrofula *noun* a disease of the lymph nodes in the neck

scroll *noun* **1** a piece of paper rolled up **2** an ornament shaped like this

scrotum *noun* the bag of skin enclosing the testicles

scrounge *verb, slang* **1** cadge **2** get by begging *noun* an attempt to beg or cadge: *on the scrounge* **scrounger** *noun*

scrub *verb* rub hard in order to clean *noun* countryside covered with low bushes

> **scrub** *verb* » scrub*s*, scrub*bing*, scrubb*ed*

scruff *noun* the back of the neck **scruffy** *adj* untidy

scrum *noun, Rugby* a struggle for the ball by the forwards of the opposing sides bunched together

scrumptious *adj, informal* delicious

scrunch *verb* crumple

scruple *noun* doubt over what is right or wrong that keeps someone from doing something *verb* hesitate because of a scruple **scrupulous** *adj* careful over the smallest details

scrutiny *noun* (*plural* **scrutinies**) careful examination, a close look **scrutinize** *verb* examine very closely

SCSI /*skoozee*/ or /*skuzee*/*abbrev*, *comput* small computer systems interface, a method of connecting a PC to peripheral devices

scuba *noun* breathing apparatus used by skin-divers

scud *verb* move or sweep along quickly: *scudding waves*

> **scud** » scud*s*, scudd*ing*, scudd*ed*

scuffle *noun* a confused fight

scull *noun* a short oar *verb* move (a boat) with a pair of these or with one oar worked at the back of the boat

scullery *noun* (*plural* **sculleries**) a room for rough kitchen work

sculptor, sculptress *noun* an artist who carves or models figures in wood, stone, clay *etc* **sculpture** *noun* **1** the art of the sculptor or sculptress **2** a piece of their work

scum *noun* **1** foam that rises to the surface of liquids **2** the most worthless part of anything: *the scum of the earth*

scunner *noun, Scot* a nuisance, a pest

scupper *noun* a hole in the side of a ship to drain water from the deck *verb* put an end to, ruin: *scupper his chances*

scurf *noun* small flakes of dead skin (*esp* on the scalp)

scurrilous *adj* insulting, abusive: *a scurrilous attack*

scurry *verb* hurry along, scamper

> **scurry** » scurri*es*, scurry*ing*, scurri*ed*

scurvy *noun* a type of disease caused by a lack of fresh fruit and vegetables

scuttle *noun* **1** a fireside container for coal **2** an opening with a lid in a ship's deck or side *verb* **1** make a hole in (a ship) in order to sink it **2** hurry along, scamper

scuzzy *adj, slang* seedy, sleazy; grubby

scythe /saidh/ *noun* a large curved blade, on a long handle, for cutting grass *etc* by hand □ *verb* cut with a scythe

SE *abbrev* south-east; south-eastern

sea *noun* **1** the mass of salt water covering most of the earth's surface **2** a great stretch of water of less size than an ocean **3** a great expanse or number: *a sea of faces* □ **sea anemone** a type of small plant-like animal found on rocks at the seashore □ **seaboard** *noun* land along the edge of the sea □ **sea dog** an old sailor; a pirate □ **seafarer** *noun* a traveller by sea, a sailor □ **seafaring** *adj* □ **seafront** *noun* a promenade with its buildings facing the sea □ **seagoing** *adj* (of a ship) sailing on the ocean □ **seagull** *noun* a type of web-footed sea bird □ **sea-horse** *noun* a type of small fish with a horse-like head and neck □ **sea level** the level of the surface of the sea □ **sea-lion** *noun* a large kind of seal the male of which has a mane □ **seaman** *noun* (*plural* **seamen**) a sailor, *esp* a member of a ship's crew who is not an officer □ **seamanship** *noun* the art of steering and looking after ships at sea □ **seaplane** *noun* an aeroplane which can take off from and land on the water □ **seascape** *noun* a picture of a scene at sea □ **seashore** *noun* the land next to the sea □ **seasick** *adj* made ill by the rocking movement of a ship □ **seaside** *noun* the land beside the sea □ **sea-trout** *noun* a type of large trout living in the sea but spawning in rivers □ **sea urchin** a type of small sea creature with a spiny shell □ **seaward** *adj* & *adv* towards the sea □ **seaweed** *noun* any of many kinds of plants growing in the sea □ **seaworthy** *adj* in a good enough condition to go to sea □ **at sea 1** on the sea **2** completely puzzled

seal[1] *noun* a furry sea animal living partly on land

seal[2] *noun* **1** a piece of wax with a design pressed into it, attached to a document to show that it is legal or official **2** a piece of wax used to keep a parcel closed **3** anything that closes tightly **4** a piece of sticky paper with a picture on it: *a Christmas seal* □ *verb* **1** mark or fasten with a seal **2** close up completely **3** make (legally) binding and definite: *seal a bargain* □ **sealing wax** a hard kind of wax for sealing letters, documents *etc*

seam *noun* **1** the line formed by the sewing together of two pieces of cloth **2** a line or layer of metal, coal *etc* in the earth □ **seamstress** *noun* a woman who sews for a living □ **the seamy side** the more unpleasant side (*eg* of life)

séance /*seh*ohns/ *noun* a meeting of people to receive messages from the spirits of the dead

seannachie /*she*nəxhi/*noun* a Gaelic storyteller

sear *verb* **1** scorch, burn **2** hurt severely

search *verb* **1** look over in order to find something **2** (with **for**) look for, seek □ *noun* (*plural* **searches**) **1** an act of searching **2** an attempt to find □ **searching** *adj* examining closely and carefully: *searching* *question* ◻ **searchlight** *noun* a strong beam of light used for picking out objects at night ◻ **search-warrant** *noun* permission given to the police to search a house *etc* for stolen goods *etc*

season *noun* **1** one of the four divisions of the year (spring, summer, autumn, winter) **2** the proper time for anything **3** a time associated with a particular activity: *football season* ◻ *verb* **1** add (salt *etc*) to improve the flavour of (food) **2** dry (wood) till it is ready for use ◻ **seasonable** *adj* **1** happening at the proper time **2** of weather: suitable for the season ◻ **seasonal** *adj* **1** of the seasons or a season **2** of work *etc*: taking place in one particular season only ◻ **seasoned** *adj* **1** of food: flavoured **2** of wood: ready to be used **3** trained, experienced: *a seasoned traveller* ◻ **seasoning** *noun* something (*eg* salt, pepper) added to food to give it more taste ◻ **season ticket** a ticket that can be used repeatedly for a certain period of time

seat *noun* **1** a piece of furniture for sitting on **2** the part of a chair on which you sit **3** the buttocks **4** a mansion **5** a place in parliament, on a council *etc* **6** the centre of some activity: *the seat of government* ◻ *verb* **1** make to sit down **2** have seats for (a certain number): *the room seats forty* ◻ **seat-belt** *noun* a belt fixed to a seat in a car *etc* to prevent a passenger from being thrown out of the seat

sebaceous *adj* secreting sebum

sebum *noun* an oily substance secreted by the skin and hair

sec *short for* **1** second **2** secretary

secateurs *noun plural* a tool like scissors, for trimming bushes *etc*

secede *verb* break away from a group, society *etc* ◻ **secession** *noun*

seclude *verb* keep (yourself) apart from people's notice or company ◻ **seclusion** *noun*

second *adj* **1** next after the first in time, place *etc* **2** other, alternate: *every second week* **3** another of the same kind as: *they thought him a second Mozart* ◻ *noun* **1** someone or something that is second **2** an attendant to someone who boxes or fights a duel **3** the 60th part of a minute of time, or of a degree (in measuring angles) **4** an article not quite perfectly made: *these gloves are seconds* ◻ *verb* **1** support, back up **2** transfer temporarily to a special job ◻ **secondary** *adj* second in position or importance ◻ **second-best** *adj* next to the best, not the best ◻ *adj* **second-hand** **1** not new; having been used by another: *second-hand clothes* **2** of a shop: dealing in second-hand goods ◻ **secondly** *adv* in the second place ◻ **second-rate** *adj* not of the best quality, inferior ◻ **second nature** a firmly fixed habit: *organizing people is second nature to her* ◻ **secondary school** a school between primary school and university *etc*

secret *adj* **1** hidden from, or not known by, others **2** secretive ◻ *noun* **1** a fact, plan *etc* that is not told or known ◻ **secrecy** *noun* the state of being secret, mystery ◻ **secretive** *adj* inclined to hide or conceal your feelings, activities *etc* ◻ **secret**

service a government department dealing with spying

secretary *noun* (*plural* **secretaries**) **1** someone employed to write letters, keep records *etc* in an office **2** someone elected to deal with the written business of a club *etc* □ **secretarial** *adj* of a secretary or their work □ **Secretary of State 1** a government minister in charge of an administrative department **2** *US* the person in charge of foreign affairs

secrete *verb* **1** hide, conceal in a secret place **2** of a part of the body: store up and give out (a fluid) □ **secretion** *noun*

sect *noun* a group of people who hold certain views *esp* in religious matters □ **sectarian** *adj* **1** of a sect **2** loyal to a sect **3** narrow-minded

section *noun* **1** a part, a division: *a section of the community* **2** a thin slice of a specimen for examination under a microscope **3** the view of the inside of anything when it is cut right through or across: *a section of a plant*

sector *noun* **1** a three-sided part of a circle whose sides are two radii and a part of the circumference **2** a part, a section

secular *adj* **1** of worldly, not spiritual or religious things **2** of music *etc*: not sacred or religious

secure *adj* **1** safe, free from danger or fear **2** confident: *secure in the knowledge that she had no rivals* **3** firmly fixed or fastened: *the lock is secure* □ *verb* **1** make safe, firm or established: *secure your position* **2** seize, get hold of: *secure the diamonds* **3** fasten: *secure the lock*

security *noun* **1** safety **2** (**securities**) property or goods which a lender may keep until the loan is paid back

secy *abbrev* secretary

sedan *noun* **1** an enclosed chair for one person, carried on two poles by two bearers (*also called*: **sedan chair**) **2** *US* a saloon car

sedate *adj* calm, serious, dignified □ **sedateness** *noun*

sedative *adj* calming, soothing □ *noun* a medicine with this effect □ **sedation** *noun* the use of sedatives to calm a patient

sedentary *adj* of a job *etc*: requiring much sitting

sedge *noun* a type of coarse grass growing in swamps and rivers

sediment *noun* the grains or solid parts which settle at the bottom of a liquid

sedition *noun* the stirring up of rebellion against the government □ **seditious** *adj* encouraging rebellion, rebellious

seduce *verb* **1** tempt (someone) away from right or moral behaviour **2** persuade (someone) to have sexual intercourse **3** attract □ **seducer** *noun* □ **seduction** *noun* □ **seductive** *adj* attractive, tempting

sedulous *adj* diligent, painstaking

see *verb* **1** have sight **2** be aware of, notice by means of the eye: *he can see us coming* **3** form a picture of in the mind **4** understand: *I see what you mean* **5** find out: *I'll see* *what is happening* **6** make sure: *see that he finishes his homework* **7** accompany: *I'll see you home* **8** meet: *I'll see you at the usual time* □ *noun* the district over which a bishop or archbishop has authority □ **seeing that** since, because □ **see through 1** take part in to the end **2** not be deceived by (a person, trick *etc*) □ **see to** attend to (the preparation of): *see to a meal*

> **see** *verb* » sees, seeing, saw, seen

seed *noun* **1** the part of a tree, plant *etc* from which a new plant may grow **2** a seed-like part of a grain or a nut **3** the beginning from which anything grows: *the seeds of rebellion* **4** a seeded player in a tournament **5** *old* children, descendants □ *verb* **1** of a plant: produce seed **2** sow **3** remove the seeds from (*eg* a fruit) **4** arrange (good players) in a tournament so that they do not compete against each other till the later rounds □ **go to seed** or **run to seed 1** of a plant: develop seeds **2** of a person, area *etc*: deteriorate, become run down

seedling *noun* a young plant just sprung from a seed

seedy *adj* **1** full of seeds **2** shabby **3** sickly, not very well

seek *verb* **1** look or search for **2** try (to do something): *seek to establish proof* **3** try to get (advice *etc*) □ **sought after** popular, much in demand

> **seek** » seeks, seeking, sought

seem *verb* **1** appear to be: *he seems kind* **2** appear: *she seems to like it* □ **seeming** *adj* apparent but not actual or real: *a seeming success* □ **seemly** *adj* suitable; decent

seen *see* **see**

seep *verb* flow slowly through a small opening, leak

seer *noun* a prophet

seersucker *noun* a lightweight ribbed cotton fabric

seesaw *noun* **1** a plank balanced across a stand so that one end of it goes up when the other goes down **2** an up-and-down movement like that of a seesaw □ *verb* **1** go up and down on a seesaw **2** move with a seesaw-like movement

seethe *verb* **1** boil **2** be very angry □ **seething** *adj*

segment *noun* **1** a part cut off **2** a part of a circle cut off by a straight line

segregate *verb* separate (someone or a group) from others □ **segregation** *noun*

seine *noun* a large type of fishing net

seismic /*saiz*mik/ *adj* of earthquakes □ **seismograph** *noun* an instrument that records earthquake shocks and measures their force

seize *verb* **1** take suddenly by force **2** overcome: *seized with fury* **3** (with **up**) of machinery: become stuck, break down □ **seizure** *noun* **1** sudden capture **2** a sudden attack of illness, rage *etc*

seldom *adv* not often, rarely: *you seldom see an owl during the day*

select *verb* pick out from several according to your preference, choose ▯ *adj* **1** picked out, chosen **2** very good **3** exclusive, allowing only certain people in ▯ **selection** *noun* **1** the act of choosing **2** things chosen **3** a number of things from which to choose ▯ **selective** *adj* **1** selecting carefully **2** of weed-killer: harmless to garden plants ▯ **selector** *noun* someone who chooses (*eg* members for a national team)

self *noun* (*plural* **selves**) **1** someone's own person **2** someone's personality, character ▯ **self-assured** *adj* trusting in your own power or ability, confident ▯ **self-centred** *adj* concerned with your own affairs, selfish ▯ **self-confident** *adj* believing in your own powers or abilities ▯ **self-conscious** too aware of your faults *etc* and therefore embarrassed in the company of others ▯ **self-contained** *adj* **1** of a house: complete in itself, not sharing any part with other houses **2** of a person: self-reliant ▯ **self-control** *noun* control over yourself, your feelings *etc* ▯ **self-defence** *noun* the defence of your own person, property *etc* ▯ **self-denial** *noun* doing without something, *esp* in order to give to others ▯ **self-effacing** *adj* keeping yourself from being noticed, modest ▯ **self-esteem** *noun* respect for yourself; conceit ▯ **self-evident** *adj* clear enough to need no proof ▯ **self-expression** *noun* expressing your own personality in your activities ▯ **self-important** *adj* having a mistakenly high sense of your importance ▯ **self-indulgent** *adj* too ready to satisfy your own inclinations and desires ▯ **self-interest** *noun* a selfish desire to consider only your own interests or advantage ▯ **selfless** *adj* thinking of others before yourself, unselfish ▯ **self-made** *adj* owing success *etc* to your own efforts: *a self-made man* ▯ **self-portrait** *noun* an artist's portrait of themselves ▯ **self-possessed** *adj* calm in mind or manner, quietly confident ▯ **self-raising flour** flour already containing an ingredient to make it rise ▯ **self-reliant** *adj* trusting in your own abilities *etc* ▯ **self-respect** *noun* respect for yourself and concern for your own character and reputation ▯ **self-righteous** *adj* thinking highly of your own goodness and virtue ▯ **self-sacrifice** *noun* the act of giving up your own life, possessions *etc* in order to do good to others ▯ **selfsame** *adj* the very same ▯ **self-satisfied** *adj* pleased, smug, satisfied with yourself ▯ **self-service** *adj* of a restaurant: where customers help or serve themselves ▯ **self-sufficient** *adj* needing no help or support from anyone else ▯ **self-willed** *adj* determined to have your own way, obstinate

selfish *adj* caring only for your own pleasure or advantage ▯ **selfishly** *adv* ▯ **selfishness** *noun* ▯

sell *verb* **1** give or hand over for money **2** have or keep for sale: *he sells newspapers* **3** be sold for, cost: *this book sells for £20* ▯ **seller** *noun* someone who sells

sell » sell*s*, sell*ing*, sold

Sellotape *noun, trademark* transparent adhesive tape, used for sticking pieces of paper together

selvage *noun* the firm edge of a piece of cloth, that does not fray

semantic *adj* relating to the meaning of words *etc*

semaphore *noun* a form of signalling using the arms to form different positions for each letter

semblance *noun* an outward, often false, appearance: *a semblance of listening*

semen *noun* the liquid that carries sperm

semester *noun, US* a term at a university *etc*

semi- *prefix* **1** half **2** *informal* partly □ **semi-detached** *adj* of a house: joined to another house on one side but not on the other □ **semi-final** *noun* the stage or match of a contest immediately before the final □ **semi-precious** *adj* of a stone: having some value, but not considered a gem

semibreve *noun, music* a whole-note (𝅝), equal to four crotchets in length

semicircle *noun* half of a circle

semicolon *noun* the punctuation mark (;)

seminal *adj* influential, important

seminar *noun* a group of students working on, or meeting to discuss, a particular subject

seminary *noun* (*plural* **seminaries**) a school or college

semiotics *noun plural* the study of signs and symbols □ **semiotician** *noun* someone who studies semiotics

Semitic *adj* Jewish

semolina *noun* the hard particles of wheat sifted from flour, used for puddings *etc*

Semtex *noun, trademark* a material used to make explosives

senate *noun* **1** the upper house of parliament in the USA, Australia *etc* **2** the governing council of some universities **3** *hist* the law-making body in ancient Rome □ **senator** *noun* a member of a senate

send *verb* **1** make (someone) go **2** have (something) carried or delivered to a place □ **sender** *noun* □ **send-off** *noun* **1** a start **2** a friendly farewell for someone going on a journey *etc* □ **send for** order to be brought

> **send** » send*s*, send*ing*, sent

senile *adj* **1** of old age **2** showing the mental feebleness of old age □ **senility** *noun*

senior *adj* older in age or higher in rank □ *noun* someone in a senior position □ **seniority** *noun* the fact of being senior

senna *noun* the dried leaves of certain plants, used as a laxative

sensation *noun* **1** a feeling through any of the five senses **2** a vague effect: *a floating sensation* **3** a state of excitement: *causing a sensation* □ **sensational** *adj* causing great excitement, horror *etc*

sense *noun* **1** one of the five powers by which humans feel or notice (hearing, taste, sight, smell, touch) **2** a feeling: *a sense of loss* **3**

an ability to understand or appreciate: *a sense of humour* **4** **(senses)** right mind, common sense: *to take leave of your senses* **5** wisdom, ability to act in a reasonable way **6** ability to be understood: *your sentence does not make sense* **7** meaning: *to what sense of this word are your referring?* □ *verb* feel, realize: *sense disapproval* □ **senseless** *adj* stunned, unconscious; foolish □ **sensor** *noun* a device that detects and measures physical changes □ **sensory** *adj* of the senses

sensible *adj* **1** wise **2** able to be felt or noticed **3** (with **of**) aware of □ **sensibility** *noun* (*plural* **sensibilities**) ability to feel, sensitivity

sensitive *adj* **1** feeling, *esp* strongly or painfully **2** strongly affected by light, movements *etc* □ **sensitivity** *noun* □ **sensitize** *verb* make sensitive (*esp* to light)

sensual *adj* **1** of the senses rather than the mind **2** indulging too much in bodily pleasures □ **sensuality** *noun* □ **sensually** *adv*

> ⚠Do not confuse: **sensual** and **sensuous**

sensuous *adj* **1** pleasing to the senses **2** easily affected through the senses □ **sensuosity** *noun* □ **sensuously** *adv*

sent *see* **send**

sentence *noun* **1** a number of words which together make a complete statement **2** a judgement announced by a judge or court □ *verb* condemn to a particular punishment

sentient *adj* thinking, reasoning

sentiment *noun* **1** a thought expressed in words **2** a show of feeling or emotion, often excessive □ **sentimental** *adj* having or showing too much feeling or emotion □ **sentimentality** *noun*

sentinel *noun* a soldier on guard

sepal *noun* one of the green leaves beneath the petals of a flower

separate *verb* **1** set or keep apart **2** divide into parts **3** disconnect **4** go different ways **5** live apart by choice □ *adj* **1** placed, kept *etc* apart **2** divided **3** not connected **4** different □ **separation** *noun* a dividing or putting apart □ **separatism** *noun* □ **separatist** *noun* someone who withdraws or urges separation from an established church, state *etc*

Sephardic *adj* relating to the Jewish people of Spain, Portugal or N Africa

sepia *noun* a brown colour

sept *noun* a division of a clan

sept- *prefix* seven

September *noun* the ninth month of the year

septet *noun* a group of seven musicians *etc*

septic *adj* of a wound: full of germs that are poisoning the blood □ **septic tank** a tank in which sewage is partially purified

> ⚠Do not confuse with: **sceptic**

septuagenarian *noun* someone from seventy to seventy-nine years old

sepulchre *noun* a tomb ▫ **sepulchral** *adj* **1** of sepulchres **2** dismal, gloomy **3** of a voice: deep, hollow in tone

sequel *noun* **1** a result, a consequence **2** a story that is a continuation of an earlier story

sequence *noun* **1** the order (of events) in time **2** a number of things following in order, a connected series

sequestered *adj* of a place: lonely, quiet

sequestrate *verb* keep apart, isolate

sequin *noun* a small round sparkling ornament sewn on a dress *etc*

sequoia *noun* a giant N American redwood tree

seraglio *noun* (*plural* **seraglios**) a harem

seraph (*plural* **seraphs** or **seraphim**) an angel of the highest rank ▫ **seraphic** *adj* like an angel

sere *adj, formal* dry, withered

serenade *noun* music played or sung in the open air at night, *esp* under a woman's window ▫ *verb* sing or play a serenade (to)

serendipity *noun* happy chance, luck ▫ **serendipitous** *adj*

serene *adj* **1** calm **2** not worried, happy, peaceful ▫ **serenity** *noun* calmness, peacefulness

serf *noun, hist* a slave bought and sold with the land on which he worked ▫ **serfdom** *noun* slavery

serge *noun* a strong type of cloth

sergeant *noun* **1** an army rank above corporal **2** a rank in the police force above a constable ▫ **sergeant-major** *noun* an army rank above sergeant

series *noun* (*plural* **series**) **1** a number of things following each other in order **2** a set of things of the same kind: *a series of books on art* ▫ **serial** *noun* a story which is published, broadcast or televised in instalments

serif *noun* a short line or stroke on the end of a printed letter

serious *adj* **1** grave, thoughtful: *serious expression on her face* **2** not joking, in earnest: *serious remark* **3** important, needing careful thought: *a serious matter* **4** likely to have dangerous results: *serious accident* ▫ **seriously** *adv* ▫ **seriousness** *noun*

sermon *noun* a serious talk, *esp* one given in church

serpent *noun, old* a snake ▫ **serpentine** *adj* like a serpent; winding, full of twists

SERPS *abbrev* state earnings-related pension scheme

serrated *adj* having notches or teeth like a saw

serried *adj* crowded together: *serried ranks*

serum *noun* **1** a clear watery fluid in blood that helps fight disease **2** a fluid injected into the body to help fight disease

serve *verb* **1** work for and obey **2** attend or wait upon at table **3** give out food, goods *etc* **4** be able to be used (as): *the cave will serve as a shelter* **5** be suitable for: *serve a* *purpose* **6** carry out duties as a member of the armed forces **7** undergo (a sentence in prison *etc*) **8** *tennis* throw up the ball and hit it with the racket to start play ▫ **serve someone right** be deserved by them

servant *noun* **1** someone paid to work for another, *esp* in helping to run a house **2** a government employee: *civil servant/public servant*

service *noun* **1** an act of serving **2** the duty required of a servant or other employee **3** a performance of (public) worship **4** use: *bring the new machine into service* **5** time spent in the armed forces **6** (**services**) the armed forces **7** (**services**) help: *services to refugees* **8** a regular supply: *bus service* **9** (**services**) public supply of water, gas, electricity *etc* **10** a set of dishes: *dinner service* ▫ *verb* keep (a car, machine *etc*) in good working order by regular repairs ▫ **serviceable** *adj* useful; lasting a long time: *serviceable clothes* ▫ **active service** service in battle ▫ **at your service** ready to help or be of use

serviette *noun* a table napkin

servile *adj* slave-like; showing lack of spirit: *a servile attitude to his employer* ▫ **servility** *noun* ▫ **servitude** *noun* slavery; the state of being under strict control

sesame *noun* a SE Asian plant whose seeds produce an edible oil

sesquicentenary or **sesquicentennial** *noun* a hundred and fiftieth anniversary

session *noun* **1** a meeting of a court, council *etc* **2** the period of the year when classes are held in a school *etc* **3** a period of time spent on a particular activity

sestet *noun* a group of six musicians *etc*

set *verb* **1** place or put **2** fix in the proper place (*eg* broken bones) **3** arrange (a table for a meal, jewels in a necklace *etc*) **4** fix (a date, a price *etc*) **5** fix hair (in waves or curls) **6** adjust (a clock or a machine *etc*) so that it is ready to work or perform some function **7** give (a task *etc*): *set him three problems* **8** put in a certain state or condition: *set free* **9** (with **off** or **out** or **forth**) start (on a journey *etc*) **10** of a jelly *etc*: become firm or solid **11** compose music for: *he set the poem to music* **12** of the sun: go out of sight below the horizon ▫ *adj* **1** fixed or arranged beforehand; ready: *all set* **2** fixed, stiff: *a set expression on his face* ▫ *noun* **1** a group of people **2** a number of things of a similar kind, or used together: *set of carving tools* **3** an apparatus: *a television set* **4** scenery made ready for a play *etc* **5** pose, position: *the set of his head* **6** a series of six or more games in tennis **7** a fixing of hair in waves or curls **8** a badger's burrow (*also called*: **sett**) **9** a street paving-block (*also called*: **sett**) ▫ **setback** *noun* a movement in the wrong direction, a failure ▫ **set-square** *noun* a triangular drawing instrument, with one right angle ▫ **setting** *noun* **1** the act of someone who or something that sets **2** an arrangement **3** a background: *against a setting of* *hills and lochs* □ **set about 1** begin (doing something) **2** attack □ **set in** begin: *winter has set in* □ **set on** attack

> **set** *verb* » sets, sett*ing*, set

sett *another spelling* of **set** (senses 8 and 9)

settee *noun* a sofa

setter *noun* a dog trained to point out game in hunting

settle *verb* **1** place in a position or at rest **2** come to rest **3** agree over (a matter): *settle the price* **4** (sometimes with **down**) become calm or quiet **5** (sometimes with **down**) make your home in a place **6** pay (a bill) **7** fix, decide (on) **8** bring (a quarrel *etc*) to an end **9** sink to the bottom □ *noun* a long high-backed bench □ **settlement** *noun* **1** the act of settling **2** a decision, an agreement **3** payment for a bill **4** money given to a woman on her marriage **5** a number of people who have come to live in a country □ **settler** *noun* someone who goes to live in a new country

seven *noun* the number 7 □ *adj* 7 in number □ **seventh** *adj* the last of a series of seven □ *noun* one of seven equal parts

seventeen *noun* the number 17 □ *adj* 17 in number □ **seventeenth** *adj* the last of a series of seventeen □ *noun* one of seventeen equal parts

seventy *noun* the number 70 □ *adj* 70 in number □ **seventieth** *adj* the last of a series of seventy □ *noun* one of seventy equal parts

sever *verb* **1** cut apart or away, break off **2** separate, part □ **severance** *noun*

several *adj* **1** more than one or two, but not many **2** various **3** different: *going their several ways* □ *pronoun* more than one or two people, things *etc*, but not a great many

severe *adj* **1** serious: *a severe illness* **2** harsh, strict **3** very plain and simple, not fancy □ **severity** *noun*

sew *verb* **1** join together with a needle and thread **2** make or mend in this way □ **sewer** *noun*

> **sew** » sew*s*, sew*ing*, sew*ed*, sewn

sewer *noun* an underground drain for carrying off water and waste matter □ **sewage** *noun* water and waste matter

sex *noun* **1** either of the two classes (male or female) into which animals are divided according to the part they play in producing children or young **2** sexual intercourse

sex- *prefix* six

sexagenarian *noun* someone from sixty to sixty-nine years old

sexism *noun* discrimination against someone on the grounds of their sex □ **sexist** *noun* & *adj*

sexology *noun* the study of human sexual behaviour □ **sexologist** *noun*

sextant *noun* an instrument used for calculating distances by means of measuring angles *eg* the distance between two stars

sextet *noun* a group of six musicians *etc*

sexton *noun* someone who has various responsibilities in a church, *eg* bellringing, gravedigging *etc*

sexual *adj* **1** of sex or gender **2** relating to sexual intercourse □ **sexuality** *noun* □ **sexually** *adv* □ **sexual intercourse** physical union between a man and a woman involving the insertion of the penis into the vagina

SF *abbrev* science fiction

SFA *abbrev* Scottish Football Association

SFX *abbrev* special effects

sgraffito *noun* decorative artwork in which layers are scraped away to reveal different colours

shabby *adj* **1** worn-looking **2** poorly dressed **3** of behaviour: mean, unfair □ **shabbily** *adv*

shack *noun* a roughly-built hut

shackle *verb* **1** fasten with a chain **2** hold back, prevent, hinder □ **shackles** *noun plural* chains fastening a prisoner's legs or arms

shade *noun* **1** slight darkness caused by cutting off some light **2** a place not in full sunlight **3** a screen from the heat or light **4** (**shades**) *informal* sunglasses **5** the deepness or a variation of a colour **6** the dark parts in a picture **7** a very small amount or difference: *a shade larger* **8** a ghost □ *verb* **1** shelter from the sun or light **2** make parts of a picture darker **3** change gradually, *eg* from one colour into another □ **shading** *noun* the marking of the darker places in a picture

shadow *noun* **1** shade caused by some object coming in the way of a light **2** the dark shape of that object on the ground **3** a dark part in a picture **4** a very small amount: *a shadow of doubt* □ *verb* **1** shade, darken **2** follow someone about secretly and watch them closely □ **shadow cabinet** leading members of the opposition in parliament

shady *adj* **1** sheltered from light or heat **2** *informal* dishonest, underhand: *a shady character*

shaft *noun* **1** anything long and straight **2** the rod on which the head of an axe, arrow *etc* is fixed **3** an arrow **4** a revolving rod which turns a machine or engine **5** the pole of a cart to which the horses are tied **6** the deep, narrow passageway leading to a mine **7** a deep vertical hole for a lift **8** a ray (of light)

shag *verb, slang* **1** have sexual intercourse **2** have sexual intercourse with □ *noun* an act of sexual intercourse

> **shag** *verb* » shag*s*, shag*ging*, shag*ged*

shaggy *adj* rough, hairy, or woolly

shagpile *adj* of a carpet: having a thick pile

shake *verb* **1** move backwards and forwards or up and down with quick, jerky movements **2** make or be made unsteady **3** shock, disturb: *his parting words shook me* □ *noun* **1** the act of shaking or trembling **2** a shock **3** a drink mixed by shaking or stirring quickly: *milk shake*

shake *verb* » shake*s*, shak*ing*, shaken, shook

shaky *adj* unsteady; trembling □ **shakily** *adv*

shale *noun* a kind of rock from which oil can be obtained

shall *verb* **1** used to form future tenses of other verbs when the subject is *I* or *we*: *I shall tell you later* **2** used for emphasis, or to express a promise, when the subject is *you, he, she, it* or *they*: *you shall go if I say you must/ you shall go if you want to* □ *see also* **should**

shallot *noun* a kind of onion

shallow *adj* **1** not deep **2** not capable of thinking or feeling deeply □ *noun* (often **shallows**) a place where the water is not deep

shalom *exclam* peace be with you, a Jewish greeting

sham *noun* something which is not what it appears to be, a pretence □ *adj* false, imitation, pretended: *a sham fight* □ *verb* pretend, feign: *shamming sleep*

sham *verb* » sham*s*, sham*ming*, shamm*ed*

shaman *noun* a tribal healer or medicine man

shamble *verb* walk in a shuffling or awkward manner □ **shambles** *noun plural*, *informal* a mess, confused disorder

shambolic *adj*, *slang* chaotic, messy

shame *noun* **1** an uncomfortable feeling caused by realization of guilt or failure **2** disgrace, dishonour **3** *informal* bad luck, a pity: *it's a shame that you can't go* □ *verb* **1** make to feel shame or ashamed **2** (with **into**) cause (someone to do something) by making them ashamed: *they shamed him into paying his share* □ **shamefaced** *adj* showing shame or embarrassment □ **shameful** *adj* disgraceful □ *adj* **shameless** *adj* feeling or showing no shame □ **put to shame** cause to feel ashamed

shammy *another spelling of* **chamois**

shampoo *verb* wash (the hair and scalp) □ *noun* **1** an act of shampooing **2** a soapy liquid used for cleaning the hair **3** a similar liquid used for cleaning carpets or upholstery

shamrock *noun* a plant like clover with leaves divided in three

shanghai *verb* **1** drug and send to sea as a sailor **2** trick into doing something unpleasant

Shangri-la *noun* an imaginary paradise

shank *noun* **1** the part of the leg between the knee and the foot **2** a long straight part (of a tool *etc*)

shank's pony walking, on foot

shan't *short for* shall not

shanty *noun* (*plural* **shanties**) **1** a roughly-made hut **2** a sailors' song □ **shantytown** *noun* an area of makeshift, squalid housing

shape *noun* **1** the form or outline of anything **2** a mould for a jelly *etc* **3** a jelly *etc* turned out of a mould **4** condition: *in good shape* □ *verb* **1** make into a certain form **2** model, mould **3** develop (in a particular way): *our plans are shaping well* □ **shapeless** *adj* having no shape or regular form □ **shapely** *adj* having an attractive shape

share *noun* **1** one part of something that is divided among several people **2** one of the parts into which the money of a business firm is divided □ *verb* **1** divide out among a number of people **2** allow others to use (your possessions *etc*) **3** have or use in common with someone else: *we share a liking for music* □ **shareholder** *noun* someone who owns shares in a business company □ **shareware** *noun* computer software that is made available for a small fee

shark *noun* **1** a large, very fierce, flesh-eating fish **2** *informal* a swindler

sharp *adj* **1** cutting, piercing **2** having a thin edge or fine point **3** hurting, stinging, biting: *sharp wind/ sharp words* **4** alert, quick-witted **5** severe, inclined to scold **6** *music* of a note: raised half a tone in pitch **7** of a voice: shrill **8** of an outline: clear □ *adv* punctually: *come at ten o'clock sharp* □ *noun, music* a sign (♮) showing that a note is to be raised half a tone □ **sharpen** *verb* make or grow sharp □ **sharpener** *noun* an instrument for sharpening: *pencil sharpener* □ **sharper** *noun* a cheat, *esp* at cards □ **sharp practice** cheating □ **sharp-sighted** *adj* having keen sight □ **sharp-witted** *adj* alert, intelligent □ **look sharp** hurry

shatter *verb* break in pieces; to upset, ruin (hopes, health *etc*)

shave *verb* **1** cut away hair with a razor **2** scrape away the surface of (wood *etc*) **3** touch lightly, or just avoid touching, in passing □ *noun* **1** the act of shaving **2** a narrow escape: *a close shave* □ **shaven** *adj* shaved □ **shavings** *noun plural* very thin slices of wood *etc*

shawl *noun* a loose covering for the shoulders

shawm *noun* an early musical instrument like an oboe

she *pronoun* a woman, girl or female animal *etc* already spoken about (used only as the subject of a verb): *when the girl saw us, she waved*

sheaf *noun* (*plural* **sheaves**) a bundle (*eg* of corn, papers) tied together

shear *verb* **1** clip, cut (*esp* wool from a sheep) **2** cut through, cut off □ **shears** *noun plural* large scissors

shear » shear*s*, shear*ing*, shorn, shear*ed*

⚠Do not confuse with: **sheer**

sheath *noun* **1** a case for a sword or dagger **2** a long close-fitting covering **3** a condom □ **sheathe** *verb* put into a sheath

shebang *noun, informal* a matter, an affair

shed *noun* **1** a building for storage or shelter: *coalshed/ bicycle shed* **2** an out-house □ *verb* **1** throw or cast off (leaves, a skin, clothing) **2** pour out (tears, blood) **3** give out (light *etc*)

sheen *noun* brightness, gloss

sheep *noun* **1** an animal whose flesh is used as food and whose fleece is used for wool **2** a very meek person who lacks confidence □ **sheep-dip** *noun* a liquid for disinfecting sheep □ **sheepdog** *noun* a dog trained to look after sheep □ **sheepish** *adj* shy; embarrassed, shamefaced □ **sheepshank** *noun* a kind of knot, used for shortening a rope □ **sheepskin** *noun* **1** the skin of a sheep **2** a kind of leather made from this

sheer *adj* **1** very steep: *sheer drop from the cliff* **2** pure, not mixed: *sheer delight/ sheer nonsense* **3** of cloth: very thin or fine □ *adv* straight up and down, very steeply □ *verb* turn aside from a straight line, swerve

⚠Do not confuse with: **shear**

sheet *noun* **1** a large piece of linen, cotton, nylon *etc* for a bed **2** a large thin piece of metal, glass, ice *etc* **3** a piece of paper **4** a sail **5** the rope fastened to the lower corner of a sail □ **sheet-anchor** *noun* a large anchor for use in emergencies □ **sheeting** *noun* any material from which sheets are made □ **sheet-lightning** *noun* lightning which appears in great sheets or flashes

sheikh *noun* an Arab chief

shekel *noun*, *hist* an ancient Jewish weight and coin

shelf *noun* (*plural* **shelves**) **1** a board fixed on a wall, for laying things on **2** a flat layer of rock, a ledge **3** a sandbank

shell *noun* **1** a hard outer covering (of a shellfish, egg, nut *etc*) **2** a husk or pod (*eg* of peas) **3** a metal case filled with explosive fired from a gun **4** a framework, *eg* of a building not yet completed or burnt out: *only the shell of the warehouse was left* □ *verb* **1** take the shell from (a nut, egg *etc*) **2** fire shells at

shellac *noun* a type of resin once used to make gramophone records

shellfish *noun* a water creature covered with a shell, *eg* an oyster, limpet or mussel

shelter *noun* **1** a building which acts as a protection from harm, rain, wind *etc* **2** the state of being protected from any of these □ *verb* **1** give protection to **2** put in a place of shelter or protection **3** go to, or stay in, a place of shelter □ **take shelter** go to a place of shelter

shelve *verb* **1** put up shelves in **2** put aside (a problem *etc*) for later consideration **3** of land: slope gently

shenanigans *noun plural, informal* trickery, mischief

shepherd, shepherdess *noun* someone who looks after sheep □ *verb* (**shepherd**) watch over carefully, guide □ **shepherd's pie** a dish of minced meat covered with mashed potatoes

sherbet *noun* **1** a fizzy drink **2** powder for making this

sheriff *noun* **1** the chief representative of a monarch in a county, whose duties include keeping the peace **2** in Scotland, the chief judge of a county **3** *US* the chief law-enforcement officer of a county

sherry *noun* a strong kind of wine, often drunk before a meal

shiatsu /shee*at*soo/ *noun* a Japanese therapy which treats illness by applying pressure to certain points of the body

shibboleth *noun* a word or attribute which identifies members of a group

> Originally a word giving membership to a group, after a Biblical story in which its correct pronunciation was used as a password

shied *past form* of **shy**

shield *noun* **1** anything that protects from harm **2** a broad piece of metal carried by a soldier *etc*as a defence against weapons **3** a shield-shaped trophy won in a competition **4** a shield-shaped plaque bearing a coat-of-arms □ *verb* protect, defend, shelter

shieling *noun* a hut used as a shelter by shepherds

shift *verb* **1** move, change the position of: *shift the furniture/ trying to shift the blame* **2** change position or direction: *the wind shifted* **3** get rid of □ *noun* **1** a change: *shift of emphasis* **2** a change of position, transfer **3** a group of workers on duty at the same time: *day shift/ night shift* **4** a specified period of work or duty **5** a loose-fitting lightweight dress □ **shiftless** *adj* having no set plan or purpose, lazy □ **shifty** *adj* not to be trusted, looking dishonest □ **shift for yourself** manage to get on by your own efforts

shiitake *noun* a dark brown Japanese mushroom

shilling *noun, Brit hist* a silver-coloured coin in use before decimalization, worth $\frac{1}{20}$ of £1 (now the 5 pence piece)

shillyshally *verb* hesitate in making up your mind, waver

> **shillyshally** » shillyshall*ies*, shillyshally*ing*, shillyshall*ied*

shimmer *verb* shine with a quivering or unsteady light □ *noun* a quivering light

shin *noun* the front part of the leg below the knee □ **shin up** climb

shindig *noun, informal* a party, a celebration

shindy *noun* (*plural* **shindies**) *informal* a noise, uproar

shine *verb* **1** give out or reflect light **2** be bright **3** polish (shoes etc) **4** be very good at: *he shines at arithmetic* □ *noun* **1** brightness **2** an act of polishing □ **shining** *adj* **1** very bright and clear **2** admired, distinguished: *a shining example*

> **shine** *verb* » shine*s*, shin*ing*, shone

shingle *noun* coarse gravel of rounded stones on the shores of rivers or of the sea □ **shingles** *noun plural* an infectious disease causing a painful rash

shinty *noun* a Scottish ball-game resembling hockey

shiny *adj* glossy, polished ◊ **shinily** *adv* ◊ **shininess** *noun*

ship *noun* a large vessel for journeys across water ◊ *verb* **1** take onto a ship **2** send by ship **3** go by ship ◊ **ship chandler** someone who deals in ship's stores ◊ **shipmate** *noun* a fellow-sailor ◊ **shipment** *noun* **1** an act of putting on board ship **2** a load of goods sent by ship ◊ **shipping** *noun* ◊ **shipshape** *adj* in good order, neat, trim ◊ **shipwreck** *noun* **1** the sinking or destruction of a ship (*esp* by accident) **2** a wrecked ship **3** ruin ◊ **shipwrecked** *adj* involved in a shipwreck ◊ **shipwright** *noun* someone who is employed to build or repair ships ◊ **shipyard** *noun* the yard in which ships are built or repaired

> **ship** *verb* » ship*s*, shipp*ing*, shipp*ed*

shire *noun* a county

shirk *verb* avoid or evade (doing your duty *etc*) ◊ **shirker** *noun*

shirt *noun* **1** a garment worn by men on the upper part of the body, having a collar, sleeves and buttons down the front **2** a similar garment for a woman

shish kebab pieces of meat and vegetables grilled on a skewer

shit *noun, taboo slang* **1** excrement, faeces **2** an unpleasant or worthless person ◊ *verb* empty the bowels ◊ *exclam* expressing anger, annoyance, displeasure *etc* ◊ **shitty** *adj* very disagreeable, unpleasant

> **shit** *verb* » shit*s*, shitt*ing*, shitt*ed* or shat

shiver *verb* **1** tremble with cold or fear **2** break into small pieces, shatter ◊ *noun* **1** the act of shivering **2** a small broken piece: *shivers of glass*

shoal *noun* **1** a group of fishes, moving and feeding together **2** a shallow place, a sandbank

shock *noun* **1** a sudden forceful blow **2** a feeling of fright, horror, dismay *etc* **3** a state of weakness or illness following such feelings **4** the effect on the body of an electric current passing through it **5** an earthquake **6** a bushy mass (of hair) ◊ *verb* **1** give a shock to **2** upset or horrify ◊ **shock-absorber** *noun* a device in an aircraft, car *etc* for lessening the impact or force of bumps ◊ **shocking** *adj* causing horror or dismay; disgusting

shod *adj* wearing shoes ◊ *verb, past form* of **shoe**

shoddy *adj* **1** of poor material or quality: *shoddy goods* **2** mean, low: *a shoddy trick*

shoe *noun* **1** a stiff outer covering for the foot, not reaching above the ankle **2** a rim of iron nailed to the hoof of a horse ◊ *verb* put shoes on (a horse) ◊ **shoehorn** *noun* a curved piece of horn, metal *etc* for making a shoe slip easily over your heel ◊ **shoelace** *noun* a cord or string used for fastening a shoe ◊ **shoemaker** *noun* someone who makes and mends shoes ◊ **on a shoestring** with very little money

> **shoe** *verb* » shoe*s*, shoe*ing*, shod

shone *past form* of **shine**

shoo *exclam* used to scare away birds, animals *etc* □ *verb* drive or scare away

shoo *verb* » shoo*s*, shoo*ing*, shoo*ed*

shoogle *verb, Scot* shake

shook *see* **shake**

shoot *verb* **1** send a bullet from a gun, or an arrow from a bow **2** hit or kill with an arrow, bullet *etc* **3** let fly swiftly and with force **4** kick for a goal **5** score (a goal) **6** of a plant: grow new buds **7** photograph, film **8** move very swiftly or suddenly **9** slide (a bolt) □ *noun* **1** a new sprout on a plant **2** an expedition to shoot game **3** land where game is shot □ **shooting-brake** *noun, old* an estate car □ **shooting star** a meteor

shoot *verb* » shoot*s*, shoot*ing*, shot

shop *noun* **1** a place where goods are sold **2** a workshop □ *verb* **1** visit shops and buy goods **2** *slang* betray (someone) to the police □ **shopkeeper** *noun* someone who owns and keeps a shop □ **shoplifter** *noun* someone who steals goods from a shop □ **shopper** *noun* someone who shops, a customer □ **shop steward** a worker elected by the other workers as their representative □ **talk shop** *informal* talk about work when off duty

shop *verb* » shop*s*, shopp*ing*, shopp*ed*

shore *noun* the land bordering on a sea or lake □ *verb* prop (up), support: *shoring up an unprofitable organization*

shorn *see* **shear**

short *adj* **1** not long: *short skirt* **2** not tall **3** brief, not lasting long: *short talk* **4** not enough, less than it should be **5** rude, sharp, abrupt **6** of pastry: crisp and crumbling easily □ *adv* **1** suddenly, abruptly: *stop short* **2** not as far as intended: *the shot fell short* □ *noun* **1** a short film **2** a short-circuit **3** (**shorts**) short trousers □ *verb* short-circuit □ **shortage** *noun* a lack □ **shortbread** *noun* a thick biscuit made of butter and flour *etc* □ **shortcoming** *noun* a fault, a defect □ **short cut** a short way of going somewhere or doing something □ **shorten** *verb* make less in length □ **shorthand** *noun* a method of swift writing using strokes and dots to show sounds (*contrasted with*: **longhand**) □ **short-handed** *adj* having fewer workers than usual □ **short list** a list of candidates selected from the total number of applicants or contestants □ **shortlived** *adj* living or lasting only a short time □ **shortly** *adv* **1** soon **2** curtly, abruptly **3** briefly □ **short-sighted** *adj* **1** seeing clearly only things which are near **2** taking no account of what may happen in the future □ **short-tempered** *adj* easily made angry □ **short-term** *adj* intended to last only a short time □ **give short shrift to** waste little time or consideration on □ **in short** in a few words □ **short of 1** not having enough: *short of money* **2** less than, not as much or as far as: *5 miles short of Inverness/£5 short of the price* **3** without going as far as: *he didn't know how to get the money, short of stealing it*

short-circuit *noun* the missing out of a major part of an intended electric circuit, sometimes causing blowing of fuses ◻ *verb* **1** of an electrical appliance: have a short-circuit **2** bypass (a difficulty *etc*)

shot *noun* **1** something which is shot or fired **2** small lead bullets, used in cartridges **3** a single act of shooting **4** the sound of a gun being fired **5** the distance covered by a bullet, arrow *etc* **6** a marksman **7** a throw or turn in a game **8** an attempt at doing something, guessing *etc* **9** a photograph **10** a scene in a motion picture ◻ *adj* **1** of silk: showing changing colours **2** streaked or mixed with (a colour *etc*) ◻ *verb, past form* of **shoot** ◻ **shotgun** *noun* a light type of gun which fires shot ◻ **a shot in the dark** a guess

should *verb* **1** the form of the verb **shall** used to express a condition: *I should go if I had time* **2** used to mean 'ought to': *you should know that already*

shoulder *noun* **1** the part of the body between the neck and upper arm **2** the upper part of an animal's foreleg **3** a hump, a ridge: *the shoulder of the hill* ◻ *verb* **1** carry on the shoulders **2** bear the full weight of (a burden *etc*) **3** push with the shoulder ◻ **shoulderblade** *noun* the broad flat bone of the shoulder

shout *noun* **1** a loud cry or call **2** a loud burst (of laughter *etc*) ◻ *verb* make a loud cry

shove *verb* push roughly, thrust, push aside ◻ *noun* a rough push

shovel *noun* a spade-like tool used for lifting coal, gravel *etc* ◻ *verb* lift or move with a shovel

show *verb* **1** allow, or cause, to be seen: *show me your new dress* **2** be able to be seen: *your underskirt is showing* **3** exhibit, display (an art collection *etc*) **4** point out (the way *etc*) **5** direct, guide: *show her to a seat* **6** make clear, demonstrate: *that shows that I was right* ◻ *noun* **1** the act of showing **2** a display, an exhibition **3** a performance, an entertainment ◻ **show business** the branch of the theatre concerned with variety entertainments ◻ **showroom** *noun* a room where goods are laid out for people to see ◻ **showy** *adj* bright, gaudy; (too) obvious, striking ◻ **show off 1** show or display (something) **2** try to impress others with your talents *etc* ◻ **show up 1** make to stand out clearly **2** expose, make obvious (*esp* someone's faults)

> **show** *verb* » shows, show*ing*, shown, show*ed*

shower *noun* **1** a short fall of rain **2** a large quantity: *a shower of questions* **3** a bath in which water is sprayed from above **4** the apparatus which sprays water for this **5** *US* a party at which gifts are given to someone about to be married ◻ *verb* **1** pour (something) down on **2** bathe under a shower ◻ **showerproof** *adj* of material, a coat *etc*: able to withstand light rain ◻ **showery** *adj* raining from time to time

shown *see* **show**

shoyu *noun* a Japanese fermented soy sauce

shrank *see* **shrink**

shrapnel *noun* **1** a shell containing bullets *etc* which scatter on explosion **2** splinters of metal, a bomb *etc*

> After Henry *Shrapnel*, 18th-century British general who invented the shell

shred *noun* **1** a long, narrow piece, cut or torn off **2** a scrap, a very small amount: *not a shred of evidence* ▯ *verb* cut or tear into shreds

> **shred** *verb* » shred*s*, shredd*ing*, shredd*ed*

shrew *noun* **1** a small mouse-like type of animal with a long nose **2** a quarrelsome or scolding woman ▯ **shrewish** *adj* quarrelsome, ill-tempered

shrewd *adj* clever, cunning

shriek *verb* make a shrill scream or laugh ▯ *noun* a shrill scream or laugh

shrift *noun*: **give someone short shrift** dismiss them quickly

> Originally a short confession made before being executed

shrike *noun* a bird which preys on smaller birds

shrill *adj* of a sound or voice: high in tone, piercing ▯ **shrilly** *adv*

shrimp *noun* **1** a small, long-tailed edible shellfish **2** *informal* a small person

shrine *noun* a holy or sacred place

shrink *verb* **1** make or become smaller **2** draw back in fear and disgust (from) ▯ *noun, informal* a psychiatrist ▯ **shrinkage** *noun* the amount by which something grows smaller ▯ **shrink-wrap** *noun* clear plastic film for wrapping, heated so that it shrinks to fit tightly ▯ *verb* wrap with this type of film ▯ **shrunken** *adj* shrunk

> **shrink** » shrink*s*, shrink*ing*, shrank, shrunk

shrive *verb, old* **1** hear a confession **2** confess

> **shrive** » shrive*s*, shriv*ing*, shrove, shrive*n*

shrivel *verb* dry up, wrinkle, wither

> **shrivel** » shrivel*s*, shrivell*ing*, shrivell*ed*

shroud *noun* **1** a cloth covering a dead body **2** something which covers: *a shroud of mist* **3 (shrouds)** the ropes from the mast-head to a ship's sides ▯ *verb* wrap up, cover

Shrove Tuesday the day before Ash Wednesday

shrub *noun* a small bush or plant ▯ **shrubbery** *noun* (*plural* **shrubberies**) a place where shrubs grow

shrug *verb* show doubt, lack of interest *etc* by drawing up the shoulders ▯ *noun* a movement of the shoulders to show lack of interest ▯ **shrug off** dismiss, treat as being unimportant

> **shrug** *verb* » shrug*s*, shrugg*ing*, shrugg*ed*

shrunk and **shrunken** *see* **shrink**

shtetl *noun, hist* a Jewish community in E Europe

shtook *adj, slang* trouble, bother

shtoom *adj, slang* quiet, silent: *keeping shtoom*

shudder *verb* tremble from fear, cold, disgust □ *noun* a trembling

shuffle *verb* **1** mix, rearrange (*eg* playing-cards) **2** move by dragging or sliding the feet along the ground without lifting them **3** move (the feet) in this way □ *noun* **1** a rearranging **2** a dragging movement of the feet

shun *verb* avoid, keep clear of

> **shun** » shun*s*, shunn*ing*, shunn*ed*

shunt *verb* move (railway trains, engines *etc*) onto a side track

shut *verb* **1** move (a door, window, lid *etc*) so that it covers an opening **2** close, lock (a building *etc*) **3** become closed: *the door shut with a bang* **4** confine, restrain in a building etc: *shut the dog in his kennel* □ **shutter** *noun* **1** a cover for a window **2** a cover which closes over a camera lens as it takes a picture □ **shut down** close (a factory *etc*) □ **shut up 1** close completely **2** *informal* stop speaking or making other noise

> **shut** » shut*s*, shutt*ing*, shut

shuttle *noun* the part of a weaving loom which carries the cross thread from side to side □ *adj* of a transport service: going to and fro between two places □ **shuttlecock** *noun* a rounded cork stuck with feathers, used in the game of badminton □ **shuttle service** a transport service moving constantly between two points

shy *adj* **1** of a wild animal: easily frightened, timid **2** lacking confidence in the presence of others **3** not wanting to attract attention □ *verb* **1** jump or turn suddenly aside in fear **2** throw, toss □ *noun* a try, an attempt □ **shyly** *adv* □ **shyness** *noun* □ **fight shy of** avoid, keep away from

> **shy** *verb* » shi*es*, shy*ing*, shi*ed*

shyster *noun, slang* a swindler

SI *abbrev, French* Système International (d'Unités), the metric unit system

Siamese *adj*: **Siamese cat** a fawn-coloured domestic cat □ **Siamese twins** twins joined by their flesh at birth

sibilant *adj* of a sound: hissing

sibling *noun* a brother or sister

sibyl *noun* a prophetess

sic *adv* so, thus (written in brackets after a word to show that it is meant to be spelt as given)

sick *adj* **1** wanting to vomit **2** vomiting **3** not well, ill **4** (with **of**) tired of □ **sick bed** or **sick room** a bed or room for people to rest in when ill □ **sicken** *verb* make or become sick □ **sickening** *adj* **1** causing sickness **2** disgusting, revolting □ **sick leave** time off work for illness □ **sickly** *adj* **1** unhealthy **2** feeble □ **sickness** *noun*

sickle *noun* a hooked knife for cutting or reaping grain, hay *etc* □ **sickle-cell anaemia** a hereditary disease in which the red blood cells are distorted in a sickle shape

side *noun* **1** an edge, border or boundary line **2** a surface that is not the top, bottom, front or back **3** either surface of a piece of paper, cloth *etc* **4** the right or left part of the body **5** a division, a part: *the north side of the town* **6** an aspect, point of view: *all sides of the problem* **7** a slope (of a hill) **8** a team or party which is opposing another ▫ *adj* **1** on or towards the side: *side door* **2** indirect, additional but less important: *side issue* ▫ *verb* (with **with**) support (one person, group *etc* against another) ▫ **sideboard** *noun* a piece of furniture in a dining-room for holding dishes *etc* ▫ **sidecar** *noun* a small car for a passenger, attached to a motorcycle ▫ **side effect** an additional (often bad) effect of a drug ▫ **sideline** *noun* an extra bit of business outside regular work ▫ **sidelong** *adj* & *adv* from or to the side: *sidelong glance* ▫ **sideshow** *noun* a less important show that is part of a larger one ▫ **sidestep** *verb* avoid by stepping to one side ▫ **sidetrack** *verb* turn (someone) away from what they were going to do or say ▫ **sidewalk** *noun*, *US* a pavement ▫ **sideways** *adv* **1** with the side foremost **2** towards the side ▫ **siding** *noun* a short line of rails on which trucks are shunted off the main line ▫ **take sides** choose to support (a party, person) against another

sidereal *adj* relating to the stars

sidle *verb* **1** go or move sideways **2** move stealthily, sneak

siege /seej/ *noun* **1** an attempt to capture a town *etc* by keeping it surrounded by an armed force **2** a constant attempt to gain control ▫ **lay siege to** besiege

siemens unit a unit of electrical conductance

sienna *noun* a reddish-brown, or yellowish-brown, pigment used in paints

sierra *noun* a range of mountains with jagged peaks

siesta *noun* a short sleep or rest taken in the afternoon

sieve /siv/ *noun* a container with a mesh used to separate liquids from solids, or fine pieces from coarse pieces *etc* ▫ *verb* put through a sieve

sift *verb* **1** separate by passing through a sieve **2** consider and examine closely: *sifting all the evidence*

sigh *noun* a long, deep-sounding breath, showing tiredness, longing *etc* ▫ *verb* give out a sigh

sight *noun* **1** the act or power of seeing **2** a view, a glimpse: *catch sight of her* **3** (often **sights**) something worth seeing: *the sights of London* **4** something or someone unusual, ridiculous, shocking *etc*: *she's quite a sight in that hat* **5** a guide on a gun for taking aim ▫ *verb* **1** get a view of, see suddenly **2** look at through the sight of a gun ▫ **sight-reading** *noun* playing or singing from music that has not been seen previously ▫ **sightseeing** *noun* visiting the chief buildings, monuments *etc* of a place

> ⚠Do not confuse with: **site** and **cite**

sign *noun* **1** a mark with a special meaning, a symbol **2** a gesture (*eg* a nod, wave of the hand) to show your meaning **3** an advertisement or notice giving information **4** something which shows what is happening or is going to happen: *signs of irritation/ a sign of good weather* □ *verb* **1** write your name on (a document, cheque *etc*) **2** make a sign or gesture to **3** show (your meaning) by a sign or gesture □ **signboard** *noun* a board with a notice □ **signpost** *noun* a post with a sign, *esp* one showing direction and distances to certain places □ **sign on** enter your name on a list for work, the army *etc*

signal *noun* **1** a gesture, light or sound giving a command, warning etc: *aid-raid signal* **2** something used for this purpose: *railway signals* **3** the wave of sound received or sent out by a radio *etc* set □ *verb* **1** make signals (to) **2** send (information) by signal □ *adj* remarkable: *a signal success* □ **signalman** *noun* someone who works railway signals, or who sends signals

> **signal** *verb* » signal*s*, signall*ing*, signall*ed*

signature *noun* **1** a signed name **2** an act of signing **3** *music* the flats or sharps at the beginning of a piece which show its key, or figures showing its timing □ **signatory** *noun* (*plural* **signatories**) someone who has signed an agreement *etc* □ **signature tune** a tune used to identify a particular radio or television series *etc* played at the beginning or end of the programme

signet *noun* a small seal, usually bearing someone's initials □ **signet ring** a ring imprinted with a signet

> ⚠Do not confuse with: **cygnet**

signify *verb* **1** mean, be a sign of **2** show, make known by a gesture: *signifying disapproval* **3** have meaning or importance □ **significance** *noun* **1** meaning **2** importance □ **significant** *adj* meaning much; important: *no significant change* □ **significantly** *adv*

> **signify** » signifi*es*, signify*ing*, signifi*ed*

silage *noun* green fodder preserved in a silo

silence *noun* **1** absence of sound or speech **2** a time of quietness □ *verb* cause to be silent □ **silencer** *noun* a device (on a car engine, gun *etc*) for making noise less □ **silent** *adj* **1** free from noise **2** not speaking □ **silently** *adv*

silhouette *noun* **1** an outline drawing of someone, often in profile, filled in with black **2** a dark outline seen against the light

> After the 18th-century French finance minister, Etienne de *Silhouette*, possibly because of his notorious stinginess

silica *noun* a white or colourless substance, of which flint, sandstone, quartz *etc* are mostly made up

silk *noun* **1** very fine, soft fibres

spun by silkworms **2** thread or cloth made from this □ *adj* **1** made of silk **2** soft, smooth □ **silken** *adj* **1** made of silk **2** smooth like silk □ **silkworm** *noun* the caterpillar of certain moths which spins silk □ **silky** *adj* like silk

silkie *noun* a mythological creature, half a human and half a seal

sill *noun* a ledge of wood, stone *etc* below a window or a door

silly *adj* foolish, not sensible

silo *noun* (*plural* **silos**) **1** a tower for storing grain *etc* **2** a pit or airtight chamber for holding silage **3** an underground chamber built to contain a guided missile

silt *noun* sand or mud left behind by flowing water □ **silt up** become blocked by mud

silver *noun* **1** a white precious metal, able to take on a high polish **2** money made of silver or of a metal alloy resembling it **3** objects (*esp* cutlery) made of, or plated with, silver □ *adj* made of, or looking like, silver □ *verb* **1** cover with silver **2** become like silver □ **silverfish** *noun* a wingless, silvery insect, sometimes found in houses □ **silver foil** or **silver leaf** silver beaten to paper-thinness, used for decoration □ **silversmith** *noun* someone who makes or sells articles of silver □ **silver wedding** a 25th anniversary of a wedding □ **silvery** *adj* **1** like silver **2** of sound: ringing and musical

simian *adj* ape-like

similar *adj* alike, almost the same □ **similarity** *noun* (*plural* **similarities**) □ **similarly** *adv* **1** in the same, or a similar, way **2** likewise, also

simile *noun* an expression using 'like' or 'as', in which one thing is likened to another that is well-known for a particular quality (*eg* 'as black as night', 'to swim like a fish')

simmer *verb* cook gently just below or at boiling-point

simnel cake a fruit cake covered with marzipan, traditionally eaten at Easter

simper *verb* **1** smile in a silly manner **2** say with a simper □ *noun* a silly smile

simple *adj* **1** easy, not difficult or complicated **2** plain, not fancy: *simple hairstyle* **3** ordinary: *simple, everyday objects* **4** of humble rank: *a simple peasant* **5** mere, nothing but: *the simple truth* **6** too trusting, easily cheated **7** foolish, half-witted □ **simpleton** *noun* a foolish person □ **simplicity** *noun* the state of being simple

simplify *verb* make simpler □ **simplification** *noun* **1** an act of making simpler **2** a simple form of anything

simplify » simplifi*es*, simplify*ing*, simplifi*ed*

simply *adv* **1** in a simple manner **2** merely: *I do it simply for the money* **3** absolutely: *simply beautiful*

simulacrum *noun* (*plural* **simulacra**) a resemblance, an image

simulate *verb* **1** pretend, feign: *she*

simulated illness **2** have the appearance of, look like ▫ **simulated** *adj* **1** pretended **2** having the appearance of: *simulated leather* ▫ **simulation** *noun*

simulcast *noun* a simultaneous television and radio broadcast of the same event

simultaneous *adj* happening, or done, at the same time ▫ **simultaneously** *adv*

sin *noun* **1** a wicked act, *esp* one which breaks religious laws **2** wrongdoing **3** *informal* a shame, pity ▫ *verb* commit a sin, do wrong ▫ **sinful** *adj* wicked ▫ **sinner** *noun* ▫ **original sin** the supposed sinful nature of all human beings since the time of Adam's sin

> **sin** *verb* » sin*s*, sinn*ing*, sinn*ed*

since *adv* **1** (often with **ever**) from that time onwards: *I have avoided him ever since* **2** at a later time: *we have since become friends* **3** ago: *long since* **4** from the time of: *since his arrival* ▫ *conj* **1** after the time when: *I have been at home since I returned from Italy* **2** because: *since you are going, I will go too*

sincere *adj* **1** honest in word and deed, meaning what you say or do, true: *a sincere friend* **2** truly felt: *a sincere desire* ▫ **sincerely** *adv* ▫ **sincerity** *noun*

Sinead /*sh*inəd/ *noun* the upper house of parliament in the Republic of Ireland

sinecure *noun* a job for which someone receives money but has little or no work to do

> Literally 'without cure', originally a paid church position which carried no responsibility for curing souls

sine qua non an indispensable condition

sinew *noun* **1** a tough cord that joins a muscle to a bone **2** (**sinews**) equipment and resources necessary for something: *sinews of war* ▫ **sinewy** *adj* having strong sinews, tough

sing *verb* **1** make musical sounds with your voice **2** utter (words, a song *etc*) by doing this ▫ **singer** *noun* ▫ **sing-song** *noun* **1** a gathering of people singing informally together **2** an up-and-down tone of voice ▫ *adj* in an up-and-down voice

> **sing** » sing*s*, sing*ing*, sang, sung

singe *verb* burn slightly on the surface, scorch ▫ *noun* a surface burn

single *adj* **1** one only **2** not double **3** not married **4** for one person: *a single bed* **5** between two people: *single combat* **6** for one direction of a journey: *a single ticket* ▫ **single-handed** *adj* working *etc* by yourself ▫ **single-minded** *adj* having one aim only ▫ **singleness** *noun* the state of being single ▫ **singly** *adv* one by one, separately ▫ **single out** pick out, treat differently in some way

singlet *noun* a vest, an undershirt

singular *adj* **1** *grammar* the opposite of **plural**, showing one person, thing *etc* **2** exceptional:

singular success **3** unusual, strange: *a singular sight* ▫ **singularly** *adv* strangely, exceptionally: *singularly ugly*

sinister *adj* suggesting evil, evil-looking

sink *verb* **1** go down below the surface of the water *etc* **2** go down or become less: *my hopes sank* **3** of a very ill person: become weaker **4** lower yourself (into): *sink into a chair* **5** make by digging (a well *etc*) **6** push (your teeth *etc*) deep into (something) **7** invest (money *etc*) into a business ▫ *noun* a basin in a kitchen, bathroom *etc*, with a water supply connected to it and a drain for carrying off dirty water *etc* ▫ **sinker** *noun* a weight fixed to a fishing line *etc*

sink verb » sink*s*, sink*ing*, sank, sunk

Sino- *prefix* relating to China or the Chinese

sinuous *adj* bending in and out, winding ▫ **sinuosity** *noun*

sinus *noun* (*plural* **sinuses**) an air cavity in the head connected with the nose ▫ **sinusitis** *noun* inflammation of (one of) the sinuses

sip *verb* drink in very small quantities ▫ *noun* a taste of a drink, a swallow

sip *verb* » sip*s*, sipp*ing*, sipp*ed*

siphon or **syphon** *noun* **1** a bent tube for drawing off liquids from one container into another **2** a glass bottle, for soda water *etc*, containing such a tube ▫ *verb* **1** draw (off) through a siphon **2** (with **off**) take (part of something) away gradually: *he siphoned off some of the club's funds*

sir *noun* **1** a polite form of address used to a man **2** (**Sir**) the title of a knight or baronet

sire *noun* **1** a male parent, *esp* of a horse **2** *hist* a title used in speaking to a king ▫ *verb* of an animal: to be the male parent of

siren *noun* **1** an instrument that gives out a loud hooting noise as a warning **2** a mythical sea nymph whose singing enchanted sailors and tempted them into danger **3** an attractive but dangerous woman

sirloin *noun* the upper part of the loin of beef

sirocco *noun* a hot dry wind blowing from N Africa to the Mediterranean coast

sirrah *noun, old* sir

sisal *noun* a fibre from a W Indian plant, used for making ropes

sister *noun* **1** a female born of the same parents as yourself **2** a senior nurse, often in charge of a hospital ward **3** a nun ▫ *adj* **1** closely related **2** of similar design or structure ▫ **sisterhood** *noun* **1** the state of being a sister **2** a religious community of women ▫ **sister-in-law** *noun* **1** the sister of your husband or wife **2** the wife of your brother or of your brother-in-law ▫ **sisterly** *adj* like a sister

sit *verb* **1** rest on the buttocks, be seated **2** of a bird: perch **3** rest on eggs in order to hatch them **4** be an official member: *sit in parliament/ sit on a committee* **5** of a court *etc*: meet officially **6** pose (for) a photographer, painter *etc* **7** take (an examination *etc*) □ **sit-in** *noun* an occupation of a building *etc* by protestors □ **sitter** *noun* **1** someone who poses for a portrait *etc* **2** a babysitter **3** a bird sitting on eggs □ **sit tight** be unwilling to move □ **sit up 1** sit with your back straight **2** stay up instead of going to bed

> **sit** *verb » sits*, sitt*ing*, sat

sitcom *noun* a television comedy series with a running theme

site *noun* a place where a building, town *etc* is or is to be placed □ *verb* select a place for (a building *etc*)

> ⚠Do not confuse with: **sight** and **cite**

sitting *noun* the state or time of sitting □ *adj* **1** seated **2** for sitting in or on **3** in office: *sitting member of parliament* **4** in possession: *sitting tenant* □ **sitting-room** *noun* a room chiefly for sitting in

situated *adj* placed

situation *noun* **1** the place where anything stands **2** a job, employment **3** a state of affairs, circumstances: *in an awkward situation*

sitz-bath *noun* a therapeutic hip-bath in hot water

six *noun* the number 6 □ *adj* 6 in number □ **sixth** *adj* the last of a series of six □ *noun* one of six equal parts □ **six-pack** *noun* a package of six cans of beer *etc* sold together □ **at sixes and sevens** in confusion

sixpence *noun*, *old* a silver-coloured coin worth $\frac{1}{40}$ of £1

sixteen *noun* the number 16 □ *adj* 16 in number □ **sixteenth** *adj* the last of a series of sixteen □ *noun* one of sixteen equal parts

sixty *noun* the number 60 □ *adj* 60 in number □ **sixtieth** *adj* the last of a series of sixty □ *noun* one of sixty equal parts

size *noun* **1** space taken up by anything **2** measurements, dimensions **3** largeness **4** a class into which shoes and clothes are grouped according to size: *she takes size 4 in shoes* **5** a weak kind of glue □ **sizeable** or **sizable** *adj* fairly large □ **size up** form an opinion of a person, situation *etc*

sizzle *verb* **1** make a hissing sound **2** fry, scorch

ska *noun* a style of Jamaican music similar to reggae

skate *noun* **1** a steel blade attached to a boot for gliding on ice **2** a rollerskate **3** a type of large flatfish □ *verb* move on skates □ **skateboard** *noun* a narrow board on four rollerskate wheels □ **skateboarding** *noun* the sport of going on a skateboard

skean-dhu /skeeən-*doo*/ *noun* a decorative dagger worn with Highland dress

skedaddle *verb, informal* run off in a hurry

skein *noun* a coil of thread or yarn, loosely tied in a knot

skeleton *noun* **1** the bony framework of an animal or person, without the flesh **2** any framework or outline ▫ *adj* of staff *etc*: reduced to a very small or minimum number ▫ **skeletal** *adj* of or like a skeleton ▫ **skeleton key** a key from which the inner part has been cut away so that it can open many different locks

skerry *noun* a reef of rock

sketch *noun* (*plural* **sketches**) **1** a rough plan or drawing **2** a short or rough account **3** a short play, dramatic scene *etc* ▫ *verb* **1** draw roughly **2** give the chief points of **3** draw in pencil or ink ▫ **sketchy** *adj* **1** roughly done **2** not thorough, incomplete: *my knowledge of geography is rather sketchy*

skew *adj* & *adv* off the straight, slanting ▫ *verb* set at a slant

skewer *noun* a long pin of wood or metal for holding meat together while roasting *etc* ▫ *verb* fix with a skewer or with something sharp

ski *noun* (*plural* **skis**) one of a pair of long narrow strips of wood or metal that are attached to boots for gliding over snow ▫ *verb* move or travel on skis

ski *verb* » ski*s*, ski*ing*, ski*ed*

skid *noun* **1** a slide sideways: *the car went into a skid* **2** a wedge put under a wheel to check it on a steep place **3** (**skids**) logs *etc* on which things can be moved by sliding ▫ *verb* **1** of a wheel: slide along without turning **2** slip sideways ▫ **on the skids** on the way down ▫ **put the skids under** hurry along

skiff *noun* a small light boat

skill *noun* **1** cleverness at doing a thing, either from practice or as a natural gift ▫ **skilful** *adj* having or showing skill ▫ **skilfully** *adv* ▫ **skilled** *adj* **1** having skill, *esp* through training **2** of a job: requiring skill

skillet *noun* a small metal pan with a long handle for frying food

skim *verb* **1** remove cream, scum *etc* from the surface of (something) **2** move lightly and quickly over (a surface) **3** read quickly, missing parts ▫ **skim-milk** *noun* milk from which the cream has been skimmed

skim » skim*s*, skimm*ing*, skimm*ed*

skimp *verb* **1** give (someone) hardly enough **2** do (a job) imperfectly **3** spend too little money (on): *skimping on clothes* ▫ **skimpy** *adj* **1** too small **2** of clothes: too short or tight

skin *noun* **1** the natural outer covering of an animal or person **2** a thin outer layer on a fruit **3** a thin film that forms on a liquid ▫ *verb* strip the skin from ▫ **skin-deep** *adj* as deep as the skin only, on the surface ▫ **skin-diver** *noun* a diver who wears simple equipment (originally someone who dived naked for pearls) ▫ **skinflint** *noun* a very mean person ▫ **skinny** *adj* very thin ▫ **by the skin of your teeth** very narrowly

skin *verb* » skin*s*, skinn*ing*, skinn*ed*

skint *adj, Brit informal* broke, without much money

skip *verb* **1** go along with a rhythmic step and hop **2** jump over a turning rope **3** leap, *esp* lightly or joyfully **4** leave out (parts of a book, a meal *etc*) □ *noun* **1** an act of skipping **2** the captain of a side at bowls *etc* **3** a large metal container for transporting refuse □ **skipping rope** a rope used in skipping

skip *verb* » skip*s*, skipp*ing*, skipp*ed*

skipper *noun* the captain of a ship, aeroplane or team □ *verb* act as captain for (a ship, team *etc*)

skirl *noun* a shrill sound, *esp* that made by bagpipes

skirmish *noun* (*plural* **skirmishes**) **1** a fight between small parties of soldiers **2** a short sharp contest or disagreement □ *verb* fight briefly or informally

skirt *noun* **1** a garment, worn by women, that hangs from the waist **2** the lower part of a dress **3** (**skirts**) the outer edge or border □ *verb* pass along, or lie along, the edge of □ **skirting** or **skirting-board** *noun* the narrow board next to the floor round the walls of a room (*also called*: **wainscot**)

skit *noun* a piece of writing, short play *etc* that makes fun of someone or event *etc*

skitter *verb* **1** skim over a surface **2** move quickly and lightly

skittish *adj* frivolous, light-headed

skittle *noun* **1** a bottle-shaped object used as a target in bowling, a ninepin **2** (**skittles**) a game in which skittles are knocked over by a ball

skive *verb*, *informal* (often with **off**) avoid doing a duty □ **skiver** *noun* a shirker

skivvy *noun*, *informal* a domestic servant, a cleaner

skua *noun* a type of seagull

skulduggery or *US* **skullduggery** *noun* trickery, underhand practices

skulk *verb* **1** wait about, stay hidden **2** move stealthily away, sneak

skull *noun* **1** the bony case which encloses the brain **2** the head □ **skullcap** *noun* a cap which fits closely to the head □ **skull and crossbones** the sign on a pirate's flag

skunk *noun* **1** a small American animal which defends itself by giving off a bad smell **2** a contemptible person

sky *noun* (*plural* **skies**) **1** the upper atmosphere, the heavens **2** the weather, the climate □ **sky-diving** *noun* jumping with a parachute as a sport □ **skylark** *noun* the common lark which sings while hovering far overhead □ **skylarking** *noun* mischievous behaviour □ **skylight** *noun* a window in a roof or ceiling □ **skyline** *noun* the horizon □ **skyscraper** *noun* a high building of very many storeys

slab *noun* a thick flat slice or piece of anything: *stone slab/ cut a slab of cake*

slack *adj* **1** not firmly stretched **2** not firmly in position **3** not strict **4** lazy and careless **5** not busy: *slack holiday season* □ *noun* **1** the loose part of a rope **2** small coal and coal-dust **3** (**slacks**) loose, casual trousers □ *verb* **1** do less work than you should, be lazy **2** slacken □ **slacken** *verb* **1** make or become looser **2** make or become less active, less busy or less fast *etc*

slag *noun* waste left from metal-smelting □ *verb*, *slang* criticize, make fun of cruelly

> **slag** *verb* » slag*s*, slagg*ing*, slagg*ed*

slain *see* **slay**

slake *verb* **1** quench, satisfy (thirst, longing *etc*) **2** put out (fire) **3** mix (lime) with water

slalom *noun* **1** a downhill, zigzag ski run among posts or trees **2** an obstacle race in canoes

slam *verb* **1** shut (a door, lid *etc*) with a loud noise **2** put down with a loud noise □ *noun* **1** the act of slamming **2** (also **grand slam**) a winning of every trick in cards or every contest in a competition *etc*

> **slam** *verb* » slam*s*, slamm*ing*, slamm*ed*

slander *noun* an untrue statement (in England, a spoken one) aimed at harming someone's reputation □ *verb* speak slander against (someone) □ **slanderous** *adj*

slang *noun* **1** popular words and phrases that are used in informal, everyday speech or writing **2** the special language of a particular group: *Cockney slang* □ *verb* scold, abuse

slant *verb* **1** slope **2** lie or move diagonally or in a sloping position **3** give or present (facts or information) in a distorted way that suits your own purpose □ *noun* **1** a slope **2** a diagonal direction **3** a point of view

slap *noun* a blow with the palm of the hand or anything flat □ *verb* give a slap to □ **slapdash** *adj* hasty, careless □ **slapstick** *adj* of comedy: boisterous, funny in a very obvious way □ *noun* comedy in this style

> **slap** *verb* » slap*s*, slapp*ing*, slapp*ed*

slash *verb* **1** make long cuts in **2** strike at violently □ *noun* (*plural* **slashes**) **1** a long cut **2** a sweeping blow

slat *noun* a thin strip of wood, metal or other material □ **slatted** *adj* having slats

slate *noun* an easily split blue-grey rock, used for roofing, or at one time for writing upon □ *adj* **1** made of slate **2** slate-coloured □ *verb* **1** cover with slate **2** say or write harsh things to or about: *the play was slated*

slattern *noun* a woman of untidy appearance or habits

slaughter *noun* **1** the killing of animals, *esp* for food **2** cruel killing of great numbers of people □ *verb* **1** kill (an animal) for food **2** kill brutally □ **slaughterhouse** *noun* a place where animals are killed in order to be sold for food

slave *noun*, *hist* **1** someone forced to work for a master and owner **2**

someone who serves another devotedly **3** someone who works very hard **4** someone who is addicted to something: *a slave to fashion* □ *verb* work like a slave □ **slavery** *noun* **1** the state of being a slave **2** the system of owning slaves □ **slavish** *adj* thinking or acting exactly according to rules or instructions

slaver *noun* saliva running from the mouth □ *verb* let saliva run out of the mouth

Slavic *adj* relating to a group of E European people or their languages, including Russian, Polish *etc*

slay *verb, formal* kill

> **slay** » slay*s*, slay*ing*, slew, slain

sleazy *adj* squalid, disreputable □ **sleaze** or **sleaziness** *noun*

sled or **sledge** *noun* a vehicle with runners, made for sliding upon snow □ *verb* ride on a sledge □ **sledgehammer** *noun* a large, heavy hammer

sleek *adj* **1** smooth, glossy **2** of an animal: well-fed and well-cared for **3** elegant, well-groomed

sleep *verb* rest with your eyes closed in a state of natural unconsciousness □ **sleeper** *noun* **1** someone who sleeps **2** a beam of wood or metal supporting railway lines **3** a sleeping car or sleeping berth on a railway train □ **sleeping bag** a large warm bag for sleeping in, used by campers *etc* □ **sleeping car** a railway coach with beds or berths □ **sleepwalker** *noun* someone who walks *etc* while asleep □ **go to sleep 1** pass into the state of being asleep **2** of a limb: become numb, tingle □ **put to sleep 1** make to go to sleep, make unconscious **2** put (an animal) to death painlessly, *eg* by an injection of a drug □ **sleep with** *informal* have sexual intercourse with

> **sleep** *verb* » sleep*s*, sleep*ing*, slept

sleepless *adj* unable to sleep, without sleep □ **sleeplessly** *adv* □ **sleeplessness** *noun*

sleepy *adj* **1** drowsy, wanting to sleep **2** looking as if needing sleep **3** quiet, not bustling: *sleepy town* □ **sleepily** *adv* □ **sleepiness** *noun*

sleet *noun* rain mixed with snow or hail

sleeve *noun* **1** the part of a garment which covers the arm **2** a cover for a gramophone record **3** a cover for an arm-like piece of machinery □ **sleeveless** *adj* without sleeves

sleigh *noun* a large horse-drawn sledge

sleight-of-hand *noun* skill and quickness of hand movement in performing card tricks *etc*

slender *adj* **1** thin, narrow **2** slim **3** small in amount: *by a slender margin*

sleuth *noun* someone who tracks down criminals, a detective

slew[1] *verb* swing round

> **slew** » slew*s*, slew*ing*, slew*ed*

slew[2] *past form* of **slay**

slice *noun* **1** a thin, broad piece of something: *slice of toast* **2** a broad-bladed utensil for serving fish *etc* □

verb **1** cut into slices **2** cut through **3** cut (off from *etc*) **4** *golf* hit (a ball) in such a way that it curves away to the right

slick *adj* **1** smart, clever, often too much so **2** smooth □ *noun* a thin layer of spilt oil

slide *verb* **1** move smoothly over a surface **2** slip **3** pass quietly or secretly □ *noun* **1** an act of sliding **2** a smooth, slippery slope or track **3** a chute **4** a groove or rail on which a thing slides **5** a fastening for the hair **6** a picture for showing on a screen **7** a piece of glass on which to place objects to be examined under a microscope □ **slide-rule** *noun* an instrument used for calculating, made up of one ruler sliding against another □ **sliding scale** a scale of wages, charges *etc* which can be changed according to outside conditions

slide *verb* » slide*s*, slid*ing*, slid

slight *adj* **1** of little amount or importance: *slight breeze/ slight quarrel* **2** small, slender □ *verb* treat as unimportant, insult by ignoring □ *noun* an insult, an offence

slim *adj* **1** slender, thin **2** small, slight: *slim chance* □ *verb* **1** make slender **2** use means (such as eating less) to become slender

slim *verb* » slim*s*, slimm*ing*, slimm*ed*

slime *noun* sticky, half-liquid material, *esp* thin, slippery mud □ **slimy** *adj* **1** covered with slime **2** oily, greasy

sling *noun* **1** a bandage hanging from the neck or shoulders to support an injured arm **2** a strap with a string attached to each end, for flinging stones **3** a net of ropes *etc* for hoisting and carrying heavy objects □ *verb* **1** throw with a sling **2** move or swing by means of a sling **3** *informal* throw

sling *verb* » sling*s*, sling*ing*, slung

slink *verb* sneak away, move stealthily

slink » slink*s*, slink*ing*, slunk

slip *verb* **1** slide accidentally and lose footing or balance: *slip on the ice* **2** fall out of place, or out of your control: *the plate slipped from my grasp* **3** move quickly and easily **4** move quietly, quickly and secretly **5** escape from: *slip your mind* □ *noun* **1** the act of slipping **2** an error, a slight mistake **3** a cutting from a plant **4** a strip or narrow piece of anything (*eg* paper) **5** a slim, slight person: *a slip of a girl* **6** a slipway **7** a thin undergarment worn under a dress, an underskirt **8** a cover for a pillow **9** *cricket* a fielding position □ **slipknot** *noun* a knot made with a loop so that it can slip □ **slipped disc** displacement of one of the discs between the vertebrae causing severe back pain □ **slipper** *noun* a loose indoor shoe □ **slippery** *adj* **1** causing skidding or slipping **2** not trustworthy □ **slip road** a road by which vehicles join or leave a motorway □ **slipshod** *adj* untidy, careless □ **slipstream** *noun* the stream of air driven back by an aircraft propeller *etc* □ **slipway** *noun* a smooth slope on which a ship is built ▫ **slip up** make a mistake ▫ **slip-up** *noun* a mistake

slip *verb* » slip*s*, slipp*ing*, slipp*ed*

slit *verb* **1** make a long narrow cut in **2** cut into strips ▫ *noun* a long narrow cut or opening

slit *verb* » slit*s*, slitt*ing*, slit

slither *verb* **1** slide or slip about (*eg* on mud) **2** move with a gliding motion ▫ **slithery** *adj* slippery

sliver *noun* a thin strip or slice

slobber *verb* let saliva dribble from the mouth, slaver

sloe *noun* the small black fruit of a blackthorn shrub, often used to flavour gin

slog *verb* work or plod on steadily, *esp* against difficulty ▫ *noun* a difficult spell of work

slog *verb* » slog*s*, slogg*ing*, slogg*ed*

slogan *noun* an easily remembered and frequently repeated phrase, used in advertising *etc*

sloop *noun* a one-masted sailing ship

slop *verb* **1** flow over, spill **2** splash ▫ *noun* **1** spilt liquid **2** (**slops**) dirty water **3** (**slops**) thin, tasteless food ▫ **sloppy** *adj* **1** wet, muddy **2** careless, untidy **3** silly, sentimental

slop *verb* » slop*s*, slopp*ing*, slopp*ed*

slope *noun* **1** a position or direction that is neither level nor upright, a slant **2** a surface with one end higher than the other, *eg* a hillside ▫ *verb* be in a slanting, sloping position

slosh *verb* **1** splash **2** *informal* hit

slot *noun* **1** a small, narrow opening, *eg* to insert coins **2** a position ▫ *verb* **1** make a slot in **2** (sometimes with **into**) find a position or place for ▫ **slot machine** a vending machine worked by putting a coin in a slot

slot *verb* » slot*s*, slott*ing*, slott*ed*

sloth *noun* **1** laziness **2** a slow-moving S American animal that lives in trees ▫ **slothful** *adj* lazy

slouch *noun* a hunched-up body position ▫ *verb* walk with shoulders rounded and head hanging

slough[1] /slow/ *noun* a bog, a marsh

slough[2] /sluf/ *noun* the cast-off skin of a snake ▫ *verb* **1** cast off (*eg* a skin) **2** of skin: come (off)

slovenly *adj noun* untidy, careless, dirty

slow *adj* **1** not fast **2** not hasty or hurrying **3** of a clock: behind in time **4** not quick in learning, dull ▫ *verb* (often with **down**) make or become slower ▫ **slowcoach** *noun* someone who moves, works *etc* slowly ▫ **slowly** *adv* ▫ **slow-motion** *adj* **1** slower than normal movement **2** of a film: slower than actual motion ▫ **slowness** *noun* ▫ **slow-worm** *noun* a snake-like, legless lizard

sludge *noun* soft, slimy mud

slug *noun* **1** a snail-like animal with no shell **2** a small piece of metal used as a bullet **3** a heavy blow ▫ **sluggard** *noun* someone who has slow and lazy habits ▫ **sluggish** *adj* moving slowly ▫ **sluggishly** *adv*

sluice *noun* **1** a sliding gate for controlling a flow of water in an artificial channel (*also called*: **sluicegate**) **2** the stream which flows through this ▫ *verb* clean out with a strong flow of water

slum *noun* **1** an overcrowded part of a town where the houses are dirty and unhealthy **2** a house in a slum

slumber *verb* sleep ▫ *noun* sleep

slump *verb* **1** fall or sink suddenly and heavily **2** lose value suddenly ▫ *noun* a sudden fall in values, prices *etc*

slung *past form* of **sling**

slunk *past form* of **slink**

slur *verb* **1** pronounce indistinctly **2** damage (a reputation *etc*), speak evil of ▫ *noun* **1** a blot or stain (on someone's reputation) **2** a criticism, an insult

slur *verb* » slur*s*, slurr*ing*, slurr*ed*

slurp *verb* drink or gulp noisily ▫ *noun* a noisy gulp

slurry *noun* **1** thin, liquid cement **2** liquid waste

slush *noun* **1** watery mud **2** melting snow **3** something very sentimental **4** sentimentality ▫ **slushy** *adj* **1** covered with, or like, slush **2** sentimental

slut *noun* a dirty, untidy woman ▫ **sluttish** *adj*

sly *adj* cunning; wily; deceitful ▫ **slyly** *adv* ▫ **slyness** *noun* ▫ **on the sly** secretly, surreptitiously

smack *verb* **1** strike smartly, slap **2** have a trace or suggestion (of): *this smacks of treason* ▫ *noun* **1** an act of smacking **2** the sound made by smacking **3** a boisterous kiss **4** a taste, a flavour **5** a trace, a suggestion **6** a small fishing vessel ▫ *adv* with sudden violence: *run smack into the door*

small *adj* **1** little, not big or much **2** not important: *a small matter* **3** not having a large or successful business: *a small businessman* **4** of a voice: soft ▫ *noun* the most slender or narrow part: *the small of the back* ▫ *adv* into small pieces: *cut up small* ▫ **small-arms** *noun plural* weapons that can be carried easily by one person ▫ **small beer** something trivial or unimportant ▫ **small hours** *noun plural* the hours just after midnight ▫ **small-minded** *adj* having narrow opinions, ungenerous ▫ **smallpox** *noun* a serious infectious illness, causing a rash of large pimples (**pocks**) ▫ **small talk** polite conversation about nothing very important

smarmy *adj* smooth in manner, unctuous, ingratiating

smart *adj* **1** clever and quick in thought or action **2** well-dressed **3** brisk **4** sharp, stinging ▫ *noun* a sharp, stinging pain ▫ *verb* **1** feel a sharp, stinging pain **2** feel annoyed, resentful *etc* after being insulted

smash *verb* **1** break in pieces, shatter **2** strike with force: *smash a ball with a racket* **3** crash (into *etc*):

the car smashed into the wall □ *noun* (*plural* **smashes**) **1** an act of smashing **2** a crash, a collision (of vehicles) **3** the ruin of a business *etc* □ **smashed** *adj, slang* drunk

smattering *noun* a very slight knowledge of a subject

smear *verb* **1** spread (something sticky or oily) **2** spread, smudge with (something sticky *etc*) **3** become smeared **4** slander, insult □ *noun* a smudge of something sticky □ **smear test** the taking of a sample of cells from a woman's cervix for examination

smell *noun* **1** the sense or power of being aware of things through your nose **2** an act of using this sense **3** something sensed through the nose, a scent □ *verb* **1** notice by the sense of smell: *I smell gas* **2** use your sense of smell on: *smell this fish* **3** give off a smell: *this room smells* □ **smelling-salts** *noun plural* strong-smelling chemicals in a bottle, used to revive fainting people □ **smelly** *adj* having a bad smell □ **smell out** find out by prying or inquiring closely

> **smell** *verb* » smell*s*, smell*ing*, smelt or smell*ed*

smelt[1] *verb* **1** melt (ore) in order to separate the metal from other material **2** *past form* of **smell**

smelt[2] *noun* a fish related to the salmon

smile *verb* **1** show pleasure by drawing up the corners of the lips **2** (sometimes with **on**) be favourable to: *fortune smiled on him* □ *noun* an act of smiling

smirch *verb* stain, soil □ *noun* a stain

smirk *verb* smile in a self-satisfied or foolish manner □ *noun* a self-satisfied smile

smite *verb* strike, hit hard □ **smitten with** affected by; strongly attracted by

> **smite** » smite*s*, smit*ing*, smitten, smote

smith *noun* a worker in metals; a blacksmith □ **smithy** *noun* (*plural* **smithies**) the workshop of a smith

smithereens *noun plural* fragments

smitten *see* **smite**

smock *noun* a loose shirt-like garment, sometimes worn over other clothes as a protection

smog *noun* thick, smoky fog

smoke *noun* **1** the cloud-like gases and particles of soot given off by anything burning **2** an act of smoking (a cigarette *etc*) □ *verb* **1** give off smoke **2** inhale and exhale tobacco smoke from a cigarette, pipe *etc* **3** cure or preserve (ham, fish *etc*) by applying smoke **4** darken (*eg* glass) by applying smoke □ **smokeless** *adj* **1** burning without smoke **2** where the emission of smoke is prohibited: *a smokeless zone* □ **smoker** *noun* **1** someone who smokes **2** a railway compartment in which smoking is allowed □ **smokescreen** *noun* anything (*orig* smoke) meant to confuse or mislead □ **smoky** *adj* **1** full of smoke **2** tasting of smoke

smolt *noun* a young salmon

smooch *verb, informal* kiss, pet

smooth *adj* **1** not rough **2** having an even surface **3** without lumps: *a smooth sauce* **4** hairless **5** without breaks, stops or jolts: *smooth journey* **6** too agreeable in manner ▯ *verb* **1** make smooth **2** calm, soothe **3** free from difficulty

smorgasbord *noun* a selection of Swedish hors d'oeuvres

smote *past form* of **smite**

smother *verb* **1** kill by keeping air from, *eg* by covering over the nose and mouth **2** die by this means **3** cover up, conceal (feelings *etc*) **4** put down, suppress (a rebellion *etc*)

smoulder *verb* **1** burn slowly without bursting into flame **2** exist in a hidden state **3** show otherwise hidden emotion, *eg* anger, hate: *her eyes smouldered with hate*

smudge a smear ▯ *verb* make dirty with spots or smears

smug *adj* well-satisfied, too obviously pleased with yourself

smuggle *verb* **1** take (goods) into, or out of, a country without paying the required taxes **2** send or take secretly ▯ **smuggler** *noun* someone who smuggles goods

smut *noun* **1** a spot of dirt or soot **2** vulgar or indecent talk *etc* ▯ **smutty** *adj* **1** dirty, grimy **2** indecent, vulgar

snack *noun* a light, hasty meal

snaffle *verb, slang* steal

SNAFU /snafoo/ *noun, US slang* chaos (*abbrev* of 'situation normal – all fucked up')

snag *noun* a difficulty, an obstacle ▯ *verb* catch or tear on something sharp

> **snag** *verb* » snag*s*, snagg*ing*, snagg*ed*

snail *noun* **1** a soft-bodied, small, crawling animal with a shell **2** someone who is very slow

snake *noun* **1** a legless reptile with a long body, which moves along the ground with a winding movement **2** anything snake-like in form or movement **3** a cunning, deceitful person

snap *verb* **1** make a sudden bite **2** (with **up**) eat up, or grab, eagerly **3** break or shut suddenly with a sharp noise **4** cause (the fingers) to make a sharp noise **5** speak sharply **6** take a photograph of ▯ *noun* **1** the noise made by snapping **2** a sudden spell (*eg* of cold weather) **3** a card-game in which players try to match cards **4** a photograph ▯ **snapdragon** *noun* a garden plant whose flower, when pinched, opens and shuts like a mouth ▯ **snapshot** *noun* a quickly taken photograph

> **snap** *verb* » snap*s*, snapp*ing*, snapp*ed*

snappy *adj* irritable, inclined to speak sharply ▯ **snappily** *adv*

snare *noun* **1** a noose or loop that draws tight when pulled, for catching an animal **2** a trap **3** a hidden danger or temptation ▯ *verb* catch in or with a snare

snarl *verb* **1** growl, showing the teeth **2** speak in a furious, spiteful tone **3** become tangled ▯ *noun* **1** a growl, a furious noise **2** a tangle, a knot **3** a muddled or confused state

snatch *verb* **1** seize or grab suddenly **2** take quickly when you have time: *snatch an hour's sleep* □ *noun* (*plural* **snatches**) **1** an attempt to seize **2** a small piece or quantity: *a snatch of music*

snazzy *adj, informal* smart, stylish

SNCF *abbrev* Société Nationale des Chemins de Fer, the French national rail service

sneak *verb* **1** creep or move in a stealthy, secretive way **2** tell tales, tell on others □ *noun* **1** someone who tells tales **2** a deceitful, underhand person

sneaky *adj* underhand, deceitful □ **sneakily** *adv*

sneer *verb* show contempt by a scornful expression, words *etc* □ *noun* a scornful expression or remark

sneeze *verb* make a sudden, unintentional and violent blowing noise through the nose and mouth □ *noun* an involuntary blow through the nose

snicker *verb* **1** snigger **2** of a horse: neigh

snide *adj* mean, malicious: *snide remark*

sniff *verb* **1** draw in air through the nose with a slight noise, *eg* when having a cold, or showing disapproval **2** smell (a scent *etc*) **3** (with **at**) treat with scorn or suspicion □ *noun* a quick drawing in of air through the nose

sniffle *noun* a light sniff, a snuffle □ *verb* sniff lightly

snifter *noun* **1** *informal* a short drink, a dram **2** a bulbous glass for drinking brandy *etc*

snigger *verb* laugh in a quiet, sly manner □ *noun* a quiet, sly laugh

snip *verb* cut off sharply, *esp* with a single cut □ *noun* **1** a cut with scissors **2** a small piece snipped off **3** *informal* a bargain: *a snip at the price*

> **snip** *verb* » snip*s*, snipp*ing*, snipp*ed*

snipe *noun* a bird with a long straight beak, found in marshy places □ *verb* **1** (with **at**) shoot at from a place of hiding **2** (with **at**) attack with critical remarks □ **sniper** *noun* someone who shoots at a single person from cover

snippet *noun* a little piece, *esp* of information or gossip

snitch *noun, informal* an informer, a tell-tale □ *verb* inform (on)

snivel *verb* **1** have a running nose, *eg* because of a cold **2** whine or complain tearfully □ *noun* **1** a running nose **2** a whine

> **snivel** *verb* » snivel*s*, snivell*ing*, snivell*ed*

snob *noun* someone who looks down on those in a lower social class □ **snobbery** *noun* □ **snobbish** *adj* □ **snobbishness** *noun*

> Originally a slang term for 'shoemaker' which changed its meaning to someone of low social class, and later to an ostentatious vulgarian

snog *verb, slang* kiss, pet

snog » snog*s*, snogg*ing*, snogg*ed*

snood *noun* a hood

snooker *noun* a game like billiards, using twenty-two coloured balls

snoop *verb* spy or pry in a sneaking secretive way ▫ *noun* someone who pries

snooty *adj* haughty, snobbish

snooze *verb* sleep lightly, doze ▫ *noun* a light sleep

snore *verb* make a snorting noise in your sleep while breathing ▫ *noun* a snorting sound made in sleep

snorkel *noun* **1** a tube with one end above the water, to enable an underwater swimmer to breathe **2** a similar device for bringing air into a submarine

snort *verb* **1** force air noisily through the nostrils **2** make such a noise to express disapproval, anger, laughter *etc* ▫ *noun* a loud noise made through the nostrils

snot *noun* mucus of the nose ▫ **snotty** *adj* supercilious

snout *noun* the projecting nose and mouth of an animal, *eg* of a pig

snow *noun* frozen water vapour which falls in light white flakes ▫ *verb* fall down in, or like, flakes of snow ▫ **snowboard** *noun* a single board used as a ski on snow ▫ **snow blindness** dimness of sight caused by the brightness of light reflected from the snow ▫ **snowdrift** *noun* a bank of snow blown together by the wind ▫ **snowdrop** *noun* a small white flower growing from a bulb in early spring ▫ **snowflake** *noun* a flake of snow ▫ **snowline** *noun* the height up a mountain above which there is always snow ▫ **snowman** *noun* a figure shaped like a human being, made of snow ▫ **snowplough** *noun* a large vehicle for clearing snow from roads *etc* ▫ **snow-shoe** *noun* a long broad frame with a mesh, one of a pair for walking on top of snow ▫ **snowy** *adj* **1** covered with snow **2** white, pure ▫ **snowed under** overwhelmed

snowball *noun* a ball made of snow pressed hard together ▫ *verb* **1** throw snowballs **2** grow increasingly quickly: *unemployment has snowballed recently*

SNP *abbrev* Scottish National Party

snub *verb* treat or speak to in an abrupt, scornful way, insult ▫ *noun* an act of snubbing ▫ *adj* of a nose: short and turned up at the end

snub *verb* » snub*s*, snubb*ing*, snubb*ed*

snuff *verb* put out or trim the wick of (a candle) ▫ *noun* powdered tobacco for drawing up into the nose ▫ **snuffbox** *noun* a box for holding snuff ▫ **snuff movie** an illegal film showing torture and the deliberate, unsuspected killing of those acting in it

snuffle *verb* make a sniffing noise through the nose, *eg* because of a cold ▫ *noun* a sniffling through the nose

snug *adj* **1** lying close and warm **2** cosy, comfortable **3** closely fitting; neat and trim ▫ **snuggle** *verb* **1** curl up comfortably **2** draw close to for warmth, affection *etc*

so *adv* **1** as shown, *eg* by a hand gesture: *so high* **2** to such an extent, to a great extent: *so heavy/ you look so happy* **3** in this or that way: *point your toes so* **4** correct: *is that so?* **5** (used in contradicting) indeed: *It's not true. It is so* ▢ *conj* therefore: *you don't need it, so don't buy it* ▢ **so-and-so** *noun*, *informal* **1** this or that person or thing **2** *euphem* used instead of a stronger insult: *she's a real so-and-so, saying that to you!* ▢ **so-called** *adj* called by such a name, often mistakenly: *a so-called expert* ▢ **so-so** *adj* not particularly good ▢ **so as to** in order to ▢ **so far** up to this or that point ▢ **so forth** more of the same sort of thing: *pots, pans and so forth* ▢ **so much for** that is the end of: *so much for that idea!* ▢ **so that** with the purpose or result that ▢ **so what?** what difference does it make? does it matter?

soak *verb* **1** let stand in a liquid until wet through **2** drench (with) **3** (with **up**) suck up, absorb ▢ **soaking** *adj* wet through ▢ *noun* a wetting, drenching ▢ **soaking wet** thoroughly wet, drenched

soap *noun* **1** a mixture containing oils or fats and other substances, used in washing **2** *informal* a soap opera ▢ *verb* use soap on ▢ **soapbox** *noun* **1** a small box for holding soap **2** a makeshift platform for standing on when speaking to a crowd out of doors ▢ **soap opera** a television series about a group of characters and their daily lives ▢ **soapsuds** *noun plural* soapy water worked into a froth ▢ **soapy** *adj* **1** like soap **2** full of soap

soar *verb* **1** fly high into the air **2** of prices: rise high and quickly

sob *verb* weep noisily ▢ *noun* a noisy weeping ▢ **sob story** a story told to arouse sympathy

> **sob** *verb* » sob*s*, sobb*ing*, sobb*ed*

sober *adj* **1** not drunk **2** serious, staid **3** not florid, unelaborate ▢ *verb* (sometimes with **up**) make or become sober ▢ **soberly** *adv* ▢ **soberness** or **sobriety** *noun* the state of being sober

sobriquet *noun* a nickname

> From a French phrase meaning literally an affectionate chuck under the chin

Soc *abbrev* Society

soccer *noun* football

sociable *adj* fond of the company of others, friendly ▢ **sociability** or **sociableness** *noun*

social *adj* **1** relating to society, or to a community: *social history* **2** living in communities: *social insects* **3** of companionship: *social gathering* **4** of rank or level in society: *social class* ▢ **social security** the system, paid for by taxes, of providing insurance against old age, illness, unemployment *etc* ▢ **social work** work which deals with the care of the people in a community, *esp* of the poor or underprivileged ▢ **social worker**

socialism *noun* the belief that a country's wealth should belong to the people as a whole, not to private owners □ **socialist** *noun* & *adj*

society *noun* **1** humanity considered as a whole **2** a community of people **3** a social club, an association **4** the class of people who are wealthy, fashionable *etc* **5** company, companionship: *I enjoy his society*

sociology *noun* the study of human society □ **sociological** *adj* □ **sociologist** *noun*

sociopath *noun* someone who hates the company of others

sock *noun* a short stocking

socket *noun* a hollow into which something is fitted: *an electric socket*

sod[1] *noun* a piece of earth with grass growing on it, a turf

sod[2] *noun, Brit slang* an obnoxious person □ **sod off** go away □ **Sod's Law** the law that the most inconvenient thing is the most likely to happen

soda *noun* **1** the name of several substances formed from sodium **2** soda-water □ **baking soda** sodium bicarbonate, a powder used as a raising agent in baking □ **soda-water** *noun* water through which gas has been passed, making it fizzy

sodden *adj* soaked through and through

sodium *noun* a metallic element from which many substances are formed, including common salt

sodomy *noun* anal intercourse □ **sodomite** *noun*

sofa *noun* a kind of long, stuffed seat with back and arms □ **sofa bed** a sofa incorporating a fold-away bed

soft *adj* **1** easily put out of shape when pressed **2** not hard or firm **3** not loud **4** of a colour: not bright or glaring **5** not strict enough **6** lacking strength or courage **7** lacking common sense, weak in the mind **8** of a drink: not alcoholic **9** of water: containing little calcium *etc* □ *adv* gently, quietly □ **soften** *verb* make or grow soft □ **soft-hearted** *adj* kind and generous □ **software** *noun*, *comput* programs *etc* as opposed to the machines (*contrasted with*: **hardware**) □ **softwood** *noun* the wood of a cone-bearing tree (*eg* fir, larch)

SOGAT *abbrev* Society of Graphical and Allied Trades

soggy *adj* **1** soaked **2** soft and wet

soi-disant *adj* pretended, would be

soil *noun* **1** the upper layer of the earth in which plants grow **2** loose earth; dirt □ *verb* make dirty

soirée /*swa*reh/ *noun* an evening get-together

sojourn *verb* stay for a time □ *noun* a short stay

solace *noun* something which makes pain or sorrow easier to bear, comfort □ *verb* comfort

solar *adj* **1** relating to the sun **2** influenced by the sun **3** powered by energy from the sun's rays □ **solar system** the sun with the planets (including the earth) going round it

sold *past form* of **sell**

solder *noun* melted metal used for joining metal surfaces □ *verb* join (with solder) □ **soldering-iron** *noun* an electric tool for soldering joints

soldier *noun* someone in military service, *esp* someone who is not an officer

sole[1] *noun* **1** the underside of the foot **2** the underside of a shoe *etc* □ *verb* put a sole on (a shoe etc)

sole[2] *adj* **1** only: *the sole survivor* **2** belonging to one person or group only: *the sole right* □ **solely** *adv* only, alone

sole[3] *noun* a small type of flat fish

solecism *noun* **1** *grammar* a improper or non-standard usage **2** a breach of good manners □ **solecistic** or **solecistical** *adj*

solemn *adj* **1** serious, earnest **2** of an occasion: celebrated with special ceremonies □ **solemnity** *noun* □ **solemnize** *verb* carry out (a wedding *etc*) with religious ceremonies

sol-fa *noun, music* a system of syllables (do, ray, me *etc*) to be sung to the notes of a scale

solicit *verb* **1** ask earnestly for: *solicit advice* **2** ask (someone for something) **3** offer yourself as a prostitute □ **solicitude** *noun* care or anxiety about someone or something

solicitor *noun* a lawyer who advises people about legal matters

solicitous *adj* **1** anxious **2** considerate, careful □ **solicitously** *adv*

solid *adj* **1** fixed in shape, not in the form of gas or liquid **2** in three dimensions, with length, breadth and height **3** not hollow **4** firm, strongly made **5** made or formed completely of one substance: *solid silver* **6** reliable, sound: *solid business* **7** *informal* without a break: *three solid hours' work* □ *noun* **1** a substance that is solid **2** a figure that has three dimensions □ **solidarity** *noun* unity of interests *etc* □ **solidity** *noun* the state of being solid

solidify *verb* make or become firm or solid

> **solidify** » solidifi*es*, solidify*ing*, solidifi*ed*

solidus *noun* a slanting stroke, a slash (/)

soliloquy *noun* (*plural* **soliloquies**) a speech made by an actor *etc* to themselves □ **soliloquize** *verb* speak to yourself, *esp* on the stage

solipsism *noun* the belief that nothing is knowable except the self □ **solipsistic** *adj*

solitaire *noun* a card-game for one player (*also called*: **patience**)

solitary *adj* **1** lone, alone **2** single: *not a solitary crumb remained*

solitude *noun* the state of being alone; lack of company

solo *noun* (*plural* **solos**) a musical piece for one singer or player □ *adj* performed by one person alone: *solo flight* □ **soloist** *noun* someone who plays or sings a solo

solstice *noun* the time of longest daylight (**summer solstice** about 21 June) or longest dark (**winter solstice** about 21 December)

soluble *adj* **1** able to be dissolved

or made liquid **2** of a problem *etc*: able to be solved ▯ **solubility** *noun*

solution *noun* **1** a liquid with something dissolved in it **2** the act of solving a problem *etc* **3** an answer to a problem, puzzle *etc*

solve *verb* **1** clear up or explain (a mystery) **2** discover the answer or solution to

solvency *noun* the state of being able to pay all debts ▯ **solvent** *adj* able to pay all debts ▯ *noun* anything that dissolves another substance

somatic *adj* relating to sleep

sombre *adj* gloomy, dark, dismal

sombrero *noun* (*plural* **sombreros**) a broad-brimmed Mexican hat

some *adj* **1** several **2** a few: *some oranges, but not many* **3** a little: *some bread, but not much* **4** certain: *some people are rich* ▯ *pronoun* **1** a number or part out of a quantity: *please try some* **2** certain people: *some won't be happy* ▯ **somehow** *adv* in some way or other ▯ **sometime** *adv* at a time not known or stated definitely ▯ **sometimes** *adv* at times, now and then ▯ **somewhat** *adv* rather: *somewhat boring* ▯ **somewhere** *adv* in some place

somebody or **someone** *noun* **1** an unknown or unnamed person: *somebody I'd never seen before* **2** an important person: *he really is somebody now*

somersault *noun* a forward or backward roll in which the heels go over the head ▯ *verb* perform a somersault

something *pronoun* **1** a thing not known or not stated **2** a thing of importance **3** a slight amount, a degree: *he has something of his father's looks*

somnambulist *noun* a sleep-walker

somnolence *noun* sleepiness ▯ **somnolent** *adj* sleepy; causing sleepiness

son *noun* a male child ▯ **son-in-law** *noun* a daughter's husband

sonata *noun* a piece of music with three or more movements, usually for one instrument

son et lumière a display of lights and sound effects, often describing a historical event

song *noun* **1** singing **2** a piece of music to be sung ▯ **songbird** *noun* a bird that sings ▯ **songster**, **songstress** *noun, old* a singer ▯ **for a song** (bought, sold *etc*) very cheaply

sonic *adj* of sound waves ▯ **sonic boom** an explosive sound that can be heard when an aircraft travels faster than the speed of sound

sonnet *noun* a type of poem in fourteen lines

sonorous *adj* giving a clear, loud sound ▯ **sonority** *noun*

soon *adv* **1** in a short time from now or from the time mentioned: *he will come soon* **2** early: *too soon to tell* **3** (with **as**) as readily, as willingly: *I would as soon stand as sit* ▯ **sooner** *adv* more willingly, rather: *I would sooner stand than sit* ▯ **sooner or later** at some time in the future

soot *noun* the black powder left by smoke □ **sooty** *adj* like, or covered with, soot

soothe *verb* **1** calm or comfort (a person, feelings *etc*) **2** help or ease (a pain *etc*) □ **soothing** *adj*

soothsayer *noun* someone who predicts the future

sop *noun* **1** bread dipped in soup *etc* **2** a bribe given to keep someone quiet □ *verb* soak (up) □ **sopping** *adj* wet through

sophism *noun* a plausible fallacy □ **sophist** *noun* □ **sophistic** *adj*

sophisticated *adj* **1** of a person: full of experience, accustomed to an elegant, cultured way of life **2** of ways of thought, or machinery *etc*: highly developed, complicated, elaborate

sophomore *noun, US* a second-year college student

soporific *adj* causing sleep □ *noun* something which causes sleep

soppy *adj* overly sentimental

soprano *noun* (*plural* **sopranos**) **1** a singing voice of high pitch **2** a singer with this voice

sorcerer, sorceress *noun* someone who works magic spells; a witch or wizard □ **sorcery** *noun* magic, witchcraft

sordid *adj* **1** dirty, filthy **2** mean, selfish **3** contemptible

sore *adj* painful □ *noun* a painful, inflamed spot on the skin □ **sorely** *adv* very greatly: *sorely in need* □ **soreness** *noun*

sorghum *noun* a grass similar to sugar-cane

sorority *noun* (*plural* **sororities**) a society of female students (*compare with*: **fraternity**)

sorrel *noun* a type of plant with sour-tasting leaves

sorrow *noun* sadness caused by a loss, disappointment *etc* □ *verb* be sad □ **sorrowful** *adj*

sorry *adj* **1** feeling regret for something you have done: *I'm sorry I mentioned it* **2** feeling sympathy or pity (for): *sorry for you* **3** miserable: *in a sorry state*

sort *noun* a kind of (person or thing): *the sort of sweets I like* □ *verb* separate things, putting each in its place: *sort letters* □ **a sort of** used of something which is like something else, but not exactly: *he wore a sort of crown* □ **of a sort** or **of sorts** of a kind, usually inadequate: *a party of sorts* □ **out of sorts** not feeling very well

sortie *noun* a sudden attack made by the defenders of a place on those who are trying to capture it

SOS *noun* **1** a code signal calling for help **2** any call for help

sot *noun* a drunkard □ **sottish** *adj* stupid with drink

sotto voce *adv* in a low voice, so as not to be overheard

soufflé /*soo*fleh/ *noun* a light, cooked dish, made of whisked egg-whites *etc*

sough *verb* of the wind: make a sighing sound

sought *past form* of **seek**

soul *noun* **1** the spirit, the part of someone which is not the body **2** a person: *a dear old soul* **3** a perfect example (of): *the soul of kindness* □ **soulful** *adj* full of feeling □ **soulless** *adj* **1** having no soul or atmosphere **2** dull, very boring

sound *noun* **1** anything that can be heard, a noise **2** a distance from which something may be heard: *within the sound of Bow Bells* **3** a narrow passage of water □ *verb* **1** strike you as being: *that sounds awful* **2** (with **like**) resemble in sound: *that sounds like Henry's voice* **3** make a noise with: *sound a horn* **4** examine by listening carefully to: *sound a patient's chest* **5** measure (the depths of water) **6** try to find out someone's opinions: *I'll sound him out tomorrow* □ *adj* **1** healthy, strong **2** of sleep: deep **3** thorough: *a sound beating* **4** reliable: *sound opinions* □ **soundproof** *adj* built or made so that sound cannot pass in or out □ *verb* make soundproof □ **soundtrack** *noun* the strip on a film where the speech and music are recorded

soup *noun* a liquid food made from meat, vegetables *etc*

soupçon /*soop*sonh/ *noun* a taste, a morsel

sour *adj* **1** having an acid or bitter taste, often as a stage in going bad: *sour milk* **2** bad-tempered □ *verb* make sour

source *noun* **1** the place where something has its beginning or is found **2** a spring, *esp* one from which a river flows

souse *verb* soak (*eg* herrings) in salted water

south *noun* one of the four chief directions, that to one's left as one faces the setting sun □ *adj & adv* to or in the south □ **south-east** (or **south-west**) the point of the compass midway between south and east (or south and west) □ *adj* in the south-east or south-west □ **southerly** *adj* **1** towards the south **2** of wind: from the south □ **southern** *adj* of, from or in the south □ **southerner** *noun* someone living in a southern region or country □ **south pole** the southern end of the imaginary axis on which the earth turns □ **southward** or **southwards** *adv* towards the south □ **sou'wester** *noun* a kind of waterproof hat

souvenir *noun* something bought or given as a reminder of a person, place or occasion

sovereign *noun* **1** a king or queen **2** *hist* a British gold coin worth £1 □ *adj* **1** supreme, highest: *sovereign lord* **2** having its own government: *sovereign state* □ **sovereignty** *noun* highest power

sow[1] *noun* a female pig

sow[2] *verb* **1** scatter (seeds) so that they may grow **2** cover (an area) with seeds □ **sower** *noun*

> **sow** » sow*s*, sow*ing*, sown or sow*ed*, sowed

soya bean or **soy bean** a kind of bean, rich in protein, used as a substitute for meat □ **soya sauce** or **soy sauce** a sauce made from soya beans used in Chinese cooking

spa *noun* a place where people go to drink or bathe in the water from a natural spring

space *noun* **1** a gap, an empty place **2** the distance between objects **3** an uncovered part on a sheet of paper **4** length of time: *in the space of a day* **5** the empty region in which all stars, planets *etc* are situated ▫ *verb* put things apart from each other, leaving room between them ▫ **spacecraft** *noun* a machine for travelling in space ▫ **spaceman, spacewoman** *noun* a traveller in space ▫ **spaceship** *noun* a manned spacecraft

spacious *adj* having plenty of room ▫ **spaciousness** *noun*

spade *noun* **1** a tool with a broad blade for digging in the earth **2** one of the four suits of playing-cards ▫ **call a spade a spade** say plainly and clearly what you mean

spaghetti *noun* a type of pasta made into long sticks

spake *verb*, *old* spoke

span *noun* **1** the distance between the tips of the little finger and the thumb when the hand is spread out (about 23 centimetres, 9 inches) **2** the full time anything lasts **3** an arch of a bridge ▫ *verb* stretch across: *the bridge spans the river*

> **span** *verb* » span*s*, spann*ing*, spann*ed*

spangle *noun* a thin sparkling piece of metal used as an ornament ▫ *verb* sprinkle with spangles *etc*

spaniel *noun* a breed of dog with large, hanging ears

spank *verb* strike with the flat of the hand ▫ *noun* a slap with the hand, *esp* on the buttocks ▫ **spanking** *noun* a beating with the hand ▫ *adj* fast: *a spanking pace*

spanner *noun* a tool used to tighten or loosen nuts, screws *etc*

spar *noun* a long piece of wood or metal used as a ship's mast or its crosspiece ▫ *verb* **1** fight with the fists **2** engage in an argument

> **spar** *verb* » spar*s*, sparr*ing*, sparr*ed*

spare *verb* **1** do without: *I can't spare you today* **2** afford, set aside: *I can't spare the time to do it* **3** treat with mercy, hold back from injuring **4** avoid causing (trouble *etc*) to ▫ *adj* **1** extra, not yet in use: *spare tyre* **2** thin, small: *spare but strong* ▫ *noun* another of the same kind (*eg* a tyre, part of a machine) kept for emergencies ▫ **sparing** *adj* careful, economical ▫ **to spare** over and above what is needed

spark *noun* **1** a small red-hot part thrown off from something burning **2** a trace: *a spark of humanity* **3** a lively person ▫ *verb* make sparks ▫ **sparking-plug** or **spark-plug** *noun* a device in a car engine that produces a spark to set on fire explosive gases

sparkle *noun* **1** a little spark **2** brightness, liveliness **3** bubbles, as in wine ▫ *verb* **1** shine in a glittering way **2** be lively or witty **3** bubble ▫ **sparkling** *adj* **1** glittering **2** witty **3** of a drink: bubbling, fizzy

sparrow *noun* a type of small dull-coloured bird ▫ **sparrowhawk** *noun* a type of short-winged hawk

sparse *adj* **1** thinly scattered **2** not much, not enough

spartan *adj* of conditions *etc:* hard, without luxury

spasm *noun* **1** a sudden involuntary jerk of the muscles **2** a strong, short burst (*eg* of anger, work) □ **spasmodic** *adj* **1** occurring in spasms **2** coming now and again, not regularly □ **spasmodically** *adv*

spastic *adj* suffering from brain damage which has resulted in extreme muscle spasm and paralysis

spat *past form* of **spit**

spate *noun* **1** flood: *the river is in spate* **2** a sudden rush: *a spate of new books*

spatial *adj* of or relating to space□ **spatially** *adv*

spats *noun plural* short gaiters reaching just above the ankle

spatter *verb* splash (*eg* with mud)

spatula *noun* a tool with a broad, blunt blade

spawn *noun* a mass of eggs of fish, frogs *etc* □ *verb* **1** of fish *etc*: lay eggs **2** cause, produce

spay *verb* remove the ovaries of (a female animal)

speak *verb* **1** say words, talk **2** hold a conversation (with) **3** make a speech **4** be able to talk (a certain language) □ **speak your mind** give your opinion openly □ **speak up 1** speak more loudly or clearly **2** give your opinion openly

> **speak** » speak*s*, speak*ing*, spoke, spoken

spear *noun* **1** a long weapon, with an iron or steel point **2** a long, pointed shoot or leaf (*esp* of grass) □ *verb* pierce with a spear □ **the spear side** the male side or line of descent (*contrasted with*: **distaff side)**

special *adj* **1** not ordinary, exceptional: *special occasion/ special friend* **2** put on for a particular purpose: *special train* **3** belonging to one person or thing and not to others: *special skills/ a special tool for drilling holes in tiles* □ **specialist** *noun* someone who studies one branch of a subject or field: *heart specialist* □ **speciality** *noun* (*plural* **specialities**) something for which a person is well-known □ **specialization** *noun* □ **specialize** *verb* work in, or study, a particular job, subject *etc* □ **specialized** *adj* of knowledge: obtained by specializing □ **specialty** *noun* (*plural* **specialties**) a branch of work in which someone specializes

species *noun* (*plural* **species**) **1** a group of plants or animals which are alike in most ways **2** a kind (of anything) □ **specie** */speeshi/ noun* gold and silver coins

specific *adj* giving all the details clearly; particular, exactly stated: *a specific purpose* □ **specifically** *adv* □ **specification** *noun* **1** the act of specifying **2** a full description of details (*eg* in a plan or contract)

specify *verb* **1** set down or say clearly (what is wanted) **2** make particular mention of

> **specify** » specifi*es*, specify*ing*, specifi*ed*

specimen *noun* something used as a sample of a group or kind of anything, *esp* for study or for putting in a collection

specious *adj* looking or seeming good but really not so good

speck *noun* **1** a small spot **2** a tiny piece (*eg* of dust) □ **speckle** *noun* a spot on a different-coloured background □ **speckled** *adj* dotted with speckles

spectacle *noun* **1** a striking or wonderful sight **2** (**spectacles**) glasses which someone wears to improve eyesight

spectacular *adj* making a great show or display; impressive □ **spectacularly** *adv*

spectator *noun* someone who watches (an event *eg* a football match)

spectre *noun* a ghost □ **spectral** *adj* ghostly

spectrum *noun* (*plural* **spectra** or **spectrums**) **1** the band of colours as seen in a rainbow, sometimes formed when light passes through water or glass **2** the range or extent of anything

speculate *verb* **1** guess **2** wonder (about) **3** buy goods, shares *etc* in order to sell them again at a profit □ **speculation** *noun* □ **speculative** *adj* speculating □ **speculator** *noun*

speculum *noun* an instrument inserted in a woman's vagina to help a doctor view her cervix *etc*

sped *past form* of **speed**

speech *noun* **1** the power of making sounds which have meaning for other people **2** a way of speaking: *his speech is always clear* **3** (*plural* **speeches**) a (formal) talk given to an audience □ **speech day** the day at the end of a school year when speeches are made and prizes given out □ **speechless** *adj* so surprised *etc* that you cannot speak

speed *noun* **1** quickness of, or rate of, movement or action **2** (*slang*) amphetamine □ *verb* **1** (*past* **sped**) (cause to) move along quickly, hurry **2** (*past* **speeded**) drive very fast in a motor-car *etc* (*esp* faster than is allowed by law) □ **speeding** *noun* driving at (an illegally) high speed □ **speed limit** the greatest speed permitted on a particular road □ **speedometer** *noun* an instrument that shows how fast you are travelling □ **speedway** *noun* a motor-cycle racing track □ **speedy** *adj* going quickly

> **speed** *verb* » speed*s*, speed*ing*, sped or speed*ed*

speedwell *noun* a type of small plant with blue flowers

speleologist *noun* someone who studies or explores caves □ **speleology** *noun*

spell *noun* **1** words which, when spoken, are supposed to have magic power **2** magic or other powerful influence **3** a (short) space of time **4** a turn (at work, rest, play) □ *verb* **1** give or write correctly the letters which make up a word **2** mean, imply: *this defeat spells disaster for us all* □ **spellbound** *adj* charmed, held by a spell □ **spelling** *noun* **1** the ability to spell words **2**

the study of spelling words correctly ▫ **spell out** say (something) very frankly or clearly

> **spell** *verb* » spell*s*, spell*ing*, spelt or spell*ed*

spelt *see* **spell**

spelunking *noun* exploring in caves as a hobby

spend *verb* **1** use (money) for buying **2** use (energy *etc*) **3** pass (time): *I spent a week there* **4** use up energy, force: *the storm spent itself and the sun shone* ▫ **spendthrift** *noun* someone who spends money freely and carelessly ▫ **spent** *adj* exhausted; having lost force or power: *a spent bullet*

> **spend** » spend*s*, spend*ing*, spent

sperm (the fluid in a male carrying) the male sex-cell that fertilizes the female egg ▫ **sperm bank** a store of semen for use in artificial insemination ▫ **sperm-whale** *noun* a kind of whale from the head of which **spermaceti**, a waxy substance, is obtained

spermatozoon *noun* (*plural* **spermatozoa**) a male sex cell contained in sperm

spermicide *noun* a substance which kills spermatozoa

spew *verb* vomit

sphagnum a kind of moss

sphere *noun* **1** a ball or similar perfectly round object **2** a position or level in society: *he moves in the highest spheres* **3** range (of influence or action) ▫ **spherical** *adj* having the shape of a sphere

sphincter *noun* a ringlike muscle which narrows an opening (*eg* the anus)

Sphinx *noun* **1** a mythological monster with the head of a woman and the body of a lioness **2** the large stone model of the Sphinx in Egypt **3** (**sphinx**) someone whose real thoughts you cannot guess

spice *noun* **1** any substance used for flavouring *eg* pepper, nutmeg **2** anything that adds liveliness, interest ▫ *verb* flavour with spice

spick-and-span *adj* neat, clean and tidy

spicy *adj* **1** full of spices **2** lively and sometimes slightly indecent: *a spicy tale* ▫ **spiciness** *noun*

spider *noun* a kind of small, insect-like creature with eight legs, that spins a web ▫ **spidery** *adj* **1** like a spider **2** of handwriting: having fine, sprawling strokes

spiel */speel/* or */shpeel/ noun*, *informal* a (long or often repeated) story or speech

spigot *noun* **1** a peg for sealing a hole **2** *US* a tap

spike *noun* **1** a pointed piece of rod (of wood, metal *etc*) **2** a type of large nail **3** an ear of corn **4** a head of flowers ▫ *verb* **1** pierce with a spike **2** make useless **3** *informal* add an alcoholic drink *esp* to a soft drink ▫ **spiked** *adj* having spikes (*esp* of shoes for running) ▫ **spiky** *adj* having spikes or a sharp point

spill *verb* (allow liquid to) run out or overflow ▫ *noun* **1** a fall **2** a thin strip of wood or twisted paper for lighting a candle, a pipe *etc* ◻ **spillage** *noun* an act of spilling or what is spilt ◻ **spill the beans** *informal* give away a secret, *esp* unintentionally

> **spill** *verb* » spill*s*, spill*ing*, spilt or spill*ed*

spin *verb* **1** draw out (cotton, wood, silk *etc*) and twist into threads **2** (cause to) whirl round quickly **3** travel quickly, *esp* on wheels **4** produce a fine thread as a spider does ◻ *noun* **1** a whirling motion **2** a ride (*esp* on wheels) ◻ **spin-doctor** *noun* someone employed by a public figure to speak to the media *etc* on their behalf ◻ **spindrier** *noun* a machine for taking water out of clothes by whirling them round ◻ **spinner** *noun* ◻ **spinneret** *noun* in a spider *etc*, the organ for producing thread ◻ **spinning wheel** a machine for spinning thread, consisting of a wheel which drives spindles ◻ **spin a yarn** tell a long story ◻ **spin out** make to last a long or longer time

> **spin** *verb* » spin*s*, spinn*ing*, spun

spina bifida a birth defect which leaves part of the spinal cord exposed

spinach *noun* a type of plant whose leaves are eaten as vegetables

spinal see **spine**

spindle *noun* **1** the pin from which the thread is twisted in spinning wool or cotton **2** a pin on which anything turns round (*eg* that in the centre of the turntable of a record-player) ◻ **spindly** *adj* long and thin

spindrift *noun* the spray blown from the tops of waves

spine *noun* **1** the line of linked bones running down the back in animals and humans, the backbone **2** a ridge **3** a stiff, pointed spike which is part of an animal's body (*eg* a porcupine) **4** a thorn ◻ **spinal cord** a cord of nerve cells in the spine ◻ **spineless** *adj* having no spine; weak

spinet *noun* a kind of small harpsichord

spinnaker *noun* a light triangular sail

spinney *noun* (*plural* **spinneys**) a small clump of trees

spinster *noun* a woman who is not married

spiral *adj* **1** coiled round like a spring **2** winding round and round, getting further and further away from the centre ◻ *noun* **1** anything with a spiral shape **2** a spiral movement **3** an increase which gets ever more rapid ◻ *verb* **1** move in a spiral **2** increase ever more rapidly

> **spiral** *verb* » spiral*s*, spirall*ing*, spirall*ed*

spire *noun* a tall, sharp-pointed tower (*esp* on the roof of a church)

spirit *noun* **1** the soul **2** a being without a body, a ghost: *an evil spirit* **3** liveliness, boldness: *he acted with spirit* **4** a feeling or attitude: *a spirit of kindness* **5** the intended meaning: *the spirit of the laws* **6** a distilled liquid, *esp* alcohol **7** (**spirits**) strong alcoholic drinks in general (*eg* whisky) **8** (**spirits**) state of mind, mood: *in high spirits* □ *verb* (*esp* with **away**) remove, as if by magic □ **spirited** *adj* lively □ **spiritual** *adj* having to do with the soul or with ghosts □ *noun* an emotional, religious song of a kind originally developed by the African American slaves □ **spiritualism** *noun* the belief that living people can communicate with the souls of dead people □ **spiritualist** *noun* someone who holds this belief

spit *noun* **1** the liquid which forms in a person's mouth **2** a metal bar on which meat is roasted **3** a long piece of land running into the sea □ *verb* (*past form* **spat**) **1** throw liquid out from the mouth **2** rain slightly **3** (*past form* **spitted**) pierce with something sharp □ **spitting image** an exact likeness □ **spittoon** *noun* a kind of dish into which you may spit

> **spit** *verb* » spit*s*, spitt*ing*, spat or spitt*ed*

spite *noun* the wish to hurt (*esp* feelings) □ *verb* annoy out of spite □ **spiteful** *adj* □ **in spite of 1** taking no notice of: *he left in spite of his father's command* **2** although something has happened or is a fact: *the ground was dry in spite of all the rain*

spittle *noun* spit

splash *verb* **1** spatter with water, mud *etc* **2** move or fall with a splash or splashes □ *noun* (*plural* **splashes**)**1** the sound made by, or the scattering of liquid caused by, something hitting water *etc* **2** a mark made by splashing (*eg* on your clothes) **3** a bright patch: *a splash of colour* □ **make a splash** attract a lot of attention

splay *verb* turn out at an angle □ **splay-footed** *adj* with flat feet turned outward

spleen *noun* **1** a spongy, blood-filled organ inside the body, near the stomach **2** bad temper

splendid *adj* **1** magnificent, brilliant **2** *informal* excellent □ **splendidly** *adv* □ **splendour** *noun*

splenetic *adj* irritable

splice *verb* **1** join (two ends of a rope) by twining the threads together □ *noun* a joint so made

splint *noun* a piece of wood *etc* tied to a broken limb to keep it in a fixed position

splinter *noun* a sharp, thin, broken piece of wood, glass *etc* □ *verb* split into splinters □ **splinter group** a group which breaks away from a larger one

split *verb* **1** cut or break lengthways **2** crack, break **3** divide into pieces or groups *etc* □ *noun* a crack, a break □ **the splits** the feat of going down on the floor with one leg stretched forward and the other back □ **splitting** *adj* of a headache: severe, intense □ **a split second** a fraction of a second □ **split your sides** laugh heartily

splutter *verb* **1** make spitting noises **2** speak hastily and unclearly

spoil *verb* **1** make useless; damage, ruin **2** give in to the wishes of (a child *etc*) and so ruin its character **3** of food: become bad or useless **4** (*past form* **spoiled**) rob, plunder ◇ *noun* (often **spoils**) plunder ◇ **spoilsport** *noun* someone who won't join in other people's fun ◇ **spoiling for** eager for (*esp* a fight)

spoil *verb* » spoil*s*, spoil*ing*, spoil*ed*

spoke *noun* one of the ribs or bars from the centre to the rim of a wheel ◇ *verb, past form* of **speak**

spoken *see* **speak**

spokesman, spokeswoman *noun* someone who speaks on behalf of others

spoliation *noun* plundering

sponge *noun* **1** a sea animal **2** its soft, elastic skeleton which can soak up water and is used for washing **3** an artificial object like this used for washing **4** a light cake or pudding ◇ *verb* **1** wipe with a sponge **2** *informal* live off money *etc* given by others ◇ **sponger** *noun, informal* someone who lives at others' expense ◇ **spongy** *adj* soft like a sponge ◇ **throw in the sponge** give up a fight or struggle

sponsor *noun* **1** someone who takes responsibility for introducing something, a promoter **2** someone who promises to pay a sum of money if another person completes a set task (*eg* a walk, swim *etc*) **3** a business firm which pays for a radio or television programme and advertises its products during it ◇ *verb* act as a sponsor to ◇ **sponsorship** *noun* the act of sponsoring

spontaneous *adj* **1** not planned beforehand **2** natural, not forced ◇ **spontaneity** *noun*

spoof *noun* a trick played as a joke, a hoax

spook *noun* a ghost ◇ **spooky** *adj* frightening

spool *noun* a reel for thread, film *etc*

spoon *noun* a piece of metal *etc* with a hollow bowl at one end, used for lifting food to the mouth ◇ *verb* lift with a spoon ◇ **spoonfeed** *verb* teach without encouraging independent thought

spoonerism *noun* a mistake in speaking in which the first sounds of words change position, as in *every crook and nanny* for *every nook and cranny*

spoor *noun* the footmarks or trail left by an animal

sporadic *adj* happening here and there, or now and again ◇ **sporadically** *adv*

spore *noun* the seed of certain plants (*eg* ferns, fungi)

sporran *noun* a small pouch worn hanging in front of a kilt

sport *noun* **1** games such as football, tennis, skiing *etc* in general **2** any one game of this type **3** a good-natured, obliging person ◇ *verb* **1** have fun, play **2** wear: *sporting a pink tie* ◇ **sporting** *adj* **1** fond of sport **2** believing in fair play, good-natured ◇ **sporting chance** a reasonably good chance ◇ **sports car** a small, fast car with only two seats ◇ **sportsman, sportswoman** *noun* **1** someone who plays sports **2** someone who shows fair play in sports **sportsmanlike** *adj*

spot *noun* **1** a small mark or stain (of mud, paint *etc*) **2** a round mark as part of a pattern on material *etc* **3** a pimple **4** a place *verb* **1** mark with spots **2** catch sight of **spotless** *adj* very clean **spotlight** *noun* a bright light that is shone on an actor on the stage *verb* **1** show up clearly **2** draw attention to **spotted** or **spotty** *adj* covered with spots **in a spot** in trouble **on the spot 1** in the place where someone is most needed **2** right away, immediately **3** in an embarrassing or difficult position

> spot *verb* » spot*s*, spott*ing*, spott*ed*

spouse *noun* a husband or wife

spout *noun* **1** the part of a kettle, teapot *etc* through which liquid is poured out **2** a strong jet of liquid *verb* pour or spurt out

sprain *noun* a painful twisting (*eg* of an ankle) *verb* twist painfully

sprang *past form* of **spring**

sprat *noun* a small fish similar to a herring

sprawl *verb* **1** sit, lie or fall with the limbs spread out widely **2** of a town *etc:* spread out in an untidy, irregular way

spray *noun* **1** a fine mist of liquid like that made by a waterfall **2** a device with many small holes (*eg* on a watering-can or shower) for producing spray **3** a liquid for spraying **4** a shoot spreading out in flowers *verb* cover with a mist or fine jets of liquid

spread *verb* **1** put more widely or thinly over an area: *spread the butter on the bread* **2** cover: *spread the bread with jam* **3** open out (*eg* your arms, a map) **4** scatter or distribute over a wide area, length of time *etc* *noun* **1** the act of spreading **2** the extent or range (of something) **3** a food which is spread on bread: *sandwich spread* **4** *informal* a large meal laid out on a table **spread-eagled** *adj* with limbs spread out **spreadsheet** *noun* a computer program with which data can be viewed on screen and manipulated

> **spread** *verb* » spread*s*, spread*ing*, spread

spree *noun* a careless spell of some activity: *a spending spree*

sprig *noun* a small twig or shoot

sprightly *adj* lively, brisk **sprightliness** *noun*

spring *verb* **1** jump, leap **2** move swiftly **3** (with **back**) return suddenly to an earlier position when released **4** set off (a trap *etc*) **5** give, reveal unexpectedly: *he sprang the news on me* **6** come from: *his bravery springs from his love of adventure* *noun* **1** a leap **2** a coil of wire used in a mattress **3** the ability to stretch and spring back **4** bounce, energy **5** a small stream flowing out from the ground **6** the season which follows winter, when plants begin to grow again **springboard** *noun* a springy board from which swimmers may dive **springbok** *noun* a type of deer found in S Africa **spring-cleaning** *noun* a thorough cleaning of a house, *esp* in the spring □ **springy** *adj* able to spring back into its former position *etc*, elastic □ **spring a leak** begin to leak □ **spring up** appear suddenly

> **spring** *verb* » spring*s*, spring*ing*, sprang, sprung

sprinkle *verb* scatter or cover in small drops or pieces □ **sprinkler** *noun* something which sprinkles water □ **sprinkling** *noun* a few

sprint *verb* run at full speed □ *noun* a short running race □ **sprinter** *noun*

sprite *noun* **1** a supernatural spirit **2** *comput* an icon which can be moved about a screen

sprocket *noun* one of a set of teeth on the rim of a wheel

sprog *noun, informal* a child

sprout *verb* **1** begin to grow **2** put out new shoots □ *noun* **1** a young bud **2** (**sprouts**) Brussels sprouts

spruce *adj* neat, smart □ *noun* a kind of fir-tree

sprung *see* **spring**

spry *adj* lively, active

spud *noun, informal* a potato

spume *noun* froth, foam

spun *past form* of **spin**

spunk *noun* **1** pluck, spirit **2** *slang* ejaculated semen

spur *noun* **1** a sharp point worn by a horse-rider on the heel and used to urge on a horse **2** a claw-like point at the back of a bird's leg **3** anything that urges someone on **4** a small line of mountains running off from a larger range □ *verb* **1** use spurs on (a horse) **2** urge on □ **on the spur of the moment** without thinking beforehand

> **spur** *verb* » spur*s*, spurr*ing*, spurr*ed*

spurious *adj* not genuine, false □ **spuriousness** *noun*

spurn *verb* cast aside, reject with scorn

spurt *verb* pour out in a sudden stream □ *noun* **1** a sudden stream pouring or squirting out **2** a sudden increase of effort: *put a spurt on*

spurtle *noun* a wooden stick for stirring porridge

sputnik *noun* a small spacecraft orbiting the earth, *orig* Russian

sputter *verb* make a noise as of spitting and throw out moisture in drops

sputum *noun* mucus and spittle from the nose, throat *etc*

spy *noun* (*plural* **spies**) someone who secretly collects (and reports) information about another person, country, firm *etc* □ *verb* **1** catch sight of **2** (with **on**) watch secretly □ **spyglass** *noun* a small telescope

> **spy** *verb* » sp*ies*, spy*ing*, sp*ied*

sq *abbrev* square

squabble *verb* quarrel noisily □ *noun* a noisy quarrel

squad *noun* **1** a group of soldiers, workmen *etc* doing a particular job **2** a group of people □ **squaddie** *noun, informal* a private, an ordinary soldier

squadron *noun* a division of a regiment, section of a fleet or group of aeroplanes ▯ **squadron leader** in the air force, an officer below a wing commander

squalid *adj* **1** very dirty, filthy **2** contemptible

squall *noun* **1** a sudden violent storm **2** a squeal, a scream ▯ **squally** *adj* stormy

squalor *noun* dirty or squalid living conditions

squander *verb* waste (money, goods, strength *etc*) ▯ **squanderer** *noun*

square 1 a figure with four equal sides and four right angles, of this shape: □ **2** an open space enclosed by buildings in a town **3** the answer when a number is multiplied by itself (*eg* the square of 3 is 9) ▯ *adj* **1** shaped like a square **2** equal in scores in a game **3** of two or more people: not owing one another anything **4** straight, level ▯ *verb* **1** make like a square **2** straighten (the shoulders) **3** multiply a number by itself **4** fit,agree: *that doesn't square with what you said earlier* **5** (with **up**) settle (a debt) ▯ *adv* **1** in a straight or level position **2** directly; exactly: *hit square on the nose* ▯ **square deal** fair treatment ▯ **square foot** or **square metre** *etc* an area equal to that of a square each side of which is one foot or one metre *etc* long ▯ **square meal** a large, satisfying meal ▯ **square root** the number which, multiplied by itself, gives a certain other number (*eg* 3 is the square root of 9)

squash *verb* **1** crush flat or to a pulp **2** put down, defeat (rebellion *etc*) ▯ *noun* **1** a crushing or crowding **2** a mass of people crowded together **3** a drink made from the juice of crushed fruit **4** a game with rackets and a rubber ball played in a walled court

squat *verb* **1** sit down on the heels **2** settle without permission in property which you do not pay rent for ▯ *adj* short and thick ▯ **squatter** *noun* someone who squats in a building, on land *etc*

> **squat** *verb* » squat*s*, squatt*ing*, squatt*ed*

squaw *noun, derogatory* **1** a Native American woman or wife **2** a woman

squawk *verb* give a harsh cry ▯ *noun* a harsh cry

squeak *verb* give a short, high-pitched sound ▯ *noun* a high-pitched noise ▯ **squeaky** *adj*

squeal *verb* **1** give a loud, shrill cry **2** *informal* inform on ▯ **squealer** *noun*

squeamish *adj* **1** easily sickened or shocked **2** feeling sick

squeegee *noun* a sponge for washing windows *etc*

squeeze *verb* **1** press together **2** grasp tightly **3** force out (liquid or juice from) by pressing **4** force a way: *squeeze through the hole in the wall* ▯ *noun* **1** a squeezing or pressing **2** a few drops got by squeezing: *a squeeze of lemon juice* **3** a crowd of people crushed together

squelch *noun* a sound made *eg* by

walking through marshy ground □ *verb* make this sound

squib *noun* a type of small firework

squid *noun* a sea animal with tentacles, related to the cuttlefish

squiggle *noun* a curly or wavy mark □ *adj* **squiggly** curly

squillions *noun plural*, *informal* a great many; millions

squint *verb* **1** screw up the eyes in looking at something **2** have the eyes looking in different directions □ *noun* **1** a fault in eyesight which causes squinting **2** *informal* a quick, close glance

squire *noun, hist* **1** a country landowner **2** a knight's servant

squirm *verb* wriggle or twist the body, *esp* in pain or embarrassment

squirrel *noun* a small gnawing animal, either reddish-brown or grey, with a bushy tail

squirt *verb* shoot out a narrow jet of liquid □ *noun* a narrow jet of liquid

Sr *abbrev* senior

SS *abbrev* steamship

St *abbrev* **1** saint **2** street **3** strait

st *abbrev* stone (in weight)

stab *verb* **1** wound or pierce with a pointed weapon **2** poke (at) □ *noun* **1** the act of stabbing **2** a wound made by stabbing **3** a sharp pain □ **have a stab at** make an attempt at

> **stab** *verb* » stab*s*, stabb*ing*, stabb*ed*

stable *noun* a building for keeping horses □ *verb* put or keep (horses) in a stable □ *adj* firm, steady □ **stability** *noun* steadiness □ **stabilize** *verb* make steady

staccato *adj* **1** of sounds: sharp and separate, like the sound of tapping **2** *also adv*, *music* (with each note) sounded separately and clearly

stack *noun* a large pile (of straw, hay, wood *etc*) □ *verb* pile in a stack

stadium *noun* (*plural* **stadiums** or **stadia**) a large sports-ground or race-course with seats for spectators

staff *noun* **1** a stick or pole carried in the hand **2** *music* a stave **3** workers employed in a business, school *etc* **4** a group of army officers who assist a commanding officer □ *verb* supply (a school *etc*) with staff

stag *noun* a male deer □ **stag party** a party for men only held the night before one of them gets married

stage *noun* **1** a platform for performing or acting on **2** (with **the**) the theatre; the job of working as an actor **3** a step in development: *the first stage of the plan* **4** a landing place (*eg* for boats) **5** a part of a journey **6** a stopping place on a journey □ *verb* **1** prepare and put on a performance of (a play *etc*) **2** arrange (an event, *eg* an exhibition) □ **stage-coach** *noun*, *hist* a coach running every day with passengers □ **stage-fright** *noun* an actor's fear when acting in public *esp* for the first time □ **stage whisper** a loud whisper □ **staging** *noun* **1** scaffolding **2** putting on the stage □ **on the**

stage in the theatre-world

stagger *verb* **1** walk unsteadily, totter **2** astonish **3** arrange (people's hours of work *etc*) so that they do not begin or end together ▢ **staggered** *adj* ▢ **staggering** *adj* astonishing

stagnant *adj* of water: standing still, not flowing and therefore not pure ▢ **stagnate** *verb* **1** of water: remain still and so become impure **2** remain for a long time in the same situation and so become bored, inactive *etc* ▢ **stagnation** *noun*

staid *adj* set in your ways, sedate

stain *verb* **1** give a different colour to (wood *etc*) **2** mark or make dirty by accident ▢ *noun* **1** a liquid which dyes or colours something **2** a mark which is not easily removed **3** something shameful in someone's character or reputation ▢ **stained glass** coloured glass cut in shapes and leaded together ▢ **stainless steel** a mixture of steel and chromium which does not rust

stair *noun* **1** one or all of a number of steps one after the other **2** (**stairs**) a series or flight of steps ▢ **staircase** *noun* a stretch of stairs with rails on one or both sides

stake *noun* **1** a strong stick pointed at one end **2** money put down as a bet **3** *hist* a post to which people were tied to be burned ▢ *verb* **1** mark the limits or boundaries (of a field *etc*) with stakes **2** bet (money) **3** risk ▢ **at stake 1** be won or lost **2** in great danger: *his life is at stake* ▢ **have a stake in** be concerned in (because you have something to gain or lose) ▢ **stake a claim** establish ownership or right (to something)

stalactite *noun* a spike of limestone hanging from the roof of a cave, formed by the dripping of water containing lime

stalagmite *noun* a spike of limestone, like a stalactite, rising from the floor of a cave

stale *adj* **1** of food: no longer fresh **2** no longer interesting because heard, done *etc* too often before **3** not able to do your best (because of overworking, boredom *etc*)

stalemate *noun* **1** *chess* a position in which a player cannot move without putting their king in danger **2** a position in an argument in which neither side can win

stalk *noun* the stem of a plant or of a leaf or flower ▢ *verb* **1** walk stiffly or proudly **2** go quietly up to animals being hunted to shoot at close range ▢ **stalker** *noun*

stall *noun* **1** a division for one animal in a cowshed *etc* **2** a table on which things are laid out for sale **3** an open-fronted shop **4** a seat in a church (*esp* for choir or clergy) **5** (**stalls**) theatre seats on the ground floor ▢ *verb* **1** of a car engine: come to a halt without the driver intending it to do so **2** of an aircraft: lose flying speed and so fall out of control **3** *informal* avoid action or decision for the time being

stallion *noun* a male horse, *esp* one kept for breeding purposes

stalwart *adj* brave, stout-hearted ▯ *noun*

stamen *noun* one of the thread-like spikes in the middle of a flower which bear the pollen

stamina *noun* strength, power to keep going

stammer *verb* **1** have difficulty in saying the first letter of words in speaking **2** stumble over words ▯ *noun* a speech difficulty of this kind

stamp *verb* **1** bring the foot down firmly on the ground **2** stick a (postage stamp) on **3** mark with a design cut into a mould and inked **4** fix or mark deeply: *forever stamped in my memory* ▯ **1** the act of stamping **2** a design *etc* made by stamping **3** a cut or moulded design for stamping **4** kind, sort: *of a different stamp* **5** a postage stamp ▯ **stamping ground** someone's favourite or habitual place to be ▯ **stamp out 1** put out (a fire) by stamping **2** suppress, crush

stampede *noun* **1** a wild rush of frightened animals **2** a sudden, wild rush of people ▯ *verb* rush wildly

stance *noun* someone's manner of standing

stanch or **staunch** *verb* stop from flowing (*esp* blood from a wound)

stanchion *noun* an upright iron bar used as a support (*eg* in windows, ships)

stand *verb* **1** be on your feet (not lying or sitting down) **2** rise to your feet **3** of an object: (cause to) be in a particular place: *it stood by the door/ stood the case in the corner* **4** bear: *I cannot stand this heat* **5** treat (someone) to: *stand you tea* **6** remain: *this law still stands* **7** be a candidate (for): *he stood for parliament* **8** be short (for): *PO stands for Post Office* ▯ *noun* **1** something on which anything is placed **2** an object made to hold, or for hanging, things: *a hat-stand* **3** lines of raised seats from which people may watch games *etc* **4** an effort made to support, defend, resist *etc*: *a stand against violence* **5** (*US*) a witness box in a law court ▯ **stand-alone** *noun* & *adj*, *comput* (of) a system, device *etc* that can operate unconnected to any other ▯ **standing** *noun* social position or reputation ▯ *adj* **1** on your feet **2** placed on end **3** not moving **4** lasting, permanent: *a standing joke* ▯ **standoffish** *adj* unfriendly ▯ **standpoint** *noun* the position from which you look at something (*eg* a question, problem), point of view ▯ **standstill** *noun* a complete stop ▯ **stand by** be ready or available to be used or help in an emergency *etc* (**standby** *noun*) ▯ **stand down** withdraw (from a contest) or resign (from a job) ▯ **stand fast** refuse to give in ▯ **stand in (for)** take another's place, job *etc* for a time (**stand-in** *noun*) ▯ **stand out** stick out, be noticeable ▯ **stand to reason** be likely or reasonable ▯ **stand up for** defend strongly ▯ **stand up to** face or oppose bravely

> **stand** *verb* » stand*s*, stand*ing*, stood

standard *noun* **1** a level against which things may be judged **2** a level of excellence aimed at: *artistic standards* **3** a large flag *etc* on a pole □ *adj* **1** normal, usual: *standard charge* **2** ordinary, without extras: *standard model* □ **standard bearer** an outstanding leader □ **standardization** *noun* □ **standardize** *verb* make all of one kind or size □ **standard lamp** a kind of tall lamp which stands on the floor of a room *etc* □ **standard of living** a level of material comfort considered necessary by a particular group of society *etc*

stank *past form* of **stink**

stanza *noun* a group of lines making up a part of a poem, a verse

staple 1 a U-shaped iron nail **2** a piece of wire driven through sheets of paper to fasten them together **3** the main item in a country's production, a person's diet *etc* **4** a fibre of wool, cotton *etc* □ *verb* fasten with a staple □ *adj* chief, main

star *noun* **1** any of the bodies in the sky appearing as points of light **2** the fixed bodies which are really distant suns, not the planets **3** an object, shape or figure with a number of pointed rays (often five) **4** a leading actor or actress or other well-known performer □ *adj* for or of a star (in a film *etc*) □ *verb* **1** act the chief part (in a play or film) **2** of a play *etc*: have as its star □ **stardom** *noun* the state of being a leading performer □ **starfish** *noun* a type of small sea creature with five points or arms □ **Stars and Stripes** the flag of the United States of America

star *verb* » star*s*, star*ring*, star*red*

starboard *noun* the right side of a ship, as you look towards the bow (or front) □ *adj*

starch *noun* (*plural* **starches**) **1** a white carbohydrate (found in flour, potatoes, bread, biscuits *etc*) **2** a form of this used for stiffening clothes □ **starchy** *adj* **1** of food: containing starch **2** stiff and unfriendly

stare *verb* look with a fixed gaze □ *noun* a fixed gaze

stark *adj* **1** barren, bare **2** harsh, severe **3** sheer: *stark idiocy* □ *adv* completely: *stark naked*

starling *noun* a common bird with dark, glossy feathers

starry *adj* full of stars; shining like stars

start *verb* **1** begin (an action): *he started to walk home* **2** get (a machine *etc*) working: *he started the car* **3** jump or jerk (*eg* in surprise) □ *noun* **1** the act of starting (*eg* on a task, journey) **2** a sudden movement of the body **3** a sudden shock: *you gave me a start* **4** in a race *etc* the advantage of beginning before, or farther forward than, others, or the amount of this: *a start of five metres*

startle *verb* give a shock or fright to □ **startled** *adj* □ **startling** *adj*

starve *verb* **1** die for want of food **2** suffer greatly from hunger **3** deprive (of something needed or wanted badly): *starved of company here* □ **starvation** *noun*

state *noun* **1** the condition (of something): *the bad state of the roads* **2** the people of a country under a government **3** (*US*) an area and its people with its own laws forming part of the whole country **4** a government and its officials **5** great show, pomp: *the king drove by in state* □ *adj* **1** of the government **2** national and ceremonial: *state occasions* **3** (*US*) of a certain state of America: *the state capital of Texas is Austin* □ *verb* tell, say or write (*esp* clearly and fully) □ **stateliness** *noun* □ **stately** *adj* noble-looking; dignified □ **statement** *noun* that which is said or written □ **state-of-the-art** *adj* most up-to-date □ **stateroom** *noun* a large cabin in a ship □ **stateside** *adj* & *adv*, *informal* of or in the United States □ **statesman** *noun* someone skilled in government □ **statesmanlike** *adj*

static *adj* not moving □ *noun* **1** atmospheric disturbances causing poor reception of radio or television programmes **2** electricity on the surface of objects which will not conduct it *eg* hair, nylons *etc* (*also called*: **static electricity**)

station *noun* **1** a building with a ticket office, waiting rooms *etc* where trains, buses or coaches stop to pick up or set down passengers **2** a place which is the centre for work or duty of any kind: *fire station/ police station* **3** rank, position: *lowly station* □ *verb* **1** assign to a position or place **2** take up a position: *stationed himself by the door*

stationary *adj* standing still, not moving

⚠Do not confuse: **stationary** and **stationery**

stationery *noun* writing paper, envelopes, pens *etc* □ **stationer** *noun* someone who sells these

statistics **1** (*noun plural*) figures and facts set out in order: *statistics of road accidents for last year* **2** (*noun sing*) the study of these: *statistics is not an easy subject* □ **statistical** *adj* □ **statistician** *noun* someone who produces or studies statistics

statue *noun* a likeness of someone or an animal carved in stone, metal *etc* □ **statuesque** *adj* like a statue in dignity *etc* □ **statuette** *noun* a small statue

stature *noun* **1** height **2** importance, reputation

status *noun* position, rank (of a person) in the eyes of others □ **status quo** the state of affairs now existing, or existing before a certain time or event □ **status symbol** a possession which is thought to show the high status of the owner (*eg* a powerful car)

statute *noun* a written law of a country □ **statutory** *adj* according to law

staunch *adj* firm, loyal; trustworthy □ *verb see* **stanch**

stave *noun* **1** a set of spaced lines on which music is written **2** one of the strips making the side of a barrel □ *verb* **1** (with **in**) crush in **2** (with **off**) keep away, delay

stave *verb* » staves, stav*ing*, stove or stav*ed*

stay *verb* **1** continue to be: *stayed calm/ stay here while I go for help*

2 live (for a time): *staying in a hotel* **3** *old* stop *noun* **1** time spent in a place **2** a rope running from the side of a ship to the mast-head **3** (**stays**) *old* corsets **stay put** remain in the same place

St Bernard *see* **Saint Bernard**

STD *abbrev* **1** subscriber trunk dialling **2** sexually transmitted disease

stead *noun* place: *she went in my stead* **stand you in good stead** turn out to be helpful to you: *his German stood him in good stead*

steadfast *adj* **1** steady, fixed **2** faithful, loyal **steadfastly** *adj* **steadfastness** *noun*

Steadicam *noun*, *trademark* a cinema camera with counter-balances to produce a smooth picture while being moved

steading *noun* farm buildings

steady *adj* **1** firm, not moving or changing **2** not easily upset or put off **3** even, regular, unchanging: *moving at a steady pace* *verb* make or become steady **steadily** *adj* **steadiness** *noun*

> **steady** *verb* » steadi*es*, steady*ing*, steadi*ed*

steak *noun* a thick slice of meat *etc* for cooking

steal *verb* **1** take (something not belonging to you) without permission **2** move quietly **3** take quickly or secretly: *stole a look at him*

> **steal** » steal*s*, steal*ing*, stole, stolen

stealth *noun* a secret way of doing, acting *etc* **stealthily** *adv* **stealthy** *adj*

steam *noun* **1** vapour from hot liquid, *esp* from boiling water **2** power produced by steam: *in the days of steam* *verb* **1** give off steam **2** cook by steam **3** open or loosen by putting into steam: *steam open the envelope* **4** move or travel by steam **steamboat** *noun* a steamer **steam-engine** *noun* an engine (*esp* a railway engine) worked by steam **steamer** *noun* a ship driven by steam **steamroller** *noun* a steam-driven engine with large and very heavy wheels, used for flattening the surfaces of roads **steamship** *noun* a steamer **steam up** of glass: become covered with condensed steam in the form of small drops of water

steamy *adj* **1** full of steam: *steamy atmosphere* **2** *informal* passionate, erotic

steed *noun*, *old* a horse

steel *noun* **1** a very hard mixture of iron and carbon **2** a bar of steel for sharpening knife blades **of steel** hard, strong: *a grip of steel* **steel yourself** get up courage (to) **steely** *adj* hard, cold, strong *etc* like steel

steep *adj* **1** of a slope: rising nearly straight up **2** *informal* of a price: too great *verb* **1** soak in a liquid **2** fill with knowledge of: *steeped in French literature*

steeple *noun* a tower of a church *etc* rising to a point, a spire **steeplechase** *noun* **1** a race run across open country, over hedges *etc* **2** a race over a course on which obstacles (*eg* walls) have been made □ **steeplejack** *noun* someone who climbs steeples or other high buildings to make repairs

steer *noun* a young ox raised for its beef □ *verb* **1** control the course of (a car, ship, discussion *etc*) **2** follow (a course) □ **steerage** *noun, old* the part of a ship set aside for the passengers who pay the lowest fares □ **steering** *noun* the parts of a ship, motor-car *etc* which have to do with controlling its course □ **steering-wheel** *noun* the wheel in a car used by the driver to steer it □ **steer clear of** keep away from

stellar *adj* of the stars

stem *noun* **1** the part of a plant from which the leaves and flowers grow **2** the thin support of a wine-glass □ *verb* **1** stop, halt: *stem the bleeding* **2** start, spring (from): *hate stems from envy*

stem *verb* » stem*s*, stemm*ing*, stemm*ed*

stench *noun* a strong unpleasant smell

stencil *noun* **1** a sheet of metal, cardboard *etc* with a pattern cut out **2** the drawing or design made by rubbing ink or brushing paint *etc* over a cut-out pattern **3** a piece of waxed paper on which words are cut with a typewriter, and which is then used to make copies □ *verb* make a design or copy in one of these ways

stencil *verb* » stencil*s*, stencill*ing*, stencill*ed*

stenographer *noun, US* a shorthand typist □ **stenography** *noun, US* shorthand

stentorian *adj* **1** of the voice: loud **2** loud-voiced

Named after *Stentor*, a loud-voiced Greek herald in the*Iliad*

⚠Do not confuse with: **stertorous**

Step *noun, trademark* a form of exercise involving stepping on and off a small platform

step *noun* **1** a movement of the leg in walking, running *etc* **2** the distance covered by this **3** a particular movement of the feet, as in dancing: **4** the sound made by the foot in walking *etc*: *heard a step outside* **5** a riser on a stair, or rung on a ladder **6** one of a series of moves in a plan, career *etc*: *take the first step* **7** a way of walking: *springy step* **8** (**steps**) a flight of stairs **9** (**steps**) a step-ladder □ *verb* **1** take a step **2** walk, move: *step this way, please* □ **step-ladder** *noun* a ladder with a support on which it rests □ **stepping-stone** *noun* **1** a stone rising above water or mud, used to cross on **2** anything that helps you to advance □ **in step 1** of two or more people walking: with the same foot going forward at the same time **2** acting *etc* in agreement (with) □ **out of step** not in step (with) □ **step up** increase (*eg* production) □ **take steps** begin to do something for a certain purpose

step *verb* » step*s*, stepp*ing*, stepp*ed*

step- *prefix* related as the result of a second marriage: *stepfather/ stepdaughter*

steppe *noun* a dry, grassy treeless plain in SE Europe and Asia

stereo *adj*, *short* for **stereophonic** ▫ *noun* (*plural* **stereos**) stereophonic equipment, *esp* a record-player and/or tape recorder, with amplifier and loudspeakers

stereo- *prefix* in three dimensions

stereophonic *adj* of sound: giving a life-like effect, with different instruments, voices *etc* coming from different directions

stereotype *noun* **1** a fixed metal plate for printing, with letters *etc* moulded onto its surface **2** something fixed and unchanging **3** a characteristic type of person ▫ **stereotyped** or **stereotypical** *adj* fixed, not changing: *stereotyped ideas*

> Originally a printing term for a fixed block of type

sterile *adj* **1** unable to have children or reproduce **2** producing no ideas *etc*: *sterile imagination* **3** free from germs ▫ **sterility** *noun* the state of being sterile

sterilize *verb* **1** make sterile **2** free from germs by boiling *etc* ▫ **sterilization** *noun*

sterling *noun* British money, when used in international trading: *one pound sterling* ▫ *adj* **1** of silver: of a certain standard of purity **2** worthy, good: *sterling qualities*

> So called after the image of a small star that was impressed on medieval silver pennies

stern[1] *adj* **1** looking or sounding angry or displeased **2** severe, strict, harsh: *stern prison sentence* ▫ **sternly** *adv* ▫ **sternness** *noun* the state or quality of being stern

stern[2] *noun* the back part of a ship

steroid *noun* any of a number of substances, including certain hormones; *see also* **anabolic steroids**

stertorous *adj* making a snoring noise

> ⚠Do not confuse with: **stentorian**

stethoscope *noun* an instrument by means of which a doctor listens to someone's heartbeats, breathing *etc*

stetson *noun* a soft, wide-brimmed hat worn traditionally by cowboys

stevedore *noun* someone employed to load and unload ships

stew *verb* cook by boiling slowly ▫ *noun* **1** a dish of stewed food, often containing meat and vegetables **2** *informal* a state of worry; a flap

steward *noun* **1** a flight attendant on an aircraft **2** someone who shows people to their seats at a meeting *etc* **3** an official at a race meeting *etc* **4** someone who manages an estate or farm for someone else

stewardess *noun* a female flight attendant (*also called*: **air hostess**)

stick *noun* **1** a long thin piece of wood; a branch or twig from a tree **2** a piece of wood shaped for a special purpose: *hockey-stick/ drumstick* **3** a long piece (*eg* of rhubarb) □ *verb* **1** push or thrust (something): *stick the knife in your belt* **2** fix with glue *etc*: *I'll stick the pieces back together* **3** be or become caught, fixed or held back: *stuck in the ditch* **4** hold fast to, keep to (*eg* a decision) □ **sticking-plaster** *noun* a kind of tape with a sticky surface, used to protect slight cuts *etc* □ **stick-in-the-mud** *noun* someone who is against new ideas, change *etc* □ **stick up for** speak in defence of

> **stick** *verb* » stick*s*, stick*ing*, stuck

stickleback *noun* a type of small river-fish with prickles on its back

stickler *noun* someone who attaches great importance to a particular (often small) matter: *stickler for punctuality*

sticky *adj* **1** clinging closely (like glue, treacle *etc*) **2** covered with something sticky **3** difficult: *a sticky problem* □ **stickiness** *noun*

stiff *adj* **1** not easily bent or moved **2** of a mixture, dough *etc*: thick, not easily stirred **3** cold and distant in manner **4** hard, difficult: *stiff examination* **5** severe: *stiff penalty* **6** strong: *stiff drink* □ **stiff-necked** *adj* proud, obstinate

stiffen *verb* make or become stiff

stifle *verb* **1** suffocate **2** put out (flames) **3** keep back (tears, a yawn *etc*) □ **stifling** *adj* very hot and stuffy

stigma *noun* **1** (*plural* **stigmata**) a mark of disgrace **2** (*plural* **stigmas**) in a flower, the top of the pistil □ **stigmatize** *verb* mark, describe as something bad: *stigmatized for life*

stile *noun* a step or set of steps for climbing over a wall or fence

stiletto *noun* (*plural* **stilettos**) **1** a dagger, or a type of instrument, with a narrow blade **2** (a shoe with) a stiletto heel □ **stiletto heel** a high, thin heel on a shoe

still *adj* **1** not moving **2** calm, without wind; quiet **3** of drinks: not fizzy □ *verb* make calm or quiet □ *adv* **1** up to the present time or the time spoken of: *it was still there* **2** even so, nevertheless: *it's difficult but we must still try* **3** even: *still more people* □ *noun* an apparatus for distilling spirits (*eg* whisky) □ **stillborn** *adj* of a child: dead at birth □ **still life** a picture of something that is not living (as a bowl of fruit *etc*) □ **stillness** *noun* the state of being still □ **stillroom** *noun* a pantry or room where drinks, food *etc* are kept

stilted *adj* stiff, not natural

stilts *noun plural* **1** long poles with footrests on which someone may walk clear of the ground **2** tall poles (*eg* to support a house built above water)

stimulant *noun* something which makes a part of the body more active or which makes you feel livelier

stimulate *verb* **1** make more active **2** encourage **3** excite

stimulus *noun* (*plural* **stimuli**) **1**

something that brings on a reaction in a living thing **2** something that rouses (someone *etc*) to action or greater effort

sting *noun* **1** the part of some animals and plants (as the wasp, the nettle) which can prick the skin and cause pain or irritation **2** the act of piercing with a sting **3** the wound, swelling or pain caused by a sting ▫ *verb* **1** pierce with a sting or cause pain like that of a sting **2** be painful, smart: *made his eyes sting* **3** hurt the feelings of: *stung by his words*

sting *verb* » sting*s*, sting*ing*, stung

stingy *adj* mean, not generous ▫ **stinginess** *noun*

stink *noun* a bad smell ▫ *verb* give out a bad smell

stink *verb* » stink*s*, stink*ing*, stank or stunk, stunk

stint *verb* allow (someone) very little: *don't stint on …* ▫ *noun* **1** limit: *praise without stint* **2** a fixed amount of work: *my daily stint*

stipend *noun* pay, salary, *esp* of a parish minister ▫ **stipendiary** *adj*

stipple *verb* paint or mark with tiny dots from a brush

stipulate *verb* state as a condition (of doing something) ▫ **stipulation** *noun* something stipulated, a condition

stir *verb* **1** set (liquid) in motion, *esp* with a spoon *etc* moved circularly **2** move slightly: *he stirred in his sleep* **3** arouse (a person, a feeling *etc*) ▫ *noun* disturbance, fuss ▫ **stirring** *adj* exciting ▫ **stir up** rouse, cause (*eg* trouble)

stir *verb* » stir*s*, stirr*ing*, stirr*ed*

stirrup *noun* a metal loop hung from a horse's saddle as a support for the rider's foot

stitch *noun* (*plural* **stitches**) **1** the loop made in a thread, wool *etc* by a needle in sewing or knitting **2** a sharp, sudden pain in your side ▫ *verb* put stitches in, sew

stoat *noun* a type of small fierce animal similar to a weasel, sometimes called an ermine when in its white winter fur

stock *noun* **1** family, race: *of ancient stock* **2** goods in a shop, warehouse *etc* **3** the capital of a business company divided into shares **4** the animals of a farm (*also called*: **livestock**) **5** liquid (used for soup) obtained by boiling meat, bones *etc* **6** a type of scented garden flower **7** the handle of a whip, rifle *etc* **7** (**stocks**) *hist* a wooden frame, with holes for the ankles and wrists, in which criminals *etc* were fastened as a punishment **8** (**stocks**) the wooden framework upon which a ship is supported when being built ▫ *verb* **1** keep a supply of (for sale) **2** supply (a farm with animals *etc*) ▫ *adj* **1** usual, known by everyone: *a stock joke* **2** usually stocked (by a shop *etc*) ▫ **stock-still** *adj* perfectly still ▫ **stocktaking** *noun* a regular check of the goods in a shop or warehouse ▫ **take stock of** form an opinion or estimation about (a situation *etc*)

stockade *noun* a fence of strong

posts set up round an area or building for defence

stockbroker *noun* someone who buys and sell shares in business companies on behalf of others □ **stock exchange 1** a place where stocks and shares are bought and sold **2** an association of people who do this □ **stock-in-trade** *noun* **1** the necessary equipment *etc* for a particular trade *etc* **2** someone's usual ways of speaking, acting *etc*: *sarcasm is part of his stock-in-trade* □ **stock market** the stock exchange; dealings in stocks and shares

stocking *noun* a close-fitting covering in a knitted fabric (wool, nylon *etc*) for the leg and foot

stockpile *noun* a store, a reserve supply □ *verb* build up a store

stocky *adj* short and stout □ **stockiness** *noun*

stodgy *adj* **1** of food: heavy, not easily digested **2** of a person, book *etc*: dull □ **stodginess** *noun*

stoic *noun* someone who bears pain, hardship *etc* without showing any sign of feeling it □ **stoical** *adj* □ **stoicism** *noun* the bearing of pain *etc* patiently

stoke *verb* put coal, wood, or other fuel on (a fire) □ **stoker** *noun* someone who looks after a furnace

stole[1] *noun* a length of silk, linen or fur worn over the shoulders

stole[2] and **stolen** *see* **steal**

stolid *adj* of someone *etc*: dull; not easily excited □ **stolidity** *noun* □ **stolidly** *adv*

stomach *noun* **1** the bag-like part of the body into which the food passes when swallowed **2** desire or courage (for something): *no stomach for a fight* □ *verb* put up with, bear: *can't stomach her rudeness*

stomp *verb* stamp the feet, *esp* noisily

stone *noun* **1** the material of which rocks are composed **2** a (small) loose piece of this **3** a piece of this shaped for a certain purpose: *tombstone* **4** a precious stone (*eg* a diamond) **5** the hard shell around the seed of some fruits (*eg* peach, cherry) **6** a measure of weight (14lb, 6.35 kilogrammes) **7** a piece of hard material that forms in the kidney, bladder *etc*, causing pain □ *verb* **1** throw stones at **2** take the stones out of fruit □ *adj* made of stone □ **Stone Age** human culture before the use of metal □ **stone-cold** *adj* very cold □ **stone-dead** or **stone-deaf** *adj* completely dead or deaf □ **stoneware** *noun* a kind of pottery made out of coarse clay □ **stonework** *noun* something that is built of stone *esp* the stone parts of a building

stony *adj* **1** like stone **2** covered with stones **3** hard, cold in manner: *stony look* □ **a stone's throw** a very short distance □ **leave no stone unturned** do everything possible

stood *past form* of **stand**

stooge *noun* someone who is used by another to do a (*usu* humble or unpleasant) job

stookie *noun, Scot* a plaster-cast for a broken limb

stool *noun* a seat without a back □

stool pigeon *slang* a police informer

stoop *verb* **1** bend the body forward and downward **2** be low or wicked enough to do a certain thing: *I wouldn't stoop to stealing* ◊ *noun* **1** the act of stooping **2** a forward bend of the body

stop *verb* **1** bring to a halt: *stop the car* **2** prevent from doing: *stop him from working* **3** put an end to: *stop this nonsense* **4** come to an end: *the rain has stopped* **5** (with **up**) block (a hole *etc*) ◊ *noun* **1** the state of being stopped **2** a place where something stops **3** a full stop **4** a knob on an organ which brings certain pipes into use ◊ **stopcock** *noun* a tap for controlling the flow of liquid through a pipe ◊ **stopgap** *noun* something which is used in an emergency until something better is found ◊ **stoppage** *noun* **1** something which blocks up (*eg* a tube or a passage in the body) **2** a halt (*eg* in work in a factory) ◊ **stopper** *noun* something that stops up an opening (*esp* in the neck of a bottle, jar *etc*) ◊ **stop press** a space in a newspaper for news put in at the last minute ◊ **stopwatch** *noun* a watch that can be stopped and started, used in timing races

> **stop** *verb* » stop*s*, stopp*ing*, stopp*ed*

store *noun* **1** a supply (*eg* of goods) from which things are taken when needed **2** a place where goods are kept **3** a shop **4** a collected amount or number ◊ *verb* put aside for future use ◊ **storage** *noun* **1** the act of storing **2** the state of being stored: *our furniture is in storage* ◊ **storehouse** or **storeroom** *noun* a building or room where goods are stored ◊ **in store for** awaiting: *trouble in store* ◊ **set (great) store by** value highly

storey *noun* (*plural* **storeys**) all that part of a building on the same floor

> ⚠Do not confuse with: **story**

stork *noun* a wading bird with a long bill, neck and legs

storm *noun* **1** a sudden burst of bad weather (*esp* with heavy rain, lightning, thunder, high wind) **2** a violent outbreak (*eg* of anger) ◊ *verb* **1** be in a fury **2** rain, blow *etc* violently **3** attack (a stronghold *etc*) violently ◊ **go down a storm** be popular or well received ◊ **storm in a teacup** a great fuss over nothing

story *noun* (*plural* **stories**) an account of an event or events, real or imaginary ◊ **storied** *adj* mentioned in stories, famous ◊ **storyboard** *noun* a series of drawings forming an outline for shooting a scene in a film

> ⚠Do not confuse with: **storey**

stout *adj* **1** fat, stocky **2** brave: *stout resistance* **3** strong: *stout walking-stick* ◊ *noun* a strong, dark-coloured beer ◊ **stout-hearted** *adj* having a brave heart ◊ **stoutness** *noun*

stove *noun* an apparatus using coal, gas or electricity *etc*, used for heating, cooking *etc* ◊ *verb, past form* of **stave**

stow *verb* **1** pack or put away **2**

fill, pack ▯ **stowaway** *noun* someone who hides in a ship in order to travel without paying a fare

straddle *verb* **1** stand or walk with legs apart **2** sit with one leg on each side of (*eg* a chair or horse)

straggle *verb* **1** wander from the line of a march *etc* **2** lag behind **3** grow or spread beyond the intended limits: *his long beard straggled over his chest* ▯ **straggler** *noun* someone who straggles ▯ **straggly** *adj* spread out untidily

straight *adj* **1** not bent or curved: *a straight line* **2** direct, frank, honest: *a straight answer* **3** in the proper position or order: *your tie isn't straight* **4** of a hanging picture *etc*: placed level with ceiling or floor **5** without anything added: *a straight vodka* **6** expressionless: *he kept a straight face* ▯ *adv* **1** by the shortest way, directly: *straight across the desert* **2** at once, without delay: *I came straight here after work* **3** fairly, frankly: *he's not playing straight with you* ▯ *noun* (with **the**) the straight part of a racecourse *etc* ▯ **straighten** *verb* make straight ▯ **straight fight** a contest between two people only ▯ **straightforward** *adj* **1** without any difficulties **2** honest, frank ▯ **straightness** *noun* the state of being straight ▯ **straight away** immediately

⚠Do not confuse with: **strait**

strain *verb* **1** hurt (a muscle or other part of the body) by overworking or misusing it **2** work or use to the fullest: *he strained his ears to hear the whisper* **3** make a great effort: *he strained to reach the rope* **4** stretch too far, to the point of breaking (a person's patience *etc*) **5** separate liquid from a mixture of liquids and solids by passing it through a sieve ▯ *noun* **1** the act of straining **2** a hurt to a muscle *etc* caused by straining it **3** (the effect of) too much work, worry *etc*: *suffering from strain* **4** too great a demand: *a strain on my patience* **5** manner: *they grumbled on in the same strain for hours* **6** a streak: *a strain of selfishness* **7** a tune **8** a kind, breed: *a strain of fowls* ▯ **strained** *adj* **1** not natural, done with effort: *a strained conversation* **2** unfriendly: *strained relations* ▯ **strainer** *noun* a sieve

strait *noun* **1** a narrow strip of sea between two pieces of land **2** (**straits**) difficulties, hardships: *dire straits* ▯ **straitened** *adj* poor and needy ▯ **straitjacket** *noun* a jacket with long sleeves tied behind to prevent a violent or insane person from using their arms ▯ **straitlaced** *adj* strict in attitude and behaviour

⚠Do not confuse with: **straight**

stramash *noun, Scot* a fuss, a commotion

strand *noun* **1** a length of something soft and fine (*eg* hair, thread) **2** *old* the shore of a sea or lake

stranded *adj* **1** of a ship: run aground on the shore **2** left helpless without money or friends

strange *adj* **1** unusual, odd: *a strange look on his face* **2** not known, seen, heard *etc* before, unfamiliar: *the method was strange to me* **3** not accustomed (to) **4** foreign: *a strange country* ◊ **strangely** *adv* ◊ **strangeness** *noun*

stranger *noun* **1** someone who is unknown to you **2** a visitor ◊ **a stranger to** someone who is quite unfamiliar with: *a stranger to hard work*

strangle *verb* **1** kill by gripping or squeezing the throat tightly **2** keep in, prevent oneself from giving (*eg* a scream, a sigh) **3** stop the growth of ◊ **stranglehold** *noun* a tight control over something which prevents it from escaping, growing *etc*

strangulate *verb* strangle, constrict ◊ **strangulation** *noun*

strap *noun* a narrow strip of leather, cloth *etc* used to hold things in place or together *etc* ◊ *verb* **1** bind or fasten with a strap *etc* **2** beat with a strap ◊ **strapping** *adj* tall and strong: *strapping young man* ◊ **straphanger** *noun* a standing passenger in a train *etc*

> **strap** *verb* » strap*s*, strapp*ing*, strapp*ed*

stratagem *noun* a cunning act, meant to deceive and outwit an enemy

strategic *adj* **1** of strategy **2** done according to a strategy: *a strategic retreat* **3** giving an advantage: *a strategic position*

strategy *noun* (*plural* **strategies**) the art of guiding, forming or carrying out a plan ◊ **strategist** *noun* someone who plans military operations

strathspey *noun* a Scottish dance tune, slower than a reel, with a dotted rhythm

stratify *verb* form layers or levels ◊ **stratification** *noun*

> **stratify** » stratifi*es*, stratify*ing*, stratifi*ed*

stratosphere *noun* the layer of the earth's atmosphere between 10 and 60 kilometres above the earth ◊ **stratospheric** *adj*

stratum *noun* (*plural* **strata**) **1** a layer of rock or soil **2** a level of society

stratus *noun* low, spread-out clouds

straw *noun* **1** the stalk on which corn grows **2** a paper or plastic tube for sucking up a drink

strawberry *noun* a type of small, juicy, red fruit or the low creeping plant which bears it ◊ **strawberry blonde** a woman with reddish blond hair

stray *verb* **1** wander **2** lose your way, become separated (from companions *etc*) ◊ *adj* **1** wandering, lost **2** happening *etc* here and there: *a stray example* ◊ *noun* a wandering animal which has been abandoned or lost

streak *noun* **1** a line or strip different in colour from that which surrounds it **2** a smear of dirt, polish *etc* **3** a flash (*eg* of lightning) **4** a trace of some quality in one's character: *a streak of selfishness* ◊ *verb* **1** mark with streaks **2** *informal* move very fast ◊ **streaked** *adj* ◊ **streaker** *noun*, *informal* someone who runs naked in public

streaky *adj* marked with streaks □ **streakiness** *noun* □ **streaky bacon** bacon with streaks of fat and lean

stream *noun* **1** a flow (of water, air, light *etc*) **2** a small river, a brook **3** any steady flow of people or things: *a stream of traffic* □ *verb* flow or pour out □ **streamer** *noun* **1** a long strip *usu* of paper, used for decorating rooms *etc* (*esp* at Christmas) **2** a narrow flag blowing in the wind □ **streamlet** *noun* a small stream □ **streamline** *verb* **1** shape (a vehicle *etc*) so that it may cut through the air or water as easily as possible **2** make more efficient: *we've streamlined our methods of paying*

street *noun* a road lined with houses *etc* □ **street cred** knowledge of current fashion, speech *etc* □ **streetwalker** *noun* a prostitute □ **streets ahead of** much better *etc* than □ **up someone's street** relating to their interests or abilities

strength *noun* **1** the state of being strong **2** an available number or force (of soldiers, volunteers *etc*) □ **strengthen** *verb* make, or become, strong or stronger

strenuous *adj* making or needing great effort: *the plans met strenuous resistance/ squash is a strenuous game* □ **strenuousness** *noun*

strep throat a severe type of throat infection

stress *noun* (*plural* **stresses**) **1** force, pressure, pull *etc* of one thing on another **2** physical or nervous pressure or strain: *the stress of modern life* **3** emphasis, importance **4** extra weight laid on a part of a word (as in *but*ter) □ *verb* put stress, pressure, emphasis or strain on

stretch *verb* **1** draw out to greater length, or too far, or from one point to another: *don't stretch that elastic too far/ stretch a rope from post to post* **2** be able to be drawn out to a greater length or width: *that material stretches* **3** (cause to) exert (yourself): *the work stretched him to the full* **4** hold (out) **5** make (something, *eg* words, the law) appear to mean more than it does □ *noun* (*plural* **stretches**) **1** the act of stretching **2** the state of being stretched **3** a length in distance or time: *a stretch of bad road* □ **stretcher** *noun* a light folding bed with handles for carrying the sick or wounded □ **stretch limo** a luxurious extra-long limousine □ **at a stretch** continuously: *working three hours at a stretch* □ **at full stretch** at the limit, using all resources

strew *verb* **1** scatter: *papers strewn over the floor* **2** cover, sprinkle (with): *the floor was strewn with papers*

> **strew** » strew*s*, strew*ing*, strew*ed*, strewn or strew*ed*

striated *adj* streaked

stricken *adj* **1** wounded **2** deeply affected (*eg* by illness) **3** struck

strict *adj* **1** insisting on exact obedience to rules **2** exact: *the strict meaning of a word* **3** allowing no exception: *strict orders* **4** severe □ **strictly** *adv* □ **strictness** *noun* □ **stricture** *noun* criticism, blame

stride *verb* **1** walk with long steps

2 take a long step **3** walk over, along *etc* ▢ *noun* **1** a long step **2** the distance covered by a step **3** a step forward ▢ **take in your stride** manage to do easily

> **stride** *verb* » stride*s*, strid*ing*, strode, stridden

strident *adj* of a sound: harsh, grating ▢ **stridency** *noun*

strife *noun* quarrelling; fighting

strike *verb* **1** hit with force **2** give, deliver (a blow) **3** knock: *to strike your head on the beam* **4** attack: *the enemy struck at dawn* **5** light (a match) **6** make (a musical note) sound **7** of a clock: sound (*eg* at ten o'clock with ten chimes) **8** (often with **off** or **out**) cross out, cancel **9** hit or discover suddenly: *strike oil* **10** take a course: *he struck out across the fields* **11** stop working (in support of a claim for more pay *etc*) **12** give (someone) the impression of being: *did he strike you as lazy?* **13** affect, impress: *I am struck by her beauty* **14** make (an agreement *etc*) ▢ **striking** *adj* **1** noticeable: *a striking resemblance* **2** impressive ▢ **strike camp** take down tents ▢ **strike home 1** of a blow: hit the point aimed at **2** of a remark: have the intended effect ▢ **strike up 1** begin to play or sing (a tune) **2** begin (a friendship, conversation *etc*)

> **strike** *verb* » strike*s*, strik*ing*, struck

string *noun* **1** a long narrow cord for binding, tying *etc* made of threads twisted together **2** a piece of wire or gut producing a note on a musical instrument **3** (**strings**) the stringed instruments in an orchestra **4** a line of objects threaded together: *string of pearls* **5** a number of things coming one after another: *string of abuse* ▢ *verb* **1** put on a string **2** stretch out in a line ▢ **stringed** *adj* having strings ▢ **string along** give false expectations to, deceive ▢ **string up** hang

> **string** » string*s*, string*ing*, strung

stringent *adj* strictly enforced: *stringent rules* ▢ **stringency** *noun* strictness

stringy *adj* **1** like string **2** of meat: tough and fibrous

strip *noun* a long narrow piece (*eg* of paper) ▢ *verb* **1** pull (off) in strips **2** remove (*eg* leaves, fruit) from **3** remove the clothes from **4** deprive: *stripped of his disguise* **5** make bare or empty: *strip the bed* ▢ **strip-cartoon** *noun* a line of drawings which tell a story ▢ **strip search** a body search of someone who has been asked to strip ▢ **striptease** *noun* an act in which a performer strips naked

> **strip** *verb* » strip*s*, stripp*ing*, stripp*ed*

stripe *noun* **1** a band of colour different from the background on which it lies **2** a blow with a whip or rod ▢ *verb* make stripes on ▢ **stripy** *adj* patterned with stripes

stripling *noun* a growing youth

strive *verb* **1** try hard **2** *old* fight

> **strive** » strive*s*, striv*ing*, strove, striven

strobe *noun* a light which produces a flickering beam

strode *past form* of **stride**

stroganoff *noun* a rich beef stew in a cream sauce

stroke *noun* **1** the act of striking **2** a blow (*eg* with a sword, whip) **3** something unexpected: *a stroke of good luck* **4** one movement (of a pen, an oar) **5** one chime of a clock **6** one complete movement of the arms and legs in swimming **7** a particular style of swimming: *breast stroke* **8** a way of striking the ball (*eg* in tennis, cricket) **9** an achievement **10** a sudden attack of illness causing paralysis □ *verb* rub gently, *esp* as a sign of affection □ **at a stroke** in a single action or effort

stroll *verb* walk slowly in a leisurely way □ *noun* a leisurely walk; an amble

strong *adj* **1** not easily worn away: *strong cloth* **2** not easily defeated *etc* **3** forceful, not easily resisted: *strong wind* **4** very healthy and robust, with great muscular strength **5** forceful, commanding respect or obedience **6** of a smell, colour *etc*: striking, very noticeable **7** of a feeling: intense: *strong dislike* **8** in number: *a workforce 500 strong* □ **strongbox** *noun* a box for storing valuable objects or money □ **stronghold** *noun* a place built to withstand attack, a fortress □ **strongly** *adv* □ **strong point** something in which a person excels □ **strongroom** *noun* a room for storing valuable objects or money □ **on the strength of** encouraged by or counting on

strop *noun* a strip of leather on which a razor is sharpened □ *verb* sharpen a razor

> **strop** *verb* » strop*s*, stropp*ing*, stropp*ed*

stroppy *adj*, *informal* quarrelsome, disobedient, rowdy

strove *past form* of **strive**

struck *past form* of **strike**

structure *noun* **1** a building; a framework **2** the way the parts of anything are arranged: *the structure of the story* □ **structural** *adj* □ **structurally** *adv*

strudel *noun* a thin pastry filled with fruit and spices

struggle *verb* **1** try hard (to do something) **2** twist and fight to escape **3** fight (with or against someone) **4** move with difficulty: *struggling through the mud* □ *noun* **1** a great effort **2** a fight

strum *verb* play (a guitar *etc*) in a relaxed way

> **strum** » strum*s*, strumm*ing*, strumm*ed*

strung *past form* of **string** □ **highly strung** easily excited or agitated

strut *verb* walk in a proud manner □ *noun* **1** a proud way of walking **2** a bar *etc* which supports something

> **strut** *verb* » strut*s*, strutt*ing*, strutt*ed*

strychnine *noun* a bitter, poisonous drug

stub *noun* a small stump (*eg* of a pencil, cigarette) □ *verb* **1** put out, (*eg* a cigarette) by pressure against something **2** knock (your toe) painfully against something

stub *verb* » stub*s*, stubb*ing*, stubb*ed*

stubble *noun* **1** the short ends of the stalks of corn left after it is cut **2** a short growth of beard

stubborn *adj* **1** unwilling to give way, obstinate **2** of resistance *etc*: strong, determined **3** difficult to manage or deal with ▯ **stubbornly** *adv* ▯ **stubbornness** *noun*

stubby *adj* short, thick and strong: *stubby fingers*

STUC *abbrev* Scottish Trades Union Congress

stucco *noun* (*plural* **stuccos**) **1** a kind of plaster used for covering walls, moulding ornaments *etc* **2** work done in stucco

stuck *past form* of **stick**

stud *noun* **1** a nail with a large head **2** a decorative knob on a surface **3** a button with two heads for fastening a collar **4** a collection of horses kept for breeding, ▯ *verb* **1** cover or fit with studs **2** sprinkle thickly (with): *the meadow is studded with flowers*

student *noun* someone who studies, *esp* at college, university *etc*

studio *noun* (*plural* **studios**) **1** the workshop of an artist or photographer **2** a building or place in which cinema films are made **3** a room from which television or radio programmes are broadcast

studious *adj* **1** studying carefully and much **2** careful: *his studious avoidance of quarrels* ▯ **studiously** *adv* ▯ **studiousness** *noun*

study *verb* **1** gain knowledge of (a subject) by reading, experiment *etc* **2** look carefully at **3** consider carefully (*eg* a problem) ▯ *noun* (*plural* **studies**) **1** the gaining of knowledge of a subject: *the study of history* **2** a room where someone reads and writes **3** a piece of music which is meant to develop the skill of the player **4** a work of art done as an exercise, or to try out ideas for a later work ▯ **studied** *adj* **1** done on purpose, intentional: *a studied insult* **2** too careful, not natural: *a studied smile*

study *verb* » studi*es*, study*ing*, studi*ed*

stuff *noun* **1** the material of which anything is made **2** cloth, fabric **3** substance or material of any kind: *what is that stuff all over the wall?* ▯ *verb* **1** pack full **2** fill the skin of (a dead animal) to preserve it **3** fill (a prepared bird) with stuffing before cooking ▯ **stuffed shirt** an inflexible, old-fashioned person ▯ **get stuffed** *slang* get lost, go away

stuffing *noun* **1** feathers, scraps of material *etc* used to stuff a cushion, chair *etc* **2** breadcrumbs, onions *etc* packed inside a fowl or other meat and cooked with it

stuffy *adj* **1** full of stale air, badly ventilated **2** *informal* dull, having old-fashioned ideas ▯ **stuffily** *adv* ▯ **stuffiness** *noun*

stultify *verb* dull the mind, make stupid

stultify » stultifi*es*, stultify*ing*, stultifi*ed*

stumble *verb* **1** trip in walking **2** walk unsteadily, as if blind **3** make mistakes or hesitate in speaking **4** (with **on**) find by chance ◊ *noun* the act of stumbling ◊ **stumbling block** a difficulty in the way of a plan or of progress

stump *noun* **1** the part of a tree, leg, tooth *etc* left after the main part has been cut away **2** *cricket* one of the three wooden stakes which make up a wicket ◊ *verb, cricket* **1** put out (a batsman) by touching the stumps with the ball **2** puzzle completely **3** walk stiffly or heavily ◊ **stumpy** *adj* short and thick ◊ **stump up** *informal* pay up

stun *verb* **1** knock senseless (by a blow *etc*) **2** surprise or shock very greatly: *stunned by the news*

stun *verb* » stun*s*, stunn*ing*, stunn*ed*

stung *past form* of **sting**

stunk *past form & past participle* of **stink**

stunt *noun* **1** a daring trick **2** something done to attract attention: *a publicity stunt* ◊ *verb* stop the growth of ◊ **stunted** *adj* small and badly shaped

stupefy *verb* **1** make stupid, deaden the feelings of **2** astonish ◊ **stupefaction** *noun*

stupefy » stupefi*es*, stupefy*ing*, stupefi*ed*

stupendous *adj* wonderful, amazing (*eg* because of size and power)

stupid *adj* **1** foolish: *a stupid thing to do* **2** dull, slow at learning **3** stupefied (*eg* from lack of sleep) ◊ **stupidity** *noun*

stupor *noun* the state of being only partly conscious

sturdy *adj* strong, well built; healthy ◊ **sturdily** *adv* ◊ **sturdiness** *noun*

sturgeon *noun* a type of large fish from which caviare is taken

stutter *verb* speak in a halting, jerky way; stammer ◊ *noun* a stammer

sty or **stye** *noun* (*plural* **sties** or **styes**) an inflamed swelling on the eyelid

Stygian *adj* hellish, infernal

style *noun* **1** manner of acting, writing, speaking *etc* **2** fashion: *in the style of the late 19th century* **3** an air of elegance **4** the middle part of the pistil of a flower ◊ *verb* call, name: *styling himself 'Lord John'* ◊ **stylish** *adj* smart, elegant, fashionable ◊ **stylized** *adj* ◊ **in style** with no expense or effort spared

stylus *noun* (*plural* **styluses**) a needle for a record-player

stymie /*stai*mee/ *verb, Scot* block, impede

Originally a golfing term for an opponent's ball in the way of your own

suave *adj* /swav/ superficially polite and pleasant, smooth

sub- *prefix* **1** under, below **2** less

than **3** lower in rank or importance

subaltern *noun* an officer in the army under the rank of captain

subconscious *noun* the contents of the mind of which someone is not themselves aware ▫ *adj* of the subconscious, not conscious or aware: *a subconscious desire for fame*

subcontract *verb* give a contract for (work forming part of a larger contract) to another company

subculture *noun* an identifiable group within a larger culture or group

subcutaneous *adj* beneath the skin

subdivide *verb* divide into smaller parts ▫ **subdivision** *noun* a part made by subdividing

subdue *verb* **1** conquer (an enemy *etc*) **2** keep under control (*eg* a desire) **3** make less bright (*eg* a colour, a light) **4** make quieter: *he seemed subdued after the fight*

subedit *verb* edit (text) at a secondary or later stage

subject *adj* **1** under the power of another: *a subject nation* **2** (with **to**) liable to suffer from (*eg* colds) **3** (with **to**) depending on: *subject to your approval* ▫ *noun* **1** someone under the power of another: *the king's subjects* **2** a member of a nation with a monarchy: *a British subject* **3** something or someone spoken about, studied *etc* **4** *grammar* the word in a sentence or clause which stands for the person or thing doing the action of the verb (*eg cat* is the subject in 'the *cat* drank the milk') ▫ *verb* (often with **to**) force to submit (to) ▫ **subjection** *noun* the act of subjecting or the state of being subjected

subjective *adj* based on personal feelings, thoughts *etc*, not impartial ▫ **subjectivity** *noun*

subjoin *verb*, *formal* add at the end, append

sub judice *adv* under consideration

subjugate *verb* bring under your power; make obedient

subjunctive *adj*, *grammar* of a verb: in a form which indicates possibility, contingency *etc* ▫ *noun* a subjunctive form of a verb

sublet *verb* let out (rented property) to another person, *eg* while the original tenant is away

sublieutenant *noun* an officer in the navy below the rank of lieutenant

sublime *adj* very noble, great or grand ▫ **sublimity** *noun*

subliminal *adj* working below the level of consciousness: *subliminal messages* ▫ **subliminally** *adv*

submachine-gun *noun* a light machine-gun fired from the hip or shoulder

submarine *noun* a type of ship which can travel under water ▫ *adj* under the surface of the sea

submerge *verb* cover with water; sink ▫ **submergence** or **submersion** *noun* ▫ **submersible** *noun* a boat that can operate under water

submit *verb* **1** give in, yield **2** place (a matter) before someone for making a judgement ▯ **submission** *noun* **1** the act of submitting **2** readiness to yield, meekness **3** an idea, statement *etc* offered for consideration ▯ **submissive** *adj* meek, yielding easily ▯ **submissively** *adv*

submit » submit*s*, submitt*ing*, submitt*ed*

subordinate *adj* (often with **to**) lower in rank or importance (than) ▯ *noun* someone who is subordinate ▯ *verb* (with **to**) consider as of less importance than ▯ **subordination** *noun*

suborn *verb* persuade (someone) to do something illegal, *esp* by bribery

subpoena *noun* an order for someone to appear in court ▯ *verb* order to appear in court

subscribe *verb* **1** make a contribution (*esp* of money) towards a charity **2** promise to take and pay for a number of issues of a magazine *etc* **3** (with **to**) agree with (an idea, statement *etc*) ▯ **subscription** *noun*

subsequent *adj* following, coming after

subservient *adj* weak-willed, ready to do as you are told ▯ **subservience** *noun*

subside *verb* **1** settle down, sink lower **2** of noise *etc*: get less and less ▯ **subsidence** *noun* a sinking down, *esp* into the ground

subsidiary *adj* **1** acting as a help **2** of less importance **3** of a company: controlled by another company

subsidy *noun* (*plural* **subsidies**) money paid by a government *etc* to help an industry ▯ **subsidize** *verb* give money as a help

subsist *verb* **1** exist **2** (with **on**) live on (a kind of food *etc*) ▯ **subsistence** *noun* **1** existence **2** means or necessities for survival

subsoil *noun* the layer of the earth just below the surface soil

substance *noun* **1** a material that can be seen and felt: *glue is a sticky substance* **2** general meaning (of a talk, essay *etc*) **3** thickness, solidity **4** wealth, property: *a woman of substance*

substantial *adj* **1** solid, strong **2** large: *a substantial building* **3** able to be seen and felt **4** in the main, but not in detail: *substantial agreement* ▯ **substantially** *adv* for the most part: *substantially the same*

substantiate *verb* give proof of, or evidence for

substantive *noun, grammar* a noun

substitute *verb* (with **for**) put in place or instead of ▯ *noun* someone or thing used instead of another ▯ **substitution** *noun*

substratum *noun* (*plural* **substrata**) **1** a layer lying underneath **2** a foundation

subsume *verb* include in something larger

subterfuge *noun* a cunning trick to get out of a difficulty *etc*

subterranean *adj* found under the ground

subtitle *noun* **1** a second additional title of a book *etc* **2** a translation of a foreign-language film, appearing at the bottom of the screen

subtle *adj* **1** difficult to describe or explain: *a subtle difference* **2** cunning: *by a subtle means* □ **subtly** *adv* □ **subtlety** *noun* (*plural* **subtleties**)

subtotal *noun* a total of one set of figures within a larger group

subtract *verb* **1** take away (a part from) **2** take away (one number from another) □ **subtraction** *noun*

suburb *noun* a residential area on the outskirts of a town □ **suburban** *adj* of suburbs □ **suburbia** *noun* the suburbs

subversive *adj* likely to overthrow (government, discipline *etc*)

subway *noun* **1** an underground crossing for pedestrians *etc* **2** an underground railway

succeed *verb* **1** (with **in**) manage to do what you have been trying to do **2** get on well **3** take the place of, follow **4** (often with **to**) follow in order (to the throne *etc*)

success *noun* (*plural* **successes**) **1** the achievement of something you have been trying to do **2** someone who succeeds **3** something that turns out well □ **successful** *adj* **1** having achieved what was aimed at **2** having achieved wealth, importance *etc* **3** turning out as planned □ **succession** *noun* **1** the act of following after **2** the right of becoming the next holder (of a throne *etc*) **3** a number of things coming one after the other: *a succession of failures* □ **successive** *adj* following one after the other □ **successor** *noun* someone who comes after, follows in a post *etc* □ **in succession** one after another

succinct *adj* in a few words, brief, concise: *a succinct reply*

succour *verb* help in time of distress □ *noun* help

succubus *noun* an evil spirit in the shape of a woman believed to have sexual intercourse with men in their sleep (*compare with*: **incubus**)

succulent *adj* **1** juicy **2** of a plant: having thick, juicy leaves or stems

succumb *verb* yield (to): *succumbed to temptation*

such *adj* **1** of a kind previously mentioned: *such things are difficult to find* **2** similar: *doctors, nurses and such people* **3** so great: *his excitement was such that he shouted out loud* **4** used for emphasis: *it's such a disappointment!* □ *pronoun* thing, people *etc* of a kind already mentioned: *such as these are not to be trusted* □ **such-and-such** *adj* & *pronoun* any given (person or thing): *such-and-such a book* □ **as such** by itself □ **such as** of the same kind as

suck *verb* **1** draw into the mouth **2** draw milk from with the mouth **3** hold in the mouth and lick hard (*eg* a sweet) **4** (often with **up** or **in**) draw in, absorb □ *noun* **1** a sucking action **2** the act of sucking

sucker *noun* **1** a side shoot rising from the root of a plant **2** a part of an animal's body by which it sticks to objects **3** a pad (of rubber *etc*) which can stick to a surface **4**

informal someone easily fooled

suckle *verb* of a woman or female animal: give milk from the breast or teat ◇ **suckling** *noun* a baby or young animal which still sucks its mother's milk

sucrose *noun* a sugar found in sugar-beet

suction *noun* **1** the act of sucking **2** the process of reducing the air pressure, and so producing a vacuum, on the surface or between surfaces

sudden *adj* happening all at once without being expected: *a sudden attack* ◇ **suddenly** *adv* ◇ **suddenness** *noun*

suds *noun plural* frothy, soapy water

sue *verb* start a law case against

suede /swehd/ *noun* a kind of leather with a soft, dull surface

suet *noun* a kind of hard animal fat

suffer *verb* **1** feel pain or punishment **2** bear, endure **3** *old* allow **4** go through, undergo (a change *etc*) ◇ **suffering** *noun* ◇ **on sufferance** allowed or tolerated but not really wanted

suffice *verb* be enough, or good enough

sufficient *adj* enough ◇ **sufficiently** *adv*

suffix *noun* (*plural* **suffixes**) a small part added to the end of a word to make another word, such as *-ness* to *good* to make *goodness*, *-ly* to *quick* to make *quickly etc*

suffocate *verb* **1** kill by preventing the breathing of **2** die from lack of air **3** feel unable to breathe freely: *suffocating in this heat* ◇ **suffocation** *noun*

suffrage *noun* **1** a vote **2** the right to vote

suffuse *verb* spread over ◇ **suffusion** *noun*

sugar *noun* a sweet substance obtained mostly from sugar-cane and sugar-beet ◇ *verb* mix or sprinkle with sugar ◇ **sugar-beet** *noun* a vegetable whose root yields sugar ◇ **sugar-cane** *noun* a tall grass from whose juice sugar is obtained ◇ **sugar daddy** an older man who lavishes money on a younger woman in exchange for companionship and, often, sex ◇ **sugary** *adj* **1** tasting of sugar **2** too sweet

suggest *verb* **1** put forward, propose (an idea *etc*) **2** put into the mind, hint ◇ **suggestion** *noun* **1** an act of suggesting **2** an idea put forward **3** a slight trace: *a suggestion of anger in her voice* ◇ **suggestible** *adj* easily influenced by suggestions

suggestive *adj* **1** that suggests something particular, *esp* sexually improper: *suggestive remarks* **2** (with **of**) giving the idea of: *suggestive of mental illness*

suicide *noun* **1** the taking of your own life **2** someone who kills themselves ◇ **suicidal** *adj* **1** of or considering suicide **2** likely to cause your death or ruin: *suicidal action*

sui generis *adj* of its own kind; unique

suit *noun* **1** a set of clothes to be

worn together **2** a case in a law court **3** *old* a request for permission to court a woman **4** one of the four divisions (spades, hearts, diamonds, clubs) of playing-cards ▯ *verb* **1** be convenient or suitable for: *the climate suits me* **2** look well on: *that dress suits you* **3** (with **to**) make fitting or suitable for: *suited his words to the occasion* ▯ **suitability** *noun* ▯ **suitable** *adj* **1** fitting the purpose **2** just what is wanted, convenient ▯ **suitcase** *noun* a travelling case for carrying clothes *etc* ▯ **suitor** *noun* a man who tries to gain the love of a woman ▯ **follow suit** do just as someone else has done

suite *noun* **1** a number of things in a set, *eg* rooms, furniture, pieces of music **2** a group of attendants for an important person

sulk *verb* keep silent because of being displeased ▯ **sulky** *adj* ▯ **the sulks** a fit of sulking

sullen *adj* angry and silent, sulky ▯ **sullenness** *noun*

sully *verb* make less pure, dirty

sully » sulli*es*, sully*ing*, sulli*ed*

sulphur *noun* a yellow substance found in the ground which gives off a choking smell when burnt, used in matches, gunpowder *etc* ▯ **sulphuric acid** a powerful acid much used in industry

sultan *noun* **1** *hist* the head of the Turkish Ottoman empire **2** an Islamic ruler

sultana *noun* **1** a sultan's wife **2** a light-coloured raisin

sultry *adj* **1** of weather: very hot and close **2** passionate, steamy

sum *noun* **1** the amount made by two or more things added together **2** a quantity of money **3** a problem in arithmetic **4** the general meaning (of something said or written) ▯ **summing-up** *noun* ▯ **sum total 1** the sum of several smaller sums **2** the main point, total effect ▯ **sum up** give the main points of (a discussion, evidence in a trial *etc*)

summary *noun* (*plural* **summaries**) a shortened form (of a story, statement *etc*) giving only the main points ▯ *adj* **1** short, brief **2** done without wasting time or words ▯ **summarily** *adv* ▯ **summarize** *verb* state briefly, make a summary of

summer *noun* the warmest season of the year ▯ *adj* of or in summer ▯ **summerhouse** *noun* a small house in a garden for sitting in

summit *noun* the highest point of a hill *etc* ▯ **summit conference** a conference between heads of governments

summon *verb* **1** order (someone) to come to you, appear in a court of law *etc* **2** (with **up**) gather up (courage, strength *etc*) ▯ **summons** *noun* (*plural* **summonses**) an order to appear in court

sumo *noun* a Japanese form of wrestling

sump *noun* **1** part of a motor-engine which contains the oil **2** a small drainage pit

sumptuous *adj* costly, splendid

sun *noun* **1** the round body in the

sky which gives light and heat to the earth **2** sunshine ▢ *verb* (with **yourself**) lie in the sunshine, sunbathe ▢ **sunbathe** *verb* lie or sit in the sun to acquire a suntan ▢ **sunbeam** *noun* a ray of light from the sun ▢ **sunburn** *noun* a burning or redness caused by over-exposure to the sun ▢ **sunburned** or **sunburnt** *adj* affected by sunburn ▢ **sundial** *noun* an instrument for telling the time from the shadow of a rod on its surface cast by the sun ▢ **sunflower** *noun* a large yellow flower with petals like rays of the sun ▢ **sunglasses** *noun plural* spectacles with tinted lenses that shield the eyes from sunlight ▢ **sunlight** *noun* the light from the sun ▢ **sunlit** *adj* lighted up by the sun ▢ **sunny** *adj* **1** full of sunshine **2** cheerful: *sunny nature* ▢ **sunrise** *noun* the rising of the sun in the morning ▢ **sunset** *noun* the setting of the sun in the evening ▢ **sunshine** *noun* **1** bright sunlight **2** cheerfulness ▢ **sunstroke** *noun* a serious illness caused by over-exposure to very hot sunshine ▢ **suntan** *noun* a browning of the skin caused by exposure to the sun

> **sun** *verb* » sun*s*, sunn*ing*, sunn*ed*

sundae *noun* a sweet dish of ice-cream served with fruit, syrup *etc*

Sunday *noun* the first day of the week, the Christian Sabbath

sunder *verb, old* separate, part

sundry *adj* several, various: *sundry articles for sale* ▢ **sundries** *noun plural* odds and ends

sung *past participle* of **sing**

sunk *adj* **1** on a lower level than the surroundings; sunken **2** *informal* defeated, done for ▢ **sunken** *adj* **1** that has been sunk **2** of cheeks *etc*: hollow

sup *verb* eat or drink in small mouthfuls

> **sup** » sup*s*, supp*ing*, supp*ed*

super *adj, informal* extremely good

super- *prefix* above, beyond, very, too

superannuate *verb* make (someone) retire from their job because of old age ▢ **superannuation** *noun* a pension given to someone retired

superb *adj* magnificent, very fine, excellent: *a superb view*

supercilious *adj* looking down on others, haughty ▢ **superciliousness** *noun*

superficial *adj* **1** of a wound: affecting the surface of the skin only, not deep **2** not thorough or detailed: *superficial interest* **3** apparent at first glance, not actual: *superficial likeness* **4** of a person: not capable of deep thoughts or feelings ▢ **superficiality** *noun* ▢ **superficially** *adv*

> ⚠Do not confuse: **superficial** and **superfluous**

superfluous *adj* beyond what is enough or necessary ▢ **superfluity** *noun*

superhuman *adj* **1** divine, godly **2** greater than would be expected of an ordinary person: *superhuman effort*

superimpose *verb* lay or place (one thing on another)

superintend *verb* be in charge or control, manage □ **superintendent** *noun* **1** someone who is in charge of an institution, building *etc* **2** a police officer above a chief inspector

superior *adj* **1** higher in place or rank **2** better or greater than others: *superior forces/ superior goods* **3** having an air of being better than others □ *noun* someone better than, or higher in rank than, others □ **superiority** *noun*

superlative *adj* **1** better than, or going beyond, all others: *superlative skill* **2** *grammar* an adjective or adverb of the highest degree of comparison, *eg* kindest, worst, most boringly

supermarket *noun* a large self-service store selling food *etc*

supernatural *adj* not happening in the ordinary course of nature, miraculous □ **supernaturally** *adv*

supernova *noun* an exploding star surrounded by a bright cloud of gas

supernumerary *adj* above the usual or required number □ *noun* (*plural* **supernumeraries**) someone beyond the required number, an extra

supersede *verb* **1** take the place of: *he superseded his brother as headmaster* **2** replace (something with something else)

supersonic *adj* faster than the speed of sound: *supersonic flight*

superstition *noun* **1** belief in magic and in things which cannot be explained by reason **2** an example of such belief (*eg* not walking under ladders) □ **superstitious** *adj* having superstitions

supervene *verb* come after or in addition

supervise *verb* be in charge of work and see that it is properly done □ **supervision** *noun* the act of supervising; control, inspection □ **supervisor** *noun*

supine *adj* **1** lying on the back **2** not showing any interest or energy

supper *noun* a meal taken in the evening

supplant *verb* take the place of somebody or of something: *the baby supplanted the dog in her affections*

supple *adj* **1** bending easily, flexible **2** of an object: bending easily without breaking □ **suppleness** *noun* □ **supply** *adv*

supplement *noun* **1** something added to supply a need or lack **2** a special section added to the main part of a newspaper or magazine □ *verb* make or be an addition to: *her earnings supplemented his income* □ **supplementary** *adj* added to supply a need; additional

suppliant *adj* asking earnestly and humbly □ *noun* someone who asks in this way

supplicate *verb* ask earnestly, beg □ **supplicant** *noun* □ **supplication** *noun* a humble, earnest request

supply *verb* **1** provide (what is wanted or needed) **2** provide (someone with something) *noun* (*plural* **supplies**) **1** an act of supplying **2** something supplied **3** a stock or store **4** (**supplies**) a stock of essentials, *eg* food, equipment, money *etc* *adj* of a teacher: filling another's place or position for a time

> **supply** *verb* » suppli*es*, supply*ing*, suppli*ed*

support *verb* **1** hold up, take part of the weight of **2** help, encourage **3** supply with a means of living: *support a family* **4** bear, put up with: *I can't support lies* *noun* **1** an act of supporting **2** something that supports **supporter** *noun* someone who supports (*esp* a football club)

suppose *verb* **1** take as true, assume for the sake of argument: *suppose that we have £100 to spend* **2** believe, think probable: *I suppose you know* **3** used to give a polite order: *suppose you leave now* **supposed** *adj* believed (often mistakenly) to be so: *her supposed generosity* **supposedly** *adv* according to what is supposed **supposing** in the event that: *supposing it rains* **supposition** *noun* **1** the act of supposing **2** something supposed **be supposed to** be required or expected to (do)

suppository *noun* (*plural* **suppositories**) a medicated swab inserted into the rectum or vagina

suppress *verb* **1** crush, put down (a rebellion *etc*) **2** keep back (a yawn, a piece of news *etc*) **suppression** *noun* the act of suppressing

suppurate *verb* of a wound: be full of, or discharge, pus

supra- *prefix* above

supreme *adj* **1** highest, most powerful: *supreme ruler* **2** greatest: *supreme courage* **supremacist** *noun* someone who believes in the supremacy of their own race *etc*: *white supremacist* **supremacy** *noun* highest power or authority **supremo** *noun* (*plural* **supremos**) *informal* a chief, a boss

surcharge *noun* an extra charge or tax

sure *adj* **1** having no doubt: *I'm sure that I can come* **2** certain (to do, happen *etc*): *he is sure to be there* **3** reliable, dependable: *a sure method* **sure-footed** *adj* unlikely to slip or stumble **be sure** see to it that: *be sure that he does it* **make sure** act so that, or check that, something is sure **sure of yourself** confident **to be sure 1** certainly! **2** undoubtedly: *to be sure, you are correct*

surely *adv* **1** certainly, without doubt **2** sometimes expressing a little doubt: *surely you won't tell him?* **3** without hesitation, mistake *etc*

surety *noun* (*plural* **sureties**) **1** someone who promises that another person will do something (*esp* appear in court) **2** a pledge, a guarantee

surf *noun* the foam made by the breaking of waves **surfboard** *noun* a long, narrow board on which someone can ride over the surf ◊ **surfer** *noun* someone who surfs ◊ **surfing** *noun* the sport of riding on a surfboard

surface *noun* the outside or top part of anything (*eg* of the earth, of a road *etc*) ◊ *verb* **1** come up to the surface of (water *etc*) **2** put a (smooth) surface on ◊ *adj* **1** on the surface **2** travelling on the surface of land or water: *surface mail*

surfeit *noun* too much of anything

surge *verb* **1** move (forward) like waves **2** rise suddenly or excessively ◊ *noun* **1** the swelling of a large wave **2** a swelling or rising movement like this **3** a sudden rise or increase (of pain *etc*)

surgeon *noun* a doctor who performs operations, often cutting the body open to examine or remove a diseased part ◊ **surgery** *noun* (*plural* **surgeries**) **1** treatment of diseases *etc* by operation **2** a doctor's or dentist's consulting room ◊ **surgical** *adj* ◊ **surgically** *adv*

surly *adj* gruff, rude, ill-mannered ◊ **surliness** *noun*

surmise *verb* suppose, guess ◊ *noun* a supposition

surmount *verb* **1** overcome (a difficulty *etc*) **2** climb over, get over ◊ **surmountable** *adj*

surname *noun* a person's last name or family name

surpass *verb* go beyond, be more or better than: *his work surpassed my expectations*

surplice *noun* a loose white gown worn by members of the clergy

⚠ Do not confuse: **surplice** and **surplus**

surplus *noun* the amount left over after what is needed has been used up ◊ *adj* left over, extra

surprise *noun* **1** the feeling caused by an unexpected happening **2** an unexpected happening ◊ *verb* **1** cause someone to feel surprise **2** come upon (someone) suddenly and without warning ◊ **take by surprise** come upon, or capture, without warning

surreal *adj* dreamlike, using images from the subconscious ◊ **surrealism** *noun* the use of surreal images in art ◊ **surrealist** *noun & adj*

surrender *verb* **1** give up, give in, yield: *surrender to the enemy* **2** hand over: *she surrendered the note to the teacher* ◊ *noun* an act of surrender, *esp* in a war

surreptitious *adj* done in a secret, underhand way

surrogate *noun* a substitute ◊ **surrogacy** *noun*

surround *verb* **1** be all round (someone or something) **2** enclose, put round ◊ *noun* a border ◊ **surroundings** *noun plural* **1** the country lying round a place **2** the people and places with which you have to deal in daily life

surtax *noun* an extra tax *esp* on income

surtitles *noun plural* a translation of an opera libretto projected on a screen above the audience

surveillance *noun* a close watch or constant guard

survey *verb* **1** look over **2** inspect, examine **3** make careful measurements of (a piece of land *etc*) ◇ *noun* (*plural* **surveys**) **1** a general view **2** a detailed examination or inspection **3** a piece of writing giving results of this **4** a careful measuring of land *etc* **5** a map made with the measurements obtained ◇ **surveyor** *noun* someone who makes surveys of land, buildings *etc*

survey *verb* » survey*s*, survey*ing*, survey*ed*

survive *verb* **1** remain alive, continue to exist (after an event *etc*) **2** live longer than: *he survived his wife* ◇ **survival** *noun* **1** the state of surviving **2** a custom, relic *etc* that remains from earlier times ◇ **survivor** *noun* someone who remains alive: *the only survivor of the crash*

sus or **suss** *verb, slang* investigate, find out ◇ **have someone sussed** understand their character, motives *etc*

susceptible *adj* **1** (with **to**) liable to be affected by: *susceptible to colds* **2** easily affected or moved ◇ **susceptibility** *noun* (*plural* **susceptibilities**)

sushi *noun* a Japanese dish of cakes of cold rice, slices of raw fish *etc*

suspect *verb* **1** be inclined to think (someone) guilty: *I suspect her of the crime* **2** distrust, have doubts about: *I suspected his air of frankness* **3** guess: *I suspect that we're wrong* ◇ *noun* someone thought to be guilty of a crime *etc* ◇ *adj* arousing doubt, suspected

suspend *verb* **1** hang **2** keep from falling or sinking: *particles suspended in a liquid* **3** stop for a time: *suspend business* **4** take away a job, privilege *etc* from for a time: *they suspended the student from classes*

suspender *noun* **1** an elastic strap to keep up socks or stockings **2** (**suspenders**) *US* braces

suspense *noun* **1** a state of being undecided **2** a state of uncertainty or worry

suspension *noun* **1** the act of suspending **2** the state of being suspended **3** the state of a solid which is mixed with a liquid or gas and does not sink or dissolve in it ◇ **suspension bridge** a bridge which is suspended from cables hanging from towers

suspicion *noun* **1** a feeling of doubt or mistrust **2** an opinion, a guess

suspicious *adj* **1** inclined to suspect or distrust **2** arousing suspicion ◇ **suspiciously** *adv*

sustain *verb* **1** hold up, support **2** bear (an attack *etc*) without giving way **3** suffer (an injury *etc*) **4** give strength to: *the food will sustain you* **5** keep up, keep going: *sustain a conversation* ◇ **sustenance** *noun* food, nourishment

suttee *noun, hist* an Indian widow who burned herself on her husband's funeral pyre

suzerain *noun* **1** a feudal lord **2** a supreme ruler ◇ **suzerainty** *noun* supreme power

svelte *adj* slender, trim

SW *abbrev* south-west; south-western

swab *noun* **1** a mop for cleaning a ship's deck **2** a piece of cottonwool used for cleaning, absorbing blood *etc* ▯ *verb* clean with a swab

> **swab** *verb* » swab*s*, swabb*ing*, swabb*ed*

swaddle *verb* wrap up (a young baby) tightly ▯ **swaddling clothes** *old* strips of cloth used to wrap up a young baby

swag *noun, Austral informal* a bundle of possessions

swagger *verb* **1** walk proudly, swinging the arms and body **2** boast ▯ *noun* a proud walk or attitude

swain *noun, old* a young man

swallow[1] *verb* **1** pass (food or drink) down the throat into the stomach **2** (with **up**) make disappear **3** receive (an insult *etc*) without objection **4** keep back (tears, a laugh *etc*) ▯ *noun* an act of swallowing

swallow[2] *noun* a bird with pointed wings and a forked tail

swamp *noun* wet, marshy ground ▯ *verb* **1** fill (a boat) with water **2** overwhelm: *swamped with work*

swan *noun* a large, stately water bird, with white feathers and a long neck ▯ **swan song** the last work of a musician, writer *etc*

swank *verb, informal* show off ▯ **swanky** *adj*

swap or **swop** *verb* give one thing in exchange for another: *swap addresses*

> **swap** or **swop** *verb* » swap*s* or swop*s*, swapp*ing* or swopp*ing*, swapp*ed* or swopp*ed*

sward *noun, old* a patch of green turf

swarm *noun* **1** a large number of insects flying or moving together **2** a dense moving crowd ▯ *verb* **1** of insects: gather together in great numbers **2** move in crowds **3** be crowded with: *swarming with tourists* **4** (with **up**) climb up (a wall *etc*)

swarthy *adj* dark-skinned

swashbuckling *adj* bold, swaggering

swastika *noun* an ancient design of a cross with bent arms, taken up as a symbol of Nazism

swat *verb* squash (a fly *etc*) ▯ *noun* an instrument for squashing insects

> **swat** *verb* » swat*s*, swatt*ing*, swatt*ed*

swatch *noun* a piece of fabric, carpet *etc* used as a sample

swath or **swathe** *noun* **1** a line of corn or grass cut by a scythe **2** a strip

swathe[1] *verb* wrap round with clothes or bandages

swathe[2] *another spelling* of **swath**

sway *verb* **1** swing or rock to and fro **2** bend in one direction or to one side **3** influence: *sway opinion* ▯ *noun* **1** a swaying movement **2** rule, power: *hold sway over*

swear *verb* **1** promise or declare solemnly **2** vow **3** curse, using the name of God or other sacred things without respect **4** make (someone) take an oath: *to swear someone to secrecy* □ **swear word** a word used in swearing or cursing □ **sworn** *adj* holding steadily to an attitude *etc*: *they had been sworn friends since childhood/ the two rivals became sworn enemies* □ **swear by** rely on, have complete faith in

> **swear** » swear*s*, swear*ing*, swore, sworn

sweat *noun* moisture secreted by the skin, perspiration □ *verb* **1** give out sweat **2** *informal* work hard □ **sweated labour** hard work for which very little pay is given □ **sweater** *noun* a jersey, a pullover □ **sweaty** *adj* wet, or stained with, sweat

swede *noun* a kind of large yellow turnip

sweep *verb* **1** clean (a floor *etc*) with a brush or broom **2** (often with **up**) gather up (dust *etc*) by sweeping **3** carry (away, along, off) with a long brushing movement **4** travel over quickly, move with speed: *a new fad which is sweeping the country* **5** move quickly in a proud manner (*eg* from a room) **6** (with **of**) clear of: *sweep the sea of enemy mines* **7** curve widely or stretch far □ *noun* **1** a sweeping movement **2** a curve, a stretch **3** a chimney sweeper **4** a sweepstake □ **sweeping** *adj* **1** that sweeps **2** of a victory *etc*: great, overwhelming **3** of a statement *etc*: too general, allowing no exceptions, rash

> **sweep** *verb* » sweep*s*, sweep*ing*, swept

sweepstake *noun* a gambling system in which those who take part stake money which goes to the holder of the winning ticket

sweet *adj* **1** having the taste of sugar, not salty, sour or bitter **2** pleasing to the taste **3** pleasant to hear or smell **4** kindly, agreeable, charming □ *noun* **1** a small piece of sweet substance, *eg* chocolate, toffee *etc* **2** something sweet served towards the end of a meal, a pudding □ **sweeten** *verb* make or become sweet □ **sweetener** *noun* **1** an artificial substance used to sweeten food or drinks **2** *informal* a bribe □ **sweetbreads** *noun plural* an animal's pancreas used for food □ **sweetcorn** *noun* maize □ **sweetheart** *noun* a lover □ **sweetmeat** *noun*, *old* a sweet, a confection □ **sweetly** *adv* □ **sweetness** *noun* □ **sweet pea** a sweet-smelling climbing flower grown in gardens □ **sweet talk** flattery, persuasion □ **sweet tooth** a liking for sweet-tasting things □ **sweet william** a sweet-smelling type of garden flower

swell *verb* **1** grow in size or volume **2** of the sea: rise into waves □ *noun* **1** an increase in size or volume **2** large, heaving waves **3** a gradual rise in the height of the ground □ *adj*, *US informal* fine, splendid □ *noun* a dandy □ **swelling** *noun* a swollen part of the body, a lump

> **swell** *verb* » swell*s*, swell*ing*, swell*ed*, swoll*en*

swelter *verb* be too hot ▯ **sweltering** *adj* very hot

swept *past form* of **sweep**

swerve *verb* turn quickly to one side ▯ *noun* a quick turn aside

swift *adj* moving quickly; rapid ▯ *noun* a bird rather like the swallow ▯ **swiftly** *adv* ▯ **swiftness** *noun*

swig *noun*, *informal* a mouthful of liquid, a large drink ▯ *verb, informal* gulp down

swig *verb* » swig*s*, swigg*ing*, swigg*ed*

swill *verb* **1** wash out **2** *informal* drink a great deal ▯ *noun* **1** partly liquid food given to pigs **2** *informal* a big drink

swim *verb* **1** move on or in water, using arms, legs, fins *etc* **2** cross by swimming: *swim the Channel* **3** float, not sink **4** move with a gliding motion **5** be dizzy **6** be covered (with liquid): *meat swimming in grease* ▯ *noun* an act of swimming ▯ **swimmer** *noun* ▯ **swimming bath** or **swimming pool** a large water-filled tank designed for swimming, diving in *etc* ▯ **swimming costume** or **swimsuit** *noun* a brief close-fitting garment for swimming in ▯ **swimmingly** *adv* smoothly, easily, successfully

swim *verb* » swim*s*, swimm*ing*, swam, swum

swindle *verb* **1** cheat, defraud **2** get (money *etc* from someone) by cheating ▯ *noun* a fraud, a deception ▯ **swindler** *noun*

swine *noun* (*plural* **swine**) **1** *old* a pig **2** *informal* a contemptible person ▯ **swineherd** *noun*, *old* someone who looks after pigs

swing *verb* **1** move to and fro, sway **2** move backwards and forwards on a swinging seat **3** turn or whirl round **4** walk quickly, moving the arms to and fro ▯ *noun* **1** a swinging movement **2** a seat for swinging, hung on ropes *etc* from a support ▯ **swing bridge** a kind of bridge that swings open to let ships pass ▯ **in full swing** going on busily

swing *verb* » swing*s*, swing*ing*, swung

swingeing *adj* very great: *swingeing cuts in taxation*

⚠Do not confuse with: **swinging**

swipe *verb* strike with a sweeping blow ▯ *noun* a sweeping blow

swirl *verb* sweep along with a whirling motion ▯ *noun* a whirling movement

swish *verb* **1** strike or brush against with a rustling sound **2** move making such a noise: *swishing out of the room in her long dress* ▯ *noun* a rustling sound or movement

switch *noun* (*plural* **switches**) **1** a small lever or handle *eg* for turning an electric current on and off **2** an act of switching **3** a change: *a switch of loyalty* **4** a thin stick ▯ *verb* **1** strike with a switch **2** turn (off or on) by means of a switch **3** change, turn: *switch jobs/ hastily switching the conversation* ▯ **switchback** *noun* a road or railway with steep ups and downs or sharp turns

◇ **switchblade** *noun* a flick-knife ◇ **switchboard** *noun* a board with equipment for making telephone connections

swither *verb* waver, oscillate

swivel *noun* a joint that turns on a pin or pivot ◇ *verb* turn on a swivel, pivot

> **swivel** *verb* » swivel*s*, swiv-ell*ing*, swivell*ed*

swiz or **swizzle** *noun, informal* a cheat, a swindle

swizzle stick a small stick used to stir drinks

swollen *adj* increased in size by swelling ◇ *verb, past form* of **swell**

swoon *verb, old* faint ◇ *noun* a fainting fit

swoop *verb* come down with a sweep, like a bird of prey ◇ *noun* a sudden downward rush ◇ **at one fell swoop** all at one time, at a stroke

swop *another spelling* of **swap**

sword *noun* a type of weapon with a long blade for cutting or piercing ◇ **swordfish** *noun* a large type of fish with a long pointed upper jaw like a sword

swore *past form* of **swear**

sworn *past participle* of **swear**

swot *verb, informal* study hard ◇ *noun* someone who studies hard

sybaritic *adj* **1** luxurious **2** fond of luxury

> After the ancient Greek city of *Sybaris* in Italy, noted for its luxury

sycamore *noun* a name given to several different types of tree, the maple, plane, and a kind of fig tree

sycophant *noun* someone who flatters others in order to gain favour or personal advantage ◇ **sycophantic** *adj*

syllable *noun* a word or part of a word spoken with one breath (*cheese* has one syllable, *but-ter* two, *mar-gar-ine* three) ◇ **syllabic** *adj*

syllabus (*plural* **syllabuses** or **syllabi**) a programme or list of lectures, classes *etc*

syllogism *noun* a combination of two propositions which lead to a third conclusion ◇ **syllogistic** *adj*

sylph *noun* **1** a type of fairy supposed to inhabit the air **2** a slender, graceful woman ◇ **sylphlike** *adj*

sylvan *adj, old* wooded

symbiosis *noun* a mutually beneficial partership ◇ **symbiotic** *adj*

symbol *noun* **1** something that stands for or represents another thing, *eg* the red cross, which stands for first aid **2** a character used as a short form of something, *eg* the signs + meaning plus, and O meaning oxygen ◇ **symbolic** or **symbolical** *adj* standing as a symbol of ◇ **symbolism** *noun* the use of symbols to express ideas *esp* in art and literature ◇ **symbolist** *noun & adj* ◇ **symbolize** *verb* be a symbol of

symmetrical *adj* having symmetry; not lopsided in appearance ◇ **symmetrically** *adv*

symmetry *noun* the equality in size, shape and position of two halves on either side of a dividing line: *spoiling the symmetry of the building*

sympathetic *adj* feeling or showing sympathy ▯ **sympathetic to** or **towards** inclined to be in favour of: *sympathetic to the scheme* ▯ **sympathetically** *adv*

sympathize *verb*: **sympathize with** express or feel sympathy (for)

sympathy *noun* (*plural* **sympathies**) **1** a feeling of pity or sorrow for someone in trouble **2** agreement with, or understanding of, the feelings, attitudes *etc* of others

symphony *noun* (*plural* **symphonies**) a long piece of music written for an orchestra of many different instruments

symposium *noun* **1** a meeting or conference for the discussion of some subject **2** a collection of essays dealing with a single subject

symptom *noun* an outward sign indicating the presence of a disease *etc*: *symptoms of measles* ▯ **symptomatic** *adj*

syn- *prefix* with, together

synagogue *noun* a Jewish place of worship

synchronize *verb* **1** happen at the same time **2** agree in time: *synchronize watches*

syncopate *verb*, *music* change the beat by accenting beats not usually accented ▯ **syncopation** *noun*

syncope *noun* the contraction of a word by omitting a letter or syllable in the middle

syndicate *noun* a number of persons who join together to manage some piece of business

syndrome *noun* a pattern of behaviour, events *etc* characteristic of some problem or condition

synod *noun* a meeting of members of the clergy

synonym *noun* a word which has the same, or nearly the same, meaning as another, *eg* 'ass' and 'donkey', or 'brave' and 'courageous' ▯ **synonymous (with)** *adj* having the same meaning (as)

synopsis *noun* (*plural* **synopses**) a short summary of the main points of a book, speech *etc*

syntax *noun* rules for the correct combination of words to form sentences ▯ **syntactic** or **syntactical** *adj*

synthesis *noun* **1** the act of making a whole by putting together its separate parts **2** the making of a substance by combining chemical elements

synthesize *verb* make (*eg* a drug) by synthesis

synthesizer *noun* a computerized instrument which creates electronic musical sounds

synthetic *adj* **1** made artificially to look like a natural product: *synthetic leather* **2** not natural, pretended: *synthetic charm* ▯ **synthetically** *adv*

syphilis *noun* an infectious disease, transmitted sexually ▯ **syphilitic** *adj*

syphon *another spelling* of **siphon**

syringe *noun* a tubular instrument

with a needle and plunger, used to extract blood, inject drugs *etc* ▯ *verb* clean out with a syringe: *needing his ears syringed*

syrup *noun* **1** a thick sticky liquid made by boiling water or fruit juice with sugar **2** a purified form of treacle

system *noun* **1** an arrangement of several parts which work together: *railway system/ solar system* **2** a way of organizing: *democratic system of government* **3** a regular method of doing something **4** the body, or its parts, considered as a whole: *my system is run down* ▯ **systemic** *adj*

systematic *adj* following a system; methodical ▯ **systematically** *adv*

T

ta *exclam, Brit informal* thanks

TAB *abbrev* typhoid-paratyphoid A and B (vaccine)

tab *noun* **1** a small tag or flap attached to something **2** a running total, a tally

tabard *noun* a short sleeveless tunic

tabby *noun* (*plural* **tabbies**) or **tabby-cat** a striped (usually female) cat

tabernacle *noun* a place of worship

tablature *noun* musical notation for the lute *etc*, with a line representing each string and letters for stopping

table *noun* **1** a flat-topped piece of furniture, supported by legs **2** a flat surface, a plateau **3** facts or figures set out in columns: *multiplication tables* ◇ *verb* **1** make into a list or table **2** put forward for discussion: *table a motion* ◇ **tablecloth** *noun* a cloth for covering a table ◇ **tableland** *noun* a raised stretch of land with a level surface ◇ **table linen** tablecloths, napkins *etc* ◇ **table tennis** a form of tennis played across a table with small bats and a light ball

tableau *noun* (*plural* **tableaux**) a striking group or scene

table d'hôte a meal of several courses at a fixed price

tablespoon *noun* a large size of spoon ◇ **tablespoonful** *noun* (*plural* **tablespoonfuls**) the amount held in a tablespoon

tablet *noun* **1** a small flat plate on which to write, paint *etc* **2** a small flat piece, *eg* of soap or chocolate **3** a pill **4** a brittle sweet made with sugar and condensed milk

tabloid *noun* a small-sized newspaper giving news in shortened and often simplified form

taboo *adj* forbidden by common consent; not approved by social custom ◇ *noun* a taboo subject or behaviour

tabor /*teh*bər/ *noun* a small kind of drum

tabular *adj* set in the form of a table

tabulate *verb* set out (information *etc*) in columns or rows

tachograph *noun* an instrument showing a vehicle's mileage, number of stops *etc*

tachometer *noun* **1** an instrument which measures speed of rotation **2** an instrument showing the speed of a vehicle's engine

tacit /*ta*sit/ *adj* understood but not spoken aloud, silent: *tacit agreement* ◇ **tacitly** *adv*

taciturn *adj* not inclined to talk ◇ **taciturnity** *noun* ◇ **taciturnly** *adv*

tack *noun* **1** a short sharp nail with a broad head **2** a sideways movement allowing a yacht *etc* to sail against the wind **3** a direction, a course **4** a rough stitch to keep material in place while sewing ▯ *verb* **1** fasten with tacks **2** sew with tacks **3** of a yacht *etc*: move from side to side across the face of the wind ▯ **change tack** change course or direction ▯ **on the wrong tack** following the wrong train of thought

tackle *verb* **1** come to grips with, deal with **2** *football etc* try to stop, or take the ball from, another player ▯ *noun* **1** the ropes and rigging of a ship **2** equipment, gear: *fishing tackle* **3** ropes and pulleys for raising heavy weights **4** an act of tackling

tacky[1] *adj* sticky, gluey

tacky[2] *adj*, *informal* shabby; vulgar, in bad taste

tact *noun* skill in dealing with people so as to avoid giving offence

tactful *adj* using tact; avoiding giving offence ▯ **tactfully** *adv* ▯ **tactfulness** *noun*

tactical *adj* **1** involving clever and successful planning **2** diplomatic, politic: *tactical withdrawal*

tactics *noun plural* **1** a way of acting in order to gain advantage **2** the art of coordinating military forces in action ▯ **tactician** *noun* someone who uses tactics skilfully

tactile *adj* of or perceived through touch

tactless *adj* giving offence through lack of thought ▯ **tactlessly** *adv* ▯ **tactlessness** *noun*

tadpole *noun* a young frog or toad in its first stage of life

tae kwon do a Korean martial art similar to karate

taffeta *noun* a thin, glossy fabric made mainly of silk

tag *noun* **1** a label: *price tag* **2** a familiar saying or quotation **3** a chasing game played by children (*also called* **tig**) ▯ *verb* put a tag or tags on ▯ **tag on to** or **tag after** follow closely and continually

tagliatelle *noun* pasta made in long ribbons

t'ai chi a Chinese system of exercise and self-defence stressing the importance of balance and coordination

tail *noun* **1** an appendage sticking out from the end of the spine on an animal, bird or fish **2** an appendage on a machine *etc*: *tail of an aeroplane* **3** the stalk on a piece of fruit **4** (**tails**) the side of a coin opposite to the head **5** (**tails**) a tailcoat ▯ *verb* **1** *informal* follow closely **2** remove the tails from (fruit *etc*) ▯ **tailback** *noun* a line of traffic stretching back from an obstruction ▯ **tailboard** *noun* a movable board at the back end of a lorry *etc* ▯ **tailcoat** *noun* a coat with a divided tail, part of a man's evening dress ▯ **tail-end** *noun* the very end of a procession *etc* ▯ **tailgate** *noun* a door at the back of a car that opens upwards ▯ **tail-light** *noun* a rear light on a vehicle ▯ **tailspin** *noun* a steep, spinning, downward dive of an aeroplane ▯ **tail-wind** *noun* a wind blowing from behind ▯ **tail off** become less, fewer or worse ▯ **turn tail** run away

tailor *noun* someone who cuts out

and makes clothes ▫ *verb* **1** make and fit (clothes) **2** make to fit the circumstances, adapt: *tailored to your needs* ▫ **tailor-made** *adj* exactly suited to requirements

taint *verb* **1** spoil by contact with something bad or rotten **2** corrupt ▫ *noun* a trace of decay or evil

tajine /ta*zheen*/ *noun* a North African stew traditionally cooked in a clay pot

take *verb* **1** lay hold of, grasp **2** choose: *take a card!* **3** accept, agree to have: *do you take credit cards?/ please take a biscuit* **4** have room for: *my car only takes four people* **5** eat, swallow **6** get or have regularly: *doesn't take sugar* **7** capture (a fort *etc*) **8** subtract: *take two from eight* **9** lead, carry, drive: *take the children to school* **10** use, make use of: *take care!* **11** require: *it'll take too much time* **12** travel by: *took the afternoon train* **13** experience, feel: *takes great pride in his work* **14** photograph: *took some shots inside the house* **15** understand: *took what I said the wrong way* **16** of a plant: root successfully **17** become popular, please ▫ **take-away** *noun* **1** a meal prepared and bought in a restaurant or shop but taken away and eaten somewhere else **2** a restaurant or shop providing such meals ▫ **taking** *adj* pleasing, attractive ▫ *noun* **1** an act of taking **2** (**takings**) money received from things sold ▫ **take account of** consider, remember ▫ **take advantage of 1** make use of (an opportunity) **2** treat or use unfairly ▫ **take after** be like in appearance or behaviour ▫ **take care of** look after ▫ **take down** write, note down ▫ **take for** believe (mistakenly) to be: *I took him for his brother* ▫ **take heed** pay careful attention ▫ **take ill** become ill ▫ **take in 1** include **2** receive **3** understand: *didn't take in what you said* **4** make smaller: *take in a dress* **5** cheat, deceive ▫ **take leave of** say goodbye to ▫ **take someone's life** kill them ▫ **taken with** attracted to ▫ **take off 1** remove (clothes *etc*) **2** imitate unkindly **3** of an aircraft: leave the ground ▫ **take-off** *noun* ▫ **take on 1** undertake (work *etc*) **2** accept (as an opponent): *take you on at tennis* ▫ **take over** take control of ▫ **take-over** *noun* ▫ **take part in** share or help in ▫ **take pity on** show pity for ▫ **take place** happen ▫ **take to 1** be attracted by **2** begin to do or use regularly: *took to rising early* ▫ **take to heart** be deeply affected or upset by ▫ **take to your heels** run away, flee ▫ **take up 1** lift, raise **2** occupy (space, time *etc*) **3** begin to learn, show interest in: *take up playing the harp*

> **take** » take*s*, tak*ing*, taken, took

talc *noun* **1** a soft mineral, soapy to the touch **2** *informal* talcum powder ▫ **talcum powder** a fine powder made from talc, used for rubbing on the body

tale *noun* **1** a story **2** an untrue story, a lie

talent *noun* **1** a special ability or skill: *a talent for music* **2** *hist* a measure of weight for gold or silver ▫ **talented** *adj* skilled, gifted

talisman *noun* an object believed

to have magic powers; a charm

talk *verb* **1** speak **2** gossip **3** give information □ *noun* **1** conversation **2** gossip **3** the subject of conversation: *the talk is of revolution* **4** a discussion or lecture: *gave a talk on stained glass* □ **talking-to** *noun* a scolding □ **talk over 1** discuss **2** persuade □ **talk round 1** discuss without coming to the main point **2** persuade □ **talk shop** *see* **shop**

talkative *adj* inclined to chatter

tall *adj* **1** high or higher than average **2** hard to believe: *tall story* □ **tallness** *noun* □ **tall order** a request to do something awkward or unreasonable

tallboy *noun* a tall kind of chest of drawers

tallow *noun* animal fat melted down to make soap, candles *etc*

tally *noun* (*plural* **tallies**) **1** an account **2** a ticket, a label **3** *old* a notched stick for keeping a score □ *verb* agree (with): *his story doesn't tally with yours*

> **tally** *verb* » tallie*s*, tally*ing*, tallie*d*

tally-ho *exclam* a cry used by fox-hunters

Talmud *noun* the basic code of Jewish civil and canon law □ **Talmudic** or **Talmudical** *adj*

tamari *noun* a concentrated soybean sauce

tamarind *noun* a tropical tree which produces long brown seed pods filled with a sweet-tasting pulp

tamarisk *noun* a bushy plant with thin branches, able to grow in dry conditions

tambourine *noun* a small one-sided drum with tinkling metal discs set into the sides

tame *adj* **1** of an animal: not wild, used to living with humans **2** dull, not exciting □ *verb* make tame, subdue

tamper *verb*: **tamper with** meddle with so as to damage or alter

tampon *noun* a plug of cotton-wool inserted into the vagina to absorb blood during menstruation

tan *verb* **1** make (animal skin) into leather by treating with tannin **2** make or become brown, *eg* by exposure to the sun □ *noun* **1** a yellowish-brown colour **2** a suntan

> **tan** *verb* » tan*s*, tann*ing*, tann*ed*

tandem *noun* a long bicycle with two seats and two sets of pedals one behind the other □ *adv* one behind the other □ **in tandem** together, in conjunction

tandoori *noun* a style of Indian cookery in which food is baked over charcoal in a clay oven

tang *noun* a strong taste, flavour or smell: *the tang of lemons*

tangent *noun* a straight line which touches a circle or curve without crossing it □ **go off at a tangent** go off suddenly in another direction or line of thought

tangential *adj* **1** of a tangent **2** peripheral, irrelevant

tangerine *noun* a small type of orange

Originally meaning 'from Tangiers', from where the fruit was exported in the 19th century

tangible *adj* **1** able to be felt by touching **2** real, definite: *tangible profits* ◻ **tangibly** *adv*

tangle *verb* **1** twist together in knots **2** make or become difficult or confusing ◻ *noun* **1** a twisted mass of knots **2** a confused situation

tango *noun* (*plural* **tangos**) a ballroom dance with long steps and pauses, originally from South America

tank *noun* **1** a large container for water, petrol *etc* **2** a heavy armoured vehicle which moves on caterpillar wheels

tankard *noun* a large drinking mug

tanker *noun* **1** a ship or large lorry for carrying liquids, *eg* oil **2** an aircraft carrying fuel

tanner *noun* someone who works at tanning leather ◻ **tannery** *noun* (*plural* **tanneries**) a place where leather is made

tannin *noun* a bitter-tasting substance found in tea, red wine *etc*, also used in tanning and dyeing

tantalize *verb* torment by offering something and keeping it out of reach ◻ **tantalizing** *adj*

tantamount *adj*: **tantamount to** coming to the same thing as, equivalent to: *tantamount to stealing*

tantrum *noun* a fit of rage or bad temper

Taoism *noun* an ancient Chinese philosophy emphasizing unity underlying all things ◻ **Taoist** *noun & adj*

tap *noun* **1** a light touch or knock **2** a device with a valve for controlling the flow of liquid, gas *etc* ◻ *verb* **1** knock or strike lightly **2** draw on, start using **3** attach a listening device secretly to (a telephone) ◻ **on tap** ready, available for use

tap *verb* » tap*s*, tapp*ing*, tapp*ed*

tapdance *noun* a dance done with special shoes that make a tapping sound ◻ *verb* perform a tapdance

tape *noun* **1** a narrow band or strip used for tying **2** a piece of string over the finishing line on a racetrack **3** a tape-measure **4** a strip of magnetic material for recording sound or pictures ◻ *verb* **1** fasten with tape **2** record on tape ◻ **tape-measure** *noun* a narrow strip of paper, plastic *etc* used for measuring distance ◻ **tape-recorder** *noun* a kind of instrument for recording sound *etc* on magnetic tape ◻ **tapeworm** *noun* a type of long worm sometimes found in the intestines of humans and animals ◻ **have someone taped** have a good understanding of their character or worth

taper *noun* **1** a long, thin kind of candle **2** a long waxed wick used for lighting oil lamps *etc* ◻ *verb* make or become thinner at one end □ **tapering** *adj*

tapestry *noun* (*plural* **tapestries**) a cloth with designs or figures woven into it, used to decorate walls or cover furniture

tapioca *noun* a starchy food obtained from the root of the cassava plant

tapir *noun* a kind of wild animal something like a large pig

tar *noun* **1** a thick, black, sticky liquid derived from wood or coal, used in roadmaking *etc* **2** *informal* a sailor □ *verb* smear with tar □ **tarred with the same brush (as)** having the same faults (as)

tar *verb* » tar*s*, tarr*ing*, tarr*ed*

taramasalata *noun* a Middle Eastern paste made from smoked cod's roe

tarantella *noun* a lively dance for pairs, originally from Naples

tarantula *noun* a type of large, poisonous spider

tardy *adj* slow; late □ **tardiness** *noun*

tare[1] *noun* the weight of a box *etc* when empty

tare[2] *noun* a weed

target *noun* **1** a mark to aim at in shooting, darts *etc* **2** a result or sum that is aimed at: *a target of £3000* **3** someone at whom unfriendly remarks are aimed: *the target of her criticism*

tariff *noun* **1** a list of prices **2** a list of taxes payable on goods brought into a country

tarmac *noun* the surface of a road or airport runway, made of tarmacadam □ *verb* surface with tarmacadam

tarmacadam *noun* a mixture of small stones and tar used to make road surfaces *etc*

tarnish *verb* **1** of metal: (cause to) become dull or discoloured **2** spoil (a reputation *etc*)

tarot /*tar*oh/ *noun* a system of fortune-telling using special cards divided into suits

tarpaulin *noun* **1** strong waterproof cloth **2** a sheet of this material

tarragon *noun* a herb used in cooking

tarry[1] *verb* **1** stay behind, linger **2** be slow or late

tarry[2] *adj* like or covered with tar; sticky

tart *noun* **1** a small pie containing fruit, vegetables *etc* **2** *informal* a prostitute □ *adj* sharp, sour □ **tartness** *noun*

tartan *noun* **1** fabric patterned with squares of different colours, traditionally used by Scottish Highland clans **2** one of these patterns: *Macdonald tartan* □ *adj* with a pattern of tartan

tartar *noun* **1** a substance that gathers on the teeth **2** a difficult or demanding person **3** a substance that forms inside wine casks □ **cream of tartar** a white powder obtained from the tartar from wine casks, used in baking

task *noun* a set piece of work to

be done ▫ **task force** a group of people gathered together with the purpose of performing a special or specific task ▫ **taskmaster** *noun* someone who sets and supervises tasks ▫ **take to task** scold, find fault with

tassel *noun* a hanging bunch of threads, used to decorate a hat *etc*

taste *verb* **1** try by eating or drinking a sample **2** eat or drink some of: *taste this soup* **3** recognize (a flavour): *can you taste the chilli in it?* **4** have a particular flavour: *tasting of garlic* **5** experience: *taste success* ▫ *noun* **1** the act or sense of tasting **2** a flavour **3** a small quantity of something **4** a liking: *taste for literature* **5** ability to judge what is suitable in behaviour, dress *etc*, or what is fine or beautiful

tasteful *adj* showing good taste and judgement ▫ **tastefully** *adv* ▫ **tastefulness** *noun*

tasteless *adj* **1** without flavour **2** not tasteful; vulgar ▫ **tastelessly** *adv* ▫ **tastelessness** *noun*

tasty *adj* having a good flavour

tat *noun* shabby articles; rubbish ▫ **tatty** *adj* shabby, tawdry

tatters *noun plural* torn, ragged pieces ▫ **tattered** *adj* ragged

tattie *noun*, *Scot* a potato

tattle *noun* gossip

tattoo *noun* **1** a coloured design on the skin, made by pricking with needles **2** a drumbeat **3** an outdoor military display with music *etc* ▫ *verb* prick coloured designs into the skin ▫ **tattooed** *adj* marked with tattoos

> From a Dutch term meaning to shut off beer taps at closing time, later applied to a military drumbeat at the end of the day

taught *past form* of **teach**

taunt *verb* tease or jeer at unkindly ▫ *noun* a jeer

> Originally a phrase *taunt for taunt*, based on the French *tant pour tant* meaning 'tit for tat'

taut *adj* **1** pulled tight **2** tense, strained

tauten *verb* make or become tight

tautology *noun* a form of repetition in which the same thing is said in different ways, *eg* 'he looked *anxious* and *worried*' ▫ **tautological** *adj*

tavern *noun*, *old* a public house, an inn

tawdry *adj* cheap-looking and gaudy

> From *St Audrey's lace*, once used to make cheap lace neckties

tawny *adj* yellowish-brown

tax *noun* (*plural* **taxes**) **1** a charge made by the government on income, certain types of goods *etc* **2** a strain, a burden: *severe tax on my patience* ▫ *verb* **1** make to pay a tax **2** to put a strain on: *taxing her strength* ▫ **taxation 1** the act or system of taxing **2** taxes ▫ **taxpayer** *noun* someone who pays taxes ▫ **tax with** accuse of

taxi *noun* (*plural* **taxis**) a vehicle

which may be hired, with a driver (*also called*: **taxi-cab**) □ *verb* **1** travel in a taxi **2** of an aeroplane: travel on the runway before or after take-off □ **taxi rank** a place where taxis park to wait for hire

> **taxi** *verb* » taxi*es*, taxi*ing*, taxi*ed*

taxidermy *noun* the art of preparing and stuffing the skins of animals to make them lifelike □ **taxidermist** *noun* someone who does this work

TB *abbrev* tuberculosis

t-cell *noun* a body cell involved in the immune system

tea *noun* **1** a plant grown in India, China *etc*, or its dried and prepared leaves **2** a drink made by infusing its dried leaves **3** a hot drink, an infusion: *beef tea/ camomile tea* **4** an afternoon or early evening meal □ **teacake** *noun* a light, flat bun □ **tea chest** a tall box of thin wood used to pack tea for export, often used as a packing case when empty □ **teapot** *noun* a pot with a spout, for making and pouring tea □ **teaspoon** *noun* a small spoon □ **teatowel** *noun* a cloth for drying dishes

teach *verb* **1** give (someone) skill or knowledge **2** give knowledge of, or training in (a subject): *she teaches French* **3** be a teacher: *decide to teach*

> **teach** » teach*es*, teach*ing*, taught

teacher *noun* someone employed to teach others in a school, or in a particular subject: *guitar teacher*

teaching *noun* **1** the work of a teacher **2** guidance, instruction **3** (**teachings**) beliefs or rules of conduct that are preached or taught

teacup *noun* a medium-sized cup for drinking tea □ **storm in a teacup** *see* **storm**

teak *noun* **1** a hardwood tree from the East Indies **2** its very hard wood **3** a type of African tree

teal *noun* a small water-bird like a duck

team 1 a group of people working together **2** a side in a game: *a football team* **3** two or more animals working together: *team of oxen* □ **team spirit** willingness to work as part of a team □ **team up with** join together with, join forces with

> ⚠Do not confuse with: **teem**

tear[1] *noun* **1** a drop of liquid from the eye **2** (**tears**) grief □ **tear gas** gas which causes the eyes to stream with tears □ **in tears** weeping

tear[2] *verb* **1** pull with force: *tear apart/ tear down* **2** make a hole or split in (material *etc*) **3** hurt deeply **4** *informal* rush: *tearing off down the road* □ *noun* a hole or split made by tearing

> **tear** *verb* » tear*s*, tear*ing*, torn, tore

tearful *adj* **1** inclined to weep **2** in tears, crying □ **tearfully** *adv*

tease *verb* **1** annoy, irritate on purpose **2** pretend to upset or annoy for fun: *I'm only teasing* **3** untangle (wool *etc*) with a comb **4**

sort out (a problem or puzzle) □ *noun* someone who teases

teasel *noun* a type of prickly plant

teaser *noun* a problem, a puzzle

teat *noun* **1** the part of an animal through which milk passes to its young **2** a rubber object shaped like this attached to a baby's feeding bottle

technical *adj* **1** relating to a particular art or skill, *esp* a mechanical or industrial one: *what is the technical term for this?/ a technical expert* **2** according to strict laws or rules: *technical defeat* □ **technically** *adv* according to the rules, strictly speaking

technicality *noun* (*plural* **technicalities**) a technical detail or point

technician *noun* someone trained in the practical side of an art

technique *noun* the way in which a process is carried out; a method

technology *noun* **1** science applied to practical (*esp* industrial) purposes **2** the practical skills of a particular civilization, period *etc* □ **technological** *adj* □ **technologically** *adv* □ **technologist** *noun*

teddy or **teddybear** *noun* (*plural* **teddies** or **teddybears**) **1** a stuffed toy bear **2** (**teddy**) a one-piece woman's undergarment

tedious *adj* long and tiresome □ **tediously** *adv* □ **tedium** *noun*

tee *noun* **1** the square of level ground from which a golfball is driven **2** the peg or sand heap on which the ball is placed for driving □ **tee up** place (a ball) on a tee

teem *verb* **1** be full: *teeming with people* **2** rain heavily

⚠Do not confuse with: **team**

teenage *adj* suitable for, or typical of, those in their teens

teenager *noun* someone in their teens

teens *noun plural* the years of age from thir*teen* to nine*teen*

teeny *adj, informal* tiny, minute

tee-shirt or **T-shirt** *noun* a short-sleeved shirt pulled on over the head

teeth *plural* of **tooth**

teethe *verb* of a baby: grow its first teeth □ **teething troubles** **1** pain caused by growing teeth **2** difficulties encountered at the beginning of an undertaking

teetotal *adj* never drinking alcohol □ **teetotaller** *noun*

TEFL /tefl/ *abbrev* teaching of English as a foreign language

tel *abbrev* telephone

tele- *prefix* at a distance

telecommunications *noun plural* the sending of information by telephone, radio, television *etc*

telecommuter *noun* someone who works at home and communicates with the office by phone, computer etc

telecottage *noun* an office building in a rural area equipped with computers *etc*

telegram *noun* a message sent by telegraph

telegraph *noun* an instrument for sending messages to a distance using electrical impulses □ *verb* send (a message) by telegraph □ **telegraphic** *adj* **1** of a telegraph **2** short, brief, concise

telekinesis *noun* the movement of objects from a distance through will-power not touch

teleology *noun* the philosophy of viewing things in terms of their purpose, not their cause

telepathy *noun* communication between people without using sight, hearing *etc* □ **telepathic** *adj*

telephone *noun* an instrument for speaking over distances, which uses an electric current travelling along a wire, or radio waves □ *verb* send (a message) by telephone □ **telephonist** an operator on a telephone switchboard

telephoto *adj* of a lens: used to photograph enlarged images of distant objects

teleprinter *noun* a typewriter which receives and prints out messages sent by telegraph

telescope *noun* a tubular instrument fitted with lenses which magnify distant objects □ *verb* **1** push or fit together so that one thing slides inside another **2** force together, compress

teletex *noun* a high-speed means of transmitting data, similar to telex

teletext *noun* news and general information transmitted by television companies, viewable only on special television sets

televise *verb* broadcast on television: *are they televising the football match?*

television *noun* **1** the reproduction on a small screen of pictures sent from a distance **2** an apparatus for receiving these pictures

teleworker *noun* someone who works from home and communicates with their employer by computer, fax *etc*

telex *noun* **1** the sending of messages by means of teleprinters **2** a message sent in this way

tell *verb* **1** say or express in words: *she's telling the truth* **2** give the facts of (a story) **3** inform, give information: *can you tell me when it's 9 o'clock* **4** order, command: *tell him to go away!* **5** make out, distinguish: *I can't tell one wine from the other* **6** give away a secret: *promise not to tell* **7** be effective, produce results: *training will tell in the end* □ **teller** *noun* **1** a bank clerk who receives and pays out money **2** someone who counts votes at an election □ **telling** *adj* having a marked effect: *telling remark* □ **all told** altogether, counting all □ **tell off** *informal* scold □ **tell on 1** have an effect on **2** give information about □ **tell tales** give away information about the misdeeds of others

tell » tell*s*, tell*ing*, told

temerity *noun* rashness, boldness

temp *abbrev* **1** temperature **2** temporary □ *noun* (*informal*) a temporarily employed secretarial worker □ *verb*, *informal* work as a temp

temper *noun* **1** habitual state of mind: *of an even temper* **2** a passing mood: *in a good temper* **3** a tendency to get angry easily **4** a fit of anger **5** the amount of hardness in metal, glass *etc* □ *verb* **1** bring (metal) to the right degree of hardness by heating and cooling **2** make less severe □ **lose your temper** show anger

temperament *noun* someone's nature as it affects the way they feel and act; disposition □ **temperamental** *adj* **1** of temperament **2** excitable, emotional

temperance *noun* the habit of not drinking much (or any) alcohol

temperate *adj* **1** moderate in temper, eating or drinking *etc* **2** of climate: neither very hot nor very cold

temperature *noun* **1** degree of heat or cold: *today's temperature* **2** a body heat higher than normal

tempest *noun* a storm, with great wind

tempestuous *adj* **1** very stormy and windy **2** passionate, violently emotional

template *noun* a thin plate cut in a design for drawing round

temple[1] *noun* a building used for public worship; a church

temple[2] *noun* a small flat area on each side of the forehead

tempo *noun* (*plural* **tempos** or **tempi**) **1** the speed at which music is played **2** the speed or rate of an activity

temporal *adj* **1** relating to this world or this life only, not eternal or spiritual **2** relating to time

temporary *adj* lasting only for a time, not permanent

temporize *verb* avoid or delay taking action in order to gain time

tempt *verb* **1** try to persuade or entice **2** attract **3** make inclined (to): *tempted to phone him up* □ **temptation** *noun* **1** the act of tempting **2** the feeling of being tempted **3** something which tempts □ **tempting** *adj* attractive

tempura *noun* a Japanese dish of fish, vegetables *etc* fried quickly in batter

ten *noun* the number 10 □ *adj* 10 in number □ **tenpin bowling** a game like skittles played by bowling a ball at ten pins standing at the end of a bowling lane

tenable *adj* able to be defended; justifiable

tenacious *adj* **1** keeping a firm hold or grip **2** obstinate, persistent, determined □ **tenaciously** *adv* □ **tenacity** *noun*

tenant *noun* someone who pays rent for the use of a house, land *etc* □ **tenancy** *noun* (*plural* **tenancies**) **1** the holding of a house, farm *etc* by a tenant **2** the period of this holding □ **tenanted** *adj* occupied, lived in

tend *verb* **1** be likely or inclined to do something: *these flowers tend to wilt* **2** move or slope in a certain direction **3** take care of, look after

tendency *noun* (*plural* **tendencies**) a leaning or inclination (towards): *tendency to daydream*

tender *adj* **1** soft, not hard or tough **2** easily hurt or damaged **3** hurting when touched **4** loving, gentle □ *verb* **1** offer (a resignation *etc*) formally **2** make a formal offer for a job □ *noun* **1** an offer to take on work, supply goods *etc* for a fixed price **2** a small boat that carries stores for a large one **3** a truck for coal and water attached to a steam engine □ **tenderfoot** *noun* an inexperienced person □ **tender-hearted** *adj* kind, sympathetic □ **tenderize** *verb* soften (meat) before cooking □ **legal tender** coins or notes which must be accepted when offered □ **of tender years** very young

tendon *noun* a tough cord joining a muscle to a bone

tendril *noun* **1** a thin curling stem of a climbing plant which attaches itself to a support **2** a curling strand of hair *etc*

tenement *noun* a block of flats

tenet *noun* a belief, opinion

tenner *noun*, *informal* a ten-pound note; ten pounds

tennis *noun* a game for two or four players using rackets to hit a ball to each other over a net □ **tennis court** a place made level and prepared for tennis

tenon *noun* a projecting part at the end of a piece of wood made to fit a **mortise**

tenor *noun* **1** a singing voice of the highest normal pitch for an adult male **2** a singer with this voice **3** the general course: *the even tenor of country life* **4** general meaning: *the tenor of the speech*

tense[1] *noun* the form of a verb that shows time of action, *eg* '*I was*' (**past tense**), '*I am*' (**present tense**), '*I shall be*' (**future tense**)

tense[2] *adj* **1** tightly stretched **2** nervous, strained: *feeling tense/tense with excitement* □ **tensile** *adj* relating to stretching □ **tension** *noun* **1** the state of being stretched **2** strain, anxiety

tent *noun* a movable shelter of canvas or other material, supported by poles and pegged to the ground

tentacle *noun* a long thin flexible part of an animal used to feel or grasp, *eg* the arm of an octopus □ **tentacular** *adj*

tentative *adj* **1** experimental, initial: *a tentative offer* **2** uncertain, hesitating: *tentative smile* □ **tentatively** *adv*

tenterhooks *noun plural*: **on tenterhooks** uncertain and very anxious about what will happen

tenth *adj* the last of ten items □ *noun* one of ten equal parts

tenuous *adj* slight, weak: *tenuous connection* □ **tenuously** *adv*

tenure *noun* **1** the holding of property or a position of employment **2** the period, or terms or conditions, of this

tepee *noun* a traditional Native American tent made of animal skins

tepid *adj* lukewarm

tequila /*təkeelə*/ *noun* a Mexican

alcoholic drink made from the agave plant

tercentenary *noun* the 300th anniversary of an event

term *noun* **1** a length of time: *term of imprisonment* **2** a division of an academic or school year: *autumn term* **3** a word, an expression: *dictionary of computing terms* **4** (**terms**) the rules or conditions of an agreement: *what are their terms?* **5** (**terms**) fixed charges **6** (**terms**) footing, relationship: *on good terms with his neighbours* ▯ *verb* name, call ▯ **come to terms** reach an agreement or understanding ▯ **come to terms with** accept, be able to live with ▯ **in terms of** from the point of view of

termagant *noun* a bad-tempered, noisy woman

terminal *adj* **1** of or growing at the end: *terminal bud* **2** of an illness: fatal, incurable ▯ *noun* **1** an end **2** a point of connection in an electric circuit **3** a computer monitor connected to a network **4** a terminus **5** an airport building containing arrival and departure areas **6** a bus station in a town centre running a service to a nearby airport

terminate *verb* bring or come to an end ▯ **termination** *noun*

terminology *noun* the special words or expressions used in a particular art, science *etc*

terminus *noun* (*plural* **termini** or **terminuses**) **1** the end **2** an end point on a railway, bus route *etc*

termite *noun* a pale-coloured wood-eating insect, like an ant

tern *noun* a type of sea bird like a small gull

terpsichorean *adj* relating to dancing

terrace *noun* **1** a raised level bank of earth **2** a raised flat place **3** a connected row of houses ▯ *verb* form into a terrace or terraces

terracotta *noun* a brownish-red mixture of clay and sand used for tiles, pottery *etc*

terra firma land as opposed to water

terrain *noun* an area of land considered in terms of its physical features: *the terrain is a bit rocky*

terrapin *noun* a small turtle living in ponds or rivers

terrarium *noun* an ornamental glass jar containing living plants *etc*

terrestrial *adj* of or living on the earth

terrible *adj* **1** causing great fear: *terrible sight* **2** causing great hardship or distress: *terrible disaster* **3** *informal* very bad: *a terrible writer*

terribly *adv*, *informal* **1** badly: *sang terribly* **2** extremely: *terribly tired*

terrier *noun* a breed of small dog

terrify *verb* frighten greatly ▯ **terrific** *adj* **1** powerful, dreadful **2** huge, amazing **3** *informal* attractive, enjoyable *etc*: *a terrific party*

> **terrify** » terrifi*es*, terrify*ing*, terrifi*ed*

territorial *adj* of, belonging to a territory ▯ **territorial waters** seas close to, and considered to belong to, a country

territory *noun* (*plural* **territories**) **1** an area of land, a region **2** land under the control of a ruler or state **3** an area allocated to a salesman *etc* **4** a field of activity or interest

terror *noun* **1** very great fear **2** something which causes great fear **3** *informal* an uncontrollable child □ **terrorize** *verb* frighten very greatly

terrorism *noun* the organized use of violence or intimidation for political or other ends □ **terrorist** *noun* someone who practises terrorism

terse *adj* using few words; curt, brusque □ **tersely** *adv* □ **terseness** *noun*

tertiary *adj* third in position or order □ **tertiary education** education at university or college level

TESL /tesl/ *abbrev* teaching of English as a second language

TESOL /*teesə*l/ *abbrev* teaching of English to speakers of other languages

TESSA /tes*ə*/ *abbrev* tax-exempt special savings account

tessera *noun* (*plural* **tesserae**) one of the small pieces making up a mosaic

test *noun* **1** a short examination **2** something done to check soundness, reliability *etc*: *ran tests on the new model* **3** a means of finding the presence of: *test for radioactivity* **4** an event that shows up a good or bad quality: *a test of courage* □ *verb* carry out tests on □ **test match** *cricket* one of a series of matches between two countries □ **test pilot** a pilot who tests new aircraft □ **test tube** a glass tube closed at one end, used in chemical tests

testament *noun* **1** a written statement **2** a will □ **Old Testament** and **New Testament** the two main divisions of the Christian Bible

testator *noun* the writer of a will □ **testatory** *adj* of a will or testament

testicle *noun* one of two sperm-producing glands enclosed in the male scrotum

testify *verb* **1** give evidence in a law court **2** make a solemn declaration of **3** (**testify to**) show, give evidence of: *testifies to his ignorance*

> **testify** » testifi*es*, testify*ing*, testifi*ed*

testimonial *noun* **1** a personal statement about someone's character, abilities *etc* **2** a gift given in thanks for services given

testimony *noun* (*plural* **testimonies**) **1** the statement made by someone who testifies **2** evidence

testis *noun* (*plural* **testes**) *formal* a testicle

testosterone *noun* the chief male sex hormone, secreted by the testicles

testy *adj* easily angered, irritable □ **testily** *adv* □ **testiness** *noun*

tetanus *noun* a disease, caused *esp* by an infected wound, causing stiffening and spasms in the jaw muscles (*also called*: **lockjaw**)

tetchy *adj* irritable, testy □ **tetchily** *adv* □ **tetchiness** *noun*

tête-à-tête /tetətet/ *noun* a private talk between two people

tether *noun* a rope or chain for tying an animal to restrict its movement ▫ *verb* **1** tie with a tether **2** limit the freedom of

Teutonic *adj* Germanic

text *noun* **1** the written or printed part of a book, not the pictures, notes *etc* **2** a printed or written version of a speech, play *etc* **3** a Biblical passage used as the basis for a sermon **4** the subject matter of a speech, essay *etc* ▫ **textbook** *noun* a book used for teaching, giving the main facts about a subject

textile *adj* of weaving; woven ▫ *noun* a woven cloth or fabric

textual *adj* of or in a text ▫ **textually** *adv*

texture *noun* **1** the quality of cloth resulting from weaving: *loose texture* **2** the quality of a substance in terms of how it looks or feels: *rough texture/ lumpy texture*

TGWU *abbrev* Transport and General Workers' Union

than *conj* & *prep* used in comparisons: *easier than I expected/ better than usual*

thane *noun*, *hist* a noble who held land from the crown

thank *verb* express gratitude to (someone) for a favour, gift *etc* ▫ **thankless** *adj* neither worthwhile nor appreciated: *thankless task* ▫ **thanks** *noun plural* gratitude; appreciation: *you'll get no thanks for it* ▫ **thanks to 1** with the help of: *we arrived on time, thanks to our friends* **2** owing to: *we were late, thanks to our car breaking down* ▫ **thank you** or **thanks** a polite expression used to thank someone

thankful *adj* grateful; relieved and glad ▫ **thankfully** *adv* ▫ **thankfulness** *noun*

thanksgiving *noun* **1** a church service giving thanks to God **2** (**Thanksgiving**) *US* the fourth Thursday of November, a national holiday commemorating the first harvest of the Puritan settlers

that *adj* & *pronoun* (*plural* **those**) used to point out a thing or person *etc* (*contrasted with*: **this**): *that woman over there/ don't say that* ▫ *relative pronoun*: *those are the colours he chose/ that's the man I spoke to* ▫ *adv* to such an extent or degree: *why were you that late?* ▫ *conj* **1** used in reporting speech: *she said that she was there* **2** used to connect clauses: *I heard that you were ill*

thatch *noun* straw *etc* used to make the roof of a house ▫ *verb* cover with thatch

thaw *verb* **1** melt **2** of frozen food: defrost, become unfrozen **3** become friendly ▫ *noun* **1** the melting of ice and snow by heat **2** a change in the weather that causes this

the *adj* **1** referring to a particular person or thing: *the boy in the park/ I like the jacket I'm wearing* **2** referring to all or any of a general group: *the horse is of great use to man*

theatre or *US* **theater** *noun* **1** a place for the public performance of plays *etc* **2** a room in a hospital for surgical operations **3** the acting profession

theatrical *adj* **1** of theatres or acting **2** over-dramatic, overdone ▯ **theatricality** *noun*

thee *pronoun, old* you (*sing*) as the object of a sentence

theft *noun* stealing

their *adj* belonging to them: *their car* ▯ **theirs** *pronoun*: *the red car is theirs*

⚠Do not confuse with: **there**

theism *noun* belief in the existence of God ▯ **theistic** or **theistical** *adj*

them *pronoun plural* **1** people or things already spoken about (as the object of a verb): *we've seen them* **2** those: *one of them over in the corner* ▯ *pronoun sing* used to avoid giving the gender of the person being referred to: *if anyone phones, ask them to leave their number*

theme *noun* **1** the subject of a discussion, essay *etc* **2** *music* a main melody which is often repeated ▯ **theme park** a public display in an open area, related to a single theme ▯ **theme song** or **theme tune** a tune that is repeated often in a film, television series *etc*

themselves *pronoun plural* **1** used reflexively: *they tired themselves out walking* **2** used for emphasis: *they'll have to do it by themselves*

then *adv* **1** at that time: *I didn't know you then* **2** after that: *and then where did you go?* ▯ *conj* in that case, therefore: *if you're busy, then don't come*

thence *adv, old* from that time or place ▯ **thenceforth** *adv* from that time onward

theocracy *noun* government of a state according to religious laws ▯ **theocratic** *adj*

theodolite *noun* an instrument for measuring angles, used in surveying

theology *noun* the study of God and religion ▯ **theologian** *noun* someone who studies theology ▯ **theological** *adj*

theorem *noun* a proposition to be proved in mathematics *etc*

theory *noun* (*plural* **theories**) **1** an explanation that has not been proved or tested **2** the underlying ideas in an art, science *etc*, compared to practice or performance ▯ **theoretical** *adj* of theory, not experience or practice ▯ **theoretically** *adv* ▯ **theorize** *verb* form theories

therapeutic *adj* **1** of therapy **2** healing, curing

therapist *noun* someone who gives therapeutic treatment: *speech therapist*

therapy *noun* (*plural* **therapies**) treatment of disease or disorders

there *adv* at, in or to that place: *what did you do there?* ▯ *pronoun* used (with *be*) as a subject of a sentence or clause when the real subject follows the verb: *there is nobody at home* ▯ **thereabouts** *adv* approximately ▯ **thereafter** *adv* after that ▯ **thereby** *adv* by that means ▯ **therefore** *adv* for this or that reason ▯ **thereof** *adv* of that ▯ **thereupon** *adv* **1** because of this or that **2** immediately

⚠Do not confuse with: **their**

theremin *noun* a device which produces vibrating synthetic sounds, used in film special effects *etc*

therm *noun* a unit of heat used in measuring gas

thermal *adj* **1** of heat **2** of hot springs

thermodynamics *noun sing* the science of the relation between heat and mechanical energy

thermometer *noun* an instrument for measuring temperature

thermonuclear *adj* relating to the fusion of nuclei at high temperatures

Thermos *noun, trademark* a kind of vacuum flask

thermostat *noun* a device for automatically controlling temperature in a room

thesaurus *noun* (*plural* **thesauri** or **thesauruses**) **1** a reference book listing words and their synonyms **2** a dictionary or encyclopedia

these *see* **this**

thesis noun (*plural* **theses**) **1** a long piece of written work on a topic, often part of a university degree **2** a statement of a point of view

thespian *noun, formal* an actor

Named after *Thespis*, founder of ancient Greek tragedy

they *pronoun plural* some people or things already mentioned (used only as the subject of a verb): *they followed the others* ◊ *pronoun sing* used to avoid giving the gender of the person being referred to: *anyone can come if they like*

thick *adj* **1** not thin, of reasonable width: *a thick slice/ two metres thick* **2** of a mixture: containing solid matter, stiff: *a thick soup* **3** dense, difficult to see or pass through: *thick fog/ thick woods* **4** of speech: not clear **5** *informal* stupid **6** *informal* very friendly ◊ *noun* the thickest, most crowded or active part: *in the thick of the fight* ◊ **thicken** *verb* make or become thick ◊ **thicket** *noun* a group of close-set trees and bushes ◊ **thickness** *noun* **1** the quality of being thick **2** the distance between opposite sides **3** a layer ◊ **thickset** *adj* **1** closely set or planted **2** having a thick sturdy body ◊ **thick-skinned** *adj* not sensitive or easily hurt

thief *noun* (*plural* **thieves**) someone who steals

thieve *verb* steal ◊ **thieving** *noun* ◊ **thievish** *adj* inclined to stealing

thigh *noun* the thick, fleshy part of the leg between the knee and the hip

thimble *noun* a small cap worn over a fingertip, used to push a needle while sewing

thin *adj* **1** not very wide between its two sides: *thin paper/ thin slice* **2** slim, not fat **3** not dense or crowded: *thin population* **4** poor in quality: *thin wine* **5** of a voice: weak, not resonating **6** of a mixture: not stiff, watery: *a thin soup* ◊ *verb* make or become thin or thinner ◊ **thinness** *noun* ◊ **thin-skinned** *adj* sensitive, easily hurt

> **thin** *verb* » thin*s*, thinn*ing*, thinn*ed*

thine *adj, old* belonging to you (used before words beginning with a vowel or a vowel sound): *thine enemies* ◊ *pronoun, old* something belonging to you: *my heart is thine*

thing *noun* **1** an object that is not living **2** *informal* a person: *a nice old thing* **3** (**things**) belongings **4** an individual object, quality, idea *etc* that may be referred to: *several things must be taken into consideration*

think *verb* **1** work things out, reason **2** form ideas in the mind **3** believe, judge or consider: *I think that we should go* **4** (with **of**) intend: *she is thinking of resigning* ◊ **think tank** a group of people who give expert advice and come up with ideas ◊ **think better of** change your mind about ◊ **think highly of** or **think much of** have a good opinion of ◊ **think nothing of 1** have a poor opinion of **2** consider as easy ◊ **think out** work out in the mind

> **think** *verb* » *thinks*, think*ing*, thought

third *adj* the last of a series of three ◊ *noun* one of three equal parts ◊ **third age** the age after retirement, early old age ◊ **third-rate** *adj* of very poor quality

thirl *verb, Scot* bind with an agreement, loyalty, love *etc*

thirst *noun* **1** a dry feeling in the mouth caused by lack of fluid **2** an eager desire (for): *thirst for knowledge* ◊ *verb* **1** feel thirsty **2** (with **for**) desire eagerly ◊ **thirsty** *adj* **1** having thirst **2** of earth: parched, dry **3** eager (for)

thirteen *noun* the number 13 ◊ *adj* thirteen in number ◊ **thirteenth** *adj* the last of a series of thirteen ◊ *noun* one of thirteen equal parts

thirty *noun* the number 30 ◊ *adj* thirty in number ◊ **thirtieth** *adj* the last of a series of thirty ◊ *noun* one of thirty equal parts

this *adj & pronoun* (*plural* **these**) **1** used to point out someone or something, *esp* one nearby (*contrasted with*: **that**): *look at this letter/ take this instead* **2** to such an extent or degree: *this early*

thistle *noun* a prickly plant with purple flowers ◊ **thistledown** *noun* the feathery bristles of the seeds of the thistle

thither *adv* to that place

thong *noun* **1** a thin strap of leather to fasten anything **2** the lash of a whip

thorax *noun* (*plural* **thoraxes** or **thoraces**) **1** the chest in the human or animal body **2** the middle section of an insect's body

thorn *noun* **1** a sharp prickle sticking out from the stem of a plant **2** a bush with thorns, *esp* the hawthorn ◊ **thorny** *adj* **1** full of thorns; prickly **2** difficult, causing arguments: *a thorny problem* ◊ **thorn in the flesh** a cause of constant irritation

thorough *adj* **1** complete, absolute: *a thorough muddle* **2** very careful, attending to every detail ▢ **thoroughbred** *noun* an animal of pure breed ▢ **thoroughfare** *noun* **1** a public street **2** a passage or way through: *no thoroughfare* ▢ **thoroughgoing** *adj* thorough, complete ▢ **thoroughly** *adv*

those *see* **that**

thou *pronoun, old* you (as the subject of a sentence)

though *conj* although: *though he disliked it, he ate it all* ▢ *adv, informal* however: *I wish I'd never said it, though*

thought *noun* **1** the act of thinking **2** something which you think, an idea **3** an opinion **4** consideration: *after much thought* ▢ *verb past form* of **think** ▢ **thoughtful** *adj* **1** full of thought **2** thinking of others, considerate ▢ **thoughtless** *adj* showing lack of thought; inconsiderate

thousand *noun* the number 1000 ▢ *adj* a thousand in number ▢ **thousandth** *adj* the last of a series of a thousand ▢ *noun* one of a thousand equal parts

thrall *noun*: **in thrall** enchanted, fascinated

thrash *verb* **1** beat severely **2** move or toss violently (about) **3** (with **out**) discuss (a problem *etc*) thoroughly **4** thresh (grain) ▢ **thrashing** *noun* a flogging, a beating

thread *noun* **1** a very thin line of cotton, wool, silk etc, often twisted and drawn out **2** the ridge which goes in a spiral round a screw **3** a connected series of details in correct order in a story ▢ *verb* **1** put a thread through a needle *etc* **2** make (your way) in a narrow space ▢ **threadbare** *adj* of clothes: worn thin ▢ **threadworm** *noun* a nematode

threat *noun* **1** a warning that you intend to hurt or punish someone **2** a warning of something bad that may come: *a threat of war* **3** something likely to cause harm: *a threat to our plans* ▢ **threaten** *verb* **1** make a threat: *threatened to kill himself* **2** suggest the approach of something unpleasant **3** be a danger to

three *noun* the number 3 ▢ *adj* 3 in number

3-D *short for* three-dimensional

threnody *noun* a lament

thresh *verb* beat out (grain) from straw

threshold *noun* **1** a piece of wood or stone under the door of a building **2** a doorway **3** an entry or beginning: *on the threshold of a new era*

threw *past form* of **throw**

thrice *adv* three times

thrift *noun* careful management of money in order to save ▢ **thrifty** *adj* careful about spending

thrill *noun* **1** an excited feeling **2** quivering, vibration ▢ *verb* **1** feel excitement **2** make excited ▢ **thriller** *noun* an exciting story, often about crime and detection ▢ **thrilling** *adj* very exciting

thrive *verb* **1** grow strong and healthy **2** get on well, be successful

thro' *short for* **through**

throat *noun* **1** the back part of the

mouth **2** the front part of the neck

throb *verb* **1** of pulse *etc*: beat *esp* more strongly than normal **2** beat or vibrate rhythmically and regularly

throb *verb* » *throbs*, throbb*ing*, throbb*ed*

throes *noun plural* great suffering or struggle □ **in the throes of** in the middle of (a struggle, doing a task *etc*)

thrombosis *noun* the forming of a clot in a blood vessel

throne *noun* **1** the seat of a monarch or bishop **2** a monarch or their power

throng *noun* a crowd □ *verb* **1** move in a crowd **2** crowd, fill (a place)

throttle *noun* the part of an engine through which steam or petrol can be turned on or off □ *verb* choke by gripping the throat

through *prep* **1** entering from one direction and out in the other: *through the tunnel* **2** from end to end, or side to side, of: *all through the performance* **3** by way of: *related through his grandmother* **4** as a result of: *through his expertise* **5** *US* from (one date) to (another) inclusive: *Monday through Friday is five days* □ *adv* into and out, from beginning to end: *all the way through the tunnel* □ *adj* **1** without break or change: *through train* **2** *informal* finished: *are you through with the newspaper?* **3** of a telephone call: connected: *I couldn't get through this morning* □ **through-and-through** *adv* completely, entirely: *a gentleman through-and-through* □ **throughout** *prep* **1** in all parts of: *throughout Europe* **2** from start to finish of: *throughout the journey* □ **throughput** *noun* an amount of material put through a process

throw *verb* **1** send through the air with force **2** of a horse: make (a rider) fall to the ground **3** shape (pottery) on a wheel **4** give (a party) □ *noun* **1** the act of throwing **2** the distance a thing is thrown: *within a stone's throw of the house* □ **throwback** *noun* a reversion to an earlier form

throw *verb* » *throws*, throw*ing*, threw, thrown

thru *US*, *informal* through

thrush (*plural* **thrushes**) **1** a type of singing bird with a speckled breast **2** a type of infectious disease of the mouth, throat or vagina

thrust *verb* **1** push with force **2** make a sudden push forward with a pointed weapon **3** (with **on, upon**) force (something, yourself) upon □ *noun* **1** a stab **2** a pushing force

thrust *verb* » thrust*s*, thrust*ing*, thrust

thud *noun* a dull, hollow sound like that made by a heavy body falling □ *verb* move or fall with such a sound

thud *verb* » thud*s*, thudd*ing*, thudd*ed*

thug *noun* a violent, brutal person

thumb *noun* the short, thick finger of the hand □ *verb* turn over (the pages of a book) with the thumb or fingers ▫ **thumbscrew** *noun, hist* an instrument of torture which worked by squashing the thumbs ▫ **rule of thumb** a rough-and-ready practical method ▫ **thumbs down** or **thumbs up** showing disapproval, or approval, of something ▫ **under someone's thumb** under their control

thump *noun* a heavy blow ▫ *verb* **1** beat heavily **2** move or fall with a dull, heavy noise

thunder *noun* **1** the deep rumbling sound heard after a flash of lightning **2** any loud, rumbling noise ▫ *verb* **1** produce the sound of, or a sound like, thunder **2** shout out angrily ▫ **thunderbolt** *noun* **1** a flash of lightning followed by thunder **2** a very great and sudden surprise ▫ **thunderclap** *noun* a sudden roar of thunder ▫ **thunderous** *adj* like thunder; very angry ▫ **thunderstruck** *adj* overcome by surprise ▫ **thundery** *adj* of weather: sultry, bringing thunder

Thursday *noun* the fifth day of the week

thus *adv* **1** in this or that manner: *he always talks thus* **2** to this degree or extent: *thus far* **3** because of this, therefore: *thus, we must go on*

thwart *verb* **1** hinder (someone) from carrying out a plan, intention *etc* **2** prevent (an attempt *etc*) ▫ *noun* a cross seat for rowers in a boat

thy *adj, old* belonging to you: *thy wife and children*

thyme *noun* a small sweet-smelling herb used for seasoning food

thyroid gland a large gland in the neck which influences the rate at which energy is used by the body

> Based on a Greek word meaning 'door-shaped', because of the shape of the cartilage in the front of the throat

tiara *noun* a jewelled ornament for the head like a crown

tibia *noun* the bone of the shin, the larger of the two bones between knee and ankle (*compare with*: **fibula**)

tic *noun* a twitching motion of certain muscles, *esp* of the face

tick[1] *noun* **1** a light mark (✓) used to mark as correct, or mark off in a list **2** a small quick noise, made regularly by a clock or watch **3** *informal* a moment: *I'll just be a tick* ▫ *verb* **1** mark with a tick **2** of a clock *etc*: produce regular ticks ▫ **ticker tape** paper tape that prints the latest news of share prices *etc* ▫ **ticking** *noun* the noise made by a clock *etc*

tick[2] *noun* a tiny blood-sucking animal

tick[3] *noun* the cloth cover of a mattress or pillow

tickle *verb* **1** excite the surface nerves of a part of the body by touching lightly **2** please or amuse

ticklish *adj* **1** sensitive to tickling **2** not easy to deal with: *ticklish problem* ▫ **tickly** *adj* ticklish

tiddly *adj* **1** slightly drunk **2** tiny

tiddlywinks *noun sing* a game in which small plastic discs (**tiddlywinks**) are flipped into a cup

tide *noun* **1** the rise and fall of the sea which happens regularly twice each day **2** *old* time, season: *Christmastide* □ **tidal** *adj* of the tide □ **tidal wave** an enormous wave in the sea often caused by an earthquake *etc* □ **tidemark** *noun* **1** a mark made by the tide at its highest point **2** a mark on the skin showing the furthest point of washing □ **tide over** help to get over a difficulty for a time

tidings *noun plural* news

tidy *adj* **1** in good order, neat **2** *informal* fairly big: *a tidy sum of money* □ *verb* make neat □ **tidily** *adv* □ **tidiness** *noun*

> **tidy** *verb* » *tidies*, tidy*ing*, tidi*ed*

tie *verb* **1** fasten with a cord, string *etc* **2** knot or put a bow in (string, shoelaces *etc*) **3** join, unite **4** limit, restrict: *tied to a tight schedule* **5** score the same number of points (in a game *etc*), draw □ *noun* **1** a band of fabric worn round the neck, tied with a knot or bow **2** something that connects: *ties of friendship* **3** something that restricts or limits **4** an equal score in a competition **5** a game or match to be played □ **tie-breaker** *noun* an extra question or part of a tied contest to decide a winner

> **tie** *verb* » *ties*, ty*ing*, ti*ed*

tier /teer/ *noun* a row of seats in a theatre *etc*, with others above or below it

tiff *noun* a slight quarrel

tig *another name* for **tag**

tiger *noun* a large animal of the cat family with a tawny coat striped with black □ **tiger lily** a kind of lily with large spotted flowers

tight *adj* **1** packed closely **2** firmly stretched, not loose **3** fitting too closely: *these jeans are a bit tight* **4** *informal* short of money **5** *informal* drunk □ **tight corner** an awkward situation □ **tight-fisted** *adj* stingy □ **tight-lipped** *adj* uncommunicative □ **tightrope** *noun* a tightly stretched rope on which acrobats perform

tighten *verb* make or become tight or tighter

tights *noun plural* a close-fitting garment covering the feet, legs and body as far as the waist

tigress *noun* a female tiger

tile *noun* a piece of baked clay *etc* used in covering floors or roofs □ *verb* cover with tiles

till[1] *noun* a container or drawer for money in a shop □ *verb* cultivate (land); plough □ **tillage** *noun* **1** the act of tilling **2** tilled land

till[2] *see* **until**

tiller *noun* the handle of a boat's rudder

tilt *verb* **1** fall into, or place in, a sloping position **2** *hist* joust **3** *hist* (with **at**) attack on horseback, using a lance □ *noun* **1** a slant **2** a thrust, a jab □ **at full tilt** with full speed and force

timber *noun* **1** wood for building *etc* **2** trees suitable for this **3** a wooden beam in a house or ship

timbre *noun* the quality of a musical sound or voice

time *noun* **1** the hour of the day **2** the period at which something happens **3** (often **times**) a particular period: *in modern times* **4** opportunity: *no time to listen* **5** a suitable or right moment: *now is the time to ask* **6** one of a number of occasions: *he won four times* **7** (**times**) multiplied by: *two times four* **8** the rhythm or rate of performance of a piece of music □ *adj* **1** of time **2** arranged to go off at a particular time: *a time bomb* □ *verb* **1** measure the minutes, seconds *etc* taken to do anything **2** choose the time for (well, badly *etc*): *time your entrance well* □ **time-honoured** *adj* respected because it has lasted a long time □ **timeless** *adj* **1** not belonging to any particular time **2** never ending: *timeless beauty* □ **timely** *adj* coming at the right moment: *a timely reminder* □ **timepiece** *noun, old* a clock or watch □ **time-sharing** *noun* **1** a system of using a computer so that it can deal with several programs at the same time **2** a scheme by which someone buys the right to use a holiday home for a specified period each year □ **timetable** *noun* a list showing times of classes, arrivals or departures of trains *etc* □ **at times** occasionally □ **do time** *slang* serve a prison sentence □ **in time** early enough □ **on time** or **up to time** punctual □ **the time being** the present time

timid *adj* easily frightened; shy □ **timidity** *noun* □ **timidly** *adv*

timorous *adj* very timid □ **timorously** *adv*

timpani or **tympani** *noun plural* kettledrums □ **timpanist** or **tympanist** *noun* someone who plays timpani

tin *noun* **1** a silvery-white kind of metal **2** a box or can made of **tinplate,** thin iron covered with tin or other metal □ *verb* **1** cover with tin **2** pack (food *etc*) in tins □ **tinfoil** *noun* □ a very thin sheet of tin, aluminium *etc* used for wrapping □ **tinny** *adj* **1** like tin **2** of sound: thin, high-pitched □ **tin-pot** *adj* feeble

tin *verb* » tin*s*, tinn*ing*, tinn*ed*

tincture *noun* **1** a slight tinge of colour **2** a characteristic quality **3** a medicine mixed in alcohol

tinder *noun* dry material easily set alight by a spark □ **tinderbox** *noun*

tine *noun* a spike of a fork or of a deer's antler

tinge *verb* **1** tint, colour slightly **2** (with **with**) add a slight amount of (something) to □ *noun* a slight amount; a hint: *tinge of pink/ tinge of sadness*

tingle *verb* **1** feel a sharp prickling sensation **2** feel a thrill of excitement □ *noun* a sharp prickle

tinker *noun* a mender of kettles, pans *etc* □ *verb* **1** work clumsily or unskilfully **2** meddle (with)

tinkle *verb* (cause to) make a light, ringing sound; clink, jingle □ *noun* a light, ringing sound

tinnitus *noun* persistent ringing in the ears

Tin Pan Alley the popular music industry, originally centred in 28th Street in New York

tinsel *noun* a sparkling, glittering material used for decoration

tint *noun* a variety or shade of a colour □ *verb* give slight colour to

tiny *adj* very small

tip *noun* **1** the top or point of something thin or tapering **2** a piece of useful information **3** a small gift of money to a waiter *etc* **4** a rubbish dump **5** a light stroke, a tap □ *verb* **1** slant **2** (with **over**) overturn **3** (with **out** or **into**) empty out or into **4** (also with **off**) give a hint to **5** give a small gift of money **6** strike lightly □ **tipster** *noun* someone who gives tips about horse-racing *etc*

> **tip** *verb* » tip*s*, tipp*ing*, tipp*ed*

tipple *verb, informal* drink small amounts of alcohol regularly □ *noun* an alcoholic drink □ **tippler** *noun*

tipsy *adj* rather drunk □ **tipsiness** *noun*

tiptoe *verb* **1** walk on your toes in order to go very quietly □ **on tiptoe** standing or walking on your toes

tirade *noun* a long, bitter, scolding speech

tire[1] *verb* **1** make or become weary **2** (with **of**) lose patience or interest in □ **tired** *adj* **1** weary **2** (with **of**) bored with □ **tireless** *adj* **1** never becoming weary **2** never resting □ **tiresome** *adj* **1** making weary **2** long and dull **3** annoying: *a tiresome child* □ **tiring** *adj* causing tiredness or weariness: *a tiring journey*

tire[2] *US spelling* of tyre

tiro or **tyro** *noun* (*plural* **tiros** or **tyros**) a beginner

tissue *noun* **1** the substance of which body organs are made: *muscle tissue* **2** a mass, a network (of lies, nonsense *etc*) **3** a paper handkerchief **4** finely woven cloth □ **tissue paper** thin, soft paper used for wrapping

tit *noun* **1** a type of small bird: *blue tit/ great tit* **2** a teat **3** *slang* a woman's breast □ **tit for tat** blow for blow, repayment of injury with injury

titanic *adj* huge, enormous

titanium *noun* a light, strong type of metal used in aircraft

titbit *noun* a tasty piece of food *etc*

titch *noun, informal* a tiny person

tithe *noun, hist* a tax paid to the church, a tenth part of someone's income or produce

titillate *verb* gently stimulate or arouse (often sexually)

> ⚠Do not confuse: **titillate** and **titivate**

titivate *verb* make smarter; improve in appearance

title *noun* **1** the name of a book, poem *etc* **2** a word in front of a name to show rank or office (*eg Sir, Lady, Major*), or in addressing anyone formally (*eg Mr, Mrs, Ms*) **3** right or claim to money, an estate *etc* □ **titled** *adj* having a title which shows noble rank □ **title deed** a document that proves a right to ownership (of a house *etc*) □ **title page** the page of a book on which are the title, author's name *etc* □ **title role** the part in a play which is the same as the title *eg Hamlet*

titter *verb* giggle □ *noun* a giggle

tittletattle *noun* gossip, idle chatter

titular *adj* **1** of or constituting a title **2** having the title without the duties of an office

tizzy *noun* a state of confusion, a flap

TLA *abbrev, comput* three-letter acronym

TLC *abbrev* tender loving care

TNT *abbrev* trinitrotoluene, a high explosive

to *prep* **1** showing the place or direction aimed for: *going to the cinema/ emigrating to New Zealand* **2** showing the indirect object in a phrase, sentence *etc*: *show it to me* **3** used before a verb to indicate the infinitive: *to err is human* **4** showing that one thing belongs with another in some way: *key to the door* **5** compared with: *nothing to what happened before* **6** about, concerning: *what did he say to that?* **7** showing a ratio, proportion *etc*: *odds are six to one against* **8** showing the purpose or result of an action: *tear it to pieces* □ *adv* almost closed: *pull the door to* □ **to and fro** backwards and forwards

toad *noun* a type of amphibian like a frog

toadstool *noun* a mushroom-like fungus, often poisonous

toady *verb* give way to someone's wishes, or flatter them, to gain favour □ *noun* someone who acts in this way

toast *verb* **1** brown (bread) by heating at a fire or grill **2** drink to the success or health of (someone) **3** warm (your feet *etc*) at a fire □ *noun* **1** bread toasted **2** the person to whom a toast is drunk **3** the drinking of a toast □ **toaster** *noun* an electric machine for toasting bread □ **toastmaster** *noun* the announcer of toasts at a public dinner □ **toast-rack** *noun* a stand with partitions for slices of toast

tobacco *noun* a type of plant whose dried leaves are used for smoking □ **tobacconist** *noun* someone who sells tobacco, cigarettes *etc*

toboggan a long, light sledge □ *verb* go in a toboggan

today *adv* & *noun* **1** (on) this day **2** (at) the present time

toddle *verb* walk unsteadily, with short steps □ **toddler** *noun* a young child just able to walk

toddy *noun* (*plural* **toddies**) a hot drink of whisky and honey

to-do *noun* (*plural* **to-dos**) a bustle, commotion

toe *noun* **1** one of the five finger-like parts of the foot **2** the front part of an animal's foot **3** the front part of a shoe, golf club *etc* □ **on your toes** alert, ready for action □ **toe the line** do as you are told

toffee *noun* a kind of sweet made of sugar and butter □ **toffee-nosed** *adj, informal* snobbish, conceited

tofu *noun* a paste of unfermented soya beans

toga *noun, hist* the loose outer garment worn by a citizen of ancient Rome

together *adv* **1** with each other, in place or time: *we must stay together/ three buses arrived together* **2** in or into union or connection: *glue the pages together* **3** by joint action: *together we can afford it*

toggle *noun* a cylindrical fastening for a coat ▯ *verb* switch quickly between two positions, states *etc* (*esp* between being on and off)

togs *noun plural, informal* clothes

toil *verb* **1** work hard and long **2** walk, move *etc* with effort ▯ *noun* hard work ▯ **toiler** *noun*

toilet *noun* **1** the act of washing yourself, doing your hair **2** a receptacle for waste matter from the body, with a water-supply for flushing this away **3** a room containing this ▯ **toiletries** *noun plural* soaps, cosmetics *etc* ▯ **toilet water** a lightly perfumed, spirit-based liquid for the skin

toilette /twa*let*/ *noun* washing and dressing

Toiseach /*tee*shəx/ *noun* the prime minister of the Republic of Ireland

token *noun* **1** a mark, a sign: *a token of my friendship* **2** a stamped piece of plastic *etc*, or a voucher, for use in place of money: *bus token/ book token* ▯ *adj* done for show only, insincere: *token gesture*

told *past form* of **tell**

tolerable *adj* **1** bearable, endurable **2** fairly good: *tolerable player* ▯ **tolerably** *adv*

tolerance *noun* **1** putting up with and being fair to people with different beliefs, manners *etc* from your own **2** ability to resist the effects of a drug *etc* ▯ **tolerant** *adj*

tolerate *verb* **1** bear, endure; put up with **2** allow ▯ **toleration** *noun*

toll[1] *noun* **1** a tax charged for crossing a bridge *etc* **2** loss, damage ▯ **take toll** cause damage or loss

toll[2] *verb* **1** sound (a large bell) slowly, as for a funeral **2** of a bell: be sounded slowly

tomahawk *noun, hist* a Native American light axe used as a weapon and tool

tomato *noun* (*plural* **tomatoes**) a juicy red-skinned fruit, used in salads, sauces *etc*

tomb *noun* **1** a grave **2** a burial vault or chamber

tombola *noun* a kind of lottery

tomboy *noun* a high-spirited active girl

tombstone *noun* a stone placed over a grave in memory of the dead person

tomcat *noun* a male cat

tome *noun* a large heavy book

tomfoolery *noun* silly behaviour

tomorrow *adv* & *noun* **1** (on) the day after today **2** (in) the future: *I'll do it tomorrow/ the children of tomorrow*

tomtit *noun* a kind of small bird

tomtom *noun* a type of drum beaten with the hands

ton *noun* **1** a measure of weight equal to 2240 pounds, about 1016 kilogrammes **2** a unit (100 cubic feet) of space in a ship ▯ **metric ton** or **metric tonne** 1000 kilogrammes

tone *noun* **1** sound **2** quality of sound: *harsh tone* **3** *music* one of the larger intervals in a scale, *eg* between C and D **4** the quality of a voice expressing the mood of the speaker: *a gentle tone* **5** a shade of colour **6** muscle firmness or strength ▢ *verb* **1** (sometimes with **in**) blend, fit in well **2** (with **down**) make or become softer **3** (with **up**) give strength to (muscles *etc*)

tongs *noun plural* an instrument for lifting and grasping coals, sugar lumps *etc*

tongue *noun* **1** the fleshy organ inside the mouth, used in tasting, speaking, and swallowing **2** a flap in a shoe **3** a long, thin strip of land **4** the tongue of an animal served as food **5** a language: *his mother tongue* ▢ **tongue-tied** *adj* not able to speak freely ▢ **tongue-twister** *noun* a phrase, sentence *etc* not easy to say quickly, *eg* 'she sells sea shells'

tonic *noun* **1** a medicine which gives strength and energy **2** *music* the keynote of a scale **3** tonic water ▢ *adj* **1** of tones or sounds **2** of a tonic ▢ **tonic water** aerated water with quinine

tonight *adv* & *noun* (on) the night of the present day

tonnage *noun* the space available in a ship, measured in tons

tonne *another spelling* of **ton**

tonsil *noun* one of a pair of soft, fleshy lumps at the back of the throat ▢ **tonsillitis** *noun* reddening and painfulness of the tonsils

tonsure *noun* **1** the shaving of the top of the head of priests and monks **2** the part of the head so shaved

too *adv* **1** to a greater extent, in a greater quantity *etc* than is wanted: *too hot to go outside/ too many people in the room* **2** (with a negative) very, particularly: *not feeling too well* (*ie* not feeling very well) **3** also, as well: *I'm feeling quite cold, too*

took *past form* of **take**

tool *noun* an instrument for doing work, *esp* by hand

toot *noun* the sound of a car horn *etc*

tooth *noun* (*plural* **teeth**) *noun* **1** any of the hard, bony objects projecting from the gums, arranged in two rows in the mouth **2** any of the points on a saw, cogwheel, comb *etc* ▢ **toothache** *noun* pain in a tooth ▢ **toothpaste** or **tooth-powder** *noun* paste or powder for cleaning the teeth ▢ **toothpick** *noun* a small sharp instrument for picking out food from between the teeth ▢ **toothsome** *adj* pleasant to the taste ▢ **tooth and nail** fiercely, determinedly

top *noun* **1** the highest part of anything **2** the upper surface **3** the highest place or rank **4** a lid **5** a circus tent **6** a kind of spinning toy ▢ *adj* highest, chief ▢ *verb* **1** cover on the top **2** rise above **3** do better than **4** reach the top of **5** take off the top of ▢ **topboot** *noun* a tall boot with a light-coloured band round the top ▢ **topcoat** *noun* an overcoat ▢ **top dog** *informal* a winner or leader ▢ **top hat** a man's tall silk hat ▯ **top-heavy** *adj* having the upper part too heavy for the lower ▯ **topmost** *adj* highest, uppermost ▯ **topnotch** *adj* of the highest quality ▯ **top-secret** *adj* (of information *etc*) very secret

top *verb* » top*s*, topp*ing*, topp*ed*

topaz *noun* a type of precious stone, of various colours

topi or **topee** *noun* a helmet-like hat used as a protection against the sun

topiary *noun* the art of trimming bushes, hedges *etc* into decorative shapes

topic *noun* a subject spoken or written about

topical *adj* of current interest, concerned with present events ▯ **topicalness** *noun*

topography *noun* the description of the features of the land in a certain region ▯ **topographical** *adj*

topple *verb* become unsteady and fall

topsyturvy *adj* & *adv* turned upside down

torch *noun* (*plural* **torches**) **1** a small hand-held light with a switch and electric battery **2** a flaming piece of wood or coarse rope carried as a light in processions ▯ *verb, slang* set fire to deliberately

tore *past form* of **tear**

toreador *noun* a bullfighter mounted on horseback

torment *verb* **1** treat cruelly and make suffer **2** worry greatly **3** tease ▯ *noun* **1** great pain, suffering **2** a cause of these ▯ **tormentor** *noun*

torn *past participle* of **tear**

tornado *noun* (*plural* **tornadoes**) a violent whirling wind that causes great damage

torpedo *noun* (*plural* **torpedoes**) a large cigar-shaped type of missile fired by ships, planes *etc* ▯ *verb* hit or sink (a ship) with a torpedo

torpedo *verb* » torpedo*es*, torpedo*ing*, torpedo*ed*

torpid *adj* slow, dull, stupid ▯ **torpidity** or **torpor** *noun* dullness

torrent *noun* **1** a rushing stream **2** a heavy downpour of rain **3** a violent flow of words *etc*: *torrent of abuse*

torrential *adj* like a torrent; rushing violently

torrid *adj* **1** parched by heat; very hot **2** very passionate: *torrid love affair*

torsion *noun* twisting; a twist

torso *noun* (*plural* **torsos**) the body, excluding the head and limbs

tortilla *noun* a Mexican flat round cake made from wheat or maize

tortoise *noun* a four-footed, slow-moving kind of reptile, covered with a hard shell ▯ **tortoiseshell** *noun* the shell of a kind of sea turtle, used in making ornamental articles ▯ *adj* **1** made of this shell **2** mottled brown, yellow and black: *a tortoiseshell cat*

tortuous *adj* winding, roundabout, not straightforward

torture *verb* **1** treat someone cruelly as a punishment or to force them to confess something **2** cause to suffer □ *noun* **1** the act of torturing **2** great suffering

Tory *noun* (*plural* **Tories**) a member of the British Conservative Party

> Originally one of a group of Irish Catholics thrown off their land who waged guerrilla war on British settlers, later applied to any royalist supporter

toss *verb* **1** throw up in the air **2** throw up (a coin) to see which side falls uppermost **3** turn restlessly from side to side **4** of a ship: be thrown about by rough water □ **toss-up** *noun* an equal choice or chance □ **toss off 1** produce quickly **2** *slang* masturbate □ **toss up** toss a coin

tot[1] *noun* **1** a little child **2** a small amount of alcoholic spirits

tot[2] *verb*: **tot up** add up

total *adj* **1** whole: *total number* **2** complete: *total wreck* □ *noun* **1** the entire amount **2** the sum of amounts added together □ *verb* **1** add up **2** amount to **3** *informal* damage irreparably; wreck □ **totally** *adv* completely

> **total** *verb* » total*s*, totall*ing*, totall*ed*

totalitarian *adj* governed by a single party that allows no rivals

totem *noun* an image of an animal or plant used as the badge or sign of a Native American tribe □ **totem pole** a pole on which totems are carved and painted

totter *verb* **1** shake as if about to fall **2** stagger

toucan *noun* a type of S American bird with a very big beak

touch *verb* **1** feel (with the hand) **2** come or be in contact (with): *a leaf touched his cheek* **3** move, affect the feelings of: *the story touched those who heard it* **4** mark slightly with colour: *touched with gold* **5** reach the standard of: *I can't touch him at chess* **6** have anything to do with: *I wouldn't touch a job like that* **7** eat or drink: *he won't touch meat* **8** concern (someone) **9** *informal* persuade (someone) to lend you money: *I touched him for £10* □ *noun* **1** the act of touching **2** the physical sense of touch **3** a small quantity or degree: *a touch of salt* **4** of an artist, pianist *etc*: skill or style **5** *football* the ground beyond the edges of the pitch marked off by **touchlines** □ **touch-and-go** *adj* very uncertain: *it's touch-and-go whether we'll get it done on time* □ **touching** *prep* about, concerning □ *adj* causing emotion, moving □ **touchstone** *noun* a test or standard of measurement of quality *etc* □ **in** (or **out of**) **touch with** in (or not in) communication or contact with □ **touch down** of an aircraft: land □ **touch off** cause to happen □ **touch on** mention briefly □ **touch up** improve (a drawing or photograph *etc*) by making details clearer *etc*

touché /too*sheh*/ *exclam* acknowledging a point scored in a game or argument

touchy *adj* easily offended □ **touchily** *adv* □ **touchiness** *noun*

tough *adj* **1** strong, not easily broken **2** of meat *etc:* hard to chew **3** of strong character, able to stand hardship or strain **4** difficult to cope with or overcome: *tough opposition* ▫ **toughen** *verb* (cause to) become tough

toupee *noun* a small wig or piece of false hair worn to cover a bald spot

tour *noun* a journey in which you visit various places; a pleasure trip ▫ *verb* make a tour (of) ▫ **tourism** *noun* the activities of tourists and of those who cater for their needs ▫ **tourist** *noun* someone who travels for pleasure, and visits places of interest

tour de force an outstanding effort or accomplishment

tournament *noun* **1** a competition involving many contests and players **2** *hist* a meeting at which knights fought together on horseback

tourniquet /*toor*nikeh/ *noun* a bandage tied tightly round a limb to prevent loss of blood from a wound

tousled *adj* of hair: untidy, tangled

tout *verb* go about looking for support, votes, buyers *etc* ▫ *noun* **1** someone who does this **2** someone who gives tips to people who bet on horse races

tow *verb* pull (a car etc) with a rope attached to another vehicle ▫ *noun* **1** the act of towing **2** the rope used for towing ▫ **towpath** *noun* a path alongside a canal used by horses which tow barges ▫ **in tow** under protection or guidance ▫ **on tow** being towed

towards or **toward** *prep* **1** moving in the direction of (a place, person *etc*): *walking towards the house* **2** to (a person, thing *etc*): *his attitude towards his son* **3** as a help or contribution to: *I gave £5 towards the cost* **4** near, about (a time *etc*): *towards four o'clock*

towel *noun* a cloth for drying or wiping (*eg* the skin after washing) ▫ *verb* rub dry with a towel ▫ **towelling** *noun* a cotton cloth often used for making towels

> **towel** *verb* » towel*s*, towell*ing*, towell*ed*

tower *noun* **1** a high narrow building **2** a high narrow part of a castle *etc* ▫ *verb* rise high (over, above) ▫ **towering** *adj* **1** rising high **2** violent: *a towering rage*

town *noun* a place, larger than a village, which includes many buildings, houses, shops *etc* ▫ **town crier** *hist* someone who made public announcements in a town ▫ **town hall** the building where the official business of a town is done ▫ **town planning** planning of the future development of a town

toxaemia *noun* poisoning

toxic *adj* **1** poisonous **2** caused by poison ▫ **toxicology** *noun*

toxin *noun* a naturally-occurring poison

toy *noun* **1** an object for a child to play with **2** an object for amusement only ▫ **toy-boy** *noun, informa* a young male companion of an older woman ◻ **toy with** play or trifle with

trace *noun* **1** a mark or sign left behind **2** a footprint **3** a small amount **4** a line drawn by an instrument recording a change (*eg* in temperature) **5** (**traces**) the straps by which a horse pulls a cart *etc* along ◻ *verb* **1** follow the tracks or course of **2** copy (a drawing *etc*) on transparent paper placed over it ◻ **traceable** *adj* able to be traced (to) ◻ **tracery** *noun* decorated stonework holding the glass in some church windows ◻ **tracing** *noun* a traced copy

trachea *noun* the windpipe

trachoma *noun* an eye disease

track *noun* **1** a mark left **2** (tracks) footprints **3** a path or rough road **4** a racecourse for runners, cyclists *etc* **5** a railway line **6** an endless band on which wheels of a tank *etc* travel ◻ *verb* follow (an animal) by its footprints and other marks left ◻ **trackball** *noun* a rotating ball in a computer keyboard which controls cursor movement ◻ **tracksuit** *noun* a warm suit worn while jogging, before and after an athletic performance *etc* ◻ **keep** or **lose track of** keep or fail to keep aware of the whereabouts or progress of ◻ **make tracks for** set off towards ◻ **track down** search for (someone or something) until caught or found

tract *noun* **1** a stretch of land **2** a short pamphlet, *esp* on a religious subject **3** a system made up of connected parts of the body: *the digestive tract*

tractable *adj* easily made to do what is wanted

traction *noun* **1** the act of pulling or dragging **2** the state of being pulled ◻ **traction engine** a road steam-engine

tractor *noun* a motor vehicle for pulling loads, ploughs *etc*

trade *noun* **1** the buying and selling of goods **2** someone's occupation, craft, job: *a carpenter by trade* ◻ *verb* **1** buy and sell **2** have business dealings (with) **3** deal (in) **4** exchange, swap ◻ **trademark** *noun* a registered mark or name put on goods to show that they are made by a certain company ◻ **trader** *noun* someone who buys and sells ◻ **tradesman** *noun* **1** a shopkeeper **2** a workman in a skilled trade ◻ **trade union** a group of workers of the same trade who join together to bargain with employers for fair wages *etc* ◻ **trade unionist** a member of a trade union ◻ **trade-wind** *noun* a wind which blows towards the equator (from the north-east and south-east) ◻ **trade in** give as part-payment for something else (*eg* an old car for a new one) ◻ **trade on** take advantage of, often unfairly

tradition *noun* **1** the handing-down of customs, beliefs, stories *etc* from generation to generation **2** a custom, belief *etc* handed down in this way ◻ **traditional** *adj* ◻ **traditionalist** *noun* someone who believes in maintaining traditions

traffic *noun* **1** the motor-cars, buses, boats *etc* which use roads or waterways **2** trade **3** dishonest dealings (*eg* in drugs) ◻ *verb* **1** trade **2** deal (in) ◻ **traffic lights** lights of changing colours for controlling traffic at road junctions or street crossings

traffic *verb* » traffic*s*, traffick*ing*, traffick*ed*

tragedy *noun* (*plural* **tragedies**) **1** a very sad event **2** a play about unhappy events and with a sad ending ◻ **tragedian** *noun* ◻ **tragic** *adj* of tragedy; very sad ◻ **tragically** *adv*

trail *verb* **1** draw along, in or through: *trailing his foot through the water* **2** hang down (from) or be dragged loosely behind **3** hunt (animals) by following footprints *etc* **4** walk wearily **5** of a plant: grow over the ground or a wall ◻ *noun* **1** an animal's track **2** a pathway through a wild region **3** something left stretching behind: *a trail of dust* ◻ **trailer** *noun* **1** a vehicle pulled behind a motor-car **2** a short film advertising a longer film to be shown at a later date

train *noun* **1** a railway engine with carriages or trucks **2** a part of a dress which trails behind the wearer **3** the attendants who follow an important person **4** a line (of thought, events *etc*) **5** a line of animals carrying people or baggage ◻ *verb* **1** prepare yourself by practice or exercise for a sporting event, job *etc* **2** educate **3** exercise (animals or people) in preparation for a race *etc* **4** tame and teach (an animal) **5** (with **on** or **at**) aim, point (a gun, telescope *etc*) at **6** make (a tree or plant) grow in a certain direction ◻ **trainee** *noun* someone who is being trained ◻ **trainer** *noun* someone who trains people or animals for a sport, circus *etc* ◻ **training** *noun* **1** preparation for a sport **2** experience or learning of the practical side of a job

trait *noun* a point that stands out in a person's character: *patience is one of his good traits*

traitor *noun* **1** someone who goes over to the enemy's side, or gives away secrets to the enemy **2** someone who betrays trust ◻ **traitorous** *adj*

trajectory *noun* (*plural* **trajectories**) the curved path of something (*eg* a bullet) moving through the air or through space

tram *noun* a long car running on rails and driven by electric power for carrying passengers (*also called*: **tramcar**) ◻ **tramline** *noun* **1** a rail of tramway **2** (**tramlines**) *tennis* the parallel lines marked at the sides of the court ◻ **tramway** *noun* a system of tracks on which trams run

trammel *noun* something that hinders movement ◻ *verb* hinder

trammel *verb* » trammel*s*, trammell*ing*, trammell*ed*

tramp *verb* **1** walk with heavy footsteps **2** walk along, over *etc*: *tramping the streets in search of a job* ◻ *noun* **1** someone with no fixed home and no job, who lives by begging **2** a journey made on foot **3** the sound of marching feet **4** a small cargo-boat with no fixed route

trample *verb* **1** tread under foot, stamp on **2** (*usu* with **on**) treat roughly or unfeelingly **3** tread heavily

trampoline *noun* a bed-like framework holding a sheet of elastic material for bouncing on, used by gymnasts *etc*

trance *noun* a sleep-like or half-conscious state

tranquil *adj* quiet, peaceful □ **tranquillity** *noun*

tranquillize *verb* make calm □ **tranquillizer** *noun* a drug to calm the nerves or cause sleep

trans- *prefix* across, through

transact *verb* do (a piece of business) □ **transaction** *noun* a piece of business, a deal

transatlantic *adj* **1** crossing the Atlantic Ocean: *transatlantic yacht race* **2** across or over the Atlantic: *transatlantic friends*

transcend *verb* **1** be, or rise, above **2** be, or do, better than

transcribe *verb* **1** copy from one book into another or from one form of writing (*eg* shorthand) into another **2** adapt (a piece of music) for a particular instrument

transcript *noun* a written copy □ **transcription** *noun* **1** the act of transcribing **2** a written copy

transept *noun* the part of a church which lies across the main part

transexual or **trans-sexual** *noun* a transvestite

transfat *noun* a type of fat found in margarine *etc* produced by artificial hardening of vegetable oil (*also called*: **trans** or **transfatty-acid**)

transfer *verb* **1** remove to another place **2** hand over to another person □ *noun* **1** the act of transferring **2** a design or picture which can be transferred from one surface to another □ **transferable** *adj* able to be transferred □ **transference** *noun*

> **transfer** *verb* » transfer*s*, transferr*ing*, transferr*ed*

transfigure *verb* change (greatly and for the better) the form or appearance of □ **transfiguration** *noun*

transfix *verb* **1** make unable to move or act (*eg* because of surprise): *transfixed by the sight* **2** pierce through (as with a sword)

transform *verb* change in shape or appearance □ **transformation** *noun* □ **transformer** *noun* an apparatus for changing electrical energy from one voltage to another

transfuse *verb* **1** pass (liquid) from one thing to another **2** transfer (blood of one person) to the body of another □ **transfusion** *noun*

transgress *verb* break a rule, law *etc* □ **transgression** *noun* the act of breaking a rule, law *etc*; a sin □ **transgressor** *noun* someone who breaks a rule, law *etc*

transient *adj* not lasting, passing □ **transience** *noun*

transistor *noun* **1** a small device, made up of a crystal enclosed in plastic or metal, which controls the flow of an electrical current **2** a portable radio set using these

transit *noun* **1** the carrying or movement of goods, passengers *etc* from place to place **2** the passing of a planet between the sun and the earth □ **transition** *noun* a change from one form, place, appearance *etc* to another □ **transitional** *adj* □ **transitory** *adj* lasting only for a short time

transitive *adj, grammar* of a verb: having an object, *eg* the verb '*hit*' in 'he *hit* the ball')

translate *verb* turn (something said or written) into another language □ **translation** *noun* **1** the act of translating **2** something translated □ **translator** *noun* someone who translates

transliterate *verb* write (a word) in the letters of another alphabet

translucent *adj* allowing light to pass through, but not transparent □ **translucence** *noun*

transmit *verb* **1** pass on (a message, news, heat) **2** send out signals which are received as programmes □ **transmission** *noun* **1** the act of transmitting **2** a radio or television broadcast □ **transmitter** *noun* an instrument for transmitting (*esp* radio signals)

> **transmit** » transmit*s*, transmitt*ing*, transmitt*ed*

transnational *noun* a company with divisions in several different countries

transom *noun* a beam across a window or the top of a door

transparency *noun* (*plural* **transparencies**) **1** the state of being transparent **2** a photograph printed on transparent material and viewed by shining light through it

transparent *adj* **1** able to be seen through **2** easily seen to be true or false: *a transparent excuse*

transpire *verb* **1** of a secret: become known **2** happen: *tell me what transpired* **3** let out (moisture *etc*) through pores of the skin or through the surface of leaves

transplant *verb* **1** lift and plant (a growing plant) in another place **2** remove (skin) and graft it on another part of the same body **3** remove (an organ) and graft it in another person or animal □ *noun* **1** the act of transplanting **2** a transplanted organ, plant *etc* □ **transplantation** *noun*

transport *verb* **1** carry from one place to another **2** overcome with strong feeling: *transported with delight* **3** *hist* send (a prisoner) to a prison in a different country □ *noun* **1** the act of transporting **2** any means of carrying persons or goods: *rail transport* **3** strong feeling: *transports of joy* □ **transportation** *noun* **1** the act of transporting **2** means of transport **3** *hist* punishment of prisoners by sending them to a prison in a different country

transpose *verb* **1** cause (two things) to change places **2** change (a piece of music) from one key to another □ **transposition** *noun*

trans-sexual *another spelling of* **transexual**

transubstantiate *verb* change into a different substance

transverse *adj* lying, placed *etc* across: *transverse beams in the roof*

transvestite *noun* someone who likes to wear clothes intended for the opposite sex

trap *noun* **1** a device for catching animals *etc* **2** a plan or trick for taking someone by surprise **3** a bend in a pipe which is kept full of water, for preventing the escape of air or gas **4** a carriage with two wheels □ *verb* catch in a trap, or in such a way that escape is not possible □ **trapdoor** *noun* a door in a floor or ceiling □ **trapper** *noun* someone who makes a living by catching animals for their skins and fur

> **trap** *verb* » trap*s*, trapp*ing*, trapp*ed*

trapeze *noun* a swing used in performing gymnastic exercises or feats

trapezium *noun* a figure with four sides, two of which are parallel

trappings *noun plural* **1** clothes or ornaments suitable for a particular person or occasion **2** ornaments put on horses

Trappist *noun* a monk of an order whose members have taken a vow of silence

trash *noun* something of little worth, rubbish □ **trashy** *adj*

trauma *noun* **1** injury to the body **2** a very violent or distressing experience which has a lasting effect **3** a condition (of a person) caused in this way □ **traumatic** *adj*

travail *noun*, *old* hard work

travel *verb* **1** go on a journey **2** move **3** go along, across **4** visit foreign countries □ *noun* the act of travelling □ **traveller** *noun* **1** someone who travels **2** a travelling representative of a business firm who tries to obtain orders for his firm's products

> **travel** *verb* » travel*s*, travell*ing*, travell*ed*

traverse *verb* go across, pass through □ *noun* **1** something that crosses or lies across **2** a going across a rock face *etc* **3** a zigzag track of a ship

travesty *noun* (*plural* **travesties**) a poor or ridiculous imitation: *a travesty of justice*

trawl *verb* fish by dragging a trawl along the bottom of the sea □ *noun* a wide-mouthed, bag-shaped net □ **trawler** *noun* a boat used for trawling

tray *noun* a flat piece of wood, metal *etc* with a low edge, for carrying dishes

treachery *noun* (*plural* **treacheries**) the act of betraying those who have trusted you □ **treacherous** *adj* **1** likely to betray **2** dangerous: *treacherous road conditions* □ **treacherously** *adv*

treacle *noun* a thick, dark syrup produced from sugar when it is being refined

tread *verb* **1** walk on or along **2** (with **on**) put your foot on **3** crush, trample under foot □ *noun* **1** a step

2 a way of walking **3** the part of a tyre which touches the ground □ **treadle** *noun* part of a machine which is worked by the foot □ **treadmill** *noun* **1** *hist* a mill turned by the weight of people who were made to walk on steps fixed round a big wheel **2** any tiring, routine work □ **tread on someone's toes** offend or upset them □ **tread water** keep yourself afloat in an upright position by moving your arms and legs

> **tread** *verb* » tread*s*, tread*ing*, trodden, trod

treason *noun* disloyalty to your own country or its government, *eg* by giving away its secrets to an enemy □ **treasonable** *adj* consisting of, or involving, treason

treasure *noun* **1** a store of money, gold *etc* **2** anything of great value or highly prized □ *verb* **1** value greatly **2** keep carefully because of its personal value: *she treasures the mirror her mother left her* □ **treasurer** *noun* someone who has charge of the money of a club □ **treasure-trove** *noun* treasure or money found hidden, the owner of which is unknown □ **Treasury** or **treasury** *noun* (*plural* **treasuries**) the part of a government which has charge of the country's money

treat *verb* **1** deal with, handle, act towards: *I was treated very well in prison* **2** try to cure (someone) of a disease **3** try to cure (a disease) **4** write or speak about **5** buy (someone) a meal, drink *etc* **6** try to arrange (a peace treaty *etc*) with □ *noun* something special (*eg* an outing) that gives much pleasure: *they went to the theatre as a treat* □ **treatment** *noun* **1** the act of treating (*eg* a disease) **2** remedy, medicine: *a new treatment for cancer* **3** the way in which someone or something is dealt with: *rough treatment*

treatise *noun* a long, detailed essay *etc* on some subject

treaty *noun* (*plural* **treaties**) an agreement made between countries

treble *adj* **1** threefold, three times normal: *wood of treble thickness* **2** high in pitch: *treble note* □ *verb* become three times as great □ *noun* **1** the highest part in singing **2** a child who sings the treble part of a song

tree *noun* **1** the largest kind of plant with a thick, firm wooden stem and branches **2** anything like a tree in shape

trefoil *noun* a three-part leaf or decoration

trek *noun* **1** a long or wearisome journey **2** *old* a journey by wagon □ *verb* **1** make a long hard journey **2** *old* make a journey by wagon

> **trek** *verb* » trek*s*, trekk*ing*, trekk*ed*

trellis *noun* (*plural* **trellises**) a network of strips for holding up growing plants

tremble *verb* **1** shake with cold, fear, weakness **2** feel fear (for another person's safety *etc*) □ *noun* **1** the act of trembling **2** a fit of trembling

tremendous *adj* **1** very great o

strong **2** *informal* very good, excellent □ **tremendously** *adv*, *informal* very

tremolo *noun* (*plural* **tremolos**) *music* rapid repetition of the same note giving a trembling sound

tremor *noun* a shaking or quivering

tremulous *adj* **1** shaking **2** showing fear: *a tremulous voice*

trench *noun* (*plural* **trenches**) a long narrow ditch dug in the ground (*eg* by soldiers as a protection against enemy fire) □ *verb* dig a trench in □ **trenchcoat** *noun* a kind of waterproof overcoat with a belt

trenchant *adj* **1** going deep, hurting: *a trenchant remark* **2** of a policy *etc*: effective, vigorous

trencher *noun*, *old* a wooden plate □ **trencherman** *noun* someone able to eat large meals: *a good trencherman*

trend *noun* a general direction: *the trend of events* □ **trendy** *adj*, *informal* fashionable

trepan *verb*, *med* remove a piece of the skull from

> **trepan** » trepan*s*, trepann*ing*, trepann*ed*

trepidation *noun* fear, nervousness

trespass *verb* **1** go illegally on private land *etc* **2** (with **on**) demand too much of: *trespassing on my time* **3** sin □ *noun* (*plural* **trespasses**) the act of trespassing □ **trespasser** *noun*

tress *noun* (*plural* **tresses**) **1** a lock of hair **2** (**tresses**) hair, *esp* long

trestle *noun* a wooden support with legs, used for holding up a table, platform *etc*

trews *noun plural* tartan trousers

tri- *prefix* three

trial *noun* **1** the act of testing or trying (*eg* something new) **2** a test **3** the judging (of a prisoner) in a court of law **4** suffering □ **on trial 1** being tried (*esp* in a court of law) **2** for the purpose of trying out: *goods sent on trial* **3** being tested: *I'm still on trial with the company* □ **trial and error** the trying of various methods or choices until the right one is found

triangle *noun* **1** a figure with three sides and three angles: △ **2** a triangular metal musical instrument, played by striking with a small rod □ **triangular** *adj* having the shape of a triangle

triathlon *noun* a sporting contest consisting of three events, often swimming, running and cycling

tribe *noun* **1** a people who are all descended from the same ancestor **2** a group of families, *esp* of a wandering people ruled by a chief □ **tribal** *adj* □ **tribesman, tribeswoman** *noun*

tribulation *noun* great hardship or sorrow

tribunal *noun* **1** a group of people appointed to give judgement, *esp* on an appeal **2** a court of justice

tribune *noun*, *hist* a high official elected by the people in ancient Rome

tributary *noun* (*plural* **tributaries**) **1** a stream that flows into a river or other stream **2** someone who gives money as a tribute

tribute *noun* **1** an expression, in word or deed, of praise, thanks *etc*: *a warm tribute to his courage* **2** money paid regularly by one nation or ruler to another in return for protection or peace

trice *noun*: **in a trice** in a very short time

triceps *noun* a muscle at the back of the arm that straightens the elbow

trick *noun* **1** a cunning or skilful action to puzzle, amuse *etc* **2** in card games, the cards picked up by the winner when each player has played a card □ *adj* meant to deceive: *trick photography* □ *verb* cheat by some quick or cunning action □ **trickery** *noun* cheating □ **trickster** *noun* someone who deceives by tricks □ **tricky** *adj* not easy to do

trickle *verb* **1** flow in small amounts **2** arrive or leave slowly and gradually: *replies are trickling in* □ *noun* a slow, gradual flow

tricolour or *US* **tricolor** *noun* the flag of France, consisting of three upright stripes of red, white and blue

tricycle *noun* a three-wheeled bicycle

trident *noun* a three-pronged spear

tried *past form* of **try**

triennial *adj* **1** lasting for three years **2** happening every third year

tries *see* **try**

trifle *noun* **1** anything of little value **2** a small amount **3** a pudding of whipped cream, sponge-cake, wine *etc* □ *verb* **1** (with **with**) act towards without sufficient respect: *in no mood to be trifled with* **2** amuse yourself in an idle way (with): *he trifled with her affections* **3** behave in a light, thoughtless manner

trifling *adj* very small in value or amount

trigger *noun* **1** a small lever on a gun which, when pulled with the finger, causes the bullet to be fired □ *verb* (with **off**) start, be the cause of, an important event, chain of events *etc*

trigonometry *noun* the branch of mathematics which has to do chiefly with the relationship between the sides and angles of triangles □ **trigonometric** or **trigonometrical** *adj*

trilby *noun* a man's hat with an indented crown and narrow brim

> So called because a hat of this shape was worn by an actress in the original stage version of George du Maurier's novel, *Trilby* (1894)

trill *verb* sing, play or utter in a quivering or bird-like way □ *noun* a trilled sound; in music, a rapid repeating of two notes several times

trillion **1** a million million millions **2** (originally *US*) a million millions

trilobite *noun* a fossil whose body forms three long furrows

trilogy (*plural* **trilogies**) a group of

three related plays, novels *etc* by the same author, meant to be seen or read as a whole

trim *verb* **1** clip the edges or ends of: *trim the hedge* **2** arrange (sails, cargo) so that a boat is ready for sailing **3** decorate (*eg* a hat) ◇ *noun* **1** the act of trimming **2** dress: *hunting trim* ◇ *adj* tidy, in good order, neat ◇ **in good trim 1** in good order **2** fit

> **trim** *verb* » trim*s*, trimm*ing*, trimm*ed*

trimming *noun* **1** a decoration added to a dress, cake *etc* **2** a piece of cloth, hair *etc* cut off while trimming

Trinity *noun* in Christianity, the union of Father, Son and Holy Ghost in one God

trinket *noun* a small ornament (*esp* one of little value)

trio *noun* (*plural* **trios**) **1** three performers **2** three people or things

trip *verb* **1** (often with **up**) stumble, fall over **2** move with short, light steps **3** (with **up**) make a mistake ◇ *noun* **1** a journey for pleasure or business **2** a light short step ◇ **tripper** *noun* someone who goes on a short pleasure trip

> **trip** *verb* » trip*s*, tripp*ing*, tripp*ed*

tripartite *adj* **1** in or having three parts **2** of an agreement: between three countries

tripe *noun* **1** part of the stomach of the cow or sheep used as food **2** *informal* rubbish, nonsense

triple *adj* **1** made up of three **2** three times as large (as something else) ◇ *verb* make or become three times as large

triplet *noun* **1** one of three children or animals born of the same mother at one time **2** three rhyming lines in a poem **3** *music* a group of three notes played in the time of two

triplicate *noun*: **in triplicate** in three copies

tripod *noun* a three-legged stand (*esp* for a camera)

triptych *noun* three painted panels forming a whole work of art

trisect *verb* cut into three ◇ **trisection** *noun*

triskaidekaphobia *noun* fear of the number thirteen ◇ **triskaidekaphobic** *adj*

trite *adj* of a remark: used so often that it has little force or meaning

triumph *noun* **1** a great success or victory **2** celebration after a success: *ride in triumph through the streets* ◇ *verb* **1** win a victory **2** rejoice openly because of a victory ◇ **triumphal** *adj* used in celebrating a triumph ◇ **triumphant** *adj* victorious; showing joy because of, or celebrating, triumph ◇ **triumphantly** *adv*

trivet *noun* a metal tripod for resting a teapot or kettle on

trivia *noun plural* unimportant matters or details

trivial *adj* of very little importance ◇ **triviality** *noun* (*plural* **trivialities**)

1 something unimportant **2** trivialness ▯ **trivialness** *noun* the state of being trivial

trod and **trodden** *see* **tread**

troglodyte *noun* a cave-dweller

trojan *noun*, *comput* a type of computer virus

troll *noun* a mythological creature, giant or dwarf, who lives in a cave

trolley *noun* (*plural* **trolleys**) **1** a small cart (*eg* as used by porters at railway stations) **2** a supermarket basket on wheels **3** a hospital bed on wheels for transporting patients **4** a table on wheels, used for serving tea *etc* ▯ **trolley-bus** *noun* a bus which gets its power from overhead wires

trollop *noun* **1** a careless, untidy woman **2** a sexually promiscuous woman

trombone *noun* a brass wind instrument with a sliding tube which changes the notes

trompe l'oeil an optical illusion

troop *noun* **1** a collection of people or animals **2** (**troops**) soldiers **3** a unit in cavalry *etc* ▯ *verb* **1** gather in numbers **2** go in a group: *they all trooped out* ▯ **trooper** *noun* a horse-soldier ▯ **troopship** *noun* a ship for carrying soldiers ▯ **troop the colours** carry a regiment's flag past the lined-up soldiers of the regiment

trope *noun* a figure of speech

trophy *noun* (*plural* **trophies**) **1** something taken from an enemy and kept in memory of the victory **2** a prize such as a silver cup won in a sports competition *etc*

tropic *noun* **1** either of two imaginary circles running round the earth at about 23 degrees north (**Tropic of Cancer**) or south (**Tropic of Capricorn**) of the equator **2** (**tropics**) the hot regions near or between these circles ▯ *adj* (also **tropical**) **1** of the tropics **2** growing in hot countries: *tropical fruit* **3** very hot

trot *verb* **1** of a horse: run with short, high steps **2** of a person: run slowly with short steps **3** make (a horse) trot ▯ *noun* the pace of a horse or person when trotting ▯ **trotters** *noun plural* the feet of pigs or sheep, *esp* when used as food

> **trot** *verb* » trot*s*, trott*ing*, trott*ed*

troubadour *noun, hist* a medieval travelling singer-musician, *esp* in France

trouble *verb* **1** cause worry or sorrow to **2** cause inconvenience to **3** make an effort, bother (to): *I didn't trouble to ring him* ▯ *noun* **1** worry, uneasiness **2** difficulty; disturbance **3** something which causes worry, difficulty *etc* **4** a disease **5** care and effort put into doing something ▯ **troubleshooter** *noun* someone whose job is to solve difficulties (*eg* in a firm's business activities) ▯ **troublesome** *adj* causing difficulty or inconvenience

trough *noun* **1** a long, open container for holding animals' food and water **2** an area of low atmospheric pressure **3** a dip between two sea waves

trounce *verb* **1** punish or beat severely **2** defeat heavily

troupe /troop/ *noun* a company of actors, dancers *etc* □ **trouper** *noun* a member of a troupe

trousers *noun plural* an outer garment for the lower part of the body which covers each leg separately □ **trouser** *adj* of a pair of trousers: *trouser leg*

trousseau *noun* (*plural* **trousseaux** or **trousseaus**) a bride's outfit for her wedding

trout *noun* a freshwater or sea (**sea-trout**) fish, used as food

trowel *noun* **1** a small spade used in gardening **2** a similar tool with a flat blade, used for spreading mortar

troy weight a system of weights for weighing gold, gems *etc*

truant *noun* someone who stays away from school *etc* without permission □ **truancy** *noun* □ **play truant** stay away from school, work *etc* without permission *etc*

truce *noun* a rest from fighting or quarrelling agreed to by both sides

truck *noun* **1** a wagon for carrying goods on a railway **2** a strong lorry for carrying heavy loads □ **trucker** *noun, US* a lorry driver □ **have no truck with** refuse to have dealings with

truculent *adj* fierce and threatening, aggressive □ **truculence** *noun*

trudge *verb* walk with heavy steps, as if tired

true *adj* **1** of a story *etc*: telling of something which really happened **2** correct, not invented or wrong: *it's true that the earth is round* **3** accurate **4** faithful: *a true friend* **5** real, properly so called: *the spider is not a true insect* **6** rightful: *the true heir* **7** in the correct or intended position □ **truism** *noun* a statement which is so clearly true that it is not worth making □ **truly** *adj*

truffle *noun* a round fungus found underground and much valued as a flavouring for food

trug *noun* a shallow basket used in gardening

trump *noun* **1** a suit having a higher value than cards of other suits **2** a card of this suit □ *verb* play a card which is a trump □ **trump card 1** a card which is a trump **2** something kept in reserve as a means of winning an argument *etc* □ **trump up** make up, invent □ **turn up trumps** play your part well when things are difficult

trumpery *noun* (*plural* **trumperies**) something showy but worthless

trumpet *noun* **1** a brass musical instrument with a clear, high-pitched tone **2** the cry of an elephant □ *verb* **1** announce (*eg* news) so that all may hear **2** to blow a trumpet

truncated *adj* **1** cut off at the top or end **2** shortened*: a truncated version*

truncheon *noun* a short heavy staff or baton such as that used by police officers

trundle *verb* wheel or roll along

trunk *noun* **1** the main stem of a

tree 2 the body (not counting the head, arms, or legs) of someone or an animal **3** the long nose of an elephant **4** a large box or chest for clothes *etc* **5** *US* the luggage compartment of a motor-car **6** (**trunks**) short pants worn by boys and men for swimming □ **trunkcall** *noun* the former name for a **national call** □ **trunk road** a main road

truss *noun* (*plural* **trusses**) **1** a bundle (*eg* of hay, straw) **2** a system of beams to support a bridge **3** a kind of supporting bandage □ *verb* **1** bind, tie tightly (up) **2** (often with **up**) prepare (a bird ready for cooking) by tying up the legs and wings

trust *noun* **1** belief in the power, truth or goodness of a thing or person **2** a task, a valuable handed over to someone in the belief that they will do it, guard it *etc* **3** charge, keeping: *the child was put in my trust* **4** arrangement by which something (*eg* money) is given to someone for use in a particular way **5** a number of business firms working closely together □ *verb* **1** have faith or confidence (in) **2** give (someone something) in the belief that they will use it well *etc*: *I can't trust your sister with my tennis racket* **3** feel confident (that): *I trust that you can find your way here* □ **trustee** *noun* someone who keeps something in trust for another □ **trustful** *adj* □ **trusting** *adj* ready to trust, not suspicious □ **trustworthy** *adj* □ **trusty** *adj* able to be depended on □ **take on trust** believe without checking or testing

truth *noun* **1** the state of being true **2** a true statement **3** the facts □ **truthful** *adj* **1** telling the truth, not lying **2** of a statement: true □ **truthfully** *adv* □ **truthfulness** *noun*

try *verb* **1** attempt, make an effort (to do something) **2** test by using: *try this new soap* **3** test severely, strain: *you're trying my patience* **4** attempt to use, open *etc*: *I tried the door but it was locked* **5** judge (a prisoner) in a court of law □ *noun* (*plural* **tries**) **1** an effort, an attempt **2** one of the ways of scoring in Rugby football □ **trying** *adj* hard to bear; testing □ **try on** put on (clothing) to see if it fits *etc* □ **try out** test by using

try *verb* » tri*es*, try*ing*, tri*ed*

tryst *noun*, *old* an arrangement to meet someone at a certain place

tsar or **tzar** or **czar** *noun, hist* the emperor of pre-revolutionary Russia

tsarina or **tzarina** or **czarina** *noun, hist* **1** the wife of a tsar **2** an empress of Russia

tsetse /*tet*si/ *noun* or **tsetse fly** an African biting fly which spreads dangerous diseases

T-shirt *another spelling* of **tee-shirt**

tsunami *noun* a large sea wave caused by an earthquake

TT *abbrev* **1** Tourist Trophy **2** tuberculin tested **3** teetotal

tub *noun* **1** a round wooden container used for washing *etc*; a bath **2** a round container for ice-cream *etc*

tuba *noun* a large brass musical

instrument giving a low note

tubby *adj* fat and round

tube *noun* **1** a hollow, cylinder-shaped object through which liquid may pass **2** an organ of this kind in humans, animals *etc* **3** a container from which something may be squeezed **4** an underground railway system **5** a cathode ray tube □ **tubing** *noun* a length or lengths of tube □ **tubular** *adj* shaped like a tube

tuber *noun* a swelling on the underground stem of a plant (*eg* a potato)

tuberculosis *noun* an infectious disease affecting the lungs

TUC *abbrev* Trades Union Congress

tuck *noun* **1** a fold stitched in a piece of cloth **2** *informal* sweets, cakes *etc* □ *verb* **1** gather (cloth) together into a fold **2** fold or push (into or under a place) **3** (with **in** or **up**) push bedclothes closely round (someone in bed) □ **tuck shop** a shop in a school where sweets, cakes *etc* are sold □ **tuck in** *informal* to eat with enjoyment or greedily

Tuesday *noun* the third day of the week

tuft *noun* a bunch or clump of grass, hair *etc*

tug *verb* **1** pull hard **2** pull along □ *noun* **1** a strong pull **2** a tugboat □ **tugboat** *noun* a small but powerful ship used for towing larger ones □ **tug-of-war** *noun* a contest in which two sides, holding the ends of a strong rope, pull against each other

> **tug** *verb* » tug*s*, tugg*ing*, tugg*ed*

tuition *noun* **1** teaching **2** private coaching or teaching

tulip *noun* a type of flower with cup-shaped flowers grown from a bulb

> Based on a Persian word for 'turban', because of the similarity in shape

tulle *noun* a kind of cloth made of thin silk or rayon net

tumble *verb* **1** fall or come down suddenly and violently **2** roll, toss (about) **3** do acrobatic tricks **4** throw into disorder □ *noun* **1** a fall **2** a confused state □ **tumbledown** *adj* falling to pieces □ **tumbler** *noun* **1** a large drinking glass **2** an acrobat □ **tumble to** understand suddenly

tumbrel or **tumbril** *noun*, *hist* a two-wheeled cart of the kind used to take victims to the guillotine during the French Revolution

tumescent *adj* swollen, enlarged

tummy *noun* (*plural* **tummies**) *informal* the stomach

tumour *noun* an abnormal growth on or in the body

tumult *noun* **1** a great noise made by a crowd **2** excitement, agitation □ **tumultuous** *adj*

tumulus *noun* an artificial mound of earth, *esp* over a tomb

tun *noun* a large cask, *esp* for wine

tuna *noun* (*plural* **tuna** or **tunas**) a large sea fish, used as food (*also called*: **tunny**)

tundra *noun* a level treeless plain in Arctic regions

tune *noun* **1** notes put together to form a melody **2** the music of a song ◇ *verb* **1** put (a musical instrument) in tune **2** adjust a radio set to a particular station **3** (sometimes with **up**) improve the working of an engine ◇ **tuneful** *adj* having a pleasant or recognizable tune ◇ **tunefully** *adj* ◇ **tuning fork** a steel fork which, when struck, gives a note of a certain pitch ◇ **change your tune** change your opinions, attitudes *etc* ◇ **in tune 1** of a musical instrument: having each note adjusted to agree with the others or with the notes of other instruments **2** of a voice: agreeing with the notes of other voices or instruments **3** in agreement (with) ◇ **to the tune of** to the sum of

tungsten *noun* an element, a grey metal

tunic *noun* **1** a soldier's or police officer's jacket **2** *hist* a loose garment reaching to the knees, worn in ancient Greece and Rome **3** a similar modern garment: *gym tunic*

tunnel *noun* **1** an underground passage (*eg* for a railway train) ◇ *verb* **1** make a tunnel **2** of an animal: burrow

tunnel *verb* » tunnel*s*, tunnell*ing*, tunnell*ed*

tunny *same as* **tuna**

turban *noun* **1** a long piece of cloth wound round the head, worn by Muslims **2** a kind of hat resembling this

turbid *adj* of liquid: muddy, clouded

turbine *noun* an engine with curved blades, turned by the action of water, steam, hot air *etc*

turbo- *prefix* using a turbine engine

turbot *noun* a type of large flat sea fish, used as food

turbulent *adj* **1** disturbed, in a restless state **2** likely to cause a disturbance or riot ◇ **turbulence** *noun* irregular movement of air currents, *esp* when affecting the flight of aircraft

turd *noun* **1** a lump of dung **2** *slang* a despicable person

tureen *noun* a large dish for holding soup at table

turf *noun* **1** grass and the soil below it **2** (with **the**) the world of horse-racing ◇ *verb* cover with turf ◇ **turf out** *informal* to throw out

turgid *adj* **1** swollen **2** of language sounding grand but meaning little, pompous

turkey *noun* (*plural* **turkeys**) a large farmyard bird, used as food

Turkish bath a type of hot air or steam bath in which someone is made to sweat heavily, is massaged and then slowly cooled

turmeric *noun* the yellow powder made from the root of a ginger-ike plant, used as a spice in curries *etc*

turmoil *noun* a state of wild, confused movement or disorder

turn *verb* **1** go round: *wheels turning* **2** face or go in the opposite direction: *turned and walked away* **3** change direction: *the road turns sharply to the left* **4** direct (*eg* attention) **5** (with **on**) to move, swing *etc*: *the door turns on its hinges* **6** of milk: go sour **7** become: *his hair turned white* **8** of leaves: to change colour **9** shape in a lathe **10** pass (the age of): *she must have turned 40* □ *noun* **1** the act of turning **2** a point where someone may change direction, *eg* a road junction: *take the first turn on the left* **3** a bend (*eg* in a road) **4** a spell of duty: *your turn to wash the dishes* **5** an act (*eg* in a circus) **6** a short stroll: *a turn along the beach* **7** a fit of dizziness, shock *etc* **8** requirement: *this will serve our turn* □ **turncoat** *noun* someone who betrays their party, principles *etc* □ **turning** *noun* **1** the act of turning **2** a point where a road *etc* joins another **3** the act of shaping in a lathe □ **turning-point** *noun* a crucial point of change □ **turnover** *noun* **1** rate of change or replacement (*eg* of workers in a firm *etc*) **2** the total amount of sales made by a firm during a certain time □ **turnpike** *noun* **1** *hist* a gate across a road which opened when the user paid a toll **2** *US* a road on which a toll is paid □ **turnstile** *noun* a gate which turns, allowing only one person to pass at a time □ **turntable** *noun* **1** a revolving platform for turning a railway engine round **2** the revolving part of a record-player on which the record rests □ **by turns** or **in turn** one after another in a regular order □ **do someone a good** (or **bad**) **turn** act helpfully (or unhelpfully) towards someone □ **to a turn** exactly, perfectly: *cooked to a turn* □ **turn against** become hostile to □ **turn down 1** say no to, refuse (*eg* an offer, a request) **2** reduce, lessen (heat, volume of sound *etc*) □ **turn in 1** go to bed **2** hand over to those in authority □ **turn off 1** stop the flow of (a tap) **2** switch off the power for (a television *etc*) □ **turn on 1** set running (*eg* water from a tap) **2** switch on power for (a television *etc*) **3** depend (on) **4** become angry with (someone) unexpectedly **5** *slang* arouse sexually □ **turn out 1** make to leave, drive out **2** make, produce **3** empty: *turn out your pockets* **4** of a crowd: come out, gather for a special purpose **5** switch off (a light) **6** prove (to be): *he turned out to be right* □ **turn to 1** set to work **2** go to for help *etc* □ **turn up 1** appear, arrive **2** be found **3** increase (*eg* heat, volume of sound *etc*) □ **turn someone's head** fill them with pride or conceit

turnip *noun* a plant with a large round root used as a vegetable

turpentine *noun* an oil from certain trees used for mixing paints, cleaning paint brushes *etc*

turpitude *noun* wickedness

turquoise *noun* a greenish-blue precious stone

> Literally 'Turkish stone', because first found in Turkestan

turret *noun* **1** a small tower on a castle or other building **2** a structure for supporting guns on a warship □ **turreted** *adj* having turrets

turtle *noun* a kind of large tortoise which lives in water ▯ **turtledove** *noun* a type of dove noted for its sweet, soft song ▯ **turtleneck** *noun* a high, round neck ▯ **turn turtle** of a boat *etc:* turn upside down, capsize

tusk *noun* a large tooth (one of a pair) sticking out from the mouth of certain animals (*eg* an elephant, a walrus)

tussle *noun* a struggle ▯ *verb* struggle, compete

tussock *noun* a tuft of grass

tutelage *noun* the state of being protected by a guardian ▯ **tutelary** *adj* protecting

tutor *noun* **1** a teacher of students in a university *etc* **2** a teacher employed privately to teach individual pupils ▯ *verb* teach ▯ **tutorial** *adj* of a tutor ▯ *noun* a meeting for study or discussion between tutor and students

tutti-frutti *noun* an Italian ice-cream containing nuts and various kinds of fruit

tutu *noun* a ballet dancer's short, stiff, spreading skirt

tuxedo *noun* (*plural* **tuxedos** or **tuxedoes**) *US* a dinner-jacket

TV *abbrev* television

TVP *abbrev* texturized vegetable protein

twaddle *noun, informal* nonsense

twain *noun, old* two ▯ **in twain** *old* in two, apart

twang *noun* **1** a tone of voice in which the words seem to come through the nose **2** a sound like that of a tightly-stretched string being plucked ▯ *verb* make such a sound

twat *noun, taboo slang* **1** the vagina **2** an idiot

tweak *verb* pull with a sudden jerk, twitch ▯ *noun* a sudden jerk or pull

tweed *noun* **1** a woollen cloth with a rough surface **2** (**tweeds**) clothes made of this cloth ▯ *adj* made of tweed

tweezers *noun plural* small pincers for pulling out hairs, holding small things *etc*

twelve *noun* the number 12 ▯ *adj* 12 in number ▯ **twelfth** *adj* the last of a series of twelve ▯ *noun* one of twelve equal parts

twenty *noun* the number 20 ▯ *adj* 20 in number ▯ **twentieth** *adj* the last of a series of twenty ▯ *noun* one of twenty equal parts

twerp *noun, informal* an idiot

twice *adv* two times

twiddle *verb* play with, twirl idly ▯ **twiddle your thumbs** **1** turn your thumbs around one another **2** have nothing to do

twig *noun* a small branch of a tree

twilight *noun* **1** the faint light between sunset and night, or before sunrise **2** the time just before or after the peak of something: *the twilight of the dictatorship*

twill *noun* a kind of strong cloth with a ridged appearance

twin *noun* **1** one of two children or animals born of the same mother at the same birth **2** one of two things exactly the same ▯ *adj* **1**

born at the same birth **2** very like another **3** made up of two parts or things which are alike ▯ **twin bed** one of two matching single beds ▯ **twin-screw** *adj* of an aeroplane: having two separate propellers ▯ **twinset** *noun* a matching cardigan and jumper

twine *noun* a strong kind of string made of twisted threads ▯ *verb* **1** wind or twist together **2** wind (about or around something)

twinge *noun* a sudden, sharp pain

twinkle *verb* **1** of a star *etc*: shine with light which seems to vary in brightness **2** of eyes: shine with amusement *etc* ▯ **twinkle** or **twinkling** *noun* the act or state of twinkling ▯ **in a twinkling** in an instant

twirl *verb* **1** turn or spin round quickly and lightly **2** turn round and round with the fingers ▯ *noun* a spin round and round

twist *verb* **1** wind (threads) together **2** wind round or about something **3** make (*eg* a rope) into a coil **4** bend out of shape **5** bend or wrench painfully (*eg* your ankle) **6** make (*eg* facts) appear to have a meaning which is really false ▯ *noun* **1** the act of twisting **2** a painful wrench **3** something twisted: *a twist of tissue paper* ▯ **twister** *noun, informal* a dishonest and unreliable person

twitch *verb* **1** pull with a sudden light jerk **2** jerk slightly and suddenly: *a muscle in his face twitched* ▯ *noun* **1** a sudden jerk **2** a muscle spasm

twitter *noun* **1** high, rapidly repeated sounds, as are made by small birds **2** slight nervous excitement ▯ *verb* **1** of a bird: make a series of high quivering notes **2** of a person: to talk continuously

two *noun* the number 2 ▯ *adj* 2 in number ▯ **two-faced** *adj* deceitful, insincere ▯ **twofold** *adj* double ▯ **two-time** *verb* have a love affair with two people at the same time

tycoon *noun* a business man of great wealth and power

> Based on a Japanese title for a warlord

tyke *noun* a dirty, ill-kempt dog

tympani, tympanist *another spelling* of **timpani**, **timpanist**

type *noun* **1** kind **2** an example which has all the usual characteristics of its kind **3** a small metal block with a raised letter or sign, used for printing **4** a set of these **5** printed lettering ▯ *verb* **1** print with a typewriter **2** use a typewriter **3** identify or classify as a particular type ▯ **typecast** *verb* give (an actor) parts very similar in character ▯ **typescript** *noun* a typed script for a play *etc* ▯ **typewriter** *noun* a machine with keys which, when struck, print letters on a sheet of paper ▯ **typist** *noun* someone who works with a typewriter and does other secretarial or clerical tasks

typhoid *noun* an infectious disease caused by germs in infected food or drinking water

typhoon *noun* a violent storm of wind and rain in Eastern seas

typhus *noun* a dangerous fever carried by lice

typical *adj* having or showing the usual characteristics: *a typical Irishman/ typical of her to be late* ▯ **typically** *adv*

typify *verb* be a good example of: *typifying the English abroad*

> **typify** » typifi*es*, typify*ing*, typifi*ed*

typography *noun* the use of type for printing ▯ **typographer** *noun* someone who sets or knows about printing type ▯ **typographical** *adj* ▯ **typographically** *adv*

tyrannical or **tyrannous** *adj* like a tyrant, cruel ▯ **tyrannize** *verb* act as a tyrant; rule over harshly ▯ **tyranny** *noun* (*plural* **tyrannies**) the rule of a tyrant

tyrant *noun* a ruler who governs cruelly and unjustly

tyre or *US* **tire** *noun* a thick rubber cover round a motor or cycle wheel

tyro *another spelling* of **tiro**

tzar, tzarina *another spelling* of **tsar**, **tsarina**

U

ubiquitous *adj* **1** being everywhere at once **2** found everywhere □ **ubiquitously** *adv* □ **ubiquity** *noun*

UCCA *abbrev* Universities Central Council on Admissions

UDA *abbrev* Ulster Defence Association

udder *noun* a bag-like part of a cow, goat *etc* with teats which supply milk

UDI *abbrev* Unilateral Declaration of Independence

UDR *abbrev* Ulster Defence Regiment

UEFA *abbrev* Union of European Football Associations

UFO *abbrev* unidentified flying object

ugli fruit a citrus fruit that is a cross between a grapefruit, a Seville orange and a tangerine

ugly *adj* **1** unpleasant to look at or hear: *ugly sound* **2** threatening, dangerous: *gave me an ugly look* □ **ugliness** *noun* □ **ugly duckling** an unattractive or disliked person who later turns into a beauty, success *etc*

UHF *abbrev* ultra high frequency

UHT *abbrev* **1** ultra-heat treated **2** ultra high temperature

uilean pipes /*oo*liən/ Irish bagpipes

ukelele /yook*əleh*lee/ *noun* a small, stringed musical instrument played like a banjo

ulcer *noun* an open sore on the inside or the outside of the body □ **ulcerated** *adj* having an ulcer or ulcers □ **ulcerous** *adj*

ult *abbrev* last month (from Latin *ultimo*): *we refer to your letter of 12th ult*

ulterior *adj* beyond what is admitted or seen: *ulterior motive*

ultimate *adj* last, final □ **ultimately** *adv* finally, in the end

ultimatum *noun* a final demand sent with a threat to break off discussion, declare war *etc* if it is not met

ultra- *prefix* **1** very: *ultra-careful* **2** beyond: *ultramicroscopic*

ultramarine *adj* of a deep blue colour

ultrasonic *adj* beyond the range of human hearing

ultraviolet *adj* having rays of slightly shorter wavelength than visible light

umber *noun* a mineral substance used to produce a brown paint

umbilical *adj* of the navel □ **umbilical cord** a tube connecting an unborn mammal to its mother through the placenta

umbrage *noun* a feeling of offence or hurt: *took umbrage at my suggestion*

umbrella *noun* an object made up of a folding covered framework on a stick which protects against rain

Literally 'little shadow' and originally used to refer to a sunshade

umlaut /*oom*lowt/ *noun* a character (¨) placed over a letter to modify its pronunciation

umpire *noun* **1** a sports official who sees that a game is played according to the rules **2** a judge asked to settle a dispute ▯ *verb* act as an umpire

umpteen *adj* many, lots ▯ **umpteenth** *adj*

Originally *umpty*, a signaller's slang term for a dash in Morse code

UN *abbrev* United Nations

un- *prefix* **1** not: *unequal* **2** (with verbs) used to show the reversal of an action: *unfasten*

unabashed *adj* shameless, blatant

unable *adj* lacking enough strength, power, skill *etc*

unaccountable *adj* not able to be explained ▯ **unaccountably** *adv*

unaccustomed *adj* not used (to)

unadulterated *adj* pure, not mixed with anything else

unanimous *adj* **1** all of the same opinion: *we were unanimous* **2** agreed to by all: *a unanimous decision* ▯ **unanimously** *adj* ▯ **unanimity** *noun*

unanswerable *adj* not able to be answered

unapproachable *adj* unfriendly and stiff in manner

unarmed *adj* not armed

unassuming *adj* modest

unattached *adj* **1** not attached **2** single, nor married or having a partner

unaware *adj* not knowing, ignorant (of): *unaware of the danger* ▯ **unawares** *adv* **1** without warning **2** unintentionally

unbalanced *adj* mad; lacking balance: *unbalanced view*

unbearable *adj* too painful or bad to be endured

unbeliever *noun* someone who does not follow a certain religion

unbending *adj* severe

unbounded *adj* not limited, very great: *unbounded enthusiasm*

unbridled *adj* not kept under control: *unbridled fury*

unburden *verb*: **unburden yourself** tell your secrets or problems to someone else

uncalled *adj*: **uncalled for** quite unnecessary: *your remarks were uncalled for*

uncanny *adj* strange, mysterious ▯ **uncannily** *adv*

uncared *adj*: **uncared for** not looked after properly

unceremonious *adj* informal, offhand

uncertain *adj* **1** not certain, doubtful **2** not definitely known **3** of weather: changeable

uncharted *adj* **1** not shown on a map or chart **2** little known

uncle *noun* **1** the brother of your father or mother **2** the husband of your father's or mother's sister ▯

Uncle Sam *informal* the United States

unclean *adj* dirty, impure

uncoil *verb* unwind

uncomfortable *adj* not comfortable

uncommon *adj* not common, strange ▯ **uncommonly** *adj* very: *uncommonly well*

uncompromising *adj* not willing to give in or make concessions to others

unconditional *adj* with no conditions attached; absolute

unconscionable *adj* more than is reasonable: *unconscionable demands*

unconscious *adj* **1** senseless, stunned (*eg* by an accident) **2** not aware (of) **3** not recognized by the person concerned: *unconscious prejudice against women* ▯ *noun* the deepest level of the mind

uncouth *adj* **1** clumsy, awkward **2** rude

uncover *verb* **1** remove a cover from **2** disclose

unction *noun* anointing; anointment ▯ **unctuous** *adj* oily, ingratiating

uncut *adj* not cut; not edited down

undaunted *adj* fearless; not discouraged

undecided *adj* not yet decided

undeniable *adj* not able to be denied, clearly true

under *prep* **1** directly below or beneath **2** less than: *costing under £5* **3** within the authority or command of: *under General Montgomery* **4** going through, suffering: *under attack* **5** having, using: *under a false name* **6** in accordance with: *under our agreement* ▯ *adv* in or to a lower position, condition *etc* ▯ **go under 1** sink beneath the surface of water **2** go bankrupt, go out of business ▯ **under age** younger than the legal or required age ▯ **under way** in motion, started

under- *prefix* **1** below, beneath **2** lower in position or rank **3** too little

underachieve *verb* achieve less than your potential

underarm *adv* of bowling *etc*: with the arm kept below the shoulder

undercarriage *noun* the wheels of an aeroplane and their supports

underclothes *noun plural* clothes worn next to the skin under other clothes

undercover *adj* acting or done in secret: *an undercover agent* (*ie* a spy)

undercurrent *noun* **1** a flow or movement under the surface **2** a half-hidden feeling or tendency: *an undercurrent of despair in her voice*

undercut *verb* sell at a lower price than someone else

underdeveloped *adj* **1** not fully grown **2** of a country: lacking modern agricultural and industrial systems, and with a low standard of living

underdog *noun* the weaker side, or the loser in any conflict or fight

underdone *adj* of food: not quite cooked

underestimate *verb* estimate at less than the real worth, value *etc*

underfoot *adj* under the feet

undergo *verb* **1** suffer, endure **2** receive (*eg* as medical treatment)

> **undergo** » undergo*es*, underго*ing*, underwent, undergone

undergraduate *noun* a university student who has not yet passed final examinations

underground *adj* **1** below the surface of the ground **2** secret, covert ▯ *noun* a railway which runs in a tunnel beneath the surface of the ground

undergrowth *noun* shrubs or low plants growing amongst trees

underhand *adj* sly, deceitful

underlay *noun* a protective layer beneath a carpet *etc*

underlie *verb* be the hidden cause or source of ▯ **underlying** *adj*

underline *verb* **1** draw a line under **2** stress the importance of, emphasize

underling *noun* someone of lower rank

undermine *verb* do damage to, weaken gradually (health, authority *etc*)

underneath *adj* & *prep* in a lower position (than), beneath: *look underneath the table/ wearing a jacket underneath his coat*

undernourished *adj* not well nourished

underpants *noun plural* underwear covering the buttocks and upper legs

under par *adj* **1** not up to the usual level **2** unwell: *feeling under par*

underpass *noun* a road passing under another one

underpay *verb* pay too little

underpin *verb* support from beneath, prop up

underplay *verb* understate, play down

underprivileged *adj* not having normal living standards or rights

underrate *verb* think too little of, underestimate

underscore *verb* underline; emphasize

undersell *verb* **1** sell for less than the true value **2** sell for less than someone else

undersigned *noun*: **the undersigned** the people whose names are written at the end of a letter or statement

undersized *adj* below the usual or required size

underskirt *noun* a thin skirt worn under another skirt

understand *verb* **1** see the meaning of **2** appreciate the reasons for: *I don't understand your behaviour* **3** have a thorough knowledge of: *do you understand economics?* **4** have the impression that: *I understood that you weren't coming* **5** take for granted as part of an agreement ▯ **understandable** *adj*

understand » understands, understand*ing*, understood

understanding *noun* **1** the ability to see the full meaning of something **2** an agreement **3** condition: *on the understanding that we both pay half* **4** appreciation of other people's feelings, difficulties *etc* ▫ *adj* able to understand other people's feelings, sympathetic

understatement *noun* a statement which does not give the whole truth, making less of certain details than is actually the case ▫ **understate** *verb*

understudy *noun* (*plural* **understudies**) an actor who learns the part of another actor and is able to take their place if necessary

undertake *verb* **1** promise (to do something) **2** take upon yourself (a task, duty *etc*): *I undertook responsibility for the food* ▫ **undertaker** *noun* someone whose job is to organize funerals ▫ **undertaking** *noun* **1** something which is being attempted or done **2** a promise **3** the business of an undertaker

under-the-counter *adj* hidden from customers' sight; illegal

undertone *noun* **1** a soft voice **2** a partly hidden meaning, feeling *etc*: *an undertone of discontent*

undertow *noun* a current below the surface of the water which moves in a direction opposite to the surface movement

undervalue *verb* value (something) below its real worth

underwater *adj* under the surface of the water

underwear *noun* underclothes

underweight *adj* under the usual or required weight

underwent *past form* of **undergo**

underworld *noun* **1** the criminal world or level of society **2** the place where spirits go after death

underwriter *noun* someone who insures ships ▫ **underwrite** *verb* **1** accept for insurance **2** accept responsibility or liability for

undesirable *adj* not wanted

undeveloped *adj* not developed

undies *noun plural, informal* underwear

undivided *adj* not split, complete, total: *undivided attention*

undo *verb* **1** unfasten (a coat, parcel *etc*) **2** wipe out the effect of, reverse: *undoing all the good I did* **3** *old* ruin, dishonour (*esp* a reputation): *alas, I am undone* ▫ **undoing** *noun* ruin, dishonour

undo » undo*es*, undo*ing*, undone, undid

undoubted *adj* not to be doubted ▫ **undoubtedly** *adj* without doubt, certainly

undreamt-of *adj* more *etc* than could have been imagined

undress *verb* take your clothes off

undue *adj* too much, more than is necessary: *undue expense* ▫ **unduly** *adv*

undulate *verb* **1** move as waves do

2 have a rolling, wavelike appearance ▫ **undulating** *adj* ▫ **undulation** *noun*

undying *adj* unending, never fading: *undying love*

unearth *verb* bring or dig out from the earth, or from a place of hiding ▫ **unearthly** *adj* **1** strange, as if not of this world **2** *informal* absurd, *esp* absurdly early: *at this unearthly hour*

uneasy *adj* anxious, worried ▫ **uneasiness** *noun*

unedifying *adj* not uplifting, degrading

unemployed *adj* **1** without a job **2** not in use ▫ **unemployment** *noun* **1** the state of being unemployed **2** the total number of unemployed people in a country ▫ **the unemployed** unemployed people as a group

unenviable *adj* not arousing envy: *unenviable task*

unequal *adj* **1** not equal; unfair: *unequal distribution* **2** lacking enough strength or skill: *unequal to the job* ▫ **unequalled** *adj* without an equal, unique

unequivocal *adj* clear, not ambiguous: *unequivocal orders*

unerring *adj* always right, never making a mistake: *unerring judgement*

UNESCO *abbrev* United Nations Educational, Scientific and Cultural Organization

uneven *adj* **1** not smooth or level **2** not all of the same quality *etc*: *this work is very uneven*

unexceptionable *adj* not causing objections or criticism

⚠ Do not confuse: **unexceptionable** and **unexceptional**

unexceptional *adj* not exceptional, ordinary

unexpected *adj* not expected, sudden

unexpurgated *adj* not censored

unfailing *adj* never failing, never likely to fail: *unfailing accuracy*

unfair *adj* not just

unfaithful *adj* **1** not true to your marriage vows **2** failing to keep promises

unfasten *verb* loosen, undo (*eg* a buttoned coat)

unfathomable *adj* not understandable, not clear

unfeeling *adj* harsh, hard-hearted

unfettered *adj* not restrained

unfit *adj* **1** not suitable **2** not good enough, or not in a suitable state (to, for): *unfit for drinking/ unfit to travel* **3** physically under par

unflagging *adj* not tiring or losing strength

unflappable *adj* imperturbable, always calm

unflinching *adj* brave, not put off by pain, opposition *etc*

unfold *verb* **1** spread out **2** give details of (a story, plan) **3** of details of a plot *etc:* become known

unforgettable *adj* unlikely to ever be forgotten; memorable

unfortunate *adj* **1** unlucky **2** regrettable: *unfortunate turn of phrase*

unfounded *adj* not based on fact; untrue

unfurl *verb* unfold (*eg* a flag)

ungainly *adj* clumsy, awkward

ungracious *adj* rude, not polite

ungrateful *adj* not showing thanks for kindness

unguarded *adj* **1** without protection **2** thoughtless, careless: *unguarded remark*

unguent *noun* ointment

unhand *verb, old* let go, release

unhappy *adj* **1** miserable, sad **2** unfortunate ▯ **unhappily** *adj* ▯ **unhappiness** *noun*

unhealthy *adj* **1** not well, ill **2** harmful to health: *unhealthy climate* **3** showing signs of not being well: *unhealthy complexion*

unheard-of *adj* very unusual, unprecedented

unhinged *adj* mad, crazy

unholy *adj* **1** evil **2** outrageous

unhorse *verb* throw from a horse

uni- *prefix* one, a single

UNICEF *abbrev* United Nations Children's Fund

unicorn *noun* a mythological animal like a horse, but with one straight horn on its forehead

uniform *adj* the same in all parts or times, never varying ▯ *noun* the form of clothes worn by people in the armed forces, children at a certain school *etc* ▯ **uniformity** *noun* sameness

unify *verb* combine into one ▯ **unification** *noun*

> **unify** » unifi*es*, unify*ing*, unifi*ed*

unilateral *adj* **1** one-sided **2** involving one person or group out of several ▯ **unilateralism** *noun* the abandoning of nuclear weapons by one country, without waiting for others to do likewise ▯ **unilateralist** *noun & adj*

uninhibited *adj* not inhibited, unrestrained

uninitiated *adj* not knowing, ignorant

uninterested *adj* not interested

> ⚠Do not confuse with: **disinterested**

uninterrupted *adj* **1** continuing without a break **2** of a view: not blocked by anything

union *noun* **1** the act of joining together **2** partnership; marriage **3** countries or states joined together **4** a trade union ▯ **unionist** *noun* **1** a member of a trade union **2** someone who supports the union of the United Kingdom ▯ **unionize** *verb* start or join a trade union ▯ **Union Jack** the flag of the United Kingdom

unique *adj* without a like or equal: *a unique sense of timing*

> ⚠Do not confuse with: **rare**

unisex *adj* of or in a style suitable for either men or women

unison *noun* **1** exact sameness of musical pitch **2** agreement, accord ◊ **in unison** all together

unit *noun* **1** a single thing, person or group, *esp* when considered as part of a larger whole: *army unit/ storage unit* **2** a fixed amount or length used as a standard by which others are measured (*eg* metres, litres, centimetres *etc*) **3** the number one ◊ **unitary** *adj* **1** forming a unit, not divided **2** using or based on units ◊ **unity** *noun* **1** complete agreement **2** the state of being one or a whole **3** the number one

unite *verb* **1** join together; become one **2** act together ◊ **united** *adj*

universe *noun* all known things, including the earth and planets ◊ **universal** *adj* **1** relating to the universe **2** relating to, or coming from, all people: *universal criticism* ◊ **universally** *adv*

university *noun* (*plural* **universities**) a college which teaches a wide range of subjects to a high level, and which awards degrees to students who pass its examinations

UNIX *noun* a type of computer operating system designed to allow multiuser access

unkempt *adj* untidy

unkind *adj* not kind; harsh, cruel

unleaded *adj* of petrol: not containing lead compounds

unleash *verb* **1** set free (a dog *etc*) **2** let loose (*eg* anger)

unleavened *adj* of bread: not made to rise with yeast

unless *conj* if not: *unless he's here soon, I'm going* (*ie* if he's not here soon)

unlike *adj* different, not similar ◊ *prep* **1** different from **2** not characteristic of: *it was unlike her not to phone*

unlikely *adj* **1** not probable: *it's unlikely that it will rain today* **2** probably not true: *an unlikely tale*

unload *verb* **1** take the load from **2** remove the charge from a gun

unlooked-for *adj* not expected: *unlooked-for happiness*

unloose *verb* **1** set free **2** make loose

unlucky *adj* **1** not lucky or fortunate **2** unsuccessful ◊ **unluckily** *adv*

unmanly *adj* weak, cowardly

unmask *verb* **1** take a covering off **2** show the true character of **3** bring to light (a plot *etc*)

unmatched *adj* without an equal

unmentionable *adj* not fit to be spoken of, scandalous, indecent

unmistakable *adj* very clear; impossible to confuse with any other: *unmistakable handwriting*

unmitigated *adj* complete, absolute: *unmitigated disaster*

unmoved *adj* not affected, unsympathetic: *unmoved by my pleas*

unnatural *adj* not natural, perverted

unnecessary *adj* not necessary; avoidable

unnerve *verb* disconcert, perturb

UNO *abbrev* United Nations Organization

unobtrusive *adj* not obvious or conspicuous; modest

unpack *verb* open (a piece of luggage) and remove the contents

unpalatable *adj* **1** not pleasing to the taste **2** not pleasant to have to face up to: *unpalatable facts*

unparalleled *adj* not having an equal, unprecedented: *unparalleled success*

unpick *verb* take out sewing stitches from

unpleasant *adj* not pleasant, nasty

unprecedented *adj* never having happened before

unpremeditated *adj* done without having been planned: *unpremeditated murder*

unprepossessing *adj* not attractive

unpretentious *adj* modest, not showy or affected

unprincipled *adj* without (moral) principles

unprintable *adj* not suitable to be printed; obscene

unquestionable *adj* undoubted, certain

unravel *verb* **1** unwind, take the knots out of **2** solve (a problem or mystery)

> **unravel** » unravel*s*, unravel*ling*, unravel*led*

unreal *adj* **1** not real, imaginary **2** *informal* amazing, incredible

unremitting *adj* never stopping, unending: *unremitting rain*

unrequited *adj* of love: not given in return, one-sided

unrest *noun* a state of trouble or discontent, *esp* among a group of people

unrivalled *adj* without an equal

unruly *adj* **1** badly behaved **2** not obeying laws or rules ◊ **unruliness** *noun*

unsavoury *adj* very unpleasant, causing a feeling of disgust

unscathed *adj* not harmed

unscrew *verb* loosen (something screwed in)

unscrupulous *adj* having no scruples or principles

unseasonable *adj* **1** of weather: not usual for the time of year **2** not well-timed

unseat *verb* **1** remove from a political seat **2** throw from the saddle (of a horse)

unseemly unsuitable, improper: *unseemly haste*

unseen *adj* not seen ◊ **sight unseen** (bought *etc*) without having been seen, at the buyer's risk

unsettle *verb* disturb, upset

unsettled *adj* **1** disturbed **2** of weather: changeable **3** of a bill: unpaid

unsettling *adj* disturbing, upsetting

unsightly *adj* ugly

unsociable *adj* not willing to mix with other people

unsolicited *adj* not requested: *unsolicited advice*

unsophisticated *adj* **1** simple, uncomplicated **2** naive, inexperienced

unsound *adj* **1** incorrect, unfounded **2** not sane

unspeakable *adj* too bad to describe in words: *unspeakable rudeness*

unstinting *adj* unrestrained, generous

unstoppable *adj* not able to be stopped

unstring *verb* remove the strings from (a musical instrument)

unstudied *adj* natural, not forced: *unstudied charm*

unsung *adj* not celebrated, neglected: *an unsung Scots poet*

unsuspecting *adj* not aware of coming danger

unswerving *adj* solid, unwavering

untenable unjustifiable: *the government's position is untenable*

unthinkable *adj* **1** very unlikely **2** too bad to be thought of

untie *verb* **1** release from bonds **2** loosen (a knot)

until *prep* up to the time of: *can you wait until Tuesday?* ▫ *conj* up to the time that: *keep walking until you come to the corner*

untimely *adj* **1** happening too soon: *untimely arrival* **2** not suitable to the occasion: *untimely remark*

unto *prep, old* to

untold *adj* **1** not yet told: *the untold story* **2** too great to be counted or measured: *untold riches*

untouchable *adj* **1** not approachable **2** not able to be equalled or surpassed ▫ *noun, old* a Hindu of very low social caste

untoward *adj* **1** unlucky, unfortunate **2** inconvenient

untrue *adj* **1** not true, false **2** unfaithful

untruth *noun* a lie ▫ **untruthful** *adj*

unusual *adj* **1** not usual **2** rare, remarkable ▫ **unusually** *adv*

unvarnished *adj* **1** not varnished **2** plain, straightforward: *the unvarnished truth*

unveil *verb* **1** remove a veil from **2** remove a cover from (a memorial *etc*) **3** bring to light, disclose

unwaged *adj* unemployed

unwarranted *adj* uncalled-for, unnecessary

unwell *adj* not in good health

unwieldy *adj* not easily moved or handled ▫ **unwieldiness** *noun*

unwind *verb* **1** wind off from a ball or reel **2** relax

unwitting *adj* **1** unintended: *unwitting insult* **2** unaware ▫ **unwittingly** *adv*

unwonted *adj* unaccustomed, not usual: *unwonted cheerfulness*

unworthy *adj* **1** not worthy **2** low, worthless, despicable **3** (with **of**) not deserving (*eg* of attention) **4** below someone's usual standard, out of character: *that remark is unworthy of you*

unwritten *adj* **1** not written down **2** of a rule, law *etc*: generally accepted

up *adv* **1** towards or in a higher or more northerly position: *walking up the hill/ they live up in the Highlands* **2** completely, so as to finish: *drink up your tea* **3** to a larger size: *blow up a balloon* **4** as far as: *he came up to me and shook hands* **5** towards a bigger city *etc*, not necessarily one further north: *going up to London from Manchester* ▯ *prep* **1** towards or in the higher part of: *climbed up the ladder* **2** along: *walking up the road* ▯ *adj* **1** ascending, going up: *the up escalator* **2** ahead in score: *2 goals up* **3** better off, richer: *£50 up on the deal* **4** risen: *the sun is up* **5** of a given length of time: ended: *your time is up* **6** *informal* wrong: *what's up with her today?* ▯ **up-and-coming** *adj* likely to succeed ▯ **on the up and up** progressing steadily, getting better all the time ▯ **up and about** **1** awake **2** out of bed after an illness ▯ **ups and downs** times of good and bad luck ▯ **up to** **1** until: *up to the present* **2** capable of: *are you up to the job?* **3** dependent on, falling as a duty to: *it's up to you to decide* **4** doing: *up to his tricks again* ▯ **up to scratch** of the required standard ▯ **up to speed** fully competent at a new job *etc*

> **up** » upp*er*, up*most* or upper*most*

upbeat *adj*, *informal* cheerful, optimistic

upbraid *verb* scold

upbringing *noun* the rearing of, or the training given to, a child

upcoming *adj* forthcoming

up-country *adv* & *adj* inland

update *verb* bring up to date ▯ *noun* **1** the act of updating **2** new information: *an update on yesterday's report*

upend *verb* turn upside down

upfront or **up-front** *adj* **1** candid, frank **2** foremost ▯ **up front** **1** at the front **2** of money: paid in advance **3** candidly, openly

upgrade *verb* **1** raise to a more important position **2** improve the quality of ▯ *noun, comput* a newer version of a software program

upheaval *noun* a violent disturbance or change

upheld *past form* of **uphold**

uphill *adj* **1** going upwards **2** difficult: *uphill struggle* ▯ *adv* upwards

uphold *verb* **1** defend, give support to **2** maintain, keep going (*eg* a tradition)

> **uphold** » uphold*s*, uphold*ing*, upheld

upholster *verb* fit (furniture) with springs, stuffing, covers *etc* ▯ **upholsterer** *noun* someone who upholsters furniture ▯ **upholstery** *noun* covers, cushions *etc*

upkeep *noun* **1** the act of keeping (*eg* a house or car) in a good state of repair **2** the cost of this

upland *noun* **1** high ground **2**

(**uplands**) a hilly or mountainous region

uplift *verb* raise the spirits of, cheer up

up-market *adj* of high quality or price, luxury

upon *prep* **1** on the top of: *upon the table* **2** at or after the time of: *upon completion of the task*

upper *adj* higher, further up ▫ *noun* **1** the part of a shoe *etc* above the sole **2** *slang* a stimulant drug ▫ **upper-case** *adj* of a letter: capital, *eg A* not *a* (*contrasted with*: **lower-case**) ▫ **upper-class** *adj* belonging to the highest social class, aristocratic ▫ **uppercut** *noun* a boxing punch which swings up from below ▫ **upper hand** advantage; dominance, control ▫ **uppermost** *adj* highest, furthest up

uppity *adj* putting on airs, haughty

upright *adj* **1** standing up, vertical **2** honest, moral ▫ *noun* an upright post, piano *etc*

uprising *noun* a revolt against a government *etc*

uproar *noun* a noisy disturbance ▫ **uproarious** *adj* very noisy

uproot *verb* **1** tear up by the roots **2** leave your home and go to live in another place

upset *verb* **1** make unhappy, angry, worried *etc* **2** overturn **3** disturb, put out of order **4** ruin (plans *etc*) ▫ *adj* distressed, unhappy *etc*, ill ▫ *noun* **1** distress, unhappiness, worry *etc* **2** something that causes distress

upset *verb* » upsets, upsett*ing*, upset

upshot *noun* a result or end of a matter: *what was the upshot of all this?*

upside-down *adj & adv* **1** with the top part underneath **2** in confusion

upstage *adv* away from the footlights on a theatre stage ▫ *adj, informal* haughty, proud ▫ *verb* divert attention from (someone) to yourself

upstairs *adv* in or to the upper storey of a house *etc* ▫ *noun* the upper storey or storeys of a house ▫ *adj* in the upper storey or storeys: *upstairs bedroom*

upstanding *adj* **1** honest, respectable **2** strong and healthy **3** *old* standing up

upstart *noun* someone who has risen quickly from a low to a high position in society, work *etc*

upstream *adv* higher up a river or stream, towards the source

upsurge *noun* a rising, a swelling up

upswing *noun* an upward or positive swing, a recovery

uptake *noun*: **quick on the uptake** quick to understand

uptight *adj* nervous, tense

up-to-date *adj* **1** modern, in touch with recent ideas *etc* **2** belonging to the present time **3** containing all recent facts *etc*: *an up-to-date account* ▫ **up to date 1** to the present time **2** containing recent facts *etc* **3** aware of recent developments

upturn *noun* a positive change, an improvement

upward *adj* moving up, ascending ◻ **upward** or **upwards** *adv* from lower to higher, up ◻ **upwardly** *adv* ◻ **upwardly-mobile** *adj* moving to a higher social status ◻ **upwards of** more than

uranium *noun* a radioactive metal

urban *adj* relating to a town or city (*contrasted with*: **rural**) ◻ **urbanization** *noun* ◻ **urbanize** *verb* make urban

urbane *adj* polite in a smooth way ◻ **urbanity** *noun* **1** smoothness of manner **2** (*plural* **urbanities**) urbane actions

urchin *noun* a dirty, ragged child

Originally meaning 'hedgehog', the prickly sense of which survives in *sea urchin*

urge *verb* **1** drive (on) **2** try to persuade: *urging me to go home* **3** advise, recommend: *urge caution* ◻ *noun* a strong desire or impulse

urgent *adj* **1** requiring immediate attention **2** asking for immediate action ◻ **urgency** *noun* ◻ **urgently** *adv*

urine *noun* the waste liquid passed out of the body of animals and humans from the bladder ◻ **urinary** *adj* ◻ **urinate** *verb* pass urine from the bladder

urn *noun* **1** a vase for the ashes of the dead **2** a metal drum with a tap, used for making and pouring out tea or coffee

US or **USA** *abbrev* United States of America

us *pronoun* used by a speaker or writer in referring to themselves together with other people (as the object in a sentence): *when would you like us to come?*

usage *noun* **1** the act or manner of using **2** the established way of using a word *etc* **3** custom, habit **4** treatment: *rough usage*

use *verb* **1** put to some purpose: *use a knife to open it* **2** bring into action: *use your common sense* **3** (often with **up**) spend, exhaust (*eg* patience, energy) **4** treat: *he used his wife cruelly* ◻ *noun* **1** the act of using **2** value or suitability for a purpose: *no use to anybody* **3** the fact of being used: *it's in use at the moment* **4** custom ◻ **no use** useless ◻ **used to 1** accustomed to **2** was or were in the habit of (doing something): *we used to go there every year*

used *adj* **1** employed, put to a purpose **2** not new: *used cars*

useful *adj* serving a purpose; helpful ◻ **usefully** *adv* ◻ **usefulness** *noun*

useless *adj* having no use or effect ◻ **uselessness** *noun*

user *noun* someone who uses anything (*esp* a computer) ◻ **user-friendly** *adj* easily understood, easy to use

usher, usherette *noun* someone who shows people to their seats in a theatre *etc* ◻ **usher** *verb* lead, convey

USSR *abbrev, hist* Union of Soviet Socialist Republics

usual *adj* **1** done or happening

most often: *usual method* **2** customary: *with his usual cheerfulness* **3** ordinary ▯ *noun* a customary event, order *etc* ▯ **usually** *adv* on most occasions

usurp *verb* take possession of (*eg* a throne) by force ▯ **usurper** *noun*

usury *noun* the lending of money with an excessively high rate of interest ▯ **usurer** *noun* a money-lender who demands an excessively high rate of interest

utensil *noun* an instrument or container used in the home (*eg* a ladle, knife, pan)

uterus *noun* (*plural* **uteri**) the womb

utilitarian *noun* concerned with usefulness, rather than beauty, pleasure *etc*

utility *noun* (*plural* **utilities**) **1** usefulness **2** a public service supplying water, gas *etc*

utilize *verb* make use of ▯ **utilization** *noun*

utmost *adj* **1** the greatest possible: *utmost care* **2** furthest ▯ **do your utmost** make the greatest possible effort

utopia *noun* a perfect place, a paradise ▯ **utopian** *adj*

> Literally 'no place', coined by Thomas More for his fictional book *Utopia* (1516)

utter[1] *verb* produce with the voice (words, a scream *etc*) ▯ **utterance** *noun* something said

utter[2] *adj* complete, total: *utter darkness* ▯ **utterly** *adv* ▯ **uttermost** *adj* most complete, utmost

U-turn *noun* a complete change in direction, policy *etc*

UVA *abbrev* ultraviolet radiation

uvula *noun* the small piece of flesh hanging from the palate at the back of the mouth

uxorious *adj* of a man: extremely fond of his wife

Uzi *noun* a type of submachine-gun

V

v *abbrev* **1** against (from Latin *versus*) **2** see (from Latin *vide*) **3** verb **4** verse **5** volume

vacancy *noun* (*plural* **vacancies**) **1** a job that has not been filled **2** a room not already booked in a hotel *etc*

vacant *adj* **1** empty, not occupied **2** of an expression: showing no interest or intelligence □ **vacantly** *adv*

vacate *verb* leave empty, cease to occupy

vacation *noun* **1** the act of vacating **2** a holiday

vaccine *noun* a substance made from the germs that cause a disease, given to people and animals to try to prevent them catching that disease □ **vaccinate** *verb* give a vaccine to, *eg* by injection into the skin □ **vaccination** *noun*

vacillate *verb* move from one opinion to another; waver □ **vacillation** *noun*

vacuous *adj* **1** empty **2** empty-headed, stupid □ **vacuously** *adv* □ **vacuousness** *noun*

vacuum *noun* a space from which all, or almost all, the air has been removed □ **vacuum cleaner** a machine which cleans carpets *etc* by sucking up dust □ **vacuum flask** a container with double walls enclosing a vacuum, for keeping liquids hot or cold

vagabond *noun* **1** someone with no permanent home; a wanderer **2** a rascal, a rogue

vagaries *noun plural* strange, unexpected behaviour: *vagaries of human nature*

vagina *noun* the passage connecting a woman's genitals to her womb □ **vaginal** *adj* of the vagina

vagrant *adj* unsettled, wandering □ *noun* a wanderer or tramp, with no settled home □ **vagrancy** *noun* the state of being a tramp

vague *adj* **1** not clear; not definite: *vague idea/ vague shape* **2** not practical or efficient; forgetful □ **vaguely** *adv*

vain *adj* **1** conceited, self-important **2** useless: *vain attempt* **3** empty, meaningless: *vain promises* □ **in vain** without success □ **vainly** *adv*

vainglorious *adj* boastful □ **vaingloriously** *adv*

valance *noun* a decorative frill round the edge of a bed

vale *noun, formal* a valley

valediction *noun* a farewell □ **valedictory** *adj* saying farewell: *valedictory speech*

valency *noun* (*plural* **valencies**) *chemistry* the combining power of an atom or group with hydrogen (*eg* in water, H^2O, oxygen shows valency two)

valentine *noun* **1** a greetings card sent on St Valentine's Day, 14 February **2** a sweetheart, a lover

valet /*valə*t/ or /*val*eh/ *noun* a manservant

valetudinarian *noun* someone who is over-anxious about their health

valiant *adj* brave □ **valiantly** *adv*

valid *adj* **1** sound, acceptable: *valid reason for not going* **2** legally in force: *valid passport* □ **validate** *verb* make valid □ **validity** *noun*

Valium *noun, trademark* a brand name for diazepam, a tranquillizing drug

valley *noun* (*plural* **valleys**) low land between hills, often with a river flowing through it

valorous *adj* brave, courageous

valour *noun* courage, bravery

valuable *adj* of great value □ **valuables** *noun plural* articles of worth

value *noun* **1** worth; price **2** purchasing power (of a coin *etc*) **3** importance **4** usefulness **5** *algebra* a number or quantity put as equal to an expression: *the value of x is 8* □ *verb* **1** put a price on **2** think highly of □ **valuation** *noun* **1** the act of valuing **2** an estimated price or value □ **value-added tax** a government tax raised on the selling-price of an article, or charged on certain services □ **valueless** *adj* worthless □ **valuer** or **valuator** *noun* someone trained to estimate the value of property

valve *noun* **1** a device allowing air, steam or liquid to flow in one direction only **2** a small flap controlling the flow of blood in the body **3** an electronic component found in older television sets, radios *etc*

vamp[1] *noun* the upper part of a boot or shoe □ *verb* **1** patch **2** play improvised music

vamp[2] *noun* a woman who sets out to attract men

vampire *noun* a dead person supposed to rise at night and suck the blood of sleeping people □ **vampire bat** a S American bat that sucks blood

van[1] *noun* a covered or closed-in vehicle or wagon for carrying goods by road or rail

van[2] *noun* short for **vanguard**

vandal *noun* someone who pointlessly destroys or damages public buildings *etc* □ **vandalism** *noun* the activity of a vandal □ **vandalize** *verb* damage by vandalism

vane *noun* **1** a weathercock **2** the blade of a windmill, propeller *etc*

vanguard *noun* **1** the leading group in a movement *etc* **2** the part of an army going in front of the main body

vanilla *noun* a sweet-scented flavouring obtained from the pods of a type of orchid

vanish *verb* **1** go out of sight **2** fade away to nothing

vanity *noun* (*plural* **vanities**) **1** conceit **2** worthlessness **3** something vain and worthless

vanquish *verb* defeat

vantage point a position giving an advantage or a clear view

vapid *adj* dull, uninteresting

vaporize *verb* change into vapour □ **vaporizer** *noun* a device which sprays liquid very finely

vapour *noun* **1** the air-like or gas-like state of a substance that is usually liquid or solid: *water vapour* **2** mist or smoke in the air

variable, variance, variation *see* **vary**

varicose vein a swollen or enlarged vein, usually on the leg

variegated *adj* marked with different colours; multicoloured

variety *noun* (*plural* **varieties**) **1** the quality of being of many kinds, or of being different **2** a mixed collection: *a variety of books* **3** a sort, a type: *a variety of potato* **4** mixed theatrical entertainment including songs, comedy, *etc*

various *adj* **1** of different kinds: *various shades of green* **2** several: *various attempts* □ **variously** *adv*

varlet *noun*, *old* a rascal

varnish *noun* a sticky liquid which gives a glossy surface to paper, wood *etc* □ *verb* **1** cover with varnish **2** cover up (faults)

vary *verb* **1** make, be, or become different **2** make changes in (a routine *etc*) **3** differ, disagree □ **variable** *adj* changeable; that may be varied □ *noun* something that varies *eg* in value □ **variance** *noun* a state of differing or disagreement □ **variant** *noun* a different form or version □ *adj* in a different form □ **variation** *noun* **1** a varying, a change **2** the extent of a difference or change: *variations in temperature* **3** *music* a repetition, in a slightly different form, of a main theme □ **at variance** in disagreement

vary » vari*es*, vary*ing*, vari*ed*

vase /vaz/ or *US* /vehz/ *noun* a jar of pottery, glass *etc* used as an ornament or for holding cut flowers

vasectomy *noun* (*plural* **vasectomies**) sterilization of a man by cutting, and removing part of, the sperm-carrying tubes

Vaseline *noun*, *trademark* a type of ointment made from petroleum

vassal *noun*, *hist* a tenant who held land from an overlord in return for certain services

vast *adj* of very great size or amount □ **vastly** *adv* □ **vastness** *noun*

VAT or **vat** *abbrev* value-added tax

vat *noun* a large tub or tank, used *eg* for fermenting liquors and dyeing

vaudeville *noun* theatrical entertainment of dances and songs, usually comic

vault *noun* **1** an arched roof **2** an underground room, a cellar □ *verb* leap, supporting your weight on your hands, or on a pole

vaunt *verb* boast

VC *abbrev* Victoria Cross

VCR *abbrev* video cassette recorder

VD *abbrev* venereal disease

VDU *abbrev* visual display unit

veal *noun* the flesh of a calf, used as food

veer *verb* **1** change direction or

course **2** change mood, opinions, *etc*

Vegan or **vegan** /*veegən*/ *noun* a vegetarian who uses no animal products

vegetable *noun* a plant, *esp* one grown for food ▢ *adj* **1** of plants **2** made from or consisting of plants: *vegetable dye/ vegetable oil*

vegetarian *noun* someone who eats no meat, only vegetable or dairy foods ▢ *adj* consisting of, or eating, only vegetable or dairy foods

vegetate *verb* **1** grow as a plant does **2** lead a dull, aimless life: *sitting at home vegetating*

vegetation *noun* **1** plants in general **2** the plants growing in a particular area

veggie *adj*, *informal* vegetarian

vehement *adj* emphatic and forceful in expressing opinions *etc* ▢ **vehemence** *noun* ▢ **vehemently** *adv*

vehicle *noun* **1** a means of transport used on land, *esp* one with wheels: *motor vehicle* **2** a means of conveying information; *eg* television or newspapers ▢ **vehicular** *adj*

veil *noun* **1** a piece of cloth or netting worn to shade or hide the face **2** something that hides or covers up ▢ *verb* **1** cover with a veil **2** hide ▢ **take the veil** become a nun

vein *noun* **1** one of the tubes which carry the blood back to the heart **2** a small rib of a leaf **3** a thin layer of mineral in a rock **4** a streak in wood, stone *etc* **5** a mood or personal characteristic: *a vein of cheerfulness* ▢ **veined** *adj* marked with veins

Velcro *noun*, *trademark* a type of fastener made of two strips of specially treated fabric which interlock

veldt /velt/ *noun*, *South African* open grass-country, with few or no trees

vellum *noun* **1** a fine parchment used for bookbinding, made from the skins of calves, kids or lambs **2** paper made in imitation of this

velocity *noun* rate or speed of movement

velour /*vəloor*/ *noun* a fabric with a soft, velvet-like surface

velvet *noun* **1** a fabric made from silk *etc*, with a thick, soft surface **2** velveteen ▢ *adj* **1** made of velvet **2** soft or smooth as velvet; silky ▢ **velvety** *adj* soft, like velvet

velveteen *noun* a cotton fabric with a velvet-like pile

venal *adj* **1** willing to be bribed **2** done for a bribe; unworthy

⚠Do not confuse with: **venial**

vend *verb* sell ▢ **vending machine** a machine with sweets *etc* for sale, operated by putting coins in a slot ▢ **vendor** *noun* someone who sells

vendetta *noun* a bitter, long-lasting quarrel or feud

veneer *verb* **1** cover a piece of wood with another thin piece of finer quality **2** give a good appearance to what is really bad ▢ *noun* **1** a thin surface layer of fine wood **2** a false outward show hiding som bad quality: *a veneer of good manners*

venerable *adj* worthy of respect because of age or wisdom

venerate *verb* respect or honour greatly ▫ **veneration** *noun* **1** the act of venerating **2** great respect

venereal disease a disease contracted through sexual intercourse

Venetian blind a window blind formed of thin movable strips of metal or plastic hung on tapes

vengeance *noun* punishment given, harm done in return for wrong or injury, revenge ▫ **with a vengeance** with unexpected force or enthusiasm

vengeful *adj* seeking revenge ▫ **vengefully** *adv*

venial *adj* of a sin: not very bad, pardonable (*compare with*: **cardinal**)

⚠Do not confuse with: **venal**

venison *noun* the flesh of a deer, used as food

venom *noun* **1** poison **2** hatred, spite

venomous *adj* **1** poisonous **2** spiteful ▫ **venomously** *adv*

vent *noun* **1** a small opening **2** a hole to allow air or smoke to pass through **3** an outlet **4** a slit at the bottom of the back of a coat *etc* ▫ *verb* express (strong emotion) in some way ▫ **give vent to** express, let out

ventilate *verb* **1** allow fresh air to pass through (a room *etc*) **2** talk about, discuss ▫ **ventilation** *noun* ▫ **ventilator** *noun* a grating or other device for allowing in fresh air

ventricle *noun* a small cavity in the brain or heart

ventriloquist *noun* someone who can speak without appearing to move their lips and can project their voice onto a puppet *etc* ▫ **ventriloquism** *noun*

Literally 'stomach speaker' and originally meaning someone possessed by a talking evil spirit

venture *noun* an undertaking which involves some risk: *business venture* ▫ *verb* **1** risk, dare **2** do or say something at the risk of causing annoyance: *may I venture to suggest* ▫ **venturesome** *adj* ▫ **venturous** *adj*

venue *noun* the scene of an event, *eg* a sports contest or conference

Venusian *adj* of the planet Venus ▫ *noun* an imaginary being from Venus

veracious *adj* truthful ▫ **veracity** *noun* truthfulness

⚠Do not confuse with: **voracious**

veranda or **verandah** *noun* a kind of terrace with a roof supported by pillars, extending along the side of a house

verb *noun* the word that tells what someone or something does in a sentence, *eg* 'I *sing*' / 'he *had* no idea'

verbal *adj* **1** of words **2** spoken, not written: *verbal agreement* **3** of verbs

verbatim *adj* in the exact words, word for word: *a verbatim account*

verbose *adj* using more words than necessary ◊ **verbosity** *noun*

verdant *adj* green with grass or leaves

verdict *noun* **1** the judge's decision at the end of a trial **2** someone's personal opinion on a matter

verdigris *noun* the greenish rust of copper, brass or bronze

verdure *noun* green vegetation

verge *noun* **1** the grassy border along the edge of a road *etc* **2** edge, brink: *on the verge of a mental breakdown* ◊ **verge on** be close to: *verging on the absurd*

verger *noun* a church caretaker, or church official

verify *verb* prove, show to be true, confirm ◊ **verifiable** *adj* able to be verified ◊ **verification** *noun*

verify » verif*ies*, verify*ing*, verif*ied*

verily *adj*, *old* truly, really

verisimilitude *noun* realism, closeness to real life

veritable *adj* **1** true **2** real, genuine

verity *noun* truth

vermicelli *noun* a type of food like spaghetti but in much thinner pieces

vermilion *noun* a bright red colour

vermin *noun plural* animals or insects that are considered pests, *eg* rats, mice, fleas *etc* ◊ **verminous** *adj* full of vermin

vermouth *noun* a kind of drink containing white wine flavoured with wormwood

vernacular *noun* the ordinary spoken language of a country or district ◊ *adj* in the vernacular

vernal *adj* of the season of spring

verruca *noun* a wart, especially on the foot

versatile *adj* **1** able to turn easily from one subject or task to another **2** useful in many different ways ◊ **versatility** *noun*

verse 1 a number of lines of poetry forming a planned unit **2** poetry as opposed to prose **3** a short division of a chapter of the Bible ◊ **versed in** skilled or experienced in

version *noun* **1** an account from one point of view **2** a form: *another version of the same tune* **3** a translation

verso *noun* the left-hand page of an open book (*compare with*: **recto**)

versus *prep* against (*short form*: **v**)

vertebra *noun* (*plural* **vertebrae**) one of the bones of the spine

vertebrate *noun* an animal with a backbone

vertex *noun* (*plural* **vertices**) the top or summit; the point of a cone, pyramid or angle

vertical *adj* **1** standing upright **2** straight up and down ◊ **vertically** *adv*

vertigo *noun* giddiness, dizziness

verve *noun* lively spirit, enthusiasm

very *adv* **1** to a great extent or degree: *seem very happy/ walk very* *quietly* **2** exactly: *the very same* ▯ *adj* **1** same, identical: *the very people who claimed to support him voted against him* **2** ideal, exactly what is wanted: *the very man for the job* **3** actual: *in the very act of stealing* **4** mere: *the very thought of blood*

vespers *noun plural* a church service in the evening

vessel *noun* **1** a ship **2** a container for liquid **3** a tube conducting fluids in the body: *blood vessels*

vest *noun* **1** an undergarment for the top half of the body **2** *US* a waistcoat

vestibule *noun* an entrance hall; a lobby

vestige *noun* a trace, an indication of something's existence

vestigial *adj* surviving only as a trace of former existence: *vestigial wings*

vestment *noun* a ceremonial garment, worn *eg* by a religious officer during a service

vestry *noun* (*plural* **vestries**) a room in a church in which vestments are kept

vet[1] *noun, informal* a veterinary surgeon

vet[2] *verb* examine, check

vet » vet*s*, vett*ing*, vett*ed*

vetch *noun* a plant of the pea family

veteran *adj* old, experienced ▯ *noun* **1** someone who has given long service **2** an old soldier **3** *US* anyone who has served in the armed forces

veterinarian *noun, US* a veterinary surgeon

veterinary *adj* relating to the treatment of animal diseases ▯ **veterinary surgeon** a doctor who treats animals

veto /*vee*toh/ *noun* (*plural* **vetoes**) **1** the power to forbid or block (a proposal) **2** an act of forbidding or blocking ▯ *verb* forbid, block

veto *verb* » veto*s*, veto*ing*, veto*ed*

Latin for 'I forbid', a phrase originally used by people's tribunes in the Roman Senate when objecting to proposals

vex *verb* annoy; cause trouble to

vexation *noun* **1** the state of being vexed **2** something that vexes

vexatious *adj* causing trouble or annoyance

VGA *abbrev, comput* video-graphics array

VHF *abbrev* very high frequency

via *prep* by way of: *travelling to Paris via London*

viable *adj* able to be managed, practicable: *viable proposition*

viaduct *noun* a long bridge taking a railway or road over a river *etc*

viands *noun plural, old* food

vibrant *adj* full of energy; lively, sparkling

vibrate *verb* **1** shake, tremble **2** swing to and fro rapidly **3** of sound: resound, ring ▯ **vibration** *noun* **1** the act of vibrating **2** a rapid to-and-fro movement ◇ **vibrator** *noun* an electrical device used for sexual stimulation ◇ **vibratory** *adj* of vibration

vicar *noun* an Anglican cleric in charge of a parish ◇ **vicarage** *noun* the house of a vicar

vicarious *adj* **1** in place or on behalf of another person **2** not experienced personally but imagined through the experience of others: *vicarious thrill* ◇ **vicariously** *adv*

vice *noun* **1** a bad habit, a serious fault **2** wickedness, immorality **3** a tool with two jaws for gripping objects firmly

vice- *prefix* second in rank to: *vice-chancellor/ vice-president*

viceroy *noun* a governor acting on royal authority

vice versa *adv* the other way round: *I needed his help and vice versa* (*ie* he needed mine)

vicinity *noun* **1** nearness **2** neighbourhood

vicious *adj* wicked; spiteful ◇ **vicious circle** a bad situation whose results cause it to get worse ◇ **viciously** *adv* ◇ **viciousness** *noun*

vicissitude *noun* **1** change from one state to another **2** (**vicissitudes**) changes of luck, ups and downs

victim *noun* **1** someone who is killed or harmed, intentionally or by accident: *victim of a brutal attack/ victim of the financial situation* **2** an animal for sacrifice ◇ **victimize** *verb* treat unjustly; make a victim of

victor *noun* a winner of a contest *etc*

victorious *adj* successful in a battle or other contest

victory *noun* (*plural* **victories**) success in any battle, struggle or contest

victuals /vitəlz/ *noun plural* food

video *adj* **1** relating to the recording and broadcasting of TV pictures and sound **2** relating to recording by video ◇ *noun* (*plural* **videos**) **1** a videocassette recorder **2** a recording on videotape **3** *US* television ◇ *verb* make a recording by video ◇ **video game** an electronically-operated game played using a visual display unit ◇ **video nasty** a pornographic or horror film on videotape ◇ **videotape** *noun* magnetic tape for carrying pictures and sound

> **video** *verb* » videos, video*ing*, video*ed*

videocassette *noun* a cassette containing videotape ◇ **videocassette recorder** a tape recorder using videocassettes for recording and playing back TV programmes

vie *verb*: **vie with** compete with, try to outdo

> **vie** » vie*s*, vy*ing*, vie*d*

view *noun* **1** a range or field of sight: *a good view* **2** a scene **3** an opinion ◇ *verb* **1** look at **2** watch (television) **3** consider ◇ **viewpoint** *noun* **1** a place from which a scene is viewed **2** a personal opinion (also

point of view) ▫ **in view 1** in sight **2** in your mind as an aim ▫ **in view of** taking into consideration ▫ **on view** on show; ready for inspecting ▫ **with a view to** with the purpose or intention of

vigil *noun* a time of watching or of keeping awake at night, often before a religious festival

vigilance *noun* watchfulness, alertness ▫ **vigilant** *adj*

vigilante /viji*lan*teh/ *noun* a private citizen who assumes the task of keeping order in a community

vignette *noun* **1** a small design or portrait **2** a short description, a sketch

vigorous *adj* strong, healthy; forceful: *vigorous defence* ▫ **vigorously** *adv*

vigour *noun* strength of body or mind; energy

Viking *noun*, *hist* a Norse invader of Western Europe

vile *adj* **1** very bad **2** disgusting, revolting ▫ **vilely** *adv*

vilify *verb* say bad things about

> **vilify** » vilifi*es*, vilify*ing*, vilifi*ed*

villa *noun* a house in the country *etc* used for holidays

village *noun* a collection of houses, not big enough to be called a town

villager *noun* someone who lives in a village

villain *noun* a scoundrel, a rascal ▫ **villainy** *noun* (*plural* **villainies**) wickedness

villainous *adj* wicked

villein *noun*, *hist* a serf

vindicate *verb* **1** clear from blame **2** justify

vindictive *adj* revengeful; spiteful

vine *noun* **1** a climbing plant that produces grapes (also **grapevine**) **2** any climbing or trailing plant

vinegar *noun* a sour-tasting liquid made from wine, beer *etc*, used for seasoning or pickling

vinery *noun* a hot-house for growing vines

vineyard /*vin*yərd/ *noun* an area planted with grapevines

vintage *noun* **1** the gathering of ripe grapes **2** the grapes gathered **3** wine of a particular year, *esp* when of very high quality **4** time of origin or manufacture ▫ *adj* **1** of a vintage **2** of wine: of a particular year **3** very characteristic of an author, style *etc*: *vintage Monty Python* ▫ **vintage car** one of a very early type, still able to run

vintner /*vit*nər/ *noun* a wine-seller

viola *noun* **1** a stringed instrument like a large violin **2** a member of the family of plants which include violets and pansies

violate *verb* **1** break (a law, a treaty *etc*) **2** harm sexually, *esp* rape **3** treat with disrespect **4** disturb, interrupt ▫ **violation** *noun* ▫ **violator** *noun*

violent *adj* **1** acting with great force: *violent storm* **2** caused by violence: *violent death* **3** uncontrollable: *violent temper* ▫ **violence**

noun great roughness and force □ **violently** *adv*

violet *noun* a kind of small bluish-purple flower

violin *noun* a musical instrument with four strings, held under the chin and played with a bow □ **violinist** *noun* someone who plays the violin

violoncello *see* **cello**

VIP *abbrev* very important person

viper *noun* **1** an adder **2** a vicious or treacherous person

virago *noun* (*plural* **viragos**) a noisy, bad-tempered woman

viral *see* **virus**

virgin *noun* someone who has had no sexual intercourse □ **the Virgin Mary** the mother of Christ

virginal[1] *adj* of or like a virgin; chaste

virginal[2] or **virginals** *noun* an early type of musical instrument, with a keyboard

virile *adj* manly; strong, vigorous □ **virility** *noun* manhood; manliness; strength, vigour

virtual *adj* in effect, though not in strict fact □ **virtually** *adv*

virtue *noun* **1** goodness of character and behaviour **2** a good quality, *eg* honesty, generosity *etc* **3** a good point: *one virtue of plastic crockery is that it doesn't break* □ **by virtue of** because of

virtuoso *noun* (*plural* **virtuosos**) a highly skilled artist, *esp* a musician □ **virtuosity** *noun*

virtuous *adj* good, just, honest □ **virtuously** *adv*

virulent *adj* **1** full of poison **2** bitter, spiteful **3** of a disease: dangerous □ **virulence** *noun*

virus *noun* (*plural* **viruses**) a germ that is smaller than any bacteria, and causes diseases such as mumps, chickenpox *etc* □ **viral** *adj* of a virus

visa *noun* a permit given by the authorities of a country to allow someone to stay for a time in that country

visage *noun* the face

vis-à-vis /veezəvee/ *prep* in relation to, compared with

viscera /*visərə*/ *noun plural* the inner parts of the body □ **visceral** *adj* **1** of the viscera **2** gory, bloody

viscid /*vis*id/ *adj* viscous

viscount /*vai*kownt/ *noun* a title of nobility next below an earl

viscountess *noun* a title of nobility next below a countess

viscous /*viskəs*/ *adj* of a liquid: sticky, not flowing easily □ **viscosity** *noun*

visible *adj* able to be seen □ **visibility** *noun* **1** the clearness with which objects may be seen **2** the extent or range of vision as affected by fog, rain *etc* □ **visibly** *adv*

vision *noun* **1** the act or power of seeing **2** something seen in the imagination **3** a strange, supernatural sight **4** the ability to foresee likely future events

visionary *adj* seen in imagination only, not real □ *noun* (*plural*

visionaries) someone who dreams up imaginative plans

visit *verb* **1** go to see; call on **2** stay with as a guest □ *noun* **1** a call at a person's house or at a place of interest *etc* **2** a short stay □ **visitation** *noun* **1** a visit of an important official **2** a great misfortune, seen as a punishment from God □ **visitor** *noun* someone who makes a visit

visor /*vaizər*/ *noun* **1** a part of a helmet covering the face **2** a movable shade on a car's windscreen **3** a peak on a cap for shading the eyes

vista *noun* a view, *esp* one seen through a long, narrow opening

visual *adj* relating to, or received through, sight: *visual aids* □ **visual display unit** a device like a television set, on which data from a computer's memory can be displayed

visualize *verb* form a clear picture of in the mind □ **visualization** *noun*

vital *adj* **1** of the greatest importance: *vital information* **2** necessary to life **3** of life **4** vigorous, energetic: *a vital personality* □ **vitality** *noun* life; liveliness, strength; ability to go on living □ **vitalize** *verb* give life or vigour to □ **vitally** *adv* □ **vitals** *noun plural*, *old* parts of the body necessary for life

vitamin *noun* one of a group of substances necessary for health, occurring in different natural foods

vitiate *verb* spoil, damage

vitreous *adj* of or like glass

vitrify *verb* make or become like glass

vitrify » vitrifi*es*, vitrify*ing*, vitrifi*ed*

vitriol *noun* sulphuric acid

vitriolic *adj* biting, scathing

vitro *see* **in vitro**

vituperate *verb* be rude to, abuse □ **vituperation** *noun* □ **vituperative** *adj* abusive, very rude

viva /*vaivə*/ *noun* an oral examination □ *verb* examine orally

vivacious *adj* lively, sprightly □ **vivaciously** *adv* □ **vivacity** *noun* liveliness, spark

vivarium *noun* a tank or other enclosure for keeping living creatures

vivid *adj* **1** life-like **2** brilliant, striking □ **vividly** *adv*

vivisection *noun* the carrying out of experiments on living animals

vixen *noun* **1** a female fox **2** an ill-tempered woman

viz *adj* namely

vizier *noun, hist* a minister of state in some Eastern countries

vocabulary *noun* (*plural* **vocabularies**) **1** the range of words used by an individual or group **2** the words of a particular language **3** a list of words in alphabetical order, with their meanings

vocal *adj* **1** of the voice **2** expressing your opinions loudly and fully □ **vocalist** *noun* a singer

vocation *noun* **1** an occupation or profession to which someone feels called to dedicate themselves **2** a strong inclination or desire to follow a particular course of action or work

vociferous *adj* loud in speech, noisy ▫ **vociferously** *adv*

vodka *noun* an alcoholic spirit made from grain or potatoes

vogue *noun* the fashion of the moment; popularity ▫ **in vogue** in fashion

voice *noun* **1** the sound produced from the mouth in speech or song **2** ability to sing **3** an opinion ▫ *verb* express (an opinion)

void *adj* **1** empty, vacant **2** not valid ▫ *noun* an empty space ▫ **void of** lacking completely

vol *abbrev* volume

volatile *adj* **1** of a liquid: quickly turning into vapour **2** of a person: changeable in mood or behaviour, fickle

volcano *noun* (*plural* **volcanoes**) a mountain with an opening through which molten rock, ashes *etc* are periodically thrown up from inside the earth ▫ **volcanic** *adj* **1** relating to volcanoes **2** caused or produced by heat within the earth

> Named after *Vulcan*, the Roman god of fire

vole *noun* any of a group of small rodents, including the water rat

volition *noun* an act of will or choice: *he did it of his own volition*

volley *noun* (*plural* **volleys**) **1** a number of shots fired or missiles thrown at the same time **2** an outburst of abuse or criticism **3** *tennis* a return of a ball before it reaches the ground ▫ *verb* **1** shoot or throw in a volley **2** return (a ball) before it reaches the ground

volt *noun* the unit used in measuring the force of electricity ▫ **voltage** *noun* electrical force measured in volts

voluble *adj* speaking with a great flow of words ▫ **volubility** *noun*

volume *noun* **1** a book, often one of a series **2** the amount of space taken up by anything **3** amount: *volume of trade* **4** loudness or fullness of sound ▫ **voluminous** *adj* bulky, of great volume

voluntary *adj* **1** done or acting by choice, not under compulsion **2** working without payment ▫ *noun* (*plural* **voluntaries**) a piece of organ music of the organist's choice played at a church service

volunteer *noun* someone who offers to do something of their own accord, often for no payment ▫ *verb* **1** act as a volunteer **2** give (information, an opinion *etc*) unasked

voluptuous *adj* full of, or too fond of, the pleasures of life

vomit *verb* throw up the contents of the stomach through the mouth ▫ *noun* the matter thrown up by vomiting

voracious *adj* very greedy, difficult to satisfy: *voracious appetite/ voracious reader* ▫ **voracity** *noun*

> ⚠Do not confuse with: **veracious**

vortex *noun* (*plural* **vortices** o

vortexes) **1** a whirlpool **2** a whirlwind

votary *noun* (*plural* **votaries**) **1** someone who has made a vow **2** a devoted worshipper or admirer

vote *verb* **1** give your support to (a particular candidate, a proposal *etc*) in a ballot or show of hands **2** decide by voting □ *noun* **1** an expression of opinion or support by voting **2** the right to vote □ **voter** *noun* someone who votes

vouch *verb* (with **for**) say that you are sure of or can guarantee: *I can vouch for his courage* □ **vouchsafe** *verb* give or grant (a reply, privilege *etc*)

voucher *noun* a paper which can be exchanged for money or goods

vow *noun* a solemn promise or declaration, *esp* one made to God □ *verb* **1** make a vow **2** threaten (revenge *etc*)

vowel *noun* **1** a sound made by the voice that does not require the use of the tongue, teeth or lips **2** the letters *a*, *e*, *i*, *o*, *u* (or various combinations of them), and sometimes *y*, which represent those sounds

vox pop public or popular opinion (from Latin *vox populi*, voice of the people)

voyage *noun* a journey, usually by sea □ *verb* make a journey

voyeur *noun* someone who gets sexual pleasure from watching other people secretly □ **voyeuristic** *adj*

VSO *abbrev* Voluntary Service Overseas

vulgar *adj* **1** coarse, ill-mannered **2** indecent **3** of the common people □ **vulgarian** *noun* □ **vulgarity** *noun* □ **vulgarly** *adv* □ **vulgar fraction** a fraction not written as a decimal, *eg* $\frac{1}{3}$, $\frac{4}{5}$

vulnerable *adj* **1** exposed to, or in danger of, attack **2** liable to be hurt physically or emotionally □ **vulnerability** *noun*

vulture *noun* a large bird that feeds mainly on the flesh of dead animals

W

wad 1 a lump of loose material (*eg* wool, cloth, paper) pressed together **2** a bunch of banknotes ▫ **wadding** *noun* soft material (*eg* cotton wool) used for packing or padding

waddle *verb* walk with short, unsteady steps, moving from side to side as a duck does ▫ *noun*

wade *verb* **1** walk through deep water or mud **2** get through with difficulty: *still wading through this book*

wader *noun* **1** a long-legged bird that wades in search of food **2** (**waders**) high waterproof boots worn by anglers for wading

wadi *noun* a rocky river-bed in North Africa, dry except in the rainy season

wafer *noun* **1** a very thin, light type of biscuit, as that eaten with ice-cream **2** a very thin slice of anything

waffle *noun* **1** *US* a light, crisp cake made from batter, cooked in a **waffle-iron 2** pointless, long-drawn-out talk ▫ *verb* talk long and meaninglessly

waft *verb* carry or drift lightly through the air or over water

wag *verb* move from side to side or up and down ▫ *noun* **1** an act of wagging **2** someone who is always joking ▫ **waggish** *adj* always joking

> **wag** *verb* » wag*s*, wagg*ing*, wagg*ed*

wage *verb* carry on (a war *etc*) ▫ *noun* (often **wages**) payment for work

wager *noun* a bet ▫ *verb* bet

waggle *verb* move from side to side in an unsteady manner ▫ *noun* an unsteady movement from side to side

wagon or **waggon** *noun* **1** a four-wheeled vehicle for carrying loads **2** an open railway carriage for goods **3** *US* a trolley for carrying food

wagtail *noun* a small black and white bird with a long tail which it wags up and down

waif *noun* an uncared-for or homeless child or animal ▫ **waifs and strays** homeless children or animals

wail *verb* cry or moan in sorrow ▫ *noun* a sorrowful cry

wain *noun*, *old* a wagon

wainscot *noun* a skirting-board

waist *noun* the narrow part of the body, between ribs and hips

waistcoat *noun* a short, sleeveles[s] jacket, often worn under an oute[r] jacket

wait *verb* **1** put off or delay actio[n] **2** (with **for**) remain in expectatio[n] or readiness for: *waiting for the bu[s] to come* **3** be employed as a waite[r] or waitress ▫ *noun* **1** a delay [2] (**waits**) singers of Christmas caro[ls] ▫ **waiting list** a list of people waitin[g] for something in order of priority □ **waiting room** a room in which to wait at a railway station, clinic *etc* □ **wait on 1** serve (someone) at table **2** act as a servant to

waiter, waitress *noun* someone whose job it is to serve people at table in a restaurant

waive *verb* give up (a claim or right) □ **waiver** *noun* **1** the act of waiving **2** a document indicating this

> ⚠Do not confuse with: **wave** and **waver**

wake[1] *verb* (often with **up**) stop sleeping □ *noun* **1** a night of watching beside a dead body **2** a feast or holiday □ **wakeful** *adj* not sleeping, unable to sleep □ **waking** *adj* being or becoming awake

> **wake** *verb* » wake*s*, wak*ing*, woken, woke or wak*ed*

wake[2] *noun* a streak of foamy water left in the track of a ship □ **in the wake of** immediately behind or after

waken *verb* wake, arouse or be aroused

walk *verb* **1** move along on foot **2** travel along (streets *etc*) on foot □ *noun* **1** an act of walking **2** a manner of walking **3** a distance to be walked over: *a short walk from here* **4** a place for walking: *a covered walk* □ **walkie-talkie** *noun* a portable radio set for sending and receiving messages □ **walking stick** a stick used for support when walking □ **walk-over** *noun* an easy victory □ **walk of life** someone's rank or occupation □ **walk the plank** *hist* be put to death by pirates by being made to walk off the end of a plank over a ship's side

Walkman *noun, trademark* a personal stereo

wall *noun* **1** a structure built of stone, brick *etc* used to separate or enclose **2** the side of a building □ *verb* (with **in, off** *etc*) enclose or separate with a wall □ **off the wall** unusual, eccentric

wallaby (*plural* **wallabies**) a small kind of kangaroo

wallet *noun* a small folding case for holding bank-notes, credit cards *etc*

wallflower *noun* **1** a sweet-smelling spring flower **2** someone who is continually without a partner at a dance *etc*

wallop *verb, informal* beat, hit □ *noun*

wallow *verb* roll about with enjoyment in water, mud *etc*

wallpaper *noun* paper used in house decorating for covering walls □ *verb* cover with wallpaper

wally /woli/ *noun* (*plural* **wallies**), *slang* a stupid or inept person

walnut *noun* **1** a tree whose wood is used for making furniture **2** the nut it produces

walrus *noun* (*plural* **walruses**) a large sea animal, like a seal, with two long tusks

waltz *noun* (*plural* **waltzes**) **1** a ballroom dance for couples with a circling movement **2** music for this dance, with three beats to each bar □ *verb* dance a waltz

WAN *abbrev, comput* wide area network

wan /won/ *adj* pale and sickly looking

wand *noun* a long slender rod used by a conjuror, magician *etc*

wander *verb* **1** roam about with no definite purpose; roam **2** go astray **3** be mentally confused because of illness *etc* □ **wanderer** *noun*

wanderlust *noun* a keen desire for travel

wane *verb* **1** become smaller (*contrasted with*: **wax**) **2** lose power, importance *etc* □ **on the wane** becoming less

wangle *verb* get or achieve through craftiness, skilful planning *etc*

wannabe *noun, informal* someone who desperately wants to be a particular thing: *filmstar wannabes*

want *verb* **1** wish for **2** need, lack □ *noun* **1** poverty **2** scarcity, lack □ **wanted** *adj* looked for, *esp* by the police □ **wanting** *adj* **1** absent, missing; without **2** not good enough **3** feeble-minded **4** (with **in**) lacking: *wanting in good taste*

wanton *adj* thoughtless, pointless, without motive: *wanton cruelty*

war *noun* an armed struggle, *esp* between nations □ *verb* (with **against**) fight in a war, make war against □ **war-cry** *noun* words shouted aloud in battle, for encouragement □ **warfare** *noun* the carrying on of war □ **warhead** *noun* the part of a missile containing the explosive □ **warlike** *adj* **1** fond of war **2** threatening war □ **warrior** *noun* a great fighter □ **warship** *noun* a ship armed with guns *etc* □ **on the warpath** in a fighting or angry mood

war *verb* » war*s*, war*ring*, war*red*

warble *verb* sing like a bird, trill □ **warbler** *noun* a type of song-bird

ward *verb* (with **off**) keep off, defend yourself against (a blow *etc*) □ *noun* **1** a hospital room containing a number of beds **2** one of the parts into which a town is divided for voting **3** someone who is in the care of a guardian □ **warden** *noun* **1** someone who guards a game reserve **2** someone in charge of a hostel or college □ **warder**, **wardress** *noun* a prison guard □ **wardrobe** *noun* **1** a cupboard for clothes **2** someone's personal supply of clothes □ **wardroom** *noun* a room for officers on a warship

-ware *suffix* manufacturec material: *earthenware/ glassware* **warehouse** *noun* a building wher goods are stored □ **wares** *nou plural* goods for sale

warm *adj* **1** fairly hot **2** of clothes keeping the wearer warm **3** of person: friendly, loving □ *verb* mak or become warm □ **warm-bloode** *adj* having a blood temperatu higher than that of the surroundin atmosphere □ **warm-hearted** *a* kind, generous □ **warmth** *noun*

warn *verb* **1** tell (someone) befor hand about possible danger, mi fortune *etc*: *I warned him about tl icy roads* **2** give cautionary advi to: *I warned him not to be late* □ **warning** *noun* a remark, notice *etc* that warns

warp *verb* **1** become twisted out of shape **2** distort, make unsound: *his previous experiences had warped his judgement* □ *noun* the threads stretched lengthwise on a loom, which are crossed by the weft

warrant *noun* a certificate granting someone a right or authority: *search warrant* □ *verb* justify, be a good enough reason for: *the crime does not warrant such punishment* □ **warranted** *adj* guaranteed □ **I warrant you** or **I'll warrant** you may be sure, I assure you

warren *noun* **1** a collection of rabbit burrows **2** a building with many rooms and passages; a maze

wart *noun* a small hard growth on the skin □ **wart-hog** *noun* a wild African pig

wary *adj* cautious, on guard □ **warily** *adv* □ **wariness** *noun*

was *past form* of **be**

wash *verb* **1** clean with water, soap *etc* **2** clean yourself with water *etc* **3** of water: flow over or against **4** sweep (away, along *etc*) by force of water □ *noun* (*plural* **washes**) **1** a washing **2** a streak of foamy water left behind by a moving boat **3** a liquid with which anything is washed **4** a thin coat of paint *etc* □ **washer** *noun* **1** someone or something that washes **2** a flat ring of metal, rubber *etc* for keeping joints tight □ **washerwoman** *noun, old* a woman who is paid to wash clothes □ **washhand basin** a bathroom sink in which to wash your hands and face □ **washing** *noun* **1** the act of cleaning by water **2** clothes to be washed □ **washing machine** an electric machine for washing clothes □ **washing-up** *noun* dishes to be washed □ **wash your hands of** have nothing further to do with □ **wash up** wash the dishes

wasp *noun* a stinging, winged insect, with a slender, yellow and black striped body

wassail *verb, old* have a convivial drinking session

waste *adj* **1** thrown away, rejected as useless: *waste paper* **2** of land: uncultivated, barren and desolate □ *verb* **1** spend (money, time, energy) extravagantly, without result or profit **2** decay or wear away gradually □ *noun* **1** extravagant use, squandering **2** rubbish, waste material **3** uncultivated land **4** an expanse of water, snow *etc* □ **wastage** *noun* **1** an amount wasted **2** loss through decay or squandering □ **wasteful** *adj* causing waste, extravagant □ **waster** or **wastrel** *noun* an idle, good-for-nothing person □ **wastepaper basket** a basket for paper rubbish □ **wastepipe** *noun* a pipe for carrying away dirty water or semi-liquid waste

watch *verb* **1** look at, observe closely **2** (often with **over**) look after, mind **3** *old* keep awake □ *noun* (*plural* **watches**) **1** the act of keeping guard **2** someone who keeps, or those who keep, guard **3** a sailor's period of duty on deck **4** a small clock worn on the wrist or kept in a pocket □ **watchdog** *noun* **1** a dog which guards a building

2 an organization which monitors business practices *etc* □ **watchful** *adj* alert, cautious □ **watchfully** *adv* □ **watchfulness** *noun* □ **watchman** *noun* a man who guards a building *etc* at night □ **watchword** *noun* a motto, a slogan

water *noun* **1** a clear, tasteless liquid which falls as rain **2** a collection of this liquid in a lake, river *etc* **3** urine □ *verb* **1** supply with water **2** dilute or mix with water **3** of the mouth: fill with saliva **4** of the eyes: fill with tears □ **water biscuit** a crisp biscuit, a cracker □ **water butt** a large barrel for rain water □ **water-closet** *noun* a toilet, a lavatory (*short form*: **WC**) □ **water-colour** *noun* **1** a paint which is mixed with water, not oil **2** a painting done with this paint □ **watercress** *noun* a plant which grows beside streams, with hot-tasting leaves which are eaten in salads □ **waterfall** *noun* a place where a river falls from a height, often over a ledge of rock □ **waterhen** *noun* a dark-coloured bird which lives near ponds or rivers □ **waterlily** *noun* a plant which grows in ponds *etc*, with flat floating leaves and large flowers □ **waterlogged** *adj* **1** filled with water **2** soaked with water □ **watermain** *noun* a large underground pipe carrying a public water supply □ **watermark** *noun* a faint design on writing paper showing the maker's name, crest *etc* □ **watermelon** *noun* a large melon with red juicy flesh and a thick, green rind □ **watermill** *noun* a mill driven by water □ **water polo** a ball-game played in a pool between teams of swimmers □ **waterproof** *adj* not allowing water to pass through □ *noun* an overcoat made of waterproof material □ **water rat** a kind of vole □ **watershed** *noun* a ridge separating the valleys of two rivers □ **watertight** *adj* so closely fitted that water cannot leak through □ **waterway** *noun* a channel along which ships can sail □ **waterwheel** *noun* a wheel moved by water □ **waterworks** *noun plural* **1** a place which purifies and stores a town's water supply **2** *euphem* the urinary system **3** *informal* tears □ **watery** *adj* **1** full of water **2** too liquid, textureless

watt *noun* a unit of electric power □ **wattage** *noun* electric power measured in watts

wattle *noun* **1** interwoven twigs and branches used for fences *etc* **2** an Australian acacia tree **3** a fleshy part hanging from the neck of a turkey

wave *noun* **1** a moving ridge on the surface of the water **2** a ridge or curve of hair **3** a vibration travelling through the air carrying light, sound *etc* **4** a hand gesture for attracting attention, or saying hello or goodbye **5** a rush of an emotion (*eg* despair, enthusiasm *etc*) □ *verb* **1** make a wave with the hand **2** move to and fro, flutter: *flags waving in the wind* **3** curl, curve □ **wavelength** *noun* the distance from one point on a wave or vibration to the next similar point □ **wavy** *adj* having waves

⚠Do not confuse with: **waive**

waver *verb* **1** be unsteady, wobble **2** be uncertain or undecided

wax 1 the sticky, fatty substance of which bees make their cells **2** a fatty substance in the ear **3** a quickly hardening substance used for sealing letters *etc* □ *adj* made of wax □ *verb* **1** rub with wax **2** grow, increase (*contrasted with*: **wane**) □ **waxen** *adj* **1** of or like wax **2** pale □ **waxworks** *noun plural* a museum displaying wax models of famous people □ **waxy** *adj* of, or like, wax

way *noun* **1** an opening, a passage: *the way out* **2** road, path **3** room to go forward or pass: *block the way* **4** direction: *he went that way* **5** route: *do you know the way?* **6** distance: *a long way* **7** condition: *in a bad way* **8** means, method: *there must be a way to do this* **9** manner: *in a clumsy way* **10** someone's own wishes or choice: *he always gets his own way* □ **wayfarer** *noun, old* a traveller on foot □ **waylay** *verb* wait for and stop (someone) □ **-ways** *suffix* in the direction of: *lengthways/ sideways* □ **wayside** *noun* the edge of a road or path □ *adj* located by the side of a road □ **wayward** *adj* wilful, following your own way □ **by the way** incidentally, in passing □ **by way of 1** travelling through **2** as if, with the purpose of: *by way of a favour* □ **in the way** blocking progress □ **make your way** go

WC *abbrev* water-closet

we *pronoun* used by a speaker or writer in mentioning themselves together with other people (as the subject of a verb): *we are having a party this weekend*

weak *adj* **1** not strong, feeble **2** lacking determination, easily persuaded **3** easily overcome: *weak opposition* □ **weaken** *verb* make or become weak □ **weakling** *noun* someone or an animal lacking strength □ **weakly** *adj* lacking strength, sickly □ **weakness** *noun* **1** lack of strength **2** a fault; a special fondness (for): *a weakness for chocolate* □ **weak-kneed** *adj* lacking determination

weal *noun* a raised mark on the skin caused by a blow from a whip

wealth *noun* **1** riches **2** a large quantity: *wealth of information* □ **wealthy** *adj* rich

wean[1] *verb* **1** make (a child or young animal) used to food other than the mother's milk **2** (with **from** or **off**) make (someone) gradually give up (a bad habit *etc*)

wean[2] /wehn/ *noun, Scot* a child

weapon *noun* **1** an instrument used for fighting, *eg* a sword, gun *etc* **2** any means of attack

wear *verb* **1** be dressed in, have on the body **2** arrange in a particular way: *she wears her hair long* **3** have (a beard, moustache) on the face **4** damage or weaken by use, rubbing *etc* **5** be damaged in this way **6** last: *wear well* □ *noun* **1** use by wearing: *for my own wear* **2** damage by use **3** ability to last **4** clothes *etc*: *school wear* □ **wearable** *adj* fit to be worn □ **wearer** *noun* □ **wearing** *adj* tiring, exhausting □ **wear and tear** damage by ordinary use □ **wear off** pass away gradually □ **wear on** become later: *the afternoon wore on* □ **wear out 1** make or become unfit for further use **2** exhaust

> **wear** *verb* » wear*s*, wear*ing*, wore, worn

weary *adj* **1** tired, having used up your strength or patience **2** tiring, boring ▯ *verb* make or become tired, bored or impatient ▯ **wearisome** *adj* causing tiredness, boredom or impatience ▯ **weary of** tired of, bored with

> **weary** » wear*ies*, weary*ing*, wear*ied*

weasel *noun* a small wild animal with a long and slender body, that lives on mice, birds *etc*

weather *noun* the state of the atmosphere, *eg* heat, coldness, cloudiness *etc* ▯ *verb* **1** dry or wear away through exposure to the air **2** come safely through (a storm, difficulty *etc*) ▯ **weatherbeaten** *adj* showing signs of having been out in all weathers ▯ **weathercock** or **weathervane** *noun* a flat piece of metal that swings in the wind to show its direction

weave *verb* **1** pass threads over and under each other on a loom *etc* to form cloth **2** plait cane *etc* for basket-making **3** put together (a story, plan *etc*) **4** move in and out between objects, or move from side to side: *weaving through the traffic* ▯ **weaver** *noun* someone who weaves

> **weave** » weave*s*, weav*ing*, wove, wov*en*

web *noun* **1** the net made by a spider, a cobweb **2** the skin between the toes of ducks, swans, frogs *etc* **3** something woven ▯ **webbed** *adj* of feet: having the toes joined by a web ▯ **webbing** *noun* a type of strong, woven tape used for belts *etc* ▯ **web-footed** or **web-toed** *adj* having webbed feet or toes

wed *verb* marry ▯ **wedlock** *noun* the state of being married

> **wed** » wed*s*, wedd*ing*, wedd*ed*

we'd *short for* **1** we would; we should **2** we had

wedding *noun* **1** marriage **2** a marriage ceremony

wedge *noun* **1** a piece of wood, metal *etc* thick at one end with a thin edge at the other, used in splitting wood, forcing two surfaces apart *etc* **2** anything shaped like a wedge ▯ *verb* **1** fix or become fixed with a wedge **2** push or squeeze (in): *wedged in amongst the crowd*

Wednesday *noun* the fourth day of the week

wee *adj, Scot* small, tiny

weed *noun* **1** a useless, troublesome plant **2** a weak, worthless person **3** (**weeds**) a widow's mourning clothes ▯ *verb* clear (a garden *etc*) of weeds ▯ **weedy** *adj* **1** full of weeds **2** like a weed **3** thin and puny, unmanly

week *noun* **1** the space of seven days from Sunday to Saturday **2** the working days of the week, not Saturday and Sunday ▯ **weekday** *noun* any day except Saturday and Sunday ▯ **weekend** *noun* the time from Saturday to Monday ▯ **weekly** *adj* happening, or done, once a week ▯ *adv* once a week ▯ *noun* (*plural* **weeklies**) a newspaper magazine *etc* coming out once a week

weep *verb* **1** shed tears **2** ooze, drip: *weeping wound* □ **weeping willow** a willow tree with drooping branches

weevil *noun* a small beetle that destroys grain, flour *etc*

weft *noun* the threads on a loom which cross the warp

weigh *verb* **1** find out how heavy (something) is by putting it on a scale *etc* **2** have a certain heaviness: *weighing 10 kilogrammes* **3** raise (a ship's anchor) **4** of burdens *etc*: press down, be heavy or troublesome **5** consider (a matter, a point) carefully **6** consider (something) mportant □ **weighbridge** *noun* a arge scale for weighing vehicles □ **veigh in** test your weight before a oxing match □ **weigh out** measure ut a quantity by weighing it on a cale

veight *noun* **1** the amount that nything weighs **2** a piece of metal veighing a certain amount: *a 100 ramme weight* **3** a load, a burden importance □ *verb* make heavy y adding or attaching a weight □ **eightless** *adj* □ **weightlessness** *oun* absence of the pull of gravity **weighty** *adj* **1** heavy **2** important

eir *noun* a dam across a stream

eird *adj* **1** mysterious, superatural **2** odd, strange

elcome *verb* **1** receive with armth or pleasure **2** accept gladly: *welcome the challenge* □ *noun* a elcoming, a warm reception □ *adj* eceived with pleasure □ **welcome to** permitted to do or take □ **you're welcome!** used in reply to an expression of thanks

weld *verb* **1** join (pieces of metal) by pressure, with or without heating **2** join closely □ *noun* a joint made by welding □ **welder** *noun*

welfare *noun* comfort, good health □ **welfare state** a country with a health service, insurance against unemployment, pensions for those who cannot work *etc*

well *noun* **1** a spring of water **2** a shaft in the earth to extract water, oil *etc* **3** an enclosed space round which a staircase winds □ *verb* (often with **up**) rise up and gush: *tears welled up in her eyes* □ *adj* in good health □ *adv* **1** in a good and correct manner: *write well* **2** thoroughly: *well beaten* **3** successfully: *do well* **4** conveniently: *it fits in well with my plans* □ *exclam* expressing surprise, or used in explaining, narrating *etc* □ **well-advised** *adj* wise □ **well-being** *noun* welfare; contentment □ **well-bred** or **well-mannered** *adj* having good manners □ **well-disposed** *adj* (with **to**) inclined to favour □ **well-informed** *adj* having or showing knowledge □ **well-known** *adj* **1** familiar **2** celebrated, famous □ **well-meaning** *adj* having good intentions □ **well-meant** *adj* rightly, kindly intended □ **well-off** *adj* rich □ **well-read** *adj* having read many good books □ **well-to-do** *adj* rich □ **well-wisher** *noun* someone who wishes someone success □ **as well as** in addition to □ **it is as well** or **it is just as well** it is a good thing, it is lucky well *adv* » better, best

we'll *short for* we will; we shall

wellingtons *noun plural* high rubber boots covering the lower part of the legs

welsh rarebit a dish made of cheese melted on toast

welt *noun* **1** a firm edging or band, *eg* on the wrist or waist of a garment **2** a weal

welter *verb* roll about, wallow □ *noun* **1** great disorder or confusion **2** a muddled mass, a jumble: *a welter of information*

wench *noun* (*plural* **wenches**) *old* a young woman, a girl

wend *verb*: **wend your way** make your way slowly

went *past form* of **go**

wept *past form* of **weep**

were *past form* of **be**

we're *short for* we are

werewolf *noun* a mythical creature which changes periodically from a human into a wolf

west *noun* one of the four chief directions, that in which the sun sets □ *adj* in the west □ *adv* to or towards the west □ **westerly** *adj* **1** lying or moving towards the west **2** of wind: from the west

western *adj* relating to, or in, the west □ *noun* a film or story about life among the early settlers in the western United States □ **westerner** *noun* someone from the west of a country □ **westernmost** *adj* most westerly □ **westward** *adj* & *adv* towards the west □ **westwards** *adv* towards the west □ **the Wild West** *hist* the western United States in the early days of its settlement

wet *adj* **1** soaked or covered with water or other liquid **2** rainy: *a wet day* □ *noun* **1** water **2** rain □ *verb* make wet □ **wet suit** a suit that allows water to pass through but retains body heat

wet *verb* » wet*s*, wett*ing*, wett*ed*

whack *noun* a loud, violent slap or blow □ *verb* slap or hit violently

whale *noun* a very large mammal living in the sea □ *verb* catch whales □ **whalebone** *noun* a light bendable substance obtained from the upper jaw of certain whales □ **whale oil** oil obtained from the blubber of a whale □ **whaler** *noun* a ship engaged in catching whales

wharf *noun* (*plural* **wharfs** o **wharves**) a landing stage fo loading and unloading ships

what *adj* & *pronoun* used to indicate something about which a question is being asked: *what day is this? / what are you doing?* □ *adj* an that: *give me what money you hav* □ *conj* anything that: *I'll take wh you can give me* □ *adj, adv* & *pronou* used for emphasis in exclamation *what ties he wears!/ what rubbish!* **whatever** *adj* & *pronoun* **1** an thing (that): *show me whatever yo have* **2** no matter what: *whatev happens* □ **whatsoever** *adj* at a *nothing whatsoever to do with me* **what about?** used in aski whether the listener would li something: *what about a glass* *milk?* ◻ **what if?** what will or would happen if : *what if he comes back?* ◻ **what with** because of: *what with having no exercise and being overweight, he had a heart attack*

wheat *noun* a grain from which the flour used for making bread *etc* is made ◻ **wheaten** *adj* **1** made of wheat **2** wholemeal ◻ **wheatear** *noun* a small bird which visits Britain in summer ◻ **wheatgerm** *noun* the vitamin-rich embryo of wheat ◻ **wheatmeal** *noun* meal made of wheat, *esp* wholemeal

wheedle *verb* beg or coax, often by flattery

wheel *noun* **1** a circular frame or disc turning on an axle, used for transporting things **2** a steering-wheel of a car *etc* ◻ *verb* **1** move or push on wheels **2** turn like a wheel or in a wide curve **3** turn round suddenly: *wheeled round in surprise* ◻ **wheelbarrow** *noun* a handcart with one wheel in front, two handles and legs behind ◻ **wheelchair** *noun* a chair on wheels for an invalid ◻ **wheelhouse** *noun* the shelter in which a ship's steering-wheel is placed ◻ **wheelie bin** a large dustbin on wheels ◻ **wheelwright** *noun* someone who makes wheels and carriages

wheeze *verb* breathe with difficulty, making a whistling or croaking sound ◻ *noun* **1** the sound of difficult breathing **2** *informal* a joke

whelk *noun* a type of small shellfish, used as food

whelp *noun* **1** a young lion **2** a puppy ◻ *verb* of a lion, dog *etc*: give birth to young

when *adv* at what time: *when did you arrive?* ◻ *adv & conj* the time at which: *I know when you left/ I fell when I was coming in* ◻ *relative pronoun* at which: *at the time when I saw him* ◻ *conj* seeing that, since: *why walk when you have a car?* ◻ **whenever** *adv & conj* **1** at any given time: *come whenever you're ready* **2** at every time: *I go whenever I get the chance*

whence *adv*, *old* from what place: *whence did you come?* ◻ *conj* to the place from which: *he's gone back whence he came* ◻ **whenceforth** *adv & conj*, *old* whence

where *adv & conj* to or in what place: *where are you going?/ I wonder where we are* ◻ *relative pronoun & conj* (in the place) in which, (to the place) to which: *go where he tells you to go/ it's still where it was* ◻ **whereupon** *adv & conj* at or after which time, event *etc* ◻ **wherever** *adv* to what place: *wherever did you go?* ◻ *conj* to any place: *wherever you may go* ◻ **wherewithal** *noun* **1** the means of doing something **2** money

whereabouts *adv & conj* near or in what place: *whereabouts is it?/I don't know whereabouts it is* ◻ *noun* the place where someone or thing is: *I don't know her whereabouts*

whereas *conj* **1** when in fact: *they thought I was lying, whereas I was telling the truth* **2** but, on the other hand: *he's tall, whereas I'm short*

wherry *noun* (*plural* **wherries**) a type of shallow, light boat

whet *verb* **1** sharpen (a knife *etc*) by rubbing **2** make (desire, appetite *etc*) keener ◊ **whetstone** *noun* a stone on which to sharpen blades

> **whet** » whet*s*, whett*ing*, whett*ed*

whether *conj* **1** either if: *whether you come or not* **2** if: *I don't know whether it's possible*

which *adj* & *pronoun* **1** used to refer to a particular person or thing from a group: *which colour do you like best?* **2** the one that: *show me which dress you would like* ◊ *relative pronoun* referring to the person or thing just named: *I bought the chair which you are sitting on* ◊ **whichever** *adj & pronoun* any (one), no matter which: *I'll take whichever you don't want/ I saw trees whichever way I turned* ◊ **which is which** which is one and which is the other: *they are twins and I can't tell which is which*

whiff *noun* a sudden puff or scent: *whiff of perfume*

while or **whilst** *conj* **1** during the time that: *while I'm at the office* **2** although: *while I sympathize, I can't really help* ◊ **while** *noun* a space of time ◊ *verb* (with **away**) to pass (time) without boredom: *he whiled away the time by reading*

whim *noun* a sudden thought or desire ◊ **whimsical** *adj* **1** full of whims, fanciful **2** humorous ◊ **whimsy** *noun* (*plural* **whimsies**) a whim

whimper *verb* cry with a low, whining voice ◊ *noun* a low, whining cry

whin *noun* gorse

whine *verb* **1** make a high-pitched, complaining cry **2** complain unnecessarily ◊ *noun* an unnecessary complaint

whinge *verb* whine, complain peevishly ◊ *noun* a peevish complaint ◊ **whingeing** *adj* ◊ **whinger** *noun*

> **whinge** *verb* » whinge*s*, whinge*ing*, whinge*d*

whinny *verb* of a horse: neigh ◊ *noun* (*plural* **whinnies**) a neighing sound

> **whinny** *verb* » whinni*es*, whinny*ing*, whinni*ed*

whip *noun* **1** a lash with a handle, for punishing, urging on animals *etc* **2** a member of parliament who sees that the members of their own party attend to give their vote when needed ◊ *verb* **1** hit or drive with a lash **2** beat (eggs, cream *etc*) into a froth **3** snatch (away, off, out, up *etc*): *whipped out a revolver* **4** move fast, like a whip ◊ **whip-hand** *noun* the advantage in a fight, argument *etc* ◊ **whippersnapper** *noun* a small, unimportant, impertinent person ◊ **whipping** *noun* a beating with a whip

> **whip** *verb* » whip*s*, whipp*ing*, whipp*ed*

whippet *noun* a breed of racing dog, like a small greyhound

whir or **whirr** *noun* a sound of fast, continuous whirling ◊ *verb* move or whirl with a buzzing noise

> **whir** *verb* » whir*s*, whirr*ing*, whirr*ed*

whirl *verb* **1** turn round quickly **2** carry (off, away *etc*) quickly ▯ *noun* **1** a fast circling movement **2** great excitement, confusion: *in a whirl over the wedding arrangements* ▯ **whirlpool** *noun* a place in a river or sea where the current moves in a circle ▯ **whirlwind** *noun* a violent current of wind with a whirling motion

whisk *verb* **1** move quickly and lightly, sweep: *their car whisked past* **2** beat or whip (a mixture) ▯ *noun* **1** a quick sweeping movement **2** a kitchen utensil for beating eggs or mixtures **3** a small bunch of twigs *etc* used as a brush

whisker **1** a long bristle on the upper lip of a cat *etc* **2** (**whiskers**) hair on the sides of a man's face, sideburns

whisky or *Irish & US* **whiskey** *noun* (plural **whiskies** or **whiskeys**) an alcoholic spirit made from grain

> Based on Scottish Gaelic *uisge beatha*, meaning 'water of life'

whisper *verb* **1** speak very softly, using the breath only, not the voice **2** make a soft, rustling sound ▯ *noun* a soft sound made with the breath

whist *noun* a type of card game for four players

whistle *verb* **1** make a high-pitched sound by forcing breath through the lips or teeth **2** make such a sound with an instrument **3** move with such a sound, like a bullet ▯ *noun* **1** the sound made by whistling **2** any instrument for whistling

whit *noun* a tiny bit: *not a whit better*

white *adj* **1** of the colour of pure snow **2** pale or light-coloured: *white wine* **3** of a pale-coloured complexion ▯ *noun* **1** something white **2** someone with a pale-coloured complexion **3** the part of an egg surrounding the yolk ▯ **white ant** a termite ▯ **whitebait** *noun* the young of herring or sprats ▯ **white elephant** something useless and costly or troublesome to maintain ▯ **white-hot** *adj* having reached a degree of heat at which metals glow with a white light (hotter than **red-hot**) ▯ **white knight** a company which comes to the aid of another facing an unwelcome takeover bid ▯ **white-knuckle** *adj* causing alarm, frightening ▯ **whiten** *verb* make or become white or whiter ▯ **whiteness** *noun* ▯ **white paper** a statement (printed on white paper) issued by the government for the information of parliament

whitewash *noun* a mixture of ground chalk and water, or lime and water, for whitening walls *etc* ▯ *verb* **1** put whitewash on **2** cover up the faults of, give a good appearance to

whither *adv & conj, old* to what place?

whiting *noun* a small type of fish related to the cod

whitlow *noun* an infected swelling beside the finger or toenail

Whitsun *noun* the week beginning with the seventh Sunday after Easter

whittle *verb* **1** pare or cut (wood

etc) with a knife **2** (with **away** or **down**) make gradually less: *whittled away his savings*

whiz or **whizz** *verb* **1** move with a hissing sound, like an arrow **2** move very fast ◊ **whiz** *noun* or **whizz kid** someone who achieves rapid success while relatively young

> **whiz** » whizz*es*, whizz*ing*, whizz*ed*

WHO *abbrev* World Health Organization

who *pronoun* **1** used to refer to someone or some people unknown or unnamed (only as the subject of a verb): *who is that woman in the green hat?* **2** *informal* used as the object in a sentence (instead of **whom**): *who did you choose?* ◊ *relative pronoun* referring to the person or people just named: *do you know who those people are?* ◊ **whoever** *pronoun* any person or people

whole *adj* **1** complete **2** all, with nothing or no one missing **3** not broken **4** in good health ◊ *noun* the entire thing ◊ **wholefood** *noun* unprocessed food produced without the aid of artificial fertilizers ◊ **wholehearted** *adj* enthusiastic, generous ◊ **wholemeal** *noun* flour made from the entire wheat grain ◊ **wholesome** *adj* giving health, healthy ◊ **wholly** *adv* entirely, altogether ◊ **on the whole** when everything is taken into account

wholesale *noun* the sale of goods in large quantities to a shop from which they can be bought in small quantities by ordinary buyers (*compare with*: **retail**) ◊ *adj* **1** buying or selling through wholesale **2** on a large scale: *wholesale killing* ◊ **wholesaler** *noun*

who'll *short for* who will; who shall

whom *pronoun* **1** used to refer to someone or some people unknown or unnamed (only as the object of a sentence): *whom did you see?/ to whom am I speaking?* **2** which person: *do you know to whom I gave it?* ◊ *relative pronoun* referring to the person or people just named: *the person whom I liked best*

whoop *noun* a loud cry, rising in pitch ◊ *verb* give a whoop ◊ **whooping-cough** *noun* an infectious disease in which violent bouts of coughing are followed by a whoop as the breath is drawn in

whore *noun*, *informal* a female prostitute

whortleberry *noun* the bilberry

whose *adj* & *pronoun* belonging to whom?: *whose handwriting is this?* ◊ *relative pronoun* of whom: *the man whose wife I know*

why *adv* & *pronoun* for which reason?: *why did you not stay?* ◊ **the whys and wherefores** all the reasons, details

wick *noun* the twisted threads in a candle or lamp which draw up the oil or grease to the flame

wicked *adj* **1** evil, sinful **2** mischievous, spiteful ◊ **wickedly** *adv* ◊ **wickedness** *noun*

wicker *adj* of a chair: made of woven willow twigs

wicket *noun* **1** a small gate or

door, *esp* in or beside a larger one **2** *cricket* the set of three stumps, or one of these, at which the ball is bowled **3** the ground between the bowler and the batsman

wide *adj* **1** broad, not narrow **2** stretching far **3** measuring a certain amount from side to side: *5 centimetres wide* ◊ *adv* **1** off the target: *the shots went wide* **2** (often with **apart**) far apart: *hold your arms wide* ◊ **wide-awake** *adj* fully awake; alert ◊ **wide-boy** *noun, slang* an astute or wily person ◊ **wide-eyed** *adj* with eyes wide open in surprise *etc* ◊ **widely** *adv* **1** over a wide area; among many: *widely believed* **2** far apart ◊ **widen** *verb* make or become wide ◊ **wideness** *noun* ◊ **wide-open** *adj* opened to the full extent ◊ **widespread** *adj* spread over a large area or among many people: *a widespread belief* ◊ **wide of the mark** off the target, inaccurate

widow *noun* a woman whose husband is dead ◊ **widower** *noun* a man whose wife is dead

width *noun* **1** measurement across, from side to side **2** large extent

wield *verb* **1** swing or handle (a cricket bat, sword *etc*) **2** use (power, authority *etc*)

wife *noun* (*plural* **wives**) **1** a married woman **2** the woman to whom a man is married

wig *noun* an artificial covering of hair for the head

wiggle *verb* move from side to side with jerky or twisting movements ◊ *noun* a jerky movement from side to side ◊ **wiggly** *adj*

wigwam *noun, hist* a conical tent of skins made by some Native Americans

wild *adj* **1** of an animal: not tamed **2** of a plant: not cultivated in a garden **3** uncivilized **4** unruly, uncontrolled **5** of weather: stormy **6** frantic, mad: *wild with anxiety* **7** of a guess *etc*: rash, inaccurate ◊ *noun* (usually **wilds**) an uncultivated or uncivilized region ◊ **wild boar** a wild type of pig ◊ **wild cat** a wild type of European cat ◊ **wildcat** *adj* of a strike: not supported or permitted by trade union officials ◊ **wildfire** *noun* lightning without thunder ◊ **wildfowl** *noun* wild birds, *esp* those shot as game ◊ **wild-goose chase** a troublesome and useless errand ◊ **wildlife** *noun* wild animals, birds *etc* in their natural habitats ◊ **like wildfire** very quickly

wilderness *noun* a wild, uncultivated or desolate region

wile *noun* a crafty trick ◊ **wily** *adj* ◊ **wilily** *adv*

will *noun* **1** the power to choose or decide **2** desire: *against my will* **3** determination: *the will to win* **4** feeling towards someone: *a sign of goodwill* **5** a written statement about what is to be done with your property after your death ◊ *verb* **1** influence someone by exercising your will: *he willed her to win* **2** hand down (property *etc*) by will **3** (*past form* **would**) also used to form future tenses of other verbs when the subject is **he, she, it, you** or **they**: *you will see me there* **4** *informal* often used for the same purpose when the subject is **I** or

we: *I will tell you later* **5** used for emphasis, or to express a promise, when the subject is **I** or **we**: *I will do it if possible* (*see also* **shall**, **would**) ◊ **wilful** *adj* fond of having one's own way; intentional: *wilful damage* ◊ **willing** *adj* ready to do what is asked; eager ◊ **at will** as or when you choose ◊ **with a will** eagerly

> **will** *verb* » will*s*, will*ing*, will*ed*

will-o'-the-wisp *noun* a pale light sometimes seen by night over marshy places

willow *noun* **1** a tree with long slender branches **2** its wood, used in cricket bats ◊ **willowy** *adj* slender, graceful

willy *noun, slang* a penis

willynilly *adv* **1** whether you wish or not **2** notwithstanding other people's feelings

> From the phrase *will I, nill I*, meaning 'whether I want or don't want'

wilt *verb* **1** of a flower or plant: droop **2** lose strength

wily *see* **wile**

wimp *noun, informal* an ineffectual person

win *verb* **1** gain by luck or in a contest **2** gain (the love of someone *etc*) by effort **3** come first in a contest **4** (often with **over**) gain the support or friendship of ◊ *noun* an act of winning; a victory ◊ **winning** *adj* **1** victorious, successful **2** charming, attractive: *winning smile* ◊ **winnings** *noun plural* money *etc* that has been won

> **win** *verb* » win*s*, winn*ing*, won

wince *verb* shrink or start back in pain *etc*, flinch: *her singing made me wince*

winceyette *noun* a type of brushed cotton cloth

winch *noun* (*plural* **winches**) **1** a handle or crank for turning a wheel **2** a machine for lifting things, worked by winding a rope round a revolving cylinder ◊ **winch up** lift up with a winch

wind[1] *noun* **1** a current of air **2** breath **3** air carrying a scent **4** air or gas in the stomach **5** the wind instruments in an orchestra ◊ *verb* put out of breath ◊ **windfall** *noun* **1** a fruit blown from a tree **2** an unexpected gain, *eg* a sum of money ◊ **wind instrument** a musical instrument sounded by the breath ◊ **windjammer** *noun* a type of sailing ship ◊ **windmill** *noun* a mill driven by sails which are moved by the wind, used for pumping water, grinding grain *etc* ◊ **windpipe** *noun* the tube leading from the mouth to the lungs ◊ **windscreen** or *US* **windshield** *noun* a pane of glass in front of the driver of a motor-car *etc* ◊ **windsurf** *verb* sail on a sailboard ◊ **windsurfer** *noun* ◊ **windsurfing** *noun* ◊ **windswept** *adj* exposed to strong winds and showing the effects of it: *windswept hair* ◊ **windward** *adj* & *adv* in the direction from which the wind blows ◊ **windy** *adj* **1** of weather with a strong wind blowing **2** of place: exposed to strong winds **get the wind up** *informal* becom afraid ◻ **get wind of** *informal* hear about in an indirect way

wind[2] *verb* **1** turn, twist or coil **2** (sometimes with **up**) screw up the spring of (a watch, clockwork toy *etc*) **3** wrap closely ◻ **winder** *noun* a key *etc* for winding a clock ◻ **winding** *adj* curving, twisting ◻ **wind up 1** bring or come to an end: *wind up a meeting* **2** *informal* annoy, tease ◻ **wind your way** make your way circuitously ◻ **wound up** tense, agitated

wind *verb* » wind*s*, wind*ing*, wound

windlass *noun* a machine for lifting up or hauling a winch

window *noun* an opening in a wall, protected by glass, which lets in light and air

wine *noun* **1** an alcoholic drink made from the fermented juice of grapes or other fruit **2** a rich dark red colour ◻ **winepress** *noun* a machine which squeezes the juice out of grapes

wing *noun* **1** one of the arm-like limbs of a bird, bat or insect by means of which it flies **2** one of the two projections on the sides of an aeroplane **3** a part of a house built out to the side **4** the side of a stage, where actors wait to enter **5** *football etc* a player positioned at the edge of the field **6** a section of a political party: *the left wing* ◻ *verb* **1** wound (a bird) in the wing **2** soar ◻ **wing commander** a high-ranking officer in the air force ◻ **winged** *adj* **1** having wings **2** swift ◻ **on the wing** flying, in motion ◻ **under someone's wing** under the protection or care of someone

wink *verb* **1** open and close an eye quickly **2** give a hint by winking **3** of lights *etc*: flicker, twinkle ◻ *noun* **1** an act of winking **2** a hint given by winking ◻ **forty winks** a short sleep

winkle *noun* a small edible shellfish (*also called*: **periwinkle**) ◻ **winkle out** force out gradually

winnow *verb* separate the chaff from the grain by wind

winsome *adj* charming

winter *noun* the cold season of the year ◻ *adj* of or suitable for winter ◻ *verb* **1** pass the winter **2** keep, feed (sheep *etc*) during the winter ◻ **winter sports** sports on snow or ice, *eg* skiing, tobogganing *etc* ◻ **wintry** *adj* **1** cold, frosty **2** cheerless, unfriendly: *a wintry look*

wipe *verb* **1** clean or dry by rubbing **2** (with **away, out, off** or **up**) clear away ◻ *noun* the act of cleaning by rubbing ◻ **wiper** *noun* one of a pair of moving parts which wipe the windscreen of a car

wire *noun* **1** a thread-like length of metal **2** the metal thread used in communication by telephone *etc* **3** *informal* a telegram ◻ *adj* made of wire ◻ *verb* **1** bind or fasten with wire **2** *informal* send a telegram **3** supply (a building *etc*) with wires for carrying an electric current ◻ **wireless** *adj* of communication: by radio waves ◻ *noun, old* a radio set ◻ **wire-netting** *noun* mesh made of wire ◻ **wiry** *adj* **1** made of wire **2** of a person: thin but strong

wise *adj* **1** very knowledgeable **2** judging rightly; sensible □ **wisdom** *noun* the quality of being wise □ **wisdom teeth** four large back teeth which appear after childhood □ **-wise** *suffix* **1** in the manner or way of: *crabwise* **2** with reference or regard to: *careerwise*

wish *verb* **1** feel or express a desire: *I wish he'd leave* **2** (often with **for**) long for, desire: *she wished for peace and quiet* **3** hope for on behalf of (someone): *wish someone luck* □ *noun* (*plural* **wishes**) **1** desire, longing **2** a thing desired or wanted: *her great wish was to live abroad* **3** an expression of desire: *make a wish* **4** (**wishes**) expression of hope for another's happiness, good fortune *etc*: *good wishes* □ **wishbone** *noun* a forked bone in the breast of fowls □ **wishful** *adj* wishing, eager □ **wishful thinking** basing your belief on (false) hopes rather than known facts □ **wish someone well** feel goodwill towards them

wishywashy *adj* **1** of liquid: thin and weak **2** feeble, not energetic or lively **3** lacking colour □ **wishy-washiness** *noun*

wisp *noun* a small tuft or strand: *a wisp of hair* □ **wispy** *adj*

wistful *adj* thoughtful and rather sad: *a wistful glance* □ **wistfully** *adv*

wit *noun* **1** (often **wits**) intelligence, common sense **2** the ability to express ideas neatly and funnily **3** someone who can do this □ **-witted** *suffix* having wits (of a certain kind): *slow-witted/ quick-witted* □ **witticism** *noun* a witty remark □ **wittingly** *adv* knowingly □ **witty** *adj* clever and amusing □ **at your wits' end** unable to solve your difficulties, desperate □ **keep your wits about you** keep alert □ **to wit** namely, that is to say

witch *noun* (*plural* **witches**) **1** a woman with magic power obtained through evil spirits **2** an ugly old woman □ **witchcraft** *noun* magic performed by a witch □ **witch doctor** someone believed to have magical powers to cure illnesses *etc* □ **witch-hazel** *noun* **1** a N American shrub **2** a healing lotion made from its bark and leaves

with *prep* **1** in the company of: *I was walking with my father* **2** by means of: *cut it with a knife* **3** in the same direction as: *drifting with the current* **4** against: *fighting with his brother* **5** on the same side as **6** having: *a man with a limp* **7** in the keeping of: *leave the keys with me*

withdraw *verb* **1** go back or away **2** take away, remove: *withdraw cash/ withdraw troops* **3** take back (an insult *etc*) □ **withdrawal** *noun* an act of withdrawing □ **withdrawn** *adj* **1** of a place: lonely, isolated **2** of a person: unwilling to communicate with others, unsociable

> **withdraw** » withdraw*s*, withdraw*ing*, with*drew*, withdrawn

wither *verb* **1** fade, dry up or decay **2** make to feel very unimportant or embarrassed: *she withered him with a look* □ **withering** *adj* **1** drying up, dying **2** of a remark *etc*: scornful, sarcastic □ **withers** *noun plural* the ridge between the shoulder bones of a horse

withhold *verb* keep back, refuse to give

> **withhold** » withhold*s*, withhold*ing*, withheld

within *prep* inside the limits of: *keep within the law* □ *adv* on the inside

without *prep* **1** in the absence of: *we went without you* **2** not having: *without a penny* **3** outside the limits of: *without the terms of the agreement* □ *adv, old* **1** on the outside **2** out-of-doors

withstand *verb* oppose or resist successfully

witness *noun* (*plural* **witnesses**) **1** someone who sees or has direct knowledge of a thing **2** someone who gives evidence in a law court **3** proof, evidence □ *verb* **1** see, be present at **2** sign your name to confirm the authenticity of (someone else's signature) **3** give or be evidence □ **witness box** the stand from which a witness in a law court gives evidence □ **bear witness** give or be evidence of: *bear witness to his character*

wizard *noun* a man believed to have the power of magic □ **wizardry** *noun* magic

wizened *adj* dried up, shrivelled: *a wizened old man*

woad *noun* **1** a blue dye **2** the plant from which it is obtained

wobble *verb* rock unsteadily from side to side □ *noun* an unsteady rocking □ **wobbly** *adj* unsteady, rocking

woe *noun* **1** grief, misery **2** a cause of sorrow, a trouble □ **woebegone** *adj* dismal, sad-looking □ **woeful** *adj* sorrowful; pitiful □ **woefully** *adv*

wolf *noun* (*plural* **wolves**) a wild animal like a dog that hunts in packs □ *verb* eat greedily: *wolfing down his food* □ **wolfhound** *noun* a large breed of dog once used to hunt wolves □ **wolfish** *adj* like a wolf □ **cry wolf** give a false alarm □ **keep the wolf from the door** keep away hunger or want

wolverine *noun* a wild animal of the weasel family

woman *noun* (*plural* **women**) **1** an adult human female **2** human females in general **3** a domestic help □ **womanhood** *noun* the state of being a woman □ **womanish** *adj* of a man: effeminate, not manly □ **womankind** or **womenkind** *noun* women generally □ **womanly** *adj* like, or suitable for, a woman

womb *noun* the part of a female mammal's body in which the young develop and stay till birth

wombat *noun* a small, beaver-like Australian animal, with a pouch

women *plural* of **woman**

won *past form* of **win**

wonder *noun* **1** the feeling produced by something unexpected or extraordinary; surprise, awe **2** something strange, amazing or miraculous □ *verb* **1** be curious or in doubt: *I wonder what will happen/ I wonder whether to go or not* **2** feel surprise or amazement (at, that) □ **wonderful** *adj* **1** arousing wonder; strange, marvellous **2** excellent □ **wonderland** *noun* a land of wonder, a fairy-like place ◇ **wonderment** *noun, old* amazement ◇ **wondrous** *adj, old* wonderful

wonky *adj, informal* not working properly, unsound

wont *adj, old* accustomed (to do something) ◇ *noun* habit: *as is his wont*

won't *short for* will not

won ton a spicy Chinese dumpling, often served in soup

woo *verb* **1** try to win the love of (someone) **2** try to gain (*eg* success) ◇ **wooer** *noun*

> **woo** » woo*s*, woo*ing*, woo*ed*

wood *noun* **1** a group of growing trees **2** the hard part of a tree, *esp* when cut for use ◇ **woodbine** *noun* the honeysuckle ◇ **woodchuck** *noun same as* **marmot** ◇ **woodcock** *noun* a game bird related to the snipe ◇ **woodcut** *noun* **1** a picture engraved on wood **2** a print made from this engraving ◇ **woodcutter** *noun* someone who fells trees, cuts up wood *etc* ◇ **wooded** *adj* covered with trees ◇ **woodland** *noun* land covered with trees ◇ **woodlouse** *noun* (*plural* **woodlice**) an insect with a jointed shell, found under stones *etc* ◇ **woodpecker** *noun* a bird that pecks holes in the bark of trees with its beak, in search of insects ◇ **wood spirit** *same as* **methanol** ◇ **woodwind** *noun* wind instruments, made of wood or metal, *eg* the flute or clarinet ◇ **woodwork** *noun* **1** the making of wooden articles **2** the wooden parts of a house, room *etc* ◇ **woodworm** *noun* the larva of a beetle that bores holes in wood and destroys it ◇ **woody** *adj* **1** like wood **2** wooded

wooden *adj* **1** made of wood **2** dull, stiff, not lively: *a wooden speech* ◇ **woodenly** *adv*

wool *noun* **1** the soft hair of sheep and other animals **2** yarn or cloth made of wool ◇ **woolgathering** *noun* day-dreaming ◇ *noun & adj* **woollen** *adj* made of wool ◇ *noun* a knitted garment made of wool ◇ **woolly** *adj* **1** made of, or like, wool **2** vague, hazy: *a woolly argument* ◇ *noun* (*plural* **woollies**) a knitted woollen garment

word *noun* **1** a written or spoken sign representing a thing or an idea **2** (**words**) talk, remarks: *kind words* **3** news: *word of his death* **4** a promise: *break your word* ◇ *verb* choose words for: *he worded his refusal carefully* ◇ **wording** *noun* choice or arrangement of words ◇ **word processor** an electronic machine, or computer program, which can store, edit and print out text ◇ **wordy** *adj* using too many words ◇ **have words** *informal* quarrel ◇ **in a word** in short, to sum up ◇ **take someone at their word** treat what they say as true ◇ **take someone's word for something** trust that what they say is true ◇ **word for word** in the exact words

wore *past form* of **wear**

work *noun* **1** a physical or mental effort to achieve or make something **2** a job, employment: *out of work* **3** a task: *I've got work to do* **4** anything made or done something produced by art, *eg* book, musical composition, painting *etc* **6** manner of working, workmanship: *poor work* **7** (**works**) a factory **8** (**works**) the mechanism (*eg* of a watch) **9** (**works**) deeds: *good works* ▯ *verb* **1** be engaged in physical or mental work **2** be employed **3** run or operate smoothly and efficiently **4** of a plan *etc*: be successful **5** get into a position slowly and gradually: *the screw worked loose* **6** organize, manage, control ▯ **workable** *adj* able to be done, practical ▯ **workaday** *adj* ordinary, unexciting ▯ **worker** *noun* someone who works at a job ▯ **working class** the social class including manual workers ▯ **working-class** *adj* ▯ **working day** or **working hours** a day or the hours that someone spends at work, on duty *etc* ▯ **working party** a group of people appointed to investigate a particular matter ▯ **workman** *noun* someone who works with their hands ▯ **workmanlike** *adj* done with skill ▯ **workmanship** *noun* **1** the skill of a workman **2** manner of making something ▯ **workshop** *noun* a room or building where manufacturing, craftwork *etc* is done ▯ **work out 1** solve **2** discover as a result of deep thought **3** of a situation: turn out all right in the end ▯ **work up** arouse, excite: *working himself up into a fury*

world *noun* **1** the earth and all things on it **2** the people of the world **3** any planet or star **4** the universe **5** a state of existence: *the next world* **6** a particular area of life or activity: *the insect world/ the world of fashion* **7** a great deal: *a world of good* ▯ **worldly** *adj* concerned with material things such as money, possessions *etc*, not the soul or spirit ▯ **worldwide** *adj* extending throughout the world ▯ *adv* throughout the world

worm *noun* **1** a small creeping animal without a backbone, often living in soil **2** *informal* a low, contemptible person **3** something spiral-shaped, *eg* the thread of a screw **4** (**worms**) the condition of having threadworms *etc* in the intestines **5** *comput* a kind of virus ▯ *verb* **1** move gradually and stealthily (in or into) **2** (with **out**) draw out (information) bit by bit

wormwood *noun* a plant with a bitter taste

worn *adj* **1** damaged by use **2** tired, worn-out ▯ **worn-out** *adj* tired, exhausted

worry *verb* **1** of a dog: shake or tear (something) with its teeth **2** annoy **3** make troubled and anxious **4** be troubled and anxious ▯ *noun* (*plural* **worries**) **1** uneasiness, anxiety **2** a cause of unease or anxiety

> **worry** *verb* » worri*es*, worry*ing*, worri*ed*

worse *adj* **1** bad or evil to a greater degree **2** more ill ▯ *adv* badly to a greater degree, more severely: *it's snowing worse than ever* ▯ **worsen** *verb* make or become worse ▯ **worse off** in a worse position, less wealthy *etc*

worship *noun* **1** a religious ceremony or service **2** deep reverence, adoration **3** a title used in addressing a mayor, provost *etc* □ *verb* **1** pay honour to (a god) **2** adore or admire deeply □ **worshipful** *adj* **1** full of reverence **2** worthy of honour

> **worship** » worship*s*, worship*ping*, worshipp*ed*

worst *adj* bad or evil to the greatest degree □ *adv* badly to the greatest degree □ *verb* beat, defeat □ **at worst** under the least favourable circumstances □ **if the worst comes to the worst** if the worst possible circumstances occur

> **worst** *verb* » worst*s*, worst*ing*, worst*ed*

worsted[1] *noun* **1** a type of fine woollen yarn **2** a strong cloth made of this

worsted[2] *past form* of **worst**

worth *noun* **1** value; price **2** importance **3** excellence of character *etc* □ *adj* **1** equal in value to **2** deserving of: *worth considering* □ **worthless** *adj* of no merit or value □ **worthwhile** *adj* deserving time and effort □ **worthy** *adj* **1** (often with **of**) deserving, suitable **2** of good character □ *noun* (*plural* **worthies**) a highly respected person: *local worthy* □ **worth your while** worth the trouble spent

would *verb* **1** the form of the verb **will** used to express a condition: *he would go if he could* **2** used for emphasis: *I tell you I would do it if possible* **3** *old* expressing a wish: *I would that he were gone*

would-be *adj* trying to be or pretending to be: *would-be actor/would-be socialist*

wound *noun* **1** a cut or injury caused by a weapon, in an accident *etc* **2** a hurt to someone's feelings □ *verb* **1** make a wound in **2** hurt the feelings of □ **wounded** *adj* having a wound, injured, hurt

WPC *abbrev* Woman Police Constable

wrack /rak/ *noun* seaweed thrown onto the shore

wraith /rehth/ *noun* an apparition of a living person, often as a warning of death

wrangle /ranggəl/ *verb* quarrel noisily □ *noun* a noisy quarrel

wrap /rap/ *verb* **1** fold or roll round: *wrap it in tissue paper* **2** (with **up**) cover by folding or winding something round □ *noun* a cloak or shawl

> **wrap** *verb* » wrap*s*, wrapp*ing*, wrapp*ed*

wrapper *noun* a loose paper cover, *eg* round a book or sweet

wrath /rath/ or /rawth/ *noun* violent anger □ **wrathful** *adj* very angry

wreak /reek/ *verb* **1** carry out: *wreak vengeance* **2** cause: *wreak havoc*

wreath /reeth/ *noun* **1** a ring of flowers or leaves **2** a curling wisp of smoke, mist *etc*

wreathe /reedh/ *verb* encircle

wreck /rek/ *noun* **1** destruction, *esp* of a ship by the sea **2** the remains of anything destroyed *esp* a ship **3** someone whose health or nerves are in bad condition ▫ *verb* destroy ▫ **wreckage** *noun* the remains of something wrecked

wren /ren/ *noun* a very small type of bird

wrench /rench/ *verb* **1** pull with a violent, often twisting, motion **2** sprain (your ankle *etc*) ▫ *noun* (*plural* **wrenches**) **1** a violent twist **2** a tool for gripping and turning nuts, bolts *etc* **3** sadness caused by parting from someone or something

wrest /rench/ *verb, formal* twist or take by force

wrestle /resl/ *verb* **1** fight with someone, trying to bring them to the ground **2** (with **with**) think deeply about (a problem *etc*) ▫ **wrestler** *noun* someone who wrestles as a sport ▫ **wrestling** *noun* the sport in which two people fight to throw each other to the ground

wretch /rech/ *noun* (*plural* **wretches**) **1** a miserable, pitiable person: *a poor wretch* **2** a worthless or contemptible person

wretched /*rechəd*/ *adj* **1** very miserable **2** worthless, very bad ▫ **wretchedly** *adv* ▫ **wretchedness** *noun*

wriggle /rigl/ *verb* **1** twist to and fro **2** move by doing this, as a worm does **3** escape (out of a difficulty *etc*)

-wright /-rait/ *suffix* a maker: *shipwright/ playwright*

wring /ring/ *verb* **1** twist or squeeze (*esp* water out of wet clothes) **2** clasp and unclasp (your hands) in grief, anxiety *etc* **3** cause pain to: *the story wrung everybody's heart* **4** force out (*eg* a promise) ▫ **wringer** *noun* a machine for forcing water from wet clothes

wring » wring*s*, wring*ing*, wrung

wrinkle /ringkl/ *noun* a small crease or fold on the skin or other surface ▫ *verb* make or become wrinkled ▫ **wrinklie** *noun, informal* an old person ▫ **wrinkly** *adj*

wrist /rist/ *noun* the joint by which the hand is joined to the arm

writ /rit/ *noun* a formal document giving an order (*esp* to appear in a law court)

write /rait/ *verb* **1** form letters with a pen, pencil *etc* **2** put into writing: *write your name* **3** compose (a letter, a book *etc*) **4** send a letter (to) **5** *comput* copy (a data file) ▫ **writer** *noun* someone who writes, an author ▫ **writing** *noun* a written text or texts ▫ **write-off** *noun* a car *etc* that has been damaged beyond repair ▫ **write down** record in writing ▫ **write off** regard as lost for ever ▫ **write up** make a written record of

write » write*s*, writ*ing*, written, wrote

writhe /raidh/ *verb* twist or roll about, *eg* in pain

wrong /rong/ *adj* **1** not correct **2** not right or just **3** evil **4** not what is intended: *take the wrong turning* **5** unsuitable: *the wrong weather for camping* **6** mistaken: *you are wrong* *if you think that* □ *noun* **1** whatever is not right or just **2** an injury done to another □ *verb* do wrong to, harm □ **wrongdoer** *noun* someone who does wrong □ **wrongdoing** *noun* □ **wrongful** *adj* not lawful or just □ **wrongly** *adv* □ **go wrong 1** fail to work properly **2** make a mistake or mistakes □ **in the wrong** guilty of injustice or error

wrote *past form* of **write**

wroth /rohth/ *noun*, *old* angry

wrought /rot/ *adj*, *old* made, manufactured □ *verb, old, past form* of **work** □ **wrought-iron** iron hammered, rather than cast, into shape □ **wrought-up** *adj* agitated, anxious

wrung *past form* of **wring**

wry /rai/ *adj* **1** slightly mocking or bitter: *wry remark* **2** twisted or turned to one side □ **wryly** *adv*

WYSIWYG *abbrev*, *comput* what *y*ou *s*ee (on the screen) *i*s *w*hat *y*ou *g*et (in the printout)

X

xenophobia *noun* hatred of foreigners or strangers ▢ **xenophobe** *noun* someone who hates foreigners ▢ **xenophobic** *adj*

Xerox *noun, trademark* **1** a photographic process used for copying documents **2** a copy made in this way ▢ *verb* copy by Xerox

Xmas *noun, informal* Christmas

X-rays *noun plural* rays that can pass through material impenetrable by light, and produce a photographic image of the object through which they have passed ▢ **X-ray** *noun* a shadow picture produced by X-rays on photographic film ▢ *verb* take a photographic image of with X-rays

xylophone *noun* a musical instrument consisting of a series of graded wooden plates which are struck with hammers

Y

yacht *noun* a sailing or motor-driven boat for racing, cruising *etc* □ **yachtsman**, **yachtswoman** *noun*

yak *noun* a Tibetan long-haired ox

yakitori *noun* a Japanese dish of grilled chicken pieces, basted with a sweet sauce

yam *noun* a tropical root vegetable, similar to a potato

Yank or **Yankee** *noun*, *Brit informal* an American

> Originally a nickname for Dutch settlers in New England in the 18th century, possibly because of the Dutch forename *Jan*

yank *verb*, *informal* tug or pull with a violent jerk □ *noun* a violent tug

yap *verb* bark sharply

> **yap** » yap*s*, yapp*ing*, yapp*ed*

yard *noun* **1** a measure of length (0.9144 of a metre, or 3 feet) **2** a long beam on a mast for spreading sails **3** an enclosed space used for a particular purpose: *railway yard/ shipbuilding yard* **4** *US* a garden □ **yard-arm** *noun* half of a yard on a mast

Yardie *noun* a member of a widespread criminal organization, based in Jamaica

yardstick *noun* **1** a standard for measurement **2** a yard-long measuring stick

yarn *noun* **1** wool, cotton *etc* spun into thread **2** one of several threads forming a rope **3** a long, often improbable, story

yarrow *noun* a strong-smelling plant with flat clusters of white flowers

yashmak *noun* a veil covering the lower half of the face, worn by Islamic women

yawl *noun* a small rowing boat or fishing boat

yawn *verb* **1** take a deep breath unintentionally with an open mouth, because of boredom or sleepiness **2** of a hole: be wide open gape □ *noun* an open-mouthed deep breath

yd *abbrev* yard(s)

ye *pronoun*, *old* you

yea /jeh/ *interj*, *old* yes

year *noun* **1** the time taken by th earth to go once round the sur about 365 days **2** the period January to 31 December **3** a perio of twelve months starting at an point **4** (**years**) age: *wise for he years* □ **yearling** *noun* a year-ol animal □ **yearly** *adj* happening ever year, or once a year

yearn *verb* **1** long (for, to do some thing *etc*) **2** feel pity or tenderne (for) □ **yearning** *noun* an eag longing

yeast *noun* a substance which causes fermentation, used to make bread dough rise and in brewing

yell *verb* give a loud, shrill cry; scream □ *noun* a loud, shrill cry

yellow *noun* the colour of gold, egg-yolks *etc* □ *adj* of this colour □ *verb* become yellow, due to ageing

yellowhammer *noun* a finch with yellow plumage

yelp *verb* give a sharp bark or cry □ *noun* a sharp bark or cry

yen[1] *noun* the standard unit of Japanese currency

yen[2] *noun, informal* a strong desire, longing: *a yen to return to Scotland*

yeoman /yohmən/ *hist* a farmer with his own land □ **yeomanry** *noun, hist* **1** farmers **2** a troop of cavalrymen serving voluntarily in the British army □ **Yeomen of the Guard** the company acting as bodyguard to the British king or queen on certain occasions

yes *interj* expressing agreement or consent □ *noun* **1** an expression of agreement or consent **2** a vote in favour

yesterday *noun* **1** the day before today **2** the past □ *adv*

yet *adv* **1** by now, by this time: *have you seen that film yet?* **2** still, before the matter is finished: *we may win yet* □ *conj* but, nevertheless: *I am defeated, yet I shall not surrender* □ **yet another** and another one still □ **yet more** still more

Yeti *noun, another name* for the **Abominable Snowman**

yew *noun* **1** a tree with dark green leaves and red berries **2** its wood

YHA *abbrev* Youth Hostels Association

yield *verb* **1** give in, surrender **2** give way to pressure or persuasion **3** produce (a crop, results *etc*) □ *noun* an amount produced; a crop □ **yielding** *adj* giving way easily

yikes *interj, Brit* goodness! heavens!

ylang-ylang /eelang-*ee*lang/ *noun* a SE Asian tree from whose flowers a fragrant oil is distilled

YMCA *abbrev* Young Men's Christian Association

yob or **yobbo** (*plural* **yobboes** or **yobbos**) *noun* a lout, a hooligan

yodel *verb* sing in a style involving frequent changes between an ordinary and a very high-pitched voice

> **yodel** » yodel*s*, yodell*ing*, yodell*ed*

yoga *noun* a Hindu system of philosophy and meditation, often involving special physical exercises

yoghurt or **yogurt** *noun* a semi-liquid food product made from fermented milk

yoke *noun* **1** a wooden frame joining oxen when pulling a plough or cart **2** a pair of oxen or horses **3** something that joins together **4** a frame placed across the shoulders for carrying pails *etc* **5** slavery, domination **6** a part of a garment fitting over the neck and shoulders **7** a part of a skirt fitting closely over the hips □ *verb* **1** put a yoke on **2** join together

yokel *noun, derog* an unsophisticated country person; a rustic

yolk *noun* the yellow part of an egg

Yom Kippur the Day of Atonement, a Jewish fast day

yonder *adv, old* in that place (at a distance but within sight) ▫ *adj* that (object) over there: *by yonder tree*

yonks *noun plural, informal* ages; a long time

yore *noun*: **of yore** *old* formerly, in times past

you *pronoun* the person(s) spoken or written to, used as the *sing* or *plural* subject or object of a verb: *what did you say?/ are you both free tomorrow?*

you'd *abbrev* **1** you would; you should **2** you had

you'll *abbrev* you will; you shall

young *adj* **1** in early life **2** in the early part of growth ▫ *noun* **1** the offspring of animals **2** (**the young**) young people ▫ **youngster** *noun* a young person

your *adj* belonging to you: *it's your life*

you're *short for* you are

yours *pronoun* belonging to you: *is this pen yours?* ▫ **Yours**, **Yours faithfully**, **Yours sincerely** or **Yours truly** expressions used before a signature at the end of a letter

yourself *pronoun* (*plural* **yourselves**) **1** used reflexively: *don't trouble yourself* **2** used for emphasis: *you yourself can't go*

youth *noun* **1** the state of being young **2** the early part of life **3** a young person **4** young people in general ▫ **youth hostel** a hostel where hikers *etc* may spend the night

youthful *adj* **1** young **2** fresh and vigorous ▫ **youthfully** *adv* ▫ **youthfulness** *noun*

you've *abbrev* you have

yo-yo *noun, trademark* a toy consisting of a reel which spins up and down on a string

yr *abbrev* year

yuan *noun* the main currency unit of The People's Republic of China

yucca *noun* a Mexican desert plant with thick spiky leaves

yucky *adj, informal* **1** disgusting, revolting **2** sickly sentimental

Yule *noun, old* Christmas ▫ **Yuletide** Christmas time

yuppie or **yuppy** *noun* (*plural* **yuppies**) a young well-paid urban professional

YWCA *abbrev* Young Women's Christian Association

Z

zabaglione *noun* a custard made with egg yolks, sugar and sweet wine

zany *adj, informal* crazy, madcap ▫ **zanily** *adv* ▫ **zaniness** *noun*

> After the name of a clownish character in the Italian *commedia dell'arte*

zap *verb* **1** strike, shoot *etc* suddenly **2** move rapidly; zip ▫ **zapper** *noun, informal* a remote control for a TV or video

> **zap** » zap*s*, zapp*ing*, zapp*ed*

zeal *noun* **1** enthusiasm **2** keenness, determination ▫ **zealous** *adj* full of zeal ▫ **zealously** *adv*

zealot /zelət/ *noun* a fanatical enthusiast

zebra *noun* a striped African animal of the horse family ▫ **zebra crossing** a pedestrian street crossing, painted in black and white stripes

zeitgeist /*zait*gaist/ *noun* the present cultural climate

zenith *noun* **1** the point of the heavens exactly overhead **2** the highest point, the peak

zephyr *noun, formal* a soft, gentle breeze

zero *noun* **1** nothing or the sign for it (0) **2** the point (marked 0) from which a scale (*eg* on a thermometer) begins ▫ **zero hour** the exact time fixed for some action ▫ **zero option** a proposal to limit or abandon the deployment of nuclear missiles if the opposing side does likewise ▫ **zero-rated** *adj* of goods: having no value-added tax

zest *noun* **1** relish, keen enjoyment **2** orange or lemon peel ▫ **zestful** *adj* ▫ **zestfully** *adv*

ziggurat *noun* a Babylonian temple in the shape of a stepped pyramid

zigzag *adj* having sharp bends or angles ▫ *verb* move in a zigzag direction

> **zigzag** *verb* » zigzag*s*, zigzagg*ing*, zigzagg*ed*

zimmer *noun, trademark* a hand-held metal frame used to give support in walking

zinc *noun* a bluish-white metal

zine /zeen/ *noun, informal* a fanzine, a special-interest magazine

zingy *adj, informal* zestful, lively

zinnia *noun* a tropical American plant of the thistle family

zip *noun* **1** a fastening device for clothes, bags *etc*, consisting of two rows of metal or nylon teeth which interlock when a sliding tab is pulled between them **2** a whizzing sound, *eg* made by a fast-flying object **3** *informal* energy, vigour ▫ *verb* **1** fasten with a zip **2** whiz, fly past at speed

> **zip** *verb* » zip*s*, zipp*ing*, zipp*ed*

zither *noun* a flat, stringed musical instrument, played with the fingers

zodiac *noun* an imaginary strip in space, divided into twelve equal parts ▢ **signs of the zodiac** the divisions of the zodiac used in astrology, each named after a group of stars

zoetrope *noun* a rotating cylinder with pictures on the inside which appear to move when viewed through slots in the side

zombie *noun* **1** a corpse reanimated by witchcraft **2** a very slow or stupid person

After the name of a voodoo snake god

zone *noun* **1** any of the five main bands into which the earth's surface is divided according to temperature: *temperate zone* **2** a section of a country, town *etc* marked off for a particular purpose: *no-parking zone/ smokeless zone* ▢ *verb* divide into zones

zonked *adj, slang* **1** exhausted **2** drunk; under the influence of drugs

zoo *noun* a place where wild animals are kept and shown to the public

zoological *adj* **1** relating to animals **2** relating to zoos; containing a zoo: *zoological gardens*

zoology *noun* the science of animal life ▢ **zoologist** *noun* someone who studies animal life

zoom *verb* **1** move with a loud, low buzzing noise **2** make such a noise **3** of an aircraft: climb sharply at high speed for a short time **4** of prices: increase sharply **5** use a zoom lens on a camera ▢ **zoom lens** *photog* a lens which makes a distant object appear gradually nearer without the camera being moved

zoon politikon a political person (literally 'animal')

Zoroastrian *noun* a member of an ancient Persian religion founded by Zoroaster ▢ *adj* of this religion ▢ **Zoroastrianism** *noun*

zucchini /zoo*kee*ni/ *noun* (*plural* **zucchini** or **zucchinis**) *US* a courgette

zydeco /*zai*dəkoh/ *noun* a percussive style of Cajun music influenced by the blues

Appendices

Punctuation Guide

capital letters

Capital letters must be used at the beginning of every sentence. Capitals are also required for the first letter of the names of people, countries, etc., and of words derived from them: *John*; *Anne*; *Sir Bernard Smith*; *Australia*; *the Australian cricket team*; *South Africa*; *a South African plant*; *Christ*; *Christian*; *Marx*; *Marxist*; *Chestnut Avenue*. Similarly, capitals must be used for the first letter of all important words in the titles of books, plays, people, organizations, and so on: *the Bay of Bengal*; *the Prince of Wales*; *Admiral of the Fleet*; *Lord Brown*; *Department of Health and Social Services*; *a book entitled The Biggest Fish in the World*. (Note that the first word of a book's or play's title must always have a capital letter also.)

When a title is hyphenated, both parts have a capital letter: *Major-General Smith*. Words which require a capital in names and titles do not of course need one in other circumstances: *the Republic of South Africa* but *South Africa is a republic*; *the President of the United States* (= a particular person) but *How many presidents of the United States have there been?*; *South America* but *the south of England*.

A few minor points are worth noting:

1. Seasons should not normally have capitals, but it may occasionally be necessary to write *Spring* rather than *spring* for the sake of clarity.
2. Many words which are in origin proper names or derived from proper names do not take a capital: *pasteurize, wellington, sandwich, watt, ampere*. In some cases, forms with and without capitals are equally correct: *plaster of paris/Paris; platonic/Platonic love*. If you are uncertain, consult a dictionary.

3. *Sir*, *Madam*, etc. should always have a capital at the beginning of a letter: *Dear Sir*.

full stop

A **full stop**, or **period**, is used to mark the end of a sentence. It is also used in abbreviations.

comma

In general, a comma marks a pause or slight break in a sentence, a less complete separation than one indicated by a semi-colon, a full stop, or brackets. The rules governing the use of the comma may seem complicated, but the complexity is more apparent than real. In certain situations a comma is obligatory; in others a comma is optional and its use is a matter of individual taste or a means of avoiding ambiguities and awkward or unclear constructions. Commas should be used sparingly: if a sentence you have written contains or seems to require a lot of commas, then the sentence is probably too long or too complex to be easily understood, and should be rewritten.

Commas are generally inserted between two or more adjectives preceding a noun: *a big, red car*; *a cold, wet, windy day*. There are, however, a number of exceptions to this rule:

1. When two adjectives together convey a single idea, they should not be separated by a comma: for example in *a great big dog*, *great* modifies *big* and serves to emphasize the bigness of the dog; similarly in *Good old Sam!*, *good* and *old* together form a single expression denoting approval or praise, and should therefore not be separated by a comma.
2. If the last adjective is more closely linked to the following noun than the other adjective(s) or if it forms a single

unit with the following noun, then it should not be preceded by a comma: *a foolish old man* (= an old man who is foolish); *a pretty little girl* (= a little girl who is pretty); *a bigger/different green pen* (= a green pen which is bigger than or different from some other green pen).

It follows from what has been said here that a comma may be appropriate in one sentence but wrong in an otherwise identical sentence, depending on the meaning to be conveyed. For example, *He bought a new, red car* means that he bought a new car which happened to be red, whereas *He bought a new red car* (with no comma) means that he already had a red car which he replaced with another red car.

(A useful test which may help you to decide whether or not to insert a comma between two adjectives is to substitute an *and* for the proposed comma: if you can put an *and* in, then put in a comma; if you can't, don't. One could not, for example, say **a great and big dog* or **Good and old Sam!*, but one could say *a cold and wet and windy day*.

3. When two or more adjectives are linked by *and*, no comma should be inserted: *a great and wise king*; *Our king is great and wise and just*. However, if the *and* links the last two adjectives in a series of adjectives otherwise separated only by commas, it also may correctly be preceded by a comma: both *a great, wise and just king* and *a great, wise, and just king* are correct. (Whichever style one chooses, one should at least try to be consistent, however.) Of course, if the last two adjectives together form a unit, a comma should not be inserted: *a big, yellow and green bus* is correct, **a big, yellow, and green bus* is not.

Essentially, the same rules as have been given above for series of adjectives apply to the insertion or omission of commas between nouns, verbs, phrases, and clauses, as can be seen from the following examples: *He washed the cups, saucers(,) and plates* (the comma between *saucers* and *and* could be omitted); *I like swimming, tennis(,) and football; She sings and dances; She sings, dances(,) and paints; She took out her keys, opened the door(,) and went in* (the longer the phrases or clauses linked, the more likely the optional comma is to be inserted).

When there is a balance or contrast between clauses linked by a conjunction, they are usually separated by a comma, but if there is a close connection between the clauses, there should be no comma: *She's a pretty girl, but not very clever; Do that again and I'll smack you!* If there is no conjunction between the clauses, a comma is usually inserted, as in *When he arrived, the children hugged him* (compare *The children hugged him when he arrived* without a comma).

Introductory words, words which form a parenthesis, or the name of the person being spoken to, should be separated from the rest of the sentence by commas: *I don't like the idea. However, you may do as you please; John, I'm pleased to say, did not take part in the prank; You, Mary, must come back tomorrow*. Notice in particular the difference between *The boy who was wearing a cap laughed* and *The boy, who was wearing a cap, laughed*: in the first sentence, the clause *who was wearing a cap* is closely linked to *boy* and serves to identify the boy concerned, whereas in the second sentence, the same clause is simply given as an additional piece of information.

A comma may be used, like a colon, before direct speech: *Peter said, 'I want to come too'*. And a comma is normally placed after *Dear Sir,* etc. at the beginning of a handwritten letter and after *Yours Sincerely*, etc. at the end of the letter, but is frequently omitted in a typewritten letter.

A comma is not needed between the month and year in

dates, nor between the number and the street name in addresses.

Special care should be taken not to separate subjects from verbs or verbs from their objects by inserting a comma between them. This is often done in an attempt to clarify the structure of a sentence, e.g. when the subject is a long and complex clause, but is not correct: for example, the comma between *killed* and *ate* in **The mouse that John's little black and white cat killed, ate the cheese* should be omitted as it divides the verb *ate* from the subject of the verb. If a sentence is so complicated as to appear to require a comma in such a position for the sake of clarity, the sentence should be rewritten.

colon

A **colon** is correctly used in a sentence when the statement that follows the colon explains, balances, or completes in some way the statement that precedes it, as in *I have something to tell you*: *John is coming tomorrow*; *This is an excellent play*: *the characters are believable, the action gripping, and the ending unexpected*; *There is just one thing I would like*: *a new car.*

A colon is also used to mark the beginning of a list of items as in *We need the following things*: *string, paper, glue, scissors, and a pencil*. Sometimes the colon preceding a list is followed by a dash (:-), especially if the list begins on a new line, but although not incorrect, this is quite unnecessary, and the dash is in general best omitted.

A third use of the colon is to introduce quoted speech, as in *John suddenly shouted: 'Look out! He's coming back!'*; a comma is also correctly used for this purpose, especially in recording casual conversation.

semicolon

A **semicolon** is used to mark a pause or break in a sentence greater than that indicated by a comma but less than the complete break marked by a full stop. It is generally used to separate parts of a sentence which are of more or less equal importance but which are not linked by a conjunction (such as *and, or, but,* etc.): *To err is human; to forgive, divine.*

There are two instances in which a semicolon may correctly be substituted for a comma:

1. If a sentence consists of a number of long clauses, themselves including several commas, the clauses may be separated by semicolons rather than commas in the interests of clarity.
2. Semicolons may be used to subdivide into groups items in a list some of which are separated by commas, since the use of commas alone might not show clearly the intended subgroupings: *Among the area's chief industries are shipbuilding, automobile engineering, and steel manufacturing; textiles and clothing; coalmining; and brewing.*

question mark

A **question** mark is used instead of a full stop to show that what comes before is a question: *what are you doing?* It is also used in round brackets to indicate uncertainty: *Tacitus, born(?) AD57.*

exclamation mark

An **exclamation mark** is used in place of a full stop to indicate an exclamation or sentence expressing strong emotion. It should not normally be used after a command unless it is needed for particular emphasis. An exclamation mark in parentheses is sometimes used to draw attention to something one finds surprising in a statement. It should be placed immediately after the word or words one wants to draw attention to, as in *Although he said he enjoyed (!) being ill, he was clearly depressed that morning.*

apostrophe

An **apostrophe** is often used to show that one or more letters or figures have been omitted from a word or number: *can't* is an abbreviation of *cannot*, *it's* of *it is*, *she'll* of *she will*, *I'd* of *I had* or *I would*, *the '30s* of *the 1930s*. Note that many words which are in origin abbreviations of longer words are now no longer written with apostrophes: *bus, flu, phone, plane.*

A further use of the apostrophe is seen in the formation of possessive nouns. The general rules which apply to the use of apostrophes with possessives are quite straightforward, but there are a few important exceptions to these rules which also must be noted. The basic rules are as follows:

> The possessive form of a noun is shown, in writing, by the addition of *'s*, as in *the child's dog; the children's dog; James's dog; Robert Burns's dog.*
>
> If the noun is plural and already ends in *s*, the apostrophe alone is used: *the boys' dog*, not **the boys's dog*. This applies also to certain expressions of time in which the time expression is treated as a possessive: *He's coming in two weeks' time.*

Notice that in all these cases, the written form of the words mirrors the spoken form: where an additional *s* is pronounced in a spoken possessive form, it is added in the written form; where no *s* is added in pronunciation, the apostrophe alone is added in the written form.

In a few exceptional cases, a singular noun ending in *s* is followed by an apostrophe alone rather than by *'s*. However, the existence of such exceptions to the general rule will not give rise to any confusion or uncertainty if it is remembered that, in such cases also, the correct written form of the words reflects the pronunciation of the spoken form. In other words, if you pronounce an *s*, write it; if you don't pronounce an *s*, don't write one. The main exceptions are names whose pronunciation with an additional *s* would be difficult or clumsy: *If you compare these two cars, you'll find that the Mercedes' engine is the more powerful.* Biblical and ancient Greek and Roman names which end in *s* can also be treated in this way, as in *Moses' laws, Xerxes' army*, but although still correct, this is not as prevalent as it used to be.

It should be noted that in certain expressions with **sake**, nouns ending in an *s* sound which by the nature of the construction ought to end in *'s* are now usually written without even an apostrophe: compare *for heaven's sake* and *for goodness sake*.

Do not use an apostrophe with possessive pronouns: the correct forms are *yours, hers, its (it's = it is), ours, theirs. One's*, however, is correct. Note also the possessive form *whose*, not **who's (who's = who is)*.

Apostrophes should not normally be used in the formation of plural nouns: plural forms such as **book's, *bag's, *lolly's* are increasingly common, and care should be taken to avoid them. An apostrophe is, however, permitted in plurals in a few specific cases, mainly for the sake of clarity:

1. An apostrophe is frequently written in the plurals of a number of, mostly short, words such as *do* (as in *do's and don'ts*), *me* (as *I feel there are two me's as the moment*), *set-to* (as in *I've had a few set-to's with him*), *he* and *she* (as in *Are the puppies he's or she's?*), but *dos, set-tos, hes* and *shes* are equally possible (*mes*

seems less acceptable than *hes* and *shes*, for no obvious reason).

2. When the word in the plural is the title of a book, play, etc *'s* is often used instead of *s* alone: *there have been three Macbeth's* (= three different versions of the play Macbeth) *performed in Edinburgh in the past six months*, but here again, *s* alone is equally permissible. *'s*, rather than *s*, is normal for the plural form of a word which is being quoted from something else, as in *There are too many that's in that sentence.*
3. *'s* should be used to form the plural of single letters and figures, as in *Dot your i's and cross your t's; Write a row of 2's, then a row of 3's.* With longer numbers, e.g. in dates, both *'s* and *s* are permissible: *Were you around in the 1930's/1930s?; How many 30's/30s are there in 240?* An *s* alone should be used to form the plural of abbreviations made up of a sequence of initial letters: the correct plural of *M.P.*, for example, is *M.P.s*, not **M.P.'s*.

quotation marks

Quotation marks are used to mark off quoted speech and to separate off or highlight words or phrases in sentences:

'Do come in,' he said.

'What does an accessary after the fact mean?'

Both single and double quotes are correct, but modern usage prefers single quotes. However, if there is a quotation or highlighted passage within another quotation, both single and double quotes must be used:

'What does "an accessary after the fact" mean?' he asked.

Punctuation marks that belong to or are part of the quoted material should be kept within the quotation marks, while other punctuation marks are placed outside the quotes. A full stop is replaced by a comma when it stands at the end of a quote which is not the end of the whole sentence. The following examples show these rules in operation:

He said: 'You must help her.'

'You must help her,' he said.

'You', he said, 'must help her.'

'You, John, must help her,' he said

'You, John,' he said, 'must help her.'

'Must I help her?' he asked.

'What do you mean by "an accessary after the fact"?' he asked.

If the end of a quotation is also the end of the sentence of which the quotation is part, there should be no full stop at the end of the sentence if there is already a full stop or other punctuation mark at the end of the quotation:

He said: 'You must help her.' is correct;

He said: 'You must help her.'. is wrong.

With question marks and exclamation marks, the rule is not absolute: for example, a sentence like

'Did he say "Are you coming?"?' she asked.

is possible, but it is generally considered preferable to omit one or other or the question marks, even though this is not strictly logical since there are two separate questions in the sentence.

dash

A **dash** is sometimes used along with a colon to introduce a list, especially if the list begins on a new line, but this is deprecated by many people and a colon alone is usually quite sufficient. A dash should certainly not be used when the list immediately follows the colon on the same line, as in *We need to buy various things: potatoes, cheese, eggs, butter, and flour* (not **...things: – potatoes,...*).

Like a colon, a dash may be used to introduce an explanation or expansion of something preceding it, as in *These are the characteristics of a good play – the characters should be believable, the action gripping, and the ending unexpected.* Two dashes may be used to mark a parenthesis or an aside, as in *His new car – a Rover, I believe – cost over £12,000.* In general, the use of dashes rather than colons or brackets in such cases gives a more informal tone to what is written.

A dash is used to introduce a summing-up of what has preceded, as in *Believable characters, gripping action, and an unexpected ending – these are the main characteristics of a good play.* And if a sentence is broken off in the middle, a dash marks the break, as in *What really annoys me is that she – but then, what's the use of talking about it?*

hyphen

For many people, hyphenation is one of the most troublesome aspects of English spelling. However, although there are certain word-types – in particular, compound nouns – in which hyphenation does not seem to follow any logical or consistent rule, there are many categories of word in which the rules are fairly clear-cut and consistent, if not entirely so, and therefore quite simple to follow.

In general, a hyphen is used to show that two or more words are to be treated as a single unit: *She is my mother-in-law*; *a good-looking, hard-working boy.* In may cases, a hyphen is so used to avoid ambiguities: compare *a little-known writer* and *a little, known writer*; *200-odd people* and *200 odd people.* The following are the most important rules of hyphenation:

1. A compound adjective consisting of two words, the second of which is a present or past participle or a word ending in *-ed*, is normally hyphenated: *good-natured*;

black-headed; *hard-wearing*; *hard-hearted*; *never-ending*; *card-carrying*; *battle-scarred*; *panic-stricken*.

When the first word of such a compound is one of the adverb **well, better, best, ill, worse, worst**, a hyphen is inserted only when the compound adjective precedes a noun, not when it occupies other positions in the sentence: *a well-known author* but *He is well known as an author* and *Well known as an author, Jim Brown is now making a name for himself as an actor*.

A past or present participle preceded by an adverb ending in *-ly* is not linked to the adverb by a hyphen in any position in the sentence: *The room is beautifully decorated*; *a beautifully decorated room*. This rule may be broken if a hyphen is needed for the sake of clarity.

2. Nouns formed from phrasal verbs (i.e. a verb plus *in, out, off*, etc.) are generally hyphenated: *take-over*; *fly-past*; *shake-up*; *share-out*; *going-over*; *passer-by*. A hyphen should not be used to join the parts of a phrasal verb itself: *We will have to share out the money*, not *...*share-out the money*. Notice the difference between *His going-over* (noun) *of the accounts was very thorough and His going over* (verb plus preposition) *the accounts caused a lot of problems*.
3. Phrases of various types, when used as adjectives and preceding the noun they qualify, require hyphens: *an up-to-date report*; *a balance-of-payments problem*; *our next-door neighbours*; *a never-to-be-forgotten experience*.
4. Numbers from 21 to 99 and fractions should be hyphenated: *twenty-three*; *fifty-six*; *one-third*.
5. Compound adjectives consisting of two simple adjectives or a noun plus an adjective are usually hyphenated when preceding a noun and often (but not always) hyphenated

in other positions (e.g. after the verb *be*): *a pitch-dark night*; *blood-red wine*; *It's pitch-dark outside*.

6. In the case of compound nouns, a comparison of the entries in two or more dictionaries will show that there are many words in which hyphenation usage is not clearly established: *coal gas* or *coal-gas*; *fire-guard* or *fireguard*. In general, a compound noun is written as two words if it is felt that the first word simply qualifies the second word like an adjective, but as a hyphenated word or a single word with no hyphen if the compound is felt to be a single lexical item denoting a particular thing or type of thing: *a bus company, trade figures* but *bus-driver, trademark*. If the 'single lexical item' type of word is well established and frequently used, and is built up from short, one-syllable words, it is likely to be written as a single word with no hyphen: *bedroom*; *bloodbath*; *teacup*. A hyphen is more likely in longer words, and where the absence of a hyphen would allow an undesirable or confusing juxtaposition of sounds or letters: *heart-throb* rather than *heartthrob*; *pole-axe* rather than *poleaxe, time-exposure* rather than **timeexposure*.

7. Prefixes like *un-, dis-, mis-, re-,* and suffixes like *-fold, -ish, -most, -ness, -ship* and *-wise*, are not normally followed, or preceded, by a hyphen. However, if the word to which a prefix is added begins with a capital letter, a hyphen is inserted: *un-English*. Note the use of a hyphen to distinguish *re-cover* (to cover again) from *recover* (to become well again), *re-count* (to count again) from *recount* (to tell), and so on, and to avoid the juxtaposition of two *e's* in *re-enter, re-elect, etc. Ex-, non-,* and *self-* are normally followed by a hyphen: *ex-wife*; *non-inflammable*; *self-respect*.

Hyphens are used to mark breaks in words not normally hyphenated, either when only part of the word is written, as in *four- or fivefold,* (where *four-* represents 'fourfold'), or at the end of a line of writing where part of the word has to be taken over to the next line. In the latter circumstance, the following rules apply:

1. If possible, split the word into logical parts in such a way that the former part suggests the whole word, or at least does not mislead the reader by suggesting the wrong word: *mis-/shapen,* not **miss-/hapen* or **misshap-/en*; *re-/install,* not **rein-/stall*; *heat-/ing* not **he-/ating.*
2. A letter that influences the pronunciation of another letter should not be separated from it at a line-break: *spe-/cial* not **spec-/ial*; *magi-/cian* not **magic-/ian.*

American English and British English

Standard American English differs from standard British English in various ways — in pronunciation, in grammar, in vocabulary, in spelling, even in punctuation. This appendix provides an overview of the most important or noticeable differences between the two standard languages.

Pronunciation

General differences in pronunciation

British English /ah/

In many words that have an /ah/ sound in British English followed by /f/, /s/, /th/, /n/ or /m/ sound, American English has an /a/, as in *after*, *banana*, *can't*, *dance*, *half*, *laugh*, *pass*, and *rather*.

British English /i/

Where British English has /i/ in final position in words such as *city* and *happy*, American English has /ee/.

British English /o/

In American English, words such as *block*, *got*, *pond*, *probable* and *top* are pronounced with an /ah/ sound. In words in which the vowel is followed by /f/, /s/, /th/, /r/, /g/ or /ng/ (eg in *coffee*, *dog*, *cross*, *forest* and *long*) a longer vowel similar to /aw/ is also common.

British English /yoo/, /yuu/

After /t/, /d/, /n/, /l/, /s/ and /th/, American English generally has /oo/ rather than /yoo/ if the vowel is stressed, eg in *duty*, *lurid*, *new*, *suit* and *tune*, but the /y/ sound is retained in unstressed syllables (eg in *menu* and *value*).

British English /iy/
In most words ending in *-ile*, American English generally pronounces the final syllable as /il/ rather than /iyl/ as in British English, eg in *futile* and *fragile*. In some words, /iyl/ is possible or required, eg in *juvenile* and *prehensile*. In general, the longer or more technical a word is, the more likely it is to be pronounced /iyl/.

British English /t/
In words such as *latter*, *metal* and *writing*, the *-tt-/-t-* is pronounced in American English with the same sound as that of the *-dd-/-d-* of *ladder*, *medal* and *riding*.

/r/
In most accents of American, /r/ is pronounced at the ends of words and before consonants. However, even in *r*-pronouncing accents, the *r* is often not pronounced when it follows an unstressed vowel and is itself followed by another *r*, eg in *governor*.

British English /ahr/ spelt -er-
In words such as *clerk* and *Derby*, where British English preserves an older pronunciation with /ahr/, American speech has /uhr/.

British English /-a-ri/
American English tends to give greater prominence than British English does to the suffixes *-ary*, *-ory* and often also *-ery*; as for example in *monetary* (BrE /-*ta*-ri/ or /-tri/, AmE /-te-ri/), *confectionery* (BrE /-*na*-ri/, AmE /-na-ri/), *obligatory* (BrE /-*to*-ri/, AmE /-taw-ri/).

British English /nt/
In American English, /t/ is often not pronounced after /n/ when what follows is an unstressed vowel, as for example

in *Atlantic*, *gentleman*, *international* and *plenty*.

Pronunciation differences in individual words

There are also many differences between British English and American English in the pronunciation of individual words. A selection of such words follows:

anti-	BrE /**an**-ti/	AmE often /**an**-tiy/
depot	BrE /**de**-poh/	AmE /**dee**-poh/
epoch	BrE /**ee**-pok/	AmE /**e**-pok/
lever	BrE /**lee**-ver/	AmE usually /**le**-ver/
leisure	BrE /**le**-zhur/	AmE usually /**lee**-zhur/
lieutenant	BrE /lef-**te**-nant/	AmE /luu-**te**-nant/
moustache	BrE /mus-**tahsh**/	AmE /**mus**-tash/
schedule	BrE /**she**-dyool/	AmE /**ske**-jool/
simultaneous	BrE /si-mul-/	AmE usually /siy-mul-/
suggest	BrE /su-**jest**/	AmE usually /sug-**jest**/
tomato	BrE /to-**mah**-toh/	AmE /to-**may**-toh/
vase	BrE /vahz/	AmE usually /vays/
vitamin	BrE /**vi**-ta-min/	AmE /**viy**-ta-min/
z	BrE /zed/	AmE /zee/
zenith	BrE /**ze**-nith/	AmE /**zee**-nith/

Grammar

Collective nouns

A singular verb is normally used with collective nouns in American English, where British English allows either a singular or a plural verb: *Our staff monitors the latest developments in language daily.*

do

American English does not use *do* as British English does in the following examples:

We don't have to go but we can do if you want (AmE *we can if you want)*
'Will you fix that for me?' 'I have done.' (AmE *I have*)

gotten

Gotten now exists in British English only in expressions such as *ill-gotten gains*. In other cases, the past participle is *got*. In American English, *gotten* is used when a process is involved (*he's gotten a new car*), but *got* when a state of possession is implied (*he's got a car*). As in British English, *he's got to go* means 'he must go', whereas *he's gotten to go* means 'he has received permission to go'.

have

The question form *Has she enough money?* is not used in American English, which uses the forms, also possible in British English, *Does she have enough money?* and *Has she got enough money?* The same applies to the negative statement form *She hasn't enough money*, as opposed to *She doesn't have enough money* and *She hasn't got enough money*.

past tense

The simple past-tense form of a verb is often used in American English where British English would use a perfect tense: *Did she leave yet?*

subjunctive verbs

After verbs, nouns and adjectives which denote requiring, demanding, ordering, urging, etc, the subjunctive is more extensively used in American English than in British

English: *We demand that she be dismissed at once; his demand that she leave immediately!; It is vital that she leave tomorrow.*

will/shall
Will is used rather than shall to form the simple future tense with first-person pronouns: *We will come back again soon.*

Vocabulary

There are many differences in vocabulary between British English and American English, of which the following is a selection:

BrE *aubergine*	AmE *eggplant*
BrE *autumn*	AmE *fall*
BrE *biscuit*	AmE *cookie*
BrE *bonnet (of car)*	AmE *hood*
BrE *boot (of car)*	AmE *trunk*
BrE *candy floss*	AmE *cotton candy*
BrE *caravan*	AmE *trailer*
BrE *car park*	AmE *parking lot*
BrE *chips*	AmE *French fries*
BrE *condom*	AmE *rubber*
BrE *cot*	AmE *crib*
BrE *courgettes*	AmE *zucchini*
BrE *crisps*	AmE *chips*
BrE *cupboard*	AmE *closet*
BrE *drawing-pin*	AmE *thumb tack*
BrE *dual carriageway*	AmE *divided highway*
BrE *first floor*	AmE *second floor*
BrE *garden*	AmE *yard*

BrE *grill*	AmE *broil*
BrE *ground floor*	AmE *first floor*
BrE *guard (on train)*	AmE *conductor*
BrE *handbag*	AmE *purse*
BrE *holiday*	AmE *vacation*
BrE *lift*	AmE *elevator*
BrE *paraffin*	AmE *kerosene*
BrE *pavement*	AmE *sidewalk*
BrE *petrol*	AmE *gas*
BrE *suppose*	AmE *guess*
BrE *sweets*	AmE *candy*
BrE *tap*	AmE *faucet*
BrE *tights*	AmE *pantyhose*
BrE *trousers*	AmE *pants*
BrE *vest*	AmE *undershirt*
BrE *waistcoat*	AmE *vest*

Spelling

General differences between British and American spelling

i) British English ***-our***
American English ***-or***

American English has ***-or*** in words such as *color*, *flavor* and *humor*. (*Glamour* and *saviour* may be spelt as in British English, however.)

ii) British English ***-re***
American English ***-er***

American English has ***-er*** in words such as *center*, *fiber*, *meter* and *theater*. But to show the hard /g/ and /k/ sounds, *acre*, *massacre*, *ogre*, etc. (Note, however, *meager*, not *meagre*.)

iii) British English ***-ll-***, ***-pp-***, ***-tt-***
American English ***-l-***, ***-p-***, ***-t-***

In inflections and derivations of words ending in *l, p*, or *t* not immediately followed by a single stressed vowel, American English generally does not double the final letter as British English does:

British English: *cancelled*, *counsellor*, *equalled*, *kidnapped*, *traveller*
American English: *canceled*, *counselor*, *equaled*, *kidnaped*, *traveler*
(but American English spells *formatting* as in British English)

Note also British English *carburettor* and *woollen*, American English *carburetor* and *woolen.*

iv) British English ***-l***
American English ***-ll***

At the ends of certain two-syllable words, American English generally has a double *l* where British English has a single *l*:

British English: *appal*, *enrol*, *fulfil*, *instil*, *skilful*
American English: *appall*, *enroll*, fulfill, *instill*, *skilfull*

v) British English ***ae/oe*** or ***e***
American English ***e***

The tendency to replace *ae* and *oe* by *e* in words from Latin and Greek is more strongly developed in American English than in British English:

British English: *aesthetic*, *amoeba*, *diarrhoea*, *foetus*, *haemoglobin*, *oesophagus*

American English (more often): *esthetic*, *ameba*, *diarrhea*, *fetus*, *hemoglobin*, *esophagus*
(but *aerobics* and *aerosol* are spelt as in British English)

vi) British English ***-ize*** or ***-ise***
American English ***-ize***

In verbs that can be spelt either *-ise* or *-ize*, the use of *-ize* is now standard in American English. Note also the spellings *analyze*, *paralyze*, etc as opposed to the British English *analyse*, *paralyse*, etc.

vii) As a rule, hyphens are used less frequently in American English than in British English,
eg *dining room* rather than *dining-room*.

Spelling differences in individual words

British English: *axe*, *catalogue*, *cheque*, *cosy*, *defence*, *draught*, grey, *jewellery*, *licence*, *moustache*, *offence*, *pyjamas*, *practice/practise*, *pretence*, *sceptic*, *sulphur*, *storey*, *tyre*

American English: *ax*, *catalog*, *check*, *cozy*, *defense*, *draft*, *gray*, *jewelery*, *license*, *mustache*, *offense*, *pajamas*, *practise*, *pretense*, *skeptic*, *sulfur*, *story*, *tire*

Punctuation

The main differences in punctuation between American and British practices are as follows:

i) **Commas between clauses:**
American English prefers some punctuation (usually a comma) between clauses in compound sentences where there is none in British English:

British English: *I was late home on Monday because I couldn't start the car.*
American English: *I was late home on Monday, because I couldn't start the car.*

ii) **Commas in lists:**
In American English, a comma is inserted before *and* in lists:
British English: *x,y and z*
American English: *x,y, and z*

iii) **Quotation marks:**
The American preference is for double quotation marks rather than single (and therefore for single quotation marks within double quotation marks for quotes within quotes). American practice also places commas and full stops (but not other punctuation marks) before quotation marks rather than after them.

British punctuation: *By an 'abstract object', McArthur means something which is 'neither spatial nor temporal'.*
American punctuation: *By an "abstract object," McArthur means something which is "neither spatial nor temporal."*

Dates

An important difference between American and British English is the way of writing dates.
In British English, '6/11/95' would mean '6 November 1995', whereas in American practice, it denotes '11 June 1995'.

Extra Spelling Guide

The following words are often misspelt when used in English:

abscess
accommodation
acquiesce
aghast
argument
asphyxiate
assassinate
attach
bachelor
beautiful
beauty
berserk
besiege
budgeted
buses
cemetery
changeable
commemorate
committee
connoisseur
conscientious
cupfuls
desiccate
detach
diaphragm
diarrhoea
diphtheria
diphthong
disappoint
dissipate
embarrass
exaggerate
exhilarate
extravagant
faeces
February
fulfil
gases
gauge
ghastly
gherkin
ghetto
ghost
government
guarantee
guard
guerrilla
(also guerilla)
haemorrhage
hangar
harass
hypocrisy
idiosyncrasy
inoculate
instal
installment
knowledgeable
lieutenant
lightning
liquefy
livelihood
manoeuvre
millionaire
nuisance
occurrence
occurred
occurring
paradigm
paraffin
parallel
paralleling
paralleled
parliament
phlegm
phlegmatic
pronunciation
publicly
questionnaire
quizzes
quizzed
quizzing
receipt
repellent
rhyme
rhythm
seize
siege
sieve
separate
skilful
sporran
supersede
tranquillity
unwieldy
wholly